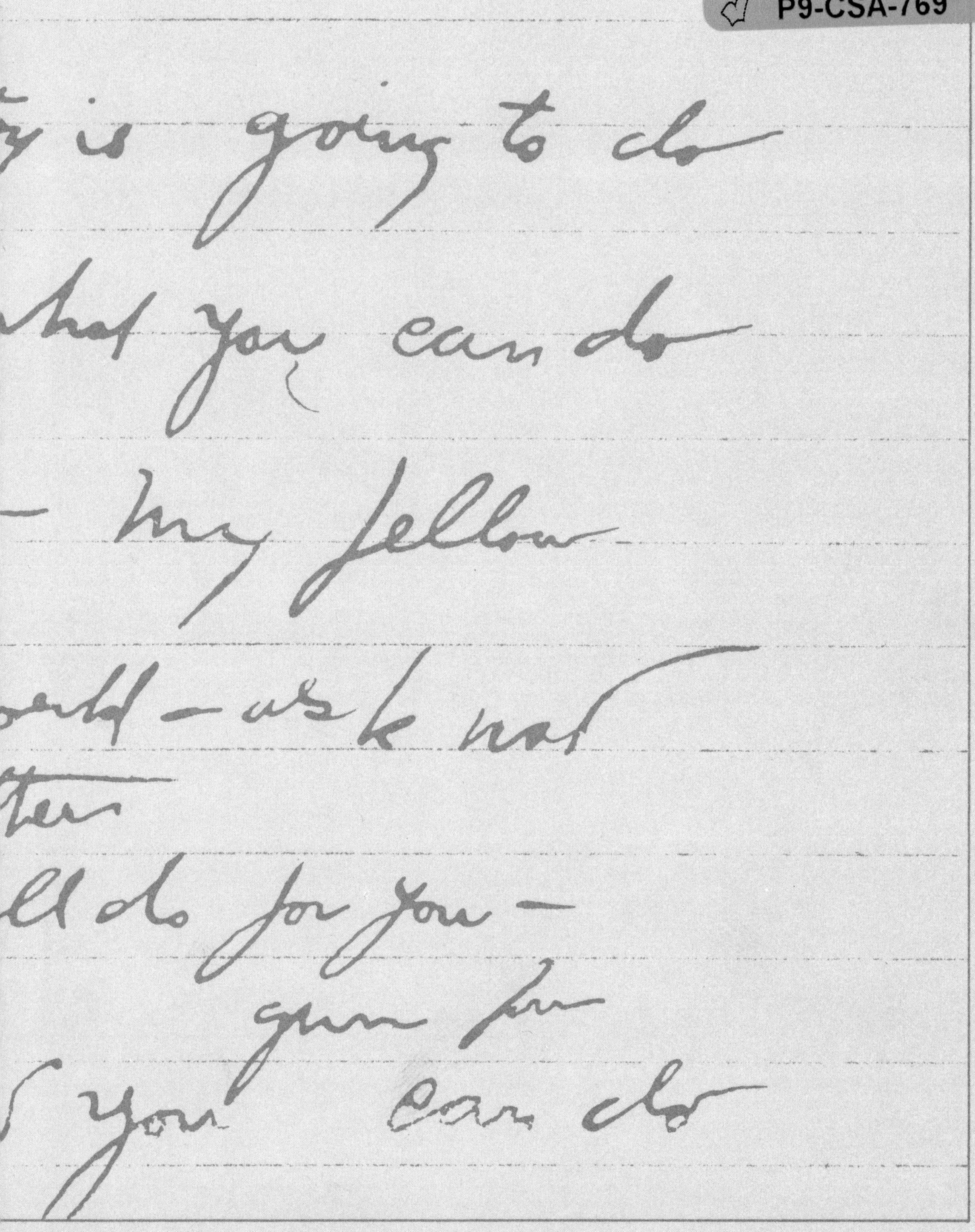
y is going to do

hat you can do

— my fellow

orld — ask not

ters

ll do for you —

[illegible] for

you can do

"LET THE WORD GO FORTH"

Books by Theodore C. Sorensen

"Let the Word Go Forth" (Editor)

A Widening Atlantic?
Domestic Change and Foreign Policy (Co-Author)

A Different Kind of Presidency:
A Proposal for Breaking the Political Deadlock

Watchmen in the Night:
Presidential Accountability After Watergate

The Kennedy Legacy

Kennedy

Decision-Making in the White House

In Berlin, 1963.

PHOTO BY ROBERT LACKENBACH/BLACK STAR.

"LET THE WORD GO FORTH"

The Speeches, Statements, and Writings of JOHN F. KENNEDY

Selected and with an Introduction by Theodore C. Sorensen

Published by
Delacorte Press
The Bantam Doubleday Dell Publishing Group, Inc.
666 Fifth Avenue
New York, New York 10103

Library of Congress Cataloging in Publication Data

Kennedy, John F. (John Fitzgerald), 1917–1963.
"Let the word go forth" : the speeches, statements, and writings of John F. Kennedy, 1947–1963 / selected and with introduction by Theodore C. Sorensen.
p. cm.
Includes index.
ISBN 0-440-50041-9
1. United States—Politics and government—1945– I. Sorensen, Theodore C. II. Title.
E838.5.K42 1988
973.92—dc19 88-15000
CIP

Manufactured in the United States of America
November 1988

10 9 8 7 6 5 4 3 2 1

BG

Designed by Giorgetta Bell McRee

NOTE

Errors in typing or transcription have been corrected. Introductory, repetitive, transitional, and other paragraphs deemed less interesting or relevant by the editor, or too outdated or partisan for inclusion, have been deleted, as have various quotations, anecdotes, and certain other portions for reasons of space and flow. State of the Union messages have been divided by subject matter. Where appropriate, these deletions have been marked with ellipses. Those seeking complete texts should contact the John Fitzgerald Kennedy Library in Boston, whose cooperation is gratefully acknowledged.

For GILLIAN

Who makes it all possible and worthwhile

Speaking in St. Paul, Minnesota, 1962.
PHOTO COURTESY CECIL W. STOUGHTON.

CONTENTS

"LET THE WORD GO FORTH"

The Inaugural Address, January 20, 1961.
PHOTO BY FRANK SCHERSCHEL, LIFE MAGAZINE © TIME INC.

INTRODUCTION

John F. Kennedy was so blessed with the gifts of reason, intellect, and vitality that eloquence came naturally to him. He believed in the power and glory of words—both written and spoken—to win votes, to set goals, to change minds, to move nations. He consistently took care to choose the right words in the right order that would send the right message. He did not regard old-fashioned eloquence as unsophisticated or unimportant, nor did he ever rise to speak in public indifferent or unprepared. In the dawn of the television era, his youthful good looks, cool confidence, and strong voice enhanced the inspirational appeal of his words; and this "style" was all-important to the continuing success of his political, legislative, diplomatic, and presidential efforts.

But he knew that words alone meant very little, that "saying so doesn't make it so." As he had planned to note in his undelivered speech in Dallas on November 22, 1963:

> Words alone are not enough. . . . Where our strength and determination are clear, our words need merely to convey conviction, not belligerence. If we are strong, our strength will speak for itself. If we are weak, words will be of no help.

Postwar Western Europe, he pointed out, had not been saved by George Marshall's speech at Harvard but by the economic recovery that the Marshall Plan sparked. His own words of warning to the Soviets over the Cuban missile crisis, he added, succeeded only because a strong and united West stood behind them.

Words and speeches, in short, were his medium, not the message. However exalted the rhetoric, he knew speeches were important only when the message was important. They were forceful only if the ideas they conveyed were forceful.

That is why accuracy, not modesty or loyalty, compels me to emphasize once again that John Kennedy was the true author of all of his speeches and writings. They set forth *his* ideas and ideals, *his* decisions and policies, *his* knowledge of history and politics. Every speech put *his* career on the line, reflecting choices for which he would be praised or blamed. Without claiming to have written every word of every draft—indeed, often generously acknowledging the assistance he received from others—he played a major role in every major speech, selecting subject matter and themes, arguments and conclusions, quotations and phrases. (The lesser talks—including some on the campaign trail, at formal dinners, or in the White House Rose Garden—were often delivered without notes or without glancing at those he had.) More importantly, he alone was responsible for the decision that lay at the heart of every major speech.

For great speeches reflect great decisions; and John F. Kennedy's greatest speeches all reflected turning points in American history for which he was responsible, including:

- his 1963 call at American University for a new look at U.S.–Soviet coexistence and a moratorium on nuclear testing in the atmosphere, the finest speech he ever gave;

- his 1963 televised address to the nation (his second most important speech, and by coincidence delivered less than thirty-three hours after his talk at American University) committing his Presidency to the abolition of all racial discrimination and segregation in this country;

- his 1961 Inaugural Address signaling the vigor and determination of our youngest elected President in history, the first to be born in this century, as he urged new national sacrifice and service;

- his 1960 campaign appeal to the Protestant clergy in Houston for an end to the unwritten rule that barred a Catholic from the White House;

- his 1962 televised declaration that the United States had spotted secret Soviet nuclear missile bases in Cuba and was determined upon their removal;

- his 1963 televised address hailing completion of the nuclear test-ban treaty, the first superpower step toward arms control; and

- his speech a few months earlier pledging this country's commitment to the freedom of millions of people gathered between the Wall and City Hall in West Berlin.

He drew strength and inspiration from his audience and surroundings in West Berlin, as he did on other historic occasions in other settings such as the U.S. Capitol, the United Nations, the Irish Parliament, Independence Hall, and the Paulskirche Assembly Hall in Frankfurt, West Germany.

Even his presidential campaign speeches offered memorable ideas—the revitalized Presidency, the Alliance for Progress, the Peace Corps, and the concept of the New Frontier itself—along with the usual partisan exhortations and platitudes.

Not surprisingly, JFK's worst major speech as President conveyed a nondecision—his televised address in August 1962 announcing that no tax cut was planned for that year.

That speech is not among those selected for this volume. Neither are others he later regretted, such as a youthful attack in the House of Representatives on President Truman's China policy, a futile presidential plea to news editors to exercise more restraint on national security stories, and a panic-inspiring emphasis on fallout shelters at the time of the Berlin crisis.

For this is not a collection, or even a representative sample, of every JFK speech or message. It is simply one man's selection of those bits and pieces in the public domain that show John F. Kennedy at his wisest, warmest, and wittiest—the most relevant for our times as well as the most eloquent, the most important in his time as well as the most inspirational, the best of his words as well as the most familiar. The objective is to gather that material in one handy volume for the first time for easy access by students of rhetoric and history, by speakers and speech writers, by those who want to remember John Kennedy better and those too young to remember him at all.

Reviewing all the words and works of Congressman, Senator, candidate, and President Kennedy was for me an exhilarating task. Reducing that vast mountain to a single volume was excruciating. Even after cutting the purely local, ephemeral, and political, even after dividing up and paring down his necessarily lengthy State of the Union addresses, a painful process of elimination remained. Space did not permit inclusion of most of the jokes, the biblical quotations, the invocations of Lincoln or Jefferson or FDR, and the references to history that made those speeches sparkle. Though he rarely spoke for more than twenty or twenty-five minutes, almost no speech could be included in full. Some important speeches and important topics could not be included at all.

Not all of the manifold subjects in which he was interested as congressman, senator, and President are of widespread interest today. It is unfortunate that long passages showing his mastery of detail and data could not be included, unfortunate that Senate speeches which produced proud legislative victories—on labor reform and the Electoral College, for example—could not be included. No doubt many readers will look in vain for a Kennedy speech that he or she particularly remembered or a Kennedy quotation especially cherished. All such errors of omission are mine.

But some of his best speeches, included here, are not particularly well remembered by Kennedy's fellow Americans. His Senate speeches on Algeria, India, and Indochina received only brief attention in this country but were widely hailed in the Third World. (It is interesting to note that JFK's best and most profound speech on Vietnam and Indochina was made while he was in the Senate, not in the White House, and that his best and most profound speech on civil rights was made in the White House, not in the Senate.) His speech to the Irish Parliament, little read here, is still revered in Dublin. His 1960 convention eve reply to former president Truman's attack on his youth and inexperience went unnoticed by many Fourth of July travelers. Two years later they also missed his 1962 Independence Day call for an Atlantic partnership that helped spur the movement toward integration in Western Europe.

Others on the list of Kennedy's best have simply been largely forgotten, including his "farewell" to the Massachusetts Legislature, his campaign-opening treatises on the Presidency, and his commencement addresses at Harvard, Yale, the University of Washington, and the University of California.

But not all are forgotten. Not since Winston Churchill (whose career and eloquence Kennedy admired equally) have any other public speaker's words and phrases become as large a part of our national memory. Those who are old enough remember how they reacted to his Cuban missile crisis TV address, how they cheered his first debate with Nixon, and how they scheduled their day around his televised press conferences. A "profile in courage" became part of our vocabulary. Humorists parody "Ich bin ein Berliner." Orators ask "not what your country can do for you . . ." Schoolchildren are assigned the Houston ministers speech. Even his quotations from John Winthrop ("a city upon a hill"), George Bernard Shaw ("Some men . . . ask why not"), and ancient Chinese proverbs ("defeat is an orphan" and "a journey of a thousand miles"), are mistakenly attributed to him.

During these last twenty-five years, no other previous president's words have been so frequently quoted, misquoted, or borrowed without attribution by politicians in both major parties.

To be sure, not everyone remembers Kennedy's speeches favorably. Some have written that his idealistic messages often set goals that could not realistically be reached in the lifetime of his audience. They are right. Others have asserted that JFK's speeches were less often interrupted by applause than were those of his successors. They are right. Critics on the right have charged that Kennedy often used Cold War rhetoric to advance liberal objectives. They also are right. Critics on the left have charged that Kennedy's tightfisted fiscal policies never matched his attacks on this country's social and economic ills. They also are right.

Still other faults can be found with the advantage of hindsight. Kennedy's Inaugural vow to "pay any price, bear any burden" reflected the Cold War atmosphere of the time (making all the more remarkable his urging the Soviets in that same speech to join in a range of peaceful pursuits). His repeated references to leadership in male terms only (e.g., "all free men are citizens of Berlin"), typical twenty-five years ago, would be unacceptable today. His speeches did not anticipate a thaw in our relations with the People's Republic of China and paid little attention to the repression in South Africa.

Moreover, much of what he did seek in these speeches and messages has never been achieved or, even worse, has been pushed further back by his successors—including his hopes for a stronger United Nations, a more cohesive Western Alliance, more foreign economic assistance, a greater emphasis on service instead of self-interest in Washington, a comprehensive ban on nuclear tests, and a free and democratic Central America.

Nevertheless, much of what he said and wrote remains valid and relevant today—on U.S.–Soviet relations and race relations, for example, expanding foreign trade and foreign aid, keeping budget deficits and price stability under control, strengthening the foreign service, and strengthening the Presidency itself.

It is not difficult to find in these speeches the beginnings of much that we take for granted today—equal rights for all Americans, the conquest of space, politics free from religious bias, federal help for higher education and the arts, the sale of American farm products to Moscow, public television, communications satellites, the Peace Corps, and much more. Perhaps his greatest legacy is the untold number of men and women, in this country and abroad, famous and obscure, who were induced to enter politics or public service by the exhortation or example of John F. Kennedy. In meeting government leaders the world around, I have frequently encountered those who have never forgotten attending one of President Kennedy's numerous sessions with foreign students gathered on the South Lawn of the White House.

Neither is it difficult to discern from these speeches what a different world we would inhabit today had John Kennedy not been cruelly cut down on November 22, 1963, at the peak of his power and prowess. Surely, as he remarked at a press conference, "life is unfair."

But John F. Kennedy was not an unhappy man. Concerned that his countrymen, unable "to see the enemy from the walls," might be unwilling to pay the price of greatness, convinced that the old ways of conventional politics and policy-making were not up to the challenge that his generation faced, his speeches often contained dire warnings and stern lectures. But they also reflected his zest for living, his love of humor and home, his pride in public service.

There is much more to a man than his speeches. As Lord Rosebery once wrote regarding the oratory of William Pitt: "It is not merely the thing that is said but the man who says it that counts, the character which breathes through the sentences." The republication here of John F. Kennedy's words cannot possibly convey in full the energy and vitality of the man, his courage as a leader, or his warmth as a friend. But they can convey his principles and his hopes; and those are worth remembering, now and for generations to come. Through his words, John F. Kennedy lives on.

The State of the Union Address, January 14, 1963.
PHOTO COURTESY CECIL W. STOUGHTON.

PART I

The Presidency

CHAPTER 1

The Inaugural Address

Aware that his words would be viewed skeptically by those in Congress and the country who thought him too inexperienced for the post, concerned by the speech only a short time earlier of Soviet Chairman Nikita Khrushchev that sounded like a call for a worldwide Communist revolution, John F. Kennedy wanted his first address as President of the United States to challenge his multiple audiences: to summon the American people to greatness, to remind free nations of their obligations, to offer the Soviet Union a choice between confrontation and cooperation, and to be his eloquent best.

We observe today not a victory of party but a celebration of freedom—symbolizing an end as well as a beginning—signifying renewal as well as change. For I have sworn before you and Almighty God the same solemn oath our forebears prescribed nearly a century and three quarters ago.

The world is very different now. For man holds in his mortal hands the power to abolish all forms of human poverty and all forms of human life. And yet the same revolutionary beliefs for which our forebears fought are still at issue around the globe—the belief that the rights of man come not from the generosity of the state but from the hand of God.

We dare not forget today that we are the heirs of that first revolution. Let the word go forth from this time and place, to friend and foe alike, that the torch has been passed to a new generation of Americans—born in this century, tempered by war, disciplined by a hard and bitter peace, proud of our ancient heritage—and unwilling to witness or permit the slow undoing of those human rights to which this nation has always been committed, and to which we are committed today at home and around the world.

Let every nation know, whether it wishes us well or ill, that we shall pay any price, bear any burden, meet any hardship, support any friend, oppose any foe, to assure the survival and the success of liberty.

This much we pledge—and more.

To those old allies whose cultural and spiritual origins we share, we pledge the loyalty of faithful friends. United, there is little we cannot do in a host of cooperative ventures. Divided, there is little we can do—for we dare not meet a powerful challenge at odds and split asunder.

To those new states whom we welcome to the ranks of the free, we pledge our word that one form of colonial control shall not have passed away merely to be replaced by a far more iron tyranny. We shall not always expect to find them supporting our view. But we shall always hope to find them strongly supporting their own freedom—and to remember that in the past, those who foolishly sought power by riding the back of the tiger ended up inside.

To those peoples in the huts and villages of half the globe struggling to break the bonds of mass misery, we pledge our best efforts to help them help themselves, for whatever period is required—not because the Communists may be doing it, not because we seek their votes, but because it is right. If a free society cannot help the many who are poor, it cannot save the few who are rich.

Let the word go forth from this time and place, to friend and foe alike, that the torch has been passed to a new generation of Americans.

To our sister republics south of our border, we offer a special pledge —to convert our good words into good deeds—in a new alliance for progress—to assist free men and free governments in casting off the chains of poverty. But this peaceful revolution of hope cannot become the prey of hostile powers. Let all our neighbors know that we shall join with them to oppose aggression or subversion anywhere in the Americas. And let every other power know that this hemisphere intends to remain the master of its own house.

To that world assembly of sovereign states, the United Nations, our last best hope in an age where the instruments of war have far outpaced the instruments of peace, we renew our pledge of support—to prevent it from becoming merely a forum for invective—to strengthen its shield of the new and the weak—and to enlarge the area in which its writ may run.

Finally, to those nations who would make themselves our adversary, we offer not a pledge but a request: that both sides begin anew the quest for peace, before the dark powers of destruction unleashed by science engulf all humanity in planned or accidental self-destruction.

We dare not tempt them with weakness. For only when our arms are sufficient beyond doubt can we be certain beyond doubt that they will never be employed.

But neither can two great and powerful groups of nations take comfort from our present course—both sides overburdened by the cost of modern weapons, both rightly alarmed by the steady spread of the deadly atom, yet both racing to alter that uncertain balance of terror that stays the hand of mankind's final war.

So let us begin anew—remembering on both sides that civility is not a sign of weakness, and sincerity is always subject to proof. Let us never negotiate out of fear. But let us never fear to negotiate.

Let both sides explore what problems unite us instead of belaboring those problems which divide us.

Let both sides, for the first time, formulate serious and precise proposals for the inspection and control of arms—and bring the absolute power to destroy other nations under the absolute control of all nations.

Let both sides seek to invoke the wonders of science instead of its terrors. Together let us explore the stars, conquer the deserts, eradicate disease, tap the ocean depths, and encourage the arts and commerce.

Let both sides unite to heed in all corners of the earth the command of Isaiah—to "undo the heavy burdens [and] let the oppressed go free."

And if a beachhead of cooperation may push back the jungle of suspicion, let both sides join in creating a new endeavor, not a new balance of power, but a new world of law, where the strong are just and the weak secure and the peace preserved.

All this will not be finished in the first one hundred days. Nor will it be finished in the first one thousand days, nor in the life of this administration, nor even perhaps in our lifetime on this planet. But let us begin.

In your hands, my fellow citizens, more than mine, will rest the final success or failure of our course. Since this country was founded, each generation of Americans has been summoned to give testimony to its national loyalty. The graves of young Americans who answered the call to service surround the globe.

Now the trumpet summons us again—not as a call to bear arms, though arms we need—not as a call to battle, though embattled we are—but as a call to bear the burden of a long twilight struggle, year in and year out, "rejoicing in hope, patient in tribulation"—a struggle against the common enemies of man: tyranny, poverty, disease, and war itself.

Can we forge against these enemies a grand and global alliance, North and South, East and West, that can assure a more fruitful life for all mankind? Will you join in that historic effort?

In the long history of the world, only a few generations have been granted the role of defending freedom in its hour of maximum danger. I do not shrink from this responsibility—I welcome it. I do not believe that any of us would exchange places with any other people or any other generation. The energy, the faith, the devotion which we bring to this endeavor will light our country and all who serve it—and the glow from that fire can truly light the world.

And so, my fellow Americans: ask not what your country can do for you—ask what you can do for your country.

My fellow citizens of the world: ask not what America will do for you, but what together we can do for the freedom of man.

And so, my fellow Americans: ask not what your country can do for you—ask what you can do for your country.

My fellow citizens of the world: ask not what America will do for you, but what together we can do for the freedom of man.

Finally, whether you are citizens of America or citizens of the world, ask of us here the same high standards of strength and sacrifice which we ask of you. With a good conscience our only sure reward, with history the final judge of our deeds, let us go forth to lead the land we love, asking His blessing and His help, but knowing that here on earth God's work must truly be our own.

The Inaugural Address
Washington, D.C.
January 20, 1961

At a Democratic fund-raising dinner one year later, Kennedy irreverently parodied his own Inaugural Address:

> We observe tonight not a celebration of freedom but a victory of party. For we have sworn to pay off the same party debt our forebears ran up nearly a year and three months ago.
>
> Our deficit will not be paid off in the next hundred days. Nor will it be paid off in the first one thousand days, nor in the life of this administration, perhaps even in our lifetime on this planet. But let us begin—remembering that generosity is not a sign of weakness and that ambassadors are always subject to Senate confirmation. For if the Democratic Party cannot be helped by the many who are poor, it cannot be saved by the few who are rich. So let us begin.

Washington, D.C.
January 20, 1962

CHAPTER 2

The Role of the President

Convinced that this country had been drifting uncertainly both at home and abroad, John Kennedy campaigned on the need to restore vigorous executive leadership in Washington. Once in the White House, he found the crises more intensive, the choices more difficult, and the criticism more inevitable than he had anticipated. By accepting both blame and brickbats with relative equanimity—particularly after the Cuban Bay of Pigs invasion fiasco early in his first year—he pleased and astonished Washington, learned from his mistakes, and built the kind of Presidency he had contemplated: dedicated, decisive, determined, and effective.

The Vital Center of Action

The modern presidential campaign covers every issue in and out of the platform from cranberries to creation. But the public is rarely alerted to a candidate's views about the central issue on which all the rest turn. That central issue . . . is not the farm problem or defense or India. It is the Presidency itself.

Of course, a candidate's views on specific policies are important, but Theodore Roosevelt and William Howard Taft shared policy views with entirely different results in the White House. Of course, it is important to elect a good man with good intentions, but Woodrow Wilson and Warren G. Harding were both good men of good intentions; so were Lincoln and Buchanan; but there is a Lincoln Room in the White House and no Buchanan Room.

The history of this nation—its brightest and its bleakest pages—has been written largely in terms of the different views our Presidents have had of the Presidency itself. This history ought to tell us that the American people in 1960 have an imperative right to know what any man bidding for the Presidency thinks about the place he is bidding for, whether he is aware of and willing to use the powerful resources of that office; whether his model will be Taft or Roosevelt, Wilson or Harding.

Not since the days of Woodrow Wilson has any candidate spoken on the Presidency itself before the votes have been irrevocably cast. Let us hope that the 1960 campaign, in addition to discussing the familiar issues where our positions too often blur, will also talk about the Presidency itself, as an instrument for dealing with these issues, as an office with varying roles, powers, and limitations.

During the past eight years, we have seen one concept of the Presidency at work. Our needs and hopes have been eloquently stated—but the initiative and follow-through have too often been left to others. And too often his own objectives have been lost by the President's failure to override objections from within his own party, in the Congress or even in his Cabinet.

The American people in 1952 and 1956 may have preferred this detached, limited concept of the Presidency after twenty years of fast-moving, creative presidential rule. Perhaps historians will regard this as necessarily one of those frequent periods of consolidation, a time to draw breath, recoup our national energy. To quote the State of the

Union message: "No Congress . . . on surveying the state of the nation, has met with a more pleasing prospect than that which appears at the present time."

Unfortunately this is not Mr. Eisenhower's last message to the Congress, but Calvin Coolidge's. He followed to the White House Mr. Harding, whose sponsor declared very frankly that the times did not demand a first-rate President. If true, the times and the man met.

But the question is what do the times—and the people—demand for the next four years in the White House?

They demand a vigorous proponent of the national interest—not a passive broker for conflicting private interests. They demand a man capable of acting as the commander in chief of the Grand Alliance, not merely a bookkeeper who feels that his work is done when the numbers on the balance sheet come out even. They demand that he be the head of the responsible party, not rise so far above politics as to be invisible—a man who will formulate and fight for legislative policies, not be a casual bystander to the legislative process.

Today a restricted concept of the Presidency is not enough. For beneath today's surface gloss of peace and prosperity are increasingly dangerous, unsolved, long postponed problems that will inevitably explode to the surface during the next four years of the next administration—the growing missile gap, the rise of Communist China, the despair of the underdeveloped nations, the explosive situations in Berlin and in the Formosa Straits, the deterioration of NATO, the lack of an arms control agreement, and all the domestic problems of our farms, cities, and schools.

This administration has not faced up to these and other problems. Much has been said—but I am reminded of the old Chinese proverb: "There is a great deal of noise on the stairs but nobody comes into the room."

The President's State of the Union message reminded me of the exhortation from *King Lear* that goes: "I will do such things—what they are I know not . . . but they shall be the wonders of the earth."

In the decade that lies ahead—in the challenging revolutionary sixties—the American Presidency will demand more than ringing manifestos issued from the rear of the battle. It will demand that the President place himself in the very thick of the fight, that he care passionately about the fate of the people he leads, that he be willing to serve them at the risk of incurring their momentary displeasure.

Whatever the political affiliation of our next President, whatever his views may be on all the issues and problems that rush in upon us, he must above all be the Chief Executive in every sense of the word. He must be prepared to exercise the fullest powers of his office—all that are specified and some that are not. He must master complex problems as well as receive one-page memoranda. He must originate action as well as study groups. He must reopen the channel of communication between the world of thought and the seat of power.

Ulysses Grant considered the President "a purely administrative officer." If he administered the government departments efficiently, delegated his functions smoothly, and performed his ceremonies of state with decorum and grace, no more was to be expected of him. But that is not the place the Presidency was meant to have in American life. The President is alone, at the top—the loneliest job there is, as Harry Truman has said.

If there is destructive dissension among the services, he alone can step in and straighten it out—instead of waiting for unanimity. If administrative agencies are not carrying out their mandate—if a brushfire threatens some part of the globe—he alone can act, without waiting for the Congress. If his farm program fails, he alone deserves the blame, not his secretary of agriculture.

"The President is at liberty, both in law and conscience, to be as big a man as he can." So wrote Professor Woodrow Wilson. But President Woodrow Wilson discovered that to be a big man in the White House inevitably brings cries of "dictatorship."

So did Lincoln and Jackson and the two Roosevelts. And so may the next occupant of that office, if he is the man the times demand. But how much better it would be, in the turbulent sixties, to have a Roosevelt or a Wilson than to have another James Buchanan, cringing in the White House, afraid to move.

For beneath today's surface gloss of peace and prosperity are increasingly dangerous, unsolved, long postponed problems that will inevitably explode to the surface.

Nor can we afford a Chief Executive who is praised primarily for what he did not do, the disasters he prevented, the bills he vetoed—a President wishing his subordinates would produce more missiles or build more schools. We will need instead what the Constitution envisioned: a Chief Executive who is the vital center of action in our whole scheme of government.

This includes the legislative process as well. The President cannot afford—for the sake of the office as well as the nation—to be another Warren G. Harding, described by one backer as a man who "would, when elected, sign whatever bill the Senate sent him—and not send bills for the Senate to pass." Rather he must know when to lead the Congress, when to consult it, and when he should act alone.

Having served fourteen years in the legislative branch, I would not look with favor upon its domination by the executive. Under our government of "power as the rival of power," to use Hamilton's phrase, Congress must not surrender its responsibilities. But neither should it dominate. However large its share in the formulation of domestic programs, it is the President alone who must make the major decisions of our foreign policy.

That is what the Constitution wisely commands. And, even domestically, the President must initiate policies and devise laws to meet the needs of the nation. And he must be prepared to use all the resources of his office to insure the enactment of that legislation—even when conflict is the result.

By the end of his term Theodore Roosevelt was not popular in the Congress—particularly when he criticized an amendment to the Treasury appropriation which forbade the use of Secret Service men to investigate congressmen.

And the feeling was mutual, Roosevelt saying: "I do not much admire the Senate, because it is such a helpless body when efficient work is to be done."

And Woodrow Wilson was even more bitter after his frustrating quarrels. Asked if he might run for the Senate in 1920, he replied: "Outside of the United States, the Senate does not amount to a damn. And inside the United States the Senate is mostly despised. They haven't had a thought down there in fifty years."

But, however bitter their farewells, the facts of the matter are that Roosevelt and Wilson did get things done—not only through their executive powers but through the Congress as well. Calvin Coolidge, on the other hand, departed from Washington with cheers of Congress still ringing in his ears. But when his World Court bill was under fire on Capitol Hill, he sent no messages, gave no encouragement to the bill's leaders, and paid little or no attention to the whole proceeding—and the cause of world justice was set back.

To be sure, Coolidge had held the usual White House breakfasts with congressional leaders—but they were aimed, as he himself said, at "good fellowship," not a discussion of "public business." And at his press conferences, according to press historians, where he preferred to talk about the local flower show and its exhibits, reporters who finally extracted from him a single sentence—"I'm against that bill"—would rush to file tongue-in-cheek dispatches, proclaiming that "President Coolidge, in a fighting mood, today served notice on Congress that he intended to combat, with all the resources at his command, the pending bill. . . ."

But in the coming years we will need a real fighting mood in the White House—a man who will not retreat in the face of pressure from his congressional leaders—who will not let down those supporting his views on the floor. Divided government over the past six years has only been further confused by this lack of legislative leadership. To restore it next year will help restore purpose to both the Presidency and the Congress.

The facts of the matter are that legislative leadership is not possible without party leadership, in the most political sense—and Mr. Eisenhower prefers to stay above politics (although a weekly newsmagazine last fall reported the startling news, and I quote, that "President Eisenhower is emerging as a major political figure"). When asked, early in his first term, how he liked the "game of politics," he replied with a frown that his questioner was using a derogatory phrase. "Being President," he said, "is a very great experience . . . but the word 'politics' . . . I have no great liking for that."

But no President, it seems to me, can escape politics. He has not only been chosen by the nation—he has been chosen by his party. And if he insists that he is "President of all the people" and should, therefore, offend none of them—if he blurs the issues and differences between the parties—if he neglects the party machinery and avoids his party's leadership—then he has not only weakened the political party as an instrument of the democratic process—he has dealt a blow to the democratic process itself.

I prefer the example of Abe Lincoln, who loved politics with the passion of a born practitioner. For example, he waited up all night in 1863 to get the crucial returns on the Ohio governorship. When the Unionist candidate was elected, Lincoln wired: "Glory to God in the highest. Ohio has saved the Nation."

But the White House is not only the center of political leadership. It must be the center of moral leadership—a "bully pulpit," as Theodore Roosevelt described it. For only the President represents the national interest. And upon him alone converge all the needs and aspirations of all parts of the country, all departments of government, all nations of the world.

It is not enough merely to represent prevailing sentiment—to follow McKinley's practice, as described by Joe Cannon, of "keeping his ear so close to the ground he got it full of grasshoppers." We will need in the sixties a President who is willing and able to summon his national constituency to its finest hour—to alert the people to our dangers and our opportunities—to demand of them the sacrifices that will be necessary. FDR's words in his first inaugural still ring true: "In every dark hour of our national life, a leadership of frankness and vigor has met with that understanding and support of the people themselves which is essential to victory."

Roosevelt fulfilled the role of moral leadership. So did Wilson and Lincoln, Truman and Jackson and Teddy Roosevelt. They led the people as well as the government—they fought for great ideals as well as bills. And the time has come to demand that kind of leadership again.

And so, as this vital campaign begins, let us discuss the issues the next President will face—but let us also discuss the powers and tools with which we must face them.

For we must endow that office with extraordinary strength and vision. We must act in the image of Abraham Lincoln summoning his wartime Cabinet to a meeting on the Emancipation Proclamation. That Cabinet had been carefully chosen to please and reflect many elements in the country. But "I have gathered you together," Lincoln said, "to hear what I have written down. I do not wish your advice about the main matter—that I have determined for myself."

And later, when he went to sign after several hours of exhausting handshaking that had left his arm weak, he said to those present: "If my name goes down in history, it will be for this act. My whole soul is in it. If my hand trembles when I sign this proclamation, all who examine the document hereafter will say: 'He hesitated.' "

But Lincoln's hand did not tremble. He did not hesitate. He did not equivocate. For he was the President of the United States.

It is in this spirit that we must go forth in the coming months and years.

National Press Club
Washington, D.C., January 14, 1960

The Leader of the Free World

I have premised my campaign on the central issue of the Presidency itself—its powers, their use and their decline. . . . For this is no mere popularity contest. We may enjoy the sideshows, the fanfare, and the headlines. But it is a President we are electing. And no Democrat can dodge the real issue of the Presidency's decline if he hopes to win in 1960. . . .

Perhaps we could afford a Coolidge following Harding. And perhaps we could afford a Pierce following Fillmore. But after Buchanan this nation needed a Lincoln—after Taft we needed a Wilson—after Hoover we needed Franklin Roosevelt. . . . And after eight years of Eisenhower, this nation needs a strong, creative Democrat in the White House.

And nowhere is this need more critical than in the conduct of our foreign affairs. For Pennsylvania Avenue is no longer a local thoroughfare. It runs through Paris and London, Ankara and Teheran, New Delhi and Tokyo. And if the soul of a journey is liberty, as Hazlitt has said, then the road from the White House that encircles the globe is freedom's way—the artery that makes all the Free World neighbors as well as allies.

And if Washington is the capital of the Free World, the President must be its leader. Our Constitution requires it—our history requires it—our very survival requires it. In foreign affairs, said the Supreme Court, "the

President alone has the power to speak or listen as the representative of this nation."

"The President alone . . ." And he is alone—at the top—in the loneliest job in the world. He cannot share this power, he cannot delegate it, he cannot adjourn. He alone is the Chief of State, not the National Security Council, Vice-President and all. He alone decides whether to recognize foreign governments, not his Senate minority leader. . . . He alone must decide what areas we defend—not the Congress or the military or the CIA, and certainly not some beleaguered generalissimo on an island domain.

If nuclear tests are to be halted—if disarmament is to become a reality—then he alone must lead the way, and not leave it to the warped judgment of the AEC [Atomic Energy Commission] and the Pentagon. And if India is to be saved—if the missile gap is to be closed—if we are to help Latin American democracies (instead of dictators)—the decision is his alone, and not that of the little men with little vision in the Bureau of the Budget.

In this 1960 campaign, four facts ought to be made clear about presidential responsibility in foreign affairs:

First, the President's responsibility cannot be delegated. For he is the one focal point of responsibility. His office is the single channel through which there flow the torrential pressures and needs of every state, every federal agency, every friend and foe.

He does not have to wait for unanimous agreement below, summed up in one-page memoranda that stifle dissent. He does not have to wait for crises to spur decisions that are long overdue. He must look ahead—and sometimes act alone—like Woodrow Wilson, locked in his study, typing his own notes to the Kaiser; or, in the words of his assistant, devouring a stack of state papers like "a starving man with a pile of flapjacks" (somewhat in contrast, I might add, to the veteran White House usher's description of Calvin Coolidge: "No other President in my time ever slept so much").

For Woodrow Wilson knew, in his own words, that in a nation's foreign affairs, the President must of necessity "be its guide—take every first step of action, utter every initial judgment . . . suggest and in large measure control its course." Thus most of the great landmarks of our foreign policy bear the name of the President who initiated them—Washington's Proclamation of Neutrality, Monroe's Doctrine, Wilson's Fourteen Points, Roosevelt's Four Freedoms, and Truman's Point Four Program.

Occasionally we remember secretaries of state as well—but usually when they overshadowed their chief: Seward for the Alaska purchase, not Andrew Johnson; Hay for the Open Door policy, not McKinley; Hughes for the Washington treaty, not Harding. . . . Certainly the President should use his secretary of state. But he should be the captain of the bridge, and not leave it to the helmsman to sail without direction. For in the words of Socrates: "If a man does not know to what port he is sailing, no wind is favorable."

Secondly, the President's responsibility cannot be abdicated to the Congress. Certainly Congress has a role in foreign affairs, constitutionally and practically. It can approve—it can appropriate. But it cannot exercise ultimate power—for it has no ultimate responsibility. It has no way of relating widely separated events, or assessing day-to-day dangers. It has no ambassadors or armies, no access to secret reports, no right to negotiate treaties or construct coalitions. We recognized this in our earliest days when we asked the king of Sweden to address no more letters "to the President and the Senate of the United States."

The President's responsibility cannot be delegated. For he is the one focal point of responsibility. His office is the single channel through which there flow the torrential pressures and needs of every state, every federal agency, every friend and foe.

For these burdens are essentially the President's—and he cannot shift his responsibility to the Congress, under the guise of bipartisanship, asking our support for an unknown policy on Quemoy and Matsu, asking our support for a Middle East doctrine that was more public relations than policy. For bipartisanship does not mean—and was never designed to mean—rubber-stamping every executive blunder without debate. . . .

No modern President of either party, of course, would deceive the Congress—like Secretary of State Webster, reportedly using his own secret map to convince the Senate that he had cheated the British in drawing the Canadian border, while at the same time Lord Ashburton was using his own secret map to convince Parliament that in reality he had cheated Webster. Nor will today's Congress and Executive actually meet in mortal combat—as Secretary of State Clay and Senator John Randolph did, when the Senate wasn't consulted on the Panama Conference, and the Senator denounced Clay's aged mother for bringing into the world "this being, so brilliant yet so corrupt, which, like a rotten mackerel by moonlight, shines and stinks."

But even today the President should be prepared to resist unwarranted congressional intrusions in foreign affairs. Above all, he must protect his Foreign Service against thoughtless congressional attacks and investigations. There are always some farm organizations looking out for their department—just as labor unions, veterans, business groups, and postal employees look out for theirs. But the Foreign Service has no pressure groups, no constituency—only the President. And the next President—a Democratic President—must champion and restore this vital agency.

Third, the President's responsibility is to all the people. He must strengthen them—and draw strength from them; educate them—and represent them; pledge his best—and inspire theirs. If he rejects "Operation Candor" as politically dangerous, if he constantly reassures an imperiled nation that all is well, if he answers all critics with an air of infallibility, or, worst of all, if he himself is not informed and therefore cannot inform the people—then the Presidency has failed the American people.

We cannot be reassured that we are building the best defense merely because we now have a general in the White House. For we have had generals in the White House before—and when Grant was asked in 1868 if he really wanted to be President, he was honest enough to reply: "No, I am a military man, not a statesman. I would just like to be Mayor of Galena long enough to build a sidewalk from my house to the station."

Our greatest foreign policy Presidents were not military men. They did not request unquestioning faith. They kept the people informed. They eloquently defined the aims and aspirations of the nation. Mr. Eisenhower's messages may be delivered in well-chosen words—but they sound more like the chairman of the board describing another profitable quarter.

There has been no willingness to say the harsh things that sometimes need to be said—to take the hard steps that may not be popular or convenient—like Thomas Jefferson, purchasing the Louisiana Territory despite outcries from the budget-cutters of his day that we could not afford $15 million for this "wilderness"—or like George Washington, standing by the Jay Treaty despite being abused, as he wrote, "in such exaggerated and indecent terms as could scarcely be applied to Nero, to a notorious defaulter or even to a common pickpocket."

Compare these Presidents to those who yielded to public pressure instead of educating it: Madison being dragged into a war he knew was unsound; McKinley being led into a war he knew was unnecessary; Harding blessing a disarmament conference he knew was unwise; Coolidge hailing a peace pact he knew was unworkable. We cannot afford in the turbulent sixties the persistent indecision of a James Buchanan, which caused Ohio's Senator Sherman to say: "The Constitution provides for every accidental contingency in the Executive—except a vacancy in the mind of the President."

In 1960 we must elect a President who will lead the people—who will risk, if he must, his popularity for his responsibility. . . .

Fourth and finally, the President's responsibility is to the Free World as well as the nation. Even before the Constitution was ratified, Jefferson predicted that "the election of a President some years hence will be much more interesting to certain nations of Europe than the election of a king of Poland ever was." And today, as the 1960 campaign begins, every nation of Europe—and the world—is in fact watching our politics and policies. As the British cartoonist David Low has said of every Free World citizen: "Fate has made us all Honorary Americans."

And thus the President of the United States—the leader of that Free World—must represent all its nations, in his every word and deed. And to them in turn his words—in his every press conference and message—represent the real "Voice of America." If they hear not one voice but many—from State, from Treasury, from Defense—they feel in doubt. And if they see him in doubt, they feel betrayed. . . .

But if the President is to be creative in foreign policy, his party must be creative. . . . Historically and inevitably the forces of inertia and reaction in the Republican Party oppose any powerful voice in the White House—Republican or Democrat—that seeks to speak for the nation as a whole. Theodore Roosevelt discovered that. Herbert Hoover discovered that and, even before he could run for President, Nelson Rockefeller discovered it. Even President Eisenhower considered forming a third party in 1954. No Republican President, no matter how dedicated, can escape the quicksand of his party's entrenched interests.

But the Democratic Party is a national party—it believes in strong leadership—and, with your help, we will give the nation that leadership in January 1961.

John Adams, our second Chief Executive, would not war with France, despite popular pressures from this young and reckless land. In this way he preserved the infant nation—he paved the way for the Louisiana Purchase—but he also insured his own bitter defeat for reelection. Yet later, as death drew near, he wrote to a trusted friend: "I desire no other inscription over my gravestone than this: 'Here lies John Adams, who took upon himself the responsibility of peace with France. . . .' "

In 1960, the next President of the United States must be prepared to take upon himself the responsibility of peace with all the world.

California Democratic Clubs Convention
Fresno, California, February 12, 1960

The Champion of Freedom

I run for the office of the Presidency not because I think it is an easy job. In many ways I think the next years are going to be the most difficult years in our history. I don't run for the office of the Presidency telling you that if you elect me life is going to be easy, because I don't think that life is going to be easy for Americans in the next decade. But I run for the Presidency because I do not want it said in the years when our generation held political power that those were the years when America began to slip, when America began to slide. I don't want historians writing in 1970 to say that the balance of power in the 1950s and the 1960s began to turn against the United States and against the cause of freedom. I don't want it said that when we held office and when we were citizens that the Russians and the Chinese Communists began to expand their power. The New Frontier is not what I promise I am going to do for you. The New Frontier is what I ask you to do for our country. Give me your help, your hand, your voice, and this country can move again.

Labor Day Campaign Kickoff
Detroit, Michigan, September 5, 1960

. . . When the Federalist Party was old and tired, Thomas Jefferson began the Democratic Party. His first action early as President was the Louisiana Purchase, against the wishes of all those who came from my own section of New England, who wanted the country to remain small, secluded, belonging to a few. Instead, he took a chance and spread the United States west, and even though when he became President the western boundary of America was Virginia, he sent Lewis and Clark all the way to the Pacific Ocean to open up the entire United States. That has been the spirit of the Democratic Party. It has been the spirit of Jackson and Roosevelt and Truman and all the rest, and that is the spirit we are going to recapture.

Campaign Remarks
Muskegon, Michigan, September 5, 1960

The Responsible Officer of Government

Q: Sir, since last Saturday a certain foreign policy situation [the failed Bay of Pigs invasion] has given rise to many conflicting stories. . . . In view of the fact we are taking a propaganda lambasting around the world, why is it not useful, sir, for us to explore with you the real facts behind this, or our motivations?

THE PRESIDENT: Well, I think, in answer to your question, that we have to make a judgment as to how much we can usefully say that would aid the interest of the United States. . . .

There's an old saying that victory has a hundred fathers and defeat is an orphan. . . .

But I will say to you, Mr. Vanocur, that I have said as much as I feel can be usefully said by me in regard to the events of the past few days. [Avoiding further] statements, detailed discussions, [is] not to conceal responsibility because I'm the responsible officer of the government—and that is quite obvious.

President's News Conference
Washington, D.C., April 21, 1961

Q: Mr. President, your brother, Ted, recently on television said that after seeing the cares of office on you, he wasn't sure he'd ever be interested in being the President. I wonder if you could tell us whether if you had it to do over again, you would work for the Presidency and whether you can recommend the job to others.

THE PRESIDENT: Well, the answer is . . . to the first is yes and the second is no. I don't recommend it to others—at least for a while.

President's News Conference
Washington, D.C., March 29, 1962

Q: Mr. President, perhaps . . . you would comment for us on the press in general, as you see it from the Presidency. Perhaps, its treatment of your administration, treatment of the issues of the day?

THE PRESIDENT: Well, I am reading more and enjoying it less . . . but I have not complained nor do I plan to make any general complaints. I read and talk to myself about it, but I don't plan to issue any general statement on the press. I think that they are doing their task, as a critical branch, the fourth estate. And I am attempting to do mine. And we are going to live together for a period, and then go our separate ways.

President's News Conference,
Washington, D.C., May 9, 1962

The Ultimate Decision Maker

WILLIAM H. LAWRENCE, AMERICAN BROADCASTING COMPANY: As you look back upon your first two years in office, sir, has your experience in the office matched your expectations? You had studied a good deal the power of the Presidency, the methods of its operations. How has this worked out as you saw it in advance?

THE PRESIDENT: . . . I would say that the problems are more difficult than I had imagined them to be. The responsibilities placed on the United States are greater than I imagined them to be, and there are greater limitations upon our ability to bring about a favorable result than I had imagined them to be. And I think that is probably true of anyone who becomes President, because there is such a difference between those who advise or speak or legislate, and between the man who must select from the various alternatives proposed and say that this shall be the policy of the United States. It is much easier to make the speeches than it is to finally make the judgments, because unfortunately your advisers are frequently divided. If you take the wrong course, and on occasion I have, the President bears the burden of the responsibility quite rightly. The advisers move on to new advice.

GEORGE E. HERMAN, COLUMBIA BROADCASTING SYSTEM: I would like to go back to the question of the consensus [on responding to Soviet missiles in Cuba] and your relationship to the consensus. You have said and the Constitution says that the decision can be made only by the President.

THE PRESIDENT: Well, you know that old story about Abraham Lincoln and the Cabinet. He says, "All in favor, say 'aye,' " and the whole Cabinet voted "aye," and then, "All opposed, 'no,' " and Lincoln voted "no," and he said, "The vote is no." So that naturally the Constitution places the responsibility on the President.

There was some disagreement with the course we finally adopted, but the course we finally adopted had the advantage of permitting other steps if this one was unsuccessful. In other words, we were starting in a sense at a minimum place. Then if that were unsuccessful, we could have gradually stepped it up until we had gone into a much more massive action, which might have become necessary if the first step had been unsuccessful. I would think that the majority finally came to accept that, though at the beginning there was a much sharper division. And after all, this was very valuable, because the people who were involved had particular responsibilities of their own; Mr. McNamara, Secretary of Defense, who therefore had to advise me on the military capacity of the United States in that area, the Secretary of State, who had to advise on the attitude of the OAS [Organization of American States] and NATO. So that in my opinion [the fact that] the majority came to accept the course we finally took . . . made it much easier. In the Cuban crisis of 1961 the advice of those who were brought in on the executive branch [side] was also unanimous, and the advice was wrong. And I was responsible. . . . No matter how many advisers you have, frequently they are divided, and the President must finally choose.

The other point is something that President Eisenhower said to me on January nineteenth [1961]. He said "There are no easy matters that will ever come to you as President. If they are easy, they will be settled at a lower level." So that the matters that come to you as President are always the difficult matters, and matters that carry with them large implications. So this contributes to some of the burdens of the office of the Presidency, which other Presidents have commented on.

It is much easier to make the speeches than it is to finally make the judgments, because unfortunately your advisers are frequently divided. If you take the wrong course, and on occasion I have, the President bears the burden of the responsibility quite rightly. The advisers move on to new advice.

SANDER VANOCUR, NATIONAL BROADCASTING COMPANY: . . . Is it true that during your first year, sir, you would get on the phone personally to the State Department and try to get a response to some inquiry that had been made?

THE PRESIDENT: Yes, I still do that when I can, because I think there is a great tendency in government to have papers stay on desks too long, and it seems to me that is really one function . . . after all, the President can't administer a department, but at least he can be a stimulant. . . .

MR. VANOCUR: You once said that you were reading more and enjoying it less. Are you still as avid a newspaper reader, magazine—I remember those of us who traveled with you on the campaign, a magazine wasn't safe around you.

THE PRESIDENT: Oh, yes. . . . It is never pleasant to be reading things that are not agreeable news, but I would say that it is an invaluable arm of the Presidency, as a check really on what is going on in the administration, and more things come to my attention that cause me concern or give me information. So I would think that Mr. Khrushchev, operating a totalitarian system—which has many "advantages" as far as being able to move in secret, and all the rest—there is a terrific disadvantage not having the abrasive quality of the press applied to you daily. . . . Even though we never like it, and even though we wish they didn't write it, and even though we disapprove, there isn't any doubt that we could not do the job at all in a free society without a very, very active press.

Now, on the other hand, the press has the responsibility not to distort things for political purposes, not to just [select] some news in order to prove a political point. It seems to me their obligation is to be as tough as they can on the administration but do it in a way which is directed toward getting as close to the truth as they can get and not merely because of some political motivation.

MR. VANOCUR: Mr. President, back before you were elected, your father used to have a favorite story he told reporters. He asked you once why do you want the job, and he cited the reasons why you shouldn't want it, and you apparently gave him an answer—I don't know whether it satisfied him, but apparently you satisfied yourself. Would you give him the same answer today after serving in this office for two years?

THE PRESIDENT: Oh, you mean "somebody is going to do it [be President]"?

MR. VANOCUR: Yes, sir.

THE PRESIDENT: Yes. I think that there are a lot of satisfactions to the Presidency, particularly, as I say, we are all concerned as citizens and as parents and all the rest, with all the problems we have been talking about tonight. They are all the problems which if I was not the President, I would be concerned about as a father or as a citizen. So at least you have an opportunity to do something about them. And if what you do is useful and successful, then of course that is a great satisfaction.

Television and Radio
Year-end Conversation with the President
Washington, D.C., December 17, 1962

The Party Leader

Our Founding Fathers did not realize that the basic fact which has made our system work was outside the Constitution. And that was the development of political parties in this country so that the American people would have the means of placing responsibility on one group, that group would have a chance to carry out its program, and the American people would have an opportunity to indicate their dissatisfaction by going to an alternative.

That system has served us well, and there is no greater responsibility in that sense that a President has, as President Truman has pointed out, than he has as a leader of a political party, and especially this political party, the oldest in the world, the oldest in our country's history.

When we stand here next to these pictures of Presidents Jefferson, Jackson, Cleveland, Wilson, Franklin Roosevelt, and Harry Truman, we are standing next to great Presidents. And we are also standing next to great party leaders who were able to use the party to carry out their programs. That is the purpose of all of our exercise. [Political power] is not an end in itself; it is a means of doing the things which this country needs in the sixties, and this country needs a lot at home and abroad.

Remarks to Members of National and State Democratic Committees at the White House Washington, D.C., January 18, 1963

The Happy President

Q: Mr. President: Just shortly after the Bay of Pigs I asked you how you liked being President, and as I remember you said you liked it better before the event. Now you have had a chance to appraise your job, and why do you like it and why do you want to stay in office four more years?

THE PRESIDENT: Well, I find the work rewarding. Whether I am going to stay and what my intentions are and all of the rest, it seems to me it is still a good many, many months away. But as far as the job of President goes, it is rewarding. And I have given before to this group the definition of happiness of the Greeks, and I will define it again: It is full use of your powers along lines of excellence. I find, therefore, the Presidency provides some happiness.

President's News Conference
Washington, D.C., October 31, 1963

CHAPTER 3

The Call to Public Service

John F. Kennedy believed there was no higher calling than politics and government. As a member of the Senate, he took special pride in recalling in his speeches and book, *Profiles in Courage,* the great senators of the past. As a candidate, he pledged a "ministry of talent" composed of the best men and women he could find, regardless of party. As President, he imbued in the career services—including a Foreign Service beleaguered by Senator Joe McCarthy and others—a new sense of pride and obligation, while simultaneously insisting upon higher ethical standards. One of his proudest achievements, the Peace Corps, exemplified his ideal of selfless, dedicated public service.

The Politician and the Intellectual

I can think of nothing more reassuring for all of us than to come again to this institution whose whole purpose is dedicated to the advancement of knowledge and the dissemination of truth.

I belong to a profession where the emphasis is somewhat different. Our political parties, our politicians, are interested, of necessity, in winning popular support—a majority; and only indirectly truth is the object of our controversy. From this polemic of contending factions, the general public is expected to make a discriminating judgment. As the problems have become more complex, as our role as a chief defender of Western civilization has become enlarged, the responsibility of the electorate as a court of last resort has become almost too great. The people desperately seek objectivity and a university such as this fulfills that function.

And the political profession needs to have its temperature lowered in the cooling waters of the scholastic pool. We need both the technical judgment and the disinterested viewpoint of the scholar, to prevent us from becoming imprisoned by our own slogans.

Therefore, it is regrettable that the gap between the intellectual and the politician seems to be growing. Instead of synthesis, clash and discord now characterize the relations between the two groups much of the time. Authors, scholars, and intellectuals can praise every aspect of American society but the political. My desk is flooded with books, articles, and pamphlets criticizing Congress. But rarely, if ever, have I seen any intellectual bestow praise on either the political profession or any political body for its accomplishments, its ability, or its integrity—much less for its intelligence. To many universities and scholars we reap nothing but censure, investigators and perpetrators of what has been called the swinish cult of anti-intellectualism.

James Russell Lowell's satiric attack more than one hundred years ago on Caleb Cushing, a celebrated attorney general and member of Congress, sets the tone: "Gineral C is a drefle smart man, he's ben on all sides that give places or pelf, but consistency still wiz a part of his plan—he's ben true to one party, that is himself."

But in fairness, the way of the intellectual is not altogether serene; in fact, so great has become popular suspicion that a recent survey of

American intellectuals by a national magazine elicited from one of our foremost literary figures the guarded response, "I ain't no intellectual."

Both sides in this battle, it seems to me, are motivated by largely unfounded feelings of distrust. The politician, whose authority rests upon the mandate of the popular will, is resentful of the scholar who can, with dexterity, slip from position to position without dragging the anchor of public opinion. It was this skill that caused Lord Melbourne to say of the youthful historian Macaulay that he wished he was as sure of anything as Macaulay was of everything.

The intellectual, on the other hand, finds it difficult to accept the differences between the laboratory and the legislature. In the former, the goal is truth, pure and simple, without regard to changing currents of public opinion; in the latter, compromises and majorities and procedural customs and rights affect the ultimate decision as to what is right or just or good. And even when they realize this difference, most intellectuals consider their chief functions that of the critic—and politicians are sensitive to critics (possibly because we have so many of them). "Many intellectuals," Sidney Hook has said, "would rather die than agree with the majority, even on the rare occasions when the majority is right."

It seems to me that the time has come for intellectuals and politicians alike to put aside those horrible weapons of modern internecine warfare, the barbed thrust, the acid pen, and, most sinister of all, the rhetorical blast. Let us not emphasize all on which we differ but all we have in common. Let us consider not what we fear separately but what we share together.

First, I would ask both groups to recall that the American politician of today and the American intellectual of today are descended from a common ancestry. Our nation's first great politicians were also among the nation's first great writers and scholars. The founders of the American Constitution were also the founders of American scholarship. The works of Jefferson, Madison, Hamilton, Franklin, Paine, and John Adams—to name but a few—influenced the literature of the world as well as its geography. Books were their tools, not their enemies. Locke, Milton, Sydney, Montesquieu, Coke, and Bolingbroke were among those widely read in political circles and frequently quoted in political pamphlets. Our political leaders traded in the free commerce of ideas with lasting results both here and abroad.

In those golden years, our political leaders moved from one field to another with amazing versatility and vitality. Jefferson and Franklin still throw long shadows over many fields of learning. A contemporary described Jefferson, "A gentleman of 32, who could calculate an eclipse, survey an estate, tie an artery, plan an edifice, try a cause, break a horse, dance a minuet, and play the violin."

Daniel Webster could throw thunderbolts at Hayne on the Senate floor and then stroll a few steps down the corridor and dominate the Supreme Court as the foremost lawyer of his time. John Quincy Adams, after being summarily dismissed from the Senate for a notable display of independence, could become Boylston Professor of Rhetoric and Oratory at Harvard and then become a great secretary of state. (Those were the happy days when Harvard professors had no difficulty getting Senate confirmation.)

I would urge that our political parties and our universities recognize the need for greater cooperation and understanding between politicians and intellectuals.

The versatility also existed on the frontier. An obituary of Missouri's first senator, Thomas Hart Benton, the man whose tavern brawl with Jackson in Tennessee caused him to flee the state, said, "With a readiness that was often surprising, he could quote from a Roman law or a Greek philosopher, from Virgil's Georgics, the Arabian Nights, Herodotus, or Sancho Panza, from the Sacred Carpets, the German reformers or Adam Smith; from Fenelon or Hudibras, from the financial reports of Necca or the doings of the Council of Trent, from the debates on the adoption of the Constitution or intrigues of the kitchen cabinet or from some forgotten speech of a deceased Member of Congress."

This link between the American scholar and the American politician remained for more than a century. Just one hundred years ago in the presidential campaign of 1856, the Republicans sent three brilliant orators around the campaign circuit: William Cullen Bryant, Henry Wadsworth Longfellow, and Ralph Waldo Emerson. Those were the carefree days when the eggheads were all Republicans.

I would hope that both groups, recalling their common heritage, might once again forge a link between the intellectual and political professions. I know that scholars may prefer the mysteries of pure scholarship or the delights of abstract discourse. But, "would you have counted him a friend of ancient Greece," as George William Curtis asked a century ago during the Kansas-Nebraska controversy, "who quietly discussed patriotism on the Greek summer day through whose hopeless and immortal hours Leonidas and his 300 stood at Thermopylae for liberty? Was John Milton to conjugate Greek verbs in his library or talk of the liberty of the ancient Shunamites when the liberty of Englishmen was imperiled?" No, the duty of the scholar, particularly in a republic such as ours, is to contribute his objective views and his sense of liberty to the affairs of his state and nation.

Secondly, I would remind both groups that the American politician and the American intellectual operate within a common framework—a framework we call liberty. Freedom of expression is not divisible into political expression and intellectual expression. The lock on the door of the legislature, the Parliament, or the assembly hall—by order of the king, the commissar, or the Führer—has historically been followed or preceded by a lock on the door of the university, the library, or the printshop. And if the first blow for freedom in any subjugated land is struck by a political leader, the second is struck by a book, a newspaper, or a pamphlet.

Unfortunately, in more recent times, politicians and intellectuals have quarreled bitterly, too bitterly in some cases, over how each group has met the modern challenge to freedom both at home and abroad. Politicians have questioned the discernment with which intellectuals have reacted to the siren call of the extreme left; and intellectuals have tended to accuse politicians of not always being aware, especially here at home, of the toxic effects of freedom restrained.

While differences in judgment where freedom is endangered are perhaps inevitable, there should, nevertheless, be more basic agreement on fundamentals. In this field we should be natural allies, working more closely for the common cause against the common enemy.

Third and finally, I would stress the great potential gain for both groups resulting from increased political cooperation.

The American intellectual and scholar today must decide, as Goethe put it, whether he is to be an anvil—or a hammer. Today, for many, the stage of the anvil, at least in its formal phases, is complete. The question he faces is whether he is to be a hammer—whether he is to give to the world in which he was reared and educated the broadest possible benefits of his learning. As one who is familiar with the political world, I can testify that we need it.

For example: The password for all legislation, promoted by either party, is "progress." But how do we tell what is progress and what is retreat? Those of us who may be too close to the issue, or too politically or emotionally involved in it, look for the objective word of the scholar. Indeed, the operation of our political life is such that we may not even be debating the real issues.

In foreign affairs, for example, the parties dispute over which is best fitted to implement the long-accepted policies of collective security and Soviet containment. But perhaps these policies are no longer adequate, perhaps these goals are no longer meaningful—the debate goes on nevertheless, for neither party is in a position to undertake the reappraisal necessary, particularly if the solutions presented are more complex to, and less popular with, the electorate.

Or take our agricultural program, for another example. Republicans and Democrats debate long over whether flexible or rigid price supports should be in effect. But this may not be the real issue at all—and in fact I am convinced that it is not, that neither program offers any long-range solution to our many real farm problems. The scholars and the universities might reexamine this whole area and come up with some real answers—the political parties and their conventions rarely will.

Other examples could be given indefinitely—where do we draw the line between free trade and protection; when does taxation become prohibitive; what is the most effective use we can make of our present nuclear potential? The intellectuals who can draw upon their rational disinterested approach and their fund of learning to help reshape our political life can make a tremendous contribution to their society while gaining new respect for their own group.

I do not say that our political and public life should be turned over to experts who ignore public opinion. Nor would I adopt from the Belgian constitution of 1893 the provision giving three votes instead of one to college graduates; or give Harvard a seat in the Congress as William and Mary was once represented in the Virginia House of Burgesses.

But, I would urge that our political parties and our universities recognize the need for greater cooperation and understanding between politicians and intellectuals. We do not need scholars or politicians like Lord John Russell, of whom Queen Victoria remarked, "he would be a better man if he knew a third subject—but he was interested in nothing but the constitution of 1688 and himself." What we need are men who can ride easily over broad fields of knowledge and recognize the mutual dependence of our two worlds.

"Don't teach my boy poetry," an English mother recently wrote the provost of Harrow. "Don't teach my boy poetry; he is going to stand for Parliament." Well, perhaps she was right—but if more politicians knew poetry, and more poets knew politics, I am convinced the world would be a little better place in which to live on this commencement day of 1956.

Harvard University Commencement
Cambridge, Massachusetts, June 14, 1956

The Senate's Distinguished Traditions

Mr. President, as chairman of the Special Senate Committee on the Senate Reception Room, established by Senate Resolution 145 of the 84th Congress, as amended, I wish to report to the Senate that our committee has completed its deliberations, and its surveys of scholarly and senatorial opinion as described in the committee report, and recommends that there be placed in the five unfilled spaces in the Senate reception room paintings portraying the following five outstanding senators of the past:

Senator Henry Clay, of Kentucky, who served in the Senate 1806–7, 1810–11, 1831–42, 1849–52. Resourceful expert in the art of the possible, his fertile mind, persuasive voice, skillful politics, and tireless energies were courageously devoted to the reconciliation of conflict between North and South, East and West, capitalism and agrarianism. A political leader who put the national good above party, a spokesman for the West whose love for the Union outweighed sectional pressures, he acquired more influence and more respect as responsible leader of the loyal but ardent opposition than many who occupied the White House. His adroit statesmanship and political finesse in times of national crisis demonstrated the values of intelligent compromise in a federal democracy, without impairing either his convictions or his courage to stand by them.

Senator Daniel Webster, of Massachusetts, who served in the Senate 1827–41, 1845–50. Eloquent and articulate champion of "Liberty and Union, now and forever, one and inseparable," he grasped in an age of divided loyalties the full meaning of the American Constitution and of the supremacy and indissolubility of the national government. Molding the symbols of the Union he cherished so strongly that neither secession nor war could break them, his steadfast courage and powerful leadership in two of the Senate's most historic and critical debates were brilliantly portrayed in orations attentively heard and eagerly read. Influential spokesman for industrial expansion, his dedication to Union above all personal and partisan considerations overshadowed the petty moral insensitivities which never compromised his national principles; and his splendid dignity and decorum elevated the status and prestige of the Senate.

Senator John C. Calhoun, of South Carolina, who served in the Senate 1832–43, 1845–50. Forceful logician of state sovereignty, masterful defender of the rights of a political minority against the dangers of an unchecked majority, his profoundly penetrating and original understanding of the social bases of government has significantly influenced American political theory and practice. Sincerely devoted to the public good as he saw it, the ultimate tragedy of his final cause neither detracts from the greatness of his leadership nor tarnishes his efforts to avert bloodshed. Outspoken yet respected, intellectual yet beloved, his leadership on every major issue in that critical era of transition significantly shaped the role of the Senate and the destiny of the nation.

Senator Robert M. La Follette, Sr., of Wisconsin, who served in the Senate 1906–25. Ceaseless battler for the underprivileged in an age of special privilege, courageous independent in an era of partisan conformity, he fought memorably against tremendous odds and stifling inertia for social and economic reforms which ultimately proved essential to American progress in the twentieth century. Determined to make law serve the rights of persons as well as property, to make government serve the interests of great social justice as well as great political parties, his constructive pioneering efforts to promote the general welfare aroused the slumbering conscience of the nation and made the Senate more responsive to it. The bitter antagonisms stirred by his unyielding opposition to international commitments and conflict were ultimately submerged by widespread admiration for his dedicated lifelong fight against political corruption and corporate greed.

Senator Robert A. Taft, of Ohio, who served in the Senate 1939–53. The conscience of the conservative movement, its ablest exponent and most constructive leader, his high integrity, analytical mind, and sheer industry quickly won him a select spot in the councils of his party and the hearts of all his colleagues. His Senate leadership transcended partisanship; his political courage and candor put principles above ambition. Dedicated to the Constitution and the American tradition of individual rights as his keen legal mind interpreted them, he demonstrated the importance of a balanced and responsible opposition in an age of powerful governments.

Speaking only for myself, I will say to the Senate that I had the most difficulty excluding from the list three other outstanding senators of the past:

George Norris, of Nebraska, one of the most courageous, dedicated men ever to sit in the Senate, and one whose influence on the public power, agricultural, labor, and political aspects of this nation will long endure.

Thomas Hart Benton, of Missouri, the great "Nestor of the Senate" from 1820 to 1850, who on more than one occasion took on the Great Triumvirate individually and collectively and bested them in the Senate itself; and Oliver Ellsworth, of Connecticut, the outstanding figure in the first Senate, who authorized the Federal Judiciary Act that will always remain a monument to his genius, and shepherded the Bill of Rights through the Senate.

Many others deserve recognition, [including]:

Alben W. Barkley, of Kentucky.
William Borah, of Idaho.
Stephen Douglas, of Illinois.
Carter Glass, of Virginia.
Justin Smith Morrill, of Vermont.
John Sherman, of Ohio.
Charles Sumner, of Massachusetts.
Lyman Trumbull, of Illinois.
Oscar Underwood, of Alabama.
Arthur Vandenberg, of Michigan.

Robert Wagner, of New York.
Thomas Walsh, of Montana.

. . . The committee has selected Senators Robert M. La Follette, Sr., of Wisconsin, and Robert A. Taft, of Ohio, as outstanding representatives of the progressive and conservative movements in the twentieth century. We realize, of course, that considerable controversy and sentiment still surround each of them; that it is impossible to prove that they deserve the honor more than Norris or Vandenberg, for example, or Borah, Carter Glass, Barkley, Wagner, Walsh, Underwood, or any among a dozen others who were seriously considered; and that whatever names are chosen from the twentieth century will appear to suffer in comparison with the Great Triumvirate.

Nevertheless, the committee believed La Follette and Taft to be the most appropriate choices under the terms of the resolution—particularly in view of the way in which they symbolized the progressive and conservative points of view on the great domestic issue that confronted the Senate during this century: the proper role of governmental activity in the economic and social life of this country.

Nevertheless, because of the controversy still surrounding the names of Taft and La Follette, it is important to recall that Clay, Calhoun, and Webster in their own times did not always enjoy the wide recognition of their talents that posterity has given them. Listen, for example, to these words spoken about Henry Clay: "He prefers the specious to the solid, and the plausible to the true. . . . He is a bad man, an impostor, a creator of wicked schemes."

Those words were spoken by John C. Calhoun, who ridiculed Clay's lack of education, moral conduct, and short temper. Daniel Webster said Clay was his "inferior in many respects"; and Andrew Jackson once characterized him as being as "reckless and as full of fury as a drunken man in a brothel." On the other hand, who was it that said that John C. Calhoun was a rigid, fanatic, ambitious, selfishly partisan, and sectional turncoat, with "too much genius and too little common sense," who would either die a traitor or a madman? Henry Clay, of course. When Calhoun boasted in debate that he had been Clay's political master, Clay retorted, "Sir, I would not own him as a slave." Both Clay and Calhoun from time to time fought with Webster; and from the other House the articulate John Quincy Adams viewed with alarm "the gigantic intellect, the envious temper, the ravenous ambition, and the rotten heart of Daniel Webster."

And yet our committee has selected Henry Clay, Daniel Webster, and John C. Calhoun—and felt it had no other choice. For over thirty years they dominated the Congress and the country, providing leadership and articulation on all the great issues of the growing nation—the tariff, fiscal policies, foreign relations, defense, internal improvements, agriculture, industrial development, westward expansion, states' rights, and slavery. From time to time they supported and opposed each other for the Presidency that each desired but never achieved. And despite whatever bitter words passed between them, their mutual respect for each other remained high. "I don't like Henry Clay," said John Calhoun, "I would not speak to him, but by God, I love him." Whatsoever Calhoun's aspirations, said Webster, "they were high, honorable, and noble. There was nothing groveling or low or nearly selfish that came near the head or the heart of Mr. Calhoun."

Henry Clay predicted that Calhoun's principles would "descend to posterity under the sanction of a great name." And whatever John Quincy Adams may have thought of Webster's "rotten heart," he considered his celebrated reply to Hayne to be the "most significant [act] since the founding of the Constitution."

This is not to say that objections cannot be raised to each of the three. Criticism of Henry Clay's moral conduct, scholarship, and political schemes may well be justified; and there are those who feel he carried the principle of compromise too far. It is true that Clay said, "It is a rule with me, when acting either in a public or a private character, to attempt nothing more than what there exists a prospect of accomplishment." And yet his spirit of compromise, in the words of Carl Schurz, "was illumined by a grand conception of the destinies of his country, a glowing national spirit, a lofty patriotism." His greatest anxiety was the preservation of the Union; and few did more to contribute toward its salvation. Abraham Lincoln called the Great Pacificator "my beau ideal of a statesman, the man for whom I fought all my humble life." An extraordinarily gifted figure, his brilliant oratorical talents, unusual vitality, and a unique gift of winning the hearts as well as the minds of his countrymen all enabled his three great compromise proposals in 1820, 1833, and 1850 to save the Union until it grew strong enough to save itself. "No other American politician," as Vernon Parrington has observed, "has been so loved by a hero-worshiping electorate—and so lovable."

Daniel Webster, it is true, portrayed, in the words of one of his intimate friends, an extraordinary "compound of strength and weakness, dust and divinity." It is true that he accepted a retainer from Nicholas Biddle of the Bank of the United States; that he accepted favors from the New England manufacturers; and that his decisions both as a senator and as a secretary of state appear to have been open to improper influence. Yet there is no serious evidence that his views on the bank, the tariff, and foreign policy would have been any different without these dubious connections—and, on the contrary, Professor Allan Nevins has written that he demonstrated more than any other colleague real insight into the problems of public finance, moderate protectionism, and international affairs. Whatever may have been petty about his financial affairs, there was nothing petty about his moral stature in times of national crisis or in his dedication to the Union.

The same answer, I believe, can be given to those objecting to the views entertained and defended by John C. Calhoun. "He was wrong," Pulitzer prize–winning historian Arthur Schlesinger, Jr., wrote us, "but he was a greater man and Senator than many people who have been right." In defending the views of his state and section on the practice of slavery, abhorrent to all of us today but a constitutionally recognized practice in his time, Calhoun was yielding to neither the pressures of expediency nor immorality—nor did his opponents at the time so regard it. Calhoun was not a proponent of disunion. Though he warned at the end of his career that secession might be the South's only means of achieving justice, he fought long and hard to keep the South in the Union.

Generally judged to be the most notable political thinker ever to sit in the Senate, whose doctrine of concurrent majorities has permanently influenced our political theory and practice, John Calhoun did more than any other senator in the nineteenth century, in the words of Professor Nevins, "to make men think clearly and carefully on fundamental political questions."

I conclude by stressing once again that I believe this project to have had for this body considerable value beyond the basic necessity for its creation. It is the committee's hope that the considerable interest evoked by this project will be of value at a time when the democratic way of life is under pressure from without and the problems and conflicting pressures involved in the political profession are frequently misunderstood within our own country. The committee has attempted in a small way to focus the nation's attention upon the Senate and its distinguished traditions, upon the high quality of men who have served in the Senate, and upon the significant role that the Senate has played in the history of our nation. The members of the special committee thus hope that an increasing awareness of national and senatorial history which should not be forgotten will be of benefit to the general public and to the Senate itself.

United States Senate
Washington, D.C., May 1, 1957

The Best People We Can Get

If we are to be successful in the days to come, if we are to implement a program for the 1960s, then we need a government that is honest, a government that is efficient, a government that is dedicated, a government that is committed solely to the public interest.

One cannot make such sweeping promises without recognizing that these promises have been made before. Every challenger for public office, especially for the Presidency, talks about a great crusade to end corruption; to obtain government clean as a hound's tooth. But experience has shown that promises are not enough. For ours is a government of men, not of promises, and some men yield to temptation. Other men lack discrimination, and other men see no wrong in pursuing their private interest in their public capacity.

The problem is not merely one of deep freezes and vicuna coats. Less flamboyant but at least equally flagrant are the cases of those who use their office to obtain contracts for firms in which they have a financial interest. Those who use their position to repay political or financial debts, those who extract [personal gain] from the information they receive, or the power they wield. These cases are not only tragic in the public sense, in terms of justice denied, of taxes wasted, of problems ignored. These tragedies have their private effects as well, for cheating in the government cannot help but affect cheating in the classroom, on the quiz show, in the expense account.

The appointment of good men, moreover, is not a matter of morality alone. It may not be unethical to appoint an ambassador who is not acquainted with the language or the problems of the countries involved, but it is harmful to the interest of our nation. It may not be immoral to appoint to key positions men drawn only from the area of private business who intend to return to that business as soon as possible. But the national interest cannot be maintained by men in our Defense Department with an average tenure of less than one year.

It may not be improper to confine presidential appointees to the members of one party, but the whole nation was the beneficiary of the service of Stimson, Knox, Forrestal, McCloy, and Lovett. Yet I cannot recall in the last eight years a single major member of my party who has been appointed to a high position in the national security field, in Defense or in State, with the exception of one man, the ambassador to Germany, Mr. David Bruce.

And if we are to open employment opportunities in this country for members of all races and creeds, then the federal government must set an example. There are twenty-six Negroes in the Foreign Service of the United States, and there are six thousand members of the Foreign Service. There is not a district judge, federal district judge, who is a Negro, in the United States, and there are more than two hundred. There are messengers, laborers, clerks, but very few heads of departments. . . . It is an interesting fact today that Africa has one fourth, or will shortly have, of all the votes of the General Assembly. And yet twenty-six Negroes, spread throughout the entire world, are speaking for us as a source of democracy in this country. I believe we can do better.

The President himself must set the key example. I am not going to promise a Cabinet post or any other post to any race or ethnic group. That is racism in reverse at its worst. So I do not promise to consider race or religion in my appointments if I am successful. I promise only that I will not consider them.

If we are going to keep the cost of living in line and protect the interest of the consumers, then those agencies which regulate the cost of the public services must be dedicated to that mission and not concern themselves with future employment or personalities. I am making no charges and mentioning no names, for history teaches us that no political party has a monopoly on honesty. Both parties attract their share of crooks and weaklings. But that does not mean that these problems are incapable of solution. That does not mean that a campaign promise is enough. A new administration must screen out those who regard government service as a door to power or wealth; those who cannot distinguish between private gain and the public interest, and those who believe that old-fashioned honesty with the public's money is both old and out of fashion. The next President himself must set the moral tone, and I refer not only to his language, but to his actions in office. For the Presidency, as Franklin Roosevelt himself has said, is preeminently a place of moral leadership. And I intend, if successful, to try to restore that leadership and atmosphere beginning in 1961.

Should I be elected President, it would be my intention to ask the ablest men in the country to make whatever sacrifice is required to bring to the government a ministry of the best talents available, men with a single-minded loyalty to the national interest, men who would regard public office as a public trust. For no government is better than the men who compose it, and I want the best, and we need the best, and we deserve the best.

It would further be my intention at the earliest possible opportunity to submit to the Congress a single comprehensive code on conflicts of interest, aimed at eliminating duplications, inadvertencies and gaps, drawing a clearer line between propriety and impropriety, and protecting the public against unethical behavior without making it impossible for the able and conscientious citizen to serve his government.

It would also be my intention, through executive orders, the appointing power and legislation, to reform and streamline our lagging administrative agencies. Of all the undiscussed problems of this campaign, one of the most important is the fact that it takes from one year to three years for a businessman, a labor union, an interest involved, to get a decision out of our national government, and justice delayed is justice denied. It would not have been necessary, perhaps, for us to have passed a labor-management reform bill a year ago if it did not require three years for the National Labor Relations Board to give the employer or the employee involved relief.

We have to do better than this if this great bureaucracy of ours, if this great government of ours, is going to function in the sixties. We have to prepare it for motion, we have to prepare it to move, we have to get the best people we can get, and then we have to organize our structure so that they can act. And that is not the situation today.

I therefore take this opportunity to give you the eight basic principles which I would use if elected President as a guide to the appointment and conduct of those who would serve in a new administration. It is not complete, but I think it does suggest at least the spirit with which we shall move.

First, no officer or employee of the executive branch shall use his official position for financial profit or personal gain, or reveal to others confidential information acquired through his position.

Second, no officer or employee shall engage in any business transactions with, or hold any financial interest in, or accept any gift, favor, or substantial hospitality for himself and his family from, any enterprise or person who is doing business or seeking to do business with that unit of the government which he serves, or is able to influence, or who is subject to regulation, investigation, or litigation under the jurisdiction of that unit. To be above criminality is not enough. Good judgment is also required.

The next President himself must set the moral tone, and I refer not only to his language, but to his actions in office. . . .

Third, all gifts which cannot appropriately be refused, such as gifts from public organizations or from foreign governments to the President of the United States, shall immediately be assigned to the Smithsonian Institution or other federal agencies for historic, scientific, or welfare use. The President must set the example. . . .

Fourth, no federal appointee to any public regulatory agency shall represent any view other than the public interest. . . . It has been unfortunate in both parties that . . . because public attention has passed away from these agencies, it is difficult to get the best talent to come to Washington and work. But we have to do it, because your future, the future of this country, is tied up with the quality of our leadership in all branches of our national service.

Fifth, no member of any such agency, and no person who assists in its decisions, shall entertain any ex parte communication from any person, including political pressure or requests originating within the executive or legislative branches. . . . And all communications from the executive branch or the legislative branch shall be made a part of the record, the public record, and every party in interest given an opportunity to reply. As Finley Peter Dunne's "Mr. Dooley" used to say, "Trust everyone, but cut the cards."

Sixth, all appointments, both high and low, will be made on the basis of ability, without regard to race, creed, national origin, sex, or occupation. Campaign contributions—and this may be bad news for us, at least for the next three weeks—campaign contributions will not be regarded as a substitute for training and experience for diplomatic positions. And appointees shall be drawn from all segments of the community, wherever the best talent can be found. This will not be a businessman's administration with "business in the saddle," as Secretary McKay [of the Interior] once described his mission. But neither will it be a labor administration or a farmers' administration. It will be an administration for and by the people.

Seventh, senior positions in the State Department, the Foreign Service, the Defense Department shall be filled by the best talent in both parties, and from the ranks of career diplomats and civil servants, and officials engaged primarily in the conduct of foreign and defense activities will not be permitted to participate actively in political campaigns. I do not want our politics colored by considerations of national security, and I do not want our national security colored by considerations of politics.

Eighth, and finally, preferences in appointments will be given to those willing to commit themselves to stay on the job long enough to learn what they must learn. The goal is a full-time effort for the full tenure of the presidential term, without regard to any prior affiliation or prospective employment. The prospects for the nation in the coming years are not easy. The tasks facing the President will not be easy, and no appointee should assume that his life will be any easier.

These eight guidelines are not a magic formula for achieving a government perfect in all its parts. All human weaknesses cannot be avoided. All errors of judgment cannot be predicted. A code of ethics by itself may be found to be either too general to be meaningful or too specific to be enforceable. But these guidelines can illustrate the atmosphere, a tone of government, an attitude which the new President must take. We emphasize this basic principle: The essence of any government that belongs to the people must lie in the biblical injunction, "No man can serve two masters, for either he will hate one and love the other, or else he will hold to one and despise the other." All America seeks a government in which no man holds to his own interest and despises the public interest, and where all men serve only the public and love that master well. . . .

I hope, in closing, that all of you who are students at this college will consider during your lifetime embarking on a career of public service. In the next ten years we are going to try to develop in this country a sense of the public interest comparable or superior to what the Soviet Union is able to develop in its country by power of the police state. How many young students at this college are willing to spend part of their lives in Africa or Latin America or Asia, are willing to spend part of their time in this college learning not merely French or Spanish or Italian, but learning some of the esoteric dialects of India or Africa, learning something about those countries, preparing themselves as doctors or teachers or engineers or scientists or nurses, or public health officials, or Foreign Service officers, to contribute part of your talents, part of the benefits of your education to society as a whole? This college was not founded and has not been maintained merely to give this school's graduates an economic advantage in the life struggle. There is a higher purpose. Professor Woodrow Wilson said that every man sent out from a college should be a man of his time as well as a man of his nation. I ask you to consider how you can best use the talents which society is now helping develop in you in order to maintain that free society. All of us are involved in the discipline of self-government. All of us in this country, in a sense, are officeholders. All of us make an important decision as to what this country must be and how it must move and what its function shall be, and what its image shall be, and whether it shall stand still, as I believe it is now doing, or whether it shall once again move forward.

Wittenberg College
Springfield, Ohio, October 17, 1960

. . . The President of the United States represents not only the Democrats of this country, he represents all of the people around the world who want to live in freedom, who look to us for hope and leadership.

I must say that if I am elected President of the United States, I am not going to attempt only to select men for positions of high leadership who happen to have the word "Democrat" after their name.

When Franklin Roosevelt became President in 1932 he selected three Republicans to be members of his first Cabinet. When President Truman was the President, he selected men like John McCloy, Robert Lovett. He kept on men like James Forrestal. He brought John Foster Dulles into the State Department to negotiate the Japanese treaty. He secured for the great positions of responsibility the best men and women he could get.

That is what we are going to do in the future. . . . In spite of all the debate between political parties, we have a common interest today to select the best people we can get, people who recognize the kind of state we live in, the kind of country we live in, the kind of world we live in; people who look to the future, who are ready to break into that future, who are ready to lead, and who want this country to move again.

Campaign Speech
Bangor, Maine, September 2, 1960

The City Upon a Hill

I have welcomed this opportunity to address this historic body and, through you, the people of Massachusetts to whom I am so deeply indebted for a lifetime of friendship and trust. For fourteen years I have placed my confidence in the citizens of Massachusetts—and they have generously responded by placing their confidence in me.

Now, on the Friday after next, I am to assume new and broader responsibilities. But I am not here to bid farewell to Massachusetts. For forty-three years—whether I was in London, or in Washington, or in the South Pacific, or elsewhere—this has been my home; and, God willing, wherever I serve, this shall remain my home.

It was here my grandparents were born—it is here I hope that my grandchildren will be born.

I speak neither from false provincial pride nor artful political flattery. For no man about to enter high office in this country can ever be unmindful of the contribution which this state has made to our national greatness. Its leaders have shaped our destiny since long before the great Republic was born.

Its principles have guided our footsteps in times of crisis as well as in times of calm. Its democratic institutions—including this historic body—have served as beacon lights for other nations as well as your sister states. For what Pericles said of the Athenians has long been true of this commonwealth:

"We do not imitate—for we are a model to others"

And so it is that I carry with me from this state to that high and lonely office to which I now succeed more than fond memories and firm friendships. The enduring qualities of Massachusetts—the common threads woven by the Pilgrim and the Puritan, the fisherman and the farmer, the Yankee and the immigrant—will not be and could not be forgotten in this nation's executive mansion. They are an indelible part of my life, my conviction, my view of the past, and my hopes for the future.

Allow me to illustrate: During the last sixty days I have been engaged in the task of constructing an administration. It has been a long and deliberate process. Some have counseled greater speed. Others have counseled more expedient tests.

For of those to whom much is given, much is required.

But I have been guided by the standard John Winthrop set before his shipmates on the flagship *Arabella* 331 years ago, as they, too, faced the task of building a new government on a new and perilous frontier.

"We must always consider," he said, "that we shall be as a city upon a hill—the eyes of all people are upon us."

Today, the eyes of all people are truly upon us—and our government, in every branch, at every level, national, state and local, must be as a city upon a hill—constructed and inhabited by men aware of their grave trust and their great responsibilities.

For we are setting out upon a voyage in 1961 no less hazardous than that undertaken by the *Arabella* in 1630. We are committing ourselves to tasks of statecraft no less awesome than that of governing the Massachusetts Bay Colony, beset as it then was by terror without and disorder within.

History will not judge our endeavors—and a government cannot be selected—merely on the basis of color or creed or even party affiliation. Neither will competence and loyalty and stature, while essential to the utmost, suffice in times such as these.

For of those to whom much is given, much is required. And when at some future date the high court of history sits in judgment on each one of us—recording whether in our brief span of service we fulfilled our responsibilities to the state—our success or failure, in whatever office we hold, will be measured by the answers to four questions:

First, were we truly men of courage—with the courage to stand up to one's enemies—and the courage to stand up, when necessary, to one's own associates—the courage to resist public pressure as well as private greed?

Secondly, were we truly men of judgment—with perceptive judgment of the future as well as the past—of our own mistakes as well as the mistakes of others—with enough wisdom to know what we did not know, and enough candor to admit it?

Third, were we truly men of integrity—men who never ran out on either the principles in which we believed or the people who believed in us—men whom neither financial gain nor political ambition could ever divert from the fulfillment of our sacred trust?

Finally, were we truly men of dedication—with an honor mortgaged to no single individual or group, and compromised by no private obligation or aim, but devoted solely to serving the public good and the national interest?

Courage—judgment—integrity—dedication—these are the historic qualities of the Bay Colony and the Bay State—the qualities which this state has consistently sent to this chamber here on Beacon Hill in Boston and to Capitol Hill back in Washington.

And these are the qualities which, with God's help, this son of Massachusetts hopes will characterize our government's conduct in the four stormy years that lie ahead.

Humbly I ask His help in this undertaking—but aware that on earth His will is worked by men, I ask for your help and your prayers, as I embark on this new and solemn journey.

Massachusetts State Legislature
Boston, Massachusetts, January 9, 1961

The Pride of a Public Career

. . . I would like to conclude with a few remarks about the state of the executive branch. We have found it full of honest and useful public servants—but their capacity to act decisively at the exact time action is needed has too often been muffled in the morass of committees, timidities, and fictitious theories which have created a growing gap between decision and execution, between planning and reality. In a time of rapidly deteriorating situations at home and abroad, this is bad for the public service and particularly bad for the country; and we mean to make a change.

I have pledged myself and my colleagues in the Cabinet to a continuous encouragement of initiative, responsibility, and energy in serving the public interest. Let every public servant know, whether his post is high or low, that a man's rank and reputation in this administration will be determined by the size of the job he does, and not by the size of his staff, his office, or his budget. Let it be clear that this administration recognizes the value of dissent and daring, that we greet healthy controversy as the hallmark of healthy change. Let the public service be a proud and lively career. And let every man and woman who works in any area of our national government, in any branch, at any level, be able to say with pride and with honor in future years: "I served the United States government in that hour of our nation's need."

State of the Union Address
The Capitol, Washington, D.C., January 30, 1961

The Peace Corps

I have today signed an executive order providing for the establishment of a Peace Corps on a temporary pilot basis. I am also sending to Congress a message proposing authorization of a permanent Peace Corps. This Corps will be a pool of trained American men and women sent overseas by the U.S. government or through private institutions and organizations to help foreign countries meet their urgent needs for skilled manpower.

It is our hope to have five hundred or more people in the field by the end of the year.

The initial reactions to the Peace Corps proposal are convincing proof that we have, in this country, an immense reservoir of such men and women—anxious to sacrifice their energies and time and toil to the cause of world peace and human progress.

In establishing our Peace Corps we intend to make full use of the resources and talents of private institutions and groups. Universities, voluntary agencies, labor unions, and industry will be asked to share in this effort—contributing diverse sources of energy and imagination—making it clear that the responsibility for peace is the responsibility of our entire society.

We will only send abroad Americans who are wanted by the host country—who have a real job to do—and who are qualified to do that job. Programs will be developed with care, and after full negotiation, in order to make sure that the Peace Corps is wanted and will contribute to the welfare of other people. Our Peace Corps is not designed as an instrument of diplomacy or propaganda or ideological conflict. It is designed to permit our people to exercise more fully their responsibilities in the great common cause of world development.

Life in the Peace Corps will not be easy. There will be no salary and allowances will be at a level sufficient only to maintain health and meet basic needs. Men and women will be expected to work and live alongside the nationals of the country in which they are stationed—doing the same work, eating the same food, talking the same language.

But if the life will not be easy, it will be rich and satisfying. For every young American who participates in the Peace Corps—who works in a foreign land—will know that he or she is sharing in the great common

task of bringing to man that decent way of life which is the foundation of freedom and a condition of peace.

Statement Released to the Press
Washington, D.C., March 1, 1961

The New Ethical Standard

No responsibility of government is more fundamental than the responsibility of maintaining the highest standards of ethical behavior by those who conduct the public business. There can be no dissent from the principle that all officials must act with unwavering integrity, absolute impartiality, and complete devotion to the public interest. This principle must be followed not only in reality but in appearance. For the basis of effective government is public confidence, and that confidence is endangered when ethical standards falter or appear to falter.

I have firm confidence in the integrity and dedication of those who work for our government. Venal conduct by public officials in this country has been comparatively rare—and the few instances of official impropriety that have been uncovered have usually not suggested any widespread departure from high standards of ethics and moral conduct.

Nevertheless, in the past two decades, incidents have occurred to remind us that the laws and regulations governing ethics in government are not adequate to the changed role of the federal government, or to the changing conditions of our society. In addition, many of the ethical problems confronting our public servants have become so complex as to defy easy commonsense solutions on the part of men of goodwill seeking to observe the highest standards of conduct, and solutions have been hindered by lack of general regulatory guidelines. As a result many thoughtful observers have expressed concern about the moral tone of government, and about the need to restate basic principles in their application to contemporary facts.

Of course, public officials are not a group apart. They inevitably

reflect the moral tone of the society in which they live. And if that moral tone is injured—by fixed athletic contests or television quiz shows; by widespread business conspiracies to fix prices; by the collusion of businessmen and unions with organized crime; by cheating on expense accounts, by the ignoring of traffic laws, or by petty tax evasion—then the conduct of our government must be affected. Inevitably, the moral standards of a society influence the conduct of all who live within it—the governed and those who govern.

The ultimate answer to ethical problems in government is honest people in a good ethical environment. No web of statute or regulation, however intricately conceived, can hope to deal with the myriad possible challenges to a man's integrity or his devotion to the public interest. Nevertheless, formal regulation is required—regulation which can lay down clear guidelines of policy, punish venality and double-dealing, and set a general ethical tone for the conduct of public business.

Such regulation—while setting the highest moral standards—must not impair the ability of the government to recruit personnel of the highest quality and capacity. Today's government needs men and women with a broad range of experience, knowledge, and ability. It needs increasing numbers of people with topflight executive talent. It needs hundreds of occasional and intermittent consultants and part-time experts to help deal with problems of increasing complexity and technical difficulty. In short, we need to draw upon America's entire reservoir of talent and skill to help conduct our generation's most important business—the public business.

Perhaps the gravest responsibility of all rests upon the office of President. No President can excuse or pardon the slightest deviation from irreproachable standards of behavior on the part of any member of the executive branch.

This need to tap America's human resources for public purposes has blurred the distinctions between public and private life. It has led to a

constant flow of people in and out of business, academic life, and government. It has required us to contract with private institutions and call upon part-time consultants for important public work. It has resulted in a rapid rate of turnover among career government employees —as high as twenty percent a year. And, as a result, it has gravely multiplied the risk of conflicts of interest while seriously complicating the problem of maintaining ethical standards. . . .

To meet this need for statutory reform, I am transmitting to the Congress a proposed Executive Employees' Standards Act—a comprehensive revision of existing conflict-of-interest statutes. I believe that this bill maintains the highest possible standards of conduct, eliminates the technical deficiencies and anachronisms of existing laws, and makes it possible for the government to mobilize a wide range of talent and skill. . . .

Ultimately, high ethical standards can be maintained only if the leaders of government provide a personal example of dedication to the public service—and exercise their leadership to develop in all government employees an increasing sensitivity to the ethical and moral conditions imposed by public service. Their own conduct must be above reproach. And they must go beyond the imposition of general regulations to deal with individual problems as they arise—offering informal advice and personal consideration. It will often be difficult to assess the propriety of particular actions. In such subtle cases honest disclosure will often be the surest solution, for the public will understand good faith efforts to avoid improper use of public office when they are kept informed.

I realize, too, that perhaps the gravest responsibility of all rests upon the office of President. No President can excuse or pardon the slightest deviation from irreproachable standards of behavior on the part of any member of the executive branch. For his firmness and determination is the ultimate source of public confidence in the government of the United States. And there is no consideration that can justify the undermining of that confidence.

Special Message to Congress on Ethics in Government
Washington, D.C., April 27, 1961

The Obligations of Citizenship

Dear Mrs. Patterson:

Many thanks for your wire of May fourth. I appreciate your interest in our nation's needs and the spirit that motivates your telegram.

Apparently the demands of the "Cold War" are not as dramatic, and thus not as well-identified, as the demands of the traditional "shooting war"—such as rationing (which we do not need), a doubling of draft quotas (which would not help), or an increase in personal income taxes (which would only impede the recovery of our economic strength).

But that does not mean that nothing is being asked of our citizens. The facts of the matter are that all the programs I am seeking—to strengthen our economy, our defenses, our image abroad, our balance of payments position and our foreign policy tools—all make demands upon one or more groups of Americans, and most often upon all Americans jointly. All of them involve some effort, some inconvenience or some sacrifice—and, indeed, they are being opposed in some quarters on that basis.

For example: I have asked that we provide a leaner, more efficient defense establishment by terminating certain projects and closing a good many bases, although there are many protests from those who want economy practiced in someone else's community. I have asked that a major effort in foreign aid to other nations be maintained for many years to come, as burdensome as some regard it. I have asked young Americans to serve without pay or comfort in a Peace Corps for underdeveloped countries; I have asked many talented individuals to give up a higher income to serve their country in public office (and not all have been willing to do so); and I have asked all government officials to give up any incompatible financial interests.

I have asked that our excise and corporation tax rates not be permitted to fall as scheduled by law—that trucking companies and jet airline companies pay a higher tax for the highways and airways they use—that our business corporations pay a higher payroll tax for improved Social Security, unemployment compensation, and health insurance—and that certain taxpayers give up their privileges of expense account living, in yachts, hunting lodges, nightclubs, and all the rest. I have asked all Americans to help meet our deficit through higher postal rates. These requests for sacrifice are being strongly resisted by some unwilling to pay the price of national greatness.

I have asked other Americans to contribute to the strengthening of our economy by paying a decent minimum wage, to give up their right to purchase as many duty-free goods when they are traveling abroad—or, if they are farmers, to accept the limitations of our feed grain program. I have asked our businessmen and labor leaders, through my Advisory Committee, to adopt price and wage levels consistent with our economic goals and need to compete; and, more directly, I have asked them to take steps that will avoid harmful work stoppages in our missile and space effort.

I have asked the newspaper industry, without much success, to exercise more self-restraint in publishing intelligence data helpful to any enemy. My messages on education, urban affairs, and natural resources have all stressed the role the local community must assume if we are to make the most of our schools, our cities, and our water and other resources. We have made clear our very strong request to employers, labor unions, and indeed all citizens for an end to racial discrimination.

I have tried to make the whole tone and thrust of this office and this administration one that will demand a higher standard of excellence from every individual in his private life—in his education, his physical fitness, his attitudes toward foreign visitors, his obligations as a citizen, and all the rest.

And finally, each time we make any move or commitment in foreign affairs, I am in need of the support of the American people, their understanding, their patience, their willingness to endure setbacks and risks and hardships in order that this country can regain leadership and initiative.

So I have asked quite a lot of the American people—and I have been gratified at their response. There is much more to be done. But I do not wish to be misinterpreted. I think we have the will as well as the resources to prevail. And I think we will.

Sincerely,
John F. Kennedy

Letter to Mrs. Alicia Patterson, Editor and Publisher, **Newsday,** *in response to her telegram questioning the sincerity of the President's Inaugural summons, May 16, 1961*

The Front Line of Service

I know that many Foreign Service officers feel (like former Marines, who believe that the old days were the best days) that the days before World War II were the golden days of the Foreign Service, that since then the Foreign Service has fallen on hard times and that there is a good deal of uncertainty about what the future may bring.

I would like to differ with that view completely. In my opinion, today, as never before, is the golden period of the Foreign Service.

In the days before the war, we dealt with a few countries and a few leaders. I remember what Ambassador Dawes said, that the job was hard on the feet and easy on the brain. Theodore Roosevelt talked about those who resided in the Foreign Service rather than working in it. We were an isolationist country, by tradition and by policy and by statute. And therefore those of you who lived in the Foreign Service led a rather isolated life, dealing with comparatively few people, uninvolved in the affairs of this country or in many ways in the affairs of the country to which you may have been accredited.

That is all changed now. The power and influence of the United States are involved in the national life of dozens of countries that did not exist before 1945, many of which are so hard-pressed.

This is the great period of the Foreign Service, much greater than any period that has gone before. And it will be so through this decade, and perhaps even more in the years to come, if we are able to maintain ourselves with success.

But it places the heaviest burdens upon all of you. Instead of becoming merely experts in diplomatic history, or in current clippings from *The New York Times,* now you have to involve yourselves in every element of foreign life—labor, the class struggle, cultural affairs, and all the rest—attempting to predict in what direction the forces will move. The ambassador has to be the master of all these things, as well as knowing his own country. Now you have to know all about the United States, every facet of its life, all the great reforms of the thirties, the forties, and the fifties, if you are going to represent the United States powerfully and with strength and with vigor. When you represent the United States today, it is not a question of being accredited to a few people whose tenure is certain, but instead, of making predictions about what will be important events, what will be the elements of power or the elements of struggle, and which way we should move. And this calls for the finest judgment.

In the Foreign Service today you have a great chance and a great opportunity. And I hope that you recognize it, and realize that on your decisions hang the well-being and the future of this country.

There is a feeling, I think, in the Foreign Service, that the State Department and the Foreign Service are constantly under attack. Well, I would give two answers to that. In the first place, the questions with which you are dealing are so sophisticated and so technical that people who are not intimately involved week after week, month after month, reach judgments which are based upon emotion rather than knowledge of the real alternatives. They are bound to disagree and they are bound to focus their attacks upon the Department of State and upon the White House and upon the President of the United States. And in addition, party division in this country, where the parties are split almost evenly, and in spite of the long tradition of bipartisanship, accentuates the criticisms to which the Department of State and the White House are subjected.

If change were easy, everybody would change. But if you did not have change, you would have revolution. I think that change is what we need in a changing world, and therefore when we embark on new policies, we drag along all the anchors of old opinions and old views. You just have to put up with it. Those who cannot stand the heat should get out of the kitchen. Every member of Congress who subjects you to abuse is being subjected himself, every two years, to the possibility that his career also will come to an end. He doesn't live a charmed life. You have to remember that the hot breath is on him also, and it is on the Senate and it is on the President, and it is on everyone who deals with great matters.

This is not an easy career, to be a Foreign Service officer. It is not an easy life. The Foreign Service and the White House are bound to be in the center of every great controversy involving the security of the United States, and there is nothing you can do about it. You have to recognize that ultimately you will be subjected, as an institution, to the criticisms of the uninformed, and to attacks which are in many cases malicious and in many cases self-serving. But either you have to be able to put up with it, or you have to pick a more secluded spot.

Personally, I think the place to be is in the kitchen, and I am sure the Foreign Service officers of the United States feel the same way. . . . I regard the office of the Presidency and the White House, and the Secretary of State and the Department, as part of one chain, not separate but united, and committed to the maintenance of an effective foreign policy for the United States of America.

Therefore, in the final analysis, it depends on you.

That is why I believe this is the best period to be a Foreign Service officer. That is why I believe that the best talent that we have should come into the Foreign Service, because you today—even more than any other branch of government—are in the front line in every country of the world.

American Foreign Service Association
Washington, D.C., May 31, 1962

CHAPTER 4

The President and Congress

Because his party suffered a net loss of twenty-two seats in the House of Representatives in the 1960 election, Kennedy was warned upon entering the White House that conservative majorities in both houses would once again defeat the Democratic agenda that had long been stifled. But Kennedy wooed his congressional friends, both battled and bargained with his foes, and appealed, when necessary, to the American people. His first year as President saw passage of most of the measures previously stalled. His three years as President produced the most new legislation since the New Deal. He did not live to sign many of his principal proposals, including pioneer measures on civil rights, taxation, and education; but, undeterred by delay and defeat, he laid the groundwork for their ultimate enactment.

The Rules Committee Battle

Q: You said in the past, sir, that the President should be in the thick of the political battle, and I wondered, sir, if you could tell us what part you're playing in the effort to expand the Rules Committee and whether you feel your domestic program—whether the success of your domestic program in part depends on expanding the Rules Committee?

THE PRESIDENT: Well, the Constitution states that each house shall be the judge of its own rules, and therefore the Speaker of the House, Mr. Rayburn, has been extremely anxious that the House be permitted to settle this matter in its own way.

But it's no secret that I strongly believe that the members of the House should have an opportunity to vote themselves on the programs which we will present. . . . I'm hopeful that whatever judgment is made by the members of the House it will permit the members to vote on these bills. This is a very difficult time in the life of our country. Many controversial measures will be presented. . . . I hope a small group of men will not attempt to prevent the members from finally letting their judgments be known.

For example, we have the housing bill which is going to come before the Congress this year. We have an aid-to-education bill. We have legislation which will affect the income of farmers. Shouldn't the members of the House themselves and not merely the members of the Rules Committee have a chance to vote on those measures? But the responsibility rests with the members of the House, and I would not attempt in any way to infringe upon that responsibility. I merely give my view as an interested citizen.

President's News Conference
Washington, D.C., January 25, 1961

The Separate Responsibilities of Each Branch

It is a pleasure to return from whence I came. You are among my oldest friends in Washington—and this House is my oldest home. It was here, more than fourteen years ago, that I first took the oath of federal office. It was here, for fourteen years, that I gained both knowledge and inspiration from members of both parties in both houses—from your wise and generous leaders—and from the pronouncements which I can vividly recall sitting where you now sit—including the programs of two great Presidents, the undimmed eloquence of Churchill, the soaring idealism of Nehru, the steadfast words of General de Gaulle. To speak from this same historic rostrum is a sobering experience. To be back among so many friends is a happy one.

I am confident that that friendship will continue. Our Constitution wisely assigns both joint and separate roles to each branch of the government; and a President and Congress who hold each other in mutual respect will neither permit nor attempt any trespass. For my part, I shall withhold from neither the Congress nor the people any fact or report, past, present, or future, which is necessary for an informed judgment of our conduct and hazards. I shall neither shift the burden of executive decisions to the Congress, nor avoid responsibility for the outcome of those decisions.

State of the Union Address
The Capitol, Washington, D.C.
January 30, 1961

Members of the Congress, the Constitution makes us not rivals for power but partners for progress. We are all trustees for the American people, custodians of the American heritage. It is my task to report the State of the Union—to improve it is the task of us all.

In the past year, I have traveled not only across our own land but to other lands—to the North and the South, and across the seas. And I have found—as I am sure you have, in your travels—that people everywhere, in spite of occasional disappointments, look to us—not to our wealth or power, but to the splendor of our ideals. For our nation is commissioned by history to be either an observer of freedom's failure or the cause of its success.

State of the Union Address
The Capitol, Washington, D.C.
January 11, 1962

The Inevitable Accord and Discord

Q: Mr. President, I understand that an exchange of letters at the summit has settled the question of the B–70 or the RS–70. Can you tell us who won what and from whom?

THE PRESIDENT: Well, I think that if you took the powers of the executive and the powers of the Congress and pushed each to its logical, or at least its possible, conclusion—not its logical but its possible conclusion—you would have, in a government of divided powers, you would have a somewhat chaotic situation. If they refused to appropriate the salary of members of the government, if we took actions which failed to consider the responsibilities of the Congress—in a country where the Constitution gives divided responsibilities we have to attempt to adjust the strong feelings on both sides.

In my opinion, there was no winner and no loser except, I think, the relations between the Congress and I think the public interest [won].

President's News Conference
Washington, D.C., March 21, 1962

Q: Mr. President, according to Dr. Gallup's latest poll, there's been a sharp rise in pro-Republican sentiment in the Middle West and a parallel or opposite drop in your popularity stock of about ten points. Do you have any explanation of your own for this phenomenon, if it is one, and does it bother you with the administration facing now a midterm election?

THE PRESIDENT: Well, I think it said I dropped personally from seventy-nine percent to sixty-nine percent. I think that if I were still seventy-nine percent after a very intense congressional session I would feel that I had not met my responsibilities. The American people are rather evenly divided on a great many issues and as I make my views clearer on these issues, of course, some people increasingly are not going to approve of me. So I dropped to sixty-nine percent, and will probably drop some more. I don't think there is any doubt of that. President Eisenhower, I think, in the November election of 1954 was down to fifty-six percent. But he survived, and I suppose I will.

President's News Conference
Washington, D.C., July 23, 1962

MR. VANOCUR: . . . How do you use the Presidency, in Theodore Roosevelt's phrase "the bully pulpit," to move these men who really are kind of barons and sovereigns in their own right up there on the Hill? Have you any way to move them toward a course of action which you think is imperative?

THE PRESIDENT: Well, the Constitution and the development of the Congress all give advantage to delay. It is very easy to defeat a bill in the Congress. It is much more difficult to pass one. . . .

It is a tremendous change to go from being a senator to being a President. In the first months, it is very difficult. But I have no reason to believe that a President with the powers of this office and the responsibilities placed on it, if he has a judgment that some things need to be done, I think he can do it just as well the second time as the first, depending of course on the makeup of the Congress. The fact is I think the Congress looks more powerful sitting here than it did when I was there in the Congress. But that is because when you are in Congress you are one of a hundred in the Senate or one of four hundred and thirty-five in the House, so that the power is so divided. But from here I look at a Congress, and I look at the collective power of the Congress, particularly the bloc action, and it is a substantial power.

Television and Radio
Year-End Conversation with the President
Washington, D.C., December 17, 1962

Q: Mr. President, you have said that you are in favor of the two-term limit to the office of the Presidency. How do you feel about former president Eisenhower's suggestion that the terms of congressmen also be limited?

THE PRESIDENT: It's the sort of proposal which I may advance in a postpresidential period, but not right now.

President's News Conference
Washington, D.C., January 24, 1963

Q: Mr. President, back on the subject of Presidential advisers, Congressman Baring of Nevada, a Democrat, said you would do much better if you got rid of some of yours—and he named Bowles, Ball, Bell, Bunche, and Sylvester.

THE PRESIDENT: Yes, he has a fondness for alliteration and for "B's." And I would not add Congressman Baring to that list as I have a high regard for him and for the gentlemen that he named. But congressmen are always advising presidents to get rid of presidential advisers. That is one of the most constant threads that runs through American history and presidents ordinarily do not pay attention, nor do they in this case.

President's News Conference
Washington, D.C., May 8, 1963

On the campaign trail.

PHOTO BY HANK WALKER, LIFE MAGAZINE © TIME INC.

PART II

The Presidential Campaign

CHAPTER 5

The Road to the White House

Unlike many who attain high public office, John F. Kennedy continued to grow in mind and spirit throughout his service in Washington. His concern for his country, his compassion for others, his judgment, his skills as a speaker and leader, all expanded in each of his seventeen years in office. His political drive and instincts were heightened as well, and he became the first to conduct a four-year quest for the Presidency. Recognizing that his youth and religion would fatally handicap his chances for a nomination decided by power brokers in a convention "backroom," he outpaced, outorganized, and outsmarted his more powerful competitors for the nomination, winning a bare majority on the first ballot. By an equally exhaustive and exhausting effort that fall, in a campaign that even included some genuinely new and worthwhile proposals, he came from behind to nose out Richard Nixon for the Presidency.

The "Parochial" Young Congressman of 1952

MR. KENNEDY: Will the gentleman tell me why you allow in this bill $80 million for Oregon, around $37 million for California, and yet you reduce so drastically the money for the New England states? Five out of the six New England states will receive no money in this bill for any project.

MR. RABAUT: The gentleman from Massachusetts, since he has been on this floor today, has been strictly parochial in his arguments and viewpoint. I have not a dime in this bill for my district or for my state except some maintenance of some small harbors, so there is nothing in it for me. But all the gentleman has talked about since he has been here is New England.

MR. KENNEDY: Does the gentleman object to that?

MR. RABAUT: No; I do not object to it, but this is not a parochial bill; this is a bill for the benefit of the United States of America.

MR. KENNEDY: The point I want to make now is that New England is a part of the United States of America, and five out of the six New England states do not receive a penny of money from this nearly half-a-billion-dollar bill.

Colloquy, Floor of the U.S. House of Representatives,
Regarding Water Projects Appropriation Bill
Washington, D.C., April 1, 1952

The "National Interest" Senator of 1954

Mr. President, I am frank to admit that few issues during my service in the House of Representatives or the Senate have troubled me as much as the pending bill authorizing participation by the United States in the construction and operation of the St. Lawrence Seaway. As you may know, on six different occasions over a period of twenty years, no Massachusetts senator or representative has ever voted in favor of the seaway, and such opposition on the part of many of our citizens and officials continues to this day. . . .

The evidence appears to be conclusive that Canada will build the seaway.

Is it in the national interest of the United States that we participate in the construction, operation, and administration of the seaway as authorized by the Wiley bill? That question has been answered in the affirmative by every President, Secretary of Army and Defense, Secretary of Commerce, National Security Council, National Security Resources Board, and other administration officials for the past thirty years, including President Eisenhower and other representatives of his administration. The President stated in that part of his message on national defense:

> Both nations now need the St. Lawrence Seaway for security as well as for economic reasons. I urge the Congress promptly to approve our participation in its construction.

Mr. President, our ownership and control of a vital strategic international waterway along our own border would be lost without passage of this bill. If Canada builds the seaway alone, it may not only be a more expensive proposition, due to the difference in topography, requiring higher tolls over a longer period of time, but the seaway will still be paid for to a great extent by the American interests whose use thereof will be many times greater than the Canadians. Thus the economy of the United States will have paid for the greater part of the seaway at a higher cost, but the U.S. government will have no voice in the decisions regarding tolls, traffic, admission of foreign ships, defense and security measures, and priorities. Inasmuch as the United States is going to benefit both economically and militarily from the construction of the seaway, and inasmuch as the Wiley bill provides that the seaway will be self-liquidating, and require comparatively small appropriations over a five-year period, I believe that our participation is in the national interest, and, therefore, should not be defeated for sectional reasons. . . .

How will the St. Lawrence Seaway help Massachusetts? There have been a great many claims advanced along the lines that it would be of help to my state; but I have studied them with care and must say in all frankness that I think they are wholly speculative at best. I know of no direct economic benefit to the economy of Massachusetts or any segment thereof from the seaway, and I have been urged to oppose the seaway on these grounds, inasmuch as the initial investment, even though repaid, will come in part from Massachusetts tax revenues. . . .

But I am unable to accept such a narrow view of my function as U.S. Senator; and in speaking on the Senate floor on behalf of the New England economy I stressed my opposition to the idea that New England's interest is best served by opposing federal programs which contribute to the well-being of the country, particularly when those programs increase the purchasing power of New England's customers. Where federal action is necessary and appropriate, it is my firm belief that New England must fight for those national policies. . . .

Moreover, I have sought the support of senators from all sections of the country in my efforts on behalf of New England, pointing out to them not only the concern which they should have for an important region in our country, but also the fact that an increase in economic activity in New England would benefit the nation as a whole. For these reasons, I cannot oppose the seaway because the direct economic benefits will go largely to the Great Lakes and Middle Western areas. I could not conscientiously take such a position, and at the same time expect support from senators in the Middle West or any other part of the country for those programs and projects of aid to New England.

The seaway is going to be built; the only question is the part we shall play in opening our fourth coastline. To those in my state and elsewhere who oppose our participation in the construction of this project for national security merely because the economic benefits go elsewhere, I would say that it has been this arbitrary refusal of many New Englanders to recognize the legitimate needs and aspirations of other sections which has contributed to the neglect of, and even opposition to, the needs of our own region by the representatives of other areas. We cannot continue so narrow and destructive a position. As was so well stated by a famous Massachusetts senator over one hundred years ago, our aim should not be "States dissevered, discordant [or] belligerent"; but "one country, one constitution, one destiny."

United States Senate
Debate on St. Lawrence Seaway
Washington, D.C., January 14, 1954

The National Convention Speaker of 1956

We have come here today not merely to nominate a Democratic candidate, but to nominate a President of the United States.

Sometimes in the heat of a political convention, we forget the grave responsibilities which we as delegates possess. For we here today are selecting a man who must be something more than a good candidate, something more than a good speaker, more than a good politician, a good liberal, or a good conservative. We are selecting the head of the most powerful nation on earth, the man who literally will hold in his hands the powers of survival or destruction, of freedom or slavery, of success or failure for us all. We are selecting here today the man who for the next four years will be guiding, for good or evil, for better or worse, the destinies of our nation and, to a large extent, the destiny of the free world.

I ask you, therefore, to think beyond the balloting of tonight and tomorrow—to think beyond even the election in November and to think instead of those four years that lie ahead, and of the crises that will come with them.

Of overwhelming importance are the ever-mounting threats to our survival that confront us abroad, threats that require a prompt return to firm, decisive leadership. Each Republican year of indecision and hesitation has brought new Communist advances—in Indochina, in the Middle East, in North Africa, in all the tense and troubled areas of the world. The Grand Alliance of the West—that chain for freedom forged by Truman and Marshall and the rest—is cracking, its unity deteriorating, its strength dissipating. We are hesitant on Suez, silent on colonialism, uncertain on disarmament, and contradictory on the other major issues of the day. . . . Once we are able to cut through the slogans and the press releases and the vague reassurances, we realize to our shock and dismay that the next four years of this hydrogen age represent the most dangerous and the most difficult period in the history of our nation.

In such a period, one man, and one man only, can bear the full and final burden of responsibility and leadership—not his Cabinet, not his assistants, not his Vice-President—only the President of the United States himself. It is for these reasons that I ask this convention in its deliberations on the Presidency to consider those four troubled years that lie ahead, and the necessity of selecting a President with the courage and the vigor and the vision equal to the task.

And consider, too, the four years that face us as a nation at home. For here, too, the absence of new ideas, the lack of new leadership, the failure to keep pace with new developments, have all contributed to the growth of gigantic economic and social problems—problems that can perhaps be postponed or explained away or ignored now, but problems that during the next four years will burst forth with continuing velocity. The problem of the nation's distressed farmers, the problem of our declining small business, the problem of our maldistribution of economic gains, the problem of our hopelessly inadequate schools, the problem of our nation's health—and many more. . . . Conferences are held, to be sure—commissions are convened—but no new steps are taken and no bold programs are effected.

Ladies and gentlemen of the convention: it is now my privilege to present to this convention, as a candidate for President of the United States . . . the man from Libertyville—the next Democratic nominee and the next President of the United States—Adlai E. Stevenson.

These are problems that cry out for solution—they cry out for leadership—they cry out for a man equal to the times. And the Democratic Party can say to the nation today—we have such a man!

We can offer to the nation today a man uniquely qualified by inheritance, by training, and by conviction, to lead us out of this crisis of complacency, and into a new era of life and fulfillment. During the past four years his wise and perceptive analyses of the world crisis have pierced through the vacillations and the contradictions of official Washington to give understanding and hope to people at home and abroad. And his eloquent, courageous, and experienced outlook on our problems here at home have stood in shining contrast to the collection of broken promises, neglected problems, and dangerous blunders that pave the road from Gettysburg to the White House.

Of course, in a democracy, it is not enough to have the right man—for first he must be elected, he must show the nation that he is the right man, he must be a winner. And I say we have a winner—in the man who became governor of this state in 1948 with the largest majority in the history of Illinois—in the man who in 1956 has shown in primary after primary that he, and only he, is the top vote-getter in the Democratic Party today.

And let us be frank about the campaign that lies ahead. Our party will be up against two of the toughest, most skillful campaigners in its history—one who takes the high road, and one who takes the low. If we are to overcome that combination in November, this convention must nominate the candidate who can best carry our case to the American people—the one who is by all odds and by all counts our most eloquent, our most forceful, our most appealing figure.

The American people saw and heard and admired this man for the first time four years ago, when, out of the usual sea of campaign promises and dreary oratory and catchy slogans, there came something new and different, something great and good—a campaign and a candidate dedicated to telling the truth. Sometimes the truth hurt—sometimes it wasn't believed, sometimes it wasn't popular—but it was always the truth, the same truth, North, South, East and West. It was a campaign that brought home to the American people two great qualities of the candidate—his natural talent for government, which had previously been demonstrated in his able, efficient, and economical administration of the state of Illinois—and, secondly, his natural talent for campaigning, for meeting people of all kinds, under all circumstances, with a zest for hard work and a will to win.

These are, as I have said, critical times—times that demand the best we have, times that demand the best America has. We have, therefore, an obligation to pick the man best qualified, not only to lead our party, but to lead our country. The nation is entitled to expect that of us. For what we do here today affects more than a nomination, more than an election—it affects the life and the way of life of all of our fellow Americans.

The time is ripe. The hour has struck. The man is here; and he is ready. Let the word go forth that we have fulfilled our responsibility to the nation.

Ladies and gentlemen of the convention: it is now my privilege to present to this convention, as a candidate for President of the United States, the name of the man uniquely qualified—by virtue of his compassion, his conscience, and his courage—to follow in the great traditions of Jefferson, Jackson, Wilson, Roosevelt, and the man from Independence. Fellow Delegates, I give you the man from Libertyville—the next Democratic nominee and the next President of the United States—Adlai E. Stevenson.

Nomination of Adlai E. Stevenson for
President of the United States
Democratic National Convention
Chicago, Illinois, August 16, 1956

The Defeated Vice-Presidential Contender of 1956

I want to take this opportunity first to express my appreciation to Democrats from all parts of the country, North and South, East and West, who have been so generous and kind to me this afternoon. I think that it proves as nothing else can prove how strong and united the Democratic Party is.

Secondly, I think what has happened today bears out the good judgment of our Governor Stevenson in deciding that this issue should be taken to the floor of the convention.

I believe that the Democratic Party will go from this convention far stronger for what we have done here today. And therefore, ladies and gentlemen, recognizing that this convention has selected a man who has campaigned in all parts of the country, who has worked untiringly for the party, who will serve as an admirable running mate to Governor Stevenson, I hope that this convention will make Estes Kefauver's nomination unanimous.

Concession of Vice-Presidential Nomination
Democratic National Convention
Chicago, Illinois, August 17, 1956

The Presidential Prospect of 1958

I have just received the following wire from my generous daddy: "Dear Jack: Don't buy a single vote more than is necessary—I'll be damned if I'm going to pay for a landslide."

I am grateful to my father for his support—but I am even more grateful to "Mr. Sam" Rayburn. At the last Democratic convention, if he had not recognized the Tennessee and Oklahoma delegations when he did, I might have won that race with Senator Kefauver—and my political career would now be over.

I have been told tonight that if I will only not reveal the truth about the members of the Gridiron Club in front of their bosses, they in turn can insure me the Democratic Presidential nomination. I am not the first politician to be thus tempted by the newspaper fraternity. When Speaker Joe Cannon half a century ago was told by the ANPA [American Newspaper Publishers Association] that, in exchange for his opposition to the newsprint tariff, the publishers would deliver him the Presidency, Speaker Cannon removed his cigar and replied: "You know, two thousand years ago or so, another fellow was tempted like this. And the tempter led him up on the highest mountaintop; and showed him all the kingdoms of the world, and all the valleys of milk and honey—and he said, 'If you will fall down and worship me, all of this will I give you.' But the truth of the matter is," Speaker Cannon went on, "he didn't own one damn inch of it." I am not sure that the members of the Gridiron Club do either. . . .

I dreamed about 1960 the other night, and I told Stuart Symington and Lyndon Johnson about it in the Cloakroom yesterday. I told them how the Lord came into my bedroom, anointed my head, and said: "John Kennedy, I hereby anoint you President of the United States." Stu Symington said: "That's strange, Jack, because I, too, had a similar dream last night, in which the Lord anointed me and declared me, Stuart Symington, President of the United States *and* outer space." And Lyndon Johnson said: "That's very interesting, gentlemen; because I, too, had a similar dream last night—and I don't remember anointing either one of you!"

We do have lots of candidates. A recent AP survey asked each senator about his preference for the Presidency—and ninety-six senators each received one vote.

The Gridiron Club
Washington, D.C., March 15, 1958

The Declaration of Candidacy in 1960

I am announcing today my candidacy for the Presidency of the United States.

The Presidency is the most powerful office in the Free World. Through its leadership can come a more vital life for our people. In it are centered the hopes of the globe around us for freedom and a more secure life. For it is in the executive branch that the most crucial decisions of this century must be made in the next four years—how to end or alter the burdensome arms race, where Soviet gains already threaten our very existence; how to maintain freedom and order in the newly emerging nations; how to rebuild the stature of American science and education; how to prevent the collapse of our farm economy and the decay of our cities; how to achieve, without further inflation or unemployment, expanded economic growth benefiting all Americans; and how to give direction to our traditional moral purpose, awakening every American to the dangers and opportunities that confront us.

I am announcing today my candidacy for the Presidency of the United States.

These are among the real issues of 1960. And it is on the basis of these issues that the American people must make their fateful choice for the future.

In the past forty months, I have toured every state in the Union and I have talked to Democrats in all walks of life. My candidacy is therefore based on the conviction that I can win both the nomination and the election.

I believe that any Democratic aspirant to this important nomination should be willing to submit to the voters his views, record, and competence in a series of primary contests. I am therefore now announcing my intention of filing in the New Hampshire primary and I shall announce my plans with respect to the other primaries as their filing dates approach.

I believe that the Democratic Party has a historic function to perform in the winning of the 1960 election, comparable to its role in 1932. I intend to do my utmost to see that that victory is won.

For eighteen years, I have been in the service of the United States, first as a naval officer in the Pacific during World War II and for the past fourteen years as a member of the Congress. In the last twenty years, I have traveled in nearly every continent and country—from Leningrad to Saigon, from Bucharest to Lima. From all of this, I have developed an image of America as fulfilling a noble and historic role as the defender of freedom in a time of maximum peril—and of the American people as confident, courageous, and persevering.

It is with this image that I begin this campaign.

Statement of Declaration for the Presidency
Washington, D.C., January 2, 1960

The Question of Age

Last Saturday one of our most dedicated and courageous Presidents gave the nation his views on the forthcoming Democratic convention. Inasmuch as Mr. Truman's remarks were directed at me, I am taking this opportunity to respond to his statement.

First, Mr. Truman suggested that I step aside as a candidate in 1960.

In response, let me say I do not intend to step aside at anyone's request.

I was the only candidate to risk my chances in all the primaries; the only one to visit every state. I have encountered and survived every kind of hazard and opposition, and I do not intend to withdraw my name now on the eve of the convention.

Secondly, Mr. Truman asserted that the convention would be controlled or prearranged.

In response, let me say to the extent that I have anything to do with it, it will be an open convention, as every convention of our broadly based party is open, even though our candidate has been selected on the first ballot in every single convention but one since 1932, including the 1948 convention, which nominated Mr. Truman.

To me, an open convention means one reflecting the free will of delegates, freely elected in contested primaries and in state conventions.

But based on my observations of him in 1952 and in 1956, and last Saturday, Mr. Truman regards an open convention as one which studies all the candidates, reviews their records, and then takes his advice.

Nevertheless, I share his hope that our convention will consider all prospective nominees, including all those he named, and some he did not name. And I hope that Mr. Truman will attend the convention, and should I be the nominee, I hope he will support me in the fall.

Third, Mr. Truman accused my supporters of using improper pressure on the delegates. Not one concrete example has ever been named. I do not want any votes that have been pressured. And the facts of the matter are that my votes come from the primaries—and I entered all that were open—and from rank-and-file Democrats who voted for me in state conventions.

The prospective candidates Mr. Truman named could have entered those primaries. Some of them were traveling widely all year, and supporting my primary opponents. But not one of them entered a primary on his own.

The other candidates also had the same opportunity as I to present their record and views to the individual delegates and state conventions. Many of them have already been properly sized up, to use Mr. Truman's words, and they have their own backers who are not, I am told, without influence and the opportunity to pressure delegates.

The heart of Mr. Truman's objection . . . is his question as to whether I am ready for the country or the country is ready for me in terms of maturity and experience.

Fourth and finally, the heart of Mr. Truman's objection, it seems, is his question as to whether I am ready for the country or the country is ready for me in terms of maturity and experience.

Let me say this as objectively as I can. I did not undertake lightly to seek the Presidency. It is not a prize or a normal object of ambition. It is the greatest office in the world . . .

My writings, addresses, and activities in foreign and domestic affairs speak for themselves, and I am willing to let our party and nation be the judge of my experience and ability.

But this much ought to be understood: If we are to establish a test for the Presidency whereby fourteen years in major elective office is insufficient experience, then all but three of the ten possibilities mentioned by Mr. Truman last Saturday must be ruled out, and every President elevated to that office in the twentieth century should have been ruled out, including the three great Democratic Presidents, Woodrow Wilson, Franklin Roosevelt, and Harry Truman himself.

And if we are to establish a so-called maturity test which finds men forty-three years of age or younger unfit for leadership, a test, by the way, not met by all those listed by Mr. Truman, and not in keeping with the constitutional test of thirty-five, which is prescribed in the Constitution, then history has repeatedly violated this principle—in the lives of President Theodore Roosevelt, Prime Minister William Pitt, and a whole host of other leaders stretching back through Napoleon to Alexander the Great.

To exclude from positions of trust and command all those below the age of forty-four would have kept Jefferson from writing the Declaration of Independence, Washington from commanding the Continental Army, Madison from fathering the Constitution, Hamilton from serving as Secretary of the Treasury, Clay from being elected Speaker of the House, and even Christopher Columbus from discovering America.

But I do not believe the American people are willing to impose any such test, for this is still a young country, founded by young men 184 years ago today and it is still young in heart, youthful in spirit, and blessed with new young leaders in both parties, in both houses of Congress, and in governor's chairs throughout the country.

The balance of power is shifting. There are new and more terrible weapons, new and uncertain nations, new pressures of population and automation that were never considered before.

The strength and health and vigor of these young men is equally needed in the White House. For during my lifetime alone four out of our seven Presidents have suffered major health setbacks that impaired at least temporarily their exercise of executive leadership. Older men may always be appointed to the Cabinet. Their wise counsel of experience will be invaluable, but then if ill health cuts short their work others may replace them. But a President is selected for four—or possibly eight—years and the voters deserve to know that his strength and vigor will remain at the helm.

So, if in the coming weeks both parties in their respective conventions should nominate candidates still in their forties, and Mr. Nixon and I, as a matter of fact, entered the Congress together fourteen years ago, the country will, I am confident, be ready for that choice.

We have had six previous Presidents in their forties and many presidential candidates, some in fact in their thirties.

It is true, of course, that almost all of the major world leaders today on both sides of the Iron Curtain are men past the age of sixty-five. It is true that the world today is largely in the hands of men whose education was completed before the whole course of international events was altered by two world wars.

But who is to say how successful they have been in improving the fate of the world? And who is to replace these men as the passage of time removes from the scene those born in the nineteenth century?

The world is changing, the old ways will not do.

The balance of power is shifting. There are new and more terrible weapons, new and uncertain nations, new pressures of population and automation that were never considered before. And in many of these new countries I have noticed, in both Africa and Asia, they are electing young men to leadership—men who are not bound by the traditions of the past, men who are not blinded by the old fears and rivalries, men who can cast off the old slogans and illusions, and suspicions.

It is time for a new generation of leadership to cope with new problems and new opportunities. For there is a new world to be won, a world of peace and goodwill, a world of hope and abundance, and I want America to lead the way to that new world.

Mr. Truman asked me if I think I am ready. I am reminded that one hundred years ago Abraham Lincoln, not yet President and under fire from veteran politicians, wrote these words: "I see the storm coming and I know His hand is in it. If He has a place and work for me, I believe that I am ready."

Today I say to you, with full knowledge of the responsibilities of that high office, if the people of the nation select me to be their President, I believe that I am ready.

Televised News Conference
New York, New York, July 4, 1960

The Final Appeal

The preconvention campaign is over. For the candidates, the hour of unity is at hand. We have all been friends for a long time. I know we always will. We have always supported our party's nominee. I know we all will in 1960.

For we are all Democrats—not northern or southern Democrats, not liberal or conservative Democrats—but Democrats by birth, conviction, and choice. We know it is neither the party of war nor the party of appeasement—our only war is against injustice, hunger, and disease—and in that war there can be no appeasement.

And we know that there is only one legitimate issue of health in this campaign—and that is the anemic health of the American economy today.

There is only one legitimate issue of age in this campaign—and that is the tragic failure of this administration to meet the needs of our older citizens, and particularly their need for medical care.

There is only one legitimate issue of creed in this campaign, and that is our devotion to the public good ahead of private interests—a creed the Republicans call creeping socialism—but FDR called it "A New Deal."

This fall will see the classic, age-old struggle—between the party of hope and the party of memory—the party of the future versus the party of the past—the party that breaks precedents versus the party that breaks promises. And every candidate here tonight joins me in one final campaign promise—we are going to win that struggle in November.

For those of you who are delegates, your hour of decision is also at hand. In the pomp and pageantry of convention politics, it is easy to forget the context of your decision: the Free World that anxiously awaits a leader—the dark clouds gathering ominously on the world horizon—the cries for help that come from around the country, from abandoned farms and mines, from overcrowded slums and schools, from the unemployed and the underpaid and the unprotected—a hundred, a thousand voices crying, here and around the world—cries that have not been heard—cries that must now be heard.

One hundred and seventy-three years ago, in another dark and uncertain hour, an earlier national convention was called—its delegates undertook to draft a new constitution. May your work as delegates here this week stand the test of time as well as theirs. May your decisions—like theirs—have meaning for future generations to come, and ignite a beacon light for all the world to see.

In the words of the poet Longfellow:

Humanity with all its fears,
With all its hopes of future years
Is hanging breathless on thy fate.

Democratic National Committee Dinner
Los Angeles, California, July 10, 1960

The Opening of the New Frontier

With a deep sense of duty and high resolve, I accept your nomination.

I accept it with a full and grateful heart—without reservation—and with only one obligation—the obligation to devote every effort of body, mind, and spirit to lead our party back to victory and our nation back to greatness.

I am grateful, too, that you have provided me with such an eloquent statement of our party's platform. Pledges which are made so eloquently are made to be kept. "The Rights of Man"—the civil and economic rights essential to the human dignity of all men—are indeed our goal and our first principles. This is a platform on which I can run with enthusiasm and conviction.

And I am grateful, finally, that I can rely in the coming months on so many others—on a distinguished running mate who brings unity to our ticket and strength to our platform, Lyndon Johnson; on one of the most articulate statesmen of our time, Adlai Stevenson; on a great spokesman for our needs as a nation and a people, Stuart Symington; and on that fighting campaigner whose support I welcome, President Harry S Truman.

I feel a lot safer now that they are on my side again. And I am proud of the contrast with our Republican competitors. For their ranks are apparently so thin that not one challenger has come forth with both the competence and the courage to make theirs an open convention.

I am telling you now what you are entitled to know: that my decisions on every public policy will be my own—as an American, a Democrat, and a free man.

I am fully aware of the fact that the Democratic Party, by nominating someone of my faith, has taken on what many regard as a new and hazardous risk—new, at least, since 1928. But I look at it this way: the Democratic Party has once again placed its confidence in the American people, and in their ability to render a free, fair judgment. And you have, at the same time, placed your confidence in me, and in my ability to render a free, fair judgment—to uphold the Constitution and my oath of office—and to reject any kind of religious pressure or obligation that might directly or indirectly interfere with my conduct of the Presidency in the national interest. My record of fourteen years supporting public education—supporting complete separation of church and state—and resisting pressure from any source on any issue should be clear by now to everyone.

I hope that no American, considering the really critical issues facing this country, will waste his franchise by voting either for me or against me solely on account of my religious affiliation. It is not relevant, I want to stress, what some other political or religious leader may have said on this subject. It is not relevant what abuses may have existed in other countries or in other times. It is not relevant what pressures, if any, might conceivably be brought to bear on me. I am telling you now what you are entitled to know: that my decisions on every public policy will be my own—as an American, a Democrat, and a free man.

Under any circumstances, however, the victory we seek in November will not be easy. We all know that in our hearts. We recognize the power of the forces that will be aligned against us. We know they will invoke the name of Abraham Lincoln on behalf of their candidate—despite the fact that the political career of their candidate has often seemed to show charity toward none and malice for all.

We know that it will not be easy to campaign against a man who has spoken or voted on every known side of every known issue. Mr. Nixon may feel it is his turn now, after the New Deal and the Fair Deal—but before he deals, someone had better cut the cards.

That "someone" may be the millions of Americans who voted for President Eisenhower but balk at his would-be, self-appointed successor. For just as historians tell us that Richard I was not fit to fill the shoes of bold Henry II—and that Richard Cromwell was not fit to wear the mantle of his uncle [sic]—they might add in future years that Richard Nixon did not measure to the footsteps of Dwight D. Eisenhower.

Perhaps he could carry on the party policies—the policies of Nixon, Benson, Dirksen, and Goldwater. But this nation cannot afford such a luxury. Perhaps we could afford a Coolidge following Harding. And perhaps we could afford a Pierce following Fillmore. But after Buchanan this nation needed a Lincoln—after Taft we needed a Wilson—after Hoover we needed Franklin Roosevelt. . . . And after eight years of drugged and fitful sleep, this nation needs strong, creative Democratic leadership in the White House.

But we are not merely running against Mr. Nixon. Our task is not merely one of itemizing Republican failures. Nor is that wholly necessary. For the families forced from the farm will know how to vote without our telling them. The unemployed miners and textile workers will know how to vote. The old people without medical care, the families without a decent home, the parents of children without adequate food or schools, they all know that it's time for a change.

But I think the American people expect more from us than cries of indignation and attack. The times are too grave, the challenge too urgent, and the stakes too high to permit the customary passions of political debate. We are not here to curse the darkness, but to light the candle that can guide us through that darkness to a safe and sane future. As Winston Churchill said on taking office some twenty years ago: If we open a quarrel between the present and the past, we shall be in danger of losing the future.

Today our concern must be with that future. For the world is changing. The old era is ending. The old ways will not do.

Abroad, the balance of power is shifting. There are new and more terrible weapons, new and uncertain nations, new pressures of population and deprivation. One third of the world, it has been said, may be free—but one third is the victim of cruel repression, and the other one third is rocked by the pangs of poverty, hunger, and envy. More energy is released by the awakening of these new nations than by the fission of the atom itself.

Meanwhile, Communist influence has penetrated farther into Asia, stood astride the Middle East, and now festers some ninety miles off the coast of Florida. Friends have slipped into neutrality—and neutrals into hostility. As our keynoter reminded us, the President who began his career by going to Korea ends it by staying away from Japan.

The world has been close to war before—but now man, who has survived all previous threats to his existence, has taken into his mortal hands the power to exterminate the entire species some seven times over.

Here at home, the changing face of the future is equally revolutionary. The New Deal and the Fair Deal were bold measures for their generations—but this is a new generation.

A technological revolution on the farm has led to an output explosion—but we have not yet learned to harness that explosion usefully, while protecting our farmers' right to full parity income.

An urban population revolution has overcrowded our schools, cluttered up our suburbs, and increased the squalor of our slums.

A peaceful revolution for human rights—demanding an end to racial discrimination in all parts of our community life—has strained at the leashes imposed by timid executive leadership.

A medical revolution has extended the life of our elder citizens without providing the dignity and security those later years deserve. And a revolution of automation finds machines replacing men in the mines and mills of America, without replacing their incomes or their training or their need to pay the family doctor, grocer, and landlord.

There has also been a change—a slippage—in our intellectual and moral strength. Seven lean years of drought and famine have withered a field of ideas. Blight has descended on our regulatory agencies, and a dry rot, beginning in Washington, is seeping into every corner of America—in the payola mentality, the expense account way of life, the confusion between what is legal and what is right. Too many Americans have lost their way, their will and their sense of historic purpose.

It is a time, in short, for a new generation of leadership—new men to cope with new problems and new opportunities.

All over the world, particularly in the newer nations, young men are coming to power—men who are not bound by the traditions of the past—men who are not blinded by the old fears and hates and rivalries—young men who can cast off the old slogans and delusions and suspicions.

The Republican nominee-to-be, of course, is also a young man. But his approach is as old as McKinley. His party is the party of the past. His speeches are generalities from *Poor Richard's Almanack.* Their platform, made up of leftover Democratic planks, has the courage of our old convictions. Their pledge is a pledge to the status quo—and today there can be no status quo.

Mr. Nixon may feel it is his turn now, after the New Deal and the Fair Deal—but before he deals, someone had better cut the cards.

For I stand tonight facing west on what was once the last frontier. From the lands that stretch three thousand miles behind me, the pioneers of old gave up their safety, their comfort, and sometimes their lives to build a new world here in the West. They were not the captives of their own doubts, the prisoners of their own price tags. Their motto was not "every man for himself"—but "all for the common cause." They were determined to make that new world strong and free, to overcome its hazards and its hardships, to conquer the enemies that threatened from without and within.

Today some would say that those struggles are all over—that all the horizons have been explored, that all the battles have been won, that there is no longer an American frontier.

But I trust that no one in this vast assemblage will agree with those sentiments. For the problems are not all solved and the battles are not all won—and we stand today on the edge of a New Frontier—the frontier of the 1960s—a frontier of unknown opportunities and perils—a frontier of unfulfilled hopes and threats.

Woodrow Wilson's New Freedom promised our nation a new political and economic framework. Franklin Roosevelt's New Deal promised security and succor to those in need. But the New Frontier of which I speak is not a set of promises—it is a set of challenges. It sums up not what I intend to offer the American people, but what I intend to ask of them. It appeals to their pride, not to their pocketbook—it holds out the promise of more sacrifice instead of more security.

But I tell you the New Frontier is here, whether we seek it or not. Beyond that frontier are the uncharted areas of science and space, unsolved problems of peace and war, unconquered pockets of ignorance and prejudice, unanswered questions of poverty and surplus. It would be easier to shrink back from that frontier, to look to the safe mediocrity of the past, to be lulled by good intentions and high rhetoric—and those who prefer that course should not cast their votes for me, regardless of party.

But I believe the times demand invention, innovation, imagination, decision. I am asking each of you to be new pioneers on that New Frontier. My call is to the young in heart, regardless of age—to the stout in spirit, regardless of party—to all who respond to the scriptural call: "Be strong and of a good courage; be not afraid, neither be thou dismayed."

For courage, not complacency, is our need today—leadership, not salesmanship. And the only valid test of leadership is the ability to lead, and lead vigorously. A tired nation, said David Lloyd George, is a Tory nation—and the United States today cannot afford to be either tired or Tory.

There may be those who wish to hear more—more promises to this group or that, more harsh rhetoric about the men in the Kremlin, more assurances of a golden future, where taxes are always low and subsidies ever high. But my promises are in the platform you have adopted; our ends will not be won by rhetoric; and we can have faith in the future only if we have faith in ourselves.

For the harsh facts of the matter are that we stand on this frontier at a turning point in history. We must prove all over again whether this nation—or any nation so conceived—can long endure; whether our society—with its freedom of choice, its breadth of opportunity, its range of alternatives—can compete with the single-minded advance of the Communist system.

Can a nation organized and governed such as ours endure? That is the real question. Have we the nerve and the will? Can we carry through in an age where we will witness not only new breakthroughs in weapons of destruction but also a race for mastery of the sky and the rain, the ocean and the tides, the far side of space and the inside of men's minds?

Are we up to the task—are we equal to the challenge? Are we willing to match the Russian sacrifice of the present for the future—or must we sacrifice our future in order to enjoy the present?

That is the question of the New Frontier. That is the choice our nation must make—a choice that lies not merely between two men or two parties, but between the public interest and private comfort—between national greatness and national decline—between the fresh air of progress and the stale, dank atmosphere of "normalcy"—between determined dedication and creeping mediocrity.

All mankind waits upon our decision. A whole world looks to see what we will do. We cannot fail their trust, we cannot fail to try.

It has been a long road from that first snowy day in New Hampshire to this crowded convention city. Now begins another long journey, taking me into your cities and homes all over America. Give me your help, your hand, your voice, your vote. Recall with me the words of Isaiah: "They that wait upon the Lord shall renew their strength; they shall mount up with wings as eagles; they shall run, and not be weary."

As we face the coming challenge, we, too, shall wait upon the Lord, and ask that He renew our strength. Then shall we be equal to the test. Then we shall not be weary. And then we shall prevail.

Acceptance of Presidential Nomination
Democratic National Convention
Los Angeles, California, July 15, 1960

The First Debate

In the election of 1860, Abraham Lincoln said the question was whether this nation could exist half slave or half free.

In the election of 1960, and in the world around us, the question is whether the world will exist half slave or half free, whether it will move in the direction of freedom, in the direction of the road that we are taking or whether it will move in the direction of slavery.

I think it will depend in great measure upon what we do here in the United States, on the kind of society that we build, on the kind of strength that we maintain.

We discuss tonight domestic issues, but I would not want any implication to be given that this does not involve directly our struggle with Mr. Khrushchev for survival.

Mr. Khrushchev is in New York and he maintains the Communist offensive throughout the world because of the productive power of the Soviet Union itself.

The Chinese Communists have always had a large population but they are important and dangerous now because they are mounting a major effort within their own country. The kind of country we have here, the kind of society we have, the kind of strength we build in the United States, will be the defense of freedom.

If we do well here, if we meet our obligations, if we are moving ahead, then I think freedom will be secure around the world. If we fail, then freedom fails.

Therefore, I think the question before the American people is: Are we doing as much as we can do? Are we as strong as we should be? Are we as strong as we must be if we are going to maintain our independence, and if we're going to maintain and hold out the hand of friendship to those who look to us for assistance, to those who look to us for survival? I should make it very clear that I do not think we're doing enough, that I am not satisfied as an American with the progress that we are making.

This is a great country, but I think it could be a greater country, and this is a powerful country but I think it could be a more powerful country.

I'm not satisfied to have fifty percent of our steel mill capacity unused.

I'm not satisfied when the United States had last year the lowest rate of economic growth of any major industrialized society in the world—

because economic growth means strength and vitality. It means we're able to sustain our defenses. It means we're able to meet our commitments abroad.

I'm not satisfied when we have over $9 billion worth of food, some of it rotting even though there is a hungry world and even though four million Americans wait every month for a food package from the government which averages five cents a day per individual.

I saw cases in West Virginia, here in the United States, where children took home part of their school lunch in order to feed their families. I don't think we are meeting our obligations toward these Americans.

I'm not satisfied when the Soviet Union is turning out twice as many scientists and engineers as we are.

I'm not satisfied when many of our teachers are inadequately paid or when our children go to school on part-time shifts. I think we should have an educational system second to none.

I'm not satisfied when I see men like Jimmy Hoffa, in charge of the largest union in the United States, still free.

I'm not satisfied when we are failing to develop the natural resources of the United States to the fullest. Here in the United States, which developed the Tennessee Valley and which built the Grand Coulee and the other dams in the northwest United States, at the present rate of hydropower production—and that is a hallmark of an industrialized society—the Soviet Union by 1975 will be producing more power than we are. . . .

I'm not satisfied until every American enjoys his full constitutional rights. If a Negro baby is born, and this is true also of Puerto Ricans and Mexicans in some of our cities, he has about one half as much chance to get through high school as a white baby. He has one third as much chance to get through college as a white student. He has about a third as much chance to be a professional man, and about half as much chance to own a house. He has about four times as much chance that he'll be out of work in his life as the white baby. I think we can do better. I don't want the talents of any American to go to waste.

I know that there are those who say that we want to turn everything over to the government. I don't at all. I want the individuals to meet their responsibilities and I want the states to meet their responsibilities. But I think there is also a national responsibility.

That argument has been used against every piece of social legislation in the last twenty-five years. The people of the United States individually could not have developed the Tennessee Valley. Collectively, they could have.

A cotton farmer in Georgia or a peanut farmer, or a dairy farmer in Wisconsin or Minnesota—cannot protect himself against the forces of supply and demand in the marketplace; but, working together in effective governmental programs, they can do so.

Seventeen million Americans over sixty-five who live on an average Social Security check of about seventy-eight dollars a month—they're not able to sustain themselves individually, but they can sustain themselves through the Social Security system.

I don't believe in big government, but I believe in effective governmental action, and I think that's the only way that the United States is going to maintain its freedom; it's the only way that we're going to move ahead. I think we can do a better job. I think we're going to have to do a better job if we are going to meet the responsibilities which time and events have placed upon us.

We cannot turn the job over to anyone else. If the United States fails, then the whole cause of freedom fails, and I think it depends in great measure on what we do here in this country.

The reason Franklin Roosevelt was a good neighbor in Latin America was because he was a good neighbor in the United States, because they felt that the American society was moving again. I want us to recapture that image. I want people in Latin America and Africa and Asia to start to look to America to see how we're doing things, to wonder what the President of the United States is doing, and not to look at Khrushchev or look at the Chinese Communists. That is the obligation upon our generation.

In 1933 Franklin Roosevelt said in his inaugural that this generation of Americans has a "rendezvous with destiny." I think our generation of Americans has the same "rendezvous." The question now is: Can freedom be maintained under the most severe attack it has ever known? I think it can be, and I think in the final analysis it depends upon what we do here. I think it's time America started moving again.

Opening Statement, First Televised
Presidential Candidates Debate
Chicago, Illinois, September 26, 1960

The Definition of Liberal

What do our opponents mean when they apply to us the label "Liberal"? If by "Liberal" they mean, as they want people to believe, someone who is soft in his policies abroad, who is against local government, and who is unconcerned with the taxpayer's dollar, then the record of this party and its members demonstrate that we are not that kind of "Liberal." But if by a "Liberal" they mean someone who looks ahead and not behind, someone who welcomes new ideas without rigid reactions, someone who cares about the welfare of the people—their health, their housing, their schools, their jobs, their civil rights, and their civil liberties—someone who believes that we can break through the stalemate and suspicions that grip us in our policies abroad, if that is what they mean by a "Liberal," then I'm proud to say that I'm a "Liberal."

But first, I would like to say what I understand the word "Liberal" to mean and explain in the process why I consider myself to be a "Liberal," and what it means in the presidential election of 1960.

In short, having set forth my view—I hope for all time—two nights ago in Houston, on the proper relationship between church and state, I want to take this opportunity to set forth my views on the proper relationship between the state and the citizen. This is my political credo:

I believe in human dignity as the source of national purpose, in human liberty as the source of national action, in the human heart as the source of national compassion, and in the human mind as the source of our invention and our ideas. It is, I believe, this faith in our fellow citizens as individuals and as people that lies at the heart of the liberal faith. For liberalism is not so much a party creed or a set of fixed platform promises as it is an attitude of mind and heart, a faith in man's ability through the experiences of his reason and judgment to increase for himself and his fellow men the amount of justice and freedom and brotherhood which all human life deserves.

I believe also in the United States of America, in the promise that it contains and has contained throughout our history of producing a society so abundant and creative and so free and responsible that it cannot only fulfill the aspirations of its citizens, but serve equally well as a beacon for all mankind. I do not believe in a superstate. I see no magic to tax dollars which are sent to Washington and then returned. I abhor the waste and incompetence of large-scale federal bureaucracies in this administration as well as in others. I do not favor state compulsion when voluntary individual effort can do the job and do it well. But I believe in a government which acts, which exercises its full powers and its full responsibilities. Government is an art and a precious obligation; and when it has a job to do, I believe it should do it. And this requires not only great ends but that we propose concrete means of achieving them.

Our responsibility is not discharged by announcement of virtuous ends. Our responsibility is to achieve these objectives with social invention, with political skill, and executive vigor. I believe for these reasons that liberalism is our best and our only hope in the world today. For the liberal society is a free society, and it is at the same time and for that reason a strong society. Its strength is drawn from the will of free people committed to great ends and peacefully striving to meet them. Only liberalism, in short, can repair our national power, restore our national purpose, and liberate our national energies. And the only basic issue in the 1960 presidential campaign is whether our government will fall in a conservative rut and die there, or whether we will move ahead in the liberal spirit of daring, of breaking new ground, of doing in our generation what Woodrow Wilson and Franklin Roosevelt and Harry Truman and Adlai Stevenson did in their time of influence and responsibility.

Our liberalism has its roots in our diverse origins. Most of us are descended from that segment of the American population which was once called an immigrant minority. Today, along with our children and grandchildren, we do not feel minor. We feel proud of our origins and we are not second to any group in our sense of national purpose. For many years New York represented the new frontier to all those who came from the ends of the earth to find new opportunity and new freedom, generations of men and women who fled from the despotism of the czars, the horrors of the Nazis, the tyranny of hunger, who came here to the new frontier in the state of New York. These men and women, a living cross section of American history, indeed, a cross section of the entire world's history of pain and hope, made of this city not only a new world of opportunity, but a new world of the spirit as well.

Tonight we salute Governor and Senator Herbert Lehman as a symbol of that spirit, and as a reminder that the fight for full constitutional rights for all Americans is a fight that must be carried on in 1961.

Many of these same immigrant families produced the pioneers and builders of the American labor movement. They are the men who sweated in our shops, who struggled to create a union, who were driven by longing for education for their children and for their children's development. They went to night schools; they built their own future, their union's future, and their country's future, brick by brick, block by block, neighborhood by neighborhood, and now in their children's time, suburb by suburb.

Tonight we salute George Meany as a symbol of that struggle and as a reminder that the fight to eliminate poverty and human exploitation is a fight that goes on in our own day. But in 1960 the cause of liberalism cannot content itself with carrying on the fight for human justice and economic liberalism here at home. For here and around the world the fear of war hangs over us every morning and every night. It lies, expressed or silent, in the minds of every American. We cannot banish it by repeating that we are economically first or that we are militarily first, for saying so doesn't make it so. More will be needed than goodwill missions or talking back to Soviet politicians or increasing the tempo of the arms race. More will be needed than good intentions, for we know where that paving leads.

In Winston Churchill's words, "We cannot escape our dangers by recoiling from them. We dare not pretend such dangers do not exist."

And tonight we salute Adlai Stevenson as an eloquent spokesman for the effort to achieve an intelligent foreign policy. Our opponents would like the people to believe that in a time of danger it would be hazardous to change the administration that has brought us to this time of danger. I think it would be hazardous not to change. I think it would be hazardous to continue four more years of stagnation and indifference at home and abroad, of starving the underpinnings of our national power, including not only our defense but our image abroad as a friend.

This is an important election. This is an important election—in many ways as important as any in this century—and I think that the Democratic Party and the Liberal Party here in New York, and those who believe in progress all over the United States, should be associated with us in this great effort.

The reason that Woodrow Wilson and Franklin Roosevelt and Harry Truman and Adlai Stevenson had influence abroad, and the United States in their time had it, was because they moved this country here at home, because they stood for something here in the United States, for expanding the benefits of our society to our own people, and the people around the world looked to us as a symbol of hope.

I think it is our task to re-create that same atmosphere in our own time. Our national elections have often proved to be the turning point in the course of our country. I am proposing that 1960 be another turning point in the history of the great Republic.

Some pundits are saying that it's 1928 all over again. I say it's 1932 all over again. I say this is the great opportunity that we will have in our time to move our people and this country and the people of the free world beyond the new frontiers of the 1960s.

Acceptance of New York Liberal Party Nomination
New York City, September 14, 1960

The Issue of Latin America

Twenty years ago this month President Franklin Roosevelt in a radio broadcast to the Western Hemisphere called upon the people of Latin America to join hands with the United States in a common struggle to keep the forces of tyranny from the shores of the Americas. "So bound together," he said, "we are able to withstand any attack from the East or the West. Together we are able to ward off any infiltration of alien political and economic ideas that would destroy our freedom and our democracy."

The nations of South America responded to Franklin Roosevelt's call. Foreign efforts to capture control of the governments of Latin America were halted. American independence was maintained. And the nations of the Western Hemisphere combined in a common effort which ultimately brought about the collapse of Nazi despotism throughout the world.

Today, once again, the independence of the Western Hemisphere is menaced from abroad. Today, once again, the combined efforts of all the American states are vital to the preservation of that independence. Today, once again, only the leadership of the United States can summon all the resources of the hemisphere to the defense of freedom. But today, unlike 1940, we have failed to exercise that leadership. Today, unlike 1940, the nations of Latin America are distrustful of our guidance, suspicious of our intentions, disillusioned by our actions. And today, unlike 1940, the forces of alien tyranny have already found their way into the Western Hemisphere—to within ninety miles of your coast—to the island of Cuba.

And this change has come about in the past eight years.

In 1953 the Republicans inherited an inter-American system in good working order. They inherited a good-neighbor policy which was more than an empty slogan. They inherited a Latin America composed of nations friendly to the United States.

But in eight short years that bright heritage, the heritage of twenty Democratic years, has been largely dissipated and destroyed, and much of the goodwill, which it took two decades to build, has been lost.

In Cuba the Communists have gained a satellite and established a base for the attempted infiltration and subversion of all Latin America. In Venezuela angry mobs have assaulted the Vice-President of the United States. In Mexico City rioting crowds have protested American policy and castigated America itself. In Panama anti-American demonstrations have imperiled the security of the Panama Canal. In Brazil, the newly elected President felt it necessary to appeal to rising anti-American sentiment in order to win the election. And every report, every broadcast, every newspaper dispatch from the south brings fresh news of unrest, of tension, of misunderstanding.

Today, time is running out for the United States in Latin America. . . .

It is time now to renew our understanding and begin to act. For although the Cold War will not be won in Latin America, it may very well be lost there.

Our first failure in Latin America has been the failure to identify ourselves with the rising tide of freedom.

Victor Hugo once wrote that no army can withstand the force of an idea whose time has come. For most of Latin America the time of freedom has come. In 1954 there were thirteen military strongmen in Latin America; today there are only five. And, if we live up to our responsibilities, in the coming months and years we may expect the elimination of all despotism in Latin America—until the American hemisphere is a free hemisphere—not partly free, not almost free, but completely free from Cape Horn to the Arctic Circle.

But the United States, the home of freedom, has been viewed far too often not as the friend of this rising tide of freedom, but as the supporter of toppling and brutal dictatorships.

In 1953 the dictator of Peru was given a medal by the United States.

In 1954 the dictator of Venezuela was awarded the Legion of Merit by our ambassador.

In 1955 our Secretary of the Navy went to Argentina and made an eloquent address comparing dictator Perón to Lincoln—to Perón's advantage.

In 1956 the dictator of Paraguay received his medal from America.

We have warmly embraced Trujillo, the brutal despot of the Dominican Republic, and recently one of our ambassadors was photographed embracing Trujillo's envoy as he was being thrown out of Nicaragua because the OAS had virtually outlawed his government.

We have dumped more than $500 million worth of arms and ammunition into Latin America over the past eight years, much of which has been used to strengthen the hand of dictatorships. And even now, despite the hard lessons of the past, our air force is planning to invite the co-dictator of Nicaragua to Washington as a guest of honor.

Although the Cold War will not be won in Latin America, it may very well be lost there.

The result of these blunders has been disaster. The people of Latin America have begun to feel that we are more interested in stable regimes than in free governments; more interested in fighting against communism than in fighting for freedom; more interested in the possible loss of our investments than in the actual loss of the lives of the thousands of young Latins who have died fighting dictators; and thus when the dictatorships fell, our actions of support were remembered, and we have been distrusted because of them.

Our second major failure in Latin America has been our failure to help the people of Latin America to achieve their economic aspirations.

Latin America is the fastest-growing area in the world. By the end of the century it will have 512 million people—more than twice as many as all of North America. And this enormous population explosion is taking place in countries where millions of people are already condemned to a life of poverty and hunger and disease; where the average family income is less than $300 a year and where population growth is outdistancing economic growth, driving this meager standard of living still lower.

Poverty is not new to Latin America. But what is new is the determination to emerge from poverty, to wipe out hunger and want, to create a modern growing economy in a small fraction of the time it took to build a modern United States or Europe.

The people of Latin America want better homes, better schools, and better living standards; they want land reform, and tax reform, and an end to the corruption which drains off a nation's resources. In short, they want a new deal for South America. And that is why in every Latin American capital there is a street or park named after Franklin Roosevelt—but I do not know of one that is named after Hoover or Coolidge or Harding or Richard M. Nixon.

The people of South America have looked to the United States—their good neighbor—the richest land on earth—for help in this great effort to develop their economy. But in the past eight years we have sent less than five percent of our economic aid to all of Latin America. We refused to enter into discussions to stabilize the commodity prices on which the Latin American economy depends, prices whose rapid fluctuation has caused the loss of more foreign exchange than all that has been gained from our total foreign-aid program. We fought the establishment of an Inter-American Bank until events forced it upon us. We ignored the President of Brazil's imaginative proposal for a large-scale "Operation Pan-America" to develop the economy of Latin America. And we had our Secretary of State leave the Inter-American Conference in 1954, after securing a resolution against Guatemala, but before the Latin American nations had been given a chance to discuss the economic problems which were the purpose of the meeting. . . .

Our third major failure in Latin America has been our failure to demonstrate America's continuing concern with the problems of the people to the south, to establish the contact between nations and people which was the essence of the good-neighbor policy.

Although Latin America is desperately in need of educated and trained men to run a modern, developing economy, in the past eight years we have brought [fewer] than four hundred students a year from all of South America to study here in the United States.

Although misunderstanding of America has been on the increase, we suspended all regular Voice of America Spanish-language broadcasts to South America between 1953 and 1959, with the exception of the six months of the Hungarian crisis. And even today, we only broadcast one hour a day. And we have also cut the number and size of all our other information programs in Latin America. Although our relations with the restless volatile nations of Latin America require the most skilled and constant attention, our diplomatic posts there have too often been viewed merely as a reward for contributions to the Republican campaign treasury, with the result that our representatives have committed blunders which have lost us respect. They have embraced doomed dictators; and they have failed to understand the rising tide of popular discontent which the Communists have so tirelessly worked to exploit.

And while we have ignored the needs of Latin America, during these last eight years of failure and defeat, the Communists have been hard at work in South America. The Soviet Union is offering programs of technical assistance, encouraging young Latins to study behind the Iron Curtain, putting more than $100 million a year into the support of local Communist parties, and offering tempting trade agreements.

When the United States refused to give Argentina credits for petroleum development, the Russians offered $100 million worth of such credits. Brazil and the Soviet Union have signed a $208 million trade agreement, and Russia has become a major importer of Uruguayan wool. Already the Soviet Union has captured one country in Latin America and is using that country as a base from which to export propaganda and revolution throughout the continent. . . .

We must end our open and warm backing of dictators. Our honors must be reserved for democratic leaders, not despots.

There is much to encourage hope in Latin America; the forces of liberal democracy are still strong and are working to create the framework of economic advance, the steady elimination of poverty and want, on which the preservation of freedom will ultimately depend. But our help and our understanding are needed; and needed now, for the time of decision in Latin America has come. And the survival of freedom in the Western Hemisphere will depend on the boldness of our programs in the years to come.

First, we need a new attitude and new approach to the nations of Latin America. Franklin Roosevelt's good-neighbor policy was a success because it demonstrated a continuing concern with hemispheric problems. But in the past eight years we have not demonstrated such concern. We have reacted to a crisis in Guatemala or a crisis in Panama or a crisis in Cuba, and then, when the crisis was over, we continued to ignore the long-range problems and needs which were at the root of all the trouble. The good-neighbor policy is no longer enough. The good-partner policy has been discredited. Our new policy can best be summed up in the Spanish words *alianza para el progreso,* an alliance for progress—an alliance of nations with a common interest in freedom and economic advance in a great common effort to develop the resources of the entire hemisphere, strengthen the forces of democracy, and widen the vocational and educational opportunities of every person in all the Americas. This policy also means constant consultation with Latin American nations on hemispheric problems, as well as on issues of worldwide significance. And it is an alliance, not merely directed against communism, but aimed at helping our sister republics for their own sake.

Secondly, we must give constant and unequivocal support to democracy in Latin America. We must end our open and warm backing of dictators. Our honors must be reserved for democratic leaders, not despots. Our ambassadors must be spokesmen for democracy, not supporters of tyrants. And we must constantly press for free elections in any country where such elections are not held. We must also strongly support the Commission on Human Rights of the OAS, a commission which can serve as a forum before which the crimes and repressions of dictators like Castro and Trujillo can be brought to the attention of all the people of Latin America.

Third, we must help provide the funds, the long-term development loans, essential to a growing economy, an economy which can raise standards of living and keep up with the population explosion, and which will also provide an increasingly important market for American goods.

Until the recent authorization of $500 million for development, nearly all our economic aid had been in the form of loans to buy American exports. As a result basic ends were ignored and a crushing burden of interest payments was imposed on Latin America. For example, Latin America will pay more in interest this year to the Export-Import Bank than the entire $500 million recently authorized by the Congress.

Future programs must emphasize the development of the basic resources on which a modern economy depends, resources like roads and power and schools, resources which private investment cannot provide; but resources which are the fundamental precondition of rising living standards. We must plan our aid in full cooperation with the Latin American states, carefully mapping the often widely varying needs of each nation, and financing a development program through the revenues of the affected nation as well as long-term loans from the United States.

In this effort we should seek the help of those of our Western allies who have historic ties with Latin America, as well as the help of the Latin American nations themselves. For there is a great deal of difference between the economic problems of Argentina, with a GNP of $500 per person, and Bolivia, with a GNP of $100 per person. And perhaps the wealthier nations of South America will be able to offer help, at least in the form of technical assistance, to the poorer countries.

Fourth, we must act to stabilize the prices of the principal commodity exports of Latin America. Almost every country in Latin America depends on one or two basic commodities for nearly all its exports, and basic commodities account for ninety percent of all South American exports. The prices of these commodities are subject to violent change. And a sudden fall can cause a decline which will sharply reduce the national income, upset the budget, and wreck the foreign-exchange position. It is plain that no program of economic development can be effected unless something is done to stabilize commodity prices. . . .

Fifth, we must encourage and assist programs of land reform. In some South American nations archaic systems of absentee ownership still keep land in the grip of a few wealthy landowners, while the mass of the people struggle for a subsistence living as tenants. This concentration of land ownership was one of the principal grievances which underlay the Cuban revolution, and which is behind most of the revolutions in modern South America.

Of course, any decision to reform the system of land ownership can only be made by the country involved. But we should always stand ready to assist them in carrying out this decision by providing technical assistance and loans, as well as helping the new landowners to set up their farms on a productive basis.

Sixth, we must act to stimulate private investment in Latin America, through improved consular services, through the basic development programs which will provide the resources which private industry needs, and by working out international agreements designed to safeguard our investments abroad. . . .

Seventh, we must expand our programs of technical assistance. We need to send an increased flow of engineers, technicians, factory managers, and others to train the Latin Americans in the techniques of modern industry and modern agriculture.

At the same time we must train more South Americans in these same skills. . . .

Eighth, we must step up our own student-exchange program, to provide education for future Latin leaders, perhaps establishing an inter-American university in Puerto Rico to which young men and women from all over the hemisphere could attend.

At the same time we must increase our sadly lagging Voice of America broadcasts, both in Spanish and in Portuguese, and all our other information programs, in order to carry the message of America to the people of Latin America.

Ninth, we must send skilled and trained men to man our diplomatic posts in Latin America, men who will be appointed not for the size of their campaign contributions, but for their interest in and knowledge of the problems of the country in which they represent the United States.

Tenth, we must make every effort to bring about some type of arms control agreement in South America, an agreement which is fully compatible with the national security needs of every nation in the hemisphere. Such an agreement would end the wasteful arms race, which now absorbs sixty percent of the budget of some Latin American nations, dissipates resources which might be used for economic development, and increases tension throughout the hemisphere. . . .

[A] program like this . . . is the ultimate answer to Castro and the Communists. For if Latin America is moving forward, if it is progressing under democratic government, then eventually the people of Cuba too will demand freedom for themselves, and Communist rule in Latin America will perish where it began—in the streets of Havana.

I believe in a Western Hemisphere where we in the United States do not speak patronizingly of "our backyard" or our "little brothers," and where the people of South America do not speak with hostility of the "colossus of the north" or shout "Yankee go home." I believe in a hemisphere of independent and free nations, sharing common traditions and goals, living in peace and mutual respect. In short, I believe in a Western Hemisphere where all people—the Americans of the South and the Americans of the North—the United States and the nations of Latin America—are joined together in an alliance for progress—*alianza para el progreso.*

Campaign Speech
Tampa, Florida, October 18, 1960

The Issue of Peace

I come here tonight and ask your support in picking this country up and moving it forward. One week from tonight the next President of the United States will be turning to the arduous task that lies ahead, the preparation of a legislative program, the selection of men and women to serve our country, and a preparation for the fight for peace abroad. But whoever our next President may be, his efforts for a successful policy abroad will depend on the men and women whom he selects to conduct that policy.

Speaking in this state a month ago, Mr. Nixon showed an incapacity to grasp the essential fact. He set up new machinery intended to win the struggle for peace and freedom. But it turned out to be nothing more than a series of conferences, committees, and goodwill tours. This should come as no surprise. For the last eight years we have faced problem after problem, and the solution to each of them has been to appoint a committee. I think it is time for action. I think it is time we met our problems.

It takes more than words, hard or soft, more than tours, more than parades, more than conferences. It takes a stronger America, militarily, economically, scientifically, and educationally. We need a stronger free world, a stronger attack on world poverty, a stronger United Nations, a stronger United States foreign policy speaking for a stronger America, and that is what we are going to get.

We can push a button to start the next war but there is no push-button magic to winning a lasting and enduring peace. To be peace loving is not enough, for the Sermon on the Mount saved its blessings for the peacemakers. The generation which I speak for has seen enough of warmongers. Let our great role in history be that of peacemakers. But in the two areas where peace can be won, in the field of disarmament and in our representations abroad, this country has been ill served.

Disarmament planning is the most glaring omission in the field of national security and world peace of the last eight years. This administration has [fewer] than one hundred people working full-time on the subject in the entire national government. This is one fifth as many government employees as take care of the cemeteries and memorials for the U.S. Battle Commission. One hundred people working for peace. As a result we have gone to every conference unprepared. Our chief negotiator admitted at the 1958 conference on preventing surprise attacks that we, and I quote him, "hadn't up to this time really given the intense study of the kind of measure which would make this . . . possible." [They] had not given intense study to the very program that they were then putting forward.

A year ago when we went to the disarmament conference, we appointed an attorney from Massachusetts to set up an ad hoc committee. That committee met for three months. It was then dismissed. Four months before the conference began we drafted an attorney from New York to head our mission.

The result was we had no program and we accepted that of the British. How could we be so indifferent to one of our great chances for peace? We are going to have to do better. If we are successful on Tuesday, we are going to set up in the national government a national peace agency, an arms research institute, to prepare the studies which are necessary, to conduct the scientific research which is essential if we are going to speak with vigor and precision in this vital area of opportunity.

Secondly, we are going to have to be better represented. We are going to have to have the best Americans we can get to speak for our country abroad. All of us have admired what Dr. Tom Dooley has done in Laos. And others have been discouraged by the examples that we read of the ugly American. And I think that the United States is going to have to do much better in this area if we are going to defend freedom and peace in the 1960s. For the fact of the matter is that out of Moscow and Peiping and Czechoslovakia and Eastern Germany are hundreds of men and women, scientists, physicists, teachers, engineers, doctors, nurses, studying in those institutes, prepared to spend their lives abroad in the service of world communism. A friend of mine visiting the Soviet Union last summer met a young Russian couple studying Swahili and African customs at the Moscow Institute of Languages. They were not language teachers. He was a sanitation engineer and she was a nurse, and they were being prepared to live their lives in Africa as missionaries for world communism.

This can only be countered by the skill and dedication of Americans who are willing to spend their lives serving the cause of freedom. The key arm of our Foreign Service abroad are the ambassadors and members of our missions. Too many ambassadors have been chosen who are ill equipped and ill briefed. Campaign contributions have been regarded as a substitute for experience. Men who lack compassion for the needy here in the United States were sent abroad to represent us in countries which were marked by disease and poverty and illiteracy and ignorance, and they did not identify us with those causes and the fight against them. They did not demonstrate compassion there. Men who do not even know how to pronounce the name of the head of the country to which they are accredited, as we saw two years ago in the case of our ambassador to Ceylon, have been sent to important countries, essential countries, in the struggle between East and West. How can they compete with Communist emissaries long trained and dedicated and committed to the cause of extending communism in those countries?

In 1958, it was reported that our ambassador to Moscow was the only American ambassador who could speak the [local] language accredited behind the Iron Curtain, only one. Only two of our nine ambassadors to the Arabic-speaking countries spoke Arabic. In eight of the twelve non-English-speaking countries of Western Europe, our ambassadors lack a workable knowledge of the language of the country to which they were accredited.

Our ambassador to Paris could not even discuss negotiations with General de Gaulle, because he lacked that skill in French. This country is going to have to do much better.

It was reported last month that seventy percent of all new Foreign Service officers had no language skill at all. Only three of forty-four

Americans in our embassy in Belgrade could speak Yugoslavian. In Athens only six of seventy-nine Americans spoke modern Greek. In New Delhi, not a single American could speak an Indian dialect fluently. We cannot understand what is in the minds of other people if we cannot even speak to them. That is why we are given tongues. Yet do you think it is possible for us, in the most deadly struggle in which freedom has ever been engaged, to win if we approach it as casually as these statistics indicate that we are?

After the key African state of Guinea, now voting with the Soviet Union in Communist foreign policy, gained its independence, a Russian ambassador showed up the next day. Our ambassador did not show up for nine months. Today, we do not have a single American diplomat in residence in six new countries of Africa which are now members of the United Nations, not a single American diplomat in residence in any of the six. Of the sixteen new African countries which were admitted to the United Nations, do you know how many voted with us on the admission of Red China? None. There are only twenty-six Negroes in the six thousand of our Foreign Service officers, and yet Africa today contains one quarter of all the votes in the General Assembly. I think we can do better.

In the two areas where peace can be won, in the field of disarmament and in our representations abroad, this country has been ill served.

I therefore propose that our inadequate efforts in this area be supplemented by a peace corps of talented young men and women, willing and able to serve their country in this fashion for three years as an alternative or as a supplement to peacetime selective service, well qualified through rigorous standards, well trained in the languages, skills, and customs they will need to know, and directed and paid by the ICA Point Four [foreign aid] agencies.

We cannot discontinue training our young men as soldiers of war, but we also want them to be ambassadors of peace. . . . General Gavin, who jumped with his division in northern France, said that no young man today could serve his country with more distinction than in this struggle for peace around the world.

This would be a volunteer corps, and volunteers would be sought among not only talented young men and women, but all Americans, of whatever age, who wished to serve the great Republic and serve the cause of freedom. Men and women who have taught, or engineers or doctors or nurses, who have reached the age of retirement, or who in the midst of their work wished to serve their country and freedom, should be given an opportunity and an agency in which their talents could serve our country around the globe.

I am convinced that the pool of people in this country of ours anxious to respond to the public service is greater than it has ever been in our history. I am convinced that our men and women, dedicated to freedom, are able to be missionaries, not only for freedom and peace, but to join in a worldwide struggle against poverty and disease and ignorance, diseases in Latin America, for example, which prevented any child in two villages in Brazil in the last twelve months from reaching one year of age.

I think this country in the 1960s can start to move forward again. We can demonstrate what a free society, freely moving and working, can do.

Archimedes said, "Give me a fulcrum and I will move the world." We in the sixties are going to move the world again in the direction of freedom and I ask your help in doing so.

Campaign Speech
San Francisco, California, November 2, 1960

The End of the Campaign

. . . I come here in the last forty-eight hours of this campaign to the greatest rally that we have had in this entire campaign, right here in this city. (It is now a quarter to three [a.m.]—Dick Nixon has been in bed for four hours. . . .)

I run as a candidate for the Presidency with a view that this is a great country, but it must be greater. I want to see us build here in this country a strong and vital and progressive society that will serve as an inspiration to all those people who desire to follow the road that we have followed. . . . We defend freedom. If we succeed here, if we can build a strong and vital society, then the cause of freedom is strengthened. If we fail here, if we drift, if we lie at anchor, if we don't provide an example of what freedom can do in the 1960s, then we have betrayed not only ourselves and our destiny, but all those who desire to be free and are not free. That is why I think this election is important. That is why this is an important campaign.

Street Rally
Waterbury, Connecticut, November 6, 1960

The margin is narrow, but the responsibility is clear . . . a margin of only one vote would still be a mandate.

Press Conference
Hyannis Port, Massachusetts, November 9, 1960

I campaigned downstate with the . . . Lieutenant Governor. Politics is a rather humbling experience. I introduced Sam Shapiro all over Illinois and I figured that I was really going to help him along, and he told me tonight that he won by 250 thousand [votes]—I grabbed Sam Shapiro's coattail and he dragged me in.

Democratic Dinner
Chicago, Illinois, April 28, 1961

I have not always considered the membership of the NAM as among my strongest supporters. . . . I recognize that in the last campaign, most of the members of this luncheon group today supported my opponent, except for a very few—who were under the impression that I was my father's son.

National Association of Manufacturers
New York, New York, December 6, 1961

There is no city in the United States in which I get a warmer welcome and less votes than Columbus, Ohio!

Democratic Dinner
Columbus, Ohio, January 6, 1962

. . . Whatever other qualifications I may have had when I became President, one of them at least was that I knew Wisconsin better than any other President of the United States. That is an unchallengeable statement. My foot-tracks are in every house in this state. . . . I suppose that there is no training ground for the Presidency, but I don't think it's a bad idea for a President to have stood outside of Maier's meat factory in Madison, Wisconsin . . . at five-thirty in the morning, with the temperature ten above.

Wisconsin Democratic Dinner
Milwaukee, Wisconsin, May 12, 1962

CHAPTER 6

The Religious Issue

No obstacle to the Presidency handicapped or antagonized John F. Kennedy more than the widespread charge that a Catholic in the White House could not uphold this country's traditional and constitutional separation of church and state and could not place the national interest ahead of the dictates of his church hierarchy. Many who recalled Al Smith's defeat in the 1928 presidential election opposed Kennedy's nomination in the belief that he was unelectable. His primary victory in West Virginia, an overwhelmingly Protestant state, silenced many of the skeptics but not the bigots, whose charges Kennedy answered in historic fashion in his September 1960 address to the Houston Ministers Association. Even then, according to the University of Michigan post-election survey, Kennedy lost at least 4.5 million Protestant Democrats. Barring a presidential candidate on religious grounds was actually ended not by Kennedy's accession to the White House office but by his conduct of that office in strict adherence to his Houston pledge.

The Responsibility of the Press

I have decided to speak with you today about what has widely been called "the religious issue" in American politics. The phrase covers a multitude of meanings. It is inaccurate to state that my "candidacy created the issue"—that, because I am replying to the bigots, I am now "running on the religious issue in West Virginia" or that my statements in response to interrogation are "fanning the controversy." I am not "trying to be the first Catholic President," as some have written. I happen to believe I can serve my nation as President—and I also happen to have been born a Catholic.

Nor am I appealing, as is too often claimed, to a so-called Catholic vote. Even if such a vote exists—which I doubt—I want no votes solely on account of my religion. Any voter, Catholic or otherwise, who feels another candidate would be a superior president should support that candidate.

Neither do I want anyone to support my candidacy merely to prove that this nation is not bigoted—and that a Catholic can be elected President. I have never suggested that those opposed to me are thereby anti-Catholic. There are ample legitimate grounds for supporting other candidates (although I will not, of course, detail them here). Nor have I ever suggested that the Democratic Party is required to nominate me or face a Catholic revolt in November.

For my religion is hardly, in this critical year of 1960, the dominant issue of our time. It is hardly the most important criterion—or even a relevant criterion—on which the American people should make their choice for Chief Executive.

The members of the press should report the facts as they find them. They should describe the issues as they see them. But they should beware, it seems to me, of either magnifying this issue or oversimplifying it.

One article, for example, supposedly summing the Wisconsin primary up in advance, mentioned the word "Catholic" twenty times in fifteen paragraphs—not mentioning even once dairy farms, disarmament, labor legislation, or any other issue. And on the Sunday before the primary, the *Milwaukee Journal* featured a map of the state, listing county by county the relative strength of three types of voters—Democrats, Republicans, and Catholics.

In West Virginia, it is the same story. As reported in yesterday's *Washington Post,* the great bulk of West Virginians paid very little attention to my religion—until they read repeatedly in the nation's press that this was the decisive issue in West Virginia. There are many serious problems in that state—problems big enough to dominate any campaign—but religion is not one of them.

For the past months and years, I have answered almost daily inquiries from the press about the religious issue. I want to take this opportunity to turn the tables—and to raise some questions for your thoughtful consideration.

First: Is the religious issue a legitimate issue in this campaign? There is only one legitimate question underlying all the rest: Would you, as President of the United States, be responsive in any way to ecclesiastical pressures or obligations of any kind that might in any fashion influence or interfere with your conduct of that office in the national interest? I have answered that question many times. My answer was—and is—*no.*

First: Is the religious issue a legitimate issue in this campaign? . . . Secondly: Can we justify analyzing voters as well as candidates strictly in terms of their religion?

Once that question is answered, there is no legitimate issue of my religion. But there are, I think, legitimate questions of public policy of concern to religious groups which no one should feel bigoted about raising, and to which I do not object to answering. But I do object to being the only candidate required to answer those questions.

Federal assistance to parochial schools, for example, is a very legitimate issue actually before the Congress. I am opposed to it. I believe it is clearly unconstitutional. I voted against it on the Senate floor this year, when offered by Senator Morse. But, interestingly enough, I was the only announced candidate in the Senate who did so. (Nevertheless I have not yet charged my opponents with taking orders from Rome.)

An ambassador to the Vatican could conceivably become a real issue again. I am opposed to it, and said so long ago. But even though it was last proposed by a Baptist President, I know of no other candidate who has been even asked about this matter.

The prospects of any President ever receiving for his signature a bill providing foreign aid funds for birth control are very remote indeed. It is hardly the major issue some have suggested. Nevertheless I have made it clear that I would neither veto nor sign such a bill on any basis except what I considered to be the public interest, without regard to my private religious views. I have said the same about bills dealing with censorship, divorce, our relations with Spain, or any other subject.

These are legitimate inquiries about real questions which the next President may conceivably have to face. But these inquiries ought to be directed equally to all candidates. I have made it clear that I strongly support—out of conviction as well as constitutional obligation—the guarantees of religious equality provided by the First Amendment; and I ask only that these same guarantees be extended to me.

Secondly: Can we justify analyzing voters as well as candidates strictly in terms of their religion? I think the voters of Wisconsin objected to being categorized simply as either Catholics or Protestants in analyzing their political choices. I think they objected to being accosted by reporters outside of political meetings and asked one question only—their religion—not their occupation or education or philosophy or income, only their religion.

Only this week, I received a very careful analysis of the Wisconsin results. It conclusively shows two significant patterns of bloc voting: I ran strongest in those areas where the average temperature in January was twenty degrees or higher, and poorest in those areas where it was fourteen degrees or lower—and I ran well in the beech tree and basswood counties and not so well among the hemlock and pine.

This analysis stands up statistically much better than all the so-called analyses of the religious vote. And so do analyses of each county based on their distance from the Minnesota border, the length of their Democratic tradition, and their inclusion in my campaign itinerary. I carried some areas with large proportions of voters who are Catholics—and I lost some. I carried some areas where Protestants predominate—and I lost some.

For voters are more than Catholics, Protestants, or Jews. They make up their minds for many diverse reasons, good and bad. To submit the candidates to a religious test is unfair enough—to apply it to the voters themselves is divisive, degrading, and wholly unwarranted.

Third and finally: Is there any justification for applying special religious tests to one office only: the Presidency? Little or no attention was paid to my religion when I took the oath as Senator in 1953—as a Congressman in 1947—or as a naval officer in 1941. Members of my faith abound in public office at every level except the White House. What is there about the Presidency that justifies this constant emphasis upon a candidate's religion and that of his supporters?

The Presidency is not, after all, the British Crown, serving a dual capacity in both church and state. The President is not elected to be protector of the faith or guardian of the public morals. His attendance at church on Sunday should be his business alone, not a showcase for the nation.

On the other hand, the President, however intent he may be on subverting our institutions, cannot ignore the Congress—or the voters—or the courts. And our highest court, incidentally, has a long history of Catholic justices, none of whom, as far as I know, was ever challenged on the fairness of his rulings on sensitive church-state issues.

Some may say we treat the Presidency differently because we have had only one previous Catholic candidate for President. But I am growing weary of that term. I am not the Catholic candidate for President. I do not speak for the Catholic Church on issues of public policy—and no one in that Church speaks for me. My record on aid to education, aid to Tito, the Conant nomination, and other issues has displeased some prominent Catholic clergymen and organizations; and it has been approved by others. The fact is that the Catholic Church is not a monolith—it is committed in this country to the principles of individual liberty—and it has no claim over my conduct as a public officer sworn to do the public interest.

So I hope we can see the beginning of the end of references to me as "the Catholic candidate" for President. Do not expect me to explain or defend every act or statement of every pope or priest, in this country or some other, in this century or the last.

I have tried to examine with you today the press's responsibility in meeting this religious issue. The question remains: What is *my* responsibility? I am a candidate. The issue is here. Two alternatives have been suggested:

1. The first suggestion is that I withdraw to avoid a "dangerous religious controversy," and accept the Vice-Presidential nomination in order to placate the so-called Catholic vote.

I find that suggestion highly distasteful. It assumes the worst about a country which prides itself on being more tolerant and better educated than it was in 1928. It assumes that Catholics are a pawn on the political chessboard, moved hither and yon, and somehow "bought off" by the party putting in the second spot a Catholic whom the party barred from the top. And it forgets, finally, that such a performance would have an effect on our image abroad as well as our self-respect here at home.

Are we going to admit to the world that a Jew can be elected mayor of Dublin, a Protestant can be chosen foreign minister of France, a Moslem can serve in the Israeli Parliament—but a Catholic cannot be President of the United States? Are we to tell Chancellor Adenauer, for example, that we want him risking his all on our front lines; but that if he were an American, we would never entrust him with our Presidency—nor would we accept our distinguished guest, General de Gaulle? Are we to admit to the world—worse still, are we to admit to ourselves—that one third of our population is forever barred from the White House?

So I am not impressed by those pleas that I settle for the Vice-Presidency in order to avert a religious spectacle. Surely those who believe it dangerous to elect a Catholic as President will not want him to serve as Vice-President, a heartbeat away from the office.

2. The alternative is to proceed with the primaries, the convention, and the election. If there is bigotry in the country, then so be it—there is bigotry. If that bigotry is too great to permit the fair consideration of a Catholic who has made clear his complete independence and his complete dedication to separation of church and state, then we ought to know it.

But I do not believe that this is the case. I believe the American people are more concerned with a man's views and abilities than with the church to which he belongs. I believe that the Founding Fathers meant it when they provided in Article VI of the Constitution that there should be no religious test for public office—a provision that brought not one dissenting vote, only the comment of Roger Sherman that it was surely unnecessary.

I am confident that the press and other media of this country will recognize their responsibilities in this area—to refute falsehood, to inform the ignorant, and to concentrate on the issues, the *real* issues, in this hour of the nation's peril.

American Society of Newspaper Editors
Washington, D.C., April 21, 1960

I sat next to Cardinal Spellman at dinner the other evening, and asked him what I should say when voters question me about the doctrine of the pope's infallibility. "I don't know, Senator," the Cardinal told me. "All I know is he keeps calling me Spillman."

Bronx Democratic Dinner
New York, New York, April 1960

The Refutation of Bigotry

I am grateful for your generous invitation to speak my views.

While the so-called religious issue is necessarily and properly the chief topic here tonight, I want to emphasize from the outset that we have far more critical issues to face in the 1960 election; the spread of Communist influence, until it now festers ninety miles off the coast of Florida; the humiliating treatment of our President and Vice-President by those who no longer respect our power; the hungry children I saw in West Virginia, the old people who cannot pay their doctor bills, the families forced to give up their farms; an America with too many slums, with too few schools, and too late to the moon and outer space.

These are the real issues which should decide this campaign. And they are not religious issues—for war and hunger and ignorance and despair know no religious barriers.

But because I am a Catholic, and no Catholic has ever been elected President, the real issues in this campaign have been obscured—perhaps deliberately, in some quarters less responsible than this. So it is apparently necessary for me to state once again—not what kind of church I believe in, for that should be important only to me—but what kind of America I believe in.

I believe in an America where the separation of church and state is absolute—where no Catholic prelate would tell the President (should he be Catholic) how to act, and no Protestant minister would tell his parishioners for whom to vote—where no church or church school is granted any public funds or political preference—and where no man is denied public office merely because his religion differs from the President who might appoint him or the people who might elect him.

I believe in an America that is officially neither Catholic, Protestant, nor Jewish—where no public official either requests or accepts instructions on public policy from the pope, the National Council of Churches, or any other ecclesiastical source—where no religious body seeks to impose its will directly or indirectly upon the general populace or the public acts of its officials—and where religious liberty is so indivisible that an act against one church is treated as an act against all.

For while this year it may be a Catholic against whom the finger of suspicion is pointed, in other years it has been, and may someday be again, a Jew—or a Quaker—or a Unitarian—or a Baptist. It was Virginia's harassment of Baptist preachers, for example, that helped lead to Jefferson's Statute of Religious Freedom. Today I may be the victim—but tomorrow it may be you—until the whole fabric of our harmonious society is ripped at a time of great national peril.

Finally, I believe in an America where religious intolerance will someday end—where all men and all churches are treated as equal—where every man has the same right to attend or not attend the church of his choice—where there is no Catholic vote, no anti-Catholic vote, no bloc voting of any kind—and where Catholics, Protestants, and Jews, at both the lay and pastoral level, will refrain from those attitudes of disdain and division which have so often marred their works in the past, and promote instead the American ideal of brotherhood.

That is the kind of America in which I believe. And it represents the kind of Presidency in which I believe—a great office that must neither be humbled by making it the instrument of any one religious group nor tarnished by arbitrarily withholding its occupancy from the members of any one religious group. I believe in a President whose religious views are his own private affair, neither imposed by him upon the nation or imposed by the nation upon him as a condition to holding that office.

I would not look with favor upon a President working to subvert the First Amendment's guarantees of religious liberty. Nor would our system of checks and balances permit him to do so—and neither do I look with favor upon those who would work to subvert Article VI of the Constitution by requiring a religious test—even by indirection—for public office. If they disagree with that safeguard, they should be out openly working to repeal it.

I want a Chief Executive whose public acts are responsible to all groups and obligated to none—who can attend any ceremony, service, or dinner his office may appropriately require of him—and whose fulfillment of his presidential oath is not limited or conditioned by any religious oath, ritual, or obligation.

This is the kind of America I believe in—and this is the kind I fought for in the South Pacific, and the kind my brother died for in Europe. No one suggested then that we might have a "divided loyalty," that we did "not believe in liberty," or that we belonged to a disloyal group that threatened the "freedoms for which our forefathers died."

And in fact this is the kind of America for which our forefathers died—when they fled here to escape religious test oaths that denied office to members of less favored churches—when they fought for the Constitution, the Bill of Rights, and the Virginia Statute of Religious Freedom—and when they fought at the shrine I visited today, the Alamo. For side by side with Bowie and Crockett died McCafferty and Bailey and Carey—but no one knows whether they were Catholics or not. For there was no religious test at the Alamo.

I believe in an America where the separation of church and state is absolute. . . . I believe in a President whose religious views are his own private affair.

I ask you tonight to follow in that tradition—to judge me on the basis of my record of fourteen years in Congress—on my declared stands against an ambassador to the Vatican, against unconstitutional aid to parochial schools, and against any boycott of the public schools (which I have attended myself)—instead of judging me on the basis of these pamphlets and publications we all have seen that carefully select quotations out of context from the statements of Catholic leaders, usually in other countries, frequently in other centuries, and always omitting, of course, the statement of the American bishops in 1948 which strongly endorsed church-state separation, and which more nearly reflects the views of almost every American Catholic.

I do not consider these other quotations binding upon my public acts—why should you? But let me say, with respect to other countries, that I am wholly opposed to the state being used by any religious group, Catholic or Protestant, to compel, prohibit, or persecute the free exercise of any other religion. And I hope that you and I condemn with equal fervor those nations which deny their Presidency to Protestants and those which deny it to Catholics. And rather than cite the misdeeds of those who differ, I would cite the record of the Catholic Church in such nations as Ireland and France—and the independence of such statesmen as Adenauer and de Gaulle.

But let me stress again that these are my views—for, contrary to common newspaper usages I am not the Catholic candidate for President. I am the Democratic Party's candidate for President who happens also to be a Catholic. I do not speak for my church on public matters—and the Church does not speak for me.

Whatever issue may come before me as President—on birth control, divorce, censorship, gambling, or any other subject—I will make my decision in accordance with these views, in accordance with what my conscience tells me to be the national interest, and without regard to outside religious pressures or dictates. And no power or threat of punishment could cause me to decide otherwise.

But if the time should ever come—and I do not concede any conflict to be even remotely possible—when my office would require me to either violate my conscience or violate the national interest, then I would resign the office; and I hope any conscientious public servant would do the same.

But I do not intend to apologize for these views to my critics of either Catholic or Protestant faith—nor do I intend to disavow either my views or my church in order to win this election.

If I should lose on the real issues, I shall return to my seat in the Senate, satisfied that I had tried my best and was fairly judged. But if this election is decided on the basis that forty million Americans lost their chance of being President on the day they were baptized, then it is the whole nation that will be the loser, in the eyes of Catholics and non-Catholics around the world, in the eyes of history, and in the eyes of our own people.

But if, on the other hand, I should win the election, then I shall devote every effort of mind and spirit to fulfilling the oath of the Presidency—practically identical, I might add, to the oath I have taken for fourteen years in the Congress. For, without reservation, I can "solemnly swear that I will faithfully execute the office of President of the United States, and will to the best of my ability preserve, protect, and defend the Constitution . . . so help me God."

Q: If this meeting tonight were held in the sanctuary of my church, it is the policy of my city that has many fine Catholics in it, it is the policy of the Catholic leadership to forbid them to attend a Protestant service. If we tonight were in the sanctuary of my church, as we are, could you and would you attend, as you have here?

SENATOR KENNEDY: Yes; I could. As I said in my statement I would attend any service that has any connection with my public office, or, in the case of a private ceremony, weddings, funerals and so on, of course I would participate and have participated. I think the only question would be whether I could participate as a participant, a believer in your faith, and maintain my membership in my church. That, it seems to me, comes within the private beliefs that a Catholic might have. But as far as whether I could attend this sort of a function in your church, whether I as Senator or President could attend a function in your service connected with my position of office, then I could attend and would attend. . . .

Q: If you are elected President, will you use your influence to get the Roman Catholic countries of South America and Spain to stop persecuting Protestant missionaries and enable them to propagate their faith as the United States gives to the Roman Catholics or any other group?

SENATOR KENNEDY: I would use my influence as President of the United States to permit, to encourage the development of freedom all over the world. One of the rights which I consider to be important is the right of free speech, the right of assembly, the right of free religious practice, and I would hope that the United States and the President would stand for those rights all around the globe without regard to geography or religion.

Q: Senator Kennedy, I have received today a copy of a resolution passed by the Baptist Pastors Conference of St. Louis, and they are going to confront you with this tomorrow night. I would like you to answer to the Houston crowd before you get to St. Louis. This is the resolution:

> With deep sincerity and in Christian grace, we plead with Senator John F. Kennedy as the person presently concerned in this matter to appeal to Cardinal Cushing, Mr. Kennedy's own hierarchical superior in Boston, to present to the Vatican Senator Kennedy's statement relative to the separation of church and state in the United States and religious freedom as separated in the Constitution of the United States, in order that the Vatican may officially authorize such a belief for all Roman Catholics in the United States.

SENATOR KENNEDY: May I just say that, as I do not accept the right of any ecclesiastical official to tell me what I shall do in the sphere of my public responsibility as an elected official, I do not propose to ask Cardinal Cushing to ask the Vatican to take some action. I do not propose to interfere with their free right to do exactly what they want. There is no doubt in my mind that the viewpoint that I have expressed tonight publicly represents the opinion of the overwhelming majority of American Catholics, and I think that my view is known to Catholics around the world.

Q: We appreciate your forthright statement. May I say we have great admiration for you. But until we know this is the position of your church, because there will be many Catholics who will be appointed if you are elected President, we would like to know that they, too, are free to make such statements as you have been so courageous to make.

SENATOR KENNEDY: Let me say that anyone that I would appoint to office as a Senator or as a President, would, I hope, hold the same view, of necessity, of living up to not only the letter of the Constitution but the spirit. I believe I am stating the viewpoint that Catholics in this country hold on the happy relationship which exists between church and state.

Q: Do you state it with the approval of the Vatican?

SENATOR KENNEDY: I don't have to have approval in that sense. I have not submitted my statement before I read it to the Vatican. I did not submit it to Cardinal Cushing. But my judgment is that Cardinal Cushing, who is the Cardinal of the diocese of which I am a member, would approve of this statement, [but] I am the one that is running for the office of the Presidency and not Cardinal Cushing and not anyone else. . . .

I guess our time is coming to an end, but let me say finally that I am delighted to come here today. I don't want anyone to think, because they interrogate me on this very important question, that I regard that as unfair questioning or unreasonable, or that somebody who is concerned about the matter is prejudiced or bigoted. I think this fight for religious freedom is basic in the establishment of the American system, and therefore any candidate for the office should submit himself to the questions of any reasonable man.

My only objection would be—my only limit to that would be—if somebody said: "regardless of Senator Kennedy's position, regardless of how much evidence he has given that what he says he means, I still would not vote for him because he is a member of that church." I would consider that unreasonable. What I would consider to be reasonable, in an exercise of free will and free choice, is to ask the candidate to state his views as broadly as possible, to investigate his record to see whether what he states he believes, and then to make an independent, rational judgment as to whether he could be entrusted with this highly important position.

I want you to know that I am grateful to you for inviting me tonight. I am sure I have made no converts to my church. But I do hope that at least my view, which I believe to be the view of my fellow Catholics who hold office, may be of some value in assisting you to make a careful judgment. Thank you.

Greater Houston Ministerial Association
Houston, Texas, September 12, 1960

The Differences From 1928

I am glad to be here at this notable dinner once again, and I am glad that Mr. Nixon is here also. Now that Cardinal Spellman has demonstrated the proper spirit, I assume that shortly I will be invited to a Quaker dinner honoring Herbert Hoover.

Cardinal Spellman is the only man so widely respected in American politics that he could bring together, amicably, at the same banquet table, for the first time in this campaign, two political leaders who are increasingly apprehensive about the November election, who have long eyed each other suspiciously, and who have disagreed so strongly, both publicly and privately, Vice-President Nixon and Governor Rockefeller.

Mr. Nixon, like the rest of us, has had his troubles in this campaign. At one point even *The Wall Street Journal* was criticizing his tactics. That is like the *Osservatore Romano* criticizing the pope. . . .

One of the inspiring notes that was struck in the last debate was struck by the Vice-President in his very moving warning to the children of the nation and the candidates against the use of profanity by Presidents and ex-Presidents when they are on the stump. (And I know after fourteen years in the Congress with the Vice-President that he was very sincere in his views about the use of profanity.) But I am told that a prominent Republican said to him yesterday in Jacksonville, Florida, "Mr. Vice-President, that was a damn fine speech." And the Vice-President said, "I appreciate the compliment but not the language." And the Republican went on, "Yes, sir, I liked it so much that I contributed a thousand dollars to your campaign." And Mr. Nixon replied, "The hell you say."

However, I would not want to give the impression that I am taking former president Truman's use of language lightly. I have sent him the following wire:

> Dear Mr. President: I have noted with interest your suggestion as to where those who vote for my opponent should go. While I understand and sympathize with your deep motivation, I think it is important that our side try to refrain from raising the religious issue.

One of the subjects that interests candidates and those who write about candidates is whether 1960 will be another 1928. I have had some interest in that question myself. Looking at the speeches of Governor

Smith in the 1928 campaign, I am struck by the continuity of the themes. The 1928 and 1960 campaigns, with all of the obvious differences, have much in common. In 1928, as in 1960, the Yankees won the pennant, the Postmaster General was promising efficient mail delivery at last, and farm purchasing power was down some twenty percent compared to eight years earlier. Three million people had left the farms in that period, just as they have in the last eight years. The stock market was unstable and two thirds of all corporate profits went to one fourth of one percent of the corporations.

In 1960, the citizens of this country face not only the great question of whether freedom will prevail, but also whether it will even endure.

In September 1928, the Republican candidate for the Presidency declared: "Real wages have improved more during the past seven and a half years than in any similar period in the history of our country." He spoke of the country's unparalleled progress. He stressed that American comfort, hope, and confidence for the future were immeasurably higher than they were seven and a half years ago.

The Democratic candidate in 1928 questioned how stable our prosperity was. He pointed to the pockets of industrial unemployment. He warned of a farm depression. He criticized administration farm vetoes. He stressed, and I quote him, "the necessity for the restoration of cordial relations with Latin America" and he called for more effective action on disarmament.

The Democratic nominee in 1928 spoke . . . about building a stronger America, strengthening not only our economy but our sense of moral purpose and our public duty. In all of these and other ways, 1960 and 1928 may be sisters under the skin.

Some say that this will also be true when the ballots are counted, that the religious convictions of the candidates will influence the outcome more than their convictions on the issues. But this is where I believe that

1928 and 1960 are very different. Regardless of the outcome, and regardless of these similarities, I do not believe the American voter in 1960 is the same as the American voter of 1928. For we live in a different world.

There are a billion more people crowding our globe, and every American can hear the rumbling of a distant drum. The next President will have a budget twenty-five times as large as that of the candidates in Al Smith's time—and he will face problems unprecedented in that time or in any time in our long history, automation and unemployment, farm surpluses and food shortages, a high cost of living in the midst of an economic slump, new nations, new leaders. The world is different across the street and on the other side of the moon. The white race is in the minority, the free-enterprise system is in the minority and the majority are looking at us harder and longer than they ever looked before.

The people who live in the tenements of Africa and Asia and Latin America want to fight their way out of the slums. The Lower East Side of the world is looking for help, and unlike 1928 the Lower East Side of the world has a voice and a vote.

"The world is large," John Boyle O'Reilly wrote, "the world is large when its weary league two loving hearts divide, but the world is small when your enemy is loose on the other side."

In 1960, as never before, our enemy is loose on the other side. In 1928 the voters perhaps could be excused for not seeing the storm coming, the Depression, the Japanese conquest of Manchuria, Hitler's rise, and all the rest. But in 1960, the citizens of this country face not only the great question of whether freedom will prevail, but also whether it will even endure. Thus, 1960 and 1928 are very different. It will be with this view of America that we shall accept the fortunes of November 8, 1960, be they favorable or unfavorable, good or bad.

The American people in 1960 see the storm coming. They see the perils ahead. 1960 is not 1928. I am confident that, whatever their verdict, Republican or Democratic, myself or Mr. Nixon, their judgment will be based not on any extraneous issue, but on the real issues of our time, on what is best for our country, on the hard facts that face us, on the convictions of the candidates and their parties, and on their ability to interpret them.

When this happens, then the bitter memory of 1928 will begin to fade, and all that will remain will be the figure of Al Smith, large against the horizon, true, courageous, and honest, who, in the words of the Cardinal, served his country well, and having served his country well, nobly served his God.

Annual Al Smith Memorial Dinner
New York, New York, October 19, 1960

The Responsibility of Parents

Q: Mr. President, in the furor over the Supreme Court's decision on prayer in the schools, some members of Congress have been introducing legislation for constitutional amendments specifically to sanction prayer or religious exercise in the schools. Can you give us your opinion of the decision itself and of these moves of the Congress to circumvent it?

THE PRESIDENT: I haven't seen the measures in the Congress and . . . would have to make a determination of what the language was and what effect it would have on the First Amendment. The Supreme Court has made its judgment, and a good many people obviously will disagree with it. . . . But I think it is important, if we are going to maintain our constitutional principle, [to]support the Supreme Court decisions even when we may not agree with them.

In addition, we have in this case a very easy remedy and that is to pray ourselves. I would think that it would be a welcome reminder to every American family that we can pray a good deal more at home, we can attend our churches with a good deal more fidelity, and we can make the true meaning of prayer much more important in the lives of all of our children. . . . I would hope that as a result of this decision that all American parents will intensify their efforts at home—and the rest of us will support the Constitution and the responsibility of the Supreme Court in interpreting it—which is theirs, and given to them by the Constitution.

President's News Conference
Washington, D.C., June 27, 1962

On the stump, 1962.
PHOTO COURTESY CECIL W. STOUGHTON.

PART III

The New Frontier

CHAPTER 7

The Restoration of Economic Growth

In 1960, America was crippled by a spreading recession, and John Kennedy campaigned on a vow "to get this country moving again." Once elected, he set out to do just that, moved by the same sense of economic justice that had sparked his plea for veterans' housing in one of his earliest speeches in Congress. Though he felt more expert regarding foreign affairs, the long hours that he invested in new or revamped economic, social, budgetary, and anti-inflationary policies helped produce this century's longest and strongest period of American economic growth.

The Angry Young Congressman

Mr. Speaker, this Congress will adjourn Saturday. It will have considered action on many matters of varying importance, but it will not have taken any action to meet the most pressing problem with which this country is now confronted—the severe ever-growing shortage of housing which faces our veterans and others of moderate income. . . .

The Bureau of the Census, in a recent survey, stated that there were 160,000 veterans of World War II in the Boston area in July of 1946. Forty-two percent of the veterans who were married among this group were living in rented rooms or doubled up. Their need is drastic. . . .

The inflated costs of building have priced new homes right out of the price level that veterans can afford to pay. This is the situation facing every veteran in this country today. It is the most important problem they face.

The majority party of this House has done nothing to help these men meet this great problem. They have spent $35 billion. They have subsidized industries. They have late this afternoon called for an investigation of the housing shortage. Since before the war ended we have been making investigations. The facts are known. This gesture by the Republican Party is a fraud—in order to draw attention away from their crass ignorance of this problem during the seven months they have been in control. They have always been receptive to the best interests of the real estate and building associations, but when it came to spending money to secure homes for the people of this country, they just were not interested.

I was sent to this Congress by the people of my district to help solve the most pressing problem facing the country—the housing crisis.

I am going to have to go back to my district Saturday, a district that sent probably more boys per family into this last war than any in the country, and when they ask me if I was able to get them any homes, I will have to answer, "not a one—not a single one."

U.S. House of Representatives
Washington, D.C., July 24, 1947

The Determined New President

The present state of our economy is disturbing. We take office in the wake of seven months of recession, three and one half years of slack, seven years of diminished economic growth, and nine years of falling farm income.

Business bankruptcies have reached their highest level since the Great Depression. Since 1951 farm income has been squeezed down by twenty-five percent. Save for a brief period in 1958, insured unemployment is at the highest peak in our history. Of some five and one-half million Americans who are without jobs, more than one million have been searching for work for more than four months. And during each month some 150,000 workers are exhausting their already meager jobless benefit rights.

Nearly one eighth of those who are without jobs live almost without hope in nearly one hundred especially depressed and troubled areas. The rest include new school graduates unable to use their talents, farmers forced to give up their part-time jobs which helped balance their family budgets, skilled and unskilled workers laid off in such important industries as metals, machinery, automobiles, and apparel.

Our recovery from the 1958 recession, moreover, was anemic and incomplete. Our gross national product never regained its full potential. Unemployment never returned to normal levels. Maximum use of our national industrial capacity was never restored.

In short, the American economy is in trouble. The most resourceful industrialized country on earth ranks among the last in the rate of economic growth. Since last spring our economic growth rate has actually receded. Business investment is in a decline. Profits have fallen below predicted levels. Construction is off. A million unsold automobiles are in inventory. Fewer people are working and the average work week has shrunk well below forty hours. Yet prices have continued to rise—so that now too many Americans have less to spend for items that cost more to buy.

Economic prophecy is at best an uncertain art—as demonstrated by the prediction one year ago from this same podium that 1960 would be, and I quote, "the most prosperous year in our history." Nevertheless, forecasts of continued slack and only slightly reduced unemployment through 1961 and 1962 have been made with alarming unanimity—and this administration does not intend to stand helplessly by.

We cannot afford to waste idle hours and empty plants while awaiting the end of the recession. We must show the world what a free economy can do—to reduce unemployment, to put unused capacity to work, to spur new productivity, and to foster higher economic growth within a range of sound fiscal policies and relative price stability.

I will propose to the Congress within the next fourteen days measures to improve unemployment compensation through temporary increases in duration on a self-supporting basis—to provide more food for the families of the unemployed, and to aid their needy children; to redevelop our areas of chronic labor surplus; to expand the services of the U.S. employment offices; to stimulate housing and construction; to secure more purchasing power for our lowest-paid workers by raising and expanding the minimum wage; to offer tax incentives for sound plant investment; to increase the development of our natural resources; to encourage price stability; and to take other steps aimed at insuring a prompt recovery and paving the way for increased long-range growth. This is not a partisan program concentrating on our weaknesses—it is, I hope, a national program to realize our national strength. . . .

We must show the world what a free economy can do.

Our national household is cluttered with unfinished and neglected tasks. Our cities are being engulfed in squalor. Twelve long years after Congress declared our goal to be "a decent home and a suitable environment for every American family," we still have 25 million Americans living in substandard homes. A new housing program under a new Housing and Urban Affairs Department will be needed this year.

Our classrooms contain 2 million more children than they can properly have room for, taught by 90,000 teachers not properly qualified to teach. One third of our most promising high school graduates are financially unable to continue the development of their talents. The war babies of the 1940s, who overcrowded our schools in the 1950s, are now descending in 1960 upon our colleges—with two college students for every one, ten years from now—and our colleges are ill prepared. We lack the scientists, the engineers, and the teachers our world obligations require. We have neglected oceanography, saline-water conversion, and the basic research that lies at the root of all progress. Federal grants for both higher and public school education can no longer be delayed.

Medical research has achieved new wonders—but these wonders are too often beyond the reach of too many people, owing to a lack of income (particularly among the aged), a lack of hospital beds, a lack of nursing homes, and a lack of doctors and dentists. Measures to provide health care for the aged under Social Security, and to increase the supply of both facilities and personnel, must be undertaken this year.

Our supply of clean water is dwindling. Organized and juvenile crimes cost the taxpayers millions of dollars each year, making it essential that we have improved enforcement and new legislative safeguards. The denial of constitutional rights to some of our fellow Americans on account of race—at the ballot box and elsewhere—disturbs the national conscience, and subjects us to the charge of world opinion that our democracy is not equal to the high promise of our heritage. Morality in private business has not been sufficiently spurred by morality in public business. A host of problems and projects in all fifty states, though not possible to include in this message, deserves—and will receive—the attention of both the Congress and the executive branch. On most of these matters, messages will be sent to the Congress within the next two weeks.

State of the Union Address
The Capitol, Washington, D.C.
January 30, 1961

The Road to Recovery

Today, I would briefly mention three areas of common concern . . . economic growth, plant modernization, and price stability.

I

First: Economic growth has come to resemble the Washington weather —everyone talks about it, no one says precisely what to do about it, and our only satisfaction is that it can't get any worse.

The economic program which I have set before the Congress is essentially a program for recovery—and I do not equate recovery with growth. But it is an essential first step. Only by putting millions of people back to work can we expand purchasing power and markets. Only by higher income and profits can we provide the incentive and the means for increased investment. And only when we are using our plants at near capacity can we expect any solid expansion.

Capacity operation is the key. No matter what other arguments or stimulants are used, the incentives for investing new capital to expand manufacturing plants and equipment are weak as long as manufacturers are operating at less than eighty percent of their capacity. From 1950 to 1958, we put only one sixth of our total output into capital formation, while Japan, Germany, Italy, the Netherlands, Canada, and Sweden were all investing one fifth or more of their total output in capital goods. So it is not surprising that each of these and other nations over the past several years have all surpassed us in average annual rate of economic growth.

I think we can do better. Working together, business and government must do better—putting people back to work, using plants to capacity, and spurring savings and investments with at least a large part of our economic gains—beginning not when our economy is back at the top, but beginning now.

II

Secondly: New plant investment not only means expansion of capacity—it means modernization as well. Gleaming new factories and headlines about automation have diverted our attention from an aging industrial plant. Obsolescence is slowing down our growth, handicapping our productivity, and worsening our competitive position abroad.

Nothing can reverse our balance of payments deficit if American machinery and equipment cannot produce the newest products of the highest quality in the most efficient manner. The available evidence on the age of our industrial plant is unofficial and fragmentary; but the trend is unmistakable—we are falling behind.

The average age of equipment in American factories today is about nine years. In a dynamic economy, that average should be falling, as new equipment is put into place. Instead, the available evidence suggests that it has been slowly rising.

Private surveys of machine tools used by manufacturers of general industrial equipment found less than half of these tools over ten years old in 1949 but two thirds over that age in 1958. Nineteen percent of our machine tools were found to be over twenty years old.

But modernization and productivity depend upon more than investment in physical resources . . . there is a direct connection between increased emphasis on education in this country and also upon increased productivity and technological change.

Meanwhile, other countries have been lowering the average age of their fixed capital. The German example is the most spectacular—their proportion of capital equipment and plants under five years of age grew from one sixth of the total in 1948 to two fifths in 1957.

All of these facts point in one direction: We must start now to provide additional stimulus to the modernization of American industrial plants. Within the next few weeks, I shall propose to the Congress a new tax incentive for businesses to expand their normal investment in plants and equipment.

But modernization and productivity depend upon more than investment in physical resources. . . . Equally essential is investment in human resources. And I think that this is obvious to those of us who have considered the problems of unemployment and depressed areas. There is no doubt that the maximum impact of a reducing economy falls upon those who are at the bottom of the educational ladder. The first people unemployed are those with the least education, the last people to be hired back are those with the least education. So there is a direct connection between increased emphasis on education in this country and also upon increased productivity and technological change.

Without strengthened programs for health, education, and science and research, the new modern plant would only be a hollow shell. Many of these programs are within the province of state and local governments. Full recovery will increase the tax revenues that they so sorely need. But the federal government will have to pay its fair share of developing these human resources.

III

Finally, government and business must turn their attention to the problem of price stability. Concern over the resumption of inflationary pressures hangs over all our efforts to restore the economy, to stimulate its growth, and to maintain our competitive status abroad. In recent days, complaints have been voiced in some quarters that this administration was not meeting its responsibilities in this area. But the facts are that, whatever one may regard our responsibilities to be, we are almost totally without direct and enforceable powers over the central problem. A free government in a free society has only a limited influence—provided that they are above the minimum—over prices and wages freely set and bargained for by free individuals and free enterprises. And this is as it should be if our economy is to remain free.

Nevertheless, the public interest in major wage and price determinations is substantial. Ways must be found to bring that public interest before the parties concerned in a fair and orderly manner.

For this reason, I have announced my determination to establish a Presidential Advisory Committee on Labor-Management Policy, with members drawn from labor, management, and the public. I want this committee to play a major role in helping promote sound wage and price policies, productivity increases, and a betterment of America's competitive position in world markets. I will look to this committee to make an important contribution to labor-management relations, and to a wider understanding of their impact on price stability and our economic health. And in this undertaking, I ask and urge the constructive cooperation of this organization and its members.

Economic growth, plant modernization, price stability—these are all intangible and elusive goals. But they are all essential to your success, and to the success of our country. Initiative, innovation, hard work, and cooperation will be required, on your part, and on ours.

But I have confidence in our nation, confidence in our economy, and confidence in your ability to meet your obligations fully. I hope that my associates and I can merit your confidence as well. For I can assure you that we love our country, not for what it was, though it has always been great—not for what it is, though of this we are deeply proud—but for what it someday can and, through the efforts of us all, someday will be.

National Industrial Conference Board
Washington, D.C., February 13, 1961

The Prudent Steward

This administration intends to adhere during the course of its term of office to the following basic principles:

1. Federal revenue and expenditure levels must be adequate to meet effectively and efficiently those essential needs of the nation which require public support as well as, or in place of, private effort. We can afford to do what must be done, publicly and privately, up to the limit of our economic capacity—a limit we have not even approached for several years.

2. Federal revenues and expenditures—the federal budget—should, apart from any threat to national security, be in balance over the years of the business cycle, running a deficit in years of recession when revenues decline and the economy needs the stimulus of additional expenditures, and running a surplus in years of prosperity, thus curbing inflation, reducing the public debt, and freeing funds for private investment.

3. Federal expenditure and revenue programs should contribute to economic growth and maximum employment within a setting of reasonable price stability. Because of the limits which our balance of payments deficit currently places upon the use of monetary policy, especially the lowering of short-term interest rates, as a means of stimulating economic growth and employment, fiscal policy—our budget and tax policies—must assume a heavier share of the responsibility.

4. Each expenditure proposed will be evaluated in terms of our national needs and priorities, consistent with the limitations and objectives described above and compared with the urgency of other budgetary requirements. We will not waste our resources on inefficient or undesirable expenditure simply because the economy is slack—nor, in order to run a surplus, will we deny our people essential services or security simply because the economy is prosperous.

5. As the nation, its needs, and their complexity continue to grow, federal nondefense expenditures may also be expected to increase, as predicted by a 1960 Bureau of the Budget study, and as indicated by the nearly forty-five percent increase from fiscal 1953 to fiscal 1961 in expenditures other than national security. But we must not allow expenditures to rise of their own momentum, without regard to value received, prospective revenues, economic conditions, the possibilities

of closing out old activities when initiating new ones, and the weight of current taxes on the individual citizen and the economy. It is my determined purpose to be a prudent steward of the public funds—to obtain a dollar's worth of results for every dollar we spend.

Special Message to Congress on Budget and Fiscal Policy
Washington, D.C., March 24, 1961

The Expansion of Opportunity

When the youngest child alive today has grown to the cares of manhood, our position in the world will be determined first of all by what provisions we make today—for his education, his health, and his opportunities for a good home and a good job and a good life.

At home, we began the year in the valley of recession—we completed it on the high road of recovery and growth. . . . At year's end the economy which Mr. Khrushchev once called a "stumbling horse" was racing to new records in consumer spending, labor income, and industrial production.

We are gratified—but we are not satisfied. Too many unemployed are still looking for the blessings of prosperity. As those who leave our schools and farms demand new jobs, automation takes old jobs away. To expand our growth and job opportunities, I urge on the Congress measures [for] Manpower Training and Development . . . Youth Employment Opportunities . . . and tax credits for investment in machinery and equipment.

Moreover—pleasant as it may be to bask in the warmth of recovery—let us not forget that we have suffered three recessions in the last seven years. The time to repair the roof is when the sun is shining—by filling . . . basic gaps in our antirecession protection. . . .

If we enact this . . . program, we can show the whole world that a free economy need not be an unstable economy—that a free system need not leave men unemployed—and that a free society is not only the most productive but the most stable form of organization yet fashioned by man.

But recession is only one enemy of a free economy—inflation is another. Last year, 1961, despite rising production and demand, consumer prices held almost steady—and wholesale prices declined. This is the best record of overall price stability of any comparable period of recovery since the end of World War II.

Inflation too often follows in the shadow of growth—while price stability is made easy by stagnation or controls. But we mean to maintain both stability and growth in a climate of freedom.

Our first line of defense against inflation is the good sense and public spirit of business and labor—keeping their total increases in wages and profits in step with productivity. There is no single statistical test to guide each company and each union. But I strongly urge them—for their country's interest, and for their own—to apply the test of the public interest to these transactions.

I am submitting for fiscal 1963 a balanced federal budget.

I am submitting for fiscal 1963 a balanced federal budget.

But a stronger nation and economy require more than a balanced budget. They require progress in those programs that spur our growth and fortify our strength. . . . a new Department of Urban Affairs and Housing . . . a new comprehensive farm program . . . a new long-range conservation and recreation program—expansion of our superb national parks and forests; preservation of our authentic wilderness areas; new starts on water and power projects as our population steadily increases; and expanded REA [Rural Electrification Administration] generation and transmission loans.

Finally, a strong America cannot neglect the aspirations of its citizens—the welfare of the needy, the health care of the elderly, the education of the young. For we are not developing the nation's wealth for its own sake. Wealth is the means—and people are the ends. All our material riches will avail us little if we do not use them to expand the opportunities of our people. . . .

To help those least fortunate of all, I am recommending a new public welfare program, stressing services instead of support, rehabilitation instead of relief, and training for useful work instead of prolonged dependency.

I am proposing a mass immunization program . . . improvements in the Food and Drug laws . . . the enactment . . . of health insurance for the aged . . . a massive attack to end adult illiteracy . . . bills to improve educational quality, to stimulate the arts . . . federally financed scholarships . . . federal aid to public school construction.

To relieve the critical shortage of doctors and dentists—and this is a matter which should concern us all—and expand research, I urge action to aid medical and dental colleges and scholarships and to establish new national institutes of health.

To take advantage of modern vaccination achievements, I am proposing a mass immunization program, aimed at the virtual elimination of such ancient enemies of our children as polio, diphtheria, whooping cough, and tetanus.

To protect our consumers from the careless and the unscrupulous, I shall recommend improvements in the Food and Drug laws—strengthening inspection and standards, halting unsafe and worthless products, preventing misleading labels, and cracking down on the illicit sale of habit-forming drugs.

But in matters of health, no piece of unfinished business is more important or more urgent than the enactment under the Social Security system of health insurance for the aged. . . . I shall recommend plans for a massive attack to end adult illiteracy . . . bills to improve educational quality, to stimulate the arts, and, at the college level, to provide federal loans for the construction of academic facilities and federally financed scholarships . . . federal aid to public school construction and teachers' salaries.

These are not unrelated measures addressed to specific gaps or grievances in our national life. They are the pattern of our intentions and the foundation of our hopes. "I believe in democracy," said Woodrow Wilson, "because it releases the energy of every human being." The dynamic of democracy is the power and the purpose of the individual, and the policy of this administration is to give to the individual the opportunity to realize his own highest possibilities.

Our program is to open to all the opportunity for steady and productive employment, to remove from all the handicap of arbitrary or irrational exclusion, to offer to all the facilities for education and health and welfare, to make society the servant of the individual and the individual the source of progress, and thus to realize for all the full promise of American life.

State of the Union Address
The Capitol, Washington, D.C.
January 11, 1962

The Preservation of Price Stability

I have several announcements to make.

Simultaneous and identical actions of United States Steel and other leading steel corporations increasing steel prices by some six dollars a ton constitute a wholly unjustifiable and irresponsible defiance of the public interest. In this serious hour in our nation's history, when we are confronted with grave crises in Berlin and Southeast Asia, when we are devoting our energies to economic recovery and stability, when we are asking reservists to leave their homes and families for months on end and servicemen to risk their lives—and four were killed in the last two days in Vietnam—and asking union members to hold down their wage requests, at a time when restraint and sacrifice are being asked of every citizen, the American people will find it hard, as I do, to accept a situation in which a tiny handful of steel executives, whose pursuit of private power and profit exceeds their sense of public responsibility, can show such utter contempt for the interests of 185 million Americans.

If this rise in the cost of steel is imitated by the rest of the industry, instead of rescinded, it would increase the cost of homes, autos, appliances, and most other items for every American family. It would increase the cost of machinery and tools to every American businessman and farmer. It would seriously handicap our efforts to prevent an inflationary spiral from eating up the pensions of our older citizens, and our new gains in purchasing power.

It would add, Secretary McNamara informed me this morning, an estimated $1 billion to the cost of our defenses, at a time when every dollar is needed for national security and other purposes. It would make it more difficult for American goods to compete in foreign markets, more difficult to withstand competition from foreign imports, and thus more difficult to improve our balance of payments position and stem the flow of gold. And it is necessary to stem it for our national security, if we're going to pay for our security commitments abroad. And it would surely handicap our efforts to induce other industries and unions to adopt responsible price and wage policies.

The facts of the matter are that there is no justification for an increase in steel prices. The recent settlement between the industry and the union, which does not even take place until July first, was widely acknowledged to be noninflationary, and the whole purpose and effect of this administration's role, which both parties understood, was to achieve an agreement which would make unnecessary any increase in prices. Steel output per man is rising so fast that labor costs per ton of steel can actually be expected to decline in the next twelve months. And in fact, the acting commissioner of the Bureau of Labor Statistics informed me this morning that, and I quote, "employment costs per unit of steel output in 1961 were essentially the same as they were in 1958."

The American people have a right to expect . . . a higher sense of business responsibility for the welfare of their country.

The cost of the major raw materials, steel scrap and coal, has also been declining, and for an industry which has been generally operating at less than two thirds of capacity, its profit rate has been normal and can be expected to rise sharply this year in view of the reduction in idle capacity. Their lot has been easier than that of one hundred thousand steelworkers thrown out of work in the last three years. The industry's cash dividends have exceeded $600 million in each of the last five years, and earnings in the first quarter of this year were estimated in the February twenty-eighth *Wall Street Journal* to be among the highest in history.

In short, at a time when they could be exploring how more efficiency and better prices could be obtained, reducing prices in this industry in recognition of lower costs, their unusually good labor contract, their foreign competition and their increase in production and profits which are coming this year, a few gigantic corporations have decided to increase prices in ruthless disregard of their public responsibilities.

The Steelworkers Union can be proud that it abided by its responsibilities in this agreement, and this government also has responsibilities which we intend to meet. The Department of Justice and the Federal Trade Commission are examining the significance of this action in a free, competitive economy. The Department of Defense and other agencies are reviewing its impact on their policies of procurement. And I am informed that steps are under way by those members of the Congress who plan appropriate inquiries into how these price decisions are so quickly made and reached and what legislative safeguards may be needed to protect the public interest.

Price and wage decisions in this country, except for a very limited restriction in the case of monopolies and national emergency strikes, are and ought to be freely and privately made. But the American people have a right to expect, in return for that freedom, a higher sense of business responsibility for the welfare of their country than has been shown in the last two days.

Some time ago I asked each American to consider what he would do for his country and I asked the steel companies. In the last twenty-four hours we had their answer. . . .

Q: Mr. President, the unusually strong language which you used in discussing the steel situation would indicate that you might be considering some pretty strong action. Are you thinking in terms of requesting or reviving the need for wage-price controls?

THE PRESIDENT: I think that my statement states what the situation is today. This is a free country. In all the conversations which were held by members of this administration and myself with the leaders of the steel union and the companies, it was always very obvious that they could proceed with freedom to do what they thought was best within the limitations of law. But I did very clearly emphasize on every occasion that my only interest was in trying to secure an agreement which would not provide an increase in prices, because I thought that price stability in steel would have the most far-reaching consequences for industrial and economic stability and for our position abroad, and price instability would have the most far-reaching consequences in making our lot much more difficult.

When the agreement was signed, and the agreement was a moderate one and within the range of productivity increases, as I've said, actually, there will be reduction in cost per unit during the next year—I thought, I was hopeful, we'd achieved our goal. Now the actions that will be taken will be—are being now considered by the administration. The Department of Justice is particularly anxious, in view of the very speedy action of the companies who have entirely different economic problems facing them than did United States Steel . . . to require an examination of our present laws, and whether they're being obeyed. . . . I'm very interested in the respective investigations that will be conducted in the House and Senate, and whether we shall need additional legislation, which I would come to very reluctantly. But I must say the last twenty-four hours indicate that those with great power are not always concerned about the national interest.

Q: In your conversation with Mr. Blough yesterday, did you make a direct request that this price increase be either deferred or rescinded?

THE PRESIDENT: I was informed about the price increase after the announcement had gone out to the papers. I told Mr. Blough of my very keen disappointment and what I thought would be the most unfortunate effects of it. And of course we were hopeful [about] other companies who, as I've said, have a different situation in regard to profits and all of the rest than U.S. Steel. . . .

I was hopeful particularly, in view of the statement in the paper by the president of Bethlehem in which he stated—though now he says he's misquoted—that there should be no price increase, and we are investigating that statement. I was hopeful that the others would not follow the example, that therefore the pressures of the competitive marketplace would bring United States Steel back to their original prices. But the parade began. But it came to me after the decision was made. There was no prior consultation or information given to the administration. . . .

Q: Mr. President, if I could get back to steel for a minute, you mentioned an investigation into the suddenness of the decision to increase prices. Did you—is the position of the administration that it believed it had the assurance of the steel industry at the time of the recent labor agreement that it would not increase prices?

THE PRESIDENT: We did not ask either side to give us any assurance, because there is a very proper limitation to the power of the government in this free economy. All we did in our meetings was to emphasize how important it was that there be price stability, and we stressed that our whole purpose in attempting to persuade the union to begin to bargain early and to make an agreement which would not affect prices, of course, was for the purpose of maintaining price stability. That was the thread that ran through every discussion which I had or Secretary Goldberg had. We never at any time asked for a commitment in regard to the terms, precise terms, of the agreement from either Mr. McDonald or Mr. Blough, representing the steel company, because in our opinion that would be passing over the line of propriety. But I don't think that there was any question that our great interest in attempting to secure the kind of settlement that was finally secured was to maintain price stability, which we regard as very essential at this particular time. That agreement provided for price stability—up to yesterday. . . .

Q: Mr. President, to carry a previous question just one step further, as a result of the emphasis that you placed on holding the price line, did any word or impression come to you from the negotiations that there would be no price increase under the type of agreement that was signed?

THE PRESIDENT: I will say that in our conversations we asked no commitments in regard to the details of the agreement or in regard to any policies [of] the union or the company—our central thrust was that price stability was necessary and that the way to do it was to have a responsible agreement, which we got.

Now, at no time did anyone suggest that if such an agreement was gained it would still be necessary to put up prices. That word did not come until last night.

President's News Conference
Washington, D.C., April 11, 1962

When a mistake has been retracted and the public interest preserved, nothing is to be gained from further public recriminations. . . . Our chief concern last week was to prevent an inflationary spiral. . . . What we attempted to do was project before the steel companies the public interest. And it was a combination of the public interest, placed upon the table in front of them, and competition which I think brought the price down. . . . Several companies refused to increase prices, and therefore competition worked its will.

President's News Conference
Washington, D.C., April 18, 1962

Later that month, at a press dinner, Kennedy parodied his own attack on big steel:

I have a few opening announcements: First, the sudden and arbitrary action of the officers of this organization in increasing the price of dinner tickets by $2.50 over last year constitutes a wholly unjustifiable defiance of the public interest. If this increase is

The Myths of Economic Debate

Let me begin by expressing my appreciation for the very deep honor that you have conferred upon me. As General de Gaulle occasionally acknowledges America to be the daughter of Europe, so I am pleased to come to Yale, the daughter of Harvard. It might be said now that I have the best of both worlds, a Harvard education and a Yale degree.

I am particularly glad to become a Yale man because, as I think about my troubles, I find that a lot of them have come from other Yale men. Among businessmen, I have had a minor disagreement with Roger Blough, of the law school class of 1931, and I have had some complaints, too, from my friend Henry Ford, of the class of 1940. In journalism I seem to have a difference with John Hay Whitney, of the class of 1926—and sometimes I also displease Henry Luce of the class of 1920, not to mention also William F. Buckley, Jr., of the class of 1950.

I even have some trouble with my Yale advisers. I get along with them, but I am not always sure how they get along with each other. I have the warmest feelings for Chester Bowles of the class of 1924, and for Dean Acheson of the class of 1915, and my assistant, McGeorge Bundy, of the class of 1940. But I am not one hundred percent sure that these three wise and experienced Yale men wholly agree with each other on every issue. So this administration, which aims at peaceful cooperation among all Americans, has been the victim of a certain natural pugnacity developed in this city among Yale men. Now that I, too, am a Yale man, it is time for peace. Last week at West Point, in the historic tradition of that academy, I availed myself of the powers of Commander-in-Chief to remit all sentences of offending cadets. In that same spirit, and in the

---

not rescinded but is imitated by the Gridiron, radio, TV, and other dinners, it will have a serious impact on the entire economy of this city.

In this serious hour in our nation's history, when newsmen are awakened in the middle of the night to be given a front-page story, when expense accounts are being scrutinized by the Congress, when correspondents are required to leave their families for long and lonely weekends at Palm Beach, the American people will find it hard to accept this ruthless decision made by a tiny handful of executives whose only interest is in the pursuit of pleasure. I am hopeful that the Women's Press Club will not join this price rise and will thereby force a rescission.

White House Correspondents and News Photographers Associations Dinner
Washington, D.C., April 27, 1962

historic tradition of Yale, let me now offer to smoke the clay pipe of friendship with all of my brother Elis, and I hope that they may be friends not only with me but even with each other. . . .

The great enemy of the truth is very often not the deliberate, contrived, and dishonest—but the myth—persistent, persuasive, and unrealistic. Too often we hold fast to the clichés of our forebears. We subject all facts to a prefabricated set of interpretations. We enjoy the comfort of opinion without the discomfort of thought.

Mythology distracts us everywhere—in government as in business, in politics as in economics, in foreign affairs as in domestic affairs. But today I want to particularly consider the myth and reality in our national economy. In recent months many have come to feel, as I do, that the dialogue between the parties—between business and government, between the government and the public—is clogged by illusion and platitude and fails to reflect the true realities of contemporary American society.

There are three great areas of our domestic affairs in which, today, there is a danger that illusion may prevent effective action. They are, first, the question of the size and the shape of government's responsibilities; second, the question of public fiscal policy; and third, the matter of confidence, business confidence or public confidence, or simply confidence in America. I want to talk about all three.

. . . Let us take first the question of the size and shape of government. The myth here is that government is big, and bad—and steadily getting bigger and worse. Obviously this myth has some excuse for existence. It is true that in recent history each new administration has spent much more money than its predecessor. Thus President Roosevelt outspent President Hoover, and with allowances for the special case of the Second World War, President Truman outspent President Roosevelt. Just to prove that this was not a partisan matter, President Eisenhower then outspent President Truman by the handsome figure of $182 billion. It is even possible, some think, that this trend may continue.

But does it follow from this that big government is growing relatively bigger? It does not—for the fact is for the last fifteen years, the federal government—and also the federal debt—and also the federal bureaucracy—have grown less rapidly than the economy as a whole. If we leave defense and space expenditures aside, the federal government since the Second World War has expanded less than any other major sector of our national life—less than industry, less than commerce, less than agriculture, less than higher education, and very much less than the noise about big government. The truth about big government is the truth about any other great activity—it is complex. Certainly it is true that size brings dangers—but it is also true that size can bring benefits. Here at Yale, which has contributed so much to our national progress in science and medicine, it may be proper for me to mention one great and little noticed expansion of government which has brought strength to our whole society—the new role of our federal government as the major patron of research in science and in medicine. Few people realize that in 1961, in support of all university research in science and medicine, three dollars out of every four came from the federal government. I need hardly point out that this has taken place without undue enlargement of government control—that American scientists remain second to none in their independence and in their individualism. . . .

I am not suggesting that federal expenditures cannot bring some measure of control. The whole thrust of federal expenditures in agriculture has been related by purpose and design to control, as a means of dealing with the problems created by our farmers and our growing productivity. Each sector, my point is, of activity must be approached on its own merits and in terms of specific national needs. Generalities in regard to federal expenditures, therefore, can be misleading—each case, science, urban renewal, education, agriculture, natural resources, each case must be determined on its merits if we are to profit from our unrivaled ability to combine the strength of public and private purpose.

Few people realize that in 1961, in support of all university research in science and medicine, three dollars out of every four came from the federal government.

Next, let us turn to the problem of our fiscal policy. Here the myths are legion and the truth hard to find. But let me take as a prime example the problem of the federal budget. We persist in measuring our federal fiscal integrity today by the conventional or administrative budget—with results which would be regarded as absurd in any business firm, in any country of Europe, or in any careful assessment of the reality of our national finances. The administrative budget has sound administrative uses. But for wider purposes it is less helpful. It omits our special trust funds and the effect that they have on our economy; it neglects changes in assets or inventories. It cannot tell a loan from a straight expenditure—and worst of all it cannot distinguish between operating expenditures and long-term investments.

This budget, in relation to the great problems of federal fiscal policy which are basic to our economy in 1962, is not simply irrelevant; it can be actively misleading. And yet there is a mythology that measures all of our national soundness or unsoundness on the single simple basis of this same annual administrative budget. If our federal budget is to serve not the debate but the country, we must and will find ways of clarifying this area of discourse.

Still in the area of fiscal policy, let me say a word about deficits. The myth persists that federal deficits create inflation and budget surpluses prevent it. Yet sizable budget surpluses after the war did not prevent inflation, and persistent deficits for the last several years have not upset our basic price stability. Obviously deficits are sometimes dangerous—and so are surpluses. But honest assessment plainly requires a more sophisticated view than the old and automatic cliché that deficits automatically bring inflation.

There are myths also about our public debt. It is widely supposed that this debt is growing at a dangerously rapid rate. In fact, both the debt per person and the debt as a proportion of our gross national product have declined sharply since the Second World War. In absolute terms the national debt since the end of World War II has increased only 8 percent, while private debt was increasing 305 percent, and the debts of state and local governments—on whom people frequently suggest we should place additional burdens—the debts of state and local governments have increased 378 percent. Moreover, debts, public and private, are neither good nor bad, in and of themselves. Borrowing can lead to overextension and collapse—but it can also lead to expansion and strength. There is no single, simple slogan in this field that we can trust.

Finally, I come to the problem of confidence. Confidence is a matter of myth and also a matter of truth—and this time let me take the truth of the matter first.

It is true—and of high importance—that the prosperity of this country depends on the assurance that all major elements within it will live up to their responsibilities. If business were to neglect its obligations to the public, if labor were blind to all public responsibility, above all, if government were to abandon its obvious—and statutory—duty of watchful concern for our economic health—if any of these things should happen, then confidence might well be weakened and the danger of stagnation would increase. This is the true issue of confidence.

But there is also the false issue—and its simplest form is the assertion that any and all unfavorable turns of the speculative wheel—however temporary and however plainly speculative in character—are the result of, and I quote, "a lack of confidence in the national administration." This I must tell you, while comforting, is not wholly true. . . . The solid ground of mutual confidence is the necessary partnership of government with all of the sectors of our society in the steady quest for economic progress.

Corporate plans are based not on a political confidence in party leaders but on an economic confidence in the nation's ability to invest and produce and consume. Business had full confidence in the administrations in power in 1929, 1954, 1958, and 1960—but this was not enough to prevent recession when business lacked full confidence in the economy. What matters is the capacity of the nation as a whole to deal with its economic problems and its opportunities. . . .

What is at stake in our economic decisions today is not some grand warfare of rival ideologies which will sweep the country with passion but the practical management of a modern economy. What we need is not labels and clichés but more basic discussion of the sophisticated and technical questions involved in keeping a great economic machinery moving ahead.

The national interest lies in high employment and steady expansion of output, in stable prices and a strong dollar. The declaration of such objectives is easy; their attainment in an intricate and interdependent economy and world is a little more difficult. To attain them, we require not some automatic response but hard thought. . . .

As we work in consonance to meet the authentic problems of our times, we will generate a vision and an energy which will demonstrate anew to the world the superior vitality and the strength of the free society.

Commencement Address, Yale University
New Haven, Connecticut, June 11, 1962

The Politics of Confidence

Q: Mr. President, a lot of people seem to feel that the idea of a Democratic administration trying to win the confidence of business is something like the Republicans trying to win the confidence of labor unions. Do you feel, sir, you are making headway in your efforts? Have you seen anything to indicate that business is coming around to your point of view on the economy and that the confidence you asked for is being restored to the marketplace?

THE PRESIDENT: Well, as I said, what is [important] is not really whether some businessmen may be Republicans—most businessmen are Republicans, have been traditionally, have voted Republican in every presidential election. But that is not the important point—whether there is political agreement.

The important point is that they recognize and the government recognizes, and every group recognizes, the necessity of attempting to work out economic policies which will maintain our economy at an adequate rate of growth. That is the great problem. . . . They feel that they would be happier if there were a Republican in the White House, but there was a Republican in the White House in 1958 and we had a recession and [again] in 1960. . . . I could be away from the scene, which might make them happy, and they might have a Republican in the White House, but the economic problems would still be there. . . .

Q: Mr. President, there is a feeling in some quarters that big business is using the stock market slump as a means of forcing you to come to terms with business. One reputable columnist, after talking to businessmen, obviously, reported this week their attitude is now, we have you where we want you. Have you seen any reflection of this attitude?

THE PRESIDENT. I can't believe I'm where business—big business—wants me.

President's News Conference
Washington, D.C., June 14, 1962

The Foundation for Freedom's Success

America has enjoyed twenty-two months of uninterrupted economic recovery. But recovery is not enough. If we are to prevail in the long run, we must expand the long-run strength of our economy. We must move along the path to a higher rate of growth and full employment. . . .

To achieve these greater gains, one step, above all, is essential—the enactment this year of a substantial reduction and revision in federal income taxes. . . .

I do not say that a measure for tax reduction and reform is the only way to achieve these goals.

No doubt a massive increase in federal spending could also create jobs and growth—but, in today's setting, private consumers, employers, and investors should be given a full opportunity first.

No doubt a temporary tax cut could provide a spur to our economy—but a long-run problem compels a long-run solution.

No doubt a reduction in either individual or corporation taxes alone would be of great help—but corporations need customers and job seekers need jobs.

No doubt tax reduction without reform would sound simpler and more attractive to many—but our growth is also hampered by a host of tax inequities and special preferences which have distorted the flow of investment.

And, finally, there are no doubt some who would prefer to put off a tax cut in the hope that ultimately an end to the Cold War would make possible an equivalent cut in expenditures—but that end is not in view and to wait for it would be costly and self-defeating. . . .

Tax reduction, alone, however, is not enough to strengthen our society, to provide opportunities for the four million Americans who are born each year, to improve the lives of thirty-two million Americans who live on the outskirts of poverty.

The quality of American life must keep pace with the quantity of American goods.

This country cannot afford to be materially rich and spiritually poor. . . .

First, we need to strengthen our nation by investing in our youth:

The future of any country which is dependent upon the will and wisdom of its citizens is damaged, and irreparably damaged, whenever any of its children is not educated to the full extent of his talent, from grade school through graduate school. Today, an estimated four out of every ten students in the fifth grade will not even finish high school—and that is a waste we cannot afford.

In addition, there is no reason why one million young Americans, out of school and out of work, should all remain unwanted and often untrained on our city streets when their energies can be put to good use. . . .

Second, we need to strengthen our nation by safeguarding its health . . . I believe that the abandonment of the mentally ill and the mentally retarded to the grim mercy of custodial institutions too often inflicts on them and on their families a needless cruelty which this nation should not endure. The incidence of mental retardation in this country is three times as high as that of Sweden, for example—and that figure can and must be reduced. . . .

We shall be judged more by what we do at home than by what we preach abroad. Nothing we could do to help the developing countries would help them half as much as a booming U.S. economy. And nothing our opponents could do to encourage their own ambitions would encourage them half as much as a chronic lagging U.S. economy. These domestic tasks do not divert energy from our security—they provide the very foundation for freedom's survival and success.

State of the Union Address
The Capitol, Washington, D.C.
January 14, 1963

CHAPTER 8

The Exploration of Space

Warned that outer space could be militarily dominated by a hostile power, concerned that the early Soviet lead in space exploration would be viewed by emerging nations as evidence of communism's success and democracy's decline, President Kennedy ascertained early in 1961 that this country would probably be unable to overtake the U.S.S.R. in any stage of the "space race" before a manned lunar landing a decade away. He thereupon proclaimed that dramatic goal as a means of focusing and mobilizing our lagging space efforts, establishing a stronger American scientific profile, and obtaining some bargaining chips for U.S.–Soviet negotiation on the exploration and governance of space.

The Adventure of Space

Since early in my term, our efforts in space have been under review. . . . We have examined where we are strong and where we are not, where we may succeed and where we may not. Now it is time to take longer strides—time for a great new American enterprise—time for this nation to take a clearly leading role in space achievement, which in many ways may hold the key to our future on earth.

I believe we possess all the resources and talents necessary. But the facts of the matter are that we have never made the national decisions or marshaled the national resources required for such leadership. We have never specified long-range goals on an urgent time schedule, or managed our resources and our time so as to insure their fulfillment.

We go into space because whatever mankind must undertake, free men must fully share. . . . I believe we should go to the moon.

Recognizing the head start obtained by the Soviets with their large rocket engines, which gives them many months of lead time, and recognizing the likelihood that they will exploit this lead for some time to come in still more impressive successes, we nevertheless are required to make new efforts on our own. For while we cannot guarantee that we shall one day be first, we can guarantee that any failure to make this effort will make us last. . . . But this is not merely a race. Space is open to us now; and our eagerness to share its meaning is not governed by the efforts of others. We go into space because whatever mankind must undertake, free men must fully share.

I therefore ask the Congress, above and beyond the increases I have earlier requested for space activities, to provide the funds which are needed to meet the following national goals:

First, I believe that this nation should commit itself to achieving the goal, before this decade is out, of landing a man on the moon and returning him safely to the earth. No single space project in this period will be more impressive to mankind, or more important for the long-range exploration of space; and none will be so difficult or expensive to accomplish. . . . But in a very real sense, it will not be one man going to the moon—if we make this judgment affirmatively, it will be an entire nation. For all of us must work to put him there. . . .

I believe we should go to the moon. But I think every citizen of this country as well as the members of the Congress should consider the matter carefully in making their judgment, to which we have given attention over many weeks and months, because it is a heavy burden, and there is no sense in agreeing or desiring that the United States take an affirmative position in outer space, unless we are prepared to do the work and bear the burdens to make it successful. If we are not, we should decide today and this year.

This decision demands a major national commitment of scientific and technical manpower, material, and facilities, and the possibility of their diversion from other important activities where they are already thinly spread. It means a degree of dedication, organization, and discipline which have not always characterized our research and development efforts. It means we cannot afford undue work stoppages, inflated costs of material or talent, wasteful interagency rivalries, or a high turnover of key personnel.

New objectives and new money cannot solve these problems. They could, in fact, aggravate them further—unless every scientist, every engineer, every serviceman, every technician, contractor, and civil servant gives his personal pledge that this nation will move forward, with the full speed of freedom, in the exciting adventure of space.

Special Address to Congress on Urgent National Needs
The Capitol, Washington, D.C. May 25, 1961

The chimpanzee who is flying in space took off at 10:08. He reports that everything is perfect and working well.

President's News Conference
Washington, D.C., November 29, 1961

The Universal Language of Space

This has been a week of momentous events around the world. The long and painful struggle in Algeria has come to an end. Both nuclear powers and neutrals labored at Geneva for a solution to the problem of a spiraling arms race, and also to the problems that so vex our relations with the Soviet Union. The Congress opened hearings on a trade bill, which is far more than a trade bill, but an opportunity to build a stronger and closer Atlantic Community. And my wife had her first and last ride on an elephant!

But history may well remember this as a week for an act of lesser immediate impact, and that is the decision by the United States and the Soviet Union to seek concrete agreements on the joint exploration of space. Experience has taught us that an agreement to negotiate does not always mean a negotiated agreement. But should such a joint effort be realized, its significance could well be tremendous for us all. In terms of space science, our combined knowledge and efforts can benefit the people of all nations: joint weather satellites to provide more ample warnings against destructive storms—joint communications systems to draw the world more closely together—and cooperation on space medicine research and space tracking operations to speed the day when man will go to the moon and beyond.

But the scientific gains from such a joint effort would offer, I believe, less realized return than the gains for world peace. For a cooperative Soviet-American effort in space science and exploration would emphasize the interests that must unite us, rather than those that always divide us. It offers us an area in which the stale and sterile dogmas of the Cold War could be literally left a quarter of a million miles behind. And it would remind us on both sides that knowledge, not hate, is the passkey to the future—that knowledge transcends national antagonisms—that it speaks a universal language—that it is the possession, not of a single class, or of a single nation or a single ideology, but of all mankind.

Address to the University of California
Berkeley, California, March 23, 1962

The New Ocean of Space

We meet at a college noted for knowledge, in a city noted for progress, in a state noted for strength, and we stand in need of all three. For we meet in an hour of change and challenge, in a decade of hope and fear, in an age of both knowledge and ignorance. The greater our knowledge increases, the greater our ignorance unfolds.

Despite the striking fact that most of the scientists that the world has ever known are alive and working today, despite the fact that this nation's own scientific manpower is doubling every twelve years in a rate of growth more than three times that of our population as a whole, despite all that, the vast stretches of the unknown and the unanswered and the unfinished still far outstrip our collective comprehension.

No man can fully grasp how far and how fast we have come, but condense, if you will, the fifty thousand years of man's recorded history in a time span of but a half century. Stated in these terms, we know very little about the first forty years, except at the end of them advanced man had learned to use the skins of animals to cover himself. Then about ten years ago, under this standard, man emerged from his caves to construct other kinds of shelter. Only five years ago man learned to write and use a cart with wheels. Christianity began less than two years ago. The printing press came this year, and then less than two months ago, during this whole fifty-year span of human history, the steam engine provided a new source of power and Newton explored the meaning of gravity. Last month electric lights and telephones and automobiles and airplanes became available. Only last week did we develop penicillin and television and nuclear power. And now if America's new spacecraft succeeds in reaching Venus, we will have literally reached the stars before midnight tonight.

This is a breathtaking pace, and such a pace cannot help but create new ills as it dispels old, new ignorance, new problems, new dangers. Surely the opening vistas of space promise high costs and hardships, as well as high reward.

So it is not surprising that some would have us stay where we are a little longer to rest, to wait. But this city of Houston, this state of Texas, this country of the United States, were not built by those who waited and rested and wished to look behind them. This country was conquered by those who moved forward—and so will space [be conquered].

If this capsule history of our progress teaches us anything, it is that man, in his quest for knowledge and progress, is determined and cannot be deterred. The exploration of space will go ahead, whether we join in it or not. It is one of the great adventures of all time, and no nation which expects to be the leader of other nations can expect to stay behind in this race for space.

We have vowed that we shall see space filled not with weapons of mass destruction, but with instruments of knowledge and understanding.

Those who came before us made certain that this country rode the first waves of the industrial revolution, the first waves of modern invention, and the first wave of nuclear power; and this generation does not intend to founder in the backwash of the coming age of space. We mean to be a part of it—we mean to lead it. For the eyes of the world now look into space, to the moon, and to the planets beyond, and we have vowed that we shall see space governed not by a hostile flag of conquest, but by a banner of freedom and peace. We have vowed that we shall see space filled not with weapons of mass destruction, but with instruments of knowledge and understanding.

Yet the vows of this nation can only be fulfilled if we in this nation are first, and, therefore, we intend to be first. In short, our leadership in science and in industry, our hopes for peace and security, our obligations to ourselves as well as others, all require us to make this effort, to solve these mysteries, to solve them for the good of all men, and to become the world's leading space-faring nation.

We set sail on this new sea because there is new knowledge to be gained, and new rights to be won, and they must be won and used for the progress of all people. For space science, like nuclear science and all technology, has no conscience of its own. Whether it will become a force for good or ill depends on man, and only if the United States occupies a position of preeminence can we help decide whether this new ocean will be a sea of peace or a new terrifying theater of war. I do not say that we should or will go unprotected against the hostile misuse of space any more than we go unprotected against the hostile use of land or sea, but I do say that space can be explored and mastered without feeding the fires of war, without repeating the mistakes that man has made in extending his writ around this globe of ours.

There is no strife, no prejudice, no national conflict in outer space as yet. Its hazards are hostile to us all. Its conquest deserves the best of all mankind, and its opportunity for peaceful cooperation may never come again. But why, some say, the moon? Why choose this as our goal? And they may well ask why climb the highest mountain. Why, thirty-five years ago, fly the Atlantic? Why does Rice play Texas?

We choose to go to the moon. We choose to go to the moon in this decade and do the other things, not because they are easy, but because they are hard, because that goal will serve to organize and measure the best of our energies and skills, because that challenge is one that we are willing to accept, one we are unwilling to postpone, and one which we intend to win. . . .

It is for these reasons that I regard the decision last year to shift our efforts in space from low to high gear as among the most important decisions that will be made during my incumbency in the office of the Presidency.

In the last twenty-four hours we have seen facilities now being created for the greatest and most complex exploration in man's history. We have felt the ground shake and the air shattered by the testing of a Saturn C-1 booster rocket, many times as powerful as the Atlas which launched John Glenn, generating power equivalent to ten thousand automobiles with their accelerators on the floor. We have seen the site where five F-1 rocket engines, each one as powerful as all eight engines of the Saturn combined, will be clustered together to make the advanced Saturn missile, assembled in a new building to be built at Cape Canaveral as tall as a forty-eight-story structure, as wide as a city block, and as long as two lengths of this field.

Within these last nineteen months at least forty-five satellites have circled the earth. Some forty of them were "made in the United States of America" and they were far more sophisticated and supplied far more knowledge to the people of the world than those of the Soviet Union.

The Mariner spacecraft now on its way to Venus is the most intricate instrument in the history of space science. The accuracy of that shot is comparable to firing a missile from Cape Canaveral and dropping it in this stadium between the forty-yard lines.

Transit satellites are helping our ships at sea to steer a safer course. Tiros satellites have given us unprecedented warnings of hurricanes and storms, and will do the same for forest fires and icebergs.

We have had our failures, but so have others, even if they do not admit them. And they may be less public.

To be sure, we are behind, and will be behind for some time in manned flight. But we do not intend to stay behind, and in this decade we shall make up and move ahead.

The growth of our science and education will be enriched by new knowledge of our universe and environment, by new techniques of learning and mapping and observation, by new tools and computers for industry, medicine, the home as well as the school. . . .

I regard the decision last year to shift our efforts in space from low to high gear as among the most important decisions that will be made during my incumbency in the office of the Presidency.

To be sure, all this costs us all a good deal of money. This year's space budget is three times what it was in January 1961, and it is greater than the space budget of the previous eight years combined. That budget now stands at $5,400 million a year—a staggering sum, though somewhat less than we pay for cigarettes and cigars every year. Space expenditures will soon rise some more, from ten cents per person per week to more than fifty cents a week for every man, woman, and child in the United States, for we have given this program a high national priority—even though I realize that this is in some measure an act of faith and vision, for we do not now know what benefits await us. But if I were to say, my fellow citizens, that we shall send to the moon, 240,000 miles away from the control station in Houston, a giant rocket more than three hundred feet tall, the length of this football field, made of new metal alloys, some of which have not yet been invented, capable of standing heat and stresses several times more than have ever been experienced, fitted together with a precision better than the finest watch, carrying all the equipment needed for propulsion, guidance, control, communications, food, and survival, on an untried mission, to an unknown celestial body, and then return it safely to earth, reentering the atmosphere at speeds of over 25,000 miles per hour, causing heat about half that of the temperature of the sun—almost as hot as it is here today—and do all this, and do it right, and do it first before this decade is out, then we must be bold. . . .

I think we're going to do it, and I think that we must pay what needs to be paid. I don't think we ought to waste any money, but I think we ought to do the job. And this will be done in the decade of the sixties. It may be done while some of you are still here at school at this college and university. It will be done during the terms of office of some of the people who sit here on this platform. But it will be done. And it will be done before the end of this decade. . . .

Many years ago the great British explorer George Mallory, who was to die on Mount Everest, was asked why did he want to climb it. He said, "Because it is there."

Well, space is there, and we're going to climb it, and the moon and the planets are there, and new hopes for knowledge and peace are there. And, therefore, as we set sail, we ask God's blessing on the most hazardous and dangerous and the greatest adventure on which man has ever embarked.

Rice University
Houston, Texas, September 12, 1962

The High Wall of Space

We have a long way to go. Many weeks and months and years of long, tedious work lie ahead. There will be setbacks and frustrations and disappointments. There will be, as there always are, pressures in this country to do less in this area as in so many others, and temptations to do something else that is perhaps easier. But this research here must go on. This space effort must go on. The conquest of space must and will go ahead. That much we know. That much we can say with confidence and conviction.

Frank O'Connor, the Irish writer, tells in one of his books how, as a boy, he and his friends would make their way across the countryside, and when they came to an orchard wall that seemed too high and too doubtful to try and too difficult to permit their voyage to continue, they took off their hats and tossed them over the wall—and then they had no choice but to follow them.

This nation has tossed its cap over the wall of space, and we have no choice but to follow it. Whatever the difficulties, they will be overcome. Whatever the hazards, they must be guarded against. With the vital help of this Aerospace Medical Center, with the help of all those who labor in the space endeavor, with the help and support of all Americans, we will climb this wall with safety and with speed—and we shall then explore the wonders on the other side.

Remarks at Dedication of Aerospace Medical Health Center
San Antonio, Texas, November 21, 1963

CHAPTER 9

The Fight for Civil Rights

Initially wary of civil rights as a political issue, John Kennedy came to recognize that the battle for equal rights and opportunity for all races was the great moral issue of our time. He forthrightly placed the Presidency at the front of that battle in a way that no twentieth-century president had done before. Shocked by the brutality endured by civil rights protesters across the nation and determined to enforce judicial orders admitting blacks to state institutions of higher learning, the President launched in mid-1963 an unprecedented and comprehensive legislative, regulatory, and educational drive to fundamentally change this country's course in black-white relations.

The American Vision

We meet on the eve of a great national convention. There our choice is more than the choice of candidates—it is the choice of party roles and responsibilities. Will we face up to the issues that face America—or will we, as Randolph said of Van Buren, "row to [our] object with muffled oars?" Will we appeal to the lowest common denominator—or will we offer leadership where leadership has so long been lacking? Will we inquire as to whether a policy is good for the North, South, East, or West—or will we know that a policy, if really good, is good for all people everywhere? And finally, will we confine our campaign to abuse of the party in power—or will we realize, to paraphrase a noted statesman, that a great "nay" is not enough—we need a mighty "yes" as well?

I hope my own views are clear. I want our party to speak out with courage and candor on every issue—and that includes civil rights. I want no compromise of basic principles—no evasion of basic controversies—and no second-class citizenship for any American anywhere in this country. I have not made nor will I make any commitments inconsistent with these objectives.

While we point with pride to the strides we have made in fulfilling our forefathers' dream of the equality of man, let us not overlook how far we still have to go. While we point with concern to denials of civil rights in one part of the country, let us not overlook the more subtle but equally vicious forms of discrimination that are found in the clubs and churches and neighborhoods of the rest of the country.

Our job is to turn the American vision of a society in which no man has to suffer discrimination based on race into a living reality everywhere in our land. And that means we must secure to every American equal access to all parts of our public life—to the voting booth, to the schoolroom, to jobs, to housing, to all public facilities including lunch counters.

Let us trust no one who offers slick and easy answers—for the only final answer will come from the work of thousands of individual answers, large and small, in the Congress, the courts, and the White House, in states and cities all over America, in the actions of brave and wise public servants, and in the reactions of determined private citizens such as yourselves.

What we are seeking, after all, is really very simple. It's merely a recognition that this is one nation and we are all one great people. Our origins may be different but our destiny is the same, our aspirations are identical. There can be no artificial distinctions, no arbitrary barriers, in securing these rights:

The right of every man to work as he wants to work, to be educated as every human being deserves to be educated, and to receive for his labor or his crops or his goods a just compensation, which he can spend as he pleases, in the nation's finest luxury store or the most modest five-and-ten.

The right of every family to live in a decent home in a decent neighborhood of his own free choice.

The right of every individual to obtain security in sickness as well as health, in retirement as well as youth.

The right of every American to think, to vote, to speak, to read, and to worship as he pleases—to stand up for his rights and, when necessary, to sit down for them.

And finally, the right of all people to be free from the tensions and terrors and burdens of war, its preparation and its consequences.

These are not minority rights or even merely civil rights—they are the goals desired and required for every American. There is nothing complicated about these goals, however difficult their achievement. There is nothing unreasonable or unusual about these goals, however much some may resist them. But they will not be achieved without leadership—moral, political, legislative, and, above all, executive leadership.

Our job is to turn the American vision of a society in which no man has to suffer discrimination based on race into a living reality everywhere in our land.

The next President of the United States cannot stand above the battle engaging in vague little sermons on brotherhood. The immense moral authority of the White House must be used to offer leadership and inspiration to those of every race and section who recognize their responsibilities. And the immense legal authority of the White House must be used to direct implementation of all constitutional rights, protection of the right to vote, fulfillment of the requirement of school desegregation, and an end to discrimination in the government's own midst—in public contracts, in employment and in all federal housing programs.

Finally, if that President is to truly be President of all the people, then he must act to bring them together to accomplish these objectives. How, without communication, can we ever proceed in democracy? There can be no progress without communication. There can be no reconciliation without meeting and talking with each other.

To be sure, there will be protest and disagreement—but if the end result is to be permanent progress instead of frustration, there must be more meetings of men and minds. And the place to begin is the White House itself, where the Chief Executive, with his prestige and influence, should exert firm and positive leadership.

Let us bear in mind that this is not merely a regional problem—it is not merely a national problem—it is international in scope and effect. For the average American of Caucasian descent does not realize that it is *he* who is a member of a minority race—and a minority religion—and a minority political system—and that he is regarded with some suspicion, if not hostility, by most of that restless, envious, surging majority. The tide of human dignity is worldwide—and the eyes of that world are upon us.

It is not enough to restate our claim to the Declaration of Independence. It is not enough to deplore violence in other lands. It is up to us to prove that our way—the way of peaceful change and democratic processes—can fulfill those goals better than any other system under the sun. It is up to us to rebuild our image abroad by rebuilding our image here at home.

The time is short—but the agenda is long. Much is to be done—but many are willing.

Francis Bacon once wrote: "There is hope enough and to spare—not only to make a bold man try—but also to make a sober-minded man believe."

My friends—if you are sober-minded enough to believe, then—to the extent that these tasks require the support, the guidance, and the leadership of the American Presidency—I am bold enough to try.

NAACP Rally
Los Angeles, California, July 10, 1960

The Standard of John C. Calhoun

For eight years . . . I have occupied the seat once held by a distinguished senator from Massachusetts, Senator Daniel Webster. He served in the time before 1850, when the Senate was at its height, and included within its ranks Cass, Clay, Douglas, Benton, and all the rest. But none of these were considered by Daniel Webster to match the talents and the character of the senator from South Carolina, John C. Calhoun. They were both born in the same year; Calhoun was a native of Abingdon, South Carolina. They both went to college in New England, one to Yale and the other to Dartmouth. They both entered Congress as young men, and they both stayed in Congress for forty years until they died, in 1850 John Calhoun, and in 1852 Daniel Webster. They worked together on foreign relations, the development of the United States, fiscal improvements. Each served in the House as well as in the Senate. Each was Secretary of State. And yet through most of their lives, they also differed on great questions. But to his dying day, Senator Daniel Webster said of John C. Calhoun, "He was much the ablest man I ever knew. He could have demolished Newton, Calvin, or Locke as a logician." He admired above all his powerful mind and his courage.

Sitting as I do in the U.S. Senate, succeeding Senator Webster, I have also admired John C. Calhoun. When I was chairman of a committee to pick five outstanding senators in the history of this country, John C. Calhoun's name led all the rest, and his portrait is now in the Senate reception room. And when I wrote a book about courageous senators, I mentioned John C. Calhoun. I am not here in South Carolina to make glittering promises or glowing predictions, but to express the hope that in 1960, South Carolina and the nation will be guided by the spirit of Calhoun and his courage. "I never know what South Carolina thinks of a measure," he once said. "I act to the best of my judgment and according to my conscience. If she approves, well and good. If she does not, and wishes anyone to take my place, I am ready to vacate. We are even."

"Are we bound in all cases to do what is popular?"

He demonstrated this in 1816 when he voted to raise the pay of congressmen from $6 a day to the munificent sum of $1,500 a year. Congressman after congressman was defeated. And yet John C. Calhoun, speaking in the House, spoke words that I invoke today. "This House is at liberty to decide on this question according to the dictates of its best judgment. Are we bound in all cases to do what is popular? Have the people of this country snatched the power of deliberation from this body? If we act in opposition to conscience and reason, are political errors, once prevalent, never to be corrected?"

That is the spirit of the Democratic Party, that is the spirit of Thomas Jefferson and Woodrow Wilson and Franklin Roosevelt and Harry Truman. Are we bound in all cases to do what is popular? In 1960, the people of the United States have a very clear choice to make between Mr. Nixon and myself. We see America in different terms, and we see the future in entirely different terms. He runs on a slogan of "You have never had it so good." I run on the slogan, "This is a great country that must be greater." I think we can do better. . . .

The test of popularity, rather than Calhoun's test of conscience, has been applied by my opponent in the sensitive area of civil rights. He makes a great show of discussing this subject when he comes south, but it is hardly the same speech he delivered in New York City last week. Up north he talks about legislation. Down here he emphasizes that laws alone are not enough. Up there he stresses how quickly he will act in all these areas. Down here he says, "I know this is a difficult problem." Up there he criticizes the Democratic Party for having nominated a southerner on the ticket. Down here he omits the civil rights plank in his own platform.

I don't think Mr. Nixon is fooling anyone, north or south. I think it is clear that, if we are to have progress in this area, and we must have progress to be true to our ideals and responsibilities, then presidential leadership is necessary so that every American can enjoy his full constitutional rights. Some of you may disagree with that view, but at least I have not changed that view in an election year, or according to where I am standing. . . .

I ask you to join us in building a stronger America, an America which will serve as an example to a watching world as we sit on a most conspicuous stage. We will give leadership if we are successful, and I can promise you this country will start to move again.

Campaign Speech
Columbia, South Carolina, October 10, 1960

The Enforcement of Court Orders

The orders of the court in the case of Meredith versus Fair are beginning to be carried out. Mr. James Meredith is now in residence on the campus of the University of Mississippi. . . .

All students, members of the faculty, and public officials in both Mississippi and the nation will be able, it is hoped, to return to their normal activities with full confidence in the integrity of American law.

This is as it should be. For our nation is founded on the principle that observance of the law is the eternal safeguard of liberty and defiance of the law is the surest road to tyranny. The law which we obey includes the final rulings of the courts, as well as the enactments of our legislative bodies. Even among law-abiding men few laws are universally loved, but they are uniformly respected and not resisted.

Americans are free, in short, to disagree with the law but not to disobey it. For in a government of laws and not of men, no man, however prominent or powerful, and no mob, however unruly or boisterous, is entitled to defy a court of law. If this country should ever reach the point where any man or group of men by force or threat of force could long defy the commands of our Court and our Constitution, then no law would stand free from doubt, no judge would be sure of his writ, and no citizen would be safe from his neighbors.

In this case in which the United States government was not until recently involved, Mr. Meredith brought a private suit in federal court against those who were excluding him from the university. A series of federal courts all the way to the Supreme Court repeatedly ordered Mr. Meredith's admission to the university. When those orders were defied, and those who sought to implement them threatened with arrest and violence, the United States Court of Appeals consisting of Chief Judge Tuttle of Georgia, Judge Hutcheson of Texas, Judge Rives of Alabama, Judge Jones of Florida, Judge Brown of Texas, Judge Wisdom of Louisiana, Judge Girwin of Alabama, and Judge Bell of Georgia, made clear the fact that the enforcement of its order had become an obligation of the United States government. Even though this government had not originally been a party to the case, my responsibility as President was therefore inescapable. I accept it. My obligation under the Constitution and the statutes of the United States was and is to implement the orders of the court with whatever means are necessary, and with as little force and civil disorder as the circumstances permit.

It was for this reason that I federalized the Mississippi National Guard as the most appropriate instrument, should any be needed, to preserve law and order while United States marshals carried out the orders of the court, and prepared to back them up with whatever other civil or military enforcement might have been required.

I deeply regret the fact that any action by the executive branch was necessary in this case, but all other avenues and alternatives, including persuasion and conciliation, had been tried and exhausted. Had the police powers of Mississippi been used to support the orders of the court, instead of deliberately and unlawfully blocking them, had the University of Mississippi fulfilled its standard of excellence by quietly admitting this applicant in conformity with what so many other southern state universities have done for so many years, a peaceable and sensible solution would have been possible without any federal intervention.

This nation is proud of the many instances in which governors, educators, and everyday citizens from the South have shown to the world the gains that can be made by persuasion and goodwill in a society ruled by law. Specifically, I would like to take this occasion to express the thanks of this nation to those southerners who have contributed to the progress of our democratic development in the entrance of students regardless of race to such great institutions as the state-supported universities of Virginia, North Carolina, Georgia, Florida, Texas, Louisiana, Tennessee, Arkansas, and Kentucky.

I recognize that the present period of transition and adjustment in our nation's southland is a hard one for many people. Neither Mississippi nor any other southern state deserves to be charged with all the accumulated wrongs of the last hundred years of race relations. To the extent that there has been failure, the responsibility for that failure must be shared by us all, by every state, by every citizen.

Mississippi and her university, moreover, are noted for their courage, for their contribution of talent and thought to the affairs of this nation. This is the state of Lucius Lamar and many others who have placed the national good ahead of sectional interest. This is the state which had four Medal of Honor winners in the Korean War alone. In fact, the Guard unit federalized this morning, early, is part of the 155th Infantry, one of the ten oldest regiments in the Union and one of the most decorated for sacrifice and bravery in six wars.

In 1945 a Mississippi sergeant, Jake Lindsey, was honored by an unusual joint session of the Congress. I close therefore with this appeal to the students of the university, the people who are most concerned.

You have a great tradition to uphold, a tradition of honor and courage won on the field of battle and on the gridiron as well as the university campus. You have a new opportunity to show that you are men of patriotism and integrity. For the most effective means of upholding the law is not the state policeman or the marshals or the National Guard. It is you. It lies in your courage to accept those laws with which you disagree as well as those with which you agree. The eyes of the nation and of all the world are upon you and upon all of us, and the honor of your university and state are in the balance. I am certain that the great majority of the students will uphold that honor.

There is, in short, no reason why the books on this case cannot now be quickly and quietly closed in the manner directed by the court. Let us preserve both the law and the peace, and then, healing those wounds that are within we can turn to the greater crises that are without and stand united as one people in our pledge to man's freedom.

Televised Address
Washington, D.C., September 30, 1962

The Right to Vote

. . . The most precious and powerful right in the world, the right to vote in a free American election, must not be denied to any citizen on grounds of his race or color. I wish that all qualified Americans permitted to vote were willing to vote, but surely in this centennial year of Emancipation all those who are willing to vote should always be permitted.

State of the Union Address
The Capitol, Washington, D.C.
January 14, 1963

The Peaceful Revolution

This afternoon, following a series of threats and defiant statements, the presence of Alabama National Guardsmen was required on the University of Alabama to carry out the final and unequivocal order of the United States District Court of the Northern District of Alabama. That order called for the admission of two clearly qualified young Alabama residents who happened to have been born Negro.

That they were admitted peacefully on the campus is due in good measure to the conduct of the students of the University of Alabama, who met their responsibilities in a constructive way.

I hope that every American, regardless of where he lives, will stop and examine his conscience about this and other related incidents. This nation was founded by men of many nations and backgrounds. It was founded on the principle that all men are created equal, and that the rights of every man are diminished when the rights of one man are threatened.

Today we are committed to a worldwide struggle to promote and protect the rights of all who wish to be free. When Americans are sent to Vietnam or West Berlin, we do not ask for whites only. It ought to be possible, therefore, for American students of any color to attend any public institution they select without having to be backed up by troops.

It ought to be possible for American consumers of any color to receive equal service in places of public accommodation, such as hotels and restaurants and theaters and retail stores, without being forced to resort to demonstrations in the street. It ought to be possible for American citizens of any color to register and to vote in a free election without interference or fear of reprisal.

It ought to be possible, in short, for every American to enjoy the privileges of being American without regard to his race or his color. In short, every American ought to have the right to be treated as he would wish to be treated, as one would wish his children to be treated. But this is not the case today.

The rights of every man are diminished when the rights of one man are threatened.

The Negro baby born in America today, regardless of the section of the nation in which he is born, has about one half as much chance of completing high school as a white baby born in the same place on the same day, one third as much chance of completing college, one third as much chance of becoming a professional man, twice as much chance of becoming unemployed, about one seventh as much chance of earning $10,000 a year or more, a life expectancy which is seven years shorter, and the prospects of earning only half as much.

This is not a sectional issue. Difficulties over segregation and discrimination exist in every city, in every state of the Union, producing in many cities a rising tide of discontent that threatens the public safety. Nor is this a partisan issue. In a time of domestic crisis men of goodwill and generosity should be able to unite regardless of party or politics. This is not even a legal or legislative issue alone. It is better to settle these matters in the courts than on the streets, and new laws are needed at every level, but law alone cannot make men see right.

We are confronted primarily with a moral issue. It is as old as the Scriptures and is as clear as the American Constitution.

The heart of the question is whether all Americans are to be afforded equal rights and equal opportunities, whether we are going to treat our fellow Americans as we want to be treated. If an American, because his skin is dark, cannot eat lunch in a restaurant open to the public, if he cannot send his children to the best public school available, if he cannot vote for the public officials who represent him, if, in short, he cannot enjoy the full and free life which all of us want, then who among us would be content to have the color of his skin changed and stand in his place? Who among us would then be content with the counsels of patience and delay?

One hundred years of delay have passed since President Lincoln freed the slaves, yet their heirs, their grandsons, are not fully free. They are not yet freed from the bonds of injustice. They are not yet freed from social and economic oppression. And this nation, for all its hopes and all its boasts, will not be fully free until all its citizens are free.

We preach freedom around the world, and we mean it, and we cherish our freedom here at home; but are we to say to the world, and, much more importantly, to each other, that this is a land of the free except for the Negroes; that we have no second-class citizens except Negroes; that we have no class or caste system, no ghettos, no master race, except with respect to Negroes?

Now the time has come for this nation to fulfill its promise. The events in Birmingham and elsewhere have so increased the cries for equality that no city or state or legislative body can prudently choose to ignore them.

The fires of frustration and discord are burning in every city, North and South, where legal remedies are not at hand. Redress is sought in the streets, in demonstrations, parades, and protests which create tensions and threaten violence and threaten lives.

We face, therefore, a moral crisis as a country and as a people. It cannot be met by repressive police action. It cannot be left to increased demonstrations in the streets. It cannot be quieted by token moves or talk. It is a time to act in the Congress, in your state and local legislative bodies and, above all, in all of our daily lives.

It is not enough to pin the blame on others, to say this is a problem of one section of the country or another, or deplore the facts that we face. A great change is at hand, and our task, our obligation, is to make that revolution, that change, peaceful and constructive for all.

Those who do nothing are inviting shame as well as violence. Those who act boldly are recognizing right as well as reality.

Next week I shall ask the Congress of the United States to act, to make a commitment it has not fully made in this century to the proposition that race has no place in American life or law. The federal judiciary has upheld that proposition in a series of forthright cases. The executive branch has adopted that proposition in the conduct of its affairs, including the employment of federal personnel, the use of federal facilities, and the sale of federally financed housing.

But there are other necessary measures which only the Congress can provide, and they must be provided at this session. The old code of equity law under which we live commands for every wrong a remedy, but in too many communities, in too many parts of the country, wrongs are inflicted on Negro citizens and there are no remedies at law. Unless the Congress acts, their only remedy is in the street.

I am, therefore, asking the Congress to enact legislation giving all Americans the right to be served in facilities which are open to the public—hotels, restaurants, theaters, retail stores, and similar establishments.

This seems to me to be an elementary right. Its denial is an arbitrary indignity that no American in 1963 should have to endure. But many do.

Next week I shall ask the Congress of the United States to act, to make a commitment it has not fully made in this century to the proposition that race has no place in American life or law.

I have recently met with scores of business leaders urging them to take voluntary action to end this discrimination, and I have been encouraged by their response. In the last two weeks over seventy-five cities have seen progress made in desegregating these kinds of facilities. But many are unwilling to act alone, and for this reason, nationwide legislation is needed if we are to move this problem from the streets to the courts.

I am also asking Congress to authorize the federal government to participate more fully in lawsuits designed to end segregation in public education. We have succeeded in persuading many districts to desegregate voluntarily. Dozens have admitted Negroes without violence. Today a Negro is attending a state-supported institution in every one of our fifty states. But the pace is very slow.

Too many Negro children entering segregated grade schools at the time of the Supreme Court's decision nine years ago will enter segregated high schools this fall, having suffered a loss which can never be restored. The lack of an adequate education denies the Negro a chance to get a decent job.

The orderly implementation of the Supreme Court decision, therefore, cannot be left solely to those who may not have the economic resources to carry the legal action or who may be subject to harassment.

Other features will also be requested, including greater protection for the right to vote. But legislation, I repeat, cannot solve this problem alone. It must be solved in the homes of every American in every community across our country.

In this respect, I want to pay tribute to those citizens, North and South, who have been working in their communities to make life better for all. They are acting not out of a sense of legal duty but out of a sense of human decency. Like our soldiers and sailors in all parts of the world, they are meeting freedom's challenge on the firing line, and I salute them for their honor and their courage.

My fellow Americans, this is a problem which faces us all—in every city of the North as well as the South. Today there are Negroes, unemployed—two or three times as many compared to whites—with inadequate education, moving into the large cities, unable to find work, young people particularly out of work and without hope, denied equal rights, denied the opportunity to eat at a restaurant or lunch counter or go to a movie theater, denied the right to a decent education. . . . It seems to me that these are matters which concern us all, not merely Presidents or congressmen or governors, but every citizen of the United States.

This is one country. It has become one country because all the people who came here had an equal chance to develop their talents.

We cannot say to ten percent of the population that you can't have that right; that your children can't have the chance to develop whatever talents they have; that the only way that they are going to get their rights is to go into the streets and demonstrate. I think we owe them and we owe ourselves a better country than that.

Therefore, I am asking for your help in making it easier for us to move ahead and to provide the kind of equality of treatment which we would want ourselves; to give a chance for every child to be educated to the limit of his talents.

As I have said before, not every child has an equal talent or an equal ability or an equal motivation, but they should have the equal right to develop their talent and their ability and their motivation, to make something of themselves.

We have a right to expect that the Negro community will be responsible and will uphold the law; but they have a right to expect that the law will be fair, that the Constitution will be color blind, as Justice Harlan said at the turn of the century.

This is what we are talking about. This is a matter which concerns this country and what it stands for, and in meeting it I ask the support of all our citizens.

Televised Address
Washington, D.C., June 11, 1963

The Role of the Military

Dear Mr. Secretary:

. . . We have come a long way in the fifteen years since President Truman ordered the desegregation of the Armed Forces. The military services lead almost every other segment of our society in establishing equality of opportunity for all Americans. Yet a great deal remains to be done. . . .

A serious morale problem is created for Negro military personnel when various forms of segregation and discrimination exist in communities neighboring military bases. Discriminatory practices are morally wrong wherever they occur—they are especially inequitable and iniquitous when they inconvenience and embarrass those serving in the Armed Services and their families. Responsible citizens of all races in these communities should work together to open up public accommodations and housing for Negro military personnel and their dependents. This effort is required by the interests of our national defense, national policy and basic considerations of human decency. . . .

I realize that I am asking the military community to take a leadership role, but I believe that this is proper. The Armed Services will, I am confident, be equal to the task. In this area, as in so many others, the U.S. Infantry motto "Follow Me" is an appropriate guide for action.

Sincerely,
John F. Kennedy

Letter to the Secretary of Defense
Washington, D.C., June 22, 1963

The Civil Rights Act of 1963

In short, the time has come for the Congress of the United States to join with the executive and judicial branches in making it clear to all that race has no place in American life or law. . . .

For these reasons, I am proposing that the Congress stay in session this year until it has enacted—preferably as a single omnibus bill—the most responsible, reasonable, and urgently needed solutions to this problem, solutions which should be acceptable to all fair-minded men. This bill would be known as the "Civil Rights Act of 1963," and would include—in addition to the aforementioned provisions on voting rights and the Civil Rights Commission—additional titles on public accommodations, employment, federally assisted programs, a Community Relations Service, and education, with the latter including my previous recommendation on this subject. In addition, I am requesting certain legislative and budget amendments designed to improve the training, skills, and economic opportunities of the economically distressed and discontented, white and Negro alike. Certain executive actions are also reviewed here; but legislative action is imperative. . . .

Events of recent weeks have again underlined how deeply our Negro citizens resent the injustice of being arbitrarily denied equal access to those facilities and accommodations which are otherwise open to the general public. That is a daily insult which has no place in a country proud of its heritage—the heritage of the melting pot, of equal rights, of one nation and one people. No one has been barred on account of his race from fighting or dying for America—there are no "white" or "colored" signs on the foxholes or graveyards of battle. Surely, in 1963, one hundred years after Emancipation, it should not be necessary for any American citizen to demonstrate in the streets for the opportunity to stop at a hotel, or to eat at a lunch counter in the very department store in which he is shopping, or to enter a motion picture house, on the same terms as any other customer. . . .

For these reasons, I am today proposing, as part of the Civil Rights Act of 1963, a provision to guarantee all citizens equal access to the services and facilities of hotels, restaurants, places of amusement, and retail establishments. . . .

This provision will open doors in every part of the country which never should have been closed. Its enactment will hasten the end to practices which have no place in a free and united nation, and thus help move this potentially dangerous problem from the streets to the courts. . . .

In order to achieve a more orderly and consistent compliance with the Supreme Court's school and college desegregation decisions, therefore, I recommend that the Congress asserts its specific constitutional authority to implement the Fourteenth Amendment by including in the Civil Rights Act of 1963 a new title. . . .

Racial discrimination in employment must be eliminated. Denial of the right to work is unfair, regardless of its victim. It is doubly unfair to throw its burden on an individual because of his race or color. Men who served side by side with each other on the field of battle should have no difficulty working side by side on an assembly line or construction project. . . .

This problem of unequal job opportunity must not be allowed to grow, as the result of either recession or discrimination. I enlist every employer, every labor union, and every agency of government—whether affected directly by these measures or not—in the task of seeing to it that no false lines are drawn in assuring equality of the right and opportunity to make a decent living. . . .

I am today proposing, as part of the Civil Rights Act of 1963, a provision to guarantee all citizens equal access to the services and facilities of hotels, restaurants, places of amusement, and retail establishments.

Many problems remain that cannot be ignored. The enactment of the legislation I have recommended will not solve all our problems of race relations. This bill must be supplemented by action in every branch of government at the federal, state, and local level. It must be supplemented as well by enlightened private citizens, private businesses, and private labor and civic organizations, by responsible educators and editors, and certainly by religious leaders who recognize the conflict between racial bigotry and the Holy Word. . . .

We will not solve these problems by blaming any group or section for the legacy which has been handed down by past generations. But neither will these problems be solved by clinging to the patterns of the past. Nor, finally, can they be solved in the streets, by lawless acts on either side, or by the physical actions or presence of any private group or public official, however appealing such melodramatic devices may seem to some. . . .

The legal remedies I have proposed are the embodiment of this nation's basic posture of common sense and common justice. They involve every American's right to vote, to go to school, to get a job, and to be served in a public place without arbitrary discrimination—rights which most Americans take for granted. . . .

I therefore ask every member of Congress to set aside sectional and political ties, and to look at this issue from the viewpoint of the nation. I ask you to look into your hearts—not in search of charity, for the Negro neither wants nor needs condescension—but for the one plain, proud, and priceless quality that unites us all as Americans: a sense of justice. In this year of the Emancipation Centennial, justice requires us to insure the blessings of liberty for all Americans and their posterity—not merely for reasons of economic efficiency, world diplomacy, and domestic tranquillity—but, above all, because it is right.

Special Message to the Congress
on Civil Rights and Job Opportunities
Washington, D.C., June 19, 1963

The March on Washington

We have witnessed today in Washington tens of thousands of Americans —both Negro and white—exercising their right to assemble peaceably and direct the widest possible attention to a great national issue . . . to secure equal treatment and equal opportunity for all without regard to race, color, creed, or nationality. . . .

Although this summer has seen remarkable progress in translating civil rights from principles into practices, we have a very long way yet to travel. One cannot help but be impressed with the deep fervor and the quiet dignity that characterize the thousands who have gathered in the nation's capital from across the country to demonstrate their faith and confidence in our democratic form of government. History has seen many demonstrations—of widely varying character and for a whole host of reasons. As our thoughts travel to other demonstrations that have occurred in different parts of the world, this nation can properly be proud of the demonstration that has occurred here today. The leaders of the organizations sponsoring the march and all who have participated in it deserve our appreciation for the detailed preparations that made it possible and for the orderly manner in which it has been conducted.

The executive branch of the federal government will continue its efforts to obtain increased employment and to eliminate discrimination in employment practices, two of the prime goals of the march. In addition, our efforts to secure enactment of the legislative proposals made to the Congress will be maintained. . . .

The cause of twenty million Negroes has been advanced by the program conducted so appropriately before the nation's shrine to the Great Emancipator, but even more significant is the contribution to all mankind.

Statement on March on Washington for Jobs and Freedom
Washington, D.C., August 28, 1963

The Long View

Q: Mr. President, this is a related question. It is about the Gallup poll. It has to do with a racial question. Agents of Dr. Gallup asked people this question: Do you think the Kennedy administration is pushing integration too fast or not fast enough? Fifty percent replied that they thought you were pushing too fast. Would you comment?

THE PRESIDENT: No, I think probably he is accurate. The fact of the matter is, this is not a matter on which you can take the temperature every week or two weeks or three weeks, depending on what the newspaper headlines might be. I think you must make a judgment about the movement of a great historical event which is taking place in this country after a period of time. You judged 1863 after a good many years—its full effect. I think we will stand, after a period of time has gone by. The fact is, that same poll showed forty percent or so thought it was more or less right. I thought that was rather impressive, because it is change; change always disturbs, and therefore I was surprised that there wasn't greater opposition. I think we are going at about the right tempo.

President's News Conference
Washington, D.C., September 12, 1963

The Final Word

. . . I pledged in 1960 that a new administration would strive to secure for every American his full constitutional rights. That pledge has been and is being fulfilled. We have not yet secured the objectives desired or the legislation required. But we have, in the last three years . . . opened more new doors to members of minority groups—doors to transportation, voting, education, employment, and places of public accommodation—than had been opened in any three-year or thirty-year period in this century. There is no uncontroversial way to fulfill our constitutional pledge to establish justice and promote domestic tranquillity, but we intend to fulfill those obligations because they are right.

Remarks intended for delivery to
Texas Democratic Dinner
Austin, Texas, November 22, 1963

CHAPTER 10

The Promotion of the Arts

President and Mrs. Kennedy sparked a revival of national interest in matters cultural and intellectual. Nobel prize winners, authors, and scholars dined in the Executive Mansion, and great American concert performers were regularly heard there. From the re-creation of the historic White House through the redesign of a fading Pennsylvania Avenue to the recognition given America's finest poets and artists, the Kennedys more by example and exhortation than by public expenditure, honored what they truly believed to be an enduring source of national pride and greatness. John Kennedy's knowledge and talent in music and painting never matched his skills as writer and orator; but in his encouragement of the arts (as in so many other areas impossible to include in this single volume), he set a standard of excellence to which all who follow might aspire.

The Liberation of the Human Mind

In 1664, Louis the Fourteenth, in his own efforts to encourage the arts, donned brilliant tights and played in a drama called *Furious Roland* before a happy court. Moreover, he drafted the highest officers of his administration for the play so that, according to an account, all clad in brilliant tights themselves, they passed before the queen and the court.

This was suggested tonight but for some reason or other the committee turned it down. But we are glad to be here in any case. . . . And we are very much indebted to all the artists who have so willingly taken part in this work tonight. For when Thomas Jefferson wrote that the one thing, which from the heart he envied certain other nations, was their art, he spoke from a deep understanding of the enduring sources of national greatness and national achievement.

But our culture and art do not speak to America alone. To the extent that artists struggle to express beauty in form and color and sound, to the extent that they write about man's struggle with nature or society or himself, to that extent they strike a responsive chord in all humanity. Today, Sophocles speaks to us from more than two thousand years. And in our own time, even when political communications have been strained, the Russian people have bought more than twenty thousand copies of the works of Jack London, more than ten million books of Mark Twain, and hundreds and thousands of copies of Hemingway, Steinbeck, Whitman, and Poe; and our own people, through the works of Tolstoy and Dostoevski and Pasternak, have gained an insight into the shared problems of the human heart. Thus today, as always, art knows no national boundaries.

Genius can speak at any time, and the entire world will hear it and listen. Behind the storm of daily conflict and crisis, the dramatic confrontations, the tumult of political struggle, the poet, the artist, the musician, continues the quiet work of centuries, building bridges of experience between peoples, reminding man of the universality of his feelings and desires and despairs, and reminding him that the forces that unite are deeper than those that divide.

Thus, art and the encouragement of art are political in the most profound sense, not as a weapon in the struggle, but as an instrument of understanding of the futility of struggle between those who share man's faith. Aeschylus and Plato are remembered today long after the triumphs of imperial Athens are gone. Dante outlived the ambitions of thirteenth-century Florence. Goethe stands serenely above the politics of Germany. And I am certain that, after the dust of centuries has passed over our cities, we, too, will be remembered not for victories or defeats in battle or in politics, but for our contribution to the human spirit.

It was Pericles' proudest boast that politically Athens was the school of Hellas. If we can make our country one of the great schools of civilization, then on that achievement will surely rest our claim to the ultimate gratitude of mankind.

Moreover, as a great democratic society, we have a special responsibility to the arts. For art is the great democrat, calling forth creative genius from every sector of society, disregarding race or religion or wealth or color. The mere accumulation of wealth and power is available to the dictator and the democrat alike. What freedom alone can bring is the liberation of the human mind and spirit which finds its greatest flowering in the free society.

Thus, in our fulfillment of these responsibilities toward the arts lies our unique achievement as a free society.

National Cultural Center Dinner
Washington, D.C., November 29, 1962

The Central Purpose of Civilization

. . . This painting is the second lady that the people of France have sent to the United States, and though she will not stay with us as long as the Statue of Liberty, our appreciation is equally great. Indeed, this loan is the last in a long series of events which have bound together two nations separated by a wide ocean, but linked in their past to the modern world. Our two nations have fought on the same side in four wars during a span of the last 185 years. Each has been delivered from the foreign rule of another by the other's friendship and courage. Our two revolutions helped define the meaning of democracy and freedom which are so much contested in the world today. Today, here in this Gallery, in front of this great painting, we are renewing our commitment to those ideals which have proved such a strong link through so many hazards.

At the same time that the creator of this painting was opening up such a wide new world to Western civilization, his fellow countryman from Italy, Columbus, was opening up a new world to a new civilization. The life of this painting here before us tonight spans the entire life of that new world. We citizens of nations unborn at the time of its creation are among the inheritors and protectors of the ideals which gave it birth. For this painting is not only one of the towering achievements of the skill and vision of art, but its creator embodied the central purpose of our civilization.

Leonardo da Vinci was not only an artist and a sculptor, an architect and a scientist, he was also a military engineer, an occupation which he pursued, he tells us, in order to preserve the chief gift of nature, which is liberty. In this belief he expresses the most profound premises of our own two nations.

National Gallery of Art
Opening of **Mona Lisa** *Exhibition*
Washington, D.C., January 8, 1963

The Fiber of Our National Life

Robert Frost was one of the granite figures of our time in America. He was supremely two things: an artist and an American. A nation reveals itself not only by the men it produces but also by the men it honors, the men it remembers.

In America, our heroes have customarily run to men of large accomplishments. But today this college and country honor a man whose contribution was not to our size but to our spirit, not to our political beliefs but to our insight, not to our self-esteem, but to our self-comprehension. In honoring Robert Frost, we therefore can pay honor to the deepest sources of our national strength. That strength takes many forms, and the most obvious are not always the most significant. The men who create power make an indispensable contribution to the nation's greatness, but the men who question power make a contribution just as indispensable, especially when that questioning is disinterested, for they determine whether we use power or power uses us.

Our national strength matters, but the spirit which informs and controls our strength matters just as much. This was the special significance of Robert Frost. He brought an unsparing instinct for reality to bear on the platitudes and pieties of society. His sense of the human tragedy fortified him against self-deception and easy consolation. "I have been," he wrote, "one acquainted with the night." And because he knew the midnight as well as the high noon, because he understood the ordeal as well as the triumph of the human spirit, he gave his age strength with which to overcome despair. At bottom, he held a deep faith in the spirit of man, and it is hardly an accident that Robert Frost coupled poetry and power, for he saw poetry as the means of saving power from itself. When power leads man toward arrogance, poetry reminds him of his limitations. When power narrows the areas of man's concern, poetry reminds him of the richness and diversity of his existence. When power corrupts, poetry cleanses. For art establishes the basic human truth which must serve as the touchstone of our judgment.

The artist, however faithful to his personal vision of reality, becomes the last champion of the individual mind and sensibility against an intrusive society and an officious state. The great artist is thus a solitary figure. He has, as Frost said, a lover's quarrel with the world. In pursuing his perceptions of reality, he must often sail against the currents of his time. This is not a popular role. If Robert Frost was much honored during his lifetime, it was because a good many preferred to ignore his darker truths. Yet in retrospect, we see how the artist's fidelity has strengthened the fiber of our national life.

If sometimes our great artists have been the most critical of our society, it is because their sensitivity and their concern for justice, which must motivate any true artist, makes him aware that our nation falls short of its highest potential. I see little of more importance to the future of our country and our civilization than full recognition of the place of the artist.

I see little of more importance to the future of our country and our civilization than full recognition of the place of the artist.

If art is to nourish the roots of our culture, society must set the artist free to follow his vision wherever it takes him. We must never forget that art is not a form of propaganda; it is a form of truth. And as Mr. MacLeish once remarked of poets, there is nothing worse for our trade than to be in style. In free society art is not a weapon and it does not belong to the sphere of polemics and ideology. Artists are not engineers of the soul. It may be different elsewhere. But in a democratic society the highest duty of the writer, the composer, the artist is to remain true to himself and to let the chips fall where they may. In serving his vision of the truth, the artist best serves his nation. And the nation which disdains the mission of art invites the fate of Robert Frost's hired man, the fate of having "nothing to look backward to with pride, and nothing to look forward to with hope."

I look forward to a great future for America, a future in which our country will match its military strength with our moral restraint, its wealth with our wisdom, its power with our purpose. I look forward to an America which will not be afraid of grace and beauty, which will protect the beauty of our natural environment, which will preserve the great old American houses and squares and parks of our national past, and which will build handsome and balanced cities for our future.

I look forward to an America which will reward achievement in the arts as we reward achievement in business or statecraft. I look forward to an America which will steadily raise the standards of artistic accomplishment and which will steadily enlarge cultural opportunities for all of our citizens. I look forward to an America which commands respect throughout the world not only for its strength but for its civilization as well. And I look forward to a world which will be safe not only for democracy and diversity but also for personal distinction.

Robert Frost was often skeptical about projects for human improvement, yet I do not think he would disdain this hope. As he wrote during the uncertain days of the Second [World] War:

Take human nature altogether since time began . . .
And it must be a little more in favor of man,
Say a fraction of one percent at the very least . . .
Our hold on the planet wouldn't have so increased.

Because of Mr. Frost's life and work, because of the life and work of this college, our hold on this planet has increased.

Amherst College
Amherst, Massachusetts, October 26, 1963

Signing the Cuban missile crisis quarantine proclamation halting the delivery of offensive weapons to Cuba, October 23, 1962.

PHOTO BY ABBIE ROWE, REPRINTED COURTESY THE JOHN FITZGERALD KENNEDY LIBRARY.

PART IV

The Pursuit of Peace and Security

CHAPTER 11

The Tide Is Turned

John F. Kennedy, as senator, candidate, and President, felt strongly that time was running out on America's necessary role as leader and defender of world freedom. In 1960, the Cold War was at a peak. The Soviet Union was flexing its military, scientific, economic, and diplomatic muscle. All prospects seemed dim for controlling the arms race, solidifying the Alliance, and preventing in the developing world the economic despair and chaos on which violence and despotism fed. In Berlin, Cuba, the Congo, Laos, Vietnam, the United Nations, the Formosa Straits, and a dozen or so other places, the new President faced mounting challenge and crisis. His speeches were designed to stir the country's conscience and awaken it to the dangers and opportunities it faced.

The Urgent Agenda

May 17, 1960, marked the end of an era—an era of illusion, the illusion that personal goodwill is a substitute for hard, carefully prepared bargaining on concrete issues, the illusion that good intentions and pious principles are a substitute for strong, creative leadership.

For on May 17, 1960, the long-awaited, highly publicized summit conference collapsed. That collapse was the direct result of Soviet determination to destroy the talks. The insults and distortions of Mr. Khrushchev and the violence of his attacks shocked all Americans, and united the country in admiration for the dignity and self-control of President Eisenhower. Regardless of party, all of us deeply shared a common disappointment at the failure of the conference. Nevertheless, it is imperative that we, as a nation, rise above our resentment and frustration to a critical reexamination of the events at Paris and their meaning for America.

For the harsh facts of the matter are that the effort to eliminate world tensions and end the Cold War through a summit meeting—necessary as such an effort was to demonstrate America's willingness to seek peaceful solutions—was doomed to failure long before the U-2 ever fell on Soviet soil. This effort was doomed to failure because we have failed for the past eight years to build the positions of long-term strength essential to successful negotiation. It was doomed because we were unprepared with new policies or new programs for the settlement of outstanding substantive issues.

Trunkloads of papers, I am told, were sent to Paris, but no new plans or positions were included. Our unwillingness to go to the summit had changed, but the steady decrease in our relative strength had not changed. Our allies and our own people had been misled into believing that there was some point to holding a summit conference, that we were prepared to say more than what changes in the status quo we would not accept, that by a miracle of personal charm and public relations the Russians could be cajoled into yielding some of their hard-won positions of strength, that we had some conception of alternative settlements that were both acceptable to us and possibly acceptable to the Soviets.

But the truth of the matter is that we were not prepared for any such negotiations and that there was no real success which the summit could have achieved, for words and discussions are not a substitute for strength—they are an instrument for the translation of strength into survival and peace.

This is the real issue of American foreign policy today, not the ill-considered timing of the U-2 or the inconsistent statements of our government. The real issue—and the real lesson of Paris—is the lack of long-range preparation, the lack of policy planning, the lack of a coherent and purposeful national strategy backed by strength.

This is an issue worthy of a great debate, a debate by the American people through the media of their political parties—and that debate must not be stifled or degraded by empty appeals to national unity, false cries of appeasement, or deceptive slogans about "standing up to Khrushchev." For the issue is not who can best "stand up to Khrushchev" or who can best swap threats and insults. The real issue is who can stand up and summon America's vast resources to the defense of freedom against the most dangerous enemy it has ever faced.

If the 1960 campaign should degenerate into a contest of who can talk toughest to Khrushchev, or which party is the "party of war" or the "party of appeasement," or which candidate can tell the American voters what they want to hear, rather than what they need to hear, or who is soft on communism, or who can be hardest on foreign aid, then, in my opinion, it makes very little difference who the winners are in July and in November, for the American people and the whole free world will be the losers.

For the next President of the United States, whoever he may be, will find he has considerably more to do than "stand up to Khrushchev," balance the budget, and mouth popular slogans, if he is to restore our nation's relative strength and leadership. For he will find himself with far-flung commitments without the strength to meet them or to back them up. He will inherit policies formed largely as reactions to Soviet action, their limits set by budgeteers without regard to world conditions or America's needs, their effectiveness often undercut by overlapping or competing agencies. He will inherit membership in alliances of uncertain stability and in international organizations of obsolete structure. He will inherit programs which have been frequently administered by shortsighted, unsympathetic men opposed to the very programs they are administering, awaiting their own return to private industry, and so lacking in compassion for our domestic needs as to be incapable of compassion for the desperate needs of the world's peoples. He will face a world of revolution and turmoil armed with policies which seek only to freeze the status quo and turn back the inevitable tides of change.

Words and discussions are not a substitute for strength—they are an instrument for the translation of strength into survival and peace.

To be sure, we have, in 1960, most of the formal tools of foreign policy: We have a defense establishment, a foreign-aid program, a Western alliance, a Disarmament Committee, an information service, an intelligence operation, and a National Security Council. But . . . we have failed to adapt these tools to the formulation of a long-range, coordinated strategy to meet the determined Soviet program for world domination—a program which skillfully blends the weapons of military might, political subversion, economic penetration, and ideological conquest. We are forced to rely upon piecemeal programs, obsolete policies, and meaningless slogans. . . . We have as our grand strategy only the arms race and the Cold War. . . .

As a substitute for policy, President Eisenhower has tried smiling at the Russians; our State Department has tried frowning at them; and Mr. Nixon has tried both. None have succeeded. For we cannot conceal or overcome our lack of purpose, and our failure of planning, by talking tough; nor can we compensate for our weaknesses by talking smoothly and by assuming that the righteousness of our principles will insure their victory. For just as we know that might never makes right, we must also remember that right, unfortunately, never makes might.

Our task is to devise a national strategy—based not on eleventh-hour responses to Soviet-created crises—but a comprehensive set of carefully prepared, long-term policies designed to increase the strength of the non-Communist world.

The hour is late, but the agenda is long.

First. We must make invulnerable a nuclear retaliatory power second to none. . . .

Second. We must regain the ability to intervene effectively and swiftly in any limited war anywhere in the world. . . .

Third. We must rebuild NATO into a viable and consolidated military force capable of deterring any kind of attack, unified in weaponry and responsibility . . . aiming beyond a narrow military alliance united only by mutual fears. . . .

Fourth. We must . . . greatly increase the flow of capital to the underdeveloped areas of Asia, Africa, the Middle East, and Latin America . . . enabling emerging nations to achieve economic as well as political independence. . . .

Fifth. We must reconstruct our relations with the Latin American democracies. . . .

Sixth. We must formulate . . . a new approach to the Middle East. . . .

Seventh. We must greatly increase our efforts to encourage the newly emerging nations of the vast continent of Africa. . . .

Eighth. We must plan a long-range solution to the problems of Berlin. . . .

Ninth. We must prepare and hold in readiness more flexible and realistic tools for use in Eastern Europe. . . .

Tenth. We must reassess a China policy which has failed dismally [and] work to improve at least our communications with mainland China. . . .

Eleventh. We must begin to develop new, workable programs for peace and the control of arms . . . to strengthen the United Nations and to increase its role in resolving international conflicts. . . .

Twelfth, and finally, we must work to build the stronger America on which our ultimate ability to defend ourselves and the free world depends . . . our own scientific effort . . . educational system . . . economy . . . equal opportunity and economic justice. . . .

I realize . . . that the length of this agenda is in sharp contrast with the rosy reassurances of the administration. "America is today," the Vice-President told his national committee Saturday, summarizing our position in the world, "the strongest country militarily, the strongest country economically, with the best educational system and the finest scientists in the world, overall." To feed that kind of diet to the American people during the coming months—to confine our national posture to one of talking louder and louder while carrying a smaller and smaller stick—is to trade the long-range needs of the nation and the free world for the short-term appearance of security.

For all America—its President, and its people—the coming years will be a time of decision. We must decide whether we have reached our limit—whether our greatness is past—whether we can go no further—or whether, in the words of Thomas Wolfe, "the true discovery of America is before us—the true fulfillment of our mighty and immortal land is yet to come."

United States Senate
Washington, D.C., June 14, 1960

The Response to Multiple Crises

I speak today in an hour of national peril and national opportunity. Before my term has ended, we shall have to test anew whether a nation organized and governed such as ours can endure. The outcome is by no means certain. The answers are by no means clear. All of us together—this administration, this Congress, this nation—must forge those answers.

To state the facts frankly is not to despair the future nor indict the past. The prudent heir takes careful inventory of his legacies, and gives a faithful accounting to those whom he owes an obligation of trust. And, while the occasion does not call for another recital of our blessings and assets, we do have no greater asset than the willingness of a free and determined people, through its elected officials, to face all problems frankly and meet all dangers free from panic or fear. . . .

No man entering upon this office, regardless of his party, regardless of his previous service in Washington, could fail to be staggered upon learning—even in this brief ten-day period—the harsh enormity of the trials through which we must pass in the next four years. Each day the crises multiply. Each day their solution grows more difficult. Each day we draw nearer the hour of maximum danger, as weapons spread and hostile forces grow stronger. I feel I must inform the Congress that our analyses over the last ten days make it clear that—in each of the principal areas of crisis—the tide of events has been running out and time has not been our friend.

In Asia, the relentless pressures of the Chinese Communists menace the security of the entire area—from the borders of India and South Vietnam to the jungles of Laos, struggling to protect its newly won independence. We seek in Laos what we seek in all Asia, and, indeed, in all of the world—freedom for the people and independence for the government. And this nation shall persevere in our pursuit of these objectives.

In Africa, the Congo has been brutally torn by civil strife, political unrest, and public disorder. We shall continue to support the heroic efforts of the United Nations to restore peace and order—efforts which are now endangered by mounting tensions, unsolved problems, and decreasing support from many member states.

In Latin America, Communist agents seeking to exploit that region's peaceful revolution of hope have established a base on Cuba, only ninety miles from our shores. Our objection with Cuba is not over the people's drive for a better life. Our objection is to their domination by foreign and domestic tyrannies. Cuban social and economic reform should be encouraged. Questions of economic and trade policy can always be negotiated. But Communist domination in this hemisphere can never be negotiated.

We are pledged to work with our sister republics to free the Americas of all such foreign domination and all tyranny, working toward the goal of a free hemisphere of free governments, extending from Cape Horn to the Arctic Circle.

In Europe, our alliances are unfulfilled and in some disarray. The unity of NATO has been weakened by economic rivalry and partially eroded by national interest. It has not yet fully mobilized its resources nor fully achieved a common outlook. Yet no Atlantic power can meet on its own the mutual problems now facing us in defense, foreign aid, monetary reserves, and a host of other areas; and our close ties with those whose hopes and interests we share are among this nation's most powerful assets.

Our greatest challenge is still the world that lies beyond the Cold War—but the first great obstacle is still our relations with the Soviet Union and Communist China. We must never be lulled into believing that either power has yielded its ambitions for world domination—ambitions which they forcefully restated only a short time ago. On the contrary, our task is to convince them that aggression and subversion will not be profitable routes to pursue these ends. Open and peaceful competition—for prestige, for markets, for scientific achievement, even for men's minds—is something else again. For if freedom and communism were to compete for man's allegiance in a world at peace, I would look to the future with ever increasing confidence.

No man entering upon this office, regardless of his party, regardless of his previous service in Washington, could fail to be staggered upon learning—even in this brief ten-day period—the harsh enormity of the trials through which we must pass in the next four years.

To meet this array of challenges—to fulfill the role we cannot avoid on the world scene—we must reexamine and revise our whole arsenal of tools: military, economic, and political.

One must not overshadow the other. On the presidential coat of arms, the American eagle holds in his right talon the olive branch, while in his left he holds a bundle of arrows. We intend to give equal attention to both.

First, we must strengthen our military tools. We are moving into a period of uncertain risk and great commitment in which both the military and diplomatic possibilities require a Free World force so powerful as to make any aggression clearly futile. Yet in the past, lack of a consistent, coherent military strategy, the absence of basic assumptions about our national requirements, and the faulty estimates and duplication arising from interservice rivalries have all made it difficult to assess accurately how adequate—or inadequate—our defenses really are.

I have, therefore, instructed the Secretary of Defense to reappraise our entire defense strategy—our ability to fulfill our commitments—the effectiveness, vulnerability, and dispersal of our strategic bases, forces, and warning systems—the efficiency and economy of our operation and organization—the elimination of obsolete bases and installations—and the adequacy, modernization, and mobility of our present conventional and nuclear forces and weapons systems in the light of present and future dangers. I have asked for preliminary conclusions by the end of February—and I then shall recommend whatever legislative, budgetary, or executive action is needed in the light of these conclusions.

In the meantime, I have asked the Defense Secretary to initiate immediately three new steps most clearly needed now:

(a) I have directed prompt attention to increase our airlift capacity . . .

(b) I have directed prompt action to step up our Polaris submarine program . . .

(c) I have directed prompt action to accelerate our entire missile program . . .

Secondly, we must improve our economic tools. Our role is essential and unavoidable in the construction of a sound and expanding economy for the entire non-Communist world, helping other nations build the strength to meet their own problems, to satisfy their own aspirations—to surmount their own dangers. The problems in achieving this goal are towering and unprecedented—the response must be towering and unprecedented as well, much as Lend-Lease and the Marshall Plan were in earlier years, which brought such fruitful results.

I intend to ask the Congress for authority to establish a new and more effective program for assisting the economic, educational, and social development of other countries and continents. That program must stimulate and take more effectively into account the contributions of our allies, and provide central policy direction for all our own programs that now so often overlap, conflict, or diffuse our energies and resources. Such a program, compared to past programs, will require

—more flexibility for short-run emergencies

—more commitment to long-term development

—new attention to education at all levels

—greater emphasis on the recipient nations' role, their effort, their purpose, with greater social justice for their people, broader distribution and participation by their people, and more efficient public administration and more efficient tax systems of their own; and

—orderly planning for national and regional development instead of a piecemeal approach. . . .

To our sister republics to the south, we have pledged a new alliance for progress—*alianza para el progreso.* Our goal is a free and prosperous

Latin America, realizing for all its states and all its citizens a degree of economic and social progress that matches their historic contributions of culture, intellect, and liberty.

This administration is expanding its Food for Peace program in every possible way. The product of our abundance must be used more effectively to relieve hunger and help economic growth in all corners of the globe.

An even more valuable national asset is our reservoir of dedicated men and women—not only on our college campuses but in every age group—who have indicated their desire to contribute their skills, their efforts, and a part of their lives to the fight for world order. We can mobilize this talent through the formation of a National Peace Corps, enlisting the services of all those with the desire and capacity to help foreign lands meet their urgent needs for trained personnel.

Finally, while our attention is centered on the development of the non-Communist world, we must never forget our hopes for the ultimate freedom and welfare of the Eastern European peoples. In order to be prepared to help reestablish historic ties of friendship, I am asking the Congress for increased discretion to use economic tools in this area whenever this is found to be clearly in the national interest.

Third, we must sharpen our political and diplomatic tools—the means of cooperation and agreement on which an enforceable world order must ultimately rest.

I have already taken steps to coordinate and expand our disarmament effort—to increase our programs of research and study—and to make arms control a central goal of our national policy under my direction. The deadly arms race, and the huge resources it absorbs, have too long overshadowed all else we must do. We must prevent that arms race from spreading to new nations, to new nuclear powers, and to the reaches of outer space. We must make certain that our negotiators are better informed and better prepared—to formulate workable proposals of our own and to make sound judgments about the proposals of others.

Our problems are critical. The tide is unfavorable. The news will be worse before it is better. And while hoping and working for the best, we should prepare ourselves now for the worst.

We cannot escape our dangers—neither must we let them drive us into panic or narrow isolation. In many areas of the world where the balance of power already rests with our adversaries, the forces of freedom are sharply divided. It is one of the ironies of our time that the techniques of a harsh and repressive system should be able to instill discipline and ardor in its servants—while the blessings of liberty have too often stood for privilege, materialism, and a life of ease.

But I have a different view of liberty.

Life in 1961 will not be easy. Wishing it, predicting it, even asking for it, will not make it so. There will be further setbacks before the tide is turned. But turn it we must. The hopes of all mankind rest upon us—not simply upon those of us in this chamber, but upon the peasant in Laos, the fisherman in Nigeria, the exile from Cuba, the spirit that moves every man and nation who shares our hopes for freedom and the future. And in the final analysis, they rest most of all upon the pride and perseverance of our fellow citizens of the great Republic.

In the words of a great President, whose birthday we honor today, closing his final State of the Union message sixteen years ago, "We pray that we may be worthy of the unlimited opportunities that God has given us."

State of the Union Address
The Capitol, Washington, D.C.
January 30, 1961

The Freedom Doctrine

The Constitution imposes upon me the obligation to "from time to time give to the Congress information of the State of the Union." While this has traditionally been interpreted as an annual affair, this tradition has been broken in extraordinary times.

These are extraordinary times. And we face an extraordinary challenge. Our strength as well as our convictions have imposed upon this nation the role of leader in freedom's cause.

No role in history could be more difficult or more important. We stand for freedom. That is our conviction for ourselves—that is our only commitment to others. No friend, no neutral, and no adversary should think otherwise. We are not against any man—or any nation—or any system—except as it is hostile to freedom. Nor am I here to present a new military doctrine, bearing any one name or aimed at any one area. I am here to promote the freedom doctrine.

I

The great battleground for the defense and expansion of freedom today is the whole southern half of the globe—Asia, Latin America, Africa, and the Middle East—the lands of the rising peoples. Their revolution is the greatest in human history. They seek an end to injustice, tyranny, and exploitation. More than an end, they seek a beginning.

Theirs is a revolution which we would support regardless of the Cold War, and regardless of which political or economic route they should choose to freedom.

For the adversaries of freedom did not create the revolution; nor did they create the conditions which compel it. But they are seeking to ride the crest of its wave—to capture it for themselves.

Yet their aggression is more often concealed than open. They have fired no missiles; and their troops are seldom seen. They send arms, agitators, aid, technicians, and propaganda to every troubled area. But where fighting is required, it is usually done by others—by guerrillas striking at night, by assassins striking alone—assassins who have taken the lives of four thousand civil officers in the last twelve months in

Vietnam alone—by subversives and saboteurs and insurrectionists, who in some cases control whole areas inside of independent nations.

With these formidable weapons, the adversaries of freedom plan to consolidate their territory—to exploit, to control, and finally to destroy the hopes of the world's newest nations; and they have ambition to do it before the end of this decade. It is a contest of will and purpose as well as force and violence—a battle for minds and souls as well as lives and territory. And in that contest, we cannot stand aside.

We stand, as we have always stood from our earliest beginnings, for the independence and equality of all nations. This nation was born of revolution and raised in freedom. And we do not intend to leave an open road for despotism.

Our patience at the bargaining table is nearly inexhaustible, though our credulity is limited . . . our hopes for peace are unfailing, while our determination to protect our security is resolute.

There is no single simple policy which meets this challenge. Experience has taught us that no one nation has the power or the wisdom to solve all the problems of the world or manage its revolutionary tides—that extending our commitments does not always increase our security—that any initiative carries with it the risk of a temporary defeat—that nuclear weapons cannot prevent subversion—that no free people can be kept free without will and energy of their own and that no two nations or situations are exactly alike.

Yet there is much we can do—and must do. . . .

In conclusion, let me emphasize one point: that we are determined, as a nation in 1961, that freedom shall survive and succeed—and whatever the peril and setbacks, we have some very large advantages.

The first is the simple fact that we are on the side of liberty—and since the beginning of history, and particularly since the end of the Second World War, liberty has been winning out all over the globe.

A second great asset is that we are not alone. We have friends and allies all over the world who share our devotion to freedom. May I cite as a symbol of traditional and effective friendship the great ally I am about to visit—France. I look forward to my visit to France, and to my discussion with a great captain of the Western world, President de Gaulle, as a meeting of particular significance, permitting the kind of close and ranging consultation that will strengthen both our countries and serve the common purposes of worldwide peace and liberty. Such serious conversations do not require a pale unanimity—they are rather the instruments of trust and understanding over a long road.

A third asset is our desire for peace. It is sincere, and I believe the world knows it. We are proving it in our patience at the test-ban table, and we are proving it in the UN, where our efforts have been directed to maintaining that organization's usefulness as a protector of the independence of small nations. In these and other instances, the response of our opponents has not been encouraging.

Yet it is important to know that our patience at the bargaining table is nearly inexhaustible, though our credulity is limited—that our hopes for peace are unfailing, while our determination to protect our security is resolute. For these reasons I have long thought it wise to meet with the Soviet Premier for a personal exchange of views. A meeting in Vienna turned out to be convenient for us both; and the Austrian government has kindly made us welcome. No formal agenda is planned and no negotiations will be undertaken; but we will make clear America's enduring concern is for both peace and freedom—that we are anxious to live in harmony with the Russian people—that we seek no conquests, no satellites, no riches—that we seek only the day when "nation shall not lift up sword against nation, neither shall they learn war any more."

Finally, our greatest asset in this struggle is the American people—their willingness to pay the price for these programs—to understand and accept a long struggle—to share their resources with other less fortunate people—to meet the tax levels and close the tax loopholes I have requested—to exercise self-restraint, instead of pushing up wages or prices, or over-producing certain crops, or spreading military secrets, or urging unessential expenditures or improper monopolies or harmful work stoppages—to serve in the Peace Corps or the Armed Services or the federal Civil Service or the Congress—to strive for excellence in their schools, in their cities, and in their physical fitness and that of their children—to take part in Civil Defense—to pay higher postal rates, and higher payroll taxes, and higher teachers' salaries, in order to strengthen our society—to show friendship to students and visitors from other lands who visit us and go back in many cases to be the future leaders, with an image of America—and I want that image, and I know you do, to be affirmative and positive—and, finally, to practice democracy at home, in all states, with all races, to respect each other and to protect the constitutional rights of all citizens.

I have not asked for a single program which did not cause one or all Americans some inconvenience, or some hardship, or some sacrifice. But they have responded and you in the Congress have responded to your duty—and I feel confident in asking today for a similar response to these new and larger demands. It is heartening to know, as I journey abroad, that our country is united in its commitment to freedom—and is ready to do its duty.

Special Address to Congress on Urgent National Needs
The Capitol, Washington, D.C.
May 25, 1961

The Great Defender of Freedom

Since the close of the Second World War, a global civil war has divided and tormented mankind. But it is not our military might, or our higher standard of living, that has most distinguished us from our adversaries. It is our belief that the state is the servant of the citizen and not his master.

This basic clash of ideas and wills is but one of the forces reshaping our globe—swept as it is by the tides of hope and fear, by crises in the headlines today that become mere footnotes tomorrow. Both the successes and the setbacks of the past year remain on our agenda of unfinished business. For every apparent blessing contains the seeds of danger—every area of trouble gives out a ray of hope—and the one unchangeable certainty is that nothing is certain or unchangeable. . . .

Yet our basic goals remain the same: a peaceful world community of free and independent states—free to choose their own future and their own system, so long as it does not threaten the freedom of others.

Some may choose forms and ways that we would not choose for ourselves—but it is not for us that they are choosing. We can welcome diversity—the Communists cannot. For we offer a world of choice—they offer the world of coercion. And the way of the past shows clearly that freedom, not coercion, is the wave of the future. At times our goal has been obscured by crisis or endangered by conflict—but it draws sustenance from five basic sources of strength:

- the moral and physical strength of the United States;
- the united strength of the Atlantic Community;
- the regional strength of our hemispheric relations;
- the creative strength of our efforts in the new and developing nations; and
- the peacekeeping strength of the United Nations.

Our moral and physical strength begins at home as already discussed. But it includes our military strength as well. So long as fanaticism and fear brood over the affairs of men, we must arm to deter others from aggression.

This nation belongs among the first to explore [space], and among the first—if not the first—we shall be. We are offering our know-how and our cooperation to the United Nations. . . . But peace in space will help us naught once peace on earth is gone. World order will be secured only when the whole world has laid down these weapons which seem to offer us present security but threaten the future survival of the human race. That armistice day seems very far away. The vast resources of this planet are being devoted more and more to the means of destroying, instead of enriching, human life.

But the world was not meant to be a prison in which man awaits his execution. Nor has mankind survived the tests and trials of thousands of years to surrender everything—including its existence—now. This nation has the will and the faith to make a supreme effort to break the log jam on disarmament and nuclear tests—and we will persist until we prevail, until the rule of law has replaced the ever dangerous use of force.

These various elements in our foreign policy lead . . . to a single goal—the goal of a peaceful world of free and independent states. This is our guide for the present and our vision for the future—a free community of nations, independent but interdependent, uniting North and South, East and West, in one great family of man, outgrowing and transcending the hates and fears that rend our age.

It is the fate of this generation . . . to live with a struggle we did not start, in a world we did not make.

We will not reach that goal today, or tomorrow. We may not reach it in our own lifetime. But the quest is the greatest adventure of our century. We sometimes chafe at the burden of our obligations, the complexity of our decisions, the agony of our choices. But there is no comfort or security for us in evasion, no solution in abdication, no relief in irresponsibility.

A year ago, in assuming the tasks of the Presidency, I said that few generations, in all history, had been granted the role of being the great defender of freedom in its hour of maximum danger. This is our good fortune; and I welcome it now as I did a year ago. For it is the fate of this generation—of you in the Congress and of me as President—to live with a struggle we did not start, in a world we did not make. But the pressures of life are not always distributed by choice. And while no nation has ever faced such a challenge, no nation has ever been so ready to seize the burden and the glory of freedom. And in this high endeavor, may God watch over the United States of America.

State of the Union Address
The Capitol, Washington, D.C.
January 11, 1962

The Tides of Human Freedom

Little more than a hundred weeks ago I assumed the office of President of the United States. In seeking the help of the Congress and our countrymen, I pledged no easy answers. I pledged—and asked—only toil and dedication. These the Congress and the people have given in good measure. And today, having witnessed in recent months a heightened respect for our national purpose and power—having seen the courageous calm of a united people in a perilous hour—and having observed a steady improvement in the opportunities and well-being of our citizens—I can report to you that the state of this old but youthful Union, in the one hundred and seventy-fifth year of its life, is good.

In the world beyond our borders, steady progress has been made in building a world of order. The people of West Berlin remain both free and secure. A settlement, though still precarious, has been reached in Laos. The spearpoint of aggression has been blunted in Vietnam. The end of agony may be in sight in the Congo. The doctrine of troika is dead. And, while danger continues, a deadly threat has been removed in Cuba.

At home, the recession is behind us. . . . In short, both at home and abroad, there may now be a temptation to relax. For the road has been long, the burden heavy, and the pace consistently urgent.

But we cannot be satisfied to rest here. This is the side of the hill, not the top. The mere absence of war is not peace. The mere absence of recession is not growth. We have made a beginning—but we have only begun.

Now the time has come to make the most of our gains—to translate the renewal of our national strength into the achievement of our national purpose.

Turning to the world outside, it was only a few years ago in Southeast Asia, Africa, Eastern Europe, Latin America, even outer space—that communism sought to convey the image of a unified, confident, and expanding empire, closing in on a sluggish America and a free world in disarray. But few people would hold to that picture today.

In these past months we have reaffirmed the scientific and military superiority of freedom. We have doubled our efforts in space, to assure us of being first in the future. We have undertaken the most far-reaching defense improvements in the peacetime history of this country. And we have maintained the frontiers of freedom from Vietnam to West Berlin.

But complacency or self-congratulation can imperil our security as much as the weapons of tyranny. A moment of pause is not a promise of peace. . . .

In short, let our adversaries choose. If they choose peaceful competition, they shall have it. If they come to realize that their ambitions cannot succeed—if they see their "wars of liberation" and subversion will ultimately fail—if they recognize that there is more security in accepting inspection than in permitting new nations to master the black arts of nuclear war—and if they are willing to turn their energies, as we are, to the great unfinished tasks of our own peoples—then, surely, the areas of agreement can be very wide indeed; a clear understanding about Berlin, stability in Southeast Asia, an end to nuclear testing, new checks on surprise or accidental attack, and, ultimately, general and complete disarmament.

For we seek not the worldwide victory of one nation or system but a worldwide victory of man. The modern globe is too small, its weapons are too destructive, and its disorders are too contagious to permit any other kind of victory.

To achieve this end, the United States will continue to spend a greater portion of its national production than any other people in the free world. For fifteen years no other free nation has demanded so much of itself. Through hot wars and cold, through recession and prosperity, through the ages of the atom and outer space, the American people have never faltered and their faith has never lagged. If at times our actions seem to make life difficult for others, it is only because history has made life difficult for us all.

But difficult days need not be dark. I think these are proud and memorable days in the cause of peace and freedom. We are proud, for example, of Major Rudolf Anderson, who gave his life over the island of Cuba. We salute Specialist James Allen Johnson, who died on the border of South Korea. We pay honor to Sergeant Gerald Pendell, who was killed in Vietnam. They are among the many who in this century, far from home, have died for our country. Our task now, and the task of all Americans is to live up to their commitment.

My friends: I close on a note of hope. We are not lulled by the momentary calm of the sea or the somewhat clearer skies above. We know the turbulence that lies below, and the storms that are beyond the horizon this year. But now the winds of change appear to be blowing more strongly than ever, in the world of communism as well as our own. For 175 years we have sailed with those winds at our back, and with the tides of human freedom in our favor. We steer our ship with hope, as Thomas Jefferson said, "leaving Fear astern."

Today we still welcome those winds of change—and we have every reason to believe that our tide is running strong. With thanks to Almighty God for seeing us through a perilous passage, we ask His help anew in guiding the "good ship *Union.*"

State of the Union Address
The Capitol, Washington, D.C.
January 14, 1963

CHAPTER 12

The National Defense

Improved photographic reconnaissance and intelligence estimates in 1961 informed President Kennedy that the most serious shortcoming in our capacity to deter a hostile assault was not a "missile gap," as his 1959 and 1960 campaign speeches had charged, but insufficient conventional forces to meet a serious challenge in Berlin and elsewhere. Maintaining strong civilian leadership and budget controls, he began a long, steady buildup of our Armed Forces. Commending their service and sacrifice, he addressed the graduating classes of all three military academies, toured U.S. installations across the country and globe, and met regularly with his principal military advisers.

The Cautious Commander-in-Chief

In my role as Commander-in-Chief of the American Armed Forces, and with my concern over the security of this nation now and in the future, no single question of policy has concerned me more since entering upon these responsibilities than the adequacy of our present and planned military forces to accomplish our major national security objectives. . . .

1. The primary purpose of our arms is peace, not war—to make certain that they will never have to be used—to deter all wars, general or limited, nuclear or conventional, large or small—to convince all potential aggressors that any attack would be futile—to provide backing for diplomatic settlement of disputes—to insure the adequacy of our bargaining power for an end to the arms race. The basic problems facing the world today are not susceptible to a military solution. Neither our strategy nor our psychology as a nation—and certainly not our economy—must become dependent upon the permanent maintenance of a large military establishment. Our military posture must be sufficiently flexible and under control to be consistent with our efforts to explore all possibilities and to take every step to lessen tensions, to obtain peaceful solutions, and to secure arms limitations. Diplomacy and defense are no longer distinct alternatives, one to be used where the other fails—both must complement each other.

The basic problems facing the world today are not susceptible to a military solution.

Disarmament, so difficult and so urgent, has been much discussed since 1945, but progress has not been made. Recrimination in such matters is seldom useful, and we for our part are determined to try again. In so doing, we note that, in the public position of both sides in recent years, the determination to be strong has been coupled with announced willingness to negotiate. For our part, we know there can be dialectical truth in such a position, and we shall do all we can to prove it in action. This budget is wholly consistent with our earnest desire for serious conversation with the other side on disarmament. If genuine progress is made, then as tension is reduced, so will be our arms.

2. Our arms will never be used to strike the first blow in any attack. This is not a confession of weakness but a statement of strength. It is our national tradition. We must offset whatever advantage this may appear to hand an aggressor by so increasing the capability of our forces to respond swiftly and effectively to any aggressive move as to convince any would-be aggressor that such a movement would be too futile and costly to undertake. In the area of general war, this doctrine means that such capability must rest with that portion of our forces which would survive the initial attack. We are not creating forces for a first strike against any other nation. We shall never threaten, provoke, or initiate aggression—but if aggression should come, our response will be swift and effective.

3. Our arms must be adequate to meet our commitments and insure our security, without being bound by arbitrary budget ceilings. This nation can afford to be strong—it cannot afford to be weak. We shall do what is needed to make and to keep us strong. We must, of course, take advantage of every opportunity to reduce military outlays as a result of scientific or managerial progress, new strategy concepts, a more efficient, manageable, and thus more effective defense establishment, or international agreements for the control and limitation of arms. But we must not shrink from additional costs where they are necessary. The additional . . . expenditures for fiscal 1962 which I am recommending today, while relatively small, are too urgent to be governed by a budget largely decided before our defense review had been completed. Indeed, in the long run the net effect of all the changes I am recommending will be to provide a more economical budget. But I cannot promise that in later years we need not be prepared to spend still more for what is indispensable. Much depends on the course followed by other nations. As a proportion of gross national product, as a share of our total budget, and in comparison with our national effort in earlier times of war, this increase in defense expenditures is still substantially below what our citizens have been willing and are now able to support as insurance on their security—insurance we hope is never needed—but insurance we must nevertheless purchase.

4. Our arms must be subject to ultimate civilian control and command at all times, in war as well as peace. The basic decisions on our participation in any conflict and our response to any threat—including all decisions relating to the use of nuclear weapons, or the escalation of a small war into a large one—will be made by the regularly constituted civilian authorities. This requires effective and protected organization, procedures, facilities, and communication in the event of attack directed toward this objective, as well as defensive measures designed to insure thoughtful and selective decisions by the civilian authorities. This message and budget also reflect that basic principle. The Secretary of Defense and I have had the earnest counsel of our senior military advisers and many others and in fact they support the great majority of the decisions reflected in this budget. But I have not delegated to anyone else the responsibilities for decisions which are imposed upon me by the Constitution.

Decisions on our participation in any conflict and our response to any threat . . . will be made by the regularly constituted civilian authorities. . . . I have not delegated to anyone else the responsibilities for decisions which are imposed upon me by the Constitution.

5. Our strategic arms and defenses must be adequate to deter any deliberate nuclear attack on the United States or our allies—by making clear to any potential aggressor that sufficient retaliatory forces will be able to survive a first strike and penetrate his defenses in order to inflict unacceptable losses upon him. As I indicated in an address to the Senate some thirty-one months ago, this deterrence does not depend upon a simple comparison of missiles on hand before an attack. It has been publicly acknowledged for several years that this nation has not led the world in missile strength. Moreover, we will not strike first in any

conflict. But what we have and must continue to have is the ability to survive a first blow and respond with devastating power. This deterrent power depends not only on the number of our missiles and bombers, but on their state of readiness, their ability to survive attack, and the flexibility and sureness with which we can control them to achieve our national purpose and strategic objectives.

6. The strength and deployment of our forces in combination with those of our allies should be sufficiently powerful and mobile to prevent the steady erosion of the Free World through limited wars; and it is this role that should constitute the primary mission of our overseas forces. Non-nuclear wars, and sub-limited or guerrilla warfare, have since 1945 constituted the most active and constant threat to Free World security. Those units of our forces which are stationed overseas, or designed to fight overseas, can be most usefully oriented toward deterring or confining those conflicts which do not justify and must not lead to a general nuclear attack. In the event of a major aggression that could not be repulsed by conventional forces, we must be prepared to take whatever action with whatever weapons are appropriate. But our objective now is to increase our ability to confine our response to non-nuclear weapons, and to lessen the incentive for any limited aggression by making clear what our response will accomplish. In most areas of the world, the main burden of local defense against overt attack, subversion, and guerrilla warfare must rest on local populations and forces. But given the great likelihood and seriousness of this threat, we must be prepared to make a substantial contribution in the form of strong, highly mobile forces trained in this type of warfare, some of which must be deployed in forward areas, with a substantial airlift and sealift capacity and prestocked overseas bases.

7. Our defense posture must be both flexible and determined. Any potential aggressor contemplating an attack on any part of the Free World with any kind of weapons, conventional or nuclear, must know that our response will be suitable, selective, swift, and effective. While he may be uncertain of its exact nature and location, there must be no uncertainty about our determination and capacity to take whatever steps are necessary to meet our obligations. We must be able to make deliberate choices in weapons and strategy, shift the tempo of our production, and alter the direction of our forces to meet rapidly changing conditions or objectives at very short notice and under any circumstances. Our weapons systems must be usable in a manner permitting deliberation and discrimination as to timing, scope, and targets in re-

sponse to civilian authority; and our defenses must be secure against prolonged re-attack as well as a surprise first strike. To purchase productive capacity and to initiate development programs that may never need to be used—as this budget proposes—adopts an insurance policy of buying alternative future options.

8. Our defense posture must be designed to reduce the danger of irrational or unpremeditated general war—the danger of an unnecessary escalation of a small war into a large one, or of miscalculation or misinterpretation of an incident or enemy intention. Our diplomatic efforts to reach agreements on the prevention of surprise attack, an end to the spread of nuclear weapons—indeed, all our efforts to end the arms race—are aimed at this objective. We shall strive for improved communication among all nations, to make clear our own intentions and resolution, and to prevent any nation from underestimating the response of any other, as has too often happened in the past. In addition our own military activities must be safeguarded against the possibility of inadvertent triggering incidents. But even more importantly, we must make certain that our retaliatory power does not rest on decisions made in ambiguous circumstances, or permit a catastrophic mistake. . . .

As a power which will never strike first, our hopes for anything close to an absolute deterrent must rest on weapons which come from hidden, moving, or invulnerable bases which will not be wiped out by a surprise attack. A retaliatory capacity based on adequate numbers of these weapons would deter any aggressor from launching or even threatening an attack—an attack he knew could not find or destroy enough of our force to prevent his own destruction. . . .

The Free World's security can be endangered not only by a nuclear attack, but also by being slowly nibbled away at the periphery, regardless of our strategic power, by forces of subversion, infiltration, intimidation, indirect or non-overt aggression, internal revolution, diplomatic blackmail, guerrilla warfare, or a series of limited wars.

In this area of local wars, we must inevitably count on the cooperative efforts of other peoples and nations who share our concern. Indeed, their interests are more often directly engaged in such conflicts. The self-reliant are also those whom it is easiest to help—and for these reasons we must continue and reshape the Military Assistance Program which I have discussed earlier in my special message on foreign aid.

The elimination of waste, duplication, and outmoded or unjustifiable expenditure items from the defense budget is a long and arduous undertaking, resisted by special arguments and interests from economic, military, technical, and other special groups. There are hundreds of ways, most of them with some merit, for spending billions of dollars on defense; and it is understandable that every critic of this budget will have a strong preference for economy on some expenditures other than those that affect his branch of the service, or his plant, or his community.

But hard decisions must be made. Unneeded facilities or projects must be phased out. The defense establishment must be lean and fit, efficient and effective, always adjusting to new opportunities and advances, and planning for the future. The national interest must be weighed against special or local interests; and it is the national interest that calls upon us to cut our losses and cut back those programs in which a very dim promise no longer justifies a very large cost. . . .

It is not pleasant to request additional funds at this time for national security. Our interest, as I have emphasized, lies in peaceful solutions, in reducing tension, in settling disputes at the conference table and not on the battlefield. I am hopeful that these policies will help secure these ends.

Special Message to Congress on Defense Policies and Principles
Washington, D.C., March 28, 1961

The Modern Military Officer

Nearly a half century ago, President Woodrow Wilson came here to Annapolis on a similar mission, and addressed the Class of 1914. That day, the graduating class numbered 154 men. There has been, since that time, a revolution in the size of our military establishment, and that revolution has been reflected in the revolution in the world around us.

When Wilson addressed the class in 1914, the Victorian structure of power was still intact, the world was dominated by Europe, and Europe itself was the scene of an uneasy balance of power between dominant figures. America was a spectator on a remote sideline.

The autumn after Wilson came to Annapolis, the Victorian world began to fall to pieces, and our world one half a century later is vastly different. Today we are witnesses to the most extraordinary revolution, nearly, in the history of the world, as the emergent nations of Latin America, Africa, and Asia awaken from long centuries of torpor and impatience.

Today the Victorian certitudes which were taken to be so much a part of man's natural existence are under siege by a faith committed to the destruction of liberal civilization, and today the United States is no longer the spectator, but the leader.

This half century, therefore, has not only revolutionized the size of our military establishment, it has also brought about a more striking revolution in the things that the nation expects from the men in our service.

Fifty years ago the graduates of the Naval Academy were expected to be seamen and leaders of men. They were reminded of the saying of John Paul Jones, "Give me a fair ship so that I might go into harm's way."

When Captain Mahan began to write in the nineties on the general issues of war and peace and naval strategy, the Navy quickly shipped him to sea duty. Today we expect all of you . . . to be prepared not only to handle a ship in a storm or a landing party on a beach, but to make great determinations which affect the survival of this country.

The revolution in the technology of war makes it necessary—in order that you, when you hold positions of command, may make an educated judgment between various techniques—that you also be a scientist and an engineer and a physicist, and your responsibilities go far beyond the classic problems of tactics and strategy.

You must know something about strategy and tactics and logistics, but also economics and politics and diplomacy and history. You must know everything you can know about military power, and you must also understand the limits of military power.

In the years to come, some of you will serve, as your Commandant did last year, as an adviser to foreign governments; some will negotiate, as Admiral Burke did in Korea, with other governments on behalf of the United States; some will go to the far reaches of space and some will go to the bottom of the ocean. Many of you, from one time or another, in positions of command or as members of staff, will participate in great decisions which go far beyond the narrow reaches of professional competence.

You gentlemen, therefore, have a most important responsibility, to recognize that your education is just beginning, and to be prepared, in the most difficult period in the life of our country, to play the role that the country hopes and needs and expects from you. You must understand not only this country but other countries. You must know something about strategy and tactics and logistics, but also economics and politics and diplomacy and history. You must know everything you can know about military power, and you must also understand the limits of military power.

You must understand that few of the important problems of our time have, in the final analysis, been finally solved by military power alone. . . . You must be more than the servants of national policy. You must be prepared to play a constructive role in the development of national policy, a policy which protects our interests and our security and the peace of the world.

Woodrow Wilson reminded your predecessors that you were not serving a government or an administration, but a people. In serving the American people, you represent the American people and the best of the ideals of this free society. Your posture and your performance will provide many people far beyond our shores, who know very little of our country, the only evidence they will ever see as to whether America is truly dedicated to the cause of justice and freedom.

In my Inaugural Address, I said that each citizen should be concerned not with what his country can do for him, but what he can do for his country. What you have chosen to do for your country, by devoting your life to the service of our country, is the greatest contribution that any man could make. It is easy for you, in a moment of exhilaration today, to say that you freely and gladly dedicate your life to the United States. But the life of service is a constant test of your will.

It will be hard at times to face the personal sacrifice and family inconvenience, to maintain this high resolve, to place the needs of your country above all else. When there is a visible enemy to fight, the tide of patriotism in this country runs strong. But when there is a long, slow struggle, with no immediate visible foe, when you watch your contemporaries indulging the urge for material gain and comfort and personal advancement, your choice will seem hard, and you will recall, I am sure, the lines found in an old sentry box at Gibraltar, "God and the soldier all men adore in time of trouble and no more, for when war is over, and all things righted, God is neglected and the old soldier slighted."

Never forget, however, that the battle for freedom takes many forms. . . . The answer to those who challenge us so severely in so many parts of the globe lies in our willingness to freely commit ourselves to the maintenance of our country and the things for which it stands.

This ceremony today represents the kind of commitment which you are willing to make. For that reason, I am proud to be here. This nation salutes you . . . and I congratulate you and thank you.

U.S. Naval Academy Commencement
Annapolis, Maryland, June 7, 1961

The Inequities of Service

Q: Mr. President, at some of our military camps there have been demonstrations by mobilized reservists, including in one case an attempted hunger strike. I wonder if you couldn't comment on these demonstrations, and couldn't you give the reservists some notion of when they might be released?

THE PRESIDENT: Well, I understand the feeling of any reservist, particularly those who may have fulfilled their duty and then they are called back. And they see others going along in normal life, and therefore they feel: how long are we going to be kept?

We will release them on the first possible date consistent with our national security. They were called up because of the crisis in Berlin, and because of the threats in Southeast Asia. And I do not think that anyone can possibly read the papers and come to the conclusion that these threats do not continue. There is no evidence that we are going to quickly reach a settlement in either one of these areas.

Life is unfair.

These reservists are doing a very important job. In my judgment, the fact they were called up and the fact they responded has strengthened the foreign policy of the United States measurably since last July and August.

Now, secondly, there is always inequity in life. Some men are killed in a war and some men are wounded, and some men never leave the country, and some men are stationed in the Antarctic and some are stationed in San Francisco. It's very hard in military or in personal life to assure complete equality. Life is unfair. . . . Some people are sick and others are well—but I do hope that these people recognize that they are fulfilling a valuable function, and that, however humdrum it is, and however much their life is disturbed and years yanked out of it, they will have the satisfaction afterwards of feeling that they contributed importantly to the security of their families and their country at a significant time.

President's News Conference
Washington, D.C., March 21, 1962

The Best Defense in the World

. . . What can we do to move from the present pause toward enduring peace? Again I would counsel caution. I foresee no spectacular reversal in Communist methods or goals. But if all these trends and developments can persuade the Soviet Union to walk the path of peace, then let her know that all free nations will journey with her. But until that choice is made, and until the world can develop a reliable system of international security, the free peoples have no choice but to keep their arms nearby.

This country, therefore, continues to require the best defense in the world—a defense which is suited to the sixties. This means, unfortunately, a rising defense budget—for there is no substitute for adequate defense, and no "bargain basement" way of achieving it. It means the expenditure of more than $15 billion this year on nuclear weapons systems alone, a sum which is about equal to the combined defense budgets of our European Allies.

But it also means improved air and missile defenses, improved civil defense, a strengthened antiguerrilla capacity and, of prime importance, more powerful and flexible non-nuclear forces. For threats of massive retaliation may not deter piecemeal aggression—and a line of destroyers in a quarantine, or a division of well-equipped men on a border, may be more useful to our real security than the multiplication of awesome weapons beyond all rational need.

State of the Union Address
The Capitol, Washington, D.C.
January 14, 1963

CHAPTER 13

The U.S.–Soviet Competition

This longest chapter in this book reflects the most important chapter in the Kennedy Presidency. That chapter began badly with an ill-conceived call to arms at Cuba's Bay of Pigs. It ended grandly with a heartfelt call for peace at the United Nations and a breakthrough sale of American wheat for Soviet consumers. In between, the world's first potential nuclear confrontation over Soviet missiles in Cuba required a steel nerve, a cool hand, and a President willing to balance deterrence with dialogue. By resolving the Cuban missile crisis with Khrushchev without firing a shot, Kennedy enormously increased his worldwide stature and confidence. As the Cold War began to recede and nuclear war no longer seemed ultimately inevitable, the first concrete measures were taken to halt not only the endless arms race but endless U.S.–U.S.S.R. belligerence.

The Real Revolution

I believe, Mr. Chairman, that you should recognize that free people in all parts of the world do not accept the claims of historical inevitability for the Communist revolution. What your government believes is its own business; what it does in the world is the world's business. The great revolution in the history of man, past, present, and future, is the revolution of those determined to be free.

Public Message to Soviet Chairman Khrushchev
after the Bay of Pigs
Washington, D.C., April 18, 1961

The Summit Encounter

I went to Vienna to meet the leader of the Soviet Union, Mr. Khrushchev. For two days we met in sober, intensive conversation, and I believe it is my obligation to the people, to the Congress, and to our allies to report on those conversations candidly and publicly.

Mr. Khrushchev and I had a very full and frank exchange of views on the major issues that now divide our two countries. I will tell you now that it was a very sober two days. There was no discourtesy, no loss of temper, no threats or ultimatums by either side; no advantage or concession was either gained or given; no major decision was either planned or taken; no spectacular progress was either achieved or pretended.

This kind of informal exchange may not be as exciting as a full-fledged summit meeting with a fixed agenda and a large corps of advisers, where negotiations are attempted and new agreements sought, but this was not intended to be and was not such a meeting, nor did we plan any future summit meetings at Vienna.

But I found this meeting with Chairman Khrushchev, as somber as it was, to be immensely useful. I had read his speeches and of his policies. I had been advised on his views. I had been told by other leaders of the West, General de Gaulle, Chancellor Adenauer, Prime Minister Macmillan, what manner of man he was.

But I bear the responsibility of the Presidency of the United States, and it is my duty to make decisions that no adviser and no ally can make for me. It is my obligation and responsibility to see that these decisions are as informed as possible, that they are based on as much direct, firsthand knowledge as possible.

I therefore thought it was of immense importance that I know Mr. Khrushchev, that I gain as much insight and understanding as I could on his present and future policies. At the same time, I wanted to make certain Mr. Khrushchev knew this country and its policies, that he understood our strength and our determination, and that he knew that we desired peace with all nations of every kind.

I wanted to present our views to him directly, precisely, realistically, and with an opportunity for discussion and clarification. This was done. No new aims were stated in private that have not been stated in public on either side. The gap between us was not, in such a short period, materially reduced, but at least the channels of communication were opened more fully, at least the chances of a dangerous misjudgment on either side should now be less, and at least the men on whose decisions the peace in part depends have agreed to remain in contact.

This is important, for neither of us tried merely to please the other, to agree merely to be agreeable, to say what the other wanted to hear. And just as our judicial system relies on witnesses appearing in court and on cross-examination, instead of hearsay testimony or affidavits on paper, so, too, was this direct give-and-take of immeasurable value in making clear and precise what we considered to be vital.

For the facts of the matter are that the Soviets and ourselves give wholly different meanings to the same words—war, peace, democracy, and popular will. We have wholly different views of right and wrong, of what is an internal affair and what is aggression. Above all, we have wholly different concepts of where the world is and where it is going.

Only by such a discussion was it possible for me to be sure that Mr. Khrushchev knew how differently we view the present and the future. Our views contrasted sharply but at least we knew better at the end where we both stood. Neither of us was there to dictate a settlement or to convert the other to a cause or to concede our basic interests. But both of us were there, I think, because we realized that each nation has the power to inflict enormous damage upon the other, that such a war could and should be avoided if at all possible, since it would settle no dispute and prove no doctrine, and that care should thus be taken to prevent our conflicting interests from so directly confronting each other that war necessarily ensued.

We believe in a system of national freedom and independence. He believes in an expanding and dynamic concept of world communism; and the question is whether these two systems can ever hope to live in peace without permitting any loss of security or any denial of the freedom of our friends. However difficult it may seem to answer this question in the affirmative as we approach so many harsh tests, I think we owe it to all mankind to make every possible effort.

That is why I considered the Vienna talks to be useful. The somber mood that they conveyed was not cause for elation or relaxation, nor was it cause for undue pessimism or fear. It simply demonstrated how much work we in the Free World have to do and how long and hard a struggle must be our fate as Americans in this generation as the chief defenders of the cause of liberty.

The one area which afforded some immediate prospect of accord was Laos. Both sides recognized the need to reduce the dangers in that situation. Both sides endorsed the concept of a neutral and independent Laos, much in the manner of Burma or Cambodia. Of critical importance to the current conference on Laos in Geneva, both sides recognized the importance of an effective cease-fire. It is urgent that this be translated into new attitudes at Geneva, enabling the International Control Commission to do its duty, to make certain that a cease-fire is enforced and maintained. I am hopeful that progress can be made on this matter in the coming days at Geneva for that would greatly improve the international atmosphere.

No such hope emerged, however, with respect to the other deadlocked Geneva conference, seeking a treaty to ban nuclear tests. Mr. Khrushchev made it clear that there could not be a neutral administrator—in his opinion—because no one was truly neutral; that a Soviet veto would have to apply to acts of enforcement; that inspection was only a subterfuge for espionage, in the absence of total disarmament; and that the present test-ban negotiations appeared futile. In short, our hopes for an end to nuclear tests, for an end to the spread of nuclear weapons, and for some slowing down of the arms race have been struck a serious blow. Nevertheless, the stakes are too important for us to abandon the draft treaty we have offered at Geneva.

The Soviets and ourselves give wholly different meanings to the same words—war, peace, democracy, and popular will. We have wholly different views of right and wrong, of what is an internal affair and what is aggression.

But our most somber talks were on the subject of Germany and Berlin. I made it clear to Mr. Khrushchev that the security of Western Europe and therefore our own security are deeply involved in our presence and our access rights to West Berlin, that those rights are based on law and not on sufferance, and that we are determined to maintain those rights at any risk, and thus meet our obligation to the people of West Berlin and their right to choose their own future.

Mr. Khrushchev, in turn, presented his views in detail, and his presentation will be the subject of further communications. But we are not seeking to change the present situation. A binding German peace treaty is a matter for all who were at war with Germany, and we and our allies cannot abandon our obligations to the people of West Berlin.

Generally, Mr. Khrushchev did not talk in terms of war. He believes the world will move his way without resort to force. He spoke of his nation's achievements in space. He stressed his intention to outdo us in industrial production, to out-trade us, to prove to the world the superiority of his system over ours. Most of all, he predicted the triumph of communism in the new and less-developed countries.

He was certain that the tide there was moving his way, that the revolution of rising peoples would eventually be a Communist revolution, and that the so-called wars of liberation, supported by the Kremlin, would replace the old methods of direct aggression and invasion.

In the 1940s and early fifties, the great danger was from Communist armies marching across free borders, which we saw in Korea. Our nuclear monopoly helped to prevent this in other areas. Now we face a new and different threat. We no longer have a nuclear monopoly. Their missiles, they believe, will hold off our missiles, and their troops can match our troops should we intervene in these so-called wars of liberation. Thus, the local conflict they support can turn in their favor through guerrillas or insurgents or subversion. A small group of disciplined Communists could exploit discontent and misery in a country where the average income may be sixty or seventy dollars a year, and seize control of an entire country without Communist troops ever crossing any international frontier. This is the Communist theory.

But I believe just as strongly that time will prove it wrong, that liberty and independence and self-determination—not communism—are the future of man, and that free men have the will and the resources to win the struggle for freedom. But it is clear that this struggle in this area of the new and poorer nations will be a continuing crisis of this decade.

Mr. Khrushchev made one point which I wish to pass on. He said there are many disorders throughout the world, and he should not be blamed for them all. He is quite right. It is easy to dismiss as Communist-inspired every anti-government or anti-American riot, every overthrow of a corrupt regime, or every mass protest against misery and despair. These are not all Communist-inspired. The Communists move in to exploit them, to infiltrate their leadership, to ride their crest to victory. But the Communists did not create the conditions which caused them.

In short, the hopes for freedom in these areas which see so much poverty and illiteracy, so many children who are sick, so many children who die in the first year, so many families without homes, so many families without hope—the future for freedom in these areas rests with the local peoples and their governments.

If they have the will to determine their own future, if their governments have the support of their own people, if their honest and progressive measures—helping their people—have inspired confidence and zeal, then no guerrilla or insurgent action can succeed. But where those conditions do not exist, a military guarantee against external attack from across a border offers little protection against internal decay.

Yet all this does not mean that our nation and the West and the Free World can only sit by. On the contrary, we have an historic opportunity to help these countries build their societies until they are so strong and broadly based that only an outside invasion could topple them, and that threat, we know, can be stopped. . . .

May I conclude by saying simply that I am glad to be home. We have on this trip admired splendid places and seen stirring sights, but we are glad to be home. No demonstration of support abroad could mean so much as the support which you, the American people, have so generously given to our country. With that support I am not fearful of the future. We must be patient. We must be determined. We must be courageous. We must accept both risks and burdens, but with the will and the work freedom will prevail.

Televised Address
Washington, D.C., June 6, 1961

The Running Tiger

Chairman Khrushchev has compared the United States to a worn-out runner living on its past performance and stated that the Soviet Union would outproduce the United States by 1970.

Without wishing to trade hyperbole with the Chairman, I do suggest that he reminds me of the tiger hunter who has picked a place on the wall to hang the tiger's skin long before he has caught the tiger. This tiger has other ideas.

I believe that we can maintain our productive development and also our system of freedom. We invite the U.S.S.R. to engage in this competition which is peaceful and which could only result in a better living standard for both of our people.

In short, the United States is not such an aged runner and, to paraphrase Mr. Coolidge, "We do choose to run."

President's News Conference
Washington, D.C., June 28, 1961

The Berlin Crisis

In consultation and full agreement with its British and French allies, and with the benefit of the views of the Federal Republic of Germany, and after consultation with the other member governments of the North Atlantic Treaty Organization, the United States on Monday delivered through its Embassy in Moscow its reply to the aide-mémoire on Germany and Berlin received from the Soviet government on June fourth. Our reply speaks for itself and advances what I believe to be an irrefutable legal, moral, and political position. In this statement I should like to convey to the American people and the people of the world the basic issues which underlie the somewhat more formal language of diplomacy.

The Soviet aide-mémoire is a document which speaks of peace but threatens to disturb it. It speaks of ending the abnormal situation in Germany but insists on making permanent its abnormal division. It refers to the four-power alliance of World War II but seeks the unilateral abrogation of the rights of the other three powers. It calls for new international agreements while preparing to violate existing ones. It offers certain assurances while making it plain that its previous assurances are not to be relied upon. It professes concern for the rights of the citizens of West Berlin while seeking to expose them to the immediate or eventual domination of a regime which permits no self-determination.

Three simple facts are clear:

1. Today there is peace in Berlin, in Germany, and in Europe. If that peace is destroyed by the unilateral actions of the Soviet Union, its leaders will bear a heavy responsibility before world opinion and history.

2. Today the people of West Berlin are free. In that sense it is already a "free city"—free to determine its own leaders and free to enjoy the fundamental human rights reaffirmed in the United Nations Charter.

3. Today the continued presence in West Berlin of the United States, the United Kingdom, and France is by clear legal right, arising from war, acknowledged in many agreements signed by the Soviet Union, and strongly supported by the overwhelming majority of the people of that city. Their freedom is dependent upon our exercise of these rights—an exercise which is thus a political and moral obligation as well as a

legal right. Inasmuch as these rights, including the right of access to Berlin, are not held from the Soviet government, they cannot be ended by any unilateral action of the Soviet Union. They cannot be affected by a so-called peace treaty, covering only a part of Germany, with a regime of the Soviet Union's own creation—a regime which is not freely representative of all or any part of Germany, and does not enjoy the confidence of the 17 million East Germans. The steady stream of German refugees from East to West is eloquent testimony to that fact.

The world knows that there is no reason for a crisis over Berlin today—and that, if one develops, it will be caused by the Soviet government's attempt to invade the rights of others.

The United States has been prepared since the close of the war, and is prepared today, to achieve, in agreement with its World War II allies, a freely negotiated peace treaty covering all of Germany and based on the freely expressed will of all of the German people. We have never suggested that, in violation of international law and earlier four-power agreements, we might legally negotiate a settlement with only a part of Germany, or without the participation of the other principal World War II allies. We know of no sound reason why the Soviet government should now believe that the rights of the Western powers, derived from Nazi Germany's surrender, could be invalidated by such an action on the part of the Soviet Union.

The United States has consistently sought the goal of a just and comprehensive peace treaty for all of Germany since first suggesting in 1946 that a special commission be appointed for this purpose. We still recognize the desirability of change—but it should be a change in the direction of greater, not less, freedom of choice for the people of Germany and Berlin. The Western peace plan and the all-Berlin solution proposed by the Western allies at Geneva in 1959 were constructive, practical offers to obtain this kind of fair settlement in Central

Europe. Our objective is not to perpetuate our presence in either Germany or Berlin—our objective is the perpetuation of the peace and freedom of their citizens.

But the Soviet Union has blocked all progress toward the conclusion of a just treaty based on the self-determination of the German people, and has instead repeatedly heightened world tensions over this issue. The Soviet blockade of Berlin in 1948, the Soviet note of November 27, 1958, and this most recent Soviet aide-mémoire of June 4, 1961, have greatly disturbed the tranquillity of this area.

The real intent of the June 4 aide-mémoire is that East Berlin, a part of a city under four-power status, would be formally absorbed into the so-called German Democratic Republic while West Berlin, even though called a "free city," would lose the protection presently provided by the Western powers and become subject to the will of a totalitarian regime. Its leader, Herr Ulbricht, has made clear his intention, once this so-called peace treaty is signed, to curb West Berlin's communications with the Free World and to suffocate the freedom it now enjoys.

The area thus newly subjected to Soviet threats of heightened tension poses no danger whatsoever to the peace of the world or to the security of any nation. The world knows that there is no reason for a crisis over Berlin today—and that, if one develops, it will be caused by the Soviet government's attempt to invade the rights of others and manufacture tensions. It is, moreover, misusing the words "freedom" and "peace." For, as our reply states, "freedom" and "peace" are not merely words—nor can they be achieved by words or promises alone. They are representative of a state of affairs.

A city does not become free merely by calling it a "free city." For a city or a people to be free requires that they be given the opportunity, without economic, political, or police pressure, to make their own choice and to live their own lives. The people of West Berlin today have that freedom. It is the objective of our policy that they shall continue to have it.

Peace does not come automatically from a "peace treaty." There is peace in Germany today even though the situation is "abnormal." A "peace treaty" that adversely affects the lives and rights of millions will not bring peace with it. A "peace treaty" that attempts to affect adversely the solemn commitments of three great powers will not bring peace with it. We again urge the Soviet government to reconsider its course, to return to the path of constructive cooperation it so frequently states it desires, and to work with its World War II allies in concluding a just and enduring settlement of issues remaining from that conflict.

Statement on Berlin Crisis
Washington, D.C., July 19, 1961

Seven weeks ago tonight I returned from Europe to report on my meeting with Premier Khrushchev and the others. His grim warnings about the future of the world, his aide-mémoire on Berlin, his subsequent speeches and threats which he and his agents have launched, and the increase in the Soviet military budget that he has announced, have all prompted a series of decisions by the administration and a series of consultations with the members of the NATO organization. In Berlin, as you recall, he intends to bring to an end, through a stroke of the pen, first our legal rights to be in West Berlin—and secondly our ability to make good on our commitment to the two million free people of that city. That we cannot permit.

We are clear about what must be done—and we intend to do it. I want to talk frankly with you tonight about the first steps that we shall take. These actions will require sacrifice on the part of many of our citizens. More will be required in the future. They will require, from all of us, courage and perseverance in the years to come. But if we and our allies act out of strength and unity of purpose—with calm determination and steady nerves—using restraint in our words as well as our weapons—I am hopeful that both peace and freedom will be sustained.

The immediate threat to free men is in West Berlin. But that isolated outpost is not an isolated problem. The threat is worldwide. Our effort must be equally wide and strong, and not be obsessed by any single manufactured crisis. We face a challenge in Berlin, but there is also a challenge in Southeast Asia, where the borders are less guarded, the enemy harder to find, and the dangers of communism less apparent to those who have so little. We face a challenge in our own hemisphere, and indeed wherever else the freedom of human beings is at stake.

Let me remind you that the fortunes of war and diplomacy left the free people of West Berlin, in 1945, 110 miles behind the Iron Curtain.

We are there as a result of our victory over Nazi Germany—and our basic rights to be there, deriving from that victory, include both our presence in West Berlin and the enjoyment of access across East Germany. These rights have been repeatedly confirmed and recognized in special agreements with the Soviet Union. Berlin is not a part of East Germany, but a separate territory under the control of the allied powers. Thus our rights there are clear and deep-rooted. But in addition to those rights is our commitment to sustain—and defend, if need be—the opportunity for more than two million people to determine their own future and choose their own way of life.

Thus, our presence in West Berlin, and our access thereto, cannot be ended by any act of the Soviet government. The NATO shield was long ago extended to cover West Berlin—and we have given our word that an attack upon that city will be regarded as an attack upon us all.

For West Berlin—lying exposed 110 miles inside East Germany, surrounded by Soviet troops and close to Soviet supply lines, has many roles. It is more than a showcase of liberty, a symbol, an island of freedom in a Communist sea. It is even more than a link with the Free World, a beacon of hope behind the Iron Curtain, an escape hatch for refugees.

West Berlin is all of that. But above all it has now become—as never before—the great testing place of Western courage and will, a focal point where our solemn commitments, stretching back over the years since 1945, and Soviet ambitions now meet in basic confrontation.

It would be a mistake for others to look upon Berlin, because of its location, as a tempting target. The United States is there; the United Kingdom and France are there; the pledge of NATO is there—and the people of Berlin are there. It is as secure, in that sense, as the rest of us—for we cannot separate its safety from our own.

I hear it said that West Berlin is militarily untenable. And so was Bastogne. And so, in fact, was Stalingrad. Any dangerous spot is tenable if men—brave men—will make it so.

We do not want to fight—but we have fought before. And others in earlier times have made the same dangerous mistake of assuming that the West was too selfish and too soft and too divided to resist invasions of freedom in other lands. Those who threaten to unleash the forces of war on a dispute over West Berlin should recall the words of the ancient philosopher: "A man who causes fear cannot be free from fear."

We cannot and will not permit the Communists to drive us out of Berlin, either gradually or by force. For the fulfillment of our pledge to that city is essential to the morale and security of Western Germany, to the unity of Western Europe, and to the faith of the entire Free World.

Soviet strategy has long been aimed, not merely at Berlin, but at dividing and neutralizing all of Europe, forcing us back on our own shores. We must meet our oft-stated pledge to the free peoples of West Berlin—and maintain our rights and their safety, even in the face of force—in order to maintain the confidence of other free peoples in our word and our resolve. The strength of the alliance on which our security depends is dependent in turn on our willingness to meet our commitments to them.

So long as the Communists insist that they are preparing to end by themselves unilaterally our rights in West Berlin and our commitments to its people, we must be prepared to defend those rights and those commitments. We will at all times be ready to talk, if talk will help. But we must also be ready to resist with force, if force is used upon us. Either alone would fail. Together, they can serve the cause of freedom and peace.

The new preparations that we shall make to defend the peace are part of the long-term buildup in our strength which has been under way since January. They are based on our needs to meet a worldwide threat, on a basis which stretches far beyond the present Berlin crisis. Our primary purpose is neither propaganda nor provocation—but preparation.

A first need is to hasten progress toward the military goals which the North Atlantic allies have set for themselves. In Europe today nothing less will suffice. We will put even greater resources into fulfilling those goals, and we look to our allies to do the same. . . .

In the days and months ahead, I shall not hesitate to ask the Congress for additional measures, or exercise any of the executive powers that I possess to meet this threat to peace. Everything essential to the security of freedom must be done; and if that should require more men, or more taxes, or more controls, or other new powers, I shall not hesitate to ask them. The measures proposed today will be constantly studied, and altered as necessary. But while we will not let panic shape our policy, neither will we permit timidity to direct our program. . . .

I am well aware of the fact that many American families will bear the burden of these requests. Studies or careers will be interrupted; husbands and sons will be called away; incomes in some cases will be reduced. But these are burdens which must be borne if freedom is to be defended—Americans have willingly borne them before—and they will not flinch from the task now.

But I must emphasize again that the choice is not merely between resistance and retreat, between atomic holocaust and surrender. Our peacetime military posture is traditionally defensive; but our diplomatic posture need not be. Our response to the Berlin crisis will not be merely military or negative. It will be more than merely standing firm. For we do not intend to leave it to others to choose and monopolize the forum and the framework of discussion. We do not intend to abandon our duty to mankind to seek a peaceful solution.

We cannot and will not permit the Communists to drive us out of Berlin, either gradually or by force.

As signers of the UN Charter, we shall always be prepared to discuss international problems with any and all nations that are willing to talk—and listen—with reason. If they have proposals—not demands—we shall hear them. If they seek genuine understanding—not concessions of our rights—we shall meet with them. We have previously indicated our readiness to remove any actual irritants in West Berlin, but the freedom of that city is not negotiable. We cannot negotiate with those who say, "What's mine is mine and what's yours is negotiable." But we are willing to consider any arrangement or treaty in Germany consistent with the maintenance of peace and freedom, and with the legitimate security interests of all nations.

We recognize the Soviet Union's historical concern about their security in Central and Eastern Europe, after a series of ravaging invasions, and we believe arrangements can be worked out which will help to meet those concerns, and make it possible for both security and freedom to exist in this troubled area.

For it is not the freedom of West Berlin which is "abnormal" in Germany today, but the situation in that entire divided country. If anyone doubts the legality of our rights in Berlin, we are ready to have it submitted to international adjudication. If anyone doubts the extent to which our presence is desired by the people of West Berlin, compared to East German feelings about their regime, we are ready to have that question submitted to a free vote in Berlin and, if possible, among all the German people. And let us hear at that time from the two and one-half million refugees who have fled the Communist regime in East Germany—voting for Western-type freedom with their feet.

The world is not deceived by the Communist attempt to label Berlin as a hotbed of war. There is peace in Berlin today. The source of world trouble and tension is Moscow, not Berlin. And if war begins, it will have begun in Moscow and not Berlin.

For the choice of peace or war is largely theirs, not ours. It is the Soviets who have stirred up this crisis. It is they who are trying to force a change. It is they who have opposed free elections. It is they who have rejected an all-German peace treaty, and the rulings of international law. And as Americans know from our history on our own old frontier, gun battles are caused by outlaws, and not by officers of the peace.

In short, while we are ready to defend our interests, we shall also be ready to search for peace—in quiet exploratory talks—in formal or informal meetings. We do not want military considerations to dominate the thinking of either East or West. And Mr. Khrushchev may find that his invitation to other nations to join in a meaningless treaty may lead to their inviting him to join in the community of peaceful men, in abandoning the use of force, and in respecting the sanctity of agreements.

While all of these efforts go on, we must not be diverted from our total responsibilities, from other dangers, from other tasks. If new threats in Berlin or elsewhere should cause us to weaken our program of assistance to the developing nations who are also under heavy pressure from the same source, or to halt our efforts for realistic disarmament, or to disrupt or slow down our economy, or to neglect the education of our children, then those threats will surely be the most successful and least costly maneuver in Communist history. For we can afford all these efforts, and more—but we cannot afford not to meet this challenge.

And the challenge is not to us alone. It is a challenge to every nation which asserts its sovereignty under a system of liberty. It is a challenge to all those who want a world of free choice. It is a special challenge to the Atlantic Community—the heartland of human freedom.

We in the West must move together in building military strength. We must consult one another more closely than ever before. We must together design our proposals for peace, and labor together as they are pressed at the conference table. And together we must share the burdens and the risks of this effort.

The Atlantic Community, as we know it, has been built in response to challenge: the challenge of European chaos in 1947, of the Berlin blockade in 1948, the challenge of Communist aggression in Korea in 1950. Now, standing strong and prosperous, after an unprecedented decade of progress, the Atlantic Community will not forget either its history or the principles which gave it meaning.

The solemn vow each of us gave to West Berlin in time of peace will not be broken in time of danger. If we do not meet our commitments to Berlin, where will we later stand? If we are not true to our word there, all that we have achieved in collective security, which relies on these words, will mean nothing. And if there is one path above all others to war, it is the path of weakness and disunity.

Today, the endangered frontier of freedom runs through divided Berlin. We want it to remain a frontier of peace. This is the hope of every citizen of the Atlantic Community; every citizen of Eastern Europe; and, I am confident, every citizen of the Soviet Union. For I cannot believe that the Russian people—who bravely suffered enormous losses in the Second World War—would now wish to see the peace upset once more in Germany. The Soviet government alone can convert Berlin's frontier of peace into a pretext for war.

The steps I have indicated tonight are aimed at avoiding that war. To sum it all up: we seek peace—but we shall not surrender. That is the central meaning of this crisis, and the meaning of your government's policy.

With your help, and the help of other free men, this crisis can be surmounted. Freedom can prevail—and peace can endure.

I would like to close with a personal word. When I ran for the Presidency of the United States, I knew that this country faced serious challenges, but I could not realize—nor could any man realize who does not bear the burdens of this office—how heavy and constant would be those burdens.

Three times in my lifetime our country and Europe have been involved in major wars. In each case serious misjudgments were made on both sides of the intentions of others, which brought about great devastation.

Now, in the thermonuclear age, any misjudgment on either side about the intentions of the other could rain more devastation in several hours than has been wrought in all the wars of human history.

Therefore I, as President and Commander-in-Chief, and all of us as Americans, are moving through serious days. I shall bear this responsibility under our Constitution for the next three and one-half years, but I am sure that we all, regardless of our occupations, will do our very best for our country, and for our cause. For all of us want to see our children grow up in a country at peace, and in a world where freedom endures. . . .

In meeting my responsibilities in these coming months as President, I need your goodwill, and your support—and above all, your prayers.

Televised Address on the Berlin Crisis
Washington, D.C., July 25, 1961

The Berlin Wall

. . . Sealing off the eastern sector of the city is . . . a direct violation of the Soviet government's commitment to "the economic and political unity of Germany" and the pledged word of the Soviet government to cooperate with the allied governments "to mitigate the effects of the administrative division of Germany and Berlin" by "facilitation of the movement of persons and goods and the exchange of information" throughout Germany, including Berlin. . . .

The United States must serve a solemn warning to the Soviet Union that any interference by the Soviet government or its East German regime with free [allied] access to West Berlin would be an aggressive act for the consequences of which the Soviet government would bear full responsibility.

Statement on Berlin Wall
Washington, D.C., August 24, 1961

NOTE: Several months later the President related to the press his deeper concerns at the time of the construction of the wall.

Q: Mr. President, criticism that we did not tear down the Berlin Wall seems to be increasing rather than declining. Just about a week ago the chairman of the Republican National Committee criticized your administration very strenuously. I don't recall that

The Continuing Dialogue

MR. ADZHUBEI: Mr. President, I am happy to get this interview from you, and I would like to tell you quite frankly that your election to the high post of President of the United States was met with great hope by public opinion in our country. In connection with this, I would like to ask you the following question—

THE PRESIDENT: May I just say that I appreciate very much your coming to the United States. I also appreciate the opportunity to talk, through you and through your newspaper, to the people of the Soviet Union. I think that communication, an exchange of views, an honest report of what our countries are like and what they want and what the people wish, is in the interests of both our countries and in the interests of peace. So we are delighted to have this opportunity.

MR. ADZHUBEI: . . . Mr. President, what do you think about the present state of Soviet–American relations, and what in your opinion must be done by the American as well as the Soviet government to improve the relations between our two countries?

THE PRESIDENT: Well, I would say that the relations today are not as satisfactory as I had hoped they would be when I first took office. In fact, one of the first things that I did on becoming President was to commit the United States to an earnest effort to achieve a satisfactory agree-

---

you've ever publicly discussed this particular phase of the question. Do you think it would be helpful for you to do so now?

THE PRESIDENT: Well, I have discussed it. I stated that no one at that time in any position of responsibility—and I would use that term—either in the West Berlin–American contingent, in West Germany, France, or Great Britain, suggested that the United States or the other countries go in and tear down the wall.

The Soviet Union has had a *de facto* control for many years, really stretching back to the late forties, in East Berlin. It had been turned over as a capital for East Germany a long time ago. And the United States has a very limited force surrounded by a great many divisions. We are going to find ourselves severely challenged to maintain what we have considered to be our basic rights—which is our presence in West Berlin, and the right of access to West Berlin, and the freedom of the people of West Berlin.

But in my judgment, I think that [such an action] could have had a very violent reaction, which might have taken us down a very rocky road. I think it was for that reason—because it was recognized by those people in positions of responsibility—that no recommendation was made along the lines you've suggested at that time.

President's News Conference
Washington, D.C., January 15, 1962

ment with the Soviet Union on the cessation of nuclear tests. As a result of that effort, at the end of March, we sent our representatives, along with Great Britain's, to Geneva for the first time with a complete treaty which we tabled for discussion. I had hoped that this would be one area where we could make real progress. It would lessen the contamination of the air, it would be a first step toward disarmament, and I felt that if we could achieve an agreement in this area, we could then move on to the other areas of disarmament which required action.

We were not successful. And, as you know, we were in fact still at the table in Geneva in August when, still negotiating, the Soviet Union resumed its tests which must have been in preparation for many months, at the very time that the conversations were going on. So that has been a disappointment.

In addition, Berlin and Germany have become, I think, areas of heightened crisis since the Vienna meeting, and I think extremely dangerous to the peace which I am sure—I know—both of our people want. . . . If we can keep the peace for twenty years, the life of the people of the Soviet Union and the life of the people of the United States will be far richer and will be far happier as the standard of living steadily rises. . . .

We want the people of the Soviet Union to live in peace—we want the same for our own people. It is this effort to push outward the Communist system, on to country after country, that represents, I think, the great threat to peace. If the Soviet Union looked only to its national interest and to providing a better life for its people under conditions of peace, I think there would be nothing that would disturb the relations between the Soviet Union and the United States.

MR. ADZHUBEI: . . . Mr. President, what is your attitude toward the idea of concluding a pact of peace between the United States and the Soviet Union? That would be a great step forward.

THE PRESIDENT: I think we should have not only an agreement between our countries, but take those steps which make peace possible. I don't think that paper, and words on paper, are as significant as looking at those areas which provide tension between our two systems and seeing if we can dispel that tension. . . .

I stated that if we had been able to get an agreement on the nuclear tests cessation, that would lead to other agreements on disarmament. . . . If we can conclude our efforts in Laos and insure a government and a country which are neutral and independent, as Chairman Khrushchev and I agreed at Vienna, then we would be able to move into other areas of tension. If we can now make an agreement on a satisfactory basis on Berlin and Germany, which is the most critical area—because it represents a matter of great interest to both our countries, and great concern to our peoples—then we could take other steps. . . .

I know that the Soviet Union suffered more from World War II than any country. It represented a terrible blow, and the casualties affected every family, including many of the families of those now in government.

I will say that the United States also suffered, though not so heavily as the Soviet Union, quite obviously. My brother was killed in Europe. My sister's husband was killed in Europe.

The point is that that war is now over. We want to prevent another war arising out of Germany. I think the important thing between the United States and the U.S.S.R. is not to create the kind of tension and pressure which in the name of settling World War II increase the chances of a conflict. . . .

I do not say that the Soviet Union is responsible for all the changes that are coming in the world. . . . People want to live in different ways. That is what we want, also. If they have a fair opportunity to make a choice, if they choose to support communism, we accept that. What we object to is the attempt to impose communism by force, or a situation where once a people may have fallen under communism the Communists do not give them a fair opportunity to make another choice. . . .

We believe that if the Soviet Union—without attempting to impose the Communist system—will permit the people of the world to live as they wish to live, relations between the Soviet Union and the United States will then be very satisfactory, and our two peoples, which now live in danger, will be able to live in peace and with a greatly increased standard of living. And I believe we have such vast economic opportunities now in both of our countries that we should consider how we can get along, and not attempt to impose our views, one on the other or on anyone else. . . .

MR. ADZHUBEI: Mr. President, since I'm talking to you in a very frank and friendly manner, I would like to ask you to imagine, at least for a moment, the following impossible thing. Imagine that you were an officer, a veteran of the Soviet Navy, who fought in World War II. You won the war, and then the very events occurred which are now taking place. One of the parts of Germany—the Federal Republic of Germany—does not recognize the borders which have been established after the war. It is again building up its armed forces. The Chancellor of that country goes to the United States to talk to the President of the United States and they have secret talks. The spirit of revanchism is very high in that part of Germany. What would your attitude be toward this, if you were a veteran of the Soviet Navy?

THE PRESIDENT: If I were a Soviet veteran, I would see that West Germany now has only nine divisions, which is a fraction of the Soviet forces. Nine divisions. It has no nuclear weapons of its own. It has a very small air force—almost no navy, I think perhaps two or three submarines. So it is not a military threat. Its nine divisions are under the international control of NATO, and subject to the command of the NATO organization, which is made up of fifteen countries of Europe which altogether have, in West Germany now, about twenty-two or twenty-three divisions—about the same number as the Soviet divisions in East Germany. So that I do not see that this country represents a military threat now to the Soviet Union, even though I recognize how bitter was the struggle in World War II—in the same way that Japan today represents no threat to the United States, even though twenty years ago there were four years of war in the Pacific against the Japanese. The power of countries changes—weapons change—science changes—without missiles, without nuclear capability, with very few divisions today, I don't believe West Germany is a military threat.

Then I would look at the power of the United States, and I would look at the power of the Soviet Union, and I would say that the important thing is for the Soviet Union and the United States not to get into a war, which would destroy both of our systems. So as a Soviet veteran, I would want the Soviet Union to reach an agreement with the United States which recognizes the interests and the commitments of the United States, as well as our own, and not attempt to enforce single-handedly a new situation upon the United States which would be against previous commitments we had made. The Soviet Union made a commitment in regard to Berlin in 1945. Germany today is divided. Germany today is not a threat to the Soviet Union militarily.

The important thing is to attempt to reach an accord which recognizes the interests of all; and I believe that can be done with respect to Germany. I recognize that there are going to be two Germanys as long as the Soviet Union believes that that is in her interest. The problem now is to make sure that, in any treaty which the Soviet Union reaches with East Germany, the rights of the other powers are recognized in Berlin. That's all we're talking about. We are not talking about encouraging revanchism, building a great German military machine, or anything else you mention. In any peace treaty which is signed with East Germany, there must be a recognition of the rights of the United States and the other powers. . . .

So, if I were a Soviet officer and wanted peace, I would think peace can be won and my country's security can be assured. The Soviet Union is a strong military power. It has great nuclear capacity. It has missiles, planes—it has a great number of divisions—it has countries associated with it. No one is ever going to invade the Soviet Union again. There is no military power that can do that. The problem is to make an agreement which will permit us to have our interests recognized, as well as yours. That should not be beyond the capacity of us both.

Chairman Khrushchev did not, nor did I, make the arrangements in 1945 in regard to Berlin. Our responsibility, given the situation, which is a difficult one, is to bring about peace, and I believe it can be done.

In short, if I were a Soviet naval officer, I would feel that the security of the Soviet Union was well protected, and that the important thing now is to reach an accord with the United States, our ally during that second war.

Interview with Aleksei Adzhubei, Editor of **Izvestia**
and son-in-law of Soviet Chairman Nikita Khrushchev
Hyannis Port, Massachusetts, November 25, 1961

The Wave of the Future

I sometimes think that we are too much impressed by the clamor of daily events. The newspaper headlines and the television screens give us a short view. They so flood us with the stop-press details of daily stories that we lose sight of the great movements of history. Yet it is the profound tendencies of history and not the passing excitements that will shape our future.

The short view gives us the impression as a nation of being shoved and harried, everywhere on the defensive. But this impression is surely an optical illusion. From the perspective of Moscow, the world today may seem even more troublesome, more intractable, more frustrating than it does to us. The leaders of the Communist world are confronted not only by acute internal problems in each Communist country—the failure of agriculture, the rising discontent of the youth and the intellectuals, the demands of technical and managerial groups for status and security. They are confronted in addition by profound divisions within the Communist world itself—divisions which have already shattered the image of communism as a universal system guaranteed to abolish all social and international conflicts—the most valuable asset the Communists had for many years.

Wisdom requires the long view. And the long view shows us that the revolution of national independence is a fundamental fact of our era. This revolution will not be stopped. As new nations emerge from the oblivion of centuries, their first aspiration is to affirm their national identity. Their deepest hope is for a world where, within a framework of international cooperation, every country can solve its own problems according to its own traditions and ideals.

It is in the interests of the pursuit of knowledge—and it is in our own national interest—that this revolution of national independence succeed. For the Communists rest everything on the idea of a monolithic world—a world where all knowledge has a single pattern, all societies move toward a single model, and all problems and roads have a single solution and a single destination. The pursuit of knowledge, on the other hand, rests everything on the opposite idea—on the idea of a world based on diversity, self-determination, freedom. And that is the kind of world to which we Americans, as a nation, are committed by the principles upon which the great Republic was founded.

As men conduct the pursuit of knowledge, they create a world which freely unites national diversity and international partnership. This emerging world is incompatible with the Communist world order. It will irresistibly burst the bonds of the Communist organization and the Communist ideology. And diversity and independence, far from being opposed to the American conception of world order, represent the very essence of our view of the future of the world.

Wisdom requires the long view. And the long view shows us that the revolution of national independence is a fundamental fact of our era. . . . The deepest hope [of new nations] is for a world where, within a framework of international cooperation, every country can solve its own problems according to its own traditions and ideals.

There used to be so much talk a few years ago about the inevitable triumph of communism. We hear such talk much less now. No one who examines the modern world can doubt that the great currents of history are carrying the world away from the monolithic idea toward the pluralistic idea—away from communism and toward national independence and freedom. No one can doubt that the wave of the future is not the conquest of the world by a single dogmatic creed but the liberation of the diverse energies of free nations and free men. No one can doubt that cooperation in the pursuit of knowledge must lead to freedom of the mind and freedom of the soul.

Beyond the drumfire of daily crisis, therefore, there is arising the outline of a robust and vital world community, founded on nations secure in their own independence, and united by allegiance to world peace. It would be foolish to say that this world will be won tomorrow, or the day after. The processes of history are fitful and uncertain and aggravating. There will be frustrations and setbacks. There will be times of anxiety and gloom. The specter of thermonuclear war will continue to hang over mankind; and we must heed the advice of Oliver Wendell Holmes of "freedom leaning on her spear" until all nations are wise enough to disarm safely and effectively.

Yet we can have a new confidence today in the direction in which history is moving. . . . We must reject oversimplified theories of international life—the theory that American power is unlimited, or that the American mission is to remake the world in the American image. We must seize the vision of a free and diverse world—and shape our policies to speed progress toward a more flexible world order.

This is the unifying spirit of our policies in the world today. The purpose of our aid programs must be to help developing countries move forward as rapidly as possible on the road to genuine national independence. Our military policies must assist nations to protect the processes of democratic reform and development against disruption and intervention. Our diplomatic policies must strengthen our relations with the whole world, with our several alliances, and within the United Nations. . . .

I am reminded of the story of the great French marshal Lyautey, who once asked his gardener to plant a tree. The gardener objected that the tree was slow-growing and would not reach maturity for a hundred years. The marshal replied, "In that case, there is no time to lose, plant it this afternoon."

Today a world of knowledge—a world of cooperation—a just and lasting peace—may be years away. But we have no time to lose. Let us plant our trees this afternoon.

University of California
Berkeley, California, March 23, 1962

The Cuban Missile Crisis

This government, as promised, has maintained the closest surveillance of the Soviet military buildup on the island of Cuba. Within the past week, unmistakable evidence has established the fact that a series of offensive missile sites is now in preparation on that imprisoned island. The purpose of these bases can be none other than to provide a nuclear strike capability against the Western Hemisphere.

Upon receiving the first preliminary hard information of this nature last Tuesday morning at 9 a.m., I directed that our surveillance be stepped up. And having now confirmed and completed our evaluation of the evidence and our decision on a course of action, this government feels obliged to report this new crisis to you in fullest detail.

The characteristics of these new missile sites indicate two distinct types of installations. Several of them include medium-range ballistic missiles, capable of carrying a nuclear warhead for a distance of more than a thousand nautical miles. Each of these missiles, in short, is capable of striking Washington, D.C., the Panama Canal, Cape Canaveral, Mexico City, or any other city in the southeastern part of the United States, in Central America, or in the Caribbean area.

Additional sites not yet completed appear to be designed for intermediate-range ballistic missiles—capable of traveling more than twice as far—and thus capable of striking most of the major cities in the Western Hemisphere, ranging as far north as Hudson Bay, Canada, and as far south as Lima, Peru. In addition, jet bombers, capable of carrying nuclear weapons, are now being uncrated and assembled in Cuba, while the necessary air bases are being prepared.

This urgent transformation of Cuba into an important strategic base—by the presence of these large, long-range, and clearly offensive weapons of sudden mass destruction—constitutes an explicit threat to the peace and security of all the Americas, in flagrant and deliberate defiance of the Rio Pact of 1947, the traditions of this nation and hemisphere, the joint resolution of the 87th Congress, the Charter of the United Nations, and my own public warnings to the Soviets on September 4 and 13. This action also contradicts the repeated assurances of Soviet spokesmen, both publicly and privately delivered, that the arms buildup in Cuba would retain its original defensive character, and that the Soviet Union had no need or desire to station strategic missiles on the territory of any other nation.

The size of this undertaking makes clear that it has been planned for some months. Yet only last month, after I had made clear the distinction between any introduction of ground-to-ground missiles and the existence of defensive antiaircraft missiles, the Soviet government publicly stated on September 11 that, and I quote, "the armaments and military equipment sent to Cuba are designed exclusively for defensive purposes," that, and I quote the Soviet government, "there is no need for the Soviet government to shift its weapons for a retaliatory blow to any other country, for instance Cuba," and that, and I quote their government, "the Soviet Union has so powerful rockets to carry these nuclear warheads that there is no need to search for sites for them beyond the boundaries of the Soviet Union." That statement was false.

This urgent transformation of Cuba into an important strategic base—by the presence of these large, long-range, and clearly offensive weapons of sudden mass destruction—constitutes an explicit threat to the peace and security of all the Americas.

Only last Thursday, as evidence of this rapid offensive buildup was already in my hand, Soviet Foreign Minister Gromyko told me in my office that he was instructed to make it clear once again, as he said his government had already done, that Soviet assistance to Cuba, and I quote, "pursued solely the purpose of contributing to the defense capabilities of Cuba," that, and I quote him, "training by Soviet specialists of Cuban nationals in handling defensive armaments was by no means offensive, and if it were otherwise," Mr. Gromyko went on, "the Soviet government would never become involved in rendering such assistance." That statement also was false.

Neither the United States of America nor the world community of nations can tolerate deliberate deception and offensive threats on the part of any nation, large or small. We no longer live in a world where only the actual firing of weapons represents a sufficient challenge to a nation's security to constitute maximum peril. Nuclear weapons are so destructive, and ballistic missiles are so swift, that any substantially increased possibility of their use or any sudden change in their deployment may well be regarded as a definite threat to peace.

For many years, both the Soviet Union and the United States, recognizing this fact, have deployed strategic nuclear weapons with great care, never upsetting the precarious status quo which insured that these weapons would not be used in the absence of some vital challenge. Our own strategic missiles have never been transferred to the territory of any other nation under a cloak of secrecy and deception; and our history —unlike that of the Soviets since the end of World War II—demonstrates that we have no desire to dominate or conquer any other nation or impose our system upon its people. Nevertheless, American citizens have become adjusted to living daily on the bull's-eye of Soviet missiles located inside the U.S.S.R. or in submarines.

In that sense, missiles in Cuba add to an already clear and present danger—although it should be noted the nations of Latin America have never previously been subjected to a potential nuclear threat.

But this secret, swift, and extraordinary buildup of Communist missiles—in an area well known to have a special and historical relationship to the United States and the nations of the Western Hemisphere, in violation of Soviet assurances, and in defiance of American and hemispheric policy—this sudden, clandestine decision to station strategic weapons for the first time outside of Soviet soil—is a deliberately provocative and unjustified change in the status quo which cannot be accepted by this country, if our courage and our commitments are ever to be trusted again by either friend or foe.

The 1930s taught us a clear lesson: aggressive conduct, if allowed to go unchecked and unchallenged, ultimately leads to war. This nation is opposed to war. We are also true to our word. Our unswerving objective, therefore, must be to prevent the use of these missiles against this or any other country, and to secure their withdrawal or elimination from the Western Hemisphere.

Our policy has been one of patience and restraint, as befits a peaceful and powerful nation which leads a worldwide alliance. We have been determined not to be diverted from our central concerns by mere irritants and fanatics. But now further action is required—and it is under way; and these actions may only be the beginning. We will not prematurely or unnecessarily risk the costs of worldwide nuclear war in which even the fruits of victory would be ashes in our mouth—but neither will we shrink from that risk at any time it must be faced.

Acting, therefore, in the defense of our own security and of the entire Western Hemisphere, and under the authority entrusted to me by the Constitution as endorsed by the resolution of the Congress, I have directed that the following initial steps be taken immediately:

First: To halt this offensive buildup, a strict quarantine on all offensive military equipment under shipment to Cuba is being initiated. All ships of any kind bound for Cuba from whatever nation or port will, if found to contain cargoes of offensive weapons, be turned back. This quarantine will be extended, if needed, to other types of cargo and carriers. We are not at this time, however, denying the necessities of life as the Soviets attempted to do in their Berlin blockade of 1948.

Second: I have directed the continued and increased close surveillance of Cuba and its military buildup. The foreign ministers of the OAS, in their communiqué of October 6, rejected secrecy on such matters in this hemisphere. Should these offensive military preparations continue, thus increasing the threat to the hemisphere, further action will be justified. I have directed the Armed Forces to prepare for any eventualities; and I trust that in the interest of both the Cuban people and the Soviet technicians at the sites, the hazards to all concerned of continuing this threat will be recognized.

Third: It shall be the policy of this nation to regard any nuclear missile launched from Cuba against any nation in the Western Hemisphere as an attack by the Soviet Union on the United States, requiring a full retaliatory response upon the Soviet Union.

Fourth: As a necessary military precaution, I have reinforced our base at Guantánamo, evacuated today the dependents of our personnel there, and ordered additional military units to be on a standby alert basis.

Fifth: We are calling tonight for an immediate meeting of the Organ of Consultation under the Organization of American States, to consider this threat to hemispheric security and to invoke articles six and eight of the Rio Treaty in support of all necessary action. The United Nations Charter allows for regional security arrangements—and the nations of this hemisphere decided long ago against the military presence of outside powers. Our other allies around the world have also been alerted.

Sixth: Under the Charter of the United Nations, we are asking tonight that an emergency meeting of the Security Council be convoked without delay to take action against this latest Soviet threat to world peace. Our resolution will call for the prompt dismantling and withdrawal of all offensive weapons in Cuba, under the supervision of UN observers, before the quarantine can be lifted.

Seventh and finally: I call upon Chairman Khrushchev to halt and eliminate this clandestine, reckless, and provocative threat to world peace and to stable relations between our two nations. I call upon him further to abandon this course of world domination, and to join in an historic effort to end the perilous arms race and to transform the history of man. He has an opportunity now to move the world back from the abyss of destruction—by returning to his government's own words that it had no need to station missiles outside its own territory, and withdrawing these weapons from Cuba—by refraining from any action which will widen or deepen the present crisis—and then by participating in a search for peaceful and permanent solutions.

This nation is prepared to present its case against the Soviet threat to peace, and our own proposals for a peaceful world, at any time and in any forum—in the OAS, in the United Nations, or in any other meeting that could be useful—without limiting our freedom of action. We have in the past made strenuous efforts to limit the spread of nuclear weapons. We have proposed the elimination of all arms and military bases in a fair and effective disarmament treaty. We are prepared to discuss new proposals for the removal of tensions on both sides—including the possibilities of a genuinely independent Cuba, free to determine its own destiny. We have no wish to war with the Soviet Union—for we are a peaceful people who desire to live in peace with all other peoples.

I call upon Chairman Khrushchev to halt and eliminate this clandestine, reckless, and provocative threat to world peace and to stable relations between our two nations.

But it is difficult to settle or even discuss these problems in an atmosphere of intimidation. That is why this latest Soviet threat—or any other threat which is made either independently or in response to our actions this week—must and will be met with determination. Any hostile move anywhere in the world against the safety and freedom of peoples to whom we are committed—including in particular the brave people of West Berlin—will be met by whatever action is needed.

Finally, I want to say a few words to the captive people of Cuba, to whom this speech is being directly carried by special radio facilities. I speak to you as a friend, as one who knows of your deep attachment to your fatherland, as one who shares your aspirations for liberty and justice for all. And I have watched and the American people have watched with deep sorrow how your nationalist revolution was betrayed—and how your fatherland fell under foreign domination. Now your leaders are no longer Cuban leaders inspired by Cuban ideals. They are puppets and agents of an international conspiracy which has turned Cuba against your friends and neighbors in the Americas—and turned it into the first Latin American country to become a target for nuclear war—the first Latin American country to have these weapons on its soil.

These new weapons are not in your interest. They contribute nothing to your peace and well-being. They can only undermine it. But this country has no wish to cause you to suffer or to impose any system upon you. We know that your lives and land are being used as pawns by those who deny your freedom.

Many times in the past, the Cuban people have risen to throw out tyrants who destroyed their liberty. And I have no doubt that most Cubans today look forward to the time when they will be truly free—free from foreign domination, free to choose their own leaders, free to select their own system, free to own their own land, free to speak and write and worship without fear or degradation. And then shall Cuba be welcomed back to the society of free nations and to the associations of this hemisphere.

My fellow citizens: let no one doubt that this is a difficult and dangerous effort on which we have set out. No one can foresee precisely what course it will take or what costs or casualties will be incurred. Many months of sacrifice and self-discipline lie ahead—months in which both our patience and our will will be tested—months in which many threats and denunciations will keep us aware of our dangers. But the greatest danger of all would be to do nothing.

The path we have chosen for the present is full of hazards, as all paths are—but it is the one most consistent with our character and courage as a nation and our commitments around the world. The cost of freedom is always high—but Americans have always paid it. And one path we shall never choose, and that is the path of surrender or submission.

Our goal is not the victory of might, but the vindication of right—not peace at the expense of freedom, but both peace and freedom, here in this hemisphere, and, we hope, around the world. God willing, that goal will be achieved.

Televised Address on Cuban Missile Crisis
Washington, D.C., October 22, 1962

Dear Mr. Chairman,

I have read your letter of October 26th with great care and welcomed the statement of your desire to seek a prompt solution to the problem. The first thing that needs to be done, however, is for work to cease on offensive missile bases in Cuba and for all weapons systems in Cuba capable of offensive use to be rendered inoperable, under effective United Nations arrangements.

Assuming this is done promptly, I have given my representatives in New York instructions that will permit them to work out this weekend—in cooperation with the Acting Secretary-General and your representative—an arrangement for a permanent solution to the Cuban problem along the lines suggested in your letter of October 26th. As I read your letter, the key elements of your proposals—which seem generally acceptable as I understand them—are as follows:

1. You would agree to remove these weapons systems from Cuba under appropriate United Nations observation and supervision; and undertake, with suitable safeguards, to halt the further introduction of such weapons systems into Cuba.

2. We, on our part, would agree—upon the establishment of adequate arrangements through the United Nations to ensure the carrying out and continuation of these commitments—(a) to remove promptly the quarantine measures now in effect and (b) to give assurances against an invasion of Cuba. I am confident that other nations of the Western Hemisphere would be prepared to do likewise.

If you will give your representative similar instructions, there is no reason why we should not be able to complete these arrangements and announce them to the world within a couple of days. The effect of such a settlement on easing world tensions would enable us to work toward a more general arrangement regarding "other armaments," as proposed in your second letter which you made public. I would like to say again that the United States is very much interested in reducing tensions and halting the arms race; and if your letter signifies that you are prepared to discuss a détente affecting NATO and the Warsaw Pact, we are quite prepared to consider with our allies any useful proposals.

But the first ingredient, let me emphasize, is the cessation of work on missile sites in Cuba and measures to render such weapons inoperable, under effective international guarantees. The continuation of this threat, or a prolonging of this discussion concerning Cuba by linking these problems to the broader questions of European and world security, would surely lead to an intensification of the Cuban crisis and a grave risk to the peace of the world. For this reason I hope we can quickly agree along the lines outlined in this letter and in your letter of October 26th.

Letter to Soviet Chairman Nikita Khrushchev
Washington, D.C., October 27, 1962

I welcome Chairman Khrushchev's statesmanlike decision to stop building bases in Cuba, dismantling offensive weapons and returning them to the Soviet Union under United Nations verification.

I welcome Chairman Khrushchev's statesmanlike decision to stop building bases in Cuba, dismantling offensive weapons and returning them to the Soviet Union under United Nations verification. This is an important and constructive contribution to peace.

We shall be in touch with the Secretary-General of the United Nations with respect to reciprocal measures to assure peace in the Caribbean area.

It is my earnest hope that the governments of the world can, with a solution of the Cuban crisis, turn their urgent attention to the compelling necessity for ending the arms race and reducing world tensions. This applies to the military confrontation between the Warsaw Pact and NATO countries as well as to other situations in other parts of the world where tensions lead to the wasteful diversion of resources to weapons of war.

Statement on Soviet Withdrawal of Missiles from Cuba
Washington, D.C., October 28, 1962

I have today been informed by Chairman Khrushchev that all of the IL-28 bombers now in Cuba will be withdrawn in thirty days. He also agrees that these planes can be observed and counted as they leave. Inasmuch as this goes a long way toward reducing the danger which faced this hemisphere four weeks ago, I have this afternoon instructed the Secretary of Defense to lift our naval quarantine.

In view of this action, I want to take this opportunity to bring the American people up to date on the Cuban crisis and to review the progress made thus far in fulfilling the understandings between Soviet Chairman Khrushchev and myself as set forth in our letters of October 27 and 28. Chairman Khrushchev, it will be recalled, agreed to remove from Cuba all weapons systems capable of offensive use, to halt the further introduction of such weapons into Cuba, and to permit appropriate United Nations observation and supervision to insure the carrying out and continuation of these commitments. We on our part agreed that once these adequate arrangements for verification had been established we would remove our naval quarantine and give assurances against an invasion of Cuba.

The evidence to date indicates that all known offensive missile sites in Cuba have been dismantled. The missiles and their associated equipment have been loaded on Soviet ships. And our inspection at sea of these departing ships has confirmed that the number of missiles reported by the Soviet Union as having been brought into Cuba, which closely corresponded to our own information, has now been removed. In addition, the Soviet government has stated that all nuclear weapons have been withdrawn from Cuba and no offensive weapons will be reintroduced.

Nevertheless, important parts of the understanding of October 27 and 28 remain to be carried out. The Cuban government has not yet permitted the United Nations to verify whether all offensive weapons have been removed, and no lasting safeguards have yet been established against the future introduction of offensive weapons back into Cuba.

Consequently, if the Western Hemisphere is to continue to be protected against offensive weapons, this government has no choice but to pursue its own means of checking on military activities in Cuba. The importance of our continued vigilance is underlined by our identification in recent days of a number of Soviet ground combat units in Cuba, although we are informed that these and other Soviet units were associated with the protection of offensive weapons systems, and will also be withdrawn in due course.

I repeat, we would like nothing better than adequate international arrangements for the task of inspection and verification in Cuba, and we are prepared to continue our efforts to achieve such arrangements. Until that is done, difficult problems remain. As for our part, if all offensive weapons systems are removed from Cuba and kept out of the hemisphere in the future, under adequate verification and safeguards, and if Cuba is not used for the export of aggressive Communist purposes, there will be peace in the Caribbean. And as I said in September, "we shall neither initiate nor permit aggression in this hemisphere."

We will not, of course, abandon the political, economic, and other efforts of this hemisphere to halt subversion from Cuba nor our purpose and hope that the Cuban people shall someday be truly free. But these policies are very different from any intent to launch a military invasion of the island.

In short, the record of recent weeks shows real progress and we are hopeful that further progress can be made. The completion of the commitment on both sides and the achievement of a peaceful solution to the Cuban crisis might well open the door to the solution of other outstanding problems.

May I add this final thought in this week of Thanksgiving: There is much for which we can be grateful as we look back to where we stood only four weeks ago—the unity of this hemisphere, the support of our allies, and the calm determination of the American people. These qualities may be tested many more times in this decade, but we have increased reason to be confident that those qualities will continue to serve the cause of freedom with distinction in the years to come.

Opening Statement, President's News Conference
Washington, D.C., November 20, 1962

The Strategy of Peace

Professor Woodrow Wilson once said that every man sent out from a university should be a man of his nation as well as a man of his time, and I am confident that the men and women who carry the honor of graduating from this institution will continue to give from their lives, from their talents, a high measure of public service and public support.

"There are few earthly things more beautiful than a university," wrote John Masefield in his tribute to English universities—and his words are equally true today. He did not refer to spires and towers, to campus greens and ivied walls. He admired the splendid beauty of the university, he said, because it was "a place where those who hate ignorance may strive to know, where those who perceive truth may strive to make others see."

I have therefore chosen this time and this place to discuss a topic on which ignorance too often abounds and the truth is too rarely perceived—yet it is the most important topic on earth: world peace.

What kind of peace do I mean? What kind of peace do we seek? Not a Pax Americana enforced on the world by American weapons of war. Not the peace of the grave or the security of the slave. I am talking about genuine peace, the kind of peace that makes life on earth worth living, the kind that enables men and nations to grow and to hope and to build a better life for their children—not merely peace for Americans but peace for all men and women—not merely peace in our time but peace for all time.

I speak of peace because of the new face of war. Total war makes no sense in an age when great powers can maintain large and relatively invulnerable nuclear forces and refuse to surrender without resort to those forces. It makes no sense in an age when a single nuclear weapon contains almost ten times the explosive force delivered by all of the allied air forces in the Second World War. It makes no sense in an age when the deadly poisons produced by a nuclear exchange would be carried by wind and water and soil and seed to the far corners of the globe and to generations yet unborn.

Today the expenditure of billions of dollars every year on weapons acquired for the purpose of making sure we never need to use them is essential to keeping the peace. But surely the acquisition of such idle stockpiles—which can only destroy and never create—is not the only, much less the most efficient, means of assuring peace.

I speak of peace, therefore, as the necessary rational end of rational men. I realize that the pursuit of peace is not as dramatic as the pursuit of war—and frequently the words of the pursuer fall on deaf ears. But we have no more urgent task.

Some say that it is useless to speak of world peace or world law or world disarmament—and that it will be useless until the leaders of the Soviet Union adopt a more enlightened attitude. I hope they do. I believe we can help them do it. But I also believe that we must reexamine our own attitude—as individuals and as a nation—for our attitude is as essential as theirs. And every graduate of this school, every thoughtful citizen who despairs of war and wishes to bring peace, should begin by looking inward—by examining his own attitude toward the possibilities of peace, toward the Soviet Union, toward the course of the Cold War, and toward freedom and peace here at home.

First: Let us examine our attitude toward peace itself. Too many of us think it is impossible. Too many think it unreal. But that is a dangerous, defeatist belief. It leads to the conclusion that war is inevitable—that mankind is doomed—that we are gripped by forces we cannot control.

We need not accept that view. Our problems are man-made—therefore, they can be solved by man. And man can be as big as he wants. No problem of human destiny is beyond human beings. Man's reason and spirit have often solved the seemingly unsolvable—and we believe they can do it again.

I am not referring to the absolute, infinite concept of universal peace and goodwill of which some fantasies and fanatics dream. I do not deny the value of hopes and dreams but we merely invite discouragement and incredulity by making that our only and immediate goal.

Let us focus instead on a more practical, more attainable peace—based not on a sudden revolution in human nature but on a gradual evolution in human institutions—on a series of concrete actions and effective agreements which are in the interest of all concerned. There is no single, simple key to this peace—no grand or magic formula to be adopted by one or two powers. Genuine peace must be the product of many nations, the sum of many acts. It must be dynamic, not static, changing to meet the challenge of each new generation. For peace is a process—a way of solving problems.

With such a peace, there will still be quarrels and conflicting interests, as there are within families and nations. World peace, like community peace, does not require that each man love his neighbor—it requires only that they live together in mutual tolerance, submitting their disputes to a just and peaceful settlement. And history teaches us that enmities between nations, as between individuals, do not last forever. However fixed our likes and dislikes may seem, the tide of time and events will often bring surprising changes in the relations between nations and neighbors.

So let us persevere. Peace need not be impracticable, and war need not be inevitable. By defining our goal more clearly, by making it seem more manageable and less remote, we can help all peoples to see it, to draw hope from it, and to move irresistibly toward it.

Second: Let us reexamine our attitude toward the Soviet Union. It is discouraging to think that their leaders may actually believe what their propagandists write. It is discouraging to read a recent authoritative Soviet text on military strategy and find, on page after page, wholly baseless and incredible claims—such as the allegation that "American imperialist circles are preparing to unleash different types of wars . . . that there is a very real threat of a preventive war being unleashed by American imperialists against the Soviet Union [and that] the political aims of the American imperialists are to enslave economically and politically the European and other capitalist countries [and] to achieve world domination . . . by means of aggressive wars."

Truly, as it was written long ago: "The wicked flee when no man pursueth." Yet it is sad to read these Soviet statements—to realize the extent of the gulf between us. But it is also a warning—a warning to the American people not to fall into the same trap as the Soviets, not to see only a distorted and desperate view of the other side, not to see conflict as inevitable, accommodation as impossible, and communication as nothing more than an exchange of threats.

No government or social system is so evil that its people must be considered as lacking in virtue. As Americans, we find communism profoundly repugnant as a negation of personal freedom and dignity. But we can still hail the Russian people for their many achievements—in science and space, in economic and industrial growth, in culture and in acts of courage.

Today the expenditure of billions of dollars every year on weapons acquired for the purpose of making sure we never need to use them is essential to keeping the peace. But surely the acquisition of such idle stockpiles—which can only destroy and never create—is not the only, much less the most efficient, means of assuring peace.

Among the many traits the peoples of our two countries have in common, none is stronger than our mutual abhorrence of war. Almost unique among the major world powers, we have never been at war with each other. And no nation in the history of battle ever suffered more than the Soviet Union suffered in the course of the Second World War. At least twenty million lost their lives. Countless millions of homes and farms were burned or sacked. A third of the nation's territory, including nearly two thirds of its industrial base, was turned into a wasteland—a loss equivalent to the devastation of this country east of Chicago.

Today, should total war ever break out again—no matter how—our two countries would become the primary targets. It is an ironic but accurate fact that the two strongest powers are the two in the most danger of devastation. All we have built, all we have worked for, would be destroyed in the first twenty-four hours. And even in the Cold War, which brings burdens and dangers to so many countries, including this nation's closest allies—our two countries bear the heaviest burdens. For we are both devoting massive sums of money to weapons that could be better devoted to combating ignorance, poverty, and disease. We are both caught up in a vicious and dangerous cycle in which suspicion on one side breeds suspicion on the other, and new weapons beget counterweapons.

In short, both the United States and its allies, and the Soviet Union and its allies, have a mutually deep interest in a just and genuine peace and in halting the arms race. Agreements to this end are in the interests of the Soviet Union as well as ours—and even the most hostile nations can be relied upon to accept and keep those treaty obligations, and only those treaty obligations, which are in their own interest.

So, let us not be blind to our differences—but let us also direct attention to our common interests and to the means by which those differences can be resolved. And if we cannot end now our differences, at least we can help make the world safe for diversity. For, in the final analysis, our most basic common link is that we all inhabit this small planet. We all breathe the same air. We all cherish our children's future. And we are all mortal.

Third: Let us reexamine our attitude toward the Cold War, remembering that we are not engaged in a debate, seeking to pile up debating points. We are not here distributing blame or pointing the finger of judgment. We must deal with the world as it is, and not as it might have been had the history of the last eighteen years been different.

We must therefore persevere in the search for peace in the hope that constructive changes within the Communist bloc might bring within reach solutions which now seem beyond us. We must conduct our affairs in such a way that it becomes in the Communists' interest to agree on a genuine peace. Above all, while defending our own vital interests, nuclear powers must avert those confrontations which bring an adversary to a choice of either a humiliating retreat or a nuclear war. To adopt that kind of course in the nuclear age would be evidence only of the bankruptcy of our policy—or of a collective death-wish for the world.

To secure these ends, America's weapons are nonprovocative, carefully controlled, designed to deter, and capable of selective use. Our military forces are committed to peace and disciplined in self-restraint. Our diplomats are instructed to avoid unnecessary irritants and purely rhetorical hostility.

For we can seek a relaxation of tensions without relaxing our guard.

And, for our part, we do not need to use threats to prove that we are resolute. We do not need to jam foreign broadcasts out of fear our faith will be eroded. We are unwilling to impose our system on any unwilling people—but we are willing and able to engage in peaceful competition with any people on earth.

Meanwhile, we seek to strengthen the United Nations, to help solve its financial problems, to make it a more effective instrument for peace, to develop it into a genuine world security system—a system capable of resolving disputes on the basis of law, of insuring the security of the large and the small, and of creating conditions under which arms can finally be abolished.

At the same time we seek to keep peace inside the non-Communist world, where many nations, all of them our friends, are divided over issues which weaken Western unity, which invite Communist intervention or which threaten to erupt into war. Our efforts in West New Guinea, in the Congo, in the Middle East, and in the Indian subcontinent, have been persistent and patient, despite criticism from both sides. We have also tried to set an example for others—by seeking to adjust small but significant differences with our own closest neighbors in Mexico and in Canada.

Speaking of other nations, I wish to make one point clear. We are bound to many nations by alliances. Those alliances exist because our concern and theirs substantially overlap. Our commitment to defend Western Europe and West Berlin, for example, stands undiminished because of the identity of our vital interests. The United States will make no deal with the Soviet Union at the expense of other nations and other peoples, not merely because they are our partners, but also because their interests and ours converge.

Our interests converge, however, not only in defending the frontiers of freedom, but in pursuing the paths of peace. It is our hope—and the purpose of allied policies—to convince the Soviet Union that she, too, should let each nation choose its own future, so long as that choice does not interfere with the choices of others. The Communist drive to impose their political and economic system on others is the primary cause of world tension today. For there can be no doubt that, if all nations could refrain from interfering in the self-determination of others, the peace would be much more assured.

This will require a new effort to achieve world law—a new context for world discussions. It will require increased understanding between the Soviets and ourselves. And increased understanding will require increased contact and communication. One step in this direction is the proposed arrangement for a direct line between Moscow and Washington, to avoid on each side the dangerous delays, misunderstandings, and misreadings of the other's actions which might occur at a time of crisis.

We have also been talking in Geneva about other first-step measures of arms control, designed to limit the intensity of the arms race and to reduce the risks of accidental war. Our primary long-range interest in Geneva, however, is general and complete disarmament—designed to take place by stages, permitting parallel political developments to build the new institutions of peace which would take the place of arms. The pursuit of disarmament has been an effort of this government since the 1920s. It has been urgently sought by the past three administrations. And however dim the prospects may be today, we intend to continue this effort—to continue it in order that all countries, including our own, can better grasp what the problems and possibilities of disarmament are.

No government or social system is so evil that its people must be considered as lacking in virtue.

The one major area of these negotiations where the end is in sight, yet where a fresh start is badly needed, is in a treaty to outlaw nuclear tests. The conclusion of such a treaty, so near and yet so far, would check the spiraling arms race in one of its most dangerous areas. It would place the nuclear powers in a position to deal more effectively with one of the greatest hazards which man faces in 1963, the further spread of nuclear arms. It would increase our security—it would decrease the prospects of war. Surely this goal is sufficiently important to require our steady pursuit, yielding to neither the temptation to give up the whole effort nor the temptation to give up our insistence on vital and responsible safeguards.

I am taking this opportunity, therefore, to announce two important decisions in this regard.

First: Chairman Khrushchev, Prime Minister Macmillan, and I have agreed that high-level discussions will shortly begin in Moscow looking toward early agreement on a comprehensive test-ban treaty. Our hopes must be tempered with the caution of history—but with our hopes go the hopes of all mankind.

Second: To make clear our good faith and solemn convictions on the matter, I now declare that the United States does not propose to conduct nuclear tests in the atmosphere so long as other states do not do so. We will not be the first to resume. Such a declaration is no substitute for a formal binding treaty, but I hope it will help us achieve one. Nor would such a treaty be a substitute for disarmament, but I hope it will help us achieve it.

Finally, my fellow Americans, let us examine our attitude toward peace and freedom here at home. The quality and spirit of our own society must justify and support our efforts abroad. We must show it in the dedication of our own lives—and many of you who are graduating today will have a unique opportunity to do, by serving without pay in the Peace Corps abroad or in the proposed National Service Corps here at home.

But wherever we are, we must all, in our daily lives, live up to the age-old faith that peace and freedom walk together. In too many of our cities today, the peace is not secure because freedom is incomplete.

It is the responsibility of the executive branch at all levels of government—local, state, and national—to provide and protect that freedom for all of our citizens by all means within their authority. It is the responsibility of the legislative branch at all levels, wherever that authority is not now adequate, to make it adequate. And it is the responsibility of all citizens in all sections of this country to respect the rights of all others and to respect the law of the land.

All this is not unrelated to world peace. "When a man's ways please the Lord," the Scriptures tell us, "he maketh even his enemies to be at peace with him." And is not peace, in the last analysis, basically a matter of human rights—the right to live out our lives without fear of devastation—the right to breathe air as nature provided it—the right of future generations to a healthy existence?

While we proceed to safeguard our national interests, let us also safeguard human interests. And the elimination of war and arms is clearly in the interest of both. No treaty, however much it may be to the advantage of all, however tightly it may be worded, can provide absolute security against the risks of deception and evasion. But it can—if it is sufficiently effective in its enforcement and if it is sufficiently in the interests of its signers—offer far more security and far fewer risks than an unabated, uncontrolled, unpredictable arms race.

The United States, as the world knows, will never start a war. We do not want a war. We do not now expect a war. This generation of Americans has already had enough—more than enough—of war and hate and oppression. We shall be prepared if others wish it. We shall be alert to try to stop it. But we shall also do our part to build a world of peace where the weak are safe and the strong are just. We are not helpless before that task or hopeless of its success. Confident and unafraid, we labor on—not toward a strategy of annihilation but toward a strategy of peace.

American University
Washington, D.C., June 10, 1963

The Nuclear Test-Ban Treaty

I speak to you tonight in a spirit of hope. Eighteen years ago the advent of nuclear weapons changed the course of the world as well as the war. Since that time, all mankind has been struggling to escape from the darkening prospect of mass destruction on earth. In an age when both sides have come to possess enough nuclear power to destroy the human race several times over, the world of communism and the world of free choice have been caught up in a vicious circle of conflicting ideology and interest. Each increase of tension has produced an increase of arms; each increase of arms has produced an increase of tension.

In these years, the United States and the Soviet Union have frequently communicated suspicion and warnings to each other, but very rarely hope. Our representatives have met at the summit and at the brink; they have met in Washington and in Moscow; in Geneva and at the United Nations. But too often these meetings have produced only darkness, discord, or disillusion.

Yesterday a shaft of light cut into the darkness. Negotiations were concluded in Moscow on a treaty to ban all nuclear tests in the atmosphere, in outer space, and under water. For the first time, an agreement has been reached on bringing the forces of nuclear destruction under international control—a goal first sought in 1946 when Bernard Baruch presented a comprehensive control plan to the United Nations.

That plan, and many subsequent disarmament plans, large and small, have all been blocked by those opposed to international inspection. A ban on nuclear tests, however, requires on-the-spot inspection only for underground tests. This nation now possesses a variety of techniques to detect the nuclear tests of other nations which are conducted in the air or under water, for such tests produce unmistakable signs which our modern instruments can pick up.

The treaty initialed yesterday, therefore, is a limited treaty which permits continued underground testing and prohibits only those tests that we ourselves can police. It requires no control posts, no on-site inspection, no international body.

We should also understand that it has other limits as well. Any nation which signs the treaty will have an opportunity to withdraw if it finds that extraordinary events related to the subject matter of the treaty have jeopardized its supreme interests; and no nation's right of self-defense will in any way be impaired. Nor does this treaty mean an end to the threat of nuclear war. It will not reduce nuclear stockpiles; it will not halt the production of nuclear weapons; it will not restrict their use in time of war.

Nevertheless, this limited treaty will radically reduce the nuclear testing which would otherwise be conducted on both sides; it will prohibit the United States, the United Kingdom, the Soviet Union, and all others who sign it, from engaging in the atmospheric tests which have so alarmed mankind; and it offers to all the world a welcome sign of hope.

For this is not a unilateral moratorium, but a specific and solemn legal obligation. While it will not prevent this nation from testing underground, or from being ready to conduct atmospheric tests if the acts of others so require, it gives us a concrete opportunity to extend its coverage to other nations and later to other forms of nuclear tests.

This treaty is in part the product of Western patience and vigilance. We have made clear—most recently in Berlin and Cuba—our deep resolve to protect our security and our freedom against any form of aggression. We have also made clear our steadfast determination to limit the arms race. In three administrations, our soldiers and diplomats have worked together to this end, always supported by Great Britain. Prime Minister Macmillan joined with President Eisenhower in proposing a limited test ban in 1959, and again with me in 1961 and 1962.

But the achievement of this goal is not a victory for one side—it is a victory for mankind. It reflects no concessions either to or by the Soviet Union. It reflects simply our common recognition of the dangers in further testing.

This treaty is not the millennium. It will not resolve all conflicts, or cause the Communists to forgo their ambitions, or eliminate the dangers of war. It will not reduce our need for arms or allies or programs of assistance to others. But it is an important first step—a step toward peace—a step toward reason—a step away from war.

Here is what this step can mean to you and to your children and your neighbors:

First, this treaty can be a step toward reduced world tension and broader areas of agreement. The Moscow talks have reached no agreement on any other subject, nor is this treaty conditioned on any other matter. Under Secretary Harriman made it clear that any nonaggression arrangements about the division in Europe would require full consultation with our allies and full attention to their interests. He also made clear our strong preference for a more comprehensive treaty banning all tests everywhere, and our ultimate hope for general and complete disarmament. The Soviet government, however, is still unwilling to accept the inspection such goals require.

No one can predict with certainty, therefore, what further agreements, if any, can be built on the foundations of this one. They could include controls on preparations for surprise attack, or on numbers and type of armaments. There could be further limitations on the spread of nuclear weapons. The important point is that efforts to seek new agreements will go forward.

But the difficulty of predicting the next step is no reason to be reluctant about this step. Nuclear test-ban negotiations have long been a symbol of East-West disagreement. If this treaty can also be a symbol—if it can symbolize the end of one era and the beginning of another—if both sides can by this treaty gain confidence and experience in peaceful collaboration—then this short and simple treaty may well become an historic mark in man's age-old pursuit of peace.

Western policies have long been designed to persuade the Soviet Union to renounce aggression, direct or indirect, so that their people and all people may live and let live in peace. The unlimited testing of new weapons of war cannot lead toward that end—but this treaty, if it can be followed by further progress, can clearly move in that direction.

I do not say that a world without aggression or threats of war would be an easy world. It will bring new problems, new challenges from the Communists, new dangers of relaxing our vigilance or of mistaking their intent.

But those dangers pale in comparison to those of the spiraling arms race and a collision course toward war. Since the beginning of history, war has been mankind's constant companion. It has been the rule, not the exception. Even a nation as young and as peace-loving as our own has fought through eight wars. And three times in the last two years and a half I have been required to report to you as President that this nation and the Soviet Union stood on the verge of direct military confrontation—in Laos, in Berlin, and in Cuba.

A war today or tomorrow, if it led to nuclear war, would not be like any war in history. A full-scale nuclear exchange, lasting less than sixty minutes, with the weapons now in existence, could wipe out more than 300 million Americans, Europeans, and Russians, as well as untold numbers elsewhere. And the survivors, as Chairman Khrushchev warned the Communist Chinese, "the survivors would envy the dead." For they would inherit a world so devastated by explosions and poison and fire that today we cannot even conceive of its horrors. So let us try to turn the world away from war. Let us make the most of this opportunity, and every opportunity, to reduce tension, to slow down the perilous nuclear arms race, and to check the world's slide toward final annihilation.

Second, this treaty can be a step toward freeing the world from the fears and dangers of radioactive fallout. Our own atmospheric tests last year were conducted under conditions which restricted such fallout to an absolute minimum. But over the years the number and the yield of weapons tested have rapidly increased and so have the radioactive hazards from such testing. Continued unrestricted testing by the nuclear powers, joined in time by other nations which may be less adept in limiting pollution, will increasingly contaminate the air that all of us must breathe.

Even then, the number of children and grandchildren with cancer in their bones, with leukemia in their blood, or with poison in their lungs might seem statistically small to some, in comparison with natural health hazards. But this is not a natural health hazard—and it is not a statistical issue. The loss of even one human life, or the malformation of even one baby—who may be born long after we are gone—should be of concern to us all. Our children and grandchildren are not merely statistics toward which we can be indifferent.

Nor does this affect the nuclear powers alone. These tests befoul the air of all men and all nations, the committed and the uncommitted alike, without their knowledge and without their consent. That is why the continuation of atmospheric testing causes so many countries to regard all nuclear powers as equally evil; and we can hope that its prevention will enable those countries to see the world more clearly, while enabling all the world to breathe more easily.

Yesterday a shaft of light cut into the darkness. Negotiations were concluded in Moscow on a treaty to ban all nuclear tests in the atmosphere, in outer space, and under water.

Third, this treaty can be a step toward preventing the spread of nuclear weapons to nations not now possessing them. During the next several years, in addition to the four current nuclear powers, a small but significant number of nations will have the intellectual, physical, and financial resources to produce both nuclear weapons and the means of delivering them. In time, it is estimated, many other nations will have either this capacity or other ways of obtaining nuclear warheads, even as missiles can be commercially purchased today.

I ask you to stop and think for a moment what it would mean to have nuclear weapons in so many hands, in the hands of countries large and small, stable and unstable, responsible and irresponsible, scattered throughout the world. There would be no rest for anyone then, no stability, no real security, and no chance of effective disarmament. There would only be the increased chance of accidental war, and an increased necessity for the great powers to involve themselves in what otherwise would be local conflicts.

If only one thermonuclear bomb were to be dropped on any American, Russian, or any other city, whether it was launched by accident or design, by a madman or by an enemy, by a large nation or by a small, from any corner of the world, that one bomb could release more destructive power on the inhabitants of that one helpless city than all the bombs dropped in the Second World War.

Neither the United States nor the Soviet Union nor the United Kingdom nor France can look forward to that day with equanimity. We have a great obligation, all four nuclear powers have a great obligation, to use whatever time remains to prevent the spread of nuclear weapons, to persuade other countries not to test, transfer, acquire, possess, or produce such weapons.

This treaty can be the opening wedge in that campaign. It provides that none of the parties will assist other nations to test in the forbidden environments. It opens the door for further agreements on the control of nuclear weapons, and it is open for all nations to sign. For it is in the interest of all nations, and already we have heard from a number of countries who wish to join with us promptly.

Fourth and finally, this treaty can limit the nuclear arms race in ways which, on balance, will strengthen our nation's security far more than the continuation of unrestricted testing. For in today's world, a nation's security does not always increase as its arms increase, when its adversary is doing the same, and unlimited competition in the testing and development of new types of destructive nuclear weapons will not make the world safer for either side. Under this limited treaty, on the other hand, the testing of other nations could never be sufficient to offset the ability of our strategic forces to deter or survive a nuclear attack and to penetrate and destroy an aggressor's homeland.

We have, and under this treaty we will continue to have, the nuclear strength that we need. It is true that the Soviets have tested nuclear weapons of a yield higher than that which we thought to be necessary, but the hundred-megaton bomb of which they spoke two years ago does not and will not change the balance of strategic power. The United States has chosen, deliberately, to concentrate on more mobile and more efficient weapons, with lower but entirely sufficient yield, and our security is therefore not impaired by the treaty I am discussing.

It is also true, as Mr. Khrushchev would agree, that nations cannot afford in these matters to rely simply on the good faith of their adversaries. We have not, therefore, overlooked the risk of secret violations. There is at present a possibility that deep in outer space, hundreds and thousands and millions of miles away from the earth, illegal tests might go undetected. But we already have the capability to construct a system of observation that would make such tests almost impossible to conceal, and we can decide at any time whether such a system is needed in the light of the limited risk to us and the limited reward to others of violations attempted at that range. For any tests which might be conducted so far out in space, which cannot be conducted more easily and efficiently and legally underground, would necessarily be of such a magnitude that they would be extremely difficult to conceal. We can also employ new devices to check on the testing of smaller weapons in the lower atmosphere. Any violations, moreover, involves, along with the risk of detection, the end of the treaty and the worldwide consequences for the violator.

Secret violations are possible and secret preparations for a sudden withdrawal are possible, and thus our own vigilance and strength must be maintained, as we remain ready to withdraw and to resume all forms of testing, if we must. But it would be a mistake to assume that this treaty will be quickly broken. The gains of illegal testing are obviously slight compared to their cost and the hazard of discovery: and the nations which have initialed and will sign this treaty prefer it, in my judgment, to unrestricted testing as a matter of their own self-interest. For these nations, too, and all nations, have a stake in limiting the arms race, in holding the spread of nuclear weapons, and in breathing air that is not radioactive. While it may be theoretically possible to demonstrate the risks inherent in any treaty, and such risks in this treaty are small, the far greater risks to our security are the risks of unrestricted testing, the risk of a nuclear arms race, the risk of new nuclear powers, nuclear pollution, and nuclear war.

This limited test ban, in our most careful judgment, is safer by far for the United States than an unlimited nuclear arms race. For all these reasons, I am hopeful that this nation will promptly approve the limited test-ban treaty. There will, of course, be debate in the country and in the Senate. The Constitution wisely requires the advice and consent of the Senate to all treaties, and that consultation has already begun. All this is as it should be. A document which may mark an historic and constructive opportunity for the world deserves an historic and constructive debate.

It is my hope that all of you will take part in that debate, for this treaty is for all of us. It is particularly for our children and our grandchildren, and they have no lobby here in Washington. This debate will involve military, scientific, and political experts, but it must not be left to them alone. The right and the responsibility are yours.

If we are to open new doorways to peace, if we are to seize this rare opportunity for progress, if we are to be as bold and farsighted in our control of weapons as we have been in their invention, then let us now show all the world on this side of the wall and the other that a strong America also stands for peace. There is no cause for complacency.

We have learned in times past that the spirit of one moment or place can be gone in the next. We have been disappointed more than once, and we have no illusions now that there are shortcuts on the road to peace. At many points around the globe the Communists are continuing their efforts to exploit weakness and poverty. Their concentration of nuclear and conventional arms must still be deterred.

The familiar contest between choice and coercion, the familiar places of danger and conflict, are all still there, in Cuba, in Southeast Asia, in Berlin, and all around the globe, still requiring all the strength and the vigilance that we can muster. Nothing could more greatly damage our cause than if we and our allies were to believe that peace has already been achieved, and that our strength and unity were no longer required.

But now, for the first time in many years, the path of peace may be open. No one can be certain what the future will bring. No one can say whether the time has come for an easing of the struggle. But history and our own conscience will judge us harsher if we do not now make every effort to test our hopes by action; and this is the place to begin. According to the ancient Chinese proverb, "A journey of a thousand miles must begin with a single step."

My fellow Americans, let us take that first step. Let us, if we can, step back from the shadows of war and seek out the way of peace. And if that journey is a thousand miles, or even more, let history record that we, in this land, at this time, took the first step.

Televised Address on Limited Nuclear Test-Ban Treaty
Washington, D.C., July 26, 1963

In its first two decades the age of nuclear energy has been full of fear, yet never empty of hope. Today the fear is a little less and the hope a little greater. For the first time we have been able to reach an agreement which can limit the dangers of this age.

The agreement itself is limited, but its message of hope has been heard and understood not only by the peoples of the three originating nations, but by the peoples and governments of the hundred other countries that have signed. This treaty is the first fruit of labor in which multitudes have shared—citizens, legislators, statesmen, diplomats, and soldiers, too.

Soberly and unremittingly this nation—but never this nation alone—has sought the doorway to effective disarmament into a world where peace is secure. Today we have a beginning and it is right for us to acknowledge all whose work across the years has helped make this beginning possible.

What the future will bring, no one of us can know. This first fruit of hope may or may not be followed by larger harvests. Even this limited treaty, great as it is with promise, can survive only if it has from others the determined support in letter and in spirit which I hereby pledge in behalf of the United States.

If this treaty fails, it will not be our doing, and even if it fails, we shall not regret that we have made this clear and honorable national commitment to the cause of man's survival. For under this treaty we can and must still keep our vigil in defense of freedom.

But this treaty need not fail. This small step toward safety can be followed by others longer and less limited, if also harder in the taking.

With our courage and understanding enlarged by this achievement, let us press onward in quest of man's essential desire for peace.

As President of the United States and with the advice and consent of the Senate, I now sign the instruments of ratification of this treaty.

Remarks upon signing the Nuclear Test-Ban Treaty
Washington, D.C., October 7, 1963

The Quest for Peace

We meet again in the quest for peace.

Twenty-four months ago, when I last had the honor of addressing this body, the shadow of fear lay darkly across the world. The freedom of West Berlin was in immediate peril. Agreement on a neutral Laos seemed remote. The mandate of the United Nations in the Congo was under fire. The financial outlook for this organization was in doubt. Dag Hammarskjöld was dead. The doctrine of troika was being pressed in his place, and atmospheric nuclear tests had been resumed by the Soviet Union.

Those were anxious days for mankind—and some men wondered aloud whether this organization could survive. But the sixteenth and seventeenth General Assemblies achieved not only survival but progress. Rising to its responsibility, the United Nations helped reduce the tensions and helped to hold back the darkness.

Today the clouds have lifted a little so that new rays of hope can break through. The pressures on West Berlin appear to be temporarily eased. Political unity in the Congo has been largely restored. A neutral coalition in Laos, while still in difficulty, is at least in being. The integrity of the United Nations Secretariat has been reaffirmed. A United Nations Decade of Development is under way. And, for the first time in seventeen years of effort, a specific step has been taken to limit the nuclear arms race.

I refer, of course, to the treaty to ban nuclear tests in the atmosphere, outer space, and under water concluded by the Soviet Union, the United Kingdom, and the United States—and already signed by nearly one hundred countries. It has been hailed by people the world over who are thankful to be free from the fears of nuclear fallout. . . .

The world has not escaped from the darkness. The long shadows of conflict and crisis envelop us still. But we meet today in an atmosphere of rising hope, and at a moment of comparative calm. My presence here today is not a sign of crisis, but of confidence. I am not here to report on a new threat to the peace or new signs of war. I have come to salute the United Nations and to show the support of the American people for your daily deliberations.

For the value of this body's work is not dependent on the existence of emergencies, nor can the winning of peace consist only of dramatic victories. Peace is a daily, a weekly, a monthly process, gradually changing opinions, slowly eroding old barriers, quietly building new structures. And however undramatic the pursuit of peace, that pursuit must go on.

Today we may have reached a pause in the Cold War—but that is not a lasting peace. A test-ban treaty is a milestone—but it is not the millennium. We have not been released from our obligations—we have been given an opportunity. And if we fail to make the most of this moment and this momentum—if we convert our newfound hopes and understandings into new walls and weapons of hostility—if this pause in the Cold War merely leads to its renewal and not to its end—then the indictment of posterity will rightly point its finger at us all. But if we can stretch this pause into a period of cooperation—if both sides can now gain new confidence and experience in concrete collaborations for peace—if we can now be as bold and farsighted in the control of deadly weapons as we have been in their creation—then surely this first small step can be the start of a long and fruitful journey.

The task of building the peace lies with the leaders of every nation, large and small. For the great powers have no monopoly on conflict or ambition. The Cold War is not the only expression of tension in this world—and the nuclear race is not the only arms race. Even little wars are dangerous in a nuclear world. The long labor of peace is an undertaking for every nation—and in this effort none of us can remain unaligned. To this goal none can be uncommitted.

The reduction of global tension must not be an excuse for the narrow pursuit of self-interest. If the Soviet Union and the United States, with all of their global interests and clashing commitments of ideology, and with nuclear weapons still aimed at each other today, can find areas of common interest and agreement, then surely other nations can do the same—nations caught in regional conflicts, in racial issues, or in the death throes of old colonialism. Chronic disputes which divert precious resources from the needs of the people or drain the energies of both sides serve the interests of no one—and the badge of responsibility in the modern world is a willingness to seek peaceful solutions.

It is never too early to try; and it's never too late to talk; and it's high time that many disputes on the agenda of this Assembly were taken off the debating schedule and placed on the negotiating table.

The fact remains that the United States, as a major nuclear power, does have a special responsibility in the world. It is, in fact, a threefold responsibility—a responsibility to our own citizens; a responsibility to the people of the whole world who are affected by our decisions; and a responsibility to the next generation of humanity. We believe the Soviet Union also has these special responsibilities—and that those responsibilities require our two nations to concentrate less on our differences and more on the means of resolving them peacefully. For too long both of us have increased our military budgets, our nuclear stockpiles, and our capacity to destroy all life in this hemisphere—human, animal, vegetable—without any corresponding increase in our security.

I have come to salute the United Nations and to show the support of the American people for your daily deliberations . . . The great powers have no monopoly on conflict or ambition. . . . Even little wars are dangerous in a nuclear world.

Our conflicts, to be sure, are real. Our concepts of the world are different. No service is performed by failing to make clear our disagreements. A central difference is the belief of the American people in self-determination for all people.

We believe that the people of Germany and Berlin must be free to reunite their capital and their country.

We believe that the people of Cuba must be free to secure the fruits of the revolution that have been betrayed from within and exploited from without.

In short, we believe that in all the world—in Eastern Europe as well as Western, in southern Africa as well as northern, in old nations as well as new—people must be free to choose their own future, without discrimination or dictation, without coercion or subversion.

These are the basic differences between the Soviet Union and the United States, and they cannot be concealed. So long as they exist, they set limits to agreement, and they forbid the relaxation of our vigilance. Our defense around the world will be maintained for the protection of freedom—and our determination to safeguard that freedom will measure up to any threat or challenge.

But I would say to the leaders of the Soviet Union, and to their people, that if either of our countries is to be fully secure, we need a much better weapon than the H-bomb—a weapon better than ballistic missiles or nuclear submarines—and that better weapon is peaceful cooperation.

We have, in recent years, agreed on a limited test-ban treaty, on an emergency communications link between our capitals, on a statement of principles for disarmament, on an increase in cultural exchange, on cooperation in outer space, on the peaceful exploration of the Antarctic, and on tempering last year's crisis over Cuba.

I believe, therefore, that the Soviet Union and the United States, together with their allies, can achieve further agreements—agreements which spring from our mutual interest in avoiding mutual destruction.

There can be no doubt about the agenda of further steps. We must continue to seek agreements on measures which prevent war by accident or miscalculation. We must continue to seek agreement on safeguards against surprise attack, including observation posts at key points. We must continue to seek agreement on further measures to curb the nuclear arms race, by controlling the transfer of nuclear weapons, converting fissionable materials to peaceful purposes, and banning underground testing, with adequate inspection and enforcement. We must continue to seek agreement on a freer flow of information and people from East to West and West to East.

We must continue to seek agreement, encouraged by yesterday's affirmative response to this proposal by the Soviet Foreign Minister, on an arrangement to keep weapons of mass destruction out of outer space. Let us get our negotiators back to the negotiating table to work out a practicable arrangement to this end.

In these and other ways, let us move up the steep and difficult path toward comprehensive disarmament, securing mutual confidence through mutual verification, and building the institutions of peace as we dismantle the engines of war. We must not let failure to agree on all points delay agreements where agreement is possible. And we must not put forward proposals for propaganda purposes.

Finally, in a field where the United States and the Soviet Union have a special capacity—in the field of space—there is room for new cooperation, for further joint efforts in the regulation and exploration of space. I include among these possibilities a joint expedition to the moon. Space offers no problems of sovereignty; by resolution of this Assembly, the members of the United Nations have forsworn any claim to territorial rights in outer space or on celestial bodies, and declared that international law and the United Nations Charter will apply. Why, therefore, should man's first flight to the moon be a matter of national competition? Why should the United States and the Soviet Union, in preparing for such expeditions, become involved in immense duplications of research, construction, and expenditure? Surely we should explore whether the scientists and astronauts of our two countries—indeed of all the world—cannot work together in the conquest of space, sending someday in this decade to the moon not the representatives of a single nation, but the representatives of all of our countries.

All these and other new steps toward peaceful cooperation may be possible. Most of them will require on our part full consultation with our allies—for their interests are as much involved as our own, and we will not make an agreement at their expense. Most of them will require long and careful negotiation. And most of them will require a new approach to the Cold War—a desire not to "bury" one's adversary, but to compete in a host of peaceful arenas, in ideas, in production, and ultimately in service to all mankind.

The contest will continue—the contest between those who see a monolithic world and those who believe in diversity—but it should be a contest in leadership and responsibility instead of destruction, a contest in achievement instead of intimidation. Speaking for the United States of America, I welcome such a contest. For we believe that truth is stronger than error—and that freedom is more enduring than coercion. And in the contest for a better life, all the world can be a winner.

The effort to improve the conditions of man, however, is not a task for the few. It is the task of all nations—acting alone, acting in groups, acting in the United Nations. For plague and pestilence and plunder and pollution, the hazards of nature and the hunger of children, are the foes of every nation. The earth, the sea, and the air are the concern of every nation. And science, technology, and education can be the ally of every nation.

We have the power to make this the best generation of mankind in the history of the world—or to make it the last.

Never before has man had such capacity to control his own environment, to end thirst and hunger, to conquer poverty and disease, to banish illiteracy and massive human misery. We have the power to make this the best generation of mankind in the history of the world—or to make it the last. . . .

But man does not live by bread alone. The members of this organization are committed by the Charter to promote and respect human rights. Those rights are not respected when a Buddhist priest is driven from his pagoda, when a synagogue is shut down, when a Protestant church cannot open a mission, when a cardinal is forced into hiding, or when a crowded church service is bombed. The United States of America is opposed to discrimination and persecution on grounds of race and religion anywhere in the world, including our own nation. We are working to right the wrongs of our own country. . . .

The United Nations cannot survive as a static organization. Its obligations are increasing as well as its size. Its Charter must be changed as well as its customs. The authors of that Charter did not intend that it be frozen in perpetuity. The science of weapons and war has made us all, far more than eighteen years ago in San Francisco, one world and one human race, with one common destiny. In such a world, absolute sovereignty no longer assures us of absolute security. The conventions of peace must pull abreast and then ahead of the inventions of war. The

United Nations, building on its successes and learning from its failures, must be developed into a genuine world security system.

But peace does not rest in charters and covenants alone. It lies in the hearts and minds of all people. And if it is cast out there, then no act, no pact, no treaty, no organization can hope to preserve it without the support and the wholehearted commitment of all people. So let us not rest all our hopes on parchment and on paper; let us strive to build peace, a desire for peace, a willingness to work for peace, in the hearts and minds of all of our people. I believe that we can. I believe the problems of human destiny are not beyond the reach of human beings.

Two years ago I told this body that the United States had proposed, and was willing to sign, a limited test-ban treaty. Today that treaty has been signed. It will not put an end to war. It will not remove basic conflicts. It will not secure freedom for all. But it can be a lever; and Archimedes, in explaining the principles of the lever, was said to have declared to his friends: "Give me a place where I can stand—and I shall move the world."

My fellow inhabitants of this planet: Let us take our stand here in this Assembly of nations. And let us see if we, in our own time, can move the world to a just and lasting peace.

United Nations General Assembly
New York, New York, September 20, 1963

The Sale of American Wheat

The Soviet Union and various Eastern European countries have expressed a willingness to buy from our private grain dealers at the regular world price several million tons of surplus American wheat or wheat flour for shipment during the next several months. They may also wish to purchase from us surplus feed grains and other agricultural commodities.

After consultation with the National Security Council, and informing the appropriate leaders of the Congress, I have concluded that such sales by private dealers for American dollars or gold, either cash on delivery or normal commercial terms, should not be prohibited by the government. . . .

The Russian people will know they are receiving American wheat. The United States has never had a policy against selling consumer goods, including agricultural commodities, to the Soviet Union and Eastern Europe. On the contrary, we have been doing exactly that for a number of years, and to the extent that their limited supplies of gold, dollars, and foreign exchange must be used for food, they cannot be used to purchase military or other equipment.

Our allies have long been engaged in extensive sales of wheat and other farm products to the Communist bloc, and, in fact, it would be foolish to halt the sales of our wheat when other countries can buy wheat from us today and then sell this flour to the Communists. In recent weeks Australia and NATO allies have agreed to sell ten million to fifteen million tons of wheat and wheat flour to the Communist bloc.

This transaction advertises to the world as nothing else could the success of free American agriculture. It demonstrates our willingness to relieve food shortages, to reduce tensions, and to improve relations with all countries. And it shows that peaceful agreements with the United States which serve the interests of both sides are a far more worthwhile course than a course of isolation and hostility.

For this government to tell our grain traders that they cannot accept these offers, on the other hand, would accomplish little or nothing. The Soviets would continue to buy wheat and flour elsewhere, including wheat flour from those nations which buy our wheat. Moreover, having for many years sold them farm products which are not in surplus, it would make no sense to refuse to sell those products on which we must otherwise pay the cost of storage. In short, this particular decision with respect to sales to the Soviet Union, which is not inconsistent with many smaller transactions over a long period of time, does not represent a new Soviet-American trade policy. That must await the settlement of many matters. But it does represent one more hopeful sign that a more peaceful world is both possible and beneficial to us all.

Opening Statement, President's News Conference
Washington, D.C., October 9, 1963

CHAPTER 14
The Western Alliance

Kennedy welcomed the political and economic integration of Western Europe as a means both of preventing any recurrence of the bitter rivalries that had produced two world wars in his lifetime and of strengthening the alliance for a rapidly changing world. Western diplomacy and trade policy, he knew, could not stand still in the face of those changes, including a resurgent Moscow and an emergent Third World. By 1963, determined to prevent any outbreak of war and any erosion of Western liberty, he sought still closer relations with his allies in a balanced use of both defense and diplomacy. His commitment to peace and security was memorably hailed in his visit to beleaguered West Berlin.

The Political-Military Link

NATO is remarkable among the alliances of history in its combination of political, military, economic, and even psychological components. What NATO is, at any time, depends not only upon its forces in being, but upon the resolution of its leaders, the state of mind of its people, and the view of all these elements which is held by those who do not always wish us well.

In this situation, it is clearly necessary that there should be close understanding between political leaders and the senior military officers. In our countries, of course, final responsibility always rests with political authorities. . . . But in NATO, from the very beginning, it has been essential that neither class of men should accept any arbitrary division of our problems into "the political" and "the military" spheres. The crucial problems have always been mixed. Political leaders have had a duty to share with their senior officers a full understanding of the political purposes of the alliance, and military leaders for their part have had to recognize that in NATO all the important military problems are political problems also.

This recognition of the interconnection between policy and force is an even more compelling necessity today, especially in all the questions which relate to the command, the deployment, and the possible use of nuclear weapons.

In the months ahead, as we share in the framing of NATO's policy and in new decisions which must guide us safely toward the future, we shall need to have the closest and most understanding communication not only from country to country, but from soldier to civilian. Political planning must be aware of military realities, and military plans in turn must be responsive to political considerations—among them such varied and important matters as resource capabilities, national attitudes, and other alliance objectives. . . . Military and political problems are not separable, and military and political men must work ever more closely together.

I hold an office which by our very Constitution unites political and military responsibility, and therefore it is no more than my duty to pledge my own best effort to keep these two kinds of problems together on my mind. I ask the same of you.

Remarks to NATO Military Committee
Washington, D.C., April 10, 1961

The Change in World Power

I do not think it altogether inappropriate to introduce myself to this audience. I am the man who accompanied Jacqueline Kennedy to Paris, and I have enjoyed it. . . .

I come on the same mission which occupied many of my predecessors, stretching all the way back to President Wilson at the conclusion of the First World War, and that is how . . . to bind more intimately for the common interest France and the United States, Europe and the United States. . . . But . . . all of the power relationships in the world have changed in the last fifteen years, and therefore our policies must take these changes into account. First is the change in Europe itself . . . its economic growth rate higher than that of the new world . . . the most outstanding example of strength through unity. . . .

> ***I am the man who accompanied Jacqueline Kennedy to Paris, and I have enjoyed it.***

The second great change is the change in weaponry. The United States no longer has a nuclear monopoly. . . . The intercontinental ballistic missile has made my own country vulnerable to attack and . . .

reinforced our view that your defense and ours are indivisible. In terms of potential destruction, Washington today is closer to Moscow than this city was to any other city in any other country before the outbreak of World War II. . . .

Third and most important is the change in the location and nature of the threat. The cause of freedom is under pressure all over the world. But because of the extraordinary rebirth of Western European strength, the struggle has been switched . . . to the whole southern half of the globe where the attack potentially comes not from massive land armies but from subversion, insurrection, and despair. Europe has conquered her own internal problems. Those that remain are on the way to solution. The time has now come for us to associate more closely together than ever in the past in a massive and concerted attack on the poverty, injustice, and oppression which overshadow so much of the globe.

Press Luncheon
Paris, France, June 2, 1961

The Trade Expansion Act

In May of 1962, we stand at a great dividing point. We must either trade or fade. We must either go backward or go forward. For more than a quarter of a century the reciprocal trade legislation fathered by Cordell Hull of Tennessee and sponsored by Franklin Roosevelt has served this country well. On eleven different occasions it has been renewed by Congresses of both parties. But that act is no longer adequate to carry us through the channels and the locks of world trade today.

For the whole pattern of trade is changing and we must change with it. The Common Market uniting the countries of Western Europe together in one great trading group indicates both a promise, and a threat, to our economy. Our international balance of payments is in deficit, requiring an increase in our exports. Japan has regained force as a trading nation; nearly fifty new nations of Asia and Africa are seeking new markets; our friends in Latin America need to trade to develop their capital; and the Communist bloc has developed a vast new arsenal of trading weapons which can be used against us. . . .

I believe that American trade leadership must be maintained and . . . furthered—and I have therefore submitted to the Congress the Trade Expansion Act of 1962.

It is not a partisan measure—its provisions have been endorsed by leaders of both parties. It is not a radical measure—its newest features merely add force to traditional American concepts. And it is not a measure favoring one section of our country over another—farm, labor, business and consumer groups, from every part of the nation, support this legislation. I am convinced that the passage of this bill is of vital importance to you and to every other American—not only to those vast numbers of people who are engaged in trade, but to every citizen: as a consumer who is concerned about the prices you must pay, as a patriot concerned about national security, as an American concerned about freedom. The basic economic facts make it essential that we pass this legislation this year.

Our businessmen, workers, and farmers are in need of new markets—and the fastest growing market in the world is the European Common Market. Its consumers will soon be nearly 250 million people. Its sales possibilities have scarcely begun to be tapped. Its demand for American goods is without precedent—if only we can obtain the tools necessary to open the door.

Our own markets here at home expand as our economy and population expand. But think of the tremendous demand in the Common Market countries, where most consumers have never had the goods which we take so much for granted. Think of the opportunities in a market where, compared to the ratio of ownership in this country, only one fourth as many consumers have radios, one seventh television sets, one fifth automobiles, washing machines, refrigerators!

Our businessmen, workers, and farmers are in need of new markets—and the fastest growing market in the world is the European Common Market. . . . Its demand for American goods is without precedent—if only we can obtain the tools necessary to open the door.

If our American producers can share in this market, it will mean more investment and more plants and more jobs and a faster rate of growth. To share in that market we must strike a bargain—we must have something to offer the Europeans—we must be willing to give them increased access to our markets. Let us not avoid the fact: we cannot sell unless we buy. And there will be those who will be opposed to this competition. But, let those who believe in competition—those who welcome the challenge of world trade, as our predecessors have done—let them recognize the value that will come from this exchange of goods. It will enrich the choice of consumers. It will make possible a higher standard of living. It will help hold the lid on the cost of living. It will stimulate our producers to modernize their products. A few—a very few—may be adversely affected, but for the benefit of those few we have expanded and refined the safeguards of the act. . . .

But let us not miss the main point: the new jobs opened through trade will be far greater than any jobs which will be adversely affected. And these new jobs will come in those enterprises that are today leading the economy of the country—our growth industries, those that pay the highest wages, those that are among the most efficiently organized, those that are most active in research and in the innovation of new products. The experience of the European Common Market, where tariffs were gradually cut down, has shown that increased trade brings employment. They have full employment in the Common Market and an economic growth rate twice that of the United States. In short, trade expansion will emphasize the modern instead of the obsolete, the strong instead of the weak, the new frontiers of trade instead of the ancient strongholds of protection.

We cannot continue to bear the burden that we must bear of helping freedom defend itself, all the way from the American soldier guarding the Brandenburg Gate to the Americans now in Vietnam, or the Peace Corps men in Colombia, unless we have the resources to finance those great expenditures which in the last year totaled over three billion dollars. Unless we are able to increase our surplus of balance of payments, the United States will be faced with a hard choice of either lessening those commitments or beginning to withdraw this great national effort.

One answer to this problem is the negative answer: raise our tariffs, restrict our capital, pull back from the world—and our adversaries would be only too glad to fill any gap that we should leave. This administration was not elected to preside over the liquidation of American responsibility. . . .

There is a much better answer—and that is to increase our exports, to meet our commitments, and to maintain our defense of freedom. I have every confidence that once this bill is passed, the ability of American initiative and know-how will increase our exports and our export surplus by competing successfully in every market of the world.

Third and last, the new trade act can strengthen our foreign policy. . . . The Alliance for Progress seeks to help these Latin American neighbors of ours. That effort must, and will, continue. But foreign aid cannot do the job alone. In the long run, our sister republics must develop the means themselves to finance their development. They must sell more of their goods on the world market, and earn the exchange necessary to buy the machinery and the technology that they need to raise their standard of living. The Trade Expansion Act is designed to keep this great market as a part of the world community, because the security of the United States is tied up with the well-being of our sister republics. . . .

For we are moving toward a full partnership of all the free nations of the world, a partnership which will have within its area ninety percent of the industrial productive power of the Free World, which will have in it the greatest market that the world has ever known, a productive power far greater than that of the Communist bloc, a trillion-dollar economy where goods can move freely back and forth. That is the prospect that lies before us, as citizens of this country, in the year 1962.

Those who preach the doctrine of the inevitability of the class struggle and Communist success should realize that . . . the great effort . . . to unify economically the countries of the Free World offers far greater promise than the sterile and broken promises of the Communist system. Against the Communist system of iron discipline, the Atlantic partnership will present a world of free choice. Against their predictions of our collapse, it will present a challenge of free nations working in harmony. . . .

In the life of every nation, as in the life of every man, there comes a time when a nation stands at the crossroads; when it can either shrink from the future and retire into its shell, or move ahead, asserting its will and its faith in an uncertain sea. I believe that we stand at such a juncture in our foreign economic policy. And I come to this city because I believe New Orleans and Louisiana and the United States choose to move ahead in 1962.

Port of New Orleans
New Orleans, Louisiana, May 4, 1962

The Atlantic Partnership

As this effort for independence, inspired by the American Declaration of Independence, now approaches a successful close, a great new effort for interdependence is transforming the world about us. And the spirit of that new effort is the same spirit which gave birth to the American Constitution.

That spirit is today most clearly seen across the Atlantic Ocean. The nations of Western Europe, long divided by feuds far more bitter than any which existed among the thirteen colonies, are today joining together, seeking, as our forefathers sought, to find freedom in diversity and in unity, strength.

The United States looks on this vast new enterprise with hope and admiration. We do not regard a strong and united Europe as a rival but as a partner. To aid its progress has been the basic object of our foreign policy for seventeen years. We believe that a united Europe will be capable of playing a greater role in the common defense, of responding more generously to the needs of poorer nations, of joining with the United States and others in lowering trade barriers, resolving problems of commerce, commodities, and currency, and developing coordinated policies in all economic, political, and diplomatic areas. We see in such a Europe a partner with whom we can deal on a basis of full equality in all the great and burdensome tasks of building and defending a community of free nations.

It would be premature at this time to do more than indicate the high regard with which we view the formation of this partnership. The first order of business is for our European friends to go forward in forming the more perfect union which will someday make this partnership possible.

A great new edifice is not built overnight. It was eleven years from the Declaration of Independence to the writing of the Constitution. The construction of workable federal institutions required still another generation. The greatest works of our nation's founders lay not in documents and in declarations, but in creative, determined action. The building of the new house of Europe has followed the same practical, purposeful course. Building the Atlantic partnership now will not be easily or cheaply finished.

But I will say here and now, on this Day of Independence, that the

United States will be ready for a Declaration of Interdependence, that we will be prepared to discuss with a united Europe the ways and means of forming a concrete Atlantic partnership, a mutually beneficial partnership between the new union now emerging in Europe and the old American Union founded here 175 years ago.

All this will not be completed in a year, but let the world know it is our goal.

In urging the adoption of the United States Constitution, Alexander Hamilton told his fellow New Yorkers "to think continentally." Today Americans must learn to think intercontinentally.

Acting on our own, by ourselves, we cannot establish justice throughout the world; we cannot insure its domestic tranquillity, or provide for its common defense, or promote its general welfare, or secure the blessings of liberty to ourselves and our posterity. But joined with other free nations, we can do all this and more. We can assist the developing nations to throw off the yoke of poverty. We can balance our worldwide trade and payments at the highest possible level of growth. We can mount a deterrent powerful enough to deter any aggression. And ultimately we can help to achieve a world of law and free choice, banishing the world of war and coercion.

For the Atlantic partnership of which I speak would not look inward only, preoccupied with its own welfare and advancement. It must look outward, to cooperate with all nations in meeting their common concern. It would serve as a nucleus for the eventual union of all free men—those who are now free and those who are vowing that someday they will be free.

On Washington's birthday in 1861 . . . President-elect Abraham Lincoln spoke in this hall on his way to the nation's capital. And he paid a brief but eloquent tribute to the men who wrote, who fought for, and who died for the Declaration of Independence. Its essence, he said, was its promise not only of liberty "to the people of this country, but hope to the world, [hope] that in due time the weights should be lifted from the shoulders of all men, and that all should have an equal chance."

On this fourth day of July 1962, we who are gathered at this same hall, entrusted with the fate and future of our states and nation, declare now our vow to do our part to lift the weights from the shoulders of all, to join other men and nations in preserving both peace and freedom, and to regard any threat to the peace or freedom of one as a threat to the peace and freedom of all. "And for the support of this Declaration, with a firm reliance on the protection of Divine Providence, we mutually pledge to each other our Lives, our Fortunes, and our sacred Honor."

Independence Hall
Philadelphia, Pennsylvania, July 4, 1962

The Exemplar of Service

Dear Mr. Monnet:

I am delighted to join my friends at Freedom House in doing honor to your great achievements. You come at a moment of high importance—and you come as the exemplar of disinterested service to Europe and to the Atlantic world.

For centuries, emperors, kings, and dictators have sought to impose unity on Europe by force. For better or worse, they have failed. But under your inspiration, Europe has moved closer to unity in less than twenty years than it had done before in a thousand. You and your associates have built with the mortar of reason and the brick of economic and political interest. You are transforming Europe by the power of a constructive idea.

Ever since the war, the reconstruction and the knitting together of Europe have been objectives of United States policy, for we have recognized with you that in unity lies strength. And we have also recognized with you that a strong Europe would be good not only for Europeans but for the world. America and a united Europe, working in full and effective partnership, can find solutions to those urgent problems that confront all mankind in this crucial time.

I have been happy, therefore, to read your statement of January 16th in which you call attention to the responsibility of Europe to share with the United States in the common defense of the West. I believe, with you, that "Americans and Europeans must recognize that neither one nor the other is defending a particular country, but that the ensemble is defending a common civilization." The United States will be true to this conviction, and we trust that it will have the support of Europeans too.

Your practical wisdom, your energy in persuasion, your tested courage, and your earned eminence in Europe are the reasons for this celebration in your honor. They are also a great resource for freedom, and I wish you many years of continued strength in your service to our cause.

Sincerely,
John F. Kennedy

Letter to Jean Monnet
Washington, D.C., January 22, 1963

The Champion of Liberty

We gather today at a moment unique in the history of the United States.

This is the first time that the United States Congress has solemnly resolved that the President of the United States shall proclaim an honorary citizenship for the citizen of another country. In enjoining me to perform this happy duty, the Congress gives Sir Winston Churchill a distinction shared only with the Marquis de Lafayette.

In proclaiming him an honorary citizen, I only propose a formal recognition of the place he has long since won in the history of freedom and in the affections of my—and now his—fellow countrymen.

Whenever and wherever tyranny threatened, he has always championed liberty. Facing firmly toward the future, he has never forgotten the past. Serving six monarchs of his native Great Britain, he has served all men's freedom and dignity.

In the dark days and darker nights when England stood alone—and most men save Englishmen despaired of England's life—he mobilized the English language and sent it into battle. The incandescent quality of his words illuminated the courage of his countrymen.

Indifferent himself to danger, he wept over the sorrows of others. A child of the House of Commons, he became its father. Accustomed to the hardships of battle, he has no distaste for pleasure.

Now his stately ship of life, having weathered the severest storms of a troubled century, is anchored in tranquil waters, proof that courage and faith and zest for freedom are truly indestructible. The record of his triumphant passage will inspire free hearts all over the globe.

By adding his name to our rolls, we mean to honor him—but his acceptance honors us far more. For no statement or proclamation can enrich his name now—the name Sir Winston Churchill is already legend.

Remarks upon signing proclamation conferring honorary citizenship on Sir Winston Churchill
Washington, D.C., April 9, 1963

The Only War We Seek

I am grateful for your invitation and I am happy to be here. I have crossed the Atlantic, some 3,500 miles, at a crucial time in the life of the Grand Alliance. Our unity was forged in a time of danger; it must be maintained in a time of peace. Our Alliance was founded to deter a new war; it must now find the way to a new peace. Our strategy was born in a divided Europe, but it must look to the goal of European unity and an end to the divisions of people and countries.

Our Alliance is in a period of transition, and that is as it should be. For Western Europe is no longer weakened by conflict, but is fast becoming a full partner in prosperity and security. Western Europe is no longer the seedbed of world war, but an instrument of unity and an example of reconciliation. And Western Europe, finally, is no longer an area in need of assistance, but can now be a source of strength to all the forces of freedom all around the globe.

I have also come to this country, the most populous in Western Europe, to express the respect of the people of the United States for the

German people's industry and their initiative, for their culture and their courage.

Here in Western Germany you have achieved a solid framework of freedom, a miracle of economic recovery, and an opportunity to express your political ideals through action in Europe and through the world.

The people of West Germany have freed themselves from the forces of tyranny and aggression. The people of the United States have now freed themselves from the long process of isolation. Together we look forward to a new future. Former foes have become faithful friends. Nations bitterly arrayed against each other have now become closely allied, sharing common values and common sentiments, as well as common interests, working within a growing partnership of equals, for peace and the common defense, on problems of trade and monetary policy, and on helping the less developed countries, and on building Western unity.

Above all, we recognize a duty to defend and to develop the long Western tradition which we share, resting as it does on a common heritage. Economically, militarily, politically, our two nations and all the other nations of the Alliance are now dependent upon one another. We are allies in the only war we seek—the war against poverty, hunger, disease, and ignorance in our own countries, and around the world.

We all know the meaning of freedom and our people are determined upon its peaceful survival and success.

My stay in this country will be all too brief, but in a larger sense the United States is here on this continent to stay. So long as our presence is desired and required, our forces and commitments will remain. For your safety is our safety, your liberty is our liberty, and any attack on your soil is an attack upon our own. Out of necessity, as well as sentiment, in our approach to peace as well as war, our fortunes are one.

Finally, I have also come to Germany to pay tribute to a great European statesman, an architect of unity, a champion of liberty, a friend of the American people—Chancellor Konrad Adenauer. Already he lives in the history he helped to make. I look forward to this visit of Chancellor Adenauer with me, with the warmth of your greeting already in my memory.

Remarks upon arrival in Germany
at Bonn-Cologne Airport, Federal Republic of Germany
June 23, 1963

The Age of Interdependence

One hundred and fifteen years ago a most learned Parliament was convened in this historic hall. Its goal was a united German Federation. Its members were poets and professors, lawyers and philosophers, doctors and clergymen, freely elected in all parts of the land. No nation applauded its endeavors as warmly as my own. No assembly ever strove more ardently to put perfection into practice. And though in the end it failed, no other building in Germany deserves more the title of "cradle of German democracy."

But can there be such a title? In my own home city of Boston, Faneuil Hall—once the meeting place of the authors of the American Revolution—has long been known as the "cradle of American liberty." But when, in 1852, the Hungarian patriot Kossuth addressed an audience there, he criticized its name. "It is," he said, "a great name—but there is something in it which saddens my heart. You should not say 'American liberty.' You should say 'liberty in America.' Liberty should not be either American or European—it should just be 'liberty.' "

Kossuth was right. For unless liberty flourishes in all lands, it cannot flourish in one. Conceived in one hall, it must be carried out in many. Thus, the seeds of the American Revolution had been brought earlier from Europe, and they later took root around the world. The German Revolution of 1848 transmitted ideas and idealists to America and to other lands. Today, in 1963, democracy and liberty are more international than ever before. And the spirit of the Frankfurt Assembly, like the spirit of Faneuil Hall, must live in many hearts and nations if it is to live at all.

For we live in an age of interdependence as well as independence—an age of internationalism as well as nationalism. In 1848 many countries were indifferent to the goals of the Frankfurt Assembly. It was, they said, a German problem. Today there are no exclusively German problems, or American problems, or even European problems. There are world problems—and our two countries and continents are inextricably bound together in the tasks of peace as well as war.

We are partners for peace—not in a narrow bilateral context but in a framework of Atlantic partnership. The ocean divides us less than the Mediterranean divided the ancient world of Greece and Rome. Our Constitution is old and yours is young, and our culture is young and yours is old, but in our commitment we can and must speak and act with but one voice. Our roles are distinct but complementary—and our goals are the same: peace and freedom for all men, for all time, in a world of abundance, in a world of justice.

I would not diminish the miracle of West Germany's economic achievements. But the true German miracle has been your rejection of the past for the future—your reconciliation with France, your participation in the building of Europe, your leading role in NATO, and your growing support for constructive undertakings throughout the world.

But Goethe tells us in his greatest poem that Faust lost the liberty of his soul when he said to the passing moment: "Stay, thou art so fair." And our liberty, too, is endangered if we pause for the passing moment, if we rest on our achievements, if we resist the pace of progress. For time and the world do not stand still. Change is the law of life. And those who look only to the past or the present are certain to miss the future.

The future of the West lies in Atlantic partnership—a system of cooperation, interdependence, and harmony whose peoples can jointly meet their burdens and opportunities throughout the world. Some say this is only a dream, but I do not agree. A generation of achievement—the Marshall Plan, NATO, the Schuman Plan, and the Common Market—urges us up the path to greater unity.

Some say that the United States will neither hold to these purposes nor abide by its pledge—that we will revert to a narrow nationalism. But such doubts fly in the face of history. For eighteen years the United States has stood its watch for freedom all around the globe. The firmness of American will, and the effectiveness of American strength, have been shown, in support of free men and free government, in Asia, in Africa, in the Americas, and, above all, here in Europe. Our commitment to Europe is indispensable—in our interest as well as yours.

For war in Europe, as we learned twice in forty years, destroys peace in America. A threat to the freedom of Europe is a threat to the freedom of America. And that is why we look forward to a united Europe in an Atlantic partnership, an entity of interdependent parts sharing equally both burdens and decisions, and linked together in the tasks of defense as well as the arts of peace.

The first task of the Atlantic Community was to assure its common defense. That defense was and still is indivisible. The United States will risk its cities to defend yours because we need your freedom to protect ours. Hundreds of thousands of our soldiers serve with yours on this continent, as tangible evidence of that pledge. Those who would doubt our pledge or deny this indivisibility—those who would separate Europe from America or split one ally from another—would only give aid and comfort to the men who make themselves our adversaries and welcome any Western disarray.

The purpose of our common military effort is not war but peace—not the destruction of nations but the protection of freedom. . . .

Second: Our partnership is not military alone. Economic unity is also imperative—not only among the nations of Europe, but across the wide Atlantic.

Indeed, economic cooperation is needed throughout the entire free world. By opening our markets to the developing countries of Africa, Asia, and Latin America, by contributing our capital and our skills, by stabilizing basic prices, we can help assure them of a favorable climate for freedom and growth. This is an Atlantic responsibility. For the Atlantic nations themselves helped to awaken these people. Our merchants and our traders plowed up their soils—and their societies as well—in search of minerals and oil and rubber and coffee. Now we must help them gain full membership in the twentieth century, closing the gap between rich and poor.

For time and the world do not stand still. Change is the law of life. And those who look only to the past or the present are certain to miss the future.

We must not return to the 1930s when we exported to each other our own stagnation. We must not return to the discredited view that trade favors some nations at the expense of others. . . . As they say on my own Cape Cod, a rising tide lifts all the boats. And a partnership, by definition, serves both partners, without domination or unfair advantage. Together we have been partners in adversity—let us also be partners in prosperity. . . .

Third and finally: Our partnership depends on common political purpose. . . . History tells us that disunity and relaxation are the great internal dangers of an alliance. Thucydides reported that the Peloponnesians and their allies were mighty in battle but handicapped by their policy-making body—in which, he related, "each presses its own ends . . . which generally results in no action at all. . . ."

Is this also to be the story of the Grand Alliance? Welded in a moment of imminent danger, will it disintegrate into complacency, with each member pressing its own ends to the neglect of the common cause? This must not be the case. Our old dangers are not gone beyond return, and any division among us would bring them back in doubled strength.

Together we must work to strengthen the spirit of those Europeans who are now not free, to reestablish their old ties to freedom and the West, so that their desire for liberty and their sense of nationhood and their sense of belonging to the Western community over hundreds of years will survive for future expression. We ask those who would be our adversaries to understand that in our relations with them we will not bargain one nation's interest against another's and that the commitment to the cause of freedom is common to us all.

All of us in the West must be faithful to our conviction that peace in Europe can never be complete until everywhere in Europe, and that includes Germany, men can choose, in peace and freedom, how their countries shall be governed, and choose—without threat to any neighbor—reunification with their countrymen.

I preach no easy liberation and I make no empty promises; but my countrymen, since our country was founded, have believed strongly in the proposition that all men shall be free and all free men shall have this right of choice.

In short, the words of Thucydides are a warning, not a prediction. We have it in us, as eighteen years have shown, to build our defenses, to strengthen our economies, and to tighten our political bonds, both in good weather and in bad. We can move forward with the confidence that is born of success and the skill that is born of experience. And as we move, let us take heart from the certainty that we are united not only by danger and necessity, but by hope and purpose as well.

For we know now that freedom is more than the rejection of tyranny —that prosperity is more than an escape from want—that partnership is more than a sharing of power. These are, above all, great human adventures. They must have meaning and conviction and purpose—and because they do, in your country now and in mine, in all the nations of the Alliance, we are called to a great new mission.

It is not a mission of self-defense alone, for that is a means, not an end. It is not a mission of arbitrary power—for we reject the idea of one nation dominating another. The mission is to create a new social order, founded on liberty and justice, in which men are the masters of their fate, in which states are the servants of their citizens, and in which all men and women can share a better life for themselves and their children. That is the object of our common policy.

To realize this vision, we must seek a world of peace—a world in which peoples dwell together in mutual respect and work together in mutual regard—a world where peace is not a mere interlude between wars, but an incentive to the creative energies of humanity. We will not find such a peace today, or even tomorrow. The obstacles to hope are large and menacing. Yet the goal of a peaceful world—today and tomorrow—must shape our decisions and inspire our purposes.

So we are all idealists. We are all visionaries. Let it not be said of this Atlantic generation that we left ideals and visions to the past, nor purpose and determination to our adversaries. We have come too far, we have sacrificed too much, to disdain the future now. And we shall ever remember what Goethe told us—that the "highest wisdom, the best that mankind ever knew," was the realization that "he only earns his freedom and existence who daily conquers them anew."

Paulskirche Assembly Hall
Frankfurt, Federal Republic of Germany
June 25, 1963

The Proudest Boast

I am proud to come to this city as the guest of your distinguished Mayor, who has symbolized throughout the world the fighting spirit of West Berlin. And I am proud to visit the Federal Republic with your distinguished Chancellor, who for so many years has committed Germany to democracy and freedom and progress, and to come here in the company of my fellow American, General Clay, who has been in this city during its great moments of crisis and will come again if ever needed.

Two thousand years ago the proudest boast was "civis Romanus sum." Today, in the world of freedom, the proudest boast is "Ich bin ein Berliner."

I appreciate my interpreter translating my German!

There are many people in the world who really don't understand, or say they don't, what is the great issue between the Free World and the Communist world. Let them come to Berlin. There are some who say that communism is the wave of the future. Let them come to Berlin. And there are some who say in Europe and elsewhere we can work with the Communists. Let them come to Berlin. And there are even a few who say that it is true that communism is an evil system, but it permits us to make economic progress. "Lass' sie nach Berlin kommen." Let them come to Berlin!

Today, in the world of freedom, the proudest boast is "Ich bin ein Berliner."

Freedom has many difficulties and democracy is not perfect, but we have never had to put a wall up to keep our people in, to prevent them from leaving us. I want to say, on behalf of my countrymen, who live many miles away on the other side of the Atlantic, who are far distant from you, that they take the greatest pride that they have been able to share with you, even from a distance, the story of the last eighteen years. I know of no town, no city, that has been besieged for eighteen years that still lives with the vitality and the force and the hope and the determination of the city of West Berlin.

While the wall is the most obvious and vivid demonstration of the failures of the Communist system, for all the world to see, we take no satisfaction in it. For it is, as your Mayor has said, an offense not only against history but an offense against humanity, separating families, dividing husbands and wives and brothers and sisters, and dividing a people who wish to be joined together.

What is true of this city is true of Germany—real, lasting peace in Europe can never be assured as long as one German out of four is denied the elementary right of free men, and that is to make a free choice. In eighteen years of peace and good faith, this generation of Germans has earned the right to be free, including the right to unite their families and their nation in lasting peace, with goodwill to all people. You live in a defended island of freedom, but your life is part of the main. So let me ask you, as I close, to lift your eyes beyond the dangers of today to the hopes of tomorrow, beyond the freedom merely of this city of Berlin, or your country of Germany, to the advance of freedom everywhere, beyond the wall to the day of peace with justice, beyond yourselves and ourselves to all mankind.

Freedom is indivisible, and when one man is enslaved, all are not free. When all are free, then we can look forward to that day when this city will be joined as one, and this country, and this great Continent of Europe, in a peaceful and hopeful globe. When that day finally comes, as it will, the people of West Berlin can take sober satisfaction in the fact that they were in the front lines for almost two decades.

All free men, wherever they may live, are citizens of Berlin, and, therefore, as a free man, I take pride in the words "Ich bin ein Berliner."

City Hall
West Berlin, Federal Republic of Germany
June 26, 1963

CHAPTER 15

The Third World

No president before or after Kennedy has matched the depth of his empathy for the struggling peoples of Latin America, Africa, and Asia, or the strength of his vow to facilitate their political and economic independence. No subsequent president fought so hard so often for development assistance, or offered so much encouragement to the United Nations. No other president welcomed so many foreign students to the White House. Kennedy's concern for the Third World's plight began during his congressional travels and developed still further in a series of scholarly Senate speeches. While, as President, he failed to make clear a realistically successful position on Vietnam, he nevertheless remained remarkably clear in not accepting the repeated recommendation that he send combat divisions and bombers to make war on behalf of a government in the south that had increasingly lost the support of its own constituents.

The Concerned Young Congressman

MR. KENNEDY: Last year when this bill was before the House, I offered a motion to cut technical assistance. But, this fall, I had an opportunity to visit . . . Southeast Asia and I think we would be making a tremendous mistake to cut this money out of the bill.

Many of us feel that the United States has concentrated its attention too much on Western Europe. We will spend several billions for Western Europe in this bill. Yet, here is an area, Asia, where the Communists are attempting to seize control, where the money is to be spent among several hundred million people, and where the tide of events has been moving against us.

The Communists are now the second largest party in India. . . . The life expectancy of people in India is twenty-six or twenty-seven years, and they are increasing at the rate of five million a year—at a rate much faster than the available food supply.

The Communists have a chance of seizing all of Asia in the next five or six years. What weapons do we have that will stop them? The most effective is technical assistance. The amount of money involved here is not sufficient to prevent their being attracted to the Communists. But it gives them some hope, at least, that their problems can be solved without turning to the Communists. We are planning to spend a very large amount of money in this area for military assistance, which is of secondary importance compared to this program. To cut technical assistance when the Communists are concentrating their efforts in this vital area seems to me a costly and great mistake.

Debate, Technical Assistance Appropriations Bill
House of Representatives
Washington, D.C., June 28, 1952

The Challenge of Imperialism: Algeria

Mr. President, the most powerful single force in the world today is neither communism nor capitalism, neither the H-bomb nor the guided missile—it is man's eternal desire to be free and independent. The great enemy of that tremendous force of freedom is called, for want of a more precise term, imperialism—and today that means Soviet imperialism and, whether we like it or not, and though they are not to be equated, Western imperialism.

Thus the single most important test of American foreign policy today is how we meet the challenge of imperialism, what we do to further man's desire to be free. On this test more than any other, this nation shall be critically judged by the uncommitted millions in Asia and Africa, and anxiously watched by the still-hopeful lovers of freedom behind the Iron Curtain. If we fail to meet the challenge of either Soviet or Western imperialism, then no amount of foreign aid, no aggrandizement of armaments, no new pacts or doctrines or high-level conferences, can prevent further setbacks to our course and to our security. . . .

There are many cases of the clash between independence and imperialism in the Western world that demand our attention. But again, one, above all the rest, is critically outstanding today—Algeria. . . .

Mr. President, the war in Algeria confronts the United States with its most critical diplomatic impasse since the crisis in Indochina—and yet we have not only failed to meet the problem forthrightly and effectively, we have refused to even recognize that it is our problem at all. No issue poses a more difficult challenge to our foreign-policy makers—and no issue has been more woefully neglected. Though I am somewhat reluctant to undertake the kind of public review of this case which I had hoped—when I first began an intensive study of the problem fifteen months ago—that the State Department might provide to the Congress and people, the Senate is, in my opinion, entitled to receive the answers to the basic questions involved in this crisis.

I am even more reluctant to appear critical of our oldest and first ally, whose assistance in our own war for independence will never be forgotten and whose role in the course of world events has traditionally been one of constructive leadership and cooperation. I do not want our policy to be anti-French any more than I want it to be antinationalist—and I am convinced that growing numbers of the French people, whose patience and endurance we must all salute, are coming to realize that the views expressed in this speech are, in the long run, in their own best interest.

I say nothing today that has not been said by responsible leaders of French opinion and by a growing number of the French people themselves.

Algeria is no longer a problem for the French alone—nor will it ever be again. . . . We have deceived ourselves into believing that we have thus pleased both sides and displeased no one with this head-in-the-sands policy.

American and French diplomats, it must be noted at the outset, have joined in saying for several years that Algeria is not even a proper subject for American foreign policy debates or world consideration—that it is wholly a matter of internal French concern, a provincial uprising, a crisis which will respond satisfactorily to local anesthesia. But whatever the original truth of these clichés may have been, the blunt facts of the matter today are that the changing face of African nationalism, and the ever-widening by-products of the growing crisis, have made Algeria a matter of international, and consequently American, concern.

The war in Algeria, engaging more than 400,000 French soldiers, has stripped the continental forces of NATO to the bone. It has dimmed Western hopes for a European common market, and seriously compromised the liberalizing reforms of OEEC, by causing France to impose new import restrictions under a wartime economy. It has repeatedly been appealed for discussion to the United Nations, where our equivocal remarks and opposition to its consideration have damaged our leadership and prestige in that body. It has undermined our relations with Tunisia and Morocco, who naturally have a sense of common cause with the aims of Algerian leaders, and who have felt proper grievance that our economic and military base settlements have heretofore required clearance with a French government now taking economic reprisal for their assistance to Algerian nationalism.

It has diluted the effective strength of the Eisenhower doctrine for the Middle East, and our foreign aid and information programs. It has endangered the continuation of some of our most strategic airbases, and threatened our geographical advantages over the Communist orbit. It has affected our standing in the eyes of the free world, our leadership in the fight to keep that world free, our prestige, and our security; as well as our moral leadership in the fight against Soviet imperialism in the countries behind the Iron Curtain. It has furnished powerful ammunition to anti-Western propagandists throughout Asia and the Middle East—and will be the most troublesome item facing the October conference in Accra of the free nations of Africa, who hope, by easing the transition to independence of other African colonies, to seek common paths by which that great continent can remain aligned with the West.

Finally, the war in Algeria has steadily drained the manpower, the resources, and the spirit of one of our oldest and most important allies—a nation whose strength is absolutely vital to the free world, but who has been forced by this exhausting conflict to postpone new reforms and social services at home, to choke important new plans for economic and political development in French West Africa, the Sahara, and in a united Europe, to face a consolidated domestic Communist movement at a time when communism is in retreat elsewhere in Europe, to stifle free journalism and criticism, and to release the anger and frustrations of its people in perpetual governmental instability and in a precipitous attack on Suez.

No, Algeria is no longer a problem for the French alone—nor will it ever be again. And though their sensitivity to its consideration by this nation or the UN is understandable, a full and frank discussion of an issue so critical to our interests as well as theirs ought to be valued on both sides of an Atlantic alliance that has any real meaning and solidarity.

This is not to say that there is any value in the kind of discussion which has characterized earlier U.S. consideration of this and similar problems—tepid encouragement and moralizations to both sides, cautious neutrality on all real issues, and a restatement of our obvious dependence upon our European friends, our obvious dedication nevertheless to the principles of self-determination, and our obvious desire not to become involved. We have deceived ourselves into believing that we have thus pleased both sides and displeased no one with this head-in-the-sands policy—when, in truth, we have earned the suspicion of all.

It is time, therefore, that we came to grips with the real issues which confront us in Algeria—the issues which can no longer be avoided in the UN or in NATO—issues which become more and more difficult of solution, as a bitter war seemingly without end destroys, one by one, the ever fewer bridgeheads of reasonable settlement that remain. With each month the situation becomes more taut, the extremists gain more and more power on both the French and Algerian sides. . . .

Instead of recognizing France's refusal to bargain in good faith with nationalist leaders or to grant the reforms earlier promised, our ambassador to the UN, Mr. Lodge, in his statement this year as previously, and our former ambassador to Paris, Mr. Dillon, in his statement last year apparently representing the highest administration policy, both expressed firm faith in the French government's handling of the entire matter. . . .

This is not a record to view with pride as Independence Day approaches. No matter how complex the problems posed by the Algerian issue may be, the record of the United States in this case is, as elsewhere, a retreat from the principles of independence and anticolonialism, regardless of what diplomatic niceties, legal technicalities, or even strategic considerations are offered in its defense. . . .

Terrorism must be combated, not condoned, it is said; it is not right to "negotiate with murderers." Yet once again this is a problem which neither postponement nor attempted conquest can solve. The fever chart of every successful revolution—including, of course, the French—reveals a rising temperature of terrorism and counterterrorism; but this does not of itself invalidate the legitimate goals that fired the original revolution. Most political revolutions—including our own—have been buoyed by outside aid in men, weapons, and ideas. Instead of abandoning African nationalism to the anti-Western agitators and Soviet agents who hope to capture its leadership, the United States, a product of political revolution, must redouble its efforts to earn the respect and friendship of nationalist leaders. . . .

The most important reason we have sided with the French in Algeria and North Africa is our reluctance to antagonize a traditional friend and important ally in her hour of crisis. . . .

The United States and other Western allies poured money and material into Indochina in a hopeless attempt to save for the French a land that did not want to be saved, in a war in which the enemy was both everywhere and nowhere at the same time.

Yet, did we not learn in Indochina, where we delayed action as the result of similar warnings, that we might have served both the French and our own causes infinitely better, had we taken a more firm stand much earlier than we did? Did that tragic episode not teach us that, whether France likes it or not, admits it or not, or has our support or not, their oversea territories are sooner or later, one by one, inevitably going to break free and look with suspicion on the Western nations who impeded their steps to independence? In the words of Turgot: "Colonies are like fruit which cling to the tree only till they ripen."

I want to emphasize that I do not fail to appreciate the difficulties of our hard-pressed French allies. It staggers the imagination to realize that France is one nation that has been in a continuous state of war since 1939—against the Axis, then in Syria, in Indochina, in Morocco, in Tunisia, in Algeria. It has naturally not been easy for most Frenchmen to watch the successive withdrawals from Damascus, Hanoi, Saigon, Pondicherry, Tunis, and Rabat. With each departure a grand myth has been more and more deflated. But the problem is no longer to save a myth of French empire. The problem is to save the French nation, as well as free Africa. . . .

Not only the French, however, needed to be convinced of the ultimate futility and cost of an Algerian-type struggle. The United States and other Western allies poured money and material into Indochina in a hopeless attempt to save for the French a land that did not want to be saved, in a war in which the enemy was both everywhere and nowhere at the same time, as I pointed out to the Congress on several occasions. We accepted for years the predictions that victory was just around the corner, the promises that Indochina would soon be set free, the arguments that this was a question for the French alone.

And even after we had witnessed the tragic consequences of our vacillation, in terms of not only Communist gains but the decimation of French military strength and political effectiveness, we still listened to the same predictions, the same promises, and the same arguments in Tunisia and Morocco. The strong pro-Western bent in each of these countries today, despite beguiling offers from the Communist East, is a tribute to the leadership of such men as Prime Minister Bourguiba, whose years in French confinement never dimmed his appreciation of Western democratic values. . . .

The time has come when our government must recognize that this is no longer a French problem alone; and that the time has passed, where a series of piecemeal adjustments, or even a last attempt to incorporate Algeria fully within France, can succeed. The time has come for the United States to face the harsh realities of the situation and to fulfill its responsibilities as leader of the free world—in the UN, in NATO, in the administration of our aid programs and in the exercise of our diplomacy—in shaping a course toward political independence for Algeria.

It should not be the purpose of our government to impose a solution on either side, but to make a contribution toward breaking the vicious circle in which the Algerian controversy whirls. . . .

The United States must be prepared to lend all efforts to such a settlement, and to assist in the economic problems which will flow from it. This is not a burden which we lightly or gladly assume. But our efforts in no other endeavor are more important in terms of once again seizing the initiative in foreign affairs, demonstrating our adherence to the principles of national independence, and winning the respect of those long suspicious of our negative and vacillating record on colonial issues.

It is particularly important, inasmuch as Hungary will be a primary issue at the United Nations meeting this fall, that the United States clear the air and take a clear position on this issue, on which we have been vulnerable in the past. And we must make it abundantly clear to the French as well as the North Africans that we seek no economic advantages for ourselves in that area, no opportunities to replace French economic ties or exploit African resources.

If we are to secure the friendship of the Arab, the African, and the Asian—and we must, despite what Mr. Dulles says about our not being in a popularity contest—we cannot hope to accomplish it solely by means of billion-dollar foreign-aid programs. We cannot win their hearts by making them dependent upon our handouts. Nor can we keep them free by selling them free enterprise, by describing the perils of communism or the prosperity of the United States, or limiting our dealings to military pacts. No, the strength of our appeal to these key populations—and it is rightfully our appeal, and not that of the Communists—lies in our traditional and deeply felt philosophy of freedom and independence for all peoples everywhere.

Perhaps it is already too late for the United States to save the West from total catastrophe in Algeria. Perhaps it is too late to abandon our negative policies on these issues, to repudiate the decades of anti-Western suspicion, to press firmly but boldly for a new generation of friendship among equal and independent states. But we dare not fail to make the effort.

"Men's hearts wait upon us," said Woodrow Wilson in 1913. "Men's lives hang in the balance; men's hopes call upon us to say what we will do. Who shall live up to the great trust? Who dares fail to try?"

United States Senate
Washington, D.C., July 2, 1957

The New Nationalism: India

Mr. President, at no time since the war has American and Western policy been so gripped by a sense of paralysis, by a waning of hope, by the loss of its compass points. More and more the thoughts of those abroad—and of Americans themselves—have been riveted on Russia's capabilities, on Russia's educational system and educational achievements, on Russia's new diplomatic and economic initiatives, on Russia's seemingly greater flexibility and power of maneuver. Less and less have we and our allies been concerned with our own capacities, our own positive objectives. . . . The uneasiness which has stirred even our closest friends is directed not against a President or secretary of state or party. In very large measure it attaches to the whole tone and thrust of our national effort in foreign policy. Indeed, we have come increasingly to doubt ourselves, to question the impact of a policy whose substance seems so very largely military, to scrutinize actions whose origins very often were in reflex to Soviet moves and transitory crises rather than rooted in a settled policy of our own.

Our sense of drift, our gnawing dissatisfaction, our seemingly hopeless predicament in reaching but the fringes of a great crisis is nowhere more evident than in our search for policies adopted effectively and concretely to the new and generally uncommitted nations which run from Casablanca to the Celebes. Over the past few years we have begun to appreciate that the tested formulas we have applied to events in Western Europe and NATO have only limited application to the broad medley of changes occurring in the uncommitted world. Though we have learned that we must come to terms with the new nationalisms, we have tended to interpret their meanings too much against the backdrop of our own historic experience on this continent and in Europe.

We have certainly begun to learn that a purely military response to the tides in the Middle East and Asia is an illusory breakwater. For military pacts and arms shipments, though sometimes a necessary instrument of national policy, are themselves new divisive forces in those areas shot through with national and regional rivalries and often lacking historic boundaries and allegiances. . . .

No thoughtful citizen can fail to see our stake in the survival of free government in India. India stands as the only effective competitor to China for the faith and following of the millions of uncommitted and restless peoples. Should India fall prey to internal disorder or disillusionment among either its masses or [its] leaders and become absorbed in the Communist system, the free world would suffer an incalculable blow. . . .

Let us not be confused by talk of Indian neutrality. Let us remember that our nation also during the period of its formative growth adopted a policy of noninvolvement in the great international controversies of the nineteenth century. Nothing serves the ultimate interests of all of the West better than the opportunity for the emergent uncommitted nations of the world to absorb the primary energies now in programs of real economic improvement.

This is the only basis on which Asian and African nations can find the political balance and social stability which provide the true defense against Communist penetration. Our friendships should not be equated with military alliances or "voting the Western ticket." To do so only drives these countries closer to totalitarianism or polarizes the world in such a way as to increase rather than diminish the chances for local war. . . .

India, for better or worse, is a world power with a world audience. Its democratic future is delicately and dangerously poised; it would be catastrophic if its leadership were now humiliated in its quest for Western assistance when its cause is good.

There is no visible political glory for either party in coming to the aid of India, particularly at a time of high taxes and pressing defense needs. The task of selling such a program to the American people is far more difficult than that of a decade ago, for we were more familiar with the people and problems of Europe, our ties were closer, their economies were more directly aligned with our own and held more certain promise of success. But the need—and the danger—are as great now as then. India today represents as great a hope, as commanding a challenge as Western Europe did in 1947—and our people are still, I am confident, equal to the effort.

I realize that it is difficult to give resonance to such words and proposals in the mood which has governed the approach to foreign aid and economic policy in both parties during the past sessions of Congress. But this mood has, in part, been induced by the persistent counsels of caution, by the lack of vision and purposefulness with which we have approached the problems of the underdeveloped world. If we are to break the aimless drifts and deadlocks in policy, if we are to regain the initiative in world affairs, if we are to arouse the decent emotions of Americans, it is time again that we seek projects with the power of stirring and rallying our hopes and energies. Once again our national interest and creative magnanimity can merge in the service of freedom.

United States Senate
Washington, D.C., March 25, 1958

The Fight for Foreign Aid

In recent years, the scale of our effort in foreign economic policy has been based upon what the administration considered to be the requirements of the domestic budgetary and political situation.

It is time now for that effort to be based upon the requirements of the international economic situation—and our own national security. Let us see exactly what is needed, when it is needed, how much of it must come from this country, and how much it will cost.

And then let us enact the program that will do the job. To do less than is needed is just as wasteful as to do more than is needed. To put it off is just as dangerous as refusing to do it at all. . . .

Congress should, of course, base its aid programs on sound criteria and productive investment. But let us remember economies need time to mature. Our own nation, in the days of its youth, sold railroad bonds to the British and other Europeans—and these were long forty- or fifty-year debentures. With the growth of our productive capacity, we gradually became a creditor nation with the ability to repay these foreign investments. . . .

I am confident that this nation can recover the initiative, that we can give to a doubting world the realization that we, and not Russia and China, can help them achieve stability and growth. We cannot be content merely to oppose what the Kremlin may propose, nor can we pretend that the East-West conflict is the only basis for our policy.

Above all, we must not resolve these difficult issues of foreign aid by perpetual postponement and compromise. There are times when it is far better to do the right thing as a result of debate and sacrifice than the wrong thing as a testimonial to national unity.

In short, it is our job to prove that we can devote as much energy, intelligence, idealism, and sacrifice to the survival and triumph of the open society as the Russian despots can extort by compulsion in defense of their closed system of tyranny. We can give a convincing demonstration that we have not a propaganda or crisis interest but an enduring long-term interest in the productive economic growth of the less developed nations. We can finally make it clear to ourselves that international economic development is not, somehow, a nagging responsibility, to be faced each year in the context of giveaways and taxes —but a vast international effort, an enterprise of positive association, which lies close to the heart of our relations with the whole free world and which requires active American leadership.

There are times when it is far better to do the right thing as a result of debate and sacrifice than the wrong thing as a testimonial to national unity.

As a nation, we think not of war but of peace; not of crusades of conflict but of covenants of cooperation; not of the pageantry of imperialism but of the pride of new states freshly risen to independence. We like to look, with Mr. Justice Holmes, beyond the vision of battling races and an impoverished earth to catch a dreaming glimpse of peace. In the words of Edmund Burke, we sit on a "conspicuous stage," and the whole world marks our demeanor. In this year and in this Congress we have an opportunity to be worthy of that role.

United States Senate
Washington, D.C., February 19, 1959

The Frontiers of Freedom

. . . No amount of arms and armies can help stabilize those governments which are unable or unwilling to achieve social and economic reform and development. Military pacts cannot help nations whose social injustice and economic chaos invite insurgency and penetration and subversion. The most skillful counterguerrilla efforts cannot succeed where the local population is too caught up in its own misery to be concerned about the advance of communism.

But for those who share this view, we stand ready now, as we have in the past, to provide generously of our skills, and our capital, and our food to assist the peoples of the less developed nations to reach their goals in freedom—to help them before they are engulfed in crisis.

This is also our great opportunity in 1961. If we grasp it, then subversion to prevent its success is exposed as an unjustifiable attempt to keep these nations from being either free or equal. But if we do not pursue it, and if they do not pursue it, the bankruptcy of unstable governments . . . and of unfilled hopes will surely lead to a series of totalitarian receiverships. . . .

I do not see how anyone who is concerned—as we all are—about the growing threats to freedom around the globe—and who is asking what more we can do as a people—can weaken or oppose the single most important program available for building the frontiers of freedom. . . .

The main burden of local defense against local attack, subversion, insurrection, or guerrilla warfare must of necessity rest with local forces. Where these forces have the necessary will and capacity to cope with such threats, our intervention is rarely necessary or helpful. Where the will is present and only capacity is lacking, our Military Assistance Program can be of help.

But this program, like economic assistance, needs a new emphasis. It cannot be extended without regard to the social, political, and military reforms essential to internal respect and stability. The equipment and training provided must be tailored to legitimate local needs and to our own foreign and military policies, not to our supply of military stocks or a local leader's desire for military display.

Special Address to Congress
The Capitol, Washington, D.C.
May 25, 1961

The Uncommitted and Underdeveloped

It is always encouraging when responsible world leaders join together to consider the problems that beset mankind. We recognize that most of the countries at Belgrade do not consider themselves committed on certain of the issues which confront us today, but we do know that they are committed to the United Nations Charter. The people of the United States share this commitment.

We know that those gathering in Belgrade are committed to finding a way to halt the waste of the earth's resources in the building of the implements of death and destruction, and the people of the United States have constantly pledged themselves to this goal.

We believe that the peoples represented at this conference are committed to a world society in which men have the right and the freedom to determine their own destiny, a world in which one people is not enslaved by the other, in which the powerful do not devour the weak. The American people share that commitment, and we have pledged the influence of this nation to the abolition of exploitation in all of its forms.

The peoples represented at Belgrade are committed to achieving a world at peace in which nations have the freedom to choose their own political and economic systems and to live their own way of life, and since our earliest beginnings this nation has shared that commitment.

All this and much more the leaders at Belgrade have in common. This and much more the people of the United States have in common with them. So for myself, and I'm sure for the American people, I express the hope that their deliberations there will bring us all nearer these goals.

Message to Belgrade Conference on Nonaligned States
Washington, D.C., August 30, 1961

Today, many Americans tend to think of developing underdeveloped countries in terms only of faraway nations. But in 1863, even measured by 1963 dollars, our own per capita income—and this should be a source of encouragement to many who are laboring with the problem of underdevelopment in far-off countries—our own per capita income was less than one dollar a day, approximately the same as Chile's. Nearly sixty percent of our labor force was engaged in agriculture, the same percentage as is today engaged in the Philippines. An estimated twenty percent of our population was illiterate, the same percentage of the population of Ceylon. Only one fifth of our 34 million people lived in towns or cities of over 5,000 in population, as is roughly true now of Turkey. In 1863, this nation had fewer railroad tracks laid than India has today, and its children had a shorter life expectancy than a child born this year in Thailand or Zanzibar.

American Bankers Association
Symposium on Economic Growth
Washington, D.C., February 25, 1963

The Future Prime Ministers

I want to welcome all of you to the White House and also to the United States. We appreciate very much your coming to this country and I am sure that you will teach us a good deal more than you can possibly learn here. . . . I am not sure it is possible to transfer the experience of any country to another country, particularly a country with inadequate resources and with inadequate skilled manpower. . . .

But . . . whatever differences there may be, what we are interested in, what I am most interested in, is the commitment to individual freedom which our country and your country permit, and the commitment to national independence. . . . I believe it is worthwhile for us to have the most intimate exchange of ideas and thoughts and hopes for the future.

So, we are very glad to have you here. I am confident I am talking to a number of future prime ministers, presidents, and others, and I just want you to know that, when you visit in that role a decade hence and the Kennedys are long gone, I am sure you will be equally welcome.

Remarks to foreign students visiting the White House
Washington, D.C., April 10, 1963

The Family of Man

I want to speak tonight very briefly . . . about the Family of Man beyond the United States. Just as the Family of Man is not limited to a single race or religion, neither can it be limited to a single city or country. The Family of Man is more than three billion strong. It lives in more than one hundred nations. Most of its members are not white. Most of them are not Christians. Most of them know nothing about free enterprise or due process of law or the Australian ballot.

If our society is to promote the Family of Man, let us realize the magnitude of our task. This is a sobering assignment. For the Family of Man in the world of today is not faring very well.

The members of a family should be at peace with one another, but they are not. And the hostilities are not confined to the great powers of the East and the West. On the contrary, the United States and the Soviet Union, each fully aware of [its] mutually destructive powers and [its] worldwide responsibilities and obligations, have on occasion sought to introduce a greater note of caution in their approach to areas of conflict.

Yet lasting peace between East and West would not bring peace to the Family of Man. Within the last month, the last four weeks, the world has witnessed active or threatened hostilities in a dozen or more disputes independent of the struggle between communism and the free world—disputes between Africans and Europeans in Angola, between North African neighbors in the Maghreb, between two Arab states over Yemen, between India and Pakistan, between Indonesia and Malaysia, Cambodia and Vietnam, Ethiopia and Somalia, and a long list of others.

In each of these cases of conflict, neither party can afford to divert to these needless hostilities the precious resources that their people require. In almost every case, the parties to these disputes have more in common ethnically and ideologically than do the Soviet Union and the United States, yet they often seem less able and less willing to get together and negotiate. In almost every case, their continuing conflict invites outside intervention and threatens worldwide escalation—yet the major powers are hard put to limit events in these areas.

As I said recently at the United Nations, even little wars are dangerous in this nuclear world. The long labor of peace is an undertaking for every nation, large and small, for every member of the Family of Man. In this effort none of us can remain unaligned. To this goal none can be uncommitted. If the Family of Man cannot achieve greater unity and harmony, the very planet which serves as its home may find its future in peril.

But there are other troubles besetting the human family. Many of its members live in poverty and misery and despair. More than one out of three, according to the FAO [Food and Agriculture Organization], suffers from malnutrition or undernutrition or both—while more than one in ten live "below the breadline." Two out of every five adults on this planet are, according to UNESCO, illiterate. One out of eight suffers from trachoma or lives in an area where malaria is still a clear and present danger. Ten million—nearly as many men, women, and children as inhabit this city and Los Angeles combined—still suffer from leprosy; and countless others suffer from yaws or tuberculosis or intestinal parasites.

If our society is to promote the Family of Man, let us realize the magnitude of our task. . . . For the Family of Man in the world of today is not faring very well.

For the blessings of life have not been distributed evenly to the Family of Man. Life expectancy in this most fortunate of nations has reached the biblical three score years and ten; but in the less developed nations of Africa, Asia, and Latin America, the overwhelming majority of infants cannot expect to live even two score years and five. In those vast continents, more than half of the children of primary school age are not in school. More than half the families live in substandard dwellings. More than half the people live on less than a thousand dollars a year. Two out of every three adults are illiterate.

The Family of Man can survive differences of race and religion. Contrary to the assertions of Mr. Khrushchev, it can accept differences of ideology, politics, and economics. But it cannot survive, in the form in which we know it, a nuclear war—and neither can it long endure the growing gulf between the rich and the poor.

The rich must help the poor. The industrialized nations must help the developing nations. And the United States, along with its allies, must do better—not worse—by its foreign-aid program, which is now being subjected to such intense debate in the Senate of the United States.

Too often we advance the need of foreign aid only in terms of our economic self-interest. To be sure, foreign aid is in our economic self-interest. It provides more than a half a million jobs for workers in every state. It finances a rising share of our exports and builds new and growing export markets. It generates the purchase of military and civilian equipment by other governments in this country. It makes possible the stationing of three and a half million troops along the Communist periphery at a price one tenth the cost of maintaining a comparable number of American soldiers. And it helps to stave off the kind of chaos or Communist takeover or Communist attack that would surely demand our critical and costly attention. The Korean conflict alone, forgetting for a moment the thousands of Americans who lost their lives, cost four times as much as our total worldwide aid budget for the current year. . . .

This is not a partisan matter. For seventeen years, through three administrations, this program has been supported by presidents and leaders of both parties. It is being supported today in the Congress by those in leadership on both sides of the aisle who recognize the urgency of this program in the achievement of peace and freedom. Yet there are still those who are unable or unwilling to accept these simple facts—who find it politically convenient to denounce foreign aid on the one hand, and in the same sentence to denounce the Communist menace. I do not say that there have been no mistakes in aid administration. I do not say it has purchased for us lasting popularity or servile satellites. I do say it is one essential instrument in the creation of a better, more peaceful world. I do say that it has substituted strength for weakness all over the globe, encouraging nations struggling to be free to stand on their own two feet. And I do not say that, merely because others may not bear their share of the burden, that is any excuse for the United States not to meet its responsibility.

To those who say foreign aid has been a failure, how can we measure success—by the economic viability of fourteen nations in Western Europe, Japan, Spain, Lebanon, where our economic aid, after having completed its task, has ended; by the refusal of a single one of the more than fifty new members of the United Nations to go the Communist route; by the reduction of malaria in India, for example, from 75 million cases to 2,000; by the 18,000 classrooms and 4 million textbooks bringing learning to Latin America under the infant Alliance for Progress?

Nearly two years ago my wife and I visited Bogotá, Colombia, where a vast new Alliance for Progress housing project was just getting under way. Earlier this year I received a letter from the first resident of this twelve hundred new home development. "Now," he wrote, "we have dignity and liberty."

Dignity and liberty—these words are the foundation, as they have been since '47, of the mutual security program. . . .

I think we can meet those obligations. I think we can afford to fulfill these commitments around the world when ninety percent of them are used to purchase goods and services here in the United States, including, for example, one third of this nation's total fertilizer exports, one fourth of our iron and steel exports around the world, one third of our locomotive exports. A cut of $1 billion in our total foreign aid program may save $100 million in our balance of payments—but it costs us $900 million in exports.

I think the American people are willing to shoulder this burden. Contrary to repeated warnings . . . I know of no single officeholder who was ever defeated because he supported this program. The burden is less today than ever before. . . .

Many members of Congress today complain that four percent of our federal budget is too much to devote to foreign aid—yet in 1951 that program amounted to nearly twenty percent of our budget—twenty percent in 1951, and four percent today. They refuse today to vote more than $4 billion to this effort—yet in 1951, when this country was not nearly as well off, the Congress voted $8 billion to the same cause. They are fearful today of the effects of sending to other people seven tenths of one percent of our gross national product—but in 1951 we devoted nearly four times that proportion to this purpose. . . .

This Congress has already reduced this year's aid budget $600 million below the amount recommended by the Clay committee. Is this nation stating it cannot afford to spend an additional $600 million to help the developing nations of the world become strong and free and independent—an amount less than this country's annual outlay for lipstick, face cream, and chewing gum? Are we saying that we cannot help nineteen needy neighbors in Latin America and do as much for the nineteen as the Communist bloc is doing for the island of Cuba alone?

Some say that they are tiring of this task or tired of world problems and their complexities, or tired of hearing those who receive our aid disagree with us. But are we tired of living in a free world? Do we expect that world overnight to be like the United States? Are we going to stop now merely because we have not produced complete success?

I do not believe our adversaries are tired and I cannot believe that the United States of America in 1963 is fatigued.

Surely the Americans of the 1960s can do half as well as the Americans of the 1950s. Surely we are not going to throw away our hopes and means for peaceful progress in an outburst of irritation and frustration. I do not want it said of us what T. S. Eliot said of others some years ago: "These were a decent people. Their only monument: the asphalt road and a thousand lost golf balls."

I think we can do better than that. . . .

It is essential, in short, that the word go forth from the United States to all who are concerned about the future of the Family of Man; that we are not weary in well-doing. And we shall, I am confident, if we maintain the pace, in due season reap the kind of world we deserve and deserve the kind of world we will have.

Remarks upon receiving Annual Family of Man Award
New York Protestant Council
New York, New York, November 8, 1963

The Alliance for Progress

One hundred and thirty-nine years ago this week the United States, stirred by the heroic struggle of its fellow Americans, urged the independence and recognition of the new Latin American republics. It was then, at the dawn of freedom throughout this hemisphere, that Bolívar spoke of his desire to see the Americas fashioned into the greatest region in the world, "greatest," he said, "not so much by virtue of her area and her wealth, as by her freedom and her glory."

Never in the long history of our hemisphere has this dream been nearer to fulfillment, and never has it been in greater danger.

The genius of our scientists has given us the tools to bring abundance to our land, strength to our industry, and knowledge to our people. For the first time we have the capacity to strike off the remaining bonds of poverty and ignorance—to free our people for the spiritual and intellectual fulfillment which has always been the goal of our civilization.

Yet at this very moment of maximum opportunity, we confront the same forces which have imperiled America throughout its history. . . .

We meet together as firm and ancient friends, united by history and experience and by our determination to advance the values of American civilization. For this New World of ours is not a mere accident of geography. Our continents are bound together by a common history, the endless exploration of new frontiers. Our nations are the product of a common struggle, the revolt from colonial rule. And our people share a common heritage, the quest for the dignity and the freedom of man.

The revolutions which gave us birth ignited, in the words of Thomas Paine, "a spark never to be extinguished." And across vast, turbulent continents these American ideals still stir man's struggle for national independence and individual freedom. But as we welcome the spread of the American revolution to other lands, we must also remember that our own struggle—the revolution which began in Philadelphia in 1776, and in Caracas in 1811—is not yet finished. Our hemisphere's mission is not yet completed. For our unfulfilled task is to demonstrate to the entire world that man's unsatisfied aspiration for economic progress and social justice can best be achieved by free men working within a framework of democratic institutions. If we can do this in our own hemisphere, and for our own people, we may yet realize the prophecy of the great Mexican patriot, Benito Juárez, that "democracy is the destiny of future humanity."

As a citizen of the United States let me be the first to admit that we North Americans have not always grasped the significance of this common mission, just as it is also true that many in your own countries have not fully understood the urgency of the need to lift people from poverty and ignorance and despair. But we must turn from these mistakes—from the failures and the misunderstandings of the past to a future full of peril but bright with hope.

Throughout Latin America, a continent rich in resources and in the spiritual and cultural achievements of its people, millions of men and women suffer the daily degradations of poverty and hunger. They lack decent shelter or protection from disease. Their children are deprived of the education or the jobs which are the gateway to a better life. Each day the problems grow more urgent. Population growth is outpacing economic growth—low living standards are further endangered—and discontent, the discontent of a people who know that abundance and the tools of progress are at last within their reach, is growing. In the words of José Figueres, "once dormant peoples are struggling upward toward the sun, toward a better life."

If we are to meet a problem so staggering in its dimensions, our approach must itself be equally bold—an approach consistent with the majestic concept of Operation Pan America. Therefore I have called on all people of the hemisphere to join in a new Alliance for Progress—*Alianza para el Progreso*—a vast cooperative effort, unparalleled in magnitude and nobility of purpose, to satisfy the basic needs of the American people for homes, work and land, health and schools—*techo, trabajo y tierra, salud y escuela.*

First, I propose that the American republics begin on a vast new Ten Year Plan for the Americas, a plan to transform the 1960s into a historic decade of democratic progress.

These ten years will be the years of maximum progress, maximum effort, the years when the greatest obstacles must be overcome, the years when the need for assistance will be the greatest.

If we are successful, if our effort is bold enough and determined enough, then the close of this decade will mark the beginning of a new era in the American experience. The living standards of every American family will be on the rise, basic education will be available to all, hunger will be a forgotten experience, the need for massive outside help will have passed, most nations will have entered a period of self-sustaining growth, and though there will be still much to do, every American republic will be the master of its own revolution and its own hope and progress.

Let me stress that only the most determined efforts of the American nations themselves can bring success to this effort. They, and they alone, can mobilize their resources, enlist the energies of their people, and modify their social patterns so that all, and not just a privileged few, share in the fruits of growth. If this effort is made, then outside assistance will give vital impetus to progress; without it, no amount of help will advance the welfare of the people.

Thus if the countries of Latin America are ready to do their part, and I am sure they are, then I believe the United States, for its part, should help provide resources of a scope and magnitude sufficient to make this bold development plan a success—just as we helped to provide, against equal odds nearly, the resources adequate to help rebuild the economies of Western Europe. For only an effort of towering dimensions can insure fulfillment of our plan for a decade of progress.

Therefore I have called on all people of the hemisphere to join in a new Alliance for Progress*—Alianza para el Progreso *—a vast cooperative effort, unparalleled in magnitude and nobility of purpose.

Secondly, I will shortly request a ministerial meeting of the Inter-American Economic and Social Council, a meeting at which we can begin the massive planning effort which will be at the heart of the Alliance for Progress.

For if our Alliance is to succeed, each Latin nation must formulate long-range plans for its own development, plans which establish targets and priorities, insure monetary stability, establish the machinery for vital social change, stimulate private activity and initiative, and provide for a maximum national effort. These plans will be the foundation of our development effort, and the basis for the allocation of outside resources.

A greatly strengthened IA-ECOSOC, working with the Economic Commission for Latin America and the Inter-American Development Bank, can assemble the leading economists and experts of the hemisphere to help each country develop its own development plan—and provide a continuing review of economic progress in this hemisphere.

Third, I have this evening signed a request to the Congress for $500 million as a first step in fulfilling the Act of Bogotá. This is the first large-scale inter-American effort, instituted by my predecessor President Eisenhower, to attack the social barriers which block economic progress. The money will be used to combat illiteracy, improve the productivity and use of their land, wipe out disease, attack archaic tax and land tenure structures, provide educational opportunities, and offer a broad range of projects designed to make the benefits of increasing abundance available to all. We will begin to commit these funds as soon as they are appropriated.

Fourth, we must support all economic integration which is a genuine step toward larger markets and greater competitive opportunity. The fragmentation of Latin American economies is a serious barrier to industrial growth. Projects such as the Central American common market and free trade areas in South America can help to remove these obstacles.

Fifth, the United States is ready to cooperate in serious, case-by-case examinations of commodity market problems. Frequent violent change in commodity prices seriously injure the economies of many Latin American countries, draining their resources and stultifying their growth. Together we must find practical methods of bringing an end to this pattern.

Sixth, we will immediately step up our Food for Peace emergency program, help establish food reserves in areas of recurrent drought, help provide school lunches for children, and offer feed grains for use in rural development. For hungry men and women cannot wait for economic discussions or diplomatic meetings—their need is urgent and their hunger rests heavily on the conscience of their fellow men.

Seventh, all the people of the hemisphere must be allowed to share in the expanding wonders of science—wonders which have captured man's imagination, challenged the powers of his mind, and given him the tools for rapid progress. I invite Latin American scientists to work with us in new projects in fields such as medicine and agriculture, physics and astronomy, and desalinization, to help plan for regional research laboratories in these and other fields, and to strengthen cooperation between American universities and laboratories.

We also intend to expand our science-teacher training programs to include Latin American instructors, to assist in establishing such programs in other American countries, and translate and make available revolutionary new teaching materials in physics, chemistry, biology, and mathematics, so that the young of all nations may contribute their skills to the advance of science.

Eighth, we must rapidly expand the training of those needed to man the economies of rapidly developing countries. This means expanded technical training programs, for which the Peace Corps, for example, will be available when needed. It also means assistance to Latin American universities, graduate schools, and research institutes.

We welcome proposals in Central America for intimate cooperation in higher education—cooperation which can achieve a regional effort of increased effectiveness and excellence. We are ready to help fill the gap in trained manpower, realizing that our ultimate goal must be a basic education for all who wish to learn.

Ninth, we reaffirm our pledge to come to the defense of any American nation whose independence is endangered. As its confidence in the collective security system of the OAS spreads, it will be possible to devote to constructive use a major share of those resources now spent on the instruments of war. Even now, as the government of Chile has said, the time has come to take the first steps toward sensible limitations of arms. And the new generation of military leaders has shown an increasing awareness that armies cannot only defend their countries—they can, as we have learned through our own Corps of Engineers, they can help to build them.

Tenth, we invite our friends in Latin America to contribute to the enrichment of life and culture in the United States. We need teachers of your literature and history and tradition, opportunities for our young people to study in your universities, access to your music, your art, and the thought of your great philosophers. For we know we have much to learn.

In this way you can help bring a fuller spiritual and intellectual life to the people of the United States—and contribute to understanding and mutual respect among the nations of the hemisphere.

With steps such as these, we propose to complete the revolution of the Americas, to build a hemisphere where all men can hope for a suitable standard of living, and all can live out their lives in dignity and in freedom.

To achieve this goal political freedom must accompany material progress. Our Alliance for Progress is an alliance of free governments, and it must work to eliminate tyranny from a hemisphere in which it has no rightful place. Therefore let us express our special friendship to the people of Cuba and the Dominican Republic—and the hope they will soon rejoin the society of free men, uniting with us in common effort.

This political freedom must be accompanied by social change. For unless necessary social reforms, including land and tax reform, are freely made—unless we broaden the opportunity for all of our people—unless the great mass of Americans share in increasing prosperity—then our alliance, our revolution, our dream, and our freedom will fail. But we call for social change by free men—change in the spirit of Washington and Jefferson, of Bolívar and San Martín and Martí—not change which seeks to impose on men tyrannies which we cast out a century and a half ago. Our motto is what it has always been—progress yes, tyranny no—*progreso sí, tiranía no!*

But our greatest challenge comes from within—the task of creating an American civilization where spiritual and cultural values are strengthened by an ever-broadening base of material advance—where, within the rich diversity of its own traditions, each nation is free to follow its own path toward progress.

The completion of our task will, of course, require the efforts of all governments of our hemisphere. But the efforts of governments alone will never be enough. In the end, the people must choose and the people must help themselves.

And so I say to the men and women of the Americas—to the *campesino* in the fields, to the *obrero* in the cities, to the *estudiante* in the schools—prepare your mind and heart for the task ahead—call forth your strength and let each devote his energies to the betterment of all, so that your children and our children in this hemisphere can find an ever richer and a freer life.

Let us once again transform the American continent into a vast crucible of revolutionary ideas and efforts—a tribute to the power of the creative energies of free men and women—an example to all the world that liberty and progress walk hand in hand. Let us once again awaken our American revolution until it guides the struggle of people everywhere—not with an imperialism of force or fear, but with the rule of courage and freedom and hope for the future of man.

Address to Latin American Diplomatic Corps
White House, Washington, D.C.
March 13, 1961

In 1934, one of the greatest of my predecessors, President Franklin Roosevelt, was the first President of the United States to visit this country. He came in pursuit of a new policy—the policy of the Good Neighbor. This policy based on the ideas of Bolívar and San Martín and Santander recognized the common interests of the American states. denied that any nation in this hemisphere had the right to impose its will on any other nation; and called for a great cooperative effort to strengthen the spirit of human liberty here in the Americas.

I am here today—the second American President to visit Colombia—in that same spirit. For our generation also has a new policy—*la Alianza para el Progreso.* Today again, that policy calls for a joint effort to protect and extend the values of our civilization—going beyond the Good Neighbor policy to a great unified attack on the problems of our age. Today again, we deny the right of any state to impose its will upon any other. And today again, these new policies are based upon the vision and the imagination of the great statesmen of Latin America. . . .

Bolívar, in a letter written when he was in exile, and the cause of liberty seemed dim, wrote: "The veil has been torn asunder. We have already seen the light and it is not our desire to be thrust back into the darkness." In our time the veil again has been torn asunder. The millions of our people who have lived in hopeless poverty—patiently suffering hunger, social injustice, and ignorance—have now glimpsed the hope of a better and more abundant life for themselves and their children. And they do not intend to be thrust back into darkness.

La Alianza para el Progreso is designed to transform this hope into a reality. It calls for a vast and immediate effort on the part of all the Americas to satisfy the basic needs of our people for work and land, and homes and schools. It expects within the next ten years—the Decade of Development—to be well on the way toward satisfying these basic needs.

Much has already been done since *la Alianza para el Progreso* was announced on March 13. And today at Techo I saw some of the results of this effort.

There President Lleras and I—in the presence of the families of hundreds of workers—dedicated a housing project in which more than 80,000 people will, for the first time, know what it will be like to live in a home in which they would want to raise their children. We also dedicated one of eighteen schools—in which 30,000 children, the most valuable asset of this hemisphere—will be given their opportunity to study and to learn, and to build their lives. . . .

Thus *la Alianza para el Progreso* is a program which is revolutionary in its dimensions. It calls for staggering efforts by us all and unprecedented changes by us all. It raises far-reaching aspirations and demands difficult sacrifices. And although we have already done much in a short time, we must do much more and act much more swiftly in the months to come. For on the success of the Alliance—on our success in this hemisphere—depends the future of that human dignity and national independence for which our forebears in every country of the hemisphere struggled.

After the American wars of independence, the President of Colombia, Santander, said: "Arms have given us independence; laws will give us freedom." These prophetic words indicate the history of our hemisphere. For our real progress has not come about through violence or tyranny, but under the guidance of democratic leaders who realized the great capacity of free society for peaceful change—men such as Franklin Roosevelt in my own country and your distinguished President in your country.

It is this knowledge and experience which is the great contribution of our nations to the other nations of the world. There are those who tell us that the only road to economic progress is by violent Communist revolution, followed by the complete subjection of man to the will of the state.

They come with banners proclaiming that they have new doctrines; that history is on their side. But, in reality, they bring a doctrine which is as old as the pharaohs of Egypt, and like the pharaohs of Egypt, doomed by history.

They promise free elections, and free speech, and freedom of religion. But once power is achieved, elections are eliminated, speech is stifled, and the worship of God is prohibited.

They pledge economic progress and increased human welfare. But they have been unable to fulfill these pledges and their failure is etched in the dramatic contrast between a free and powerful and prosperous Western Europe and the grim, drab poverty of Communist Eastern Europe, or the hunger of China, or the wall which separates West Berlin from East Berlin. The fact is that the wall and the rifle squads of the last twelve months have shown us again—if we did not need to be shown—that when such doctrines have had to face the united will of free men, they have been defeated.

We are a young and strong people. Our doctrines—the doctrines lit by the leaders of your country and mine—now burn brightly in Africa and Asia and wherever men struggle to be free. And here in our own hemisphere we have successfully resisted efforts to impose the despotisms of the Old World on the nations of the New.

Today we face the greatest challenge to the vitality of our American revolution. Millions of our people—scattered across a vast and rich continent—endure lives of misery. We must prove to them that free institutions can best answer their implacable demand for social justice, for food, for material welfare, and above all, for a new hope—for themselves and for their children. And in so proving the blessings of freedom in Latin America, we will be teaching the same lesson to a watchful and impatient world.

We in the United States have made many mistakes in our relations with Latin America. We have not always understood the magnitude of your problems, or accepted our share of responsibility for the welfare of the hemisphere. But we are committed in the United States—our will and our energy—to an untiring pursuit of that welfare and I have come to this country to reaffirm that dedication.

The leaders of Latin America, the industrialists and the landowners, are, I am sure, also ready to admit past mistakes and accept new responsibilities. For unless all of us are willing to contribute our resources to national development, unless all of us are prepared not merely to accept but initiate basic land and tax reforms, unless all of us take the lead in improving the welfare of our people, that leadership will be taken from us and the heritage of centuries of Western civilization will be consumed in a few months of violence.

This is the message I bring to those of us who are here tonight—and I am grateful that I have had an opportunity to be with you.

But I also want to talk to those beyond this dinner table, and beyond this room, and this old house. And that message is for the millions of people in a thousand cities and villages throughout the mountains and lands of our hemisphere. To all of them—to the workers, to the *campesi-*

nos on the farms, to the women who toil each day for the welfare of their children—to all we bring a message of hope. Every day, every hour, in my country and in this country, and in all the countries of this hemisphere, dedicated men and women are struggling to bring nearer the day when all have more to eat, and a decent roof over their heads, and schools for their children—when all will have a better and more abundant life to accompany that human dignity to which all men are entitled, and that love of freedom to which all of us are committed by our inheritance and our desire. And tonight, here in this old city, I pledge to you the commitment of the United States of America to that great cause.

State Dinner
Bogotá, Colombia, December 17, 1961

I want to tell you how welcome you are to the White House. I think this is the most extraordinary collection of talent, of human knowledge, that has ever been gathered together at the White House, with the possible exception of when Thomas Jefferson dined alone. . . .

I know that the Nobel prize does not have any geographic or national implications. Mr. Nobel in his will, in fact, made it very clear . . . that no attention would be paid to nationality. . . .

But I think we can take some satisfaction that this hemisphere . . . has permitted the happy pursuit of knowledge and of peace; and that over forty percent of the Nobel prizes in the last thirty years have gone to men and women in this hemisphere.

And of particular pleasure today is the fact that thirteen Nobel prizes for peace have gone to those who live in this hemisphere. . . .

So I hope that you will join me in drinking to the Nobel prize winners of this year and other years—and, perhaps more widely, to all those people everywhere whom they serve.

White House Dinner
Honoring Western Hemisphere Nobel Prize Winners
Washington, D.C., April 29, 1962

In 1825 a son of El Salvador and citizen of Central America—Antonio José Canas—the first minister accredited by the United Provinces of Central America to the United States, delivered an invitation to Secretary of State Henry Clay. He asked him to send representatives to the first Inter-American Congress at Panama, a meeting at which, he said, the struggling new nations of the hemisphere "might consider upon and adopt the best plan for defending the states of the New World from foreign aggression, and . . . raise them to that elevation of wealth and power, which, from their resources, they may attain."

Today, 138 years later, we are gathered in this theater in pursuit of those same goals: the preservation of our independence, the extension of freedom, and the elevation of the welfare of our citizens to a level as high as "from our resources" we can attain. And today I have come from the United States at the invitation of a Central America which, with Panama, is rapidly attaining a unity of purpose, effort and achievement which has been unknown since the dissolution of that earliest federation.

That early conference did not achieve all its goals. But from it flowed the dream and creation of Bolívar, Canas, and José Cecilio de Valle of Costa Rica—the dream which became the inter-American system . . . the most successful, the most fruitful, and the most enduring international order in the history of the world.

Every effort to reimpose the despotisms of the Old World on the people of the New has ultimately been beaten back. . . . This system has maintained an unmatched record of peaceful relations among its members. There have been occasional conflicts to mar this record. But nowhere else have nations lived as neighbors with so little hostility and warfare. And today the principles of nonintervention and the peaceful resolution of disputes have been so firmly imbedded in our tradition that the heroic democracy in which we meet today can pursue its national goals without an armed force to guard its frontiers. In few other spots in the world could this be said today.

We have not attained this strength by merely trying to protect what was already won, to preserve the gains of the past, to maintain the status quo. If these were our system's goals, it would inevitably have crumbled as old orders crumbled. Instead it has survived, prospered, and grown despite wars and revolutions, despite changing ideologies and changing technologies, despite shifts in power and shifts in wealth—because it has been itself an instrument of change, profound revolutionary change, which has molded the history of this hemisphere and shaped the thinking of men seeking freedom and dignity in all lands. . . .

In the two-year period beginning July 1, 1961, under programs supported by the United States as part of its contribution to the Alliance, almost 3,000 new classrooms will have been built in the nations represented here today; . . . 2 million more books to children hungry for learning.

In the fifty years following its creation, the inter-American system worked to establish the political equality and national dignity of all its members, to extend political democracy and to strengthen the principle that no nation should forcibly impose its will upon another. These goals have been largely met. The equality of sovereign states is accepted by all. Intervention and force have been renounced. Machinery of peaceful settlement has been strengthened. Democracy rules in most of our lands. It will ultimately prevail over the last vestiges of tyranny in every land in this hemisphere. . . .

Today we are faced not merely with the protection of new nations, but with the remolding of ancient societies—not only with the destruction of political enemies, but with the destruction of poverty, hunger, ignorance, and disease—not alone with the creation of national dignity but with the preservation of human dignity.

To meet this enormous challenge, the peoples of the Americas have fashioned an *Alianza para el Progreso,* an alliance in which all the American states have mobilized their resources and energies to secure land for the landless, education for those without schools, and a faster rate of economic growth within a society where all can share in the fruits of progress. Here in Central America we have already begun to move toward the goals of the *Alianza*. . . .

In the two-year period beginning July 1, 1961, under programs supported by the United States as part of its contribution to the Alliance, almost 3,000 new classrooms will have been built in the nations represented here today; almost a million new books have been distributed; and tomorrow we will begin to distribute more than *2 million more books to children hungry for learning.* But much more remains to be done.

Some 7,600 new homes will have been built during this two-year period under *Alianza* programs in these nations—but much more remains to be done.

Three quarters of a million children will have been fed, but many are still hungry.

Six thousand new teachers have been trained, as well as many thousands of agricultural workers, public health and other public administrators. Still more are needed.

Yet we cannot be, and I know none of us are, satisfied with the progress we have made. Peoples who have waited centuries for opportunity and dignity cannot wait much longer. And unless those of us now making an effort are willing to redouble our efforts, unless the rich are willing to use some of their riches more wisely, unless the privileged are willing to yield up their privileges to a common good, unless the young and the educated are given opportunities to use their education, and unless governments are willing to dedicate themselves tirelessly to the tasks of governing efficiently and developing swiftly, then, let us realize, our *Alianza* will fail, and with it will fail the society of free nations which our forefathers labored to build. . . .

At the very time that newly independent nations rise in the Caribbean, the people of Cuba have been forcibly compelled to submit to a new imperialism, more ruthless, more powerful, and more deadly in its pursuit of power than any that this hemisphere has ever known. Just when it was hoped that Cuba was about to enter upon a new era of democracy and social justice, the Soviet Union, through its Cuban puppets, absorbed the Cuban nation into its empire. . . .

I am hopeful that at this meeting we will again increase our capacity to prevent the infiltration of Cuban agents, money, and propaganda. We will build a wall around Cuba—not a wall of mortar or brick or barbed wire, but a wall of dedicated men determined to protect their freedom and their sovereignty. And in this effort, as in all the other necessary efforts, I can assure you the United States will play its full part and bear its full burden.

In 1822, Bolívar, the father of the inter-American system, said this: "United in heart, in spirit and in aims, this Continent . . . must raise its eyes . . . to peer into the centuries which lie ahead. It can then contemplate with pride those future generations of men, happy and free, enjoying to the full the blessings that heaven bestows on this earth, and recalling in their hearts the protectors and liberators of our day."

My friends and colleagues; today we meet, representing seven of the great republics of America, united in spirit and in aims. We are confident of our ultimate success in protecting our freedom, in raising the living standards of our citizens, in beginning a new era of hope in American history. Secure in that confidence, we, too, can look forward to other centuries knowing that our descendants may also gratefully recall in their hearts the "protectors and liberators" of our day.

Conference of Central American Republics
San José, Costa Rica, March 18, 1963

The New Nations of Africa

For almost a century the course of the European empire had moved southward—along the coast of Africa, and around the Cape of Good Hope to the east. With the discovery of America, the kings, the generals, and the traders turned westward, leaving Africa to become the neglected and undeveloped province of a few European nations.

Today, more than four centuries later, the work of Columbus is being reversed. The nations of the West once more look toward Africa. And Africa itself is struggling for the freedom and the economic progress which centuries of neglect have denied it.

But if the voyages of Columbus led to history's retreat from Africa, they also were the first step toward the emergence of modern Africa.

For it was in the new world of Columbus that man began his first rebellion against control by ancient empires. In 1776, the year of the American Revolution, Tom Paine wrote that "A flame has arisen not to be extinguished."

Today that same flame of freedom burns brightly across the once "dark continent," creating new nations—driving old powers from the scene—and kindling in the African people the desire to shape their own destinies as free men. In 1953, three nations of Africa south of the Sahara were independent; today there are nineteen free nations. And freedom soon will cover the whole continent.

Each of these newly emerging African nations has, in varying degree, the same basic problems, the same needs, and the same dangers. And in each of them wait the same tireless and implacable agents of communism—watching for the opportunity to transform hunger, or poverty, or ignorance into revolt and Communist domination.

The new nations of Africa are determined to emerge from the poverty and hunger which now blanket much of that vast continent.

They are determined to build a modern and growing economy with a constantly rising standard of living. They are determined to educate their people—maintain their independence—and receive the respect of all the world.

There can be no question about this determination. The only real question is whether these new nations will look West or East—to Moscow or Washington—for sympathy, help, and guidance in their great effort to recapitulate, in a few decades, the entire history of modern Europe and America.

I believe that if we meet our responsibilities—if we extend the hand of friendship—if we live up to the ideals of our own revolution—then the course of the African revolution in the next decade will be toward democracy and freedom, rather than toward communism and slavery.

For it was the American Revolution—not the Russian—which began man's struggle for national independence and individual liberty. When the African National Congress in Northern Rhodesia called for reform and justice, it threatened a "Boston Tea Party," not a Bolshevik bomb plot. African leader Tom Mboya invokes the "American Dream"—not the Communist Manifesto. And in the most remote bushlands of central Africa there are children named Thomas Jefferson and George Washington—but there are none named Lenin or Stalin or Trotsky.

And our ties with Africa are not merely the ties of history and spirit. For our goals for today's Africa are the goals of the Africans themselves.

We want an Africa where the abysmally low standard of living is constantly rising—where industry and business are growing—where malnutrition and ignorance are disappearing.

And this is what Africa wants.

We want an Africa which is made up of a community of stable and independent governments—where the human rights of Negroes and white men alike are valued and protected—where men are given the opportunity to choose their own national course, free from the dictates or coercion of any other country.

We want an Africa which is not a pawn in the Cold War—or a battleground between East and West.

And this, too, is what the African people want.

And none of these goals is a goal of the Communists—who wish only to perpetuate the want and chaos on which Communist domination can be built.

Under such circumstances we would suppose that there was no place for communism in Africa—and that the new nations of Africa would increasingly look to the West and to America for help.

But the harsh facts of the matter are that the cause of freedom has been steadily losing ground in Africa—and communism has been gaining. . . .

We have lost ground in Africa because we have neglected and ignored the needs and the aspirations of the African people—because we failed to foresee the emergence of Africa and ally ourselves with the cause of independence—and because we failed to help the Africans develop the stable economy and the educated population on which their growth and freedom depend. And today we are still making the same mistakes and experiencing the same failures.

Although Africa's single greatest need is for educated men—men to man the factories, staff the government, and form the core of the educated electorate on which the success of democracy depends, we have done almost nothing to help educate the African people. There are only a handful of college graduates in the entire continent and less than one percent of all Africans who enter primary grades ever finish high school. Yet today we are aiding [fewer] than two hundred African students to study in this country—we are supplying virtually no books or teachers to Africa—and [fewer] than five percent of all our foreign technical assistance goes to Africa south of the Sahara. . . .

Although Africa is the poorest and least productive area on earth, we have done little to provide the development capital which is essential to a growing economy. Through the end of 1957 we had granted Africa less than two tenths of one percent of all our foreign assistance. And in 1959 Africa received only two percent of all the money spent by the Development Loan Fund, a fund specifically created to help underdeveloped countries.

The only real question is whether these new nations [of Africa] will look West or East—to Moscow or Washington—for sympathy, help, and guidance in their great effort to recapitulate, in a few decades, the entire history of modern Europe and America.

Although by 1952 it was obvious that the new African nations would be a growing force on the world scene, we ignored these nations until events forced them upon us. Our State Department did not even establish a Bureau of African Affairs until 1957—and that same year we sent more Foreign Service officers to West Germany than [to] all of Africa. Even today, barely five percent of our Foreign Service personnel is stationed in Africa—and five newly independent countries have no representation at all. . . .

These failures, and many more like them, this record of neglect and indifference, of failure and retreat, has created a steady decline of American prestige in Africa—and a steady growth of Soviet influence.

If we are to create an atmosphere in Africa where freedom can flourish, where long-enduring people hope for a better life for themselves and their children, where men are winning the fight against ignorance and hunger and disease, then we must embark on a bold and imaginative new program for the development of Africa.

First, to meet the need for education we must greatly increase the number of African students—future African leaders—brought to this country for university training. But training new leaders is not enough. We must help the African nations mount a large-scale attack on mass ignorance and illiteracy through the establishment of a multination African educational development fund [and] send an increasing stream of experts and educators—engineers and technicians—to train Africa in the tools of modern production and science, and in the skills and knowledge essential to the conduct of government.

Second, we must use our surpluses and our technology to meet the critical African need for food. Three quarters of the African people struggle to survive on subsistence farms, and malnutrition is Africa's greatest health problem. Our agricultural experts must train African farmers to use modern methods to increase food production—freeing labor and capital for industry, and putting an end to hunger. . . .

Third, we must provide the development capital which alone can transform limited resources into a higher standard of living for the African people . . . long-term capital loans essential to develop the roads, the power, the water, the hospitals, and . . . stimulate private investment. . . .

Fourth, we must make the United Nations the central instrument of our effort in Africa . . . to build a strong and free Africa, rather than use African nations as pawns in the Cold War. . . .

Fifth, we must ally ourselves with the rising tide of nationalism in Africa . . . the most powerful force in the modern world . . . because these are our historic principles. . . .

Sixth, we must wipe out all traces of discrimination and prejudice against Negroes at home. . . . Every instance of racial intolerance, every act of hatred or bigotry, which takes place in America, finds its way to the front pages of African newspapers. . . . More than six hundred African and Asian students cannot find decent housing—here in New York—because of their color. And African diplomats have similar difficulties finding homes in Washington. What picture of America will these leaders and future leaders bring back to their own land? . . .

In a recent film, *The Defiant Ones,* two men—a white man and a Negro —chained together, fall into a deep pit. The only way out is for one to stand on the shoulders of the other. But, since they were chained, after the first had climbed over the top of the pit, he had to pull the other out after him, if either one was to be free.

Today, Africa and America, black men and white men, new nations and old, are bound together. Our challenges rush to meet us. If we are to achieve our goals—if we are to fulfill man's eternal quest for peace and freedom—we must do it together.

National Council of Women
New York, New York, October 12, 1960

Q: Mr. President, your roving ambassador to Africa has been widely criticized for some of the statements he has made, that is, Mr. Williams, including the one of "Africa for the Africans," and the like. Do you find any validity in this criticism, and would you consider that his tour of Africa has been a plus for United States policy?

THE PRESIDENT: I think Governor Williams has done very well. I am wholly satisfied with his mission. It's a very difficult one. . . .

The statement "Africa for the Africans" does not seem to me to be a very unreasonable statement. He made it clear that he was talking about all those who felt that they were Africans, whatever their color might be, whatever their race might be. I do not know who else Africa should be for.

President's News Conference
Washington, D.C., March 1, 1961

The War in Indochina

Mr. President, the time has come for the American people to be told the blunt truth about Indochina.

I am reluctant to make any statement which may be misinterpreted as unappreciative of the gallant French struggle at Dien Bien Phu and elsewhere; or as partisan criticism of our Secretary of State just prior to his participation in the delicate deliberations in Geneva. Nor, as one who is not a member of those committees of the Congress which have been briefed—if not consulted—on this matter, do I wish to appear impetuous or alarmist in my evaluation of the situation.

But to pour money, material, and men into the jungles of Indochina without at least a remote prospect of victory would be dangerously futile and self-destructive. Of course, all discussion of "united action" assumes the inevitability of such victory; but such assumptions are not unlike similar predictions of confidence which have lulled the American people for many years and which, if continued, would present an improper basis for determining the extent of American participation.

Despite this series of optimistic reports about eventual victory, every member of the Senate knows that such victory today appears to be desperately remote, to say the least, despite tremendous amounts of economic and materiel aid from the United States, and despite a deplorable loss of French Union manpower. The call for either negotiations or additional participation by other nations underscores the remoteness of such a final victory today, regardless of the outcome at Dien Bien Phu. It is, of course, for these reasons that many French are reluctant to continue the struggle without greater assistance; for to record the sapping effect which time and the enemy have had on their will and strength in that area is not to disparage their valor. If "united action" can achieve the necessary victory over the forces of communism, and thus preserve the security and freedom of all Southeast Asia, then such united action is clearly called for. But if, on the other hand, the increase in our aid and the utilization of our troops would only result in further statements of confidence without ultimate victory over aggression, then now is the time when we must evaluate the conditions under which that pledge is made.

I am frankly of the belief that no amount of American military assistance in Indochina can conquer an enemy which is everywhere and at the same time nowhere, "an enemy of the people" which has the sympathy and covert support of the people.

Moreover, without political independence for the Associated States, the other Asiatic nations have made it clear that they regard this as a war of colonialism; and the "united action" which is said to be so desperately needed for victory in that area is likely to end up as unilateral action by our own country. Such intervention, without participation by the armed forces of the other nations of Asia, without the support of the great masses of the people of the Associated States, with increasing reluctance and discouragement on the part of the French—and, I might add, with hordes of Chinese Communist troops poised just across the border in anticipation of our unilateral entry into their kind of battleground—such intervention, Mr. President, would be virtually impossible in the type of military situation which prevails in Indochina.

This is not a new point, of course. In November of 1951, I reported upon my return from the Far East as follows:

> In Indochina we have allied ourselves to the desperate effort of a French regime to hang on to the remnants of empire. There is no broad, general support of the native Vietnam government among the people of that area. To check the southern drive of communism makes sense but not only through reliance on the force of arms. The task is rather to build strong native non-Communist sentiment within these areas and rely on that as a spearhead of defense rather than upon the legions of General de Lattre. To do this apart from and in defiance of innately nationalistic aims spells foredoomed failure.

In June of last year, I sought an amendment to the Mutual Security Act which would have provided for the distribution of American aid, to the extent feasible, in such a way as to encourage the freedom and independence desired by the people of the Associated States. My amendment was soundly defeated on the grounds that we should not pressure France into taking action on this delicate situation; and that the new French government could be expected to make "a decision which would obviate the necessity of this kind of amendment or resolution." The distinguished majority leader [Mr. Knowland] assured us that "We will all work, in conjunction with our great ally, France, toward the freedom of the people of those states."

Every year we are given three sets of assurances: First, that the independence of the Associated States is now complete; second, that the independence of the Associated States will soon be completed under steps "now" being undertaken; and, third, that military victory for the French Union forces in Indochina is assured, or is just around the corner, or lies two years off. But the stringent limitations upon the status of the Associated States as sovereign states remain; and the fact that military victory has not yet been achieved is largely the result of these limitations. Repeated failure of these prophecies has, however, in no way diminished the frequency of their reiteration, and they have caused this nation to delay definitive action until now the opportunity for any desirable solution may well be past.

To pour money, material, and men into the jungles of Indochina without at least a remote prospect of victory would be dangerously futile and self-destructive.

It is time, therefore, for us to face the stark reality of the difficult situation before us without the false hopes which predictions of military victory and assurances of complete independence have given us in the past. The hard truth of the matter is, first, that without the wholehearted support of the peoples of the Associated States, without a reliable and crusading native army with a dependable officer corps, a military victory, even with American support, in that area is difficult if not impossible, of achievement; and, second, that the support of the people of that area cannot be obtained without a change in the contractual relationships which presently exist between the Associated States and the French Union.

If the French persist in their refusal to grant the legitimate independence and freedom desired by the peoples of the Associated States; and if those peoples and the other peoples of Asia remain aloof from the conflict, as they have in the past, then it is my hope that Secretary Dulles, before pledging our assistance at Geneva, will recognize the futility of channeling American men and machines into that hopeless internecine struggle.

The facts and alternatives before us are unpleasant, Mr. President. But in a nation such as ours, it is only through the fullest and frankest appreciation of such facts and alternatives that any foreign policy can be effectively maintained. In an era of supersonic attack and atomic retaliation, extended public debate and education are of no avail, once such a policy must be implemented. The time to study, to doubt, to review, and revise is now, for upon our decisions now may well rest the peace and security of the world, and, indeed, the very continued existence of mankind. And if we cannot entrust this decision to the people, then, as Thomas Jefferson once said: "If we think them not enlightened enough to exercise their control with a wholesome discretion, the remedy is not to take it from them but to inform their discretion by education."

United States Senate
Washington, D.C., April 6, 1954

I want to make a brief statement about Laos. It is, I think, important for all Americans to understand this difficult and potentially dangerous problem. In my last conversation with General Eisenhower, the day before the inauguration, on January 19, we spent more time on this hard matter than on any other thing. And since then it has been steadily before the administration as the most immediate of the problems that we found upon taking office.

Our special concern with the problem in Laos goes back to 1954. That year at Geneva a large group of powers agreed to a settlement of the struggle for Indochina. Laos was one of the new states which had recently emerged from the French Union and it was the clear premise of the 1954 settlement that this new country would be neutral—free of external domination by anyone. The new country contained contending factions, but in its first years real progress was made toward a unified and neutral status. But the efforts of a Communist-dominated group to destroy this neutrality never ceased.

In the last half of 1960 a series of sudden maneuvers occurred and the Communists and their supporters turned to a new and greatly intensified military effort to take over. . . .

In this military advance the local Communist forces, known as the Pathet Lao, have had increasing support and direction from outside. Soviet planes, I regret to say, have been conspicuous in a large-scale airlift into the battle area—over one thousand sorties since last December 13, plus a whole supporting set of combat specialists, mainly from Communist North Vietnam, and heavier weapons have been provided from outside, all with the clear object of destroying by military action the agreed neutrality of Laos.

It is this new dimension of externally supported warfare that creates the present grave problem. The position of this administration has been carefully considered and we have sought to make it just as clear as we know how to the governments concerned.

Laos is far away from America, but the world is small.

First, we strongly and unreservedly support the goal of a neutral and independent Laos, tied to no outside power or group of powers, threatening no one, and free from any domination. Our support for the present duly constituted government is aimed entirely and exclusively at that result. And if in the past there has been any possible ground for misunderstanding of our desire for a truly neutral Laos, there should be none now.

Secondly, if there is to be a peaceful solution, there must be a cessation of the present armed attacks by externally supported Communists. If these attacks do not stop, those who support a truly neutral Laos will have to consider their response. The shape of this necessary response will, of course, be carefully considered, not only here in Washington, but in the SEATO conference with our allies which begins next Monday.

SEATO—the Southeast Asia Treaty Organization—was organized in 1954, with strong leadership from our last administration, and all members of SEATO have undertaken special treaty responsibilities toward an aggression in Laos.

No one should doubt our resolution on this point. We are faced with a clear and one-sided threat of a change in the internationally agreed position of Laos. This threat runs counter to the will of the Laotian people, who wish only to be independent and neutral. It is posed rather by the military operations of internal dissident elements directed from outside the country. This is what must end if peace is to be achieved in Southeast Asia.

Thirdly, we are earnestly in favor of constructive negotiation among the nations concerned and among the leaders of Laos which can help Laos back to the pathway of independence and genuine neutrality. We strongly support the present British proposal of a prompt end of hostilities and prompt negotiation. We are always conscious of the obligation which rests upon all members of the United Nations to seek peaceful solutions to problems of this sort. We hope that others may be equally aware of this responsibility.

My fellow Americans, Laos is far away from America, but the world is small. Its two million people live in a country three times the size of Austria. The security of all Southeast Asia will be endangered if Laos loses its neutral independence. Its own safety runs with the safety of us all—in a real neutrality observed by all.

I want to make it clear to the American people and to all of the world that all we want in Laos is peace, not war; a truly neutral government, not a Cold War pawn; a settlement concluded at the conference table and not on the battlefield.

Our response will be made in close cooperation with our allies and the wishes of the Laotian government. We will not be provoked, trapped, or drawn into this or any other situation; but I know that every American will want his country to honor its obligations.

Opening Statement, President's News Conference
Washington, D.C., March 23, 1961

MR. CRONKITE: Mr. President, the only hot war we've got running at the moment is of course the one in Vietnam, and we have our difficulties there, quite obviously. . . .

THE PRESIDENT: I don't think that unless a greater effort is made by the government to win popular support that the war can be won out there. In the final analysis, it is their war. They are the ones who have to win it or lose it. We can help them, we can give them equipment, we can send our men out there as advisers, but they have to win it, the people of Vietnam, against the Communists.

We are prepared to continue to assist them, but I don't think that the war can be won unless the people support the effort and, in my opinion, in the last two months, the government has gotten out of touch with the people.

The repressions against the Buddhists, we felt, were very unwise. Now all we can do is to make it very clear that we don't think this is the way to win. It is my hope that this will become increasingly obvious to the government, that they will take steps to try to bring back popular support for this very essential struggle.

MR. CRONKITE: Do you think this government still has time to regain the support of the people?

THE PRESIDENT: I do. With changes in policy, and perhaps with personnel, I think it can. If it doesn't make those changes, I would think that the chances of winning it would not be very good.

Interview, Walter Cronkite
CBS Television News
Washington, D.C., September 2, 1963

We would expect to withdraw a thousand men from South Vietnam before the end of the year . . . as the training intensifies and is carried on in South Vietnam.

President's News Conference
Washington, D.C., October 31, 1963

The United Nations

We must increase our support of the United Nations as an instrument to end the Cold War instead of an arena in which to fight it. In recognition of its increasing importance and the doubling of its membership

—we are enlarging and strengthening our own mission to the U.N.;

—we shall help insure that it is properly financed;

—we shall work to see that the integrity of the office of the Secretary-General is maintained.

And I would address a special plea to the smaller nations of the world —to join with us in strengthening this organization, which is far more essential to their security than it is to ours—the only body in the world where no nation need be powerful to be secure, where every nation has an equal voice, and where any nation can exert influence not according to the strength of its armies but according to the strength of its ideas. It deserves the support of all.

State of the Union Address
The Capitol, Washington, D.C.
January 30, 1961

We meet in an hour of grief and challenge. Dag Hammarskjöld is dead. But the United Nations lives. His tragedy is deep in our hearts, but the task for which he died is at the top of our agenda. A noble servant of peace is gone. But the quest for peace lies before us.

The problem is not the death of one man—the problem is the life of this organization. It will either grow to meet the challenges of our age, or it will be gone with the wind, without influence, without force, without respect. Were we to let it die, to enfeeble its vigor, to cripple its powers, we would condemn our future.

For in the development of this organization rests the only true alternative to war—and war appeals no longer as a rational alternative. Unconditional war can no longer lead to unconditional victory. It can no longer serve to settle disputes. It can no longer concern the great powers alone. For a nuclear disaster, spread by wind and water and fear, could well engulf the great and the small, the rich and the poor, the committed and the uncommitted alike. Mankind must put an end to war —or war will put an end to mankind.

So let us here resolve that Dag Hammarskjöld did not live, or die, in vain. Let us call a truce to terror. Let us invoke the blessings of peace. And, as we build an international capacity to keep peace, let us join in dismantling the national capacity to wage war.

This will require new strength and new roles for the United Nations. For disarmament without checks is but a shadow—and a community without law is but a shell. Already the United Nations has become both the measure and the vehicle of man's most generous impulses. Already it has provided—in the Middle East, in Asia, in Africa this year in the Congo—means of holding man's violence within bounds.

Every man, woman, and child lives under a nuclear sword of Damocles, hanging by the slenderest of threads, capable of being cut at any moment by accident or miscalculation or madness.

But the great question which confronted this body in 1945 is still before us: whether man's cherished hopes for progress and peace are to be destroyed by terror and disruption, whether the "foul winds of war" can be tamed in time to free the cooling winds of reason, and whether the pledges of our Charter are to be fulfilled or defied—pledges to secure peace, progress, human rights, and world law.

In this hall, there are not three forces, but two. One is composed of those who are trying to build the kind of world described in Articles I and II of the Charter. The other, seeking a far different world, would undermine this organization in the process. . . .

However difficult it may be to fill Mr. Hammarskjöld's place, it can better be filled by one man rather than by three. Even the three horses of the troika did not have three drivers, all going in different directions. They had only one—and so must the United Nations executive. To install a triumvirate, or any panel, or any rotating authority, in the

United Nations administrative offices would replace order with anarchy, action with paralysis, confidence with confusion. . . .

To give this organization three drivers—to permit each great power to decide its own case, would entrench the Cold War in the headquarters of peace. Whatever advantages such a plan may hold out to my own country, as one of the great powers, we reject it. For we far prefer world law in the age of self-determination, to world war, in the age of mass extermination.

Today, every inhabitant of this planet must contemplate the day when this planet may no longer be habitable. Every man, woman, and child lives under a nuclear sword of Damocles, hanging by the slenderest of threads, capable of being cut at any moment by accident or miscalculation or madness. The weapons of war must be abolished before they abolish us.

Men no longer debate whether armaments are a symptom or a cause of tension. The mere existence of modern weapons—ten million times more powerful than any that the world has ever seen, and only minutes away from any target on earth—is a source of horror and discord and distrust. Men no longer maintain that disarmament must await the settlement of all disputes—for disarmament must be a part of any permanent settlement. And men no longer pretend that the quest for disarmament is a sign of weakness—for in a spiraling arms race, a nation's security may well be shrinking even as its arms increase.

For fifteen years this organization has sought the reduction and destruction of arms. Now that goal is no longer a dream—it is a practical matter of life or death. The risks inherent in disarmament pale in comparison to the risks inherent in an unlimited arms race. . . .

In short, general and complete disarmament must no longer be a slogan, used to resist the first steps. It is no longer to be a goal without means of achieving it, without means of verifying its progress, without means of keeping the peace. It is now a realistic plan, and a test—a test of those only willing to talk and a test of those willing to act.

Such a plan would not bring a world free from conflict and greed—but it would bring a world free from the terrors of mass destruction. It would not usher in the era of the superstate—but it would usher in an era in which no state could annihilate or be annihilated by another. . . .

I therefore propose . . . that disarmament negotiations resume promptly, and continue without interruption until an entire program for general and complete disarmament has not only been agreed but has been actually achieved.

The logical place to begin is a treaty assuring the end of nuclear tests of all kinds, in every environment, under workable controls. The United States and the United Kingdom have proposed such a treaty that is reasonable, effective, and ready for signature. We are still prepared to sign that treaty today.

We also proposed a mutual ban on atmospheric testing, without inspection or controls, in order to save the human race from the poison of radioactive fallout. We regret that that offer has not been accepted. . . .

To destroy arms, however, is not enough. We must create even as we destroy—creating worldwide law and law enforcement as we outlaw worldwide war and weapons. . . .

For peace is not solely a matter of military or technical problems—it is primarily a problem of politics and people. And unless man can match his strides in weaponry and technology with equal strides in social and political development, our great strength, like that of the dinosaur, will become incapable of proper control—and like the dinosaur, vanish from the earth.

As we extend the rule of law on earth, so must we also extend it to man's new domain—outer space.

All of us salute the brave cosmonauts of the Soviet Union. The new horizons of outer space must not be driven by the old bitter concepts of imperialism and sovereign claims. The cold reaches of the universe must not become the new arena of an even colder war.

To this end, we shall urge proposals extending the United Nations Charter to the limits of man's exploration in the universe, reserving outer space for peaceful use, prohibiting weapons of mass destruction in space or on celestial bodies, and opening the mysteries and benefits of space to every nation. . . .

But the mysteries of outer space must not divert our eyes or our energies from the harsh realities that face our fellow men. Political sovereignty is but a mockery without the means of meeting poverty and illiteracy and disease. Self-determination is but a slogan if the future holds no hope. . . .

The first threat on which I wish to report is widely misunderstood: the smoldering coals of war in Southeast Asia. South Vietnam is already under attack—sometimes by a single assassin, sometimes by a band of guerrillas, recently by full battalions. The peaceful borders of Burma, Cambodia, and India have been repeatedly violated. And the peaceful people of Laos are in danger of losing the independence they gained not so long ago.

No one can call these "wars of liberation." For these are free countries living under their own governments. Nor are these aggressions any less real because men are knifed in their homes and not shot in the fields of battle.

The very simple question confronting the world community is whether measures can be devised to protect the small and the weak from such tactics. For if they are successful in Laos and South Vietnam, the gates will be opened wide.

The United States seeks for itself no base, no territory, no special position in this area of any kind. We support a truly neutral and independent Laos, its people free from outside interference, living at peace with themselves and with their neighbors, assured that their territory will not be used for attacks on others, and under a government comparable (as Mr. Khrushchev and I agreed at Vienna) to Cambodia and Burma.

But now the negotiations over Laos are reaching a crucial stage. The cease-fire is at best precarious. The rainy season is coming to an end. Laotian territory is being used to infiltrate South Vietnam. The world community—and all those who are involved—must recognize that this potent threat to Laotian peace and freedom is indivisible from all other threats to their own.

To this end, we shall urge proposals extending the United Nations Charter to the limits of man's exploration in the universe, reserving outer space for peaceful use, prohibiting weapons of mass destruction in space or on celestial bodies.

Secondly, I wish to report to you on the crisis over Germany and Berlin. This is not the time or the place for immoderate tones, but the world community is entitled to know the very simple issues as we see them. If there is a crisis it is because an existing peace is under threat, because an existing island of free people is under pressure, because solemn agreements are being treated with indifference. Established international rights are being threatened with unilateral usurpation. Peaceful circulation has been interrupted by barbed wire and concrete blocks.

One recalls the order of the Czar in Pushkin's *Boris Godunov:* "Take steps at this very hour that our frontiers be fenced in by barriers. . . . That not a single soul pass o'er the border, that not a hare be able to run or a crow to fly."

It is absurd to allege that we are threatening a war merely to prevent the Soviet Union and East Germany from signing a so-called treaty of peace. The Western Allies are not concerned with any paper arrangement the Soviets may wish to make with a regime of their own creation, on territory occupied by their own troops and governed by their own agents. No such action can affect either our rights or our responsibilities.

If there is a dangerous crisis in Berlin—and there is—it is because of threats against the vital interests and the deep commitment of the Western powers, and the freedom of West Berlin. We cannot yield these interests. We cannot fail these commitments. We cannot surrender the freedom of these people for whom we are responsible. A "peace treaty" which carried with it provisions which destroy the peace would be a fraud. A "free city" which was not genuinely free would suffocate freedom and would be an infamy.

For a city or a people to be truly free, they must have the secure right, without economic, political, or police pressure, to make their own choice and to live their own lives. And as I have said before, if anyone doubts the extent to which our presence is desired by the people of West Berlin, we are ready to have that question submitted to a free vote in all Berlin and, if possible, among all the German people.

The elementary fact about this crisis is that it is unnecessary. The elementary tools for a peaceful settlement are to be found in the Charter. Under its law, agreements are to be kept, unless changed by all those who made them. Established rights are to be respected. The political disposition of peoples should rest upon their own wishes, freely expressed in plebiscites or free elections. If there are legal problems, they can be solved by legal means. If there is a threat of force, it must be rejected. If there is desire for change, it must be a subject for negotiation and if there is negotiation, it must be rooted in mutual respect and concern for the rights of others.

The Western powers have calmly resolved to defend, by whatever means are forced upon them, their obligations and their access to the free citizens of West Berlin and the self-determination of those citizens. This generation learned from bitter experience that either brandishing or yielding to threats can only lead to war. But firmness and reason can lead to the kind of peaceful solution in which my country profoundly believes.

We are committed to no rigid formula. We see no perfect solution. We recognize that troops and tanks can, for a time, keep a nation divided against its will, however unwise that policy may seem to us. But we believe a peaceful agreement is possible which protects the freedom of West Berlin and allied presence and access, while recognizing the historic and legitimate interests of others in assuring European security. . . .

The events and decisions of the next ten months may well decide the fate of man for the next ten thousand years. There will be no avoiding those events. There will be no appeal from these decisions. And we in this hall shall be remembered either as part of the generation that turned this planet into a flaming funeral pyre or the generation that met its vow "to save succeeding generations from the scourge of war."

In the endeavor to meet that vow, I pledge you every effort this nation possesses. I pledge you that we shall neither commit nor provoke aggression, that we shall neither flee nor invoke the threat of force, that we shall never negotiate out of fear, we shall never fear to negotiate.

Terror is not a new weapon. Throughout history it has been used by those who could not prevail, either by persuasion or example. But inevitably they fail, either because men are not afraid to die for a life worth living, or because the terrorists themselves came to realize that free men cannot be frightened by threats, and that aggression would meet its own response. And it is in the light of that history that every nation today should know, be he friend or foe, that the United States has both the will and the weapons to join free men in standing up to their responsibilities.

But I come here today to look across this world of threats to a world of peace. In that search we cannot expect any final triumph—for new problems will always arise. We cannot expect that all nations will adopt like systems—for conformity is the jailor of freedom, and the enemy of growth. Nor can we expect to reach our goal by contrivance, by fiat, or even by the wishes of all.

But however close we sometimes seem to that dark and final abyss, let no man of peace and freedom despair. For he does not stand alone. If we all can persevere, if we can in every land and office look beyond our own shores and ambitions, then surely the age will dawn in which the strong are just and the weak secure and the peace preserved.

Ladies and gentlemen of this Assembly, the decision is ours. Never have the nations of the world had so much to lose, or so much to gain. Together we shall save our planet, or together we shall perish in its flames. Save it we can—and save it we must—and then shall we earn the eternal thanks of mankind and, as peacemakers, the eternal blessing of God.

United Nations General Assembly
New York, New York, September 25, 1961

I see little merit in the impatience of those who would abandon this imperfect world instrument because they dislike our imperfect world. For the troubles of a world organization merely reflect the troubles of the world itself. And if the organization is weakened, these troubles can only increase. We may not always agree with every detailed action taken by every officer of the United Nations, or with every voting majority. But as an institution, it should have in the future, as it has had in the past since its inception, no stronger or more faithful member than the United States of America. . . .

No policeman is universally popular—particularly when he uses his stick to restore law and order on his beat. Those members who are willing to contribute their votes and their views—but very little else—have created a serious deficit by refusing to pay their share of special UN assessments. Yet they do pay their annual assessments to retain their votes—and a new UN bond issue, financing special operations for the next eighteen months, is to be repaid with interest from these regular assessments. This is clearly in our interest.

State of the Union Address
The Capitol, Washington, D.C.
January 11, 1962

Q: Mr. President, Senator Jackson says that this administration and the last have been putting too much stock in the United Nations and that a strong Atlantic Community offers the best avenue to peace. What is your view on this?

THE PRESIDENT: I see nothing contradictory in a strong Atlantic Community and the United Nations. Nor is there anything contradictory in a strong Organization of American States and the United Nations. In fact, the United Nations, when it was written in 1945, gave room for these regional organizations, of which there are a great many and of which the United States is a member. I support the United Nations very strongly, and I think the American people do, not because its power is unlimited [but] because we believe that it serves the interests of the United States. . . .

Now, I would be very unhappy if the United Nations were weakened or eliminated. You would have a great increase in the chances of a direct confrontation in someplace like the Congo between the great powers. It might involve the United States directly and perhaps the Soviet Union on the other side. The United Nations serves as a means of channeling these matters, on which we disagree so basically, in a peaceful way. But that doesn't suggest that we have to choose between the Atlantic Community and the United Nations. We believe in the Atlantic Community; we are committed to strengthening it. . . . And we also support the United Nations.

President's News Conference
Washington, D.C., March 21, 1962

The Little Nations

. . . I am deeply honored to be your guest in the free Parliament of a free Ireland. If this nation had achieved its present political and economic stature a century or so ago, my great grandfather might never have left New Ross, and I might, if fortunate, be sitting down there with you. Of course, if your own President had never left Brooklyn, he might be standing up here instead of me! . . .

The White House was designed by James Hoban, a noted Irish-American architect, and I have no doubt that he believed by incorporating several features of the Dublin style he would make it more homelike for any President of Irish descent. It was a long wait, but I appreciate his efforts. . . .

I am proud to be the first American President to visit Ireland during his term of office, proud to be addressing this distinguished assembly, and proud of the welcome you have given me. My presence and your welcome, however, only symbolize the many and enduring links which have bound the Irish and the Americans since the earliest days.

Benjamin Franklin—the envoy of the American Revolution who was also born in Boston—was received by the Irish Parliament in 1772. It was neither independent nor free from discrimination at the time, but Franklin reported its members "disposed to be friends of America. By joining our interest with theirs," he said, "a more equitable treatment . . . might be obtained for both nations."

Our interests have been joined ever since. Franklin sent leaflets to Irish freedom fighters. O'Connell was influenced by Washington, and Emmet influenced Lincoln. Irish volunteers played so predominant a role in the American army that Lord Mountjoy lamented in the British Parliament that "we have lost America through the Irish." John Barry, whose statue we honored yesterday and whose sword is in my office, was only one who fought for liberty in America to set an example for liberty in Ireland. Yesterday was the 117th anniversary of the birth of Charles Stewart Parnell—whose grandfather fought under Barry and whose mother was born in America—and who, at the age of thirty-four, was invited to address the American Congress on the cause of Irish freedom. "I have seen since I have been in this country," he said, "so many tokens of the good wishes of the American people toward Ireland." And today, eighty-three years later, I can say to you that I have seen in this country so many tokens of good wishes of the Irish people toward America.

And so it is that our two nations, divided by distance, have been united by history. No people ever believed more deeply in the cause of Irish freedom than the people of the United States. And no country contributed more to building my own than your sons and daughters. They came to our shores in a mixture of hope and agony, and I would not underrate the difficulties of their course once they arrived in the United States. They left behind hearts, fields, and a nation yearning to be free. It is no wonder that James Joyce described the Atlantic as a bowl of bitter tears, and that an earlier poet wrote, "They are going, going, going, and we cannot bid them stay." . . .

There are those who regard this history of past strife and exile as better forgotten. But, to use the phrase of Yeats, let us not casually reduce "that great past to a trouble of fools." For we need not feel the bitterness of the past to discover its meaning for the present and the future. And it is the present and the future of Ireland that today holds so much promise to my nation as well as to yours, and, indeed, to all mankind. . . .

George Bernard Shaw, speaking as an Irishman, summed up its approach to life: Other people, he said, "see things and say: 'Why?' . . . But I dream things that never were and I say: 'Why not?' "

Eighty-three years ago, Henry Grattan, demanding the more independent Irish Parliament that would always bear his name, denounced those who were satisfied merely by new grants of economic opportunity. "A country," he said, "enlightened as Ireland, chartered as Ireland, armed as Ireland and injured as Ireland will be satisfied with nothing less than liberty." And today, I am certain, free Ireland—a full-fledged member of the world community, where some are not yet free, and where some counsel an acceptance of tyranny—free Ireland will not be satisfied with anything less than liberty.

I am glad, therefore, that Ireland is moving in the mainstream of current world events. For I sincerely believe that your future is as promising as your past is proud, and that your destiny lies not as a peaceful island in a sea of troubles, but as a maker and shaper of world peace.

For self-determination can no longer mean isolation; and the achievement of national independence today means withdrawal from the old status only to return to the world scene with a new one. New nations can build with their former governing powers the same kind of fruitful relationship that Ireland has established with Great Britain—a relationship founded on equality and mutual interests. And no nation, large or small, can be indifferent to the fate of others, near or far. Modern economics, weaponry, and communications have made us realize more than ever that we are one human family and this one planet is our home.

Across the gulfs and barriers that now divide us, we must remember that there are no permanent enemies. Hostility today is a fact, but it is not a ruling law. The supreme reality of our time is our indivisibility as children of God and our common vulnerability on this planet.

Some may say that all this means little to Ireland. In an age when "history moves with the tramp of earthquake feet," in an age when a handful of men and nations have the power literally to devastate mankind, in an age when the needs of the developing nations are so staggering that even the richest lands often groan with the burden of assistance —in such an age, it may be asked, how can a nation as small as Ireland play much of a role on the world stage?

I would remind those who ask that question, including those in other small countries, of the words of one of the great orators of the English language:

> All the world owes much to the little "five feet high" nations. The greatest art of the world was the work of little nations. The most enduring literature of the world came from little nations. The heroic deeds that thrill humanity through generations were the deeds of little nations fighting for their freedom. And oh, yes, the salvation of mankind came through a little nation.

Ireland has already set an example and a standard for other small nations to follow.

This has never been a rich or powerful country, and yet, since earliest times, its influence on the world has been rich and powerful. No larger nation did more to keep Christianity and Western culture alive in their darkest centuries. No larger nation did more to spark the cause of independence in America, indeed, around the world. And no larger nation has ever provided the world with more literary and artistic genius.

This is an extraordinary country. George Bernard Shaw, speaking as an Irishman, summed up its approach to life: Other people, he said, "see things and say: 'Why?' . . . But I dream things that never were and I say: 'Why not?' "

It is that quality of the Irish—that remarkable combination of hope, confidence, and imagination—that is needed more than ever today. The problems of the world cannot possibly be solved by skeptics or cynics whose horizons are limited by the obvious realities. We need men who can dream of things that never were, and ask why not. It matters not how small a nation is that seeks world peace and freedom, for, to paraphrase a citizen of my country, the humblest nation of all the world, "when clad in the armor of a righteous cause, is stronger than all the hosts of Error."

Ireland is clad in the cause of national and human liberty with peace. To the extent that the peace is disturbed by conflict between the former colonial powers and the new and developing nations, Ireland's role is unique. For every new nation knows that Ireland was the first of the small nations in the twentieth century to win its struggle for independence, and that the Irish have traditionally sent their doctors and technicians and soldiers and priests to help other lands to keep their liberty alive.

At the same time, Ireland is part of Europe, associated with the Council of Europe, progressing in the context of Europe, and a prospective member of an expanded European Common Market. Thus Ireland has excellent relations with both the new and the old, the confidence of both sides, and an opportunity to act where the actions of greater powers might be looked upon with suspicion.

The central issue of freedom, however, is between those who believe in self-determination and those in the East who would impose on others the harsh and oppressive Communist system; and here your nation wisely rejects the role of a go-between or a mediator. Ireland pursues an independent course in foreign policy, but it is not neutral between liberty and tyranny and never will be.

For knowing the meaning of foreign domination, Ireland is the example and inspiration to those enduring endless years of oppression. It was fitting and appropriate that this nation played a leading role in censuring the suppression of the Hungarian revolution. For how many times was Ireland's quest for freedom suppressed only to have that quest renewed by the succeeding generation?

Those who suffer beyond that wall I saw on Wednesday in Berlin must not despair of their future. Let them remember the constancy, the faith, the endurance, and the final success of the Irish. And let them remember, as I heard sung by your sons and daughters yesterday in Wexford, "the boys of Wexford, who fought with heart and hand, to burst in twain the galling chain and free our native land."

The major forum for your nation's greater role in world affairs is that protector of the weak and voice of the small, the United Nations. From Cork to the Congo, from Galway to the Gaza Strip, from this legislative assembly to the United Nations, Ireland is sending its most talented men to do the world's most important work—the work of peace.

In a sense, this export of talent is in keeping with an historic Irish role —but you no longer go as exiles and emigrants but for the service of your country and, indeed, of all men. Like the Irish missionaries of medieval days, like the "wild geese" after the Battle of the Boyne, you are not content to sit by your fireside while others are in need of your help.

Nor are you content with the recollections of the past when you face the responsibilities of the present. Twenty-six sons of Ireland have died in the Congo; many others have been wounded. I pay tribute to them and to all of you for your commitment and dedication to world order. Their sacrifice reminds us all that we must not falter now. . . .

I speak of these matters today, not because Ireland is unaware of its role, but because I think it important that you know that we know what you have done. And I speak to remind the other small nations that they, too, can and must help build a world peace. They, too, as we all are, are dependent on the United Nations for security, for an equal chance to be heard, for progress toward a world made safe for diversity.

The peacekeeping machinery of the United Nations cannot work without the help of the smaller nations, nations whose forces threaten no one and whose forces can thus help create a world in which no nation is threatened. Great powers have their responsibilities and their burdens, but the smaller nations of the world must fulfill their obligations as well.

A great Irish poet once wrote: "I believe profoundly . . . in the future of Ireland . . . that this is an isle of destiny, that that destiny will be glorious . . . and that when our hour is come, we will have something to give to the world."

My friends: Ireland's hour has come. You have something to give to the world—and that is a future of peace with freedom.

Irish Parliament
Dublin, Ireland, June 28, 1963

CHAPTER 16

The Uses and Limits of Power

John Kennedy shied away from all attempts to fix an ideological label on him, but "principled pragmatist" or "idealist without illusions" would not have offended him. With the detached objectivity that enabled him to analyze his own country's and administration's strengths and weaknesses, he recognized that a new war, particularly a nuclear war, would represent not a noble cause but the failure of all his aspirations. He did not confuse strength with force or peace with weakness. He knew that the superpowers had to find a more rational means than armed conflict of settling their very real differences. In this, as in so many other ways, his wisdom deserves remembering today.

The Role of Negotiations

In 1961 the world relations of this country have become tangled and complex. One of our former allies has become our adversary—and he has his own adversaries who are not our allies. . . .

We increase our arms at a heavy cost, primarily to make certain that we will not have to use them. We must face up to the chance of war, if we are to maintain the peace. We must work with certain countries lacking in freedom in order to strengthen the cause of freedom. We find some who call themselves neutral who are our friends and sympathetic to us, and others who call themselves neutral who are unremittingly hostile to us. And as the most powerful defender of freedom on earth, we find ourselves unable to escape the responsibilities of freedom, and yet unable to exercise it without restraints imposed by the very freedoms we seek to protect.

We cannot, as a free nation, compete with our adversaries in tactics of terror, assassination, false promises, counterfeit mobs and crises.

We cannot, under the scrutiny of a free press and public, tell different stories to different audiences, foreign and domestic, friendly and hostile.

We cannot abandon the slow processes of consulting with our allies to match the swift expediencies of those who merely dictate to their satellites.

We can neither abandon nor control the international organization in which we now cast less than one percent of the vote in the General Assembly.

We possess weapons of tremendous power—but they are least effective in combating the weapons most often used by freedom's foes: subversion, infiltration, guerrilla warfare, civil disorder.

We send arms to other peoples—just as we send them the ideals of democracy in which we believe—but we cannot send them the will to use those arms or to abide by those ideals.

And while we believe not only in the force of arms but in the force of right and reason, we have learned that reason does not always appeal to unreasonable men, that it is not always true that "a soft answer turneth away wrath," and that right does not always make might.

In short, we must face problems which do not lend themselves to easy or quick or permanent solutions. And we must face the fact that the

United States is neither omnipotent nor omniscient—that we are only six percent of the world's population—that we cannot impose our will upon the other ninety-four percent of mankind—that we cannot right every wrong or reverse each adversity—and that therefore there cannot be an American solution to every world problem.

These burdens and frustrations are accepted by most Americans with maturity and understanding. They may long for the days when war meant charging up San Juan Hill—or when our isolation was guarded by two oceans—or when the atomic bomb was ours alone—or when much of the industrialized world depended upon our resources and our aid. But they now know that those days are gone—and that gone with them are the old policies and the old complacencies. And they know, too, that we must make the best of our new problems and our new opportunities, whatever the risk and the cost.

But there are others who cannot bear the burden of a long twilight struggle. They lack confidence in our long-run capacity to survive and succeed. Hating communism, yet they see communism in the long run, perhaps, as the wave of the future. And they want some quick and easy and final and cheap solution—now.

There are two groups of these frustrated citizens, far apart in their views yet very much alike in their approach. On the one hand are those who urge upon us what I regard to be the pathway of surrender—appeasing our enemies, compromising our commitments, purchasing peace at any price, disavowing our arms, our friends, our obligations. If their view had prevailed, the world of free choice would be smaller today.

On the other hand are those who urge upon us what I regard to be the pathway of war: equating negotiations with appeasement and substituting rigidity for firmness. If their view had prevailed, we would be at war today, and in more than one place.

It is a curious fact that each of these extreme opposites resembles the other. Each believes that we have only two choices: appeasement or war, suicide or surrender, humiliation or holocaust, to be either Red or dead. Each side sees only "hard" and "soft" nations, hard and soft policies, hard and soft men. Each believes that any departure from its own course inevitably leads to the other: one group believes that any peaceful solution means appeasement; the other believes that any arms buildup means war. One group regards everyone else as warmongers, the other regards everyone else as appeasers. Neither side admits that its path will lead to disaster—but neither can tell us how or where to draw the line once we descend the slippery slopes of appeasement or constant intervention.

In short, while both extremes profess to be the true realists of our time, neither could be more unrealistic. While both claim to be doing the nation a service, they could do it no greater disservice. This kind of talk of easy solutions to difficult problems, if believed, could inspire a lack of confidence among our people when they must all—above all else—be united in recognizing the long and difficult days that lie ahead. It could inspire uncertainty among our allies when above all else they must be confident in us. And even more dangerously, it could, if believed, inspire doubt among our adversaries when they must above all else be convinced that we will defend our vital interests.

We must face the fact that the United States is neither omnipotent nor omniscient—that we are only six percent of the world's population . . . and that therefore there cannot be an American solution to every world problem.

The essential fact that both of these groups fail to grasp is that diplomacy and defense are not substitutes for one another. Either alone would fail. A willingness to resist force, unaccompanied by a willingness to talk, could provoke belligerence—while a willingness to talk, unaccompanied by a willingness to resist force, could invite disaster.

But as long as we know what comprises our vital interests and our long-range goals, we have nothing to fear from negotiations at the appropriate time, and nothing to gain by refusing to take part in them. At a time when a single clash could escalate overnight into a holocaust of mushroom clouds, a great power does not prove its firmness by leaving the task of exploring the other's intentions to sentries or those without full responsibility. Nor can ultimate weapons rightfully be employed, or the ultimate sacrifice rightfully demanded of our citizens, until every reasonable solution has been explored. "How many wars,"

Winston Churchill has written, "have been averted by patience and persisting good will! . . . How many wars have been precipitated by firebrands!"

If vital interests under duress can be preserved by peaceful means, negotiations will find that out. If our adversary will accept nothing less than a concession of our rights, negotiations will find that out. And if negotiations are to take place, this nation cannot abdicate to its adversaries the task of choosing the forum and the framework and the time. . . .

No one should be under the illusion that negotiations for the sake of negotiations always advance the cause of peace. If for lack of preparation they break up in bitterness, the prospects of peace have been endangered. If they are made a forum for propaganda or a cover for aggression, the processes of peace have been abused.

But it is a test of our national maturity to accept the fact that negotiations are not a contest spelling victory or defeat. They may succeed—they may fail. They are likely to be successful only if both sides reach an agreement which both regard as preferable to the status quo—an agreement in which each side can consider its own situation to be improved. And this is most difficult to obtain.

But, while we shall negotiate freely, we shall not negotiate freedom. Our answer to the classic question of Patrick Henry is still no—life is not so dear, and peace is not so precious, "as to be purchased at the price of chains and slavery." And that is our answer even though, for the first time since the ancient battles between Greek city-states, war entails the threat of total annihilation, of everything we know, of society itself. For to save mankind's future freedom, we must face up to any risk that is necessary. We will always seek peace—but we will never surrender.

In short, we are neither "warmongers" nor "appeasers," neither "hard" nor "soft." We are Americans, determined to defend the frontiers of freedom, by an honorable peace if peace is possible, but by arms if arms are used against us. . . .

University of Washington
Seattle, Washington, November 16, 1961

The Voices of Extremism

In the most critical periods of our nation's history, there have always been those on the fringes of our society who have sought to escape their own responsibility by finding a simple solution, an appealing slogan or a convenient scapegoat.

Financial crises could be explained by the presence of too many immigrants or too few greenbacks. War could be attributed to munitions makers or international bankers. Peace conferences failed because we were duped by the British, or tricked by the French, or deceived by the Russians. It was not the presence of Soviet troops in Eastern Europe that drove it to communism, it was the sellout at Yalta. It was not a civil war that removed China from the Free World, it was treason in high places.

At times these fanatics have achieved a temporary success among those who lack the will or the wisdom to face unpleasant facts or unsolved problems. But in time the basic good sense and stability of the great American consensus has always prevailed.

Now we are face-to-face once again with a period of heightened peril. The risks are great, the burdens heavy, the problems incapable of swift or lasting solution. And under the strains and frustrations imposed by constant tension and harassment, the discordant voices of extremism are once again heard in the land. Men who are unwilling to face up to the danger from without are convinced that the real danger is from within.

They look suspiciously at their neighbors and their leaders. They call for "a man on horseback" because they do not trust the people. They find treason in our churches, in our highest court, in our treatment of water. They equate the Democratic Party with the welfare state, the welfare state with socialism, socialism with communism. They object quite rightly to politics intruding on the military—but they are very anxious for the military to engage in their kind of politics.

But you and I—most Americans, soldiers and civilians—take a different view of our peril. We know it comes from without, not within. It must be met by quiet preparedness, not provocative speeches. And the steps taken this year to bolster our defenses—to increase our missile forces, to put more planes on alert, to provide more airlift and sealift and ready divisions, to make more certain than ever before that this nation has all the power that it will need to deter any attack of any kind —these steps constitute the most effective answer that can be made to those who would sow the seeds of doubt and of hate.

So let us not heed these counsels of fear and suspicion. Let us concentrate more on keeping enemy bombers and missiles away from our shores, and concentrate less on keeping neighbors away from our shelters. Let us devote more energy to organizing the free and friendly nations of the world, with common trade and strategic goals, and devote less energy to organizing armed bands of civilian guerrillas that are more likely to supply local vigilantes than national vigilance.

Let our patriotism be reflected in the creation of confidence in one another, rather than in crusades of suspicion. Let us prove we think our country great, by striving to make it greater. And, above all, let us remember, however serious the outlook, however harsh the task, the one great irreversible trend in the history of the world is on the side of liberty—and we, for all time to come, are on the same side.

California State Democratic Party Dinner
Los Angeles, California, November 18, 1961

Q: Mr. President, a number of your right-wing critics say that your foreign policy is based on a no-win policy in the Cold War. Would you address yourself to this charge?

THE PRESIDENT: Well, of course, every American . . . wants the United States to be secure and at peace, and wants the cause of freedom around the world to prevail. . . . And what we are anxious to do, of course, is . . . permit what Thomas Jefferson called the disease of liberty to be caught. . . . . We want to do that, of course, without having a nuclear war. Now, if someone thinks we should have a nuclear war in order to win, I can inform them that there will not be winners in the next nuclear war, if there is one, and this country and other countries will suffer very heavy blows. So that we have to proceed with responsibility and with care in an age where the human race can obliterate itself. The objective of this administration, and I think the objective of the country, is to protect our security, keep the peace, protect our vital interests, and make it possible for what we believe to be a system of government which is in accordance with the basic aspirations of people everywhere to ultimately prevail. That is our objective and that's the one that we shall continue.

President's News Conference
Washington, D.C., February 14, 1962

Those self-appointed generals and admirals who want to send someone else's son to war ought to be kept at home by the voters and replaced in Washington by someone who understands what the twentieth century is all about.

. . . This is no time, in 1962, for rash talk which strengthens the claims of our adversaries. This is no time for confused and intemperate remarks on the part of those who have neither the facts nor the ultimate responsibility.

This is the time for a man who talks softly, but who'll also carry a big stick. . . . Those self-appointed generals and admirals who want to send someone else's son to war and who consistently vote against the instruments of peace ought to be kept at home by the voters and replaced in Washington by someone who understands what the twentieth century is all about.

Indianapolis Airport
Indianapolis, Indiana, October 13, 1962

Q: Mr. President, in some of our major cities, John Birch or right-wing-type groups have been organizing boycotts against stores which carry imports from so-called Iron Curtain countries, and in some cases intimidating the stores. The State Department suggests that this is contrary to our policy of encouraging nonstrategic trade with those countries. I wonder if you share that view about those boycotts?

THE PRESIDENT: Yes. I think that it harasses merchants and I don't think it carries on much of an effective fight against the spread of communism. If they really want to do something about the spread of communism, they will assist the Alliance for Progress, for one thing, or they will encourage their children to join the Peace Corps, or they will do a good many other things which are very greatly needed. They will be generous to students who come to the United States to study, and show them something of America. Those are the things that really make a difference, not going down and, because some merchant happens to have Polish hams in his shop, saying he is unpatriotic. That doesn't seem to me to be a great contribution in the fight against communism.

President's News Conference
Washington, D.C., December 12, 1962

The Unfinished Agenda

Ignorance and misinformation can handicap the progress of a city or a company, but they can, if allowed to prevail in foreign policy, handicap this country's security. In a world of complex and continuing problems, in a world full of frustrations and irritations, America's leadership must be guided by the lights of learning and reason—or else those who confuse rhetoric with reality and the plausible with the possible will gain the popular ascendancy with their seemingly swift and simple solutions to every world problem.

There will always be dissident voices heard in the land, expressing opposition without alternatives, finding fault but never favor, perceiving gloom on every side and seeking influence without responsibility. Those voices are inevitable.

But today other voices are heard in the land—voices preaching doctrines wholly unrelated to reality, wholly unsuited to the sixties, doctrines which apparently assume that words will suffice without weapons, that vituperation is as good as victory and that peace is a sign of weakness. At a time when the national debt is steadily being reduced in terms of its burden on our economy, they see that debt as the greatest single threat to our security. At a time when we are steadily reducing the number of federal employees serving every thousand citizens, they fear those supposed hordes of civil servants far more than the actual hordes of opposing armies.

We cannot expect that everyone, to use the phrase of a decade ago, will "talk sense to the American people." But we can hope that fewer people will listen to nonsense. And the notion that this nation is headed for defeat through deficit, or that strength is but a matter of slogans, is nothing but just plain nonsense.

I want to discuss with you today the status of our strength and our security . . . strength and security are not easily or cheaply obtained, nor are they quickly and simply explained. There are many kinds of strength and no one kind will suffice. Overwhelming nuclear strength cannot stop a guerrilla war. Formal pacts of alliance cannot stop internal subversion. Displays of material wealth cannot stop the disillusionment of diplomats subjected to discrimination.

Above all, words alone are not enough. The United States is a peaceful nation. And where our strength and determination are clear, our words need merely to convey conviction, not belligerence. If we are strong, our strength will speak for itself. If we are weak, words will be of no help.

I realize that this nation often tends to identify turning points in world affairs with the major addresses which preceded them. But it was not the Monroe Doctrine that kept all Europe away from this hemisphere—it was the strength of the British fleet and the width of the Atlantic Ocean. It was not General Marshall's speech at Harvard which kept communism out of Western Europe—it was the strength and stability made possible by our military and economic assistance.

In this administration also it has been necessary at times to issue specific warnings—warnings that we could not stand by and watch the Communists conquer Laos by force, or intervene in the Congo, or swallow West Berlin, or maintain offensive missiles on Cuba. But while our goals were at least temporarily obtained in these and other instances, our successful defense of freedom was due not to the words we used, but to the strength we stood ready to use on behalf of the principles we stand ready to defend.

A nation can be no stronger abroad than she is at home. Only an America which practices what it preaches about equal rights and social justice will be respected by those whose choice affects our future.

This strength is composed of many different elements, ranging from the most massive deterrents to the most subtle influences. And all types of strength are needed—no one kind could do the job alone. Let us take a moment, therefore, to review this nation's progress in each major area of strength.

First . . . the strategic nuclear power of the United States has been so greatly modernized and expanded in the last one thousand days, by the rapid production and deployment of the most modern missile systems, that any and all potential aggressors are clearly confronted now with the impossibility of strategic victory—and the certainty of total destruction—if by reckless attack they should ever force upon us the necessity of a strategic reply. . . .

But the lessons of the last decade have taught us that freedom cannot be defended by strategic nuclear power alone. We have, therefore, in the last three years accelerated the development and deployment of tactical nuclear weapons . . . radically improved the readiness of our conventional force . . . and . . . moving beyond the traditional roles of our military forces . . . achieved an increase of nearly six hundred percent in our special forces—those forces that are prepared to work with our allies and friends against the guerrillas, saboteurs, insurgents, and assassins who threaten freedom in a less direct but equally dangerous manner.

But American military might should not and need not stand alone against the ambitions of international communism. Our security and strength, in the last analysis, directly depend on the security and strength of others, and that is why our military and economic assistance plays such a key role in enabling those who live on the periphery of the Communist world to maintain their independence of choice. Our assistance to these nations can be painful, risky and costly, as is true in Southeast Asia today. But we dare not weary of the task. For our assistance makes possible the stationing of 3.5 million allied troops along the Communist frontier at one tenth the cost of maintaining a comparable number of American soldiers. A successful Communist breakthrough in these areas, necessitating direct United States intervention, would cost us several times as much as our entire foreign-aid program, and might cost us heavily in American lives as well. . . .

And reducing the economic help needed to bolster these nations that undertake to help defend freedom can have the same disastrous result. . . .

I have spoken of strength largely in terms of the deterrence and resistance of aggression and attack. But, in today's world, freedom can be lost without a shot being fired, by ballots as well as bullets. The success of our leadership is dependent upon respect for our mission in the world as well as our missiles—on a clearer recognition of the virtues of freedom as well as the evils of tyranny.

That is why our Information Agency has doubled the shortwave broadcasting power of the Voice of America and . . . taken a host of other steps to carry our message of truth and freedom to all the far corners of the earth.

And that is also why we have regained the initiative in the exploration of outer space, making an annual effort greater than the combined total of all space activities undertaken during the fifties . . . and making it clear to all that the United States of America has no intention of finishing second in space. . . .

There is no longer any fear in the free world that a Communist lead in space will become a permanent assertion of supremacy and the basis of military superiority. There is no longer any doubt about the strength and skill of American science, American industry, American education, and the American free enterprise system. . . .

Finally, it should be clear by now that a nation can be no stronger abroad than she is at home. Only an America which practices what it preaches about equal rights and social justice will be respected by those whose choice affects our future. Only an America which has fully educated its citizens is fully capable of tackling the complex problems and perceiving the hidden dangers of the world in which we live. And only an America which is growing and prospering economically can sustain the worldwide defenses of freedom, while demonstrating to all concerned the opportunities of our system and society.

It is clear, therefore, that we are strengthening our security as well as our economy by our recent record increases in national income and output. . . .

My friends and fellow citizens: I cite these facts and figures to make it clear that America today is stronger than ever before. Our adversaries have not abandoned their ambitions, our dangers have not diminished, our vigilance cannot be relaxed. But now we have the military, the scientific, and the economic strength to do whatever must be done for the preservation and promotion of freedom.

That strength will never be used in pursuit of aggressive ambitions—it will always be used in pursuit of peace. It will never be used to promote provocations—it will always be used to promote the peaceful settlement of disputes.

We in this country, in this generation, are—by destiny rather than choice—the watchmen on the walls of world freedom. We ask, therefore, that we may be worthy of our power and responsibility, that we may exercise our strength with wisdom and restraint, and that we may achieve in our time and for all time the ancient vision of "peace on earth, goodwill toward men." That must always be our goal, and the righteousness of our cause must always underlie our strength. For as was written long ago, "except the Lord keep the city, the watchman waketh but in vain."

Remarks prepared for delivery at
Dallas Trade Mart Luncheon (undelivered)
November 22, 1963

Meeting the press.
PHOTO COURTESY CECIL W. STOUGHTON.

SOURCES

PART I THE PRESIDENCY

CHAPTER 1 *The Inaugural Address*

The Inaugural Address, Washington, D.C., January 20, 1961, "Public Papers of the Presidents: John F. Kennedy" (hereafter cited as Public Papers), 1961, pp. 1–3.

FOOTNOTE: Excerpt from remarks to a Democratic fund-raising dinner on the first anniversary of the Inaugural, Washington, D.C., January 20, 1962, ibid., 1962, pp. 40–41.

CHAPTER 2 *The Role of the President*

The Vital Center of Action:
National Press Club speech, Washington, D.C., January 14, 1960, "John Fitzgerald Kennedy, A Compilation of Statements and Speeches made During his Service in the United States Senate and House of Representatives," 88th Congress, 2d Session, Senate Document No. 79 (hereafter cited as Senate Document No. 79), pp. 1106–1109.

The Leader of the Free World:
California Democratic Clubs Convention, Fresno, California, February 12, 1960, from the John Fitzgerald Kennedy Library collection of various Kennedy speech files (hereafter cited as "Collection"), speech text, pp. 2–23.

The Champion of Freedom:
Labor Day campaign kickoff speech, Detroit, Michigan, September 5, 1960, "The Speeches, Remarks, Press Conferences, and Statements of Senator John F. Kennedy, August 1 through November 7, 1960," Report of the U.S.

Senate Committee on Commerce, Subcommittee on Freedom of Communications, 87th Congress, 1st Session, Report 994 (hereafter cited as Senate Report No. 994), p. 113.

Campaign remarks, Muskegon, Michigan, September 5, 1960, ibid., p. 120.

The Responsible Officer of Government:
The President's news conference, Washington, D.C., April 21, 1961, Public Papers, 1961, pp. 312–313.

The President's news conference, Washington, D.C., March 29, 1962, ibid., 1962, p. 276.

The President's news conference, Washington, D.C., May 9, 1962, ibid., p. 376.

The Ultimate Decision Maker:
Television and radio year-end conversation with the President, Washington, D.C., December 17, 1962, ibid., pp. 889–891, 903.

The Party Leader:
Remarks to members of National and State Democratic Committees, Washington, D.C., January 18, 1963, ibid., 1963, pp. 50–51.

The Happy President:
The President's news conference, Washington, D.C., October 31, 1963, ibid., p. 830.

CHAPTER 3 *The Call to Public Service*

The Politician and the Intellectual:
Harvard commencement address, Cambridge, Massachusetts, June 14, 1956, Senate Document No. 79, pp. 1035–1037.

The Senate's Distinguished Traditions:
Remarks to U.S. Senate on selection of portraits of outstanding senators, U.S. Senate, Washington, D.C., May 1, 1957, ibid., pp. 486–494.

The Best People We Can Get:
Campaign speech, Wittenberg College, Springfield, Ohio, October 17, 1960, Senate Report No. 994, pp. 634–638.

Campaign speech, Bangor, Maine, September 2, 1960, ibid., pp. 82–83.

The City Upon a Hill:
Farewell address to Massachusetts State Legislature, Boston, Massachusetts, January 9, 1961, Collection, Text, pp. 1–3.

The Pride of a Public Career:
State of the Union Address, the Capitol, Washington, D.C., January 30, 1961, Public Papers, p. 27.

The Peace Corps:
Statement upon the establishment of the Peace Corps, Washington, D.C., March 1, 1961, ibid., pp. 134–135.

The New Ethical Standard:
Special message to Congress on Ethics in Government, Washington, D.C., April 27, 1961, ibid., pp. 326–327, 330, 333–334.

The Obligations of Citizenship:
Letter to Mrs. Alicia Patterson, editor and publisher of *Newsday,* May 16, 1961, ibid., pp. 376–378.

The Front Line of Service:
Remarks to the American Foreign Service Association, Washington, D.C., May 31, 1962, ibid., 1962, pp. 532–534.

CHAPTER 4 *The President and Congress*

The Rules Committee Battle:
The President's news conference, Washington, D.C., January 25, 1961, Public Papers, 1961, p. 11.

The Separate Responsibilities of Each Branch:
State of the Union Address, the Capitol, Washington, D.C., January 30, 1961, ibid., p. 19.

State of the Union Address, the Capitol, Washington, D.C., January 11, 1962, ibid., 1962, p. 5.

The Inevitable Accord and Discord:
The President's news conference, Washington, D.C., March 21, 1962, ibid., p. 260.

The President's news conference, Washington, D.C., July 23, 1962, ibid., p. 573.

Television and radio year-end conversation with the President, Washington, D.C., December 17, 1962, ibid., pp. 892, 894.

The President's news conference, Washington, D.C., January 24, 1963, ibid., 1963, p. 95.

The President's news conference, Washington, D.C., May 8, 1963, ibid., p. 375.

PART II THE PRESIDENTIAL CAMPAIGN

CHAPTER 5 *The Road to the White House*

The "Parochial" Young Congressman of 1952:
Colloquy on House floor regarding Water Projects Appropriation Bill, House of Representatives, Washington, D.C., April 1, 1952, Senate Document No. 79, pp. 111–112.

The "National Interest" Senator of 1954:
Remarks during Senate debate on St. Lawrence Seaway, U.S. Senate, Washington, D.C., January 14, 1954, ibid., pp. 271–276.

The National Convention Speaker of 1956:
Nomination of Adlai E. Stevenson for Presdent of the United States, Democratic National Convention, Chicago, Illinois, August 16, 1956, Collection, Text, pp. 1–4.

The Defeated Vice-Presidential Contender of 1956:
Conceding the Vice-Presidential nomination, Democratic National Convention, Chicago, Illinois, August 17, 1956, Collection, Official Proceedings of the Democratic National Convention, 1956, p. 482.

The Presidential Prospect of 1958:
Remarks to the Gridiron Club, Washington, D.C., March 15, 1958, Collection, Text, pp. 1–2.

The Declaration of Candidacy in 1960:
Statement of Declaration for the Presidency, Washington, D.C., January 2, 1960, Collection, Text.

The Question of Age:
Nationally televised news conference, New York, New York, July 4, 1960, *The New York Times,* July 5, 1960, p. 1, col. 8.

The Final Appeal:
Remarks to Democratic National Committee Dinner on convention eve, Los Angeles, California, July 10, 1960, Collection, Text, pp. 1–2.

The Opening of the New Frontier:
Acceptance of presidential nomination, Democratic National Convention, Los Angeles, California, July 15, 1960, Collection, Text, pp. 1–7.

The First Debate:
Opening statement, first televised presidential candidates debate, Chicago, Illinois, September 26, 1960, Senate Report No. 994, Part 3.

The Definition of Liberal:
Acceptance of New York Liberal Party nomination, New York, New York, September 14, 1960, ibid., pp. 239–242.
The Issue of Latin America:
Campaign speech, Tampa, Florida, October 18, 1960, ibid., pp. 1159–1166.

The Issue of Peace:
Campaign speech, San Francisco, California, November 2, 1960, ibid., pp. 863–866.

The End of the Campaign:
Campaign remarks, street rally, Waterbury, Connecticut, November 6, 1960, ibid., p. 912.

Press conference, Hyannis Port, Massachusetts, November 9, 1960, Collection.

Democratic Dinner, Chicago, Illinois, April 28, 1961, Public Papers, 1961, p. 339.

National Association of Manufacturers, New York, New York, December 6, 1961, ibid., pp. 773–774.

Ohio Democratic Dinner, Columbus, Ohio, January 6, 1962, ibid., 1962, p. 1.

Wisconsin Democratic Dinner, Milwaukee, Wisconsin, May 12, 1962, ibid., p. 389.

CHAPTER 6 *The Religious Issue*

The Responsibility of the Press:
American Society of Newspaper Editors, Washington, D.C., April 21, 1960, Collection, Text, pp. 1–8.

Bronx County Democratic Dinner, New York, New York, April 1960, Collection.

The Refutation of Bigotry:
Greater Houston Ministerial Association, Houston, Texas, September 12, 1960, Senate Report No. 994, pp. 208–218.

The Differences From 1928:
Annual Al Smith Memorial Dinner, New York, New York, October 19, 1960, ibid., pp. 666–669.

The Responsibility of Parents:
The President's news conference, Washington, D.C., June 27, 1962, Public Papers, 1962, pp. 510–511.

PART III THE NEW FRONTIER

CHAPTER 7 *The Restoration of Economic Growth*

The Angry Young Congressman:
Statement on House floor, U.S. House of Representatives, Washington, D.C., July 24, 1947, Senate Document No. 79, pp. 9–11.

The Determined New President:
State of the Union Address, the Capitol, Washington, D.C., January 30, 1961, Public Papers, 1961, pp. 19–20, 22.

The Road to Recovery:
National Industrial Conference Board, Washington, D.C., February 13, 1961, ibid., pp. 87–89.

The Prudent Steward:
Special message to Congress on Budget and Fiscal Policy, Washington, D.C., March 24, 1961, ibid., p. 221.

The Expansion of Opportunity:
State of the Union Address, the Capitol, Washington, D.C., January 11, 1962, ibid., pp. 5–9.

The Preservation of Price Stability:
The President's news conference, Washington, D.C., April 11, 1962, ibid., pp. 315–319, 321.

The President's news conference, Washington, D.C., April 18, 1962, ibid., pp. 331, 335.

Footnote: Remarks at White House Correspondents and News Photographers Association Dinner, Washington, D.C., April 27, 1962, ibid., pp. 344–345.

The Myths of Economic Debate:
Commencement address, Yale University, New Haven, Connecticut, June 11, 1962, ibid., pp. 470–475.

The Politics of Confidence:
The President's news conference, Washington, D.C., June 14, 1962, ibid., pp. 491–492.

The Foundation for Freedom's Success:
State of the Union Address, the Capitol, Washington, D.C., January 14, 1963, ibid., 1963, pp. 12–15.

CHAPTER **8** *The Exploration of Space*

The Adventure of Space:
Special address to Congress on Urgent National Needs, the Capitol, Washington, D.C., May 25, 1961, Public Papers, 1961, pp. 403–405.

The President's news conference, Washington, D.C., November 29, 1961, ibid., p. 761.

The Universal Language of Space:
University of California, Berkeley, California, March 23, 1962, ibid., 1962, p. 264.

The New Ocean of Space:
Rice University, Houston, Texas, September 12, 1962, ibid., pp. 668–671.

The High Wall of Space:
Dedication of Aerospace Medical Health Center, San Antonio, Texas, November 21, 1963, ibid., 1963, p. 883.

CHAPTER **9** *The Fight for Civil Rights*

The American Vision:
NAACP rally, Los Angeles, California, July 10, 1960, Collection, Text, pp. 1–3.

The Standard of John C. Calhoun:
Campaign speech, Columbia, South Carolina, October 10, 1960, Senate Report No. 994, pp. 548–551.

The Enforcement of Court Orders:
Televised address to the nation, Washington, D.C., September 30, 1962, Public Papers, 1962, pp. 726–728.

The Right to Vote:
State of the Union Address, the Capitol, Washington, D.C., January 14, 1963, ibid., 1963, p. 14.

The Peaceful Revolution:
Televised address to the nation, Washington, D.C., June 11, 1963, ibid., pp. 468–471.

The Role of the Military:
Letter to the Secretary of Defense, Washington, D.C., June 22, 1963, ibid., p. 496.

The Civil Rights Act of 1963:
Special message to the Congress on Civil Rights and Job Opportunities, Washington, D.C., June 19, 1963, ibid., p. 483.

The March on Washington:
Statement on March on Washington for Jobs and Freedom, Washington, D.C., August 28, 1963, ibid., p. 645.

The Long View:
Excerpt, the President's news conference, Washington, D.C., September 12, 1963, ibid., p. 677.

The Final Word:
Remarks intended for delivery to Texas Democratic Dinner, Austin, Texas, November 22, 1963 (undelivered), ibid., pp. 896–897.

CHAPTER **10** *The Promotion of the Arts*

The Liberation of the Human Mind:
National Cultural Center Dinner, Washington, D.C., November 29, 1962, Public Papers, 1962, pp. 846–847.

The Central Purpose of Civilization:
National Gallery of Art, Opening of *Mona Lisa* Exhibition, Washington, D.C., January 8, 1963, ibid., 1963, p. 5.

The Fiber of Our National Life:
Amherst College, Amherst, Massachusetts, October 26, 1963, ibid., pp. 816–818.

PART **IV** THE PURSUIT OF PEACE AND SECURITY

CHAPTER **11** *The Tide Is Turned*

The Urgent Agenda:
Speech on Senate floor, the Capitol, Washington, D.C., June 14, 1960, Senate Document No. 79, pp. 926–934.

The Response to Multiple Crises:
State of the Union Address, the Capitol, Washington, D.C., January 30, 1961, Public Papers, 1961, pp. 19, 22–28.

The Freedom Doctrine:
Special address to Congress on Urgent National Needs, the Capitol, Washington, D.C., May 25, 1961, ibid., pp. 396–398, 405–406.

The Great Defender of Freedom:
State of the Union Address, the Capitol, Washington, D.C., January 11, 1962, ibid., 1962, pp. 9–12, 15.

The Tides of Human Freedom:
State of the Union Address, the Capitol, Washington, D.C., January 14, 1963, ibid., 1963, pp. 11–12, 15, 18–19.

CHAPTER 12 *The National Defense*

The Cautious Commander-in-Chief:
Special message to Congress on Defense Policies and Principles, Washington, D.C., March 28, 1961, Public Papers, 1961, pp. 229–233, 236–238, 240.

The Modern Military Officer:
United States Naval Academy Commencement, Annapolis, Maryland, June 7, 1961, ibid., pp. 447–448.

The Inequities of Service:
The President's news conference, Washington, D.C., March 21, 1962, ibid., 1962, pp. 259–260.

The Best Defense in the World:
State of the Union Address, the Capitol, Washington, D.C., January 14, 1963, ibid., 1963, p. 18.

CHAPTER 13 *The U.S.–Soviet Competition*

The Real Revolution:
Public message to Soviet Chairman Khrushchev after the invasion of the Bay of Pigs, Washington, D.C., April 18, 1961, Public Papers, 1961, p. 287.

The Summit Encounter:
Televised report to the American people on the U.S.–U.S.S.R. summit in Vienna, Washington, D.C., June 6, 1961, ibid., pp. 442–446.

The Running Tiger:
The President's news conference, Washington, D.C., June 28, 1961, ibid., p. 478.

The Berlin Crisis:
Statement on the Berlin crisis, Washington, D.C., July 19, 1961, ibid., pp. 521–523.

Televised address to the American people on the Berlin crisis, Washington, D.C., July 25, 1961, ibid., pp. 533–540.

The Berlin Wall:
White House statement on the Berlin Wall, Washington, D.C., August 24, 1961, ibid., pp. 568–569.

Footnote: Excerpt from the President's news conference, Washington, D.C., January 15, 1962, ibid., 1962, pp. 20–21.

The Continuing Dialogue:
Interview by Aleksei Adzhubei, editor of *Izvestia* and son-in-law of Soviet Chairman Khrushchev, Hyannis Port, Massachusetts, November 25, 1961, ibid., 1961, pp. 741–751.

The Wave of the Future:
University of California, Berkeley, California, March 23, 1962, ibid., 1962, pp. 265–266.

The Cuban Missile Crisis:
Televised address to the American people on the Cuban missile crisis, Washington, D.C., October 22, 1962, ibid., pp. 806–809.

Letter to Soviet Chairman Khrushchev, Washington, D.C., October 27, 1962, ibid., pp. 813–814.

Statement on Soviet withdrawal of missiles from Cuba, Washington, D.C., October 28, 1962, ibid., p. 815.

Opening statement, the President's news conference, Washington, D.C., November 20, 1962, ibid., pp. 830–831.

The Strategy of Peace:
Commencement address, American University, Washington, D.C., June 10, 1963, ibid., 1963, pp. 460–464.

The Nuclear Test-Ban Treaty:
Televised address to the American people on the Limited Nuclear Test-Ban Treaty, Washington, D.C., July 26, 1963, ibid., pp. 601–606.

Remarks upon signing the Nuclear Test-Ban Treaty, Washington, D.C., October 7, 1963, ibid., pp. 765–766.

The Quest for Peace:
General Assembly of the United Nations, New York, New York, September 20, 1963, ibid., pp. 693–698.

The Sale of American Wheat:
Opening statement, the President's news conference, Washington, D.C., October 9, 1963, ibid., pp. 767–768.

CHAPTER 14 *The Western Alliance*

The Political-Military Link:
NATO Military Committee, Washington, D.C., April 10, 1961, Public Papers, 1961, p. 255.

The Change in World Power:
Press luncheon, Paris, France, June 2, 1961, ibid., pp. 429–431.

The Trade Expansion Act:
Port of New Orleans, New Orleans, Louisiana, May 4, 1962, ibid., 1962, pp. 359–361.

The Atlantic Partnership:
Independence Hall, Philadelphia, Pennsylvania, July 4, 1962, ibid., pp. 538–539.

The Exemplar of Service:
Letter to Jean Monnet, Washington, D.C., January 22, 1963, ibid., 1963, p. 72.

The Champion of Liberty:
Remarks upon signing proclamation conferring honorary citizenship on Sir Winston Churchill, Washington, D.C., April 9, 1963, ibid., pp. 315–316.

The Only War We Seek:
Remarks upon arrival in Germany, Bonn-Cologne Airport, Federal Republic of Germany, June 23, 1963, ibid., pp. 497–498.

The Age of Interdependence:
Paulskirche Assembly Hall, Frankfurt, Federal Republic of Germany, June 25, 1963, ibid., pp. 516–521.

The Proudest Boast:
West Berlin City Hall, June 26, 1963, ibid., pp. 524–525.

CHAPTER 15 *The Third World*

The Concerned Young Congressman:
Debate on Technical Assistance Appropriation Bill, House of Representatives, Washington, D.C., June 28, 1952, Senate Document No. 79, p. 120.

The Challenge of Imperialism: Algeria:
Address to the Senate on imperialism and Algeria, U.S. Senate, Washington, D.C., July 2, 1957, ibid., pp. 511–514, 518–521, 523, 528, 530.

The New Nationalism: India:
U.S. Senate, Washington, D.C., March 25, 1958, ibid., pp. 591–608.

The Fight for Foreign Aid:
U.S. Senate, Washington, D.C., February 19, 1959, ibid., pp. 789–797.

The Frontiers of Freedom:
Special address to Congress on Urgent National Needs, the Capitol, Washington, D.C., May 25, 1961, Public Papers, 1961, pp. 399–400.

The Uncommitted and Underdeveloped:
Message to the Belgrade Conference of Nonaligned States, Washington, D.C., August 30, 1961, ibid., p. 573.

Remarks to American Bankers Association Symposium on Economic Growth, Washington, D.C., February 25, 1963, ibid., 1963, p. 210.

The Future Prime Ministers:
Remarks to a group of foreign students visiting the White House, Washington, D.C., April 10, 1963, ibid., p. 319.

The Family of Man:
Remarks upon receiving the annual Family of Man Award, New York Protestant Council, New York, New York, November 8, 1963, ibid., pp. 839–842.

The Alliance for Progress:
Address to Latin American Diplomatic Corps, White House, Washington, D.C., March 13, 1961, ibid., 1961, pp. 170–175.

State Dinner, Bogotá, Colombia, December 17, 1961, ibid., pp. 811–814.

Remarks at White House Dinner honoring Western Hemisphere Nobel prize winners, Washington, D.C., April 29, 1962, ibid., 1962, p. 347.

Conference of Central American Republics, San José, Costa Rica, March 18, 1963, ibid., 1963, pp. 264–267.

The New Nations of Africa:
National Council of Women, New York, New York, October 12, 1960, Senate Report No. 994, pp. 567–571.

The President's news conference, Washington, D.C., March 1, 1961, Public Papers, 1961, p. 139.

The War in Indochina:
Speech on Senate floor, U.S. Senate, Washington, D.C., April 6, 1954, Senate Document No. 79, pp. 284–292.

Opening statement, the President's news conference, Washington, D.C., March 23, 1961, Public Papers, 1961, pp. 213–215.

Interview by Walter Cronkite on CBS Television, September 2, 1963, ibid., 1963, pp. 651–652.

The President's news conference, Washington, D.C., October 31, 1963, ibid., p. 828.

The United Nations:
State of the Union Address, the Capitol, Washington, D.C., January 30, 1961, Public Papers, 1961, p. 26.

General Assembly of the United Nations, New York, New York, September 25, 1961, ibid., pp. 618–626.

State of the Union Address, the Capitol, Washington, D.C., January 11, 1962, ibid., 1962, pp. 10–11.

The President's news conference, Washington, D.C., March 21, 1962, ibid., pp. 254–255.

The Little Nations:
Irish Parliament, Dublin, Ireland, June 28, 1963, ibid., 1963, pp. 535–539.

CHAPTER 16 *The Uses and Limits of Power*

The Role of Negotiations:
University of Washington, Seattle, Washington, November 16, 1961, Public Papers, 1961, pp. 725–727.

The Voices of Extremism:
California State Democratic Party Dinner, Los Angeles, California, November 18, 1961, ibid., pp. 735–736.

The President's news conference, Washington, D.C., February 14, 1962, ibid., 1962, p. 141.

Campaign remarks, Indianapolis, Indiana, October 13, 1962, ibid., p. 772.

The President's news conference, Washington, D.C., December 12, 1962, ibid., pp. 872–873.

The Unfinished Agenda:
Remarks prepared for delivery at Dallas Trade Mart Luncheon (undelivered), November 22, 1963, ibid., 1963, pp. 891–894.

Defending his program, May 22,1963.
PHOTO BY ABBIE ROWE, COURTESY THE JOHN FITZGERALD KENNEDY LIBRARY.

INDEX

for freedom

the same hig

sacrifice and

and will h

you. ~~I to~~

were & ~~disagree~~

P9-CRL-561

Accounting Standards in Evolution

Ross M. Skinner

Holt, Rinehart and Winston of Canada, Limited

Canadian Cataloguing in Publication Data

Skinner, Ross M.
Accounting standards in evolution

Includes index.
ISBN 0-03-922001-X

1. Accounting. I. Title.

HF5635.S58 1987 657'.044 C87-093161-X

Publisher: Richard Kitowski
Publishing Services Manager: Karen Eakin
Editorial Co-ordinator: Edie Franks
Copy Editor: Anne Stilman
Cover Design, Typesetting and Assembly: Cundari Group Ltd.
Printing and Binding: John Deyell Company

Printed in Canada
2 3 4 5 91 90 89 88

Preface

This book has three principal objectives. The first is to recount in an organized fashion the standards that govern financial reporting today. The second is to explain why they take the form that they do—that is, to explore the general theory underlying today's standards and the particular thinking that has influenced the form taken by individual standards. The third is to evaluate the standards and underlying theory critically—to appraise strengths and weaknesses with a view to stimulating discussion and possible improvement.

Forty years ago, when I entered accounting practice, we were still fighting battles to require a systematic provision for depreciation regardless of whether a year's results were good or bad and to prevent the charging of arbitrary provisions for "reserves" against income. Now, forty years later, the issues have changed radically but the struggle for better financial reporting continues. Accounting standards today cover much more territory and deal with much more complex issues. Yet no one would claim that we are close to resolving all possible points of contention. Accounting standards have evolved over time and will continue to evolve—hence the title of this book.

My strong belief is that an understanding of the past development of ideas will help us in the present and future. All of us have our ingrained mind-sets, and it is instructive to look back to see how much of previous conventional wisdom appears strange in retrospect. That is why Part I of this book consists of an excursion, unfortunately all-too-brief, through the history of accounting. Accountants, and particularly those involved in setting accounting standards, would do well to devote more time to the study of the history of their discipline and the way it has responded to changes in its environment.

Part II, the longest part of this book, examines the state of current accounting standards. The majority of these standards spring from practice and are described, somewhat misleadingly, as "generally accepted accounting principles." That description is misleading because, not infrequently, those responsible for setting accounting standards prescribe treatments that are substantially contrary to existing practice. That fact suggests that standard-setters have some conceptual framework in their minds which they use to arrive at their recommendations. It is apparent that the theory of historical cost accounting provides much of that framework. Historical cost accounting reached its zenith of acceptance and respect around 1960. Yet, even at the height of its influence, it never came close to providing answers to all financial reporting questions. It was oriented to business organizations and had little to say about the accounting of nonbusiness entities and governments. Among business organizations, it concentrated on product-handling industries and was poorly adapted to the financial reporting needs of such important sectors of the economy as financial institutions, investment companies, service industries, and the extractive industries. Because of these and other shortcomings, we stand on shaky ground in attempting to improve existing accounting standards. The final chapter of Part II contains some suggestions for doing so without radical departure from the basic approach of historical cost accounting.

Part III chronicles the efforts made to replace or revise historical cost accounting so as to better portray the effects of changing prices in financial reports. By now it is clear that those efforts have failed. There are several contributing reasons.

One important reason is that accounting theoreticians could not agree on the superiority of any one model for price-change accounting. Their disagreements were fundamental, extending even to their premises as to the objectives of financial reporting. On the practical side, preparers of financial statements were uneasy about the degree of value estimation required in most models of price-change accounting and users of financial statements evinced a lack of interest in the whole subject. In view of the likelihood of a repetition of price instability at some future time—whether five, ten, or twenty-five years hence—standard-setters would do well to ponder the lessons of this experience and be better prepared to act another time.

Periodically, the gaps and weaknesses in historical cost accounting stimulate accountants to wonder if we could articulate a better conceptual framework. The first chapter of Part IV builds upon the literature in this field to suggest a structure of thought. Although such an exercise has value, not too much can be expected from it. No matter how clear the objectives of financial reporting, it will always be necessary to make significant trade-offs between the information that is desired and the information achievable with reasonable reliability of measurement. Thus, it seems likely that accounting standards will have to continue to deal with issues in considerable detail rather than be confined to broad statements of principle.

The final chapter in the book deals with the mechanics of setting accounting standards. Several different arrangements are possible. The claim of the accounting profession for primacy in the task rests upon its competence and experience in dealing with financial reporting issues. Yet, the record suggests that standard-setting requires some measure of legal support to be workable. To deserve such support the profession must be seen to be acting in the public interest and must perform effectively. While the CICA performance has been creditable, improvements could be made in dealing with emerging issues and monitoring the performance of standards already issued. Some action is also necessary to stem the proliferation of accounting methods in Canada attributable to the fact that new U.S. practices are usually accepted here without question. Meeting these demands might require modification of the existing standard-setting structure.

This book could not have been completed without the support and assistance of my firm, Clarkson Gordon. I am particularly grateful for suggestions and critical comments on drafts of large sections of the book by partners of the firm, D.W. Lay, and J.A. Milburn. Drafts of individual chapters also benefited materially from the comments of H. Bierman, Jr., G.W. Braum, H.F.C. Graham, D.A. Leslie, L.S. Rosen, J.N. Ross, W.G. Ross, W.K. Strelioff, and some fifteen members of the National Accounting Standards department of Clarkson Gordon. Karen Montano both commented on content and provided major assistance in editing. The last word, appropriately, belongs with Pearl Newbold. Without her cheerful dedication and superb efficiency at the word processor I might never have reached the end of this work.

Toronto 1986 R.M. Skinner

Ross M. Skinner

A chartered accountant since 1949, Ross Skinner joined the firm of Clarkson Gordon in 1945 and became a partner in 1954. He served as National Director of Accounting Standards for the firm for fifteen years and although officially retired, he remains active in the field of accounting research and standards.

His love of the profession is demonstrated by his involvement over the years. He has been a member of, and chaired, many professional and academic committees, including the Accounting and Auditing Research Committee of the Canadian Institute of Chartered Accountants and the Financial Disclosure Advisory Board of the Ontario Securities Commission.

Accounting Standards in Evolution is the latest in a long line of prestigious accomplishments. As an author of accounting and auditing textbooks and articles, Ross Skinner is unsurpassed in Canada. Among his works are *Analytical Auditing, Accounting Principles: A Canadian Viewpoint, Pension Accounting,* and *Canadian University Accounting. Accounting Standards in Evolution* will undoubtedly become the authoritative accounting reference text in Canada.

Ross Skinner was recognized for his outstanding achievements by the conferring of an honorary doctorate in 1979 by Brock University. In 1984, he was awarded the highest honor of the Institute of Chartered Accountants of Ontario: the Award of Outstanding Merit, and in 1985, the Certificate of Merit of the Canadian Institute of Chartered Accountants. In 1987, he was appointed Adjunct Professor and Director of the Centre for Accounting Studies in the Faculty of Management Studies at the University of Toronto.

Contents

Abbreviations

The following abbreviations are used in this book:

Accounting and business terms

ACM	Actuarial cost method
AFUDC	Allowance for funds used during construction
CCA	Capital cost allowance (chapter 14)
CCA	Current cost accounting (chapters 29, 30)
COP	Current operating profit
CRVA	Current realizable value accounting
CVA	Current value accounting
D&D	Depletion and depreciation
DCF	Discounted cash flow
EPS	Earnings per share
EV	Economic value
FIFO	First in, first out
GAAP	Generally accepted accounting principles
HOPAM	Higher of proceeds and market value
ITC	Investment tax credit
LIFO	Last in, first out
LOCAM	Lower of cost and market value
MWCA	Monetary working capital allowance
NRV	Net realizable value
R&D	Research and development
RC	Replacement cost
RCA	Replacement cost accounting
SAR	Stock appreciation right
SCF	Statement of cash flow
SCFP	Statement of changes in financial position
SFAS	Statement of financial accounting standards (U.S.)
SSAP	Statement of standard accounting practice (Great Britain and Ireland)
VF	Value to the firm

Institutions and associations

AAA	American Accounting Association
AIA	American Institute of Accountants (former name of AICPA)
AICPA	American Institute of Certified Public Accountants
AISG	Accountants International Study Group
APB	Accounting Principles Board (U.S., 1959 to 1973)
CAP	Committee on Accounting Procedure (U.S., 1939 to 1959)
CICA	Canadian Institute of Chartered Accountants
CIPREC	Canadian Institute of Public Real Estate Companies
FASB	Financial Accounting Standards Board (U.S., 1973—)
IASC	International Accounting Standards Committee
IFAC	International Federation of Accountants
NYSE	New York Stock Exchange
SEC	Securities and Exchange Commission (U.S.)

References to professional literature

The content of this book does not take into account professional recommendations subsequent to:

- Release No. 50 of the *CICA Handbook,* dated April 1986.
- Statement of Financial Accounting Standards No. 88 by the FASB, dated December 1985.

Chapter One

Introduction

Accounting is a practical occupation. It has little point unless it serves a purpose. Some people—a small minority—find some satisfaction in the symmetry of a balanced set of accounts. But for most people the value in accounting lies in the information it conveys.

That information may be simple—perhaps no more than a record of wealth, of property owned and debts owed. A mere record of wealth at a particular date, however, is no more than an inventory. Compare inventories of wealth at two different dates and you have additional information—an indication of managerial stewardship, especially important when management is separated from ownership. Add a record of inflows and outflows of cash, goods, and services in the period; thereby a basis is laid for control of the steward and his subordinates. Analyze the inflows and outflows in terms of causes and effects, and you have an explanation of the sources of gain or loss. Consider the relationship of past gains and losses to conditions prevailing when they were incurred, and you have a basis for predicting consequences of future actions.

Thus, accounting results may furnish information useful for decision making by management or by others with an interest in the reporting entity. Take this one step further to aggregate the financial information reported by significant entities or subsets of entities within a society, and you may have information relevant to social policies. Entity accounting data may also be used directly as instruments of social policy—as in the application of income and other taxes, price regulation, and so on.

Two conditions give rise to accounting in its various forms. The first is the existence of some need for information that may be satisfied by accounting records. The second is the development of means and techniques for satisfying such needs. By way of analogy, we know that certain problems theoretically solvable by mathematical methods could not in practice be attempted until the computational power of the computer became available. In the same way we can say that applications of accounting were limited to listings of goods until coined money became available and was adopted as a unit of account. It is evident that if we seek an explanation of why we account as we do, we should first look to economic history for the answer.

Our review of history starts with a paradox. Accounting in some form can be traced back in various civilizations for over six thousand years. In our own western civilization accounting has been widespread for over five hundred years. Yet it is only in the last fifty to one hundred years that accountants have felt a need to work out a theory of accounting. The explanation of this paradox is simple. Successful accomplishment in any activity requires understanding of the task and mastery of techniques required to carry it out. Where the task is clear, interest is restricted to techniques. So long as the accounting goal was merely to keep records, accounting instruction concentrated on "how to do it." When a financial reporting objective—an information communication goal—was added to the record-keeping function, the task of accounting became more difficult, and a theory to guide its methods became necessary.

Since roughly 1850, accounting has increasingly been used to provide information for decisions rather than merely to provide a record of property owned and transactions in property. Two branches of accounting have emerged in this period, distinguishable by the type of decision made. *Management accounting* is concerned with the production and interpretation of information that will be useful for an entity's internal decisions about investment, production, pricing, marketing, and so on. *Financial reporting*, on the other hand, is concerned with the production and interpretation of information for use by persons outside the entity. One very important purpose of financial reporting is to facilitate decisions by outside parties whether to invest in the entity or provide credit to it.

The stress on the informational uses of accounting transforms it from a mere technique (albeit one of considerable practical importance) into a discipline that needs to be understood at a conceptual level. We need to know not just how to account, but why we account. This is particularly true of financial reporting. Management of an entity is in the fortunate position of being able to specify the information it wants to aid efficient operation. Good management accounting, therefore, rests upon an appreciation of the information needed to optimize management performance. Financial accounting, in contrast, addresses a much more diffuse audience—all those outside an entity who have some legitimate interest in its financial progress and well-being.

Determination of who those people are and the selection of the information that is beneficial for them to receive require a conceptual framework that was lacking in 1850. Gradually, over the next one hundred years, customary modes of financial reporting emerged and were eventually dignified by the name "generally accepted accounting principles." From roughly 1930 on, societies of professional accountants, frequently urged on by governments or government agencies, attempted to codify such principles in order to remove inconsistencies and conflicts and to encourage improvement in financial reporting. Over a period of time the constitution of the professional committees created for this purpose has tended to be modified so as to be more widely representative. At the same time the committees' recommendations have been increasingly recognized as being authoritative, so that it has become possible to describe these committees or boards as standard-setting bodies and their recommendations as standards of financial reporting. In effect, the determination of accounting principles by a process of acceptance has been largely superseded by organized standard-setting efforts.

The primary purpose of this book is to describe present-day accounting standards and to evaluate them in conceptual terms. Part I of the book is devoted to a history of the evolution of accounting, from a collection of recording techniques rationalized by the invention of double entry to a sophisticated communication device using the medium of financial statements and reports. Part II discusses existing accounting practices as influenced by history and current thought and evaluates them on their merits. Part III reviews the various proposals that have been made to deal more effectively with the impact of changing prices. Part IV attempts to present a conceptual framework for financial reporting and discusses the institutions needed to develop and maintain effective accounting standards.

Part One

The Historical Development of Accounting

Chapter Two

The Record-Keeping Function of Accounting

Accounting is concerned in essence with wealth. Wealth, that is to say an accumulation of goods beyond immediate human needs, is the basis of civilization. It is not surprising, then, to find some form of accounting associated with the most ancient of recorded civilizations.

Three periods in the development of accounting can be discerned. In the first, from 4000 B.C. up to A.D. 1300, the record-keeping aspect was predominant. Accumulations of wealth require control, and for this some form of accounting is essential. The second period, from about 1300 up to 1850, was marked by the spread of commerce. With widespread commerce the need for adequate records grew. The distinguishing feature of this period was that accounting records became capable of dealing with masses of data and summarizing them so as to facilitate the business carried on. This period may still be called a record-keeping stage, but the advances implicit in the technique of double entry mark the era as one of systematized bookkeeping rather than one of mere record keeping. The double-entry technique was further important in that it was capable of extension and refinement so as to meet the needs of the third era, from 1850 to the present.

The groundwork for this final period was laid by the vast surge of economic activity in the preceding century known as the Industrial Revolution. The emergence of large-scale enterprise required the mobilization of large capital sums, which in turn led to the separation of the functions of ownership and management and to increasing use of the legal institution of the limited liability company. In time, accounting played its part by becoming a source of information about costs and profits to assist management. Also, through financial statements it became a means of communicating information to investors, creditors, and others who were separate from internal management but entitled to reports on enterprise progress. The development of accounting as an information source is described beginning in chapter 3.

Preconditions of accounting

Certain attainments of civilization were necessary before even the simplest accounting record could exist. Further advances in skills and institutional arrangements were necessary for advanced forms. The following were among the more important preconditions for accounting with any degree of sophistication.

Literacy

People must be able to read and write in order to keep records of any length. Thus, in the earliest civilizations accounting was largely limited to those institutions, such as the church and government, that represented repositories of the literary arts or could afford to employ clerks drawn from the limited section of the population that could read and write. There were, however, some ways to cope with the problem of illiteracy. In Babylonia scribes were used to make records of contracts, receipts, etc. These could be said to be the earliest public accountants. In pre-Norman England and in mediaeval times generally, accountability was fulfilled largely by oral communication of activities and results. An audit—literally a hearing—was performed mainly by evaluating the reasonableness of such reports.

An efficient numbering system

Any accounting record beyond the simplest lists and records of individual transactions entails addition and subtraction. Widespread facility in these skills, in turn, depends upon an adequate numbering system. The Arabic numbering system, familiar to us, did not become widely known in European civilizations until at least the thirteenth century A.D. Even then, the use of Roman numerals in record keeping continued to be common for many years.

The Arabic system has "place-value," meaning that its numbers can be arrayed in columns. Thereby, addition or subtraction is made easy by beginning with the extreme right-hand column and moving progressively to the left. To achieve place-value (given the usual decimal base), it was necessary to have nine numerical symbols for the figures one to nine and a zero cipher which could be combined with each of the other numbers to yield ten, twenty, and so on. The end result is that in any whole number the right-hand symbol stands for the number of units, the next left symbol for the number of tens, the next left for the number of hundreds, and so on indefinitely. (Extension to the right of the decimal point follows the same rules.)

Many ancient numbering systems had no zero and had varying quantities of numerical symbols.[1] The Romans used seven basic symbols; one of the major Greek systems had twenty-eight. With few symbols, numbers were long — in Roman notation the number 3,878 is written MMMDCCCLXXVIII. With a greater number of symbols the typical length of numbers can be reduced, but at the expense of making the system harder to learn. The impediment to arithmetical operations caused by lack of place-value could be overcome in computations by the use of the abacus, which was common in ancient civilizations. The important point for accounting, however, was that without place-value in written figures there was no incentive to put figures in columns and to separate the record of opposites (cash receipts and payments; amounts receivable and payable). Thus, the primitive numbering systems in the ancient world meant primitive accounting.

Writing materials

Until recently, extensive account keeping has depended upon supplies of inexpensive writing material. Paper was invented in China in the second millenium B.C., but not introduced to Europe until the twelfth or thirteenth century A.D. Before the availability of paper a variety of writing materials was used to keep accounts. The Babylonian civilizations relied on clay tablets. Egypt benefited from the use of a much less cumbersome material—papyrus—from at least 3000 B.C., and potsherds were also often used for brief accounts after the conquest by Alexander the Great in the fourth century B.C. From that time, for about one thousand years, papyrus became the main writing material for important documents in Greek and Roman civilization. Some temple or government accounts were inscribed on stone or other durable material, but wooden tablets coated with wax were widely used for everyday accounts. These were convenient because they could be erased and reused. Parchment was also used to some extent and became the more common material toward the end of the Roman Empire. However, not until the introduction of paper was there a relatively inexpensive and convenient writing material. As a consequence, accounting and documentation in the ancient world were cramped and limited.

Money

The idea of coinage, that is, the issuance of pieces of valuable metal stamped by government authority as a guarantee of purity and weight, was conceived in China in the second millenium B.C. Coined money came into use in the Mediterranean world around the seventh century B.C. The existence of a standard medium of exchange was vital to any advanced development of accounting, for without it accounts could consist only of records of individual contracts and inventories of property by quantities. Once money had become available as a "unit of account," it was possible to represent diverse kinds of property by numbers and thus, by a process of valuation, derive totals for capital, profits, and so on.

The invention of coined money, however, did not result in widespread improvements in accounts for many hundreds of years. The existence of many states and principalities, each with its own coinage, presented a problem in recording accounts using any one currency as the unit of account. (The problem of foreign currency translation is indeed an ancient one.) In addition, the valuation process required when money is used as a common unit of account depends to a considerable extent on the existence of widespread market exchange values. Thus the realization of the full potential for accounting from the invention of money had to await the commercial expansion that marked the end of the Middle Ages.

The age of record keeping

We must now examine how accounting developed to satisfy the need for records. From the earliest times there was a need for a record of incomplete transactions. A narrative description of the transaction, set down in chronological order, was the natural form of record. Frequently, when a loan was made or credit given or accepted, space was left below the original transaction record to record its ultimate completion. These simple records of transactions, however, did not provide the summarization and classification of data necessary for usefulness in the management of affairs. This lack of summarization is the primary reason why we classify the ancient age of record keeping separately from the age of bookkeeping that began about A.D. 1300.

Accounting for control

Apart from the record-keeping aspect, the major use of accounts in the initial era was that of control. Substantial accumulations of wealth always require administration. This meant that property owners had to employ servants to look after their affairs, and those so entrusted needed to be made accountable for property passing through their hands. Governments, in particular (perhaps because the rulers, unlike today, had a personal interest in the result) took care to control tax receipts and keep accurate records of other receipts and disbursements. Perhaps the most sophisticated government accounting system of ancient times was achieved in China during the Chao Dynasty (1122–256 B.C.). The system in use exhibited a full accounting cycle, marked by budgeting, responsibility accounting by funds, interim and annual reporting, audits, and a triennial examination of the effectiveness of each government agency.[2]

Whether the entity was a government, a religious institution, a private estate, or simply a household, the elements of control were the same. These were the creation of records of transactions (with varying degrees of support documentation), sometimes a separation of functions so as to achieve internal control, and an audit. The audit, in essence, was a review of the records by the owner, or by officials sufficiently informed to assess their probable accuracy. In the absence of detailed documentation the principal audit technique was that of interrogation.

This accounting framework persisted through the Middle Ages and beyond. English manorial accounting has given us a name for it—stewardship accounting—from the title of the official responsible for the business affairs of the manor. The "Charge and Discharge" statement was developed as the form of the steward's account. This statement recorded the amount the steward was charged for, namely property in his hands at the beginning of the period and any natural increase in property. Amounts deemed to be discharges of his responsibility included expenses of the manor, payments to the owner of the manor, and losses of property from natural causes. The steward remained accountable for any balance not discharged. Chatfield points out that it was in the steward's interest to minimize the receipts for which he was responsible and maximize the report of expenses and losses. To this he attributes the origin of the doctrine of conservatism in accounting.[3]

The stewardship form of accounting persisted long after the widespread adoption of double-entry accounting for commercial use. Indeed, in important aspects it underlies government accounting and nonprofit-organization accounting today. It is also interesting to note that in earliest times there was little difference in objectives and concepts between public and private accounts. It was the desire to compute costs and profits that set private accounting on a separate path.

The evolution of bookkeeping

By A.D. 1300 most of the conditions for accounting progress had been fulfilled. Paper was becoming available. Coined money was in common use as a medium of exchange. The Arabic numerical notation was being introduced. Finally, the development of Mediterranean commerce enhanced the demand for good records. In the two centuries before 1300 the Crusades had opened up the Middle East to trade, and silks, spices, and other eastern products created a demand for European goods in exchange. Italy was in the best position to take advantage of the trading opportunities, and Venice and Genoa established themselves as entrepôts in the trade between Europe and the East. Italians, especially the Florentines, also became the world's bankers. In all this they were helped by advances in business organization, such as the invention of bills of exchange and the use of credit. The time was ripe for the first major advance in accounting.

- The widespread development of credit and banking made it convenient to have continuous records of amounts due to and from other parties, rather than separate records for each transaction entered into and its settlement. In these individual accounts it was convenient and natural to separate opposites—loans and repayments, deposits and withdrawals. The resulting "bilateral form" of account reflected the concept of duality in the form of debits and credits.
- The Italians developed the practice of trading through overseas consignment agents. An agent is accountable to his principal for the goods consigned to him and proceeds from their sale. The balancing of goods unsold and sales proceeds (represented either by accounts receivable or cash collected) with the obligation to the principal also provided a natural illustration of the concept of duality embodied in double entry.
- As the form of business evolved from a series of isolated ventures to a continuing enterprise, a new concept of a business as an entity with an existence separate from that of its owners began to take root. When a long-term business was conducted in partnership form, accounting for capital also gained in importance because each partner had to be credited with his proper share of profits.

Thus we can see the elements of double-entry bookkeeping drawing together as a natural outcome of early business conditions. The concept of capital, required in the case of continuing partnerships, confirmed the basic equilibrium of double entry. The maintenance of equilibrium, in practice, required the opening of nominal accounts for revenues and expenses. This represented in the long run the great potential of the double-entry system, namely its ability to distinguish and analyze the elements of profit and loss and thus explain the change in capital from time to time.

Early forms of bookkeeping

This potential was not realized immediately. Early trading firms typically operated in separate ventures. Records of venture costs and receipts had been kept together well before the introduction of double entry. It was natural to continue with the venture as the focus of nominal accounts in a double-entry system, particularly since ship captains or other parties were frequently entitled to share in the profits of individual ventures. In contrast, the need for periodic reckonings of profit of the business as a whole was much smaller for many businesses. Typically, a ledger was not closed and balanced except when a new one was to be opened or on special occasions such as the death of a partner. Owners were able to keep on top of their businesses by dint of personal contact, following the results of ventures, and reading the ledgers themselves.

There were some exceptions. Surviving records of banking and manufacturing companies of Florence provide evidence of a more advanced technique. The Medici bank, for example, required annual balance sheets (essentially listings of account balances) from its nine branches in Italy and abroad and used these as a means of control, especially watching for doubtful accounts receivable and excessive loans.[4] Examples can also be found of financial statements displaying such accrual techniques as prepayments, depreciation accounting, and allowances for taxes and contingencies.

Double-entry accounting is associated with the name of Friar Luca Pacioli and his treatise on bookkeeping. This was one of five sections in his book *Summa de Arithmetica, Geometria, Proportioni et Proportionalita,* published in 1494. This date is more than 150 years after the time of the earliest surviving set of accounts identified as a complete double-entry system. It is evident that Pacioli did not invent the system; rather, he described it as actually practised in his day. Since much of his experience was in Venice, his treatise reflected practices of that centre and came to be known as "the method of Venice." In particular, it described venture accounting, and, although Pacioli recommended annual balancing to help detect errors, he never mentioned periodic financial statements. The contribution of Pacioli was that he made knowledge of the method of Venice widespread. The *Summa* was translated into several languages, and foreign accounting treatises for hundreds of years tended to be copies of Pacioli's work or copies of copies.

From the fifteenth century on, the advantage in trading and commerce moved from the Mediterranean to the Atlantic as discoveries widened the horizons of western civilization. Spain and Portugal led in the sixteenth century, to be succeeded by England and the Low Countries as maritime power shifted northward. The method of Venice followed the spread of commerce. Although, inevitably, adaptations and improvements were made over the course of time, the record-keeping uses of accounts remained primary.

The organization of English trade and commerce, A.D. 1300–1800

The five centuries from 1300 to 1800 saw an expansion of trade and commerce that created a need for new forms of business organization. That same expansion also eventually created a need for financial reports to organize the information from a set of accounts and to provide a succinct means of conveying information to parties at interest. In fact, the development of financial reporting is closely linked with the emergence of the modern business corporation, with its limited liability and transferable shares. Since financial reporting traditions in the English-speaking countries have their origin in the development of the corporation in England in the nineteenth century, we turn now to a description of the organization of English commerce leading up to that century.

Forms of business organization

Apart from the individual proprietorship, several forms of organization of commercial activity can be traced from early times in England. A form of partnership existed in the thirteenth and fourteenth centuries in the "Societas," firms of Italian financiers operating in England. The basic concept of the corporation as an artificial person was also recognized in the common law at that time, although not in connection with commercial activity. The Church, the Town, and the Guild were all recognized as entities independent of their members, capable of owning property in their own right and having perpetual existence. Members, being separate persons in law from the corporation, had no direct claim on its property nor any personal liability for its debts.

The extension of this concept to business ventures did not take place until later, and at first only on a restricted basis. Most large corporations up to the end of the seventeenth century were established by royal charter, such as the Russia Company (1555), the East India Company (1600), and the Hudson's Bay Company (1670). (These are short forms of the companies' names; their full legal names were much longer.) Often these charter companies were given monopolies to trade in a certain area or in certain products and in some cases took on obligations in return, such as the promotion of colonization. They did not necessarily receive all the attributes that characterize corporations today; for example, the privilege of limited liability for shareholders was not invariable.

Such a company might evolve over a period of time from a loose umbrella covering a recurring series of self-liquidating ventures to a permanent entity possessed of substantial assets in the form of ships, trading posts, and inventories. The East India Company, for example, originally raised capital (the joint stock) for each voyage separately. At the end of each voyage the property was divided among the subscribing venturers. As the company acquired more permanent property, it became increasingly difficult to identify assets with individual voyages, and it became necessary to allocate them (and hence profits) among voyages. Beginning in 1613 the problem of allocation was lessened by raising capital subscriptions for four-year terms, one quarter to be paid up each year. In 1657 the principle of permanently invested capital and transferable shares was adopted. As a result, future distributions no longer represented divisions of assets at the conclusion of a venture, but rather "dividends" paid from profits.[5] The change, however, did not mean the end of venture or voyage accounting. It was still possible to base profit computation on the results of completed voyages together with allowances for administrative expenses and asset valuations outside the voyage accounts.

Some chartered companies were "regulated," meaning that membership was restricted to merchants who had been apprenticed to the trade. This limitation hampered the raising of capital, so that such companies tended to lose out over time to companies organized on the joint-stock principle. The term "joint stock" simply referred to the contribution of the members to finance the company which, depending on the participation arrangements, might take the form of cash or assets (such as ships) for use in the venture.

The great majority of business ventures, of course, were not carried on by chartered corporations. The idea of contributions to a joint stock—in effect, a pooling of assets—was adopted by unincorporated companies as well as corporations. English privateering activity in the late 1500s, for example, was largely carried on by joint-stock companies. In effect, these were informal extended partnerships, and their exact legal status was nebulous. At first, most such companies were engaged in foreign trading activity. Later, as domestic enterprise grew in scale, the joint-stock concept was adopted for such diverse activities as mining, water supply, insurance, and banking.

The South Seas Bubble

Transfers of interests in joint-stock companies were permitted, and in time a market for shares developed. Stock jobbers were active in the market, and company promoters used it to raise capital. Commercial publication of share prices commenced in 1692. As in any unregulated market there was some fraud and deceit, and share prices fluctuated widely. Scott reports that, for the most part, company flotations before 1700 were reasonable speculations.[6] Failures, nevertheless, tended to be blamed on what was called the "pernicious art of stock jobbing" and cast a shadow on the whole concept of joint-stock companies.

From 1690 to 1720, periods of boom and crisis succeeded each other in the market, culminating in a major crash in 1720. The crash is associated with the South Seas Company, which was organized in 1711. At that time the market price of government debt was severely depressed. The company had two objectives: one was to obtain a government monopoly on trade to South America; the other was to acquire government debt cheaply, thereby establishing a firm base of assets. The idea was that the company would accept all unfunded government debt (debt that did not have a specific revenue source earmarked for its repayment) at par in subscription for its shares. The theory was that ownership of that debt by the company would provide it with an undoubted "fund of credit" against which it could borrow to finance its activities.

This plan was implemented, and the company operated relatively uneventfully for several years. But in 1719, a company promotion boom began in England on a highly speculative basis. Shares in new companies were issued with as little as one-eighth of one percent paid up on the par value. As the boom progressed, the stated objects of many of the companies became increasingly improbable, so that skeptical observers referred to them as "bubble companies."

The promoters of the South Seas Company evidently decided to take advantage of the speculative fever. In early 1720 they successfully competed with the Bank of England (then privately owned) to win the right to undertake a new scheme involving the national debt. The scheme called for the company, as before, to buy in outstanding government debt (this time funded debt) in return for subscriptions to its shares. If, for example, the South Seas stock stood at a premium of twenty-five percent over par, it would issue *eight* £100 par value shares for each £1,000 bond, crediting capital account with £1,000. But since £1,000 represented the par value of *ten* shares, the government permitted the company to make up the difference by selling two extra shares to the public. The company paid the government a bonus on selling these shares and recorded the remainder of the proceeds as gain.

This government-abetted scheme for share price inflation through treating capital proceeds as income met with ill-deserved success. The company's shares advanced rapidly in price as soon as it obtained the right to undertake the debt conversion operation. This meant that it had to issue substantially fewer shares for each £1,000 bond acquired and consequently had more bonus shares to sell independently for its and the government's gain. That very success created problems, however, for there was not enough cash in the country available for investment to buy up the bonus shares. The answer to that problem was simple. The shares were sold for very little cash down; credit was extended for the remainder of the price, the shares themselves being accepted as security.

Yet cash was still tight, especially since so many other companies were selling shares at the same time. To eliminate this competition the company encouraged Parliament to pass the so-called "Bubble Act." This act, effective June 24, 1720, prohibited the offering of shares for public subscription by a company that did not have a charter or that had a charter for activities other than those for which it was raising money. Two months later, the South Seas Company instigated legal action against four other companies for contravention of the Bubble Act. The result was unfortunate. A rapid fall in the price of shares of the companies attacked resulted in margin calls. These triggered liquidation of shareholdings, thereby putting pressure on the share prices of all companies, including the South Seas Company. In the space of less than two months the company's shares fell from a peak price of £1,000 to £180. The rapid collapse of the boom left the fledgling capital market, as so often since, sadder but not permanently wiser.

The stagnation of accounting

The aftermath of the bubble period was a prolonged distrust of joint-stock companies. It was felt that the extravagant promotions proved that investors not personally involved in company activity would fail to invest wisely. Moreover, managers of such companies were bound to be inefficient since their own financial interest was not at stake. The dominant thinking in Parliament was that joint-stock companies should be discouraged, and incorporation granted only in cases where capital requirements were very large and limited liability essential. Types of enterprise qualifying under these criteria included such public works as canals, bridges and docks, companies undertaking long and continuing risks such as life insurance, financial institutions such as banks, and companies engaged in foreign trade. The result of this thinking, together with strict enforcement of the Bubble Act, was to hamper the issuing of capital at the very time when the new enterprises springing up might have found a developed capital market most useful. Thus the new textile companies, mines, foundries, metal-working companies, and potteries remained largely in private hands until well into the nineteenth century.

There was little in this history to forward the development of financial reporting. Company charters could contain clauses requiring regular audit and financial reporting to shareholders. Clauses might also state that dividends were to be paid only out of profits and specify the nature of reserves that could be withheld from distributable profits. None of these clauses, however, were standardized or mandatory. As for business in private hands, the old accounting traditions were sufficient, and little organized thought was given to accounting's potential as a source of information for management and decision making. Chatfield sums up the state of eighteenth-century accounting as follows:

> *[T]he eighteenth century merchant still valued it [double-entry bookkeeping] chiefly for its ability to bring order to his accounts. Most problems we associate with profit finding and asset valuation concerned him hardly at all. Without the paraphernalia of accruals, matching, or periodic reckonings, his venture accounts measured the results of particular operations, while paging through the ledger gave him some idea of overall activity. But he developed neither a clear concept of income nor systematic procedures for judging the success or failure of his business over a period of time. Public investment in firms was rare, a tradition of accountability to outsiders was lacking, and financial statements were of minor importance. It was the Industrial Revolution, not the bookkeeping innovations preceding it, which drew out accountancy's analytical potential.*[7]

Summary

As a practical art, accounting responds to needs. The existence of wealth creates a need for records to serve as a control over those entrusted with it. Trade creates a need for records of unsettled transactions. We therefore find some form of accounting records associated with early civilization — as far back as six thousand years ago.

Record keeping requires both skills and facilitating conditions. Clerks must be literate; an efficient numbering system and cheap writing material are necessary for extensive records; and a standard of value in the form of money is essential to any large-scale records because of the need for some common unit of account.

The spread of commerce after the Crusades vastly increased the importance of good business records. As the leaders in trade and banking the Italians pioneered advances in record keeping, and the concept of double entry evolved naturally out of the need for records of continuing business relationships. For the most part, however, such relationships did not include the provision of capital for a business on a long-term basis by parties not involved in running it. Instead, outside financing tended to be for individual ventures, resulting in profit reporting on a venture-by-venture basis, rather than for regularly established periods of time.

Double entry, in its venture accounting version, accompanied the spread of commerce throughout Europe. As the scale of business activity grew, a need developed for a better-capitalized and more permanent form of business organization than the trading ventures typical of early commerce. The English corporation authorized by royal charter provided one means of meeting this need. The evolution of private joint-stock enterprises into companies with transferable shares, plus the development of a market for exchange of shares around 1700, represented another. The collapse of the South Seas Bubble in 1720 and the consequent restrictive legislation, however, set back for a century the development of this logical means of raising capital. Accounting might have been expected to free itself from the traditional venture accounting approach more quickly had it not been for this restriction on the form of business organization. As it was, accounting remained largely frozen in its previous mold until well into the nineteenth century.

References

[1]For a full and interesting discussion see G.E.M. de Ste. Croix, "Greek and Roman Accounting," in *Studies in the History of Accounting*, ed. A.C. Littleton and B.S. Yamey (London: Sweet & Maxwell, 1956), pp. 14-74, especially from p. 50 on.

[2]See M. Chatfield, *A History of Accounting Thought*, rev. ed. (Huntington, N.Y.: Robert E. Krieger Publishing Co., 1977), pp. 8-9.

[3]Ibid., p. 29.

[4]See R. de Roover, "The Development of Accounting Prior to Luca Pacioli According to the Account-books of Medieval Merchants," in *Studies in the History of Accounting*, ed. Littleton and Yamey, pp. 151-52.

[5]Chatfield, op. cit., pp. 79-80.

[6]W.R. Scott, *The Constitution and Finance of English, Scottish and Irish Joint-Stock Companies to 1720,* 3 vols. (Cambridge: Harvard University Press, 1912; reprint ed., New York: Peter Smith, 1951), chap. 18.

[7]Chatfield, op. cit., p. 61.

Chapter Three

Emergence of the Financial Reporting Function

The quickening of the pace of economic development from about 1750 on has become known as the Industrial Revolution. This era saw the transformation of manufacturing from localized activities producing simple goods into large-scale production, centralized in factories and using paid labour. This change was fundamental. Where formerly much of business, especially foreign trade, was carried on in the form of separate ventures, now the characteristics of continuous production, a large work force, and large capital investment were more compatible with the modern accounting concept of the "going concern."

As the scale of enterprise grew and with advances in technology, particularly the application of steam power, the limitations on company financing caused by restrictions on incorporation became increasingly unsatisfactory. In 1825 the English Bubble Act was repealed. The act of repeal made it possible to spell out the degree of limitation of liability in company charters, but that still left the status and powers of joint-stock companies in doubt. In 1837, incorporation became easier as the system of incorporation by letters patent was adopted. The Joint Stock Companies Act of 1844 went still further, by granting a general power to incorporate by registration. An 1855 act permitted all registered companies to obtain limited liability. At that date it can be said that the corporation in its modern legal form had evolved.

Large-scale continuing enterprise also meant changes in relations with investors if the enterprise was widely owned. Where previously profit sharing could be accomplished merely by dividing up the assets of completed ventures, a more regular process of distribution was now called for. Dividends could only be paid with assets deemed surplus to business needs. This did not mean that dividends could be paid only out of profits, although there was obviously some connection. A firm exploiting a wasting asset such as a coal mine, for example, might reasonably pay out all receipts in excess of those required for its running expenses and for maintaining the operation until the workings were exhausted. In any event, cash available for dividends would be greater when times were good than when they were bad. Inevitably, there was an association in the public mind between dividends and profitability, with the result that the size of dividends paid might well affect the value of an interest in a company. Obviously, in the absence of financial reporting the opportunities for manipulation of public opinion through manipulation of dividends were very great. Thus, the first major opportunity for accounting to serve a wider interest than that of owner-managers arose with the transformation of business activity into going concerns.

The corporation and financial reporting

The companies act of 1844 introduced two significant requirements. First, a "full and fair" balance sheet was to be presented at each ordinary meeting of shareholders. Second, auditors were to be appointed and their report on the balance sheet was to be read at the meeting. In the same year the Joint Stock Banking Act required that a bank incorporated under it provide an annual audited balance sheet and profit and loss account. The following year, the Companies Clauses Consolidation Act, applicable to the public-utility type of corporation chartered by a special act of Parliament, included audit and financial reporting requirements in model clauses of company regulations. The act also provided that no dividend should be paid by those companies out of capital.

These acts represented the first acknowledgement of a public interest in financial reporting and audit. The legislation, however, proved ineffective. It did not specify the minimum contents of the balance sheet; it said nothing about the basis of valuation of assets and liabilities; and it did not set out in detail the auditor's duties. It did not even require that the statutory balance sheet relate to the date of the shareholders' meeting. It was easy to evade the intent of the legislation, even to the point of filing identical statements year after year or fabricating them for the purpose of filing with the Registrar.

When legislation on companies was next revised in 1855 and 1856, the issue was faced as to whether to strengthen the regulation of accounts and audit or to drop the mandatory requirements. The laissez-faire attitude of the times apparently persuaded Parliament that financial reporting could be left as a matter to be settled between a company and its shareholders. The mandatory reporting and audit provisions were dropped, not to be revived until 1900. The 1856 Joint Stock Companies Act, however, encouraged good financial reporting with a model set of company articles, including enlightened provisions with respect to the accounts to be kept, the audit, and the forms of the balance sheet and the statement of income and expenditure to be laid before the annual general meeting. The model articles also provided that dividends should not be payable except out of profits. The directors, however, might set aside reserve funds out of profits to meet possible contingencies, for equalizing dividends, or for repairing and maintaining the works. The reference to reserves may have been unfortunate in that it did not answer the question whether the provision for such reserves might be deducted in determining *reported* profits and, if so, whether the provisions needed to be disclosed.

Many companies did provide audited financial statements to shareholders as suggested by the model articles in the 1856 and subsequent acts. In addition, legislation passed during the nineteenth century to regulate special types of companies such as banks, insurance companies, railroads, and gas companies usually required the provision of audited financial statements, sometimes semiannually rather than annually. Thus, company accountants and auditors had to wrestle with questions of valuation of assets and computation of profits. Legislation or an individual company's articles might require a full and fair financial statement and might prohibit the payment of dividends except out of profits, but it was left to the accountant and management to say what those terms meant.

It must be remembered that there was no cohesive public accounting profession much before 1880. The Edinburgh Society of Accountants became the first "chartered accountants," receiving a royal charter in 1854. Local societies were formed in a number of centres in ensuing years, and in 1880 a merger of English societies resulted in the Institute of Chartered Accountants in England and Wales. Up till that time accountants often offered a variety of services such as that of appraiser, actuary, and estate executor, in conjunction with public accounting. Bankruptcies and liquidations constituted their chief source of work. Since there was often a whiff of fraud about business failures, it was natural to appoint individuals with such skills to make special investigations or to conduct audits of companies on behalf of creditors or shareholders. Nevertheless, auditing, as such, was not their main line of business, and no established body of knowledge had been built up covering audit reports on financial statements. The mediaeval tradition of the audit as a check against fraud and error led to detailed checks of the recorded transactions. But there were no understood audit requirements specifically designed to support reports on the fairness of financial statements.

Bases of nineteenth-century financial reports

In the face of this void in accounting theory, financial reporting for corporations developed on an ad hoc basis. There were two distinct strands of development. The so-called "double-account" basis of accounting and financial reporting was associated with large, public-service companies. Other types of enterprise, which were generally denied the right to incorporate until after the repeal of the Bubble Act, continued the accounting tradition of privately owned business in previous centuries. This tradition, although never highly codified, called for the production of a balance sheet (if any financial report at all was required) reporting assets and liabilities valued on whatever basis seemed reasonable.

The requirement of the English legislation that corporations produce financial reports led to the notion that the answers to questions of accounting rested with the law, and with the courts on matters of detail. It was possible to deduce the existence of a "capital maintenance" doctrine under the law, and that provided some guidance to accounting evolution. By the end of the century, however, decisions of the courts had destroyed that doctrine. Financial reporting for corporations was left where it started out—without any real theory to guide it.

The "double-account" form of financial statement

As already noted, the Companies Clauses Consolidation Act of 1845 set out audit and financial reporting requirements for the public-utility type of company incorporated by special act of Parliament. The fundamental concept of the special-act companies was that capital subscribed was to be spent in construction of a facility to be maintained in the public service permanently. All necessary expenditures to operate and maintain the facility were to be met from revenue so as to ensure perpetual service. This led naturally to a division in the balance sheet. The "capital" section recorded the presumed permanent fixed capital assets and capital subscribed, while the "revenue" section recorded the assets and liabilities associated with day-to-day operations, or "circulating capital" as it was called. Similarly, a distinction was made between profits, representing the excess of operating revenues over operating expenditures, and "capital" gains and losses, being the results of any disposition of capital assets.

The problems associated with the double-account system are particularly well illustrated in railroad accounting. The railway age in Great Britain can be said to have begun about 1830 with the successful development of the steam locomotive. There was a burst of railway promotion in 1835 and 1836 and again in the mid-1840s.

In those years, about one thousand companies were promoted and five thousand miles of track completed. In only a few short years, however, railway shares fell out of favour among investors, and many companies found it necessary or advisable to institute enquiries into alleged fraud or abuse in the previous promotional period. Construction booms and periods of financial stringency alternated for the next two decades.

The double-account concept applied to the new railways led to questions that can be categorized under two main headings: (1) How should one distinguish between expenditures chargeable to capital and those chargeable to revenue account? and (2) Is a provision for depreciation of capital assets a necessary charge in determining operating profits?

Under the first heading, there were several practical questions (some of them with a very modern sound).

- What should be done with interest paid on loans (and, until prohibited in 1847, on shareholders' capital) during construction? Most companies charged such interest to capital. Some, but not all, companies divided interest between revenue and capital when some branch lines were still under construction.
- Might capital expenditures be charged to revenue account? In the late 1840s, when railway shares were out of favour with investors, several companies "closed their capital accounts." This meant that capital expenditure had to be written off to revenue account unless specially authorized by the shareholders. Such policies usually had to be abandoned in a few years since they made major line extensions or other capital improvements impossible, or they prevented a regular dividend policy, or both. Nonetheless, the fact that the accounting for capital expenditure was considered optional indicated that the accounting was regarded more as a matter of financial policy than as a matter of proper profit and asset reporting.
- Might a portion of the cost of capital asset replacements be charged to capital? On this question, practice varied among companies. At least some companies capitalized the cost of betterments (although this created the problem of distinguishing between normal repairs and betterments). Beyond this, some companies also accepted the idea of capitalizing the increase in cost of a replacement over the original capitalized cost of the asset replaced, even though no betterment was involved. Other companies charged all replacements to revenue account.
- Might current repairs be capitalized? Although there could be little rationale for such a practice, it does not appear to have been uncommon, at least in the early years of railway promotion.

Initial consideration of depreciation was confused by a conflict between two interpretations of the reason for depreciation accounting. On the one hand, depreciation could be conceived of as a necessary charge against revenue in order to allow for the regular consumption of capital through use. On the other hand, depreciation accounting could be regarded as merely the name given to the process of valuing capital assets. From the latter valuation perspective, there was no depreciation unless there was a decline in the market value of the asset. In one extreme case, fixed assets were written up rather than depreciated, with the credit being carried to revenue account.

The valuation notion was superseded at a fairly early date, to be replaced by the idea of depreciation as a means of (1) providing on a regular basis for the inevitable decline in serviceability of capital assets and (2) creating a fund for their replacement. Since rolling stock clearly had limited life, a depreciation provision was at first thought desirable for it. But then, since rolling stock was replaced regularly, it was felt the cost of replacements could be absorbed as they occurred and depreciation accounting was not required. Opinions about depreciation accounting for rails developed in the opposite direction. At first it was thought that proper maintenance would make rails last so long that depreciation was not worth consideration. Then opinion shifted. Since rails were replaced only at extended intervals, a depreciation fund was seen as desirable for them.

Unfortunately, a depreciation provision was seen more as a matter of business policy than as a principle of accounting. This view probably was encouraged by statutory references to reserve funds "for maintaining and repairing the works" — something that directors might (or might not) set aside along with reserves for contingencies and for equalizing dividends. Some companies dropped depreciation provisions in the promotional period of the mid-1840s, but many commenced them after the shakeout in the late 1840s. In a few years most discontinued them again, having found them inadequate to meet replacements. The general contention of railroad management was that the soundest course was to charge replacements against revenue when required. This, of course, made it crucial that a proper distinction be made between new construction and replacement expenditures — a distinction which it may be doubted was actually achieved in practice. Also, replacement accounting encouraged management to smooth reported results simply by varying the amount of replacement expenditures. In the extreme, replacements too long postponed could lead to the failure of the railway, a fate that was not uncommon.

Clearly the accounting practices of the railways were inconsistent to the point of chaos. The situation was so unsatisfactory that Parliament, in the Regulation of Railways Act of 1868, was moved to impose uniform financial reporting and audit provisions on the railways, notwithstanding its general reluctance to interfere with the internal affairs of companies. The reporting system that was adopted confirmed the double-account system but did nothing to solve the question of the distinction between capital and revenue. In fact, the system probably encouraged, although it did not compel, the use of replacement accounting instead of depreciation accounting. Thus, the inconsistencies and inadequacies of railroad accounting continued.[1]

Financial reporting for ordinary companies

For other, less capital-intensive enterprises, there was no special theory to guide financial reporting. Rather, the natural approach was to provide a valuation of individual assets and liabilities. The important statement was a listing of these valuations—a balance sheet. Accumulated profit (the amount divisible among partners or owners) was represented by the excess of net assets over the capital committed previous to the reporting date. The chief problems were to provide fair valuations for the balance sheet items and to see that none was omitted. The growth in scale of enterprise increased this difficulty, and the emerging accounting profession had to ponder several vexing questions.

- How might values be found for inventory? When productive processes became extended it was no longer possible to refer to market prices for substantial portions of the inventory. This problem was met by the development of cost accounting, largely in the last quarter of the century.[2] Costs useful for management purposes could be adopted as a reasonable basis of valuation for financial accounting as well.
- Was it reasonable to take into account fluctuations in the market value of working capital items? There was no "realization" rule in previous accounting traditions, and accountants did not think it wrong in principle to record assets at market value even though such value was above cost. But values that went up could also come down. Morever, in those days dividends paid were closely associated with the amount of profits reported. A realization test not only would lessen uncertainty about valuations but also would ensure that profits reported were in liquid form, thereby facilitating payment of the dividend suggested by the profit figure. For such practical reasons, accountants in time came to advocate the rule of valuation at lower of cost and market.
- How about fluctuations in value of fixed assets, including investments? Again, since the previous tradition was a valuation tradition, accountants could not say that revaluation of fixed assets was wrong. They did, however, come to the view that to be continually writing such assets up and down was not a useful practice in a going concern and could be misleading. Their conservative instinct was satisfied by the idea that long-term assets need only be written down for value changes that appeared to be relatively permanent.
- Was it necessary to provide for depreciation with respect to the wearing out of long-term assets used in production? Accountants were quick to adapt the valuation idea to a belief in a depreciation provision, even though fluctuations in value could reasonably be ignored. Much of the discussion revolved around practical questions. How was it possible to estimate useful life? Should depreciation be heavy when repairs and maintenance were light? The discussion was at a level that would not be out of place today, and an excellent theoretical exposition on depreciation was published as early as 1890.[3]
- Should goodwill be valued and should purchased goodwill be amortized? Instinctively, accountants were against the valuation of goodwill. Sentiment was mixed on the question of amortization.
- Was it proper to create reserves out of profits and subsequently restore them to profits for the purpose of equalizing reported profits and dividend payments? If so, what disclosure must be given? It is probably fair to say that not all accountants were opposed to the desire to report profit figures indicative of long-term earning power. But there was a natural concern about the obvious dangers of misrepresentation. Unfortunately, the very wording of the model articles in the 1856 and 1862 companies acts seemed to encourage such reserves, and judicial dicta in dividend cases certainly did not discourage them.

Profit measurement and the doctrine of capital maintenance

It is clear from the literature of the time that English accountants took a very legalistic view of financial reporting. The requirements to provide full and fair reports and to ascertain profits distributable as dividends were embodied in companies acts or clauses in a company's articles. Therefore the form and content of financial statements were ultimately matters for the law to decide. (An alternative interpretation—that what was a fair financial report, or what was profit, should be determined on economic principles—seems not to have been considered.)

The historical business tradition, stemming from the days when business consisted of a series of ventures, was that profits should be distributed when determined. It became English practice for company shareholders to approve the final dividend at the annual general meeting of the company. It was desirable, therefore, that the financial statements presented to the annual meeting should display the surplus that was distributable. If the law had anything to say on that subject, it was important for accountants to discover it.

There were grounds for believing that the law did control the amount distributable as dividends. One of the long-standing concerns about the granting of limited liability to companies had been that creditors might be damaged by fraudulent or negligent dissipation of company assets. A possible answer to this lay in the existence of shareholders' capital as a margin of safety, but this was effective only so long as the capital was maintained. It could be inferred that the law required such capital maintenance as the price of limited liability. First, limited companies had to state in their initial Memorandum of Association the amount of their proposed registered capital, while companies without limited liability did not have to do so. Second, while a limited liability company might subsequently increase or consolidate the existing capital, it was prohibited from reducing it. Finally, since a company's Memorandum of Association declared that capital was to be applied to the purposes of the business, it was reasoned it would be beyond the power of the directors to return it to the shareholders. This reasoning was reinforced by the specific provisions respecting reduction of capital introduced into the 1867 and 1877 companies acts. If dividends were permitted to reduce capital, these provisions would have been unnecessary and meaningless.

Early court cases dealing with the legality of dividends upheld the capital maintenance doctrine. These cases also held that valuations upon which directors made their dividend decisions must be neither negligently made nor fraudulent and, in a sketchy way, began to give some guidance on valuation questions. By the last quarter of the nineteenth century, the emerging accounting profession might reasonably consider its task to be that of achieving a better definition of distributable profits within the framework of the law. The prevailing thinking is illustrated by an excerpt from a paper read by Ernest Cooper in 1888 to the CA Students Society of London:

> *Numerous questions arise upon the valuation of assets.... One matter I think it is of great importance for auditors as well as directors to bear carefully in mind [is] that the law itself or knowledge of the law in regard to accounts of Companies is ... in an extremely imperfect state. Many practices of Companies in regard to their accounts, I think we may assume, will in course of time, come up for consideration by the Judges, with whom, of course, and not with accountants, must rest the ultimate decision of doubtful points arising upon accounts.*[4]

Collapse of the capital maintenance doctrine

Three cases in the short period of ten years rudely disrupted the accountants' understanding of the state of the law. The first and most important of these was the case of Lee v. Neuchatel Asphalte Co. decided by the Court of Appeal in

1889.[5] The company was formed in 1873 as an amalgamation of six others, its business being to exploit a mining concession held for a limited period of years. The articles of the company provided that profits should be applied to dividends, except that before recommending any dividend the directors might set aside, out of profits, a reserve fund for contingencies, dividend equalization, or repairing or maintaining works connected with the business. The question in the case was whether there could be said to be distributable profits without provision for exhaustion of the capital asset (the mining concession).

The judges who decided the case agreed upon the result but for contradictory reasons. Cotton L.J. noted that the capital subscribed included the mining concession. No provision for exhaustion was required because the concession was still held and had increased in value. Lopes L.J. stressed the inherently wasting character of the mining concession and held there was no obligation to recoup the cost of such wasting assets before distribution of dividends.

The opinion of Lindley L.J. was the most sweeping of the three rendered. There was nothing in the companies acts "about how dividends are to be paid, nor how profits are to be reckoned; all that is left ... to the commercial world." Similarly there was nothing requiring capital to be made up if lost. "If they [businessmen] think their prospects of success are considerable, so long as they pay their creditors, there is no reason why they should not go on and divide profits ... although every shilling of the capital may be lost." There was nothing in the acts to show "what is to go to capital account or what is to go to revenue account.... [B]usinessmen very often differ in opinion about such things." All that the previous cases had decided was that "You must not have fictitious accounts. If your earnings are less than your current expenses, you must not cook your accounts so as to make it appear that you are earning a profit, and you must not lay your hands on your capital to pay dividends."

The decision in the case of Verner v. The General and Commercial Investment Trust (Limited)[6] followed naturally from the reasoning in Neuchatel. The company was organized to make investments in stocks and debentures but not to trade as a jobber or broker. Its investments were speculative in character and, at the time of the case, market value was below cost by £246,000. (Total issued capital was £600,000.) Of this amount it was considered that £75,000 was unlikely to be recovered within a reasonable time. Current investment receipts, however, exceeded administration expenses and debenture interest expense, so that there were liquid funds from which a dividend could be paid. It was held that since the company still held the assets in which its capital had been invested, the dividend could not be said to be paid out of capital. It was not necessary to recoup the loss in value of such assets before payment of dividends. What was necessary was that the dividend could be paid without reduction of the amount of "circulating capital" (presumably at the beginning of the fiscal year). This was the same as saying that there had to be an excess of receipts over ordinary expenses in the given year out of which the dividend could be paid.

The final case was *in re* National Bank of Wales Limited.[7] In this case it had been found upon liquidation of the bank that substantial advances made to customers and certain directors were worthless. It was apparent in hindsight that profits in certain years had been deliberately overstated because of the failure to write off or make provision for bad and doubtful accounts. A director of the bank, John Cory, was sued by the liquidator for restitution of funds on the grounds (inter alia) that dividends had wrongfully been paid out of capital while he was a director. On appeal, it was held that the dividends were not paid out of capital on the peculiar reasoning that the capital was already lost by reason of the fact the debts were bad. On further appeal to the Privy Council, the decision was upheld on different grounds. The issue of whether dividends had been paid out of capital was thus left unresolved. Two judges went out of their way to dissociate themselves from some of the sweeping generalizations of the Appeal Court. Unfortunately, however, they did not clearly indicate their own views, stating merely that the question was difficult and had to be dealt with case by case.

These three cases effectively destroyed the capital maintenance doctrine and with it the accountants' assumption that the law provided a conceptual framework for accounting. The literature of the last decade of the nineteenth century reflects their consternation, as evidenced by the following extract from another paper by Ernest Cooper:

> *Six years ago ... I read a paper at a Meeting of your Society entitled 'What is Profit of a Company?'*
>
> *... It seems as though the state of matters in regard to Profit, which in 1888 was doubt and uncertainty, is in 1894 something like confusion.*
>
> *Unless I am misinformed, Counsel and Solicitors are in doubt how to advise upon questions connected with preparing Balance Sheets and ascertaining Profit.*
>
> *... It has been held that Directors paying a Dividend do so at their peril if they have not a Balance Sheet showing the true state of the Company* (Rance's case, *6 Ch. 104). They expose themselves to the terrible penalties that Judges have attached to Sec. 165 of the Companies Act 1862.... Within the last few months a Judge has stated that Auditors are sufficiently Officers of a Company in his view to bring them within this section. If he be right, the already sufficient responsibilities and anxieties of an Auditor will be extended beyond those known to any trade or profession.*[8]

Summary

The new enterprises that developed in the Industrial Revolution were of a different character from the trading ventures of earlier centuries. The new industries required increasingly large amounts of capital, employed a large work force, and operated continuously. Venture accounting was no longer suitable for them, but it was not necessarily clear what should succeed it.

Although long delayed by the disillusionment caused by the South Seas Bubble, reform of corporations legislation eventually took place in the nineteenth century to meet the needs of the new enterprises. The legislation created or enhanced a demand for financial reports, a demand that accountants and accounting theory were quite unprepared to meet.

In the absence of a cohesive theory, financial reporting developed in an ad hoc fashion. A particular form of reporting had grown up in one sector—that of capital-intensive companies providing essential public services in transportation and public utilities. This reporting system—the double-account system—emphasized the distinction between the supposedly permanent capital investment and the operating costs to run it. This distinction was artificial; few forms of investment are permanent, and there is no clear dividing line between assets with a short and a long life. As a result, the system faced difficulty in classifying costs incurred as between capital and revenue accounts. Neither was there a good understanding of the need to recognize depreciation of capital assets. When depreciation was recognized at all, it was thought of more as an expedient to facilitate replacement than as a requirement for measuring profit and financial position.

With respect to other forms of business, accountants tended to think of financial statements as a report on valuations. Practical problems, however, suggested modification of the simple valuation approach. As production processes became more complicated, cost was easier to compute than value to account for inventory in non-marketable form. As for fixed assets, mere fluctuations in value seemed irrelevant to a going concern. The need for depreciation was also in question here. Finally, the proper accounting for reserves held back from distributable profits was an open question.

Accountants looked to the courts to provide precedents that would help them resolve financial reporting issues. The belief that it was illegal to reduce capital provided support both for conservatism in valuations of circulating assets and for appropriate provisions for depreciation of capital assets or for other losses. Three cases respecting the legality of dividends toward the end of the nineteenth century shattered that belief. Without it, accountants were left with no real theory of financial reporting. They knew that assets and liabilities had to be reported and valued and profit had to be measured, but they had been left with no theory as to how to do it.

References

[1]See the summing up by H. Pollins, "Aspects of Railway Accounting Before 1868," in *Studies in the History of Accounting*, ed. A.C. Littleton and B.S. Yamey (London: Sweet & Maxwell, 1956), especially pp. 353-54.

[2]For an excellent history, see M.C. Wells, *Accounting for Common Costs* (Urbana, Ill.: Center for International Education and Research in Accounting, 1978).

[3]O.G. Ladelle, "The Calculation of Depreciation," in *The Late Nineteenth Century Debate over Depreciation, Capital and Income*, ed. R.P. Brief (New York: Arno Press, 1976). (First published in *The Accountant*, November 29, 1890 and December 6, 1890.)

[4]E. Cooper, "What is Profit of a Company?" in *Late Nineteenth Century Debate*, ed. Brief. (First published in *The Accountant*, November 10, 1888, pp. 740-46.)

[5]Lee v. Neuchatel Asphalte Company (1889) 41 Ch.D. 1. (Reprinted in *Late Nineteenth Century Debate*, ed. Brief.)

[6]Verner v. The General and Commercial Investment Trust (Limited) (1894) 63 Ch.D. 456. (Reprinted in *Late Nineteenth Century Debate*, ed. Brief.)

[7]*In re* National Bank of Wales Limited (1899) 2 Ch.D. 629 and Dovey V. Cory (1901) AC. 477.

[8]E. Cooper, "Chartered Accountants and the Profit Question," in *Late Nineteenth Century Debate*, ed. Brief. (First published in *The Accountant*, November 24, 1894, pp. 1033-43.)

Chapter Four

Financial Accounting in the Twentieth Century

To this point our description of the modern history of accounting has been limited to developments in the United Kingdom. This is legitimate since the situation in North America was very similar. The accounting profession developed first in England and Scotland, and many accountants from there visited the Americas to audit the accounts of enterprises financed by British capital. A considerable number remained to mingle with local accountants in establishing the profession in North America.

In spite of the fact that corporations legislation in the United States typically had nothing to say about financial reporting or audit, the development of accounting in that country in the nineteenth century was very similar to that in England. Chatfield points out one difference.[1] Relatively more of the financing of American companies consisted of short-term bank credit rather than the issuance of capital stock. Bankers looked to working capital as the prime security for their loans. Accordingly, audits for credit purposes naturally concentrated on the balance sheet position and, in particular, on working capital rather than on profit. The idea of conservatism in the valuation of working capital was thus reinforced.

The leading edge of advances in accounting shifted from England to the United States in the twentieth century. The U.S. emerged from World War I as a creditor nation and undoubtedly the most powerful of the world's economies. Its new status was reflected in a burgeoning capital market that enhanced the need for sound financial reporting. At the same time, American universities were the first to recognize accounting as an academic study, and it became a principal subject in the early business schools. Acceptance of accounting as an academic discipline introduced a more conceptual and critical approach to its study, which balanced and enriched its pragmatic orientation.

As described in the previous chapter, the collapse of the capital maintenance doctrine left financial reporting with little conceptual basis. Storey recounts that the void was filled by the proposition that most business undertakings had become going concerns and, therefore, their assets should be reported in a balance sheet at "going-concern value."[2] That value depended upon the nature of the asset. Those assets *with which* business was carried on—the fixed assets—should be valued at cost reduced by an appropriate allowance for consumption of utility over their useful lives. Fluctuations in market or realizable value could be ignored because the fixed assets of a going concern would not be sold. On the other hand, assets such as inventory and accounts receivable *in which* the business was conducted—the "floating" or "circulating" assets—should be valued at realizable value because realization was the whole purpose for which those assets were held.

The going-concern concept provided a satisfactory guide to practice except in one respect. Conservative accountants did not like the idea of reporting inventory at realizable values above cost when realization lay in the future. It was, therefore, widely accepted that a valuation basis of the lower of cost and realizable value was preferable.

Accountants' beliefs as to the basis of good accounting in the early twentieth century can be summarized in the following statements:

- The balance sheet is the most important financial report.
- The balance sheet is basically a statement of asset values and liabilities.
- Cost is a satisfactory basis of valuation for assets held for use or sale, except that depreciation of fixed assets should be allowed for and inventory should be written down to realizable value if below cost.

These beliefs did not answer all questions. Accountants were confused about whether capital gains or losses were part of income and about the definition of income in general. They did not know whether, or how, to account for goodwill. In addition, they were in no position to impose their ideas of accounting theory upon managements of companies, especially in the absence of any clear legal support. The following aspects of practice were particularly troublesome:[3]

- Many companies periodically would write up (or, less frequently, write down) their fixed assets on the basis of appraisals. So long as the balance sheet was regarded as a valuation statement, this was hard to resist.
- Many company managements resisted the idea that depreciation was a necessary expense of earning income and must be recorded systematically. Management tended to look on depreciation as a discretionary reserving of profits against ultimate replacement of plant. Such reserves could be varied in amount depending on whether times were good or bad.
- Some prosperous companies considered it proper to create "secret reserves" by understating assets or overstating liabilities, with consequent reduction in profits reported. Although the practice was conservative, its arbitrary aspects concerned anyone interested in fair financial reporting. The situation was even worse if, in some subsequent year, the reserves were released, thereby overstating profits reported at that time. That result was definitely unconservative, but management could always argue that reserves were intended to protect "against a rainy day." If it was proper to create them, it must be proper to use them when the rainy day arrived.

Pressures for improvements in financial reporting

As time passed, the contradictions and inconsistencies in corporate financial reporting became less and less tolerable, and the forces making for change became more insistent. Some of the forces for change in the United States were as follows:

- The income tax legislation of the early part of the century created a need for good accounting records and provided a stimulus to some change in theory. Basically, it shifted attention from the balance sheet to measurement of income. It was advantageous for tax purposes to establish that income arose only upon realization and also to accept the necessity for depreciation as a charge in determining income earned. The need for an objective basis for taxation also emphasized actual transactions, rather than valuations, as a basic ground-work for financial reporting. Thereby impetus was given to the adoption of the cost principle for valuation of assets.

- Certain government agencies became interested in good financial reporting as an aid to the granting of credit and thereby to the expansion of business and investment. At the request of the Federal Trade Commission, the American Institute of Accountants (AIA) prepared a guide to audit entitled *Uniform Accounting*. This 1917 statement suggested formats for the balance sheet and income statement. It was reissued with revisions and under new titles in 1918 and again in 1929 and 1936, the final version being entitled *Verification of Financial Statements*.
- The New York Stock Exchange (NYSE), as the primary market for publicly traded securities, also was influential. Listed companies were required to submit financial statements to shareholders from the early 1920s, although these did not have to be audited until 1933.

Although constructive, these efforts might well be characterized as "too little and too late." There was little accounting progress during the prosperous 1920s. Then the stock market crash of 1929 and the ensuing Great Depression provided a much more compelling impetus toward the improvement of financial reporting. Rightly or wrongly, inadequate financial reporting received some of the blame for the market excesses before the crash and the subsequent losses. An AIA Committee on Co-operation with the NYSE was formed in 1930. In 1933 it recommended six accounting principles. Five of these were accepted by the NYSE; the unfortunate exception was the suggestion that companies should disclose the accounting methods employed by them—a most desirable rule given the alternatives possible in accounting practice. These five, plus one other, were formally adopted by the AIA membership in 1934.[4] These so-called "basic principles" in fact represented attempts to curb the worst excesses of 1920s accounting and came nowhere near to providing a rounded framework for good accounting practice.

A more powerful stimulus for change was conceived in 1933. In that year, the federal government enacted the Securities Act to regulate the issuance of new securities to the public. In the following year, the Securities and Exchange Act was enacted to regulate trading in public securities markets, and the Securities and Exchange Commission (SEC) was set up as the regulating body. The threat of government intervention galvanized the accounting profession to organized action to promote improvements in accounting principles. In the event, the SEC resolved by a narrow margin to devote its efforts to regulation of disclosure in prospectuses and annual financial statements and to rely on the profession for improvements in accounting measurements.

Establishing the direction of change

The pressure for reform faced the accounting profession with a dilemma. There was no body with both the power and capability to mandate comprehensive change in financial reporting. The SEC had been given authority over the financial reporting of public companies but lacked the means, on its own, to enforce a whole new model of financial reporting. Corporation management, which has the responsibility to prepare financial reports, is invariably interested primarily in its own situation and lacks the energy to consider an overall theory of financial reporting. Moreover management, almost inevitably, is inclined to favour accounting practices that do not overly restrict its freedom to report as it thinks best. Auditors and the professional societies of accounting have ample reason to desire a well-defined accounting theory and clear-cut guidelines based upon it. But auditors (at least, the auditors of the 1930s and 1940s) also lacked the power and perhaps the will to develop and enforce a well-defined accounting theory and tight accounting standards. The responsibility for financial reports lay in the first instance with management. The auditor was in no position to say what must be done—merely what might not be done under pain of a qualified report. Moreover, many auditors and accountants believed that, in view of the complexity and variety in forms of business enterprise, rules of general application could not be set out except in the most abstract terms.

The practical result of this was that the accounting profession, with continual prodding by the SEC, tried to achieve reform in little steps rather than by dramatic changes. From the outset the position was adopted that prescription of all-embracing accounting rules was undesirable. Rather, each corporation should adopt those reporting practices best suited to its individual circumstances, provided those practices were "generally accepted" and/or had "substantial authoritative support." (The latter phrase was used by the SEC in 1938 to describe accounting practices that would be acceptable in financial statements filed with it.)

The primary need seen by the American Institute was to narrow areas of difference and inconsistency in accounting practices and to further the development and recognition of generally accepted accounting principles. For this purpose, reference to the institute membership as a whole, as was done in 1934, was too cumbersome, and occasional special committees were not sufficient. In 1939, a standing Committee on Accounting Procedure (CAP) was set up with the objective of issuing bulletins to the membership on accounting matters.

In spite of the notion of the overriding importance of what came to be known as generally accepted accounting principles (GAAP), the fact that a committee could express preferences and give guidance logically implied that there was some underlying accepted theory of accounting. In its introductory bulletin the CAP had this to say:

> *The committee regards corporation accounting as one phase of the working of the corporate organization of business, which in turn it views as a machinery created by the people in the belief that, broadly speaking, it will serve a useful social purpose....*
>
> *... In the last forty years the outstanding change in the working of the corporate system has been an increasing use of it for the purpose of converting into liquid and readily transferable form the ownership of large, complex, and more or less permanent business enterprises. This development ... [has led] to the creation of new controls, revisions of the law, and a reconsideration of accounting procedure.*
>
> *As a result of this development in the field of accounting, problems have come to be considered more from the standpoint of the current buyer or seller in the market of an interest in the enterprise than from the standpoint of a continuing owner....*

One manifestation [of this development] ... has been a demand for a larger degree of uniformity in accounting....

Other phases have been increased recognition of the significance of the income statement, with a resulting increase in the importance attached to conservatism in the statement of income, and a tendency to restrict narrowly charges to earned surplus. The result of this emphasis upon the income statement is a tendency to regard the balance-sheet as the connecting link between successive income statements and as the vehicle for the distribution of charges and credits between them.... [T]his concept ... should not obscure the fact that the balance-sheet has significant uses of its own.[5]

The concept of the primacy of the income statement filled the vacuum left by the loss of faith in balance sheet valuations. It was observed in the depression period that stock prices responded more to reported income than to balance sheet book values. But income had to be defined in a certain way to avoid the valuation problem. Income tax law, by which income was seen basically as an excess of measurable receipts over expenses, provided a possible answer. Income was to be based on actual business transactions. It should not be considered earned until revenue was "realized" and costs pertaining thereto were matched. This implicit conceptual framework was supported by academic writing of the time—in particular, the American Accounting Association's *Tentative Statement of Accounting Principles Underlying Corporate Financial Statements*, issued in 1936. The same ideas were strongly encouraged by the SEC.

Further support for the emphasis on the income statement came in 1940, with the publication by the American Accounting Association of a monograph by W.A. Paton and A.C. Littleton. In their preface the authors said:

We have attempted to weave together the fundamental ideas of accounting rather than to state standards as such. The intention has been to build a framework within which a subsequent statement of corporate accounting standards could be erected. Accounting theory is here conceived to be a coherent, coordinated, consistent body of doctrine which may be compactly expressed in the form of standards if desired.[6]

This work was broadly in tune with the thinking of the times. Merely by its existence as a well-reasoned exposition, it was to be enormously influential. Its important feature was that it was not merely an organized recital of accounting practice. Instead, it provided an approach to building a conceptual framework that has been followed, with variations, in many subsequent publications.

Paton and Littleton suggested that the most important accounting responsibility of a modern corporation was to provide information to investors, present and prospective, who were not familiar with its affairs as insiders. They further suggested that a large corporation was a quasi-public institution having broad responsibilities: to employees for fair wages and working conditions, to customers for fair prices and good service, and to government and to society for taxes. Because of this broad accountability and the need to avoid bias in favour of one interest or another, a consistent framework of accounting standards was needed. Standards were seen as statements giving broad guidance to the presentation of accounting facts. Standards were not intended to be detailed rules. They should, however, be orderly and internally consistent; they should be in harmony with observable conditions; and they should be impartial.

The basic concepts suggested by the authors and some of the implications they deduced from them are listed below.

- A business undertaking is an entity in its own right, separate from its proprietors or investors or other interested parties. The focus of interest, then, is on the assets within the enterprise rather than on the increases or decreases in proprietorial equity. From this it was argued that the "price aggregates" (costs of assets, etc.) involved in entity transactions form the proper base for its accounting, and the main accounting responsibility is to trace the flow of price aggregates through the entity.
- Continuity of enterprise is the typical experience; hence, accounting may normally assume a "going concern." It follows from this that financial statements for a part of the life of a business are provisional in character. It was also argued that the continuity characteristic of business makes "earning power" the most significant determinant of enterprise value. Hence the income statement is the most important accounting report. Each statement, however, should be considered only as part of a series covering a number of years, in view of its tentative nature.
- Money-price is the common denominator by which diverse objects can be expressed homogeneously in the accounts, even though service potentials are the significant elements behind the accounts. Since all transactions are expressed in the related "price aggregates," unity is achieved in the accounting. Hence, the concepts of cost, revenue, asset, liability, etc. are all aspects of the single subject matter—the exchange transaction.
- Business activity consists of transforming inputs (materials, labour, etc.) into outputs representing new combinations with new utilities. Input costs can be seen as "attaching" to outputs. Hence assets can be recorded at cost, leaving the recognition of value added from activity until "realization." At that time, the gain can be objectively measured.
- Costs measure effort and revenues measure accomplishment. Ideally, income reported would represent revenues realized less the costs contributing to the revenues. For practical reasons it is not possible to trace all costs to revenue. Hence, some costs must be matched with time periods rather than directly with realized revenue. The precise basis of matching with time periods (e.g., in the case of depreciation) is of minor importance, so long as it is reasonable on a long-run basis and any corrections are clearly disclosed when recognized.
- Accounting should be based on verifiable, objective evidence to the extent possible.

Inevitably there were many who disagreed with some of the detailed prescriptions of Paton and Littleton, but the broad framework of ideas was appealing. Both the emphasis on the income statement and the idea that accounting was a process of allocation of objectively determined price aggregates, guided by the ideal of matching cause and effect, appealed to accountants seeking some theoretical justification for avoiding the slippery process of value estimation.

From GAAP to accounting standards

For the better part of five decades, professional committees or boards with more or less independent status have laboured to give guidance to the goal of better accounting. The American lead in appointing a standing committee was followed shortly by other countries. The English Institute of Chartered Accountants in 1942 appointed a committee to issue technical recommendations. The Committee on Accounting and Auditing Research of the Canadian Institute of Chartered Accountants commenced work in 1946. Broadly similar committees are at work now in many countries. In addition, there now exists an International Accounting Standards Committee, sponsored by professional societies in a large number of countries, that issues statements with a view to promoting "harmonization" of financial accounting standards internationally.

The United States experience

The United States experience has gone through three distinct periods. Each of the first two periods ended with a sense of disillusionment and a determination to do better. Both times a strong element in the disillusionment was a sense that the committee or board involved had spent most of its time "fighting brush fires" and that its recommendations lacked any substantial conceptual base. In each case the succeeding board was given a mandate to engage in more basic research and build a "conceptual framework," within which individual recommendations were expected to fit in a logical, internally consistent fashion.

The CAP lasted twenty years. In that period it issued fifty-one bulletins, including eight on accounting terminology. Many important issues were dealt with, including such subjects as allocation of income tax cost, treatment of costs associated with pension plans, and accounting for business combinations. In retrospect, it is clear that the committee's work suffered from the strong emphasis on "general acceptance." The belief that accounting standards could not be imposed but must develop through acceptance made the committee timid, so that very often its opinions were expressed as preferences rather than positive recommendations. Often, also, practice in a particular area would stretch criteria suggested by the CAP. For example, in business combinations the committee suggested that "pooling of interests" accounting was appropriate when equity interests of both combining parties continued after a merger and when all the circumstances indicated that it was a real sharing of interests and not simply an acquisition of one party by the other. If one combining interest was "minor," it was to be presumed the merger was not a pooling. Nevertheless, over a period of time, practice came to accept pooling accounting when one of the combining interests was even less than five percent of the other. As a result of these problems, in the end it could be said that the committee failed to achieve its objective of reducing inconsistency in practice, even though its analysis and recommendations were valuable in themselves.

The proposed solution was to bring theory and research to bear on the problems of practice. The CAP was replaced by the Accounting Principles Board (APB), which was to be supported by a Director of Research and a greatly expanded program of research studies. The first charge upon the research division was to draw up a new conceptual framework and suggest its broad implications for financial accounting. This was seen as involving two phases. There was to be identification of a few postulates of accounting—observations to be taken as given. Then, broad principles were to be enunciated, flowing from and consistent with the postulates.[7]

The attempt was not a success. The statement of postulates seemed innocuous—almost a statement of self-evident concepts lacking any strong guidance for practical standards. The statement of broad principles suffered from a different criticism—it gave unwelcome guidance. Both statements were thought by the APB to be "too radically different from present generally accepted accounting principles for acceptance at this time."[8] In addition, there was considerable doubt whether the proposals in the studies could be implemented without too great a loss of objectivity. The board commissioned a new study to catalogue accounting principles that were thought to be generally accepted, with the idea that this might give a lead to further research better adapted to the needs of practice.[9] A few years later, the board itself issued a statement organizing and summarizing what it considered to be the existing status of GAAP.[10]

In the meantime, having rejected the proposed new conceptual framework, the APB was forced to take up where the CAP had left off. Almost immediately it ran into heavy weather. The Revenue Act of 1962 introduced a new tax concession in order to stimulate economic activity—the investment tax credit. Accounting for the tax reduction resulting from this credit raised completely new issues. There was a sharp split in opinion among board members as to the best accounting, and its recommendation received only the minimum support required for issuance under its voting rules. That split in opinion was duplicated in industry. The SEC refused to support the majority recommendation of the board. Thus, the board was faced with a situation where its implicit conceptual framework was inadequate, general acceptance could not be found for *any* single position, and its authority was under attack. It was forced to retreat and accept a diversity of accounting methods for the tax credit.

Thereafter, for a time the board seemed to settle down. Research studies on more specific subject areas began to appear and, although not always followed in board pronouncements, at least helped the board to arrive at reasoned conclusions on the issues. Over a period of some twelve years the board issued thirty-one "Opinions." Many of the subjects had previously been dealt with by the CAP, but with a greater background in the complex issues involved the board was able to provide more positive and more detailed guidance. At least part of the reason for detailed and specific rules was the desire to avoid the erosion of standards that previously had resulted from the stretching of criteria expressed in general terms.

The complexity of the issues dealt with by the APB had certain consequences. One was a lack of unanimity within the board itself on many issues. Compromises often had to be made to obtain the two-thirds majority necessary to approve issuance of an opinion. In addition, the variety in possible views increased the opportunity for parties with a vested interest to lobby board members on behalf of their point of view. On occasion, lobbying also went over the heads of the APB in attempts to persuade the SEC and Congress that they should overrule the board. The politicized atmosphere surrounding certain highly charged issues revealed an apparent weakness in the composition of the board. The majority of the members of the board were partners of auditing firms. It appeared to cynical observers that these members were open to pressures from important clients that might affect the independence of their opinions. The compromises necessary to obtain agreement on complex questions reinforced that impression, even though there was never any solid evidence to support it. Moreover, the compromises emphasized the absence of a thorough conceptual framework to support the board's opinions.

In an attempt to solve this problem, the institute, by now renamed the American Institute of Certified Public Accountants (AICPA), decided to make a more formal effort to get back to first principles. A study on the objectives of financial statements was commissioned. About the same time, the profession relinquished its sole responsibility for the appointment of the standard-setting board and joined with other private-sector associations to sponsor a new board—the Financial Accounting Standards Board (FASB). This new board was urged to arrive at some agreed-upon conceptual framework with all deliberate speed.

In the course of this history a little-noted evolution took place. As previously indicated, the CAP did not regard itself as legislating accounting principles; it merely provided informal guidance. The ultimate test of a principle was general acceptance. This attitude continued through the early years of the APB. However, the investment tax credit debacle was very damaging to the APB's prestige and threatened its claim to give informed guidance. The reaction in the profession was to close ranks. In 1964, Council of the AICPA attempted to add weight to the APB's opinions by adopting a resolution that institute members should ensure that any departure from the board's opinions be specifically disclosed, either in footnotes to the financial statements or in the audit reports of members. A few years later, the authority of the APB's opinions was further strengthened. The AICPA's Code of Ethics was amended to make it a contravention of ethics to issue an unqualified audit report on financial statements not in conformity with a specific APB recommendation, unless the departure was necessary to make the statements not misleading.

After the APB was dissolved, the FASB was recognized as its successor for the purpose of application of the code of ethics. The FASB was further strengthened by an announcement of the SEC in 1973 that it would regard accounting practices contrary to FASB promulgations as lacking in substantial authoritative support. As a result of these developments, the recommendations of the APB and then the FASB became much more than guidance to good practice: they became effectively the only acceptable practice. This was a change of overwhelming importance. General acceptance, as a justification of an accounting principle, was valid only where the boards had not made a specific recommendation. When a firm recommendation was issued, it became, ipso facto, a rule of practice. Accounting *standards,* arrived at by a quasi-legislative procedure, thus tended to replace accounting *principles,* recognized as a result of general acceptance.

From 1973 onwards, the FASB has issued statements, interpretations of statements, and technical bulletins at a rate almost three times as fast as that of the APB. The outpouring of recommendations has led preparers and users alike to complain about "standards overload." The complaints have been reinforced by the fact that the board has continued the APB tradition of highly detailed rule making. Yet it is not clear what the FASB could have done differently, given the ever-increasing complexity of business arrangements and the lack of consensus on criteria of good financial reporting.

In spite of the great importance assigned to the conceptual framework project, the FASB took a long time to bring it to fruition. Six Statements of Financial

Accounting Concepts were issued over the period from 1978 to 1985. These statements have been highly abstract in character. In spite of their generality it is apparent that consensus was difficult to attain and that this difficulty increased as the statements progressed closer to providing guidance to actual accounting. A number of observers have expressed disappointment with the potential usefulness of the statements for improvement in practice.

The Canadian experience

Like the CAP, the Canadian Committee on Accounting and Auditing Research began with the goal of influencing practice by argument and persuasion. In its early years, several of the committee's bulletins dealt with good disclosure in financial statements and prospectuses. This was a difference from the United States, where disclosure matters were largely left to the SEC. The Canadian committee was on occasion venturesome, providing guidance on new issues earlier than in the United States. Two examples were Bulletin 10 in 1954, which provided the first formal advocacy of the idea of income tax allocation in relation to differences between accounting depreciation and tax capital cost allowances, and Bulletin 21 in 1965, which first spelled out certain fundamental assumptions necessary for pension cost accounting.

Not surprisingly, the Canadian committee's recommendations cover much the same subjects as the American. More often than not American recommendations on a specific issue are released before the Canadian material. Inevitably there tend to be similarities in their conclusions—which reflect in some measure consultation between the standard-setting bodies. Some Canadians also feel that, in view of the linkages between the U.S. and Canadian capital markets, Canadian financial reporting practice cannot be markedly different from that of the United States. This sentiment is generally supported by Canadian companies registered with the SEC, who dislike being forced to disclose differences between Canadian accounting practices followed in their financial statements and corresponding U.S. practices. This does not mean there are no differences between Canadian and U.S. accounting standards. On the contrary, the final Canadian position often differs from that of the U.S. in points of detail. But there is a tendency to adopt the broad outline of the U.S. position and confine differences to specific secondary issues.

The Canadian recommendations are distinctive in that they are normally shorter and less detailed than the American. In part this simply reflects the fact that the all-volunteer Canadian committee does not have the resources to explore every subject to the same extent as does the FASB. In part also, it reflects a distinctive Canadian policy of leaving more room for the exercise of professional judgment as to the best accounting in each situation. There are both advantages and disadvantages to the policy. It can be easier to see the framework of principle behind more generally stated recommendations; also, it is certainly easier to adapt to special circumstances if one is not confined by a rigid set of rules. On the other hand, professional judgment cannot operate in a vacuum. There has to be understanding of and agreement with the concepts underlying an accounting standard as a basis for professional judgment. The problem with this is that accounting standards are often required because such agreement is lacking. We shall return to this subject in Part IV.

It is the practice of the Canadian profession to periodically review its efforts toward the encouragement of good accounting. In 1968, membership in the committee was broadened to include representatives of other bodies interested in financial reporting. The former series of individual bulletins was transformed into a "Handbook" with a logically organized structure. In 1973 the committee was split into two committees, one for accounting and one for auditing, and the accounting committee was organized in sections so as to enlarge the number of subjects that could be under consideration at any one time. Steps were also taken to obtain broader "exposure" of committee recommendations before their adoption was voted upon. This evolutionary process contrasts to a degree with the U.S. history of terminating one committee and making a fresh start with a new body. Canadian experience is also different in that the function of standard setting is still under the sponsorship of the accounting profession, rather than being carried on under the aegis of an independent foundation as is the case in the United States.

There has been the same transition in Canada in the nature of professional statements. In the early years, they merely represented guidance to good practice; now they have become mandatory standards to be observed. The mechanism of the evolution, however, has been somewhat different. From an early date, the Canadian profession followed the practice of making recommendations with respect to financial disclosure provisions to the legislature concerned, whenever companies acts were in the process of revision. The most noteworthy success along these lines came in 1953 when the Ontario corporations act was completely revised. The profession persuaded the government of the day to incorporate into the Act the provisions of the first CICA bulletin on financial disclosure virtually in their entirety. As companies acts in the other provinces and in the federal jurisdiction came under review, there was a tendency to pick up provisions from other Canadian statutes. In this way the legal impact of the CICA recommendations on financial disclosure spread through much of the country.

The next step in the transition from generally accepted principles to accounting standards came in 1968 when the new *CICA Handbook* was adopted. The committee on its own volition (but following the precedent established by the AICPA council) adopted a recommendation that any departure from its recommendations should be specifically disclosed in notes to the financial statements or, failing that, in the auditor's report. The obvious intention was to encourage adherence to committee recommendations. The committee, however, did not suggest or intend that other accounting practices, if properly supported, could not be considered acceptable, and disclosure of a departure from the recommendations was not considered tantamount to qualification of the audit report.

This understanding was upset by forces outside the profession. In 1972, the securities administrators of several Canadian provinces announced National Policy No. 27. This stated that the securities administrators would regard *CICA Handbook* pronouncements as "generally accepted accounting principles" as that term was used in either securities legislation or companies legislation. At first, it was not clear that the administrators would not also accept alternative practices that had substantial support—the policy statement did not say that CICA pronouncements were the *only* generally accepted accounting principles—but subsequent commission actions have led to that conclusion. In a number of cases, commissions have questioned whether individual company reporting practices were in compliance with CICA recommendations and have required future compliance. As a result of this policy, the *CICA Handbook* has, in effect, taken on the status of law with respect to most filings under the jurisdiction of provincial securities acts. In 1975, the same result was brought about with respect to annual financial statements for companies under federal jurisdiction, as a result of the inclusion of a reference to the *CICA Handbook* in the regulations to the new Canada Business Corporations Act. Several provinces have also amended their companies legislation to this effect.

The result of this development has been that the recommendations of the Accounting Standards Committee (as it is now called) in the *CICA Handbook* have quasi-legislative status. That gives them greater authority than those of professional committees or independent boards in almost any other country. In one way, this is very desirable. On the other hand, there are also pitfalls. There is a tendency to read quasi-legislative standards legalistically; therefore, it is important that the intent and meaning of the standards be unmistakably clear. There is also a danger that when the standards cannot be ignored, attempts will be made to upset them by lobbying government. The best defence against this lies in the quality of the standards themselves. It is vital that they be well reasoned and demonstrably designed to achieve fair financial reporting. It is important, also, that each standard be seen as part of a cohesive whole. A sound conceptual framework strengthens each individual standard. When one gets down to the detail of individual issues in the real world, these objectives can be very difficult to achieve.

International accounting standards

The development of financial accounting standards has followed broadly similar lines in many other countries. Detailed description is beyond the scope of this book. Reference should be made, however, to efforts that have been put forth to harmonize accounting standards across many countries.

An initial cooperative step was taken with the formation of the Accountants' International Study Group by the U.S., Canadian, and British professions to conduct a series of comparative studies of accounting practices in the three countries. A more ambitious effort began with the formation of the International Accounting Standards Committee (IASC) in 1973. This committee was initially sponsored by accounting institutes in nine countries, and the number participating has now grown to several times the original number. The purpose of the IASC has been "to formulate and publish in the public interest, standards to be observed in the presentation of audited financial statements and to promote their worldwide acceptance and observance."[11]

A large number of International Accounting Standards have already been issued. The internationalization of the accounting profession was carried a step further with the formation of the International Federation of Accountants (IFAC) in 1977. This body is sponsored by many of the same institutes as is the IASC, but the membership is not identical. The two bodies, however, have agreed to cooperate. In effect, the IASC acts as the delegated representative of the IFAC with respect to accounting standards.[12]

A strong motivation for the development of international standards lies in the internationalization of the capital markets. If investors worldwide need to compare and make sense of prospectuses and annual reports of companies from different parts of the world, common standards of financial reporting are highly desirable. Multinational companies, for their part, would find their financial reporting function much less costly and less of a nuisance if the accounting results of all their operating units could be kept on the same basis. Then they could flow into the consolidated financial statements with little adjustment required for differences in accounting policies.

There are, however, substantial difficulties in the way of international harmonization. Different countries have different tax and corporations legislation and different forms of government regulation that may impede harmonization. There is also the question of the degree to which local accounting standards *should* change. It is conceivable that standards designed for use in well-developed, public capital markets may be less valuable where there is no such market. It may be that a case can be made for the coexistence of international and local standards in some countries, but little investigation has been made of this question.

Difficulties also occur in the process of formulation of international standards. Where so many countries sponsor this work, it is obvious that no one country can have more than one or two delegates participating in the international standard-setting deliberations. Inevitably, international standards have had and will continue to have a large degree of compromise. Considerable flexibility is allowed in order to avoid forcing changes on important constituent members or running the risk of loss of their support. Yet such compromise inevitably weakens the effect of the proposed international standards.

Then there is the problem of achieving compliance with the standards. The IASC sponsor from each country has committed itself to support and encourage adoption of IASC standards. Yet there is a question how effective this support can be. In the United States (the most influential member), the sponsoring body is the American Institute of Certified Public Accountants, which has no control over the actions of the FASB or the SEC, the bodies that set the standards for the U.S. In Canada, support of the IASC takes the form of a CICA commitment to consider IASC pronouncements as they emerge. If there are significant differences from Canadian practice not justified by differences in the Canadian environment, a project is initiated to modify the *CICA Handbook* unless there is disagreement with the IASC recommendation. A separate CICA publication is available comparing IASC standards with Canadian practice. The Toronto Stock Exchange (and a number of stock exchanges in other countries) have lent support by urging listed companies either to state that their accounting policies comply with international accounting standards or to disclose differences therefrom.

It remains to be seen whether the accounting profession worldwide will have sufficient commitment and coherence to achieve international standards that really overcome the existing marked differences in financial reporting practices from country to country. As time has passed, however, the IASC has tackled increasingly difficult subjects in some depth. As it has done so, it has acquired increasing respect and influence.

Summary

Financial accounting entered the twentieth century with little in the way of a theoretical basis. The balance sheet was considered the most important statement and was considered a valuation statement. The use of cost as a starting point for valuation, however, was supported on practical grounds. Accountants disliked appraisals of fixed assets and believed that depreciation should be provided as a systematic amortization of cost. They also disliked the provision of secret reserves and, even more, their undisclosed release. Nevertheless, undesirable accounting practices persisted until well on in this century in the face of the relative weakness of the accounting profession.

The introduction of the income tax in the United States created greater interest in the measurement of income and gave a practical impetus to the development of the realization rule for revenue recognition and to the recognition of depreciation accounting. Certain government agencies and the New York Stock Exchange also made efforts to improve the standard of financial reporting. The depression of the 1930s and the formation of the Securities and Exchange Commission provided a considerably stronger impetus for improvement. The accounting profession was faced with the need to become more forceful in its ideas and actions or risk subordination to government regulation of financial reporting.

By this time the groundwork had been laid for a more comprehensive theory of financial accounting based on the deemed primacy of the income statement. The theory that came to be known as "historical cost accounting" was expounded in academic writing that has proved to be highly influential in shaping accounting practice. Essential elements of this theory are the propositions (1) that accounting should be based on price-aggregates resulting from bargained exchanges, and (2) that income can be appropriately measured by recognizing revenue when realized and matching incurred costs with recognized revenue. Matching is achieved largely by means of attaching costs to cost objects, such as inventory or fixed assets, that are written off as sold or consumed. Although no statement of the historical cost theory was officially adopted by the practising profession at the time, the influence of the theory permeated the detailed recommendations of professional committees from the 1930s onward.

The profession attempted to make progress through a program of gradualism. It was believed that a comprehensive set of rules for accounting would be far too inflexible to meet the variety of circumstances encountered in business, and that generally suitable accounting practices would emerge, with a little guidance from the profession, by a process of general acceptance. A standing Committee on Accounting Procedure was establshed in 1939 in the United States to make recommendations designed to achieve greater uniformity in practice. Similar bodies were established subsequently in a number of other countries.

The American experience has been that such bodies tend to get caught up in individual issues and, perhaps, do not "see the forest for the trees." There have been, as a result, recurring cries for more attention to be paid to the theoretical basis of financial reporting. It was found also that a committee recommendation did *not* automatically become generally accepted. Some suggestions have been stretched so far beyond their intent as to produce absurd results. Because of this, recommendations tend to become more detailed and more categorical as time goes on. External authority has also been added to professional recommendations through required disclosure of departures from them and through SEC support. Finally, the Financial Accounting Standards Board was set up independent of the profession.

Canadian experience has not been as turbulent as the American. Standard setting has remained under the wing of the profession, and its authority has been reinforced by official recognition under securities and corporations legislation. There has been the same tendency to proliferation of standards (not surprisingly since the same economic influences exist in Canada as in the United States). No conceptual framework statements have been attempted at an official level, although a research study was completed in 1980.

An International Accounting Standards Committee was founded in 1973 and is now sponsored by well over fifty countries. The committee has made a significant contribution with limited resources, but the task of achieving true international harmonization is a very difficult one.

References

[1]M. Chatfield, *A History of Accounting Thought*, rev. ed. (Huntington, N.Y.: Robert E. Krieger Publishing Co., 1977), pp. 1-7.

[2]R.K. Storey, "Revenue Realization, Going Concern and Measurement of Income," *The Accounting Review*, April 1959, pp. 232-38.

[3]These and other shortcomings were denounced in W.Z. Ripley, *Main Street and Wall Street* (Boston: Little, Brown & Co., 1927).

[4]The six principles, in brief, were:

- Unrealized profit should not be credited to income.
- Charges belonging in income account should not be charged to capital surplus.
- Surplus of a subsidiary earned before acquisition is not part of consolidated earned surplus.
- When a company has acquired its own stock and not cancelled it, dividends on that stock do not form part of its income.
- Amounts receivable from officers, employees, and affiliated companies must be shown separately in the balance sheet.
- If stock is issued to acquire property and some stock is donated back to the company, the par value of the stock issued cannot be treated as cost of the property nor can proceeds from the resale of the stock be credited to surplus.

The full text of these principles may be found in American Institute of Accountants, Committee on Accounting Procedure, *Restatement and Revision of Accounting Research Bulletins*, Accounting Research Bulletin No. 43 (New York: AIA, 1953).

[5]American Institute of Accountants, Committee on Accounting Procedure, *General Introduction and Rules Formerly Adopted*, Accounting Research Bulletin No. 1 (New York: AIA, 1939), subsequently consolidated in Introduction and Chapter 1 of *Restatement and Revision of Accounting Research Bulletins*, Accounting Research Bulletin No. 43 (New York: AIA, 1953).

[6]W.A. Paton and A.C. Littleton, *An Introduction to Corporate Accounting Standards*, Monograph No. 3 (AAA, 1940), p. ix.

[7]The resulting publications were M. Moonitz, *The Basic Postulates of Accounting*, Accounting Research Study No. 1 (New York: AICPA, 1961) and R.T. Sprouse and M. Moonitz, *A Tentative Set of Broad Accounting Principles for Business Enterprises*, Accounting Research Study No. 3 (New York: AICPA, 1962).

[8]AICPA, APB, *Statement by the Accounting Principles Board*, APB Statement No. 1 (New York: AICPA, 1962).

[9]P. Grady, *Inventory of Generally Accepted Accounting Principles for Business Enterprises*, Accounting Research Study No. 7 (New York: AICPA, 1965).

[10]AICPA, APB, *Basic Concepts and Accounting Principles Underlying Financial Statements of Business Enterprises*, APB Statement No. 4 (New York: AICPA, 1970).

[11] See IASC, *Preface to Statements of International Accounting Standards* (London: IASC, 1978), par. 3.

[12]For a description of international developments and some evaluation of the prospects see J.P. Cummings and M.N. Chetkovich, "World Accounting Enters a New Era," *Journal of Accountancy*, April 1978, pp. 52-61. Also see two papers in *Papers Presented at the 1977 Accounting Research Convocation on the Subject of Patterns of Change*, ed. J.J. Davies (University, Alabama: Graduate School of Business Administration, University of Alabama, 1977). W.D. Hall: "Establishing Standards for International Financial Reporting," pp. 95-106, and G.G. Mueller, "International Accounting Standards," pp. 107-32.

Part Two

Accounting Standards Today

Chapter Five

Historical Cost Accounting

Part I has described how the need for communication through financial reports evolved in the middle of the nineteenth century and how accountants and managements groped their way over a long period toward forms of reports acceptable for that purpose. The notions of capital maintenance and going concern provided some guidance in dealing with the difficult questions of valuation of assets and liabilities, but a well-articulated theory of financial reporting did not emerge until well on in the twentieth century. From the 1930s onward the application of the theory has developed and been continuously modified to meet new situations.

The objective of Part II of this book is to describe today's accounting standards and explain how they fit within the basic historical cost accounting theory. This chapter begins with a recapitulation of the basic tenets of historical cost accounting. We then consider some gaps in the theory and areas that need clarification. We proceed to discuss one major stumbling block to its implementation that helps to explain why quite specific accounting standards are both necessary and difficult to achieve.

The groundwork is then laid for succeeding chapters. Since the basic data for historical cost accounting are provided by exchange transactions, we analyze and classify the types of transactions engaged in by an entity and other events that may affect its financial position and results of operations. We then discuss the nature of the issues that must be addressed in the course of taking the input provided by transactions and other events and interpreting it so as to arrive at the figures for assets, liabilities, revenues, and expenses that appear in financial reports.

Elements of historical cost accounting

The theory that developed in the 1930s and has been refined and extended in succeeding decades rests on the following assumptions:

- Measurement of results of operations for a period has been accepted as the primary goal of financial reports. Observation of reactions of the capital markets and other interested parties to accounting reports suggests that information as to income earned in a period has more significance for investment and other decisions than has the information reported in a balance sheet.
- Cost is the attribute of assets used as the primary basis for recording in the accounts. In this way, the uncertainties associated with a valuation approach to accounting for assets are largely avoided. In certain cases, however, when the values of assets have fallen below amounts currently realizable or recoverable from future operations, write-downs are to be made and loss recognized, notwithstanding the uncertainty attaching to the valuation process.
- Revenue from productive activity is to be recognized as having been earned when (1) its amount is fixed by contract or by transaction with an outside party,4 (2) its collectibility is reasonably assured or reasonable allowances can

be made for noncollectibility, and (3) the commitments undertaken by the enterprise in return for the revenue have been substantially fulfilled. In the case of businesses that sell goods, the normal revenue recognition point is the point of sale. Assets recorded when revenue is recognized are measured at estimated realizable value.

- Costs incurred for assets are to be recognized as expenses as the usefulness of the asset expires. When an item of inventory is sold, it is obvious that its usefulness to the vendor has expired and expense (the cost of goods sold) must be recognized. In other cases the expense recognition point is far from obvious. The problem of expense recognition has often been expressed as the problem of "matching" costs with revenues. This description is appropriate to recognition of cost of goods sold and other sales-related costs but not to the treatment of other types of costs. Hence the more general term "expense recognition" is preferable.
- Windfalls (the receipt of unearned benefits) are recognized only when realized. Casualties (costs or losses incurred without compensating benefit) are recognized generally when they become probable and can be measured with reasonable reliability.

"Historical cost accounting" is called by that name since the primary basis of measurement of assets held for productive activities (including the earning of rental or investment income) is their original or "historical" cost. A more broadly descriptive term might be "transaction-based accounting," since the primary measurement basis for *both* assets held for productive activities and liabilities incurred is their value at the time of the transaction by which they were acquired or incurred.

The reliance on exchange transactions to provide the source figures for assets, liabilities, revenues, and expenses represents a basic break from the previous valuation system of accounting. The orientation to bargained transactions provides the foundation for the claim that the historical cost system is "objective." It is a reasonable assumption that a bargained transaction between an entity and outsiders represents good evidence of the value of the good or thing received by the entity at the time of the transaction. Thus, transaction-based figures should also be useful at or near the time of the transaction.

In the course of the accounting, however, initially recorded figures are subject to a variety of adjustments. Various costing methods may be used to calculate the total cost of an asset manufactured internally. Depreciation or amortization is recorded to allow for gradual consumption of the utility of assets held for use over a period of time. A judgment-based allowance for uncollectible amounts reduces the transaction figure for accounts receivable. Write-downs of other assets under the rule of "lower of cost and market" are made in various circumstances. Such judgment-based adjustments must be taken into account in assessing the overall objectivity of the historical cost system.

In addition, the gain in objectivity in the historical cost theory is attained only at the expense of some loss of realism. Because revenue recognition rules are tied to external transactions, an enterprise cannot take account of the value added by its productive activity before such revenue transactions occur. Other improvements in the well-being of an enterprise also cannot be recognized. For example, the discovery of mineral or oil and gas reserves by a company in the extractive industries, the natural growth of timber reserves in a forest products company, or a gain in the value of assets because of market price changes are not taken into account under the historical cost system. Finally, the historical cost theory, as customarily applied, does not allow for the fact that the value of the currency in which transactions are measured changes over time.

Unclear areas in historical cost theory

There are certain matters on which writers on accounting theory have not reached a consensus and which have not been extensively addressed by authoritative accounting recommendations. To begin with, financial reports deal with the resources and operations of a specific reporting entity. We need to ask what criteria determine how we define the entity that is to report. Second, historical cost accounting theory suggests that one of the most important objectives of accounting is to measure income. If we are going to measure income, it would seem we need to have a clear idea of what income is. Third, we find the term "accrual accounting" used frequently in accounting literature as a form of shorthand describing the totality of present-day accounting standards. It may be useful to explore what accrual accounting means. Finally, it may be useful to examine what is, or ought to be, the impact of uncertainty on accounting measurements, since uncertainty about the future is pervasive in the real world.

The concept of the accounting entity

The core function of financial reporting is to report wealth and changes in wealth over time. We cannot begin to account, however, unless we have a clear definition of the entity for which we are accounting. There are two aspects to the question of entity. The first is that of defining the boundaries of the entity itself. What criteria are there to tell us what resources and transactions belong to the entity furnishing a financial report? The second aspect is that of determining what is the focus of interest in the report. To use the common expression, what is the bottom line? or perhaps we should say, whose is the bottom line? If we aim to report income and wealth, we must ask whose income and whose wealth we are reporting.

The boundaries of an entity. In a modern society, wealth is owned by individuals, business partnerships or associations, business corporations, nonprofit organizations, and governments. It would be natural to look to ownership as the determining factor in defining an accounting entity. But, while ownership is an important factor, it is not the only factor. We have little difficulty in visualizing Kovac's Fruit Store as an entity in its own right apart from the Kovac family. The essential point, in this example, is that we can recognize the fruit store as a separate function or activity. The transactions in which it engages—the buying and selling of fruit, the payment of wages and other operating expenses—can be distinguished from the personal transactions of Mr. Kovac. This capability of separation is the key to an accounting entity. Economic resources and obligations can be identified with the entity, and we can define boundaries so that records may be designed to keep track of flows of resources across its boundaries.

To a considerable degree, the choice of accounting entity is a matter of convenience. In fact, there may be overlaps in defined entities. While a group of companies is treated as one entity in consolidated financial statements, a single corporation within the group can also be reported on as an entity, and its separate statements are relied upon for income tax, credit agreements, or other purposes.

Flexibility in choice of entity is obviously desirable for special purposes. One would expect some theory, however, to tell us how the entity should be defined for the purpose of financial reports to the public. Unfortunately, no such theory exists in complete form. The question has been tackled in the context of consolidation accounting—the most significant area for business accounting — but there is virtually no guidance for nonprofit organizations. A university, for example, whose primary functions are teaching and research, may carry on a wide variety of other activities—bookselling and publishing, operation of hospitals, medical and dental clinics, theatres, sporting facilities, and so on. It is not clear to what extent the assets, liabilities, revenues, and expenses of such facilities must be included in the public financial report of the university or what criteria should control the decision. The problem of entity definition is even more acute in government, where an activity may be treated as a separate entity simply because of the structure of the legislation authorizing it. Such gaps in accounting theory are symptomatic of the fact that financial accounting theory has concentrated mainly on the problems of business accounting.

The focus of interest in financial reports. We must also ask what is to be the primary focus of interest in entity financial statements. Consider Kovac's Fruit Store. The person primarily interested in its financial statements will be Mr. Kovac himself. (Of course, his banker, and perhaps others, will be interested as well.) He will want to know details about his investment in the business and what has been its profit and cash flow. In other words, the person who has most at stake in the success of the business is the proprietor, and his interest is "proprietary." Consequently, the focus of interest in the income statement will be the profit accruing to the proprietor after all other claims on revenues are satisfied. The focus of interest in the balance sheet will be the residual left over after all claims on assets are deducted.

Compare Kovac's Fruit Store with a large multinational corporation. Many people besides its shareholders have a major stake in the activities and well-being of such a corporation. Its management and employees often have a more enduring stake than an individual small shareholder, who may buy in today and sell out in six months. The financial interest of bondholders, bankers, and other creditors may be almost as great as that of the shareholders and usually will be concentrated in fewer hands. The taxation authorities of several countries have a stake in the corporation's activities and its reporting of them. The communities in which its plants are located have a stake in whether it operates in a safe and socially responsible fashion. Realistically speaking, the shareholders of such a corporation are only one of a number of constituencies that have an interest in the corporation.

In the light of this, many accounting theorists think that a nonproprietary view should govern financial reporting. Under the so-called "entity" viewpoint, the principal accounting focus of interest is upon the resources entrusted to the entity itself and the changes in them over the accounting period, not upon the interests of the various constituencies. Reporting the actual distribution of entity operating income among its claimants, including the income tax authorities, various classes of creditors, and the several classes of shareholders, is considered of secondary importance.

The point of view taken—proprietary or entity—can affect the way the accounting is performed, including the form of presentation of the financial statements.[1] Some examples are as follows:

- When a corporation is formed there are certain costs of incorporation. Since the corporate form of organization is presumably an advantageous way to organize the ownership interest, the proprietary viewpoint would treat such costs as assets. Since the costs do not in themselves contribute to the successful operation of the actual business carried on, the entity viewpoint would write off such costs as representing an effective reduction of the resources under the control of the entity.
- A corporation may receive a government subsidy that induces it to undertake investment in plant that it would not otherwise undertake. From a proprietary point of view, the investment involved is the net amount after the subsidy, and that net amount should be recorded as the cost of the plant. From an entity point of view, the assets under the corporation's control have been increased by a plant with a certain gross cost, and arguably that is what it should account for.
- From a proprietary point of view, interest paid on debt and income taxes represent expenses because they reduce the income available for the proprietary interest. From an entity point of view, taxes and interest represent distributions of its income from operations like dividends, rather than expenses required to earn entity income.
- A corporation may purchase or redeem outstanding debt securities for less or more than their carrying value on the books. From the proprietary point of view, a gain or loss has been realized that forms part of the reported income for the proprietor(s). From an entity point of view, there is no gain or loss but merely a rearrangement of claims upon it.

By and large, today's accounting standards for business enterprises adopt the proprietary point of view. This may be partly attributable to the evolution of accounting from the position where its primary objective was a report to owners. The emphasis is reinforced by the major influence upon accounting of regulation in the interests of full and fair disclosure to the capital markets. As a practical matter the financial information prepared on the proprietary basis and suitable for security holders may well contain all or nearly all the information that it is reasonable to require in general purpose financial reports.

Nonbusiness organizations are a different matter. As noted, there exists no strong theory to indicate what ought to be the boundaries of the reporting entity for them. Standards for financial reporting of nonbusiness organizations are in a relatively primitive state and have yet to address this question.

The meaning of income in accounting

As already stated, historical cost accounting theory adopted the measurement of income as its primary objective. Most of us have some idea of income in our minds and feel no strong need for explanation of the concept. Simply from the derivation of the word, one might think that income is something that comes in and hence should be observable (perhaps as a flow of cash). A little thought, however, serves to dispel that notion. If a person receives cash on loan, she does not have income. On the other hand, the salary received in cash by an employee may well be less than his income because of various deductions made by the employer or because some income is received in nonmonetary form.

Thus the concept of income is more complicated than might appear at first sight. Indeed, we have different implicit concepts for income from labour and income from capital. If you buy a fixed-term annuity, for example, you divide the annuity payments that come in into two portions, one representing return of the capital invested and the remainder considered to be income. On the other hand, if you invest time and effort in a professional education such as medicine, you do not divide the subsequent net proceeds from your practice into a portion representing return of your investment and a remainder representing income. The moral of this is that income is whatever we say it is. It is an artificial concept, not a real world phenomenon. If we say that measurement of income is the primary objective of accounting, we ought to make explicit what we mean by the term income. In logic, it has to be defined before we can measure it.

Formal attempts to define income, especially in the works of economic theorists, almost always involve some notion of capital maintenance. A popular definition of income for a business (adapted from economic theory) is that income for a period is that amount which can be distributed by a business and yet leave it as well off at the end of the period as it was at the beginning. There are severe problems in making this definition operational for the purpose of income measurement.

- In the first place, well-offness is a subjective concept. It depends upon expectations as to the future, and expectations can change with time. If one's resources have not changed but expectations as to future cash inflows from them have changed over a period, it must be decided whether that change in expectations is or is not part of the income to be measured for the period.
- In any event, expectations are not something that themselves can be measured. Any practical measurement of income must look for objective surrogates for expectations. An obvious choice of surrogate lies in market values for resources and claims upon them. Since market values are based on collective expectations, however, any income measurement based on market values necessarily includes the effect of changes in expectations. Two other difficulties are mentioned below.
- Market values for assets that represent fixed claims to money consist of the present value of the future money claims when discounted at a market rate of interest. Market values of other assets, being largely based on expectations of future cash flows, are also affected indirectly by going rates of interest. The general level of interest rates can change over a period. Hence, some changes in market values over a period will be attributable to changes in interest rates rather than to changes in the assets' collective ability to generate cash flows. If income measurement is based on market values, it will necessarily include the impact of changing interest rates. Some people, at least, would prefer a definition of income based solely on changes in prospects for distributable cash flows, rather than including within income the extraneous impact of changing interest rates.
- It is common knowledge that the value of a business as a whole will be different from the sum of the values of its identifiable assets less liabilities. If one wishes a measure of well-offness, it is the value of the business as a whole that is relevant (except when sale of the net assets individually would bring more than the business, in which case the business ought to be liquidated).

Unfortunately, any estimation of the value of a business as a going concern is considered too subjective for purposes of income measurement. The customary recourse—that is, valuing the assets and liabilities individually to arrive at a measure of well-offness—necessarily means that the measurement of income is less than ideal. (This problem is known as the "aggregation problem" and will be encountered repeatedly in accounting contexts.)

- Measures of net resources, and hence income, are necessarily made in monetary terms so that one can arrive at one total representing a whole portfolio of different kinds of resources. But the real value of money—that is, its purchasing power or command over goods—itself changes over time. Thus, increases in values in monetary terms over a period do not necessarily correspond with real increases in well-offness. Many believe that income ought to be defined in real terms. That is to say, any measure of income based on nominal valuations in money ought to be deflated or inflated to compensate for changes in the purchasing power of money. Measurement of changes in purchasing power, however, itself creates a number of difficult conceptual and practical problems.

The problems in measurement of what might be considered an ideal definition of income have been such that the ideal has clearly not been influential in the development of accounting practice. Instead, the historical cost accounting theory has not gone much beyond the idea that income is the excess of revenues over the expenses of earning those revenues. To measure income for a period one must first decide what are the revenues for a period and the expenses applicable to those revenues. In other words, accounting income is defined in procedural terms rather than conceptual terms. It depends upon the conventions adopted for recognition of revenue and expense, rather than such conventions being deduced from the ideal concept of income. This pragmatic approach leaves room for much confusion as to what really are the esssential concepts of income, revenue, and expense in historical cost accounting.

In the first place, there has been confusion as to when income emerges in the course of business activity. Under the ancient venture accounting tradition, there was no income until the venture was completed. Later, when business became more continuous in character, Adam Smith, the father of classical economics, suggested that income should not be considered to exist until realization through sale. In contrast, the valuation approach to accounting for ordinary nineteenth century business enterprise stipulated no such requirement for income recognition.

The increasing emphasis on realization in the twentieth century was primarily supported by considerations of convenience and income tax advantage, rather than by theoretical considerations. As a result, exceptions to the realization emphasis could be admitted. George O. May wrote:

> *Manifestly, when a laborious process of manufacture and sale culminates in the delivery of the product at a profit, that profit is not attributable, except conventionally, to the moment when the sale or delivery occurred.*[2]

Hence, realization is not an essential characteristic of accounting income but rather merely a convenient criterion for recognition that may be abandoned when considered appropriate. A striking example is provided by the treatment of long-term construction contracts. It is generally conceded that significant distortion in reported income can occur if income recognition is left until the date of completion of the contract. The significance of this example lies in the fact that it is by no means easy, as a practical matter, to evaluate contract performance at some interim date before completion. Yet the perceived distortion of income if such is not done has allowed the realization principle to be disregarded in this case. In short, although people seem to have some implicit notions about income, the lack of an agreed definition encourages inconsistent accounting and makes it difficult to arrive at cohesive accounting standards for the historical cost model.

Meaning of the term "accrual accounting"

The term accrual accounting is frequently encountered in accounting literature. Sometimes it is accompanied by modifiers, as in the phrases "full accrual accounting" or "modified accrual accounting," but rarely is their precise meaning explained. Sometimes accrual accounting is used as a synonym for income accounting under the historical cost model; at other times it is used differently. The result is undesirable confusion.

In a discussion of the objectives of business enterprise accounting the Financial Accounting Standards Board (FASB) described accrual accounting thus:

> *Accrual accounting attempts to record the financial effects on an enterprise of transactions and other events and circumstances that have cash consequences for an enterprise in the periods in which those transactions, events, and circumstances occur rather than only in the periods in which cash is received or paid by the enterprise.... It recognizes that ... operations of an enterprise during a period, as well as other events that affect enterprise performance, often do not coincide with the cash receipts and payments of the period.*[3]

This description draws a sharp contrast between cash basis accounting and accrual accounting. The precise interpretation of accrual accounting, however, depends critically on the period in which transactions, events, and circumstances are deemed to "occur." The FASB definition gives no guidance as to how this is determined.

The FASB has also described accrual accounting in the context of nonbusiness organizations. The description is almost identical with that quoted above for business enterprises, merely substituting some words to recognize the service goal of the nonbusiness organization. A footnote keyed to the description states:

> *This paragraph is not intended to prejudge specific recognition and measurement issues involved in applying accrual accounting in the nonbusiness area. For example, whether certain inflows of financial resources, such as taxes, grants, and contributions, should be recognized in the period when a claim arises, when they are received, when they are appropriated for use, when they are used, or when other events occur, is beyond the scope of this Statement.*[4]

Again it is not clear—in fact the FASB specifically withholds guidance—when transactions and events are deemed to "occur." That is left to be determined by individual accounting conventions generally accepted for the type of entity being reported upon. Once again, as was the case with accounting income, the concept is determined by the procedures rather than the procedures being determined by the concept.

The result of this is much confusion in accounting literature, particularly in the area of nonbusiness organizations. There is a strong tradition in some types of nonbusiness entities of using the term accrual accounting to describe an accounting basis that recognizes revenues (and the related monetary asset) and expenditures (and the related monetary liability) at the time a legal claim arises. On this basis, transactions and events are deemed to "occur" not when cash changes hands but when a cash payment becomes assured by a contractual commitment. Since the financial effect is recorded at the time of performance, this form of accrual accounting means that costs of tangible or intangible assets acquired to render future service are written off as acquired rather than as the services of the asset are consumed.

So long as different accounting practices are considered appropriate for business and nonbusiness organizations the same term—accrual accounting—should not be used to describe both sets of practices. The simplest cure to this problem would be to attach a descriptive modifier to the word "accrual." For example, nonbusiness organizations might be said to be using "contractual accrual accounting." Business organizations might be described as using "benefit accrual accounting" because accruals in business accounting are based on the idea of assigning transaction results to the period of benefit or sacrifice associated with the transaction.

Accounting conflicts stemming from uncertainty

Measurement of income under the historical cost model requires a classification of results of transactions as between assets, liabilities, revenues, and expenses. In the presence of uncertainty it is difficult to formulate standards for classification of transaction results and to make individual classification decisions. The difficulty in obtaining consistent treatment has been exacerbated by a little-recognized split in accountants' attitudes. On the one hand, there are those who instinctively wish to minimize uncertainty. Their attitude tends to be "expense all costs when incurred unless they can be clearly shown to have future benefit."[5] On the other hand there are those who feel that measurement of income requires a rigorous association of costs and revenues. Thus, a business that makes a product for sale and recognizes revenue at point of sale should strive to find ways to associate a high percentage of costs with inventory in order to effect a matching with sales revenue.

As a result, some standards seem to be greatly influenced by the matching ideal while others are very much influenced by the desire to minimize the use of estimates and allocations through sticking close to cash accounting. For example, in the United States the concentration on full absorption inventory costing in preference to direct costing represents a victory for the full allocation approach. On the other hand, the preference of the FASB for successful efforts accounting over full cost accounting for deferred exploration and development costs in the oil industry represents the "stick-to-cash" attitude. Of course the circumstances, including the degree of uncertainty involved, are different in these two issues. But the traditional historical cost model does not tell us just how the ideal of matching should be reconciled with uncertainty.

In the early period of the historical cost model a pattern developed for solution of some questions of classification of results of transactions. Because of the overriding stress laid on measurement of income, the natural question for classification purposes was: Is the charge or credit related to that transaction or event all attributable to this year's income? If the answer to that question was no, very often the procedure adopted was to "defer" the cost or revenue to fall into the income measurement of future years. Because of the articulation of the balance sheet and income statement, these deferred items necessarily were treated as assets or liabilities. And because it was rarely clear in such cases to what period the items did relate, their subsequent amortization to income was frequently arbitrary.

Such looseness did not escape criticism. A natural focus for criticism was the deferred items reported as assets and liabilities in the balance sheet. What was the real nature of the asset or liability in question? It was often hard to say and because of this they were dubbed by one writer "what-you-may-call-its"—a fair description.[6]

The idea that financial accounting depends basically on identification and measurement of revenues and expenditures for a period and that the balance sheet consists of the residuals of the income measurement process has been called the "Revenue and Expense viewpoint." A contrasting approach has developed in recent years under the name of the "Asset and Liability viewpoint."[7] Under this viewpoint, no cost may be deferred by the matching process unless there is strong evidence that the asset recorded probably will result in receipt of a benefit in future. Similarly, no credit may be deferred unless there is good evidence it represents a probable future sacrifice.

The treatment of research and development (R&D) costs provides one example of a switch from one viewpoint to the other in accounting standards. Up to about 1975, one would ask the question with respect to R&D costs: Are these costs intended to produce revenues of the period in which they are incurred? Since the answer would usually be no, it was considered perfectly proper to defer R&D costs when incurred and amortize them over some presumed period of future benefit (which in most cases was fairly arbitrary). In the mid-1970s, however, accounting standards were revised. Research costs (and in the United States, development costs also) are always to be written off because of lack of assurance as to commercial results. Deferral of development costs is permitted only if several tests are met indicating a considerable degree of certainty as to future benefit.

In a world of certainty, there would be no conflict between the Asset and Liability viewpoint and the Revenue and Expense viewpoint. It is only when uncertainty enters the picture that confusion arises. It may be noted that the insistence under the Asset and Liability viewpoint that only clearly identifiable and measurable assets be recorded is conservative in effect—which is one reason it has been urged. The same test applied to liabilities, however, is the opposite of conservative, and this is potentially dangerous as enterprises undertake more and more commitments and obligations to be fulfilled in future. In any event, it is not clear at present that either the Revenue and Expense viewpoint or the Asset and Liability viewpoint is predominant in accounting standards and practice. This confusion is a source of weakness in the application of the historical cost theory.

The matching problem in historical cost accounting

The core of the historical cost theory is the idea that bargained transaction amounts (hence, objectively determined amounts) can be attributed to periods so as to measure income. The idea of matching is customarily expressed in terms of matching costs with realized revenues. It should be recognized, however, that the realization convention is itself merely a device to attribute revenues to accounting periods. Thus, a more general description of the historical cost approach is that it represents a way to measure income for a period by attributing (matching) both revenue transactions and cost transactions to periods.

There are problems in attributing one event to a time period or associating events with each other. The following discussion of types of attribution may clarify the matter.[8]

- One-to-one attribution. There is little or no problem in associating single events or transactions when one can observe the link between them. For example, if one buys a single pig, there is no problem in saying that the cost of the pig is $X, the observed purchase price. If one sells the same pig for $Y, it is similarly obvious what the revenue from the sale is. It logically follows that the profit from the sale of the pig is $Y minus $X.
- Many-to-one attribution. There is also little problem in attributing many subjects or events to one object if there is a connection directly traceable between each of the subjects and the object. For example, if one can observe materials being cut for a product and labour being expended in its fabrication, we can say that the materials and labour are attributable to the product and its cost cannot be less than the sum of the costs of the material and labour.
- One-to-many attribution. There is, however, a severe problem in attributing one subject to several objects. Suppose the pig purchased for $X is butchered and the various parts sold. It is well known that there is no way to demonstrate what is the cost of a side of bacon or any other product of that pig. There is one "joint" cost of all the meat and other products obtained from the pig, and there is no way to prove what is the cost of a particular portion of the meat. There are several conventions that can be devised for attributing a cost. For example, if the pig weighed 200 kilos at purchase, one could say that the cost per kilo is $X/200 and if a piece of bacon weighs 2 kilos, its cost is $2X/200. The "joint costing" approach would attribute cost to a particular portion of meat by saying that its cost is determined by computing the percentage of its sale price to the total sale price of all the products from the pig and applying that percentage to the total cost of the pig. A "by-product costing" approach would assume that the cost of the less important products was equal to the revenue realizable from them, leaving a net cost to be assigned to the other, more important products on some other basis. The point is that one or more of these conventions may seem to be reasonable in particular circumstances but none can be proven to be correct to the exclusion of any other approach.
- Many-to-many attribution. It must be obvious that if the partitioning of one subject among many objects is impossible to measure, the attribution of many subjects jointly to many objects will be equally impossible to demonstrate. As an example, factory overhead will consist of many types of cost—indirect labour, power, heat, repairs and maintenance, depreciation, and so on. Attribution of these costs to the many products produced by the factory requires costing conventions. Many conventions may look more or less reasonable; none can be proved to be superior to any competitor.

Under income accounting theory the matching process frequently requires one-to-many or many-to-many attributions. Because no one attribution method can be proved to be exclusively correct, it can be predicted that a variety of methods will tend to be found in practice for each such matching situation. Accounting standard setters are faced with the decision whether to permit diversity in practice in each such situation or to impose a single more or less arbitrary solution in the interests of comparability.

Historical cost accounting and generally accepted accounting principles

The discussion so far might be taken to suggest that problems in accounting practice all result from limitations, shortcomings, or ambiguities in the historical cost accounting theory. Things are not quite as simple as that. It will be recalled from chapter 4 that early committees set up by the accounting profession to investigate problem areas did not consider themselves as setting standards in accordance with a theory of accounting. The authority of their recommendations, they believed, would stem only from general acceptance.

Successors of the early committees have acquired much greater authority. Their pronouncements now set standards, rather than being mere recommendations or statements of preference. Nevertheless, the tradition of the overriding importance of general acceptance remains powerful. That tradition manifests itself in two ways. First, standard-setting bodies hesitate to suggest a standard that is contrary to entrenched practice, even when the standard is clearly consistent with the requirements of historical cost accounting theory. Second, practice in new situations is not necessarily guided by theory. The question asked by those responsible for financial reporting when faced with a new problem is not necessarily, what does accepted theory call for? It is just as likely to be, what are other people doing?

The present situation is that the test for use of an accounting method ostensibly remains general acceptance, rather than conformity with fundamental financial reporting theory. The term "general acceptance" is used in audit reports and has been adopted by legislation or regulations governing financial reporting. Use of the term is a source of confusion. In a new situation, obviously there is no generally accepted principle. If different entities adopt different policies, there is no mechanism for judging which is generally accepted. (In practice, it is not impossible that all will be considered generally accepted.) On the other hand, a recommendation of a standard-setting body is automatically deemed generally accepted to the exclusion of other practices, no matter how unpopular the recommendation is.

This situation provides part of the reason why some people urge the development of an explicit conceptual framework for financial reporting. It is not so much that there is a need to modify accounting theory but simply to make clear the theory we have. These sentiments were behind the commissioning of American Institute of Certified Public Accountants (AICPA) Research Study No. 7 by Paul Grady and Accounting Principles Board (APB) Statement No. 4 on concepts and accounting principles (referred to in chapter 4). The influence of these studies, however, has been less than it might have been because they have never been adopted as the official position of accounting standard setters. Thus the ambiguities in generally accepted accounting practice continue, and constant effort is required to check inconsistencies in practice.

The implementation of historical cost accounting

As has been indicated, the historical cost theory tries to avoid a valuation approach to financial reporting. To accomplish this, it relies, in the first instance, upon transactions to furnish measurements of assets, liabilities, revenues, and expenses. It also relies mainly upon transactions to signal when assets, liabilities, revenues, and expenses are to be recognized. Transactions with outsiders, however, are not sufficient to provide information on all changes in financial position that ought to be recorded. Production activity, for example, may have significant impact on the well-being of an entity before culminating in a transaction with an outsider. Other events, some fortuitous, may also have significant impact on entity resources. The following tabulation is an attempt to provide a comprehensive classification of the transactions and events that result in changes in entity resources.[9] This classification provides a background for discussion in the remainder of Part II of this book.

I. Transactions and events that give rise to inflows or outflows of assets and liabilities to or from the entity.

   A. Exchange transactions with other parties in which each party receives and gives up something of value.

      1. Operating transactions. These consist of purchases, sales, and barters of goods or services (including services rendered for wages) in the normal course of active operations. In purchase and sale transactions there is an active party who performs by delivering goods or services and a passive party whose obligation is simply to make payment. To a financial institution that is in the business of accepting funds from the public (by way of deposits, insurance premiums, etc.) and investing, such borrowing and investment transactions might also be considered part of normal operations.
      2. Passive investment transactions. These consist of purchases or sales of investments acquired for the production of income, where the purchaser does not acquire a right to manage or significantly influence the management of the investment. Also included is the receipt of investment returns in the form of interest, etc.
      3. Financing transactions. These are borrowings from or loans to others. The essential element of a financing transaction is the promise of one party to pay cash to the other in future.
      4. Settlement transactions. These are collections or repayments flowing from obligations arising out of other transactions or events. In most cases they consist simply of payment of cash in satisfaction of a previously incurred obligation.
      5. Advance payments. These are payments made as full or partial settlement of obligations not yet incurred.

B. Nonreciprocal transfers to or from other parties
   1. Capital transactions. These are contributions or withdrawals of capital by owners or payments of a return (e.g., dividends) to owners.
   2. Other. These include taxes, gifts, thefts, fines, settlements of threatened or actual lawsuits, and so on.

II. Transactions and events that give rise to changes in assets and liabilities held.
   A. Productive activities. These include manufacturing, processing, distribution, packaging, trading, growing things, extraction of minerals, and service activities of all kinds. They also include the discovery of valuable assets where discovery activities are planned.
   B. Changes in values of assets and liabilities as a result of market conditions or interest rate changes.

III. Completely fortuitous events involving creation or destruction of assets or changes in their value while held.
   A. Windfalls. These consist of completely unplanned accessions of assets or changes in the value of assets owned. An example would be discovery of valuable gravel deposits under land acquired for other purposes.
   B. Casualties. These are fortuitous losses of assets or incurrences of liabilities. Examples would include loss or damage to assets from fire, flood, earthquakes, etc.

Inspection of this classification of transactions and events helps one to visualize the problems in representing them faithfully in financial reports. Those problems will be of two sorts—determining when to recognize the events and choosing appropriate bases to measure the events.

- In general, these problems are least difficult in exchange transactions (category I, A above) particularly when the exchange involves an immediate payment of cash. The exchange event is usually readily observable, and the consideration in the exchange usually provides an appropriate measurement basis.
- Nonreciprocal transfers (category I, B) may or may not be easy to account for. Capital transactions are straightforward if the transfer is in cash. Depending on their particular circumstances, other nonreciprocal transfers may present problems in timing of recognition as well as measurement.
- It is difficult to know when to recognize the results of productive activities (category II, A) because they are normally continuous. Measurement is also difficult owing to the lack of exchange prices.
- Changes in values of assets when held (category II, B) are sometimes easy to measure (for example, when the commodity measured is of a standard type and good markets for it exist). More often they are difficult to measure because of incomplete markets and lack of assurance that the commodity in question could be or would be sold at market prices.
- Windfalls (category III, A) are quite likely to be difficult to measure. It may also be difficult to know when to recognize them.
- Casualties (category III, B) are likely to be easy to recognize because the loss is observable. Measurement requires a valuation process.

The task of historical cost accounting is to devise workable methods for interpreting operating transactions and peripheral activities or other events in terms of assets and liabilities to be reported from time to time and revenue, expense, gain, and loss attributable to specific periods. Guidance is required to answer the following broad questions:

- What events or transactions give rise to the initial recognition of assets, liabilities, and capital contributions in the accounts? In other words, when does an accountable event occur?
- How are the transaction amounts to be measured for the purpose of recording them?
- What are the conditions that justify recognition of revenue as earned?
- On what basis are costs incurred to be recognized as expenses? This question resolves itself into two subquestions:
  - Where a productive process has occurred so that the assets acquired in transactions with outside parties (including labour and overhead services among assets acquired) have been transformed or partially transformed into a product or service suitable for sale, how shall the costs of the factors of production be assigned or aggregated into the cost of the work in process or finished product?
  - On what basis shall the cost of product or other costs not treated as product costs be recognized as expenses because their capacity for contribution to future revenue has expired or partially expired?
- How should expense be recognized when obligations are undertaken in present operations that will probably result in costs in future periods?

It will be observed that these broad decision areas are expressed largely in terms of an entity that manufactures, processes, or distributes a product. The historical cost accounting theory has concentrated largely on this type of entity and has very little to say about nonbusiness organizations. It also has little to say about questions that arise for business entities that do not conform to the pattern of a product-handling business. Some types of financial institutions, extractive companies, real estate companies, investment enterprises, brokers, and traders all have significant accounting problems for which the historical cost model has limited relevance. As a result, the accounting practices of these entities have tended to develop through general acceptance within the industries themselves. In recent years more attention has been paid to their needs, but it is still difficult to fit some of their accounting practices within any recognized conceptual framework of accounting.

In the following two chapters, approaches to the initial recognition and measurement of exchange transactions, nonreciprocal transfers, and windfalls and casualties will be dealt with. Several succeeding chapters will deal, in essence, with recognition and measurement of the results of productive activity. Under the historical cost theory, this is usually discussed under the headings "Recognition of Revenue," "Matching of Costs," and "Loss Recognition." In each case, questions of recognition and measurement are dealt with together. Since the historical cost theory ignores price changes of assets and liabilities while held (except for loss recognition in some cases), discussion of accounting for changes in the values of assets and liabilities is reserved for Part III.

While accounting standards governing the recognition and measurement of operating revenues and expenses and peripheral gains and losses cover the majority of transactions and events to be accounted for, there are a large number of individual situations that must also be dealt with. For example, there must be an agreed approach to financial reporting when two entities are combined and to the production of consolidated financial statements thereafter. Standards must be settled for expressing foreign currency amounts in terms of the currency used for financial reporting. Accounting for passive investments represents a separate area of interest. Investment accounting is just one of the problems encountered in financial institutions, and, in general, these bear little relationship to problems encountered in industrial and commercial concerns. Accounting for nonbusiness organizations and governments also has developed along different lines from accounting for business enterprises. In addition, many questions arise with respect to the presentation of financial statements, the disclosure required therein, and supplementary information that may be presented to assist analysis. These special accounting areas are dealt with in the later chapters of Part II.

Summary

The outlines of the historical cost accounting theory were clear by the 1930s. Since that time, the theory has been continuously developed and modified to meet new situations. Its elements are: belief in the importance of income measurement; reliance on cost as the primary basis of reporting assets acquired for sale or use; recognition of revenue as earned based on substantial completion of effort and assurance, usually contractual, of collection of proceeds; and recognition of expense as benefits from costs incurred are consumed.

Although the outlines of the theory are clear, there are certain issues it does not deal with. For example, there are no clear criteria for defining the boundaries of activities that should be covered by the financial report of a given entity. Nor is there any theory to suggest the appropriate focus of interest in such a report. In business accounting, there tends to be a "proprietary" focus. Some writers feel that focus is inappropriate for large corporations because many parties besides shareholders have a stake in such an entity. The suggested alternative focus is the net resources entrusted to the corporation and resource flows before distributions to the various stakeholders. Such an "entity" focus also seems more appropriate for nonbusiness organizations.

A more serious deficiency is the lack of any clear accounting theory as to how income should be defined. For example, traditional accounting practice stresses that income should be "realized," but the exceptions allowed prove that this is a rule of convenience rather than a fundamental characteristic of the concept of income. As a result, clear criteria governing the recognition of earned revenue or income are difficult to arrive at.

When an entity keeps track of and reports on assets and liabilities other than on a cash basis, it is said to have adopted accrual accounting. Unfortunately, this term is used very imprecisely. In particular, its usage by nonbusiness organizations tends to be different from that of business organizations. If several different varieties of accrual accounting continue to be accepted, the names given to the several versions ought to be differentiated to avoid confusion.

Historical cost accounting avoids the uncertainties of valuations largely by relying on amounts established in bargained transactions. In so doing, it runs into uncertainties of another kind. The results of transactions must be classified — asset or expense, revenue or liability. The essence of assets and liabilities lies in the fact that they represent expectations of future benefit or future sacrifice. Since the future is uncertain, accountants must take a position: Shall they aim for best estimates at the risk of considerable error, or shall they bias standards toward hard facts, adopting the position that revenue and expense should be reported at or near the time of cash flows, except when there is very strong evidence that the revenue is earned or expense incurred in some other period? The development of an accounting standard often suffers from a tug-of-war between these two points of view.

Even without uncertainty as to future, the assignment of results of transactions to accounting periods—the problem of matching—would suffer from a severe technical problem. Frequently in accounting a single subject must be allocated among several objects. There is no single method for making such an allocation that can be shown to be superior to all possible competing methods. Allocation methods may seem intuitively reasonable, but the superiority of one over another cannot be scientifically demonstrated. Accounting standard-setters are faced with a choice when allocations are required. Either no standard allocation method is provided, in which case there is a high probability that different entities will use different methods in similar circumstances; or a standard allocation method is adopted in the interests of promoting comparability, but it is inevitably arbitrary.

In the face of these theoretical and practical difficulties, the task of accounting standards has been to devise workable ways to implement the historical cost theory. Standards must answer these questions: When should a transaction or event first be recognized in the accounts? How should amounts involved in transactions be measured? When should revenue from sale or services be recognized? How should costs incurred be attached to cost objects such as inventory or fixed assets? On what basis should expense be recognized as the benefits from such cost objects are consumed? How should expense be recognized for costs to be incurred in future because of obligations arising from present activities?

Accounting standard-setting bodies have developed within a tradition that holds that the ultimate test of accounting policies is general acceptance. Thus, although accounting development has undoubtedly been significantly influenced by the historical cost accounting theory, it is not always clear that that theory should be the controlling influence on a proposed standard if generally accepted practice is at variance with the theory. This ambiguity tends to make the setting of consistent standards more difficult than it otherwise would be.

In addition, it must be noted that the historical cost model is directed primarily at dealing with the straightforward operating activities of an industrial or commercial enterprise. The legal and economic environments pose many questions to which the historical cost theory provides no answer. How does one merge the figures of businesses entering into a business combination? What kind of report or reports should be issued for an affiliated group of companies? How does one report business done in foreign currencies? Still other questions are posed in accounting for specialized types of enterprise such as financial institutions, extractive industries, and nonbusiness entities. Standard answers to these questions stem from experience rather than theory. Finally, accounting standards are required for presentation and disclosure in financial reports. To date, these seem to be based less on theory than on common sense.

References

[1]It is an oversimplification to talk of only two points of view with respect to the accounting entity. Meyer identified some eight different concepts in three broad categories. See P.E. Meyer, "The Accounting Entity," *Abacus*, December 1973, pp. 116-26. In addition, the significance of the fundamental view taken of the entity to the form of accounting to be adopted is often debatable. For examples of conflicting reasoning, compare opinions expressed in T.A. Lee, "The Accounting Entity Concept, Accounting Standards, and Inflation Accounting," *Accounting and Business Research*, Spring 1980, pp. 176-86, with those expressed in F.A. Bird, L.F. Davidson, and C.H. Smith, "Perceptions of External Accounting Transfers Under Entity and Proprietary Theory," *The Accounting Review*, April 1974, pp. 233-44.

[2]G.O. May, *Financial Accounting: A Distillation of Experience* (New York: Macmillan Co., 1943; reprint ed., Houston: Scholars Book Co., 1972), p. 30.

[3]FASB, *Objectives of Financial Reporting by Business Enterprises*, Statement of Financial Accounting Concepts No. 1 (Stamford: FASB, 1978), par. 44.

[4]FASB, *Objectives of Financial Reporting by Nonbusiness Organizations*, Statement of Financial Accounting Concepts No. 4 (Stamford: FASB, 1980), par. 50, n. 23.

[5]H.W. Bevis, *Corporate Financial Reporting in a Competitive Economy* (New York: Macmillan Co., 1965), pp. 97-100.

[6]R.T. Sprouse, "Accounting for What-You-May-Call-Its," *Journal of Accountancy*, October 1966, pp. 45-53.

[7]For a more extended discussion of these two viewpoints, see FASB Discussion Memorandum *Conceptual Framework for Financial Accounting and Reporting: Elements of Financial Statements and Their Measurement* (Stamford: FASB, 1976), pp. 37-40.

[8]The discussion in this section is stimulated by the published work of Arthur L. Thomas. His most complete exposition of the problems with matching is to be found in the series Studies in Accounting Research published by the American Accounting Association. His two studies (Nos. 3 and 9 in the series) are entitled *The Allocation Problem in Financial Accounting Theory* (AAA, 1969) and *The Allocation Problem: Part Two* (AAA, 1974). Anyone wishing a simpler expression of his ideas may see papers by him entitled "The FASB and the Allocation Fallacy," *Journal of Accountancy*, November 1975, pp. 65-68; "Matching: Up from Our Black Hole," in *Accounting for a Simplified Firm Owning Depreciable Assets: Seventeen Essays and a Synthesis Based on a Common Case*, ed. R.R. Sterling and A.L. Thomas (Houston: Scholars Book Co., 1979) pp. 11-33; and *Joint-Cost Allocation Revisited*, Occasional Paper No. 20 (Lancaster, England: International Centre for Research in Accounting, University of Lancaster, 1980). Exchanges of differing views between Thomas and two commentators are to be found in *The Accounting Review* (L.G. Eckel, "Arbitrary and Incorrigible Allocations," *The Accounting Review*, October 1976, pp. 764-77, and A.L. Thomas, "Arbitrary and Incorrigible Allocations: A Comment," *The Accounting Review*, January 1978, pp. 263-69), and in *CAmagazine* (S. Himmel, "Financial Allocations Justified," *CAmagazine*, October 1981, pp. 70-73, and A.L. Thomas, "Why Financial Allocations Can't Be Justified," *CAmagazine*, April 1982, pp. 28-32). Professor Thomas' analysis leads him to the conclusion that the matching concept is so incapable of implementation as to be meaningless. This is a more extreme conclusion than that reached by the author of this book.

[9]This classification scheme is adapted from L.T. Johnson and R.K. Storey, *Recognition in Financial Statements: Underlying Concepts and Practical Conventions* (Stamford: FASB, 1982), chap. 8.

Chapter Six

Initial Recognition and Measurement of Accountable Events

A transaction-based accounting system must have rules to determine when transactions and other events will receive initial recognition in the accounts. Income accounting provides a set of rules for allocating revenues and expenses to accounting periods, and in the process these rules affect the recognition and measurement of various assets and liabilities. Operating transactions, however, often take place before it is appropriate to recognize any revenue or expense consequences. In addition, a large number of nonoperating transactions and events must be accounted for. Accordingly, there must be accounting standards to govern the initial recognition and measurement of all these "accountable events," quite separate from standards for measuring income. Discussion of these initial standards is the purpose of this chapter.

Initial recognition of transactions

To deduce a set of logical recognition rules one should ask: What is it about assets and liabilities that makes it important to bring them into account in financial statements? With respect to assets, the historical tradition was that the accounts provided a summary of property owned. The emphasis on ownership provided a recognition rule—recognize a transaction at the time that legal title to the asset is obtained. In the modern accounting period, however, the strict emphasis on legal position has been reduced. Financial statements are supposed to provide useful information. From a user point of view, the important characteristic of an asset is not whether the entity has legal title to it but whether the entity bears the risk and is in a position to reap the rewards from possession of the asset. This test of asset recognition is supported by the fact that it simplifies matters to be able to recognize a transaction when an observable physical act—such as delivery—takes place. That act is suitable as a test of recognition of asset disposal by the vendor as well, since delivery is a solid indicator of performance.

To users of financial statements, the importance of liabilities lies in the amount and timing of their claims on liquid assets of an entity. When a liability is incurred for purchase of an asset that will itself yield a cash inflow in the near term, the impact of the transaction on liquidity may be relatively unimportant. Thus, transaction recognition rules can be based on other criteria. On the other hand, when a contract creates a liability that will have to be substantially paid down before the asset involved produces a comparable cash inflow, it is more important that the liability be recognized. This accounts for the customary practice of recording liabilities for capital work in process as work progresses rather than upon completion and turnover of the asset and for the further emphasis on disclosure of commitments. It does not, however, provide clearly defined guidance to the timing of formal recognition of liabilities since, in a broad sense, the liability arises as soon as a contract is signed, even though it may be completely unperformed.

The result of all the foregoing is that the rules for initial recognition of transactions are not well defined. It can be said that a transaction should not be recognized later than the time of performance (or substantial performance) by the vendor or the time when the contract liability could have a significant impact on the liquidity of the entity in the near future. A legal transfer of title test is still used for some transactions in practice, but the more widespread criterion for recognition is that of complete or substantial performance under the contract.

The following discussion deals with different types of transactions in more detail.

Initial recognition of operating transactions

What constitutes "performance"—the dominant criterion for recognition of operating transactions—needs to be interpreted. Consider a simple case, for example, that of manufacture and sale of a commodity. From the purchaser's point of view, it is convenient to recognize the transaction when the commodity is actually delivered because delivery provides firm evidence of the vendor's performance. That recognition point also makes sense since that is the time when the purchaser has the opportunity to use the commodity and should become accountable for it. From the vendor's point of view, the situation may not be so clear. The most convenient time to record the sale is usually the point of shipment; however, the product risk and reward will not completely pass until delivery. Nevertheless, the point of shipment from the plant is normally a satisfactory practical basis for recognizing the sales transaction. In short, ideally the exchange should be recognized at the time of effective transfer of risk and reward associated with the thing exchanged. In practice, the recognition point may be modified slightly to facilitate convenient and consistent recording. In any event, accounting for the exchange is likely to be based upon an observable physical act.

In the case of ordinary plant and equipment bought in completed form, practice is mixed. Frequently the purchase transaction is not recognized until delivery, just as is the case with inventory. In Canada, however, the right to claim tax allowances rests upon title to the assets, rather than on possession or use. For this reason, the practice of recording capital asset purchases upon transfer of title before delivery is fully accepted.

A performance test can also be applied with respect to the acquisition of services. For example, if an independent consultant is engaged to render a report, a logical recognition point would be the date of delivery of the report. On the other hand, if the consultant is engaged simply to render advice, the obligation should be recognized progressively as service is rendered. In practice, it is a common (although not completely logical) practice to recognize the obligation for all services performed and record the expense even though the benefit of the service has not yet been received.

Initial recognition of nonoperating exchanges and other accountable events

In financing and investment transactions by industrial, commercial, and service enterprises—that is, the issuance of debt securities or the making of loans—there is usually little lapse of time between the effective date of the contract and the transfer of funds. Therefore, although recording at the contract date is considered technically correct, a delay until cash is paid or received is of little significance unless a reporting period-end intervenes.

Nonreciprocal transactions that are the subject of contract, such as share capital issues or reductions, are likewise recorded when legally effective. (In an unincorporated entity, where capital contributions and withdrawals are decided upon informally, recognition would be given only as they occur.) Dividends become an enforceable debt when declared and therefore are recognized by the payor at the declaration date.

The various types of taxes payable should be recognized not later than the date on which they become payable. Income accounting standards, however, normally require recognition of accrued taxes earlier as the obligation builds up.

More or less fortuitous nonreciprocal transfers are recognized not later than the time the transfer takes place. If it appears probable at some earlier date that a nonreciprocal payment will be required, it may be recognized at that earlier date (see discussion of contingencies in chapter 9). Damages and penalties imposed in a lawsuit, for example, should be estimated and provided for in advance of judgment if it seems probable that they will be imposed and a reasonable estimate can be made.

Casualties—the destruction or damage of existing assets—can only be recognized as they occur, by write-downs or write-offs of the assets. Windfalls, in contrast, are not recognized when they occur, on the general grounds of conservatism. Instead, recognition is delayed until realization by way of receipt of a legal claim or cash. Significant unrecognized windfalls should be disclosed on much the same basis as contingent assets.

Advance payments and settlement transactions are, naturally, recognized at the time of cash payment.

Recognition of events that occur subsequent to the date of the financial statements

Questions arise as to the recognition in financial statements of events that occur after the end of the period but before the financial statements are finalized. Examples of such post-balance sheet events are:

- There is a sharp decline in price of a major inventory commodity that indicates that the realizable value of inventory on hand at the year-end is below its cost at that date.
- A bankruptcy of a debtor occurring after the year-end suggests that the allowance for uncollectible accounts with respect to amounts owing by that debtor at the year-end is inadequate.
- A contract for sale of a division of the business or a significant portion of productive assets is closed after the period-end.

Whether and how such post-balance sheet events should be accounted for in period-end statements depends upon a fundamental distinction in their nature. Certain events occurring after the year-end, such as the first two above, cast light on the estimates made in accounting for assets and liabilities existing at the year-end. It is natural and logical that the subsequent information be taken into account to make sure the estimates in the financial statements are the best possible. On the other hand, other subsequent events, such as the last-mentioned above, have nothing to do with the position at the year-end. Such events cannot be used to change the accounting otherwise required for assets and liabilities that do exist at the year-end. They may, however, be of such importance that they should be disclosed in the financial statements to make the statements as useful as possible.

The merits of the latter conclusions are open to debate. For example, a not uncommon situation is that of disposal of a significant investment or a significant productive asset just after the year-end for a substantial gain. It may even be that the contract for disposal of the asset is in existence at the year-end but the closing date is after the year-end. In such a case it is arguable that the year-end financial position is portrayed more usefully for readers if the subsequently completed transaction is formally recognized.

Nevertheless, accounting principles do not permit the recording of gain in such a case. The reason for this is that it would be difficult to know where to stop if some subsequent events were recognized in financial statements but not others. It may be clear that inclusion of the subsequent transaction would be useful in one case, but other cases would be less clear and confusion would inevitably result. On a pragmatic basis, accountants think it better to stick to the letter of the rule and thereby avoid the need for making fine, and inevitably inconsistent, distinctions between one situation and another. If the rule is that assets are carried at cost before realization and generally accepted accounting principles state that realization occurs at the time of closing the contract, then the asset must be carried at cost even though the subsequent completion of the closing is perfect evidence of a higher value.

Disclosure is possible to mitigate the severity of this rule. Where subsequent events have a significant impact on financial position, such events not only may, but should, be disclosed. In most cases, such disclosure is given by footnote to the financial statements. Where, however, the subsequent events represent a significant departure from normal operating transactions and their impact is extreme, it would be good practice to provide pro forma figures incorporating the effect of the subsequent transactions, either in a footnote or in an extra column beside the historical transaction figures.

Executory contracts

Now that the transfer of legal title test has been largely abandoned in favour of an economic significance test for recognition, it is pertinent to inquire more closely into the possible indicators of economic significance. Even a short-term contract—say one for the purchase of goods—may involve several events. The purchase order is placed or a contractual relationship otherwise established. The vendor manufactures the goods. Depending upon the terms of the contract and the actions of the vendor, legal title may pass while the goods are at the vendor's plant or upon shipment from it. Delivery to the purchaser occurs. Finally, the purchaser completes the contract by payment. The question is, at what point in that array of events does economic significance arise?

In accounting, a contract under which neither party has performed or one in which the portion of the contract obligation remaining unperformed by each party is equal is known as an executory contract. There is no doubt that the existence of executory contracts can be significant to an entity's financial position. A company with lots of orders on hand to give assurance of activity that will cover its fixed costs is usually (assuming the order prices are compensatory) in a better position than one with little work ahead of it. Moreover, noncancellable contracts at fixed prices transfer the risk of price fluctuations to the purchaser.

The question of executory contracts has become of greater importance because of the increasing tendency in business to enter into long-term contractual arrangements. Obviously, the potential economic significance of a long-term contract is greater than that of a short-term contract:

These points seem important from the point of view of the purchaser under a long-term contract:

- The contract will usually involve a minimum monetary commitment year by year, for example, under basic rental clauses or "take-or-pay" clauses for products or "throughput agreements" with a transportation or processing facility. These minimum commitments are very similar to fixed commitments for debt charges and thus are an important factor in assessing the solvency of an enterprise.
- Some contracts are for the services of an asset in being—typically in the case of long-term leases. If such leases cover virtually the whole useful life of the asset, there is very little difference in economic significance between them and an instalment purchase of the asset. Yet not only is the balance sheet portrayal different between an owned asset and a leased asset that is not capitalized, the expense recognition is typically different as well, since depreciation and interest connected with an owned asset are rarely equivalent to rental on a leased asset (see chapter 7).
- Long-term contracts for product are often akin to a long-term commodity speculation. In addition, if the contract is long enough, it may be sufficient to recoup the whole cost of a plant built by the vendor to produce the product and may consume the whole useful life of such plant. In that case, the contract for the product in substance buys the plant just as much as would a direct lease of the plant for its full economic life.

Similarly, the existence of a long-term contract has important economic significance to the vendor of products or services.

Given that commitments under long-term contracts can be so significant, the question for accounting standards is not whether financial statements should in some way disclose their significance but rather how that disclosure may best be achieved—whether by formal recognition of the contract rights and obligations among the assets and liabilities of the entity or by other means. The possibilities seem to be the following:

- At one end of the scale, the present value of all contractual rights and obligations could be recognized as assets and liabilities as soon as they become firm and noncancellable. This would be in accordance with a fundamental definition of an asset as an expectation of future benefit arising from present conditions (the contract) and of a liability as an expectation of future required sacrifices arising from present conditions. Since contract rights and obligations are part of financial position in this widest sense, it could be argued that they should be recorded in the balance sheet. Mere disclosure in a footnote, unread by many users of financial statements, would not carry the same weight. In addition, valuation of rights under unperformed contracts would force consideration of the need for provisions for loss. Such need can easily be overlooked when commitments are not formally recorded.

- Against this extreme position, it may be argued that it would be confusing to mix up in one statement assets that are employed in earning a return and other assets that have yet to become available to the purchaser. An intermediate position, then, would be to recognize contract rights and obligations with respect to assets actually in being and rendering service. This would support the practice of capitalizing leases that are in substance purchases of assets. It could also support a practice of capitalizing the rights to property use inherent in all leases.
- At the other end of the scale would be a policy of reliance on full disclosure with respect to all contractual rights and obligations that are unperformed, rather than the formal incorporation of capitalized present values in the balance sheet. This policy has the virtue of flexibility, in that the disclosure could be tailored to fit the circumstances. It would also avoid the difficulty of determining which contracts should be capitalized and the almost inevitable inconsistency in capitalizing some and not others that are quite similar. Proponents of the efficient markets hypothesis would also argue that disclosure (including quantification of capitalized values if desired) would be just as effective as inclusion in the balance sheet in providing information to the capital markets.

Until recently, accepted practice relied entirely on the disclosure approach with respect to commitments, and what disclosure was provided was uneven. Within the past ten years capitalization of leases that could be considered equivalent to purchases of assets was required. In 1981 the FASB made more explicit the requirement for disclosure of unconditional purchase obligations for goods or services, including disclosure of the minimum amounts required to be paid under such contracts and their timing. Disclosure is also required of actual amounts paid (including any excess over minimum requirements) in periods covered by the financial report.[1]

Transaction measurement

The reliance of the historical cost model on transactions has been explained by the fact that such reliance helps to solve the measurement problem. "Fair value" is customarily defined as the price at which a commodity would be exchanged by a willing buyer and a willing seller, neither of whom is under any compulsion to make the exchange. This idea of fair value underlies accounting's reliance on bargained exchanges as the initial basis of measurement of assets and liabilities. In addition, the exchange value has the great advantage for accounting purposes of being verifiable.

The importance to the historical cost system of getting a proper measurement of the exchange value cannot be overstated. If the consideration in a sale transaction is not fairly measured, profit will be directly misstated as a result. Likewise, if the cost of an asset acquired in a purchase transaction is not fairly stated, all subsequent measurements using that cost figure will be distorted.

In the majority of transactions the consideration given or received is cash payable immediately or in the near future. In these circumstances, the use of the exchange price for measurement is the most satisfactory general rule. But some transactions do not call for a cash price or a price fairly equivalent to a cash price. For those cases, accounting needs rules for translating the transaction consideration into its equivalent in terms of a cash value at the transaction date. These rules are discussed in succeeding sections.

Delayed payment transactions

Where a contract itself provides that there shall be a discount from the contract price for payment in cash within a certain short period, it is obvious that the fair value of the rights exchanged under the contract is the cash amount after discount, not the contract price. In such cases the best accounting treatment is to record sales revenues and purchase costs as the net cash figure. If the discounts happen not to be taken by the purchaser, the extra amount ultimately paid should be recorded as an item of financial revenue (by the vendor) or financial expense (by the purchaser).

Where payment is not called for within a short period of time after performance and the contract does not provide a reasonable rate of interest on the contract price for the delay in cash payment, it is clear that the transaction is not fairly measured at the contract price. The task then becomes one of finding a fair valuation for the transaction.[2]

- Occasionally a note payable or other debt security given by the purchaser as consideration may have an observable market value that can be used to value the transaction.
- Occasionally also the goods or services sold in the transaction can be independently valued. There may, for example, be an established market for such goods or services from which a current price can be obtained. Alternatively, the vendor may offer the goods for sale both for a cash price and on delayed credit terms. If so, the cash price (if that price is taken by a sufficient number of purchasers to evidence that it is realistic) can be used to value the credit transaction.
- If neither of these approaches provides a reliable value, the debt can be valued by "imputing," on a judgment basis, the interest rate that would be negotiated on an arm's-length basis for a debt instrument of equivalent quality. Factors to be considered in selecting the imputed interest rate would include the credit standing of the debtor as evidenced by the interest rate paid on other borrowings, and the repayment and other terms of the debt, including the collateral given.

When a monetary asset or liability is recorded at a figure different from its stated principal amount because of delayed payment terms, it will be necessary to amortize the difference over the period to payment, so that the asset or liability will be recorded at face value at maturity. The accepted way to do this is called the "effective-yield" method. The imputed interest rate is applied to the opening book value of the asset or liability each period and interest revenue or expense is recognized. When the transaction has been valued directly by either of the first two methods above (that is, not using an imputed interest rate), it will be necessary to calculate the effective interest rate implied by the difference between the contract price and the cash-equivalent valuation used in the accounting.

Transactions and nonreciprocal transfers that are nonmonetary

When no monetary consideration is involved in a transaction or other accountable event, the measurement problem becomes even more difficult.

Nonmonetary exchanges are commonly known as "barter" transactions. In such transactions the fair values of the things exchanged are not evident from the transaction itself, as would be the case if cash were the consideration. The old joke about the child who sold her dog for $50,000 and took back two $25,000 cats in payment illustrates the point.

Once again an attempt must be made to record the transaction at fair value. The general rule is that a barter transaction should be recorded at the fair value of the thing acquired or the fair value of the thing disposed of, whichever can be estimated more reliably.

There may be various indicators of fair value. The best indicator, of course, would be a market price derived from an active market for freely exchangeable goods. In the absence of such market prices, regular price quotations by the buyer or seller for goods or services similar to those involved in the exchange may furnish evidence of value. Such evidence, however, isn't always persuasive. For example, a television station might well sell unused advertising time to a newspaper in return for advertisements displayed in the paper. Neither party might be willing to buy advertising from the other independently at normal rates, but each may think it worthwhile to incur the little additional extra cost in running an advertisement for the other in return for what it gets. In such a case, a valuation of the transaction at a figure as low as the incremental cost of running the advertisement would reflect the economics of the situation.

Nonreciprocal transfers such as the receipt or disbursement of a gift or dividend in kind may also be nonmonetary. Once again, fair value recording of the transaction is necessary to achieve fair presentation, difficult though that may be.

Nonreciprocal transfers involving the issuance or reacquisition of share capital are similar to exchanges in that the share capital issued or reacquired can be viewed as being sold or bought. Thus, when such transfers involve the exchange of shares for nonmonetary consideration, the fair value of the transaction may be evidenced by quoted market values for the shares at or about the time of the transaction. Some caution is required if a sizable block of shares is involved, since quoted values for small numbers of shares traded on an exchange may be an unreliable indicator of the price at which a large block of shares would trade.

There are certain exceptions to the general rule that nonmonetary transactions and transfers should be recorded at fair value:[3]

- Where fair value is not determinable within reasonable limits—that is, when there is a major uncertainty about the realizability of any fair value figure that might be assigned—the transfer is recorded at the carrying value of the asset given up by the entity for the lack of any better alternative.
- Where the asset given up is part of the normal operating assets of the enterprise, consideration must be given to the possibility of conflict with the accepted rules for the measurement of income. For example:
  - Revenue is often not recognized until near the culmination of an earning process. Accordingly, if a product held for sale is swapped for other inventory or rights to acquire other inventory in the same line of business, the transaction should not be recognized at fair value and revenue should not be recorded.
  - Assets held for use in the production of goods or services by an enterprise are rarely written down and never written up (in the absence of appraisals, see chapter 11). If, therefore, such productive assets are simply exchanged for assets of the same general type, performing the same function or employed in the same line of business, it would be quite inconsistent to record fair values at that time when nothing had changed insofar as the basic operations were concerned. (One may add that frequently it is difficult to determine the fair values in such exchanges and that criteria are lacking to judge whether assets exchanged should be considered similar.)
- If an exchange is partly for cash and partly nonmonetary, some realization of gain or loss may be recorded by the recipient of the cash in the above two situations.
- Where nonmonetary assets are spun off to owners as part of a plan of reorganization, liquidation, or division of a going concern (and not merely as a dividend) or where a previous business combination is, in effect, reversed, the nonreciprocal transfer is accounted for on the basis of the recorded values of resources transferred, not fair value. Although inconsistent with the treatment of dividends in kind, this is a common sense rule, probably justified on cost-benefit considerations.

The fact that the exchange of productive property for similar productive property does not generate a gain or loss prompts a question. Suppose productive property is destroyed or expropriated and the insurance or expropriation proceeds are, after an interval but as soon as possible, reinvested in replacement property. The receipt of proceeds is a monetary transaction, but from the standpoint of the entity the conversion into money is involuntary and is rectified by restoration of the previous position as soon as possible. Except for this involuntary event, no gain or loss would have been recorded and the productive plant carrying value would have been unaffected. As on so many occasions, this situation forces a choice between two accounting standards that appear to be relevant:

- On the one hand, it can be argued that involuntary conversions of productive plant should not be considered realizations if reinvestment of the monetary proceeds in similar plant occurs. So far as possible, the business has been continued as it would have been if there were no interruption. Therefore, the historical record of results and the trends from year to year will best be portrayed by accounting that ignores the involuntary interruption.

- On the other hand, it can be argued that the general rule is that monetary exchanges provide evidence of fair value that should not be ignored in accounting. It is always desirable that the figures for assets and liabilities be as close to a current fair value as possible. Under historical cost accounting, recognition of changes in fair value is delayed in practice until transactions provide objective evidence of the change. But there is no justification for delaying recognition beyond that point.

The latter viewpoint is the one that is accepted.[4]

Basket transactions

Transactions in which more than one right or thing is bought or sold for a single negotiated price are known generally as "basket" transactions. Whether the transaction is a purchase or a sale, there is an accounting problem in attributing a price to the several things bought or sold. Since this is a "one-to-many" attribution, there is no single demonstrably correct answer to this problem (see chapter 5).

The problem is that the price negotiated for the basket of assets will rarely be exactly equal to the sum of estimates of fair value for each asset individually. Depending on the circumstances, any of the following approaches to attribution of the total price could appear reasonable:

- The total price might be divided up among individual items in proportion to the estimated fair value of the individual items.
- A purchaser who bought the basket with the aim of keeping some assets and disposing of others for whatever they would fetch might attribute estimated realizable value to the latter (or actual realized value if known soon enough) and allocate the remaining purchase price to the assets to be retained, in proportion to their fair values.
- When a purchase price (including the value of liabilities assumed, if any) is less than the sum of estimated fair values, a purchaser might assign the estimated fair value as the cost of assets whose values are the most reliably measurable and reduce or eliminate the estimated fair values of other assets so that the total values assigned make up the total purchase price.
- Where the purchase price of the assets of a business purchased as a going concern exceeds the sum of estimated fair values of identifiable assets purchased (less values of liabilities assumed where applicable), the excess may be assigned to general goodwill.

The most commonly encountered basket purchase situation is that in which one business acquires the assets or shares of another in a "business combination." In such a case (as will be described more fully in chapter 18), the approach taken is one of the last two described above.

In the ordinary basket transaction, the vendor does not usually have an accounting problem since no purpose is served by ascertaining the gain or loss on each individual item sold and there is therefore no need to allocate the sale price. The vendor does, however, need to allocate the price when the things sold represent different types of future claims upon him. Typically, this occurs when a company sells different securities for one price. A conceptually similar problem exists when securities with hybrid characteristics (for example, convertible debentures) are sold.

- Different types of securities may be issued as a unit for one price, for example 100 preferred shares with 10 common shares or a $1,000 debenture with 10 common shares. In such a case, the consideration should be divided in accordance with the relevant fair value of each security at the date of issuance. This accounting rule is reinforced in Canada by legal requirements that the shares be issued for a consideration equal to their fair value.
- Securities (usually debentures or preferred shares) may also be issued with detachable warrants entitling the holder to buy a given number of common shares at a stated price for a given period. The holders of these warrants have a call upon the company for common shares and that call has a value. Faithful representation requires that the proceeds from issuance be allocated to the warrants and the other securities in accordance with the fair value of each type of security at the date of issue.[5] Unfortunately, it is not uncommon in Canada to credit the whole of the proceeds to the issued security and ignore the existence of the warrants, except for footnote disclosure. When the related security is debt, this erroneous practice will have the result of understating the effective interest cost in future.
- Securities (usually debentures or preferred shares) may also be issued that are convertible into other securities (usually common shares) on stated terms. The holders of such convertible securities thus have two rights—the right to receive interest and payment of principal at maturity (or equivalent rights for preferred shares) and the right to convert into common shares. The latter right has a value in itself, which is evidenced by the fact that the convertible security will be issuable at a lower yield rate (i.e., at a higher price) than would another security of the same issuer similar in all respects except for the conversion privilege. The exercise of one right, however, extinguishes the other. In particular, exercise of the conversion privilege extinguishes the right to receive further payments on the debt or preferred shares. One view is that because the conversion rights are not separable from the security, the consideration received for convertible securities should be entirely assigned to the debt or preferred share category so long as the conversion right has not been exercised. This view has been accepted in practice.[6] As in the case of securities sold with detachable warrants, the result of this practice is that the cost to service the convertible security in terms of interest or dividend yield is understated. An alternative (and better) view is that the conversion privilege has a distinct value, that such value can be estimated with reasonable reliability, and that faithful representation of the security issued requires the separation of proceeds into amounts attributable to its separate elements.[7]

Related-party transactions; non-arm's-length transactions; economic dependence

In the real world, parties to exchanges are not always independent; there may be some relationship between them that gives them a common interest. This fact casts doubt on the assumption of the historical cost system that exchange prices are good indicators of fair value and hence undermines the potential usefulness of financial statements produced following that system. In addition, the possibility of arbitrary changes in the conditions of related-party transactions from time to time means that current financial statements may be less reliable as a basis for prediction of the future.

Where a relationship between parties affects their dealings, transactions between them are said to be not at arm's-length. Particular transactions may fail to be at arm's-length because all those concerned with the bargaining for that transaction have a common interest, even though the parties are otherwise unrelated. More commonly, a relationship between parties that causes them not to deal at arm's-length is not confined to a particular deal or situation but rather is capable of affecting all their dealings with each other. In accounting, parties are said to be "related" if one party has the ability to control or significantly influence the operating and financial decisions of the other, or if each of the parties is subject to the control or significant influence of another party.[8]

When parties are related, accounting must be concerned with the possibility that their transactions are not priced on the same basis that they would be if their dealings were fully at arm's-length. Another way of putting this is to say that the substance of the transactions may not be fully indicated by their form. Thus, an overly high price for goods or services sold by one party to another may, in substance, embody a gift or subsidy from the buyer to the vendor.

The definition of relationship in terms of *ability* to control or *significantly* influence another party means that it will not always be clear whether parties are related. One party may be able to control another without having a legal right to do so. And significant influence is, of course, a matter of degree. In practice the most difficult situations to judge will be those where an individual has some form of control or influence over another individual or a corporation. The *CICA Handbook* recommendation does not specifically refer to "significant influence" in the case of the individuals.[9] It is well known, however, that a company can often be effectively controlled with a shareholding that is much less than fifty percent. In any event, the inclusion of the term "significant influence" in the general definition of the term "related party" strongly suggests that individual shareholdings that represent less than legal control of a corporation may yet give rise to related-party status. In the United States a "principal owner," defined as someone (whether individual or corporation) who owns over ten percent of the voting interest, is deemed to be related to a corporation.[10]

The existence of transactions with related parties obviously creates a problem for an accounting system that relies on exchange prices for its measurements. Since the basic desire is to report transactions at fair value, one might think that amounts involved in transactions with related parties should be adjusted, where necessary, to prices that would be equivalent to those that would be arrived at between willing buyers and sellers bargaining on an arm's-length basis. Yet the historical cost system was prompted largely by the desire to avoid the need for valuation judgments in accounting.

Even if revaluations were made so as to identify subsidy elements in related-party transactions, the possibility would remain that, without the existence of related parties, other transactions might have taken place (for example, sales orders might not have been diverted to a third related party). Also, some transactions that did take place might not have occurred. To adjust the actual record for transactions that would have taken place but did not because of the related-parties situation or that did take place but would not have in the absence of the relationship would be speculative in the extreme. It is true that, if possible, such adjustment might provide information valuable in judging the economic viability of the entity on its own. On the other hand, it would obscure the picture of the activity of the entity as it actually took place and ignore the fact that resources owned and claims upon them and (usually) the taxable income are all based on the transactions that actually took place.

As a practical matter, most accountants hesitate to espouse an attempt to restate related-party transactions to fair values. The Accountants International Study Group (AISG) had this to say:

> *[I]t often is impossible to establish what would have been the terms of any non-arm's length transaction had it been bargained on an arm's length basis, because no comparable transactions may have taken place and, in any event, the transaction might never have taken place at all if it had been bargained using different values. Consideration must be given, however, to the need to disclose the existence and details of the related party transactions so as to achieve fair presentation in the financial statements.*[11]

In the face of the practical difficulty in requiring wholesale restatements of transactions with related parties, accounting standards have focussed on disclosure issues. Disclosure could be designed to cover one or all of the following: the fact that relationships with other parties exist that could have an impact on transactions of the reporting entity; the identity of parties who should be considered related to the reporting entity; and practical details about transactions that have actually occurred with related parties.[12]

Every reporting entity has some related parties, even if they are only its management personnel. It does not seem helpful to require disclosure of the obvious. Debate has, therefore, focussed on the desirability of disclosing the existence of parties controlling or controlled by the reporting entity or controlled in common with it. International Accounting Standard No. 24 requires disclosure of control relationships whether or not there have been transactions between the related parties.[13] The Canadian standard does not require disclosure of control relationships in the absence of actual transactions between the reporting entity and interests controlled by it or controlling it. Although one might think identification of controlling interests or, at least, disclosure of their existence could frequently be of great importance, particularly in the case of public companies, the fact is that the legal permissibility of nominee shareholdings in Canada makes it impossible to enforce such disclosure.

It is agreed that there should be description of the nature and extent of any related-party transactions, of any balances due to or from related parties at the period-end and settlement terms (if not apparent), and of the nature of the relationships. (Once again, controlling interests hiding behind nominee shareholdings can evade such disclosure requirement if they are unknown to management.) Compensation arrangements with management, expense allowances, and the like are exempted from disclosure. (Legislation requires that some details of management remuneration and directors' fees be disclosed in proxy requests sent to shareholders.)

Although the extent of related-party transactions can often be inferred from their recorded dollar amounts, that will not always be true. Services may be rendered to related parties without a compensatory charge or without any charge at all. In such cases, some other means—presumably descriptive wording—must be adopted to indicate the extent of the transactions in question. When transactions with related parties are made on the same terms as transactions with unrelated parties under similar conditions, the fact that they are on a basis equivalent to arm's-length transactions is considered proper disclosure. If, however, there are no similar independent transactions to provide objective evidence, it is considered improper to make such a representation.

Although major customers or suppliers or other parties having a business relationship with an entity are often in a position to exert significant influence upon it, such parties are by convention not considered to be "related parties." Nevertheless, the Canadian standard requires disclosure of "economic dependence" where operations reflect a significant amount of business done with or through such parties.

A final admonition is that, although there are many situations in which related-party transactions are accounted for without adjustment to reflect their substance, the possibility of manipulation of accounting results by means of such transactions cannot be ignored. In the case of transactions involving capital contributions, corroborative indicators that transaction values are fair values are important. In the case of regular operating transactions, disclosure of their existence and extent is normally considered sufficient. Disclosure of the effect of any change in the basis upon which such transactions are made from one period to another is also desirable, and is required in U.S. practice.[14]

Disclosures may not be enough, however, for transactions that occur irregularly. Suppose, for example, that the entire inventory of an entity were sold to a related party just before the year-end and gain recorded. Unless there were a basic change in the manner of carrying on the business (which would be apparent within a short period of time after the sale), the transaction would appear to be a sham and should not be accounted for in accordance with its form. There are too many possible forms of sham transactions to permit accounting rule making that addresses every one. Accountants must apply common sense and professional judgment in examining transactions with related parties to decide whether financial statements incorporating their effects can be considered fairly presented, even with maximum disclosure.

Summary

Since the historical cost accounting system relies mainly on exchange transactions to provide data entering into the accounts, it is vital to understand when a transaction should first be recognized in the accounts and how it should be measured. There must be a similar understanding with respect to recognition and measurement of any other "accountable events."

Accounting practices governing initial recognition have developed largely through tradition, and a clear, authoritative, statement of criteria for initial recognition is not to be found in the professional literature. Historically, since a balance sheet was regarded as a statement of property owned and legal claims, it was thought that the proper test for initial recognition was the legal position. When was title transferred in an asset purchase? When did a liability become legally enforceable? Today, we think more in terms of accounting's objective of providing useful information. We wish to know what assets are actually on hand, capable of being managed for profit. We also wish to know what claims exist that may significantly affect the liquidity of the entity. In general terms, then, the governing rule is that a transaction should be recognized at the time the purchaser receives the asset that is the subject of the transaction or at the time when the liability to the vendor can have a significant impact on the purchaser's liquidity, whichever is earlier.

It is often asked whether a significant transaction or event that takes place after a fiscal period-end, but before the financial statements are issued, should be reflected in those financial statements. The answer is suggested by common sense. First, a subsequent event may cast light on the probable accuracy of estimates made in valuing assets and liabilities that are presented or disclosed in the period-end financial statements. If so, the estimate should be adjusted in accordance with the new information. On the other hand, when a subsequent event is completely independent of the previous period, no adjustment should be made to the period-end financial statements. Financial statements are intended to be a record, as factual as possible, of what has actually occurred up to the reporting date. Finally, subsequent events that have significant impact on financial position should be disclosed as part of the supplementary financial information provided.

Every sizable entity is, at all times, enmeshed in a web of contractual relationships with other parties that are not yet fully performed. The existence of these executory contracts can have a significant effect on the well-being of an entity. Three possible approaches to reporting the existence of these contracts can be visualized. First, amounts involved in the contracts could be discounted to a present value and that value recorded as both asset and liability in the balance sheet. Second, a capitalization policy could be followed when the contract covers an asset in being, whose services are currently being enjoyed by one of the contracting parties. Finally, information about executory contracts could be provided in a supplementary note to the financial statements. In today's practice, the third approach is predominant. Capitalization of amounts in long-term contracts is followed in the single case of long-term leases of property, when the lease is deemed virtually equivalent to an instalment purchase of the property.

One simple principle ought to govern the measurement of amounts involved in transactions. Since transactions provide the basic input to accounting, it is obvious that the measurement of amounts involved should be realistic in relation to values at the time of the exchange. Measurement difficulties may be encountered in several situations.

- If the settlement date of a transaction is delayed for a significant period, good accounting requires that the nominal amount of the transaction be discounted unless the contract provides for interest at a commercial rate.
- Nonmonetary exchanges or barter transactions also require estimation of the equivalent cash value involved in the transaction. That value is usually established by reference to the fair value of the thing given up or the fair value of the thing received in the exchange, whichever is more clearly evident. There are two exceptions to this fair value rule: (1) if the value of neither of the things exchanged can be measured with a reasonable degree of satisfaction, and (2) if the assets exchanged represent similar productive assets, so that the exchange cannot be regarded as the culmination of an earnings process.

- Certain types of exchanges are called basket transactions, because they involve the purchase or sale of several things for one price. These transactions present a problem in allocating the purchase or sale price among its components. The basis of allocation of the total price should be reasonable. In business combinations, accounting standards spell out the basis in some detail. Basket sales of securities, that is, the sale of two or more separately identifiable securities, such as debentures and stock purchase warrants sold together, are dealt with less clearly in accounting standards. In Canada, illogically, the total price received is not always separated into components. Convertible securities are even more difficult to account for. Here, only one security is sold for a single price, but the security contains rights beyond those embodied in a nonconvertible security. Unless the conversion right is separately accounted for, the effective interest cost or dividend yield on a convertible security will be understated. In spite of this, present accounting standards do not require separate accounting for the conversion rights.

Transactions between related parties create a considerable problem for fair transaction measurement. When one party is able to exercise significant influence over another, it is often not possible to tell whether the transaction is fairly priced or even whether it would have taken place at all in the absence of the relationship. Ideally, nominal amounts in related party transactions should be remeasured and the adjusted values (where adjustment is necessary) should form the basis of the accounting. In practice, accountants consider the task of remeasurement too subjective to be attempted. Instead, accounting standards call for disclosure of the existence of transactions involving related parties and the amounts involved therein as shown by the records.

References

[1]See FASB, *Disclosure of Long-term Obligations,* Statement of Financial Accounting Standards No. 47 (Stamford: FASB, 1981).

[2]In the United States, a valuation approach has been required for delayed payment transactions since 1971 as a result of APB, *Interest on Receivables and Payables,* Opinion No. 21 (New York: AICPA, 1971). In Canada there has been no equivalent official recommendation. In its absence, occasional examples may be encountered of delayed payment amounts being recorded at face value rather than fair value. The practice, however, should no longer be regarded as generally accepted.

[3]These exceptions are set out more fully in APB, *Accounting for Nonmonetary Transactions,* Opinion No. 29 (New York: AICPA, 1973).

[4]Involuntary conversions are discussed in FASB, *Accounting for Involuntary Conversions of Nonmonetary Assets to Monetary Assets: An Interpretation of APB, Opinion No. 29,* Opinion No. 30 (Stamford: FASB, 1979).

[5]See APB, *Accounting for Convertible Debt and Debt Issued with Stock Purchase Warrants,* Opinion No. 14 (New York: AICPA, 1969), pars. 11-15.

[6]The Accounting Principles Board reversed itself on this issue between Opinion No. 10 (*Omnibus Opinion - 1966*) and Opinion No. 14 (*Accounting for Convertible Debt*). The arguments are discussed in paragraphs 1-10 of the latter Opinion.

[7]The value of the conversion privilege may be estimated by estimating the value of the security as it would be without the privilege and comparing that value with the actual market value at date of issue. Such a subjective valuation could be tested by valuation models based on the application of theories developed for the valuation of contingent claims (which are primarily used in estimating the value of options). See R.D. King, "The Effect of Convertible Bond Equity Values on Dilution and Leverage," *The Accounting Review,* July 1984, pp. 419-31. If a convertible debenture were valued on such a basis at its date of issue, there would exist, in all probability, a discount from its face value. This discount logically should be fully amortized by the time the debenture is converted into common shares, if the true cost of the debt is to be reported during the period it is outstanding as debt. Since the conversion date is unknown until it occurs, some assumption would need to be made as to this date, and the subjectivity of this would trouble some accountants. See M.J. Stephens, "Inseparability and the Valuation of Convertible Bonds," *Journal of Accountancy,* August 1971, pp. 54-62.

[8]CICA, "Related-Party Transactions—Disclosure Considerations," *CICA Handbook,* Section 3840 (Toronto: CICA), par. 03. See also IASC, *Related Party Disclosure,* International Accounting Standard No. 24 (London: IASC, 1984), par. 4.

[9]*CICA Handbook,* Section 3840, par. 04(b).

[10]FASB, *Related Party Disclosures,* Statement of Financial Accounting Standards No. 57 (Stamford: FASB, 1982), par. 24e.

[11]AISG, *Related Party Transactions* (Toronto: AISG, 1978), par. 15.

[12]These different aspects are thoroughly reviewed in chapters 7 to 9 of a CICA Research Study by A.K. Mason, *Related Party Transactions* (Toronto: CICA, 1979).

[13]IASC, *Related Party Disclosure,* par. 24.

[14]FASB, *Related Party Disclosures,* par. 2c.

Chapter Seven
Accounting for Leases

Chapter 6 addressed the problems in accounting for long-term commitments in general. One particular class of commitment has received more attention than any other. From the post-World War II period the practice of leasing capital assets required for a business, rather than owning them, has expanded many times over. Several factors have contributed to this growth. As a substitute for ownership, a lease generally provides all of the financing for an asset. Thus, a lessee can conserve its equity for the purpose of financing working capital or other assets. A lessor often has a stronger credit rating than a lessee and may be willing to share the benefits of lower financing costs. A lessor may also be able to utilize tax benefits in connection with the property leased, whereas a lessee may not have enough taxable income to do so immediately or may be a nontaxable entity. Finally, to the extent that lease financing is "off balance sheet," lessees have felt their financial position appears stronger, with consequent favourable impact on their credit rating and cost of capital.

Accountants have long felt concern that accounting for leased property in accordance with its legal form might not portray the economic substance of an entity's financial position. More specifically, these have been the concerns:

- Fixed payments due under a lease commitment can be equally or more onerous than payments due on debt. Yet, at one time the former did not show as a liability on the balance sheet while the latter did. The essential question is: What is the nature of a liability for accounting purposes? Is it purely a matter of legal form? Or should the term "liability" for accounting purposes be assumed to include any obligation that requires a fixed series of payments in future?
- A lease contract may be the equivalent of a conditional or instalment sale of the asset leased. This is often obvious where the lessee has an option to purchase the asset at the termination of the lease for consideration that is clearly a bargain. It may also be indicated when the lease contains bargain renewal options, or where its noncancellable term covers what may reasonably be expected to be the economic life of the asset. If a lease is in substance an asset purchase, failure to show the asset in the balance sheet may conceal the full investment risk of the company and will certainly distort any comparisons with other companies of the rate of return on assets. This distortion is compounded by the different ways of accounting for the expenses of ownership between leased and purchased assets. Suppose, for example, that an asset having a five-year life with no expected salvage value can be bought for $5,000 or rented for $1,278 a year, payable in advance. If the asset is bought out of the proceeds of debt bearing interest at 14% and if depreciation is on the straight-line basis, the first year's ownership cost will be $1,000 in depreciation (an operating expense) and $700 in interest (a financial expense). This contrasts with the rental expense of $1,278 under the lease alternative, which would be reported entirely as an operating expense. Under the ownership alternative the interest expense will decline as

> the debt is paid off, and thus the total ownership costs will show a declining pattern. The rental expense, however, will remain constant. If, therefore, leasing and purchasing are merely two different ways to get exactly the same thing—the use of the asset over its economic life—the difference in manner of reporting ownership costs is very questionable.

The initial response of the profession to these concerns was to require expanded disclosure of lease commitments by lessees. In addition, capitalizing the initial present value of the lease payments as an asset and obligation was recommended where it was clearly evident that the lease was in substance a purchase.[1] Practice was slow to accept that recommendation, preparers of financial statements being reluctant to lose the supposed advantages of off-balance-sheet financing. As a result, more recent accounting standards for lease accounting have attempted to be much more specific as to the criteria that mark a lease as being in substance a purchase and sale of property.

The concept underlying present lease standards—that leases that are in substance purchases and sales of property should be so accounted for—is not the only possible concept. Some accountants have suggested that the purchase-equivalent character of a lease is not the important one in terms of business economics. An entity acquires an asset not for the joys of ownership but rather for the service it will yield. The essential characteristic of a leased asset is its ability to render valuable service, and that is provided (for a limited period) by short-term leases as well as leases that cover the economic life of the property. By this reasoning, then, it would be appropriate to recognize the present value of lease rentals (less any portion of the rentals required to cover lessor services) as an asset and obligation at the inception of all leases. Such an approach would also have the practical merit of avoiding the necessity of spelling out criteria for the identification of leases to be capitalized—criteria that are inevitably difficult to implement.

Lease accounting terminology

Under present standards, leases that transfer "substantially all benefits and risks incident to ownership of the property leased" are given the following names:

- From the viewpoint of the lessee, such a lease is called a "capital lease."
- From the viewpoint of a lessor who simply buys an asset for the purpose of leasing—that is, an investor in leases—such a lease is called a "direct financing lease."
- From the viewpoint of a lessor who is a manufacturer or dealer in particular types of assets and who uses leases as a medium for disposing of assets for profit, such a lease is called a "sales-type lease."

Leases classified as direct financing leases and sales-type leases from the viewpoint of the lessor are both capital leases from the viewpoint of the lessee. The three categories will be referred to collectively hereafter as "ownership leases."

A lease that does not qualify as an ownership lease is called an "operating lease" by both lessor and lessee.

Several special terms have been defined to facilitate implementation of lease accounting standards. These are described as follows.

Bargain purchase option. This is an option granted to the lessee to purchase the property leased that appears, at the inception of the lease, to be so favourable that its exercise ultimately is reasonably assured.

Contingent rentals. These are rentals whose amount is determined by factors other than the passage of time. A definition is provided for contingent rentals because a rental that may or may not have to be paid is not considered sufficiently certain to figure in amounts recorded for lease assets and obligations capitalized in a balance sheet. Contingent rentals may be based on percentages of sales or intensity of use of the property leased. The *CICA Handbook* refers to rentals based on the prime interest rate or price indexes as being contingent, as well. The FASB provides that lease payments dependent upon an existing index or rate, such as the Consumer Price Index or the prime bank lending rate, are to be regarded as a fixed rental based on the index or rate existing at the lease inception. Changes in rentals resulting from deviations (plus or minus) in these amounts are regarded as contingent. Since lease rentals tied to the prime rate or a price index are certainly not going to fall to zero during a lease, the FASB approach makes better sense than does a literal interpretation of the CICA definition.

Executory costs. These are costs pertaining to the property leased that will be paid in future, such as property taxes, insurance, or costs of cleaning and maintenance. Unless the lessee bears such costs, rentals must cover them, and only the net rental after deduction of such costs, and perhaps a profit element thereon, can be considered payment for use of the property.

Initial direct costs. These are costs, such as commissions and legal fees, that are incurred by the lessor at the inception of a lease and are directly traceable to the negotiation and execution of the lease.

Interest rate implicit in the lease. This is the discount rate required to be applied to (1) "minimum lease payments" (defined below) excluding any portion attributable to executory costs and profit thereon, and (2) any estimated residual value of the leased property that is not included in minimum lease payments, so that the sum of the discounted present value of these two items is equal to the fair value of the property leased at the inception of the lease. This implicit rate must be calculated by trial and error, a process that can be facilitated by computer programs, programmable calculators, or interpolation from a precalculated table.[2]

Lease term. This is the noncancellable term of the lease plus further periods for which the terms and conditions of the lease establish reasonable assurance at its inception that the lessee will exercise renewal privileges for those periods. The lease term as defined, however, does not extend beyond the date upon which a bargain purchase option becomes exercisable.

Lessee's incremental borrowing rate. This is the hypothetical rate of interest the lessee would have had to pay if he had purchased, rather than leased, the property and borrowed the money necessary to pay for it. For the purpose of estimating this hypothetical rate, it is assumed that the debt is repayable over a term similar to that of the lease and with security to the lender equivalent to that which the lessor possesses under the lease.

Leveraged lease. This is a lease involving three parties—the lessee, the lessor, and a third party financier whose payment comes from the lease rentals but who has no recourse against the lessor for nonpayment. Such an arrangement has substantial tax advantages to the lessor in the United States, but these are not available in Canada. As a result such leases are not common in Canada and are not dealt with in its accounting standards.

Minimum lease payments. From the lessee's point of view, minimum lease payments comprise minimum rentals called for by the lease over its term together with (1) any guarantee given by the lessee or a related party of the residual value of the property reverting to the lessor at the end of the lease term, and (2) any penalty payable by the lessee for failure to renew or extend the lease at the end of its term. From the lessor's point of view, minimum lease payments comprise the foregoing plus any guarantee of residual value that is provided by a financially capable third party who is unrelated to both the lessor and lessee.

Criteria for identification of ownership leases

How does one identify a lease that conveys substantially all the benefits and risks incident to ownership? Several criteria are given in the standards.[3]

- If, in all probability, the lessee will ultimately obtain title to the property in accordance with the lease, it is obviously an ownership lease. That occurs when the lease actually conveys title at the end of the lease term or when it grants an option to buy the property at some time during the lease that appears to be such a bargain that its exercise is reasonably assured.
- If the lease term is such that the lessee may expect to obtain substantially all of the economic benefits from the property, even though it will not result in transfer of title, the lease is also to be considered an ownership lease. For this purpose, it is suggested that a lease that covers 75% of economic life in terms of elapsed time will usually be considered to convey substantially all of the asset's economic benefits.
- If the lease provides the lessor with some assurance of recovery of his investment in the leased property together with some return on investment over and above the recovery, the lease is also to be considered an ownership lease. Such assurance is considered to be provided when the present value of the minimum lease payments at the inception of the lease (excluding any portion of the rentals required to cover "executory costs") equals substantially all (usually taken as 90% or more) of the fair value of the leased property.

The last of these three tests is the most complicated. In order to apply it a lessor must calculate the "interest rate implicit in the lease." The end result of this test is that, for the lessor, the present value of the unguaranteed residual value at the lease inception may not exceed 10% of the fair value of the property.

The application of the test by the lessee differs from that of the lessor. If his "incremental borrowing rate" is lower than the interest rate implicit in the lease or if it is not possible to ascertain or make a reasonable estimate of the rate implicit in the lease, the incremental borrowing rate is used.

It may be noted that if the first criterion is met it is unnecessary to consider the other criteria. The latter are applicable only to leases that leave a residual property right to the lessor. Both of the last two criteria are attempts to measure whether the unguaranteed residual right is so significant that the lease should not be considered as a substantial transfer of all risks and rewards to the lessee. The second criterion is written from the viewpoint of the lessee, who may not have all the information necessary to apply the third criterion with confidence. The third criterion is written from the viewpoint of the lessor. Both criteria are supposed to be applied, however, and if either is met the lease is to be treated as an ownership lease, not an operating lease.

Ownership leases — lessor accounting

It should be noted first that, for lessor accounting only, a lease must pass two further tests in order to qualify for accounting as an ownership lease.

- If the lessor has exposure to further costs—for example, by way of guarantee of asset performance or guarantee against obsolescence—that are not collectible from the lessee or others, the amount of such costs must be capable of reasonable estimation so that provision may be made for them in recording income.
- Similarly, the credit risk should be normal in the circumstances so that reasonable allowances for uncollectibility can be made.

If these tests are not met, the lease may not be classified and accounted for as an ownership lease. As a result, it is possible that a lease that is treated as a capital lease by the lessee will be treated as an operating lease by the lessor.

Income accounting by lessors

The basic idea in accounting for direct financing leases is that income is to be recognized over the lease term so as to yield a constant rate of return on the unamortized balance of the asset. Initially, the lease asset is recorded at a net amount equal to the net investment in the lease at the time of its inception. That net amount, however, is divided into two elements: (1) the gross amount over the lease term of the minimum lease rentals less the portion thereof deemed to relate to executory services, together with the estimated residual value of the property; and (2) a deduction for unearned income to reduce the gross figures to the net investment figure. As rentals are received they are deducted from the figure of gross rentals receivable, and a transfer is made from unearned income to earned lease income in an amount equal to the precalculated rate of return applied to the opening net carrying value of the asset. For reasons to be given shortly, that precalculated rate of return will not necessarily be equal to the "interest rate implicit in the lease" as that term was defined previously.

A simplified example — use of pretax interest rate

A simplified example will illustrate the accounting. Suppose:

- A lessor buys a piece of equipment for $50,000 and immediately leases it on a direct financing lease.

- The lessor is entitled to an investment tax credit (ITC) of 15% or $7,500 on the asset.
- The lease term is eight years and the expected residual value at that time is $10,000 of which $8,000 is guaranteed by the lessee.
- The annual rental is $6,913 payable in advance.

In this example, what is the "interest rate implicit in the lease" as defined by accounting standards? According to the definition given earlier (which is the definition provided in the *CICA Handbook*) that rate is 6.994%, as shown by the following tabulation:

Present value of eight lease payments of $6,913 discounted at 6.994%	$44,177
Present value of residual value of $10,000 (including guaranteed and unguaranteed portions)	5,823
Fair value of property	$50,000

The FASB standard, in contrast, directs that any ITC expected to be realized by the lessor should be deducted from the fair value of the property for the purpose of estimating the implicit interest rate. Since the ITC in this example is $7,500, we must find the interest rate that produces a present value of lease payments and residual value of the property equal to $42,500. That interest rate is 12.0%.

The FASB approach appears more reasonable. The ITC is so closely associated with the investment in the lease that it is unrealistic to leave it out of the calculation of the effective rate of return on the lease. Also, such treatment is consistent with the 1985 change in the *CICA Handbook* requiring that ITCs be credited against related asset costs. However, even the FASB calculation could be considered open to criticism if the benefit from the ITC is received later than the time of the original investment. For the purposes of our illustrations, for example, assume that the ITC is realized at the end of year 1. In that case, the interest rate that would equate the present value of all the cash inflows connected with the lease (other than income tax on the lease earnings) with the fair value of the property would be 11.415%, not 12.0%. For purposes of all our subsequent illustrations we shall base the implicit interest rate on the timing and amounts of all the cash flows connected with the lease, not just some of them. We shall, however, provide two sets of calculations—the first excluding actual income tax recoveries and payments as they are affected by accelerated capital cost allowances, and the second including such income tax effects. The *CICA Handbook* contemplates that either of these two approaches may be used in lease accounting.

The pretax cash flows in our example are scheduled in Table 7-1. The balance sheet figures at the inception of the lease and one year later are shown in Table 7-2.

An allowance for uncollectible payments would also be made for the lease portfolio as a whole, to the extent required.

Since the lease rentals are in advance, the net investment of $50,000 is immediately reduced by the first payment of $6,913. The transfer from unearned to earned income for the year, then, will be 11.415% of ($50,000–$6,913) = $4,918, reducing unearned income to $17,886.

Table 7-1

Pretax Cash Inflow (Outflow) by Period

	At Lease Inception (January 1)	Year 1	2	---- 7	8	Total
Cost of equipment	($50,000)					($50,000)
Investment tax credit		$7,500				7,500
Net investment						42,500
Rentals	6,913	6,913	$6,913	$6,913		55,304
Residual value					$10,000	10,000
Total inflows						65,304
Unearned income						$22,804

Table 7-2

Makeup of Lease Asset in Balance Sheet

	Lease Inception — January 1 (Before first rental receipt)	Year 1, December 31
Minimum lease payments (at inception — total rentals of $55,304 plus guaranteed residual value of $8,000)	$63,304	$56,391
Estimated unguaranteed residual value	2,000	2,000
	65,304	58,391
Less unearned income	22,804	17,886
Net investment in lease (after investment tax credit)	$42,500	$40,505
Investment tax credit receivable	$ 7,500	

The constant rate of return used for income recognition purposes in this illustration is 11.415%, the previously calculated implicit interest rate. That rate will often not be appropriate for income recognition purposes. The existence of "initial direct costs" is the usual reason for this. The standards provide that such costs should be expensed as incurred and an equal amount of initial unearned lease income should be recognized as earned immediately, so as to offset the expense. Obviously, if this is done, the income recognition rate must be reduced accordingly so that there can be recognition of a constant rate of return for the remaining lease term. In the preceding illustration, if unearned income at the lease inception were drawn down to cover initial direct costs of $2,500, the rate of income recognition subsequently would have to be reduced to 9.705% to permit complete amortization of the investment in the lease down to the residual value of $10,000.

At the inception of the lease, the portion of the net investment attributable to the estimated future residual value is that future amount discounted at the income recognition rate. In this case, that would be $10,000 discounted for eight years at 9.705% = $4,766. Since the accounting ends up with $10,000 on the books at the end of the lease term, it is obvious that the original amount of $4,766 has been "accreted" at the interest rate of 9.705%. The standards require that the estimate of residual value be reviewed regularly and that, if a reduction in the estimate is made, an appropriate adjustment should be made to the net carrying value of the lease. The amount of that adjustment depends upon the accreted amount of the residual value at the time of change in estimates.

For example, suppose that three years after the inception of our illustrative lease the estimated residual value were reduced from $10,000 to $8,000 (the floor guaranteed by the lessee). The accreted amount of the residual value at that point, at the 9.705% interest rate, would be $\$4{,}766(1.09705)^3 = \$6{,}293 = \$10{,}000/(1.09705)^5$. The revised amount should be $\$8{,}000/(1.09705)^5 = \$5{,}035$. The indicated loss of $1,258 would be recognized by reducing the unguaranteed residual value asset by $2,000 and reducing the unearned income by $742.

The foregoing example does not illustrate the treatment of executory costs. Where a lessor has such an obligation, an estimate must be made of the payments to be incurred. If the service giving rise to the executory costs is significant, the lessor should also allow a profit margin thereon on a reasonable basis. The total of the estimated costs and profit margin of each period should be deducted from the gross rentals, for the purpose of calculating the interest rate implicit in the lease and determining the total amount of minimum lease rentals to be recorded as an asset at the inception of the lease. It is then necessary, subsequently, to split rentals received between the portion to be treated as a reduction of minimum lease payments receivable and the remainder to be treated as service revenue.

Apart from the possible recognition of profit in relation to the executory costs, the total income from the lease is attributed to accounting periods on the basis of the calculated constant rate of return. Such a basis of income recognition is consistent with the view of a lease as a financing vehicle, since it is traditional accounting practice for investments in financial assets such as annuities, long-term bonds, etc. It will be noted that no profit is attributed to the effort involved in lease-related activities, such as negotiating the lease or arranging realization of the residual value. That result occurs because the prescribed accounting allows only for the recovery of costs in the treatment of initial direct costs and in the calculation of estimated residual value. Nevertheless, the example illustrates once again that when income is earned in different activities undertaken over more than one period, the allocation of income to periods is arbitrary to some degree.

Since the constant rate of return is a pretax rate of return, an appropriate income tax charge must be accounted for. Assuming the lessor continues to be taxed on the basis of asset ownership, his actual taxes payable will be considerably affected by the timing of capital cost allowance. It will be necessary, therefore, to use tax allocation accounting to maintain the standard rate of tax expense in relation to the pretax income reported from the lease.

Use of after-tax interest rate

In Canada, a different basis of accounting for a lease is also available that takes account, in its approach to income recognition, of the income tax advantages of leasing. The essential concept is that the lessor is interested in after-tax returns. Accordingly, it is more faithful to the economics of leasing to calculate the effective after-tax rate of return on the lease investment and recognize income at that rate, rather than use a pretax rate.

This concept may be illustrated using the facts in the previous example but incorporating income taxes in the illustration. For this purpose it is assumed that:

- The income tax rate is 45%.
- The investment tax credit is deducted from the capital cost of the asset for the purpose of calculating capital cost allowance. Capital cost allowance is allowed at the rate of 50% of the equipment cost on a straight-line basis.
- The lessor has enough income from other sources to absorb all tax deductions arising from the lease, even though the lease rentals themselves are insufficient to do so in the first two years.

The taxable income and tax are scheduled in Table 7-3. The cash flows are scheduled in Table 7-4.

On the basis of assuming that the lessor's investment in the equipment, the initial direct costs, and the first rental payment take place on January 1 in year 1 and all other cash flows take place effectively at the end of the year (lease rentals on January 1 of the following year), the implicit after-tax rate of return can be calculated at 8.5037%. On this basis, the after-tax income from the lease to be reported is found by applying the constant rate of 8.5037% to the unamortized balance of investment from time to time. In the first year, for example, the income would be 8.5037% of $45,587 = $3,877. The unamortized balance at the end of year 1 would be $45,587 plus $3,877 minus the cash flow of $21,990 = $27,474. Income for the second year would be 8.5037% of $27,474 = $2,336, and so on. The incomes to be recorded year by year, compared with the incomes recorded using the pretax rate as previously described, are shown in Table 7-5.

There clearly can be a substantial difference in the income reported year by year on the two bases, even though both are founded on the use of a constant rate of return. Which is superior? It can be argued that the method using the after-tax rate is a more faithful representation of the economics of the lease. Properly understood, a rate of return is an expression stating the relationship between cash flows and cash investment on a basis allowing for the time value of money. Since an entity's well-being depends upon the return it can retain after tax, the relevant rate of return should not ignore the impact of tax law upon the timing of cash flows.

There is a problem, however, in fitting income recognition based on an after-tax rate of return into an accounting presentation framework that traditionally shows tax expense separate from other revenues and expenses. Moreover, even though the calculation of the after-tax return is based on a figure of net investment in the lease from time to time—that is, the net investment after deducting deferred taxes—the *CICA Handbook* specifically requires that deferred taxes be presented separately in the balance sheet. How may this be done? One approach is to gross up the scheduled after-tax return using the standard tax rate (in our example 45%). Thus, in year 1 of the lease the after-tax return of $3,877 would be shown as

Table 7-3

Taxable Income and Tax by Period

	Year 1	2	3	----	7	8	Total
Annual rentals	$ 6,913	$ 6,913	$6,913		$6,913	$ 6,913	$55,304
Initial direct costs	(2,500)						(2,500)
Capital cost allowance, 50% of $42,500	(21,250)	(21,250)					(42,500)
Recaptured capital cost allowance						10,000	10,000
Taxable (loss)/income	(16,837)	(14,337)	6,913		6,913	16,913	20,304
Tax (recovery)/payable at 45%	($ 7,577)	($ 6,452)	$3,111		$3,111	$ 7,611	$ 9,137

Table 7-4

After-tax Cash Inflow (Outflow) by Period

	At Lease Inception (January 1)	Year 1	2	3	----	7	8	Total
Cost of equipment	($50,000)							($50,000)
Initial direct costs	(2,500)							(2,500)
Investment tax credit		$ 7,500						7,500
Rentals	6,913	6,913	$ 6,913	$6,913		$6,913		55,304
Residual value							$10,000	10,000
Income tax		7,577	6,452	(3,111)		(3,111)	(7,611)	(9,137)
	($45,587)	$21,990	$13,365	$3,802		$3,802	$ 2,389	$11,167

Table 7-5

Comparison of Reported Income Using Pretax and After-tax Rates of Return

Year	Based on Constant Pretax Return of 9.705%		Based on Constant After-tax Return of 8.5037%
	Pretax Income	After-tax Income (55% of pretax)	
1	$ 4,425	$ 2,434	$ 3,877
2	3,455	1,900	2,336
3	3,119	1,715	1,398
4	2,751	1,513	1,194
5	2,347	1,291	972
6	1,904	1,047	732
7	1,418	780	471
8	885	487	187
	$20,304	$11,167	$11,167

$3,877/0.55 = $7,049 on a pretax basis. The tax expense reported would be the difference of $3,172. Since the actual tax related to the lease is a recovery of $7,577 in that year, a deferred tax provision of $10,749 must be made. Table 7-6 shows the full schedule of figures reported for pretax income from the lease, tax expense, and the deferred tax transfers required to show that tax expense figure.

It will be noted that in this example the first year pretax income reported of $7,049 exceeds the actual lease rental payment of $6,913 by $136. That means that it is actually necessary to write up the net investment in the lease on the asset side of the balance sheet by $136. The true figure of the net unrecovered investment, of course, is the asset figure less the deferred tax balance, and it is on this net figure that the 8.5037% after-tax return is calculated. It is evident that the calculation of the pretax income based on the standard tax rate of 45% is highly artificial, as is the calculation of deferred tax which is dependent upon that pretax figure.

An alternative after-tax basis

An alternative basis of presentation can be developed based on the following reasoning.[4] Cash flows from a lease are required to (1) recover the original investment, (2) provide an after-tax return to the lessor (at the rate of 8.5037% in our example), and (3) constitute a fund for payment of taxes. The recognition of tax expense that is required in the first year is that percentage of pretax income that would have to be funded (and subsequently accumulated at the after-tax rate of return on the lease). The tax expense recorded in the second year should be the same percentage of pretax income *plus* an amount equivalent to interest on the hypothetical fund for payment of future taxes, and so on year by year.

The key problem is to calculate the percentage of pretax income that is sufficient to fund all tax payments in the manner described. That percentage can be

Table 7-6

Calculation of Pretax Income and Deferred Taxes

	Year								
	1	2	3	4	5	6	7	8	Total
After-tax scheduled income	$ 3,877	$2,336	$1,398	$1,194	$ 972	$ 732	$ 471	$ 187	$11,167
Gross-up to pretax (÷ 0.55)	7,049	4,247	2,542	2,172	1,767	1,331	856	340	20,304
Tax expense to be reported	3,172	1,911	1,144	978	795	599	385	153	9,137
Actual tax (recovery)	(7,577)	(6,452)	3,111	3,111	3,111	3,111	3,111	7,611	9,137
Deferred tax: provision	$10,749	$8,363							19,112
draw-down			$1,967	$2,133	$2,316	$2,512	$2,726	$7,458	$19,112

determined as follows. Calculate the present value at the inception of the lease of the after-tax returns to be reported under it (as tabulated in the right-hand column of Table 7-5) based on the lease rate of return of 8.5037%. Calculate also the present value at the lease inception of the actual tax recovered or paid each year (as shown in the fourth line of Table 7-6). Those present values will amount to $8,970 and $1,910 respectively. The present value of the *pretax* lease income is the sum of these figures: $8,970 + $1,910 = $10,880. Therefore, the effective tax burden is $1,910/$10,880 = 17.55%. This tells us that, with the generous capital cost allowances assumed in this case, the taxpayer is as well off with a 45% tax rate as he would be if the rate were only 17.55% applied to the pretax income reported under the lease.

Space precludes a full illustration here of the income statement presentation. The interested reader can make the necessary calculation of the tax provisions (and resulting deferred tax provisions and draw-downs year by year) using the 17.55% tax rate and adding interest to accumulated deferred tax balances at the rate of 8.5037%. It is evident that this method, in effect, calculates deferred taxes on a discounted basis—a practice that is prohibited by the *CICA Handbook*. However, when the lease accounting is based on the use of an after-tax rate of return, it is only consistent in logic that every element in the net investment in the lease, including the deferred taxes, be reported on a discounted basis. The presentation previously described, under which the figure of undiscounted deferred tax was backed into, is artificial and inconsistent with the economics of the lease.

Sales-type leases

In a sales-type lease the present value of minimum lease payments (after allowance for executory costs and related profit) is recorded as an asset and credited to sales revenue. The previous carrying value of the property leased, less the present value of any unguaranteed residual value therein, is written off as cost of sales. Thus the initial investment in the lease recorded in the balance sheet consists of the present value of the minimum lease payments and the present value of the unguaranteed residual value, just as in the case of the direct financing lease. The subsequent accounting is exactly the same as for the direct financing lease except that an amount equal to initial direct costs is not transferred from unearned to earned income at the lease inception. With sales-type leases initial direct costs are deemed to represent costs that should be set off against profit to be recorded on the sale of the property, rather than against the profits subsequently recorded from the lease.

The lessor under both direct financing and sales-type leases discloses in the financial statements the net investment in the leases and finance income therefrom. Disclosure is also to be made of the accounting basis used in recognizing income. If the balance sheet is classified, the current portion of the investment in the lease is classified as a current asset.

Ownership leases — lessee accounting

The lessee under a capital lease must record the lease as though he had bought an asset and undertaken a debt equal to the purchase price. As noted earlier, the deemed purchase price is the capitalized value of the minimum lease payments less the amount deemed applicable to executory services, determined by discounting them at the interest rate implicit in the lease or the lessee's incremental borrowing rate, whichever is lower.

Depreciation is written on the capital value of the leased asset using the lessee's customary depreciation methods. When the lease is capitalized because it transfers title to the asset or probably will do so at the end of the lease term, the depreciation period will be the assumed useful life of the asset, consistent with the lessee's depreciation policy for similar owned assets. If the lease is capitalized because it fits either of the other two criteria for capitalization—i.e., it covers more than 75% of the estimated economic life of the asset, or the present value of minimum lease payments exceeds 90% of fair value—the asset must be fully amortized over the lease term even though that term is shorter than its estimated useful life. It may be, however, that amortization of the asset need not reduce the asset to zero at the end of the lease term. The minimum lease payments that form the basis of the amount capitalized include the amount of any guarantee of the residual value by the lessee or a related third party. That means that, at the end of the lease term, the accounts will still show a liability for this guarantee. If the asset retains that much residual value to the lessor, the lessee will not be called upon to make good on the guarantee. Hence, so long as it can be assumed that the lessor will realize at least the guaranteed residual value, amortization of the asset by the lessee need only reduce its carrying value at the end of the lease term to that guaranteed residual value figure. Then, when the lessor realizes the residual value, the lessee can offset the carrying value against the recorded liability for the guarantee.

Rental payments, excluding the portion accounted for as executory costs, will be accounted for partly as interest on the debt obligation and partly as repayment of principal. The interest portion will be calculated at the rate assumed in capitalizing the asset. In this way, the debt will be amortized down to the residual guarantee amount by the rental payments.

Financial statement disclosure is required with respect to assets capitalized under leases and their amortization in a manner broadly consistent with disclosure given to fixed assets. Disclosure is also required of capitalized lease obligations separate from other long-term obligations and of details of future minimum lease payments for each of the next five years and in aggregate. Where a classified balance sheet is presented, the current portion of long-term lease obligations must be classified among current liabilities.

Operating leases

In contrast to ownership leases, accounting for operating leases contains few problems. In most cases rentals payable are equal amounts per period over the lease term and will be accounted for as revenue (by the lessor) and expense (by the lessee) on a straight-line basis consistent with the payment terms. Even if rentals are not constant over the lease, the standards suggest that revenue and expense should be recognized on the straight-line basis unless circumstances suggest otherwise. (For example, if the asset's service declines sharply with age, a declining rental would be perfectly logical.)

Initial direct costs incurred by a lessor with respect to an operating lease should be deferred and amortized in proportion to revenue recognition. The lessor also must disclose rental income recorded for the year and the cost and accumulated depreciation of property held for leasing. (The *CICA Handbook* encourages additional disclosure such as information as to the amount of contingent rentals received or paid. The FASB standard *requires* all the additional disclosure that is merely suggested by the *CICA Handbook*.)

Because of the commitment aspect, lessees disclose future minimum lease payments required on operating leases for each of the next five years and in aggregate (excluding, if desired, leases that are for less than one year at the date of their inception).

Special problems in lease accounting

A variety of questions come up in the course of lease accounting because of the special circumstances of particular leases or because of changes that can be negotiated in lease agreements after their initiation. These questions are dealt with here briefly, largely based on guidance provided in FASB material.

Renewals, modifications, and terminations of leases

All renewals, extensions, or changes in the provisions of an existing lease give rise to a new agreement. The classification of that new agreement (as an operating or ownership lease) is established in accordance with the criteria previously explained. When a previous ownership lease is reclassified as an operating lease, the net investment in the lease (in the case of a lessor) or related asset and obligation (in the case of a lessee) are written off. The lessor also reinstates the leased asset among the recorded tangible assets at its original cost, fair value, or present carrying amount of the investment in the lease, whichever is lowest. Thus, the lessor may have to recognize a loss on the lease change. The lessee may show either a loss or gain on write-off of the lease asset and obligation.

Where the classification of an ownership lease does not change, asset and obligation balances related to the original lease are not written off but rather are adjusted to take account of the new lease provisions in order to be appropriately amortized over the remaining term of the new lease. This is achieved as follows:

- A lessor adjusts the balance of minimum lease payments and estimated residual value to amounts appropriate under the new lease conditions. The net amount of the adjustment is carried to unearned income account. The lessor then calculates a new lease interest rate that results in revenue recognition and amortization of the lease receivables so as to leave the correct residual value on the books at the end of the lease.
- A lessee adjusts the balance of the obligation under the lease to the present value of the remaining minimum lease payments under the modified lease agreement. The amount of the adjustment is carried to the asset account with subsequent depreciation being adjusted accordingly. The FASB directs that the interest rate used in calculating present value be the same as the

interest rate used in accounting for the lease obligation as it was originally recorded. Presumably this is because the previous lease balances are not written off at the time of the lease change, so that the accounting is affected both by the previous and new lease provisions. The *CICA Handbook* is silent on this point.

The *CICA Handbook* provides no guidance on accounting for the case where a previous sales-type lease is reclassified as a direct financing lease. The FASB directs that it be treated in the same way as a previous direct financing lease that continues to be so classified under its new terms. This seems reasonable since, after its initial recording, a sales-type lease is accounted for in exactly the same way as a direct financing lease. On the other hand, when a direct financing lease is replaced by a sales-type lease, the balance of net investment in the previous lease plus the residual value of the asset forms the "cost" to be written off in accounting for the new lease.

Terminations of leases before conclusion of the original agreement are dealt with in the same manner as changes in leases from ownership leases to operating leases. That is, previous balances relating to the lease asset are written off the books, the lessor reinstates the property among his tangible recorded assets, and the net adjustment is carried to income.

It may be noted here that FASB instructions for dealing with lease changes are far more complicated than those in the *CICA Handbook*. The most important difference is that when a lease is reclassified from an ownership lease to an operating lease, the FASB directs that the previous lease accounting be carried on until the end of the term of the original lease, with the result that gains and losses resulting from the change in lease terms are not recognized at the time of change.

Sale or assignment of lease rights or sale of leased property by lessor

When a lessor assigns his interest in an ownership lease or sells the property so leased, accounting for the transaction follows the normal course. When the property leased is sold, the entire net investment in the lease and residual value (if any) is written off against the sales proceeds. When the lease rentals are assigned without sale of the property, the write-off against sales proceeds excludes any residual property values on the books.

Usually, sale of property that has been leased out on an operating lease or of property that is intended to be leased out by the purchaser on an operating lease is also treated as a normal sale. If, however, the vendor retains substantial risks of ownership (e.g., by an agreement to reacquire the property upon certain events), the sale in legal form is not accounted for as a sale. Instead, the proceeds are recorded as an amount borrowed, carrying a notional interest rate estimated to be equivalent to that which the vendor would pay for debt with an equivalent degree of risk. Rentals on the property (whether received directly by the purchaser or received and passed on by the vendor) give rise to an entry by the vendor crediting an equal amount as rental revenue, charging interest expense on the borrowing at the notional rate, and reducing the recorded liability for the difference. Since the property ostensibly sold is still on the books of the vendor, depreciation is recorded so as to write off the asset over the period of time estimated to be required to fully amortize the borrowing.

Subleases

When a lessee subleases property, he looks upon the sublease agreement as would any lessor and accounts for it in accordance with the approaches already described. The fact that there is a sublease does not affect his accounting for the obligation he has to the primary lessor. However, a sublease may have almost the effect of a lease termination. When a lease is amended, with the participation of the lessor, so that the sublessee becomes the primary obligor, it is reasonable (and the FASB specifically recommends) that the lessee treat the original lease as terminated and account for any secondary obligation he may retain on the same basis as any other contingency.

Sale-leaseback transactions

To understand the accounting for sale and leaseback transactions, one has to understand their economics. If the leaseback to the vendor-lessee covers virtually the entire economic life of the property (as it often does), it is evident that the purchaser-lessor does not really have the risks and rewards of the property. Rather, his position is more like that of a lender to the lessee on the security of the property. In this situation, there is no reason why the sale price of the property should be a realistic indicator of its fair value. If the vendor-lessee is a good credit risk, the sale price in the agreement (in essence, a borrowing) could be much more than the fair value of the property. This fact influences the lessee's accounting. He accounts for the lease obligation and lease asset following the standard approaches already described. However, because of the uncertainty as to the significance of the sale price, he does not recognize profit or loss on the sale. Instead, the nominal profit or loss is deferred and amortized to income on the following basis:

- When the lease is treated as a capital lease,
  - If the lease is for land only, the amortization is on a straight-line basis over the term of the lease. The end result of this accounting is strange and probably unintended by the standard-setters. The land sold and leased back is in the possession of the vendor-lessee uninterruptedly. As a result of this accounting, however, by the end of the lease term it has been written up by the difference between the ostensible sale price and its pre-lease carrying value, with the credit going to income over the period of the lease.
  - If the lease covers land and buildings, amortization is proportionate to the depreciation of the buildings.
  - If the lease covers other depreciable assets, the amortization is proportionate to their depreciation.
- If the lease is treated as an operating lease, the amortization is in proportion to rental payments over the term of the lease.

The logic of the requirement for full deferral of gain on sale and leasebacks under short-term operating leases is dubious. If the operating lease is short-term, the purchaser-lessor has taken on distinct risks associated with the property and is therefore unlikely to have paid more than a fair price for it.

The lessor's accounting in a sale and leaseback transaction contains no modifications of the normal lease accounting rules.

Leases between related parties

When ownership type leases exist between related parties and separate financial statements are issued for each party, it may be difficult to know what is the fairest accounting. Because of the relationship between the parties, contractual lease arrangements may often be so easily altered that an ownership lease has little more force and effect than an operating lease. The FASB advises that recognition of leases between related parties should be modified as necessary to conform to economic substance. But there may well be little hard evidence as to just what is economic substance. In practice, as in the case of most other related-party transactions, it will usually be necessary to report the lease transactions in accordance with their form, with disclosure of the relationship between the contracting parties and the existence and amount of lease flows between them.

Accounting for real estate leases

Real estate leases in many cases are more significant to the financial position and results of operations of an entity than any other class of lease. At the same time, they present the most difficulties in following lease accounting standards. These difficulties include the following:

- One lease frequently covers more than one type of asset—land, buildings, and sometimes equipment as well.
- Rentals often cover services to be performed by the lessor as well as payment for the use of property.
- Some portion of the rental is often not a fixed amount but rather varies in step with some escalation factor or index.
- A real property lease may not be for an entire identifiable property unit but rather may be for a part only—such as a store in a shopping centre or a floor in an office building.

These problems must be approached along the lines of "peeling the onion."

The first complication to be dealt with is the separation of any components of the lease that do not represent real estate property. Thus, if equipment is included in property leased, an estimate of the rentals applicable to it must be made, difficult though that may be. These estimated rentals and the equipment leased are accounted for as though they constituted a separate and distinct lease.

The second complication lies in the estimate of amounts included in the lease for executory costs. If the latter costs involve significant effort by the lessor, it is reasonable to assume that an allowance for profit should be included in the estimates—that is, the estimate of executory costs should produce a figure equivalent to what the lessee would have to pay to have the services performed by a third party.

After these allocations, one is left with the rentals applicable solely to the land and buildings leased. These may include rentals that are fixed in amount and "contingent rentals." Only the fixed rentals are included in the figure of minimum lease payments that is used as one of the tests in deciding if a lease is an ownership lease and that forms the basis of amounts recorded as assets and liabilities in such leases.

Leases of land and buildings together for periods of, say, forty or fifty years present complications. If title is transferred at the end of the lease or there is a bargain purchase option, the lessee will account for the lease as an ownership lease. In such a case there must be an allocation of the capitalized value of the asset between the portions attributable to the land and the building in order that depreciation accounting may be based on the latter only. This allocation is made in proportion to the fair values of the two components at the inception of the lease.

When title transfer does not take place at the end of a lease of land and buildings, there will often be cases where substantially all the benefits and risks of building ownership have been transferred, but, because of its perpetual life, the same is not true of the land. In such cases there must be some standard approach to classification of the lease.

When the fair value of the land is minor in relation to the total fair value of the leased property at the lease inception (the FASB suggests where land value is less than twenty-five percent of the whole), the land and building are considered as a single unit for the purpose of classifying the lease, and the economic life of the building is taken as the economic life of the unit. Accordingly, if the lease is classified as an ownership lease, the lessee will depreciate the whole asset over the lease term. The lessor will account for the lease as for any other lease involving a single asset.

When the fair value of the land is significant in relation to the total fair value of the leased property at the inception, the two components are considered separately for the purposes of lease classification and accounting. For this purpose, the net rentals are allocated to the two components. This enables classification of the building component of the lease either as an ownership or an operating lease and accounting for it accordingly. The land component is accounted for as an operating lease.

The *CICA Handbook* recommendation is that the net rentals be allocated between land and building components in proportion to their fair values. This is not logical since the rental applicable to the building must cover both return on investment and depreciation of the asset, while the rental applicable to the land need cover a fair return only. The FASB avoids this objection by stipulating that the fair rental for the land is to be taken as a product obtained by multiplying its fair value by the lessee's incremental borrowing rate. The remainder of the minimum lease payments is then attributed to the building.[5]

A lease of part of a building or part of a larger whole, such as a shopping centre, theoretically should be looked at as a lease of land and buildings, since the building could not exist without the land upon which it is located. It is also possible that such a lease may cover most of the economic life of the building component and hence should be capitalized. There are peculiar difficulties in so doing, however, since it may be very hard to estimate costs or fair values of the property leased or even to make a reasonable assumption as to how much land should be attributed to the premises leased.

The complications in implementing accounting standards with respect to real estate leases represent a source of weakness. It is clear that most lessees prefer not to recognize the capitalized value of leases in their balance sheet. First, it puts debt on the balance sheet that they fear may be adverse to their credit rating. Second, it tends to require greater charges to income in the early years of the lease than the straight rental amount. Finally, the more complicated accounting makes work. If the standards were to say, simply, that leases should be capitalized where they convey substantially all the benefits and risks of ownership in the property, the recommendation would be too vague to be implemented uniformly and, in view of the resistance by financial statement preparers, would be unlikely to achieve its objective. Accordingly, the standards have attempted to introduce quantitative guidelines for capitalization where leases do not transfer title to the property or contain bargain purchase options. Unfortunately, these guidelines simply provide signposts for those who are minded to avoid capitalization of their leases.[6]

Summary

Leases were traditionally considered to be executory contracts. As such, lease rentals were recognized as revenue or expense only as the lessee used the assets leased, which usually coincided fairly closely with rental payment dates. With the great expansion of the leasing industry, doubts began to be expressed that this accounting was satisfactory. While a long-term lease could have much the same economic effect as a purchase of an asset wholly financed by debt, the two transactions might be accounted for very differently.

To avoid this, accounting standards have been developed with the general intent that leases that transfer "substantially all the benefits and risks of ownership" (referred to here as "ownership leases") should be accounted for differently from other "operating leases." The standards have provided criteria for making the distinction between the two types of leases. These have had to be spelled out in quantitative terms to make them workable.

A lessor who has put property out under an ownership lease is considered to have sold the property or at least sold most of the valuable rights inherent in it. Accordingly, lessor accounting is designed to show as an asset not the property itself but rather the present value of lease rentals receivable (together with any residual property value after the lease expiration). Income accounting follows the approach ordinarily used for interest-bearing investments, rather than the approach used for operating assets. This means that the implicit rate of interest provided by the lease rentals must be calculated. That return can be calculated on a pretax or after-tax basis, and in Canada either rate may be used to govern income recognition, even though the resulting pattern of income over the lease lifetime may be quite different. A lessor who is simply an investor in ownership leases is said to enter into "direct financing leases." A lessor who is a manufacturer or dealer in the property leased may record a profit when property is rented under an ownership lease; such leases are called "sales-type leases."

A lessee who rents property under an ownership lease (called a "capital lease" in this case) records the present value of the lease rentals as though it were tangible property purchased, financed by debt. Again, an interest rate must be selected to make this calculation, and for this purpose the lessee will use his "incremental borrowing rate," unless he knows the interest rate implicit in the lease and it is lower. Normal depreciation accounting and debt accounting procedures are followed thereafter with respect to the assets and liabilities recorded.

Many technical problems are encountered as a result of changes in leases, subleases, sale and leaseback transactions, and so on. These are dealt with in detail in the accounting standards. Especially in the real estate industry, complexities in leases make it quite difficult to apply the lease accounting standards.

At best, lease accounting standards have been a qualified success. There has been basic opposition to them from those who desire to preserve the presumed advantages of off-balance-sheet financing. Opposition is reinforced by the apparent complexity of the lease accounting standards and, especially in smaller owner-operated businesses, the perception that lease capitalization does not provide information to help manage the business. The decision to restrict capitalization to those leases that are substantially equivalent to ownership forced very detailed rule making upon the standard-setters, because "substantially equivalent" is such a fuzzy concept. When rules are detailed and are interpreted literally, it is easy to frustrate their intention by structuring transactions so that they just fail to meet criteria specified in the rules. Lease accounting has suffered from this problem in practice, particularly in the case of real estate leases.

An alternative approach to lease accounting could be based on the proposition that entities buy productive assets chiefly for the services obtainable from them. A lease is equivalent to a purchase except that access to the services is acquired for a limited period of time only, rather than for the asset's lifetime. If the essence of an asset lies in the services it can provide, it is arguable that all leases should be capitalized, not just those that are equivalent to the acquisition of lifetime services. This concept is simpler in essence than that embodied in today's standards but would present its own implementation problems. Chief among these would be the problem of providing a logical and workable basis for discounting lease rentals for the purposes of capitalization.

It seems probable that a concept of capitalizing all leases (with the exception of very short leases) would not be readily accepted. If a well-thought-out standard were in place dealing with the disclosure of all commitments, as was suggested in chapter 6, it might be that the additional information provided by capitalization of lease contracts would be so small as not to be worth the effort involved.

References

[1]See recommendations in American Institute of Accountants Committee on Accounting Procedure Bulletin No. 38, *Disclosure of Long-term Leases in Financial Statements of Lessees* (New York: AIA, 1949), subsequently consolidated in Chapter 14 of *Restatement and Revision of Accounting Research Bulletins*, Accounting Research Bulletin No. 43 (New York: AICPA, 1953). See also *Reporting of Leases in Financial Statements of Lessee*, APB Opinion No. 5 (New York: AICPA, 1964).

[2]See two articles in *Journal of Accountancy*, May 1980 issue: E. Obersteiner and P.J. Jalics, "Determining Implicit Interest," pp. 34-36, and M. Masoner and J.A. White, "Implicit Interest Rate Table," pp. 36-44.

[3]See CICA, "Leases," *CICA Handbook*, Section 3065 (Toronto: CICA), par. 06.

[4]This approach to lease reporting on an after-tax basis is stimulated by work done by J.A. Milburn Ph.D., FCA, in exploring the subject of discounted deferred tax accounting.

[5]This and certain other detailed issues in lease accounting are discussed in R. Brault, N. Chlala, and L. Ménard, "Accounting for Leases: Why Canadian Standards Don't Measure Up," *CAmagazine*, December 1985, pp. 42-51.

[6]Research shows that some businesses have shifted their pattern of asset acquisition from leasing to buying as a result of the introduction of lease capitalization standards. It also indicates that existing leases have been renegotiated and new leases have been structured to avoid the necessity of capitalization. See A.R. Abdel-khalik, *The Economic Effects on Lessees of FASB Statement No. 13, Accounting for Leases* (Stamford: FASB, 1981). See also R.F. Selby, "Controlling the Financial Impact of Long-term Leases," *CAmagazine*, May 1979, pp. 28-31; R.F. Selby, "Real Estate Leases: An Accounting Dilemma," *CAmagazine*, October 1980, pp. 53-56; and R. Dieter, "Is Lessee Accounting Working?" *The CPA Journal*, August 1979, pp. 13-19.

Chapter Eight

Income and Revenue Recognition

In an exchange economy, the goal of productive activity is to sell a product or service for more than its cost of production. As explained in chapter 5, present-day accounting measures income as the difference between costs (sacrifices) and revenues (benefits). On this basis, if one visualizes a business in the form of a single venture, income over its entire lifetime will be the difference between cash receipts (excluding capital paid in) and cash disbursements (excluding capital withdrawn or return on capital, such as dividends, paid out).[1] It is natural, therefore, to think of revenue as an inflow of assets (ultimately cash) in exchange for the product of the enterprise.

This discussion oversimplifies matters. An enterprise may receive cash other than in exchange for product or service, or as a capital contribution. For example, if some asset were destroyed by fire, the insurance proceeds would not represent payment for the productive activity of the enterprise. It is still true that over the lifetime of an enterprise the excess of cash receipts over cash disbursements (excluding cash associated with capital transactions) will equal the net gain. But that net gain will consist of (1) the excess of revenues from productive activity over costs of earning those revenues, and (2) miscellaneous gains or losses on events or activities that are not part of the main activity of the enterprise.

When we speak of the lifetime of an enterprise from initial cash investment to ultimate cash realization, it is possible to talk solely about movements in cash. When we account for a period shorter than the enterprise lifetime, we have a problem. At any given point of time the enterprise will have delivered product or services for which it has not yet received payment. Conversely, it may have received payment for which it has not yet satisfied its obligation to deliver. It will also have incurred other costs and acquired rights or things that may reasonably be expected to be rewarded by the receipt of cash in a future exchange transaction. Moreover, it may not yet have paid for goods or services it has received. Thus, estimation of income for a period is considerably more difficult than determination of income for a completed business lifetime. Such estimation requires that noncapital cash inflows of past, present, and future periods be assigned to periods in which they are "earned." Similarly, noncapital cash outflows of past, present, and future periods must be assigned to the period in which any benefit from them is used up. That is, the goal of income accounting under the transaction-based model is to provide rules for assigning revenues and expenses from operating transactions and gains and losses from peripheral activities to accounting periods.

Because income accounting associates cash flows with time periods, it automatically results in recognizing assets and liabilities. For example, a cash receipt today associated with revenue of a future period must be recorded as unearned revenue—a liability to deliver product or service in the future. A cash disbursement today associated with revenue of future periods must be recorded as an asset—an expectation of future benefit. In other words, asset and liability recognition (and changes in assets and liabilities previously recognized) can result from income accounting conventions as well as the conventions governing initial recognition of assets and liabilities discussed in previous chapters.

The bulk of this chapter will discuss the recognition of revenues earned from operations. Gain and loss recognition will be referred to at the end of the chapter.

Recognition of earned revenues

Until quite recently, it was customary to think of recognition of earned revenue and income as being synonymous with *realization*. One of the dictionary meanings of the term "realize" is the conversion of property into money. That definition emphasizes both the idea of an exchange and of a liquid asset received in exchange (strictly speaking, cash itself).

Historically, conservatism and the desire for certainty reinforced the emphasis in accounting on exchange for a liquid asset. The exchange test reduced uncertainty as to the amount of revenue to be recognized. It also reduced uncertainty as to the amount of expenses incurred to earn the revenue, since frequently most of a vendor's work has been performed before the product is sold. The liquid asset criterion also meant that proceeds would be more easily measurable. The result of all these influences tended to focus attention on point of sale as the criterion par excellence for revenue recognition. Thus, in 1934, the membership of the American Institute of Accountants formally adopted the following rule:

> *Unrealized profit should not be credited to income account.... Profit is deemed to be realized when a sale in the ordinary course of business is effected, unless the circumstances are such that the collection of the sale price is not reasonably assured.*[2]

This simple rule seemed quite satisfactory for the majority of situations for many years. Where it was not—notably in the case of long-term construction contractors—generally accepted practice developed alternatives that dealt with the particular problem. In the late 1960s and early 1970s, this happy situation began to break down. Several contributing causes can be discerned.

- The rule that revenue was earned at point of sale was essentially based on a stereotype of a business making a standardized product for a mass market, on a more or less regular basis, with few obligations after sale. That image had never fitted construction contractors, and it became less and less realistic as a description of much modern business activity. The growth of the service sector of the economy alone saw to that.
- In the business stereotype, sale came near the end of the business activity, when most costs had been incurred. Measurement uncertainties were thereby minimized. In some industries, business practices changed and developed so this was no longer true. The sale might come early on, leaving substantial obligations on the vendor for future performance. Worse, the sale itself might involve significant uncertainties as to collection. In these circumstances, sale was not a good basis for triggering revenue recognition.
- In many types of business, one sales price might cover several products or

services. Even a business manufacturing a straightforward product was apt to have to provide increasingly complex warranties or other services. One price received for a bundle of products or services raises the question whether one revenue recognition point is satisfactory or whether allocation of revenue to work performed is required.

By 1970, some modification of previously accepted ideas had occurred. It was no longer believed that revenue could be recognized only in exchange for a liquid asset. (The treatment of barter transactions described in chapter 6 illustrates this point.) It was also felt that a sale was not, by itself, sufficient for revenue recognition—there had to be performance by the vendor as well. The accepted rule was stated by the Accounting Principles Board (APB) as follows:

> *Revenue is generally recognized when both of the following conditions are met: (1) the earning process is complete or virtually complete, and (2) an exchange has taken place.*[3]

The traditional exception for long-term contractors was also acknowledged.

Since 1970 practice has continued to develop, and considerable study has been given to special situations. The result has been the development of further exceptions to the sales basis of revenue recognition, some inconsistencies between rules applied in different situations, and some difficulty in seeing a common rationale for revenue recognition.

We can identify three broad approaches to the recognition of revenue. The first may be called the "critical event" approach.[4] Under this approach, the revenue from product sale or service is recognized in full at the time of one selected critical event. (The 1934 American Institute rule indicated that sale was ordinarily deemed to be that critical event.) Certain accounting results flow from this approach. Certain assets, such as accounts receivable or accrued revenue, are recognized and measured at the amount of revenue received or to be received. Any costs previously recorded as assets that are deemed applicable to that revenue must be written off. Costs to be incurred after the critical event that are applicable to the revenue must be estimated, and expense and liability recorded.

The second approach to revenue recognition is the "accretion" approach. Under this approach, revenue is deemed to be earned over the whole period of productive activity and is recognized gradually on some basis that relates to accomplishment. The asset recognized is accrued revenue, measured at a reasonable proportion of the ultimate amount of revenue to be received. Costs that are deemed to be associated with the ultimate product or service sold are generally written off when incurred, since the accrued revenue stands as the asset recorded in their place. Other costs, such as costs of fixed assets, are written off as their benefits are consumed in operations.

A third approach represents an extension of the other two. When one sale price conveys several distinguishable benefits to the customer, the total revenue is allocated among the distinctive products or services. Then, the amount allocated to each such product or service is recognized as earned on either the critical event or accretion approach.

The feasibility of each of these approaches depends to a considerable extent upon the time when a revenue transaction takes place. If a transaction is not contracted until late in the production cycle, recognition usually must be based upon the critical event approach (with some small possibility of revenue allocation to after-sale activities). If the revenue-producing contract is entered into early, however, any of the three approaches—critical event, revenue accretion, and revenue allocation—becomes possible.

The critical event approach

As just explained, when a revenue transaction does not occur until late in the production cycle of a business, the critical event approach is almost always followed. The reason is that until that time the amount of revenue can rarely be estimated with reasonable confidence, and hence the income cannot be measured satisfactorily. This clue suggests that the basic criterion for selection of the precise critical event is the removal of uncertainty. That criterion usually suggests point of sale as the critical event for revenue recognition when the revenue transaction occurs late in the cycle of productive activity, but other critical events are conceivable. These will be reviewed first in the following discussion.

Revenue recognition at completion of production. Long-standing practice has sanctioned the recognition of revenue and profit before sale (at the time of completion of inventory ready for sale) in a limited number of situations. As a matter of mechanics this is accomplished by valuing the completed inventory at net realizable value while writing off production costs.

Early accounting literature provided two justifications for this practice. First, in a few cases (precious metals were cited as an example) where there were no substantial selling costs and the price was stable, there could be relative certainty as to the amount of revenue and profit as soon as production was completed and its cost was known. Second, in some industries more than one product was produced by a common production process or from common materials, and in this situation the joint-costing problem (a one-to-many attribution) meant that presumed cost figures for inventory were highly arbitrary.

Today, there is hardly any industry—certainly not the production of precious metals—that can confidently count upon receipt of a fixed predetermined price for all its output (in the absence of long-term sales contracts). Nevertheless, there remain enterprises—including the precious metal producers—where there is a well-established market for the product, and selling is not a major activity of the enterprise.

In practice, therefore, instances are still found where end-product inventory is valued at estimated realizable values and revenue recognized accordingly. In Canada, these include some base metal mining companies where several metals are produced from complex ores. (To the extent possible, revenue recognized with respect to production on hand at a year-end is based on amounts actually realized after the year-end.) In the United States, however, the general practice of mining companies is to value product at some estimate of cost, and many Canadian companies follow suit.

Recognition of revenue at completion of production, although rare, has merit, especially in those industries where expenditure of effort is not necessarily highly correlated with value of production from one period to the next. Such conditions are found, for example, in agriculture and the extractive industries. The chief limitation on the method's use lies in the inability to reasonably predict values for product. The importance of that limitation may vary from one industry to another or even between different types of operation within an industry.

Revenue recognition at completion of a venture. There are times when an enterprise is undertaken, costs are incurred, and revenues come in, but whether the final result will be a profit or loss is shrouded in uncertainty until near the end of the venture. In circumstances such as these, the businessman may revert to one of the earliest forms of accounting—"venture" accounting or "voyage" accounting. Under this approach, all costs and revenues of the venture are entered in one account and carried forward as a net figure in the balance sheet (subject to write-downs if losses appear probable). The accumulated venture balance is not closed out until the venture is completed and all revenues and costs are known. This form of accounting was widely used in trading ventures from the middle ages onward and persists today in the accounting of tramp freighter companies. The "completed contract" method of accounting for contractors may be regarded as a variant of it. In general, the venture basis of accounting has application where the business carried on naturally consists of a small number of projects and where the final total cost or revenue associated with any project is highly speculative, so that early experience gives no assurance as to the final result.

Revenue recognition at point of sale. Point of sale is a satisfactory point for revenue recognition in a large number of situations because, when sale occurs, the amount of revenue can usually be estimated with fair certainty. Also, costs applicable to the revenue are largely known. A further idea implicit in the selection of sale as the recognition point is that of customer satisfaction. Consider the case of a standard product made under conditions in which costs are well controlled and highly predictable. From the standpoint of the vendor the hardest job may be to get the order; once that is done he may be able to estimate his profit with a high degree of certainty. In spite of that, many accountants feel that profit is not earned and therefore revenue should not be recognized until the vendor has delivered the product or service the customer is buying. This is the idea implicit in one of the tests stated by APB Statement No. 4, quoted previously, that "the earnings process is complete or virtually complete."

Comments made in chapter 6 as to recognition and measurement of transactions are relevant to sales transactions. That is, the criterion for recognition should be performance rather than the legal test of transfer of title. Also, the sales revenue to be recognized should allow for trade and quantity discounts, cash discounts, and discounts for substantial delay in collection.

Recognition of revenue as earned requires the coincident recognition of expenses of earning that revenue, so that a proper income figure emerges. Costs that are directly related to sales (for example, cost of goods sold and sales commissions) must be identified and written off. A suitable basis must also be in place for writing off other costs incurred before sale that are not directly traceable to particular sales (for example, costs of fixed assets used in administration). Finally, expense must be recognized for after-sale costs, such as warranties. Such provisions can present great difficulty since the amount of after-sale costs is not known but rather must be estimated. In spite of this difficulty, recognition of any material amount of such costs at the time that revenue is recognized is required for fair income reporting.

Uncertainties with respect to recognition of revenue at point of sale include uncertainty whether all receivables will be collected, uncertainty as to the possibility of returns by customers, and uncertainty as to the amount of claims for substandard or damaged goods. Gross revenue recorded should be reduced by allowances for all these possibilities, based on informed estimates and past experience.

The impact of major uncertainty. Ordinarily, as just described, allowances are made for the possibilities of return, nonpayment, etc., in recording revenue. Upon occasion, however, the inability to estimate with reasonable assurance the dollar impact of transactions that will not be consummated is justification for delaying recognition of earned revenue beyond the usual recognition point.[5] The accounting reaction to such uncertainty may take various forms.

- A sale for accounting purposes is supposed to transfer substantially all the benefits and risks pertaining to ownership of the property. If the sales contract is so loosely drawn or the business policy of the vendor is so flexible that the transaction does not, in substance, transfer ownership, the transaction is more like an option or consignment than a sale. In these circumstances, the sale transaction is simply not accounted for. Any cash received is treated merely as a deposit that may be applied when recognition of the transaction becomes justified.
- Where the principal uncertainty concerns collectibility, the traditional approach has been to recognize the sale but defer recognition of the profit. This may be achieved by one of three methods:
  - The instalment basis of accounting calls for transfer of previously deferred profit to income as cash is received, in the proportion that the cash receipt bears to the total sale price. Some writers suggest this procedure is illogical in that it determines the amount of profit to be taken up on each instalment on the basis of a total sale price that is uncertain of collection. With respect to any individual transaction, this objection is correct. The objective of the procedure, however, is merely to restrain recognition of profit to allow for some unknown percentage of uncollectibles and, when applied to sales transactions in the aggregate, may (or may not) arrive at a reasonable result.
  - The cost-recovery basis of accounting is still more conservative than the instalment basis. Under cost recovery, all cash collections are credited against the asset account until the cost of the asset sold is completely recaptured. Thereafter, further cash collections are all profit. The fact that, under this method, profit recognition does not take place until well after sale, makes it rather unsatisfactory from the standpoint of income measurement, and it is very rarely encountered in practice.
  - In the case of sales of services, if no costs have been deferred as an inventory of work done on service contracts, the above two methods of delayed profit recognition cannot be used. In their place, under conditions of great uncertainty, revenue can be recorded on a simple cash collection basis, rather than when billed.

It is obvious that after-sale costs present another difficulty in that their amount cannot be completely known at the point of sale. The more demanding that after-sale activities are and the further in the future that they will occur, the greater the uncertainty. Uncertainty will also be greater in new situations—for example, uncertainty as to warranty costs for a new-technology product. Severe difficulties in estimation of after-sale costs (if, for example, it is thought the variance in possible warranty costs could be enough to wipe out the profit) may be grounds for postponement of recognition of revenue and profit on the whole transaction.

The accretion approach

The simplest example of the accretion approach is furnished by accounting practice with respect to investments carrying a fixed rate of interest. Where interest is an important element of enterprise income, especially in the case of financial intermediaries or other entities holding large investment portfolios, the standard practice is to recognize interest revenue as it accretes over time. Wherever material, revenue will be recorded on the effective-yield method whereby interest at the rate stated in the security is modified by amortization of any premium or discount from face value implicit in its acquisition price. The key to the use of the accretion approach in this case is the promise of a fixed return on a time basis. Revenue from other investments, such as dividends on stocks, is customarily not recorded until entitlement to it arises. (One could argue that accretion of dividends on secure preferred stocks would provide a fairer presentation.)

A second major example of the accretion approach is furnished by accounting practice with respect to long-term construction contracts. An accretion basis of accounting for such contracts developed quite early, for several reasons:

- Since the contract was signed before any work was done, recognition of revenue at point of sale made no sense.
- When contracts were long-term in nature and irregular in their incidence, waiting until completion to recognize revenue and profit provided a very misleading picture of activity and results of operations.
- Because a contract price was arrived at before work was done, one major uncertainty that ordinarily dictates delay in revenue recognition was not present. (It may be noted, however, that because of the possibility of "change notices," "extras," performance bonuses, or penalties, etc., the total revenue that will be received on a contract is rarely completely certain.)

As a result of these considerations it became accepted practice for long-term construction contractors to record revenue on the so-called "percentage-of-completion" basis. (That title is only loosely descriptive. The basic objective is to record revenue in step with contractor performance. Performance may be measured in various ways, only some of which fit the description of percentage-of-completion.)

Originally the percentage-of-completion method was considered only as an acceptable alternative to the completed contract method. Now, U.S. literature suggests that the percentage-of-completion method is preferable (except for a business consisting of repetitive short-term contracts) and should be used, unless there are inherent hazards outside normal business risks that make estimates on particular contracts unreliable. Poor estimating procedures and poor quality of field reporting and job costing raise problems for financial reporting and auditing but are not considered, in themselves, as hazards that make the completed contract method of reporting preferable.[6]

Depending on the circumstances of the business and the contract, one of several approaches can be used to measure the contractor's performance. These can be classified broadly as "output methods" and "input methods." Output methods base the amount of revenue to be recorded on some measure of accomplishment.

Costs incurred to accomplish the measured output are identified and matched with revenue; thus it is essential to keep cost records that can be related to accomplishment. Input methods look at costs or efforts expended and express them as a percentage of total estimated costs or efforts to arrive at the percentage of contract revenue to be recognized. A more detailed discussion follows.

Output methods

- If a contract specifies a price per unit produced or delivered, revenue recognition on the basis of units shipped is similar to normal procedures for recognition at point of sale.
- Contracts that pay on the basis of units of work done, for example, quantities of pavement laid or earth excavated or dredged, can also be dealt with on a unit basis.
- It may be possible to specify milestones in contract achievement for the purposes of revenue recognition—for example, stages of construction of a building—and revenue can be recognized based on architects' or engineers' certificates. If this method is used, however, there must be confidence that the revenue accrued at each milestone represents a fair recompense for that stage of work. The payment called for by the contract for each stage is not necessarily a good measure of accomplishment. Often contract payments will be loaded at the front end to assist the financing of the contractor.

Input methods

- Input methods generally fit the description of percentage of completion. They may differ in the indicators of completion that they use. A very commonly used indicator is that of costs incurred on the contract. Total revenues are estimated, total costs are estimated, and revenue earned is recognized as that percentage of total estimated revenue that the actual costs incurred to date represent of total estimated costs. For the purpose of this calculation it is important to exclude from actual costs those that do not represent actual performance, such as payments made to subcontractors who have not yet performed. The cost basis of measurement may also be modified when it is felt that some costs do not provide good indicators of performance. For example, if it is felt that materials acquisition or subcontracting do not involve the same effort as work performed directly by the contractor, they may be excluded from costs used in measuring percentage of performance. Alternatively, an arbitrary, low margin of profit may be applied to them and the remainder of the contract price be recognized on the basis of the percentage of completion indicated by other costs.
- Another way to refine percentage-of-completion methods is to base percentages of completion on what are regarded as key indicators, such as labour hours, labour dollars, machine hours, etc.

There is a method of revenue recognition that falls between the percentage-of-completion approach and the completed contract approach. Under the completed contract approach, no revenue is recognized at all until the contract is complete or substantially complete. Correspondingly, no contract costs are written off until that time. Period costs that cannot be clearly related to contracts, however, continue to be written off. As a result, in any period when contract completions are unusually high or low, period costs may appear very much out of line with the apparent volume of business activity as indicated by contract costs recognized as expenses. To avoid this, a contractor who cannot recognize contract profit under the percentage-of-completion method, perhaps because of considerable uncertainty as to the total amount of revenue or costs, but who has some assurance that there will be no loss may use a percentage-of-completion accounting approach with a zero estimate of profit. In this way, a reasonable impression of activity on contracts is portrayed in the income statement, but the principle that profit should not be recognized in the face of inherent uncertainty is respected.

This discussion is not exhaustive. A variety of revenue recognition methods may make sense in particular contract situations. In addition, many enterprises do not recognize revenue and profit on contracts until they are some distance into the contract, when estimates of total costs and revenues have become more reliable. The important point of principle, however, is that where an earnings process is extended over a long period, revenue recognition at a critical event simply fails to portray reasonably the activities going on. This point is most obvious in relation to contracting enterprises but is applicable in concept to any type of enterprise. Thus there has been a tendency for the accretion approach to revenue recognition to become more widely used whenever the amount of revenue can be established at the outset.

The revenue allocation approach

Earlier, reference was made to the necessity of making provision for after-sale costs (such as warranty costs) when revenue is recognized at a critical event. The existence of after-sale costs gives rise to a conceptual question in revenue recognition. Should all the sale revenue be recorded at the point of sale and provision made simply for the future costs to be incurred? Or should the sales price itself be apportioned, part to be assigned as revenue of the period of sale and part to be deferred to the future period, in an amount sufficient to allow a profit to be reported in that period on the work done by the vendor in fulfilling his obligation? More generally, can there be multiple revenue recognition points tied to distinguishable segments of the vendor's performance?

Application of the accretion concept represents one response to the problem of revenue recognition when major activity occurs after the sale price is established. But, in complex situations, allocation of revenue represents an alternative that may be exercised in conjunction with an accretion approach or a critical event approach. For example, suppose in the real estate industry a condominium project were sold with the sale price covering property management services for a stated period after sale. Because of the absence of separate compensation for the property management function, the sale price should be allocated between the two functions. In this case, the sale price allocated to the property management function would be recognized as revenue on the accretion approach as that function was performed. The sale price allocated to the condominium units would, in Canada, be recognized when the purchaser is in a position to occupy the unit—a critical event. In the United States, revenue from the sale of land and the construction could, if circumstances permit, be recognized by stage of completion.

Basis of revenue allocation. A serious problem in any scheme for allocation of revenue is that of pricing the various functions to which revenue is allocated. No general criteria have been stated in accounting standards. Bases of allocation have been developed for individual situations, especially in the financial services industry, that are not necessarily consistent in terms of their underlying concepts.

It would seem, a priori, that the best basis for allocation of revenue to functions would be prices established by the marketplace for those functions if they are independently performed. Unfortunately, such prices are likely to be available only in a minority of situations. Something equivalent may be available for financial service companies, however. For example, if a company is making a loan or investment that entails certain associated tasks, a market rate of interest may be capable of being observed that can be taken as the price for the pure function of "renting" the money.

If independently established prices are not available, it may be possible to simulate them by estimating what would provide a reasonable margin over costs of providing each function, given the capital investment required for performance of the function and the risks involved. Caution needs to be exercised to ensure that revenue allocated to functions performed first is conservatively estimated, so that a reasonable profit remains for later functions.

In a number of cases, revenue is allocated to some functions in an amount equal to the cost of performing them, leaving the remainder of the revenue to be allocated to later functions. This cost-recovery basis of allocation is similar in concept to by-product costing for inventory. There could be two motives for such an approach. First, allocation on a cost-recovery basis to functions performed in the early stages may be desired to be conservative, leaving the profit element to be recognized in later stages closer to the culmination of the earning process. Second, the cost-recovery basis may be used for functions that are considered secondary in character, reserving profit recognition for the activities that are considered more important. One possible test of the relative importance of various functions could be that of customer interest in the result. For example, a loan may involve significant activities and costs in terms of appraisal of security and obtaining legal and other documentation. Yet it is the use of the money loaned that the customer is interested in. There is some intuitive appeal, therefore, to the idea that the revenue is primarily earned over the loan period and is only secondarily related to the loan origination.

If a cost-recovery approach is adopted, a decision must be made as to whether the revenue allocated will be equal to directly traceable costs only or may be calculated on a full costing basis, that is, including an allowance for fixed overheads. In a number of cases only directly traceable costs are included—a conservative approach.

It may be noted that the same result, from the standpoint of income reported, can be obtained in relation to secondary functions by simply deferring the costs in question until the major revenue recognition point(s) without any revenue allocation to the minor activity. There is no obvious basis for preferring one of these expedients over the other; both are found in practice in different contexts.

Some examples in practice of revenue allocation are described below.

- A sales finance company will initially record amounts recoverable on loans at their gross amount reduced by an allowance for unearned income to the net amount advanced on the loan. Then a transfer from unearned income to earned income of an amount equal to loan acquisition costs may be made, leaving the remainder of the unearned income to be recognized on a yield basis or equivalent over the term of the loan.

- In the United States a more complicated method of revenue recognition for finance companies has been advocated. Under the so-called "combination method," a portion of unearned income equal to the costs of borrowed funds plus a profit margin thereon is recognized on the effective-yield method. The remainder of initially unearned income is recognized as revenue over the loan life in step with costs incurred for acquisition, servicing, and collection.[7] In effect, the accretion approach of revenue recognition is followed, but with separate bases of accretion for each of the functions to which the sales price is allocated.
- Allocation to revenue of loan commitment fees can be even more complicated. U.S. practice for savings and loan associations is guided by recommendations of an AICPA committee.[8] An amount equal to directly traceable underwriting costs is recognized as revenue immediately. To the extent that the fee is a payment for earmarking funds to be lent, it is deferred and amortized over the loan commitment period. To the extent that the fee represents payment to the lender for undertaking an interest rate risk (by guaranteeing the loan rate), the fee is deferred until draw-down of the loan. If at that time the market interest rate is higher than the contract interest rate, the deferred fee is amortized over the loan period as an adjustment of the effective yield. On the other hand, if the contracted rate is equal to or higher than the market interest rate at the loan date or if the loan is not drawn down, the commitment fee is taken into income at that time. Finally, to the extent that the fee is regarded as an adjustment of loan yield, it is deferred and amortized over the combined commitment and loan period, on a straight-line basis for the commitment period and as an adjustment of effective yield over the loan period. These rules are complex. They illustrate use of the underlying principle of revenue allocation even at the expense of some apparent loss of objectivity.

Treatment of initial fees

The practice in some industries of charging an initial fee at the inception of service and subsequently continuing service fees may in some cases interrelate with the question of revenue allocation. One danger needs to be guarded against. It may be that an initial fee and continuing service charges are enough, taken together, to fairly compensate the service provided, but the continuing service charge alone is inadequate to be fair compensation for continuing service efforts. In effect, part or all of the initial charge is required to recompense the continuing activity. The following paragraphs review several situations in which initial fees are charged.

An initial fee may be charged to cover initial costs required to provide a customer with access to continuing service. An example of such a charge might be an installation charge for cable TV. When the fee is reasonable in relation to the costs and effort involved in providing access, there should be no objection to recognizing revenue from the charge and writing off the related costs at completion of the work for which the fee is charged. It should be clear, however, that the fees for continuing service will be adequate so that it can stand on its own feet.[9]

In another case, an initial fee may be charged merely to help the service provider finance the requisite capital investment. Such might be the case, for example, in a sports or fitness club. The accounting for that initial fee would depend upon its nature. If the fee is refundable when a member withdraws, it should be treated as a deposit. If it is not refundable, it may logically be taken into income, but if the fee is paid on a once-and-for-all basis a precise indicator of the appropriate revenue recognition period is lacking. In those circumstances, amortization over the average duration of a membership would seem to be appropriate. (Clubs that use fund accounting—see chapter 25—are likely to exclude initial fees from operating income.)

Loan origination fees. Such fees charged by a financial institution provide a good example of the questions associated with accounting for initial fees. The following considerations are relevant:

- If the lender provides services that are valuable in themselves to the vendor as an incidental to making the loan, it can be argued that the initial fee is for those services and revenue should be recognized.
- If revenue is recognized on this basis, it should be evident that the interest rate to be charged over the loan lifetime is normal for the risk involved, and the origination fee is not, in substance, an interest prepayment.
- Even though the lender is not providing special services to the borrower, there may well be costs associated with the loan origination. Some institutions avoid depressing reported income by recognizing revenue from loan origination fees in order to offset the estimated direct costs of executing the loan. A similar effect on income can be achieved by deferring such loan costs for amortization over the lives of the loans.

It is not clear that any one accounting treatment is predominant in Canadian financial institutions. Practices for savings institutions in the United States are currently (1986) under review by the Financial Accounting Standards Board (FASB).

Franchising. Another accounting area that has given problems in the past is that of recognition of revenue from initial franchise fees. A franchise arrangement commonly calls for payment of an initial franchise fee and continuing fees. The former may cover the right to use the franchise name and various set-up services provided by the franchisor, such as help in site selection, management training, facility design, etc. The latter may cover the right to use the franchise name as well as continuing services by the franchisor.

In the past, problems have been encountered in accounting for initial fees because it was not clear when the fee was earned by the franchisor; sometimes fees were not payable in full immediately, and there was doubt as to their ultimate collectibility; and finally, inadequate financial statement presentation and disclosure of initial fees might conceal their nonrecurring nature. As franchising spread as a form of business, franchisors commonly recognized revenue from initial franchise fees at the time of sale, although other recognition bases were used to some extent, such as recognition at time of cash collection or when the franchisee opened for business. After some experience it became clear that recognition at time of sale was too early in many cases. Present recommended practice is as follows:[10]

- First, it must be considered whether continuing franchise fees are likely to be sufficient in relation to future services to be provided by the franchisor.

If not, an appropriate portion of the initial fee should be deferred and amortized over the life of the franchise so as to cover continuing services with a reasonable profit allowance.

- In addition, if any part of the fee is for tangible property, that part must be separated out and treated as revenue from the sale of assets.
- The remainder of initial franchise fees is to be recognized when the franchisor has substantially performed all services called for, any obligation to refund cash or forgive receivables has expired, and no other conditions or obligations exist. There is a presumption that substantial performance will not have been completed before the franchisee has opened for business.
- In unusual cases where the collection period for franchise fees is extended and collectibility cannot be estimated with reasonable assurance, revenue is to be recognized on either the instalment or the cost-recovery basis.
- Should the franchisor have an option to purchase a franchisee business and there is an understanding or probability that he will do so, initial franchise fee revenue is to be completely deferred to be applied against the franchisor's investment in the outlet if, as, and when it occurs.

Some special industry situations

An appendix to an International Accounting Standard provides a useful recapitulation of revenue recognition practices in a number of common situations.[11] The following paragraphs supplement that discussion.

The real estate industry. Enterprises in the real estate industry often engage in transactions of great complexity that provide practical tests of the general principles of revenue recognition. There are several major problem areas. First, a sales transaction in form may be little different from an option. The buyer may have so little stake in the property that he may feel free to "walk away" from it if its value drops or other difficulties occur. Second, a vendor may retain obligations in connection with property sold so that he remains exposed to some risks pertaining to the property. Third, a vendor may undertake commitments to perform other services after sale as part of the inducements for the sale. Fourth, one contract may cover not only the transfer of property but also the responsibility to construct improvements. The response to these various conditions may take the form of postponement of recognition of sale, making provision at time of sale for future service costs, or, in some fashion, apportioning the sale price so that revenue and profit are recognized in instalments or by stages of completion.

In Canada, accounting problems of the real estate industry have been studied and recommendations made by the Canadian Institute of Public Real Estate Companies (CIPREC).[12] With respect to revenue recognition, the recommendations are along the following lines:

- Revenue from land sales is recognized when the vendor has fulfilled all his obligations, which is normally at the time title passes. Vendor obligations will typically include such matters as registering a plan of subdivision and letting contracts for land servicing. At the time of revenue recognition the purchaser should have made a down payment in cash, or given consideration of equivalent value, or have given a strong covenant, so that there is a high degree of assurance that the purchaser is committed to the property. The appropriate revenue recognition date will often be indicated by the date when interest begins to run on the purchaser's unpaid balance. Substantial uncertainties as to future costs to be incurred, the financial capability of the purchaser, or a variety of other factors may well suggest that recognition of the sale should be postponed. A small down payment and an extended series of payments at low interest suggest recognition of profit on the instalment basis of accounting rather than full recognition immediately.

- Sales of houses and commercial or industrial buildings are normally recognized when title passes at closing. Sales of condominium units may be recognized when arrangments are made to permit and require the purchaser to buy, finance, and occupy the unit, even though it may not be possible for legal title to pass until some later date.

It will be noted that no mention is made of recognition of revenue and profit in accordance with the percentage of completion of vendor obligations. Where a real estate company constructs a building for a single purchaser, however, that accounting would be permissible, just as it would be for any general contractor.[13]

In the United States, a much more detailed set of accounting standards has been enunciated for transactions involving real estate.[14] These standards provide a considerable variety of rules for revenue recognition, depending on the circumstances, but are so worded as to leave less room for judgment than do the CIPREC recommendations.

Revenue from service transactions. In the past few decades the performance and sale of services has formed an increasing percentage of business activity. Yet much of accounting literature is still written as though business activity mainly consisted of the manufacture and sale of tangible products. Accordingly, there has been a tendency for accounting practices for service industries to develop and become generally accepted within the narrow context of the industry itself, with little concern for consistency with what is done in other industries. Some of the inconsistencies in practices for recognition of initial revenue, described earlier, represent examples.

The essential problem in service industries, as in any other business, is to relate revenues with the periods in which they are deemed earned and associate costs appropriately with either recognized revenues or time periods. With respect to cost association, however, many service industries have a particular problem. It is difficult to identify costs that are equivalent to costs of inventory in a manufacturing entity. There may be no directly traceable material and labour costs. Also, because there is not a factory separate from the office, it is difficult to separate general and administration costs from costs that might be treated as overhead costs on inventory. Hence the automatic association of costs of goods sold with sales revenue that is found in manufacturing industries is lacking in many service industries. Consider an advertising agency that earns commissions on advertising placed. Where services such as research, art work, copywriting, and production are not covered by specific charges, how are they to be associated with commissions earned?

In view of the wide variety of service activities, it is not surprising that a variety of revenue recognition methods is found. The following discussion is largely based on suggestions in an FASB "Invitation to Comment."[15]

- Many service activities consist of the performance of a single act, for example, repair of appliances or sale of property by a real estate broker. The only possible revenue recognition point in such a case is that of point of sale, which often will coincide with or be close to cash collection. In such cases, direct costs of making the sale are often small in relation to the ongoing costs of facilities required to do business. In any case, direct sale costs are incurred virtually instantaneously with the sale (for example, sale commissions), while other costs bring no benefit unless there are sales. Accordingly, it usually makes sense to charge all costs to expense as they are incurred. If, however, costs are incurred that are directly related to revenue that will be recognized in future, they may be deferred.

- By extension, if the service activity performed consists of a series of acts, but one act among them represents the culmination of performance and is much more significant than other acts, revenue can be recognized at the time of the culminating act, usually the point of sale or execution of service. All costs that cannot be directly related to future revenue are expensed.
- By further extension, if the service provided consists of a series of activities, but the activities and their duration are not well defined, it may be impractical to recognize revenue at any time other than when it becomes billable. Again, although work in process represents an asset, costs are usually written off to expense as incurred because the asset is of indeterminate value.
- In contrast, when the service activities are well defined and revenue is known or capable of estimation within reasonable limits, an accretion basis of revenue recognition becomes both feasible and the most faithful representation of the activity portrayed. If, for example, the service consists largely of making facilities available for a fee (as in a club or health spa), it makes sense to recognize revenue as earned on a time basis and write off all costs as incurred.
- Some services, such as maintenance and repair of appliances or office equipment, may also be offered for a flat fee for a given contract period. Revenue from service contracts would normally be recognized rateably over the life of the contract in the absence of a better basis of recognition. Common sense should govern, however. For example, if the typical contract term is three years and experience indicates that the costs of repair service tend to increase over the three years, it would be sensible to recognize contract revenue in a rising pattern over its duration.
- In other situations, the service performed may be more variable over time. If revenue tends to vary with direct effort, however, it may be possible to accrue revenue as performance proceeds. In a public accounting firm, for example, if recovery rates per hour can be reasonably estimated, earning activity is fairly portrayed by valuing hours accumulated in work in process at estimated recoverable amounts (allowing an appropriate discount for expected delays in collection) and writing off costs as incurred. In effect, inventory is carried at estimated realizable value. This approach may also be applicable in legal firms and some consulting practices. In situations that are basically similar but where revenue recoveries are more difficult to estimate, the approach may be varied by valuing work in process at a cost rate per hour. Putting some value on work in process, where billing and realization are delayed, is likely to provide a better portrayal of income and financial position than would a system of writing off all costs when incurred and recognizing revenue only when billed.

- In still other situations, services are contracted for in advance covering specified work—for example, architectural or engineering project services. In such cases, accounting that is very similar to that described previously for construction contractors may be followed.
  - When a sales value can be assigned reasonably objectively to specific activities, revenue may be recognized as the activities are performed.
  - Alternatively, the direct costs of contract performance may be accumulated and revenue recognized in the proportion that performance costs to date bear to total estimated cost on the service contract. (Reference is made here to the accumulation of direct costs, whereas in construction contract accounting, a very considerable amount of indirect costs is likely to be accumulated by contracts. The difference may be explained by the facts that (1) in service industries a high proportion of cost will be salary costs that can be treated as direct, and (2) remaining costs are likely to be of a general and administrative nature whose allocation to contracts would be arbitrary at best.) If neither of these approaches is possible but activity is fairly even over the contract period, revenue can be recognized on a simple straight-line approach.
- The usual condition holds that revenue recognition should be postponed if collectibility cannot be estimated with reasonable certainty.

Recognition of gain and loss on peripheral transactions

As noted at the beginning of this chapter, an entity engages from time to time in sales or other transactions that are not part of its normal operations. Such peripheral transactions include the disposition of assets purchased for use and not for resale, liquidation or refinancing of debt, and so on. Since these transactions are not undertaken with a view to satisfying customer needs, the criterion of whether the proceeds have been earned is usually irrelevant. Instead, gain or loss will be recognized using the traditional test of realization, that is, when cash or promises to pay cash are exchanged. (If the consideration is a promise to pay cash, the usual caveat as to collectibility applies.) In some circumstances loss (but not gain) will be recognized even though realization has not taken place.

The fact that recognition of gain or loss takes place at the time of realization may, on occasion, encourage entities to sell assets or extinguish liabilities in order to recognize gains that otherwise would not be reported under the historical cost system. This possibility is an inevitable accompaniment of the historical cost accounting basis. The possibility, however, does give rise to concern that recognition of gain at realization could be used to manipulate reported results. What if a subsequent transaction puts the vendor in exactly the same situation as he was before the sale? What if the sale is consummated in a manner that leaves the vendor exposed to some risks in relation to the property sold?

- One possible means of manipulation is a sale of an asset with execution of a simultaneous repurchase agreement at the sale price. It is clear in such a case that the sale is a sham; there has been no realization in substance and no gain should be recognized. Financial institutions may engage in such sale and repurchase transactions not so much with the aim of recording gains as with the aim of "window dressing" their balance sheets at a period-end to show a more liquid position or a different distribution of assets than that resulting from their actual operations. Although the ability to mislead in this form of window dressing is usually less serious, its patent dishonesty nevertheless makes it objectionable.

- The treatment of gain or loss on extinguishment of debt when such extinguishment is accomplished with the proceeds of a new issue of debt is a question that has divided accountants for many years. Debt refunding may become attractive for various reasons. For example, it may be thought that interest rates will rise in future and therefore extending the maturity date of existing debt is desirable. If interest rates at the date of refunding are below the interest rate on the outstanding debt, a premium will be required to redeem that outstanding debt (in the absence of a right to call it). In such a case, some accountants have felt it erroneous to record a loss on the debt redemption when the refunding operation as such is considered desirable. Moreover, it is pointed out that if the loss were deferred and amortized over the remaining term of the debt redeemed, that amortization, together with the interest costs (at the lower rate) on the new debt, would merely approximate the interest costs that would have been paid had the old issue been left outstanding. Accepted accounting practice on this issue has varied over the years. It is now thought, however, that bygones should be bygones and gain or loss with respect to an issue of debt that is retired should not be deferred.[16]
- In recent years a question has arisen as to accounting for debt extinguished if the debtor retains some obligations with respect to it. Suppose, for example, a debtor is legally released from the primary obligation on real estate debt because that obligation is assumed by the purchaser of mortgaged property, but the original debtor remains secondarily liable. In such a case, it is reasoned that the debtor's position has changed from that of being a direct debtor to that of an entity subject to a contingent liability. Thus, unless the exercise of the guarantee is likely, the debt should be treated as extinguished when the debtor ceases to be primarily liable, and gain or loss on the extinguishment should be recorded.
- A further question has arisen in the United States. Suppose a debtor sets aside securities in trust to meet all obligations with respect to outstanding debt. May the trust assets be offset against the outstanding debt for balance sheet presentation purposes, and may gain be recognized for the difference between the carrying value of the trust securities and the recorded amount of the debt? The FASB has ruled with respect to such "in substance defeasance" that, with proper disclosure, the transaction may be accounted for as though the debt were extinguished; accordingly, gain may be recognized. To qualify for such treatment, however, the chance of the debtor being called upon to make good on the debt, other than from the trust assets, must be remote. To ensure this, the assets must be irrevocably placed in the trust, they must be monetary assets in the same currency as the debt, and they must be essentially risk-free. Also, cash flows from the trust assets must approximately coincide in timing and amount with scheduled interest and principal payments on the debt.[17]

- Companies in certain types of industries, in the course of their business, build up portfolios of amounts receivable that are collectible in instalments with interest. Such companies may wish, from time to time, to sell such portfolios for the purpose of freeing up cash for other investment, often retaining an obligation to administer and collect the amounts receivable. Provided that servicing costs of the portfolio are adequately covered by a separate fee arrangement or by an allocation of the purchase price to that end and provided the purchaser has no recourse against the vendor under guarantees of the amounts receivable, it is clear that the sale of a portfolio can be regarded as a completed transaction and gain or loss recorded. What, however, is the position if the purchaser does have recourse to the vendor should some of the receivables prove uncollectible? The FASB has ruled that such a sale with recourse should be treated as a realized transaction under certain conditions. These are that the transferor does not have an option to repurchase the receivables nor the purchaser a right to resell them (other than under the recourse provision), and that the transferor can reasonably estimate the allowance required for uncollectible amounts. A sale is to be recognized even if the sale price is subject to change by a provision in the contract tying the purchaser's effective income to a floating interest rate.[18] If these conditions are not fulfilled, however, the transaction is not to be treated as a sale, and the proceeds paid by the purchaser are to be treated as loan financing.

Two of the FASB recommendations seem questionable or likely to be difficult to apply. When the purchase price of receivables with recourse is structured so that the purchaser is guaranteed a floating rate of interest, it is questionable that the sales price should be considered as known. Indeed, rather than giving up the risks associated with the accounts receivable, the vendor appears to have taken on the risk of changes in the interest rate. The "in substance defeasance" recommendations seem more supportable in theory. The practical requirement that the trust assets be essentially risk-free, however, means that a very little difference in the quality of the security available can make the difference between recognition and nonrecognition of gain. It is doubtful that what is really a very selective application of current value accounting represents an improvement on a consistent application of the realization test.

Summary

In the early days of the historical cost accounting model, revenue recognition did not present serious problems. The basic idea that revenue should be recognized only when realized—that is, when an exchange transaction was consummated in which the consideration was a liquid monetary asset—seemed capable of dealing with the vast majority of situations. Recognition of revenue with respect to a single contract extending over a long period of time was considered a special case that could be dealt with by a special approach—percentage-of-completion accounting.

As the variety in forms of business organization has grown, experience has shown that several revenue recognition approaches are needed to permit faithful representation of business activity. The criteria governing when each approach should be adopted are, in some respects, still unclear. The following are the main ideas.

Three possible approaches may be taken to revenue recognition: the critical event approach, the revenue accretion approach, and the revenue allocation approach. The approach that is taken in practice is significantly influenced by the point in the cycle of productive activity at which a revenue contract is entered into.

When a sale contract is not made until most productive effort has taken place, revenue is ordinarily recognized at the time of a "critical event." The criteria governing the selection of that critical event are that it should represent the time when the significant risks and rewards from ownership of the asset sold have been transferred to the purchaser and that there is not significant remaining uncertainty as to the consummation of the sale, collectibility of the consideration, or remaining costs to be incurred to fulfill the vendor's obligations. Normally that critical event is the point of delivery by the vendor under a sales contract, provided there is little doubt as to acceptance by the customer. Other critical event recognition points are used in a minority of cases.

Measurement of the amount of revenue recognized follows the standard procedure for transaction measurement—that is, revenue should be recognized at its cash value equivalent at the date of recognition.

If some costs required to fulfill a contract obligation will be incurred after the critical event recognition point, a liability for them must be accrued in order to provide a proper measure of income. Indeed, when major efforts remain to take place after an initial revenue recognition point, it would probably be better to follow the revenue allocation approach, allocating the total contract revenue between an amount to be recognized at the initial recognition point (such as sale) and a remainder to be recognized upon completion of the subsequent activities or as they are performed, in accordance with the circumstances.

Great uncertainty as to consummation of sales transactions, collectibility of proceeds, or amount of future costs to be incurred to satisfy post-sales obligations causes postponement of the critical event or deferment of the net income recorded on the sale. If the amount of returns or future costs is unpredictable but could be large, the critical event should be postponed. If the uncertainty relates to future collectibility, the sale may be recognized but its income results deferred, to be recognized subsequently on the instalment or cost-recovery basis.

When a sale contract is settled before an extended production or service process, great uncertainty as to costs may lead to postponement of revenue recognition until some subsequent critical event (such as completion of the work—the completed contract basis of recognition). Frequently, however, it will be preferable to recognize some revenue as work proceeds, either on the accretion approach or the revenue allocation approach.

The accretion approach may be used when revenue can be related to some reasonable indicators of progress. Such indicators may consist of output measures, in which case it is necessary to be able to relate costs incurred to the several outputs. Indicators may also be input measures—measures of effort or costs. When these are used, the contract revenue is recognized in proportion to the percentage of inputs accomplished up to the reporting date to the total expected consumption of inputs.

The revenue allocation approach requires the identification of several functions covered by the single contract price and allocation of some revenue to each function. The revenue allocated to each function is recognized as earned either on the critical event basis or the accretion basis, as seems most appropriate. Ideally, the amount of revenue allocated to each function is based on prices for the function if it were performed independently. If such prices are not available, the allocation becomes based more on judgment. One expedient is to allocate to minor functions only sufficient revenue to cover costs traceable to performance of those functions.

Treatment of an initial fee charged when a continuing relationship is set up with a customer depends upon the circumstances. When the initial fee is for identifiable services and is reasonable in amount, it may be recognized as though it were a separate revenue transaction. In other cases, the initial fee may be a separate charge that simply provides additional revenue to cover continuing service cost. In such cases, the fee, if not refundable, can be recognized as revenue over the estimated service period for the customer or club member in question. In still other cases, an initial fee may cover some specific services but may be unreasonably high in relation to the value of those services, so that it appears, in substance, to be merely a different way of charging for continuing services. If the fee for continuing services does not appear to be adequate compensation, some or all of the initial fee should be deferred for amortization against revenue recognized over the estimated period of continuing service.

Revenue from property owned, such as interest and dividends on securities, royalties, and rentals, is recognized on different bases, depending on the circumstances. Revenue from interest and rentals, for example, is recognized on the accretion approach in proportion to time elapsed. Revenue from dividends is recognized on a critical event basis—the event being the declaration of the dividend. Revenue from royalties is recognized as it accrues in accordance with the terms of the rental agreement.

References

[1]This proposition is demonstrated by R.K. Storey, "Cash Movements and Periodic Income Determination," in *Financial Accounting Theory: Issues and Controversies*, ed. S.A. Zeff and T.F. Keller (New York: McGraw-Hill Book Co., 1964), pp. 46-53. Storey points out that the proposition is true only if profit is deemed satisfactorily measured by the net increment in cash. If profit were deemed to be the excess of purchasing power received over purchasing power invested and prices were not stable over the period of measurement, the proposition would no longer be true.

[2]American Institute of Accountants, Committee on Accounting Procedure, "Rules Adopted by Membership," Chapter 1A in *Restatement and Revision of Accounting Research Bulletins*, Accounting Research Bulletin No. 43 (New York: AIA, 1953), par. 1.

[3]AICPA, APB, *Basic Concepts and Accounting Principles Underlying Financial Statements of Business Enterprises*, APB Statement No. 4 (New York: AICPA, 1970), par. 150.

[4]The term "critical event" was coined in an article by J.H. Myers, "The Critical Event and Recognition of Net Profit," reprinted in *Financial Accounting Theory*, ed. Zeff and Keller, pp. 54-59. Myers proposed criteria for identification of the point of revenue recognition, but these have not been adopted in accounting standards.

[5]See FASB, *Revenue Recognition When Right of Return Exists*, Statement of Financial Accounting Standards No. 48 (Stamford: FASB, 1981). SFAS 48 emphasizes as well the requirement that risks in connection with the property sold be effectively transferred.

[6]See AICPA, *Accounting for Performance of Construction-Type and Certain Production-Type Contracts,* Accounting Standards Division Statement of Position No. 81-1 (New York: AICPA, 1981), especially pars. 23-25. This statement provides a very useful discussion of all aspects of contract accounting.

[7]AICPA, Committee on Finance Companies, *Audits of Finance Companies,* Industry Audit Guide (New York: AICPA, 1973).

[8]AICPA, Committee on Savings and Loan Associations, *Savings and Loan Associations,* rev. ed., Audit and Accounting Guide (New York· AICPA, 1979).

[9]In American practice, cable TV hook-up revenue is recognized only to the extent that it reflects direct selling costs. Any remainder of the hook-up charge is deferred to be amortized over the estimated average lifetime of a subscriber connection. Initial subscriber installation costs are capitalized and depreciated in a normal fashion. Costs of disconnecting and reconnecting are charged to expense when incurred. See FASB Statement of Financial Accounting Standards No. 51, *Financial Reporting by Cable Television Companies* (Stamford: FASB, 1981).

[10]See CICA Accounting Guideline, "Franchise Fee Revenue," July 1984, in *CICA Handbook* (Toronto: CICA). See also FASB, *Accounting for Franchise Fee Revenue,* Statement of Financial Accounting Standards No. 45 (Stamford: FASB, 1981).

[11]See IASC, *Revenue Recognition,* International Accounting Standard No. 18 (London: IASC, 1982).

[12]Canadian Institute of Public Real Estate Companies, *Recommended Accounting Practices for Real Estate Companies,* 2nd ed. (Toronto: CIPREC, 1980). Reference should also be made to National Policy No. 5 of Canadian securities regulatory authorities, entitled *Recognition of Profits in Real Estate Transactions.*

[13]See CICA Research Study, *Accounting for Real Estate Development Operations* (Toronto: CICA, 1971).

[14]See FASB, *Accounting for Sales of Real Estate,* Statement of Financial Accounting Standards No. 66 (Stamford: FASB, 1982).

[15]See FASB Invitation to Comment, *Accounting for Certain Service Transactions* (Stamford: FASB, October 23, 1978).

[16]AICPA, APB, *Early Extinguishment of Debt,* APB Opinion No. 26 (New York: AICPA, 1972).

[17]FASB, *Extinguishment of Debt: An Amendment of APB Opinion No. 26,* Statement of Financial Accounting Standards No. 76 (Stamford: FASB, 1983).

[18]FASB, *Reporting by Transferors for Transfers of Receivables with Recourse,* Statement of Financial Accounting Standards No. 77 (Stamford: FASB, 1983).

Chapter Nine

Expense Recognition; Accrued Liabilities; Contingencies; Non-cash Executive Compensation

In the previous chapter we introduced the subject of periodic income measurement by reviewing accounting standards for recognition of revenue as earned. In this chapter we begin consideration of standards for matching expenditures with revenues (or with accounting periods) in order to arrive at a net period income figure. To put that in another way, we are about to address the subject of recognition of "expense."

Let us begin with some comments on terminology.

- In a purchase transaction, the purchaser gives "consideration" in exchange for the goods or services acquired. The consideration represents the sacrifice in the transaction, which may consist of payment of money or the giving up of some other valuable commodity or the assumption of a liability.
- The term "cost" represents the value of the consideration given. In a fair exchange it may be presumed that it will also approximate the value of the thing acquired. Cost is also used in somewhat different senses. For example, in addition to the sense of acquisition cost, it may be used to mean manufactured cost, that is, the sum of acquisition costs of material, labour, and overhead that is deemed (by the costing system in use) to be required to produce a commodity.
- The term "expenditure" is used to describe a purchase transaction. To make an expenditure is to make a payment of cash or equivalent or to incur a contractual liability. Expenditure is often used almost interchangeably with cost to mean the value of consideration.
- The term "expense" refers to the consumption of the benefit obtained from goods or services owned. In historical cost accounting, expense is measured by the cost of the goods or services consumed (cost being used in the sense of acquisition cost or manufactured cost, as the case may be). Cost can also be used in a third sense (that is, in addition to the two already mentioned) to mean the same thing as expense. Thus we may speak of cost of operations for a period instead of expense for a period.

In this chapter we shall use "expenditure" to mean the act of consummating a purchase of goods or services. When the word "cost" is used, the sense in which it is used will be apparent from the context.

Expenditures are made to acquire benefits in the form of goods or services. With a few exceptions (expenditure on land is one), the benefits received from expenditures are sooner or later entirely consumed. As those benefits are consumed we wish to recognize expense. The benefits received from the majority of expenditures will be consumed either at the time of or subsequent to the transaction. There are a number of cases, however, when an entity will receive and consume benefits in return for an obligation to make future expenditures. In such cases expense must be recognized at the time of benefit consumption, and a figure representing the obligation is "accrued" in the balance sheet. These considerations have significance for the meaning we attach to the word "liability" in accounting.

Chapter 6 has indicated that a liability is recognized by one party to a transaction when the other party has performed part or all of his obligation without receiving the consideration contracted for. In addition, as just noted, there are occasions when an entity will receive benefits in return for obligations that are not yet contractual liabilities to known parties. For example, a company undertaking a quarrying operation might be required, as a condition of its licence to operate, to rehabilitate the site of operations after completion of quarrying. Such an undertaking to make future expenditures is a liability for accounting purposes just as much as is a contractual liability. The key question is when such a liability and the related expense should be recognized. In the case of the quarrying operation, the probable future cost can be regarded as the cost of a licence to do business that accrues over the lifetime of the project. In more general terms, we can say that future obligations attributable to business being done and the related expense are to be accrued (recognized) as the benefit in exchange for the undertaking (the benefit being the right to do business in our quarrying example) is received.

Upon occasion, also, an entity discovers it has or may have an obligation to make payments, which may or may not be attributable to specific aspects of its operations, but which were not previously foreseen. Although the obligation, in some sense, must have arisen out of operations prior to the date of discovery, no benefit from the payment will be discernible at the time of discovery. When recognized, therefore, the amount charged against income does not represent an expense recognized in relation to benefit consumed, but simply a loss. The obligation to make payment is also a liability for accounting purposes but, to the extent it is uncertain, it is customarily known as a contingent liability.

In this chapter we wish to discuss standards for recognition of expenses and unforeseen losses. We shall divide our discussion into three sections:

- Recognition of expense and liability with respect to expenditures made to acquire goods and services. Our discussion in this chapter will be general. In chapters 10 to 12 we shall delve more thoroughly into the subjects of inventory accounting, fixed asset accounting, intangible asset accounting, and expense recognition with respect to those assets.
- Recognition of expense and accrued liabilities with respect to obligations that entail future expenditures. We shall discuss some examples in this chapter but reserve detailed exploration of the complex issues in pension accounting for chapter 13.
- Recognition of loss and liabilities with respect to obligations arising out of past operations that were unforeseen at the time the operations were going on.

We shall end the chapter with discussion of an unsolved issue in expense recognition—that is, the question of how to account for employee compensation in the form of stock options or their equivalent.

Expenditures to acquire goods and services

Recognition of expense with respect to goods and services acquired involves several decisions. These are: (1) the subdivision of expenditure amounts between "period costs" and costs attaching to assets, (2) the selection of "cost objects" to be recorded as assets, (3) the choice of methods for attaching costs to assets, and (4) the choice of methods for measuring expense to be recognized with respect to assets sold or assets whose usefulness has otherwise expired.

Recognition of expense for period costs

The first decision occurs at the time an expenditure takes place. Some expenditures, such as sales commissions, will be clearly applicable to revenue currently being recognized as earned and thus should be recorded as expense immediately. Most other expenditures will be undertaken in the hope and expectation of contributing to future revenue. Ideally, all costs in such transactions would be carried forward as costs of identifiable product or service projects and be recognized as expense when revenue therefrom is recognized. Unfortunately, this ideal is unattainable for several practical reasons. For example, planning and research activities, although clearly applicable to hoped-for future revenue, may well not be capable of association with existing products or service categories. In this situation, there is likely to be much less assurance that these expenditures will benefit future operations. In addition, many services acquired, such as administrative services, although necessary, have a very indirect connection with specific earned revenues. Finally, many expenditures will have transitory benefits and will be recurrent in nature, so that expense figures reported for a going concern will be very little different if they are written off as incurred, rather than deferred and matched with earned revenues on some more precise basis. For these several reasons—uncertainty of future benefit, remoteness from direct productive activity, or short-lived character of benefit—it is accepted that many expenditures should be recognized as expense as soon as incurred. The costs involved are known as "period costs" because they are written off in the period they are incurred.

In addition to outlays with transitory or uncertain benefits, there is a class of expenditures from which clear benefit may be perceived over a future period but which should nevertheless be written off when incurred. For example, many companies in the early 1980s adopted early retirement plans whereby employees were offered incentives to retire within a certain period. It was easy to see future benefit from this policy—reduction in payroll costs after the retirement, reducing the drag of older employees on productivity, greater flexibility in promotion policy, and so on. Yet the costs of the program should be recognized as expense immediately, rather than be deferred.[1] The benefit that the entity gains from the program lies in the liquidation of an obligation it has to existing employees. The cost of paying someone not to work is not a positive contribution to future operations.

There is a simple test to distinguish whether such an expenditure relates to the future or the past. If a new company would not have to make the same expenditure as an existing company, the latter's cost is a legacy from the past, not an investment in the future. Ideally, it should have been accrued over the service period of the employees taking early retirement. Since it was not, it must be written off when it finally becomes clear that it will be incurred.

Selection of cost objects

If an expenditure is not to be recognized as a period cost, a second decision arises. The cost in question must be associated with some cost object that will be recorded as an asset. The question is: What are the criteria that guide the selection of cost objects?

- The most obvious cost object, of course, is a tangible good to be sold or wrought into a good to be sold in future.
- Where the product of the business is service rather than a tangible good, it may still be possible, if costs can be associated with particular revenue contracts, to record an asset category similar in nature to tangible inventory. Thus a consulting engineering or architectural firm may accumulate salary costs as contract work in process for specific jobs or clients.
- Other tangible goods may be acquired for use rather than for sale. Plant and equipment or inventories of supplies are examples. Rarely is there doubt that the cost of such items may be treated as an asset and carried forward for matching against future revenues.
- Payments are often made to suppliers of goods or services in advance of the receipt of those items. The fact that something is yet to be received ordinarily justifies the treatment of prepayments (prepaid insurance, prepaid rent, etc.) as assets.
- Sometimes purchases consist of intangible property such as a licence or legal right. If the intangible is well defined and benefit from its use can be controlled, it is just as clearly a potential source of future revenue as any tangible productive asset like machinery and equipment.
- If, however, the cost incurred does not give rise to a well-defined contractual or property right, the case is more doubtful. Consider costs incurred for advertising and promotion. Undoubtedly the expenditure is incurred in the hope that future revenue will be enhanced. But how successful will the promotion be? And how long will the benefit last? The fuzziness of the matching concept is epitomized by the name given to such intangible cost objects. When carried forward, they are called simply "deferred costs" rather than by a name, like plant and equipment or prepayments or patent rights, that independently describes what the nature of the asset is.

Deferred costs provide the best example of the problem of allocation of expenditures to periods of benefit. In principle there is no difference, for the purpose of income measurement, between the cost of a tangible asset that contributes to the production of future revenue and any other expenditure that has the same result. Yet accountants are instinctively wary of treating the latter as assets. The primary reason for this is the uncertainty as to the extent to which such expenditures will produce revenue. To lessen that concern, some accountants have advocated that costs be carried forward only with respect to assets that are severable from the enterprise.

Costing of assets

After the selection of cost objects is settled, there remains the problem of assignment of costs to the cost objects. For something acquired in an exchange transaction, the cost is simply the sacrifice made in the exchange. In most cases that sacrifice can be measured in terms of the amount payable in the transaction. As we have seen already, however, if the transaction does not require immediate payment of cash, the proper measure of the cost or sacrifice is the cash-equivalent price that would be required at the acquisition date.

This uncomplicated concept of cost does not carry through to the "cost" of an asset emerging from a production process. The accountant thinks of the cost of a manufactured product as being the sum of the acquisition costs of all its components. That description begs the question of what are the components of a manufactured product. Some costs, such as raw materials, are traceable directly to individual units of product. Some costs vary in amount with the volume of production but cannot be traced directly to individual products. Some costs are required to provide productive capacity but are fixed in amount even though the volume of production varies quite widely. In general, only a minority of costs are traceable directly to units of product, and other costs must be *allocated* on some basis to provide a figure of cost per unit of product.

For accounting purposes, the historical cost of an asset that is fabricated rather than purchased outright in an exchange transaction is the sum of the acquisition costs of the components deemed to have entered into the asset under the costing system in force. Obviously the significance of such a figure of cost depends upon the validity of the costing system. Possible costing elements are reviewed below.

- For tangible goods there is always the cost of materials embodied in the good. Although the actual material embodied represents an absolute minimum cost figure, there may be a question whether the cost of scrap material resulting from trimming or production errors should be included as part of the cost of the good. Possibly an allowance for a standard amount of scrap may be counted as part of the product cost with any excess being treated as expense. In some instances there is a further problem when a single source of raw material eventually gives rise to a number of products. Examples of such "joint" products include a variety of refined products derived from crude oil, a number of metals obtained from complex ore bodies, and various cuts of meat, hides, and other products obtained from a single animal slaughtered. In all these cases, as soon as more than a single output emerges from the production process, material costs cannot be traced to individual outputs because tracing the costs to a product involves a one-to-many allocation.
- Labour that is directly expended in fabrication of a product can be visualized as embodied in it, just as are materials. The direct costs of material and labour are known as "prime costs," as distinguished from other costs of production known as "overhead costs."
- Certain types of overhead costs tend to vary with the volume of production, while other types are relatively fixed in amount over a considerable range of production. Still others may be described as "semivariable"—that is, they may have both fixed and variable components, or they may increase in steps at given volume points but remain relatively constant between steps.

If the amount of a given cost is highly correlated with the quantity of production, that is evidence that the cost is caused by the act of production and therefore can legitimately be counted as a product cost. Moreover, the higher the correlation with production volume, the more likely it is that reasonable ways can be found to trace the costs to the product.

- Fixed overhead costs are often described as "capacity costs," in that the cost is incurred in order to provide the facilities or capacity to produce or render service, while additional variable costs must ordinarily be incurred to make the product. Some capacity costs, such as the cost of plant and equipment, may be described as "sunk costs" or unavoidable costs since, once incurred, they are unalterable. Other capacity costs, such as regular maintenance costs or rentals, are recurring and may be more controllable. By definition, fixed costs cannot be traced to the output of production processes. As a consequence, if they are to be attached to cost objects such as inventory or self-constructed fixed assets, some relatively arbitrary allocation basis must be found.
- Overhead costs are customarily classified as manufacturing, selling, and general and administrative costs. In principle, the attachment of costs to cost objects should not depend on how the cost is described but rather on whether a relationship can be established between it and the cost object. In practice, however, it is usually assumed that a cost that is described as general and administrative is inherently indirect and cannot reasonably be associated with such cost objects as inventory or self-constructed fixed assets. Occasional exceptions to this rule are justified, for example, in accumulating costs applicable to contracts in process where the contract price specifically allows for recovery of general and administrative costs.
- Thus far, only costs incurred in consideration for the acquisition of goods or services have been described. These are distinguishable by their nature from costs of financing or cost of capital, that is, from payments made or other rewards given to suppliers of capital for the use of their funds. In accounting (with the exception of regulated industries), only costs associated with outstanding debt are treated as "financing costs." Such financing costs include not only interest at the stipulated rate but also amortization of costs of issue and premium or discount in the issue price of the debt.

What then are the criteria that are, or ought to be, used to attach costs to cost objects? The most obvious criterion is that of causation. If it can be shown that a cost had to be incurred to produce the cost object, then it is logical that such cost should be deemed to be a cost *of* the object. The strength of the demonstration that a cost had to be incurred, however, varies with the circumstances. In some cases—for example, the prime costs of material and direct labour—we can observe that the cost is necessary to the product, for without it there is no product. When it can be shown that a given cost varies in step with the volume of production, the proof of a causal connection is also strong. In the usual case, however, a given cost (for example, power) contributes to a variety of products; hence, it is difficult to allocate the cost incurred among individual units of product. Often the problem can be lessened by making additional measurements (for example, metering power usage by production runs). It then becomes a cost/benefit question whether the additional measurement is worthwhile. Usually a basis of allocation can be found that represents an acceptable compromise between accuracy in tracing and cost of tracing.

When a cost does not vary with volume of output, the problem becomes much more difficult. Simple reasoning may tell us that costs of capacity to produce must precede production, so that one can say the former is caused by the latter. Because the cost precedes production, however, there is no measuring device that can establish direct causation between the output and the capacity cost, and there is no way to demonstrate how much of the capacity cost is caused by individual products. Where causation cannot be traced, it cannot be used to guide the allocation of cost to the product, and some other basis of allocation must be used. Two general bases are found. Frequently allocations are based on some indicator of intensity of activity—such as direct labour cost, hours worked, or machine hours consumed. Less frequently allocation may be based on value of output—as when joint costs are allocated in proportion to the selling price or net contribution margin of the products.

Two major issues have arisen as to techniques of attaching costs to cost objects. First, there is the question whether costs allocated to a given object should be restricted to variable costs (direct costing), or whether they should include an allocated portion of fixed overhead costs (absorption costing or full costing). Second, there is the question whether financing costs may, in any circumstances, be attributed to a cost object. In practice, the answer to both these questions is "it depends." That answer will be discussed in greater detail in subsequent chapters.

Recognition of expense as assets are consumed

Once costs are attached to cost objects, some system must be in place to recognize expense as the benefit from the asset is consumed. With respect to product costs there must be a partitioning of costs between those applicable to revenue currently being recognized and those applicable to revenue yet to be recognized. In the ordinary case of sale of goods, this means that costs must be identified with goods as they are produced, so that subsequently there can be a division between cost of goods sold and cost of goods still on hand.

In the case of tangible or intangible capital assets held for use rather than sale, there is no periodic disposition of part of the asset to provide a basis for distinguishing between costs to be written off and costs that retain their asset status. Because of this, some scheme of amortization of assets' costs must be adopted to portray the periodic consumption of their usefulness. That scheme will inevitably be arbitrary but is supposed to meet the test of being "systematic and rational." The same test applies to the write-off of deferred costs. What appears to be systematic and rational will depend on the circumstances.

Costs carried forward as prepayments are simply written off as the service that has been prepaid is received.

The reduction of asset valuations by depreciation, amortization, or reduction of amounts prepaid is not necessarily synonymous with recognition of expense in the period of write-off. The amounts written off may be classified as overhead costs that will, under the costing system in force, be allocated to cost of inventory or other assets currently being produced. Eventually, however, all costs incurred for assets with limited economic life must be recognized as expense in some period.

Recognition of accrued liabilities and related expense

Recognition of expense with respect to costs to be incurred in future arising out of current operations can present severe measurement problems. Sometimes the problem is one of estimating how many people will qualify for future payment. For example, this question arises with respect to pension or other employee benefits that are payable only if employees survive or fulfill certain vesting conditions. Costs to be recorded depend on estimation of probabilities and thus often will be calculated by actuaries. Sometimes the problem also involves estimates of the future costs of making good on the obligation. Thus, estimates of future warranty costs require not only estimates of how many claims will be made but also estimates of the cost of repairing or otherwise making good on the claims. Engineering judgment may be required in these estimates. Sometimes estimates are required of major work that must be done in future—for example, making good the environmental damage resulting from current operations. Estimates of such future costs may be based on previous experience but can be very difficult when extensive experience is lacking, as in the case of decommissioning costs for nuclear reactors.

Various references in accounting literature suggest that where the probable amount of future costs cannot be "reasonably estimated," a liability need not be formally recorded. Instead, disclosure is to be made of the existence of the liability where material. This state of affairs is rather unsatisfactory. First, the decision whether an amount can be reasonably estimated is subjective, and there is danger that judgment might be biased by a desire to omit liabilities in order to present a better picture of financial condition. Second, the omission of any estimate of a material liability necessarily means that reported income and shareholders' equity are misstated. If the liability actually exists, the one thing that is known for sure is that its amount is not zero.

Two important conceptual questions affect the amount of expense and accrual to be recognized in any particular case. First, there is the question whether the amount of expected future costs should be discounted to a present value at the reporting date. Second, one must consider the impact of inflation on estimates of costs to be incurred in future. Should the expense today reflect estimated future costs expressed in nominal dollars that are expected to have a very different purchasing power from that of today's dollar? These two questions are interrelated.

Discounting the liability

When an obligation will not need to be satisfied until some time in the future, it is natural to ask whether the estimated cost of that obligation should be discounted when it is first recognized in the accounts. It was noted earlier that discounting is required in measuring purchase or sale transactions carrying delayed payment terms. The same logic supports the application of a discount factor to amounts of future costs to be recognized in connection with current operations. Except in the case of pension cost accounting, however, this refinement has not been widely adopted. The period to maturity of many accruals, of course, is sufficiently short that the discount factor is unimportant.

If an accrual of future cost is to be discounted when first recognized, a discount rate must be selected. A rate of interest accessible to the entity through borrowing could be selected on the basis that incurring an obligation to be liquidated in future is in effect the same as borrowing. In the alternative, one might reason that the cost to be accrued currently should not be greater than the sum that, invested in a sinking fund, would compound to equal the amount due at maturity. The indicated interest rate, then, would be that which could be earned on a safe investment. Whatever the rate selected, the liability initially recognized on a discounted basis would have to be accreted at that rate until maturity to cover the estimated cost at that time.

Allowing for price changes in future cost provisions

In some cases, future costs to be incurred will be determined by a formula so that the amount of cost is fixed in terms of a dollar amount. In many situations, however, there will be no formula. The cost will simply be the amount required to perform certain services or to complete a particular project. Any proper estimate of that cost must take into account inflationary impacts on costs between the recognition date and the maturity date. The difficulty is that an accurate forecast of inflation or of specific price changes over any extended period of time is hard to achieve.

Consider a hypothetical example. Operations today result in an obligation to perform specified work five years hence. If that work were performed today it would cost $1 million. At a current market rate of interest of, say, 10%, the present value of $1 million five years hence is only about $621,000. However, because of expected inflation the cost will probably be much more five years hence. If the amount of expense recognized today is only $621,000 and that amount is accreted at 10%, the accrued liability after five years will be only $1 million. By that time the cost to discharge the obligation might have risen to, say, $1,340,000 (a figure implying an annual rate of price increase of about 6%). Clearly the initial expense recognized is inadequate in this case. If the obligation is to be discounted using a market rate of interest, the future cost must be estimated at the number of dollars it will take to discharge it at future cost levels, not present cost levels.

The trouble with this is that many people are reluctant to estimate the cost of work to be done some considerable time in the future. They may well object: That future cost will depend upon the rate of inflation between now and then, and who can forecast that? They might even go so far as to argue that the future cost cannot be "reasonably estimated," and therefore nothing should be accrued.

Fortunately, an expedient is available to avoid such an irrational result. A well-established theory in economics holds that the actual interest rate at any particular time represents a combination of a "real" interest rate and the anticipated rate of inflation over the term for which the nominal interest rate is quoted. Thus if the annual interest rate is 10% and the anticipated annual inflation rate is 6% a year, the real interest rate may be calculated as 1.10/1.06 − 1 = 0.037736 or 3.77%. An accountant faced with an argument that it is impossible to estimate future costs may ask instead for an estimate of the cost that would be incurred if the obligation were discharged immediately. In our example that estimate would be $1 million. The accountant would then discount that figure at 3.77% and recognize as expense the present value of about $831,000. Subsequently that figure would be accreted at the nominal interest rate of 10%. This would arrive at an accrued obligation figure of about $1,340,000 five years hence.

This expedient may appear to be a trick done with smoke and mirrors, and to some extent it is. The onus is transferred to the accountant to make an assumption as to inflation expectations (in this example 6%) in order to derive the estimated "real" rate of interest of 3.77%. In the absence of indexed securities trading in the market there will be no extrinsic evidence as to the real rate of interest; only the nominal rate of interest can be observed. Nevertheless, there have been economic studies that have estimated the historical medium-to-long-term interest rates in Canada as being in the neighbourhood of 3%. This approximate level is borne out by British government experience with the issuance of indexed bonds. Thus the accountant is not completely without a basis for selection of the real interest rate to be used. In any event, it would be far better accounting to make an accrual for future costs based on discounting at almost any reasonable estimate of real interest rates than it would be to ignore the liability altogether. In addition, as the obligation comes closer to maturity it is always possible to modify the amount of the accrual as its probable ultimate amount becomes less uncertain.

This basic approach could be extended to more complex situations, but it is beyond the scope of this book to discuss them in depth.

Accounting practice in accruals of future costs

Despite the undisputed theory of historical cost accounting requiring expense recognition and liability accrual for future payments or sacrifices attributable to the earning process up to the financial reporting date, practice has almost always lagged in making the necessary accruals. Sometimes the explanation is that no one seriously thinks of the financial consequences at the time that new obligations are undertaken or imposed. Initially, also, it may be clear that the amounts of accruals would be immaterial in any event. Hence, expenses are accounted for on the cash basis because it is easier to do so, and because it makes little difference to the financial position and results reported. Subsequently, as the business grows, the unaccounted-for liability may become more material in the balance sheet. Even then, it may still be possible to argue that since the increase in the liability in any given year is immaterial to income reported, it need not be accrued.

Finally, when the undisclosed liability becomes uncomfortably large, it is possible for a business to look at the financial reports of other companies, ascertain that they too do not accrue for the same type of obligation and, therefore, argue that it is "generally accepted" to account for such obligation on a cash basis, no matter what accounting theory says. In that situation, the only effective way to rectify accounting practice across the board is to have accounting standard-setters address the issue and state that the cash basis of accounting for the cost in question should no longer be considered acceptable. Unfortunately, by that time many companies have a strong vested interest in nondisclosure of the accumulated obligation, and many imaginative arguments may be made as to why the liability cannot be accurately estimated, how costly it will be to account for it on the accrual basis, or what serious economic consequences will follow from any requirement to implement proper accrual accounting.

Warranty costs. An early example of the failure to apply accrual accounting in a new situation is provided by warranty obligations. When products were simple and the rule of "caveat emptor" prevailed in commercial practice, costs of product claims after sale were small. Gradually, however, companies began introducing product warranties, first in the area of consumer durables and then more broadly.

The legal background also gradually changed to provide more protection to buyers, so that today few suppliers of goods are not at risk with respect to future claims for inadequate product quality. Some companies made provision for estimated future warranty costs as soon as they adopted a formal warranty policy. Others did not, and the failure was widespread throughout the 1940s and later. Over a long period of time, however, accrual accounting for warranty costs gained ground, so that today we can say that provision for warranty obligations is required both by accounting theory and generally accepted practice. In this case, the universal practice is to base the provision on estimates of future costs, not discounted.

Project obligations. Costly obligations to be performed some considerable time in the future have already been mentioned. Two examples are the obligation of a strip-mining operation to restore the environment after completion of mining and the obligation of an electricity generating utility to dismantle a nuclear power plant at the end of its service period. In both instances it is clear that the future cost is attributable to the minerals or energy produced over the lifetime of the operation. Not to accrue for that cost over that lifetime would seriously misstate the profitability of the operation. Moreover, in the case of the electrical utility it would lay the burden of those costs not on the customers who benefited from the service, but on future generations of customers or (in a privately owned utility) on the shareholders.[2]

Employee benefits. Several questions in liability accounting have originated with fringe benefits promised to employees. A long-standing example is provided by vacation pay. Long before there were any legal requirements on the subject, many companies adopted policies of providing paid vacations to employees who met minimum service requirements and were still employed at the time that vacations might be taken. For companies with a calendar year-end and a vacation qualification year stretching from, say, May 1 to April 30, that meant that many employees had earned, through their service to the fiscal year-end, the greater part of the vacations to which they would become entitled the following May 1.

It could be argued, of course, that if an employee does not continue in service until the following April 30 she will receive nothing, and therefore there is no liability at the preceding December 31. The other view is that the vacation policy was adopted by the employer as part of the employee compensation package. The employee earns her vacation by service throughout the vacation qualification year; therefore, the liability should be accrued over that period. The fact that some employees may not qualify for vacation because of subsequent termination does not mean that a vacation liability is not accruing. An allowance for vacations that will not be taken can be built into the calculation of the accrual. That is, the problem is one of measurement of the liability, not a question whether a liability exists. In past practice, some companies accounted for vacation pay on an accrual basis but many accounted for it only on a cash basis—probably because it was considered immaterial, but possibly also because of a belief that it was not a recordable liability.

In 1980 the FASB addressed the issue of accounting for payments for "compensated absences." By this term the board meant to include all payments by employers to employees for periods in which the employee did not render service, such as vacation periods, periods when the employee was absent because of illness, and paid holidays.[3] The board, in essence, confirmed the description of an accounting liability set out earlier. The employer's obligation to pay for such compensated absences should be accrued if (1) the employee had a right because of service rendered up to the financial reporting date to receive compensation while absent for some reason in the future, and (2) the earned right could be carried forward to one or more future periods or had vested in the employee or might vest in future.

Benefits to retired employees. In recent years many employers have adopted policies, formal or informal, of providing welfare benefits for retired employees such as dental or medical benefits or death benefits. Unless administered in conjunction with a company pension plan, the cost of such benefits has, to date, almost always been recorded on a cash basis rather than an accrual basis. Since it is clear that benefits to retired employees must be attributable to service performed before retirement, it would seem on the face of it that accrual accounting should be performed for such benefits, just as it is for pension benefits. An estimate of cost on a full accrual basis for benefits commonly offered in the United States was in excess of five percent of payroll, compared with costs that might be recognized on a cash basis in the early stages of such plans in the neighbourhood of one percent of payroll.[4] (In Canada, the availability of medical coverage under government plans should mean that the problem of postretirement welfare benefits is less severe than in the United States, although no studies are available to confirm this.) At the time of writing, the FASB has the issue of postretirement welfare benefits on its active agenda and as an interim step has required disclosure of details concerning these benefits.[5]

Finally, the subject of employer accounting for costs and liabilities under pension obligations has been a difficult one for many years. The issues are so complex that the subject deserves a chapter to itself. (See chapter 13.)

Recognition of loss on unforeseen liabilities

Occasionally an entity becomes subject to a liability that is completely unforeseen. Formal recognition of such a liability requires recognition of a loss as well (although occasionally the loss may be recoverable from some third party). Standards for accounting for such unforeseen losses are known under the title of accounting for contingencies. As will be seen in the following discussion, the concept of a contingency is not very clearly defined.

The meaning of a contingency

The Canadian definition of a contingency is as follows:

> *A contingency is defined as an existing condition or situation involving uncertainty as to possible gain or loss to an enterprise that will ultimately be resolved when one or more future events occur or fail to occur. Resolution of the uncertainty may confirm the acquisition of an asset or the reduction of a liability or the loss or impairment of an asset or the incurrence of a liability.*[6]

Fairly similar definitions are found in the FASB Statement of Financial Accounting Standards No. 5 and in International Accounting Standard No. 10.[7] Some observations on this definition are as follows:

- There is an emphasis on a condition or situation *existing* at the financial reporting date that has potential for gain or loss. The term "existing" implies that contingencies requiring accounting consideration arise solely from business done to date, the assets and liabilities associated therewith, and transactions to which an entity is committed at the reporting date. Mere intentions to undertake future risks do not represent accounting contingencies.
- The reference to uncertainty as to possible gain or loss adds little by itself. Any human activity is uncertain. The definition goes on to speak of uncertainty "that will ultimately be resolved" by future events. Since uncertainties with respect to individual aspects of activity must be resolved eventually, it is not clear what these words add to the definition. Comments below on the contrast between the CICA and FASB discussions of contingencies suggest that the two bodies are interpreting these words differently.

Are these definitions helpful? One test is to see how clearly they apply to particular situations. For example, both the *CICA Handbook* and FASB Statement No. 5 distinguish between uncertainties that meet the definition of contingencies and normal uncertainties in accounting estimates. Both state that amounts owing for services received are not contingencies even though the amount owing has to be estimated. Consistent with this, the CICA material suggests that provisions for warranties "are not usually regarded as contingencies." In contrast, the FASB suggests that these are contingencies, since a claim must be made to fix the obligation and presumably this is the future event that resolves the contingency. Similarly, the CICA material suggests that losses from doubtful accounts are not contingencies, whereas the FASB statement says that they are, since there is initially doubt as to the collectibility of the accounts.

The common definition of the CICA and the FASB apparently conceals an unstated difference in concept. The CICA concept seems to be that uncertainties associated with revenues and expenses recognized in the course of normal business merely constitute, so to speak, normal estimation difficulties. The term "contingencies" is restricted to conditions that may lead to gains and losses, but such gains or losses are outside the normal run of business activity, are not expected at the time the original condition arises, and hence are essentially not foreseeable or measurable at that time. The FASB concept is much broader and seems to embrace all uncertainties created by the possibility of future actions by parties outside the entity, even though an estimate of the effects of such actions is part of the normal process of revenue and expense accounting.

The accounting treatment of contingencies

The acknowledgement given to contingencies (however defined) in financial statements may take one of two forms: (1) an allowance for estimated loss or gain, or (2) disclosure of the possibility of gain or loss without formal recognition of an estimated amount. In this section, the more common case of loss contingencies will be described first. Then, for convenience, we shall discuss gain contingencies even though they do not fit the main theme of the chapter—expense and loss recognition. (In some cases a contingency may have characteristics of both a loss and gain contingency. For example, a lawsuit with claim and counterclaim may go either way.)

Implicit within the accounting standards dealing with loss contingencies is a division of uncertainty into two categories, namely event uncertainty—what is the probability of the adverse future event—and measurement uncertainty—what will be the loss if the adverse event occurs. Determination of the accounting treatment depends upon judgments on both these matters.

Implicit within the accounting standards dealing with loss contingencies is a division of uncertainty into two categories, namely event uncertainty—what is the probability of the adverse future event—and measurement uncertainty—what will be the loss if the adverse event occurs. Determination of the accounting treatment depends upon judgments on both these matters.

Event uncertainty. Under the first category a judgment must be made as to the probability of occurrence of the adverse event. According to the *CICA Handbook* the probability of an event may be deemed to be (1) likely, or having a high chance of occurrence, (2) unlikely, or having a slight chance of occurrence, or (3) not determinable. The third subdivision apparently covers the situation where no judgment as to probability is made (presumably on the grounds that there is no evidence or experience upon which a judgment can be made).

This is a confusing classification. To begin with, it is not exhaustive. There must be a great many situations where a probability is determinable but it falls between a "high" and a "slight" chance of occurrence. Moreover, all judgments about future events are inherently uncertain and hence could be said to be "not determinable." If one assumes that judgments can be made, it is hard to believe that a knowledgeable person has no idea whatsoever of the possible outcome of existing conditions. Many people are instinctively unwilling to quote odds on an uncertain outcome, but that is a different thing from saying that the outcome is not determinable.

The FASB description of probabilities of event occurrence is clearer than the Canadian. According to the FASB, the whole range of possibilities may be subdivided between events that are "probable," "reasonably possible," and "remote." Unless the *CICA Handbook* intended the words "not determinable" to be equivalent to the FASB category of "reasonably possible," the Canadian description of event uncertainty is incomplete.

Measurement uncertainty. A judgment must also be made as to whether the loss, if it should occur, is reasonably capable of estimation. There are several possible situations. The amount of loss could be one particular figure with little chance of variance, plus or minus. The amount of possible loss could fall into a wider range but with one figure within that range clearly more probable than others. The amount of possible loss could fall into a wide range with no one figure within that range considered more likely than any other. It is even possible that there could be two quite likely figures of loss, widely separated in amount. For example, it might appear that a lawsuit is likely to be lost, but the likely damages could differ substantially depending on whether actions of the plaintiff are deemed to have contributed to the loss.

Accounting for loss contingencies

The prescribed accounting treatment in Canada, based on the foregoing judgments, is as follows:

- If a loss (by impairment of asset or requirement for future payment) is considered likely and its amount is reasonably capable of estimation,
  - Accrue the estimated amount of loss where a point estimate of loss has been made.
  - If one particular estimate of loss within the possible range is considered a better estimate than any other, accrue that amount. Disclose, by footnote to the financial statements, the exposure to loss above the amount accrued.
  - Accrue the *minimum* estimate of loss where there is a range of possible loss but no amount appears a better estimate than any other. Disclose the exposure to loss above the amount accrued.
- If a recovery related to the loss is likely (for example, a recovery from a third party with respect to a guarantee), the loss to be accrued is reduced by the likely recovery amount.
- If a loss is considered likely but its amount is not reasonably capable of estimation, disclose the existence of the contingent loss and state that an estimate of loss cannot be made.
- If a loss is possible but its likelihood is not determinable, disclose the existence of the contingent loss and its amount or the fact that its amount is not determinable.

Because of its confused description of event uncertainty, the *CICA Handbook* is unclear as to the case where the probability of a loss can be determined and that probability falls between the likely and unlikely categories. In practice, the existence of such a contingency would be disclosed (and is required in the U.S. under the FASB standard).

In addition, where a loss might be significant in relation to the whole financial position, it would be good practice to make disclosure even though the probability of such loss is slight. By long tradition, also, guarantees or similar obligations are disclosed as contingent liabilities even though a call to make good under the guarantee would not always be significantly adverse to the financial position.

Gain contingencies

Unlike the case of loss contingencies, the asset (or reduction of liability) associated with a gain contingency is never accrued in the financial statements. (The accrual of estimated recoveries from income tax loss carryforwards that are "virtually certain" is an exception to this rule.) The reason given for the asymmetrical treatment of contingent gains and losses is that accrual of contingent gains would offend the realization convention. In place of recognition by accrual, accounting standards call for footnote disclosure of the existence of likely contingent gains, prohibit disclosure of unlikely contingent gains, and permit but do not require disclosure of contingent gains where their likelihood is not determinable. As with the case of loss contingencies, footnote disclosure, if given, should include an estimate of the amount or a statement that an estimate cannot be made.

General risks vs. specific risks

It is uncontentious that general risks attributable to the business carried on are not required to be described in financial statements. This is a common sense conclusion. Uncertainty is pervasive, and the user of financial statements ought to be presumed to have sufficient acquaintance with the world to know that. That being said, it is a different situation when a general business risk threatens to become an immediate claim or risk. Accounting standards do list as contingencies such items as threat of expropriation of assets, threatened litigation, and possible claims or assessments. Where a general business risk has resulted in a foreseeable claim or loss, management must exercise its judgment as to whether the risk is sufficiently slight to permit ignoring it or whether it must be disclosed and/or a loss accrued.

Some issues in contingency accounting

Adverse consequences from disclosure. It is often feared that disclosure of a loss contingency may increase the probability of its occurrence. Where a risk exists that an outside party may assert a claim against an entity and it is thought that such a claim, if asserted, would be successful, management must weigh the probability of assertion of the claim. If it is probable that the claim will be made, it may be possible to accrue for the loss in a way that does not call attention to the contingency. If the loss accrual is unusual and sufficiently material, however, it will be difficult to disclose that fact without alerting possible claimants to their position. Moreover, when accrual is not made for the full loss exposure, the disclosure called for by the contingency standards may also alert possible claimants. Unfortunate though this result may appear to the reporting entity, published accounting standards leave little alternative to disclosure in the interests of fair financial reporting.

Reserves for contingencies. Some decades ago some entities followed the practice of creating and maintaining arbitrary "reserves for contingencies" that were partially justified on the proposition that any entity is faced with the possibility of unforeseeable losses merely by being in business. It could then be claimed that the possibility of unasserted claims was covered and no special disclosure was required should their assertion become probable. This is no longer possible, since the arbitrary creation of such reserves is too open to abuse.

Reserves for self-insurance. Some entities also used to create "reserves for self-insurance" by charges against income. The reasoning was that an enterprise that did not carry normal insurance because its risks were sufficiently spread to "self-insure" would show a different pattern of income from companies that did insure, even though their financial position and income potential were essentially the same. The noncomparability would arise because the income reported by the self-insurer would appear better (through the lack of insurance premium expense) in periods when no losses were incurred but would appear worse in other periods when losses were incurred, even though over a period of years the two practices balanced out.

These reserves are no longer considered acceptable. The general feeling is that reserves for self-insurance understate the equity position when no loss has occurred. This is obviously so, since a company would be free to place insurance at any time, thereby removing the need for the reserve. It is further felt that recording charges to income for self-insurance costs (considered equivalent to insurance premiums) is "what if" accounting that does not correspond with the facts. Authoritative statements do, however, encourage (but do not require) that an entity make disclosure of its exposure if it does not carry insurance against a material risk that normally would be covered.

Reserves for catastrophes. Many casualty insurance companies at one time followed the practice of maintaining "reserves for catastrophes," on reasoning somewhat similar to that used by non-insurance companies to justify reserves for self-insurance. The reasoning was that some types of insurance losses may be bunched at particular times by reason of a single event (a catastrophe), such as a hurricane striking a populated but unprotected area. Such catastrophic losses occur irregularly so that loss amounts are not level from year to year. Premiums, on the other hand, are designed to cover such losses on average over a period of years. It used to be argued that a better portrayal of income is achieved by accruing reserves in years when losses are unusually light and drawing them down in heavy loss years. This practice has also been discontinued on the grounds that the reserves did not represent real liabilities.

Accounting upon resolution of a contingency. Since contingencies, by definition, are related to "an existing condition," it is natural to ask whether losses recognized upon resolution of the contingency or adjustments of any initial accruals should be accounted for as prior period adjustments (to be discussed in a subsequent chapter). The FASB prohibits prior period adjustment treatment, partly on the grounds that it would be inconsistent to prohibit initial accrual of losses that are probable (on the grounds they are not reasonably capable of estimation) and then, on resolution of the contingency, require that the loss be attributed to the earlier period.[8] The *CICA Handbook* position is less rigid because its definition of a prior period adjustment is much looser. It does, however, require that disclosure given to the contingency before its resolution indicate whether the gain or loss on settlement is expected to be treated as an item of income in the period of settlement or as a prior period adjustment. It seems likely that this requirement is an attempt to discourage unbalanced reporting whereby gains are treated as items of current income and losses as prior period adjustments.

That the requirement is necessary at all indicates the great difficulty of distinguishing items that should be and should not be treated as prior period adjustments. Although not mentioned in the Canadian accounting standard, there appears to be a common sense practice that is widely followed. If the contingency arises as part of the normal recurring business of an entity, a charge or credit upon its resolution will be treated as an income item. If contingencies are not the normal consequence of the kind of business carried on, large gains or losses on settlement will be treated as prior period adjustments (although small adjustments are likely to be carried to current income).

Critique and summary of contingency accounting

It is evident from the foregoing that accounting standards dealing with contingencies have not succeeded in eliminating confusion. The clearest illustration of this lies in the fact that the CICA and FASB, although providing virtually identical definitions of a contingency, have such different concepts of what they are talking about.

It may be concluded that uncertainty is pervasive, and attempts to fit it into neat categories are likely to be confusing. It may be possible to deal with uncertainty in individual standards for revenue and expense recognition and provide a catch-all standard for losses and gains from uncertainty, as the CICA standard attempts. Alternatively, it may be possible to enunciate a general standard for all accounting recognition and estimation problems under uncertainty, as the FASB standard comes close to doing.

If one were looking for guidance to the treatment of uncertainty in general, the present contingency standards have little merit. The injunction not to provide for probable losses if their amount is not reasonably capable of estimation invites avoidance of accruals. It is less and less likely to lead to a fair presentation of income and financial position in a world where business enterprise is increasingly bound up in obligations and commitments to be satisfied in future. The prohibition of accrual of reasonably possible (but less than likely) losses that can be readily estimated is likewise dangerous. The requirement to use the lowest possible figure where a range of loss is possible completes the overturn of the long-standing tradition of conservatism.

In contrast to the treatment of loss contingencies, the failure to permit accrual of probable contingent gains is consistent with the historical tradition of conservatism. It is, however, inconsistent within itself since a probable contingent gain may be recognized if it reduces the amount accrued for a related contingent loss, but not otherwise.

The usefulness of the guidance provided by existing standards is further lessened by the use of verbal descriptions of degrees of probability. The CICA's definition states that a future event is likely if its chance of occurrence is high and unlikely if its chance of occurrence is slight. The reference to "chance of occurrence" clearly implies that a judgment as to degree of probability is to be made. Would everyone agree with the meaning and, specifically, the degree of probability of such terms as "likely," "high chance of occurrence," "unlikely," and "slight chance of occurrence"?

The author's expectation is that people would disagree over quite a wide range as to probabilities to be assigned to verbal descriptions, and this expectation is supported by research in the field of communication.[9] If standard-setters wish to make their intentions clear, it is suggested that they should (1) conduct more extensive research among persons having a stake in financial reporting as to their understanding of verbal expressions of likelihood and (2) explain the guidance in the standards in more precise terms. For example, a standard might say: by "likely" we mean that the probability of occurrence is 75% or more. This would avoid the possibility that two individuals (say, a statement preparer and auditor) might both make the same judgment as to probability of loss—say, it is 70%—but disagree whether such probability is "likely."

Also, standard-setters might well review their instructions as to measurement of losses to be recorded because they are considered likely. For example, when a range exists as to the likely loss amount and no one estimate within the range is more likely than any other, it seems irrational to accrue the minimum estimate, rather than the central estimate in the range. In the more common case where a probability distribution of estimated loss follows a normal curve, the central estimate will also be the most likely estimate and therefore the amount accrued. A more difficult situation occurs when a probability distribution is skewed, that is, when the range of possible loss is quite wide but the probabilities are concentrated at one end of the range. In such a case, the median estimate of loss will not be the most probable loss estimate.

Whatever the decision on loss accrual, there remains the problem of providing adequate disclosure of the range of possible loss. More research could be done to assist standard-setters in giving guidance on how the dispersion of possibilities can best be communicated. A priori, it seems desirable to convey some idea of the range of possible loss, and of the most likely loss when that figure departs significantly from the central point of the range.

It may be noted that the possibility that amounts can be estimated only within a range is a very serious one for accrual accounting in general. Often the problem is mitigated by the law of large numbers. That is, when a single risk may have a wide range of possible outcomes, it will nevertheless be found that the outcomes of a large number of similar risks will average out to a figure that is predictable within a narrow range. Thus, it is possible to estimate fairly accurately the survival contingencies (and based on this, the pension costs) of a large employee group. But if one executive or small group of executives is given entitlement to a deferred pension, the ultimate cost may vary in quite a wide range. Should accounting therefore ignore the cost of deferred executive compensation as the contingency standards might suggest? It is submitted that in such a case recording the expected value of the obligation (perhaps based on the potential cost to insure the risk) and recording gain or loss for the difference between the expected and actual outcome when it occurs would be better accounting than ignoring the obligation initially on the grounds of uncertainty. Disclosure could then be concentrated on the possible variance of the estimate, if material, rather than having to carry the burden of informing the reader both of the existence of the deferred compensation claim and of the difficulty in measuring it precisely.

The difference between U.S. and Canadian standards with respect to prior period adjustments highlights a final source of confusion in the contingency standards. In dealing with the treatment of contingent losses from pending or threatened litigation, the FASB speaks of "the period in which the underlying cause ... occurred."[10] Notwithstanding the words "underlying cause," there is to be no accrual of possible loss in the period of underlying cause unless it is both probable and reasonably capable of estimation. The meaning of probable is merely defined as "likely to occur," which certainly means a probability of over 50% and perhaps much higher. (The equivalent Canadian guidance defines "likely" as having a high chance of occurrence.) Moreover, when the loss does occur, Statement of Financial Accounting Standards No. 16 prohibits it from being attributed to the period of underlying cause by means of treating it as a prior period adjustment.

It seems that, by this, the FASB is providing a rule for allocation of losses to periods. Unless losses are deemed "probable" in the period of underlying cause, they are to be attributed to the period when they become probable. Let us apply this rule (as the FASB implicitly or explicitly does) to other situations that the board also regards as contingencies. Unless losses with respect to accounts receivable collection or product warranties are probable and reasonably capable of estimation, the loss contingency is not to be accrued. If it is assumed that "probable" means having a 60% or more chance of occurrence (a possible interpretation), losses will not be attributed to the period of underlying cause in many situations when they will occur. Such a rule seriously undermines both the objective of fair income determination and the tradition of conservatism. (It must be acknowledged that the board suggests that if there is significant uncertainty as to collection of receivables or assertion of warranty claims and, in the latter case, if the range of possible loss is wide, there may be questions whether revenue should be recognized in full on the related sale transaction.[11] It is not definite, however, that inability to accrue the loss prevents recognition of revenue.)

Based on the foregoing, it is suggested that accounting guidance to the treatment of uncertainty needs to be thought through and substantially revised. It is suggested that guidance should be along the following lines:

- As at present, there should be no obligation to make special disclosure of ordinary business risks to which an enterprise is exposed. If a particular risk, however, becomes more than usually threatening, disclosure should be required. Beyond this, accrual of loss may be required along the lines described below. It is inevitable that judgment must be exercised to determine exactly when and how disclosure should be made.
- It will be convenient to deal differently with risks incidental to the normal recurring operations of the business and other risks of loss that occur irregularly, if at all, and whose occurrence cannot be assumed at the time of the initial event that gives rise to the risk.
- The possibility of loss associated with the first type of risk should be allowed for in the period when the associated revenue is recognized as earned—which may be taken as the period of underlying cause. The problem is a pure estimation problem. In principle, the most likely estimate of loss should be accrued. Additional disclosure is required if there is a wide dispersion in possible loss figures. If the uncertainty is so great that an estimate cannot be made within reasonable limits and if the possible loss is material to the financial position or income reported, profit on the related business transactions should not be recognized but rather should be deferred with disclosure of the related material loss contingency. In short, either accrue for losses with respect to known risks, or do not record any profit. Since the most likely estimate is accrued at the time of underlying cause, subsequent changes in estimates must reflect new information and should not be treated as prior period adjustments.
- In the case of the second type of risk, where loss is not a normal presumption at the time the risk condition arises and therefore no reasonable estimate of loss can be made (or the initial estimate is zero), accrual of loss should be made at the time that the most likely value of the loss becomes material. Disclosure is required before that time if material losses are possible, unless the probability of their occurrence is remote (say, less than ten percent).
- A loss that could be very material in relation to shareholders' equity should be disclosed even if its probability of occurrence is thought to be as low as five percent.

Non-cash executive compensation

Over the years companies have developed a variety of ways of compensating key employees other than by means of cash payment. Typically, compensation plans are in some way related to the company's stock. Putting stock in the hands of employees is one way of stimulating them to identify the company's interests with their own. Making their compensation related to changes in the market value of the company stock may have even more direct motivational effect. But if these plans are motivational, they obviously must carry with them benefits to the employees. That naturally raises the question of who pays for those benefits. If plans represent a form of incentive compensation, one must naturally consider what their cost is to the employer. Under the principles developed in this chapter, expense ought to be recognized by the company in relation to that cost, and the obligation ought to be recognized at the time the employee service is rendered. Unfortunately, it has proved very difficult to arrive at a basis for making such recognition.

We shall begin our discussion by describing several common types of plans, consider how they benefit employees, and whether, in each case, such benefits represent a measurable cost that is or ought to be recognized for accounting purposes.

Survey of employee stock or stock-price-related plans

Stock bonuses. A simple way to achieve stock ownership by employees who are deemed significant contributors to a company's success is to pay performance bonuses in the form of stock rather than cash. The benefit to the employee is obviously the value of the stock. The cost to the company is not a direct cash cost, but rather the sacrifice of the opportunity to sell the shares for cash, and the resultant dilution of other shareholders' interest in the company. Since stock issued must be recognized at fair market value at the issue date, the cost of the compensation must be recorded and would be expensed (usually immediately) just as would a cash bonus.

Non-interest-bearing stock purchase loans. Employees receive benefits if shares are issued to them under an ownership plan and they are given extended loans to pay for them that are non-interest bearing or carry an interest rate that is low by normal commercial standards. The compensatory nature of such plans is often indicated by the fact that they are restricted to key employees. What is the nature of the benefit, however? On the surface, it is the receipt of a low-interest or no-interest loan. The benefit to the employee and cost to the company can be quantified by discounting the loan. The difference between the face amount of the loan and its discounted value would represent a measure of the inherent compensation expense. In such a case, however, it might well be argued that the employee's commitment to buy stock provides motivation, especially over the period elapsing till he is entitled to take the stock down and sell it. Thus the compensation expense should be deferred initially and recognized over that period. If that is done, the expense recognized might merely offset the income recognized, as the amount receivable increases from its original discounted amount to its full face value.

It is conceivable that this superficial view of the employee benefit is not completely correct. There have been occasions when companies whose stocks have declined greatly in price have forgiven employee loans on account of stock purchases. It may be, therefore, that a stock purchase plan is really intended as a means of giving employees a call on the stock, which will be exercised if the price goes up, but which does not involve a risk to the employee if the share price declines. (Some plans are formally structured to avoid the risk of share price decline by allowing employees to subscribe for convertible preferred shares that will have a floor redemption price even though the common stock declines in price.) If that is the plan's substance, recording the stock as issued against a loan receivable (which may never be collected) is misleading. The plan is much more akin to a stock option plan. A more effective presentation in all the circumstances would be to credit the capital stock account (as is required because the stock is legally issued) but to deduct the loan receivable from shareholders' equity.

Executive stock options. The most popular form of stock-related incentive compensation is the simple stock option. Typically, an employee is given an option for a limited period, say five to ten years, to acquire stock in the company at an exercise price that is usually close to the market price at the date the option is granted. The option right is not assignable and is usually contingent upon the employee's continued employment with the company. Since the option exercise price is at, or only slightly below, the market value at the date the option is granted, there is little, if any, assured benefit to the employee from the plan. Nevertheless, the employee who is granted the option undoubtedly receives something of value. What he receives is the right to profit if the shares appreciate in value during the option period. Given the tendency of share prices to fluctuate and a long-term rising price trend for most shares, there is a high probability that the market value of shares will rise above the exercise price at some time over an option period that is as long as five to ten years. As in the case of a stock bonus plan, the cost to the company of a stock option lies in the sacrifice of the opportunity to sell the shares for cash at the current market price instead of the exercise price and the dilution of the shareholders' equity as a result. In spite of this, in Canada no attempt is made to recognize compensation cost in connection with stock option plans.

Phantom plans, stock appreciation rights, and tandem plans. A "phantom" stock plan simulates the effect of a stock option without actually requiring the issuance of stock. Instead of granting the employee an option on a given number of shares, the company will credit her with an equivalent number of phantom shares. At any time after the employee's rights become exercisable, the value of her phantom shares may be computed, and the employee is permitted to request payment for her accumulated rights. A phantom plan also has the flexibility to simulate a stock purchase plan financed by a shareholder loan. Under such a variation, the employee is credited with phantom dividends equal to cash dividends paid on the real stock from time to time, together with interest on the phantom accumulation. After her rights become exercisable, the employee is entitled to receive the full amount notionally to her credit—i.e., the notional market value of her phantom shares together with accumulated dividends and interest.

In another variation of the phantom plan, "stock appreciation rights" (SARs) are granted the employee giving him a right to receive the appreciation in price of a given number of shares over the plan period. Phantom plans and SARs differ from the plans they simulate in that their cost is eventually represented by a real cash outflow rather than by dilution of the equity of other shareholders. Accordingly, it is not possible to avoid accounting for the associated cost. Thus there is, in Canada, a fundamental conflict between accounting for phantom plans and for other types of stock-related incentive plans. The conflict is even more vividly illustrated in the case of "tandem plans." Under this type of plan, the employee accumulates rights calculated in the same way as in a phantom plan. The specific terms of the plan, however, may provide that the employer has an option to satisfy the obligation by payment of cash or issuance of stock of equivalent value, or that the employee may elect whether to receive cash or stock.

Accounting for stock-price-related plans

Canadian standard-setters have simply not addressed these conceptual discrepancies in generally accepted accounting principles. U.S. standard-setters have been more venturesome, as will be seen from the discussion below. For convenience, we shall deal first with a straightforward stock option plan.

Accounting for stock options. The initial conceptual question is whether *any* expense needs to be recognized for an option plan, considering that the company parts with no resources under it. A superficial interpretation of the entity theory of accounting might suggest that since the compensation is paid for by the other shareholders through dilution of the value of their shares, rather than by the entity itself, it need not be recorded. But this would be mistaken. If the entity issued shares or warrants to acquire assets without paying cash, even the entity theory would require recognition of the transaction in order to make the entity accountable for the assets. Issuance of a stock option is similar to issuance of a warrant, and employee services represent valuable consideration for which the entity should be accountable just as much as for tangible assets. The question, therefore, is not whether to recognize compensatory stock option contracts, but how.

A second question—when to recognize the option transaction—is more difficult. There are several possible dates, including the date at which the option right is granted to the employee, the date at which his entitlement to it vests (for example, he may have to remain with the company for a period to retain the right), the date at which the right first becomes exercisable (which may sometimes be later than the vesting date), or the date when the option is actually exercised.

The last date may be dismissed fairly easily. Once the employee has an unfettered right to exercise the option, his position is like that of an investor (specifically a holder of a share warrant), and the variation in the value of the option after that date cannot reasonably be considered compensation expense. Extension of the same line of thinking suggests the grant date as the proper time for recognition. What the employee receives for his services is a right to acquire shares. Both the employer and employee presumably have some idea of the value of that right when it is granted and that is the amount of compensation. Some people might, however, argue for the vesting date or exercisable date on the grounds that the compensation is contingent until then. In its consideration, the U.S. Accounting Principles Board was convinced by the arguments in favour of the grant date.[12]

A third question centres on how to measure the value of the option right at the grant date. The APB decided that it should be measured as the difference between the market value of the stock option at the grant date and the exercise price of the option. Since most options in the United States were granted at or near the current market price, this practically meant that no expense was recognized in most cases. In other words, the accounting standard had the effect that compensation expense was not recognized for schemes that had been concluded to be compensatory in nature.

This answer is clearly wrong in theory, but the board based its position largely on practical grounds. Stock options normally have restrictions and conditions at the grant date, and are not transferable. As a result, there are no market prices to establish the value of such restricted options, and the board preferred to base measurement on the more objective evidence of market prices for the shares. Some accountants think this answer is a bad one since it is definitely biased in omitting any valuation of a right that clearly has some value. To rectify this, the usual suggestion is that the models used in finance theory for estimating the value of traded warrants or options be used, modified to allow for the reduction in value of employee options resulting from the restrictions contained within them.[13] Doubts as to the practicality of this solution are still widespread.

A final question concerns the allocation of the cost that is recognized to periods when it is deemed earned by the employee. This is governed by the facts of the case, and little guidance was provided by the APB. Option rights could be deemed to have been awarded as compensation for past services only, in which case the expense would be recognized in full at the date of grant. When a cost is recognized with respect to current and future services, however, the unamortized amount thereof is not carried as an asset but rather is deducted from shareholders' equity.

In the final result, although the APB addressed the issues with respect to stock option plans, its decision to measure the value of option compensation on the basis of the market value of the stock at the date of grant virtually eliminated the practical impact of its deliberations.

Accounting for stock appreciation rights. Subsequent to the APB deliberations, plans based on SARs multiplied and it became necessary for the FASB to develop rules for their treatment.[14] The board decided that the liability for SARs must be accrued over the service period covered by the plan (presumed to be the period till the rights vested, in the absence of any other indication). The amount to be accrued at any given time would be based on the worth of the SARs if they were to be exercised at the current market price, and the cost resulting from recording that target was to be prorated over the service period.

Reliance on the current market price for recognition of the accrued liability necessarily means wide fluctuations in its amount as the stock price fluctuates. That, in turn, means wide fluctuations in expense to be recognized each period. Indeed, if there were a sharp drop in stock price from one reporting period to another, the expense recorded could be negative. The resulting fluctuations in reported expense figures have naturally drawn criticism. But even more serious is the discrepancy between the treatment of ordinary stock options and SARs. Essentially, the wide difference in results occurs because the compensation is measured at the grant date for stock options and ultimately at the exercise date for SARs. Yet the problem is not easy to solve.[15]

Quite apart from measurement difficulties there are certain conceptual issues to be sorted out. Consider SARs. At the time a stated number of SARs are granted to an executive, a certain expectation exists as to possible appreciation in the stock price and, therefore, the amount the executive will be paid upon exercise of her rights. That amount, discounted for uncertainty, could be thought of as her compensation. At the exercise date the stock price will normally be different from that expected. Suppose it is much higher. What is the nature and explanation of the extra amount that must be paid by the company? There are two possible explanations.

- One explanation is that the higher stock price is attributable to the employee's efforts. Therefore, even though the incentive scheme was unexpectedly successful, it is proper to treat the high cash payments required entirely as compensation expense. The chief accounting problem is to find a reasonable basis for accrual of that expense over the period between the date the SARs were granted and their exercise date. If this explanation is accepted, however, one must consider its significance for the treatment of incentive stock options. Unless the grant of a stock option to an employee can be shown to be substantially different in character from that of the grant of SARs (which seems unlikely), their accounting ought to be consistent. Thus it would be necessary to recognize compensation expense for the full excess of the market price of shares optioned at the exercise date over the exercise price of the option.

- An alternative hypothesis is that changes in the share price after the grant date are affected by so many events that it is unreasonable to attribute them to the efforts of one or more specific employees. Even though the intent of providing compensation related to the share price is to motivate the employee, the compensation element is restricted to the value that the employee and employer together see in it at the date the right is granted. If this hypothesis is accepted, a grant of SARs would be thought of as equivalent to a cash payment of compensation to the employee at the grant date and a simultaneous payment by the employee to the company of the same amount in return for a call option on the company's stock at its price on the grant date. The amount recognized as compensation would then be determined by the value of that hypothetical option at the grant date. This accounting would be consistent with accounting for ordinary employee stock options if the latter were valued as an option and not merely by taking the difference between the exercise price and the grant date share price. A consistency problem could arise subsequently, however, if the SARs were paid off at a price higher than the value assigned to the call on the stock. The ordinary stock option, when exercised, is recorded at the option price received and requires no further charge to income when exercised. To create consistency between option accounting and accounting for SAR payments in this case, one of two alternatives would have to be adopted:
  - The excess of the SAR payment over compensation expense recognized at the grant date would be written off as a capital transaction. The result would be the same as if stock had actually been issued at the grant date price and immediately repurchased by the company for cancellation at the current market price.
  - Alternatively, when normal stock options are issued they would be recorded at the current value of the option at the issue date. The difference between this amount and the excess of the value of the stock at the exercise date over the option price would be charged to income. This charge would not, however, be regarded as compensation expense, but rather as the loss to the company from granting options to buy its stock. For further consistency this new basis of accounting would have to be extended to other calls existing on the company's stock—such as calls resulting from outstanding warrants to buy stock.

It seems unlikely that any of these possible accounting approaches would enlist general support at this time. Yet it seems that one of them has to be adopted to cure the present conceptual inconsistencies between accounting for ordinary stock options and accounting for SARs. In addition, even if agreement were reached on the preferable conceptual approach, the practical problem of providing realistic valuations of options and SAR rights at the grant date would remain.

Summary

Measurement of periodic income under the historical cost accounting model requires that expenditures on goods and services be recognized as expense in those periods when the benefit from the goods and services is used up. A particular reporting period may be benefited by expenditures made in prior periods, expenditures of the current period, or even expenditures that will not take place until future periods. When a benefit is received in the current period in return for an obligation to be satisfied by future expenditures, the necessary expense recognition is achieved by "accruing" the liability. For accounting purposes, that accrual is as much a liability at a particular reporting date as is the contractual liability for goods and services already received.

We shall deal first with expenditures made prior to the reporting date. Several stages are involved in the process of expense recognition.

- First, "period costs" incurred are written off to expense as the expenditure takes place. The justification is that their benefit is short-lived or that reasonable assurance is lacking as to revenues after the reporting date attributable to the expenditure.
- Second, "cost objects"—what we customarily think of as assets—must be identified.
- Third, costing methods must be adopted to associate costs incurred with cost objects. A long-standing debate exists over whether a "full costing" or "absorption costing" approach should be adopted or whether costs attached to assets should be confined to costs that are fairly directly traceable to the object—the "direct costing" approach. There has also been some division of opinion whether financing costs, such as interest, may be treated as part of the cost of an asset while it is being constructed or made ready for service. It now seems accepted that financing costs may be attached to assets when a connection can be traced.
- The final stage is the recognition of expense as an asset's benefit is used up. For inventories, this requires a method for allocating costs previously attached to the inventories as between costs applicable to goods sold or scrapped and costs applicable to goods still on hand. For other assets that are largely consumed in use rather than being sold, some "systematic and rational" basis must be adopted for amortizing cost to expense over the asset's useful life.

When a liability accrues in a period—that is, when operations of a period have benefited in return for an obligation to make expenditures in future—the measurement of the expense and the accrued liability can be difficult. People may be reluctant to make an estimate of costs far in the future because of changes in prices over the period. The question also arises whether the future costs should be discounted in recognizing expense currently. Theory provides a yes answer to that question, and that may help the other difficulty. So far as expense recognition is concerned, approximately the same answer should result from (1) estimating the future costs in terms of dollars of future purchasing power and discounting it to a present value at nominal rates of interest, and (2) estimating the cost of the future work in terms of current prices and discounting that at a "real" interest rate.

While this is what theory prescribes, practice in accounting for future obligations is quite mixed. Obligations for pensions are recognized on a discounted basis, but most other obligations are not. It is not unusual for entities to fail to accrue properly for obligations arising under new business arrangements. A statement in an accounting standard of the general principles would be useful.

Liabilities that are unforeseen frequently arise in the ordinary course of operations. When first noticed, they often appear to be only possible, not a certainty—in which case they are known as contingencies. There is some confusion in accounting literature as to whether any accrual that is not for a fixed amount or any judgment-based allowance, such as an allowance for doubtful accounts, is a contingency. A narrower concept of a contingency distinguishes it from normal estimation problems such as those just described. Instead, a contingency is thought of as some condition involving the possibility of gain or loss that had its origin in previous operations but that was completely unexpected when those operations and activities took place. This latter concept appears to be the more useful.

Recognition of a liability and consequent loss with respect to a contingency (once it is realized that it exists) depends upon a judgment as to how likely the loss is and whether a reasonable estimate can be made of its amount. The guidance given in accounting standards as to both of these judgments is poorly worded and is biased toward nonrecognition of the loss. This shortcoming may be partially overcome by required disclosure, but, even here, more thought needs to be given to effective ways to convey to statement readers the range of possible outcomes of the contingency.

In contrast to contingent losses, recognition of a gain under a contingency is not to take place before realization. Disclosure of the contingent asset before realization is also restricted to the more likely cases.

Executive compensation plans by means of stock options represent one form of future obligation undertaken in return for services. This obligation and the related expense have traditionally not been recognized at the time the option is granted or over the period that it matures. Canadian accounting standards have ignored the problem, while U.S. standards have addressed it but have been unable to provide a satisfactory answer. The difficulty is that it is hard to provide an objective measurement of the value of the compensation at the time it is earned by the executive. This issue has grown more pressing with the development of compensation plans that reward the executive in the same way as stock options but pay that reward in cash rather than stock. When cash is paid, some accounting must be given for the full payment, including that portion of the reward attributable to appreciation in the stock price after the compensation award was granted. This is fundamentally in conflict with accounting for stock options, where the appreciation in stock prices after the date of grant is ignored. For various reasons, however, it is very difficult to resolve this conflict in accounting.

References

[1]See FASB, *Employers' Accounting for Settlements and Curtailments of Defined Benefit, Pension Plans and for Termination Benefits*, Statement of Financial Accounting Standards No. 88 (Stamford: FASB, 1985).

[2]This issue has been addressed in the context of nuclear power costs in K.H. Chan and T.T. Cheng, "The Recovery of Nuclear Power Plant Decommissioning Costs by Public Utilities," *Journal of Accounting Auditing & Finance*, Winter 1984, pp. 164-77.

[3]See FASB, *Accounting for Compensated Absences*, Statement of Financial Accounting Standards No. 43 (Stamford: FASB, 1980).

[4]P.A. Gewirtz, M.H. Greene, and W. Napoli, Jr., "The Unexpected Benefit Obligations," *Financial Executive*, January 1982, pp. 11-15.

[5]FASB, *Disclosure of Postretirement Health Care and Life Insurance Benefits*, Statement of Financial Accounting Standards No. 81 (Stamford: FASB, 1984).

[6]CICA, "Contingencies," *CICA Handbook*, Section 3290 (Toronto: CICA), par. 02.

[7]FASB, *Accounting for Contingencies*, Statement of Financial Accounting Standards No. 5 (Stamford: FASB, 1975) and IASC, *Contingencies and Events Occurring after the Balance Sheet Date*, International Accounting Standard No. 10 (London: IASC, 1978).

[8]FASB, *Prior Period Adjustments*, Statement of Financial Accounting Standards No. 16 (Stamford: FASB, 1977), par. 37.

[9]See, for example, G.R. Chesley, "Interpretation of Uncertainty Expressions," *Contemporary Accounting Research*, Spring 1986, pp. 179-99. See also G.R. Chesley and H.A. Wier, "The Challenge of Contingencies: Adding Precision to Probability," *CAmagazine*, April 1985, pp. 38-41.

[10]FASB, *Accounting for Contingencies*, par. 33.

[11]Ibid., pars. 23, 25.

[12]See APB, *Accounting for Stock Issued to Employees*, Opinion No. 25 (New York: AICPA, October 1972).

[13]See, for example, J.J. Weygandt, "Valuation of Stock Option Contracts," *The Accounting Review*, January 1977, pp. 40-51 and R.J. Sokol, "Using Classic Financial Tools to Analyze Deferred Compensation," *CAmagazine*, February 1983, pp. 52-57.

[14]See FASB, *Accounting for Stock Appreciation Rights and Other Variable Stock Option or Award Plans: An Interpretation of APB Opinions No. 15 and 25*, Interpretation No. 28 (Stamford: FASB, 1978).

[15]The following articles are critical of the failure by the FASB to reconcile its treatment of stock options and stock appreciation rights: W.A. Wallace, "The Effects of Delays by Accounting Policy-Setters in Reconciling the Accounting Treatment of Stock Options and Stock Appreciation Rights," *The Accounting Review*, April 1984, pp. 325-41, and P.B. Thomas and L.E. Farmer, "Accounting for Stock Options and SARs: The Equality Question," *Journal of Accountancy*, June 1984, pp. 92-98. It is notable that neither article attempts to propose a solution.

Chapter Ten

Inventory and Cost of Sales

Inventory accounting presents some very debatable issues both in the aspect of costing the asset and in the aspect of determining cost of sales. In the former category there is a long-standing controversy over the merits of direct costing as against full absorption costing. This issue has never been conclusively settled, although interest in it seems to have lessened in the last two decades. In the latter category there has been the issue of what is the proper cost flow assumption for determining cost of sales—first in, first out (FIFO) or last in, first out (LIFO). This issue, likewise unsettled, took on greater importance under the inflationary conditions beginning in the 1970s, since inflation tends to widen the impact of choice of one method over the other.

Cost attachment to inventory

Years ago it was quite common to find manufactured goods costed at "prime cost"—that is, including the cost of materials and direct labour only. Of course, at that time manufacturing processes were simple and such costs constituted a high percentage of total costs. With increasing mechanization and complexity of production processes, overhead costs became more and more important, a trend that has continued till this day. It was only natural, therefore, that systems should be developed for attaching overhead costs to products. Costing systems were probably developed primarily for purposes such as assisting in product-pricing decisions. Once available, however, they could be, and were, used for financial reporting purposes as well.

Since cost systems were devised and adopted by individual businesses or industries, it was inevitable that there should be differences between them. When professional accounting societies began making recommendations to guide financial reporting practice, an important goal was to narrow the gap between prime costing methods, still found in practice, and highly developed sophisticated costing systems providing a reflection or "absorption" of all costs pertaining to manufacturing. It was relatively easy to conclude that the exclusion of all overheads from a cost calculation was likely to result in a figure quite unrepresentative of the sacrifice and effort in the ordinary process of manufacture. It was less easy to obtain agreement beyond that.

Full absorption costing vs. direct costing

For more than twenty years from about 1940, a vigorous debate raged between supporters of "full absorption costing" and those of "direct costing." The absorption-costers held, in general, that every cost that could be identified as being necessary for production must find its way into the unit cost figure for individual products. The direct-costers, in contrast, saw a distinction between costs of providing capacity to produce, which were essentially fixed over wide ranges of production, and actual costs of production, which tended to vary with the volume of production activity. The important arguments are summarized below.

On behalf of direct or variable costing

- By definition, costs that are already fixed are not pertinent to any decision that management might take, such as a decision as to volume of production or price of product. The only information that is relevant to a decision is information as to its impact on costs and revenues. There is no impact on costs that are already fixed; hence it is argued it is unlikely that it will be useful to include fixed costs in figures reported as assets.
- A division of costs between fixed and variable is necessary to find the volume break-even point in a business. By the same token, a division between variable costs of goods sold and fixed manufacturing and other costs will provide a better portrayal of margins achieved on sales and hence will produce an income statement more useful for financial analysis.
- Revenue is recognized in most cases upon completion of performance. Income accounting requires that costs applicable to the completed performance be written off when revenue is recognized, and that costs carried forward in inventory be restricted to those clearly identifiable with future revenue. If fixed costs are included in inventory, one will find that during years of inventory buildup less than twelve months' fixed costs will be included in cost of sales, while in years when inventory is reduced, more than twelve months' fixed costs will be absorbed. As a result, periodic profits reported will not reflect the results of completed performance only but will also be affected by inventory buildups and draw-downs. This confuses the financial report and even provides an opportunity to manipulate profits by building up inventory when it is desired to bolster the reported results.

On behalf of full absorption costing

- The full absorption case rests essentially on the proposition that costs that are necessarily incurred in production should be reflected in the cost assigned to products in inventory. If this is not done, a shift in production technology from a variable cost to a fixed cost (say, a substitution of machinery for labour) will have the strange result that the apparent product cost will go down by the full amount of the variable cost eliminated.
- In rebuttal to the direct costing argument—there is nothing wrong with reported profit being influenced by inventory buildup. Profit is earned by all activity, not just by sale. It would be bad management to build up inventory if it could not be sold, since carrying unsold inventory costs money. Hence, if a company is producing rapidly and building up inventory, it is a fair assumption that its prospects are good, and this can reasonably be reflected in reported profits.

An interesting resolution to this controversy was suggested in an article published in 1962.[1] The authors based their case on the proposition that the economic attribute of an asset is its ability to bring in future benefit. Thus a cost incurred should be treated as an asset only if it has a favourable effect on expected future costs or future revenues. On this basis, variable costs would always be carried forward since, if they had not been expended, it would be necessary to incur them again to have product for sale. The future economic benefit from fixed costs is more debatable. If future orders can be readily filled from future production, then fixed costs incurred in the past, such as depreciation, have no favourable effect on future revenues and should not be carried forward. On the other hand, if product must be on hand to make sales possible (for example, because current production cannot meet demand), then all costs incurred and associated with the product may legitimately be treated as part of the inventory asset.

This situation-specific basis of inventory valuation (called by its authors "relevant costing") has not received recognition in authoritative recommendations. Perhaps this has been because the method might be thought too subjective, or perhaps because overall principles of inventory costing have not received serious consideration for a long time. Since most businesses require a certain stock of inventory at all times to avoid lost revenue from stockouts, it would seem that most of the time the relevant costing basis would require recognition of fixed costs in inventory with respect to at least part of the inventory. To facilitate application of the relevant costing concept, it might be provided that each business should establish minimum inventory quantities suitable to its circumstances. Then fixed costs would be included in inventory only up to the minimum quantities established, with variable costing being applied to inventory held above those quantities. This proposal would greatly reduce the danger of manipulation. In addition, it would be consistent with the second sentence in the following recommendation on inventory costing from the *CICA Handbook*:

> *Usually expenditures arising out of abnormal circumstances, such as rehandling of goods and idle facilities, are not included. Similarly, in some cases, a portion of fixed overhead is excluded where its inclusion would distort the net income for the period by reason of fluctuating volume of production.*[2]

The principal authoritative recommendations on inventory costing in North America may be found in Accounting Research Bulletin No. 43 of the AICPA, issued in 1953, and *CICA Handbook* Section 3030. On the matter of assignment of overhead costs to inventory, both the American and Canadian pronouncements contain some rather vague language. It has been stated that the intention of Bulletin 43 was to prescribe full absorption costing only. A different interpretation, however, can be drawn from its wording "exclusion of all overheads from inventory costs does not constitute an accepted accounting procedure."[3]

Unfortunately, there are few recent surveys of inventory-costing practice to prove what are generally accepted applications of the authoritative recommendations. A U.S. survey of manufacturing firms conducted in 1972 showed that a majority of firms did not treat all indirect production costs as components of inventory cost, notwithstanding the emphasis in the United States on full absorption costing.[4] (Pressure by the Internal Revenue Service in favour of absorption costing may have changed this picture since 1972.) A Statistics Canada survey in 1975 showed that 27% of companies in manufacturing industries used direct costing methods.[5] (Unfortunately the study did not ascertain whether such methods were used for internal purposes, for external reporting purposes, or for both.) On the evidence available, it cannot be said that direct costing is contrary to generally accepted accounting principles in Canada. The following are some impressions as to prevailing Canadian practice.

- It is clear that costing inventory at prime cost is contrary to generally accepted accounting principles if variable overhead costs are significant in amount, as they usually are. There probably are cases where a direct or variable costing approach is rigorously followed. Much more common, however, are cases where some indirect production costs, but not others, are allocated to inventory. Depreciation on manufacturing plant and equipment is a common exclusion from allocated costs. In general, there is much variation in practice from one enterprise to another.
- It is now generally recognized that it is wrong to calculate an indirect cost figure per unit of inventory on the basis of the actual amount of such costs for a period divided by the actual quantity of inventory units produced, regardless of whether production is high or low. Such a practice has the nonsensical result of showing a high per-unit cost when volume of production is low and a low cost when production is high, in spite of the fact that the cost is largely fixed. To avoid this, it is necessary to determine a standard or representative per-unit cost from time to time, based on an estimate of the normal or planned production capacity of the plant. Then, in periods when production is low, the amount of indirect costs allocated to inventory will be less than the actual incurred costs, and the difference (the cost "unabsorbed") will be written off as a period expense attributable to unused capacity. Occasionally, in periods of abnormally high activity, actual overhead costs may be "overabsorbed" using the standard rate per unit for allocation to inventory. In such cases it is accepted that the amount overabsorbed should be apportioned between inventory on hand at the end of the period and cost of goods sold, so as to avoid overstating the actual cost of goods in inventory.
- It is permissible, where indirect or fixed overhead costs are allocated to inventory, to allocate such overheads only with respect to minimum quantities and to include variable overhead costs only in inventory above the minimum.
- Very few enterprises would consider any costs initially classified as general and administrative to be included in overheads allocated to inventory, because such costs are generally thought to be too remote from the production process. If, however, it can be shown that a given administration cost is caused by manufacturing activity and some reasonable basis for associating it with inventory can be found, there is no theoretical reason why it should not be allocated to inventory.

What rule should be adopted if it were desired to standardize practice? The answer might depend upon the objective. One possible aim might be to report an inventory cost as close as possible to its fair value. If so, full absorption costing would be preferable. Another aim might be to minimize distortion of income reported. If so, there would be at least some cases in which a full costing approach would be better than direct costing. Those cases can be identified by irregularity in the pattern of revenue recognition. If revenue is recognized on the critical event basis at or near completion of earning activity and the business is such that these completion dates occur at irregular intervals (for example, in businesses that do work to order rather than producing standard goods with a fairly steady pattern of sales), it is best to associate as much cost as possible with work in process. This will avoid the misleading picture conveyed by substantial overhead cost write-offs in periods when productive activity on incomplete projects is at a high level but little revenue is being recognized on completed projects. Of course, in these same circumstances distortion of income may be even more effectively avoided if it is possible to adopt the accretion approach to revenue recognition.

On the other hand, a direct costing approach saves work and is more easily defended against the charge that the allocation of overheads to individual products is highly arbitrary. It is also less likely to create problems in income reporting when inventory is overstocked. Moreover, whenever revenue is recognized on a more or less regular basis, consistent use of direct costing will normally produce an income figure not materially different from that produced under absorption costing. From a practical standpoint, therefore, there may be little harm in the present situation, where enterprises are free to choose inventory costing methods ranging from direct costing to full absorption costing, as their circumstances suggest.

Interest as an element for inventory cost

Full discussion of the possible allocation of financing costs to cost objects is reserved for the next chapter, since the question arises most frequently in connection with self-constructed fixed assets. Allocation of interest cost to inventory, so that it is absorbed through the cost of sales account rather than through direct write-off, would not greatly affect results reported in most circumstances and would make work. Nevertheless, in principle, if financing costs can be directly traced to inventory, there is no reason why they should not be deferred as part of the cost accumulated in inventory up to the time it is ready for sale. In practice, interest is inventoried by land developers and, on infrequent occasions, by contractors.

Inventory costing — contractors

This section on cost attachment may be concluded with brief reference to certain specialized industry practices. It has already been noted that when revenue recognition is irregular, a full cost approach is desirable. This is borne out by the practice of contractors who do not use the accretion (percentage-of-completion) basis of revenue recognition. In some cases contract prices may be established so as to cover specific named costs plus an allowance for profit or margin. In those cases contract costing should at least accumulate costs that are specifically designated for recovery in the contract price. Such costs may include an allowance for general and administrative costs which will accordingly be inventoried.

May costs be carried forward in contract work in process if they are not covered in the scheduled costs reimbursable? That depends on the circumstances. Provided there are reasonable bases for allocation of a given cost to the contract and provided the contract price allows sufficient margin to recover such costs, there is no reason for not inventorying them. Where contracts are not fully financed by purchaser prepayments, there will normally also be some interest costs if the contract is of any duration. It will usually be possible to trace interest costs to the contracts causing it, and it is therefore appropriate to treat such interest as a contract cost. In practice, however, most contractors continue with the long-established practice of treating all interest as a period expense.

Costing real estate inventories

Real estate developers who buy land, service it, obtain approval of plans of subdivision, and sell lots or lots and houses together are carrying on an activity with some similarity to the manufacture of a product. Correspondingly, the land acquired for this purpose, whether raw or developed, is similar to the inventory of a manufacturer. Because real estate projects are long in development and revenue from sale is irregular, a full costing basis is highly appropriate for them. Accounting practices recommended by the Canadian Institute of Public Real Estate Companies include the following. Preacquisition costs incurred in seeking out land for development may be initially treated as deferred charges. Then when land is acquired, an appropriate portion of the deferred charges may be capitalized as part of the land cost. (If the acquisition effort is abandoned, the deferred costs should be written off at that time.) General and administrative cost should be departmentalized and either charged directly (if possible) or allocated on a reasonable basis to acquisition, development, and construction activities. Carrying costs (interest and real estate taxes) should also be capitalized. Interest capitalized is restricted to actual interest, whether directly incurred for the project or allocated out of the general interest cost borne by the company. Imputed interest on equity may not be capitalized. It is also recommended that the cost of issues of bonds and debentures that finance specific developments should be included in the costs of those developments.[6]

Finding cost of goods sold or of goods consumed in manufacturing

Inventory costing conventions attribute costs incurred to goods on hand. When the goods are made to order, costs are likely to be assigned to individual units or job lots. When goods are made for stock, costs are likely to be allocated to production runs, from which unit costs can be derived by dividing the run cost by the quantity produced. However unit cost is determined, there are likely to be differences in the unit cost assigned to goods produced at different times. When goods are sold, the question arises: What is the correct figure to be recognized as cost of goods sold? A similar question occurs with respect to raw materials or supplies bought at different times. When they are put into production or consumed in production the question is: What is the right cost figure to enter in the costing system for raw material or supplies consumed?

The flows of cost factors that are assumed in answer to these questions fall into two broad categories. One set of cost-flow assumptions visualizes costs incurred as attaching to specific physical units of goods, so that costs are automatically known and absorbed when goods are sold or consumed. Other cost-flow assumptions consider it unimportant to associate costs closely with specific units of product, but rather give priority to writing off inventory costs incurred against revenues on a basis thought to best portray the income earned on completed transactions.

Expense recognition based on physical flow of goods

Specific identification. The most easily understood method of finding cost of sales is that of "specific identification." If the cost of each unit of inventory has been determined and particular goods sold are specifically identified, the cost to be written off seems obvious. This method is invariably used when goods in inventory are costly and highly individual in character. That is, it is used generally for luxury items or "big ticket" items, such as art objects, jewellery, automobiles in the hands of dealers, and so on. Its use makes sense because both the cost and the sale price will be highly influenced by individual features of the thing sold. By specific identification the vendor is enabled to pinpoint her successes and failures in acquisition of goods and, thereby, improve her judgment. Specific identification is also used for goods made to the customer's order. Once again, special features ordered by the customer may have influenced the cost, and it is useful for the vendor to be able to compare actual results with those expected when a price was quoted on the job.

FIFO. Where goods dealt in are interchangeable or easily replaceable (the majority of business situations), the arguments for specific identification are less strong. Nevertheless, the basis of expense recognition is still supposed to be "matching costs with revenues." Many accountants instinctively feel that matching is logically achieved by recognizing the cost of the actual goods sold or consumed as the amount to be written out of inventory. Much of the time this desire encounters a practical difficulty. For many goods, one unit is indistinguishable from another. In these circumstances it will not be worth the effort to keep track of costs for individual units of inventory. Other goods may not be completely interchangeable but are of so low a value that again it is not worth keeping track of costs on an individual unit basis. In both these cases, the cost of goods actually consumed will not be known.

In the case of perishable goods, it can safely be assumed that an attempt will be made to dispose of the earliest goods received or produced before later goods. Thus it can be assumed that costs applicable to unsold goods on hand are the latest costs incurred, and therefore the write-off of costs from inventory should be on the FIFO convention. Even when goods are not very perishable, management will generally tend to move goods on a first in, first out basis. Thus the FIFO convention is very widely used, basically because in most cases it is likely to conform to the natural physical flow of goods. (There may be some situations where plant layout does not conduce to a FIFO movement of nonperishable goods. Even so, the FIFO convention may be used simply because it makes reported results more comparable to those of other entities.)

Expense recognition based on other cost-flow assumptions

Average cost. The interchangeable character of many types of inventory leads to still another cost-flow assumption. Where a collection of identical or nearly identical goods has been acquired at varying prices, it seems reasonable to think of a total cost applicable to all the units held and an average price per unit. That average cost can then be written off as units are sold or consumed. When more goods are acquired for inventory, their cost is added to the pool of costs remaining in inventory, and a new average is struck. This method has some appeal as a reflection of the homogeneous character of goods in inventory. It involves more computational work than FIFO, however, and often will produce results little different from FIFO. Hence it is less widely used.

Base stock. A radically different approach was developed around 1900 under the name of the "base stock" method. The concept underlying this method was that any ongoing business must hold minimum quantities of inventory that do not vary greatly in composition from one period to the next. One could say, then, that these basic quantities are more akin to a fixed asset than to inventory that will be sold or consumed. If so, it was considered undesirable to attach different costs to the base amount from time to time, just as it would be undesirable to continuously revalue fixed assets held. To initiate this method, inventory held was divided into two components. The fixed component consisted of defined minimum quantities valued at cost at the date of initiation of the method or at an arbitrary figure deemed likely to be as low as cost might drop to at any time in future. Quantities in excess of the defined minimum quantities were considered to be true inventory, to be accounted for by using any of the accepted cost-flow assumptions.

The base stock method was criticized on various grounds. Valuation of the fixed component at arbitrary, low prices was said to be a departure from the historical cost principle. The selection of basic quantities was also arbitrary. In addition, there was no automatic mechanism whereby the defined base stock could change as different goods were added to inventory and others were phased out. As a result, the method was really only workable for a business engaged in processing a staple commodity, such as lead, copper, or sugar. On top of this, the method was disallowed early on for taxation purposes in the United States (and later in the United Kingdom and Canada), which greatly reduced its practical appeal.

LIFO. The place of base stock was taken by the LIFO cost-flow assumption. LIFO is quite similar to base stock in its practical effect, although supported by a different theory. The concepts underlying LIFO, as it was originally conceived, are as follows. There are certain businesses, for example, base metal processors, oil refiners, and tanners, that process a primary commodity that is subject to wide swings in price over short periods of time. To protect itself against such price gyrations, a business may set selling prices so as to recover the current replacement cost of the commodity plus what is, in effect, a processing charge to reward the business for its effort. The most appropriate cost figure to match against the selling price, therefore, is a current cost, and the latest cost incurred provides the best approximation to a current cost. Since costs recognized as cost of sales are always the latest costs, it follows that inventory on hand is carried at the earliest cost incurred (at or subsequent to the effective date of adoption of the LIFO method).

There are a number of practical flaws in the LIFO method.

- If prices are changing rapidly in either direction, the cost of the most recent purchase may not be very close to the current cost at the time of sale. The method works best, therefore, when an enterprise reorders at regular and frequent intervals and maintains inventory quantities at a fairly constant level, rather than speculating in price movements by stocking up when prices are low and vice versa.
- Sometimes it may be impossible to maintain inventory quantities at a level amount for reasons beyond the control of the enterprise. For example, a strike

in the plants of a major supplier may cause a reduction in the stock of the enterprise. Under such conditions "involuntary liquidation" of inventory occurs, and goods sold are costed at prices increasingly remote in time so that they bear no relation to current prices. Thus the method fails in its objective.

- The same results can occur when an enterprise phases out some existing products or lines of business in a "voluntary liquidation." Old costs are matched against current revenues.
- The LIFO method was intended to cope with the distorting effect of *fluctuations* in acquisition prices of inventory. The idea was that, as acquisition prices rose, LIFO would reflect the higher costs of sales sooner than FIFO; the converse would occur when prices fell, but over a complete cycle of price movement the amount charged to cost of sales would be the same under the two methods. This idea ignored the possibility of a long-term trend in prices, such as has been experienced over the last fifty years. When the long-term price trend is rising, LIFO tends to charge more to expense than does FIFO, and correspondingly the valuation of inventory on hand tends to be lower. The net result is that income reported by companies using the LIFO method is not comparable, even over a complete business cycle, with that reported by companies under the FIFO method. Also, the inventory figure reported in the balance sheet of companies using LIFO tends to be grossly undervalued in terms of current conditions.

In brief, the LIFO idea represents an attempt to make the figure of cost of sales a better representation of the current sacrifice involved to earn revenue than is achieved by other cost-flow assumptions. That objective is worthwhile, but it is not always attained because of the problem of inventory liquidation. In addition, LIFO provides a very poor representation of the worth of inventory on hand for balance sheet purposes. In essence, LIFO is an attempt to adopt replacement cost accounting for the income statement but not for the balance sheet. That peculiar characteristic was forced by the need to argue that the method represented merely a variant of the historical cost system and thus was acceptable for taxation purposes. In fact, because the inventory carrying values in the balance sheet may represent costs incurred many years ago, the method is fundamentally incompatible with other applications of historical cost accounting, as well as being an inadequate substitute for replacement cost accounting. Nevertheless, it is possible to argue that, with all its conceptual faults, the use of LIFO accounting for inventory produced a better representation of income in the inflationary period of the 1970s and early 1980s than did any other available method. That it was an inadequate substitute for a well-thought-out system of accounting for price change does not detract from the fact that it was the only accepted way to cope with the problem.

There are two approaches to the implementation of LIFO. The older, "specific goods" approach prices goods on hand at the end of the year at the cost figure at which the same or similar goods were carried at the beginning of the year, up to the quantities held in the previous year. Any addition to quantities held over the previous year-end, or goods held that were not in stock at the previous year-end, are costed at their acquisition price in the current year. The similarity of goods held at the beginning and end of the fiscal year is crucial to the successful application of the specific goods method. A business that is continually changing from one product to another is, in effect, making voluntary liquidations of the discontinued products, so that older costs, rather than current costs, are charged to cost of sales with respect to such products.

This liquidation problem is reduced under the application of "dollar value" LIFO, but the extent of the reduction may depend upon the specific way it is applied. To implement dollar value LIFO, it is first necessary to divide the inventory into pools of costs, for the purpose of developing price ratios applicable to each pool that measure the change between current-year cost and base-year cost. (Base year is the year of adoption of LIFO.) Pools of costs may include all inventories in a "natural business unit." Alternatively, "multiple pools" may be developed by product line, with separate pools for raw material, work in process, and finished goods in each product line. To lessen the exposure to the voluntary liquidation problem, it is desirable to have as few pools as possible, and for this purpose the natural business unit approach is generally preferable.

There are many other points of detail that arise in the application of the LIFO method. Since LIFO is little used in Canada because its use is not permitted for tax purposes, these are not reviewed here. Those interested may refer to U.S. literature and U.S. tax regulations for further information.[7]

Certain aspects of costing sales under contracts

Apart from general issues involved in the choice of cost-flow assumptions, special problems may be found in particular industries. Industries that contract to produce a quantity of high-value products, such as aircraft or aircraft components, may use an accounting method that falls between the completed contract method and percentage-of-completion accounting. That is to say, revenue may be recognized and applicable costs written off for each unit of product shipped, rather than only upon completion of the contract. In effect, the product unit is treated as though it were a small contract in itself, accounted for on the completed contract basis.

There is no problem in this if the costing system is capable of providing a cost figure for each unit completed and that cost is recognized as the cost to be matched with the unit sale proceeds. There is, however, a more sophisticated basis of costing units sold that may be applied in industries to which the "learning curve" applies. The learning curve is a phenomenon first observed in airframe manufacturing but applicable to other industries as well. What has been observed is that in a demanding manufacturing process the direct labour required and perhaps some other manufacturing costs as well tend to decrease for each succeeding unit of production in a reasonably predictable fashion over an extended period of time. As a result of this learning effect, the first units produced in a production series will have a considerably higher cost, and later units a considerably lower cost, than the average for the whole production run. Because of this phenomenon, some companies relieve the inventory of accumulated costs at an estimated average cost per unit for each unit completed, rather than at the actual cost. As the production run progresses, the actual experience is checked to see if the forecast productivity gains are actually being achieved, and adjustments are made to the costing-out rate where necessary.

There are some dangers with this system.

- If revenue billable for succeeding units in the production run is reduced to reflect the learning effect, it is wrong to cost units completed on this method. Recognition of the learning curve can be in revenue or in costs but not both.

- If there are interruptions to the production schedule, the learning effect is also interrupted. Should such interruptions occur, through strikes or for other reasons, it is vital that recalculations be made of costs expected over the future of the contract, and that loss be recognized, so that the revised chargeout rate per unit (the revised average cost) can absorb all the costs carried forward in inventory.

This description has been written in terms of an average chargeout rate for a specific contract. There are industries (again the aircraft industry is an example) where a given product may be expected to be manufactured over an extended period of years under a number of individual contracts for different customers. Thus the learning effect may continue through several contracts, including contracts not yet signed at the time early contracts are commenced. In this situation, an entity may adopt the "program costing" approach. An assumption is made as to the total number of units that will be produced under all contracts in the program, future as well as present, and an estimated average cost is struck assuming the learning effect. This average cost is used as a chargeout rate from the beginning. Since all the productivity gains will not be realized within the early contracts, it is obvious that such a chargeout rate will not absorb all costs incurred in those contracts, and some will remain in inventory to be absorbed as part of the cost of future contracts.

Clearly the risk of error is much higher under program costing. First, the number of units to be sold in the program can only be an estimate, rather than being a number determined by a contract. Second, there is the possibility that sales prices in later, follow-on contracts may have to be reduced because of competition, etc. Third, in a very long program there could be a time when costs level off and this must be allowed for. Finally, the risk of interruption or delays in the production schedule disrupting the learning curve is greater the longer the program. The method should be used, therefore, only with the utmost caution.[8]

Costing retail land sales

Determining costs of units of land sold out of a land subdivision also presents complicated problems.

- It is necessary to estimate all costs that will be incurred under the developer's obligation to complete work for the subdivision as a whole. Any future carrying costs to be capitalized must also be estimated in order to arrive at a total estimated pool of costs for the subdivision.
- Proceeds of land sold or to be sold at less than fair value pursuant to agreements with governments are treated as reductions of the pool of costs. Hence, any future proceeds of this nature must be estimated.
- Should there be any servicing costs incurred for the joint benefit of later stages in a large development (for example, oversized sewers or water mains), the extra cost expended for the benefit of the later stages is removed from the pool and deferred, to be charged against such stages.
- The net pool of costs must then be apportioned to units sold. If all units are alike, the unit cost is calculable by straight division. If the land is basically

sold for one type of use (for example, residential or commercial) but the sizes of the units vary, costs may be allocated on an area or foot-front basis. Where the units for sale have a different value, however, a more satisfactory way to apportion costs is on the "net-yield" basis, whereby the amount of cost assigned to each unit sold is proportional to its sale price, expressed as a percentage of the anticipated total proceeds from all units.

- The expectation may be that sales prices for units to be sold later will be higher than those sold earlier. If this is the case but the market value used in the calculation of costs per unit sold is a current value rather than an estimate of ultimate proceeds, it may be reasonable to omit future estimated carrying costs from the pool of costs being allocated. The justification would be that future increases in sales realization (not taken into account in the calculation) are expected to cover future carrying costs.

Summary

Costing assets and subsequently finding ways to recognize expense as the asset value is consumed represent the key questions in inventory accounting. The choice between direct costing and full absorption costing has been argued principally in the context of inventories, although it also is pertinent to other types of assets constructed internally. The second problem—that of appropriate recognition of cost of sales as revenue is recognized—is unique to inventories.

Full absorption costing provides a balance sheet carrying value closer to fair value than does direct costing. It is particularly suitable in a business with an irregular pattern of revenue recognition. A modification of this method, to restrict capitalization of fixed overheads to minimum inventory quantities, has theoretical justification and prevents manipulation of income through overstocking inventory. Direct costing, on the other hand, has practical merits. It is simpler to apply and can be helpful in analyzing factors that have influenced operating results. In practice, inventory costing methods used by enterprises often represent compromises between the two approaches, rather than being entirely one or the other.

Several methods of costing goods sold are found in practice. When goods are produced to order, costs are usually accumulated by order or by job and there is little problem in associating costs with revenue. The same is frequently true in the case of contracts for services. Likewise, when goods sold represent high value items with individual characteristics, the costing system usually provides for specific identification of costs with individual inventory items.

The difficult problems in recognition of cost of goods sold arise when the inventory consists of interchangeable items. In such cases, even though goods on hand may have been acquired at different costs, there is little point in keeping careful track of actual cost incurred for specific units of inventory. Accordingly, some assumption as to flow of cost factors must be made when the goods are sold to permit recognition of expense.

The most common assumption is that the cost to be recognized as cost of goods sold consists of the earliest costs in inventory (the FIFO assumption). The assumption has appeal because it is probably consistent with the physical movement of goods in most businesses.

A second assumption is that an average of costs accumulated for all units of goods that are "fungible" or interchangeable represents a reasonable figure of cost to be recognized as each unit is sold. This assumption has appeal because the use of an average figure seems compatible with the interchangeable character of the goods.

A third assumption (the LIFO assumption) recognizes the most recent cost incurred as the cost to be assigned to cost of goods sold. The rationale for this is that the most recent cost is the best representation of the sacrifice made to earn revenue. Unfortunately, the actual application of LIFO is such that it often does not succeed in matching a current cost against revenue recognized. The problem is that LIFO is supposed to be an application of historical cost accounting, and it is difficult, perhaps impossible, to ensure that some historical cost can be found that is equivalent to a current cost. There is, in fact, an inherent conflict between the conceptual justification of LIFO and the historical cost accounting theory.

Specialized inventories present special problems in costing work in process and determining the cost of units sold. These problems are solved within the general framework of inventory accounting while having regard to the special characteristics of the industry.

References

[1]G.H. Sorter and C.T. Horngren, "Asset Recognition and Economic Attributes—The Relevant Costing Approach," *The Accounting Review*, July 1962, pp. 391-99.

[2]CICA, "Inventories," *CICA Handbook*, Section 3030 (Toronto: CICA), par. 03.

[3]American Institute of Accountants, Committee on Accounting Procedure, "Inventory Pricing," chapter 4 in *Restatement and Revision of Accounting Research Bulletins*, Accounting Research Bulletin No. 43 (New York: AIA, 1953), par. 5.

[4]S. Landekich, "Cost Allocations to Inventory," *Management Accounting*, March 1973, pp. 51, 72.

[5]Statistics Canada, *Inventory Accounting Methods in Manufacturing Industries, 1975*, No. 31-524 Occasional (February 1978).

[6]See Canadian Institute of Public Real Estate Companies, *Recommended Accounting Practices for Real Estate Companies*, 2nd ed. (Toronto: CIPREC, 1980).

[7]See, for example, two articles by B.N. Schwartz and M.A. Diamond, published in the *The CPA Journal*. The first is "Is 'Dollar-Value' LIFO for You?" July 1980, pp. 33-40, and the second is "Dollar-Value LIFO for Manufacturers or Processors," July 1981, pp. 31-37. A number of debatable points have also been covered in an "Issues Paper" prepared by the Task Force on LIFO Inventory Problems, Accounting Standards Division of the AICPA, and presented by the Accounting Standards Executive Committee to the Financial Accounting Standards Board, *Identification and Discussion of Certain Financial Accounting and Reporting Issues Concerning LIFO Inventories* (New York: AICPA, November 30, 1984).

[8]For a general discussion of accounting methods relying on the learning curve, see N. Baloff and J.W. Kennelly, "Accounting Implications of Product and Process Start-Ups," *Journal of Accounting Research*, Autumn 1967, pp. 131-43, and W.J. Morse, "Reporting Production Costs That Follow the Learning Curve Phenomenon," *The Accounting Review*, October 1972, pp. 761-73.

Chapter Eleven

Fixed Assets and Depreciation

This is the first of two chapters dealing with accounting for assets held for use in operations rather than for sale. In this chapter we deal with property, plant, and equipment (commonly called "fixed assets"). In the next we discuss accounting for intangible assets.

For fixed assets the accounting problems reduce to two basic issues: how to find the cost of assets and how to recognize expense as the benefits from the costs incurred expire. The latter problem does not apply to an asset such as land so long as its continued economic usefulness remains a reasonable presumption.

Cost attachment

The fundamental principle for costing property, plant, and equipment is clear. All costs actually incurred and necessary for the acquisition of the asset and making it ready to serve should be capitalized. The difficulties come in the practical application of this principle.

Assets purchased externally

The majority of fixed assets are purchased from external sources. The chief element of cost, then, is the invoiced price less any applicable cash or trade discounts. The chief costing problem lies in ensuring that costs incidental to acquisition and costs of making the asset capable to serve are capitalized. With respect to land and buildings, such costs include any costs of options to buy the property that were exercised, commissions if any, legal fees, land survey costs, etc. With respect to equipment, costs include all customs duties and taxes, transportation inward, insurance in transit, foundations and installation costs, and other charges for testing and preparation.

Assets purchased as replacements

Certain questions arise when an asset replaces one previously owned. If the previous asset is traded in on the new one, the only objective figure in the exchange is the cash paid out over and above the trade-in allowance. Often a trade-in allowance is inflated, with a compensatory inflation in the contract price for the new asset. When it is suspected this may have happened, a realistic trade-in price should be substituted in the accounting to avoid inflating the cost of the new asset and misstating the gain or loss on the asset traded in. When a realistic trade-in value cannot be estimated, the entity may adopt the neutral procedure of recognizing no gain or loss on the asset disposed of. This will mean that the new asset will be costed at the sum of the cash price paid and the net book value of the asset traded in.

A second question relates to the costs of removal of the asset replaced. Although some accounting literature suggests that removal costs may be added to the cost of the replacement asset (or any excess of removal costs over salvage may be so added), this is clearly wrong in principle. The cost of restoring a site to its original condition represents a cost applicable to the service of the asset retired. Only the cost that would be necessarily incurred to install a new asset, whether or not it replaced a previous asset, is properly capitalized.

Additions and renovations

Difficult practical problems can arise when additions or renovations are made to an existing asset (most often a building).

- The cost of a straight *addition* to a building should, of course, be capitalized. Unfortunately, an addition often involves damage to the existing structure that must be made good. Ordinarily it can be accepted that virtually all such cost may be capitalized since it is a necessary consequence of management's decision to undertake the addition. The work, however, may restore the existing premises to a better condition than they were in previously (e.g., simply by leaving them in a freshly painted condition). In general, if work has been done that would have been done in any event (e.g., repainting) and the work would have been treated as expense, an appropriate estimate of that part of the cost of the addition should be written off.
- An improvement that leads to a better quality of service without extending asset life may be called a *betterment*. For example, air-conditioning added to a building would be a betterment. Costs necessarily incurred for betterments should be capitalized, except for amounts that may qualify as expenses on the same basis as described above.
- Costs may also be incurred that increase *the capacity* of an asset for service without increasing the quality of service. Such costs are similar in economic effect to an addition. Sometimes the increased capacity is represented by an increased volume capability and sometimes by an extension of service life at the existing capacity. If costs are capitalized when service life is extended, care should be taken to adjust the depreciation rate accordingly. A possible alternative would be to leave the rate unchanged but charge the additional cost against the previously accumulated depreciation.
- Improvements are often difficult to distinguish from major repairs. In fact, one project may have characteristics of both. In such a case, it is necesary to apportion the cost based on informed estimates.
- In addition, depending on one's point of view, a major repair may be viewed either as a repair or a replacement. For example, a new roof may be viewed as a repair to a building or a new asset in itself. The proper accounting for such major repairs must tie in with the depreciation policy, as will be described subsequently.

In short, given expenditures may have characteristics both of asset addition and asset repair and maintenance. The logic of the situation dictates the appropriate accounting in such a case—usually an apportionment of cost between that estimated to represent an addition or improvement that should be capitalized, and that estimated to be maintenance or repair. The apportionment usually must be made on an estimated basis, for which purpose expert advice may be required.

Capitalized costs are usually added to the asset account, but in some cases charging them against accumulated depreciation is logical.

Self-constructed assets

The primary attribute of cost — that it represents a sacrifice of money or money's worth — is reasonably evident when management makes an outside purchase. Such purchase costs can also be taken as evidence of value received, since management has discretion whether or not to incur them. The situation is less clear when an entity constructs plant or equipment for its own account. The doubt has manifested itself (as was true for inventory) in debates over the merits of direct costing versus full costing and over the propriety of including interest as part of an asset cost.

Basis of costing. The general arguments for and against direct or variable costing and for and against full costing need not be repeated here. It may be, however, that there is an argument favouring variable costing for plant and equipment construction that is not applicable to inventories. Recall that to produce goods for sale it is necessary to have capacity to produce as well as to incur costs for materials, labour, etc. Since management would not have invested in capacity to produce unless it thought full costs could be recovered with a profit, the fact of investment suggests (unless the decision was unwise) that the value of goods produced will be at least equal to full cost most of the time. But once production cost is in place, the cost is sunk. A decision to use the productive capacity for some purpose other than production of goods for sale—e.g., production of capital goods for one's own use—does not carry any such implication that value is expected to exceed full cost. Provided there is spare capacity, a decision to produce an asset for one's own use is justified provided its value in use will be in excess of the variable cost attributable to its production. The conservative view, therefore, is that only variable costs should be capitalized with respect to self-constructed assets unless the decision to construct them has caused the loss of other valuable production.

Practice with respect to capitalization of costs of self-constructed assets varies. Those companies that rarely construct capital assets for their own use are likely to follow a variable costing approach or relevant costing (see chapter 10). Those companies that regularly produce their own capital assets may well follow their normal inventory costing procedures. Doubts as to the value of capital assets produced in such a situation would probably be smaller since the assets are likely to be similar to assets produced for sale. As with inventories, allocation of general and administrative costs to the asset is rare. Exceptions are found in industries that are continually building for their own account. Some public utilities or real estate companies, for example, may be said to be in the business of construction as well as their primary business. In such cases, self-constructed assets may include an allocation or direct charging of such costs as those of the engineering department, construction office, and appropriate other general and administrative costs.

Construction inefficiencies. Costs of self-constructed assets (or assets acquired under a cost-plus contract) lack the certainty in amount provided by a fixed price contract. Accordingly there is greater danger that such an asset may not be worth its cost, especially in the case of projects involving technically difficult construction.

Accounting literature generally warns that extraordinary costs owing to inefficiency or bad luck should not be capitalized. Examples of such costs might include extra costs attributable to strikes, fires, flood, etc. In practice, however, it may be difficult to quantify such costs or losses. For example, a variety of extra costs may be caused by construction delays. Yet some such delays may be no surprise in a complex project. It seems unreasonable to require that costs of routine inefficiency (which would be covered by an allowance for contingencies in a contractor's bid) must be identified and written off. Even strike costs may be offset in part if it is reasonable to assume that it would have been necessary to pay higher employment costs without the strike. In short, the identification of costs of inefficiency is subject to reasonable judgment, and immediate write-off needs to be considered only where major problems in construction have occurred.

Capitalization of financing costs. When an asset is self-constructed (or when a major asset is acquired from a contractor), it is normally necessary to make payments to meet costs before the asset is ready for service. Financing must be obtained for such payments and costs (interest, etc.) will be incurred on such financing. Several questions arise in relation to such financing costs. May they be considered part of the cost of the asset financed? If so, on what basis are they to be attached to the asset? If costs of debt during construction are treated as part of the asset cost, should there be a cost imputed to the use of equity capital as well?

The early view in accounting, for the most part, was that debt costs were a necessary expense of borrowing and no more. Interest was payable for the use of money for a period and consequently was required to be treated as an expense in the period it accrued. The contrary view was that accounting should look to what the money was borrowed for in order to decide how interest costs should be accounted for. If borrowed money was used in construction, the cost of that borrowing during the construction period could be recovered from revenues only after the plant went into service. Accordingly, a proper matching required that such interest cost be treated as part of the plant cost, so that it would become part of depreciation expense matched against plant revenues.

Until 1979 there was no authoritative accounting guidance on the subject of capitalization of interest. In the absence of such guidance, practice was mixed. Most companies did not capitalize interest costs in any circumstances. There was a tendency, however, for companies engaged in major construction projects to capitalize interest with respect to such projects. Where interest was capitalized, in general it was restricted to interest directly traceable to the project. The assumption was that only interest with respect to increases in borrowing subsequent to the initiation of the project should be capitalized, and then only to the extent that borrowing increases were less than the accumulated amount of project expenditures from time to time.

In 1979, the FASB released Statement of Financial Accounting Standards No. 34, *Capitalization of Interest Cost*, to standardize U.S. accounting in this area. The board introduced several new ideas.

- Interest cost is a necessary part of the cost of *acquiring* an asset if a period of time is required to get it ready for use. Therefore, interest not only may be capitalized during that period, it must be capitalized.
- In practice, rigorous application of the test that interest should be capitalized

during any long period of acquisition would necessitate capitalization of interest in many situations (e.g., where inventories are long in production or maturation). Because of the turnover of assets, a change to a policy of capitalization of interest would often have little impact on income reported. The board therefore concluded that capitalization of interest should take place only with respect to an asset that represents a discrete project for which costs are separately accumulated and where the amount of interest is likely to be significant. In the case of inventory, interest capitalization is to be restricted to industries such as heavy contractors, shipyards, etc.

- The basic objective of interest capitalization is to record the sacrifice involved in construction. That sacrifice includes not only the additional interest cost on borrowing caused by the project but also any additional return forgone because the construction project was undertaken. The benefit of such other return, in the absence of construction, would accrue to the equity. Although such sacrifice is undoubtedly part of the economic cost of the asset, the board concluded that capitalization of such a return would be outside the historical cost model. The reasoning was that the cost would have to be "imputed," rather than being a cost resulting from an exchange transaction.
- The board found a compromise answer, however. It observed that in the absence of construction the funds tied up in it would be available to retire existing debt. Interest on that debt represents the result of an exchange transaction. Therefore it is legitimate to capitalize, as a cost of construction, not only interest on debt incurred subsequent to the date construction commences, but also the "avoidable" cost of interest on debt that has been incurred previous to construction but that theoretically might be paid off were it not for the construction. The total amount capitalized is not permitted to exceed total debt interest recorded, in order to maintain the premise that only costs actually incurred in an exchange transaction may be capitalized.

The board was fairly flexible with respect to the precise manner of determining the interest to be capitalized. An average rate of interest can be used, calculated on a judgment-based selection of borrowings deemed applicable. Alternatively, the board permits the use of interest on borrowing subsequent to the date of construction specifically deemed to be for the construction. In that case, interest with respect to any excess of construction expenditures over deemed specific borrowings may be capitalized at the average rate for all other borrowing deemed to be applicable.

As is apparent, the board's conclusions were highly pragmatic. Moreover, the logic is necessarily strained by the board's unwillingness to modify what it conceives to be the framework of the historical cost model. The recommendations are in serious conflict with normal practice in Canada up to 1979. Since U.S. precedents are normally considered authoritative in Canada (in the absence of a contrary CICA recommendation), the FASB recommendations have been, or are likely to be, adopted by some Canadian companies, thereby enlarging the existing diversity in practice in this area.

A criticism may be made of any capitalization method that restricts amounts capitalized to actual interest incurred. The asset cost recorded will differ depending upon the way it is financed. The use of equity financing results in no cost capitalization directly. In contrast, the higher the percentage of debt, the more the cost of the asset will appear to be. The FASB procedure lessens the force of this criticism, since its general effect will be to capitalize more interest than was the practice prior to SFAS No. 34.

The only way to avoid these criticisms completely, while still maintaining the principle that an asset's acquisition cost includes the cost of financing it, is to recognize an imputed cost with respect to equity capital and capitalize an overall cost of capital with respect to all asset acquisition expenditures. Some accountants argue forcefully that such a procedure would provide a better representation of the economics of investment.[1] It is acknowledged, however, that adoption of that procedure would raise consequential questions as to the treatment of the credit arising from capitalization (is it income for the equity?) and as to the treatment of costs of capital bound up in holding assets as opposed to merely constructing them. In present practice an overall cost of capital figure is capitalized only by regulated public utilities and in a few analogous situations, and then only during the construction or acquisition period. This divergence from normal GAAP is justified on the basis that it conforms to the way that regulators calculate the rate base upon which a return on capital is calculated for recovery (along with other costs) from tariffs for service.

If interest is capitalized on construction in process, at what point does capitalization cease? The general rule is that capitalization should cease as soon as the asset is substantially complete and capable of operation at a reasonable level of capacity. That means that testing and trial runs should be complete. When an asset becomes ready to render service in stages, capitalization of interest on the costs of each stage (a calculation that will often require apportionment of total cost to stages on some reasonable basis) ceases when each stage is ready. If, however, the effective service capacity of one stage or unit depends upon completion of another stage, capitalization continues until that other stage is complete and it is possible to render a saleable service.

Expense recognition — depreciation

Except in the case of land, the usable life of any tangible asset must come to an end sooner or later. An ultimate limit is imposed by deterioration of the asset through wear and tear or exposure to the elements. Thus there is a physical boundary to asset life. More important, however, is the boundary imposed by obsolescence. An asset may continue to be perfectly fit for its original intended use and yet have lost all its value except as scrap. Obsolescence may be caused by technological advances whereby some other asset will perform the function better. It may also be caused by shifts in the business environment. Demand for the output of the asset may disappear, or changes in volume may make some other scale of production facility less costly per unit of output.

Because a fixed asset has a limited life, its cost (less ultimate net salvage, if any) is an expense required to earn income over its lifetime. Determination of income for a period less than the asset lifetime requires some decision as to how much of that expense is applicable to each period under review. The objective of depreciation accounting, as customarily stated, is to allocate the cost less salvage value of fixed assets over their useful lives in a systematic and rational fashion. That definition suggests examination of what is meant by "salvage value," "useful life," and "systematic and rational."

Interrelationship between depreciation and other costs of plant service

An initial comment should be made on the objective of depreciation accounting as set out above. Acquisition cost and salvage proceeds are not the only costs or cost recoveries associated with the services of plant and equipment. There are ancillary costs required to obtain their services, including running costs, repairs and maintenance, and costs pertaining to ownership. Income accounting, in principle, requires that all the costs of plant and equipment services be accounted for in a systematic and rational fashion. That broader objective may be achieved by logical treatment of ancillary costs on their own, or by modifying depreciation accounting to take the pattern of other costs into consideration. Either way, their essential interconnection should not be ignored.[2]

Major repairs or replacements illustrate the interconnection. As mentioned earlier, often components of a larger unit require renovation or replacement one or more times during the lifetime of the major unit. Roofs, wiring, and plumbing require renewal in buildings. Steel-making furnaces require relining. Ships require quadrennial as well as annual surveys. All these represent costs of obtaining property services that occur irregularly and may distort average costs of operation if written off to expense as incurred. What expense recognition method would be "systematic and rational" for them? Various approaches are found in practice.

- When a structure has major components that require renewal before the end of the life of the structure itself, the depreciation rate may be established at a higher figure than would be applicable to the shell alone. When components are replaced, the cost may be charged against the accumulated depreciation, with the expectation that after these charges the depreciation accumulated will be an appropriate amount to absorb the write-off of the cost of the structure at the end of its life.
- A more precise alternative would be to capitalize the cost of components separately from that of the shell and apply different depreciation rates to each in order to recognize their different useful lives. This approach has the practical difficulty that the cost of the components separately will probably not be known at the date of first acquisition.
- The provision for major repairs or replacement of components can be separated from depreciation accounting by charging expense and crediting a provision (liability account). This is done commonly with respect to the cost of relining steel furnaces and the cost of quadrennial surveys for ships.
- Alternatively, major repairs or component replacement costs can be accounted for by deferring their costs when incurred and amortizing the cost over the period to the next expected repair date or the end of service life of the related asset. This approach avoids the need for estimates of future costs. Both this method and the previous one are deficient in that provision for major repairs is missed out for one period in their service life. Under the previous method there is no provision in the final period before scrapping. Under this method there is no provision in the first period after acquisition.
- Finally, major repairs and replacements may simply be written off when incurred if their probable amount in any particular year is unlikely to be such as to severely distort the recorded total of expenses.

All these approaches are found in practice in particular situations.

Salvage as a factor in the depreciation base

The base for calculation of depreciation, according to the standard definition, is historical cost less "salvage." Several comments may be made.

First, the proceeds obtainable from an asset depend upon the date at which it is disposed of and generally decline with age. The salvage figure obviously should be an estimate of proceeds at the actual date of disposal. Thus the estimate of salvage must correlate with the estimate of asset life.

The actual salvage proceeds, of course, will be affected by price changes between the date an asset is acquired and its disposal date. Does an estimate of salvage require a forecast of inflation over the period to disposal of the asset? If so, it is conceivable that the estimated salvage proceeds could exceed the original cost of the asset and no depreciation at all would be recognized. That possibility suggests the answer. It makes no sense to subtract estimates of future depreciated dollars from historical dollar costs in finding a figure for depreciation. To avoid this, the estimate of salvage proceeds should be guided, where possible, by disposal values of comparable assets at the date of the acquisition.[3]

Must costs of removal of the asset be offset against estimated salvage proceeds? In general, the answer is yes. The cost of restoring the surroundings to the conditions they were in before the asset was acquired is logically part of the cost of the asset services, and should be recognized as expense in its service period.

What should be done if removal costs exceed salvage proceeds? Should the depreciation charge be increased so that accumulated depreciation at the end of the asset life will be enough to absorb both the write-off of the asset cost and the cost of removal in excess of salvage? Where the excess removal costs are small, such a procedure may be perfectly satisfactory as a practical matter. There may be situations, however, where removal costs are extremely major. In such a case it would be technically better accounting to provide for the expected future cash outflow as a liability, rather than as an accumulation of depreciation. The subject of accruals for future expenditures is discussed in chapter 9.

In many situations the amount of net salvage will be immaterial, and extreme efforts to attain precision in estimates are not warranted in view of the more important uncertainty as to useful life. In practice, careful consideration of salvage amounts is largely restricted to public utility companies. Salvage is usually allowed for, implicitly or explicitly, in the case of automotive-type equipment, but many companies ignore net salvage altogether in their depreciation calculations for other plant.

The meaning and estimation of useful life

As already suggested, the usual life of an asset comes to an end as a result of physical deterioration or for economic reasons. But many types of assets pass through several hands before being abandoned or scrapped at the end of their physical or economic life. From the standpoint of the first owner, however, an asset's useful life is over when he sells it. One is left with the rather ordinary conclusion that the "useful life" over which cost less net salvage value is to be allocated cannot be longer than the period of ownership. May it be shorter? It may be if the owner fails to recognize that the economic value of the asset has expired. For example, an asset may be taken out of service and held, ostensibly as standby, even though the likelihood of future reactivation is small. Indeed, if management is not alert, an asset may sometimes remain in service and yet contribute nothing to net cash returns. Ordinarily, however, one should be able to presume that an asset whose economic life has ended will shortly be scrapped or otherwise disposed of.

The estimation of length of useful life, therefore, reduces to an estimate of how long the asset will be held, subject to caution concerning the possibility of complete obsolescence prior to the end of the normal holding period. Since the asset retirement date lies in the future, the estimate cannot be more than an informed guess. Past experience with similar types of assets provides some guidance. Where the main cause of retirement is physical deterioration, the past experience may be a very good guide. Studies of certain categories of public utility plant, for example, have yielded statistics that show that retirements take place in relatively well-defined patterns, and "survival curves" are constructed on much the same principle as mortality tables used in life insurance. Asset lives for assets that are more individual in character and assets that are more subject to obsolescence are less predictable. Helpful industry-wide studies are sometimes available. An entity must also bear in mind its own replacement policy, the possible impact of its maintenance policy on length of life, and the possibility of acceleration in the rate of obsolescence in the future. In the end, however, estimates can only be a matter of judgment. Once made, estimates of useful life and salvage should be reviewed regularly and amended when necessary. Conditions change, and depreciation accounting should adapt to those changes.

The foregoing represents the theory with respect to estimation of useful lives. Practice is somewhat different. Apart from public utilities, most companies pay little attention to the estimation of useful lives but rather tend to follow past practices and accepted norms. Much of practice can be traced back to the influence of income taxation. The imposition of a tax on business income was a great stimulus to depreciation accounting. When it came to saving taxes businessmen could see the merits of the concept of depreciation, even though many had been unenthusiastic when it was simply a question of financial reporting. As a result of negotiation between taxpayers and taxation officials there grew up in Canada, in the twenty years after the imposition of income taxes, a recognized schedule of depreciation rates allowable for tax for various broad asset categories, mostly on the straight-line basis.

These rates implied conservative estimates of asset lives for the most part and were widely adopted for financial reporting purposes. Subsequently, in 1949, the taxation system changed to provide for "capital cost allowances" on the declining-balance basis, generally at rates double those previously allowed on the straight-line basis. Many companies adopted the declining-balance basis so as to stay in conformity with tax calculations, but over the years since then tended to drift back to the straight-line pattern. Either way, the rates used have been consistent with short asset lives.

The meaning of "systematic and rational"

Given estimates of salvage value and useful life, the final step in depreciation accounting is to select a pattern for allocation of the depreciable base over the useful life. This is achieved typically by applying a mathematical formula or convention. The use of a formula makes an allocation method "systematic." The important question, however, is, what makes it rational? Strangely, there is virtually no discussion of criteria for rational allocation methods in authoritative accounting literature. It appears that a method will be considered rational if it strikes an ordinary observer as being reasonable in the circumstances. By this test a variety of depreciation patterns have gained acceptance and may be applied virtually interchangeably, even though the resulting figure of depreciation may be quite different depending on the method adopted. The following discussion reviews some suggestions as to criteria of rationality.

Depreciation based on asset contributions to net revenue. It is an elementary observation that investment in property, plant, and equipment is made in the expectation that asset services will result in a net cash inflow over a period of years. It seems logical, therefore, that depreciation expense reported should be in some way proportional to the "net revenue contribution" (NRC) expected from the asset—that is, the revenue to be received from the asset's output less related expenses.

There are at least two ways in which a depreciation pattern could be based upon a series of forecast NRCs for an asset.[4] Under the simplest approach, the amount of cost recognized as depreciation for a period would be proportional to the fraction that that period's expected NRC formed of total expected NRCs for all periods. Consequently, the operating profit margin after depreciation recorded would be an unchanging percentage of NRC period by period (assuming actual NRCs turned out to be as forecast). Also, the depreciation pattern over the asset lifetime would be modelled upon the forecast pattern of NRCs. Thus, if NRCs were expected to be constant over the asset lifetime, the depreciation pattern would be straight-line.

A second approach might be considered more consistent with the economics of investment. Explicit recognition would be given to the fact that, because of the time value of money, NRCs to be realized in the more distant future are less valuable than those to be realized in the nearer future. The economic significance of future NRCs at any point of time may be measured by their discounted present value; therefore, a logical depreciation pattern would be one that results in the net carrying value of the asset declining in step with the present value of the estimated future NRCs. Such a depreciation pattern is said to be "time-adjusted." If the NRCs are expected to be constant over the asset's lifetime, the reported net carrying value of the asset would decline in the same fashion as does the value of an annuity—slowly at first and with increasing rapidity as time passes.

Unfortunately, it is virtually impossible to make objective estimates of NRCs. The reason is that it is usually impossible to make accurate subdivisions of net revenue amongst the various assets that work together to produce revenue in total. Thus, historical evidence to provide any basis for estimates of the NRC of a single asset is usually lacking. Nor can one use capital budgeting estimates as a basis for estimates of NRCs. For, if a capital budgeting estimate is made to assist a decision whether to buy a single asset, it will take into account the *incremental* cash flows that will be caused by the investment. Incremental cash flows normally will be bonused by the existence of other assets previously acquired and therefore cannot be attributed solely to the new asset.[5] On the other hand, when a capital budgeting forecast is made for a whole new project, the NRCs will be attributable to all the assets required for the project, which normally will have various useful lives, and it will be impossible to say how much of the total project NRC is attributable to each asset.[6]

Depreciation based on the decline in asset market value. It has been said that depreciation is intended to provide a rational allocation of asset cost over its service life;

it is not intended as a valuation of the asset. This proposition needs some examination. Since the cost of an asset is normally a market price at the date of acquisition and salvage proceeds represent a market price, one is entitled at least to ask why a depreciation pattern consistent with the decline in market value for used assets would not be rational.

One traditional concern has been that market values fluctuate. Since a fixed asset is acquired for use and not for sale, it is argued such fluctuations are irrelevant. In addition, even if prices did not fluctuate, there might be a general inflationary or deflationary trend in prices that would be reflected in market values. Such a trend, it may be argued, should not be reflected in an historical cost accounting system.

These arguments carry considerable weight without being totally conclusive. It is possible to conceive of a typical decline in asset value with use and age that would occur in the absence of temporary price fluctuations or inflationary or deflationary price trends. Depreciation based on such a decline would probably be little different from a depreciation pattern based on the present values of NRCs, since market prices of used assets must be governed by estimates of NRCs.

One point that would need to be clarified, should such an approach be implemented, would be the question whether the typical decline in market value used to guide the depreciation pattern should be based upon buying prices for used assets or selling prices. If it could be assumed that the entity would replace the asset if it did not have it, the buying price would seem to be the logical value until the forecast year of disposal. If, however, an asset were acquired with the expectation that its function would not be replaced at the end of its service period, a switch to a selling value should occur at some earlier time.

A serious practical objection to basing depreciation on market values for used assets lies in the lack of available information as to typical used market values. The difficulty is twofold. For some, perhaps many, types of assets there may be no real market from which price information can be derived. Such exchanges of used assets as take place represent isolated deals. For other types of assets relatively active markets exist, but there is no organized source of information concerning the prices at which exchanges are taking place. It is apparent that considerable research would be necessary to provide an adequate base of information to support depreciation patterns that could be deemed to simulate typical market value declines in a steady-price economy.[7]

Depreciation based on physical output. A third, initially appealing approach to depreciation accounting is to make the periodic asset cost write-off proportional to the consumption of its capacity to serve. The application of this method requires estimates of quantities of output over the asset life rather than net revenue contributions. Since output should produce net revenue, however, the difference in thinking between this approach and that which recognizes depreciation expense proportional to NRCs may be more apparent than real. If the NRC of a unit of output is constant over the asset's life, the two methods are essentially the same. On the other hand, if the NRC is not constant per unit of output, the logic of recognizing expense in step with units consumed becomes less appealing. In essence, the service-capacity basis of recognition is justifiable mainly as a basis of approximating the effects of an allocation based on NRC.

Summary of criteria for rational depreciation. After discussing possible objectives for depreciation accounting, Lamden, Gerboth, and McRae suggested the following criteria for a rational depreciation method:[8]

- The depreciation allocation should be proportional to some measure of the asset's contribution to the business (an NRC approach).
- The depreciation allocation should be proportional to the incidence of events contributing to the exhaustion of asset usefulness (a service-capacity approach).
- Depreciation should result in measuring the decline in asset value in conformity with the values a rational purchaser would assign to the remaining service potential of the asset from time to time over its life (an asset valuation approach).
- The depreciation allocation should tend to equalize the sum of depreciation and other asset-related costs year by year (an NRC approach).
- The depreciation allocation should result in reporting, other things being equal, a constant rate of return on the net recorded investment in the asset (a time-adjusted NRC approach).

As may be seen, these criteria merely summarize the various approaches discussed above. The authors recognized that the objectives contain some degree of conflict. In the final analysis depreciation methods remain primarily a matter of convention, and alternatives persist in similar circumstances. The difficulty is that, even if there were full agreement upon the objectives of depreciation, factual information required to implement a method designed to achieve those objectives is usually lacking.

Conventional depreciation patterns

Conventional depreciation patterns may be classified as straight-line methods, unit-of-output methods, declining-charge methods, and increasing-charge methods.

The straight-line pattern. The simplest and most common depreciation pattern is the straight-line pattern. The annual depreciation amount is found by dividing the estimated number of periods of useful life into the depreciation base (cost less net salvage).

The straight-line pattern is sometimes thought to be justified by the fact that it results in recording a constant margin on net revenue. In fact, that result is unlikely to be achieved. There are probably relatively few instances in which the revenue contribution of an asset does not decline with age (owing to operating inefficiences, greater downtime, etc.) while its repair and maintenance costs go up with age. A more likely justification for the straight-line pattern is that it represents a compromise between the conflicting arguments favouring decreasing- and increasing-charge methods. It also has the virtue of simplicity in calculation.

Unit-of-output pattern. The pattern known by the name of "unit-of-output" depreciation is also essentially a straight-line method. The amount of depreciation for each unit of output is found by dividing the depreciable base by the estimated quantity of output over the asset's useful life.

The unit-of-output pattern is most appropriate where the quality of service of an asset does not deteriorate with use, maintenance costs do not increase, and the useful life of the asset is largely determined by rate of usage rather than passage of time.

Decreasing-charge patterns. There are at least three variations of decreasing-charge patterns. Under the "diminishing-balance" method, a rate of depreciation is struck that is applied to the opening carrying value of the asset for each period (cost less depreciation accumulated in previous periods) so as to reduce the carrying value to estimated salvage value at the end of the asset's life. As the net undepreciated balance declines progressively, so does the amount of the periodic depreciation charge. In practice, this formula is rarely used. Instead, one of the following two methods is normally applied.

The "sum-of-the-years'-digits" method is a method whereby the depreciation for a particular year of an asset's life is a fraction of the depreciable base. The denominator of the fraction is the sum of the digits in the asset's expected life. The numerator is the reverse digit to the actual year in the life. That is to say, in the first year of a ten-year life asset the numerator is ten, in the second year it is nine, and so on. This method is rarely found in Canada but is more common in the United States because of its acceptance for tax purposes there.

The "double-declining-balance" pattern is a diminishing-balance method where the depreciation rate set (applicable to the progressively declining undepreciated balance) is double what would appear to be the appropriate straight-line rate. The simple doubling of the straight-line rate is arbitrary. It became customary because that is the basis adopted for tax purposes when the capital cost allowance system was introduced in 1949. This method never completely writes off the asset and thus is bound to contain some error when applied to assets that have no net positive salvage value. It is conceivable that some other arbitrarily selected rate (say 150% of straight-line rates) might produce results that looked more reasonable for some types of assets.

Increasing-charge patterns. There are two increasing-charge depreciation methods that are essentially the same mathematically, but are explained by somewhat different processes of reasoning.

The annuity method is based on the idea that the real economic cost of asset use must include a charge for cost of the capital tied up in the asset. Thus, the depreciation charge for an owned asset should be equivalent to what would have to be paid in rent for the same asset if it were not owned. (Another term for such a depreciation charge is "rental value.") On the other hand, the benefits of ownership should also be reflected by reporting a credit for interest or return on the capital tied up in the asset. The level annual rental value charge and the decreasing credit for interest return on the decreasing book value of the asset result in a net charge that increases over time. In presentation in financial statements the two components may be separated or combined.

What governs the choice of interest rate? The annuity pattern of depreciation is often advocated on the basis that it will report a constant rate of return on the undepreciated asset balance when the annual NRCs of the asset are constant over its life. If this is the objective, then the interest rate must be the internal rate of return of the asset, that is, the rate of interest that, when applied to discount the annual NRCs and the ultimate asset salvage value, will make the sum of their two present values equal to the original asset cost. On the other hand, if the objective is, say, to provide a charge for rental value that is equivalent to the rental that would be charged by a lessor, an approximation of cost of capital would represent a logical rate of interest.

A provision for depreciation under the sinking-fund method similarly consists of two components. The basic component is the level annual sum that would have to be deposited in a sinking fund to accumulate at interest to the amount of the depreciable base at the end of an asset's life. The second component is the charge for interest that must be added on the increasing balance of the notional sinking fund each year (assuming an actual sinking fund is not created).

The concept of the sinking-fund depreciation pattern is that maintenance of capital requires recognition of asset consumption in the determination of income but that, where revenues at least cover expenses, the amount of depreciation will be represented by cash recovered from revenue. It is unreasonable to think that such cash will not itself earn income (or return the capital advanced to buy the asset) until it comes time to replace the asset depreciated. Thus the depreciation charge can properly increase in step with the presumed earnings on such assets. With this background of thinking, the interest rate assumed for sinking-fund depreciation purposes could logically be an approximation of the rate that can be earned on asset reinvestment. Alternatively, to the extent that assets are financed by debt and cash inflows from revenue equivalent to the depreciation amount are used to pay down debt, the interest rate on the debt would be a logical rate to use in the sinking-fund calculation.

In spite of the differences in concept, it may be noted that if the same interest rate is used, the net depreciation charge under both the annuity and sinking-fund methods will be the same. One other practical characteristic of these increasing-charge methods should be noted. The longer the asset life and the higher the interest rate assumed, the more the depreciation provision will be concentrated in the latter portion of the life. Table 11-1 shows the amount of cost to be written off in the last 20% of an asset's life (in this example assuming no salvage) for varying lives and interest rates. At a 15% rate of interest, note that 75% of the cost of a 50-year asset remains to be amortized in the last ten years of its life.

It is apparent that increasing-charge depreciation methods are extremely vulnerable to errors in life estimates for such longer asset lives. In practice,

Table 11-1

Net Book Value of Asset Remaining under Increasing-Charge Depreciation Methods after Asset Life Is 80% Expired

	Remaining Book Value to be Depreciated in Last 20% of Asset Life under Increasing-Charge Depreciation, Assuming Interest Rates of:		
Estimated Full Asset Life	**5%**	**10%**	**15%**
10 years	24%	28%	32%
25 years	31%	42%	52%
50 years	42%	62%	75%

increasing-charge depreciation methods are little used in Canada except in the case of real estate companies and a few utility companies. The CIPREC manual suggests an arbitrary limitation of the interest assumption to 4-6%.

It should be emphasized that reliance on the objective of reporting a constant rate of return on an asset (assuming NRCs could be estimated on a reasonable basis) does *not* necessarily imply the use of the annuity or sinking-fund pattern of depreciation. The time-adjusted depreciation pattern that will be consistent with the goal of reporting a constant return on investment depends directly on the amounts of NRCs year by year over the asset's life. To show this, Table 11-2

Table 11-2

Patterns of Depreciation That Will Yield a Constant Rate of Return on an Asset, Given Different Rates of Decline in Net Revenue Contributions

	Period				
	1	2	3	4	5
		Annuity Pattern			
Net revenue contribution	$ 2,511	$ 2,511	$ 2,511	$ 2,511	$ 2,511
Depreciation	1,511	1,662	1,828	2,011	2,212
Net income	1,000	849	683	500	299
Net book value of asset, beginning of year	$10,000	$ 8,489	$ 6,828	$ 5,000	$ 2,989
Rate of return on asset	10%	10%	10%	10%	10%
		Straight-Line Pattern			
Net revenue contribution	$ 2,844	$ 2,660	$ 2,475	$ 2,291	$ 2,106
Depreciation	1,844	1,844	1,844	1,844	1,844
Net income	1,000	816	631	447	262
Net book value of asset, beginning of year	$10,000	$ 8,156	$ 6,311	$ 4,467	$ 2,622
Rate of return on asset	10%	10%	10%	10%	10%
		Declining-Balance Pattern (40% rate)			
Net revenue contribution	$ 5,000	$ 3,000	$ 1,800	$ 1,080	$ 648
Depreciation	4,000	2,400	1,440	864	518
Net income	1,000	600	360	216	130
Net book value of asset, beginning of year	$10,000	$ 6,000	$ 3,600	$ 2,160	$ 1,296
Rate of return on asset	10%	10%	10%	10%	10%

presents an example of an asset costing $10,000 with a useful life of five years and with salvage value of $778 at the end of that period. Three different patterns of NRCs over its life are shown along with the depreciation patterns required to produce a constant return on investment over the lifetime of the asset.

This calculation shows that, even if the objective of reporting a constant rate of return on the asset is accepted, that objective does not imply the choice of one depreciation pattern in particular. It all depends on the pattern of the asset's NRCs over its life. Moreover, even though NRC patterns can never be known with certainty, a calculation such as the foregoing, showing the NRCs implied by each depreciation pattern, can be an aid to judgment. For example, few assets are likely to have level NRCs over their whole life. Thus the annuity pattern will almost always be unreasonable. The straight-line calculation, in contrast, appears more likely. The declining-balance pattern also could be applicable for some assets, although the rate of decline in implied NRCs shown in this table looks extreme.

Probabilistic depreciation

Uncertainties inherent in estimates of useful life and salvage, especially the former, have a bearing on the choice of depreciation pattern. One cannot be sure what is the appropriate figure to use as an estimate of useful life. Indeed, a company that owns a number of assets of the same general type is likely to find that some last longer and some expire earlier than the best estimate of life expectancy. For example, suppose a company buys eight assets for $1,000 each that will probably be retired (with no net salvage) at year-ends shown in the following list: year 8, one asset; year 9, two; year 10, two; year 11, two; and year 12, one. Since the average probable life is 10 years, the normal straight-line depreciation write-off would be $800 per annum. In fact, however, with perfect foreknowledge annual depreciation should be as follows: the eight-year asset, $125; the nine-year assets, $222.22; the ten-year assets, $200; the eleven-year assets, $181.82; and the twelve-year asset $83.33. Thus the straight-line depreciation for the group as a whole should be: for the first eight years, $812.37; in year nine, $687.37; in year ten, $465.15; in year eleven, $265.15; and in year twelve, $83.33. If this pattern of higher depreciation in the first several years tailing off toward the end is correct for a group of assets, then it must also be correct for a single asset, given the uncertainty that always exists as to estimated useful life. In the normal situation a refinement to use such "probabilistic depreciation" would probably be immaterial when weighed against the range of judgment possible in choice of depreciation method and the estimates of all kinds entering into the depreciation calculation. In cases where depreciation judgments are made more scientifically, however, the adjustment to probabilistic depreciation may properly be taken into account.[9]

As a final point on depreciation patterns, it should be noted that the patterns described above are not the only possible ones. Those patterns have become established because each embodies a simple mathematical formula that undeniably makes the pattern "systematic" (if not necessarily "rational"). There is no logical reason, however, why they should not be adapted or combined if the result appears more rational than that yielded by conventional patterns. For example, a declining-balance pattern could be adopted for the first fraction of an asset's life, with a switch to straight-line for its remaining years, or vice versa.[10]

Some practical issues in depreciation accounting

A number of practical points in depreciation accounting are discussed below.

Commencement of depreciation. An initial question is, at what time following the acquisition of the asset should depreciation accounting begin? If depreciation is calculated on the unit-of- production basis (implying that wear and tear is the chief cause of loss of useful life), depreciation obviously begins when the asset begins to render service. In the majority of cases, however, where depreciation is tied to the passage of time, the answer is somewhat different. The theory is that depreciation should begin when the asset is capable of rendering service, whether it does so or not. As a practical matter, companies follow two or three shortcuts with respect to depreciation on new assets routinely acquired. A half-year's depreciation may be written in the year of addition and one-half year's at the end, or a full year's depreciation in the first year and none in the year of disposal, or the reverse. These shortcut approaches are, however, acceptable only because their deviation from a policy of accruing depreciation on new assets from their individual ready-to-serve date is immaterial. Depreciation should begin on major new additions at the proper date, regardless of the existence of any shortcut policy on routine purchases.

Depreciation on large capital projects begins after completion of testing and trial runs—that is, it coincides with the date when interest capitalization ceases. Any incidental revenue before that ready-to-serve date should be treated as a reduction of asset cost. An exception is indicated where a major asset inevitably goes through a load buildup period. In such a case there are good grounds for phasing in the full depreciation accrual, simply to fulfill the objective of relating depreciation to the asset's net revenue contribution. Such a procedure has some precedent in major new public utility construction but is less likely to be justified in the plant expansion of ordinary industries. When adopted, the depreciation buildup should be proportional to the faster of the actual or planned load buildup. The failure of load to grow as planned is not an excuse for failure to accrue depreciation.

Depreciation on idle plant. May depreciation be suspended when plant is idle by reason of a strike or other causes? If depreciation were primarily a function of wear and tear, the argument for suspension would be a strong one. However, to the extent that obsolescence is the primary factor in determining economic life, an asset loses value whether or not it is used. Thus, it is the normal practice to continue the standard depreciation write-off during the period of idleness. If plant units are taken out of service and held as standby, depreciation is also continued. Depreciation may be discontinued on plant taken out of service with a view to sale. In this situation such plant held for realization should be segregated from the plant in use on the balance sheet, its value should be written down to estimated realizable value, and that valuation should be kept under review as time passes to see whether further write-downs are necessary.

Individual asset vs. group depreciation. There may be some question whether assets are considered as a group or individually for depreciation purposes. Ordinarily, assets are classified in similar-life groups to facilitate the calculation of depreciation. That does not necessarily imply that the accumulated depreciation is not, in principle, applicable to individual assets. It is common practice, when an individual asset is disposed of, to calculate the depreciation that must have been accumulated with respect to it and to recognize gain or loss for the difference between the asset's net book value and proceeds on disposal. An alternative approach is to consider the accumulated depreciation as being applicable to the entire group or class of assets, in which case no gain or loss would be recognized on disposal of an individual asset. Instead, the asset cost would be written off against the accumulated depreciation account and the proceeds of disposal would be credited to that account. Especially when there are only a few assets in a class or group, however, care must be taken to see that the balance of accumulated depreciation after a disposal is not unreasonably high or low in relation to the cost and remaining lives of assets still in service. The group or "bulk" reserve approach, as it is called, is found most frequently in conjunction with a declining-balance depreciation pattern but may be applied to other patterns as well.

Depreciation adjustments. In theory, estimates of useful lives used for depreciation purposes should be kept under regular review to see whether changes in them should be made. The question arises, if a change in useful life is indicated, should a recalculation of previously accumulated depreciation be made and an adjustment made to income account currently, or as a prior period adjustment? The answer is no. The estimation process in accounting is inherently uncertain. Changes made in estimates may themselves prove to be in error. Accordingly, the generally accepted approach is that changes in estimates should not result in a restatement of previously reported results. Instead, a change in estimate should be made through current income if it applies to a short-life asset or liability (e.g., a changed estimate affecting profit reported on a contract in process) or prospectively if it applies to a longer-life asset or liability. Thus the suggested practice would be to adjust the depreciation rate so as to cause the depreciable base to be fully provided for at the end of asset lives as re-estimated. An exception would be made if it were estimated that depreciation as newly calculated could not be recovered from net revenues over the remaining lives. In such a case, an immediate write-down to recoverable values would be called for.

Unfortunately, only a minority of companies have a practice of making serious reviews of their depreciation policies from time to time. As a result, it is not unknown for companies to discover, too late, that depreciation has been significantly overprovided or underprovided. For example, a company might find that significant assets will be fully depreciated within a year or two, even though many years of useful life remain. To adjust the depreciation provision prospectively in such a case may result in subsequent figures of depreciation that are completely unrepresentative of any reasonable figure. The technically correct treatment in such a case would be to recognize that an error was made in previous years when the useful life should have been, but was not, re-estimated. Correction of this failure requires restatement of the accumulated depreciation to the amount it would have been had this error not been made, and correction of the figures for any previous years being reported.[11] A failure to account for foreseeable changes in useful life in prior years, however, should not be confused with an unusual event that has caused one or more assets to become obsolete in the current year. Any loss of value attributable to the latter cause should be recorded as an expense of the year in which the obsolescence occurred.

Appraisals of fixed assets

The recording of fixed assets in balance sheets on the basis of appraised value rather than cost was common before the development and spread of the historical cost model in the 1930s and 1940s. The gradual acceptance of cost-based accounting and the active opposition to appraisals by the Securities and Exchange Commission led to the virtual disappearance of the use of appraisals in the United States. An important factor in such disappearance, also, was undoubtedly the lack of confidence by accountants in the reliability of appraisals, coupled with the fact that different approaches to appraisal values are possible, some of which at least are unsuitable for financial reporting purposes. It was not until 1965, however, that the Accounting Principles Board was prepared to state positively that property, plant, and equipment should not be written up by an enterprise to reflect appraisal or current values above cost.[12]

In other English-speaking countries, notably the United Kingdom and Australia, the practice of making regular valuations of property, plant, and equipment for financial statement purposes is common. In the 1970s, inflation in those countries tended to be somewhat higher than in North America but the difference was not extreme.

Canada falls somewhere between the other Commonwealth countries and the United States in its practice. The CICA Committee on Accounting and Auditing Research clearly tried to discourage the use of an appraisal basis for valuation for fixed assets when it said, "The writing up of fixed asset values should not occur in ordinary circumstances."[13] That statement originated in Bulletin 11 issued in 1955, at which time CICA recommendations did not have the influence they have today. As a consequence, the practice of restating fixed assets on the basis of appraisals from time to time continues to be accepted, although used by a minority of companies. In 1955, over 25% of the companies covered in a survey of financial reporting practice by public Canadian companies disclosed some or all property valued on an appraisal basis. That percentage steadily declined over the years after 1955, levelling off to a figure of about 5% in the late 1970s.[14] Included in the latter percentage, however, are a few examples of companies that have recently restated fixed assets at appraisal values. It appears, then, that valuation of fixed assets on the basis of appraisals continues to be regarded as acceptable. In contrast, the CIPREC manual recommends that its members not disclose appraisal values of real estate in financial statements or notes thereto, "because appraisal values are highly variable and fluctuate widely over time."[15] Another consideration applicable to real estate companies is that part of their real estate holdings are inventory, and even properties held for income are frequently sold, so that the character of real estate company holdings is somewhat different from that of fixed assets held for use in the normal manufacturing or trading company.

The authoritative literature is clear that if appraised values for depreciable assets are incorporated in the balance sheet, depreciation thereafter must be based on such values. One cannot logically argue that appraisal values are more relevant than historical costs yet continue to base depreciation upon the latter.

It must be conceded that the inclusion of appraised values for property, plant, and equipment in the balance sheet is inconsistent with the historical cost model, just as is LIFO accounting for inventory. The justification, if any, for both these departures from strict theory is found in the presumption that the resulting figures are more relevant. Particularly in the case of long-lived property, historical costs can become quite unrepresentative of current economic values, and depreciation charges based thereon are likely to be unsatisfactory for any realistic portrayal of income. On the other hand, the accountant's traditional suspicion of appraisal values is not without foundation. Appraisals may be conducted for many purposes and may use different criteria of value—current market value, long-term fair value, physical capacity to serve, and so on. If appraisals are to be used in accounting, the basis of appraisal value needs to be defined. For property, plant, and equipment held for use, the basis presumably should be the reproduction cost of the property less allowance for physical and functional depreciation (i.e., obsolescence). Difficulties in estimating such a depreciated current cost are discussed in Part III.

Summary

As with inventory, there are two basic issues in fixed-asset accounting—determining the cost of the assets, and finding a basis for recognition of expense as their value is consumed.

Most fixed assets are acquired by external purchase. The principal problem for such assets is to make sure that costs incidental to the acquisition are capitalized. When improvements are made to existing assets, there also can be difficulties in differentiating betterments from repairs, but these are solved in accordance with the facts of the case. Self-constructed assets present some conceptual problems with respect to capitalization of overheads and of financing costs during construction. All variable costs of construction including variable overheads should always be capitalized, but there is some inconsistency in practice beyond that. Canadian practice accepts that costs of debt financing construction may be capitalized but does not require it across the board. Formerly, the amount of financing cost capitalized was restricted to the increase in interest costs incurred during the construction period. A FASB recommendation has broadened the basis of capitalization by permitting capitalization of all interest that would be "avoidable" if construction had not taken place.

Measurement of periodic income requires recognition of depreciation expense on a systematic and rational basis over the estimated useful life of all property, plant, and equipment having limited lives. The amount to be recognized as depreciation over that lifetime (the depreciation base) is the original cost less the expected net salvage proceeds on disposal after deducting any costs of removal.

Logically, all costs associated with the service of a fixed asset should be recognized as expense in a systematic and rational fashion over the asset's useful life. Depreciation accounting, however, normally deals only with the original cost less salvage. Other costs that are associated with plant service but that occur irregularly should be dealt with on a basis compatible with depreciation accounting, if material. A variety of ways exist, for example, to spread the cost of major repairs and renewals over a reasonable period.

Depreciation patterns are supposed to recognize expense over an asset's useful life in a "systematic and rational" pattern. Patterns used in practice generally follow some mathematical formula such as the straight-line basis. Accordingly, a depreciation pattern can be said to be "systematic." Unfortunately, it is more difficult to ensure that a pattern is rational. There are several possible criteria for rationality, but it is usually very difficult or impossible to apply these criteria effectively. In practice, entities tend to follow customary depreciation patterns, often influenced by patterns and life estimates allowed for income tax purposes.

In Canada, carrying values of fixed assets are, on infrequent occasions, restated on the basis of appraisals. If appraisal figures have been recognized, depreciation accounting is based thereon. Restatement on the basis of appraisals is essentially inconsistent with the historical cost model of accounting, just as is LIFO accounting for inventory.

References

[1]See, for example, R.N. Anthony, *Tell It Like It Was: A Conceptual Framework for Financial Accounting* (Homewood, Ill.: Richard D. Irwin, 1983).

[2]For a lucid explanation, see W.T. Baxter, *Depreciation* (London: Sweet & Maxwell, 1971).

[3]One must note, of course, that if this course is followed and salvage amounts do rise because of inflation, a gain will be shown upon disposal of the asset. Unfortunately, it is inevitable under historical cost accounting that "fictitious" holding gains will appear in income somewhere under inflationary conditions. The argument here is that it is better to concentrate them under the heading "gain on disposal of fixed assets" at the end of the asset's life than to reduce annual depreciation so that it is far removed from a current cost of rendering service, even in the first year of service.

[4]The differences between the two approaches are well described in O. Johnson, "Two General Concepts of Depreciation," *Journal of Accounting Research*, Spring 1968, pp. 29-37.

[5]The point is well argued in F.K. Wright, "Towards a General Theory of Depreciation," *Journal of Accounting Research*, Spring 1964, pp. 80-90, especially from p. 88 on.

[6]See also Baxter, op. cit.; Wright, op. cit.; and W.T. Baxter and N.H. Carrier, "Depreciation, Replacement Price and Cost of Capital," *Journal of Accounting Research*, Autumn 1971, pp. 189-214.

[7]One early attempt to estimate typical declines in used asset values is found in chapter 5 of G. Terborgh, *Realistic Depreciation Policy* (Chicago: Machinery and Allied Products Institute, 1954). A more recent work is Study No. 7 in the series Studies in Accounting Research of the American Accounting Association, C.R. Beidleman, *Valuation of Used Capital Assets* (AAA, 1973). After an examination of used market prices for selected types of equipment in the categories of railroad cars, fork lift trucks and machine tools, Beidleman made several significant observations: (1) asset useful lives are significantly longer than those customarily used for accounting purposes, (2) salvage may be quite significant in amount, (3) age is the single most important factor explaining declines in asset lives, thereby suggesting it is appropriate to base depreciation patterns on age, and (4) value tends to drop off in a gentle declining-balance pattern. Significantly, the statistical significance of Beidleman's observations was improved when market prices were deflated by price indexes. It should be remembered, of course, that past results are only a guide to the future. A quickening in the pace of technological advance could change both asset lives and the rate of decline in asset values.

[8]C.W. Lamden, D.L. Gerboth, and T.W. McRae, *Accounting for Depreciable Assets*, Accounting Research Monograph No. 1 (New York: AICPA, 1975).

[9]Literature on this subject includes two articles by Y. Ijiri and R.S. Kaplan, "Probabilistic Depreciation and Its Implications for Group Depreciation," *The Accounting Review*, October, 1969, pp. 743-56, and "Sequential Models in Probabilistic Depreciation," *Journal of Accounting Research*, Spring 1970, pp. 34-46. See also F.C. Jen and R.J. Huefner, "Depreciation by Probability-Life," *The Accounting Review*, April 1970, pp. 290-98, and R.A. Friberg, "Probabilistic Depreciation with a Varying Salvage Value," *The Accounting Review*, January 1973, pp. 50-60. Terborgh, op. cit., chapter 8, identified the problem with an average service life assumption in 1954. If an entity does not insure its assets against loss (i.e., if it acts as a "self-insurer"), the possibility of casualty losses can also be factored into a probabilistic depreciation pattern. See R.J. Huefner, "Alternative Approaches to Casualty Loss Recognition," *Financial Management*, Spring 1975, pp. 50-56.

[10]Along the same lines, an ingenious application of the declining-charge idea to units of production depreciation is suggested in J.R. Williams, "Time and Use Depreciation," *Management Accounting*, January 1972, pp. 28-30.

[11]See CICA, "Accounting Changes," *CICA Handbook*, Section 1506 (Toronto: CICA), pars. 25-29.

[12]AICPA, APB, *Status of Accounting Research Bulletins*, APB Opinion No. 6 (New York: AICPA, 1965), par. 17.

[13]CICA, "Fixed Assets," *CICA Handbook*, Section 3060 (Toronto: CICA), par. 01. The origin of this recommendation may be found in Bulletin No. 11, *Surplus*, issued in 1955 by the Committee on Accounting and Auditing Research of the CICA. That Bulletin said, "Unless replacement cost accounting becomes generally acceptable, the writing up of fixed asset values should not occur in ordinary circumstances and should be discouraged. It is recognized that there may be exceptions ... [in enumerated circumstances]."

[14]See the biennial surveys published by the CICA under the title *Financial Reporting in Canada* (Toronto).

[15]Canadian Institute of Public Real Estate Companies, *Recommended Accounting Practices for Real Estate Companies*, 2nd. ed. (Toronto: CIPREC, 1980), par. 600.01.

Chapter Twelve
Accounting for Intangibles

A second category of assets held for use rather than sale may be described under the general title "intangibles." Under this heading we include "deferred charges," specific types of intangibles such as patent rights or franchises, and general intangible value commonly known as "goodwill." The accounting use of the term "intangible assets" is somewhat narrower than one might expect from the ordinary meaning of the words. From their dictionary meaning, for example, we might think that accounts receivable or investments in securities are intangible assets since they have no corporeal existence beyond writing on a piece of paper. In accounting, however, the term intangible asset is generally reserved for assets acquired for the production of operating income and excludes assets, such as accounts receivable, that result from the earning of revenue.

The nature and classification of intangibles

If one accepts the general definition of an asset as any right or condition that carries with it an expectation of future benefit, it is clear that intangibles can be assets just as much as tangibles like inventory or plant and equipment. A patent in a drug company or a brand name in a cosmetic company are as important to the production of revenue as any of the physical assets. There are, in fact, a large number of intangible factors that may enhance an entity's well-being. Table 12-1 sets out typical sources of intangible benefit to an entity, the embodiment of the intangible, and the specific activity that may help to create the intangible asset.

Examination of this table leads to the question: For accounting purposes, which of these intangible assets should be classified as deferred charges, which as identifiable intangibles, and which as general goodwill? For example, if institutional advertising builds goodwill, should the asset be classified as deferred advertising or goodwill? If research efforts result in a patentable product, is the asset deferred research cost or patents?

The concept of goodwill

One hundred years ago, business goodwill was thought of very much as its name suggests—the advantage to a business of kindly feelings toward it, especially on the part of customers. Originally, goodwill was thought to pertain directly to the personality and skill of the owner. Later it was realized that to a considerable degree goodwill attached to the business itself and represented part of its value that could be realized if the business were sold. In addition, the concept of goodwill tended to broaden beyond that of mere customer loyalty. If goodwill represented a value transferable with the business, it was natural to think of it as comprehending all intangible factors that could lead to profits above those that might normally be expected from investment in the tangible assets of the business.

Recognition that goodwill existed posed a problem for accountants. Were there

Table 12-1

Some Elements of Goodwill

Source of Goodwill	Embodiment of Goodwill	Activity Creating Goodwill
Favourable attitudes Customer loyalty Supplier loyalty Employee loyalty Good governmental relationship Good credit standing		Advertising Circulation promotion (publishers, cable-TV) Charitable and community activity Personnel and benefits programs Skilled management Successful business operation
Competitive advantage Exclusive rights to do business Desirable products Brand recognition	Franchises, licences Patents, copyrights, agreements Trademarks	Lobbying R&D, contacts with artists, etc. Marketing, product-launch activities
Technological know-how Secret manufacturing processes Skilled work force		Development activities R&D Staff training
Going concern value		Organization, start-up activities

circumstances in which goodwill should be recognized as an asset of the business? How could it be measured if it was recognized? Once goodwill was defined as representing the totality of intangible factors beneficial to a business, a means of estimating its value became possible. The future level of profitability of the business could be forecast, and then a fair return on the fair value of the tangible assets of the business could be estimated. Subtracting the latter figure from the forecast profits left a figure of excess or "super" profits, which could be presumed to be attributable to intangible goodwill. Discounting these expectations of excess profits (for as long as they could be expected to persist) would yield a present value that could be considered to be the value of goodwill. Of course, such a value estimate is highly subjective.

Even when the balance sheet was thought of as a listing of values, accountants were never predisposed in favour of recording goodwill in the accounts. Recognition of the value of goodwill as it grew would be to take credit for unrealized profit, and, in any event, the method of valuation was very speculative. General acceptance of the historical cost system settled the question decisively. Since goodwill could not be associated with an exchange transaction, it could not be recognized.

There is one exception to that general statement. Whenever one business purchases another, it inevitably pays for any goodwill that may exist, along with other assets. In such a basket purchase of assets the total purchase cost (including the value of liabilities assumed) must be assigned to individual assets acquired to enable subsequent accounting. Accounting standards call for estimation of the fair value of all the identifiable assets acquired, and assignment of the excess of the total purchase price over the sum of such fair values to goodwill. Thus, purchased goodwill is treated as a "master valuation account"—the difference between values of assets individually and in the aggregate. (The opposite case, where the sum of fair values of identifiable assets exceeds the total purchase price, will be discussed later in this chapter.)

The present situation, then, is that goodwill is defined as the summation of all intangible factors that add value to a business (except for identifiable intangibles to be discussed below). However, goodwill as such is not accounted for under the historical cost system except on occasions when it is purchased in a business combination transaction. Present accounting for goodwill is thus internally inconsistent. The treatment of identifiable intangibles creates other inconsistencies.

Identifiable intangibles

As the middle column of Table 12-1 illustrates, some aspects of overall intangible value take specific forms. Typically, those specific intangibles are associated with legal or contractual rights. As such, they can often be bought or sold separately from the particular business entity. For example, a company might patent a process and sell the patent to another company for exploitation, perhaps retaining a royalty right—another intangible asset. Because such intangibles can be bought, there are occasions when they will be recognized as assets under historical cost accounting, just as is a purchased tangible asset. But this results in two further inconsistencies in accounting: (1) an inconsistency between the treatment of purchased identifiable intangibles and the treatment of internally developed identifiable intangibles, and (2) a possible inconsistency between the treatment of identifiable intangibles acquired in a business combination and those purchased separately.

The first inconsistency may be illustrated by patents. If a valuable patent is purchased from another party, its cost will be capitalized, to be amortized over its period of usefulness. If the same patent is developed through internal research efforts, the costs of that research will be written off as incurred. The explanation for this anomaly is evident. In contrast to the case of self-constructed tangible assets, there is much less certainty that a valuable intangible asset can be created by internal effort. Thus, the accepted accounting practice is to write off research and development costs having such an objective, at least until a degree of success has been achieved that is deemed sufficient to capitalize the costs. (See subsequent discussion of research and development costs.)

The second inconsistency likewise may be traced to practical causes. Accounting standards for business combinations that are accounted for as basket purchases call for the total purchase cost to be allocated among individually identifiable assets, with any excess over the sum of their fair values being reported as goodwill. In effect, the definition of goodwill as representing the totality of all intangible factors advantageous to a business is modified to exclude intangible factors that can be separately identified. It can be argued that it is logical that an identifiable intangible asset acquired in a business combination should be accounted for on the same basis as one acquired by individual purchase. Implementation of this instruction, however, can encounter severe practical problems. Most businesses do have some patent, franchise, or contract rights that unquestionably have value.

But there rarely, if ever, are markets for such highly individual intangible assets. Thus, such assets cannot be valued directly. Neither can the total purchase price for all assets be allocated to individual assets in proportion to their contribution to net cash flow, because the attribution of cash flows to individual assets requires a one-to-many allocation that is impossible to make.[1] For these reasons, many purchasers do not make a serious attempt to allocate costs in a business combination to specific intangible assets but rather lump all intangibles under the heading of goodwill.

Yet another inconsistency in practice stems from confusion as to just what is an identifiable intangible. It has been suggested above that identifiable intangibles represent specific legal or contractual rights that can be bought or sold separately from the business entity. Some businessmen interpret the word "identifiable" differently—if one can put a name to an intangible factor, that is enough to consider it as identifiable. Thus, "circulation lists" of a publisher or "licences" of a cable-TV company are considered as identifiable intangibles and receive all or most of the allocation of cost that otherwise would be described as goodwill. In reality, the essential character of such intangibles is indistinguishable from that of goodwill—both contribute to the superior earning power of the enterprise. Yet the accounting for them may be different depending upon what they are called. The cost of identifiable intangibles is not always required to be amortized (in Canada), but purchased goodwill must be amortized.

Deferred charges

It was stated earlier that goodwill is not recorded under historical cost accounting unless it is purchased. This statement is not strictly accurate when we consider certain individual components of goodwill. It often happens that a business incurs material amounts of costs on an irregular basis that are expected to benefit one or more future periods as well as the current period. It has become generally accepted that in some such situations costs may be "deferred" for amortization against future periods of benefit. In a sense, such deferred costs represent identifiable aspects of the composite intangible that is goodwill. They are identifiable by the common sense test that they require a significant expenditure that is reasonably expected to bear fruit in future periods.

Since expectations become progressively less certain of realization as the forecast time span lengthens, deferred charges are almost invariably amortized over a relatively short period. Some accountants may see a distinction between deferred charges and goodwill on this basis. Deferred costs are expected to bring relatively short-term benefits; goodwill is generally more long-lasting. The distinction, however, is not sharply marked.

To sum up the foregoing discussion on the nature of intangibles:

- Many intangible factors may contribute to the earnings and success of the business. One of these factors is usually customer loyalty. The term goodwill, however, is not restricted to that factor and is now used in accounting to comprehend the value of all intangible factors favourable to a business (apart from specific identifiable factors).
- Goodwill builds up or declines in value in a business almost insensibly. Certain costs may appear designed to build goodwill—e.g., advertising, some staff training expenses, etc.—but goodwill is likely to be built as much by

quality of product and service as by direct outlays. As a practical matter it is impossible to value goodwill objectively in the absence of a sale of the business. It is also impossible to identify all costs that contribute to the development of goodwill and only to goodwill. Accordingly, the historical cost model does not attempt to cost and record goodwill built up internally. If certain cost outlays appear likely to result in future intangible benefits, those costs may be recorded as "deferred charges"—e.g., deferred advertising—but they are not called goodwill because at best they are only a part of the overall goodwill. Goodwill as such is recorded only when purchased as part of the assets of a business acquired.

- Specific identifiable intangible factors acquired in a business combination are supposed to be accounted for separately from goodwill. This requirement creates a problem not encountered when a specific intangible is purchased by itself. First, there is the question of what is meant by an identifiable intangible. Second, there is the problem of assigning part of the overall purchase cost to identifiable intangibles when there is no market for such intangibles. For these reasons, present accounting practice for so-called identifiable intangibles is inconsistent and unsatisfactory.

Accounting for recorded intangibles

As with other assets, two questions have to be resolved in accounting for recorded intangibles: What is the cost of the asset, and on what basis should it be written off? These will be covered in the discussion below of individual classes of intangibles.

Deferred charges

It is not possible to catalogue all the different types of costs incurred for services that may carry intangible benefits over several future periods. The types mentioned below represent those that are most commonly considered for deferment, but the comments are not exhaustive.

Advertising. Advertising expenditures, in some industries at least, have a very direct relationship to future sales. It is natural, therefore, to at least consider the deferment of advertising costs for write-off over some period of expected future benefit. In fact, it is acknowledged that for interim financial reporting purposes, a proper portrayal of income may require some spreading of advertising expenses over the fiscal year.[2] Nevertheless, the carryforward of deferred advertising costs at a fiscal year-end is rare. In part, that is because the period of future benefit would normally be short and the amounts deferrable relatively immaterial. There may also be a feeling that advertising is a normal cost of business maintenance that should be expensed as incurred. Finally, the period of benefit is uncertain, and the study required to improve estimates of the duration of benefit from advertising may be felt to be not worth the trouble.[3] Cost deferment is likely to occur, therefore, only in relation to unusually expensive programs that are undertaken irregularly—say a new product launch—and then the amortization period will be short.

Product development. Product development costs are incurred regularly in many industries in significant amounts. Often they are expensed when incurred because they are regarded simply as necessary costs of staying in business. If there is any variation in the level of development costs, however, an entity may wish to follow a policy of deferral and amortization in order to portray income more effectively. In the automobile industry, for example, tooling and development for new models may be accumulated at the time of model change for amortization over the new model production period. Similarly, in other consumer durable industries, major product development costs may be deferred for amortization over product life cycles of varying lengths. Product development costs, as here described, are to be distinguished from development costs of new products (to be discussed subsequently) as that term is used in the phrase "research and development."

Plant renovation. Occasionally a manufacturing company may undertake a plant renovation that is primarily to make the workflow and handling more efficient, rather than to add new equipment. Since such a program may be costly and undertaken only infrequently, it may be felt that it is proper to spread the cost over several fiscal periods. Any such costs deferred should be restricted to costs directly traceable to the program and should not represent normal maintenance deferred from previous years. In practice the period of amortization is arbitrary, but it is generally acknowledged it should be short in view of the intangible nature of the benefit. A three-year amortization period is common.

Start-up costs. Any enterprise that grows in discrete units will often experience a reasonably well-defined set of "start-up" costs with each new unit. For example, a financial institution opening a new branch, a motel chain opening a new motel, and a fast-food chain opening a new restaurant may all have a well-developed pattern of saturation advertising, entertainment for local dignitaries, gifts to attract customers, and so on, all to start business flowing. Some but not all enterprises in this position accumulate and defer such start-up costs. Since the period of benefit is indefinite, the amortization period selected is arbitrary. An amortization period of sixty months is common, but anything beyond that would generally be considered excessive.

Initial losses. Initial losses are a feature of many project start-ups, as much as special start-up costs. The fact is that when a branch is opened, a new plant constructed, or a new venture undertaken, it often takes some time to reach a profitable level of activity. Moreover, in planning the project such initial losses may well have been allowed for in the project evaluation. In an economic sense, then, start-up period losses may be regarded as part of the investment necessary to get a project up and running. For this reason, companies sometimes feel it would be proper to defer start-up losses for write-off against subsequent hoped-for profits, and two or three Canadian companies actually adopted this practice in the 1960s. The practice did not catch on, however. Capitalization of losses, rather than costs, was inconsistent with the historical cost model, and in any event there was no particular reason to believe the amount of start-up losses incurred was equivalent to the going concern value created. It is now generally accepted that deferral of losses, whether start-up or otherwise, is not permissible.

Financing costs. When an entity raises financing in the form of debt or capital stock, various costs are normally experienced, including legal fees, prospectus costs, commissions to selling agents, and so on. The benefit from these costs is obviously the use of funds obtained through the financing. It is appropriate, therefore, to defer such costs and amortize them over the period for which the funds are available. In the case of costs related to debt financing, the amortization may be accomplished, along with that of any discount or premium on the issue, through recognition of the debt costs on the "effective-yield" method. That is, interest and amortization expense together are recognized as expense at a constant yield rate on the balance of debt and unamortized costs outstanding from time to time. Issue costs related to capital stock are more difficult because there is no fixed term to the financing. Common, although not completely logical, practice is to write such costs off against retained earnings at the time they are incurred. An acceptable alternative is to carry them unamortized as a deferred asset. Where preferred shares have a probable redemption schedule, there is an argument for amortizing their issue costs over that schedule. The amortization expense should be grouped with preferred share dividends to record the effective cost of the shares.

Research and development. An increasingly important category of cost that confers intangible benefits is that identified by the name of research and development (R&D). There is no better example of a cost incurred for future intangible benefit, nor is there a better example of the difficulty in accounting for intangibles.

The problem begins with definitions. Research costs are defined for accounting purposes as investigatory costs undertaken in the hope of gaining new scientific or technical knowledge. They include costs up to the stage where new products or processes or significant improvements to existing products and processes are conceived of as being feasible. Development activities are concerned with the translation of ideas into usable results. They include testing and evaluation of alternative possibilities, design, construction and testing of prototypes and pilot plants, and (in Canada but not in the United States) market research delineating the potential market before commercial production.

Costs of R&D are to be determined by approaches that are generally similar to those used in costing inventory—including the allocation of overheads where applicable. In Canada, fixed assets and specific intangibles acquired for a single R&D project and with no expected alternative use are to be capitalized. Depreciation written thereon over the life of the project is to be classified as R&D. In the United States, if the fixed asset or intangible has no future use beyond the project for which it is acquired, its entire cost is to be classified as R&D upon acquisition.

In practice, considerable difficulty may be experienced in distinguishing between costs of research and costs of development since these activities tend to run into each other. Care also needs to be taken in classifying costs where people normally engaged in research and development work are used in what is essentially a production operation, especially in the start-up and debugging stages.

Historically, practice has varied in the accounting treatment of R&D costs. Income accounting theory calls for their deferment for amortization over periods of presumed future benefit, and a minority of companies have followed this practice. Many companies have not, however, for a variety of reasons. The benefits from research costs especially and from new product or process costs to a degree are speculative. If only three projects out of ten will prove successful, many accountants and businessmen feel that no costs should be carried forward since the odds on any individual project are that it will fail. They are unimpressed with an argument that all costs may be properly carried forward because it is necessary to try ten projects to get three successes. The unpleasant surprise when losses have to be recognized on large unsuccessful projects seems to outweigh the unpleasantness of regular absorption of costs not related to current income. Even when projects are successful, the appropriate period for amortization and its pattern (declining-balance or straight-line) are usually matters for guesswork. Finally, many established companies look on R&D costs as part of the regular recurring costs of maintaining the business that should be absorbed regularly, much like general and administrative costs.

Because of the lack of uniformity in practice, accounting standard-setters looked at the problem in the 1970s. On the basis of the uncertainty of success with respect to any individual research or development project, the FASB espoused the extreme position by requiring that all R&D costs be written off to expense at the time they are incurred.[4] The CICA has been somewhat less conservative in recommending that development costs (but not research costs) be deferred under certain conditions.[5] The conditions are that it be "demonstrated" that the product or process is technologically feasible, the enterprise intends to continue to the stage of selling or using the output, the market for it or use for it is clearly defined, and the enterprise is able to obtain the resources necessary to complete the project.

Thus the CICA has made a trade-off between faithful representation of the purpose for which the costs were incurred and reliability of asset measurement. It has attempted to stick a little more closely to the theory of income accounting at the expense of some inevitable lack of uniformity in accounting. Whether it is "demonstrated" that a product or process is feasible and financeable will to some degree be a matter for judgment and, if judgment turns out to be incorrect, there will inevitably be some unpleasant surprises.

It is necessary to amortize any costs that have been deferred coincident with the start of commercial production, preferably on the basis of projected sales or use of the product or process. Also required is a regular review of the unamortized balance of deferred costs and write-off of any portion deemed not recoverable from time to time. Despite the differences between U.S. and Canadian standards, at least some costs clearly incurred for future benefit will be charged to expense immediately in both countries. In these circumstances, the standards properly call for full disclosure of amounts of R&D costs incurred and written off.

Computer software costs. The difficulty in defining cut-off points for determination of costs to be written off and costs to be capitalized is well illustrated by the experience in applying R&D standards to the production of computer software. The problem here is that, although some steps in the production of computer software are like R&D, they also are an integral part of the production of the product. Specifically, there is not usually a prototype stage the completion of which serves as a relatively clear signal of the end of the development stage. In addition, it is not so clear whether computer software under development is a new or significant improvement, within the meaning of the R&D standards. Many computer software products may represent merely minor improvements or adaptations of existing products and technology; others may be deemed significant. A further anomaly lies in the fact that purchased computer software is automatically capitalized under ordinary accounting principles, whereas the costs of internally developed software might be largely written off under the application of the R&D standards.

After extended deliberation the FASB provided a standard to guide practice in

1985.[6] The standard provided decision rules (1) to distinguish costs deemed to be research and development from those deemed to be production costs (to be capitalized as assets), and (2) to distinguish between initial production costs to be recorded as a capital asset (and subsequently amortized) and other recurring production costs to be treated as inventory.

Costs are to be written off as research and development expense up to the time that technological feasibility is demonstrated. The primary indicator of technological feasibility is the completion of detail program design. That design must be complete and in accordance with product specifications. If any further development features are high-risk because they incorporate novel or untried functions, the uncertainties must have been resolved by coding and testing beyond the program design stage. It must also be established that the enterprise has the necessary capability to produce the product. In cases where production plans do not include a detail program design stage, technological feasibility is not considered established until there exists a tested working model consistent with the product design.

After technological feasibility is deemed established, costs of producing the software documentation and training materials are to be capitalized. If the software is to become part of another product or process, however, capitalization is not to begin until that other product or process has emerged from the R&D stage. Capitalization of cost ceases and amortization begins when the product is available for general release. Amortization for a period is to be based upon the ratio of current revenue from the product to the total of current and anticipated future revenue. The figure of amortization is not to be less, however, than a figure arrived at by spreading the unamortized balance of cost equally over the estimated remaining life of the product, including the period being reported upon. In addition, costs carried forward for a product at the beginning of production and at any time subsequently are to be written down if they exceed estimated future net revenues realizable from the product after allowance for all production costs and maintenance and customer support costs.

Costs of duplicating the software, documentation, training material, and other costs involved in sale and distribution of the product are to be accounted for as inventory.

Purchased software acquired for sale or lease is to be accounted for on a basis consistent with internally developed software. That is, if the technological feasibility of the purchased software is not established, the cost must be written off. An exception is made if some or all of the cost of that software may be attributed to an alternative future use. In that case, the appropriate portion of the cost may be capitalized and amortized over the period of use.

Under the general R&D standard in Canada, development costs may not be carried forward unless the product is technologically feasible (and also meets tests of market and financial feasibility). Practice with respect to deferment of computer software development costs has tended to become more conservative over time, indicating that an increasingly stringent interpretation of feasibility has been adopted in practice. It may be that Canadian practice will adopt the FASB definition of technological feasibility for computer software, thereby leading to cross-border harmonization of accounting practice in this area.

Development-stage companies. The problem of cost deferment is at its most acute in entities that are in a preoperating stage (including enterprises formed to explore for minerals or oil and gas that have not yet gone into production). Since there is no revenue from operations, it is an elementary observation that all costs are being incurred in the hope of future benefit. Traditional accounting practice has been based on this observation and has treated all costs as deferred charges (other than costs that can be assigned to specific assets such as fixed assets or inventory acquired in anticipation of operations). Any incidental revenue received during the preoperating period is normally credited against the single amount carried forward as deferred preoperating costs. Sometimes this practice is varied (not very logically) by excluding general and administrative costs or interest expense from the deferred preoperating costs.

The total deferred costs continue to accumulate (without an effective recoverability test since recoverability is usually virtually impossible to estimate in the preoperating stage) until the enterprise commences operations and reaches what is felt to be a commercial operating level. There should be a control, however, to the effect that if operations are commenced and take longer than expected to reach a commercial or profitable level, deferment of net costs should cease and the transition to normal profit and loss accounting should be made.

There are several difficulties with this traditional basis of accounting. The first is the difficulty just mentioned in establishing the transition point from the development-stage accounting to regular income accounting. The second is the problem of disposing of the deferred preoperating costs. In the mining industry, the exploration and any preliminary development costs are assigned to areas of interest and are written off if and when a decision is made to abandon efforts in the area. (Abandonment may be signalled by allowing mining claims to lapse, but a write-off of exploration costs may be required before that date since the effective interest in an area may lapse yet claims be maintained in good standing on a purely speculative basis.) Where exploration and development costs in an area are carried through to production, amortization (depletion) begins on a unit-of-production basis. Selection of a unit rate of amortization is usually difficult since mineral reserves may not be adequately delineated at the outset. In companies outside the extractive field, there is neither a basis for write-off of preoperating costs before production nor any particularly logical basis for amortization after commercial operations commence. In practice, the amortization period chosen is virtually completely arbitrary and is likely to be selected on the basis of being the maximum amount of write-off that can be covered by profits reported in the first few years.

If development-stage accounting is logical at all, it should be logical for some new projects of established operating companies as well as for new companies. There is nothing to stop a going concern from embarking on a new business venture that, if undertaken by an entirely new company, would be accounted for using development-stage accounting. Some going concerns do, in fact, use accounting equivalent to development-stage accounting when undertaking completely new projects. Others, however, continue with normal accounting, thereby absorbing as current expenses costs that do not relate to their revenue-producing activities.

In short, it can be said that accounting for ventures in the development stage is shot through with inconsistencies and anomalies and is difficult to fit into the normal income accounting framework. The FASB addressed these inconsistencies shortly after it dealt with research and development costs.[7] In essence, the board decided to eliminate distinctive accounting practice for development-stage enterprises and apply to them the same accounting standards applicable to operating enterprises. Because of the normal inability to establish recoverability of preoperating costs and because much of the activity of development-stage enterprises consists of raising financial resources, planning, and research and development, the board's decision meant that most costs for such enterprises, except for tangible assets, are written off when incurred.

In these circumstances, the board called for special disclosure in the financial statements. The statements are to be described as those of an entity in the development stage and are to describe the nature of the development-stage activity. The deficit is to be described as having been accumulated in the development stage. The income statement and statement of changes in financial position are to show separately the cumulative amounts of revenue, expense, etc. since the inception of the enterprise. An analysis of shareholders' equity from inception is to be provided showing, inter alia, dates and details of each issue of equity securities, distinguishing those issued for cash and those issued for other consideration, the nature of any non-cash consideration, and the basis for assigning dollar amounts to it. In this fashion, the board has avoided the well-nigh impossible task of determining whether costs incurred in the development-stage activities have produced equivalent value so as to justify their asset status. In Canada, however, in the absence of a specific standard on the subject, traditional practice as described earlier is still generally accepted.

Identifiable intangibles

As already described, identifiable intangibles may be acquired by purchase or developed through internal effort. In general, only very directly traceable costs, such as legal fees for patent applications, should be capitalized for self-developed identifiable intangibles. For this reason they do not constitute a significant accounting problem.

Amortization of the cost of purchased or internally developed identifiable intangibles should, in theory, take place over their economic life. In some cases, as in patents, the duration of the legal life puts a maximum on the economic life of the asset. The economic life may nevertheless be shorter than the legal life, and amortization should be over the shorter period if past experience with similar assets or other evidence so indicates. In other cases a legal right, such as a licence, may be of short duration, but if the right is renewable without charge and normally without difficulty, the economic life may be indefinite as a practical matter. Generally accepted accounting principles in Canada permit but do not require the amortization (over an arbitrary period) of intangible assets with an indefinite life. If circumstances suggest a limit to the life of an intangible previously not amortized, amortization should begin. In the absence of any indication that declining-balance amortization is appropriate, a straight-line amortization pattern is usually used. In the United States, it is felt that no intangible asset has indefinite life, and amortization is required over a maximum period of forty years for all intangibles (unless acquired before November 1, 1970) where a shorter period of life is not indicated.[8]

Goodwill

From the earlier discussion it will be apparent that goodwill cannot be fully accounted for within the historical cost model because it is largely not the result of a cost outlay. It is not surprising that generally accepted accounting principles do not permit attempts to cost or value general goodwill as it grows or diminishes during the conduct of the business.

Even if accounting were to adopt a valuation approach in place of the historical cost model, accounting for the value of goodwill would be very difficult. The reason is that goodwill is inseparable from the business carried on. Firm evidence of its value, then, is to be found only when the business is sold. Some think that a value can be derived from the market value of the outstanding securities of an entity. It is not clear, however, that market values for trades in a company's securities can properly be translated into a valuation of the entity as a whole. In any event, that basis of valuation is only available for the minority of entities whose securities are publicly traded. For the rest, valuation of goodwill would be almost completely subjective.

As a practical matter, therefore, under almost any system of accounting one can think of, it would be preferable to ignore goodwill. But there is one situation in which it cannot be ignored—that is, the situation when one entity purchases another. The problem, then, is what to do with the cost of the goodwill purchased. The problem has been debated for more than three-quarters of a century, and no one yet has come up with an answer satisfactory to everyone. There are three main proposals for accounting for goodwill purchased in a business combination. The basis for each and the objections to each are set out briefly below.

- Possibly the simplest approach would be to write off purchased goodwill at the date of acquisition against any surplus account that is available—in most cases retained earnings. The argument for this is that the end result would be consistent with the treatment of internally generated goodwill. The latter is not accounted for (and any cost incurred in generating it is written off). Hence the former should be written off as well. It is sometimes argued, also, that goodwill is not an asset of the entity: the entity cannot manage goodwill or realize upon it by selling it. Rather, goodwill is an asset only to the owners of the enterprise and should be accounted for by them rather than by the entity.[9] The objection to these arguments is that if management of an entity has bought an asset, it should be accountable for it. If goodwill is not of permanent life, its cost should be amortized against income. Otherwise the performance of the management will be made to look unduly favourable. A management that builds a business and bears the start-up costs and probable period of losses or low profits will suffer in comparison with a management that buys a business as a going concern with an established level of profitability. Also, in some situations the proposed accounting will be impossible, or at the least disadvantageous, because the acquiror will not have enough surplus to absorb the write-off of the goodwill or because of the severe effect on its debt/equity ratio. For these reasons, it is almost inevitable that some other approach would have to be allowed in addition to the apparently simple approach of immediate write-off of goodwill.
- A directly opposite approach is to capitalize the cost of purchased goodwill and leave it unamortized unless or until the business to which it is related is sold or the goodwill independently appears to be losing or to have lost its value. The argument for this is that normally the goodwill of a business is being maintained by current operations. This is true just as much of a new business acquired as of a business that has been under the direction of

management for some time. Nonamortization of purchased goodwill, therefore, makes earnings of a purchasing company comparable with those of other companies that have not made acquisitions. Some of the same objections apply to this suggestion as to the first. Without amortization of goodwill, the increase in reported earnings as a result of the business acquired can give a misleading picture of management's performance. Also, management will be tempted to bias the allocation of the purchase price toward goodwill and away from other assets if goodwill does not have to be amortized. Moreover, no asset except land lasts forever. If not amortized, there is a distinct possibility that an entity will discover, too late, that it has a worthless asset in its balance sheet.

- An intermediate position is that in which goodwill is capitalized upon acquisition but then is amortized over a period deemed appropriate in the circumstances but with an outside limit. This approach involves acceptance of the proposition that no intangible asset lasts forever. Indeed, if one considers the fact that an acquired business is likely to have made a variety of outlays with future intangible benefit, that the value of those intangible benefits is probably reflected in the overall goodwill payment, and that the duration of some of those elements is quite short, a fairly rapid amortization of goodwill would be justified. The objection to this is the argument that goodwill, whether short-term or long-term, is probably being maintained in current operations. Moreover, as a practical matter the period or pattern for amortization is usually extremely arbitrary. Many entities choose to amortize purchased goodwill over the forty-year maximum permitted by accounting standards even though common sense tells us that its economic life will be much shorter in most cases. Thus the amortization charged against income will be, for the most part, a meaningless figure. The chief virtue of this approach is that it gets a dubious asset off the balance sheet, while the length of amortization period tends to ensure that income distortion, if any, is minimized.

Negative goodwill

Inspection of the earlier display of factors that may be advantageous to a business suggests that a number of factors may be disadvantageous almost as easily as advantageous. For example, a management may be incompetent rather than efficient. A work force may be untrained, surly, and uncooperative rather than skilled and hardworking. Because of these negative intangible factors, it is as easy for a business to realize less than a normal return on its tangible assets as it is to earn above average returns. Hence it is not inappropriate to think of "negative goodwill" as the summation of all the adverse intangible factors bearing on a business, just as we think of positive goodwill as the summation of favourable factors.

We have already noted that it is a practical impossibility to value positive goodwill. Ordinarily one cannot even identify all the intangible factors that constitute goodwill, let alone value them objectively. So it is also with negative goodwill. Ordinarily it must be left to the reader of financial statements to deduce the existence of positive or negative goodwill from an entity's success in achieving revenues and controlling costs. But, as with positive goodwill, negative goodwill may manifest itself when a business is purchased by another entity. When this occurs it is as difficult to know how to account for negative goodwill as it is for positive goodwill.

The amount of negative goodwill at the time of a purchase may be established by comparing the purchase price of the business acquired (including the value of liabilities assumed) with the sum of the fair values of its assets taken individually. If the situation were a mirror image of that of positive goodwill, one might say that negative goodwill was the allowance made in the purchase price for the disadvantageous factors impinging on the business acquired. Then one might argue it would be logical to record the assets required at their individual fair values and record the difference between the sum of these fair values and the purchase price as a deferred credit, to be amortized to income over the duration of the period during which the adverse factors are expected to persist.

Although the foregoing explanation and proposed treatment for negative goodwill are not illogical, there are two other possibilities. It may be that the purchaser of the business was a good negotiator or was lucky and made a "bargain purchase." That is to say, he genuinely acquired a business with good prospects for less than it was worth. Some might discount this possibility on the grounds that independent parties acting in their own interests are likely to strike a fair price without undue advantages to one side or the other. No doubt this is so in the majority of cases, but any accountant with wide experience will know it is not true universally. The fact is that the purchase and sale of a business does not take place every day, and mistakes may be made in bargaining through inexperience. True bargain purchases do happen (just as people often pay too much to acquire a business). If it could be proved that a business has been purchased at a bargain, some might argue that the logical treatment would be to take the credit for negative goodwill into income immediately in the period of purchase.

There is a third possible explanation for negative goodwill: that it results from an overvaluation of the net assets of the business acquired. Valuation of the individual assets of a going concern is a difficult art because many of them are in a semimanufactured state or a used condition and there rarely are good markets for such assets from which prices can be derived. Thus the apparent negative goodwill may simply be the amount of asset overvaluation. If so, the credit balance might be handled by subtracting it from the valuations placed on the assets.

Thus, there are three possible treatments for negative goodwill: (1) treat it as a price allowance because of subnormal profit expectations and bring it into income over the period in which the profits are expected to remain subnormal, (2) treat it as the result of a bargain purchase and credit it to income immediately upon acquisition, or (3) treat it as resulting from valuation errors and deduct it from the estimated fair values of the individual identifiable assets, probably beginning with those for which the valuation is most uncertain.

Accounting standards for business combinations have chosen the third of these approaches. If the initial valuation of assets of an entity acquired indicates negative goodwill, the CICA recommends that the credit be used to reduce the valuations previously assigned to identifiable nonmonetary assets, allocating the reduction among individual assets according to circumstances.[10] The American standard limits the application of the credit to noncurrent assets (excluding long-term investments in marketable securities) and treats any excess as a deferred credit.[11]

These recommendations generally espouse the most conservative procedure. They also tend to limit manipulation of accounting for business combinations since any overvaluation of nonmonetary assets acquired beyond a certain point will be cancelled out by the credit back of negative goodwill. A rigorous application, however, can lead to a misleading portrayal of financial position and results of operations in the case of a true bargain purchase. The complete elimination of property, plant, and equipment values, as sometimes occurs, is often indisputably wrong by any sensible judgment and can lead to overstated income through understated depreciation in subsequent years. The Canadian practice of taking any further reduction against inventory values has an even more absurd effect on the cost of sales figure in the next accounting period. In this respect, the American arbitrary rule seems better than the Canadian.

Summary

Intangibles do not represent a homogeneous class of asset. To understand the accounting for intangibles it is first necessary to review the types of assets that are accounted for.

- By a process of evolution, the term "goodwill" has come to stand for the totality of intangible factors that add value to a business enterprise. It is not a specifically recognizable asset like other assets, but rather an omnibus term embracing a wide variety of beneficial intangible factors, some of which are quite unrelated to others.
- In a few cases, specific embodiments of intangible value are identifiable because they represent valuable rights, usually legal or contractual, that can be controlled by the entity. Identifiable intangibles such as patents, licences, franchises, royalty agreements, etc. can often be bought and sold, sometimes separately from the business carried on.
- In several other cases, one can be reasonably sure that some fairly well defined expenditure will be repaid by intangible rewards in future, but those rewards are inseparable from the business carried on. Thus, advertising may produce customer loyalty, and costs of opening a new branch or sales outlet may result in building a base of customers. Such assets essentially represent components of overall goodwill.

Certain inconsistencies in the accounting for intangibles result partly from differences in their inherent character, partly from difficulty in measuring their cost, and partly from confusion as to their appropriate classification.

- Overall goodwill is created as much, if not more, by the efficient operation of a business as it is by any identifiable expenditure. Accordingly, it is universally accepted that it is impossible to put a value on goodwill created through regular operations. On the other hand, when one business acquires another, part of the purchase consideration inevitably relates to the goodwill of the latter; hence it is not possible to avoid accounting for purchased goodwill.
- Even though the growth of overall goodwill is not accounted for, it is generally accepted that costs incurred to create subcomponents of goodwill may be "deferred" for future write-off at a time closer to that when the benefit from the expenditure is received.
- While purchase costs of identifiable intangibles that can be separated from a business are capitalized, internal costs to produce a similar specific intangible are unlikely to be capitalized because it is difficult to trace those

costs to the intangible right. In one case, that of patent rights, today's accounting standards prohibit capitalization of most of the research and development costs required to produce the ultimate asset.

- Standards for accounting for acquisition of a business require that *identifiable* intangibles acquired with the business be allocated a portion of the cost of purchase, separate from any residual cost attributed to goodwill. Unfortunately, because of the lack of markets for such specialized assets there is rarely objective evidence upon which to base an allocation of cost to them. Thus, in practice the standard instructions are often ignored.
- On the other hand, owing to the lack of a rigorous definition of what is an "identifiable" intangible, it is possible in the case of some business purchases to call the general goodwill of a business acquired by some other name, such as circulation lists, and thereby treat it as an identifiable intangible.

Today's practice with respect to intangibles that are accounted for as assets may be summarized as follows:

- Purchase costs for identifiable intangibles that can be bought and sold individually are capitalized. If a purchased intangible is considered to have indefinite life, the cost need not be amortized. If its useful life (which may be shorter than its legal existence) is considered to be limited, amortization must be recognized.
- Certain types of expenditures that clearly carry substantial intangible future benefits may be recorded as assets and described as "deferred" costs in the balance sheet. There is no clear basis for differentiating what types of costs should be treated as deferred. Frequently the period of future benefit from such expenditures is indeterminate. Accordingly, the period over which they are amortized to income seems to be determined more by industry practice than by any rigorous assessment of period of benefit. The period of amortization is usually relatively short.
- When one business acquires another, any cost identified as the cost of purchased goodwill is recorded as an asset and is supposed to be written off over its period of benefit but, in any event, over a period not exceeding forty years. The judgment as to duration of the benefit from purchased goodwill is almost always arbitrary.

In a business combination, the sum of the fair values of the assets acquired not infrequently exceeds the sum of the purchase price paid and liabilities assumed. In different situations there are different possible explanations for the existence of such "negative goodwill." To improve consistency in the accounting, however, the standard approach is to reduce the values that otherwise would be assignable to nonmonetary assets acquired, thereby eliminating the figure of negative goodwill.

References

[1]Notwithstanding this difficulty, some authors have argued for separate valuation of specific intangibles. See J.R. Campbell and J.D. Taylor, "Valuation of Elusive Intangibles,"

CAmagazine, May 1972, pp. 39-46, and J.L. Vaughan, Jr., "Give Intangible Assets Useful Life," *Harvard Business Review*, September-October 1972, pp. 127-32. Tax advantages to separate accounting for specific intangibles provide at least part of the motivation for the authors' proposals.

[2]See Accounting Principles Board (APB), *Interim Financial Reporting*, APB Opinion No. 28 (New York: AICPA, 1973), par. 16d.

[3]For a contrary view, see D.L. Flesher, *Accounting for Advertising Assets* (University, Miss.: Bureau of Business and Economic Research, School of Business Administration, University of Mississippi, 1979). The author suggests that deferral and amortization of advertising costs could make a material difference to the figures reported where marketing is the major activity of an entity. Methods of estimating the duration of benefit from advertising based on past experience are also described. The methods, however, are not wholly convincing.

[4]FASB, *Accounting for Research and Development Costs*, Statement of Financial Accounting Standards No. 2 (Stamford: FASB, 1974).

[5]CICA, "Research and Development Costs," *CICA Handbook*, Section 3450 (Toronto: CICA).

[6]See FASB, *Accounting for the Costs of Computer Software to Be Sold, Leased, or Otherwise Marketed*, Statement of Financial Accounting Standards No. 86 (Stamford: FASB, 1985).

[7]See FASB, *Accounting and Reporting by Development Stage Enterprises*, Statement of Financial Accounting Standards No. 7 (Stamford: FASB, 1975).

[8]AICPA, APB, *Intangible Assets*, APB Opinion No. 17 (New York: AICPA, 1970).

[9]See G.R. Catlett and N.O. Olson, *Accounting for Goodwill*, Accounting Research Study No. 10 (New York: AICPA, 1968).

[10]CICA, "Business Combinations," *CICA Handbook*, Section 1580 (Toronto, CICA), par. 44.

[11]AICPA, APB, *Business Combinations*, APB Opinion No. 16 (New York: AICPA, 1970), par. 87.

Chapter Thirteen

Accounting for Pension Costs and Obligations

Pension plans adopted by employers are of two broad types: "defined contribution" plans and "defined benefit" plans. Under a defined contribution plan, the amount contributed by the employer is established by a set formula such as a percentage of the employee's salary. The amount accumulated for each employee over the years, together with investment earnings added, provides a fund from which an annuity can be bought at retirement. The amount of the annuity depends on the earnings achieved on contributions before retirement and the rates at which annuities can be bought at retirement. Thus, the employee does not have assurance as to the amount of pension to be received.

In contrast, under a defined benefit plan the employer provides a formula for calculating the pension benefits to be paid after retirement. The formula is usually related to years of service and often also to wage levels while employed. The employer is then expected to provide the promised benefits. Usually regular contributions to a separate pension fund will be made to ensure that money will be available at retirement, but completely unfunded plans are possible in some jurisdictions.

For the most part, defined contribution plans do not present particular accounting problems. If the formula calls for employer contributions on a regular predetermined basis, the expense each period is simply the required contribution with respect to that period. The accounting problems that arise with respect to defined benefit plans will be discussed in the remainder of this chapter.

Defined benefit plans

There are three dominant types of defined benefit plans, classified according to the formula by which the pension benefits are calculated. "Flat-benefit" plans promise employees a given amount of monthly benefit after retirement for each year of service. This type of plan is usually established as a result of union negotiations. "Career-average" plans promise a unit of benefit expressed as a percentage of salary for each year worked. Thus, for service in a particular year an employee earns an annual pension of, say, 2% of salary in that year. Alternatively it could be said that the employee earns a pension of 2% of total earned salary over her career, or 2% times average salary during the career times the number of years of service—hence the name "career-average." This type of plan was originally adopted mainly for white-collar workers.

Finally, there are plans that base the benefit upon salary in the last year of the employee's service or the average of the last three or five or ten years or perhaps an average of the three or five mostly highly paid years in her career. Thus, the benefit formula could be 1.5% of average salary in the last five years of service times the number of years of service. These "best-pay" or "final-pay" plans will be referred to under the latter name hereafter. Final-pay plans were originally devised for executives who might be expected to experience a steep rise in earnings over their careers and who would therefore find a pension based on average career earnings to be much lower than their earnings level just prior to retirement. With the inflationary trends in the last twenty years, the same could be said of the pattern of most employees' earnings over their lifetime, and final-pay plans have become much more widely adopted.

It was not until after World War II that pension plans became widely adopted. A typical plan covering clerical workers around 1950 was the career-average plan providing benefits of 1.5% or 2% of salary. The interest assumption used in costing that benefit was in the range of 3.5% to 4.5% (in Canada) and the calculated cost (at the 2% benefit level) was 10% of salary, 5% met by employee contributions and 5% met by the employer. When final-pay plans were introduced for more highly paid employees, the benefit level was commonly 1.5% of the final pay for each year of service. This was calculated to cost a little more (as a percentage of salary) than a 2% career-average plan. Flat-benefit plans negotiated with unionized employees initially provided for low monthly benefits of, say, $2.00 for each year of service. Benefits were, however, regularly reviewed as part of the contract bargaining process and tended, if anything, to rise faster than did direct wages.

The evolution of pension accounting

The interest of accounting authorities in pension plans in the postwar period was initially restricted to a narrow question. When a plan was first adopted it was customary to grant some benefit entitlement to long-service employees, even though their previous employment gave them no right to a pension. Such "past service" had a cost, and it was customary for employers to make supplemental payments into the new pension fund over a period of perhaps ten years to cover that cost. What was the proper accounting treatment for past-service cost?

Many Canadian companies followed the practice of recording a liability for the full amount of past service and, since it was "past," charged the cost against retained earnings. Others followed the traditional cash basis of accounting for pension costs and simply wrote past-service contributions off as paid over the ten-year period. In the United States, however, the Committee on Accounting Procedure of the American Institute of Accountants reasoned that an employer would not voluntarily assume an obligation for past service unless future benefit was expected. Thus, the cost should be written off as expense over current and future years when the benefit might be deemed received.[1]

It was not until the mid-1960s that Canadian and U.S. statements were issued dealing with all problem areas in pension accounting. These statements introduced some order into accounting practice but did not solve all problems. Flexibility was allowed in the choice of actuarial methods and assumptions, which allowed numerous inconsistencies in accounting to grow over time.

The history of pension plans since 1950 helps one understand the problems. As previously noted, around 1950 pension plans were costed assuming that investment returns of 3.5% to 4.5% could be achieved. At that time interest yields on Government of Canada securities were around 3% to 3.5%, so that the pension cost interest assumption was closely in tune with current investment yields. Throughout the 1950s and early 1960s interest rates tended to creep up. The result was a tendency for a surplus over obligations to build up in pension plans. These surpluses permitted relatively painless improvements in benefits, including more widespread adoption of final-pay benefit formulas.

Then, in the late 1960s, inflation began to gallop and continued to do so through much of the 1970s. Increases in wage and salary rates meant continuous and strong increases in the money amounts of pension obligations under final-pay plans. Investment returns, on the other hand, lagged. Although over the long term the nominal rate of return on investments tends to increase or decrease so as to remain above the inflation rate, in the short term fund assets may be locked into low yields on fixed-return securities. In addition, inflation tends to depress the market values of both bonds and stocks.

Thus, pension funds found themselves with obligations soaring and asset values increasing slowly or even declining, so that huge deficits began to appear in actuarial valuations of final-pay plans. Flat-benefit and career-average plans were in better shape, except that their fixed formula benefits began to look inadequate in the face of inflation. Hence there was a tendency to update benefits, and the resulting past-service obligations had to be dealt with. From 1950 on there had been a tendency for actuaries to revise their interest assumptions for valuation purposes following, but lagging behind, changes in market interest rates. In the 1970s that tendency became more marked in the face of the huge unfunded positions opening up in plan valuations.

In the first half of the 1980s the picture changed again. The rate of inflation declined, and the rate of wage and salary increases for a time fell below the rate of inflation. Interest rates, however, stayed well above the rate of inflation so that funds not locked in to low-yield securities could achieve rates of return well above the rates assumed for actuarial valuation purposes. In the early 1980s, the typical actuarial interest rate assumption had increased to the neighbourhood of 6.5%; at the same time, yield rates on Government of Canada long-term bonds were around 15%. The interest rate assumption had clearly come adrift from any correspondence with current market conditions. The result was an in-built tendency for surpluses to appear in successive plan valuations. These could be used by employers to improve benefits or reduce contributions and expense recognized, or could even be withdrawn with consequent recognition of gain.

The elements of pension cost calculations

Accountants have traditionally relied upon actuaries to furnish estimates of pension cost for a period. Actuaries, in turn, have developed such estimates primarily to guide the rate or amount of contributions to be made to funds set up for payment of future benefits. There are three basic elements in actuarial calculations. First, there must be an estimate of what benefit payments will be made in future with respect to members of the plan. Second, since it is agreed that costs to be incurred in future must be discounted, there must be a basis for selecting a discount rate. Third, some method must be adopted for attributing the total benefits that ultimately will be paid to the periods in which they are earned.

Estimation of ultimate benefit payments

In order to calculate future benefits payable to pension plan members, estimates must be made of a number of variables. Mortality in the employee group must be estimated. Some estimate must also be made of the ages at which employees will choose to retire. Withdrawals before retirement from causes other than death, such as employee disability or resignation, must be estimated. Withdrawals must also be separately characterized as between those that occur before vesting and after vesting. Salary escalation must be estimated for final-pay plans. All these estimates are customarily known as "actuarial assumptions." An interest rate to discount estimated future costs is also customarily selected, or at least recommended, by the actuary and is also called an actuarial assumption. It is different in character from other actuarial assumptions, however. Other assumptions form the basis of estimating ultimate pension outlays. The interest assumption enters into the translation of that estimated outlay into a periodic cost figure to be recognized as it accrues. The choice of interest rate is discussed further in the next section.

Actuarial assumptions differ in nature, one from another. The fundamental assumption of mortality rates and the assumption of disability rates depend largely on physical constraints inherent in mankind and on the physical environment. Experience over time and observation of trends should enable quite reliable long-term predictions. Assumptions as to retirement ages are less reliable, being dependent on social trends and conditions specific to the employer that may change from time to time. Assumptions of turnover in employment are likewise affected, but to a greater degree, by both these factors. The actuary can look to experience in the past in the particular work force, but cannot be confident that the future will be similar to the past. Even less certainty can be felt about the so-called economic assumptions. These consist of (1) the assumption of salary escalation required when actuarial cost methods incorporating salary projection are used, (2) the assumption of rate of return on pension fund assets—conventionally called the "interest" assumption—used in discounting pension obligations to present values at the reporting date, and (3) the several assumptions required to predict the level of governmental postretirement assistance where plan benefits are "integrated" with government benefits.

The interest assumption

Actuaries tend to think of the interest assumption as an assumption of what monies set aside in the pension fund can earn over the long term. This thinking is tied in to the prefunding objective that has traditionally been the main concern of actuaries. They have no independent theory as to the interest assumption applicable to an *unfunded* pension obligation, but merely a general (and sound) conviction that obligations not payable until the future are less burdensome than obligations payable currently.

In estimating the future rate of return on investments, actuaries have traditionally taken a long view. Pension obligations stretch far into the future. The funds required to meet those obligations will come partly from assets on hand, but also very largely from reinvestment of earnings. Thus, the discount rate assumed depends only in part on the apparent rate of return on existing pension fund assets. To a considerable degree it depends on the returns available on funds that will be reinvested in future, which is very largely a guess. (To the extent that zero coupon bonds or stripped coupons are available to produce funds required at maturity of the obligation, guesswork is removed. The limited supply of such securities, however, makes complete reliance upon them as evidence of investment returns unreliable.) For these reasons actuaries have traditionally used an interest assumption considered to be representative of long-term rates of return, and have changed it only infrequently. Stability in the interest assumption has practical advantages, since it tends to stabilize the employer's contributions to the pension fund with respect to the current service of employees. Accountants have historically accepted actuarial calculations as the basis of their figures, and thus implicitly have accepted the actuary's interest assumption.

Acceptance of the actuarial approach has meant concealing an economic fact in the accounting. If the benefit earned in a year is a fixed dollar amount determined by the pension formula, the real cost *does* vary from year to year depending on the level of interest rates, rather than being the constant amount that results from an unchanging actuarial interest assumption. The variation in real cost could easily be seen if an employer followed a practice of buying deferred annuities to cover each employee's pension entitlement as it was earned. The cost of the annuities bought each year would vary directly with the interest rate. In addition, acceptance of actuarial figures means acceptance of the effects of arbitrary changes in the interest assumption. From around 1970 onward, such changes became much more common, even though the rate assumed was supposed to be long-term.

Allocation of future benefit costs to periods

To derive a pension cost attributable to employee service in a given period, there must be some way of assessing how much of the full pension obligation at retirement is attributable to work done in that particular period. In straight mathematical terms, there are an infinite number of ways to assign a discounted amount to periods so that it will accumulate with interest to the full estimated liability at employee retirement dates. The possible methods range from making full provision for the future liability at the date an employee joins the pension plan (called initial funding by actuaries), to making provision only on the date the employee retires (terminal funding).

Actuaries have developed a variety of standard patterns for the allocation of future costs to service years, known as "actuarial valuation methods" or "actuarial cost methods" (ACMs). The latter term will be used hereafter. (Unfortunately, actuarial—and accounting—terminology is not standardized in pension matters. Common equivalent terms will be set out in the discussion below.) Some common ACMs used in calculating a cost for current service (also known as "normal cost") are described below.

- One *family* of ACMs is called "accrued benefit" methods (also known as "unit credit" or "single premium" methods). The basic idea underlying this family is that benefits earned to date by employees—or accrued benefits—can be derived from the plan benefit formula. Those accrued benefits can be valued at their discounted present value at the financial reporting date, and the increase in that accrued liability over the period is the pension cost to be allocated to the period.

- The first method in the accrued benefit family of methods, known as the "accumulated benefit" method, is based directly on current entitlements under the pension formula. For example, in a career-average plan, the pension entitlement might increase by 2% of the current year's salary each year. Thus, the pension cost for the year is simply the present value of a pension of 2% of the year's salary, reduced by the probabilities of not qualifying for the pension owing to death, withdrawal before vesting, etc. (Allowances for such probabilities in the cost calculation are known as "decrements.") In contrast, in a final-pay plan the accumulated benefit at any point of time is based on the latest year's salary. Thus, the cost for the latest year is the yearly benefit entitlement rate (such as 1.5% of salary) applied to the latest year's salary, *plus* a catch-up of previous years' earned entitlements to the latest year's salary level (all modified by the applicable decrements).
- Two methods in the accrued benefit family depart from strict adherence to rights currently earned under the pension formula. Both methods "project" the change in earned entitlement amounts that will occur in future as a result of increases in salary before retirement. Then those projected entitlement amounts (less allowances for decrements) are allocated to years of service on one of two bases. An equal amount may be assigned to each year of service, or, an amount may be assigned based on the proportion that the current year's salary is of the anticipated career salary. The method by which the projected benefit is allocated evenly over years of service (before discounting) is known as the "projected benefit method prorated on services" and the other as the "projected benefit method prorated on salaries." (The FASB refers to these two methods as the "benefit/years-of-service" method and the "benefit/compensation" method. The two methods are also known by actuaries as "modified accrued benefit" methods or as the "accrued benefit method with salary projection.")
- A second *family* of ACMs is known as "level contribution" methods. (A common actuarial description for this family is "projected benefit" or "level premium" methods. They are *not*, however, the same as the "projected methods" just described.) The level contribution family of methods does not go through the step of finding an amount of benefits deemed to be earned or accrued at a financial reporting date and valuing that obligation. Rather, it takes the estimated benefit to be earned over an employee's career and spreads the discounted cost thereof over the service period, as a level cost for each year or as a level percentage of salary. The FASB describes these methods as the "cost/years-of-service" method and the "cost/compensation" method. Various actuarial approaches within this family of methods are known as "entry age normal," "individual level premium," "attained age normal," and "aggregate."

The primary concern of actuaries is that the necessary fund be built up by the time employees retire. It does not matter to the actuary how much is contributed in a particular year, provided the ACM meets the retirement fund objective. Hence, actuarial science does not provide any theory that is helpful in meeting the accounting objective of measuring income for a period. The existence of a wide variety of ACMs that could be selected almost at will together with the acceptance by accountants of amounts funded as a measure of expense for a year was an important reason why the measurement of periodic pension cost was not comparable from company to company under accounting standards in effect before 1987.

The impact of choice of discount rate and ACM on pension cost calculations

The choices made in the areas just discussed can have a material impact on pension cost calculations accepted for accounting purposes, but generalizations as to the impact are not simple. With respect to the choice of ACM, it must be remembered that if the interest rate assumption is held constant all methods must show an identical accumulated liability for any given employee by the time he or she reaches retirement age. That is to say, if one ACM recognizes less expense than another in the early years of an employee's career, it must make it up in later years. Thus, whether the application of one ACM results in a higher or lower expense figure than another for a particular year depends upon the age distribution of the whole active plan membership and upon the length of time the plan has operated. If the plan is just starting, the level contribution methods will show a considerably higher annual expense figure than an accrued benefit method. If the plan has been in operation for some time and the membership group is old, the reverse will be true.

One can say, however, that as long as there are some plan members who have not yet reached retirement, the accumulated liability recorded under a level contribution approach will always be higher than that under an accrued benefit approach (again given the use of the same interest assumption). That follows from the fact that level contribution ACMs charge more to expense in the early years of an employee's career, so that other ACMs must always be in a position of needing to catch up. (In speaking of accumulated liability here we are referring to the liability recognized *before* deduction of pension fund assets.) This has significance when a plan is adopted or amended. The past-service obligation taken on by the employer will be measured at a different amount depending upon the ACM used. This obviously has some impact on the way expense is recognized subsequently.

The choice of interest rate also has the effect of shifting among years the amount of expense recognition with respect to an individual employee. Choice of a higher rate of interest results in lower expense recognition in the earlier years of an employee's career and the need to recognize greater interest expense (as part of the pension cost figure) in later years, after retirement as well as before. Again, the effect on total expense to be recognized in a year for a given plan depends to some degree on the age distribution of the plan members. The impact of the choice of interest rate also differs between ACMs, being relatively more important when the level contribution method is used than when an accrued benefit ACM is used. Nevertheless, as a broad generalization it can be stated that the choice of interest rate is material.

There is a long-standing actuarial rule of thumb that a change of 1% in the interest assumption will change the expense recognized for a typical plan population in the neighbourhood of 20% to 25%. This percentage might be about a third lower for plans valued under the accrued benefit method. In final-pay plans, changes in the interest assumption might well be accompanied by an offsetting change in the salary escalation assumption. If so, the impact of the interest rate change would be cut roughly in half. (The offset is not complete because a change in the salary escalation adjustment only applies up to employees' retirement dates, while a change in the interest assumption affects the calculations after retirement as well.)

Issues in pension accounting

Practice in recognizing pension obligations and periodic pension cost up to the mid-1980s relied almost completely upon the amounts funded as determined by customary actuarial methods, even though it has long been understood that the objective of setting aside assets in a pension fund and that of measuring pension cost for a period and accrued to date are quite different. This situation will probably change with the introduction of new standards in Canada and the United States that first take effect in late 1987.[2] (The effective date is postponed by two years for nonpublic enterprises that sponsor no defined benefit pension plan with more than one hundred participants.) These two standards are referred to hereafter as the 1987 standards.

Issues dealt with in these standards are explained below. One observation may help in understanding these issues. Pension cost for a period has traditionally been thought of and accounted for as one single amount. In reality, it is made up of several different components. There is the service cost component—i.e., the present value of benefits earned by plan members for service during the year. (It would not be unreasonable to restrict the term "pension cost for the period" to this component alone.) There is also the interest cost to be added to the liability for pension benefits previously accrued. Offsetting this, there is the actual return on pension fund assets for the year. There is also the amount of cost attributed to the year with respect to any plan changes that have granted benefit entitlements to employees with respect to service prior to the change. Then there is the recognition given to experience gains and losses or to adjustments that have been made to the calculation of pension liability because of changes in actuarial assumptions. Finally, under the 1987 standards there will also be amortization of any initial underfunded or overfunded position recognized at the time the new recommendations come into effect.

The issues will be discussed under the following headings:

- The nature of an employer's obligation for pensions
- Specification of benefits upon which recognition of the pension liability and periodic cost is based
- The choice of an ACM
- The choice of an interest rate
- Accounting for past-service cost
- Accounting for pension fund investments
- Accounting for experience gains and losses and changes in actuarial assumptions
- Recognition of a minimum liability
- Transition to the new accounting basis
- Curtailments and settlements of pension obligations; special termination benefits
- Pension plan disclosure
- Evaluation of the 1987 standards.

The nature of an employer's obligation for pensions

If one goes back far enough in history one finds that the grant of a pension was usually a mark of favour by an monarch or nobleman to an artist or other retainer. Favours given can be withdrawn and this ex gratia characteristic carried over to pensions when first granted by corporations. Since there was no firm commitment, it was natural that pension payments should be treated as expense on a "pay-as-you-go" basis.

That pensions paid to retired employees are mere acts of beneficence lacks credibility in a business setting. There are too many advantages to a business from the adoption of a pension policy—the reduction of employee turnover and hence training costs, the freedom to retire older employees who otherwise might be a drag on productivity, and so on. Thus, the idea grew that a pension policy adopted by a business could be considered part of the consideration for services of employees—a form of wage that was deferred to the employee's postretirement years. When pension plan terms came to be included as a subject in collective bargaining, that view could hardly be denied—at least for those plans. It is not so clearly evident that plans for white-collar employees represent a bargain struck between the employees and employers in the market for labour services. Yet indirectly it must be so. Consider a businessman who has no pension plan hiring clerical help. He may well hear a desirable candidate say: "I'd like to work for you but I can't afford to pass up the pension and other benefits I can get from X corporation." If people act in their own best interests, the businessman has no option but to provide competitive fringe benefits or else pay a higher direct wage.

Even if pensions are regarded as a form of deferred wage explicitly or implicitly bargained with the employees, there remains the question of exactly what is the bargained transaction. It is customary for many funded pension plans to contain a clause to the effect that the employer is entitled to terminate the plan, and in that event the liability is limited to amounts that have been contributed to the pension fund. Almost all plans also contain a clause to the effect that an employee's entitlement to receive benefits under the plan formula does not "vest" (i.e., does not become an absolute right) until she has put in a prescribed number of years of service. Because of these considerations, accountants with a legalistic bent of mind take one of two positions:

- The pension liability is determined by the amount an employer actually puts in to the pension fund. Essentially, this is equivalent to a cash basis of recording pension cost. Since an employer normally has some discretion in funding policy, this basis gives him the opportunity to choose the level of cost to be recorded in any given period. Recent legislation in some jurisdictions (e.g., the United States and Ontario) makes the employer liable for certain minimum amounts if the fund is insufficient. Liability recognition based on a contractual or legal position would have to take this into account and could require a considerable amount of work to calculate.
- The pension obligation to an individual employee is only contingent before vesting. Since vesting is a necessary condition for the ultimate liability, no cost should be recorded until vesting occurs.[3] With respect to any individual employee this view means that a large amount of liability (and presumably expense) would be recorded in the year of vesting. For a large employee group as a whole, however, such "spikes" would tend to average out.

It should be noted that in both these cases the recognition of pension cost is not tied directly to service put in by the employee. In the latter case no cost (or expense) is recognized in the prevesting period. In the former case the connection between employee service and cost recognition is quite indirect.

A third position is that the key event in triggering recognition of a liability should be that transaction or event by which the accounting entity receives performance or value in satisfaction of its obligation. Since a pension is regarded as part of employee compensation, it follows under this view that cost should be recognized as the employee puts in service. It may be that some employees will not receive their pensions because their employment is terminated before vesting. But this is a problem in *estimating* the amount of the employer's liability that can be solved on the basis of past experience and judgment, just like the problem of estimating future warranty costs. Only in this way can cost be recorded at the time necessary for sensible income accounting. This is in accordance with our discussion in chapter 9 of the nature of liabilities in accounting.

The important contribution of the accounting standards adopted in the 1960s was the recognition of this point. At that time it was argued that, once adopted, a business could not easily abandon a pension plan. Since accounting assumes a business will continue as a going concern in the absence of evidence to the contrary, it must also be assumed that it will need satisfied employees; hence, its pension arrangements cannot be unilaterally terminated notwithstanding its technical right to do so. This position is confirmed in the 1987 standards.

Specification of benefits upon which recognition of the pension liability and periodic cost is based

The general principle that liability should be accrued currently for future pension costs attributable to current employee service raises the question of what future pension amounts are so attributable. There are two aspects to this question. First, what basis is there for estimating future benefits that will be granted in return for service today? Second, is it legitimate to be conservative in the estimation of the amount of such benefits in view of the fact that many variables affect just who will qualify for pensions and for how long?

Expected benefits. The standard actuarial answer to the first of these questions has been that the benefit formula stated in the pension plan provides the basis for estimating the future liability for service up to a particular plan valuation date. That answer seems logical on the face of it. If a pension plan is regarded as a contract for deferred wages, one would think that the terms of the contract must govern the liability.

It can be observed, however, that employers often amend plans to improve benefits. When they do, it is quite customary to grant improvements in benefits in respect of "past service." That is, with no further service (except when some time remains to vesting of improved benefits), members of the plan at the time of the amendment receive an increase in their entitlements. Not infrequently, improvements in benefits are extended to plan members who have already retired. Benefit improvements granted with respect to past service stimulate a question. If there was no obligation to improve benefits before the amendment, how can the benefit improvements attributed to past service be explained? There are two possible answers. The first is that even though the benefit improvement is calculated by reference to past service, it really is given as part of the consideration for future service. As reported previously, that was the reasoning of the first U.S. recommendation on pension accounting. The second is that there is an unwritten understanding between employer and employees—a sort of implied contract—that when plan benefits are improved there will be no discrimination between members' service before and after the date of the amendment.

The latter possibility is not unthinkable. Consider, for example, an employee who joined the company at age 45 in 1965, a period when there had been a very low inflation rate (2% a year on average) for over ten years. The employee reckons that the company's career-average pension plan, along with other resources, will provide an adequate retirement income. But in the twenty years from 1965 to 1985 the purchasing power of the dollar drops to almost one-quarter of its level in 1965 (an average annual rate of inflation over the period of 7%). Consider also that the company's contributions to the pension plan were expected to earn 5% to 6% in 1965, but because of rises in interest rates associated with inflation between 1965 and 1985 the money funded in 1965 earns much more than the originally assumed rate of return. Is it unreasonable that the employee might expect, and the employer might feel some obligation to grant, an increase in pension under the circumstances? In fact, surveys consistently show a majority of employers do increase pensions to retired employees in inflationary conditions (although normally by a percentage that is below the rate of inflation).[4,5]

The essential question is: If pension entitlements represent deferred wages, what is the employees' and employer's understanding of the entitlement involved? The pension plan provides a formula expressed in nominal dollars. But perhaps there is an understanding as well that the employer will supplement the pension if needed so that it will really perform its function of supporting the employee's living standard after retirement. If so, that future sacrifice on the part of the employer is actually attributable to the service of the employee while employed, and should be allowed for in the accrual at that time. The trouble is, of course, that there is no clear and unequivocal commitment on the part of the employer to maintain the purchasing power of pension income. As indicated, many employers do improve the pension amounts, but few have kept up with inflation and some have made no improvement at all. Clearly, accounting for unstated moral obligations is very difficult—any assumption as to what an individual employer will do in future, in the absence of a contractual or statutory obligation, can be very much a guess.

Probably because of this uncertainty, the 1987 accounting standards take the position that the plan formula ordinarily is the basis for estimating pension benefits earned at a valuation date. The FASB does acknowledge the possibility that an employer may have a commitment to future amendments (as evidenced by a past history of making such amendments). If so, the accounting should be based on that substantive commitment and its existence and nature is to be disclosed.[6] The *CICA Handbook* could be interpreted to allow the same accounting. A pension plan is defined as any arrangement "contractual or otherwise." The reference to "otherwise" could permit accruals for future benefit improvements based on evidence similar to that suggested by the FASB. However, the wording of the standards does not seem strong enough to *force* recognition of probable future amendments, even though a plan has a regular history of amendments.

Estimation of benefit amounts. Based on the benefit formula assumed, actuarial assumptions as to mortality, withdrawals, and so on are applied to estimate actual dollar amounts of benefits. It is generally thought that actuaries in the past have tended to err on the conservative side in their assumptions. The 1987 accounting standards suggest that this is to stop. Each assumption is to be a "best estimate" of the most likely future result. Moreover, the assumptions are described as reflecting management's judgment. Although, no doubt, management will rely on actuarial advice as it has in the past, the final responsibility is management's.

The choice of an ACM

From the earlier discussion it can be seen that the choice of ACM, like the choice of the interest assumption, can have a significant effect on the amount of pension liability and periodic pension expense reported. The question is: Is one method more rational than another for the purpose of measuring income? Or might it be found that different ACMs are appropriate for different types of plans?

One answer to these questions is derived from a simple line of thinking. If the benefit entitlement earned by an employee or employee group for a given year's service is known, the calculation of its cost and the accrued liability seem straightforward. Actuarial assumptions are required as to future events that may affect the ultimate benefit payouts, but the cost for the year is the discounted present value of the best estimates of those future payouts.

This argument leads to the use of the accumulated benefit ACM (the pure form of the accrued benefit family of methods) for both the flat-benefit plan and the career-average plan. In spite of the "career-average" name given to the latter type of plan, its formula actually gives a specific discrete benefit (e.g., 2% of the current year's salary) for each year of service. The treatment of the final-pay plan is more debatable. Strict reliance on the pension plan formula indicates that the benefit earned in each and every year is a percentage of final salary. Therefore, the cost of the benefit earned each year must reflect what that final salary will be. The ACM that achieves this is the projected benefit method prorated on services.

It can be seen that a key issue in the selection of an ACM is whether complete reliance ought to be placed upon a plan's benefit formula to determine pension costs for a given year's service. Doubts have often been expressed on this score. Many hold the view that a benefit formula is designed to provide a reasonable pension in relation to the service performed by an employee throughout an entire career, but should not be interpreted as measuring the portion of the benefit "earned" by an employee in any particular year. From this, they argue that any method that systematically recognizes an adequate amount of pension cost is satisfactory. Level contribution ACMs are as good as any other, and the level percentage of payroll method is intuitively appealing.[7]

The 1987 standards have prescribed the use of the accumulated benefit ACM for the flat-benefit plan and the projected benefit method prorated on services for career-average and final-pay plans. The fact that the plan formula is relied upon to provide the unit of benefit to be attributed to each year of service was influential in this decision. It is not clear, however, why it was considered logical to assume salary projection for the career-average plan.

The choice of an interest rate

In traditional actuarial practice, the interest rate used to discount the pension obligation has been the long-term expected rate of return on pension fund assets. The result of this is that, so long as the estimated rate is unchanged, an experience gain or loss will develop over each period between valuations of pension fund assets and obligations equal to the difference between (1) the interest added at the standard rate to the amount of the obligation over the period and (2) the actual return on the pension fund assets over the period (which depends to some extent on the basis of valuation adopted for the assets).

Historically, there have been wide variations in the interest assumptions used by actuaries for different plans. Although some of this disparity might be attributed to different yields on assets held by different plans, it is doubtful that such differences provide a complete explanation. Changes in the interest assumption were also being made more frequently as time went on, no doubt largely in response to the volatility in interest rates in the early 1980s. As a result, figures of pension expense and unfunded obligation (where reported) were not comparable between companies and were inconsistent between years within a single company. (Differences in ACMs used and changes in ACMs were also significant contributors to noncomparability and inconsistency.)

The CICA and the FASB have parted company in dealing with the interest assumption in their 1987 standards, with the CICA clinging to the traditional actuarial approach. With respect to actuarial assumptions in general, the *CICA Handbook* states: "The assumptions would take into account the actual experience of the plan and, in recognition of the long-term nature of the plan, expected long term future events, without giving undue weight to recent experience."[8] That description sounds very much like the traditional actuarial approach to the choice of interest rate. However, as noted previously, actuaries began changing the interest assumption much more frequently from about 1970 onwards—a practice inconsistent to a degree with the idea of a long-term assumption. It remains to be seen whether the "best estimate" interest assumption under the new standard will be any more stable over time and comparable among different enterprises than interest assumptions were previously.

The FASB has made a radical break with past tradition in SFAS No. 87. This statement introduces two interest rate assumptions in place of the traditional assumption of one long-term rate. First, there is a discount rate to be used in valuing the obligation and calculating the interest expense related to that obligation in the ensuing reporting period. That rate is to be a best estimate of the interest rate that would be implicit in the price of annuities purchased to settle the obligation if such annuities were purchased at the valuation date. That is to say, the rate is a current rate and may be expected to vary from one annual valuation date to another. Second, there is to be a determination of an expected long-term rate of return on plan assets. That rate of return is to be applied to a "market-related" valuation of plan assets to determine the investment earnings component of pension cost in the next reporting period. Certain accounting consequences of this change in interest rate treatment are important.

- The valuation of the pension fund obligation disclosed as supplementary information will become more volatile than it was under previous accounting practice because of the regular re-estimation of the current interest rate obtainable for settlement of the obligation.
- The current-service cost component of periodic pension cost will also become more volatile for the same reason.

- The interest cost component of periodic pension cost will also be affected. However, in this case the volatility will be dampened by the effect of changes in the interest assumption on the valuation of the obligation. The higher the rate, the lower the value of the obligation, and vice versa. Thus, if the interest assumption is raised, the higher rate will be applied to a lower obligation figure, which will tend to stabilize the periodic interest cost component.
- Because the expected rate of return on assets is supposed to be a long-term rate, one might expect that it will be changed infrequently, and then only by small amounts. If a stable rate of return were applied to pension fund assets valued at market value, the volatility in market values of assets from year to year would also introduce a corresponding volatility into the investment return component of periodic pension cost. To reduce this effect, the board has decided that "market-related" values of assets shall be used for this purpose, rather than fair values at the valuation date. The meaning of the term market-related will be discussed subsequently.
- The decision to use a long-term return assumption and market-related values for measurement of the investment return component of periodic cost posed a problem for the FASB in view of its belief that market-related values were less relevant information than current fair values for the plan assets. To minimize this lack of informativeness, the board decided that, even though the investment return component was *measured* on the basis just described, the figure that should be *disclosed* was the actual return on plan assets for a period, based upon the fair value of plan assets at the beginning and end of the period. In order to balance this disclosure with the total of periodic pension cost charged against income, the difference between the actual return on plan assets and the return measured using the long-term return assumption is required to be added to the figure disclosed for other components of periodic pension cost: namely, amortization of experience gains and losses, amortization of prior-service cost, and amortization of the net obligation or asset existing at the date of transition to the new accounting basis. (These items will be discussed subsequently.)

The interest rate used to discount the pension obligation ideally should be estimated by ascertaining interest rates implicit in current prices for annuity contracts that could settle the obligation. Alternatively, annuity rates may be estimated by looking to returns currently available on high-quality fixed-income investments over the term to maturity of the obligation and rates expected to be available for reinvestment of investment earnings during that term.

Comment. In previous practice the long-term rate of return assumed by actuaries could be, and often was, biased towards conservatism. This practice resulted in building a larger pension fund than otherwise required, thereby protecting employee interests. It also protected employers from possible unpleasant surprises and, once a cushion was built into the fund, gave them greater opportunity to alter funding contributions and expense recognized from one year to another by changing the interest assumption. In addition, it had the practical effect of allowing employers to prefund and preexpense future benefit improvements, an option that was quite desirable under conditions of rapid inflation.

The instruction in the 1987 standards that actuarial assumptions—including the interest assumption—be best estimates appears to foreclose this possibility. If the interest rate assumed is the best estimate of the long-run rate of return, the amount of pension cost accrual should be just enough to allow for benefits already promised; there will be no room for benefit improvement (unless, as previously noted, employers are prepared to admit they have an unwritten commitment to make future improvements). It is just conceivable that this change in accounting standards may inhibit improvements in pension benefits because of the unwillingness of employers to acknowledge large changes in the pension liability on an irregular basis. On the other hand, that possibility rests on an assumption that the best estimate of the long-run rate of return will be evident within a narrow range. The author's opinion is that there will continue to be quite a broad range in "best" estimates of long-run rate of return, and therefore the opportunity for conservative bias will remain.

The FASB decision to use an interest rate reflecting current conditions for recognition of the current-service cost component and the interest cost component of pension expense will make the expense recognized more volatile than it is under the CICA standard. Both standards apply a long-run investment return assumption, but the FASB applies that rate to the market-related values of actual fund assets, while the CICA, in effect, applies it to an amount equal to the pension liability. The results of the two methods for this component will therefore be different whenever the CICA measure of the pension liability differs from the market-related value of the fund assets. When a plan is overfunded on the CICA basis of measurement, the FASB method will show a higher credit to expense than the CICA method, and vice versa.

Accounting for past-service cost

When a pension plan is initially adopted, or when a plan is amended to improve benefits, it is customary to award some entitlement to benefits to members at the time of the adoption or amendment, based on their service previous to that date. Thus, no further performance is required from such employees to earn those benefits (except that of remaining in service until they vest). The proper accounting for such "past-service" benefits has been a matter of considerable debate. Should a liability be recorded with respect to the benefit entitlements granted, or at least the vested portion thereof, at the date of grant? How should the cost of past-service benefits be matched to accounting periods?

The issue of immediate liability recognition. The answer to the question whether liability recognition is required at the date of adoption or amendment logically rests upon the accepted accounting definition of a liability. Some argue that the liability should be recognized because it represents a probable future sacrifice attributable to past transactions or events, the event in this case being the employer's grant of the past-service entitlement.[9] This argument is reinforced by the observation that, if there were two otherwise identical companies but one had just adopted a pension plan while the other had had one in existence for some time, it would be necessary to record the past service of the former in order to show the financial position of the two on a comparable basis.

One basis for rebuttal to these arguments depends upon close examination of the nature of the plan adoption or amendment. Is it an event of a kind that should trigger liability recognition? Consider that entities regularly sign contracts that call for future payments but do not record the liability until there is performance by the other party. Has there been performance in the case of the grant of past-service benefits? The fact that the benefit is calculated on the basis of *past* service suggests that performance has occurred and the liability should be recognized. The same logic, however, might dictate that the cost be written off immediately. Accounting authorities have rejected that position. They have traditionally argued that past service, in spite of its name, is really granted with respect to the future service of the employee group. If the expense should be recognized in future, it is argued that the liability accrual need not be recognized until then.

The 1987 CICA standard appears to have accepted the latter position. In contrast, the FASB position straddles the two arguments. The board holds that when a plan amendment grants past service, the employees have performed all the services required to be entitled to benefits. Therefore, there is a substantive liability. The board also believes that employers obtain future economic benefits from such plan amendments. In other words, by granting past-service benefits the employer has bought an intangible asset akin to goodwill. The board, however, decided to continue the past practice in pension accounting of delaying recognition of certain events. Recognition of a liability for past service and the corresponding intangible asset is not to take place at the time of a plan introduction or amendment. Under certain conditions (to be discussed subsequently) a minimum liability is to be recognized with respect to all the obligations of the plan. The obligation for past service is a factor in the calculation of that minimum liability.

The period of amortization of past-service cost. Obviously, if the cost of past-service benefits is attributed to future service periods, it remains necessary to decide over how many periods the cost should be recognized. The "future economic benefits" to the employer are thought to stem chiefly from the incentive effect of plan amendments upon the employee. Logically the cost recognition period should relate to the length of time in which the incentive effect of the plan adoption or amendment persists. Unfortunately, there is absolutely no available evidence as to the typical duration of the incentive or as to how it diminishes with time.

The 1987 standards suggest that it is reasonable to relate the past-service cost associated with a plan initiation or amendment to the remaining service life of the employee group covered at the time of the initiation or amendment. The standards differ somewhat in their recommendations as to how this might be done. The difference can be illustrated by a simplified example. Suppose an employee group at the time of a plan amendment consisted of 55 employees, 10 of whom were expected to retire after 1 year, 9 after 2 years, 8 after 3 years, and so on down to one at the end of the tenth year. The total number of service-years in this example would be 220, of which 55 would occur in the first year, 45 in the second year, and so on.

The FASB method prescribes minimum amortization of 55/220 = 25% of the plan amendment cost in the first year, 45/220 = 20.5% in the second year, and so on. The declining-balance pattern of amortization seems quite appropriate, since almost certainly any motivational effect of a plan amendment is greatest just following the date of the amendment. To reduce computations, however, the FASB is prepared to accept any amortization method that absorbs the cost of the past service more rapidly than this formula indicates.

The CICA suggests amortization of the past-service cost in a "rational and systematic" manner over an appropriate period, normally the "expected average remaining service life of the employee group." The term "average" means the weighted average service life per employee—i.e., 220/55 = 4.0 years in our previous illustration. What pattern of amortization would be "rational" could also be debated. Since use of an average period rather than the full period of remaining service life is somewhat arbitrary in itself, it could be argued that either a declining-balance or straight-line pattern of amortization is reasonable. It is hard to see, however, that an increasing-charge pattern could ever be rational, considering that the motivational impact of a plan amendment is bound to decline with time.

The CICA suggestion is more conservative than that of the FASB, since the CICA uses an average remaining service life while the FASB recommendation is related to the full remaining service life. As noted, however, the FASB permits faster amortization for convenience. In addition, both standards contemplate that there may be circumstances, such as a history of regular plan amendments, that indicate that the period of economic benefit from an amendment is shorter than the remaining service life of an employee group. In these circumstances, amortization ought to be accelerated.

Comment. It is expected that for most plans the average remaining service life, however computed, will fall in the range of ten to twenty years. In the author's opinion, such a period is far longer than the period over which the motivational impact of most plan amendments may be expected to last, although it is perhaps not inappropriate for amortization of past service granted when a plan is first introduced. The author's skepticism as to period of benefit is particularly strong when plan amendments merely go some distance to restoring the purchasing power of benefits previously earned that has been eroded by inflation. His belief, therefore, is that very frequently the amortization period should be short.

Accounting for pension fund investments

The choice of a method to account for pension plan obligations represents the essence of the pension accounting problem. When the plan is unfunded it represents the whole of the problem. But if a plan is funded, the accepted accounting treatment is to charge the contributions to the fund against the recorded liability. One might infer from this treatment that funding liquidates the liability and therefore there should be no further concern about the accounting for the fund investments. In practice the facts are otherwise. Unless the employer discontinues the plan, a residual responsibility remains for payment of the benefits promised. The assets set aside in the fund will help meet that responsibility, but if they are lost or the fund makes a lower return than expected, the employer makes up the difference. Because of this effect on the financial position of the employer, there is a strong argument in logic that the gross pension obligation and the pension fund assets should both be displayed in the employer's balance sheet.[10] In this way, the full liability that the employer is insuring would be clearly disclosed, and the pension fund assets for which he bears the ultimate risk (and shares the rewards) would be displayed also. A segregation of the assets and obligations to indicate the dedication of the former to the latter would, of course, be desirable.

Following this line of thought, one might well ask: Why do we need to consider accounting for pension fund investments as part of the pension accounting problem? The dominant basis of accounting for other long-term investments in other circumstances is the basis of cost (or amortized cost in the case of fixed-interest securities). Why should not this basis be used for pension fund securities as well? One answer is that for investments other than fixed-yield securities, much of the return hoped for will take the form of capital gain. If the pension obligation figure is accreted at a hoped-for investment yield including capital gains, it is inconsistent not to recognize accretion in capital value of pension fund assets as it occurs.

The need for compatibility between the valuations of pension plan obligations and pension plan assets may be illustrated by a hypothetical case. Suppose it is estimated that the portion of a plan's obligations maturing twenty years hence will amount to $100,000, and suppose high-quality zero coupon bonds are held in an equal face amount. The position, thus, is completely in balance. As long as the estimated obligation remains unchanged and the bonds are still held, it will remain so. Suppose further that the bonds have just been acquired at a cost of $14,864—that is, on a 10% yield basis—and that the obligation has been discounted at 10% as well, so that the current valuations correctly reflect the fully funded position. Now consider how the fund assets and obligations are to be valued at the next valuation date. In the normal course the valuation of the $100,000 obligation will be accreted at 10 percent to amount to $16,350 because it is one year closer to maturity. But suppose also that interest rates have fallen from 10% to 9% in the intervening period. If the discount rate is dropped to 9% the obligation will now be valued at $19,449. But if the bonds held are valued at amortized cost they will only amount to $16,350, and the valuation will show a net experience loss of $3,099. To avoid this result the bonds need to be valued at current market price rather than amortized cost. Since bonds sell on a yield basis, their current market value should have appreciated to the $19,449 figure.

The lesson is that if pension obligations are discounted at current interest rates, the correct basis of valuation for interest-bearing investments will be current market value. The connection is not so obvious for investments that do not carry fixed interest rates. Nevertheless, one can argue that the general tendency of high interest rates is to depress the value of all assets and that of low interest rates is to enhance them, so that the valuation of other assets at current market value also seems quite appropriate if liabilities are valued at current interest rates.

What if pension obligations are discounted at long-term average rates of return rather than at interest rates current at the valuation date? In such a case, a valuation of pension fund assets at current market values would be inconsistent, but the appropriate alternative is not immediately obvious. Presumably the objective should be to state the assets at a figure consistent with the long-term yield expected to be obtained from them. For a portfolio of fixed-interest securities, the traditional accounting basis of amortized cost or the "deferral and amortization" approach (see discussion in chapter 16) could be considered appropriate. For equity securities, some carrying value that reflects the expected long-term return (with such return including anticipated capital gains) would be logical. However, there is always the possibility that expectations may not be fulfilled. A compromise that retains some tie to actual experience is to value such securities at a moving average of market values over a recent period of years. If there is a long-term trend in the prices of securities held, such a moving average will give it some recognition, with a lag determined by the length of the averaging period.

The 1987 CICA standard calls for the use of "market-related values" for pension fund assets. That term is not rigidly specified. It is defined as being either current market value (or an approximation thereto when market prices are not available), or a value that is adjusted to market over a period not to exceed five years. No distinction is made in the standard between fixed-interest debt securities and equity securities. All are to be valued at market-related values.

The 1987 FASB standard embodies a conflict. The pension obligation is revalued at current interest rates each year. This suggests that pension fund assets should be valued at market value at the same date, and, in fact, they are so valued for the purpose of measuring the fund surplus or deficiency at the valuation date. On the other hand, the return on investment component of pension cost is to be based on an assumed long-term rate of return applied to market-related values of the assets. Ordinarily, one would expect that the opening valuation of fund assets plus the return thereon accounted for as a component of the periodic pension cost, together with contributions to and payments out of the fund for the year, would equal the closing valuation of fund assets. For that equation to work, the assets would have to be valued at market-related values rather than current fair values. To reconcile the use of current values in the valuation position and of market-related values for income measurement purposes, the board has determined that the difference between the actual return on fund assets and the investment return component of periodic pension cost shall be treated as an experience gain or loss, recognition of which is delayed.

Comment. Both the CICA and FASB standards contain compromises in this area. A logical, consistent basis of valuation of pension plan obligations and assets is obtained when obligations are valued using current interest rates, and assets are valued at current fair values. This accounting basis, however, can produce very volatile figures for pension expense from year to year. The CICA standard has continued with the traditional view that pension expense should not be volatile because a pension plan is expected to be a long-term continuing arrangement. To implement this view, the CICA has called for the use of an estimated long-term rate of return in discounting the pension obligation. Correspondingly, it permits the use of "market-related" values for assets rather than current fair values. This seems to be a reasonable compromise, even though estimation of both long-term rates of return and market-related asset values is subject to a considerable degree of arbitrariness. It is not clear, however, why amortized costs, or a valuation based on the deferral and amortization of gains and losses, would not be preferable to market-related values for a portfolio of secure-quality fixed-interest securities.

The FASB compromise is extremely uneasy. The board has been unwilling to give up the greater relevancy of figures for the pension obligation and current-service cost measured using current interest rates. It likewise believes that current fair values of fund assets are more relevant than any other possible basis of valuation, but it has been unwilling to extend that belief into a requirement that the investment return component of pension expense reflect the unrealized gains and losses that result from valuation at fair value. The result has been that the board has ridden at least two horses, using fair values for disclosure of the pension fund position, calculating the pension cost component based on an assumed long-run rate of return applied to market-related asset values, and reconciling the conflict by burying the difference between the investment return on the fair value basis and the return on the other basis in experience gains and losses.

Accounting for experience gains and losses and changes in actuarial assumptions

Actuarial assumptions traditionally represent estimates of what the experience will be on average with respect to the various factors affecting pension costs, not what experience will be in any given short period. Some assumptions (especially the economic assumptions) are little more than guesses based on past experience, and could prove to be substantially in error over the whole period required to discharge the pension obligations to an existing employee group. For both these reasons, any valuation of pension plan liabilities and assets will show differences between their actual amounts at the valuation date and the amounts they would have been had the actuarial assumptions proved to be exactly fulfilled in the period since the last valuation. These differences are known as "experience gains and losses."

All actuarial assumptions are tentative, even those that are not related to unpredictable economic factors such as interest rates. It is not surprising, therefore, that actuaries occasionally change their assumptions. The result, of course, is an increase or decrease in the calculated value of the plan obligations, and consequently an increase or decrease in plan surplus or deficit. It is conceivable that assumptions might be different for the future than for the past yet both be well founded. It seems more likely, however, that changes in assumptions will be based on the fact that previous assumptions have not been borne out by experience. If so, it might seem desirable that the surplus or deficit created by the change in valuation basis (not to mention the surplus or deficit attributable to the inappropriate assumptions of the past) should be absorbed as quickly as possible. The whole matter is so nebulous, however, that both the CICA and the FASB have decided there need be no distinction between the treatment of changes in actuarial assumptions and of experience gains or losses.

A decision is required whether to recognize periodic experience gains and losses in pension costs, and if so, how. One possible argument is that, since actuarial assumptions are supposed to be "best estimates" and the latest actuarial valuation should provide the best data, any experience gain or loss should be recognized as part of pension cost immediately it is determined. A diametrically opposed argument may be made, however, based on the observation that most actuarial assumptions are long-term in nature. If the assumptions are accurate in the long term, experience gains and losses calculated in individual valuations will cancel out over time and no recognition should be given to them in the short term.

The 1987 CICA standard has taken the straightforward but arbitrary position that experience gains and losses and the effect of changes in actuarial assumptions shall be amortized to income over the expected average remaining service life of the employee group. For experience gains and losses only, the standard suggests that a shorter amortization period may be appropriate in some circumstances, but gives no clue as to what those circumstances are.

The FASB standard calls for quite different treatment. To begin with, the FASB calls for annual plan valuations. These are necessary under its scheme to enable calculation of the interest cost on the obligation and the current service cost to be recognized in the next accounting period. These annual valuations will disclose a difference between plan obligations and the fair value of plan assets. That difference may be composed in part of the unamortized balance of past-service cost and of the difference that existed at the date of the transition to accounting on the basis of the 1987 standard. The remainder will be the experience gain or loss accumulated since that standard came into effect.

Part of that remainder will be represented by the difference between the current fair value of plan assets and their market-related values. This asset component of experience gain and loss will automatically be taken care of by the fact that market-related values of plan assets will be continuously adjusted toward market value over a maximum five-year period. The other part of the remaining difference will represent experience gain and loss attributable to the valuation of the pension obligation. This will have been caused by normal deviations of actual experience from mortality and other assumptions, and also by the effect of using a current discount rate each year that may be different from the one used in the previous valuation. Once this liability part of the experience gain and loss is established, recognition of gain or loss in income is governed by the so-called "corridor approach." Under this approach, no amortization to income is required so long as the accumulated experience gain or loss at a valuation date is less than ten percent of the greater of (1) the pension obligation value, and (2) the fair value of the plan assets at that date. If an excess exists, amortization of the excess is to begin based on the average remaining service period of active plan members. The calculation is made independently each year based on figures in the latest valuation. Thus, the accumulated experience gain or loss can easily be outside the corridor in one year and not in the next.

This corridor formula establishes a minimum only for amortization of accumulated experience gain or loss. An enterprise is to be permitted to use any systematic method of amortization provided it is used consistently, it treats gains and losses similarly, and its use is disclosed. However, the minimum amortization amount calculated under the corridor formula must be recognized in any year when it exceeds the amount required to be amortized by the system otherwise in force.

Comment. There is a considerable difference in the apparent philosophy underlying the approaches taken in the two standards. The corridor approach adopted by the FASB seems to suggest that experience gains and losses are expected to cancel out over time. Only when the accumulated amount becomes substantial is amortization required as a precaution against continuing error. The CICA approach, in contrast, seems more concerned that a persistent error could be present. If it is, it is better to begin amortization early rather than late. In this sense the CICA method could be considered more conservative than that of the FASB.

Recognition of a minimum liability

Because the cost of past-service amendments is recognized on an amortized basis, and the same is true for net experience losses and any net liability existing at the date of transition to the 1987 accounting standards (see next section for discussion), the full gross obligation with respect to pensions will not normally be reflected in any figure of net pension asset or liability recorded in the balance sheet. Such delayed recognition of part of the pension obligation has been traditional in pension accounting, and is continued in the Canadian 1987 standard.

The FASB has also adhered to delayed recognition for the most part, but has taken a small step toward recognition of a minimum liability in some circumstances. Details of the calculation will not be set out here other than to say it is based on the use of an "accumulated benefit" ACM for all plans, which minimizes the amount of the liability. If the gross obligation so calculated exceeds the amount of the plan assets, a minimum liability is to be recorded in the balance sheet. An intangible asset may be recognized to balance the minimum liability up to the amount of any remaining unamortized balance of past-service cost. If the minimum liability figure exceeds such unamortized past-service cost, the difference (net of deferred taxes) is to be charged as a separate reduction of shareholder's equity.

It seems doubtful that this complicated accounting conveys worthwhile information.

Transition to the new accounting basis

Ordinarily, when a change in accounting basis is made, it is desirable to make a retroactive adjustment to results previously reported in order to show trends in the figures on the new basis of accounting. It is impractical to do this for pension accounting because of the amount of recalculation that would be required. Accordingly, the 1987 standards have adopted a compromise. The amounts of the pension obligation and of the plan assets are to be calculated on the new basis of accounting. The net underfunded or overfunded position shown on the new basis of calculation is to be compared with the net accrued pension liability or prepaid pension asset recognized under the previous basis of accounting. The difference becomes an unrecognized transition asset or liability to be amortized over future years.

The CICA standard calls for amortization of that transition asset or liability "normally" over the expected average remaining service lives of employees. There is no indication of what circumstances would call for an abnormal basis of amortization. The FASB chooses the same normal amortization period, but permits an arbitrary fifteen-year period if that is longer. Also, if most of the plan participants are inactive, the amortization period used is to be the average future life expectancy of those participants.

Curtailments and settlements of pension obligations; special termination benefits

The accounting methods discussed so far assume, in essence, that a pension plan, once adopted, continues in a routine fashion indefinitely. In particular, the delay in recognition of experience gains and losses, of past-service cost, and of the transition asset and liability are founded on the view that the pension plan will continue to operate on a steady keel, so that it is legitimate to smooth out the reporting of its financial consequences. While this assumption is not unreasonable most of the time, there are occasions when sharp discontinuities occur in pension plans, including the ultimate discontinuity of plan termination.

There are two significant types of discontinuity in pension plans—a plan "settlement" and a "curtailment."

- A settlement is any irrevocable event by which the employer or the plan is relieved of the primary obligation to pay the promised benefits and also is relieved of significant risks in relation to the obligation or to the assets used to make settlement.
- A curtailment is an event that significantly reduces the expected years of future service of employees or eliminates the expectation of earning future benefits for a significant number of employees. Thus, a curtailment might result from a plant closing with resulting termination of employment or from adoption of an early retirement program that significantly reduces the future years of service of the employees taking early retirement.

If a plan is completely terminated and the accrued obligation has been transferred to other parties, both a curtailment and a settlement have taken place.

A settlement consists of the discharge of some or all of an employer's obligation existing under a pension plan. The consideration for that discharge may differ from the amount of obligation as previously calculated, so that a question of gain or loss recognition arises. In contrast, when a curtailment occurs there is no settlement of the liability, but there is nevertheless likely to be a change in the calculated amount of the pension obligation. For example, employees who terminate their employment before the expected retirement date may lose some unvested benefits that have been allowed for in the liability calculation. Also, in a final-pay plan, their ultimate pensions will be based upon salaries at the time of the termination, rather than the presumably higher salaries they would have received had they stayed until normal retirement age. The recalculation of the pension obligation as a result of a curtailment also raises the question of gain or loss recognition.

Gain or loss calculated on the basis of a comparison of the calculated obligation before and after the events of settlement or curtailment does not tell the whole story. We must remember that the amount of the obligation as calculated immediately before the settlement or curtailment may have been affected by events that have not yet been reflected in the accounts. For example, the calculated obligation may have been increased by a plan amendment granting past service benefits, the cost of which has not yet been fully amortized against income. Similarly, there may exist an unrecognized balance of transition asset or liability, or an unrecognized balance of experience gain or loss that occurred after the transition to the new accounting basis called for by the 1987 standards. These unrecognized balances have a bearing on the amount of gain or loss to be recognized upon a settlement or curtailment.

The FASB provides much more detailed guidance than does the CICA for the accounting treatment of settlements and curtailments.[11] Accordingly, the FASB recommendations will be taken as the foundation of the following discussion, but reference to any apparent difference in the CICA thinking will be made where necessary.

It is worth noting at the outset two assumptions that appear to underlie the FASB recommendations:

- At the time of the transition to the 1987 standards, a net unrecognized asset or liability position with respect to the pension plan will have resulted from recalculations on the new accounting basis. The FASB assumes that if that transition difference was a liability, it may reasonably be attributed to plan amendments granting past service prior to the date of the transition. On the other hand, if the transition recalculation showed a transition asset, it may be assumed that all past service prior to the transition date was taken care of, and the transition asset stems from experience gains or excess recognition of pension expense.
- It is assumed that settlement of the employer's obligation for pension benefits without termination of the plan or curtailment of future employee service should not affect any future benefits the employer may have expected from past-service costs undertaken previously because the employees remain with the company. Thus, there is no need to take unrecognized past service into account when recording gain or loss on settlement. On the other hand, a curtailment does affect the employer's expectation of future benefit from previous grants of past service because the future years of service to be received from employees is reduced or eliminated in a curtailment.

Accounting for settlements. A settlement may result from direct transfers of assets to employees to discharge the obligation to them, or from the purchase of annuities to meet the obligation. An annuity may be participating or nonparticipating. Some participating annuities may make the employer subject to additional payment for adverse deficiencies, or otherwise expose the employer to continuing risks with respect to satisfaction of the obligation. If they do, the purchase of those annuities cannot be regarded as a settlement. More limited participation rights do not prevent settlement accounting, but the FASB is not explicit as to where the dividing line should be drawn.

The elements of gain or loss to be recognized upon complete settlement of a pension plan obligation are as follows:

- Any difference between the calculated amount of the obligation before settlement and the consideration given for the settlement. (Under the FASB standard, this difference should be nonexistent since the obligation at any particular time is supposed to be calculated based on the amount required to settle it. Under the CICA approach, however, a difference is likely.)
- Any experience gain or loss accumulated since transition to the new standard that has not been amortized to income in that period (including any experience gain or loss resulting from recalculation of the net obligation at its settlement amount immediately before the settlement)
- Any transition *asset* remaining unamortized at the settlement date.

Note that under the FASB approach an unrecognized transition *liability* is not an element to be taken into account in computing settlement gain or loss. This rests on the assumption, already mentioned, that any such liability is likely to be caused in large part by the grant of past-service benefits prior to the date of transition. This assumption, of course, will be inaccurate in some cases. A transition liability could also represent unrecognized experience losses or even past underfunding. The CICA standard is not explicit on the treatment of a transition asset or liability. A possible inference from the rather loose wording of *Handbook* paragraph 3460.53 is that it was intended that *both* transition assets and liabilities should be taken into account in computing gain or loss upon settlements.

When a settlement is effected through a participating annuity, the cost of the participation feature will be recorded as an asset. (The remaining cost of the annuity is, in effect, written off against the liability that is discharged.) The employer remains at risk with respect to realization of the value of the participation feature. For this reason, the FASB requires that any gain to be recognized upon settlement be reduced by the amount of cost assigned to the participation feature. (If there is a loss recognized on settlement, however, it does not have to be increased by the cost of the participation feature.)

A settlement may cover only part of an employee's existing pension obligation. For example, annuities might be purchased to cover vested benefits only, or to cover benefits accrued based on present salaries but not on projected salaries. If the settlement is partial, the second and third elements of gain or loss listed above (experience gain or loss and unamortized transition asset) are to be prorated according to the reduction in the calculated amount of the pension obligation resulting from the settlement. If, as aforesaid, an annuity participation right has been purchased, its value is to be subtracted from the maximum gain on these two elements before proration of that gain.

In order to reduce the effort required to comply with this accounting, the FASB has conceded that employers may adopt a policy (to be followed consistently) of not recognizing gain or loss where the cost of a year's settlements is less than the sum of the service cost and interest components of periodic pension cost for that year.

Accounting for curtailments. When a curtailment occurs, two aspects must be considered. First, the fact that the number of years of future service of employees is curtailed means that benefits previously expected from past-service plan amendments are no longer to be expected. Therefore, if the cost of such amendments made previously has not yet been fully recognized, recognition must be accelerated. The FASB requires that a loss be recognized with respect to the previously unrecognized past-service cost, in the proportion that the reduction in expected future years of service is of the previously expected total future years of service. Any transition liability still unrecognized at the curtailment date is considered tantamount to past service and therefore is to be treated on the same basis—i.e., a loss is to be recognized.

Curtailment will also result in a change (usually a reduction) in the measured amount of the pension obligation. In isolation, that change can be considered a gain or a loss. However, we cannot ignore the interaction with other elements in our pension calculations. For example, the measured amount of the pension obligation before the curtailment might have shown the impact of an experience loss. If that experience loss has not been fully recognized for accounting purposes, by the same token the reduction of the measured obligation as a result of the curtailment should not be fully recognized as a gain. Accordingly, the FASB instructions are as follows:

- For the purpose of these computations, combine the figure of unrecognized experience gain or loss subsequent to the transition with the figure of any unamortized transition *asset*. The total is regarded for this purpose as the net unrecognized experience gain or loss with respect to the plan. (Recall that a transition *liability* is regarded, in contrast, as equivalent to unrecognized past service.)
- If there is an apparent gain on remeasurement of the pension obligation after curtailment, reduce it by any net experience *loss* (as adjusted by the unamortized transition asset, as just described). In other words, if there is a gain on obligation remeasurement, recognize that gain. However, the amount recognized is to be reduced by any net unrecognized experience *loss* but is not to be increased by any net unrecognized experience *gain*.
- If there is an apparent loss on remeasurement of the pension obligation, reduce it by any net experience *gain*. In other words, recognize any loss on obligation measurement. However, reduce the loss recognized by any unrecognized net experience *gain*, but do not increase it by a net experience *loss*.

It should be noted that if the curtailment results from an early retirement plan and that plan includes an offer of special retirement benefits, any increase in the plan obligation resulting from such benefits is not included in this calculation, but is accounted for separately, as described subsequently under the caption "termination benefits."

These FASB instructions regarding computation of gain or loss with respect to curtailments are complex. In contrast, the *CICA Handbook* says that gains or losses are to be recognized on curtailments, but provides little guidance (in paragraph 3460.53) on how such gains or losses are to be determined. In particular, it is not apparent how one should compute the portion of unrecognized experience gain or loss, or the transition asset or liability that should be recognized at the time of a curtailment. Various approaches could be taken. In view of this confusion, it is the author's opinion that an entity should not be criticized for following FASB guidance in this area.

Losses determined on the above basis are to be recognized in income as soon as it is probable that a curtailment will occur and its effects can be reasonably estimated. Estimated gains on curtailment, in contrast, are not to be recognized until the employee retirements take place or the plan suspension or amendment is adopted. This is the normal approach taken under accounting standards for contingencies. The *CICA Handbook* suggests this approach for settlements as well as for curtailments.

Termination benefits. Termination benefits may be offered to employees as part of a pension plan, or separately. A scheme of termination benefits may be agreed upon to take effect upon certain events, such as a plant closing ("contractual termination benefits"). A loss should be accrued for such benefits when payment becomes probable and their amount is reasonably capable of estimation. On other occasions, "special termination benefits" may be offered for a short term only. The liability and loss for these are to be recognized when the employees accept the offer and the amount can be estimated. The situations that give rise to payments of termination benefits may also give rise to curtailment accounting with respect to the pension plan.

Pension plan disclosure

The 1987 FASB standard has prescribed disclosure for defined benefit plans that is considerably expanded over that previously required.

- A description of the plan(s), including employee groups covered, type of benefit formula, funding policy, types of assets held, significant nonbenefit liabilities, and nature and effect of significant matters affecting comparability of information for periods presented. Disclosure of the benefit formula is particularly useful since flat-benefit and career-average plans are more likely to be upgraded (with consequent increases in cost) than final-pay plans.[12]
- An analysis of the pension cost for the period as among (1) the service cost component, (2) the interest cost component, (3) the actual return on assets, and (4) the aggregate of the amortization of unrecognized past-service cost, experience gain and loss, and transition asset or liability, together with the difference between the actual return on assets for the year and the expected long-term return on assets.
- A reconciliation of the net pension liability or prepayment reported in the balance sheet (as well as any additional minimum liability) with the following off-balance-sheet figures pertaining to the plan and its accounting:
  — The fair value of plan assets

- The projected benefit obligation, disclosing the amount of obligation calculated on the accumulated benefit basis and the amount of vested benefits
- The amount of unrecognized past-service cost
- The amount of unrecognized gain or loss from experience or changes in actuarial assumptions
- The amount of remaining transition asset or liability.

- The weighted-average assumed discount rate and rate of compensation increase used to measure the projected benefit obligation and also the weighted-average expected long-term rate of return on plan assets.
- If applicable, details concerning securities of the employer and related parties held by the pension plan and details of annual benefits covered by annuities issued by the employer and related parties, and certain other details explaining the application of the standard.

The disclosure of the economic assumptions (the second to last disclosure noted above) is particularly valuable. Disclosure of the sensitivity of pension liabilities and costs to changes in those assumptions, as proposed in the exposure draft for this statement, would have been even more valuable but was dropped on the grounds of its costliness.

For defined contribution plans, a description of the plans is required together with comment on any significant matters affecting comparability of information for periods presented. The annual cost recognized is also to be disclosed.

For defined benefit plans, the 1987 CICA standard, in sharp contrast to the FASB standard, requires only that disclosure be given of the present value of accrued pension benefits and, separately, the value of pension fund assets. (Presumably "value" refers to market-related values used in the accounting, but that is not made clear.) Some additional items are mentioned as something companies "may wish to disclose." For defined contribution plans, disclosure of the present value of any future past service contributions to be made by the employer is all that is required.

Comment. The FASB disclosures will add greatly to the information available and the understanding of statement readers who have some familiarity with the working of pension plans. It seems likely that serious analysts will soon equip themselves to grasp the significance of the disclosures, to the extent that they are not so equipped already. The disclosure required by the CICA, in contrast, is notable only for its brevity. This is all the more disturbing when it is considered that the discount rate used to calculate the pension obligation and the current-service cost—a key assumption—will be a much "softer" figure under the CICA standard than it is under the FASB's. Realistically speaking, an estimate of the future long-term rate of return on investments is anybody's guess. In contrast, the rate at which obligations could currently be settled, which is called for in the FASB standard, is capable of being supported by evidence. (The major impact of variation in the choice of discount rate will be recalled from earlier discussion in this chapter.) The inadequate CICA disclosure is all the harder to understand because it so clearly contravenes the golden rule that disclosure should always be made when material accounting estimates are subject to a high degree of judgment.

Evaluation of the 1987 standards

The problem of accounting for pension costs and obligations represents a severe test of the practicality of recognizing and measuring future costs attributable to past and present operations. The 1960s accounting standards were founded on the belief that actuarial science provided answers to the measurement problem. The renewed interest in the problem in the 1980s was associated with the realization that actuarial approaches were in some respects inconsistent with accounting concepts and objectives, particularly the objective of providing a rational and *systematic* approach to measuring pension cost period by period. There is too much scope within actuarial methods for arbitrary decisions and inconsistent application from period to period to meet that objective.

Extensive discussion and research preceded the 1987 standards and identified the key issues. With this background, the standard-setters arrived at a number of decisions.

- The basic concept that pension benefits are attributable to service rendered during an employee's working career and that accordingly the liability should be recognized then, was reaffirmed. Unfortunately, since it was decided that plan improvements after retirement should normally not be anticipated in the accounting, this objective literally cannot be achieved.
- There was some acknowledgement of the proposition that an employer might have an unwritten commitment to make benefit improvements, and, if so, the cost recognized for a period could be based upon expected benefit improvements. This was not strongly urged, however, and its application is likely to be uneven. Most enterprises will continue to look only to promises currently embodied in their pension plan formulas as a basis for the accounting.
- Standard methods were adopted for allocation of employee entitlements to future benefits under a plan to the periods in which they are deemed earned. Although the reasons for choosing one actuarial cost method over another remain debatable, the decision to select just one among possible alternatives represents a major break from past tradition, and this will help the comparability of accounting from one enterprise to another.
- The requirement that actuarial assumptions be "best estimates" is also a break from past tradition. The requirement is particularly important with respect to the investment return or "interest" assumption, which has often been biased conservatively in the past. In view of the fact that assumptions as to the future are always speculative, it remains to be seen whether this change will have significant practical impact.
- A normal basis for recognition of the cost of amendments to pension plans has been recommended. This normal basis almost certainly extends the amortization period long beyond the possible benefit from the amendment, but there are no studies available to suggest a more reasonable period. Shorter amortization is permissible in somewhat vaguely defined circumstances. The present variability in the write-off period for the cost of plan amendments is, therefore, likely to continue.
- The CICA and FASB have recommended quite different bases for treatment of experience gains and losses and of the effect of changes in actuarial assumptions. There is no obvious reason to prefer one basis over the other since it is difficult to be other than arbitrary in this area.
- The CICA choice of a "market-related" basis of valuation of pension fund assets seems reasonable in the context of its other decisions, although it is not clear why that basis needs to be extended to fixed-interest securities.

- The FASB has made the most radical break from previous tradition in its prescription of an interest rate reflecting current conditions to be used in valuing the gross pension obligation and calculating the interest accrual thereon in the next accounting period. To be consistent with this basis of valuing the pension obligation, the board has been required to prescribe a current fair value basis for pension fund assets. It has, in effect, adopted current value accounting for the off-balance-sheet figures of pension plan assets and liabilities. These valuations have significance for the measurement of pension cost attributed to a period. The adoption of current values, without other changes, would introduce great volatility into the figure of periodic pension expense. To limit this, the board has adopted an uneasy compromise for measurement of the investment return component of pension expense, a compromise that is very hard to rationalize.
- The FASB has introduced significant improvements in disclosure with respect to pension plans and their accounting. These, plus the standardization of actuarial cost methods, are by far the most important advances in the new standard. The disclosure requirements of the CICA, in contrast, are grossly inadequate.

The FASB has stated its belief that its recommendations are probably not the final step in the evolution of more useful pension accounting. That belief is almost certainly correct, although it is doubtful that accounting for a cost so dependent upon estimates of future events can ever be made a matter of routine. The 1987 standards have tackled one major source of variability in pension cost accounting by standardizing the choice of actuarial cost method. The attempt to standardize actuarial assumptions by prescribing that they be "best estimates" is likely to be less successful. The FASB requirement to use a current interest rate for valuing the pension obligation eliminates part of the problem associated with different assumptions of interest rates, at the expense of introducing greater volatility into the periodic pension cost figure. It remains to be seen whether that result will prove acceptable. It may be that a better way to produce some comparability between enterprises with respect to the interest assumption would have been merely to require disclosure of amounts of pension costs and obligations using an arbitrarily selected, but representative, benchmark rate of interest.

Summary

Recognition of cost and a liability for future payments under a pension plan presents the most difficult of problems in a difficult accounting area—that of making appropriate provision for uncertain future cash payments resulting from obligations arising out of current operations.

A key factor in understanding the conceptual issues and arriving at conclusions on them is the realization that periodic pension cost, as customarily reported, is an amalgam of several conceptually distinct measurements, including (1) the cost attributable to current service of the employees for the period, (2) interest added to pension obligations previously recognized, (3) earnings recognized on investments held in any separate pension fund, (4) cost to be recognized from plan changes that grant benefit entitlements for past service, and (5) adjustments to previously recorded figures to allow for experience different from that upon which previous measurements were based and for changes in estimates of the future.

The principal issues in pension cost accounting are reviewed below.

- The first requirement is an estimate of the future benefit payments that will arise from employee service over their careers. In principle, accounting standards recognize that future benefits paid may result from unwritten commitments by the employer, and these may be greater than those embodied in a formal pension plan document. In practice, however, the accounting standards emphasize reliance on the express plan formula as it exists from time to time. There is a trade-off here between the reliability of the figures and the relevance of estimates embodying likely future improvements to benefits. In the real world a plan with a rigidly stated formula—such as a flat-benefit or career-average plan—may end up, as a result of regular benefit improvement, providing much the same ultimate pension as a final-pay plan with its more open-ended formula. The unfortunate result of reliance on express plan formulas in the accounting is that costs assigned to periods for these different plan formulas will be quite different in amount.
- In view of the very long lapse of time between employee service and payment of benefits, estimates of future benefits and of future returns attainable on pension plan investments are subject to considerable uncertainty. In spite of this, accounting standards hold that estimates should be "best estimates," rather than having a conservative bias. Because of the wide range possible in judgments as to some of these variables—especially the average long-run investment return to be expected—the requirement to use best estimates may not accomplish much by way of standardizing practice.
- Some method is required for allocating the discounted amount of future benefit payments to years in which they are deemed earned by employees. There are a large number of actuarial cost methods that provide for such allocation, most of which can meet the test of being rational and systematic. To promote uniformity in practice, the 1987 accounting standards have adopted one stated method to be applied to each particular pension plan formula.
- In the selection of a discount rate to be applied in recognizing the present cost of future benefits, the CICA follows traditional actuarial practice in basing the rate on some estimate of the long-run average rate of return on fund investments. The 1987 FASB standard has broken new ground in requiring that the pension obligation be revalued each year at a discount rate reflecting current conditions, and that cost attributed to employee service in the ensuing year be discounted using the same rate.
- Since plan amendments granting benefit improvements for past service are usually not anticipated in the accounting, there must be some basis for recognizing their cost when they do occur. The 1987 accounting standards suggest amortization in relation to the expected remaining service life of the employee group in the normal situation. The CICA is more conservative than the FASB in the precise manner of amortization suggested. Both standards leave room for more rapid amortization when such is deemed appropriate.

- In principle, the method of valuation of pension fund assets should be compatible with the interest rate used to discount the plan obligation. The CICA prescribes valuation of pension fund assets at market-related values—a basis allowing for some smoothing of the effect of fluctuations in market value—which can be considered compatible with the use of an estimated long-term average rate of investment return for discounting the plan obligation. The FASB prescribes the use of a current fair value for valuing pension fund assets which is compatible with the use of a discount rate reflecting current conditions in valuing the pension fund obligation. In an uneasy compromise, however, the FASB bases the calculation of the investment return component of annual pension cost upon an estimate of long-term rate of return, and this is applied to a separate valuation of pension fund assets, on the basis of market-related values.
- Periodic revaluations of pension plan obligations reveal experience gains and losses—differences between the calculated present value of the obligation and the figure it would be at the date of valuation if the assumptions upon which previous cost and liability accruals had been based were borne out by experience. Differences also arise as a result of changes from time to time in the best estimates of future experience. In view of the fact that valuations of pension plan obligations themselves rest upon assumptions as to future experience, and that future experience is likely to deviate in some respect from the assumptions, it is not thought necessary to continuously adjust pension obligations and costs recognized as indicated by the latest valuation data. However, to avoid the possibility of a growing divergence between the position revealed by successive valuations and the obligation accounted for, some amortization of differences is considered desirable. The basis of amortization is necessarily highly arbitrary. The CICA and FASB have chosen different arbitrary methods.
- Because adjustments to measured plan obligations resulting from plan amendments and experience gains and losses are not given immediate recognition, there will be occasions when something akin to an "off-balance-sheet liability" exists. The FASB requires recognition of a minimum amount of liability offset by an intangible asset and, on occasion, a direct reduction of shareholders' equity. Since the minimum liability is calculated on a different basis from that used to measure the pension obligation for other purposes, it is extremely doubtful that this accounting has any information value.
- Discontinuities in pension plans resulting from significant curtailments in expected future employee service, or settlements in whole or in part of plan obligations, give rise to recalculation of the amount of pension obligations and immediate recognition of gain or loss. The FASB standard gives detailed guidance as to how this should be done.
- The FASB prescribes extensive disclosure in connection with pension plans and the accounting performed for them. This disclosure will give great help to a skilled statement analyst in understanding the significance of pension plan commitments and costs. The disclosure required by the CICA standard, in contrast, is minimal.

References

[1]American Institute of Accountants, Committee on Accounting Procedure, *Pension Plans—Accounting for Annuity Costs Based on Past Services,* Accounting Research Bulletin No. 36 (New York: AIA, 1948), subsequently consolidated in *Restatement and Revision of Accounting Research Bulletins,* Accounting Research Bulletin No. 43 (New York: AIA, 1953), Chapter 13A.

[2]See CICA, "Pension Costs and Obligations," *CICA Handbook,* Section 3460 (Toronto: CICA), and FASB, *Employers' Accounting for Pensions,* Statement of Financial Accounting Standards No. 87 (Stamford: FASB, 1985).

[3]See the argument of L. Lorensen and P. Rosenfield in "Vested Benefits—A Company's Only Pension Liability," *Journal of Accountancy,* October 1983, pp. 64-76.

[4]See, for example, *Report on Survey of Pension Plans in Canada,* 6th ed. (Toronto: Financial Executives Institute Canada, 1983), pp. 33-34, and "The Effectiveness of Current Ad Hoc Indexing of Pensions," *The Mercer Bulletin,* February 1984, pp. 1-2.

[5]If it were thought justified in theory to attempt to anticipate future plan improvements to the extent that they merely kept up with inflation, one way to perform the calculation would be to apply a real interest rate to discount the obligation estimated under the present benefit formula. The reasoning would be similar to that set out in chapter 9 suggesting the use of real interest rates in discounting future cost accruals. This approach would avoid the necessity of making subjective estimates of future inflation rates. Unfortunately, it has a weakness inasmuch as one may not be justified in assuming that the present pension plan formula would be as generous if the benefits promised were actually indexed. See R.M. Skinner, *Pension Accounting: The Problem of Equating Payments Tomorrow with Expenses Today* (Toronto: Clarkson Gordon, 1980), chap. 10.

[6]FASB, *Employers' Accounting for Pensions,* par. 41. The author predicts that this accounting will be rarely, if ever, followed because employers will be unwilling to acknowledge unwritten commitments.

[7]These propositions concentrate entirely on pension cost in isolation. But pension costs are only one element in the total compensation of employees. Total compensation will be established by negotiation in the labour market. An exploratory conceptual analysis makes some intriguing suggestions as to how this market might work. Under different scenarios, different ACMs would be logical. Unfortunately, the empirical research necessary to determine which scenario(s) applies in the real world has not been performed. See J.E. Pesando and C.K. Clarke, *Economic Models of the Labour Market: Their Implications for Pension Accounting,* Studies in Canadian Accounting Research (Canadian Academic Accounting Association, 1983). For a condensed version of the study by the authors, see "Economic Models of the Labour Market and Pension Accounting: An Exploratory Analysis," *The Accounting Review,* October 1983, pp. 733-48.

[8]*CICA Handbook,* Section 3460, par. 16.

[9]See, for example, T.S. Lucas and B.A. Hollowell, "Pension Accounting: The Liability Question," *Journal of Accountancy,* October 1981, pp. 57-66.

[10]See, for example, J.L. Treynor, P.J. Regan, and W.W. Priest, Jr., *The Financial Reality of Pension Funding under ERISA* (Homewood, Ill.: Dow Jones-Irwin, 1976).

[11]FASB, *Employers' Accounting for Settlements and Curtailments of Defined Benefit Pension Plans and for Termination Benefits,* Statement of Financial Accounting Standards No. 88 (Stamford: FASB, 1985). As the title implies, this standard covers accounting for special termination benefits, whether these are offered as part of a pension plan or outside it.

[12]The Financial Executives Institute Canada study, *Report on Survey of Pension Plans in Canada,* p. 34 indicates that voluntary increases in pensions to retired members of career-average plans tend to be higher than those of other plans.

Chapter Fourteen

Accounting for Government Assistance

In a modern state no enterprise can avoid the pervasive influence of government. It has been said that the power to tax is the power to destroy. It might also be said that the kindly sun of government beneficence can breathe life into new enterprise and revivify the failing. No one can doubt that government taxation, direct and indirect, and government assistance, also direct and indirect, are material to the financial well-being of an enterprise.

As previously described, the historical cost system rests upon a foundation of bargained transactions in which the accounting entity knows what it is getting in return for payments made and knows what it is sacrificing in return for payments received. The absence of free bargaining in most transactions with government means that the general theory of the historical cost system provides little guidance for their accounting. As a result, accounting standards have developed largely on an ad hoc basis to meet individual issues as they arise. In this chapter we deal with issues in two broad areas of government relations: accounting for direct government assistance to business and accounting for indirect government assistance through the income tax system.

Accounting for direct government assistance

In the past twenty-five years there has been a proliferation of government programs providing assistance to private business. Direct assistance may take at least two different forms. First, governments may give outright grants or subsidies. Second, governments may provide assistance by providing service at less than market rates—for example, providing loans at low interest rates. Or a government may simply refrain from charging a normal impost on particular enterprises—for example, a municipality may agree not to charge taxes for a period to new industry locating within its boundaries. Variations of these basic types of direct assistance are also possible. For example, a grant may be repayable if qualifying conditions are not fulfilled, or a loan may be made forgivable upon fulfillment of given conditions.

Conceptual questions

Before the last quarter century a business entity rarely received contributions from anyone who did not have a financial interest in it. Typically, any contributions received without an obvious quid pro quo represented donations from shareholders—people who were benefited by the financial well-being of the business. Accordingly, the logical accounting treatment was to treat such contributions as capital receipts; they clearly were not part of any earning process.

The key conceptual question with respect to government assistance is whether it too should be treated as a capital receipt or whether, in some fashion, it should should be a factor in income accounting. The arguments in favour of treating government assistance as a capital contribution are:

- The costs incurred by an entity represent the results of bargained exchanges. It would be wrong to distort the portrayal of actual asset cost and expense by offsetting grant proceeds against them.
- Government grant programs may well be temporary. It would be preferable to portray operating results on a stand-alone basis to help evaluation of the long-term viability of the entity.
- Government grants are paid gratuitously and are in no sense earned. Therefore they should not affect reported income.
- Government grants can be regarded merely as a substitution for financing from other sources and therefore should be accounted for as financing.

The arguments in favour of taking grant proceeds into account in income determination are as follows:

- Accounting traditionally is concerned with reporting the results of the commitment of resources by the owners of the entity. It is the *net* cost of assets and the *net* expenses borne by the owners that is of interest in evaluating the success or otherwise of their investment. It does not distort what actually happened to show net costs in this way. As for portrayal of long-term viability, management will make future investment decisions in the light of conditions prevailing in the future. There is no requirement to replace existing investment if it is not profitable. Therefore, there is no requirement to show the results of existing investment as if it had not been subsidized merely because future replacement of investment might not be eligible for subsidy.
- Government assistance is not truly gratuitous since an entity must take certain actions or fulfill certain conditions to qualify for assistance. Fulfillment of the qualifications for assistance usually involves costs that are taken into account in the determination of income. From the viewpoint of reporting on the progress of the enterprise itself, it is important to take the assistance into account as well as the costs. The conditions imposed for the receipt of government assistance normally provide adequate guidance for recognizing the impact of the assistance on income. The assistance should be recognized in income in step with the expenses that are offset or the revenues that are subsidized by the government program.

Grants and subsidies

The question of accounting for government assistance was first addressed in Canada in 1967 in the context of government grants to subsidize qualified investment in plant and equipment. The CICA recommendation was two-pronged. If an enterprise would have made a qualified investment even without the stimulus of the grant, it was to be treated as contributed capital (not income). On the other hand, if the enterprise would not have made the investment without the grant, the grant proceeds were to be credited against the cost of the assets subsidized.

In this way their carrying value would not be above the amount of sacrifice voluntarily made by the entity, and thus could be presumed to be the equivalent of an economic value evidenced by a bargained transaction.

This solution proved to be unworkable. The accounting treatment depended upon what management claimed was a determining factor in its decision. Since the grant was available in any case, management had to exercise its imagination as to whether it would have made the investment without the grant. In practice, the basis of accounting adopted seemed to conform more to the end result desired than to what appeared to be the economics of the situation.

As a result, the CICA re-examined the question some years later. By that time the variety of government assistance programs had greatly increased, so that it was necessary to consider more than just investment subsidies. This time it was decided to follow the proprietary theory completely. From the standpoint of an owner deciding whether to make an investment or incur some other expenditure, it is the *net* cost that is relevant to the decision whether the expenditure is worthwhile. If government assistance is available, it is logical to take it into account in the expenditure decision. It follows that the best accounting for proceeds from government assistance is to offset them against the cost or costs with which they are associated. The credit for the assistance received then flows into income automatically, as the net cost is recognized in expense in accordance with normal income determination rules.

Implementation of this approach to accounting for government assistance requires determination of the essential nature of the assistance. That nature is normally indicated by the conditions imposed for qualification for assistance.

- If the assistance is intended to supplement revenue, it should be credited to revenue (as an item of other income) as conditions for receipt of assistance are fulfilled.
- If the assistance is designed to subsidize costs that will be treated as period costs, it should be offset against them as they are expensed. Assistance received in advance of the expensing of related costs should be treated as a deferred credit to be matched with actual cost outlays as they are written off to expense in future.
- If assistance is tied to expenditure on fixed assets, two treatments are permissible. The amount of assistance may be deducted directly from the recorded cost of the fixed assets and depreciation based on the net amount. Alternatively, the assistance amount may be treated as a deferred credit and amortized to income in step with depreciation written on the related assets.

In practice it is not always easy to distinguish just how a particular type of government assistance should be reflected in income. When a grant is tied to a particular type of cost, there is a strong presumption that the grant should be reflected in income in step with the recognition of that cost as expense. For example, if a grant is a percentage of expenditures on scientific research or pollution control, it is clear that the purpose of the program is to reduce the cost of making those particular expenditures. If a grant is a percentage of investment in plant and equipment in a particular location, it is clear that the appropriate treatment of the grant is a reduction of fixed asset costs. Even though the program's objective may be to create employment in a particular area, the fact is that it achieves that aim by reducing the cost of investment in that area.

The situation is more obscure when eligibility for government assistance is not conditional upon specific monetary expenditure by the entity within a clearly defined time period. For example, a grant intended to stimulate employment might be conditioned upon achieving a given level of employment and maintaining it for at least three years. One might argue in such a case that the grant could be amortized to income over the three years, since it becomes unconditional at the end of that time. On the other hand, if fixed investment had to be made to create those jobs, and especially if that investment could not readily be disposed of if the venture were closed down, one might argue that, in substance, qualification for the government assistance put the entity at risk over the lifetime of the investment. Hence, the grant should be reflected in income over that lifetime.

Since there is a wide variety in terms and conditions possible in government assistance programs, it is very difficult to suggest accounting rules appropriate to every circumstance. In general, however, whenever doubt exists it can be suggested that if it appears that achievement of the government support required a long-term investment, then the credit arising from the receipt of that support is best amortized over the lifetime of the venture.[1]

Conditions applicable to government assistance programs may also introduce an element of uncertainty into the accounting. If the entity has fulfilled the important conditions required to achieve the objectives of the program, and has reasonable assurance of fulfilling the remaining conditions, it is considered proper to accrue the estimated amount of assistance receivable and begin accounting for its income effect. Similarly, if assistance has been received but may be required to be repaid if the entity does not continue to fulfill certain conditions, income accounting may proceed provided there is reasonable assurance those continuing conditions will be met. Finally, certain assistance may be provided in the form of loans that will be forgiven over a period of time if the entity continues to fulfill specific conditions. Assuming there is reasonable assurance at the outset that the conditions will be fulfilled, the forgivable loan is tantamount to a grant, and may be so accounted for so long as the qualifying conditions continue to be fulfilled.

In assessing an entity's operations it is useful to know the extent to which income and financial position reported have been affected by government assistance, and especially the extent to which support currently being credited to income account will be discontinued in future without compensating reduction in costs or in revenues. The *CICA Handbook* calls for disclosure of a considerable amount of detail with respect to grants received, their terms and conditions, and any contingent liability for repayment.

There is a technical question not dealt with in the CICA recommendations. If a grant does not reduce the tax basis of a fixed asset but its amount is credited against the carrying value of the asset on the books, the total capital cost allowance claimable over the asset's life will exceed its initial carrying value. Under a different government program a grant might be used to reduce the tax basis of the asset. In that case, if the grant is taken to a deferred credit account, the tax basis will be less than the carrying value of the asset. In both these cases the difference between the initial tax and accounting basis for the asset will create difficulty for the operation of tax allocation accounting (to be discussed in the next chapter). As a practical matter, it seems most convenient to credit a grant to the deferred credit account when it does not reduce the tax basis and credit it against the fixed asset cost when it does. It would be objectionable, however, to have inconsistent statement presentation just because grants are received that have different tax treatment. To achieve consistency in such a case, it is suggested that any balance of deferred credits related to grants be deducted from the fixed asset carrying value in the presentation of the balance sheet.

Concessionary arrangements

Indirect subsidies may be given by different levels of government in many different ways. For example, a senior government might make low-cost financing available for entities setting up business in a depressed area. Or, a municipality may commit itself to remission of taxes for a fixed period to induce industry to locate within its boundaries. It is extremely difficult to account for such forms of government assistance in a manner that is consistent with the treatment given outright grants or subsidies.

Consider a municipality that gives a business a ten-year remission of real property taxes. The form of assistance is a tax remission, but the purpose is to induce investment in the community. It is normally at the point of the initial investment decision that the availability of the assistance affects management decision making. It would be logical, therefore, to capitalize the present value of the government assistance as an asset at the time the investment is undertaken, and treat the offsetting credit as a reduction in fixed asset cost or a deferred credit, just as if the municipality had given a direct subsidy.

In practice this degree of sophistication in accounting is not attempted, no doubt partly because of the difficult estimates that would be required of capitalized value and appropriate amortization period. Government assistance received by way of concessions is normally accounted for just as it is received. That is to say, actual interest paid on low interest loans is charged to expense, or realty tax expense is simply not recorded if none is charged under a concessionary arrangement. Accordingly, where government concessions are material to results reported, it is important to disclose their amount and the future period for which they will continue.

Government assistance through the income tax system

One particular form of concessionary assistance occasionally used in Canada in the past has been the so-called "income tax holiday." For example, new mines used to be free from income tax for the first three years after the beginning of commercial production. In such a case it would have been difficult, if not impossible, to place a value on the concession at the commencement of operations. In contrast, another program briefly in effect in the early 1970s allowed a new enterprise in a depressed area the choice of a stated subsidy against fixed asset costs or a three-year income tax holiday. In that case, a company electing the tax holiday could have recorded an asset for the amount equal to the fixed asset subsidy it might have had—crediting fixed asset cost for the value of the subsidy—and subsequently recorded a gain or loss on its decision, depending upon whether the tax avoided under the holiday exceeded or fell short of the recorded asset. No one adopted this decision-oriented—and possibly embarrassing to management—basis of accounting.

These two different income tax concessions stimulate consideration of a conceptual question. There is little question that when a government program gives an enterprise a choice between an outright grant or taking an equivalent amount as a reduction in taxes payable, the tax reduction, if taken, is in substance a grant. Thus, if a given program grant would be treated as a reduction in fixed asset cost, an equivalent tax reduction taken under the same program should be credited to fixed assets. Correspondingly, the tax expense for the period is recorded as if there had not been a tax reduction.

The case is more debatable when government assistance is available *only* in the form of a credit against income taxes payable. In that case there are two necessary conditions to receipt of the assistance—fulfillment of the program qualifications, and the earning of taxable income. This is a specific example of a general problem in accounting. When two or more events are necessary to one outcome, which event shall be regarded as predominant so as to form the basis of accounting recognition of the outcome? An answer has already been suggested for bargained exchanges. For example, in chapter 13 it was suggested that future pension cost must be estimated and provided for at the time employee service is received because that is the time the reporting entity receives the benefit it bargained for in the exchange. Income tax, however, is a nonreciprocal transaction between the government and the taxpayer. Thus, the timing of value given or value received as a test for recognition of revenue and cost is not directly applicable.

In this situation, two competing views are held. Under one viewpoint, because the transaction is nonreciprocal the expense for income tax is whatever amount results from the law and regulations adopted by the government. If the government permits special tax reductions in special circumstances, these represent merely "a selective reduction in tax rate." The reduction should "flow through" to net income reported in the year when the reduction is effective. Under the other viewpoint, it is pointed out that the availability of the tax concession normally affects the taxpayer's bargaining in other transactions. The receipt of the tax concession is almost always conditional upon the taxpayer undertaking other actions. Thus, the tax reduction ought to be accounted for as a direct offset to the costs incurred in the other transactions undertaken to meet the government conditions.

This fundamental question in tax accounting has never been addressed in isolation on its merits. Instead, questions have arisen in the context of accounting for individual tax incentives and have been answered, either through the development of practice or through specific accounting standards, in ways that have not always been consistent. We discuss a few specific cases below. Note that tax incentives can take the form of deductions from taxable income in excess of actual costs incurred (thereby reducing net tax by the amount of the extra deduction multiplied by the applicable tax rate) or can be direct credits against tax otherwise payable.

Tax incentives through deductions from taxable income

Extra tax deductions from taxable income are sometimes provided by simply factoring up a cost that otherwise would be deductible at its actual amount. For example, Canadian tax law at one time allowed a deduction for scientific research expenditures of 150% of their actual cost. So long as such factored-up expenditures are written off in the accounts in the same year as the tax deduction is taken, any method of accounting for the tax saving has the same effect on net income after tax. Under the flow-through approach, tax expense is reported in the income statement at its actual reduced amount and the expenditures that gave rise to the extra tax reduction are reported at their actual amount. Alternatively, the tax reductions resulting from the extra deductible amount could be treated on a basis equivalent to a government grant. To accomplish this the amount of the tax reduction would have to be calculated and reported income tax increased, while the actual expense that qualified for the extra tax reduction would be reduced. In practice, this refinement in accounting is not normally performed. Flow-through accounting is followed automatically although, in view of the lack of impact on the reported income figure, it may be doubted that much thought has been given to the desirability of a different form of presentation.

The situation is less straightforward when an extra tax allowance is granted for capital expenditures. For example, some years ago a qualified investment within a given period gave rise to a right to claim capital cost allowance (CCA) based on 115% of the cost of the asset. This provision was intended to stimulate capital investment. Accounting for the incentive on a basis fully consistent with that for direct capital assistance would have required that an amount equivalent to the present value of the extra capital cost allowance be credited against the asset account (or treated as a deferred credit) and be brought into income in step with depreciation on the asset. Because of the extra record-keeping complications that this would cause, however, the general practice was simply to allow the tax reduction from the extra capital cost allowance to flow through to income.[2]

Now that the CICA has issued new standards for treatment of investment tax credits (see next section), a flow-through treatment in a situation similar to that just described would be inconsistent.

Direct credits against taxes payable

One of the most hotly debated issues in accounting in the last twenty-odd years has been that of the treatment of tax credits allowed in consideration for investment in qualifying assets. This debate was first joined in the United States in 1962. The Internal Revenue Code permitted an "investment credit" against taxes payable equal to a percentage of the cost of certain depreciable assets acquired after 1961. The immediate question was, when should the reduction be taken into income?

Some felt that it could be treated as income immediately—the flow-through basis. Others thought that since it stemmed from investment in depreciable assets, it should be reflected in income in step with depreciation written on the assets. There was also a modification of the flow-through method. As originally enacted, any tax credit taken reduced the tax basis (undepreciated capital cost in Canadian terms) of the assets. It was identical in effect, therefore, to a 100% claim of CCA up to the amount of the tax credit without corresponding depreciation being written in the accounts. Under tax allocation principles (see next chapter) the difference in timing of the reduction of tax and book values should lead to recognition of a deferred tax credit recorded at the current rate of tax. Thus, it was proposed that the amount of the investment credit should be apportioned. Fifty-two percent (the then-current rate of tax) should be credited to deferred taxes. Forty-eight percent could flow through immediately to income.

The opinion of American accountants on this issue was sharply divided. A majority of the Accounting Principles Board favoured the deferral and amortization approach to recognizing the credit in income. However, two phenomena previously almost unknown were to frustrate a standard embodying the majority opinion. Deferral and amortization was hotly opposed by certain industrial interests. A lobby was organized to go over the heads of the board to the Securities and Exchange Commission in an attempt to persuade the commission not to enforce the board's opinion. Deferral and amortization was also opposed by the U.S. Treasury Department on the grounds that such an accounting rule would reduce the incentive to business to take advantage of the program and thereby would tend to frustrate its aims. This was the first important occasion on which an argument was made that accounting standards should be determined, not necessarily by the criterion of fair presentation, but rather by the criterion of their expected "economic consequences."

The significance of an economic consequences argument in this case should be understood. If the flow-through method provided the most faithful presentation of the effect on income and wealth of the investment credit, then there was no need to argue that it had favourable economic consequences. It would be justified on its own merits. It is only when the flow-through method was *not* the best method to achieve accounting objectives (or in the unlikely event that there was no basis for determining the best method) that possible economic consequences needed to be marshalled in its support. In effect, the Treasury Department was taking the relatively cynical position that fair financial reporting to creditors, owners, and the capital markets generally should take second place to the presumed economic policy objectives of government.

The economic consequences argument also needed to be examined on its own merits. In deciding on capital expenditures, most enterprises go through a "capital budgeting" exercise to determine whether the proposed expenditure meets certain criteria. For example, incremental cash receipts and outlays that are forecast as a result of operation of a proposed capital asset may be discounted by the current weighted-average cost of capital to see whether the net present value equals or exceeds the cost of the proposed asset. If it does not, the investment is rejected. Consider the simplified example in Table 14-1 of such an appraisal for an asset costing $100,000. (All cash flows are assumed to take place at the end of the year. The weighted-average cost of capital is taken as 15% after tax.)

Since the total net present value of the forecast cash flows at $98,107 is less than the asset cost of $100,000, the project will be rejected. An investment credit even as low as 5%, however, would bring the present value of cash flows over $100,000 and cause acceptance of the project. In other words, the availability of government assistance changes the economics of the project and should stimulate investment *regardless of the accounting*. Some might argue that some managements may be sufficiently incompetent as not to make such an analysis. Or, it might be felt that management with incentive compensation contracts tied to reported accounting earnings would be motivated to make uneconomical investments merely to take advantage of the boost in earnings from flow-through accounting. If either of these is correct, prohibition of flow-through accounting would dampen the potential stimulative effect of the investment tax credit. It is hard to believe, however, that sound public policy can be based upon inducing unsound private decisions.

These considerations were not strongly urged in 1962 or even since that time. Under political pressure, the Securities and Exchange Commission failed to support the Accounting Principles Board in its proposed accounting standard and forced the board to adopt a permissive stance. A subsequent effort by the board in 1971 met with further lobbying, which culminated in a Congressional prohibition of any attempt to prescribe a single method of accounting in the financial

Table 14-1

Illustration of Project Evaluation by Discounting Cash Flows

	Year 1	Year 2	Year 3	Year 4	Year 5	Total
Pretax incremental cash flows	$49,000	$44,000	$34,000	$20,000	$ 9,000	
Income tax after maximum CCA	4,050	9,000	8,820	5,112	1,717	
Net operating cash flows	44,950	35,000	25,180	14,888	7,283	
Salvage proceeds					7,776	
Net cash return	$44,950	$35,000	$25,180	$14,888	$15,059	
Present value factor	.8696	.7561	.6575	.5718	.4972	
Present value of cash flows	$39,087	$26,465	$16,556	$ 8,512	$ 7,487	$98,107

reports of entities to be filed with government agencies. As a result, accounting practice for the investment tax credit in the United States is still optional. The vast majority of companies follow the flow-through method.

Investment tax credits were introduced in Canada a few years after their introduction in the United States. The CICA gave consideration to their accounting in connection with projects on income tax accounting and government grant accounting. Each time it backed off from making a recommendation, in view of the controversy on the subject so evident in the United States. Finally it became clear that standards for accounting for direct government assistance were open to serious attack unless logical consistency could be achieved between the accounting for government assistance effected through the tax system and directly.[3] In essence the CICA adopted the following convincing reasoning:

- The historical cost accounting system calls for accrual accounting when cash flows fall into periods other than those to which they may be reasonably attributed in accordance with their underlying economic causes.
- It is inconsistent with the historical cost model of accounting to record gains merely because assets have been acquired.
- Government assistance pinpointed to specific situations and rendered through the tax system is not fundamentally different in character from direct government grants.

Accordingly, investment tax credits should be deducted from the related investment in fixed assets or treated as deferred credits to be amortized to income on the same basis as the related assets.[4]

Summary

This chapter deals with accounting aspects of government assistance to private enterprise by way of direct grants or subsidies or assistance granted on special conditions through reductions in income tax.

The basic issue in accounting for direct government assistance is whether such assistance should be treated as a capital contribution, or whether it should enter into income accounting. Today's accounting standards are firmly based upon the proprietary viewpoint; thus, any contributions from parties other than shareholders must be reflected in income sooner or later. That settled, the accounting resolves itself into a question of how government assistance should be reflected in income.

- All selective government assistance is granted based on conditions to be fulfilled by the grantee. Fulfillment of these conditions normally involves costs to the grantee. A logical basis for accounting for the government assistance, therefore, is to reflect it in income at the same time as the related costs are written off. This can be achieved by crediting the grant proceeds against the costs in the first instance leaving only the net cost to be written off as expense, or by treating the grant proceeds as a deferred credit when first received and amortizing that credit to income in step with the expensing of the related costs.
- Assistance granted by government is not always expressed as conditional upon monetary expenditure. It may be based upon attainment by the grantee of some nonmonetary objective. In such a case, judgment must be exercised as to the proper basis for recognition of the assistance proceeds in income. If the grant has the result of involving the enterprise in capital investment, as often it will, it would be logical to amortize the grant in step with the amortization of the investment.
- Governments may provide assistance through remission of normal imposts, rather than through a direct payment to the grantee. Logically, the value of such assistance should be treated in the same fashion as a direct subsidy. In practice it is not. Expense reported is simply lower than it otherwise would be. Where this is the case, it is important that financial statements disclose the existence and amount of the special assistance and its termination date.

Government assistance may also be given indirectly by selective tax deductions or tax credits, rather than by direct grant. The grantee in such a case must have taxable income in order to take advantage of the assistance. Because of this, there has been debate whether the benefit of the tax concession should be reported in income as the tax reductions are achieved—the so-called "flow-through" basis of accounting—or whether the income tax expense should be "normalized" to the figure it would have been without the special concessions. The credit resulting from the normalization entry is then treated in the same fashion as would a credit from direct government assistance. This latter position has been accepted in Canada in the case of accounting for the investment tax credit, effective in 1985. To be logical, any other form of special concession granted through the income tax system should henceforth be treated in a compatible fashion.

References

[1]This problem is discussed in *CICA Handbook* "Accounting for Government Assistance," Section 3800, par. 12 (Toronto: CICA). The guidance given by that paragraph is quite general and it is possible that it might be interpreted differently from the opinions here expressed.

[2]See "New CCA Base: 115% of Cost," *Canadian Chartered Accountant*, March 1971, pp. 152-53.

[3]See R.H. Crandall, "Government Intervention— The PIP Grant Accounting Controversy," *Cost and Management*, September-October 1983, pp. 55-59.

[4]See CICA, "Investment Tax Credits," *CICA Handbook*, Section 3805 (Toronto, CICA).

Chapter Fifteen

Accounting for Income Tax Expense

Since the early 1950s the whole area of accounting for income tax of corporations has been an extremely contentious subject. The debate revolves around the question of income tax allocation. Is income tax a cost whose recognition as expense can be allocated between periods, like other costs, for the better portrayal of income? If allocation is performed, what is its conceptual basis, and how is it to be implemented?

A few accounting writers suggest that income tax is not an *expense* of earning income but rather is a *distribution* of income after it has been earned. From this they argue that distributions are what they are and cannot be allocated. To support the argument, it is pointed out that income tax is not voluntarily undertaken, is not in any direct way a payment for services, and is unlike other expenses in that it can be negative. These observations are true, and it is certainly open to someone to define income tax as a distribution and not an expense. That, however, does not end the matter so long as one objective of accounting is to report how much income accrues to the owners of a company. If, for example, pretax income this year contains elements that will be taxed next year, what is the best way to measure the owners' share in that reported pretax income? It is at least arguable that one must deduct not only the actual tax payable this year, but also the additional tax that will probably be payable next year because of transactions that are reported as part of this year's income. The allocation of income tax expense among accounting periods, it is clear, stems from the proprietorial emphasis in generally accepted accounting principles.

The idea of allocation of income tax expense begins with what is known as "intraperiod allocation," and this will be discussed first. Then we shall discuss the enormously complicated subject of "interperiod allocation" and conclude with the specific topic of accounting for tax loss carrybacks and carryforwards.

Intraperiod tax allocation

The intraperiod allocation question may be traced back to a time when it was common to record some gains or losses through the retained earnings account rather than through the income account. Under the "current operating performance" concept, the aim was to portray net income as including only revenues, expenses, or gains and losses that might be considered a reflection of the operating performance of the entity for the year. Recording unusual or "nonoperating" gains or losses in income, it was thought, would "distort" the record of performance; hence, such items could be credited or charged directly to retained earnings account.

If the gains or losses excluded from the income statement had income tax effects, confusion was possible. For example, suppose a loss charged to retained earnings was deductible for tax purposes. If the income tax figure in the income statement was reported as reduced, the net income after tax would be higher than otherwise and would not be truly representative of the current operating performance. To prevent this, Bulletin No. 23 of the American Institute of Accountants' Committee on Accounting Procedure, issued in 1944, recommended that the actual tax payable should be apportioned. An amount equal to the tax effect (reduction or increase) attributable to the gain or loss excluded from ordinary income should be reported together with that gain or loss (usually netted from it). The tax expense remaining after adjustment for that partition should be reported as the normal tax provision in the current operating section of the income statement.[1]

Subsequent to 1944, accounting standards have evolved so that certain other credits or charges (such as the net results of a discontinued business or "extraordinary items") may be reported in the income statement after the figure of normal operating income but before net income. Other special items may be reported in the retained earnings statement (prior period adjustments or effects of accounting changes), or there may be capital transactions with tax effects charged or credited directly to retained earnings or to other accounts in the shareholders' equity. The 1944 recommendation of intraperiod allocation has been logically extended to these cases.

The general principle now is that any tax effects (reduction or increase) associated with gains and losses reported in the income statement after the income tax expense line, or in other statements that portray the change in shareholders' equity over the accounting period, should be reported together with those special items. The figure for normal tax expense in the income statement is increased or reduced to compensate. The amount of the tax effect attributable to the special items is computed on a "with-and-without" basis—that is, by calculating what the tax expense would have been without the special items and comparing that figure with actual tax expense.

Interperiod tax allocation

Bulletin 23 was also the first authoritative accounting statement to suggest what we now know as interperiod tax allocation. By the time it was issued, the emphasis on "matching" revenues and costs to achieve a proper measure of income was resulting in recognition of an increased number of deferred charges in the balance sheet. Usually, costs treated as deferred charges were claimable for tax purposes only in the year incurred. Consequently, if income taxes were charged to income without allocation between accounting periods, tax expense reported would appear unnaturally low in relation to pretax income when deferred charges were incurred, and unnaturally high in subsequent periods when the deferred charges were written off. The same logic that suggested that income tax expense could be allocated between the income statement and retained earnings suggested allocation among different periods. The bulletin recommended that an amount equal to the tax reduction attributable to the deferred cost should be added to the actual tax payable for the year to arrive at a proper expense figure, and should be credited to the deferred charge account. Thereafter, the deferred charge, net of the tax reduction, would be amortized in the normal fashion.

The year 1954 saw the beginning of the enduring debate over tax allocation in both Canada and the United States. In the latter country, the Revenue Act of 1954 gave permission for the use of accelerated patterns of depreciation (such as the sum-of-the-years'-digits method) for tax deduction calculations. In Canada, the declining-balance basis for capital cost allowance (that is, an accelerated write-off pattern) had been adopted with the new Income Tax Act in 1949. A Canadian company was not permitted, however, to take advantage of the faster tax write-offs unless it also wrote depreciation of the same amount in its books. That requirement was rescinded in 1954. In that year, then, in both countries the possibility arose of significant continuing differences between depreciation written on the books and depreciation (or capital cost allowance) claimed for tax purposes. Notwithstanding, since tax allowances continued to be restricted to the historical cost of assets acquired, the tax payable from earnings over the lifetime of any individual asset (assuming no change in rates of tax in the period) would be the same in aggregate as it was before. The acceleration of depreciation allowances for tax purposes simply meant that less tax would be paid in the early years of an asset's life and more in the later years. In these circumstances it was asked: Would it not be best from an accounting point of view to "defer" the tax reduction resulting from tax allowances in excess of book depreciation on assets, and to credit those tax reductions back against tax expense in those future years when tax allowances were less than book depreciation? In this way, one could match the tax effect of capital cost allowances with depreciation written in the accounts.

This question was far more important in Canada than in the United States. The new tax system applied the declining-balance basis to all assets, not just to assets acquired after the effective date of the new law as in the United States. In addition, Canadian taxpayers could claim capital cost allowance on the cost of all assets to which title had been acquired (including the cost of assets still under construction). Thus, without interperiod tax allocation, reported tax expense in Canada could be reduced and reported profits increased by the mere act of acquiring assets. To the CICA that idea was repugnant, particularly when the reduction in tax was almost certain to be followed by later increases because of the steady diminution in tax deductibility of the asset. In Bulletin No. 10, the CICA Accounting and Auditing Research Committee expressed a strong preference for interperiod tax allocation to solve this problem. In the United States the Committee on Accounting Procedure took up a compromise position at first, but four years later changed its mind and recommended the position preferred in Canada.

A substantial minority of companies (about one-third) were not convinced by the argument for interperiod tax allocation. As a result, conflicting accounting presentations continued for some years. Then, in 1967, by which time official institute recommendations had acquired more authority, both the CICA and the U.S. Accounting Principles Board issued new statements. The statements withdrew sanction for the flow-through or "taxes payable" method of recording income tax expense and prescribed a "comprehensive tax allocation" approach. The basis of that approach, and possible variations in its application, will now be described.

Comprehensive tax allocation

Comprehensive tax allocation is based upon the idea that most revenues earned by a business are included in taxable income sooner or later, and most costs incurred are allowed as deductions sooner or later. There are, however, differences in the timing of recognition of some revenues and expenses for accounting and tax purposes. These differences can make actual taxable income for a given year differ sharply from the accounting income reported for that year. Thus, the actual tax payable may not be a fair presentation of the real burden of taxes on that reported accounting income. To resolve this, the idea of comprehensive tax allocation is that (with the exception of a few items that never enter into taxable income) each dollar of revenue reported for accounting purposes can be considered as bearing a tax charge, and each dollar of expense reported for accounting purposes can be considered as being entitled to a tax reduction. To the extent that there are differences in any given year in the timing of recognition of revenues and expenses for accounting and tax purposes, the resulting effects on tax payable (whether an increase or decrease in tax) can be deferred (and treated as deferred charges or deferred credits in the balance sheet), to be brought back into the figures of tax expense in future years when the timing differences reverse.

To understand the method fully, we need to examine closely certain ideas underlying it and certain issues in its application. We therefore deal below with (1) the causes of differences between accounting income before tax and taxable income, (2) the nature of so-called permanent differences, (3) the nature of so-called timing differences, (4) differences in the concept of the assets and liabilities recognized as a result of the allocation process, (5) how additions to and withdrawals from deferred taxes are calculated, (6) the balance sheet classification of deferred taxes, and (7) the treatment of deferred tax with respect to timing differences whose reversal is indefinite.

Differences between accounting and taxable income. The whole idea of the allocation of income tax expense among accounting periods depends upon the assumption that the revenues and costs that enter into the determination of taxable income are the same revenues and costs that are reported as elements of accounting income. Some writers dispute this assumption. They argue that the tax law is now so full of provisions designed to provide administrative convenience or special incentives that it has lost all connection with accounting income.

The strength of this argument depends upon the facts. It is conceivable that accounting and income taxation could lose touch. For example, if the tax law were to adopt a new definition of income (perhaps more explicitly designed to avoid the taxation of real capital in the guise of income during inflation) while accounting clung to the historical cost model, the two systems might be very difficult to reconcile. Or, if the tax system made a large number of modifications over the years to the definition of taxable revenues and taxable deductions, such changes might, on a cumulative basis, add up to a system recognizably different from the accounting model.

It is doubtful that history to date supports such a conclusion. At its inception in English-speaking countries, income tax legislation basically adopted business accounting practices. In time, the extension of income taxation has influenced accounting practice in view of the convenience in not being required to keep duplicate records. Both historical cost accounting and tax laws place a high value on the objectivity of actual transactions as a basis for income determination. In Canada, evidence of the similarity of the two systems is provided by the fact that the computation of taxable income in a corporate tax return begins with the words "income shown by the financial statements" and continues with the adjustments (relatively few in number) to arrive at taxable income. It could not be set up in this way if there were not a large degree of common ground between the two systems. Let us, then, consider the nature of the adjustments reconciling accounting and taxable income to see how they are handled under comprehensive tax allocation.

Permanent differences. To begin with, there is a small class of differences between accounting and taxable income caused by items entering into the calculation of one that have no counterpart in the other.

- Items affecting taxable income that have no counterpart in accounting income include a variety of incentives provided from time to time through the tax system.
- Items affecting accounting income that have no counterpart in taxable income include the nontaxable portion of capital gains, tax-free dividends received from other Canadian corporations, and the nondeductible portion of expense recognized for amortization of goodwill.

These differences are collectively known as "permanent differences," in contrast to the more common timing differences. The term "permanent" tends to be misleading. It simply means that the item in question is unique to the tax system or the accounting system, as the case may be. It does not mean that a tax concession with no accounting counterpart is necessarily permanent or irrevocable within its own system. For example, in the United States an investment tax credit can be partially recovered by the government if a qualifying asset is not held for stated periods of time.

Accordingly there should be no presumption that the cash effect of a given tax incentive does not need allocation just because it has no accounting counterpart. As previously discussed, it is now thought that the investment tax credit should be allocated. In general, every income tax concession needs to be examined individually to see whether its cash consequences need to be allocated in the interest of fair financial reporting, whether or not the concession can be associated with a specific accounting expense.

Timing differences. Timing differences between accounting and taxable income can be classified on the basis of whether the difference relates to a revenue item or to an expense item, and also on the basis of whether the recognition of the item for accounting purposes precedes or follows its recognition for tax purposes. This provides four different categories. Table 15-1 sets out a number of examples in each category. The table also expands on the character of each timing difference listed, and lays the groundwork for some points to be discussed subsequently.

- Column (1) lists the related asset or liability for each timing difference. The related asset or liability is the balance sheet item that is charged or credited when recording the particular revenue or expense that gives rise to a timing difference between tax and accounting. For example, revenue from instalment sales is taxed at a different time from that at which it is recognized in the accounts. The instalment account receivable is the asset recorded when the revenue is recognized. Accordingly, that receivable is the asset that is related to the deferred tax recorded. It will be noted that no related asset or liability is shown in Table 15-1 for certain types of timing difference. This generally occurs when the tax legislation is following a different basis of income measurement from that used in the accounts, rather than being a

Table 15-1

Summary of Accounting/Tax Timing Differences

Type of Timing Difference	Related Asset/Liability (1)	Cause of Reversal (2)	Reversal Predictable or Indefinite? (3)	Future Effect on Tax (4)
A. Revenue/income recorded before taxed				
Instalment sales	Instalment accounts receivable	Cash collection	Predictable	Tax payable when cash collected
Percentage-of-completion contract income	—	Completion of contract	Predictable	Tax payable when contract complete
Unremitted profits of foreign investee	Equity-accounted investment; nil in consolidation	Remittance of profits	Indefinite	Tax payable when profits remitted
B. Expense recorded before tax deduction				
Warranty costs	Warranty liability	Specific costs incurred	Predictable	Tax deduction when costs incurred
Deferred compensation	Compensation liability	Compensation paid	Predictable	Tax deduction on payment
LIFO cost of sales in excess of FIFO	—	FIFO exceeds LIFO	Indefinite	Tax deduction if reversal
C. Expense recorded after tax deduction				
Various prepayments or deferred charges	Prepaid or deferred asset	Asset amortized	Predictable	Tax payable on future net cash recovery from asset
Capital cost allowance in excess of depreciation	Depreciable assets	Depreciation catches up to capital cost allowance	Predictable (for individual assets)	Tax payable on future net cash recovery from asset
D. Revenue/income recorded after taxed				
Intercompany profits eliminated on consolidation	—	Goods sold to outsiders	Predictable	Tax reduced by previous step-up in asset tax basis
Customer prepayments on subscriptions or contracts	Unearned revenue	Revenue recognition requirement fulfilled	Predictable	Tax reduced to extent of expenses to be incurred to earn revenue

simple case where the tax recognition is on a cash basis and the accounting recognition on an accrual basis.

- Column (2) sets out the causes of reversal of the timing difference. Several timing differences occur because the taxation system clings to a cash basis for recognition of certain revenues and expenses while accounting is on an accrual basis. If the accounting accrual precedes the cash effect, the reversal occurs when the cash transaction takes place (for example, when warranty costs are actually experienced). If the cash effect precedes the accounting accrual, the reversal occurs when the accounting accrual entry is made (for example, when a deferred cost is amortized to expense). Other timing differences reverse when the income measurement convention used for accounting purposes catches up with that used for tax purposes or vice versa.
- Column (3) indicates whether the timing of reversal is predictable or indefinite. In most cases it is predictable, especially those cases where the timing differences result from a cash basis recognition for tax purposes and an accrual basis recognition for accounting purposes. However, when a different income measurement basis is used, as in the case of the use of LIFO accounting for financial reporting and FIFO for tax purposes, the time of reversal (if any) is indefinite.
- Column (4) describes how future tax will be affected by reversals of timing differences.

As indicated, there are very few situations where the timing of reversal is indefinite. Income earned by foreign subsidiaries or investees is recognized by the investor under consolidation or equity accounting when earned by the foreign entity, but withholding tax (and domestic income tax when applicable) is not payable until earnings are remitted. Sometimes also a company obtains tax deductions with respect to the capital cost of an asset that will not be charged off to income unless it is sold. For example, if interest is capitalized as part of the cost of land acquired that is not held for sale, and that interest reduces taxes, the reversal of the timing difference will not occur unless the land is sold.

Conceptual basis for assets and liabilities resulting from tax allocation. Over the years three different ways to implement tax allocation have been suggested. Each of these methods suggests a different concept of the deferred tax balances that appear in the balance sheet.

- The deferral method. This method rests upon the implied identification of each accounting revenue with a tax charge and each accounting expense with a tax reduction, as described earlier. Suppose a particular item of revenue or expense enters into taxable income in a different period from that in which it enters into reported accounting income. Then the associated tax charge or tax reduction is moved from reported tax expense of the period of taxation to the reported tax expense of the period in which the revenue or expense item is recognized for accounting purposes. This allocation of tax charges or tax reductions results in deferred debits or credits in the balance sheet. These are regarded primarily as adjustments required to achieve a better matching of tax expense with pretax reported accounting income. No particular effort is made to explain the nature of these deferred assets and liabilities.

- The accrual method. This method does attempt to explain the balance sheet amounts that result from interperiod allocation. A recorded liability is held to represent the future tax burden that is attributable to timing differences, while a recorded asset is held to represent future tax advantages attributable to timing differences. Since those advantages or that burden will be realized in the future, their amounts depend upon the tax rates that will exist in future. Accordingly, it is held that the balances should be calculated originally and subsequently recalculated based on best estimates of tax rates that will exist in future when the timing differences reverse.
- The net-of-tax method. This method focusses attention not so much on the future tax effects of timing differences as on the valuation of assets and liabilities associated with timing differences. For example, if provision is made for future warranty costs in recording income from goods sold but the costs are not deductible until paid, it is suggested that the amount of provision can be reduced because of the expectation of an offsetting tax deduction. Or, if capital cost allowance is taken in excess of normal depreciation in the accounts, addtional depreciation would be written because the prospects for the after-tax cash return from an asset are reduced by using up its tax deduction potential. From this explanation it can be seen that the net-of-tax method is not really a *tax* allocation process. Rather, it is a modification of other accounting conventions to allow for the effects of income tax treatment on asset and liability valuation. That is to say, the tax expense line in the income statement would remain at the amount of tax payable for the year. An amount *equal to* the tax charges and tax reductions caused by timing differences would be taken into account as an adjustment to normal depreciation expense, warranty cost provision, etc. recorded elsewhere in the income statement. (Some accountants, however, would prefer to apply the net-of-tax method differently. In order to preserve the normal percentage relationship between pretax income and tax expense reported in the income statement, they would "normalize" the tax expense figure for charges and credits associated with timing differences. The offsetting credits and debits, however, would be taken as adjustments to the associated asset and liability accounts in the balance sheet. Although it is obviously illogical to debit tax expense and credit accumulated depreciation, for example, it is argued that such a presentation would improve reader understanding of the fundamental elements of income and financial position.)

The deferral method is the approach that was authoritatively approved in Canada and the United States in 1967. In the 1960s, it was generally accepted that if matching in the income statement were properly achieved, one need not be concerned with the resultant deferred charges or credits in the balance sheet. Correct matching would automatically mean that deferred charges represented future benefits in some sense, and deferred credits represented some form of future sacrifice or disadvantage. Since that time, accounting theorists have placed increasing emphasis on a balance sheet point of view. They have been sharply critical of deferred charges and credits on the grounds that they are "uninterpretable"—that is (it is asserted), no one knows what they mean. That criticism has focussed particularly on deferred tax credits, which in the past twenty years have tended to increase in amount relative to the size of shareholders' equity. A subsequent section will analyze this issue in greater depth.

Computation of additions to and withdrawals from deferred taxes. Significant complications arise in the implementation of tax allocation accounting on the deferred approach. The essential idea may be illustrated by reference to instalment sales. Suppose an instalment sale of $1,000 is made in year 1 and cash is collected on it in year 2, so that it becomes taxable in that year. Suppose, further, that the basic tax rate in both years is 46%, but in year 2 only there is a 5% surcharge, making the actual tax cost 48.3%. In year 1, $460 in deferred taxes is recognized by charging tax expense and crediting deferred taxes. In year 2, actual tax of $483 becomes payable on the transaction; $460 is withdrawn from the deferred tax account to offset the expense, leaving $23 to be borne by current income.

This is a consequence of the deferral approach. The actual tax rate applicable in the year the timing difference originates is used in recording the original deferred tax. This rate may well be different from that applicable in the year the timing difference reverses, leaving the difference in tax cost to affect tax expense reported in the year of draw-down. This problem is not serious if tax rate changes are small; it can produce peculiar figures for tax expense when they are large. In particular, management of a small business may arrange to claim maximum discretionary tax allowances, such as capital cost allowances, when taxable income is above the annual limit for the small business tax rate reduction. The timing difference so created is then eliminated in less profitable years by underclaiming the discretionary allowance and thereby reversing the timing difference. The result is that the tax expense reported in the year of reversal is unnaturally lowered. That effect can be explained and even rationalized as representing a deferral of recognition of the effects of tax planning until realization, but non-accountants tend to find it confusing.

Now suppose that a second instalment sale of $1,000 takes place in year 2 with the tax falling into year 3 when collection takes place. What happens to the deferred tax figures? Under the "gross change" approach, an amount of $460 would be drawn down from the deferred tax with respect to the timing difference that originated in year 1 (as before), and tax expense would be charged with $483 with respect to the timing difference originating in year 2. Under the "net change" approach, the originating and reversing timing differences in year 2 would be offset, so that the opening balance of $460 in the deferred credit account would be carried forward. Thus, the two possible approaches to dealing with timing difference reversals also tend to produce inconsistent results when tax rates change from year to year.

Next, suppose that the originating timing difference in year 1 represents an excess of capital cost allowance over straight-line depreciation on a fixed asset newly acquired, rather than on an instalment sale. If one wished to follow the gross change method, it would be necessary to assume when that timing difference—the excess capital cost allowance—reversed. Capital cost allowance could continue to exceed depreciation on the same asset for several years, depending upon the tax class of the asset. One must have some basis for assuming when the timing difference arising in year 1 reverses. One possible assumption would be a FIFO assumption that reversal occurs for the first time when depreciation exceeds capital cost allowance on the asset, and the earliest reversal should be applied to the earliest originating difference. (Other assumptions are conceivable.) Now suppose that several different assets acquired in year 1 have different rates of depreciation and/or capital cost allowance. To apply the gross change method would require keeping records of differences by different classes of assets and, in order to allow for possible tax rate changes from year to year, by different years of acquisition. The record-keeping complexity insures that the gross change method is not adopted in practice, at least for this type of timing difference.

Is it necessary to account separately for deferred taxes with respect to each type of timing difference? Where the net change method is used, reversals of timing differences in some categories, notably differences between capital cost allowance and depreciation, will occur only infrequently, while in other situations reversals may occur much more frequently. Some separate accounting by types of timing difference is required because the accounting standards require separation of deferred taxes into long-term and short-term categories for balance sheet presentation purposes (see discussion below). Apart from this, net change accounting often is applied across categories within the long- or short-term classification so as to offset the total of all types of originating timing differences with the total of all reversals.

When the net change approach is adopted, whether by type of timing difference or overall, one is likely to experience several years in succession when deferred taxes increase, each year's provision possibly being at a different tax rate. When a draw-down is required, then, there will be a question of what rate should be used for draw-down, since it will not be possible to identify a specific year of origin applicable to the net amount drawn down. The assumption must be arbitrary. In practice, in Canada, the rate used is the average rate applicable to the total timing differences represented by the deferred tax balance at the time of draw-down.

The amount of deferred tax applicable to an originating timing difference is supposed to be calculated by computing the taxes payable for the period as they would be "with and without" the difference in question. There can be a difficulty in some circumstances, however, if there is more than one type of timing difference and separate deferred taxes are calculated for each type. For example, suppose a business is utilizing its small business rate reduction to the limit and would be paying some tax at full rate without the effect of timing differences. It may be that each type of timing difference affects taxable income by less than the amount of income subject to the high tax rate, but that all types of timing differences together reduce taxable income below the point where it is covered by the small business deduction. Then the with-and-without calculation applied to each type of timing difference by itself will indicate tax deferred at full rates, but the same calculation applied to the total of timing differences will show some reduction at lesser rates. In such a case, the actual total tax reduction obtained must be apportioned among the types of timing difference.

In brief, the theory of tax allocation under the deferral approach visualizes that timing differences of all types are regularly arising and, in due course, reverse themselves. The theory visualizes identification of the actual effect on taxes payable of each originating timing difference and deferral of the effect, to be restored to tax expense at the time the particular timing difference reverses. For various reasons, such identification of specific tax effects with specific timing differences is highly impractical. The Canadian approach, whereby originating and reversing timing differences in a year and across asset categories are offset, with only the net change being accounted for, saves much work but represents merely an approximation to the result called for by the theory. The approximation could be improved if tax effects were calculated by separate category of timing difference, but even that refinement is not regularly found in practice.

Balance sheet classification of deferred taxes. In view of the somewhat nebulous character of deferred tax debit or credit balances carried forward in the balance sheet, confusion can easily arise as to where they should be presented in a classified balance sheet—whether they should be shown as current or noncurrent. The CICA suggests a decision rule—deferred tax balances should be classified as current or noncurrent depending upon the classification of the asset or liability to which they relate.[2]

Column (1) of Table 15-1 indicates that deferred tax cannot always be related to a specific asset or liability. The FASB has provided an answer to this problem.[3] Where there is not a relationship between deferred tax reversals and an asset or liability, one should look directly to the estimated date of reversal and classify the deferred tax as current if the reversal is within one year of the financial reporting date, and noncurrent if it is not. The general principle can be summed up thus: A deferred tax balance should be regarded as current if it will reverse and thereby have an impact on the taxable income calculation within one year of the reporting date. Where the reversal date of deferred tax with respect to a particular type of timing difference is indefinite, any deferred tax provided would normally be classified as noncurrent.

Accounting for deferred taxes when reversal is indefinite. A more important question with respect to timing differences whose reversal is indefinite is whether deferred taxes should be recorded at all. In practice, such cases are dealt with on a situation-specific basis. For example, in Canada, deferred tax is to be accrued with respect to unremitted earnings of subsidiaries or equity-accounted investees only to the extent that it is reasonable to assume it will be remitted. On the other hand, Canadian practice is to allow for deferred taxation with respect to a timing difference arising from claiming interest for tax purposes that is capitalized as part of the cost of land not held for sale. That timing difference will reverse only if the property is sold. (If the land is sold, the reversal of the timing difference will be taxed only at capital gains rates even though the original tax reduction was at ordinary income rates. Under a rigorous application of the deferral approach to tax allocation, the latter amount of tax should be deferred originally. In practice, sometimes only the lesser capital gains tax liability is provided.)

Objections voiced to comprehensive tax allocation

The debate over the allocation of tax expense has raged for thirty years. In that period few have changed their opinions. The issue provides classic proof of the impossibility of "general acceptance" as a means of resolving difficult questions of accounting principle. Participants in the debate typically argue from different premises and, not surprisingly, arrive at different conclusions. The accounting literature cited in the bibliography provides extensive examination of the debate. The principal arguments of the opponents of comprehensive tax allocation will be reviewed here, proceeding from the simplest to the more complex.

Income tax allocation obscures management performance. A few accountants argue that reporting tax expense as the amount actually payable accurately portrays management's skill or otherwise in minimizing taxes. This is a shallow argument. Unless future years' income tax rates are expected to be higher than the current year's rates by more than the after-tax rate of interest obtainable, management would be foolish not to claim every possible deduction it can for tax purposes as early as possible. Thus, ordinarily there is no real skill involved in making the right choices in filing income tax returns, to the extent that choices exist at all. (Many differences between tax and accounting income are prescribed by law and are not a matter of choice.)

Income taxes are indivisible. Some argue from the premise that taxes paid result from a process of applying a statutory tax rate to a figure of *net* taxable income. Therefore, they reason that no individual revenue or individual cost can be related in isolation to the figure of tax expense. It is contrary to the nature of income tax to attribute parts of it to individual items of revenue or cost recognized for accounting purposes (notwithstanding that it can often be shown that had the enterprise not incurred a particular cost or become entitled to proceeds from a particular revenue transaction, the net tax would have been a different figure).[4]

This argument is basically an argument against *any* allocation in accounting reports. If it is wrong to discover a relationship between net taxable income and certain costs and revenues, and hence between taxable income and the periods in which those costs and revenues are reported, it must be equally wrong to, say, discover a relationship between the cost of a fixed asset and the period in which it renders service. That fixed asset cost is just as indivisible as is income tax expense. What the argument overlooks is the accounting purpose of providing useful information. The whole basis of income accounting is to provide information beyond that provided by a mere recital of cash receipts and payments or of legally determined rights and obligations. To argue that income tax allocation is illegitimate because it requires a division of cost is to argue that a very high percentage of existing accounting conventions are illegitimate.

Taxes payable accounting assists the prediction of future cash flows. Others have argued that investors and other users of financial statements are interested in future cash flows and would be better served by reporting taxes at the amount assessable, since that represents cash payable in or soon after the fiscal year.

This argument is simply an assertion that future cash flows will look like cash flows in the most recent period—an argument that is unsubstantiated and extremely dubious. It is clearly false with respect to isolated timing differences that affect taxes payable in one direction in one year and in the opposite direction in a subsequent year. But even beyond this, the argument is either illogical or incomplete. If one year's actual cash flows are the best evidence of future cash flows, why not just present a cash statement? Why not, for example, write off investment in plant on a cash basis? If the answer is that capitalization and amortization of plant cost provide a better estimate of average future cash flows to be expected, how does one distinguish between plant cost allocation and income tax allocation in this respect? If expenditures on plant are uneven, it seems probable that tax deductions with respect to capital expenditures will likewise be uneven—although possibly to a lesser degree. In short, this argument, like the one preceding, is really saying that the whole present system of income accounting is wrong and should be changed to a cash basis statement.

Income tax allocation assumes future events. A number of opponents of tax allocation have argued as follows. A reversal of a timing difference does not have a tax effect unless there is taxable income at the time of the reversal. The existence of taxable income at that time will depend (largely) on future revenues and future costs. Therefore the tax effect of the reversal is contingent upon future events, and thus that reversal impact is not properly an asset or liability before that time. To put the point another way—an asset or liability at a particular date may be defined as a probable future cash flow attributable to past events (up to the reporting date). The tax impact of timing difference reversals depends upon two classes of events that occur in sequence: the originating events, and the reversing events that affect future taxable income. The argument is that an asset or a liability can be recognized only when *all* the events necessary to the cash flow concerned have occurred. Until that time the asset or liability is contingent only.[5]

To evaluate this argument, consider the nature of liabilities. The amount of warranty costs depends upon future events. The amount of pension cost also depends upon future events. Consider too that the revenue ultimately obtained from sales on credit depends upon future events (collection of receivables). The crucial question for accounting is *which* event triggers recognition of revenues, costs, and associated assets and liabilities. Once that is decided, the rest of the problem is measurement. Tax allocation proponents argue that tax is the joint result of the earning of revenue that is taxable and the incurrence of cost that is deductible. Once that is admitted, it logically follows that for accounting purposes it is basically sensible and informative to report the resulting (probable) tax expense flowing from revenues and costs in the same period as that in which accounting recognizes them in income.

But, the opponents of tax allocation object, in no other case is the occurrence of the future event dependent upon future revenue earning activity of the company.[6] Warranty claims are made, pensions are paid, and accounts receivable are collected regardless of whether the enterprise makes a profit in the future. There is a conclusive answer to this argument. It may be true that some cost and revenue allocations to periods are based on future events other than those related to future earnings, but that is far from universally true. In fact, the realization of virtually every asset carried at cost or some derivative of cost in the balance sheet—assets such as inventory, plant and equipment, and various intangibles—is dependent upon future transactions and, if a profit cannot be assumed, the assets are written down.

This argument is particularly apropos in relation to fixed assets, because the most controversial and most material aspect of tax allocation accounting relates to the timing differences between depreciation on fixed assets and capital cost allowances. Consider depreciable plant carried in the balance sheet at, say, $10 million whose undepreciated capital cost for tax purposes has been reduced to, say, $6 million. The plant book value of $10 million implies an expectation that at least $10 million can be recovered from future revenues over and above amounts required to cover other costs of earning that revenue. If that expectation is fulfilled, taxable income over that period will be at least $4 million (because capital cost allowance claims with respect to the plant are restricted to $6 million). There are, of course, uncertainties since the future is always uncertain. But at least we can say this. If we knew that future revenue activities could recover only $6 million from the present plant, then we should have increased depreciation to date and thereby we would have eliminated the timing difference. If we knew the future operations would recover $10 million with respect to the plant, we could be sure the reversal of the timing difference would generate taxable profit and, for the reasons given above, it is logical to relate that tax cost to the earlier periods when the excess capital cost allowance was taken. (This argument ignores the separate question of whether reversals of timing differences are indefinitely postponed by new originating differences. This will be addressed shortly.)

Deferred taxes are not liabilities. A considerable number of writers have argued that deferred tax credits are not liabilities as that term is used in accounting. (Presumably they would also argue that deferred tax debits are not assets, but that question typically receives less attention.)

There are at least three separate and distinct reasons given for arguing that deferred tax credits are not liabilities. The first is the argument that they are not true liabilities because they are dependent upon future events. That has been discussed in the immediately preceding section. The second argument is based on a definition of accounting liabilities as future sacrifices attributable to events up to the reporting date and concludes that at least some deferred taxes do not fit this definition. We shall postpone discussion of this point for the moment and take it up subsequently in a section discussing the essential character of deferred taxes. The third argument holds that deferred tax credits cannot be liabilities because (for the most part) they are never paid off. This is known as the permanent deferral argument and is discussed immediately below.

Many timing differences never reverse. The application of tax allocation requires some kind of judgment as to when timing differences reverse. A clear basis for determining when a reversal occurs is therefore necessary. For example:

- If revenue is recognized on instalment sales before it is taxed, does that timing difference reverse when the revenue enters into taxable income (e.g., when cash is collected), or may the assumption of reversal be nullified by a subsequent originating timing difference?
- If taxes are paid on sales of goods that are still in inventory in a consolidated group of companies, should one assume that the timing differences reverse when a sale to an outside party triggers accounting recognition of profit? Or is that reversal cancelled by the fact that tax is prepaid on further intercompany sales of goods still in inventory?

Most, but not all, accountants believe that future originating timing differences do *not* nullify scheduled reversals of existing timing differences that take place in a clear-cut fashion, as in these particular examples. The majority is not nearly as large, however, when it comes to reversal of timing differences between booked depreciation and amortization of plant for tax purposes. This is where the controversy over tax allocation becomes most acute.

Since income tax amortization of plant is typically limited to cost, it is clear that, for a single asset, tax amortization in excess of book depreciation must have completely reversed by the time the asset is fully depreciated. Yet most opponents of comprehensive tax allocation argue that reversals do not take place because one can normally count upon excess tax amortization on new plant assets being available to offset the reversal on older assets. That is to say, reversal does take place for a single asset company that does not plan to buy additional assets until replacement is due but does not take place in the more normal situation of a company that has a number of assets at various stages in their life cycle and is continually buying new assets. In effect, in the latter case, the whole is considered to be different from the sum of its parts.

The argument that timing differences with respect to amortization of fixed assets do not normally reverse is simple. Most companies are going concerns. Most going concerns are continually replacing their fixed assets and a majority are growing—i.e., adding to their net capital stock. In addition, with exceptions in some individual industries, if inflation is more than moderate, new assets are likely to cost more than those they replace. For all these reasons, in the absence of significant changes in tax law, the net amount claimable for tax purposes is likely to rise over the long term, and net reductions in the excess of amounts claimed over depreciation written are likely to occur rarely and not in significant amounts. In these circumstances, if tax allocation accounting is followed, the balance of deferred tax credits will tend to show a steady increase. From this it is reasoned that the "liability" for deferred taxes is not a true liability because it is never paid off. A number of empirical studies have been made over the years that confirm that deferred tax credits in the aggregate have shown a long-term tendency to increase, and reductions in any particular year have been infrequent and relatively small in relation to increases.

It must be conceded that the observation that the total amount of deferred taxes should not be expected to decrease markedly is correct. In a completely stationary state, every figure of revenue and expense of a business would be stationary on both the accounting and tax bases of recognition (and every figure of revenue and expense for a period would also be equal to the cash inflows and outflows for the period, regardless of what systems of depreciation and inventory cost flows were used). Since, in our economy, most businesses are growing rather than stationary or declining (especially in nominal dollar terms), we should expect net increases in deferred tax to be the normal rule, not net reductions. The empirical studies, therefore, did not add to our knowledge; they simply confirmed what we should already have known. The more serious objection to these studies, however, is that they are irrelevant unless it can be shown that it is proper, in accounting for tax effects, to lump together assets not yet acquired with assets held.

To answer this question, a simple test can be made. Ask any rational businessman whether he would pay as much (as an investment to produce income) for an asset that is not claimable for tax purposes as he would for a physically identical asset that is deductible. He will surely say that he would not. Then ask him if it would change his opinion if he knew that he would be purchasing additional pieces of equipment that were fully tax deductible. Again, if he is rational, it would not. The point is that there is no connection between the first purchase decision and subsequent decisions. There is no basis whatsoever for assuming that the tax status of the second and subsequent assets has anything to do with the first. This is even more true when it is a question of lumping together asset acquisitions that have not yet taken place with those that have. Historical cost accounting is limited to recognizing the effects of transactions that have taken place. It is fundamentally in error to take into account future transactions that are not the consequence of past transactions in any way.

In the last analysis, the answer to the tax allocation controversy should be sought in the economics of business and investment. If it is true that no rational businessman would pay as much for an asset that is not deductible for tax purposes as he would for one that is deductible, why should not some expense be recognized in the period when an asset is stripped of part of the value received in exchange for the cost incurred? Opponents of tax allocation have never answered this question. If it cannot be answered, all other arguments, such as those as to the semantic meaning of a liability in accounting or the indivisibility of income tax, however plausible they may seem in isolation, must be regarded as suspect.

Partial tax allocation

In practice, few opponents of comprehensive tax allocation favour a complete flow-through approach whereby tax expense recorded is exactly the amount of tax expected to be assessed for a given year. Most accept that some timing differences between accounting income and taxable income warrant recognition through tax allocation procedures. There is no consensus, however, on exactly how such "partial allocation" should be implemented. The British system and some possible alternatives are outlined below.

Partial allocation in the United Kingdom and Ireland. A new Statement of Standard Accounting Practice—SSAP No. 15—for deferred taxes was issued effective in 1979 but revised in May 1985.[7] As revised, the standard calls for recognition of deferred taxes in relation to originating timing differences, based on forecasts of whether a liability or asset will "crystallize" within a foreseeable period. Future asset acquisitions are taken into account in assessing the likelihood of a crystallization of liability. The foreseeable period may be relatively short—say, three to five years—if timing differences recur regularly but may need to be extended if significant reversals in subsequent years are a reasonable possibility. Timing differences are to be looked at on a combined basis in judging whether net reversals are likely. The accrual approach is to be used in recognizing deferred tax assets or liabilities so that these have to be revalued with changes in tax rates.

Other possibilities in partial allocation. In its original version, SSAP No. 15 indicated that one particular type of timing difference should be assumed to be short-term, so that deferred taxes should always be recognized with respect to it. The timing differences in question were those resulting from the recognition of certain revenues or expenses on an accrual basis for accounting purposes and on a cash basis for tax purposes. With respect to other types of timing differences, recognition of deferred taxes was not required unless it was foreseeable that their cumulative net amount was likely to decrease in future.

Beechy discusses a number of other bases for implementing partial allocation, and favours an approach that would recognize deferred tax only with respect to nonrecurring (probably more accurately described as irregularly occurring) timing differences. Since he believes deferred taxes are not liabilities, he concludes that the deferral approach, not the accrual approach, should be used in recognizing them.[8]

Evaluation of tax allocation

The preceding discussion has dealt extensively with the arguments in the tax allocation debate because the issue has been so controversial for so long. The discussion has suggested that the arguments against comprehensive tax allocation have counterarguments at every point. That does not mean, however, that comprehensive tax allocation as it is now practised is necessarily the best conceivable way to account for timing differences between accounting and taxable income. Many people are confused as to the real nature of deferred tax debits and credits appearing in the balance sheet as a result of tax allocation. A good accounting practice should be seen to correspond with the economic substance of events affecting an enterprise. It is perfectly reasonable, therefore, to feel that deferred tax charges and credits in the balance sheet should be explainable in terms of real economic phenomena. It is appropriate to examine the balance sheet effects of comprehensive tax allocation, therefore, to see if they can be properly described as something more understandable than mere deferments.

The essential character of deferred taxes. At several points in previous chapters we have referred to the essential character of an asset as lying in an expectation of future inflow of cash or equivalent benefit resulting from events prior to the reporting date. Similarly, a liability has been defined as an expectation of future outflow of cash or equivalent sacrifice attributable to events prior to the reporting date. To test whether the deferred tax debits and credits resulting from tax allocation are "interpretable," we can examine how well they stand up to these definitions. For this purpose, refer again to Table 15-1.

- Timing differences falling into category A (revenue or income recognized in the accounts before being fully taxed) will result in future taxes payable, everything else being equal, with one possible exception. The exception is unremitted profits of subsidiaries or equity-accounted investees. Future tax in that case will be avoided or postponed if the profits are not remitted.
- Timing differences falling into category B (expense recognized before being deductible for tax purposes) will probably result in future tax reductions, again with one possible exception. Realization of the future tax reduction does depend upon the existence of taxable profits in future. Where the existence of such profits is in doubt, the deferred tax asset itself is in doubt. Consistent with this, today's accounting standards require that deferred tax debits pass the test that there be reasonable assurance as to realization. The exception referred to above in this category is the timing difference that results from the excess of cost of sales on the LIFO basis used for accounting over cost of sales on the FIFO basis used for taxation. The considerable uncertainty as to future reversal of that timing difference militates against recognition of the resulting deferred tax as an asset.
- Timing differences falling into category C (expense recorded for accounting purposes after being deductible for tax purposes) all result in future taxes payable with a high degree of probability. It can be assumed first, that the related asset would not be recognized as such unless future net cash returns from its use were at least capable of recovering its carrying value. If that assumption is correct, we can be sure that future taxes will be payable since the tax basis of the asset is less than its carrying value in the accounts. It requires a probability of future losses to negate that assumption, and any such assumption of persisting future losses would raise serious question as to the propriety of carrying the asset at its existing book value.
- Timing differences falling into category D (revenue or income recognized after being taxed) need individual consideration. The case of profits taxed on intercompany sales of goods that are still in the inventory of the purchaser is relatively straightforward. The goods will ultimately be sold or written off, and the tax basis, as stepped up by the intercompany sale, will represent

a deduction for tax purposes. Only if the purchasing company is unlikely to have taxable profits is there doubt as to the realizability of the deferred tax asset.

- The case of customer prepayments taxed when received but treated as unearned revenue for accounting purposes (also in category D) is somewhat less clear. The cash effects on the revenue side of the transaction have already occurred—cash has been received from the customer and tax has been paid. But, for accounting purposes, the revenue is not regarded as earned; to be consistent, therefore, recognition of the related tax cost is also deferred. One might argue that since there are no future cash effects under the revenue transaction, no liability should be recorded for the unearned revenue and no asset for the related tax. This, however, would ignore the fact that an obligation remains in return for the revenue receipt. A sacrifice of inventory, or a future expenditure, will be required to satisfy the obligation, and these in turn will qualify as tax deductions. Thus there will be future cash-equivalent outflows and tax reductions as a result of the unearned revenue. They need not, however, be exactly equal in amount to the unearned revenue and deferred tax debit recorded. It is clear that the difference is attributable to the profit (or occasionally loss) element in the unearned revenue recorded. In other words, unearned revenue under income accounting rules does not exactly fit the definition of a liability if it is rigidly defined as an expectation of an *equal* future outflow of cash or equivalent. Correspondingly, the deferred tax related to unearned revenue will not exactly fit a definition of an asset as an expectation of an equal future cash inflow. But both the liability and asset recorded will reflect *some* expectation of future cash outflows and savings; the deviation from the normal definition of an asset or liability is minor.

Let us sum up this analysis. Deferred tax credits with respect to timing differences in categories A and C are recognized in situations in which future taxes will be payable with a high degree of probability. The only possible exception is the case where the date of reversal of the timing difference is indefinite. Thus deferred tax credits have economic substance and fit an appropriate definition of a liability as a probable future sacrifice arising from present conditions.

Deferred tax debits with respect to timing differences in categories B and D do represent real economic phenomena in the shape of future tax reductions. They do not represent an expected future cash inflow, but rather a reduction in probable future taxes. If an asset is rigorously defined as an expected future inflow of cash or cash equivalent, these tax reductions do not qualify under the definition. However, it is at least arguable that a reduction in an amount that otherwise will be payable in future is an asset, just as much as a direct inflow of cash. In the case of taxes paid on customer prepayments received and treated as unearned, the future tax reduction may be different than the amount of deferred tax recorded, but that difference will ordinarily be minor.

No assumption as to future profits is required with respect to deferred tax credits. If future operations are at a break-even, tax will be payable when the timing difference is reversed. The deferred tax credits are fully consistent with that portion of the definition of a liability that limits the cause of the liability to events prior to the reporting date. In contrast, realization of deferred tax debits does depend upon the earning of future profits. To this extent, an argument can be made that deferred tax debits are not assets because they are not *solely* attributable to events that have taken place prior to the reporting date. In this case, once again we have a situation where a single result—the future tax reduction—is dependent upon two preconditions: the previous prepayment of tax, and the subsequent existence of taxable profits against which to set off the costs not previously allowed for tax. The tax allocation standard in existence today has chosen to recognize an asset with respect to future tax reductions, provided there is reasonable assurance as to their realizability.

We can conclude that if a rigorous definitional test is imposed to determine whether deferred tax credits are liabilities, all such credits pass the test except those resulting from timing differences whose reversal is uncertain. In their case, some further event may be required to cause the reversal. Some accountants might consider that to be grounds for not treating such deferred taxes as a liability. Others would take the probability of reversal as the determining factor for recognition. As we have seen previously, practice in recognizing deferred tax credits from timing differences with indefinite reversal varies depending upon the type of timing difference.

There is more doubt whether deferred tax debits pass a rigorous definitional test for recognition as assets. Their dependence upon the earning of future taxable profits would rule them out unless the dominant accountable event is considered to be the initial prepayment of tax. Today's tax allocation standards have taken the latter position because it is considered to result in a fairer portrayal of income.

In any event, it is clear that both deferred tax credits and deferred tax debits that have predictable reversal dates are interpretable in terms of future cash effects. The former will increase the amount of taxes payable in future. The latter will reduce the amount of taxes payable in future. Because deferred tax credits and debits can be interpreted as future cash effects, the accrual approach to measurement seems more justified than the deferral approach. Only occasionally, however, will there be reliable evidence as to what future tax rates will be.

Comprehensive tax allocation as presently practised in the United States and Canada uses the deferral approach rather than the accrual approach. That approach is also applied in practice in a manner that intermingles originating and reversing timing differences occurring within an accounting period and sometimes intermingles various types of timing differences. Although this broad-brush approach seems less than ideal, it is conceivable that its convenience in implementation justifies the resulting approximations and occasional distortions.

The use of discounting in tax allocation accounting. Over the years a number of writers have suggested that deferred tax balances resulting from tax allocation accounting should be reported on a discounted basis.[9] Accounting standard-setters have never pursued this possibility intensively. It seems likely that the long-standing controversies over the merits of any tax allocation made the standard-setters wary of introducing yet another complication. But the failure to use some form of discounting may well significantly reduce the fairness of the portrayal of income tax expense under the tax allocation approach. Lengthy postponement of tax liabilities is equivalent to a significant reduction in the effective tax rate. Present accounting practices fail to come to grips with this issue.

Most timing differences are fairly short-term in nature, so that discounting for them might not be important as a practical matter. The principal area where discounting would have a significant impact is that of differences between accounting depreciation and amounts claimed for capital cost allowances. Several issues would have to be addressed in working out a discounting approach in this area.

To begin with, the concept of tax allocation would have to be agreed upon. Discounting is consistent in logic with the accrual approach since it is based upon anticipation of the impact on future taxes payable of timing difference reversals. Discounting would not be consistent with the deferral approach unless that approach is considered merely a practical approximation to the accrual approach. Many would argue that discounting also has no place in net-of-tax accounting. On the surface that is true, since amortization of fixed asset cost is normally considered merely a mechanical spreading of cost. Time-adjusted depreciation patterns as described in chapter 11, however, embrace an interest factor, and it may be that our mechanical depreciation allocations are effectively approximations to the more scientifically determined time-adjusted methods. Thus, net-of-tax accounting and explicit recognition of a discount factor are not necessarily incompatible.

Application of discounting techniques would require a solution to two conceptual issues. The first involves finding a rationale for selection of an interest rate. A second is to find a rationale for determination of the time when timing differences reverse, in view of the fact that capital cost allowance on many assets will exceed depreciation for several years before it reverses. Most accountants probably would make an arbitrary assumption that the first reversals apply to the first originating timing differences, but other assumptions are possible. Further exploration of the conceptual issues and practical problems in discounted tax allocations would be too extensive for this book. We leave the subject, then, with the observation that the application of discounting in tax allocation would probably improve the economic realism of the figures, but would be complex and almost certainly would extend the boundaries of the existing debate.

Accounting treatment of loss carrybacks and carryforwards

Under income tax law, losses for a year determined under tax rules may be offset against taxable profits earned within a carryback period and, if not fully offset, the remainder may be applied against taxable profits earned within a specified carryforward period. (Under the rules in Canada at time of writing the carryback period is three years and the carryforward period is seven years.) In periods when losses are incurred, therefore, tax recoveries will be realized if taxable profits were earned within the carryback period. There is also a possibility of future tax reductions for losses not offset against profits earned in the carryback period.

The fact that losses of one period can affect taxes assessed with respect to another period raises the question whether tax allocation accounting is required. If the decision is that allocation is required, it must be noted that the tax system provides for carryback and carryforward of *taxable* losses, whereas tax allocation accounting is concerned with the relationship of tax expense reported to *accounting income*. Thus, any tax allocation for loss transfers between periods must take into account not only the cash effect of transfers of taxable losses, but also any related effects on timing differences between taxable and accounting income. To simplify discussion of the issues, we shall deal first with the need for tax allocation for loss effects assuming no timing differences exist, and then consider the interaction of tax allocation for losses and for other timing differences.

Tax allocation for loss carrybacks and carryforwards

A loss carryback or carryforward causes a reduction in tax assessed in the year to which it is applied. In what year should that reduction be reflected? If tax expense were calculated on a flow-through basis, the answer would be straightforward. The tax recovered from losses carried back would be recognized in the year of recovery—i.e., the year of loss. The tax reduction in years to which the loss is carried forward would also be reflected in the year of recovery, but those years would be profit years, not the year of loss.

The acceptance of tax allocation theory as it has previously been explained leads to a different result. Apart from permanent differences between accounting and taxable income, tax expense is supposed to be directly related to pretax accounting income. Therefore, if there is a pretax accounting loss, the impact of that loss on taxes payable must be reflected in the tax expense (or recovery) reported for the year of loss. The application of this basic principle to loss carrybacks and loss carryforwards, however, differs to a degree because of the uncertainty that exists with respect to realization of carryforwards.

There is little problem with loss carrybacks. The tax recovery from a loss carryback is a known figure (except for the usual uncertainties with respect to taxes not yet assessed) and therefore can be readily recognized in income of the loss year. Tax recoveries from loss carryforwards are a different matter since there may be great uncertainty whether sufficient profits can be earned within the carryforward period to absorb all the losses carried forward. The uncertainty is emphasized by the fact that loss carryforwards exist only where taxable profits (if any) of the loss carryback period have been insufficient to cover them. In view of this uncertainty, current accounting standards permit recognition of an asset for loss carryforwards only if there is "virtual certainty" of their recovery.

It is clear that virtual certainty cannot exist where a loss has been incurred in the normal course of operations and the loss has been too large to be covered by the carryback provision. Thus, for virtual certainty to exist, (1) the loss must be clearly traceable to an identifiable cause that has been eliminated and is not expected to recur, (2) there is a record of profitability on normal operations that should be capable of absorbing the loss carryforward, and (3) there is assurance beyond reasonable doubt that taxable income can be generated within the loss carryforward period to absorb the actual tax loss.

One question that sometimes arises is whether one can look to the record of profitability and prospect of taxable income in other companies within a related group of companies to provide the required level of assurance. The reasoning is that such a group can often arrange to transfer profitable operations into a loss company to absorb loss carryforwards. The U.S. literature suggests that it would be appropriate to take account of this possibility only when specific plans are adopted for reorganization so as to take advantage of the loss.

In the infrequent case where an asset is recognized with respect to a tax loss carryforward, the literature suggests the use of the expected rate of tax in the loss recovery period (if such a rate has been enacted) to measure the benefit. Any subsequent change in that rate is accounted for as an adjustment affecting income in the year of change.

If the virtual certainty test is not met in the year of loss, the standards call for delay in recognition of the tax benefit until actual realization, notwithstanding that conditions may change so that there may appear to be virtual certainty in some intervening year. A realized benefit from the carryforward is to be presented in the income statement as an "extraordinary item."

The interaction between timing differences and tax loss carryforwards

Tax allocation theory presumes that readers of financial statements are interested in future tax benefits or sacrifices with respect to accounting revenues, expenses, and losses recognized up to the reporting date. Future tax benefits include any actual reduction in future taxes arising from losses carried forward and utilized within the allowable period. They also include benefits from taxes paid in advance on certain revenues, or from taxes paid but deferred because certain expenses recognized for accounting were not deductible for tax but will be allowed in later years. If loss carryforwards calculated under the tax law are doubtful of realization within the carryforward limit, there may also be doubt as to realization of the other tax benefits.

Conversely, deferred tax credits may have been recognized with respect to future adverse effects on taxes resulting from reversals of timing differences. If future profits cannot be assumed, these adverse effects disappear. Thus, it would be inconsistent to continue to treat them as liabilities and at the same time deny asset status to tax loss carryforwards on the grounds of doubt as to the realization of future profit. Accounting for tax losses carried forward thus interacts with accounting for timing differences.

Arriving at the accounting entries to portray the end result of this interaction can be quite complex. An orderly approach is suggested below.

1. Record any changes in deferred tax balances resulting from timing differences that have had an effect on actual taxes in the current year (the loss year). Even though a tax loss exists, there can be adjustments to deferred tax balances in the year. For example, if an accounting profit of $100,000 is shown, but timing differences of $150,000 produce a taxable loss of $50,000, deferred taxes would be recorded with respect to $100,000 of the timing differences.
2. Record the actual amount of tax recoverable as a result of the tax loss carryback, and credit tax expense of the loss year.
3. If changes have been made to previous years' timing differences in refiling tax returns for the loss carryback years (for example, capital cost allowance claims have been reduced to maximize taxable income of those years), adjust the recorded deferred tax balances and credit tax expense in the loss year.
4. At this point assessment of loss carryforward accounting begins. Consider two possible situations:
   a) Deferred tax debits from previous years remain on the books. There have also been timing differences in the current year that would have produced deferred tax debits, except that they served only to reduce the taxable loss rather than having an actual tax effect. There is also a residual

loss carryforward. The last two items both have a potentially beneficial effect with respect to future tax expense, and together they may be called the "accounting loss carryforward."

b) Deferred tax credits from previous years remain on the books. There may also be timing differences in the current year that would have produced additional deferred tax credits, except that they served only to increase the taxable loss rather than having an actual tax effect. There is also the residual tax loss carryforward. In this case the "accounting loss carryforward" is the amount of the tax loss carryforward *minus* the amount of timing differences for which deferred tax credits have not been booked.

It should be apparent that, under tax allocation theory, it is the accounting loss carryforward that is the more significant figure for the purpose of income measurement and financial statement disclosure. This is most easily seen with respect to situation (b) above. In that case, if the tax loss carryforward is realized in full by application against future taxable income (and had not previously been recorded as an asset), the resulting credit must be allocated in part to deferred taxes to pick up the effect of the timing differences, with the remainder flowing through to income in the year of realization.

5. In situation (a) it is necessary to assess whether there is virtual certainty of realization of the benefit from the tax loss carryforward within the period permitted by law. If there is, the estimated future recoverable tax may be recognized as an asset, and tax expense in the loss year credited. Consideration must also be given to the recoverability of benefit from timing differences not booked as deferred tax debits because they have not had an effect on actual taxes. If there is "reasonable assurance" as to the recovery of benefit from such timing differences, they too may be recognized (by charging deferred tax debits and crediting tax expense in the loss year). In determining reasonable assurance, the period of reversal of the timing differences must be taken into account. If the reversal is within management's discretion (as in the case of differences between depreciation and capital cost allowance), the test may be somewhat less demanding than the virtual certainty requirement for recognition of the potential recovery from the tax loss carryforward. If the reversal is automatic (for example, it relates to revenues taxed in advance that will be recognized in accounting income of the following year), it may be just as hard or harder to be sure of recovery of benefit as it is for actual tax loss carryforwards. The *CICA Handbook* requires that deferred tax debits from previous years be written off (as an extraordinary loss) if deferred tax debits with respect to timing differences in the loss year are not recorded.[10]

6. In situation (b) it is also necessary to assess whether there is virtual certainty of realization of the benefit of the tax loss carryforward within the permitted period. If there is such virtual certainty, an asset should be recorded and tax expense of the loss year credited for the amount of the *accounting loss carryforward* only. (If the full tax loss carryforward were recognized as an asset, the portion represented by timing differences in the loss year would have to be credited to deferred income taxes.) Even if there is not virtual certainty as to recovery of the tax loss carryforward, it is necessary to consider the status of any deferred income tax credits

> from prior years that are on the books. If taxable profits cannot be assumed within the loss carryforward period, it follows that timing difference reversals within that period will suffer no penalty. Therefore, it is appropriate to draw down from recorded deferred income tax credits amounts equivalent (at the tax rates used in recording the deferred credits) to the lesser of the accounting loss carryforward and the maximum amount of reversals of timing differences that can occur within the tax loss carryforward period.

To the extent that a tax loss carryforward is not recognized on the grounds of lack of virtual certainty, the *CICA Handbook* requires disclosure of its amount, excluding any portion that would be credited to deferred taxes if realized, together with the expiration dates of the loss carryforward(s). Also required is disclosure of the amount of deferred tax debits that have not been recognized but could be if there were reasonable assurance of their recovery.[11] In effect, the accounting loss carryforward is to be disclosed, but it is also to be made clear how much of that is represented by tax directly recoverable within the loss carryforward period under the operation of the tax law.

One final observation may be made. The present accounting standard is based on acceptance of the proposition that the dominant accounting event in this case is the incurrence of the loss. The result is that tax loss recoveries are attributed to the year of loss, subject to the virtual certainty constraint for loss carryforwards. Realization of loss carryforwards depends upon the earning of future taxable profits. Under the more stringent definition of an asset described earlier—that an asset recognized must be attributable to events up to the reporting date and only such events—a loss carryforward asset could not be recorded except to the extent that it was assured by reversals within the carryforward period of deferred tax credits existing at the reporting date.

Disclosure with respect to income tax generally

For a variety of reasons, tax expense reported for a period may differ from the figure one would expect based on pretax accounting income. The actual tax rate may differ from the normal rate because of the small business deduction or because income is earned abroad and taxed at different rates. Permanent differences between accounting and taxable income may result from the operation of tax or other legislation. Losses may be incurred that are not subject to tax allocation because of lack of virtual certainty, and so on. Taxes payable will also usually differ from tax expense reported because of timing differences between taxable and accounting income. A serious analyst of the financial statements may well wish to know what are the causes of the differences in both these categories. The analyst may base his assessment of the quality of the reporting entity on predictions of one or both of income to be reported and cash flow to be reported in the next few years. It makes a difference to those predictions whether differences in both categories are likely to persist. For example, if changes in income tax or other legislation are likely to occur, an analyst estimating future after-tax income will need information to help estimate the impact of these events. Or, if the analyst is trying to estimate the operating cash flow available to meet debt commitments in the near future, timing difference effects that will sharply reverse within that period are relevant to his analysis.

There is a strong case, therefore, for disclosure of details reconciling accounting income, tax expense reported under tax allocation procedures, and taxes payable for a period. Disclosures reconciling pretax accounting income and tax expense reported have been required in the United States for many years, but have been required in Canada (and then only for public companies) only since 1984. To date, so far as North America is concerned, only companies reporting to the United States Securities and Exchange Commission are required to provide information as to the types of timing differences that have resulted in deferred tax provisions or draw-downs in the reporting year.

Summary

Accounting for income tax expense has been a highly debatable subject for many years. Income for a period subject to tax is not calculated in exactly the same fashion as income for the same period calculated in accordance with accounting standards. To a high degree each calculation is based upon the same material—transactions engaged in by the entity. But the two calculations may allocate the revenues and expenses flowing from these transactions to different periods. This fact gives rise to the basic question: Must the figure of tax expense reported in accounting statements of income be the amount of tax as assessable for that year? Or, may the tax expense assessable for a year be allocated among accounting periods to correspond with the way revenues and expenses that make up taxable income are reported as elements of accounting income?

The idea that the figure of tax assessable for a period was divisible began with proposals for "intraperiod allocation." Some costs and revenues that enter into taxable income for a period may be classified for accounting purposes as extraordinary items in the income statement, or be charged or credited to retained earnings account or to a contributed capital account. It is generally accepted that the tax effects of revenues and expenses reported outside ordinary income should not be included with ordinary tax expense but rather should be reported in the same place as the revenue or expense item with which they are associated. Such intraperiod allocation of tax expense assists the analysis of financial statements and is not contentious.

"Interperiod tax allocation," that is, allocation of elements of tax assessable for one year to one or more other years, may be regarded as only an extension of the idea of intraperiod allocation. Most accountants believe that interperiod tax allocation is justified when an identifiable revenue or expense is recognized in a clear-cut fashion in one period for accounting purposes and another for the purposes of taxation, especially when the lapse of time between recognition for the two purposes is short. It is when timing differences between accounting and tax recognition of revenues and expenses are recurring or reverse only over a considerable period of time that a marked division of opinion occurs. Some accountants believe the fairest portrayal of income occurs when "comprehensive tax allocation" is performed that takes account of all timing differences. Others believe that there should be only "partial tax allocation" for certain types of timing differences. Today's accounting standards espouse comprehensive tax allocation.

Many objections have been made to the concepts of comprehensive tax allocation, especially with respect to timing differences represented by the excess of capital cost allowance taken for tax purposes over depreciation written on plant for accounting purposes. Among other things, it is argued in this case that new plant assets acquired will entitle an entity to more capital cost allowances with the very probable result that, in the aggregate, the timing differences will never reverse. As a result, the balance of the deferred tax credit will never decline, and it cannot be regarded as a true liability.

The heart of this argument lies in the assumption that it is proper to offset capital cost allowances on plant yet to be acquired against deficiencies in capital cost allowances on assets currently held. This assumption is fundamentally in error. In the first place, accounting should not be affected by transactions that have not yet taken place—the future plant acquisitions. In the second place, there is no way to rationalize why the tax status of a future plant acquisition has anything to do with the tax status of existing plant.

The following observations can be made about deferred tax balances:

- When the reversal period is predictable, deferred tax credits are associated with increases in future taxes, even in the absence of future transactions, and hence represent real liabilities.
- When the reversal period is predictable, deferred tax debits are associated with future reductions in taxes (with a minor exception). The realization of those future reductions, however, depends upon the earning of profits in future. If it is believed that the future tax reduction should be reported in the same period as that in which the expense or revenue giving rise to that reduction was reported (as is the basis of present accounting standards), the deferred tax should be recorded as an asset so long as its recovery is probable. On the other hand, if one believes that an asset should never be recorded that can be realized only by means of profits arising from subsequent transactions, deferred tax debits should not be recorded unless covered by recorded deferred tax credits.
- When the reversal of a timing difference is not predictable, it is open to question whether deferred taxes should be recorded with respect to it.

The fact that recorded deferred tax credits and debits stand for real impacts on future taxes payable suggests that they should be measured at future tax rates to the extent possible. That means adoption of the accrual approach to tax allocation, rather than the deferral approach. In economic terms, a strong argument can also be made for discounting the future tax impacts, but a number of conceptual and practical problems would need to be solved to accomplish that end.

Loss years result in tax recoveries, not tax expense. Under present accounting standards, the credit for those recoveries is deemed to be applicable to the year of loss, not the year when the recovery is realized. When recoveries of taxes paid in previous years are made as a result of loss carrybacks there is no problem — the year of recovery and the year of loss are the same. Loss carryforwards are a different matter. In a minority of cases the future tax recovery is anticipated and an asset is recorded in the loss year. This is supposed to take place only in unusual circumstances when the future recovery can be said to be virtually certain. If an asset is not recorded in the loss year, any recovery of taxes from the loss carry-forward in future years is treated as an item of extraordinary income in the year of recovery.

There is a connection between the accounting for existing deferred tax balances and tax loss carryforwards. If the tax loss carryforward is not recognized as an asset because of lack of virtual certainty of future taxable profits, it is necessary to take a hard look at existing deferred tax debits, because their realization also depends upon future profits. On the other hand, when deferred tax credits exist, some favourable future result is assured. Either taxable profits will be earned, thereby resulting in recovery of the tax loss carryforward, or else reversals of timing differences will occur without penalty. To recognize this situation, draw-downs of deferred taxes may be recorded in the year of loss to the extent of the lesser of the amount recoverable from the loss carryforward and the reversals of deferred taxes scheduled to occur in the carryforward period.

References

[1]American Institute of Accountants, Committee on Accounting Procedure, *Accounting for Income Taxes*, Accounting Research Bulletin No. 23 (New York: AIA, 1944), subsequently consolidated in Chapter 10B of *Restatement and Revision of Accounting Research Bulletins*, Accounting Research Bulletin No. 43 (New York: AIA, 1953).

[2]CICA, "Corporate Income Taxes," *CICA Handbook*, Section 3470 (Toronto: CICA), pars. 23-24.

[3]See FASB, *Balance Sheet Classification of Deferred Income Taxes: An Amendment of APB Opinion No. 11*, Statement of Financial Accounting Standards No. 37 (Stamford: FASB, 1980).

[4]This argument along with others is reviewed in T.H. Beechy, *Accounting for Corporate Income Taxes: Conceptual Considerations and Empirical Analysis* (Toronto: CICA, 1983), chap. 2.

[5]See P. Rosenfield and W.C. Dent, "No More Deferred Taxes," *Journal of Accountancy*, February 1983, pp. 44-55.

[6]See Beechy, op. cit., chap. 2, par. 51.

[7]Institute of Chartered Accountants in England and Wales, *Accounting for Deferred Tax*, rev., Statement of Standard Accounting Practice No. 15 (London: ICAEW, 1978, revised 1985).

[8]Beechy, op. cit., chaps. 2 and 11.

[9]For an early example, see H.A. Black, *Interperiod Allocation of Corporate Income Taxes*, Accounting Research Study No. 9 (New York: AICPA, 1966).

[10]*CICA Handbook*, Section 3470, par. 52.

[11]Ibid., par. 54.

Chapter Sixteen

Accounting for Portfolio Investments, Options, Futures, and Swaps

To this point in Part II we have concentrated on the accounting issues associated with active business operations. In this chapter we turn our attention to passive investments. By the term "passive" we mean that the investor's actions with respect to such investments are limited to decisions whether or when to buy or sell. Such passive investments are beginning to be called "portfolio investments" in accounting literature. In a subsequent chapter we shall discuss investments in subsidiary and affiliated companies upon whose operations the investor can exercise significant influence.

In recent years the possibilities for investment and speculation have been greatly expanded by the emergence of a wide variety of exchange-traded options and futures contracts. Frequently, a decision to invest in these instruments is influenced by an investor's holdings of other investments. It follows that accounting for options and futures cannot be considered in isolation from accounting for more conventional forms of investment. While options and futures contracts are often used to hedge investment or financing risks, they may also be used to hedge certain operating risks. Hedges will also be covered in the discussion in this chapter.

Yet another hedging medium has become very widely used in the short space of a few years. This medium is the "swap" contract. There are two basic types of swaps — the "interest-rate swap" and the "foreign currency swap." Only the first of these will be discussed in this chapter. At the time of writing, swap contracts are not traded on an exchange, but a secondary market for them appears to be developing.

Accounting for portfolio investments

Portfolio investments may have a wide variety of legal characteristics, and these have significance for their accounting. A broad distinction may be made between investments with debt characteristics and investments with equity characteristics, using the terms "debt" and "equity" without strict regard to their legal definitions.

Investments with debt characteristics are those in which the amount and timing of payments to the holders, including return of principal, are fully, or close to fully, specified. This class of investment includes treasury bills, promissory notes, bonds, debentures, annuities, mortgages, leasehold interests, and term preferred shares. Investments with equity characteristics provide no firm promise of payment but hold out the promise of gain to the holder. These investments include common shares, preferred shares, precious metals, and real estate. As in any classification scheme, there are several borderline cases. For example, a preferred share without any participation right is like a fixed-term security except for the lack of a firm redemption date. A significant mandatory redemption provision moves a preferred share even closer in its investment characteristics to debt. Convertible bonds have characteristics of both debt and equity securities, either of which may be dominant at a particular time.

Yet another group of financial instruments might be considered equity securities but have significant characteristics that set them apart. We refer to options, futures contracts, and rights or warrants to buy other securities. The significant characteristic of options is that the sole source of their value is the right to acquire another asset. That value will inevitably disappear if the option is not exercised by its expiry date. The significant characteristic of a futures contract is that it is a commitment that can be favourable or unfavourable depending on movements in price of the subject of the contract. Accounting for options and futures is discussed in specific terms subsequently, but much of that discussion is pertinent to stock rights and warrants as well.

There is also a question whether real estate owned should be considered a passive investment or whether management responsibilities may make it effectively an active business operation. Even if it is considered to be a passive investment, it differs from most other investments in that it will be necessary to recognize depreciation in relation to any limited-life improvements of the property. If it is not considered a passive investment, either inventory accounting or fixed asset accounting may be applicable depending upon the circumstances. (See chapters 10 and 11.)

Investment accounting for the ordinary business

Current accounting practice is fairly well established for investments by the ordinary business. In the case of financial institutions and nonprofit organizations, however, accounting for investments is less uniform and tends to vary from one type of entity to another. We shall first discuss accepted accounting practice for investments by ordinary businesses.

Generally accepted investment accounting in the normal business enterprise is highly influenced by the balance sheet classification of the investment. However, it is not always entirely clear whether a particular investment should be classified as current or noncurrent.

- Liquidity is a prerequisite for investments classified as current. Some investments, such as treasury bills, call loans, and short-term deposits are liquid because they have early maturity dates or are callable. Other investments are liquid because active markets exist for them. Marketability is facilitated when property is fungible, as is the case with shares of a corporation. Investments with individual characteristics such as mortgages and real estate are less likely to be readily marketable. Although liquidity is a prerequisite for classification of an investment as a current asset, not all liquid investments are so classified.
- The final classification of liquid investments rests upon management intention with respect to the investment. Unfortunately there is some variation in the interpretation of the intention test. It is clear that if management in-

tends to hold a security for the long term, it should be classified as long-term. Likewise, if management intends to sell the security in the short term it should be classified as current. The problem comes when management has no fixed intention with respect to a liquid security. Should it be classified as current because there is no firm intention to hold it, or should it be classified as long-term because there is no firm intention to sell it? Some enterprises classify all liquid investments as current, in order to maximize the apparent working capital and working-capital ratio. Others that have a well-established investment policy classify all investments bought following their policy as long-term, leaving only temporary investments of cash that is surplus to current business needs to be classified as current. In such cases, the portfolio as a whole is regarded as being held for the long term, even though some securities within it are temporary in nature. Because of this uncertainty in basis of classification, it is possible that a management could decide to reclassify some of its investment portfolio as short-term should it appear that reported working capital needed bolstering. Conversely, cases have occurred where investments have been reclassified from the current to the long-term category in order to avoid a write-down to market under the more stringent valuation rules applicable to current assets.

Accounting for investments classified as current. The fundamental accounting basis for investments, as for other assets, is cost. Because current assets should not be carried above realizable value, however, the valuation basis for current investments is lower of cost and market (LOCAM). There may be no market for certain short-term investments, but their early maturity or other facilities for realizing or borrowing upon the asset usually mean that cost may be considered to be market. For other securities, market means the figure realizable at the financial reporting date and is not affected by changes in market quotations subsequent to that date (although occasionally subsequent changes could be sufficiently material to require disclosure). The LOCAM test may be applied by individual security or by the whole portfolio classified as current. If securities have been written down, and their market value subsequently recovers, practice is mixed with respect to reversal of the write-downs.

Accounting for investments classified as noncurrent. Again, the fundamental basis for valuation of investments is cost. It is generally accepted that investments classified as long-term need not be written down when market value is below cost; presumably the basis is the belief that recognition of fluctuations in market value of an investment held for the long term would not improve reporting of income. If the value of one or more individual securities has suffered an impairment that is other than temporary, however, those individual securities should be written down. It is matter for judgment when that condition exists. The words "other than temporary" unfortunately are sufficiently vague to allow for considerable variability in judgment. At one time, accounting literature used to speak of the need for write-down when values were "permanently impaired." That test did not produce very useful accounting, since it was hard to be sure of permanent impairment in investment value short of bankruptcy of the security issuer. The present wording suggests that write-downs should be made when value recovery is not foreseeable apart from wishful thinking. The following conditions suggest a value decline that is more than temporary:

- Severe losses incurred by the investee and/or continued losses or low profits for a period of years.
- A prolonged period in which the quoted market value of the security is less than its carrying value. (Declines in value of fixed-maturity securities need not be taken into account if the decline is the result of general market conditions — e.g., a rise in interest rates — and it is not expected the security will be disposed of before maturity.)
- Financial difficulties suffered by the investee.

This list is not all inclusive. When such indicators of impairment persist for three or four years there is a presumption that a value decline is other than temporary, which may be rebutted only by very persuasive evidence.[1] The estimated length of time before an investment can be expected to recover its value may also be a factor in determining the need for write-down. If management intends to sell a security in the near future, or if it may be required to liquidate its portfolio because of needs for cash, it may be necessary to write down the security or portfolio merely because recovery cannot be expected before realization.

When a write-down appears necessary, a judgment is required as to the amount of write-down. In practice, the test used in writing down values for long-term assets is "recoverable value." Recoverable value simply means the cash that can be got out of the asset with little regard to the length of time taken to recovery.[2] That test appears to leave some room for reasonable estimates of recovery in value before disposition if the current value appears to be abnormally depressed. To improve the reliability of accounting it would seem desirable to use a less speculative figure. For investments, at least, if a write-down is necessary there hardly seems a better test of value than the amount estimated to be actually realizable at the financial reporting date.

Once a long-term investment is written down, the reduced carrying value cannot be written up again before disposal.

Accounting for investments in unclassified balance sheets. It is normal in some types of industry to present balance sheets in which assets are not classified as current or noncurrent. In such cases, it frequently will be appropriate to follow the investment accounting basis just described for investments classified as noncurrent. In some situations, however, when investments are expected to be held only for the short term, it will be reasonable to account for the holdings or some of them on a straightforward LOCAM basis.

Investments generally. As is true for other monetary assets, income is recognized on fixed-term interest-bearing securities on the basis of their "effective yield." The effective yield is a calculated figure for each such security that represents a constant periodic rate of return on its carrying value over its entire life. To be conservative, the effective yield is calculated to the call date when a premium is paid and to the maturity date when a purchase is made at a discount.

To recognize the effective yield in income, it is necessary to amortize any difference between the original purchase price of the security and its ultimate redemption price in such a way that the sum of the cash yield and amortization in each period equals the income figure produced by applying the effective yield rate to the opening carrying value of the investment. Thus, when it is said that such securities are carried at cost, it must be understood that cost means amortized cost. An exception may be made for temporary holdings or for securities held primarily as trading assets, since amortization for the short holding period is likely to be immaterial in relation to the ultimate gain or loss recorded on disposal.

The use of a constant yield rate to govern recognition of income is arbitrary. A reduction in the income rate recognized as an investment approaches maturity, although also arbitrary, would be more consistent with the fact that short-term interest rates in the market tend to be lower than long-term rates. However, the accepted constant return assumption is convenient and corresponds with the normal way that investment yields are quoted in the marketplace.

When a particular security in a portfolio has been acquired in several lots at different times and different costs and subsequently part but not all of the holding is sold, the question arises as to what cost should be assigned to the part of the holding sold. The *CICA Handbook* recommendation in this case is to apply the average unit cost of all purchases in costing the securities sold.[3] Since all securities are identical no matter when acquired, this is obviously the sensible answer. In the United States, flexibility is permitted in cost-flow assumptions to permit conformity with the options available for taxation purposes.

Quoted market values should be disclosed (if available) whether the investments are classified as current or long-term. When only part of the portfolio has a quoted market value, the carrying value of that part should be disclosed in conjunction with the market value. Occasionally a holding of a particular security is so large that quoted market price may not be closely indicative of realizable value for the block. In such cases, it is good practice to add a caution that quoted market value may not be representative of realizable value.

U.S. practice. Because of the introduction of SFAS No. 12 in 1975, U.S. accounting practice for marketable securities is considerably different from normal Canadian practice.[4] Different rules apply to holdings of equity securities classified as current assets and holdings classified as long-term investments. Transfers between the two categories must be valued at lower of cost and market at the date of transfer, with any loss being recorded as if it were realized. Both categories are to be valued at a period-end at the lower of aggregate cost and aggregate market. A write-down (or a write-up on subsequent recovery to not more than aggregate cost) is reflected in net income for the current-asset category but is taken directly to shareholders' equity for long-term investments. If a decline in value of an individual long-term security is considered other than temporary, however, it is to be written down and the write-down treated as a loss charged to net income.

Investment accounting in specialized situations

In several specialized situations, accounting practice for investments may deviate from the standard approach just described. Usually, the deviation has developed because some alternative accounting practice appears to be better suited to the particular situation. Unfortunately, clear criteria have not been developed to determine which accounting methods are best for particular situations. The result has been diversity in practice, with some entities in specialized situations adopting special accounting practices for investments, and others in the same situations following more or less the standard approach. The following describes some of the reasons for the development of specialized accounting.

- In some cases the ready realizability of investments is of supreme importance to any assessment of an entity's financial position. The volatile nature of the business of investment dealers and brokers, for example, makes the cashable status of their assets and liabilities by far the most relevant financial information for them. Only such values provide a good portrayal of liquidity and solvency of the enterprise. A smoothed portrayal of income from their investments is of lesser interest since, for the most part, income from investments while held will be overshadowed by gains and losses in trading. Cashable values are also important to open-end investment funds because participants have a right to redemption of their position at current net asset values upon very short notice. However, closed-end investment funds also commonly use market value accounting, indicating that market values are considered important for investment companies even when liquidity is not the prime concern.
- In other cases, the predominant sentiment is directly opposite. When an investment portfolio is not likely to be liquidated there may well be greater interest in an accounting basis that reports earnings from investments on a smooth basis from year to year — representative of the long-term rate of return — than in the reporting of a figure that fluctuates widely from period to period because of realized and unrealized gains and losses. Some examples of situations that create a desire for a smooth figure of reported investment income and asset values are as follows:
  - A large endowment fund or pool of trust funds in a charitable or educational entity pays out its income each year to support the activities for which the funds were donated or collected. An accounting basis that provides a smooth measure of income facilitates budgeting for such activities.
  - A life insurance company has policy obligations that will require the disbursement of funds over many years into the future. These obligations are valued by discounting actuarial estimates of future payments using standard interest rates intended to represent attainable long-run investment returns with a margin for safety. A large portion of the investments held to fund the obligations consists of fixed-interest securities. If interest rates rise significantly, the market values of these fixed-interest securities will decline. Thus, a loss would be shown on a market value basis of accounting. The rise in interest rates, however, is favourable, not unfavourable. Higher interest rates will enhance the future cash flow from reinvestment of investment earnings, thereby making it easier to meet policy obligations to the extent that those obligations are fixed in monetary terms. The general point is that it would be misleading to value assets at market value without also revaluing policy obligations at current interest rates. Regular revaluation of both assets and liabilities would increase the accounting cost, and might confuse readers of the statements because of the volatility of figures reported, without providing a significantly better portrayal of operations. Similar arguments may be made for pension plans or other financial institutions with long-term liabilities.[5]
  - Even financial institutions whose obligations are largely short-term see arguments against a market value accounting basis for investments. In a financial institution, total assets may be twenty times or more the amount of shareholders' equity, and most of the assets will be investments in one form or another. If all investments are valued at market value, a

decline of little more than five percent in value over a period could wipe out the reported equity. Since market values can easily change by much more than this over a one-year period, financial institutions fear that adoption of market value accounting could have a serious effect on depositor and investor confidence. In addition, the ease of valuation of assets would vary from one type of asset to another. Estimates of current values for some types of investments could be quite speculative. Omission of significant amounts of investments from the market valuation basis because of difficulty in valuation could be criticized as being inconsistent if there was reason to believe their fair value was significantly different from book value. Some would also argue that market values do not form a satisfactory basis for accounting because they do not really represent realizable values but would be interpreted as such. They are not realizable because disposal of an investment portfolio of significant size by an institution would itself depress the market values.

Thus, in those industries categorized by large investment portfolios we have sharply divergent tendencies. Some situations lead to reliance on current market values as the exclusive basis for investment carrying value. Other situations lead to exactly the opposite position — a desire to exclude the effects of fluctuating market values from carrying values. In the latter situation, some are satisfied with the standard basis of accounting for ordinary business entities — based on LOCAM or amortized cost less allowances for investment impairments that are other than temporary. Others would prefer to go even further and develop accounting bases that provide a measure of periodic income considered more representative of average long-term investment performance. Two such methods will be discussed shortly — the "deferral and amortization" basis of accounting for fixed-interest securities, and the "moving-average market value" basis for equity securities.

Trading portfolios in financial institutions. If one accepts the suggestion that different accounting for investments is justified by differences between long-term and short-term objectives, it follows that an entity such as a financial institution may have two pools of investments accounted for differently because of the different investment objectives for the two pools. Any such segregation would have to be based on management intention.

One might at first think that it would be difficult to prove intention. But that is not necessarily so. In the first place, the officers responsible for the trading portfolio may be different from those responsible for long-term investment policy. If so, intent may be demonstrated initially by identifying the persons who authorized the purchase of securities and by the portfolio to which the securities are assigned on the books. Subsequently, the distinction can be maintained by requiring that any transfers between portfolios be accounted for at market value, with gain or loss being recorded according to the rules applicable to the selling portfolio. In such cases, the trading portfolio is logically accounted for on a market value basis, with value changes being immediately recognized in income. The long-term portfolio would be accounted for on whatever basis is selected as most appropriate for long-term investments.

Deferral and amortization. The amortized cost basis of accounting provides a smooth portrayal of investment income from debt securities, provided all securities are held to maturity. But even in portfolios held for the long term, some buying and selling before maturity usually takes place in the interests of improving investment performance. From the viewpoint of any individual security, recognition of gain or loss on disposal before maturity is necessary to complete the record of investment performance. From the perspective of a portfolio as a whole, when proceeds from sales are regularly reinvested a different view of performance is possible.

At October 1, 1985, Government of Canada 10% bonds maturing October 1, 1995 were quoted at $95.90 to yield 10.68% to maturity. At the same date, Government of Canada 14% bonds maturing October 1, 2006 were quoted at $120.90 to yield 11.37%. Suppose a portfolio held bonds of the first of these issues acquired at par, so that income reported on the cost basis of accounting was $50 each half-year for each $1,000 bond. Suppose further that the first issue was sold and the proceeds reinvested in the second. Ignoring transaction costs, under cost-based accounting a loss of $41 would be recognized on the sale of each $1,000 bond and the income for the next half-year would rise to 11.37% of $959/2 = $54.52 — an increase in income of $4.52. At first sight, the gain in reported income might appear to be simply the result of investing in a higher-yielding bond. But the difference in annual yield on the two securities at the trade date was only 11.37% - 10.68% = 0.69%. We should have expected the increase in income for the half year, therefore, to be only 0.69% of $959/2 = $3.31.

To understand this, consider what would have happened had the original issue been sold and the proceeds reinvested in an identical issue. As before, a loss of $41 would be recognized on sale. Thereafter (again ignoring transaction costs), income reported for the next half year would rise to 10.68% of $959/2 = $51.21. Thus, taking a loss on the security sold boosts the income reported thereafter even though there has been absolutely no change in the composition of the portfolio. While the illustration of sale and repurchase of identical securities is unrealistic, the point it makes is of general application. A loss taken currently will simply increase future reported portfolio income over the term to maturity of the security sold, and conversely.[6]

The purpose of the deferral and amortization approach is to avoid this discontinuity in income reporting. In our example, the investment in the issue maturing in 1995 has an influence on income right up to that maturity date regardless of whether the issue was sold or held. For if the security is sold, a sacrifice of principal has to be taken that reduces the higher yield rate obtainable on reinvestment. If that loss of principal is taken into account, the real increase in yield over the period to 1995 is limited to the difference between the yield obtainable on the replacement issue and the yield implicit in the market price of the issue sold. To portray this in the accounting, it is necessary to defer the loss on the issue sold and amortize that loss so that it is fully absorbed by the time the issue would have matured had it been held. To be strictly consistent with accounting on the effective-yield basis for amortization of premiums and discounts on securities purchased, the amortization of the loss should be on a sinking-fund pattern. (While this example describes deferment of a loss, the same principle holds in relation to a gain.)

Deferral and amortization accounting does not take into account the possibility that a decline in value of a debt security may be specifically attributable to a decline in its quality, rather than to changes in the general level of interest rates. If adopted, therefore, it is necessary to have some sort of safeguard that calls for direct write-down against income of securities when a decline in value is other than temporary. If the portfolio is sold out or shrinks significantly, it also would not seem reasonable to continue to carry forward the full amount of deferred gains or losses. This effectively means that the deferral and amortization accounting approach is not appropriate except for well-established portfolios with reasonable assurance of continuity.

Moving-average market values. Let us turn now to investments in common stocks. It is well known that the return expected from investment in common stocks comes partly from dividends and partly from increases in the market value of the stock. It is total performance that counts. The cost method of accounting for such investments, therefore, fails to recognize an intrinsic part of the investment performance until the stock is sold. Since stocks may be held for a long time, this is an important shortcoming of the cost approach for accounting for equities. The use of market values is one possible response to this shortcoming. People who stress the importance of long-term investment performance, however, object to basing the accounting on every fluctuation in market value. Managers of large portfolios are unable to take full advantage of short-term price changes because of the size of their holdings, and even smaller portfolios are likely to be deterred by the transaction costs associated with trading in and out of the market. Accordingly, there is a desire to record equity investments at values that are representative of current conditions without necessarily using the quoted market values that happen to exist on the last day of the quarter or the year being reported on and only on that day. There is also a desire to reflect as income a figure that shows the investment performance averaged out over a period, not a figure that would be materially influenced — some may say distorted — by the fact that the market happens to be unusually high at the beginning of the period and unusually low at the end, or conversely.

One suggested accounting method is based on the idea that market prices, although following a long-term upward trend, display a cyclical pattern around the trend line over approximately a five-year period in response to the business cycle. The idea, then, is that equity securities in the portfolio may be carried at a five-year moving average of market prices, and in this way fluctuations of balance sheet values and reported income will be dampened.[7]

One question that has been asked is whether moving-average or similar valuations are suggested merely for the purpose of smoothing income fluctuations, or whether they have any real economic significance. It has been argued that a moving-average price is an estimator of future net realizable value from an investment and, on average, is superior for this purpose to spot market prices that are capricious in the short run.[8] This contention has been hotly disputed on a priori grounds supported by empirical evidence. It is pointed out that evidence shows no correlation between past price movements in a stock and future price movements. Movements in stock prices from day to day form a "random walk" — if prices go up for several days in a row there is no more reason to expect they will go up (or down) tomorrow than to expect that four heads shown on four tosses of a coin will be followed by another head (or a tail). The inference is that movements in prices respond to new information only and respond very quickly. At any given time, therefore, the current market price should be the best indicator of future realizable values discounted at the market's required rate of return. This argument was supported by a study showing that current market prices surpassed five-year moving averages as a predictor of prices one year later.[9] A rebuttal to this argument referred to an unpublished study arriving at the opposite conclusion.[10] It would seem that this is a question that ought to be capable of resolution through empirical research — although perhaps more exhaustive than the studies referred to.

Conflicting arguments over investment accounting methods

The arguments against the cost or LOCAM basis of accounting have been more vigorous in the case of investments than they have been for any other category of asset. No doubt the reason is that well-developed securities markets provide much better evidence of value for a high proportion of investments than is available for other asset categories. The criticisms of cost-based methods of accounting for investments are as follows:

- Reliance on historical cost detracts from comparability between companies. Two entities theoretically could hold exactly the same portfolio, yet show very different amounts for the asset because the securities were acquired at different times.
- With respect to investments in equity securities, the normal expectation is that the reward for investment will be received in the form of both dividends and capital gains. If the latter source of gain is not recognized until realized, the portrayal of investment performance will be obscured.
- In general, the realization convention has an erratic effect on reported income and return on investment. On top of this, when the market value of securities held has risen considerably above cost, management is able to manipulate reported income merely by its decisions to sell or not to sell out of the portfolio.
- On the other hand, when market values are significantly below cost, management may be deterred from selling investments because of the desire not to "take a loss." Accounting can thus inhibit investment policy.
- Finally, the judgment whether a particular investment has suffered a reduction in value that is other than temporary is highly subjective. That subjectivity adds to the possibility of manipulation of reported results, and compounds the problem of lack of comparability.

The principal objections made to adoption of a market value basis of accounting as an alternative to cost-based accounting are as follows:

- Difficulties in valuation. Although active markets provide reliable prices for a wide variety of investments, quoted prices will not always be conclusive evidence of value. Values of large blocks of shares, for example, may be more or less than prices indicated by trading in small lots. Likewise, prices in thinly traded markets may be unreliable. Beyond this, estimates of value for highly individual types of investments may be difficult to obtain and unreliable. When prices are difficult to obtain, accounting on a value basis not only may be unreliable but also will be more costly.
- Inconsistency in accounting basis. Some accountants argue that it would be

inconsistent to adopt market value accounting for investments and not for other categories of assets. Also, as discussed earlier, market value accounting for investments would, in some situations, logically need to be associated with current value accounting for liabilities.

- Effect on reported income. Perhaps the most strongly held argument against market value accounting for investments is the contention that when investment portfolios are long-term, market value fluctuations introduce erratic gains and losses into reported income. These are considered essentially meaningless by an enterprise that, by the nature of its business, must remain close to fully invested at all times. This view is particularly strongly held by financial institutions that are highly leveraged by deposit liabilities or other forms of liability to the public.

The deferral and amortization method of accounting for portfolios of debt securities and the moving-average market value basis for equity securities both represent attempts to overcome disadvantages of cost-based accounting approaches while avoiding or mitigating the full impact of a straight market value approach on periodic income reporting. The deferral and amortization approach is simply a modest extension of cost-based accounting. One of its chief practical advantages is that for the fixed-income portfolio it removes the possibly distorting effect of cost-based accounting on investment decisions resulting from the reluctance to sell securities when sale requires recognition of a loss. Its chief disadvantage is that its use is limited to fixed-interest securities and to situations where the portfolio is likely to be a stable or steadily growing amount. If an entity holds a substantial amount of equity securities as well as debt securities, some method that smooths the recording of gain or loss on the equity portfolio would be logically consistent with the use of deferral and amortization for the debt portfolio.

The chief merit of the moving-average market value basis for equity securities is that it may provide some recognition of the capital gain component of return on equity securities — a very important component — without waiting for realization. The chief criticism is that the precise basis of application of moving-average methods (e.g., the selection of length of period for averaging) can vary and must be selected arbitrarily. It is also argued that the resulting balance sheet valuations are meaningless and therefore inferior to actual market values.

A moving-average technique could be used for debt security portfolios as well as equity portfolios. If the predominant investment policy for debt securities is to hold them to maturity or for long periods, one could argue that the deferral and amortization method is preferable. On the other hand, active trading in the debt portfolio would lend more support to a moving-average approach.

A compromise that permits the use of market values in the balance sheet but excludes market fluctuations from income is suggested by a CICA research study on portfolio investments.[11] Income would be reported on whatever long-term basis is selected. The balance sheet valuation of investments would be at market value. The difference between that value and the carrying value that would be consistent with the long-term income recognition basis would be treated as a separate category of shareholders' equity.

It is suggested that standard-setters should consider questions in the following order in an attempt to resolve these conflicting practices.

- First, is there sufficient justification for some departure from traditional historical cost accounting in the case of investments? There are strong arguments that there is. Reliable market prices are available for a high proportion of investments, and a reliable current market value is much more relevant information than historical cost. This is particularly so if turnover of the whole or a significant part of the portfolio is a practical possibility. If so, the current market value would seem to be the best basis for reporting investment performance. If market value accounting were adopted for portfolio investments, some thought would be appropriate to the presentation of results. It would seem desirable to segment the balance sheet and income statement more clearly than is now done in order to segregate operating and investment assets and the income therefrom. It might even be desirable to present two income statements, to help overcome the aversion of many corporate managements to variable figures of earnings per share. If the figure of earnings per share from operations were to retain the degree of stability it now has, it might be possible to accept a presentation of return on passive investments that reflects the variability inherent in market prices.

- Second, if a market value basis is adopted for investment portfolios for most entities, must it be extended to all? Standard-setters should consider carefully the reasons why some entities on their own have adopted market value accounting, even when it was clearly contrary to the ordinary accepted position, while other types of entity have a record of strong resistance to the merest suggestion that the market value basis should be adopted (a resistance that becomes overwhelming if it is proposed that unrealized changes in market value be reflected through income). It is possible to have some sympathy with such resistance for entities that, as a practical manner, do not have the ability to liquidate entire holdings of investments because their investments are, in effect, operating assets, the majority of which must be held to produce a steady stream of income to meet expenses.
- Third, if a market value basis is not adopted for some entities, are there accounting bases that are better than LOCAM for the portrayal of income from large investment portfolios? Any such possible bases are best considered within the context of specific industry situations.

Accounting for options and futures contracts

In recent years there has been a significant expansion in the activities of organized exchanges beyond dealings in the traditional instruments of bonds, stocks, and commodity contracts. These new market activities have opened new possibilities for investment, speculation, and hedging of risks. Accounting issues, have arisen that are new to some extent but also are related to issues in accounting for investments. Various practices have developed to deal with these issues, but no authoritative guidance has been developed in Canada. In the United States a recent standard on accounting for futures contracts has tackled some but not all of the questions.[12] The following discussion is exploratory to a considerable extent.

The new instruments fall into two broad classes, options contracts and futures contracts, which are similar in some characteristics and different in others. The holder of an option has a right, but not an obligation, to buy or sell a specific property at a given price. The seller or "writer" of the option has the obligation to deliver or purchase the security in question, but only if the optionee demands it. In contrast, a futures contract represents a firm commitment on the part of the buyer and seller of the contract to purchase or sell the subject of the contract at a future date specified in the contract.

An extremely important use of both options and futures contracts is to offset or "hedge" risks inherent in business or investment operations. Accounting for the contracts is affected by their use as hedges. It will be convenient, therefore, to provide some discussion of risk and hedging before the discussion of the accounting for these instruments.

Risk and hedging

All property is at risk of some sort. There is the risk of physical loss through fire, theft, accident, and so on. The risk of such losses can be lessened by preventive measures, and, to the extent it cannot be avoided completely, it may be shared through insurance. Property is also exposed to the risk of change in value over time. Risk is not simply confined to assets owned. It may pertain to liabilities undertaken to finance assets as well, and also to commitments to acquire assets or to undertake obligations. For convenience hereafter we shall use the general term "position at risk" to include all sources of risk, whether pertaining to assets, liabilities, or commitments.

Value changes in assets held for personal enjoyment or consumption may occur simply because of changes in public taste. For most positions at risk in a business, however, value changes are the result of one of three factors: (1) changes in the expected amount of cash inflow or outflow associated with the risk position, (2) changes in the degree of certainty of the inflows or outflows, and (3) changes in the general level of interest rates resulting in changes in the capitalized value of expected cash flows. In the case of certain assets and liabilities, cash inflows and outflows are established by contract; in accounting, these are conventionally called monetary assets and liabilities. Monetary asset and liability positions are subject to the second and third types of risks described above, but not the first. Hedges of risk positions in monetary assets and liabilities are often called hedges of interest-rate risk. Since the current interest rate determines the value of such asset and liability positions, however, hedges of interest-rate risks are simply a particular form of hedge of value.

The basic purpose of hedging is to achieve risk minimization. A risk position is hedged when the same cause that triggers an unfavourable change in its value will cause a favourable change in the value of some other position. For example, if a financial institution's portfolio of interest-bearing investments is financed by interest-bearing liabilities of the same amount and duration, a rise in the general level of interest rates will decrease the value of both the asset and liability positions by approximately equal amounts. On the other hand, if the position is unbalanced in either amount or duration, the entity is exposed to risks of changes in interest rates that adversely affect value. Sometimes an entity can arrange its affairs so as to be in a naturally hedged position, as in the case just described. In other cases, an entity will buy hedging instruments such as options or futures contracts whose value varies with changing conditions in a direction opposite to the adverse value changes in the position it is desired to hedge. As will be described, a futures contract used as a hedge will offset both favourable and adverse changes in the value of the position hedged. In contrast, beyond a certain point an option does not offset a favourable change, even though it does fully offset unfavourable changes (at the price of the option premium).

For a hedge to be completely effective, adverse value changes in the position at risk must be fully compensated for by favourable value changes in the hedging instrument. Such "perfect" hedges may be difficult to achieve. A perfect hedge is achieved when the subject of the hedging instrument is identical with the risk position hedged, and a long position in one is offset by a short position in the other. Thus, sale of a futures contract on some commodity can provide a perfect hedge of the risk of ownership of that same commodity. But options or futures contracts are not available for all types of positions that one might desire to hedge. For example, interest-rate futures contracts are available only for a few standard securities. Thus, there usually will not be an exact match between the position at risk and a contract purchased or sold as a hedge.

When a hedging instrument is based on a property that is not identical with the position at risk, but whose value tends to vary in step with that of the position hedged, the hedge is known as a "cross-hedge." Sometimes, also, price changes in the subject of the futures contract may correlate with that of the thing hedged but their amplitude may be less or more. In such cases a "hedge ratio" may be worked out. That is, if the value of a futures contract (say) is expected to change by lesser amounts than that of the position hedged, the dollar amount of the contract might be established at (say) 1.2 times the dollar value of the position hedged. The relationship between the amount of hedging instruments required and the position hedged may also be affected by differing tax treatments. It may take more or less of the hedging instrument to offset the after-tax impact of price changes in the position hedged if one is subject to capital gains treatment and the other to ordinary income treatment.

Finally, it may be noted that a hedging instrument itself may contain risks, even though its subject is identical with that of the position hedged. For example, the price set in a futures contract for delivery will not be identical with the spot price of the underlying property at the time the contract is bought or sold (the difference is known as "basis"). Over the duration of the futures contract, that basis or spread between the future price and the spot price may change. Thus, the value of the contract may not change so as to fully compensate for changes in the value of the underlying commodity. In addition to the possibility of loss from this "basis risk," there are costs involved in hedging, such as commissions to brokers and carrying costs with respect to margin requirements.

Accounting for options

An option is a right given by one party to another to buy or sell the property described in the option at a stated price at the discretion of the option holder within a stated period. (This describes an "American" option. A different form of option, known as the "European" option, allows the buyer to exercise the right of purchase only at the end of the option period.) Our primary concern in this section is with options traded on organized exchanges. Options on listed stocks have been traded for a number of years. Options on foreign currencies and a variety of other forms of property have been listed for trading more recently. For convenience, the discussion below will refer to options on listed stocks, but similar considerations apply to other exchange-traded options.

There are two basic types of traded stock options. In a "call" option the buyer has a right to require the option writer to sell a specific stock at a given exercise (or "striking") price at any time up to the expiry date of the option. In a "put" option the buyer has the right within the option period to require the option writer to buy the stock in question at the exercise price. To acquire these rights, the buyer of an option pays a price that is established through trading in the exchange. When the option is first written, the exercise price will usually be set above the current market price of the stock in the case of a call and below it in the case of a put. Such options are described as "out-of-the-money." Subsequently, during the option period the market price of the stock may change so that the option is "in-the-money." That is to say, a security that is "called" could be resold immediately for more than the exercise price, or a security that is "put" could be repurchased at the same time for less than the exercise price. In practice, most options (other than those that expire worthless) are not exercised, but rather are closed out by making a sale or purchase of an identical option with the two positions being offset by the exchange.

The holder of an option cannot lose more than was paid for it. An option buyer gains if its quoted value rises. That generally occurs with a call option when the stock price rises and with a put option when the stock price falls. The attraction is that the gain may be large relative to the cost of the option if the stock price changes by a large amount. In return for the option price the writer of an option is exposed to greater risk, since the loss, when the stock price rises above the call price or falls below the put price, is limited only by the possible extent of the stock price change within the option period. The writer may be "covered" or hedged against this risk, however, if he owns the stock that is callable under the option or is short the stock that may be put to him under a put option. His loss then is simply the sacrifice of part of the gain he would have had in the absence of the option. A covered option writer, in effect, is wagering that the price of the stock will not move sufficiently up under a call option or down under a put option to cost him money. If his wager pays off he is in pocket by the option price.

Several factors determine the value of an option right to a holder from time to time. For an option that is out-of-the-money, the longer the period to expiry, the more valuable the option will be. Also, the greater the volatility of the stock price, the more valuable the option will be, since the chance of significant gain as a result of the stock price rising above the exercise price (for a call) or falling below it (for a put) is thereby enhanced. As the stock price moves to approach the exercise price, the option value obviously will increase, and when the option is well in-the-money, its value will change virtually dollar for dollar with changes in the stock price. Because of the interaction of these factors, the value of an option can change substantially over its lifetime. At the expiry date obviously it becomes zero.

Accounting for options must be looked at from the viewpoint of both the option holder and the option writer. Both puts and calls must be considered. Finally, one must take into account whether or not the option writer or holder has a position in the stock that is the subject of the option, so that the option is a hedge against loss. Thus, eight possibilities need to be looked at.

Speculative options

The simplest situations to consider are those where neither the holder nor the writer of the option has a position in the stock that is the subject of the option.

That is to say, the option position is unhedged. We shall consider first the position of the holder.

Accounting by the holder — unhedged puts and calls. When the holder acquires an option and does not have a position in the related security, the option is clearly speculative. The holder has paid a price. The only possibility of gain is an increase in the option value before it expires. Three bases of accounting may be considered.

- The cost basis. This basis is unsatisfactory because the option is bound to become worthless at its expiry date. It would seem ridiculous to carry it at full cost right up to that date and then suddenly be forced to write it off. Moreover, the probable volatility in option values means that cost is likely to be an irrelevant figure within a very short time after its acquisition.
- The LOCAM basis. This basis is somewhat more acceptable since it would preclude reporting the asset at a figure above realizable value and it is consistent with the valuation basis of short-term assets generally. But it would still result in carrying values that have no significance much of the time.
- The market value basis. This is the only basis of valuation that is continuously relevant. It is also the only basis that faithfully represents the outcome of the speculative decision to acquire the right.

The latter arguments are similar to those made in favour of reporting marketable securities at market value. They are, however, even stronger for options than for marketable securities, because options cannot in any sense be said to have been acquired for the production of income rather than gain, and uncovered options cannot be said to have any part in a long-term investment strategy. It is hard to avoid a conclusion that speculative activity is best portrayed by valuing speculative option positions at market, regardless of the manner in which other assets and liabilities are reported.

It makes no difference to these conclusions whether the options are puts or calls.

Accounting by the writer — unhedged puts and calls. The writer of an uncovered option is in a mirror-image position to that of the purchaser. Instead of a right, the writer has an obligation for which a fee (the option price) has been received. The accounting possibilities are as follows:

- Record the option price as a liability until the option is closed out or expires. This basis would be unsatisfactory because the liability figure would become uninformative as the option price changes. The practice would also ignore losses (which might be major) before realization.
- Record the option obligation at the higher of the proceeds received and the current market price (hereafter, for convenience, referred to as HOPAM). This basis would be an improvement because it would not ignore apparent losses. The delay in recognition of any gain until realization would mean that results of the speculation would not be reported currently.
- Adjust the option obligation continuously to its market price. This basis would provide the best measure of the obligation since it would represent the figure at which the obligation could be settled on a continuing basis. It also would provide the most current and best measure of the result of the speculative decision to write the option.

Once again a market value basis of accounting seems best when a position is taken purely for speculative purposes. This conclusion would apply equally to put and call options.

Hedged options

An initial generalization with respect to hedged options seems obvious. If the investments that hedge the option position are accounted for on a market value basis, there is no question but that the option position should also be valued at market. This applies both to the option holder and the option writer. It is only when investments are not accounted for at market that questions arise.

Accounting by the holder — hedged call options. Consider first a call option that hedges a short position in the stock. In such a case, the holder is hoping to profit from a decline in the market price of stock that he is short, but by purchasing the call has limited his potential loss should the stock rise. The best answer in this case appears to be based on the presumption that the entire position is speculative. The only source of gain on a short position is a decline in the market value of the stock. The holding of the related call option limits the potential loss from a stock price rise but does not change the inherent speculative character of the activities. The best accounting, therefore, would be the market value basis for *both* the short position in the stock and the call option.

Accounting by the holder — hedged put options. Are the conclusions similar for a put option? In this case it may be arguable that the stock is held as an investment for the purpose of income and gain, but that the holder is willing to bear a cost to obtain some protection against a decline in its value. The accounting that seems appropriate varies, however, depending upon (1) whether the option is in-the-money or out-of-the-money when purchased, (2) whether the option is acquired at the same time as the stock or at some later date when the market price of the stock has moved away from its book value, and (3) whether the stock is accounted for at cost or LOCAM.

Consider, first, options that are out-of-the-money when purchased. Assume also, to begin with, that the related stock is accounted for at cost (unless long-term impairment has been suffered). It would be wrong to merge the option cost with the carrying value of the stock since the option has a limited life while the stock does not. Instead, the option cost should be carried as a separate asset, and it seems reasonable to begin to amortize it over the period to its expiry date. Amortization is logical even if the option's market value rises after acquisition, since a rise in the value of the option suggests a deterioration in the prospects for the underlying stock. If the latter deterioration is not to be recognized on the grounds that it may not become realized, it seems consistent to assume that the appreciation in the option value may also disappear before realization.

Subsequent to its acquisition (1) the option may be exercised (if the stock price declines below the exercise price of the put), (2) the option may be sold, or (3) it may expire. If the option is exercised when some balance of its cost remains unamortized, the loss on the option should be reported as an adjustment of the gain or loss on disposal of the stock. (There could be a gain on the stock even though the exercise of the put suggests a decline in the stock price. This could occur if the option was not acquired until some time after the stock, at which time the stock price had appreciated above its cost.)

If the option is sold at a figure that does not recover amortized cost, the loss should be recognized. The decision to hedge the downside risk on the stock has been terminated, and it is appropriate to write off the full cost of that decision. If the option is sold at a profit, the accounting is more debatable. A gain on the option suggests a deterioration in the stock price — the risk that was hedged by the option. If the carrying value of the stock is above its market price at the time the option is sold, it would seem reasonable to apply the gain on the option to reduce the carrying value of the stock to that market price. Any excess gain on the option may reasonably be recognized in income.

The foregoing discussion was based on the assumption that the underlying stock was accounted for at cost. If, instead, the accounting basis was LOCAM, one complication is added. One must consider how that basis is affected by changes in the market value of the option from time to time. The answer is that when a LOCAM test is applied to the stockholding on an item-by-item basis, it should take into account the option as well, because of the fact that the market value of the stock and the option tend to move in opposite directions. For example, suppose a stock is bought at $105 and simultaneously a put option is acquired for $5 with an exercise price of $100 (thereby limiting total potential loss on the position to $10). Subsequently, the stock price falls to $98 but the option price rises to $10 at a time when the option carrying value has been amortized down to $4. Thus the book value of the position is $105 + $4 = $109. If the LOCAM test is applied separately, carrying values would be written down to $98 + $4 = $102. But the combined market value would be $98 + $10 = $108. In this situation the write-down should be restricted to $1.

A further complication is added if the option is in-the-money when purchased. Consider a put option purchased that is related to a stock owned with a carrying value of $35. The current market value of the stock at the date of purchase is $33, the exercise price is $35, and the option costs $6. It would be unreasonable to amortize the entire $6 over the period to expiry of the option because, if the market price of the stock remains the same over the period, $2 will be recoverable by closing out the option just before its expiry. It would be equally unreasonable to add the $2 to the cost of the stock since the stock is already carried above market value, and in any event, the $2 is *not* part of the cost of the stock. A possible solution is to separate the option price into two parts — $4 to be accounted for on an amortized basis and $2 representing the in-the-money position. The latter asset would be carried unamortized before realization. It would, however, have to be included as part of cost in the application of the LOCAM test for the combined stock and option position.

Accounting by the writer — covered call options. Suppose a call is sold on a stock owned. One might argue that so long as the exercise price of the call is above the carrying value of the stock, the price received for the option is an assured gain. But that would not portray the economics of the situation. A stock that has limited upside potential because it is callable is not worth as much as a stock not subject to call. If the sale of the option were to be recognized as a realization, it would be necessary to offset some part of the cost of the stock against it to measure the gain, if any, realized. It would be more realistic to treat the option proceeds as an advance payment for the call right, representing revenue earned only over the period the call is outstanding. On that basis, if the option period is short enough to foresee a steady diminution in risk over the period, then the proceeds could be amortized to income over the period of the option. (Again, any portion of the proceeds attributable to the option being in-the-money should be accounted for separately and not be amortized.) In the alternative, it could be argued that deferral of income recognition until expiry or other settlement of the option would be more consistent with the realization emphasis implicit in accounting for the related stock at cost or LOCAM.

The option right will be extinguished as a result of (1) exercise by the holder, (2) repurchase by the writer, or (3) expiry. If the option is exercised, the credit balance(s) remaining in the accounts with respect to the option should be written off to income along with the gain or loss recorded on disposal of the stock. If the option is repurchased, the gain or loss should be recognized in income except that, to the extent the carrying value of the stock is above current market price, the gain on the option should be used to write down the stock. If the option simply expires, the unamortized portion of the option price, if any, should be taken into income.

If the related stock is accounted for on the LOCAM basis, the existence of the call option should be taken into account in the LOCAM calculation. Since the option represents an obligation, not an asset, the test that is applicable to it alone is HOPAM, not LOCAM. To arrive at the correct result, however, the two should be regarded as one position. For example, suppose the carrying amounts of the stock and call option are $96 and $5 respectively and their market values at the reporting date are $106 and $11. The LOCAM figured for the stock by itself is $96, and the HOPAM figure for the option is $11, which would require a loss to be recognized on the latter of $6. If the position is looked at on a combined basis, however, the net carrying value is $96 – $5 = $91 and the net market value is $106 – $11 = $95. No loss recognition is required.

Accounting by the writer — covered put options. The risk of the writer under a put option may be covered by a short position in the stock. (This is a somewhat unlikely combination of positions.) The put option by itself would be a purely speculative position. Likewise, a short sale by itself is purely speculative. The speculative character is not changed by the existence of the two positions together; there is simply a change in the dimensions of the speculation. Accordingly, the best accounting basis for the two positions is market value, with changes in value being immediately recognized in income.

Accounting for futures contracts

As noted already, the difference between a futures contract and an option contract lies in the fact that the former binds *both* buyer and seller according to its terms. The commitment is two-sided, whereas only the seller is obligated under an option and then only if the buyer chooses to exercise it.

The contracts differ also in that the purchaser *buys* his option right, and thereafter there is no further cash movement associated with the contract unless it is exercised or closed out. In contrast, nothing is paid initially on a futures contract price but both buyer and seller are required to put up margin through the broker with the exchange as a guarantee of performance. Thereafter, as the market value of the contract changes day by day, the contract is "marked to market." This means that if the value of the contract advances, the seller must put up a "variation margin" equal to the difference between the original contract price and the current value, while the buyer is entitled to withdraw a like amount (and conversely if the value of the contract declines). Because the contract is regularly marked to market in this way, no additional cash need flow between buyer and seller through the exchange when the contract is closed out before delivery. At the time of close-out the parties are entitled to withdraw their margins plus gains from marking to market not previously withdrawn (if any).

As futures markets have expanded, the concept that they deal in contracts for a rigorously defined, deliverable commodity has also been stretched. Interest-rate futures contracts, for example, are quoted based upon delivery of defined securities such as a nine-percent coupon Government of Canada bond maturing in eighteen years from the contract maturity date. But delivery requirements may be satisfied through delivery of a longer-term bond or a bond with a different coupon rate with appropriate adjustment in price.

A more extreme departure from the basic concept is found in contracts for stock-index futures. Buyers and sellers of these contracts are, in effect, making bets on the future course of the stock market as a whole. If the contract goes full term, the bets are paid off in dollars, not in a deliverable commodity, with the number of dollars being established by the difference between the actual index value at the contract maturity date and the index value stated in the contract. (Most contracts, however, would be closed out before maturity.) It thus appears that any variable that can be measured in a fashion generally accepted as satisfactory could be made the subject of exchange-traded futures contracts if there is enough interest to make trading in the contract economic.

Speculative futures contracts

As with options, a futures contract entered into as a speculation is best accounted for on a current value basis. The results of the speculation are best portrayed if the resulting adjustments to current value are reported in income as they occur. It could be argued that when an investment portfolio is reported on a LOCAM basis it would be consistent to defer gains until settlement of the futures contract. The FASB has rejected this argument on the grounds that futures contracts are different in character from investments.

Futures contracts that are hedges

When contracts are entered into as hedges of risk positions, it is generally considered that accrued gains and losses on contracts should not be taken directly to income. The somewhat imperfect character of hedges in the real world, however, and a certain fuzziness in the concept of hedging combine to make it very difficult to give completely satisfactory accounting guidance. In general, the accounting for a hedge varies depending upon whether the hedge is of a commitment or whether it is of an existing asset or liability position. In the latter case, the accounting may also vary so as to make sense in combination with the accounting for the related asset or liability. A number of specific situations are discussed below.

Hedge of an existing asset. The simplest situation to consider is that of a trader or investor in commodities or securities that are financed entirely by equity. Such an entity is directly at risk from changes in the prices of its assets. It may well be possible to sell futures contracts that provide effective hedges against price changes in individual assets for the duration of the futures contract — commodity futures or interest-rate futures as applicable. If the accounting basis for the assets is market value, the logical accounting basis for the futures contracts would also be market value. In this way, gains and losses recognized on changes in market value of the assets is offset by losses and gains recorded on the futures contracts, and the net result would properly portray the effect of the hedge.

Many entities (including some traders and dealers) do not use a market value basis of accounting, but rather use the LOCAM basis. In such a case the logical accounting for the futures contract changes. Consider the purchase of a long-term bond recorded at cost and simultaneous sale of an interest-rate futures contract. If the market value of that bond falls, there should be a compensating gain on the futures contract. When the futures contract is closed out, that gain could be credited to the carrying value of the bond as though it were an adjustment of its cost. The result, if the hedge is effective, is that the revised carrying value should be very close to the market value of the bond. That seems sensible since the purpose of the hedge is to protect against changes in the price of the bond. If the bond investment is accounted for on an amortized basis, the credit of the futures contract gain to the asset will mean an adjustment in the rate of amortization. Technically that adjustment should take place as the gain accrues, but for convenience it may be delayed until realization.

Suppose, however, that the hedge was not put on when the bond was bought. Suppose the bond was bought at $100, rose in price to $105, at that point was hedged by a futures contract, and thereafter fell again to $100 at which time the futures contract was closed out. If the contract was a perfect hedge, a gain of $5 would have been accumulated and treatment of that gain as an adjustment of the bond carrying value would reduce that carrying value to $95. That does not seem quite so sensible. The carrying value has been adjusted *away* from market value rather than towards it as in the previous example.

The point is, of course, that a hedge preserves the value of the asset *at the time the hedge contract is entered into*. Hedging, if successful, ensures that any excess of market value over book value of the property at the date the hedge is entered into will be preserved so long as the hedge is in existence. The somewhat odd result here in essence is attributable to the fact that the LOCAM basis of accounting does not permit recognition of gain before realization. Since the futures contract is identified as a hedge of the bond investment, and that investment has not been sold, gain cannot be recognized in income. To avoid recognition, the gain on the futures contract is credited to the book value of the asset hedged.

Hedge of existing liability. Now consider the same trader or investor, but this time assume the asset position is partly financed by fixed-interest debt with a fixed term to maturity. The economic position of the equity is now influenced not only by changes in the market value of the assets but also by changes in the fair value of the debt. Even if the debt is not redeemable before maturity, it would normally be possible for the entity to buy securities that could meet all the debt obligations (so that the position would be tantamount to debt redemption), and it is highly unlikely that the cost of those securities would equal the book value of the debt.

The risk to the equity position attributable to the debt may already be hedged if some of the assets of the entity are reasonably equivalent interest-bearing securities. If not, the purchase of an interest-rate futures contract could hedge the debt position, and the question of appropriate accounting arises. In this situation it is not customary accounting to adjust debt book values to current values even if the assets are carried on a market value basis. Therefore the question of recording the futures contract at market does not arise. Instead, on reasoning similar to that for hedges of interest-bearing assets, gain or loss on the contract could be treated as an adjustment of the premium or discount inherent in the debt carrying value. As in the case of the hedged bond investment, future amortization of the debt premium or discount after adjustment would have to be recalculated so that the gain or loss on the hedge would, in effect, be recognized in income over the term to maturity.

Hedges of net asset and liability positions. Some financial intermediaries are particularly vulnerable to risk from asset price changes, both because they may be faced with sudden requirements for liquidity and because their licence to do business under regulation typically depends upon maintenance of a margin of safety between asset values and liabilities. Hedging risk positions may be very desirable in this situation but the entity needs to be careful of the point made earlier — certain of the asset and liability positions may naturally hedge each other so that further hedging by futures contracts would increase risk. In particular, interest-bearing liabilities and interest-bearing assets can hedge each other against value changes attributable to changes in the general level of interest rates.

The mere existence of interest-bearing assets and liabilities acquired at the same time does not necessarily mean that a perfect natural hedge exists. If, for example, the asset matures in fifteen years and the debt matures in five years, the asset may well be worth less than its face value at the time the debt must be paid off. Even if the maturity dates of the asset and liability are the same, interest-rate risk will not be completely eliminated if the timing of the cash flows connected with the asset and liability is different. For example, suppose a purchase of a ten-year bond bearing semiannual coupons is financed by a ten-year zero-coupon liability. Most of the amount payable at maturity of the latter will represent accrued interest. To meet that liability, much of the interest received on the bond investment will have to be accumulated. If interest rates fall over the ten years, the amount accumulated will fall short of the amount required to pay off the zero-coupon liability. In technical terms, the asset and the liability do not have the same "duration" even though the maturity dates are the same, because the cash receipts from the investment will be received earlier, on average, than the cash payable on the liability.

This situation suggests that a financial institution should look to its future cash inflows and outflows attributable to its entire portfolios of assets and liabilities to assess its interest-rate risk position and determine appropriate hedges for the risk. Unfortunately, hedging on such a "macro" basis makes it very difficult to follow the accounting approaches described previously — that is, to associate specific hedges with specific asset and liability positions so that gains and losses on the hedging instruments are used to adjust the carrying value of specific assets and liabilities, with subsequent amortization to income.

Hedges of commitments. An entity may be exposed to risks as a result of commitments as well as positions in presently owned assets or liabilities. A financial intermediary, for example, under some conditions might be willing to make mortgage loan commitments at fixed interest rates several months before the money is to be advanced.

By so doing it exposes itself to the risk that the mortgages receivable may not be worth face value at the time they are acquired because of changes in interest rates after the commitment was undertaken. An interest-rate futures contract can hedge this risk. The logical accounting would be to treat any gain or loss on such hedge contracts as an adjustment to the carrying value of the mortgages, to be amortized to income over the period the mortgages are outstanding.

Likewise, an ordinary operating business may undertake commitments for various reasons. For example, to assure supply a business may place fixed-price orders for crucial raw materials for future delivery. Since the commitment price is fixed, there is a risk that the market price may be lower at the actual delivery date, giving competitors an advantage. To offset this risk the business might sell a futures contract for the commodity in question. Deferral of gain or loss on the futures contract and treating it as an adjustment of the purchase cost when delivery is taken would correct the purchase price to approximate market at the delivery date and give proper recognition to the intention of the hedge. (It may be noted that long-standing accounting tradition requires that purchase commitments be taken into account as though they were inventory on hand in applying the LOCAM test to inventory. Purchase commitments that have been hedged in the manner described from their inception may be excluded from this calculation.)

Anticipatory hedges

If a fixed-price commitment to buy can be hedged, what about a situation in which future purchases are certain or probable but there is no commitment? Manufacturing enterprises are virtually certain to be buying their basic raw materials on a regular basis once they have invested their resources to commence business. Some financial intermediaries such as life insurance companies are virtually assured of a regular inflow of funds requiring investment. In these situations, an enterprise may wish to "lock in" current prices for future material prices or "lock in" current yields on interest-bearing investments.

That can be done, some think, by buying commodity futures or interest-rate futures. A futures purchase in such a situation has been called an "anticipatory hedge," and it is argued that when a business is highly likely to buy the item in question because of the circumstances of the business, an anticipatory hedge should be accounted for as if it were simply an alternative to a fixed purchase commitment. To achieve this, no gain or loss on the hedge would be recognized in income. Rather, changes in the value of the futures contract would be deferred and ultimately treated as an adjustment to the cost of the item deemed hedged.

This position is open to question. An alternative basis of accounting would record the purchase of the property in question at its actual cost and recognize gain or loss on the futures contract as though it were speculative. It is arguable that this would be a more faithful representation of the economic performance of the business and the results of management decision making. The property purchased would be recorded at its actual cost — a basis more comparable with that of other entities. The result of management's good (or bad) decision making in buying the futures contract would be recorded separately.

A possible objection to such accounting lies in the argument that buying the futures contract is equivalent to making a fixed-purchase-price commitment. Both have the effect of fixing in advance the amount of dollars required to purchase the needed asset. This argument does indeed suggest the desirability of consistency in the accounting. Consistency could be achieved in another way, however, when a commodity is acquired on a fixed-price basis in accordance with a commitment entered into before it was necessary. When quantities to be purchased are freely available in the spot market so that it is feasible to delay a purchase commitment until near the time of delivery, it could be informative to record the purchase at the current market price at the time orders would have had to be placed for delivery, and treat the difference between that figure and the fixed-price contract figure as a gain or loss attributable to the decision to contract early.

The strongest argument for hedge accounting for a futures contract in a raw material of a business is that the business must regularly purchase that commodity. That argument does not apply with nearly the same force to the case of financial intermediaries. While it will often be true that such companies have a regular inflow of funds requiring them to invest, their choice of acceptable investment vehicles may be quite wide. They may, as a matter of policy, wish to put a certain portion of their funds in interest-bearing securities. They may also, at any given time, wish to lock in interest rates for future purchases by buying interest-rate futures contracts. When the future arrives, however, the investment in the securities previously intended may well not be the best choice available out of the spectrum of possible investments and still less would be the choice if the actual cost figure were as high as a figure of current market price plus loss on the futures contract. The argument in favour of anticipatory-hedge accounting in this business situation, therefore, is even weaker than it is for a business buying a futures contract in a commodity it has to acquire.

FASB recommendations for accounting for futures contracts

The FASB guidance for accounting for futures contracts is along the following lines:

- An initial decision must be made whether the futures contract qualifies as a hedge. These are the criteria for qualification:
  - The position (asset, liability, or commitment) deemed hedged is exposed to price (or interest-rate) risk and is actually contributing to the overall risk of the entity. That is to say, the risk is not already hedged by the existence of other assets, liabilities, or commitments.
  - The futures contract is designated as a hedge of a specific risk exposure (the designation and basis of the hedge should be documented).
  - There is a clear economic relationship between the subject of the futures contract and the thing hedged. At the outset of the hedge, past experience must indicate that high correlation of price change is probable.
- If a contract does not qualify as a hedge, it should be accounted for at market value with gains and losses as the contract is marked to market being taken directly to income. This is not considered inconsistent with a LOCAM basis of accounting for investments owned by the same entity, since it is held that futures contracts are different in character from investments. In addition, the cash payable or receivable from the exchange as a result of daily marking to market of a futures contract can be considered to be realization of gains and losses.
- Even if a contract is considered a hedge, it should be accounted for on a market value basis if the asset or liability or commitment hedged is also accounted for on the basis of market value. Gains and losses recognized on

one position will offset losses or gains recognized on the other, which faithfully represents the purpose and economics of a hedge.

- When a contract hedges a position not accounted for at market, different accounting applies. First, where the futures contract hedges a specific item that is deliverable (that is, the futures contract is not a cross-hedge — a contract for delivery of something not identical to the item hedged) and it is probable that the hedged item and the futures contract will be retained to the delivery date specified in the contract, the difference between the futures contract price and the fair value of the item hedged (the "basis") *may* be amortized to income over the life of the contract. Except for this possible separate treatment of basis, any gain or loss on the contract should be regarded as an adjustment of the carrying value of the item hedged. The adjusted value will be subject to evaluation under the LOCAM test if that test is applicable to that item.
- When an item hedged is accounted for on an amortized basis (that is, differences between face value and carrying value are amortized to income over its period to maturity), adjustments of carrying value for gains and losses on futures contracts must also be amortized. While theoretically this amortization should begin as soon as the gain or loss occurs (that is, daily), as a practical matter it may be delayed until the time the futures contract is closed out.
- Futures contracts that are not related to existing asset, liability, or firm commitment positions may nevertheless be accounted for as hedges (i.e., anticipatory hedges) if they meet the hedge qualification criteria referred to above, and if
  - the significant characteristics of the anticipated exposed position (expected dates of transactions, type of commodity or financial instrument involved, expected quantity involved, and term to maturity [if a financial instrument]) are identified; and
  - there is a high level of assurance that the anticipated transactions will occur, as evidenced by such factors as the frequency of similar transactions in the past, the commitment of resources to the activity so that the proposed transactions are in the normal course, and so on.
- The market value of a futures contract designated as a hedge should continue to exhibit a high correlation with the market value of the item hedged. If it fails to do so, hedge accounting should be discontinued, and any difference between price changes on the contract and market value changes on the items hedged should be written off.
- When futures contracts have been accounted for as hedges, disclosure should be made of the nature of assets, liabilities, firm commitments, or anticipated transactions hedged and the method of accounting for the futures contracts. (Disclosure of accounting for speculative contracts would presumably be included in the general description of accounting policies if material.)

Evaluation of accounting for hedges through futures contracts

It is apparent that accounting for futures contracts as hedges is complex and may not be fully satisfactory. Two or three areas need further consideration. First, it is not clear how effectively interest-rate futures contracts can hedge individual monetary investment or liability positions. Accordingly, hedge accounting based on matching hedge contracts with individual positions may not work well. Second, the accounting for "basis" risk in futures contracts is not well specified and may need further thought. Third, the idea of accounting for anticipatory hedges is questionable. It is usually considered that undertaking a fixed-price commitment for future delivery creates risk exposure. Such exposure can be created, for example, by placing a firm order with a supplier of materials before necessary. Identical exposure can be created by buying a futures contract. If that is so, it is hard to see why the futures contract should be regarded as a hedge, whether anticipatory or otherwise. Rather, it seems to be a speculation on which gain or loss should be recognized as it occurs. If this is conceded, of course, it follows that when a firm order is entered into with a supplier before necessary, that too is a speculation that should lead to gain or loss recognition. This is not the customary accounting now, with the exception of loss recognition on inventory commitments.

Accounting for interest-rate swaps

A swap is a bilateral agreement (between so-called "counterparties") to exchange cash payments at specified future dates. In an interest-rate swap the future payments are tied to stated interest rates or standard interest-rate definitions, such as the prime rate. In the simplest type of swap two counterparties agree to swap interest payments on identical principal amounts of debt. This does not mean that each pays the interest on the other party's debt. Rather, it means that each pays to the other party an amount equal to the interest that the other must pay to its creditors.

In practice, swap contracts are likely to be arranged with a bank or other financial intermediary standing between the two parties. That is, each party will contract with the bank, not directly with the other party. A possible motive for an interest-rate swap could be to exchange a fixed-rate interest obligation for a floating-rate obligation, or conversely. Such an exchange might reduce risk for both parties. For example, the party with a fixed-interest obligation might have assets producing income tied to floating rates, while the other party may be in the opposite situation. The number of possible advantages expands when obligations in different currencies are swapped (to be discussed further in chapter 20). For example, a company may be able to borrow more cheaply for the long term in a foreign currency, and then by a swap may cover its foreign currency risk exposure. Finally, a swap contract may be used to speculate as well as to shed risk. For example, a company with no debt might agree to swap a floating-rate interest payment obligation for a fixed-rate obligation if it thought interest rates were likely to increase.

Accounting for speculative swap contracts

When a speculative swap is entered into, the rights acquired and obligations undertaken are presumably of equal value. An argument could be made that these rights and obligations are very similar to investments and debt obligations, and therefore should be recognized as assets and liabilities in the balance sheet. In practice, however, they are not so recognized, which may be considered to be consistent with the accepted accounting treatment for futures contracts and for commitments generally. Fees paid or to be paid for the contract may reasonably be amortized over its life.

As time passes and conditions change, the value of the rights swapped will change, and one will ordinarily become more valuable than the other, at least temporarily. If, as has been argued, speculative positions are best valued on a mark-to-market basis, the swap commitments should likewise be valued and gain or loss recognized. In the absence of a quoted market value, a contract could be valued by calculating the excess or shortfall of the future stream of payments versus the future stream of receipts, assuming continuation of present conditions (e.g., the present difference between the fixed- and floating rate payments) and discounting the net stream to a present value.

Accounting for matched swap contracts

When a swap contract is effectively substituted for an identified existing asset or obligation, the swap is said to be matched. The prime concern, when a matched swap exists, is proper disclosure of the related asset or obligation. For example, if the contract has the effect of converting floating rate debt into fixed-rate debt, that fact needs to be disclosed, including the newly effective fixed rate. It should not be implied, however, that the actual debt obligation outstanding is at a fixed rate, since the swap contract will normally be subject to early termination in some circumstances. The existence of special covenants under the contract (if significant) and the possibility of early termination should be disclosed.

A swap contract is likely to call for a lump sum payment from one party to the other in the event of early termination. Likewise, a sale of a favourable swap position can produce a gain. If the contract terminated or sold has been accounted for as matching an existing asset or obligation, the question arises as to the treatment of the gain or loss on termination or sale. Different opinions are held on this. The prevailing sentiment in the United States appears to be that such gain or loss should be deferred and amortized over the shorter of the period to the end of the swap contract or the position with which it was previously matched.

A swap contract may be less than a perfect match for the interest-bearing asset or obligation with which it is linked. For example, if a primary obligation carrying a floating rate is matched with a swap contract that exchanges a floating-rate commitment for a fixed-rate commitment, but the floating-rate commitment in the swap contract is defined differently from the floating rate under the primary obligation, the match may be imperfect. It is necessary to be careful in such a case that the disclosure of the debt obligation and swap contract does not imply that the effective interest cost has become completely fixed by the swap arrangement. (It is conceivable, if the variable rate under the swap contract departed significantly from the primary obligation rate and looked likely to continue to do so, that loss recognition would be appropriate.)

A swap may also be less than a perfect match for a floating-rate demand obligation if the amount of that primary obligation varies from time to time — perhaps on a seasonal basis. If the unmatched position becomes significant and persists for significant periods of time, consideration will have to be given to treating the swap contract as at least partly speculative.

The variety in possible forms of swap contracts continues to increase so that their recognition in accounting needs to be considered almost on a case-by-case basis. The general principles that have developed so far seem to be as follows: Commitments under swap contracts that are purely speculative need to be valued upon some basis and gain and loss recognized when they become unbalanced. On the other hand, when swap contracts are matched with existing balance sheet positions the problem is largely one of giving appropriate disclosure to the changes in terms and risks of those positions because of the swap contract. Since swap contracts are not always perfect matches, it is necessary to be on the alert to the need for special accounting recognition with respect to the unmatched aspects of the contract.

Summary

In the ordinary business, accounting for portfolio investments is significantly influenced by their classification in the balance sheet.

- Investments classified as current are typically carried at LOCAM. "Market" means realizable value at the reporting date. The market test may be applied to each individual security or, probably more commonly, in the aggregate for the entire portfolio classified as current. A holding that has been written down may subsequently be written up to cost if market recovers.
- Investments classified as noncurrent may also be described as being carried at LOCAM. In this case, however, the meaning of market is the looser term "recoverable value," and a write-down is made only when it is considered that the decline in value is other than temporary. The test is applied by individual security, rather than by the holding in the aggregate, and a write-down, when made, may not be reversed before realization.

Some industries follow accounting practices that differ from those described above, for reasons peculiar to their specialized situations.

- Investment companies and brokers and dealers in securities generally value all investments at market value or estimated fair value where market prices are not available, recognizing both realized and unrealized gains and losses in income.
- Certain financial institutions may wish to treat realized gains and losses on fixed-term securities on the "deferral and amortization" basis. That is to say, realized gains and losses are initially deferred and are amortized to income over the term to maturity of the security sold.
- Certain financial institutions may also wish to adjust carrying values of equity securities to a moving average of market values over a specific period, recognizing the net effect of these adjustments together with realized gains and losses in income.

None of the above methods of investment accounting is given any recognition in the *CICA Handbook*. However, the existence of specialized industry situations may permit a conclusion that the methods are generally accepted in the context of that industry. It is clear that the market value basis for investment companies and brokers and dealers is generally accepted as appropriate to the industry characteristics. The deferral and amortization method may also be considered generally accepted in restricted circumstances, based on its use in some situations and on support for it in influential accounting literature. Moving-average valuation bases for equity securities, or other accounting methods having similar objectives, are little used, and it is doubtful that they can be considered generally accepted.

Accounting for options and futures contracts depends upon whether they represent speculation or whether they hedge risk positions in some other asset or liability. If options and futures are speculative, they should be accounted for on a market value basis with adjustments to market being reflected in current income. In addition, if they hedge another risk position, but that position is accounted for at market value, the hedging options or futures contracts should also be accounted for at market value. Accounting for other hedge positions is described below.

Premiums paid or received with respect to options bought or written should be allocated between an amount equal to the in-the-money status of the option when purchased (if any) and the remainder. The latter amount should be amortized over the remaining term of the option. If the position hedged by the option is liquidated before the option expires, any balance(s) of premium remaining unamortized should be written off as an adjustment to the gain or loss on the position hedged. If the option position is closed out on its own before its expiry date, gain or loss can be recognized except that gain should be used to write down the position hedged to the extent that its book value is above market at that date.

Gain or loss recorded on the mark-to-market basis for a futures contract hedging an asset or liability position should apply against the carrying value of the position. In practice, the gain or loss may be deferred until close-out of the contract and applied to the asset at that time.

Gain or loss on a futures contract hedging a purchase commitment is deferred until the asset is purchased. At that time, the gain or loss is used to adjust the carrying value of the asset acquired.

There is precedent for treating a futures contract as an anticipatory hedge — that is, treating it as though it were a hedge of a future transaction that is expected but not a firm commitment. It is questionable whether such accounting provides the best representation of management decision making.

If futures contracts are to be accounted for as hedges, it is important that they be identified as such and that there be evidence that they will be effective as hedges. The FASB has provided detailed recommendations to guide the accounting.

Accounting for interest-rate swaps is still in a development stage in view of the relative novelty of these arrangements and their evolving character. Most swap contracts to date are entered into to change the risk characteristics of associated assets or liabilities recorded in the balance sheet. Accounting recognition given to these matched contracts consists mainly of disclosure of their important provisions and the effect they have in changing the effective interest income or expense of the related position. Swap contracts can also be speculative, in which case the preferable accounting treatment is to recognize gain or loss as it accrues.

References

[1]CICA, "Long-term Investments," *CICA Handbook*, Section 3050 (Toronto: CICA), pars. 27-33. See also an Auditing Interpretation by the Staff of the Auditing Standards Division of the AICPA, "Evidential Matter for the Carrying Amount of Marketable Securities," published in the *Journal of Accountancy*, April 1975, pp. 69-70.

[2]This meaning, which is assigned to the term "recoverable value" in practice, is in conflict with the recent use of a similar term in *CICA Handbook*, Section 4510, "Reporting the Effects of Changing Prices," par. 15(e). There, "recoverable amount" may be either the net realizable value of an asset or its "value in use." The latter term describes a discounted figure.

[3]*CICA Handbook*, Section 3050, par. 35.

[4]FASB, *Accounting for Certain Marketable Securities*, Statement of Financial Accounting Standards No. 12 (Stamford: FASB, 1975).

[5]A recent CICA research study advocates, however, the use of market values for assets in pension plan financial statements *and also* valuation of liabilities at current values. See *Financial Statements for Pension Plan Participants* (Toronto: CICA, 1984).

[6]For a fuller illustration of this effect, see R.M. Skinner, "Accounting for Profits and Losses on Investments," *Canadian Chartered Accountant*, April 1961, pp. 327-33, and M. Moonitz, "Accounting for Investments in Debt Securities," in *Essays in Honor of William A. Paton*, ed. S.A. Zeff, J. Demski, and N. Dopuch (Ann Arbor, Mich.: Division of Research, Graduate School of Business Administration, University of Michigan, 1979), pp. 57-72. It should be added that, although Moonitz agrees that no profit or loss occurs at the date one debt security is exchanged for another, he is an advocate of market value based accounting rather than "deferral and amortization" accounting.

[7]The operation of moving-average methods is more fully explained in the CICA Research Study, *Accounting for Portfolio Investments* (Toronto: CICA, 1984).

[8]W.J. Morris and B.A. Coda, "Valuation of Equity Securities," *Journal of Accountancy*, January 1973, pp. 48-54.

[9]See W.H. Beaver, "Reporting Rules for Marketable Equity Securities," *Journal of Accountancy*, October 1971, pp. 57-61, and "Accounting for Marketable Equity Securities," *Journal of Accountancy*, December 1973, pp. 58-64.

[10]See letter to the editor by Morris and Coda in *Journal of Accountancy*, December 1973, pp. 36-38.

[11]*CICA, Accounting for Portfolio Investments.*

[12]FASB, *Accounting for Futures Contracts*, Statement of Financial Accounting Standards No. 80 (Stamford: FASB, 1984).

Chapter Seventeen

Recognition of Gains and Losses; Statement Presentation of Gains and Losses and Other Accounting Adjustments; Accounting for Capital

Previous chapters have dealt with the recognition and measurement of normal recurring operating and investment transactions. We now come to consideration of the accounting recognition given to unplanned gains and losses, occasional adjustments in accounting, and capital transactions. First, we deal with accounting for gains and losses that interrupt the smooth pattern of recognition of revenues and expenses. Then we turn to the financial statement classification and disclosure of these gains and losses, and to the statement presentation of other adjustments to carrying values of assets and liabilities resulting from various types of accounting changes. In the third major section we discuss the accounting for the ownership interest in an entity, with particular emphasis on capital transactions and capital gains and losses. We comment also on a few types of gain or loss or adjustment that are credited or charged to the ownership interest without being clearly identified as either income or capital.

Gain and loss recognition

Gains and losses to be discussed in this chapter fall into two broad categories:

- Losses to be recognized with respect to operating assets when the normal expense recognition rules are inadequate (e.g., write-downs of inventory).
- Gains and losses resulting from transactions or events that are peripheral or merely incidental to the main business activity of the entity.

The first category above might have been dealt with in earlier chapters dealing with individual assets. Discussion has been consolidated here, however, to see to what extent practices in recognition of losses are consistent, one with another.

Recognition of loss on asset write-downs

When, as often happens, the market value or value in use of an asset appears to be less than its carrying value on the books, what should be done? Given the emphasis in historical cost accounting theory upon measurement of the results of completed earnings transactions, it might be argued that nothing should be done because realized income is most accurately portrayed simply by matching costs actually incurred with resulting proceeds.

On the other hand, it can be argued that expense recognition is essentially a process of writing off costs whose benefit has expired. If a cost incurred cannot be recovered from future revenue, its benefit has clearly expired and it should be written off.

Two conflicting concepts underlie these arguments. One is a concept of a business as consisting of a series of overlapping ventures. The focus of accounting is on the individual venture (investment in product), and the emphasis is on portraying the outcome of complete ventures. The other is a concept of a business as one integrated and continuing venture. The ceiling valuation of all assets committed to the venture is cost. That cost is to be reduced and expense recognized whenever its benefit expires — whether it clearly applies to revenue recognized already or whether its benefit has been lost for some other reason.

The historical development of accounting practice has supported the latter point of view. Increasingly complex business processes made it convenient to use cost as a basis for valuation of productive assets. The nineteenth-century dividend cases did not require that capital be maintained but did suggest that circulating capital should not be valued above realizable value. The use of financial statements for credit purposes made lower of cost and market (LOCAM) a widely accepted basis of asset valuation. The advent of the income tax established the principle of realization for income tax (meaning that assets could not be valued above cost before realization). It also provided an incentive to write down assets below cost when possible. Thus, LOCAM became well established as the basis for valuation of working capital, although accounting for investment in fixed and other assets has remained more doubtful.

Several issues require clarification in relation to recognition of losses on assets held. Precisely how is market value or realizable value or recoverable value to be interpreted? Must there be an examination of the relationship between cost and market value for each individual asset or may it be accomplished by groups of assets? Once assets have been written down, may they be written up again if market value recovers? These issues will be discussed in the context of individual asset categories.

Inventories

The meaning of "market". In Canada, there have been no CICA recommendations as to the meaning of "market" in the phrase "lower of cost and market," but practice is fairly well established.[1] Since inventory is acquired for resale, the relevant market price is a selling price. Also, the price that is relevant is not necessarily the quoted selling price for goods at the financial reporting date, but rather the actual price that will be achieved on sales after the period-end. Market is thus taken as realizable value less costs that would directly and necessarily be incurred to effect a sale. Because of this emphasis on an actual cash value for the inventory, it would be logical to discount the estimated net proceeds should realization be likely to be delayed. For inventory that will turn over within a normal short period, however, this refinement is ignored.

Inventory held that is not ready for sale, such as work in process and raw materials, is more difficult to value at net realizable value because both the ultimate sales price and costs to complete and sell are less certain. For these reasons, the interpretation of the term "market" may shift to replacement cost for raw materials, plus manufacturing costs incurred to date for work in process in the early stages. Reliance on replacement cost is based on an expectation that selling prices will tend to move in step with replacement costs. When that is not a reasonable expectation a write-down to replacement cost may not be required. Conversely, a write-down may be required when ultimate realizable value has obviously declined even though replacement costs have not declined.

In a majority of business situations a profit margin over replacement cost is available, so that inventory written down to replacement cost will normally yield a margin. Inventory written down just to realizable value, however, will not yield a margin. One could therefore argue that the use of realizable value as a test for market for one section of inventory and replacement cost for another is inconsistent. In practice, however, that inconsistency exists. The accepted idea is that inventory need not be written down so far as to assure a profit in the following accounting period. The use of replacement cost for valuation of raw materials and work in process in its early stages is merely an expedient.

The valuation of inventory of retailers represents an exception to the statement that the term market ordinarily means net realizable value. In many retail enterprises it would be an unreasonably onerous task to price all items of inventory on hand at their specific cost. It is therefore accepted that cost or LOCAM may be estimated by the "retail method" of inventory valuation. Under this method, inventory is first priced on the basis of selling prices marked on the product, and a percentage deduction is made from the total selling price for the inventory (or for major groupings of inventory) to reduce to cost or LOCAM.

The percentage deduction is developed from stock purchase records priced at both cost and retail. If the retail prices used in this calculation are modified to allow for mark-ups and mark-downs subsequent to purchase of the stock, the percentage arrived at will represent the average gross profit realized on sale. Application of this percentage to inventory priced at retail at any particular date should reduce it to approximate cost. On the other hand, if retail prices in the calculation are not adjusted for subsequent mark-downs, a larger percentage will be developed that represents a normal or target gross profit. If this percentage is applied to items in inventory that have been marked down from their original selling price, those items will be priced below cost, and the inventory as a whole can be described as being priced, on average, at the lower of cost and selling price less a normal percentage margin. That percentage must cover selling costs. Since these represent a much higher proportion of total cost in a retailer than in most other industries, this departure from the use of straight net realizable value is less important than it might seem at first sight.[2]

In the United States, in contrast to Canada, replacement cost is taken as the dominant interpretation of market price. This is qualified by a provision that an inventory item need not be written down as far as replacement cost if that would yield more than the normal profit margin on estimated selling price. On the other hand, if replacement costs remain equal to or above historical cost but selling prices decline, the inventory must be written down if historical cost exceeds net realizable value. Thus, for much of the time the American rule will cause write-downs to allow a profit margin in the next accounting period, but that will not always be the case.

Application of the market test. In both countries the most common practice is to compare cost and market prices for individual inventory items in applying the LOCAM test. When this is done, the figure to which an inventory item is written down is assumed to be its "cost" so long as the item continues to be held. That is to say, an item cannot be written down in one period and then, if still on hand at the end of the next, be written back up. A considerably less common practice is to compare the aggregate cost of inventory with aggregate market value for each natural product division in the inventory rather than item by item. If this is done, the net write-down is not attributed to specific products, and it is therefore more difficult to prevent a write-down in one period being offset by a recovery in net realizable value in the next.

United States literature also states that if a business is expected to lose money for a sustained period, the inventory need not be written down to offset a loss inherent in subsequent operations. The logic of this rule seems questionable. What it seems to say is that if conditions are so bad that much of the inventory is costed above net realizable value, write-downs need not be made, but if conditions are not so bad they should be made. At the very least, special disclosure should be made if an entity adopts this departure from normal valuation practice.

Although purchase commitments for inventory are not recorded in the formal accounts, the tradition of conservatism calls for a provision for loss on the same basis as would be required if the goods on order had been received. Similarly, when a contractor estimates that losses will be incurred on a contract in hand, a full provision for the estimated loss on the total contract is to be made even though the contract is incomplete at the reporting date.

Fixed assets

Property, plant, and equipment held for use is at the opposite extreme from inventory held for sale. Declines in value as a result of use should be allowed for by a systematic depreciation provision over the estimated useful life of the asset. That leaves the accountant with the question of what to do when it appears, as occasionally happens, that the carrying value of the property, plant, and equipment is impaired and unlikely to recover.

Are write-downs necessary? Authoritative accounting literature is ambivalent on this question. On the one hand, the accountant's conservative instinct urges him to record all losses that have been suffered even though realization has not taken place. On the other hand, several considerations give him pause. The chief problem is to estimate a figure of value recoverable from an asset. Unless it is obviously near the end of its physical life, one often cannot be sure that economic conditions will not change so as to give it a new lease on life. In addition, since future cash flow is the product of many resources working together, it is hard to assign impairment of value to specific assets unless they are distinguishable in some way. (For example, it might be evident that a whole plant or division is obsolete.) In view of the subjectivity of estimates of recoverable value, there could be abuses. A management, particularly one newly placed in charge, might wish to write down assets sharply (the so-called "big bath" treatment) to relieve future reported income of some of the burden of depreciation. Consequently, the present accounting position is well summarized as follows:

> In unusual circumstances *persuasive evidence may exist of impairment of the utility of productive facilities indicative of an inability to recover cost although the facilities have not become worthless. The amount at which those facilities are carried is* sometimes *reduced to recoverable cost and a loss recorded prior to disposition or expiration of the useful life of the facilities.*[3] (emphasis added)

Basis for write-downs. If property, plant, and equipment is to be written down when value is impaired, it is necessary to decide what is appropriate as a new basis of valuation. An estimate of the net amount realizable on disposition seems inappropriate if the value in use of the asset (the estimated net present value of future cash flows from the asset) is higher. A reduction to value in use, however, means that (if the new valuation is accurate) future operations may be expected to show a profit after depreciation on the new carrying value. Moreover, the amount of that profit will be determined by the discount rate assumed in the calculation of net present value. Many accountants feel that there is no need to charge operations today to allow a profit to be recorded in future. Therefore, the reduction in carrying value need only be to the recoverable amount, that is, to the amount of cash that actually will be recovered from use (or sale) of the asset in future, without any discounting.

Investments

Chapter 16 has discussed accounting for portfolio investments. In brief, it may be stated here that marketable securities classified as current assets are written down when their market value at a period-end is materially below cost. Where investments are classified as long-term, however, an individual investment holding is to be written down only when its realizable value has suffered a decline below carrying value that is considered to be "other than temporary." This applies to an investment in common shares that is large enough to carry significant influence upon the investee (and therefore is accounted for on the equity basis of accounting) as well as to ordinary portfolio investments.

Special situations

Disposal of part of a business. Occasionally an enterprise sells or plans to sell the assets and undertaking of a substantial portion of its business as a unit, or discontinues a substantial division. This unusual event raises several questions as to recognition, measurement, and reporting of such transactions.

The first question relates to the recognition date. If it is not certain that the division will be disposed of, no accounting action will be taken except in the infrequent case where assets would be written down even in the absence of a disposal. On the other hand, if a formal plan of disposal of a division has been adopted, that decision makes a future gain or loss probable; hence, an estimate needs to be made of that future gain or loss. In that estimate it is necessary to consider not only the probable net proceeds of asset disposal but also the possibility of cash operating losses for the period until the disposal can be concluded.

Consistent with the general treatment of contingencies, recognition of loss is required when it is anticipated; recognition of gain is delayed until realization. This approach is applied to disposal proceeds of assets and prospective operating results taken together. That is to say, losses on asset disposal may be offset by expected profits during the period up to disposition, and conversely. The income statement presentation of gains or losses on disposal of part of the business will be discussed in a subsequent section.

Reorganizations and quasi-reorganizations. On rare occasions a company that is in financial difficulties may go through a reorganization in which creditors and shareholders may accept a reduction in their rights and claims upon the company, and assets are written down to values considered more realistic in the situation. A quasi-reorganization is similar except that it does not involve the creditors. Instead, it takes place after formal approval by the shareholders, usually involving a reduction of legal capital. In both cases, any write-down of assets must be applied first to eliminate retained earnings (if any). Thereafter, the write-downs (plus any existing deficit) are applied against contributed surplus created by reductions in the claims of shareholders or creditors. To show that the enterprise has had a "fresh start," disclosure is made for a period of ten years after the readjustment that the balance in retained earnings account (or deficit) was accumulated since the date of the reorganization.

Statement presentation of gains, losses, and other adjustments

The gains and losses just discussed result from deviations from the normal planned course of operations or from incidental and possibly nonrecurring activity. There is naturally a question as to how such gains and losses can best be reported in financial statements to assist readers in assessing just what has happened. The same question arises with respect to all sorts of other adjustments, such as adjustments to correct errors, adjustments of past figures in the light of new information, or adjustments resulting from accounting changes — such as changes in estimates or in accounting policies. All of these are discussed in this section.

Extraordinary and unusual items

Chapter 5 described the early development of the historical cost theory with its emphasis on income measurement based on actual transactions. Despite the emphasis on income measurement there was no clear idea in those years of just what should be included in income. There existed a strong tradition, derived from English law, of a distinction between capital gain and income. The classic example is that of the tree and its fruit. The tree is a capital asset and the fruit the income derived from it. Correspondingly, proceeds from sale of fruit were income but from the sale of the tree were capital, i.e., not income. Following this legal precedent, accounting reports often excluded so-called capital gains or losses from the figure of income reported and, instead, charged or credited them directly to "capital reserves" or simply to the earned surplus account.

This legally derived point of view was quite acceptable to accountants. The accountant's interest in income measurement stemmed from its usefulness in indicating the earning power of a business — the source of capital value. Accordingly, many accountants felt that it was important that the reported income figure be normal, not "distorted" by unusual events or transactions. Under this view not only capital gains or losses could be excluded from income, but also gains and losses from windfalls, casualties, or other unexpected events. This "current operating performance" viewpoint on income measurement was completely acceptable in the 1930s and 1940s when the historical cost theory gained its ascendency.

At the same time, an opposing viewpoint was held that subsequently gained strength. Under the "all-inclusive" view, emphasis was laid upon the idea of the statement of income as providing a complete historical record, year by year, of the results of operations. It was considered fruitless, and possibly misleading, to filter out gains and losses thought to be nonoperating or nonrecurring. It was argued that if gains and losses can happen once, they can happen again. In any event, their existence is part of the record of performance. Given adequate disclosure, statement readers can make their own decision as to whether a gain or loss should be considered a factor in recurring earning power.

The passage of time disclosed the weakness in the notion of current operating performance. Its implementation required a decision in every unusual case whether a gain or loss should be reported as part of income or not. Such classification distinctions are always difficult at the borderline. In practice, the result of the classification uncertainties, as demonstrated by several studies, was that losses excluded from income far exceeded gains so excluded.

This suggestion of bias in the accounting was naturally disturbing. In an effort to rectify the situation, the U.S. Committee on Accounting Procedure in 1947 attempted to define and limit the items that could be excluded from reported income.[4] The committee's advice was as follows. First, capital transactions *must* be excluded from reported income. Second, material extraordinary items — defined as being items that in the aggregate are clearly not identifiable with or do not result from the usual or typical business operations of the period — *ordinarily* should also be excluded. Examples of such items were (1) charges or credits relating to operations of prior years, (2) gains or losses on the sale of assets not acquired for resale, (3) losses of a type not usually insured against, except where such losses are a recurrent hazard, (4) the write-off of intangibles, and (5) the write-off of unamortized bond discount or premium and bond issue expenses upon early retirement or refunding of a debt issue.

One can immediately see the questions. If materiality is to be judged in the aggregate, two dissimilar items, each material in itself, would be offset and not disclosed. Was that right? Is it right to exclude charges or credits relating to prior periods if such represent adjustments of previous years' estimates that tend to recur regularly because of the uncertainty inherent in the business carried on? If there is a gain or loss on disposition of fixed assets, might not the gain or loss really represent an adjustment of prior years' depreciation? Should that be excluded from reported income? The reference to a "recurrent hazard" suggests that gains or losses from ordinary business risks should be reported through income even if material, but the outcome of extraordinary (or unforeseen?) risks should not be. Is it possible to make such a distinction? Risk is a fact of business life, and the range of possibility from extremely remote to highly likely is continuous. The word "recurrent" helps, but is one talking of recurrence every second year, every fifth year, or every tenth year? Opinions might differ.

As a result of such uncertainties, inconsistent practice continued. The Accounting Principles Board addressed the question again in 1966 and moved further towards the all-inclusive position, although with some compromises.[5] The compromises were that "prior period adjustments" (a relatively new term) were to continue to be excluded from reported income. Other extraordinary items, although now to be included in net income reported for a year, were to be identified and reported on an after-tax basis at the end of the statement of income, clearly segregated from ordinary income for the year. An attempt was also made to provide a more rigorous definition of both prior period adjustments (see further discussion below) and extraordinary items. In 1969, the CICA adopted the American recommendations with minor changes in wording only, and these form the basis of our present standards.[6]

The basic criterion of an extraordinary item is that a reasonable person would not take it into account as a recurring factor in evaluating the operations and worth of an enterprise. To meet this criterion, an item should be not typical of normal business operations and not expected to recur regularly over a period of years. Both these characteristics are required. For example, even though a gain or loss is not typical of normal business operations, it would not be excluded if it occurred with some regularity. Specific examples of extraordinary items cited in the CICA recommendations are:

- Gain or loss on sale or discontinuance of a significant segment of a business or a whole plant
- Gain or loss on sale of an investment not acquired with the intention of resale
- Gain or loss on expropriation of properties or from other governmental or regulatory intervention.

It is recognized that what is extraordinary to one company may be ordinary to another. A large diversified company may encounter almost any of these conditions with some regularity in various segments of its operations. This fact suggests that the concept of risks outside normal business operations is not very sound. If any of these gains or losses occur with some regularity in a large enough enterprise, one can hardly consider the risks as something outside normal operations. In other words, frequency of occurrence seems to be the real operational test. This test probably corresponds more closely with an ordinary person's concept of the term "extraordinary." For example, if an enterprise with a limited number of major customers suffers a material bad debt loss on the bankruptcy of one of them, management and users of financial statements are likely to regard that as extraordinary, regardless of whether bad debt losses are typical of normal business operations.

The accounting standards of the latter part of the 1960s did not succeed in eliminating criticisms about inconsistency in the treatment of extraordinary items.[7] Whereas formerly the criticisms mainly concerned their total exclusion from income, now the criticism lay in their classification. The underlying cause, however, was the same. Where there is a continuous shading of colour from white at one end to black at the other, it is notoriously different to express in words just where in the grey area white should be deemed to have become black.

The U.S. Accounting Principles Board tried again in 1973.[8] The board emphasized that an event or transaction had to meet *both* the tests of abnormality in relation to the ordinary activities of the enterprise and infrequency of occurrence to qualify as extraordinary. Only three examples of extraordinary items were mentioned. These were gains or losses resulting from (1) a major catastrophe such as an earthquake, (2) an expropriation, or (3) a prohibition under a new law or regulation. The board also removed one of the events previously most frequently classified as extraordinary by prescribing separate accounting for gain or loss on disposal of a segment of a business. (Disposal of a line of business that is less than a segment did not qualify as extraordinary because it could not be considered abnormal in relation to ordinary and typical business activities.)

The result of these new recommendations, together with indications of close monitoring of extraordinary items by the Securities and Exchange Commission, was a sharp reduction in the number of extraordinary items reported. Other U.S. accounting standards, however, require certain items to be classified as extraordinary, namely, the realization of the benefit of an income tax loss carryforward, gain or loss on extinguishment of debt other than on acquisition of debt to meet one-year sinking-fund requirements, and the write-off of interstate operating rights of Motor Carriers consequent upon deregulation in 1980.[9] With the possible exception of the last, none of these meet the basic criteria for extraordinary items. The anomalous position now is that most items now reported as extraordinary do not fall within the basic criteria stated; thus the attempt to facilitate better understanding of results of operations by this classification of results has become ineffective. Because of the 1973 changes in the United States, the Canadian standard, which was modelled on the previous U.S. standard, is now different from the present U.S. standard. The Canadian standard remains subject to the difficulties in interpretation that caused the change in the United States.

Statement presentation of discontinued operations

There are significant differences between the United States and Canada in the income statement presentation of discontinued operations.

United States treatment. To begin with, the U.S. standard makes a distinction not made in Canada between discontinuance or disposal of a "segment" of a business and discontinuance or disposal of less than a segment.[10] A segment is defined as a component whose activities represent a separate major line of business or class of customer. Because of this definition, a disposal of a particular product line or a particular plant, when other product lines or plants in the same business or selling to the same class of customer continue, would not constitute disposal of a segment.

When a complete segment of a business is discontinued, ordinary income is to be subdivided between income from continuing operations and income from the discontinued segment. The latter is to show the following separately (on an after-tax basis):

- Gain or loss from operations before the formal decision to discontinue or dispose of the segment (the measurement date).
- Estimated net *loss* (if any) on disposal of the assets of the segment and on operations subsequent to the measurement date (to the extent operating profit/loss can be estimated with reasonable accuracy — ordinarily expected to be for a period no longer than one year). The estimate of profit/loss on subsequent operations is to be disclosed.

Previous years' operating figures are to be restated to break out the profit or loss on the segment for comparison.

The results of disposal of assets or an undertaking constituting less than a line of business cannot be treated as either a discontinuance of business or an extraordinary item. They may, if material, be given special disclosure as a component of ordinary continuing income before tax.

Canadian treatment. In Canada, gain or loss on sale or discontinuance of a whole plant or a significant segment of a business is to be reported as extraordinary. This differs from the U.S. treatment in that (1) disposals of less than a segment can qualify for special treatment, and (2) that special treatment consists of inclusion among extraordinary items, rather than reporting on discontinued operations separately.

As is the case in the United States, the possible operating profit or loss over any remaining period required to close out the operation should be taken into account in determining the net extraordinary loss recorded (at the date of the discontinuance decision) or gain (at realization). However, operations *before* the formal discontinuance decision are part of regular operations and therefore cannot be grouped with the discontinuance gain or loss as is done in the United States. Nevertheless, separate disclosure of past profit/loss from discontinued operations (to the extent it can be accurately identified) has merit for analytical purposes and should be encouraged.

Unusual items

Both in Canada and the United States, items forming part of ordinary operations that are "unusual" in nature or infrequent in occurrence are to be reported as separate components of ordinary income or given special footnote disclosure. Such items should not be hard to identify even though judgment is required. Generally, any revenue or expense that stands out from a trend established over the most recent years should be reviewed for special disclosure. In addition, all material gains or losses on peripheral activities should be reviewed for frequency of occurrence.

Given adequate disclosure of all unusual items, one may question whether there is any great advantage to the segregation of defined extraordinary items, particularly if the definition of "extraordinary" does not coincide with what the ordinary financial statement reader would understand by that word.

Prior period adjustments

In spite of the shift toward the all-inclusive income statement in the 1960s, prior period adjustments were to continue to be excluded from reported income. That exclusion was potentially dangerous since many figures in financial statements are subject to uncertainty when first reported. The intention was that items excluded from the current year's income should be restricted to the results of events that not only had their roots in the past but also were not attributable to any business done in the current year. That test led to the following criteria, all of which have to be satisfied to permit classification of the item as a prior period adjustment:[11]

- The item must be specifically identified with and directly related to business activities of particular prior periods.

- It must not be attributable to economic events occurring subsequent to those periods.
- It must depend primarily on decisions or determinations by persons other than management.
- It could not reasonably be estimated prior to such decisions.

The first of these criteria is intended to ensure that an item treated as a prior period adjustment cannot in any way be regarded as a reward for current period activity or a cost associated with current period activity. The key word in the second criterion is "economic." For every prior period adjustment there must be some event in the current period that triggers recognition. Otherwise the adjustment would have been fully accounted for previously. What narrows the field is the exclusion of economic events — i.e., presumably events or transactions in the course of the business carried on or developments in its economic environment that have an impact on its financial position. These exclusions are reinforced by the third criterion — the management decision aspect. If management has played much part in the outcome of the event in question, it seems that such outcome must be in part attributable to its activity in the current period and, in many cases, will have the aspect of planned economic activity as well. The fourth criterion differentiates a prior period adjustment from a correction of an error but otherwise has little operational significance.

The standards suggest that true prior period adjustments are rare. Two examples cited in the Canadian literature are nonrecurring settlements of income taxes, and settlements of claims arising from litigation. Even here the application of the criteria is not beyond dispute. For example, payment of additional income taxes established by a court judgment certainly qualifies as a prior period adjustment since it clearly relates to prior years and is determined by a body independent of management. It has been argued, however, that additional income taxes settled out of court would not qualify as a prior period adjustment, because settlement required the active involvement of management. The distinction between the two events makes little common sense. It well illustrates the difficulty, however, in making crystal-clear definitional classifications.

In 1977 the FASB moved even further toward the all-inclusive income concept by restricting prior period adjustment treatment to two items: (1) corrections of errors of prior years, and (2) a specific item resulting from business combination accounting — namely, adjustments consequent upon recovery of preacquisition tax loss carryforwards of subsidiary companies.[12]

Error corrections. In Canada, the correction of an error from previous years is described as an accounting change rather than a prior period adjustment, but nonetheless is treated in the same fashion as the latter. An error may be purely mechanical in nature, such as an error in arithmetic, or may be a bad estimate based on ignorance or misinterpretation of information available at the reporting date. The availability of information is crucial. Accounting estimates are continually revised in subsequent periods based on new information. Such revisions are not considered corrections of errors, because the original estimates must be considered correct if they were based on all the information available at the time.

Prior period adjustments and corrections of errors are treated as follows:

- The adjustment is charged or credited to retained earnings.

- Income and retained earning balances for all prior years presented are restated for the adjustment.
- Adequate explanations are given of the adjustment or correction.

Accounting changes

Reported figures may be affected by accounting changes as well as real events or transactions. Accounting changes may be classified as (1) changes in accounting estimates, (2) changes in accounting policies, and (3) changes in the definition of the accounting entity covered by the financial report.

Changes in accounting estimates. Many estimates are required in accounting because of the uncertainty inherent in the real world — such as estimates of the service lives of fixed assets, of salvage values, of realizable values of inventory, of recoverable values of accounts receivable, and of amounts that will be payable under warranties. No matter how careful these estimates, revisions to some of them will prove necessary from time to time. If the estimates were originally made in an unbiased fashion, revisions must be the result of subsequent experience, new developments, or new information. It is accepted, therefore, that revisions should not give rise to restatement of results previously reported.

If the estimate relates to a specific amount receivable or payable, the effect of the changed estimate is absorbed immediately in the income of the year of change. On the other hand, if the estimate has to do with amortization of a long-lived asset, the effect of a correction is spread over the current and future periods. The difference in treatment is probably pragmatic. Estimates of the duration of a long-lived asset may well be uncertain even when updated, and may be subject to additional revisions in future. It is thought best to mitigate the effect of such uncertainties by spreading any adjustments so far as possible. (This represents the author's interpretation of the rather uninformative, if not circular, advice given in paragraph 24(b) of Section 1506 of the *CICA Handbook*.)

Broadly speaking, a similar treatment is adopted for estimates of long-term liabilities. Changes in actuarial assumptions, for example, are amortized over a period relating to the remaining service lives of employees at the time of the change. Revisions in the amount of foreign currency debt (which revisions may be regarded as revised estimates of amounts payable at maturity) are spread over the period remaining to maturity. On the other hand, increases in a provision for estimated losses should not be delayed when there is little continuing uncertainty as to their amount. If, for example, early losses on a product with a five- or ten-year warranty indicate much poorer expectations than were originally anticipated, the required increase in provision should be recognized immediately, not phased in. Similarly, provisions for contingent losses, where made, are regularly revised based on best estimates.

Changes in accounting estimates are sufficiently common that there is no general rule requiring their disclosure. If a change qualified as an "unusual item," however, or if the change could have a material effect on reported results in future years, it should be disclosed.

Changes in accounting policies. Changes in accounting policies are less frequently encountered than changes in accounting estimates. Where more than one accounting policy is possible in given circumstances, an entity is expected to have chosen that which seems most suitable to it. The term "accounting policies" is interpreted broadly to include methods of application. Thus, depreciation accounting as a policy embraces both the general principle that plant and equipment should be amortized over its estimated useful life and the use of straight-line or accelerated patterns in the application of that policy.

A new accounting policy is sometimes adopted prospectively with no change to previous accounting. For example, a change to an accelerated depreciation pattern might be adopted for application only to assets acquired after the date of change. More often, however, changes in accounting policies are made retroactive, thereby changing the carrying amounts of assets and liabilities on hand. When this occurs, two possibilities are conceivable. The amount of the adjustment could be taken to income account or direct to retained earnings without restatement of prior years' earnings figures. Alternatively, previous years' earnings could be restated so far as they are presented, with consequential adjustment of balances of retained earnings for each year presented.

The primary argument against restatement is that it may reduce public confidence in the financial statements. On the other hand, on the assumption the new accounting policy is considered preferable, it seems more useful to readers of financial statements to report figures for all years on the new basis, so that comparisons between years are facilitated and distortion of trends is prevented. This position is accepted in Canada, and restatement is recommended (in a manner similar to that for prior period adjustments).[13]

Exceptions are made on practical grounds in two situations. First, it may be impossible to know what the figures would have been at the beginning of the year of change if the new accounting policy had been effective. Second, there may be situations where the amount of the adjustment at the beginning of the year of change is known, but limitations in the accounting records make it very difficult or impossible to reconstruct figures on the new basis beyond that point. For example, a contractor switching from a completed contract basis of profit recognition to a percentage-of-completion basis might find that records required to assess percentage of completion were unavailable earlier than the first of the year of change.

Accordingly, Canadian practice can now be summarized as follows:[14]

- Changes in accounting policy that concern assets or liabilities on hand before the effective date of change should be applied retroactively if possible. If so applied, reported financial statement figures presented for years before the year of change should be restated, again if possible.
- The nature of any change in accounting policy should be described. This should be supplemented by disclosure of its impact on figures presented which, depending upon the case in hand, can usefully be crystallized in terms of its after-tax impact on net income, earnings per share, or on working capital. In all cases, the disclosure of impact should deal with the impact on the current period (indicating, for example, whether and by how much the net income for the year has been increased or decreased by the change compared with what it would have been under the previous policy). Where previous years' figures have been restated, that fact should be made clear along with similar disclosure of the impact.
- Where a change in accounting policy has *not* been applied retroactively, that fact should be disclosed. Where it has been applied retroactively but previous

year's figures have *not* been restated, that also should be disclosed. In that case the cumulative adjustment to the opening balance of retained earnings should be clearly disclosed.

- Disclosure of changes in accounting policy should not be confined to those that have a material effect in the year of change if the effect is likely to be material in future.

This policy requires interpretation in a number of areas.

- An entity may be accounting for certain items of revenue or cost on a simple basis (such as the cash basis) because they are immaterial. If they subsequently become material, adoption of a more careful accounting policy is not regarded as a change in accounting policy. In general, adoption of a new accounting policy because of new conditions or because of entry into a new line of business is not considered a change in accounting policy.
- It is sometimes argued that an accounting change is not a change in accounting policy, or even a change in method of application of an accounting policy but is merely a "refinement" introduced in the interests of more accurate accounting. For example, suppose overhead in inventory has been calculated heretofore on the basis of a plant-wide allocation rate but departmentalization now permits a more accurate assignment of overheads to various product lines. It can be argued that there is no change in accounting objective or principle here. The calculation has simply been refined. If material, of course, the change should be disclosed fully as an "unusual item" affecting income, so that the only real question ought to be whether reference to the change needs to be included in the auditor's report. Opinions differ on this point. The author prefers the simple viewpoint that any change in figures reported that is not caused by real changes in the business done, but merely by changes in the way it is accounted for, should be described as a change in accounting policy. The term "refinement" should be reserved for an immaterial change.
- Not infrequently, changes in the classification of assets, liabilities, revenues, or expenses in the financial statement are made from one period to another. On the theory that accounting includes recording, classifying, reporting, and interpreting the results of economic events, it can be argued these classification changes are also changes in accounting policy. Certainly rules for classification of current assets and current liabilities are conventionally considered to be accounting principles. Nevertheless, accepted standards see a distinction between recording and measurement on the one hand and presentation in the financial statements on the other. Thus, reclassification is not regarded as a change in accounting policy. To improve comparability, however, previous years' financial statements are reclassified to conform with the latest year reported where possible.
- Occasionally, there can be difficulty in distinguishing between accounting policy changes and changes in estimates. Indeed, an accounting policy change can substitute for a change in estimate. It is generally considered that, where there is doubt as to the type of accounting change, its treatment as a change in estimate should be preferred to treatment as a change in policy. This preference is presumably based on the desire to make sure that cur-

rent income reported includes all the effects of changes triggered by current experience. In individual cases, however, judgment may well be very difficult.

In view of the disadvantages to chopping and changing in financial reporting, there is a general presumption that accounting policies should be applied without change year after year. American standards go further and provide that a change in policy may only be made to a policy considered preferable in the circumstances, and that the auditor should specifically state his approval of the change. This requirement is supplemented by a SEC requirement that registrants file notice of accounting policy changes accompanied by the audit firm's statement that it considers the change to be preferable. This counsel of perfection is well intentioned but of doubtful effectiveness. As an example, many accountants consider LIFO accounting to be fundamentally inconsistent with the historical cost accounting model. Yet it is not known that any auditor withheld approval of the many changes to LIFO accounting that have occurred since the date of APB Opinion No. 20. The reason is simple. The very existence of alternative accounting policies is prima facie evidence that standard-setters are unable to specify the circumstances in which each of the competing policies is applicable. If standard-setters cannot accomplish this task, it is unreasonable to expect individual auditors or members of management to succeed where they have failed.

Changes in reporting entity. The third category of accounting change — namely, a change in the reporting entity — occurs much less frequently. Such a change may be caused by a change in circumstances. For example, when two entities combine in a pooling of interests, the new entity is deemed a continuation of both of the preceding entities; their histories should therefore be combined. A change in entity may also result from a change in judgment. For example, management may decide that a significant subsidiary, previously excluded from consolidation on the grounds of incompatibility of operations with the parent, should now be accounted for within the consolidation. Whether resulting from a change in circumstances or a change in judgment, the accounting follows the standard practice for changes in accounting policy. That is, the change is applied retroactively with restatement of any figures for prior periods that are presented.

Suppose an investment in a forty-percent-owned company has been carried on the equity basis of accounting and this year is consolidated because acquisition of additional shares has given the parent company majority control. Should the consolidation be given retroactive treatment? The technical answer is no since equity accounting was, and continues to be, appropriate for the position as it was at the previous year-end. It would be common sense, however, to present pro forma consolidated figures for purposes of comparison (omitting the previously reported figures if permissible under the law) as an aid to reader comprehension.

Consider also a situation where a previously consolidated subsidiary is sold during the year. In this case the change in entity is not an accounting change but a real event. Nevertheless, it would be useful to restate the previous years' figures so that the subsidiary is removed from the consolidation and recorded on the basis of equity accounting. Investments that are held on a temporary basis should not be consolidated; the subsequent disposition of the subsidiary provides evidence that the holding, at least in the most recent years, could be considered as temporary.

Accounting for capital

Capital transactions

The one thing that has always been agreed upon in accounting is that there is a distinction between the nature of capital transactions and income transactions. The essential idea is simple. One cannot make a gain or loss on dealing with oneself. Therefore, no matter how narrowly or how broadly the concept of income is defined, there will be some "capital transactions" that lie outside it.

It is necessary, however, to have a clear idea of what constitutes a capital transaction. The following are the principal varieties:

- Transactions in which capital is contributed to an entity or withdrawn from it are capital transactions. In a business corporation this would include the subscription of capital in return for shares. It would also include forfeiture of shares by a shareholder, redemption of shares according to the terms of their issue, or purchase of shares by the corporation on the open market.
- Payments of costs and expenses in connection with the issuance of capital are likewise regarded as capital transactions. Gains and losses on redemption of capital or on purchase and resale of shares are excluded from income since they are part of a capital transaction.
- Payment of a return on capital, such as dividends, is also a capital transaction.
- Under Canadian tax law, part of the income tax paid by a Canadian controlled private company is refundable to the company in an amount equal to twenty-five percent of any dividend paid by the company (up to the amount of refundable tax previously paid). The effect is that if a company pays a dividend equal in amount to its income after tax (excluding the refundable tax), then all the refundable tax will be recovered. One way of looking at the refundable tax is that it is not an income tax on the company, but rather an advance payment of tax that will become payable by the shareholder if and when income earned by the company is passed on to the shareholder in the form of dividends. The CICA has therefore recommended that the refundable tax paid by the company be treated as a capital transaction and charged against retained earnings — that is, as a payment not to shareholders but on account of shareholders.[15]
- In those rare cases where a business combination is treated as a pooling of interests, the theory is that the merged company is in substance a continuation of all the preceding companies entering into the merger. As a result, the previous financial histories of the combining companies are added together as representing the history of the pooled entity, and the assets and liabilities of each component at the time of the combination are added together at their existing carrying values to form the statement of financial position of the combined entity. There are always some expenses directly attributable to any combination and the question arises of how these should be reported. Since they are attributable to the combination, they are clearly not part of the income history of any component before combination. On the other hand, since the combined entity is considered to be merely a continuation of the previous components, neither do the expenses represent a

cost of earning income after the combination. The solution adopted to this dilemma is to treat the expenses as capital transactions and charge them directly to retained earnings.[16]

- Provisions or releases of "reserves" on a discretionary basis are also regarded as capital in nature and hence do not affect reported income.
- Adjustments made upon quasi-reorganization of a company (see earlier discussion) are also treated as though they were capital transactions. This accepted accounting practice is based on custom rather than on any rigorous conceptual justification.

From the foregoing it is evident that a clear concept of exactly what is capital is an essential underpinning to the concept of a capital transaction. The concept of capital is very broad under the entity theory — consisting of all financing provided to an entity other than that provided as a result of the excess of revenues over operating expenses. The concept of capital under the proprietary viewpoint is limited to capital furnished by the proprietor or partners in an unincorporated entity, or to equity shares as defined by law in a corporation. A third interpretation, also consistent with the proprietory concept, would be even narrower. Capital could be restricted to the residual equity — e.g., in a corporation, share capital that carries a right to participation in residual income and residual assets on liquidation after all fixed amount claims of other security holders are satisfied.

As a matter of history, accounting has adopted the second of these viewpoints under the influence of legal concepts of corporation capital. Since fixed-claim preferred shares are very different in essential character from common shares, it is arguable that either of the other two concepts would be superior. Some consequences of this choice for the distinction between income and capital transactions and some other debatable points are discussed below.

- Issuance and redemption or repurchase of debt securities are, under the present proprietary definition, not capital transactions. Consequently, expenses and discounts or premiums on issue of such securities must be absorbed in income (by amortization) along with interest costs. Also, gains and losses on retirement must be reported as income. In contrast, payments of costs of issue of preferred shares and gains and losses on their redemption or repurchase are capital transactions and must be excluded from income.
- This distinction between debt and preferred shares can become blurred by special provisions of the latter. For example, preferred shares that are retractable on specific dates at the option of the holder lack some of the characteristics of capital, which is commonly thought of as being permanent in nature. The situation is even worse with "term preferred" shares which have a fixed redemption date. The SEC has ruled that such shares cannot be grouped with permanent capital in a balance sheet (even though dividends on them continue to be treated as capital transactions); the CICA, however, has done no more than urge disclosure of the special characteristics of the shares.[17]
- In Canada, there is a lack of clear guidance as to the accounting treatment of warrants to buy shares. As noted in chapter 6, when detachable warrants are issued in conjunction with another security such as debentures, some companies may not estimate proceeds attributable to the warrants and account for them separately. Others follow the required American practice and

separate the proceeds. The question then is, should these proceeds be treated as capital? If not, and if the warrants were to expire worthless, the gain would have to be treated as income, as would any gain or loss that might occur on buying in the warrants before exercise. The more logical treatment, in view of the fact that warrant proceeds are received only in the hope of acquiring a capital interest eventually, would be to treat warrants as capital, and if they expire without exercise to transfer the proceeds to contributed surplus. It would be wrong, however, to credit them to contributed surplus before they expire because that would suggest that the proceeds represent part of the equity attributable to the existing common shares, not the new shares that will be issued upon exercise.

- A company with a subsidiary company usually reports on a consolidated basis. That is, the assets and liabilities reported by the parent company include both those directly owned or owed by it and those attributable to its subsidiaries. If the parent company owns less than one hundred percent of the subsidiary's common shares, it nevertheless accounts for one hundred percent of the carrying value of the subsidiary's assets and liabilities in the consolidation, together with a figure of "minority interest" representing the proportionate share of the outside shareholders in the book value of the subsidiary's net assets. Is that minority interest equivalent to capital of the parent company (perhaps like a special kind of preferred share)? Such an interpretation is possible in theory, but is not at present a generally accepted accounting principle. If it were, the issue of shares by the subsidiary to a minority interest would be regarded as a capital transaction, not giving rise to gains or losses to be reported as income. Instead, present practice is to treat such dispositions in consolidated statements as de facto dispositions of the parent company's investment in the subsidiary giving rise to an income gain or loss (see chapter 19).

Accounting for proprietary equity

Under the proprietary viewpoint, all income is considered to accrue to the legal equity, subject to the claims of prior ranking capital. We can see, then, that the total ownership interest recorded in a balance sheet (the difference between assets and liabilities) comes basically from two sources — capital transactions and accumulated retained income. How then is capital portrayed in a balance sheet?

Balance sheet portrayal. There are two partially conflicting ideas that influence the presentation. One (and this is the older, more traditional idea) is that the balance sheet of a corporation should show its legal capital. The legal capital is the amount that cannot be reduced (except by losses) without formal proceedings. By inference, an excess of net assets over legal capital must be distributable in the absence of other impediments.

The other idea is that the balance sheet presentation of capital should preserve the record of the source of the capital. That is to say, there should be a basic distinction between capital arising from capital transactions and capital arising from the accumulation of income not distributed.

Accounting standards favour the second concept — that elements of capital should be classified by source rather than by legal status.[18] Implementation of this preference, however, is not necessarily clear-cut.

- Cash dividends paid, although a capital transaction, are customarily charged against retained earnings. The common view is that dividends represent a distribution of earnings. It is possible in law, however, to pay dividends out of contributed surplus. Is there any accounting rule that requires that dividends be charged to retained earnings (where such exist)? Such a rule would be tantamount to saying that for accounting purposes a corporation cannot return capital even though in law it may. The need for such an accounting rule is not obvious. Provided the directors explicitly determine that a dividend represents a distribution of contributed surplus and provided the shareholders are informed that it is not a distribution of earnings, there seems to be no objection to treatment of the dividend in accordance with its legal form.
- Stock dividends, unlike ordinary dividends, do not involve any disposition of the net assets of an entity. If one is interested in portraying the source of the net assets (capital transactions or retained earnings), does it make sense to change that portrayal where there has been no change in the assets? To justify the change, one has to visualize a notional payment of cash on the dividend and concurrent subscription for additional stock by the shareholders. Since it is not at all sure that shareholders would reinvest given the choice, this interpretation seems somewhat fanciful (see further discussion of stock dividends below).
- When a company redeems or purchases shares for cancellation (a capital transaction), the cost must be allocated among whatever components of shareholders' equity are shown in the balance sheet. Various bases of allocation are described in the *CICA Handbook*.[19] A method is favoured that would reduce capital attributed to the same class of shares, pro rata, absorb any excess against contributed surplus to the extent it arises from transactions in the same class of shares, and charge any remaining excess to retained earnings.
- When a company issues shares, there usually are some expenses of issue that are treated as a capital transaction because they are a necessary incidental to raising capital. The preferable accounting treatment would be to show the net proceeds of issue after expenses as the capital attributable to the issue. The legal capital, however, is often the consideration actually received from the shareholders. It has been customary not to report capital issued at an amount less than the legal capital. Accordingly, share issue expenses are commonly written off directly to retained earnings or carried as a deferred asset.

In view of these uncertainties in classification, one is bound to question whether it is all worthwhile. Is any user's decision influenced by the division between reported capital and accumulated retained earnings? Does any financial ratio depend upon that split? It has been argued that the reader will be able to tell from the split whether capital has been raised largely from capital contributions or whether retained earnings have been significant. While that is true, is it important? A history of earnings and dividends for the last five to ten years, usually readily available, has far more significance to the financial statement user than any accumulated retained earnings figure in the balance sheet. In the author's opinion, the portrayal of capital in a balance sheet would be improved by the following principles:

- Remove all preferred stock and other capital elements not representing residual equity from the total of shareholders' equity and display them separately. If dividends on preferred shares are cumulative, however, appropriate the correct amount from retained earnings to be grouped with preferred share capital in the balance sheet.
- Report one figure for total residual equity. Disclose any information pertaining thereto that is deemed relevant, such as the amount thereof that is free from restriction on distribution and, if significant, an indication of the nature of the restriction — the existence of legal capital, covenants in loan agreements, etc.
- Provide a statement or statements tracing the changes in all items of residual equity over the reporting period from capital issues, repurchases, or retirements; from exercise of warrants, options, or conversion privileges; from earnings for the period; from dividends declared; and from any other capital transactions.
- Disclose additional information deemed relevant in the same way as at present, including the number of shares outstanding and changes therein, all terms and conditions attaching to preferred shares, details of commitments to issue shares upon exercise of outstanding conversion, option, or warrant rights, details of any share transactions or non-cash consideration, and so on.

Specific issues in capital accounting. The following comments deal with a few specific situations in accounting for capital.

A stock split clearly has no significance other than to the number of shares outstanding. Each shareholder has exactly the same proportionate interest in the company after the split as she had before. There is no reason, therefore, to change the balance sheet display of capital for a stock split other than to adjust the figures given for the number of shares outstanding.

A common shareholder's proportionate interest in a company is likewise unaffected by a dividend paid entirely in stock. Stronger arguments are made for accounting recognition in this case, however, and greater consideration is required.

- Consider the (rare) case of a dividend paid in stock (either additional preferred shares or common shares) on a preferred share. In this case the relative interests of the preferred and common shareholders are clearly altered by the dividend. Proper accounting would therefore require crediting capital of the appropriate category for the value of the stock issued and charging retained earnings.
- Now consider the case where a dividend in the form of preferred stock is paid to common shareholders. The claim of each shareholder upon the assets of the company is not altered by the dividend, since what she gains through holding preferred shares she loses in her residual equity claim. The form of her interest has, however, changed. It would seem right in this case, then, to credit preferred share capital for the value of the shares issued and reduce common equity. There could be a theoretical argument that all the elements of common equity should be reduced proportionately, but in practice the entire dividend would be charged to retained earnings.
- We come now to the most common case — that of a dividend in common stock paid to the common shareholders. Here the effect is exactly the same as a split of common stock. Yet the accounting practice is different. Why?

The only authoritative statement is found in the U.S. Accounting Research Bulletin No. 43.[20] There it was argued that a shareholder looks upon stock dividends as a distribution of corporate earnings in an amount equivalent to the fair value of the shares. That impression is reinforced (it was said) by the fact that little change in the market value of the shares is usually observable after the dividend. Accordingly, the fair value of shares issued as a stock dividend should be capitalized where those conditions hold. The bulletin suggested that stock dividends in an amount less than twenty or twenty-five percent of the outstanding shares were unlikely to materially affect their market value. (It may be doubted that that conclusion would be valid today.) Until recently, stock dividends were relatively rare in Canada and practice did not necessarily follow American precedent. It was common to capitalize a stock dividend at the minimum amount permitted by law. In some jurisdictions, at least, the directors now have discretion to establish the minimum amount to be added to stated capital.

- In the 1980s in Canada, stock dividends have become more common for tax reasons. A number of companies have split their common shares into two classes that are freely interchangeable, one of which pays dividends in cash and the other of which pays dividends in stock having a market value equivalent to the cash dividends. In these cases, the stock dividend is invariably capitalized at its cash-equivalent value. The fact that shareholders have the right to choose between a cash and stock dividend makes the latter in substance equivalent to payment of a cash dividend. (This tax treatment was altered in 1985.)

Treasury stock purchases. When a corporation purchases its own shares but does not immediately cancel them, several questions arise. The first concerns the treatment of their cost in the balance sheet — should it be shown as a reduction of shareholders' equity, or as an asset? There are several arguments against treatment as an asset (and to some degree against allowing the shares to continue in the figures of shares outstanding). The shares should not continue to be shown as issued because they carry none of the normal rights pertaining to share ownership — to receive dividends, to vote for directors, or to receive distributions in liquidation. The cash paid for the shares is effectively withdrawn from the entity. This is evidenced by the fact that the "asset" could not earn income. There can only be a gain or loss on its resale. Against this, there is the fact that a company that regularly invests in equity shares will find its own shares to be a competitor for investment funds and may acquire them merely because they appear to be better value than other securities, with the full intention of reselling them when advantageous. Some writers also argue that when a company buys its own shares in anticipation of using them to meet commitments to sell shares under warrants, options, or conversion rights, they are more of the character of operating assets than capital reductions. These arguments suggest that the treatment of purchased shares might depend upon intention as to their use.

Although open to debate, the generally accepted practice now is to treat a company's own shares acquired as a reduction of shareholders' equity. The possibility of resale or reuse of the shares is, however, influential in the treatment in the shareholders' equity section of the cost of shares purchased. Two possibilities exist. One is to account for shares acquired as though they were retired, and to write off the cost against the elements of shareholders' equity. If the shares were then resold, the sale would be accounted for as a new issue (the two-transaction method). The other possibility is to deduct the cost of the shares from the total of shareholders' equity. No gain or loss would be recorded as such until the shares were resold or a decision made that they should be cancelled. In effect, the failure to cancel is seen as evidence of intent to resell and gain or loss recognition is postponed until such sale takes place (the one-transaction method). The latter method is the one recommended in Canada.[21] American practice is similar but greater flexibility in treatment is possible.

Other adjustments to owners' equity

We have described how recorded capital is affected directly by capital transactions and indirectly by income transactions that end up in the retained earnings account. We are left with some odds and ends that do not fit under this dichotomy. By and large they represent the fruit of compromise — an agreement that some changes in assets and liabilities should be recorded, but ducking the issue of whether the change is capital or income in character. Since they represent compromises, not much can be said about their logic.

- Appraisal increase credits are still shown in some balance sheets. Revaluation of long-term assets represents a hangover from a time before the general acceptance of the historical cost model. In Canada the practice has become rare and in the United States nonexistent under the pressure of the SEC, but in Britain and Australia it flourishes. Once assets are written up in a revaluation, the question of disposition of the credit arises. It cannot be taken to income because it is not realized through an exchange with outside parties. The compromise solution has been to show the credit as a separate item in shareholders' equity. Since depreciation on the written-up assets must be based upon the new values, it is permissible (but not required) to make a regular transfer from the appraisal increase credit account to retained earnings of an amount equal to the extra depreciation written because of the revaluation.[22]
- In the United States, there is a somewhat similar practice with respect to long-term investments in marketable equity securities. For balance sheet purposes a long-term portfolio of equity securities is required to be valued at the lower of its aggregate cost and market value. Unrealized fluctuations in market value, however, are to be kept out of reported income. This is achieved by carrying any unrealized write-down in a year, or recovery of a previous year's write-down, to a special account that is reported as a separate element in shareholders' equity.
- Translation of the accounts of a foreign subsidiary for purposes of inclusion in a parent company consolidation is discussed in chapter 20. When the subsidiary operates relatively independently of the parent, its "functional currency" is considered to be different from that of the parent. Its basic financial position and results of operation are reported in its functional currency, and thus must be translated into that of the parent company for purposes of consolidation. That translation is performed using the current exchange rate at the balance sheet date for the subsidiary's balance sheet position, and the average exchange rate for the year for the subsidiary's income to be included in consolidated income. If the exchange rate used for translation changes over the course of the year, a gain or loss results from this

translation process. For example, suppose a wholly owned U.S. subsidiary reports a net equity of $100 at the beginning of a year, earns $5 during the year, pays no dividends, and ends the year with an equity of $105. Assume the exchange rate for the U.S. dollar in terms of Canadian dollars is 1.33 at the beginning of the year, 1.37 on average during the year, and 1.40 at the end of the year. The net assets of the subsidiary would be included in the Canadian parent company's position at the beginning of the year at Canadian $133 and the income at $5 x 1.37 = $6.85, for a total of $139.85. However, the closing balance sheet of the subsidiary would show a translated net asset position of $105 x 1.40 = $147. The apparent gain on translation of $7.15 would not be taken to income but rather would be carried as a separate line component in shareholders' equity. (A loss would be treated identically.) It will be noted that a gain indicates a strengthening of the functional currency of the subsidiary vis-à-vis the reporting currency of the parent, and a loss indicates a weakening. Gains and losses on translation of foreign investees carried on the equity basis of accounting are similarly treated.

- U.S. standards require that the liability recognized with respect to a pension plan be not less than the excess of the present value of pension obligations measured by the accumulated benefit method over the fair value of the pension fund assets. That minimum liability recognized is to be balanced by an intangible asset up to the amount of any prior service cost from a plan amendment not yet recognized in income. An excess of the minimum liability over the latter amount is to be recorded as a separate component (a reduction) of shareholders' equity.

Summary

This chapter deals with three broad subject areas: (1) standards for recognition of loss on asset write-downs and in certain special situations, (2) statement presentation of gains and losses of all types, and (3) statement presentation of owners' equity, especially in corporations.

The historical cost accounting theory holds that cost should be retained as the basis for valuation of assets held for sale or production of income only so long as the benefit from that cost has not expired. Normal expense recognition conventions are supposed to allow for write-off of cost as benefits are consumed, but occasionally it becomes necessary to recognize further loss. The basis of that recognition differs to some extent from one category of asset to another.

- It is accepted that inventory, as a current asset, should not be carried at an amount above its net realizable value. For practical reasons, replacement cost is taken as a proxy for realizable value for raw materials and work in process at early stages of production. The exact manner of application of the lower of cost and market rule may vary to some extent. Once an item of inventory is written down, that write-down may not be reversed before disposal.
- In theory, a long-term asset should be written down if a decline in value below book value is expected to be "other than temporary." This test is particularly difficult to apply in the case of property, plant, and equipment

continuing in use. In practice, the decision whether, and by how much, such assets should be written down, is highly judgmental. If the decision is that an asset should be written down, it seems to be accepted that it is permissible merely to reduce the book value to "recoverable value," i.e., the amount that is estimated could be recovered in cash from future operations without any discount for delay in realization. (It is questionable that this is a satisfactory basis of valuation.) The need for write-downs may be considered on an individual asset basis, but in practice whole groupings of assets, such as a whole plant or division, are likely to need write-down if any are to be written down. Once made, write-downs are not reversed before disposal of the assets.

- Marketable securities carried as current assets must be written down when market value is below cost. The market value used is the value at the year-end since that is equivalent to realizable value at that date. The test may be applied by individual security or for the portfolio as a whole. Practice is mixed as to whether values are written up to cost if the market value subsequently recovers.
- The book value of long-term investments is written down only if a decline in value is considered to be other than temporary. The test is applied by individual security. Written-down values are considered to represent a new cost figure and write-downs cannot be reversed before realization.

It has long been understood in accounting that capital transactions, in essence transactions with owners, and consequential expenditures, should never be reported as part of income. At one time, under the "current operating performance" idea, it was thought that the results of a variety of other transactions should also be excluded from the report of income for a period in order to enhance its usefulness as an indicator of operating results ordinarily to be expected. Faced with great difficulty in making a clean distinction between ordinary and other transactions and events, accounting standards have, over a long period of time, moved away from the current operating performance concept toward the "all-inclusive" concept. The latter concept holds that virtually every transaction or event other than capital transactions is part of the income history of an enterprise and should be reported through income sooner or later. The present position is as follows:

- Gains and losses in capital transactions — nonreciprocal transactions with owners — continue to be excluded from income. Depending upon the situation, they may be credited or charged directly to a capital surplus account.
- Income reported is to be all-inclusive with a few exceptions.
  - Gains or losses recognized in the current year but solely attributable to the activities of prior years may be treated as prior period adjustments. When recognized, they are credited or charged to retained earnings and previous years' figures of income are restated.
  - Errors in previous years' accounts discovered in a current year require adjustments that are akin to gains and losses. The adjustments are treated on the same basis as prior period adjustments.
  - Changes in accounting policies, if applied retroactively, also produce adjustments to be treated on a basis similar to prior period adjustments. Special disclosure is to be given to emphasize the effect of the change in

policy on the current year and on restated figures for prior periods. Some accounting policy changes are applied only prospectively, but these too require special disclosure.

- Understanding of results reported in income for a year is to be enhanced in two ways:
  - Gains and losses that are not typical of normal business activity, that are not expected to recur regularly, and that are not considered as factors that would be important in an evaluation of the ordinary operations of the enterprise are to be shown separately, net of tax, at the foot of the income statement.
  - Gains and losses that are typical of normal business activity but that are unusual, because of their size or infrequency of occurrence, should be given special disclosure.

  Whether the idea of separate reporting of extraordinary items is a good one is questionable. To avoid abuse it is necessary to define the term "extraordinary" narrowly. It then does not coincide with what most statement readers would consider extraordinary.

Some confusion exists as to the presentation of owners' equity in the balance sheet — particularly the shareholders' equity of a corporation. Should the legal capital (the amount that cannot be distributed to owners without formal proceedings for reduction of capital) be shown separately, or should capital be classified by source — that is, distinguishing between capital contributed and accumulated retained earnings? Accounting standards generally espouse the latter idea, but there are difficulties. For example, a stock dividend, if any amount is capitalized, transfers accumulated earnings to capital. On the other hand, an ordinary dividend may in some circumstances be charged to a contributed capital account.

It is doubtful that there is much significance to the subclassification of shareholders' equity. The significant figure is the total claim on the net assets of the business of each class of capital. In some circumstances it is also useful to know that portion of the residual equity that could not be distributed by way of dividends for whatever reason — because it is legal capital, because of covenants in trust indentures, and so on.

In recent years there have been a few uneasy compromises resulting in accounting entries being treated neither as income nor as capital. It has been desired to report assets and liabilities on a current basis of valuation for the balance sheet, but not to treat changes in those current values as income. Thus, the effect of those adjustments has been carried as a separate element of shareholders' equity. No theory exists to rationalize such treatment.

References

[1]A research study was published in 1963 — G. Mulcahy, *Use and Meaning of "Market" in Inventory Valuation* (Toronto: CICA, 1963).

[2]For a more complete description of the finer points in the retail method of inventory valuation, see B.J. Bunton and R.J. Sycamore, "What's Wrong with the Retail Method," *CAmagazine*, October 1981, pp. 40-47.

[3]AICPA, APB, *Basic Concepts and Accounting Principles Underlying Financial Statements of Business Enterprises,* APB Statement No. 4 (New York: AICPA, 1970), par. 183, principle M-5C.

[4]See American Institute of Accountants, Committee on Accounting Procedure, *Income and Earned Surplus,* Accounting Research Bulletin No. 32 (New York: AIA, 1947), subsequently consolidated in *Restatement and Revision of Accounting Research Bulletins,* Accounting Research Bulletin No. 43 (New York: AIA, 1953), chap. 8.

[5]AICPA, APB, *Reporting the Results of Operations,* APB Opinion No. 9 (New York: AICPA, 1966).

[6]CICA, "Extraordinary Items," *CICA Handbook,* Section 3480 and "Prior Period Adjustments," *CICA Handbook,* Section 3600 (Toronto: CICA, both sections as amended in 1971).

[7]See, for example, L.A. Bernstein, "Extraordinary Gains and Losses — Their Significance to the Financial Analyst," *Financial Analysts Journal,* November-December 1972, pp. 49-52, 88-90; M.J. Amenta, "Unsettled Issues and Misapplications of APB Opinion No. 9 as to Treatment of Extraordinary Items," *The CPA Journal,* August 1972, pp. 640-43, 664; and W. Langdon, "Abuse of the Extraordinary Item," *Cost and Management,* November-December 1973, pp. 53-55.

[8]AICPA, APB, *Reporting the Results of Operations — Reporting the Effects of Disposal of a Segment of a Business, and Extraordinary, Unusual and Infrequently Occurring Events and Transactions,* APB Opinion No. 30 (New York: AICPA, 1973).

[9]See APB, *Accounting for Income Taxes,* Opinion No. 11 (New York: AICPA, 1967); FASB, *Reporting Gains and Losses from Extinguishment of Debt: An Amendment of APB Opinion No. 30,* Statement of Financial Accounting Standards No. 4 (Stamford: FASB, 1975); and FASB, *Accounting for Intangible Assets of Motor Carriers: An Amendment of Chapter 5 of ARB No. 43 and an Interpretation of APB Opinions 17 and 30,* Statement of Financial Accounting Standards No. 44 (Stamford: FASB, 1980), respectively.

[10]AICPA, APB, *Reporting the Results of Operations* (1973).

[11]*CICA Handbook,* Section 3600.

[12]See FASB, *Prior Period Adjustments,* Statement of Financial Accounting Standards No. 16 (Stamford: FASB, 1977).

[13]CICA, "Accounting Changes," *CICA Handbook,* Section 1506 (Toronto: CICA).

[14]United States practice is more mixed. In Opinion No. 20, the Accounting Principles Board recommended that adjustments caused by accounting policy changes (with a few exceptions) be included in income of the year of change as a "catch-up" adjustment. See AICPA, APB, *Accounting Changes,* Opinion No. 20 (New York: AICPA, 1971). Figures for prior years reported for comparative purposes would not be restated, but additional pro forma figures of net income and earnings per share would be supplied to show what the figures would have been had the new accounting policy been in effect previously. Where subsequent APB Opinions or FASB statements have required changes in established accounting policies, however, retroactive treatment, rather than a catch-up adjustment, has been required in the majority of cases.

[15]CICA, "Corporate Income Taxes — Additional Areas," *CICA Handbook,* Section 3471 (Toronto: CICA).

[16]CICA, "Business Combinations," *CICA Handbook,* Section 1580 (Toronto: CICA) par. 72.

[17]See CICA Accounting Guideline, "Term-preferred Shares," December 1977, in *CICA Handbook* (Toronto: CICA).

[18]See CICA, "Surplus," *CICA Handbook,* Section 3250 (Toronto: CICA).

[19]See CICA, "Share Capital," *CICA Handbook,* Section 3240 (Toronto: CICA) pars. 13-18.

[20]CICA, American Institute of Accountants, Committee on Accounting Procedure, "Stock Dividends and Stock Split-Ups," in *Restatement and Revision of Accounting Research Bulletins,* Accounting Research Bulletin No. 43 (New York: AIA, 1953) chap. 7B.

[21]See CICA, "Share Capital," *CICA Handbook,* Section 3240 (Toronto: CICA) pars. 6-11. These recommendations predate changes in corporations legislation in some jurisdictions that require that shares repurchased be cancelled or restored to the category of authorized but unissued, thereby reducing stated capital. In effect the change in the law makes a dead letter of the accounting recommendations in those jurisdictions.

[22]See CICA, "Appraisal Increase Credits," *CICA Handbook,* Section 3270 (Toronto: CICA).

Chapter Eighteen

Accounting for Business Combinations

At some point in their history many enterprises acquire the assets and undertaking of another business entity through direct purchase or, indirectly, through purchase of a majority of the controlling shares of the other entity. Some acquirers make many acquisitions over a period of years. Such acquisitions of one operating business by another unrelated entity are known as "business combinations."

The proper approach to accounting for business combinations was a matter of great debate prior to the early 1970s. It was common for a purchaser to record the assets and liabilities of the entity purchased at their carrying value in the books of the latter. The difference between the aggregate of those carrying values and the purchase price was recorded as a separate asset (often called goodwill) or, if negative, as a separate component of shareholders' equity. Thereafter, this "purchase discrepancy" might or might not be amortized to income. Alternatively, the purchase discrepancy could be written off to retained earnings at the time of acquisition.

This accounting for acquisitions had no theoretical justification. The purchaser's cost had no necessary relationship to book values of the vendor established, perhaps years earlier, in exchanges with other parties. What was relevant to the purchaser was the cost to him of what he had acquired. That was more likely to be related to current values of assets and liabilities than to the vendor's book values. Moreover, it made no sense to write off part of the cost paid in an arm's-length transaction immediately the deal was consummated. Nevertheless, these approaches to accounting for business combinations had the merit of simplicity and ease of implementation and were widely used.

Effective in 1974 the *CICA Handbook* prescribed new methods for business combination accounting that were more in tune with the economic substance of such transactions. The method usually applicable is known as "purchase accounting." Purchase accounting is considered appropriate whenever one of the constituents entering into a combination can be identified as the acquirer.

When one entity pays cash or other monetary consideration for the assets or shares of the other, the entity paying the consideration is obviously the acquirer. However, combinations may also be effected by exchanges of shares, statutory amalgamations, formation of a new company to acquire the shares of both constituents, and so on. In such cases one must look to who ends up with control of the combined entity in order to identify the acquirer. For example, if a small company issued three times the number of its existing outstanding shares to acquire all the shares of a larger company, the former shareholders of the latter would end up with three-quarters of the voting shares of the combined entity. In such a "reverse takeover," the company that ends up as the parent company in legal form is not the acquirer for accounting purposes.

If the shareholders of one of the combining entities end up with more of the voting shares than do those of the other entity, the former would normally be regarded as the acquirer. If, however, the balance is relatively even (say, fifty-five to forty-five or closer), other indicators should be considered. For example, if the smaller constituent is owned by a tightly knit group while the share ownership of the other is widely dispersed, the dominant interests in the smaller may well end up effectively controlling the merged entity. Representation on the board of directors after the merger, and the holders of important management positions may also give a good indication of who was the influential party in the combination. In rare cases these indicators fail, and it is apparent that the combination is a true partnership merger. In such cases "pooling of interests" accounting (discussed further below) is followed rather than purchase accounting.

Purchase accounting

Purchase accounting simply follows the normal approach to accounting for a basket purchase, with refinements to allow for the complexities of a business combination. The main problems to be addressed in purchase accounting are (1) valuation of the consideration given for the business acquired, (2) allocation of its cost among the various assets and liabilities acquired, (3) treatment of the purchase discrepancy between the net aggregate value assigned to the assets and liabilities and the net cost, and (4) disclosure required in financial statements after the combination.

Valuation of the consideration

The aggregate cost of the net assets acquired in a business combination accounted for as a purchase is the value of the consideration given. A valuation problem arises only when the consideration given is in the form of assets other than cash (almost always securities). If securities issued provide a fixed yield in the form of interest or preference dividends and do not have other unusual characteristics, a valuation based upon the market values of the securities about the time of issue or the current market values of similar securities should be reasonably satisfactory. It is important that such evaluation be made. It is wrong to value the securities issued at their par or face value if their contractual interest or dividend rate is different from market yield rates.

Valuation of common stock issued to effect an acquisition may present more of a problem. To measure the sacrifice involved in the consideration given, one would ideally like to know the cash-equivalent value of the shares issued. The current quoted market price at the acquisition date represents evidence of current value and is often used to cost the acquisition, but there can be reasons to justify a somewhat different valuation. For example, a large block of shares will not necessarily command the same price as smaller lots customarily traded on the market, especially if the current market price is exceptionally high or low in relation to the representative market price and trend therein over the longer term. In subjective terms, the company's sacrifice can best be expressed as an estimate of what net consideration it might receive either in a public or private issue of an equivalent number of shares.

The situation is still more difficult if the shares of the acquirer are not quoted. Corporations law requires that the directors place a stated value on shares issued equal to the value of the consideration received for them. But valuing a business acquired may be very difficult. The calculations and judgments made by the acquirer in deciding to make an offer should be helpful and may be the only evidence available. Unfortunately, since the vendor and purchaser have not agreed upon the value, such estimates are much less persuasive evidence than would be an agreed-upon cash price. Detailed evaluations of assets acquired will be required for the next step in the accounting, and may be helpful in giving some very rough indication of aggregate value. Since, however, the valuation of goodwill and most other intangible assets is highly, if not wholly, a matter of judgment, individual asset valuations will rarely produce a total figure acceptable as the total value to be applied to the deal.

In spite of all these difficulties, valuation of the consideration given is a necessary starting point in accounting for the purchase transaction.

Correlation of valuation of consideration and effective accounting date for an acquisition. Income reported by an acquirer is affected in two ways by a business combination. First, the acquirer records income from the business acquired from the date of acquisition. Second, the acquirer suffers a loss of income or additional expense because of the consideration given up for the business acquired. Alternatively, if the consideration given takes the form of additional shares issued, there will not be any direct offset to the increase in income from the business acquired but there will be a dilution of earnings per share of the acquirer.

Fair income reporting requires that there be coordination of these income effects. It would be misleading to start recognizing income from the business acquired before recognizing any expense or dilution of earnings per share from the consideration given up, or vice versa. Care must be taken in the accounting to avoid this lack of coordination. In particular, attention must be paid to the choice of date when it is proper for a purchaser to start recognizing income from the business acquired.

When the business combination consists of a purchase of assets of a going concern rather than shares in a company, there is little doubt about that choice. The effective date in economic terms is the date upon which the acquirer comes into possession of the property and is in a position to enjoy its rewards. It is when the combination takes the form of an acquisition of shares (either in a takeover bid or a negotiated deal) that the effective date is more open to question. In this case the record of the acquiree's operations continues uninterrupted. From the purchaser's point of view, it is very convenient to pick a month-end or quarter-end as the effective date of acquisition for accounting purposes. In this way he can minimize the work involved in cutting off and verifying the asset position in the midstream of operations. When the effective date of acquisition is somewhat arbitrarily set, however, it is important that other aspects of the transaction be selected or calculated so as to be consistent with it.

- Sometimes the consideration payable under the purchase agreement varies with the amount of working capital or equity reported by the acquiree at a given date. It is usually logical that that date should be selected as the effective date of acquisition for the acquirer's accounting.
- Sometimes the agreement prohibits payment of dividends or adjusts the purchase price for any dividends paid after a given date. Such terms suggest that the purchase is effective by that date.
- Since the relationship of dividend record dates to the closing date will determine whether the vendor shareholders or the acquirer receive dividends, the

closing date is important. If the effective date chosen for accounting precedes the record date of a dividend going to vendor shareholders, that dividend must be treated as a liability when the purchaser allocates the purchase consideration among the assets and liabilities of the business acquired (for the purpose of consolidation or equity accounting).
- If the valuation of the consideration is based upon quoted share prices in a particular period, it would be inconsistent to choose an effective accounting date that does not fall within that period.

Once the effective date of acquisition for accounting purposes is known, it is necessary to achieve logical consistency with the valuation of the consideration. Thus (subject to materiality considerations), if the consideration takes the form of a cash payment made before the effective accounting date, the out-of-pocket acquisition cost should be increased by capitalization of actual or imputed interest between the payment date and the effective accounting date. Likewise, if payment is not made until after the effective accounting date, the payment should be allocated partly to imputed interest expense, with the remainder being treated as the acquisition cost. Equivalent accounting is required if the consideration takes the form of an interest-bearing security but the date upon which interest begins to accrue on the security does not coincide with the effective accounting date for the acquisition. (Any imputation of interest would be at an after-tax rate, since imputed interest would not be recognized for income tax purposes.) Finally, if the consideration given is in the form of common shares, the calculation of earnings per share for the issuer in the period of acquisition should assume that the shares were issued at the effective accounting date for the acquisition.

Contingent consideration. Sometimes the consideration promised in an acquisition is adjustable depending upon future events. The *CICA Handbook* suggests that if the outcome of such contingencies can be determined "beyond reasonable doubt," the acquisition should be recorded on the expected outcome basis.[1] Since the adjustment clause in the contract probably reflects different views by the vendor and purchaser as to the probable future outcome, it is likely that the criterion "beyond reasonable doubt" will rarely be fulfilled at the acquisition date. In that case the accounting, when the outcome of the contingency is known, depends upon the type of adjustment clause.

- An adjustment clause may provide that additional consideration shall be given if earnings are maintained or increased in a specified future period. Such a clause probably indicates some doubt as to the earning power of the business acquired. When that doubt is resolved favourably, the additional consideration under the adjustment clause is regarded as part of the payment for the acquisition, and therefore requires adjustment of the values recorded for the net assets acquired in the combination (frequently an addition to the figure of goodwill).
- Alternatively, an adjustment may depend upon the future market price of the shares issued by the acquirer. For example, assume an acquirer issued 100,000 shares at a time when the value of the shares issued was $40 each, with a guarantee of a share price of $45 one year later. If the market price does not reach $45 at the specified date, more shares will be issued to make the value $4.5 million. That is, if the market price remains at $40 a share

it will be necessary to issue another 12,500 shares. In such a case the guaranteed value is regarded as the value of the acquisition ($4.5 million in this example). Therefore, the acquisition should be recorded originally at that cost and resolution of the contingency should merely require a change in the number of shares recorded as issued, not a change in the value placed on the acquisition.

Allocation of cost of an acquisition

The valuation of the consideration establishes the aggregate cost of the assets less the liabilities acquired or assumed in the business combination. It is then necessary to allocate that cost to individual assets and liabilities. This is not an easy task. The aggregate value of a business undertaking is rarely equal to the sum of its individual identifiable assets and liabilities. In addition, acquirers rarely make valuations of all individual assets and liabilities in arriving at their acquisition decision. (Even if they wished to, they would normally be unable to do so except in very approximate terms because of lack of detailed information about the vendor's assets and liabilities before the acquisition is consummated.)

Some businessmen wonder why an allocation of purchase price is necessary, seeing that valuations of individual assets and liabilities did not enter into their decision process. The answer is simple. The accounting process depends entirely on tracking individual assets and liabilities and changes in them. An investment in a going concern is an investment in assets having varying useful lives. Accounting must separate the future cash flow from the investment into the portion that represents recovery of investment and the portion that represents pure gain, in order to measure the success of the investment and its financial position period after period.

The acquirer might then ask: Why do I need to change the valuations of assets and liabilities that were on the books of the acquiree? If I made an investment decision on the basis of these figures, why should I now change them? The answer again is simple. It is true that the *cash flow* from the assets of the acquiree should be unaffected by the acquisition as such (although subsequent management decisions will obviously have an impact). But if the acquirer paid more for those assets than the original owner, more of that cash flow will represent recovery of investment to the acquirer than it did to the original owner. If the acquirer wants to assess the result of *his* investment decision, he must take into account the cost of the investment to *him*, not to the previous owner.

Allocation bases. How should the acquirer's cost be assigned to the individual assets and liabilities acquired? Naturally one expects the allocation to have some relationship to the current or fair value of the individual assets and liabilities. But, as already noted, the amount of the consideration is unlikely to equal the sum of those fair values.

Several methods of allocation might be possible, of which we shall mention two. As a first step, both methods would find the gross cost of the assets by adding the estimated present value of any liabilities assumed to the value of the net consideration given. Under the first method, that gross cost would be allocated to each individual asset category (including goodwill) in proportion to the estimated fair value of each category. Thus, if the estimated fair values of all assets totalled $14 million but the gross investment cost was only $12 million, each asset category would be assigned a cost of 12/14 of its estimated fair value. The second method rests upon an assumption that estimates of the fair values of different asset categories have varying reliability. Therefore, the identifiable assets are arranged in order of reliability of valuation, and cost is assigned equal to the fair value of each asset, starting with the most reliable, until the total cost is accounted for. If the purchase price exceeds the estimated fair value of all the identifiable assets, the residual is assigned to goodwill. This "residual" method is the one required by current accounting standards.

Value estimation. Numerous problems of detail arise in estimating the fair values of liabilities and of identifiable assets. The general principles may be summarized in a few statements.

- It is important that both liabilities and assets be valued. The overall acquisition cost is determined by the value of the debt and preferred share obligations assumed, as well as the amount of cash paid or value of common shares issued. Debt or preferred shares assumed should *not* be recorded at face value if they could be discharged for less or, if they could not be discharged, if they could be fully serviced (principal and interest) by purchasing safe investments at a cost lower than the face value of such securities.
- Monetary liabilities and assets are valued at the amount of future cash payable or receivable from them, discounted at an interest rate appropriate to the risk characteristics of the item. If the monetary asset or debt is marketable, the market price will provide direct evidence of the discounted present value.
- Nonmonetary assets and liabilities present more of a problem. Nonmonetary obligations require an estimate of the future cost of fulfilling the obligation. In strict theory, that future cost should include a reward for effort in discharging the obligation (or should represent an amount equivalent to that which would have to be paid to some other party in order to assume the obligation) and that amount should be discounted to present value at the acquisition date.
- Nonmonetary assets held for sale should, where possible, be valued at estimated selling price, less allowance for any costs to be incurred in completing and selling the product, and less a reasonable allowance for profit with respect to effort required and delay in realization. When an estimate of realizable value is too speculative, however, as in the case of an inventory of raw materials, replacement costs may be used. Nonmonetary assets not held for sale should be valued at estimated replacement cost for similar capacity.

CICA Handbook Section 1580 provides recommendations which, although generally in line with these principles, could be interpreted differently on points of detail. The recommendations should be referred to for guidance in specific situations.

At this point, recall that estimation of the fair values of assets and liabilities is only the first step in arriving at an allocation of the purchaser's cost. Several problems are commonly encountered in making allocations of the cost of an acquisition.[2]

- To be truly realistic the allocation should identify assets or liabilities that are valuable but not on the books of the acquiree. For example, if the going rental rate for rented premises changes substantially, a long-term lease of premises taken out at previous rental rates may acquire considerable value or represent a considerable burden. Also, the acquiree may have substantial obligations with respect to severance indemnities or postretirement employee benefits that are not recognized in its accounts. The possibility of such situations should be taken into account in the process of allocating the cost of an acquisition.

- When a business combination is effected through acquisition of shares, several problems relate to differences between the tax status of the assets and liabilities acquired and their fair values at the time of acquisition. To begin with, even if the fair value of an asset or liability were exactly the same as its book value on the books of the acquiree, its tax basis might be different, as evidenced by a deferred tax balance on the acquiree's books. In economic terms, the fair value of an asset or liability is its fair value as it would be if the tax basis were the same amount, plus or minus the *present value* of the future tax effect caused by any difference in tax basis. Since the latter adjustment is on a present value basis, it will not equal the deferred taxes recorded on the books of the acquiree. Notwithstanding, for convenience in future accounting the *CICA Handbook* recommends that deferred tax balances of the acquiree be carried forward unchanged into the consolidated financial statements. In contrast, U.S. practice is to estimate the asset's fair value with due allowance for its tax basis and not to carry forward deferred tax balances.
- In practice, of course, the fair value of the asset at the acquisition date is unlikely to equal the acquiree's book value. The *CICA Handbook* prescribes that the additional difference in value attributable to the lack of tax basis should not be recognized through the deferred tax account but rather should be recognized by adjustment of the carrying value of the asset in the combination. As a result, much of the supposed convenience from carrying forward deferred tax balances disappears.
- An acquiree will sometimes have a loss carryforward for tax purposes that is not recorded as an asset on its books because it is not "virtually certain" of recovery. Such a loss carryforward, however, may have a real value simply because there is a good chance of recovery, a chance that may well be enhanced by actions of the acquirer. The recommendation is that the recoverable value of a tax loss carryforward (discounted as appropriate) be recorded as an asset if there is a "reasonable assurance" of realization of its benefits. If not recorded at the time of acquisition because of lack of that assurance, any subsequent realization is treated as extraordinary income, not an adjustment of values at the time of acquisition. (U.S. standards treat the subsequent recovery as a retroactive adjustment of the purchase consideration.)
- Several questions come to mind if the acquiree has a defined benefit pension plan that will continue after the acquisition.
  - Sometimes a business combination results in an equalization of pension plan benefits offered to employees of the combined entities. If such equalization is reasonably certain to occur and will involve increased costs, any increase in obligation attributable to employees of the constituent taken over should be allowed for in the valuation.

- Frequently, part of the unfunded obligation with respect to the acquiree's pension plan will be attributable to improvements of benefits for prior service that have not yet been recognized as expense on the grounds that such improvements produce benefits to be received in future years. An acquirer should be very skeptical of his ability to realize those benefits. Generally the full amount of the unfunded liability should be recognized at the acquisition date without any offset for unrecognized prior service.
- As we have seen in chapter 13, the 1987 pension accounting standards call for the accounting recognition of pension obligations normally to be based on the plan formula. The current value of future benefits promised under the plan would be best approximated by discounting them at interest rates equivalent to those that could be obtained on a purchase of annuities to fund the benefits, or rates of return obtainable on high quality investments that might be used to fund the benefits. If this valuation basis is used for pension obligations assumed, the logically consistent basis for pension fund assets taken over would be current market value. (The acquirer's balance sheet, of course, would record only the net amount of pension obligation or asset.)
- Although this basis of valuation of pension obligations and assets is consistent with the principles of business combination accounting, one must also consider its compatibility with pension accounting standards. It appears unlikely at the time this is written that the Canadian 1987 pension accounting standard will result in pension valuations consistent with those just stated. If differences do exist there is, at least, an argument that, for consistency and future accounting convenience, pension obligations and assets taken over in an acquisition may be valued based on methods and assumptions compatible with those used in accounting for the acquirer's own plans.[3]

- The *CICA Handbook* suggests the valuation of intangible assets "which can be identified and named."[4] As is argued in chapter 12, many more intangible factors can be identified and named than can be valued on any reasonable basis. Valuation of specific intangible factors acquired in a business combination should be restricted to those assets whose utility can be transferred to other parties independent of the business and therefore have some hope of a value in exchange. Even for these, hard evidence should be available to justify the basis of valuation.

In view of the occasionally severe difficulties in valuation, it may take several months to a year before a cost can be allocated on the basis of reasonably satisfactory evidence. Initial allocations, therefore, must be regarded as tentative and subject to adjustment when all the necessary information is obtained.

There is an underlying conflict running through this discussion of the allocation of purchase cost. The allocation is based on current values of assets and liabilities and includes all elements of value, as it must since the purchase price presumably takes all elements of value into account. In contrast, normal accounting conventions are not based on current values and do not provide continuous accounting for all elements of value, but rather expense many such elements as period costs when they are incurred. Thus, if the assets and liabilities of the acquiree are originally taken into account largely on an all-inclusive current value basis, there will be discontinuities thereafter as the accounting reverts to the normal practice.

For example, the valuation of inventory is supposed to be based on estimated selling price less estimated cost of disposal and a reasonable allowance for selling effort. This basis of valuation means that manufacturing profit earned by the vendor is included in the valuation of inventory taken over. But normal accounting conventions do not permit taking credit for manufacturing profit before realization. This means that when the inventory of the acquiree is sold, the profit reported will be a selling profit only; on the other hand, when replacement inventory is manufactured, no manufacturing profit element will be recognized. In that sale period, therefore, profit of the business taken over will be understated compared with what will be shown subsequently as normal accounting conventions become effective. Similarly, discrepancies may occur if tools and dies are recorded originally as assets and subsequently written off, if pension accounting is not handled consistently, and so forth. One possible way to lessen this problem would be to permit valuation of assets and liabilities of the acquiree on a basis compatible with the accounting methods used by the acquirer for recognizing its assets and liabilities. It is probable that this approach is taken by many acquirers in practice, in spite of the recommendations in current accounting standards.

This problem of discontinuity in accounting becomes particularly acute when the acquiree is a financial institution. The assets and liabilities of such an institution may contain thousands of interest-bearing contracts. If these are individually revalued at interest rates prevailing at the acquisition date, the change in amortization schedules thereafter would require virtually a complete rewriting of the records of the acquiree. In the circumstances, the only practical solution would seem to be to accept the acquiree's accounting figures but to calculate a valuation override for interest-bearing assets unmatched by liabilities of similar term or for abnormal interest rate spreads on matched assets and liabilities. That valuation account would then be amortized appropriately to postacquisition income over the duration of the interest-bearing contracts. Non-interest-bearing assets and liabilities would be valued under normal approaches.

Accounting for purchase discrepancies

Purchased goodwill. If any part of the purchase price remains unallocated to identifiable assets, that residual is assigned to goodwill. Chapter 12 has discussed the different possible ways to account for goodwill arising on acquisition. Present standards require that it be amortized over its estimated life, not to exceed forty years. In view of the nebulous nature of goodwill it is usually impossible to make any very close estimate of its reasonable life. Most acquirers use the maximum forty-year amortization period even though one's subjective opinion might suggest such a period is usually too long in our ever-changing business environment.

Negative discrepancies. Where a negative purchase discrepancy falls out from the valuation of the net assets of the acquiree, the *CICA Handbook* directs that it be allocated so as to reduce the values assigned to individual nonmonetary assets. The selection of nonmonetary assets is to be based on judgment but usually would begin with the intangibles, followed by the fixed assets. There have been cases where such application of a negative purchase discrepancy has produced patently absurd results. Fixed assets and even inventory have been required to be written off, even though the previous operations of the acquiree have reported profits after normal charges for depreciation and cost of sales. Such cases represent true bargain purchases. Accounting standards would do well to permit the carryforward of the acquiree's book values in such exceptional cases, particularly for inventory, perhaps treating unapplied negative purchase discrepancy as a component of shareholders' equity.

Acquisitions disclosure

Accounting standards call for disclosure of pertinent details about business acquisitions, including a description of the business acquired and the percentage interest held in voting shares (where the acquisition is effected through a share purchase). The effective date of acquisition and the period for which the results of the acquiree are included in the income statement of the acquirer are also to be disclosed.

Financial details of the acquisition are to be disclosed, including (1) details of the fair value of the consideration given, (2) the total amount assigned to all assets excluding goodwill, (3) the amount assigned to goodwill and its proposed amortization period, (4) the amount assigned to total liabilities of the acquiree, and (5) the minority interest in net assets. For the purpose of tie-in with information in the statement of changes in financial position, it is useful to provide additional detail as to categories of assets acquired. All this information can be compactly presented in the so-called "acquisition equation," which details the assets acquired less liabilities and minority interest, if any, and balances them with the consideration given. A description of any contingent consideration and its amount is also to be disclosed.

Supplemental pro forma disclosure of results of operations on a combined basis from the beginning of the year of acquisition is also considered very desirable to aid investment analysis in the year of acquisition and comparison in the next year.

Pooling of interests accounting

As noted at the beginning of this chapter, pooling of interests accounting is followed when none of the constituents entering into a business combination can be identified as the dominant party. The theory of pooling accounting, then, is that the former constituents have simply agreed to share their interests and therefore no new basis of accountability should arise. The mechanics are very simple. The accounting policies of the constituents entering into the combination must first be conformed. After this is done, the balances of assets, liabilities, and equity of the constituents (as adjusted) are simply added together to form the balance sheet of the combined entity. Since the combination is deemed to be a continuation of the previous constituents, the income figures previously reported by the separate constituents (after restatement for accounting policy changes) are likewise added together to provide an earnings history for the combined entity.

In theory, the capital, contributed surplus, and retained earnings accounts of the constituents would also be added together to form the elements of shareholders' equity reported by the combined entity. Depending upon the way the combination is consummated, however, the legal capital of the continuing entity may be greater than the sum of the shareholder capital amounts previously reported by the constituents. If it is desired to report the amount of stated capital on the face of the balance sheet, it is necessary, when this occurs, to transfer contributed surplus (if any), and often retained earnings as well, to capital account.

United States standards have taken a different direction from the Canadian in distinguishing between cases where purchase and pooling of interests accounting is used. In essence, the U.S. standard is based on the concept that if a combination is effected through an exchange of voting shares only and there are no direct or collateral arrangements to bail out the shareholders of one or the other of the constituents, the combination should be treated as a pooling of interests. This general idea is supported by a series of detailed rules designed to prevent what is really a purchase qualifying for pooling accounting.[5] These apparently have not prevented abuses.[6]

Some accountants have suggested that a pooling of interests is a significant event and should not be accounted for merely by carrying forward the reported accounting figures for the constituents of the combination. Instead, they advocate "new entity" accounting whereby all the assets and liabilities of the merged entities are valued at fair value at the date of the combination. Under a variant of this, all the assets except goodwill would be valued for inclusion in the balance sheet. This method, although at least as logical in theory as conventional pooling accounting, would compound the valuation difficulties present in purchase accounting and has drawn little support.

Other issues related to business combinations

"Push-down" accounting

When an acquisition takes the form of a purchase of shares of an acquiree, the purchasing accounting standard applies only to the valuation of assets and liabilities in the parent company's consolidated financial statements. Purchase accounting rules do not speak to the effect of the combination, if any, upon the accounting of the newly acquired subsidiary.

Suppose the new parent has acquired one hundred percent of the voting common shares of the acquiree and no outstanding public interest remains in it in the form of debt securities, preferred shares, or other securities. It may well be convenient for the new parent to "push down" to its new subsidiary the values it has allocated to assets and liabilities in order to facilitate the future consolidation of financial statements. Beyond the question of convenience, however, there is a question of principle. Since evidence of the current value of the assets and liabilities of the subsidiary has been provided by an independently bargained exchange transaction, would it be better accounting to report on that basis in the subsidiary's financial statements for all public reporting purposes after the acquisition? The U.S. Securities and Exchange Commission has advocated this position.[7] It seems to make common sense and, based on U.S. precedent, can be considered within generally accepted accounting principles to do so.

Questions begin to arise when the acquiree is not wholly owned by its parent, or when there are publicly held securities in it that have priorities over its common shares. Why should the financial reports to the minority interest or to such security holders be influenced by a transaction in which neither they nor the reporting entity itself participated? Is the discontinuity in reporting of depreciation, amortization, etc., justified? What is the impact on covenants in debt indentures based on generally accepted accounting principles if there is a radical change in measurements of the asset and liability positions? Beyond this, there is a general question — if one type of transaction external to an entity causes an adjustment of the measurement basis of its assets and liabilities, are there other transactions that logically might have a similar result? For example, a "leveraged buy-out" of an entity is likely to be based on a current value assessment of its financial position.[8] Should there be a change in basis of measurement whenever there is a significant change in the controlling ownership of an entity, or is this merely a selective (and somewhat haphazard) application of current value accounting?

Accounting standards have not addressed these questions in any organized fashion. It is doubtful that clear criteria could be drawn to distinguish cases where a new basis of accounting should be adopted. Also, since adoption of new bases of accounting would not affect the values of assets and liabilities for tax purposes, better guidance would be necessary for dealing with differences between accounting values and tax values than is now found in the business combination standard. On balance, it seems likely that application of push-down accounting in the absence of a general acceptance of current value accounting ought to be extremely limited.

Non-arm's-length business combinations

Accounting standards for business combinations specifically disclaim any attempt to give guidance to combinations that involve the transfer of net assets or exchanges of shares between entities under common control. Bases permissible for such transactions depend, therefore, on general acceptance, and practice is far from standardized. The following commentary will present the author's opinions on preferable practice.

Sale of an unincorporated business by an individual to a wholly owned company, amalgamation of two companies wholly owned by another company or by an individual, or sale of an operating division by a parent company down to a wholly owned subsidiary all represent rearrangements of the legal interests of the controlling entity without significant economic substance. Because the rearrangements lack economic substance, a change in basis of measurement for assets and liabilities involved is generally not appropriate (so long as historical cost accounting is the general rule).

Instead, what has been called "continuity of interest" accounting is appropriate. The carrying values of assets and liabilities transferred from one legal entity to another should not change. For example, an amalgamation of two companies under common control, although not technically a pooling of interests, would be accounted for using an approach identical to pooling of interests accounting. Or, if shares of a wholly owned subsidiary corporation are issued to its parent in consideration for a business acquired, the shares issued should be recorded at an amount equal to the parent's carrying value of the net assets acquired.

Even if the consideration paid by the acquirer in such a case is cash, the transaction cannot, in logic, be accounted for based on the cash amount. Suppose, for example, a subsidiary 100% owned by another corporation buys a business for $150,000 cash from that other corporation, and the net assets transferred have a book value of $100,000. Continuity of interest accounting prevents the net assets acquired being accounted for at more than $100,000. To balance the transaction, the extra $50,000 should be treated by the acquiring subsidiary as though it were a dividend. Probably many accountants will balk at this suggestion. But what is the alternative? Shall all non-arm's-length transfers of business undertakings be reported at fair value? Or shall we quietly forget the precept that substance should govern form in the accounting? In this case, for example, suppose the acquiring subsidiary actually did pay a dividend of $50,000 and then bought the net undertaking for its book value of $100,000. Would anyone argue that the net assets should be recorded at $150,000? If not, what is the difference between the two forms of transactions in their end result?

Certain explanatory comments need to be added, however.

- When corporations legislation establishes the stated capital of a company as an amount equal to the fair value of consideration received, a problem will be encountered similar to that described above under pooling of interests accounting. If stated capital is to be reported in the equity section of an acquiring corporation, it may be necessary to capitalize surplus. Alternatively, disclosure may be made that the legal capital is different from the amount reported as capital for accounting purposes.
- If the tax basis of net assets transferred remains the same as it was in the hands of the vendor, deferred tax accounts should be transferred unchanged. On the other hand, if the tax basis is changed as a result of the transaction, the deferred tax accounts may well need to be adjusted. Under continuity of interest accounting it is appropriate to look at tax allocation on a combined basis. That is to say, if one subentity reduces tax by selling assets below their previous tax basis, it would be appropriate for the buying subentity to recognize deferred tax accordingly in its accounts.
- Continuity of interest accounting does not preclude the use of appraisal accounting *after* a transaction if it would otherwise be acceptable. That is to say, although continuity of interest accounting prevents the establishment of a new accounting basis merely as a result of the amount of consideration arbitrarily set in a non-arm's-length agreement, there is no bar to any accounting that would be acceptable in the absence of the transaction.
- Disclosure is required of related party transactions (see chapter 6). That disclosure would be a logical place to explain any accounting peculiarities created by differences in the measurements used in the continuity of interest accounting and those applicable for taxation or for determining the amount of legal capital.

The foregoing description of continuity of interest accounting has been predicated on the assumption that there has been no change in the interests of the proprietors of the entities entering into the combinations. If that condition does not hold, the basis of continuity of interest accounting — no change in economic substance — may be overturned. Consider the following possible situations.

- A parent company sells an operating division to a fifty-five percent-owned subsidiary.
- A group of individuals forms a company and sells a going business to it in return for shares, preparatory to a significant offering of shares by that company to the public or to outside interests.

The first of these situations would simply be a large-scale related-party transaction. The directors of the subsidiary would have a duty to be satisfied that the purchase price did not exceed fair value for the business acquired. Normal Canadian practice would be to record this transaction at its agreed value and provide details in the disclosure of related-party transactions. (In the parent company consolidated financial statements, profit recorded on the intercompany transaction would be eliminated, as will be described in the next chapter.)

In the second case, there should be evidence of value to support the original issue of shares to the group of owners. The successful marketing of shares to outside interests subsequently may be regarded as confirmation of the valuations included in the financial statements and disclosed in the share offering document. (If the valuations implied higher amortization of expense, etc., the previous earnings history of the business transferred would have to be appropriately modified by pro forma adjustments for the purpose of the selling document with respect to the shares.)

Although not well articulated in accounting standards, the common thread in these examples is that when new parties acquire an interest in a business undertaking, the most useful accounting presentation for them will be one that is based on values current at the date of their acquisition of an interest — the values upon which their investment was presumably predicated. In many transactions, this proposition comes into conflict with the notion that when parties at interest do not change, the accounting measurement basis should not change. No authority in Canada has stated how large an outside interest introduced must be to justify the abandonment of the continuity of interest principle and introduction of a new basis of accounting. It is not even clear that there must be a change in ownership interest. For example, suppose a business undertaking is transferred to a new corporation in return for shares, and a substantial issue of debt securities is made, secured only by the assets of the company. Would that justify a new accounting basis for the net assets transferred to the company? These issues, in present practice, are faced on a case-by-case basis.

The suggestions stated above with respect to the use of "continuity of interest" accounting need to be viewed in the context of the general approach to accounting for related-party transactions. At present, no Canadian accounting standard addresses the question of *measurement* of related party transactions; *disclosure* considerations only are dealt with in *CICA Handbook* Section 3840. The general practice with respect to related-party transactions in the normal course of business seems to be to record such transactions on the basis of their contract amount, relying on disclosure to alert the reader to the possibility that these may not be equivalent to independently bargained values.

Chapter 6 suggests, however, that transactions out of the usual course of business should be given special consideration. Non-arm's-length business combinations fall squarely into this category, and the preceding comments deal with that situation. In addition, this category probably applies to many transactions whereby controlling interests sell major assets to corporations under their control, taking advantage of Section 85 of the Income Tax Act to specify tax values for the property transferred different from the amount stated in the transaction. Accounting practice with respect to these "Section 85 rollovers" is highly confused. Some accountants advocate accounting on the basis of fair value if reasonably determinable.[9] Some would use the actual stated exchange figure, following the form of the transaction. Some would use predecessor book values. A rule consistent with the suggestion above with respect to non-arm's-length business combinations would be to use predecessor book values (adjusted as appropriate for taxation differences resulting from the transaction) unless there is a significant change in ownership interests.

Summary

A business combination occurs when an existing entity, or a new entity, acquires control over one or more other existing entities. In Canada, whenever a dominant party in a combination can be identified (the acquirer), a business combination is accounted for by the "purchase" method. In essence, the purchase method simply spells out how this particularly complex form of "basket purchase" of assets (and assumption of liabilities) is to be accounted for.

The application of purchase accounting presents several problems.

- The first problem is that of measurement of the purchase consideration. The basic accounting principle that a transaction should be measured at its cash-equivalent value at the transaction date is applicable. This means that a fair value must be assigned to non-cash consideration. Depending on the circumstances, contingent consideration may require assignment of additional cost to the purchase at the time of the transaction or, more likely, at some later date.
- The second problem, and a major one, is that of assignment of the value of the consideration to the various assets acquired and liabilities assumed. In this connection, it is necessary to take into account the possible existence of assets and liabilities that are not on the books of the acquiree. A fair value must be assigned to any liabilities assumed. The sum of those liability valuations plus the value of the consideration given represents the gross cost to be allocated to the assets. Then, a fair value is estimated for the assets — a difficult problem for assets not regularly traded in a market. A fair value that would be arrived at in an ordinary exchange should be adjusted to allow for any difference between the tax basis of assets and liabilities and the fair values so estimated.
- When the sum of estimated fair values is compared with the gross purchase consideration there usually will be a "purchase discrepancy" — a difference, plus or minus, between the sum of fair values and the gross cost. If the gross cost is greater than the identifiable assets, the positive purchase discrepancy is considered to be goodwill. If the purchase discrepancy is negative — that is, the sum of the estimated fair values of assets exceeds the gross cost — the discrepancy is judgmentally applied so as to reduce the cost assigned to nonmonetary assets. When the purchaser has made an advantageous acquisition, this procedure can, upon occasion, produce subsequent expense figures that, when those costs are written off, are unrepresentative of expense to be expected in continuing operations.

A purchaser's first financial statements after an acquisition are expected to provide relatively full details of the acquisition and its manner of accounting.

A simpler accounting approach known as "pooling of interests accounting" is followed when an acquirer cannot be identified in a business combination. This approach simply calls for adding together the assets, liabilities, and equity of each of the combining entities (after any adjustments necessary to make their accounting policies conform). In effect, the entities combined are treated as though they always had been combined. Consistent with this, the historical earnings records of the combining entities are added together to provide an earnings history for the newly combined entity.

Suggestions have been made that, after a purchase of another company, the new parent company's costs (as determined by the allocation process) should be "pushed down" onto the books of the subsidiary. When the subsidiary is wholly owned and there are no significant outside interests that have a financial stake in it (for example, holders of preferred shares or debt), this suggestion has a great deal of merit. If other parties have a right to financial reports from the subsidiary, however, the change in its basis of accounting after the combination is harder to justify.

The combination of businesses under common control is a frequently encountered example of a "related party transaction." If no new stake-holders are being brought into the picture, the fact of the combination does not justify the use of a new basis of accounting. Instead, the use of "continuity of interest" accounting — a method similar to pooling of interests accounting — is appropriate. If new financial interests acquire a stake in the combination at the same time, however, there is more rationale for a new basis of accounting.

References

[1]CICA, "Business Combinations," *CICA Handbook*, Section 1580 (Toronto: CICA), par. 33.

[2]A useful description of the process of making an allocation may be found in T.M. Bartlett, Jr., W.W. Kingsbery, and C. Toder, "Problems in Accounting for a Business Purchase," *Financial Executive*, April 1973, pp. 52-68.

[3]This was the suggestion in APB, *Business Combinations*, Opinion No. 16 (New York: AICPA, 1970), par. 88h., n. 13. However, this is now superseded in the United States because the FASB 1987 standard on pension accounting calls for pension obligation and asset measurement at fair value.

[4]*CICA Handbook*, Section 1580, par. 45(e).

[5]AICPA, APB, *Business Combinations*, pars. 45-48.

[6]Some examples are given in S.P. Gunther, "Lingering Pooling Problems," *The CPA Journal*, June 1973, pp. 459-64. See also J.C. Anderson and J.G. Louderback, III, "Income Manipulation and Purchase-Pooling: Some Additional Results," *Journal of Accounting Research*, Autumn 1975, pp. 338-43.

[7]See SEC, *The Application of the "Push Down" Basis of Accounting in the Separate Financial Statements of Subsidiaries Acquired In Purchase Transactions*, Staff Accounting Bulletin No. 54 (Washington: SEC, November 3, 1983). See also J.M. Sylph, "Push Down Accounting: Is the US Lead Worth Following?" *CAmagazine*, October 1985, pp. 52-55.

[8]See discussion in M.E. Cunningham, "Push-Down Accounting: Pros and Cons," *Journal of Accountancy*, June 1984, pp. 72-77.

[9]J.M. Sylph and E.G. Percival, "Accounting Options for Section 85 Rollovers," *CAmagazine*, July 1981, pp. 42-47.

Chapter Nineteen
Accounting for Intercorporate Investments

In many business combinations the acquiring company does not buy the assets of the business acquired directly but rather buys a majority of the shares of the company holding the assets. In addition, many companies choose to set up separate subsidiaries to carry on various aspects of their business or to operate in different geographical regions. Some companies, indeed, may be purely holding companies with little in the way of assets outside their investments in subsidiary or affiliated companies.

Consolidated financial statements

How should a parent company report its investment in one or more subsidiaries in its financial statements? Conceivably it might record such investments at a figure representing the cost invested in them and report as income from them merely the amount of dividends received. Such a basis of accounting was widely used some decades ago. The objections to it are obvious from a simple example. Suppose an operating company took a major division of its business and sold it to a subsidiary company in return for all its shares. Nothing would have happened in substance. Yet, if the investment in the subsidiary were accounted for on the cost basis, the financial statements of the parent would lose a great deal of information. The individual assets, liabilities, revenues, and expenses of the subsidiary would no longer be reported in the financial statements of the parent. Income reported from the subsidiary could be varied almost at will merely by the parent company's decision to cause its subsidiary to declare or withhold the declaration of dividends. The idea of consolidated financial statements to overcome these disadvantages was adopted by some North American companies even before 1900 and was widespread before there were any accounting standards on the subject. Today, standards have been developed applicable to all companies, and have contributed to a large measure of consistency in practice.

The concept of consolidation

A consolidated basis of accounting has been said to be desirable when a group of companies constitutes an economic unit. Just what constitutes an economic unit is not entirely clear from the words themselves. Does it mean the operations carried on by members of the group must be complementary in some way? It does not mean that in practice, since some "conglomerates" presenting consolidated financial statements carry on completely unrelated types of business within the group. Does it mean that top management of the group is able to manage the resources of components of the group to the best advantage of the group as a whole? That is nearer to the mark, but it is still necessary to know what is meant by management of resources. In many groups the main functions of top management are restricted to making investment decisions, allocating financial resources, raising additional financing where necessary, and monitoring the performance of the chief divisional executives without interfering with their operating decisions.

The idea of an economic unit thus leads naturally to adoption of *control* as the primary criterion for consolidation. A second criterion is that of ownership. Management is accountable to owners for resources entrusted to it. Consolidation accounting generally provides a fuller accountability for resources than does investment accounting. For the most part, these two criteria reinforce each other since control goes with ownership — at least ownership of voting shares. There are, however, some conflicts and uncertainties.

- Suppose Company P owns 60% of the common shares of Company S which owns 60% of the common shares of Company A. The beneficial interest of Company P in the net assets and income of Company A is only 36%. That is, if all the income of Company A were distributed or all its assets were distributed in liquidation, and the amounts were paid on by Company S to its shareholders, Company P would receive only 36%. Yet there is no doubt that Company P is firmly in control of the management of Company A's resources.
- To make the example more extreme, suppose the capital structure of each of Company S and Company A consisted of voting common shares to the extent of 20% of the common equity and nonvoting shares to the extent of 80%. Suppose also that Company S owned all the voting shares and none of the nonvoting shares of Company A, and Company P's ownership of Company S was similar. Then Company P would have absolute control of the resources of Company A but only a 4% beneficial interest in them. Some accountants think consolidation accounting inappropriate in such a case.
- On the other hand, a subsidiary company might be wholly owned but be subject to debt covenants that might be so constraining that the exercise of parent company control is rather limited in scope.

The *CICA Handbook* combines the criteria of control and ownership in its rules governing consolidation practice. All subsidiaries are normally consolidated, but the term "subsidiary" is defined as being a company in which another company *owns* directly or indirectly a majority of shares carrying the right to elect at least a majority of the members of the board of directors.[1] This definition lays stress on control, but it is control exercised through the means of voting share ownership, not through other means. When the mechanical application of this rule does not accord with the basic criteria, however, exceptions are to be made.

- If control is likely to be temporary because of a planned disposition of a subsidiary, that subsidiary should not be consolidated.[2]
- If increases in the subsidiary equity are unlikely to accrue to the parent or if the parent's control is seriously impaired, as when a subsidiary is in receivership or bankruptcy, it should not be consolidated.[3] (In such cases recognition of impairment in value of the investment that is shown after deconsolidation would almost certainly be required as well.)

The consolidation rule is also subject to two exceptions on pragmatic grounds:

- In Canada, the financial statements of banks and life insurance companies follow bases of accounting that are inconsistent in some respects with generally accepted accounting principles. In particular, under the influence of regulation the accounting of these institutions may be more conservative than would be required for a fair portrayal of income or may be designed to smooth the figure of reported income over a period of years. Unless the financial statements of such subsidiaries can be modified to conform with generally accepted accounting principles (and it may not be clear what modifications should be made to accomplish this), they are not to be included in the parent company consolidation but rather are to be accounted for by a modified form of the equity method. This simply means that the investment in the subsidiary will be carried at cost plus the parent's share of its undistributed reported earnings (notwithstanding that those earnings are not determined in accordance with generally accepted accounting principles) plus or minus normal adjustments for amortization of any purchase discrepancies, etc., that would be made in applying the equity method of accounting. This compromise is clearly a choice between evils. Lacking a good measure of the performance of the subsidiary, a poor measure is considered better than mere adherence to the cost basis of investment accounting.
- An exception to the rules requiring consolidation is also allowed "when the financial statement components of a subsidiary are such that consolidation would not provide the more informative presentation to the shareholders of the parent company."[4] The *CICA Handbook* amplifies this vague guidance by indicating that there may infrequently be circumstances where "a subsidiary's financial statement components may be so dissimilar to those of the other companies in the group that their inclusion in the consolidated financial statements would provide a form of presentation which may be difficult to interpret."[5] This amplification is itself vague. The author believes that it refers particularly to the problem caused by consolidation of a financial intermediary with an ordinary nonfinancial company. In a financial institution the liabilities to the public and others may be twenty to thirty times the amount of its equity. In an ordinary company, in contrast, a debt/equity ratio of one to one is considered quite high. Consolidation of the balance sheet and income statement of two such dissimilar entities makes it hard to apply the conventional tools of financial analysis that would be applied to either separately. Yet this problem is present to some degree in most consolidations. A consolidation of a manufacturing enterprise and a retail enterprise will also upset expected financial ratios. The *CICA Handbook* suggests that it is rare that full consolidation of all subsidiaries will not be the more informative presentation. The author believes, to the contrary, that a set of financial statements excluding some subsidiaries from consolidation, if accompanied by financial statements of the subsidiaries not consolidated, will often be more informative than a fully consolidated statement. Accordingly he does not know what criteria to use to interpret the CICA recommendation.

This last point suggests that consolidation is a means of presentation that has distinct disadvantages as well as advantages. It is not just that consolidation of components in different lines of business distorts financial ratios. Consolidation may also conceal aspects of the legal position that are significant to the financial position. Many writers have pointed out that creditors cannot depend on consolidated financial statements to indicate the safety of their position, since their claim (in the absence of cross guarantees) is restricted to the assets of the individual legal entity to which they have advanced credit. Shareholders may also be misled. For example, consolidation of healthy subsidiaries with a parent company in a weak working capital position may conceal the real risks of the latter, for assets of the subsidiaries may be tied up by contracts or debt covenants and thus may be unavailable at short notice to stave off insolvency of the parent. If earnings are mainly in the subsidiaries, it also may be difficult to pass cash up to the parent company to meet its interest or dividend requirements.[6]

There are various possibilities for overcoming these difficulties, but none is without some objection.

- Financial statements may be presented on a "consolidating" basis. Such statements look very like a consolidation worksheet, presenting in columns side by side the figures of the individual parent and subsidiary companies, adding across (after adjustments and eliminations) to the consolidated figures. Consolidating statements are highly revealing to a serious analyst, but their very wealth of information generally makes them too overpowering for the ordinary financial statement reader.
- Financial statements may be presented on an unconsolidated basis (with the investment in subsidiaries accounted for on the equity basis) with supplementary statements provided for at least the major subsidiaries. To tie in with the parent company's figure of investment on the equity basis, it would be desirable that the figures of the subsidiary be stated on the "push-down" basis. To amplify the presentation, the main financial statements could also show fully consolidated figures side by side with the unconsolidated parent company figures. As with consolidating financial statements, the principal objection to this solution is the increased complexity of the financial presentation.
- Reliance could be placed on "segment information" pertaining to the different lines of business carried on within the group to supply the additional information as to financial position and operations of components of the group. (See discussion of segment disclosure in chapter 22.) This solution is reasonably satisfactory when different lines of business are generally carried on in different subsidiaries. It does not meet the problem when the natural divisions between segments do not correspond very closely to the boundaries of the corporations within which the various segment activities are carried on.

The conclusion must be that there is no one basis of presentation that is perfectly adapted to provide in simple form all needed information about complex groupings of corporations and activities. Full consolidation is a somewhat artificial device for presenting information about a complex organization in a compact form. When supplemented by segment disclosure, it is a satisfactory basis of general purpose reporting for most groups of corporations most of the time. It is conceivable that other devices might be equally satisfactory for general use. In any case, specific additional information may well be desirable in individual cases.

Possible bases for implementation of consolidation

There are several conceivable ways of putting together figures in a consolidation. A choice is required whenever there is a minority interest in a subsidiary. The choice affects two aspects of the consolidated financial statements: (1) the valuation of assets and liabilities of the subsidiary included in the consolidated statements, and (2) the figure ascribed to minority interest in the consolidation. The difference will be illustrated by the following simple example. Company P buys 70% of the common shares of Company S for $84,000. The net asset position of Company S at the date of acquisition is summarized in Table 19-1.

Table 19-1

Net Assets of Company S at Acquisition

	Book Value	Fair Value	Excess of Fair Value
Working capital	$50,000	$ 50,000	–
Fixed assets	30,000	50,000	$20,000
	$80,000	$100,000	$20,000

Since 70% of the fair value of the net assets of Company S is $70,000, there is a purchase discrepancy of $14,000 inherent in the price of $84,000, and this is considered to be goodwill.

- Under the entity concept of accounting, the primary focus of interest is on the resources under the control of the entity. Claims upon those resources by the various sources of capital are of lesser concern. An entity concept of consolidation would therefore wish to show the subsidiary assets in consolidation at a figure based on their fair value at the date of acquisition. Since the parent company paid $84,000 for a 70% interest, the fair value of all the assets must be $120,000. The identifiable assets would be included in the consolidation at $100,000, goodwill at $20,000, and minority interest at $36,000 (30% of $120,000). Consistent with the entity concept, the share of the minority interest in the earnings of the subsidiary would not be reported as a deduction in the consolidated income statement but rather as a distribution of consolidated income. Also the minority interest would be reported in the balance sheet as a different form of equity, rather than something completely outside the consolidated equity.
- Under the proprietary concept of accounting, the primary interest lies in reporting to the shareholders of the parent company. (Minority shareholders in the subsidiary should be satisfied by the report of the subsidiary itself.) The 70% interest of the parent company in the assets of the subsidiary should therefore be recorded at the parent company's cost, but the 30% interest still held by the minority shareholders need only be recorded at the book values used in reporting to them. Thus the identifiable assets of the sub-

sidiary would be included in the consolidation at $94,000 (70% of $100,000 plus 30% of $80,000), goodwill at $14,000, and minority interest at $24,000. This concept is also known as the "parent company" approach to consolidation. In the consolidated income statement, to be consistent with a strict proprietary viewpoint, the share of the minority interest is deducted in arriving at consolidated earnings and the minority interest itself is excluded from shareholders' equity in the balance sheet.

- A compromise approach, leaning rather more closely to the entity approach, is known as the "parent company extension" approach. Under this basis the identifiable assets are included in the consolidation at their fair value of $100,000. Goodwill, however, is restricted to the excess of the parent company's cost over its share of fair value — i.e., $14,000 — and the minority interest is reported at its share of the fair value of the assets excluding goodwill, namely $30,000. This approach may be rationalized in several ways. Since the statement is intended for the shareholders of the parent company and not for the shareholders of the subsidiary, there is no reason to base the minority interest figure on the book values applied in reporting to them alone. Instead it seems more logical to show their interest at values that are relevant to the parent company shareholders. Thereby one avoids the rather strange mixed asset carrying values, consisting of 70% at a current figure of cost and 30% at figures established in transactions by the subsidiary at earlier dates. The restriction of the reported goodwill to the parent company's cost may be justified by the argument that there may be a value to control as such that would be included in the parent company's cost, and it cannot be assumed that there is a corresponding value to the minority interest.

The *CICA Handbook* recommends the use of the parent company concept of consolidation — the second of the three described above. This choice is explainable on practical grounds. The net assets included in the consolidation are to be reported at the parent company's cost, and the asset carrying values must be derived from an allocation of that cost. When a parent company acquires shares in a subsidiary in a series of transactions (a step-by-step purchase) the value of the subsidiary's assets may change between one step and the next, and consequently the cost for a (say) 20% interest in them is likely to change from one step to the next. If the cost basis of accounting is to be retained, the cost incurred in earlier steps cannot be written up (or down) to the level of the cost incurred in the latest step. If it is not logical to write up the parent company's earlier cost in consolidation, it cannot be logical to write up the minority interest — at least not after the first step in the acquisition. Thus, mixed asset valuation bases are inevitable in step acquisitions unless one adopts a form of current value accounting. This being so, the continuance of reporting minority interest at subsidiary book values seems less irrational and has the merit of practical convenience.

Still another possibility for consolidation remains. Consolidated statements could be prepared on a basis known as "proportionate consolidation" or "pro rata consolidation." Under this concept, the minority interest in assets and liabilities of the subsidiary is completely disregarded. If the parent company has a beneficial interest of 70% in the subsidiary, it merely takes up 70% of the valuation of its assets and liabilities, which is arrived at in the usual way by allocating the parent company's cost grossed up to 100% basis. Similarly, in the income statement 70%

of the revenues and expenses of the subsidiary are included line by line in the consolidated figures. In this manner the minority interest does not appear anywhere in the consolidated financial statements. There is consequently no question as to how it should be valued. This pro rata concept is consistent with the overall proprietary approach to accounting — perhaps more so than the parent company concept now in use. It might be criticized on the grounds that inclusion of only the parent company share of the subsidiary's assets, liabilities, revenues, and expenses in the consolidated financial statement conflicts with the idea of the entire group being one economic unit. That objection seems to be well founded. But, given that consolidation accounting is an artificial procedure in any event, the simplicity and practicality of pro rata consolidation make it a method with some attraction.

Accounting for changes in the parent company's interest

We shall now proceed to a brief discussion of some technical details encountered in consolidation accounting using the parent company concept. First we shall deal with changes in the investing company's interest in another company.

Step acquisitions. As already observed, consolidation accounting normally commences when the parent company has acquired more than 50% voting control of a subsidiary. Control may be acquired, however, only after a series of acquisitions. A small interest in a company may be acquired initially simply as an investment. Subsequently more may be acquired so that the investor begins to have "significant influence" over the investee, even though outright voting control is not held. Further acquisitions may then push the interest held over the 50% level at which consolidation is in order.

If majority control were acquired in one step, the procedure would be straightforward. As already described, the cost of the investment would be allocated taking into account the fair values of the subsidiary's assets and liabilities at date of acquisition. But in a step-by-step acquisition the cost of the investment has been incurred at several dates, and the fair values of the subsidiary's assets and liabilities will have been different at each date. How is the aggregate of such costs to be assigned to assets and liabilities and dealt with thereafter in the consolidation? In principle the answer is simple. The cost of a 10% acquisition (say) is dealt with in exactly the same way as the cost of a 55% acquisition. That is, a 10% cost is allocated taking into account fair values at the date the interest is acquired and enters into consolidation accounting based on those values. If fractional interests are acquired in several steps, each is dealt with in this way. Thus, in consolidation, the parent company's share of assets and liabilities of the subsidiary will be recorded based on allocations of costs incurred by the parent at several different dates, while the minority interest share of the subsidiary's net assets will always be based on the subsidiary's book values, as they exist from time to time.

This general principle encounters some practical difficulties in application. As noted, before control is acquired blocks of shares may have given the investor influence but not control, and before that, blocks may have been acquired only for investment purposes. If shares acquired give the investor significant influence, "equity accounting" for them is required thereafter. As will be described subsequently, equity accounting is similar to consolidation in requiring allocation of the investment cost over the investee's net asset position at the date of acquisition. Thus, if equity accounting is already being performed for blocks of shares held, the acquisition of another block giving control creates no new problems with respect to previous holdings. But, if the first one or two blocks of shares acquired are accounted for as portfolio investments, there will have been no allocation of cost at their acquisition dates, and it rarely, if ever, will be possible to make a good allocation retroactively. In these circumstances, it is accepted that the cost of blocks of shares held before significant influence is acquired should be added to the cost of the newly acquired shares when equity accounting first becomes appropriate, and that such total cost be allocated based on fair values at that date.

Dispositions of parent company shareholdings. When a parent company sells some of its shares in a subsidiary but retains control, those shares will be costed at their average carrying value under equity or consolidation accounting, and gain or loss will be recorded by the parent accordingly. In the consolidated financial statements there is a rather peculiar result of such a sale. Although the consolidated balance sheet still includes *all* the assets and liabilities of the subsidiary, the values attaching to them will change. That is because of their mixed basis of valuation — part at the parent company's cost and part at the minority interest value (based on book values in the accounts of the subsidiary). If the balance between the parent company and minority interest share changes, the carrying values change in consolidation.

Once the parent company sells enough shares to lose control, of course, consolidation of the subsidiary ceases, and its assets and liabilities disappear line by line from the consolidated figures. If significant influence is retained, the remaining investment in shares reverts to the equity accounting basis. As soon as the sale of shares drops the holding below the level at which equity accounting is appropriate, the carrying value of any remaining shares held is treated as though it represented "cost," and normal cost-based investment accounting follows from then on.

Share issues and repurchases by a subsidiary. From a consolidated point of view, an issue of shares by a subsidiary company to the public has the same result as a sale by the parent company of some of its holdings in the subsidiary. After the issue there are more assets within the consolidated group, but the parent company's interest in the assets held by the subsidiary is decreased while that of minority shareholders is increased. The amount per share received by the subsidiary on the share issue may be more or less than the parent company's carrying value per share at the date of the subsidiary share issue. If it is more, the parent company will gain more from the increase in the subsidiary's total assets than it loses from the dilution of its equity in the subsidiary, and conversely. Thus it will have a gain or loss to record.

There is a debatable point here. If the parent company's invested cost is deemed to include a premium for control (accounted for as goodwill) that is exclusive to the parent, that particular portion of the investment is not diluted by the subsidiary's share issue so long as control is retained. That suggests that the proceeds per share received by the subsidiary from the share issue to outsiders could actually be less than the parent company's carrying value per share without there being a loss to the parent. A similar point arises if the parent sells some shares in the subsidiary without selling control. Perhaps some proportion of the parent company's carrying value theoretically need not be costed out against the sales proceeds. The *CICA Handbook*, however, recommends the recognition of disposal of goodwill as an intrinsic part of the sale in this situation (see Section 1600, paragraph 47).

When additional shares of a partly owned subsidiary become available for purchase, a parent company may be in a position to buy them itself or to cause the subsidiary to buy in those shares. From the group point of view, the effect is the same. Resources within the group are reduced by buying up the subsidiary shares, and the parent company's percentage interest is increased. Accordingly, a purchase of minority interest shares by the subsidiary itself is accounted for in consolidation just as though it were a step acquisition by the parent company.[7]

Mechanics of consolidation

Various technical problems occur in the mechanics of consolidation that will be touched on only briefly here.

- Ideally the fiscal period of a subsidiary to be consolidated will coincide with that of the parent. It is accepted, however, that statements with fiscal period-ends up to three months apart may be consolidated. If such a gap exists, intercompany transactions between the statement dates must be examined to ensure that appropriate eliminations, adjustments, and disclosures are made.
- Ideally, also, accounting policies of a subsidiary should be consistent with those of its parent. There may, however, be disadvantages to a newly acquired subsidiary in changing its policies to conform with those of the parent, especially if a minority interest exists or if the subsidiary operates in a foreign country in which its accounting methods are the norm or perhaps are legally required. It is therefore accepted that a subsidiary's accounting policies need not be changed or adjusted for the purposes of consolidation so long as they are policies that would be acceptable in the country of the parent company. If not changed, however, disclosure of the accounting policies used in the consolidated financial statements will become more complex.
- A number of adjustments are required in the consolidation process. There must be elimination of the balance representing the investment in the subsidiary in the books of the parent company, substituting for it the net assets of the subsidiary and the minority interest. In the course of the elimination, any differences between subsidiary asset and liability values and the allocation of the parent company's purchase cost at the time of acquisition must be allowed for, as well as amortization or write-off of these differences against earnings reported subsequent to the acquisition. Finally, since the consolidated financial statements treat the group of companies as one entity, there must be elimination of the effects of intercompany transactions upon figures in the financial statements of the individual entities being consolidated. All these types of adjustments are described in standard accounting textbooks.
- One conceptual issue must be resolved in relation to the treatment of profit on intercompany sales when a minority interest exists in one or the other of the parties to a transaction. In a "downstream" sale (from parent company to subsidiary) it could be argued that the parent company has realized profit to the extent of the minority interest's share of the transaction. Like-

wise, in an "upstream" sale (from subsidiary to parent) it could be argued that the minority interest, as an outside party to the transaction, should be credited with its share of the profit for purposes of its valuation in the consolidated financial statements. Both these views are rejected in practice. Since the parent company is considered in control of all transactions, all profit effects are to be eliminated. In the case of an upstream sale, the elimination carries through to the share of the minority interest in the profit that has been recorded in the subsidiary's accounts.

- Preferred shares of subsidiary companies that are held by outsiders are classified as part of the minority interest. Hence, preferred dividends paid to that minority interest should be deducted in the consolidated *income* statement as part of the minority interest entitlement. If a subsidiary has failed to pay dividends on cumulative preferred shares held by minority shareholders, provision for those dividends also should be deducted in the consolidated income statement, even though such a provision is not recognized in the income statement of the subsidiary.
- Upon occasion, operating losses or consolidation adjustments, if applied in the normal fashion, would turn the minority interest share of equity into a negative figure. Unless minority shareholders have given guarantees, they cannot be forced to contribute additional amounts to cover subsidiary losses. Accordingly, losses that are charged to the minority interest should be limited to an amount that would reduce it to zero. Beyond that point, the parent company must recognize one hundred percent of the losses as its own for purposes of consolidation. Of course, if the parent company decides it will not give further support to the subsidiary, it need not provide for the losses. In such a case it must remove the subsidiary from the consolidation, because its failure to give support will result in loss of control.

Consolidation where reciprocal shareholdings exist

Occasionally subsidiary companies hold common shares in their parent company. When they do, the preparation of consolidated financial statements becomes more complicated, and great care is necessary to achieve a correct presentation. A simple example is considered below.

The following transactions occur at the launching of two new enterprises:

- Company P is incorporated and issues 2,400 shares to the public for $240,000 cash.
- Company P invests $80,000 in 800 shares of a subsidiary company (Company S) to carry on a separate business. Company S also issues 200 shares to the public for $20,000 cash.
- Company S is issued 600 shares of Company P for $60,000 cash.

Table 19-2 shows the balance sheets of the two companies and the consolidated balance sheet of Company P after these inaugural transactions.

Table 19-2

Inaugural Balance Sheets of Company P and Company S

Individual Company Balance Sheets

		Company P	Company S
Cash		$220,000	$ 40,000
Investment in Company S		80,000	
Investment in Company P			60,000
		$300,000	$100,000
Capital — Company P	3,000 shares	$300,000	
Capital — Company S	1,000 shares		$100,000
		$300,000	$100,000

Consolidated Balance Sheet — Company P

Cash			$260,000
Minority interest in Company S			$ 20,000
Capital	3,000 shares	$300,000	
Less shares held within group	600 shares	60,000	240,000
			$260,000

It will be noted that the investment by Company S in shares of Company P is not treated in the consolidated balance sheet as an asset. Since Company S is controlled by Company P, the intercompany share issue could be regarded as merely shifting assets from one pocket to another. The identical end position might have been achieved had Company P originally issued 3,000 shares to the public and Company S bought back 600 of these shares. In that case it could be interpreted that Company S acted, in effect, as agent for Company P in buying Company P shares. Thus the accounting followed is the same as that which occurs when a company buys in its own shares.

Let us consider now the result that would follow if earnings of the two companies subsequent to acquisition were fully distributed. To make this calculation we must remember that an initial distribution by Company P would go 80% to its public shareholders and 20% to Company S. The latter portion would be redistributed by Company S, 20% to its minority shareholders and 80% back to Company P. Upon receipt of that redistribution (equal to 16% of the initial distribution), Company P would again pay it out, 80% to its public shareholders and 20% to Company S, and so on. In the end result, the public shareholders of Company P would receive considerably more than 80% of Company P's earnings. Similarly, the minority shareholders of Company S effectively have a somewhat greater than 20% interest in its earnings.

Since the consolidated balance sheet shows the shares in Company P held by

Company S as a deduction from consolidated shareholders' equity, rather than as being outstanding, the consolidated income reported should relate only to the remaining shareholders — that is the public shareholders — of Company P. We want to know the portion of the earnings of both Company P and Company S that accrue to the public shareholders of Company P. Because of the revolving nature of distributions of earnings of the two companies as described above, a special calculation is required to find these amounts.

Let A = the portion of distributions by Company P that accrues to the public shareholders of Company P.

Let B = the portion of the distributions by Company S that accrues to the public shareholders of Company P.

In calculating A we will remember that:

1. 80% of Company P's own earnings goes directly to the public shareholders on the first distribution.
2. 20% of that first distribution goes to Company S. The portion of any distributions from Company S that will reach the public shareholders of Company P has already been defined as B.

In calculating B we will remember that any distribution from Company S to Company P will be passed on to the public shareholders of Company P in the defined proportion A.

Therefore,

$$A = .8 + .2B \qquad (1)$$
$$B = .8A \qquad (2)$$

Substituting (2) into (1) and simplifying

$$A = .8 + .16A = .952381$$

Therefore,

$$B = .761905$$

The proportions of the distributions of Company P and Company S that accrue to the minority interest in Company S are the complements of A and B, or 4.7619% and 23.8095% respectively. (These proportions could also be derived by setting up equations in a fashion analogous to the above.)

Suppose that over a period of years Company P earns $300,000 and Company S earns $160,000. The individual company balance sheet positions are shown in Table 19-3, based on the assumption that no dividends are distributed in that period.

Table 19-3

Balance Sheets Showing Retained Earnings

	Company P	Company S
Sundry assets	$520,000	$200,000
Investment in Company S	80,000	
Investment in Company P		60,000
	$600,000	$260,000
Capital — Company P	$300,000	
— Company S		$100,000
Retained earnings	300,000	160,000
	$600,000	$260,000

To prepare a consolidated balance sheet we need to know the distribution of accumulated earnings. Table 19-4 shows that distribution, based on the percentages derived above.

Table 19-4

Entitlement to Post-inaugural Earnings of Company P and Company S

Earnings of	Public Shareholders of Company P	Minority Interest in Company S
Company P — $300,000	$285,714	$14,286
Company S — $160,000	121,905	38,095
	$407,619	$52,381
Add minority interest in Company S capital		20,000
Total minority interest		$72,381

The consolidated balance sheet of Company P is shown in Table 19-5.

It will be noted that the consolidated balance sheet cannot be prepared in the normal way whereby the minority interest is based on the book figures of equity in the subsidiary company's balance sheet. Instead it is necessary first to calculate the split of combined post-acquisition profits between the public shareholders of Company P and the minority shareholders of Company S, as illustrated. Once this is done, the calculation hangs together. In this case, for example, the consolidated equity of Company P amounts to $647,619, which represents the equity applicable to the 80% of its shares that are held by the public. Accordingly, the

Table 19-5

Consolidated Balance Sheet — Company P

Sundry assets			$720,000
Minority interest in Company S			$ 72,381
Shareholders' equity			
Capital	3,000 shares	$300,000	
Consolidated retained earnings		407,619	
		707,619	
Less shares held within group	600 shares	60,000	647,619
			$720,000

20% of its shares held by Company S should be worth one-quarter or $161,905. Together with the other assets in Company S, that makes a total equity in that company of $361,905. The 20% interest in it held by its minority shareholders is therefore valued at one-fifth or $72,381.

There often will be complications in dealing with reciprocal shareholdings beyond those illustrated in this simple example. For example, the date at which the subsidiary acquires shares in the parent may precede the date when the parent acquires control of the subsidiary. Allowing for this complication, the rules generally applicable may be described as follows:

- The minority interest shown in the consolidated balance sheet at the date of acquisition by the parent will equal its percentage share of the shareholders' equity shown by the subsidiary's accounts at that date. Thereafter, that figure of minority interest will be changed by allocations of profits determined using the formulas that have been illustrated.
- At the time of the business combination, it will be necessary, as usual, to allocate the purchase cost of the parent company to the net assets of the subsidiary at that date. Since the shares held by the subsidiary in its new parent form part of these assets, they too must be assigned a fair value, which may be different from their carrying value in the books of the subsidiary.

An alternative presentation. A number of Canadian companies take an alternative approach to presentation of consolidated statements when interlocking shareholdings are present. This approach is based on an implicit assumption that the subsidiary company has paid a dividend in kind of its shareholdings in the parent company just before consolidation. In effect, this solves the interlocking share problem by assuming it away.

For example, suppose in the previous illustration it is assumed for consolidation purposes that Company S has paid a dividend of its 600 common shares in Company P so that 120 shares are transferred to the minority interest and 480 shares are received by Company P. Once this assumption is made, it is no longer necessary to calculate Company P's share of Company S's earnings through the use of simultaneous equations. Company P's share of Company S's earnings will be recorded simply at 80% of $160,000 or $128,000. Table 19-6 shows the consolidated balance sheet of Company P at the inaugural date and after the earnings period using this alternative approach.

Table 19-6

Consolidated Balance Sheet — Company P
(Alternative method)

		Inaugural Date		Showing Retained Earnings	
Sundry assets			$260,000		$720,000
Minority interest in Company S			$ 8,000		$ 40,000
Shareholders' equity					
Capital	3,000 shares	$300,000		$300,000	
Consolidated retained earnings				428,000	
		300,000		728,000	
Less shares held within group	480 shares	48,000	252,000	48,000	680,000
			$260,000		$720,000

The essence of the difference between the standard presentation method and this alternative lies in the net number of shares deemed to be still outstanding. Under the standard method, the full 600 shares held by Company S are treated as reacquired. Under the alternative method, only 480 shares are deemed reacquired, the other 120 having been deemed to be distributed to the minority interest (thereby reducing the obligation shown to it).

A comparison of statistics under the two methods is shown in Table 19-7.

Table 19-7

Comparison of Figures Under Two Consolidation Methods

	Standard Method	Alternative Approach
Company P shares — net deemed outstanding	2,400	2,520
Shareholders' equity — Company P		
At inaugural date	$240,000	$252,000
Per share	$100.00	$100.00
Post-inaugural earnings	$407,619	$428,000
Per share	$169.84	$169.84

The "equity" basis of accounting

If consolidation accounting is required for investments that represent ownership of more than 50% of the voting equity in another company, what basis is appropriate for smaller holdings? For many years the only alternatives to consolidation accounting for investments in common shares were the traditional cost, or lower of cost and market, bases of accounting.

In the course of time it became clear that cost-based accounting did not provide the fairest presentation for significant holdings of shares in other companies. In today's economy, most companies retain a substantial part of their earnings to finance growth. Accordingly, dividends received from such companies provide only a partial measure of the performance of the investment. Hence, reporting the investment at cost is likely to provide a poor measure of the real value of the investment if some time has elapsed since it was acquired. In addition to this, it is clear that companies can often be effectively controlled by shareholdings of less than 50% of the voting shares. When other shareholdings are widely dispersed, the dominant shareholder is often in a position to buy enough additional shares very quickly to obtain actual control. When he is in this position, control will effectively be conceded to him even though the ownership is something less than 50% of the voting shares. With shareholdings progressively less than 50%, the possibility of another party bidding to acquire control of the investee becomes greater, and the ability of management to resist the wishes of a single large shareholder also becomes greater. Nevertheless, holders of large blocks of shares are likely to retain significant influence over the direction and management of a company.

In the late 1960s and early 1970s a new basis of investment accounting, known as equity accounting, became popular for large blocks of shares, as a halfway point between ordinary cost-based investment accounting and consolidation accounting. The equity basis of accounting, like the cost method, records the investment as a single figure on the asset side of the balance sheet and income from the investment on a single line in the income statement. The basis of measurement of the investment is, however, changed. The income attributable to a major investor following equity accounting is computed in exactly the same way as is income for the majority interest in a consolidation.

That is to say, an investor who uses equity accounting must make an allocation of investment cost on the basis of fair values of the assets and liabilities of the investee at the date of acquisition. Subsequently it adjusts its share of income reported by the investee to amortize any differences between the investee's book values for assets and liabilities and the allocation implicit in the investor's purchase price. The carrying value of the asset on the equity basis of accounting begins at cost, is increased by the investor's share of the profit or loss of the investee calculated as just described, and is reduced by any dividends paid by the investee. Occasionally, also, the investor may have to record its share of prior period adjustments or capital transactions reported by the investee. On this basis the carrying value of the investment is equal to the aggregate of the investor's net interest in the assets and liabilities of the investee after adjustments similar to those that would be made in consolidation.

In essence, then, the equity method of accounting is firmly based on the concepts of consolidation accounting, so that it is sometimes called "one-line consolidation." That description is apt, except that the investor's share of extraordinary items, prior period adjustments, or capital transactions of the investee are not recorded on the same line as income from the investee but rather are reported according to their nature, as they would be if they were the result of the investor's own transactions.

The attempt to tie in with consolidation accounting has one anomalous result. A profit taken on a downstream sale (say, of inventory) from the investor to the investee will be recorded through the normal sales and cost of sales accounts of the investor. If the item sold is still in the inventory of the investee at the year-end, the profit will normally be eliminated through reducing the figure of income picked up with respect to the investee, even though the investee did not record that income. (*CICA Handbook*, Section 1600, paragraph 78, provides some flexibility to avoid this result.) In passing, it may be noted that some Canadian companies eliminate only the investor's share of profit on downstream sales when the item sold is still among the investee's assets. This deviation from the rules applicable to consolidation accounting follows U.S. practice. The difference from consolidation accounting receives some justification from the fact that the investor does not control the investee outright but only has "significant influence."

As indicated, equity accounting is considered appropriate when the investor does not have actual control but does have significant influence upon the investee. The existence of significant influence may be indicated by such factors as representation on the board of directors, material intercompany transactions or operating links, and so on. On the other hand, an investor may take quite a passive interest in an investee and yet still be deemed to have significant influence because of the potential inherent in any large ownership interest.

The authoritative standards suggest that there should be a presumption of significant influence when the shareholding is 20% or more and a presumption of lack of influence below that level. Both of these presumptions are open to rebuttal by other evidence. For example, even if a holding is over 20%, the existence of another investor having a large block of shares would create some doubt. That doubt might be set at rest by evidence of more active influence such as representation on the board. However, if an investor is frozen out by hostile interests or is unable to obtain any consideration greater than that to which any shareholder is entitled, a lack of significant influence would be demonstrated. One practical test of significant influence lies in the investor's ability to obtain sufficient information from the investee on a timely basis to perform equity accounting.

Reciprocal shareholdings — equity accounting

There are a number of cases in Canada where two companies each hold substantial blocks of shares in the other and it is clear that each has significant influence on the affairs of the other. Thus equity accounting seems appropriate for the interlocking shareholdings. The application of equity accounting in this case is based on the general principles already illustrated for consolidation accounting, but there are some new aspects.

As was described in the discussion of consolidation accounting, it is possible to take two approaches. First, the earnings attributable to each company may be calculated using simultaneous equations in the manner previously illustrated. The resulting distribution of earnings will represent the earnings attributable to the public's holding of shares — that is, it will exclude earnings attributable to the interlocking shareholdings. Since, contrary to the position in consolidation accounting, neither company will show its interest in its own shares held by the other company as having been reacquired, it is necessary to show earnings figures in relation to all the shares outstanding, not just the shares in the hands of the public. Accordingly, the earnings distribution calculated by the simultaneous equations must be grossed up for each company. For example, if 80% of a company's shares are held by the public and the earnings from the two companies applicable to these shares are calculated as $60,000, the total earnings to be reported by the company would be 100/80 of $60,000 = $75,000.

Under an alternative approach, an initial assumption is made (for purposes of calculation only) that each company has paid out a dividend in kind of its shareholdings in the other company. On this assumption, each company can recognize its share of earnings from the other assets of the other company in direct proportion to its percentage shareholding in that company. The income reported by each company will be less than the earnings reported as described in the previous paragraph but, when divided by the reduced number of shares deemed to be outstanding, will yield an identical figure of earnings per share. This method simplifies the calculation of the income pick-up but raises a question about the presentation of the balance sheet. If the assumption underlying this presentation is that a company's own shares have been dividended back to it, should the investment in the other company and its own shareholders' equity both be reduced to reflect the assumed dividend and shares reacquired? If that is not done, there will be an inconsistency between the logic of the presentation of the balance sheet and the income statement. On the other hand, some may question that the balance sheet should reflect a reacquisition of shares that has not taken place.

This problem is only an aspect of a larger problem in statement presentation. In each case, the bottom line figure of earnings represents a company's share of earnings on its own assets (a share that is less than 100% because of the interlocking shareholdings) plus its share of the other company's earnings. The income statement, however, will report 100% of the sales, expenses, and operating income of the company carrying on the activity, and the difference between that operating income figure and the bottom line of income reported (which difference could be negative) will be reported as though it were income attributable to the investment in the other company. This presentation is rather unsatisfactory and could be misleading to anyone trying to analyze and project the profitability of each company. It appears impossible to cure this deficiency without reporting the earnings of both companies in the financial statements of each company and indicating the significance of each earnings stream to the bottom line for each particular company based on the effect of the intercompany shareholdings.

Accounting for joint ventures

An increasingly common form of business operation, especially in certain industries, is the joint venture. A joint venture often is incorporated but may also be a partnership or some other unincorporated arrangement. Hence this part of this discussion is not limited just to intercorporate investments.

In very broad terms, the business motivation for a joint venture is the desire to share the risks and rewards of the venture. In risky types of enterprise, joint ventures are one means whereby venturers can spread their risks rather than put all their eggs in one basket. In other cases, venturers may pool resources in order to be able to afford a facility that none would find economical on its own.

From the accounting standpoint, the important characteristic of a joint venture is that it is under joint control.[8] Normally there will be a formal agreement that establishes that joint control. For operational purposes the agreement overrides differences in ownership interest. Thus, even if one venturer holds a majority share of a project, it still should be accounted for as a joint venture if the actual control is joint. As an investment, therefore, the joint venture falls somewhere between a subsidiary that is controlled by the investor alone and a large shareholding that gives the holder significant influence but not control.

Before there were any authoritative statements on joint venture accounting, three bases of accounting for joint ventures were found in practice — the cost basis, the equity basis, and proportionate or pro rata consolidation. The last of these was particularly common in certain industries where venturers held undivided interests in assets of the venture.

Equity accounting for joint ventures has been criticized on the grounds that it fails to show details of assets and liabilities over which the investor has (joint) control and of the revenues and expenses associated therewith. A company that carried on all its business in the form of joint ventures could have just one line in each of its financial statements — investment in joint ventures in the balance sheet and net income from joint ventures in the income statement. On the other hand, the proportionate consolidation method has been criticized because it adds together the directly owned assets and liabilities of the investor with a pro rata share of indirectly controlled assets and liabilities of one or more joint ventures. To cure this, the "expanded equity" basis of presentation has been proposed whereby the pro rata share of assets, liabilities, revenues, and expenses of joint ventures would be included in the financial statements but segregated from the corresponding items pertaining to the direct activities of the investor. Some compression would be required under this basis to avoid overly cumbersome financial statements. For example, the direct current assets of the investor could be set out in the normal fashion followed by one figure described as "investor share of net current assets of joint ventures."[9]

The *CICA Handbook* has recommended the equity basis of accounting as the basic method of accounting for investments in joint ventures. Proportionate consolidation is allowed as an alternative when "a significant portion of the venturer's activities is carried out through joint ventures."[10] The logic of this is not impressive. If proportionate consolidation is a valid method of accounting, it is not clear why it should cease to be valid if the joint venturer carries on a lot of other activities directly. In any case, opinions may well vary as to the meaning of "significant portion."[11]

In addition, where proportionate consolidation is followed, the *CICA Handbook* calls for disclosure in summary form of the venturer's share of the assets, liabilities, income, and expense of the joint ventures, normally on a combined basis. Also, where proportionate consolidation is not followed but might have been because the joint ventures represent a significant portion of the venturer's activities, the same disclosure is to be made.[12]

Although the basic method for accounting for a joint venture is stated to be the equity method, the *CICA Handbook* gives special consideration to downstream transactions between the investor and the joint venture, and makes recommendations that are not identical to those applicable in the ordinary form of equity accounting.

- When assets are sold or transferred to a joint venture in exchange for a capital interest in it, no gain or loss is to be recognized at the time of transfer.
- On the other hand, when an ordinary business transaction takes place and the substance of the transaction is such that a gain or loss has occurred
  - gain may be recognized to the extent of the interests of other venturers not affiliated with the investor; and
  - loss must be recognized in full.[13]

Finally, contrary to the normal practice in equity accounting for investments in non-subsidiaries, provision is to be made for any income taxes that might be payable on joint venture earnings not yet remitted.[14]

Summary

When a parent and subsidiary company relationship is established, whether as a result of a business combination or otherwise, it is now accepted that the parent company should prepare its financial statements on a consolidated basis thereafter. The basic concept is that entities under common ownership and control form one economic unit, which should accordingly report on a unified basis. The primary criterion for consolidation is the existence of control effected through ownership, direct or indirect, of a majority of the voting shares of the subsidiary.

There are different possible ways to apply consolidation accounting. The "parent company" concept is used in practice. Under that concept, when a minority interest exists, the figure attributed to the minority interest in the consolidation represents its percentage share of the book value of the equity shown by the subsidiary. As a result of this treatment, the net assets of the subsidiary included in the consolidation are valued on the basis of the parent company's cost determined at the time of the business combination (see chapter 18) to the extent of the parent company's percentage interest in the net assets, and at the subsidiary company's book value to the extent of the minority interest percentage. Other possible concepts of consolidation base the valuation of the minority interest and of the subsidiary's net assets entirely (with the possible exception of goodwill) upon the parent company's acquisition cost and the distribution of that cost among the assets and liabilities.

Another possible basis for consolidation accounting is that of proportionate or pro rata consolidation. On this basis, the consolidated financial statements reflect only the parent company's share of the assets, liabilities, revenues, and expenses of the subsidiary, and the valuation of those items is determined initially by the allocation of the parent company's cost in the business combination. In this way, the issue of presentation of minority interest is avoided entirely. The proportionate consolidation method is not used in consolidation practice today but is used to some extent in joint venture accounting.

While consolidated financial statements do present information in a compact form, they are not without disadvantages. When the asset and debt structures of the parent and one or more subsidiary companies are different, the act of adding them together in consolidation tends to average out and obscure many of the ratios customarily relied upon for financial analysis. In extreme cases this is considered a reason for not presenting consolidated financial statements. In addition, the averaging out of ratios such as working capital or interest coverage can obscure real financial weakness in the parent company.

There are a large number of technical questions that arise in the application of consolidation accounting. These are discussed in works devoted to the subject and are not dealt with in any great detail in this chapter.

Equity accounting is a derivative of consolidation accounting that was developed for cases where an investor had an investment position that gave it significant influence over another entity but not majority voting control. In this situation, it was considered that the normal accounting basis whereby an investment in equity shares is carried at original cost failed to portray the real performance of the investment satisfactorily. The equity method records such significant investments at their original cost to the investor, increased by its share of earnings of the investee subsequent to the date of acquisition determined as they would be if the subsidiary's financial statements were adjusted for purposes of consolidation with the investor, and reduced by cash dividends paid by the investee. The investment is presented on one line in the investor's balance sheet, and its share of income for a period is reported on one line in the income statement (with the exception of its share of extraordinary items). For this reason, the method is sometimes known as "one-line consolidation."

Equity accounting is also used, with some slight modifications, for investments in joint ventures. Another method sometimes used is proportionate consolidation, already described. A joint venture is characterized by agreement among the venturers that gives them all a share in control. Because of that control feature, it is considered that the performance of an investment in a joint venture is better portrayed in the financial statements of a venturer by a method that recognizes the joint venture's earnings as they accrue, rather than as they are remitted to the venturer.

References

[1]CICA, "Long-term Investments," *CICA Handbook*, Section 3050 (Toronto: CICA), pars. 03-06.

[2]Ibid., par. 10.

[3]Ibid., par. 08.

[4]Ibid., par. 14.

[5]Ibid., par. 13.

[6]For a detailed discussion and skeptical view of the advantages claimed for consolidation accounting, see R.G. Walker, "An Evaluation of the Information Conveyed by Consolidated Statements," *Abacus*, December 1976, pp. 77-115.

[7]CICA, "Consolidated Financial Statements," *CICA Handbook*, Section 1600 (Toronto: CICA) par. 48.

[8]See CICA, "Investments in Corporate and Unincorporated Joint Ventures," *CICA Handbook*, Section 3055 (Toronto: CICA) pars. 03-06.

[9]For a good discussion of these ideas, see D.L. Reklau, "Accounting for Investments in Joint Ventures - A Reexamination," *Journal of Accountancy*, September 1977, pp. 96-103, and R. Dieter and A.R. Wyatt, "The Expanded Equity Method — An Alternative in Accounting for Investments in Joint Ventures," *Journal of Accountancy*, June 1978, pp. 89-94.

[10]*CICA Handbook*, Section 3055, par. 11.

[11]The compromise may be explained by events during the development of the recommendations. At an early stage in its deliberations the committee favoured the proportionate consolidation method as the basic method of accounting for investments in joint ventures. It is reported that a large company was concerned with the amount of debt it would have to report on this basis and threatened a legal challenge if the recommendations went through. The Canada Corporations Act required that the income statement show income from different classes of investment each on one line. The proposed accounting would not do that and thus might not have been in compliance with the act. Such a challenge could not be mounted today under the Canada Business Corporations Act.

[12]*CICA Handbook*, Section 3055, par. 26.

[13]Ibid., pars. 16 to 22. There is some confusion in these paragraphs because the italicized recommendation in paragraph 22 seems to contradict or at least ignore the advice in paragraph 18 on transfers of assets in return for a capital interest.

[14]Ibid., par. 24.

Chapter Twenty

Foreign Currency and Financial Reporting

The history of accounting practice and accounting standards in relation to business done in foreign currencies has been confused and controversial. Part of the problem is that it is difficult to understand the economic forces that determine exchange rates. Part also lies in the fact that the relative importance of different aspects of those forces changes over time.

Three sets of issues will be discussed in this chapter. The first set concerns the choice of reporting currency by an entity that conducts operations in more than one currency. The second concerns the accounting by an entity for transactions — purchases, sales, investments, and borrowing — conducted by it in a currency other than its reporting currency. The third concerns the translation for the purpose of incorporation in the parent entity's financial statements of the separate financial statements of a branch or subsidiary that are maintained in a different currency. (By extension, these same issues are applicable to equity accounting or proportionate consolidation for an investment in a foreign joint venture or other investee, since these methods are based on the same concepts as consolidation accounting.) Before discussing these accounting issues it may be helpful to provide some background on determinants of currency exchange rates.

Determinants of currency exchange rates

In the period since 1944 there have been two distinct international systems for managing currency relationships. In 1944, the Bretton Woods agreement produced a system whereby the governments of major trading nations undertook to maintain the price of their currencies in U.S. dollars at "pegged" or fixed rates, with narrow fluctuations permitted around those rates. The resultant stabilization of exchange rates simplified the accounting problem of translating amounts expressed in foreign currency and enabled simple solutions that would work most of the time.

There were two major accounting problems related to foreign currency in this era. First, the pegged rate for any particular currency might get out of line with basic economic conditions from time to time, eventually forcing a change in the official pegged rate — devaluation of currency downward or revaluation upward in terms of the U.S. dollar. Whenever such a change occurred, there was always some confusion and debate as to its accounting consequences, which would be settled one way or another (not necessarily consistently by all companies affected), and the accounting would then settle down again. Second, there was the ever-present question of how to translate currencies of countries outside the Bretton Woods system for the purpose of consolidation or equity accounting. This was particularly troublesome with respect to the currencies of those countries experiencing rapid inflation. Normally those currencies exhibited a progressive and often severe weakening trend against those of the more stable industrialized countries.

The general solution in this case was to distinguish between assets and liabilities that were deemed to hold their essential economic value regardless of the value of the currency of the country of residence — to be translated at historical exchange rates, and other assets and liabilities that were assumed to be exposed to risk of changes in the currency value — to be translated at current rates.

In the early 1970s the Bretton Woods system collapsed. In essence, the underlying economic influences determining the relative values of currencies became too volatile and too strong to be confined within a system of government-determined, infrequently changed, pegged rates. In addition, as the necessary adjustments were made, first to a new schedule of fixed rates (the Smithsonian agreement) and then to a system of largely floating rates, it became apparent that the U.S. dollar (and Canadian dollar) had become overvalued at the previous fixed rates. The increase in frequency and magnitude of changes in currency exchange rates thereafter triggered closer examination of accounting bases for translation and the reported gains and losses that resulted from exchange movements. The result was a widespread feeling that accounting did not properly portray the exposure to foreign exchange risk in foreign operations. Much study and debate ensued, resulting initially in accounting standards that did not stand the test of usage, and then in the early 1980s in revised standards that are now in force.

Freely floating exchange rates present a serious problem for accounting in that the current level of rates at any time will be subject to both short-term and long-term influences. In the resulting rate volatility it can be very difficult to detect what ought to be considered the fundamental value of one currency in terms of other currencies. There are two simple theories that suggest how exchange rates should be expected to change over time. The purchasing power parity theory argues that one country's currency should be expected to weaken in terms of that of another country if prices in its economy are rising faster than prices in the other country. The rationale is simple. If prices are rising rapidly in one country, that should tend to penalize its exports and encourage imports. Changes in the balance of trade will change the supply of and demand for its currency in the exchange markets and tend to drive its exchange rate down.

A different theory, the interest rate parity theory, is based on the connection between interest rates and exchange rates. If exchange rates were really expected to remain steady, it would pay investors to move funds from countries with low interest rates to those with higher rates (assuming the level of investment risk is perceived as being equal). That movement should tend to reduce interest rates in the recipient country and raise them in the country that is exporting capital. The movement should continue until an equilibrium position is reached. An ideal equilibrium would exist if risk-adjusted interest rates in each country were equal and their currency exchange rate steady. So far as capital movements are concerned, however, the situation would also be in equilibrium if relatively higher interest rates in one country were just sufficient to compensate for the rate of decline in the exchange value of its currency.

The balance of payments between two countries is customarily subclassified as (1) flows attributable to trade in goods and services, (2) capital flows, and (3) official financing by way of movements in government foreign exchange reserves or central bank borrowings (or repayments) from other central banks or the International Monetary Fund (IMF). The purchasing power parity theory concentrates on the current balance of trade as the primary influence on foreign exchange rates. The interest rate parity theory concentrates on capital flows. Other structural factors, such as (1) the rise in imported oil prices owing to the OPEC cartel in the 1970s, (2) the oil price decline with the weakening of the cartel in the early 1980s, and (3) changes in the international competitiveness of industry in individual countries, are also important. The multiplicity of influences on exchange rates makes it difficult to be sure what forces are responsible for changes in exchange rates from time to time. By the same token it is difficult to be sure that accounting policies dependent on shifting exchange rates are always consistent with fundamental long-term economic forces. For a closer look at exchange rates as they exist from time to time we shall now turn to a brief discussion of the foreign exchange markets.

Markets for currencies of important trading nations are well developed. In the market, "spot" exchange rates are quoted for settlement in two business days. The spot exchange rates are determined by demand and supply for the currencies in question which, as just discussed, result basically from trading transactions, capital movements, and occasional government intervention in the exchange markets.

Anyone who enters into commitments that will involve the purchase or sale of a foreign currency at some future date is exposed to the risk of loss if there is an adverse movement in exchange rates between the commitment date and the future settlement date. To limit the risk it is possible to enter into "forward" contracts, generally with a bank or other financial institution, to buy or sell the committed foreign currency amount at the future settlement date for a stated price. That forward exchange rate tends to be the spot rate plus or minus the interest differential between the interest rate available on the currency bought and that applicable on the currency sold over the period of the contract.

To understand why, consider a foreign currency debt payable six months hence. The debtor could buy the requisite foreign currency at the spot rate with funds borrowed in domestic currency. He could then make a six-month loan of the foreign currency. At the end of the six months, proceeds from repayment of the loan would provide the foreign currency to meet the account payable. During the six months the debtor would have received interest on the foreign currency loan and paid interest on his domestic currency borrowing. Incurring this differential in interest would have enabled him to cover his foreign currency debt without buying the currency forward. Because this possibility exists, arbitrage will tend to ensure that the forward contract will be priced on the basis of the spot currency price plus or minus the interest differential as described (together with any charge for service by the financial institution arranging the forward contract).

Since interest differentials tend to reflect the relative strength of the two currencies, there will be a general tendency for spot rates to move in the direction of the forward rates over a period. Because of the many factors that may influence an exchange rate in the short term, however, it is unlikely that the spot rate at the end of a forward contract will be exactly equal to the forward rate at the inception of the contract.

The elimination of exposure to risk of loss is known as "hedging" the risk. A foreign exchange risk exists whenever the domestic currency equivalent of a future cash flow in a foreign currency could be affected by exchange rate changes. Such future cash flow may result from an existing monetary asset or liability (such as an account receivable or payable) or from an existing commitment. In economic terms the exposure to risk is hedged if the loss from an adverse exchange movement on an existing monetary position or commitment is offset by gain on some other instrument or security resulting from the same exchange movement. Different types of instruments are available to hedge foreign exchange risk, each with its own characteristics and costs.

- As already explained, one can enter into a forward contract to buy or sell a specified amount of foreign currency at a specified future date for a specified price in domestic currency.
- Foreign currency futures are like forward contracts in that they represent a contract to buy or sell a specified amount of foreign currency at a specified price at a future date. But they differ from forward contracts in several respects. First, they are not tailored to the settlement of a specific commitment as is usually the case with a forward contract. Rather, they are expressed in standard round amounts maturing after a preset time period. Second, futures contracts are entered into with an exchange rather than being a contract directly between two parties. The exchange is responsible for keeping purchase and sale contracts in balance. To protect its position, the exchange pursues a policy of "marking to market" the contracts. That is, as the foreign exchange rate changes from day to day, each contracting party pays or receives amounts to or from the exchange so as to make up the difference between the spot price and the contract price so long as the contract is outstanding. Finally, the contracts are usually closed out before their maturity date rather than being settled by actual receipt or payment of the foreign currency amount specified in the contract. A buyer of a currency futures contract incurs the cost of broker's commission. That cost is modified by interest lost or gained on amounts paid to or received from the exchange as the result of the mark-to-market procedure while a contract is outstanding.
- Foreign currency options, like futures contracts, are traded on an exchange. Foreign currency options give the holder the right to "call" or "put" a specified amount of foreign currency for a specified price during the option period. A person wishing to hedge against loss on payment commitments in a foreign currency would buy a call option. A put option hedges against loss on amounts collectible in the foreign currency. A buyer of a foreign currency option pays a price, the amount of which varies with the level of the option exercise price. Thus, if the option exercise price is more favourable than the spot price for the currency at the date the option is bought (i.e., the option is "in-the-money"), the price of that option will naturally be higher than that of an option where that is not true (one that is "out-of-the-money"). The true premium inherent in an option price thus could be said to be the price paid minus the amount by which the option is in-the-money at the purchase date or plus the amount by which the option is out-of-the-money at that date. When an option is used as a hedge against a foreign currency risk exposure, the loss from an exchange rate movement adverse to the exposed position should be covered by the gain on the foreign currency option. The price paid for this coverage is the premium paid for the option. On the other hand, if the exchange rate moves in a direction that is favourable to the exposed position, the premium paid for the option will be lost but the most that can be lost is the price paid for it. Therefore an option, unlike a forward or futures contract, can prevent loss (beyond the premium amount) but does not necessarily preclude gain. Accordingly, as one might expect, the premium paid for an option is higher than the commission that would be payable on a futures contract of equivalent amount.

- The three preceding foreign currency contracts are typically available only for relatively short periods. A foreign currency swap agreement, in contrast, may cover periods ranging from two to three years up to ten years or even longer. This extension of term plus the greater simplicity of the swap make it a significant addition to possible currency hedging arrangements. Swaps are commonly used, in effect, to convert existing debt obligations from one currency to another. They differ from pure interest-rate swaps in that they can offset the risk on principal payment as well as on interest payments. They can embrace interest-rate risk protection as well as foreign currency risk protection, since the interest obligations exchanged can be from a fixed to a floating rate of interest as well as being from one currency to another. Thus, they are extremely flexible instruments. Swap contracts that represent mere exchanges of currencies today with an agreement to re-exchange at specified rates in future are also common. In substance these provide risk protection similar to a long-dated forward exchange contract. Swap contracts facilitate the exploitation of anomalies in the foreign exchange and capital markets. For example, a borrower may at times be able to get significantly better interest rates in relation to its creditworthiness in the Eurocurrency market than at home. A swap contract can then shed the foreign currency risk taken on without necessarily wiping out all the interest-rate advantage. A risk is assumed, however, that the other party to the swap may not perform if the exchange rate moves adversely to its interest. The reliability of that party is thus important. Swap contracts may also be helpful in overcoming other problems such as lack of available credit in local markets, foreign exchange controls, and taxation anomalies.[1]

We turn now to a discussion of the accounting issues.

The choice of reporting currency

The fact that there is a choice of the currency to be used in financial reports may seem strange. Most people probably assume that an entity reports in the currency of the jurisdiction in which it is incorporated, or if not incorporated, where its management and control resides. That assumption is valid in the vast majority of situations. Yet Canadian accountants are aware of a number of Canadian companies that report in U.S. dollars, and a limited number of multinational corporations that report in a currency other than that of the jurisdiction in which the parent company is incorporated. There must be some justification for these departures from normal practice, but what is it? Accounting standards give no guidance on this subject, and accounting literature is sparse.[2]

Consider these possible situations:

- A company is incorporated and majority-owned in Canada but carries on all its business operations in the United States. Apart from a bank account and a few investments, all assets and liabilities are held in the United States.
- A company incorporated and wholly owned in Canada carries on all its operations in Argentina and, as above, holds almost all its assets in that country. There is, however, a significant amount of debt payable in Canadian dollars.

- A multinational corporation is incorporated in Luxembourg, has business operations widely spread around the world outside North America, and is listed on all the major stock exchanges in the world. The nationality of its shareholders is also diverse, the largest single group being U.S. shareholders holding thirty-nine percent of the outstanding common shares.

Opinions might well differ as to the most useful and understandable reporting currency in these situations. Here are some factors that would influence opinions.

- The starting point for many accountants would be the country of incorporation. If substantial operations are carried on there or substantial ownership is located there, the jurisdiction of incorporation might well be decisive, all other factors being equal. But a company can be incorporated in a jurisdiction largely as a matter of legal convenience or for taxation reasons. These are factors that have little significance to the objective of useful and understandable financial reporting. Hence, one may conclude that the country of incorporation is not a significant consideration in itself. It may be used as a sort of "tie breaker" if the merits of the currency of the country of incorporation and one or more other currencies are evenly balanced.
- The currency in which transactions are denominated, in contrast, is a highly important factor. This factor, however, needs some interpretation. Consider a Canadian company in a resource industry conducting all its operations in Canada but selling virtually all its production abroad at prices set in U.S. dollars. The majority (in number) of its transactions are conducted in Canadian dollars — all its purchases and payroll — and basic records except for sales and accounts receivable are kept in Canadian dollars. That might suggest that the financial statements should be expressed in Canadian dollars. On the other hand, the ultimate source of profits is sales in U.S. dollars, and the company may even have a policy of paying dividends in U.S. dollars, to save conversion costs for those shareholders who wish to receive payment in that currency. In such a case, the choice of reporting currency as between the Canadian dollar and U.S. dollar may be relatively evenly balanced.
- If there is a significant amount of debt outstanding, the currency in which the bulk of the debt is denominated has some importance to the decision. Since coverage of debt interest is an important aspect of financial reporting, it will be less confusing to have the debt interest reported as an unchanging figure year by year so long as the debt itself is unchanged. This is important not only to the debt holders themselves but also for analysts wishing to assess the financial risk of the company.
- A multinational company with operations scattered around the world may find that no one currency stands out as the one in which the majority of its operations are carried on. Various other considerations then receive added importance. For example, if many more shareholders reside in one of the countries in which there are significant operations than in any of the others, the currency of that country might well be a logical choice for the reporting currency.
- The choice of currency might also be strongly influenced by the relative strength and stability of each of the possible contenders. Where a choice exists, a country with restrictions on currency convertibility should be

avoided. Also, the currency of a country with low, or no more than moderate, inflation is preferable. A currency suffering rapid depreciation in value represents a poor choice of reporting currency for anyone not familiar with its history.

- The U.S. dollar is a strong contender for selection by any multinational company when no other currency is the predominant choice. As a reserve currency, and one in terms of which most other currencies are quoted in the foreign exchange markets, the U.S. dollar is the best known of all the world currencies. It also has had the advantage historically of a low rate of inflation relative to most (but not all) other countries. As an alternative it may be that, at some future date, multinational corporations will wish to report in an artificial currency that represents an average of a "basket" of currencies, such as the Special Drawing Rights established by the IMF or the European Currency Unit (ECU) for countries whose operations are concentrated in Europe. At present, however, these artificial currencies are not sufficiently well known to the public at large to serve as a satisfactory basis for financial reporting.

The foregoing suggests that there are times when the choice of reporting currency is not an automatic or mechanical choice. The currency in which most business is carried on by the entity must be a strong contender, but other factors are also important. In the end, the financial statements must be understandable by those who are expected to use them.

Choice of reporting currency and choice of GAAP

One question may arise. Is there any implication that accounting principles used in a financial report must be those of the country whose currency is adopted as the unit of measurement? For example, if a Canadian company reports in U.S. dollars, is there an implication that it follows U.S. generally accepted accounting principles? There is no recognized rule that the choice of accounting principles depends upon the choice of reporting currency, or vice versa. Nevertheless, in view of the possibility of confusion on this point, it is highly desirable, if not essential, that a company not reporting in the currency of its own jurisdiction should disclose very clearly that its accounting principles are determined by practice in its own country. This is particularly important when a substantial body of its shareholders resides in the country whose currency it uses as the unit of measurement.

Accounting for transactions in foreign currency

Any enterprise may have transactions denominated in a currency other than its reporting currency. (Hereafter such currencies will be referred to as foreign currencies. For a Canadian company using the U.S. dollar as its reporting currency, transactions in Canadian dollars would, by this definition, be regarded as foreign currency transactions.) Three issues will be discussed in relation to foreign currency transactions: (1) At what exchange rate shall these transactions be recorded initially in the accounts kept in the reporting currency? (2) What is to be the valuation basis of assets and liabilities denominated in foreign currency subsequent to the transaction date that gives rise to them? (3) On what basis shall exchange rate gains and losses on assets and liabilities denominated in foreign currency be recognized in income? These issues will be discussed for operating transactions separate from investment and borrowing transactions. For convenience, the discussion will initially be limited to unhedged positions in foreign currency and then will consider the effect of hedging.

Accounting for operating transactions in foreign currency

For a variety of competitive and commercial reasons an entity may wish to, or have to, enter into purchase and sale transactions that are denominated in a foreign currency. When it does, certain questions must be answered. At what figure in domestic currency should the transaction be booked? How should the exposure to foreign currency risk affect the accounting? How and when should the gains or losses resulting from that risk be reflected in the accounts? The answers to these questions must fit on a time scale running from the date the entity becomes committed to a contract in foreign currency through the date when the transaction is first recognized in the accounts, subsequent financial reporting dates while the account payable or receivable arising from the transaction is still outstanding, and finally the date when settlement occurs.

Consider the accounting for a Canadian company's commitment, entered into on June 30, for a shipload of product from France with delivery scheduled for approximately November 30 and settlement in francs two months after delivery. It should be clear that the Canadian company is exposed to the risk of changes in the exchange rate for French francs as soon as it is committed to the purchase. Suppose it does not hedge that risk but simply pays the amount of Canadian dollars required to settle the liability at its due date. The amount of dollars paid can be thought of as, in part, payment for cost of product and, in part, gain or loss on the foreign exchange risk. If it is desired to account strictly in accordance with management's decision making, these elements must be separated.

One simple way to do so would be to record the purchase at the commitment date valued at the forward exchange rate for the settlement date. If a forward contract was not actually entered into, there would be a difference between the booked amount and the actual settlement cost which would represent the realized gain or loss on the foreign currency risk undertaken. At any financial reporting date prior to settlement, an unrealized foreign exchange gain or loss would exist with respect to the commitment because of exchange rate changes since it was taken on. The amount of that gain or loss could be measured by calculating the domestic currency equivalent of the foreign currency obligation at the forward exchange rate prevailing on the reporting date. The difference between that calculated amount and the figure at which the commitment was originally recorded would be the gain or loss to be recognized in income.

Early recognition of commitments in foreign currency, in the manner just described, could be difficult if the commitments were so long-term that reliable figures for the forward exchange rates could not be obtained. Perhaps for this reason, accounting standards have chosen to adhere more closely to the normal practice for domestic transactions. That is to say, the transaction is recognized at the performance date rather than at the commitment date. When recognized, the foreign currency amount of the transaction is translated at the spot exchange rate at that date. At any subsequent reporting date before settlement, the foreign currency payable or receivable is translated at the then-current spot rate and foreign exchange gain or loss recognized even though unrealized. Final gain or loss is recognized on settlement. If there are many transactions in a foreign currency it is acknowledged that the use of average exchange rates or approximations to ease the burden of record keeping is satisfactory.[3]

As we shall see later, when a commitment is hedged by a forward contract or other instrument, the transaction is measured at the exchange rate locked in by that instrument at the *commitment* date. Accordingly, there is a fundamental inconsistency in the measurement of cost in such transactions depending upon whether or not they are hedged.

Accounting for investments or borrowing denominated in a foreign currency

An entity may also borrow money in a foreign currency or invest in an interest-bearing security denominated in a foreign currency. If it does, it is exposed to an exchange risk on the transaction, and the question arises as to how and when any gains or losses on such positions should be recognized. (Operating transactions that give extended terms to the buyer have a similar impact. An account payable due in instalments is tantamount to a direct borrowing, and an account receivable collectible in instalments is equivalent to an investment in a security that matures in instalments.) The discussion below will concentrate on direct borrowing in a foreign currency. With correction for differences in circumstances, the reasoning applied to accounting for a foreign currency borrowing can be applied to accounting for an amount receivable in foreign currency.

Two questions arise with respect to accounting for borrowing in a foreign currency. At what amount should it be reported in the entity's domestic currency balance sheet? Also, if adjustments are made from time to time in the carrying value of that borrowing, when and how should such adjustments be recognized in income? (If adjustments are recognized in income as they occur, income reported could be significantly affected by unrealized gains and losses that might well be reversed before maturity.)

The traditional accounting basis for foreign currency debt left its balance sheet carrying value unchanged from the figure of proceeds originally received from the borrowing until the debt became a current liability. Today's accounting standards have progressed beyond traditional accounting. It is now felt that since current exchange rates must be regarded as more relevant than past rates, the translation of the face amount of the foreign currency debt into domestic currency should always be at the current rate.

That leaves the question whether the consequential adjustments should be part of income in the periods when the exchange rates change. The United States position is that adjustments should be recognized in income immediately. The Canadian standard has compromised. That compromise is understandable when it is remembered that foreign currency borrowings are far more important to Canadian companies than to U.S. companies, in view of the smaller capital market in Canada. Given the volatility of foreign exchange rates under a floating-rate system, immediate recognition of unrealized gains or losses on adjustments of foreign currency debt to current rates could, in some companies, swamp reported operating income, especially in quarterly financial statements. Many believe that it is fundamentally misleading to permit what may be mere fluctuations in exchange rates to have this effect.

The Canadian compromise takes this form:[4]

- As noted already, debt is translated at the rate current at the financial reporting date since no other rate is considered equally relevant. If the debt has a "fixed or ascertainable life," resulting adjustments in carrying value are treated as deferred charges or deferred credits. Adjustments with respect to debt that has no ascertainable life, or debt classified as a current liability, are to be recognized in income immediately.
- Adjustments deferred are amortized over the remaining term of the debt if it has a fixed or ascertainable life extending beyond the end of the next fiscal year.

Meaning of "ascertainable life." The meaning of the term "ascertainable life" is obscure. It was probably inserted to take care of such situations as bank loans that, although in demand form, have a schedule for repayment that is understood between the borrower and the bank. To have any meaning, a stretch-out of amortization over a presumed ascertainable life should be based on some external evidence, such as an understanding with the borrower, and should not be based merely on management's expectations as to future availability of cash for debt reduction.

Basis of amortization. The precise method of amortization over the remaining term of the debt is also not specified. Three possible bases of amortization over the remaining lifetime have been explored in the literature.[5] Because these proposals are all based on prospective amortization, as required by the *CICA Handbook*, they all suffer from a flaw. That is to say, the impact of a given change in exchange rates on amortization for the period, and thus on income, is much greater if it occurs near the end of the debt life than if it occurs near the beginning.

One minor point may be noted. In a serial debt issue, the number of years to maturity varies for each instalment of principal. In such a case, it is necessary to treat the amount maturing at each separate date as though it were a separate debt issue for the purpose of calculating the amount of amortization to maturity.

Renegotiation of foreign currency debt. If foreign currency debt is settled before maturity, any unamortized balance of deferred debit or credit with respect to that debt is to be written off. The *CICA Handbook*, however, makes an exception in unspecified circumstances "when a renegotiation of the terms and conditions ... may not constitute a settlement."[6] In such a case the deferred charge or credit remaining is to be amortized over the life of the renegotiated debt.

The first question to be asked about this provision is: What constitutes renegotiation? Can it be "*re*negotiation" if a completely new lender takes over the position of the lender being paid off? That might not seem unreasonable if, for example, it resulted simply from a company changing bankers without significant other changes in the debt characteristics. Can it be called renegotiation if debt in one currency is paid off with proceeds from borrowing in another currency? On the face of it that would seem unreasonable, but some might argue that some currencies are so closely linked that substitution of one for the other without major change in terms of the debt can be regarded as a renegotiation rather than a settlement. Is there any limit to changes in debt terms? For example, if the maturity date is extended from five years to ten or twenty years, or if there is a substantial change in the security supporting the debt, or if the interest rate is changed from fixed to floating or the reverse, can that still be regarded as renegotiation? Without a better explanation of the meaning of the term "renegotiation," the answers to these questions are matters of opinion.

A second question concerns the merits of the instruction to amortize the deferred debit or credit remaining at the time of renegotiation over the duration of the renegotiated debt. If the new debt has a shorter maturity than that replaced, most would agree that the amortization should be revised so that any deferred debit or credit is fully amortized when the debt is finally retired. The position when the maturity date of debt is extended upon renegotiation is more debatable. At the time the original debt was issued the company undertook an exposure to foreign exchange risk for the original term of the debt. At the time of renegotiation, the actual result of that risk bearing to that date was indicated by the current exchange rate. The CICA intention was that any adjustment required as a result of changes in the exchange rate should be regarded as an adjustment of the direct interest cost on the debt and thus should be spread over its term. The question is whether that term for amortization should be altered because the debt maturity has been extended.

In the author's opinion it should not be. It should be clear that if one is borrowing in a foreign currency, the exchange risk is greater when the borrowing is for five years (say) than when it is for six months. By extending the term to maturity by renegotiating debt, an entity assumes a *greater* exposure to foreign exchange risk than it had before. It flies in the face of logic that by increasing its exposure to foreign exchange risk an entity should reduce its recognition of loss (or gain) with respect to past foreign exchange risk taking.

Evaluation of Canadian treatment of foreign currency investment or borrowing. When a company invests in a foreign currency monetary asset or incurs a foreign currency monetary liability, it exposes itself to risk from changes in the exchange rate with respect to that currency. The result of that risk must be recognized in income at some time. One way to do so is to continuously restate the carrying value of the asset or liability to an amount equal to its face amount in foreign currency translated at the exchange rate current at the reporting date and to recognize the adjustment in income immediately as a gain or loss.

The CICA has rejected this treatment, largely because fluctuations in exchange rates could have a significant impact on periodic income reported and yet be meaningless if they were to cancel out over the term to maturity of the asset or liability. However, almost certainly there will be *some* gain or loss because of exchange rate movements over that time, so that some method must be adopted for recognition of that amount in income. The CICA considers that such gain or loss is inherently part of the return on the asset or the cost of the debt over its life, and therefore it should be amortized in some way over that period. Unfortunately, even if it is conceded that gain or loss should be amortized, the approach suggested by the CICA is open to severe criticism.

- If the ultimate foreign currency gain or loss is regarded as an adjustment of the yield on the investment or the effective cost of the debt, that adjustment applies over the whole contract period of the asset or liability. It does not just apply to the period remaining after a movement in the exchange rate occurs. Thus prospective amortization of the effect of exchange rate changes is inconsistent with the basic rationale for amortization.

- That conclusion is reinforced by consideration of the economics of the case. Let us ask ourselves whether the probability of gain and of loss on foreign exchange is evenly balanced when a Canadian company borrows abroad at a lower interest rate than that obtainable at home. The interest rate parity theory, referred to earlier, tells us that it is not. If the risk were evenly balanced, everyone (except those with a high aversion to risk) would borrow abroad to take advantage of the lower interest rate. That would result in a quick equalization of interest rates. If that equalization has not occurred, it must be presumed that the probability is that exchange losses will occur when an entity borrows abroad.
- How, then, might amortization be applied from the beginning? Consider a Canadian company borrowing abroad. At the time of borrowing it could be estimated what rate of interest would have had to be paid on borrowing on equivalent security at home. Interest expense might then be recorded at that estimated domestic rate, with the excess over the actual foreign interest rate being credited to the liability account. Then, to the extent that differences arose from time to time between that carrying value for the liability and its principal amount translated at current exchange rates, those differences could be amortized over the period to debt maturity. If the interest rate parity theory is broadly accurate, this treatment would minimize differences to be amortized and provide a better portrayal of annual debt cost. (Before adoption, however, it would be wise to research how well this method — and possibly competing ones — would work under actual conditions.)

The suggested CICA treatment of deferred debits or credits at the time of debt renegotiation seems particularly unfortunate. If it is correct that entities will normally borrow in a foreign currency principally to take advantage of lower interest rates and that those lower rates will be associated with foreign exchange losses, there will be deferred exchange losses more often than deferred exchange gains. If this is so, the CICA standard is unconservative at every point. First, it does not provide from the inception of the borrowing for the probable strengthening of the foreign currency vis-à-vis the domestic currency that economic theory suggests is to be expected. Second, it has chosen (perhaps understandably) not to recognize the loss in full when the exchange rate does change. Third, amortization of the deferred loss is prospective only and therefore tends to push off recognition of the loss so that it is piled on top of further losses that are likely to occur in future. Finally, companies are able to take advantage of an undefined notion of renegotiation to push loss recognition still further into the future.

Accounting for speculative foreign currency contracts

Foreign currency contracts (forward exchange contracts, currency futures contracts, and currency options) have been described earlier. These contracts may be used to hedge an existing exposure to foreign exchange risk. Accounting in that situation will be discussed subsequently. Equally, they may be used for speculation on foreign exchange movements. That is, if a foreign exchange risk exposure does not exist, the purchase of a foreign exchange contract will create such an exposure.

When an entity has committed itself to a foreign exchange contract for speculative purposes, there is little doubt that the most informative accounting for the results of that decision to speculate is to recognize gain or loss as the value of the contract changes. That accounting is required by U.S. standards. On outstanding forward exchange contracts the gain or loss is measured at any given reporting date by multiplying the foreign currency amount contracted for by the difference between the forward rate available to the contract termination date as at the reporting date and the forward rate in the contract. If the speculation takes the form of a futures contract, the entity will have paid or received variation margin on the contract subsequent to taking it on, and that margin will measure the gain or loss that has accrued. If the speculative medium is an option, the gain or loss will be indicated by market quotations on the options. (With respect to forward exchange contracts, one might note that the cash gain or loss based on changes in the forward exchange rate will not take place until the contract maturity date. One might argue, therefore, that a discounted figure based on the difference in forward rates would better represent the economic gain or loss, especially on long-dated contracts.)

The *CICA Handbook* does not speak directly to the question of accounting for speculative foreign exchange contracts. The U.S. standard practice is acceptable in Canada and preferable to any other basis, such as one that recognizes losses immediately but defers gains until realization.

Hedges of exposure to foreign currency risk on transactions

As explained earlier, an economic hedge exists when the foreign exchange risk on one position is offset by an equal and opposite risk on another position. That is, if a change in the exchange rate occurs, it will be favourable to one and adverse to the other with the net effect being zero.

Positions exposed to foreign exchange risk include monetary assets or liabilities denominated in a foreign currency, firm commitments to pay or receive foreign currency in the future, and the several types of foreign currency contracts if they are acquired for speculation as described in the preceding section.

Any position which, standing by itself, is exposed to foreign exchange risk can serve as a hedge of another risk in the same foreign currency that takes the opposite direction. For example, an entity can be naturally hedged if its activities are such that its accounts receivable and accounts payable in a particular foreign currency are approximately equal in amount most of the time. Or, if an entity has some positions at risk that are not naturally hedged, it can arrange one or more foreign currency contracts to accomplish a balanced risk position. As we shall see shortly, the CICA has extended the idea of hedging instruments to include, in some circumstances, expected but not assured future cash flows in the foreign currency.

The amount of foreign exchange risk is a function of the time to settlement of the asset, liability, or commitment in the foreign currency. A foreign currency account receivable and account payable of equal amount are naturally hedged in economic terms so long as both are outstanding. Once one position becomes liquidated, the other becomes unhedged from that time forward. Likewise, the exchange risk will be only partially hedged if the opposing positions at risk are unbalanced in amount.

It is an objective of current accounting standards to account for foreign currency positions that are fully hedged in such a fashion that no net foreign exchange gain or loss will be reflected in income. The question that arises is: How shall the accounting be arranged so as to avoid recognition of gain or loss on perfectly hedged positions when the exchange rate moves and yet provide the best possible balance sheet portrayal of foreign currency positions? In general, four possibilities exist for avoiding gain or loss recognition on hedges, as described below. Accounting practice must select from among these alternatives.

1. The position at risk can be regularly revalued at current exchange rates. If the hedging medium is an asset or liability recorded in the balance sheet, it too can be regularly revalued. Or, if the hedging medium is a foreign currency contract that is treated as executory (that is, it does not result in recognized balance sheet assets and liabilities), a net contract value (positive or negative) resulting from exchange rate movements can be calculated at each reporting date and recognized as an asset or liability. The amount of any adjustments in carrying values of positions at risk and their hedging mediums would be carried directly to income where they would offset each other, so that no net gain or loss would be reported. Alternatively, the adjustments could be carried to a "suspense account" with the same effect; however, it would then become necessary to maintain a continuous analysis of that suspense account to ensure appropriate write-off of any balance that might result from a hedge that was imperfect.
2. Recognition of exchange rate changes can be omitted both with respect to the position at risk and the hedging instrument until one of them is realized.
3. The position at risk can be regularly revalued but changes in the value of the hedging medium ignored. In this case the amount of the regular adjustment to the carrying value of the position at risk would have to be deferred until settlement of the hedging medium, at which time the gain or loss on that medium and the accumulated deferred gain or loss on the position at risk would be offset.
4. Changes in the value of a position at risk can be ignored but changes in the value of the hedging instrument be recognized. In this case the amount of the adjustment to the latter would have to be deferred until such time as the effect of exchange rate movements on the position at risk came to be recognized. That might occur, for example, on the occasion of recognition of a transaction resulting from a foreign currency commitment previously unrecorded.

From the standpoint of faithful representation of all foreign currency positions in the balance sheet, the approach described under the first point above seems to be preferable. Consistent recognition on a current basis of the effect of exchange rate changes on all foreign currency positions would also avoid the necessity of recognition of deferred gains and losses and might avoid the confusion possible as a result of treating the effect of exchange rate changes differently for one position from that of another. Under the point 1 approach whereby all adjustments are recognized in income, a perfect hedge will result in no net effect on income, while an imperfect hedge will result in some net gain or loss, which will be appropriately recognized as it occurs.

One modification of this approach has to be made, however, to give effect to the intention of the Canadian standard with respect to a long-term investment or borrowing in foreign currency. If such a position is only partially hedged, it will be necessary to apportion the adjustment to its carrying value so that only the hedged proportion is taken to income while the remainder is deferred and amortized on a basis consistent with that previously described for unhedged positions. (Alternatively, some might interpret the *CICA Handbook* to suggest that the amount of any adjustment to a long-term monetary asset [or liability] and to a position identified as hedging it should be netted against each other and any net excess of the asset [or liability] adjustment should be deferred to be amortized to income in future. This would have the effect of including any differences resulting from imperfections in the hedge in the amount to be amortized in future.)

In spite of the apparent superiority of the first approach based on regular revaluation of all foreign currency positions, it is not required by the standards or adopted in practice in all situations. The following are the exceptions:

- A commitment to make a purchase or sale is not recognized in accounting until performance. Present standards do not suggest any change in this for commitments in a foreign currency, nor do they suggest recognition of any value (positive or negative) with respect to a foreign currency commitment when the exchange rate changes. Accordingly, the treatment of the effect of exchange rate movements on a position hedging a foreign currency commitment must be made to conform. Either no adjustment will be recognized for the effect of foreign exchange movements on the hedging medium before the commitment becomes a recognized transaction, or else the gain or loss resulting from such adjustment must be deferred until the transaction recognition date. The emphasis in the published accounting standards is on the latter treatment. Monetary items in a foreign currency are always to be adjusted to their equivalent at current exchange rates, and it appears that is the intention for foreign currency contracts as well. In practice, however, a forward contract hedging a commitment might be left unrecognized until the commitment becomes a transaction, for reasons of convenience.
- As will be discussed shortly, the *CICA Handbook* visualizes some situations in which a position at risk may be hedged by a nonmonetary asset or a future revenue stream. In such a case, it is virtually impossible to revalue the supposed hedging medium for exchange rate changes. Hence, when the position at risk is a monetary asset or liability, the approach described in point 3 above is adopted. If the position deemed to be hedged is a commitment, the approach described in point 2 would have to be adopted.

Because of the deferment of gain or loss in some cases and the complete omission of recognition of a commitment and its hedging instrument in others, accounting standards seek to ensure that the hedge is genuine and will continue to be effective over the hedge period. To be considered effective, it must seem probable at the outset that the value of the hedging instrument will change with changing exchange rates so as to offset the impact of those rate changes on the position hedged. If the hedging instrument is for a shorter period than the position hedged, the *CICA Handbook* seems to suggest that the management must have an intention of renewing the hedge up to the settlement date of the position hedged in order to justify deferment of gain or loss.[7] The FASB, in contrast, has concluded (correctly, in the author's opinion) that if an economic hedge exists, accounting should reflect that fact and there need not be any linkage of the date of the hedging instrument and the position hedged.[8] The standards require that management identify the existence of the hedge at its outset in order to follow hedge accounting.[9]

When gain or loss is being deferred on a presumed hedge, a problem may arise if hedge accounting must be discontinued before its originally expected date. The recommended treatment is as follows. If (1) a hedging instrument matures before settlement date of the position hedged and is not renewed, or (2) the hedging instrument is disposed of before that date, or (3) hedge accounting is discontinued because the hedge appears not to be effective, any cumulative gain or loss deferred up to the date of such event is to continue to be deferred until recognition date for the transaction hedged and then will be used to adjust the transaction measurement in the manner previously described.[10] By extension of the same reasoning, one may infer that if gain or loss was not currently being recognized and deferred on a hedging instrument, such as a forward contract, and the contract was terminated before the commitment became a recognized transaction, it would be reasonable to defer the gain or loss on the hedging instrument at the time of termination, to be merged with the transaction recognition subsequently.

When gain or loss is deferred, care must be observed in implementing hedge accounting because it is often not possible to match all the terms and conditions of a position at risk with a hedging instrument. For example, if the hedging instrument is for a larger foreign currency amount than a commitment hedged, the gain or loss recorded on the hedging instrument as the exchange rate changes must be apportioned so that deferment is restricted to the amount applicable to the foreign currency amount of the commitment. Similarly, if a hedge extends beyond the transaction recognition date, deferment of gain or loss must cease at that date.

When a hedging medium consists of a foreign currency contract, there will be certain costs related to the contract, and the accounting becomes somewhat more complicated than it is for a hedge based solely on foreign currency monetary assets and liabilities. The general objective is that costs of hedging should be written off to expense over the lifetime of the hedging contract if the position hedged is a monetary asset or liability. On the other hand, if it is a commitment that is hedged, the costs of hedging are considered to be an adjustment of the transaction hedged. Accordingly, they should be deferred if incurred before recognition of the transaction and at that time should be merged with the cost or revenue recognized on the transaction. These general principles may be implemented in somewhat different fashion for different types of hedging contracts.

- On forward exchange contracts the cumulative gain or loss at any time can be calculated by comparing the current spot rate of exchange with the spot rate at the time the contract was entered into. The difference in those two rates multiplied by the foreign currency amount of the contract is the gain or loss on a cumulative basis. This contract value is recognized period by period as the exchange rate moves by recording an accrued asset or liability with respect to the contract. This, however, does not take care of the difference between the spot rate at the inception of the contract and the forward rate contracted for at which it will be settled. That difference may be regarded as the cost (or proceeds, because it can be negative) from hedging. The difference is amortized over the lifetime of the contract. The amortization is carried to income on a regular basis if the position hedged is a monetary asset or liability and is deferred for subsequent inclusion in the transaction amount recognized if the position hedged is a commitment. Similar accounting is followed for swap contracts, which, in this situation, are tantamount to long-term forward exchange contracts.

- On a foreign currency futures contract the holder will pay or be entitled to receive variation margin. That margin is calculated by tracking the changes in the spot exchange rate after the contract is entered into. Recognition of the variation margin as an asset or liability (or as cash payments are made or cash is received with respect to it) automatically causes recognition of gain or loss. That gain or loss is deferred if it relates to a commitment; otherwise it is recognized in income. Brokers' commissions on a futures contract are payable upon settlement. Thus, the commission cost should be accrued over the life of the contract with the amount of the accrual being charged to income or deferred as has been described for forward exchange contract costs.
- No authoritative guidance has been provided with respect to a hedge in the form of a foreign currency option contract. The following observations may suggest a reasonable basis of accounting for a call option hedging a payment obligation. Mirror image observations might be made about a put option hedging a future foreign currency cash receipt.
  - At the time a call option is bought, there will be a certain relationship between the strike price (i.e., the exercise price) under the option and the spot price for the foreign currency. If the strike price is below the spot price, the option is "in-the-money." The true premium paid for the currency risk aspect of the option is thus the actual premium less the in-the-money portion. Conversely, if the strike price is above the spot price, the spot price has to rise by that difference before the option becomes worth anything at its expiry date. Thus one can say that the true measure of the option cost in this case is the actual premium paid plus the excess of the strike price over the spot price when the contract is acquired.
  - Consider an option that is out-of-the-money when bought and is intended to hedge a monetary liability. To the extent the foreign currency value rises, the liability will become more onerous — that is, a loss will have to be recorded on it. There will be no offsetting gain on the option until the spot price rises to the strike price, but thereafter the gain in the in-the-money value of the option will match the loss on the liability. If the option is exercised to provide the foreign currency required when the obligation falls due, the net loss to be absorbed will be the loss on the obligation not covered while the spot price was rising to the strike price, plus the actual premium paid for the option.
  - Now consider an option that is in-the-money when bought. As the foreign currency value rises, the loss on the liability will be exactly offset by the gain in the in-the-money value of the option. Upon exercise, the full in-the-money value of the option will be recovered, including the amount existing when the option was acquired, and therefore the net cost of hedging will be the original actual premium less the portion thereof that was in-the-money at the acquisition date.
  - Consider next the effect of declining spot prices over the period of the option. The burden of the liability hedged will decline as the spot price

declines. If the option is in-the-money when bought, the in-the-money value will decline, offsetting the gain on the liability, but only up to the point where that in-the-money value is wiped out. Once that point is reached, the option will be allowed to expire so long as the currency spot price does not recover. Thus the real cost of the hedge is again the actual premium paid less the portion that was in-the-money at the acquisition date.

- It follows from the foregoing that if an option used for hedging is an exact match for the position hedged in terms of amount and duration, the following would be a reasonable way to account for an option hedging a monetary asset or liability.
  - First, the original premium paid for the option would be recorded in two parts. One part would be a calculated amount representing the true premium — that is, the actual premium paid minus the acquisition date in-the-money position or plus the excess of the strike price over the spot price at the acquisition date. The other part recorded would be the difference between the actual premium paid and the true premium. This could be regarded as the intrinsic contract value and would be positive if the contract was in-the-money and negative if it was out-of-the-money — that is, if the strike price exceeded the spot price at acquisition.
  - Second, the true premium would be amortized to income over the life of the contract, representing the cost of maintaining a hedged position.
  - Third, changes in the contract value would be recorded regularly based on changes in the spot price for the currency, *except* a cumulative loss on the option would not be recorded beyond the amount that it was originally in-the-money. The effect of recognition of gain or loss on the option in income would be to offset the gain or loss on the position hedged, except that because the option loss is limited to the original in-the-money amount, a net gain could be achieved if the currency spot rate falls far enough.

If the option contract were hedging a commitment, rather than a monetary asset or liability, the foregoing procedures would be modified to defer both the gain and loss recognized on the contract and the amount of amortization written on the true premium. At the date of recognition of the transaction resulting from the commitment, such deferred balances would be merged with the cost or revenue recorded on the transaction.

These procedures are complex. It may be noted that the balance of the unamortized true premium on the books plus or minus the contract value based on the regular adjustments for spot rate changes would not remain equal to the quoted market value of the contract from time to time, although the difference would not be expected to grow too large. Thus, should the contract be terminated before the hedging position, there would be a further gain or loss to be dealt with. It would not be unreasonable to regard this as an adjustment of the effective contract cost. If this is agreed, however, a simpler accounting basis is possible. That is, rather than go through the complications of regular revaluations of the contract and amortization of the true premium, it would be possible simply to record changes in the market value of the contract as they occur. If the contract hedges a monetary asset or liability, these changes could be taken to income where they would provide a rough offset to the loss recognized on the position hedged, or to a gain up to the loss limit provided by the original in-the-money position. If hedging a commitment, the gain or loss on the option contract would be deferred to be merged with the transaction cost or revenue when recognized. It should be noted that if the option is for a larger foreign currency amount than the commitment hedged, the gain or loss deferred should be restricted to the proportion equivalent to the commitment amount percentage of the option amount.

Hedging with nonmonetary assets. The *CICA Handbook* indicates that a nonmonetary asset held that will (with reasonable assurance) be converted into sufficient foreign currency at the date of settlement of a liability in the same currency can be viewed as a hedge.[11] It is hard to be sure what was meant by this. One may suppose that a situation was visualized in which an entity owns a portfolio of stocks traded on a foreign exchange or a piece of real estate located in the foreign country which it intends to sell and use the proceeds to liquidate the liability deemed hedged.

In any event, if such a position can be identified there is an accounting problem because the carrying value of the nonmonetary asset will not be continuously adjusted for exchange rate changes. Consequently, it is necessary to defer the gains or losses recognized on the regular adjustment to the current exchange rate of the liability deemed hedged. When the asset is sold, what is to become of that deferred gain and loss? The only apparent way to avoiding reporting it as a foreign exchange gain or loss seems to be to treat it as an adjustment of the proceeds of sale from the asset and thereby as a factor in the net gain or loss reported on that sale.

One may ask: What happens if it turns out that the asset in question is not sold at the time the liability is liquidated? Based on the proposition that the liability and nonmonetary asset did hedge each other, it could be argued that continued deferral of the gain or loss until eventual sale of the asset would be appropriate. This would be consistent with continued deferral of gain or loss when a hedging instrument related to a commitment is terminated before the commitment matures.

The logic of all this is highly questionable. The CICA recommendation overlooks the essential nature of a hedging instrument, namely that its value can be *relied upon* to fluctuate proportionate to changes in the foreign exchange rate. That simply cannot be said about a portfolio of stocks, a piece of real estate, or any other nonmonetary asset. Thus, in the author's opinon, a nonmonetary asset can never be shown to be an effective hedge of a foreign exchange risk.

Revenue-stream hedges. The *CICA Handbook* also speaks of a future revenue stream in a foreign currency as a possible hedge of foreign currency obligations. This suggestion also raises many questions. In the first place, one needs to understand what is meant by a "revenue stream." The term "revenue" is by itself confusing in this context. Revenue is an accrual accounting term. Debt is not paid with revenue; it must be paid with cash. The *CICA Handbook* really means cash flow from sales or services in this context. But then consider a case in which sales revenue in the foreign currency is partly used to cover operating expenses in that currency. It is obvious that only the *net* cash stream is available to meet the foreign currency obligation.

Even then a question may be asked. Suppose a Canadian company obtained all its revenues in U.S. dollars but incurred all its ordinary running expenses in

Canada. The money must come from somewhere to pay those expenses. Hence it is arguable that only the amount of U.S. dollar cash flow not required to meet Canadian operating expenses should be regarded as available to meet the U.S. dollar debt. Alternatively, it might be considered acceptable to regard all the U.S. dollar net cash flow as available to meet U.S. dollar debt if it is reasonable to expect that Canadian dollar borrowing will be incurred to finance Canadian dollar operating costs.

The *CICA Handbook* is silent on this point. Consider, however, the general instruction that there should be reasonable assurance that a hedge will be effective in order for hedge accounting to be applied. This could be taken to mean that if all the projected U.S. dollar cash flow is designated as a hedge of U.S. dollar debt, there must be reasonable assurance that the U.S. cash flow *will* be held in U.S. dollar assets to meet U.S. debt service costs and that Canadian dollar borrowing can and *will* be implemented to meet the Canadian dollar costs. In practice, this might well mean that the maximum that could be designated as a hedge is the net cash flow from operations, expressed in U.S. dollars, regardless of where the operating costs were incurred.

A second problem with a hedge in the form of a revenue stream is that of timing. Cash flow from operations comes in a more or less continuous stream; debt is paid off all at once or in blocks at specific dates. One of the conditions for an *effective* hedge of this kind, then, is that the cash flow in the foreign currency be accumulated in cash, or an asset easily convertible to cash, so that it is actually available to pay off the debt when required. If this is not done, there will inevitably be a net deferred loss or gain on the debt when it is paid off, and the required write-off of that deferred amount will be proof that the hedge was not effective.

It should be evident that in order to provide reasonable assurance that a revenue-stream hedge will be effective, it will be necessary to make a forecast of the amount of foreign currency that will be available from that stream and will actually be used or set aside to meet the debt obligations as they arise. That forecast must take into account not only forecast net income and charges against that income that will not require an outlay of cash but also income taxes and capital expenditures or other investments expected during the forecast period. If all the foreign currency cash flow from operations will be absorbed by new investment, it cannot hedge the risk exposure on the existing debt.

Some margin for error should be allowed in the forecast. If the foreign currency appreciates, that appreciation may not only increase the burden of the foreign currency debt but may also damage the competitiveness of business that is conducted in that currency. In addition, all business is uncertain and forecasts may go very wrong. What margin for error is allowed will be a matter for judgment in the particular circumstances of each case, but the risk must not be underrated if there is to be reasonable assurance of the effectiveness of the hedge.

If the forecast shows an apparent margin of net foreign currency receipts over debt requirements, it may be asked whether the entity can pick and choose which years' net cash flows shall be deemed to hedge the debt. To take an extreme case, suppose a debt matures five years hence and the forecast shows a net cash flow in foreign currency in each year, over and above the amount required to take care of the debt interest, that is sufficient to meet the requirement for retirement of debt principal. May the entity pick the revenue of the last year as the hedge of the debt principal? The *CICA Handbook* does not deal with this point, but some cautions should be expressed.

First, the further into the future that the forecast extends, the less assurance there can be as to its accuracy. Thus, other things being equal, the margin for error allowed in the forecast should be much greater in the fifth-year than in the first year. It may be that the uncertainty is sufficiently great that there cannot be reasonable assurance of the hedge effectiveness in that year almost regardless of the size of the future foreign currency cash flow that is forecast.

Second, as will be described more fully below, revenue-stream hedge accounting calls for the foreign currency net cash flow to be translated at the exchange rate applicable at the time the hedge was designated. Consider a case where the foreign currency is strengthening at a rate of ten percent a year or roughly sixty percent over five years. If only the fifth-year cash flow is designated as a hedge, the income figures for years one to four will all be translated at exchange rates current in those years, while some part of the revenue in the fifth-year will be translated at an exchange rate in effect five years earlier. Not only will this distort the true trend in revenues, it will also, in effect, load the entire exchange loss with respect to the debt principal into just one year out of the five years that the debt is outstanding. This can hardly be said to be good accounting.

The manner of application of revenue-stream hedge accounting is not immediately obvious from the *CICA Handbook* description. An example wherein cash flow from a U.S. branch of a Canadian enterprise is designated as a hedge of U.S. dollar debt owed by that enterprise will illustrate the principle. Suppose that a revenue-stream hedge is designated in 19x0 against a five-year borrowing of U.S. $2,500,000. Suppose also, that the gross revenue in 19x1 in the United States is forecast to be $10 million and that after meeting all operating and investment requirements, U.S. $500,000 will be available in cash to be held against future debt liquidation. Suppose further that the exchange rate was $1.00 U.S. = $1.30 Canadian when the hedge was designated in 19x0 and $1.00 U.S. = $1.40 Canadian in 19x1.

The suggestion is that "the amount included in the determination of net income of future periods would be the foreign currency amount translated at the exchange rate in effect when the revenue stream is identified as a hedge."[12] What this vague instruction appears to mean is that a portion of the U.S. dollar revenue for 19x1 is to be translated at the rate of $1.30, rather than the current exchange rate of $1.40. In our example, revenue of U.S. $500,000 will be translated at $1.30 into Canadian $650,000, while the remainder of the revenue of U.S. $9,500,000 will be translated using the $1.40 rate. This translation procedure will result in a credit of $50,000, which will be recorded as a deferred exchange adjustment (credit) partly offsetting the debit deferred exchange adjustment arising upon translation of the debt at the 19x1 exchange rate.

This illustration would be less complex if the revenue-stream hedge consisted simply of the net return from an investment in the United States, rather than the cash flow from a business operation. The principle involved is the same, however. One starts with the amount of cash flow that is presumed to hedge the debt obligation (and that is being accumulated for that purpose). Net income or revenue from the foreign source that is reported for the period must be, in effect, misstated by being translated at the exchange rate applicable when the hedge was designated, rather than at the exchange rate in the year it was earned. Since the increase in foreign currency assets accumulated as a result of that net income or revenue will be translated at the correct rate, a difference appears as the result of translation, which will be deferred to offset the deferred exchange gain or loss on the item hedged.

During the period the hedge is intended to be outstanding, there must be regular reviews to see that it remains effective. It is equally important to see that foreign currency assets are actually set aside, as planned, so as to be available for ultimate liquidation of the debt. It must be remembered that if these assets are not set aside, future exchange gains and losses with respect to them will not be realized. Hence, there will be nothing to offset the gains and losses on the debt, and the hedge will not have been effective.

There are several objections to revenue-stream hedge accounting. The most obvious is that it misstates the revenue derived from foreign source assets. It can hardly be argued that revenue is as fairly portrayed when translated at an exchange rate in effect several years earlier as when it is translated at the exchange rate in effect at the time when it is earned. In addition, there is an undesirable degree of flexibility in revenue-stream hedge accounting. It is optional whether or not a hedge is designated (which is true of hedge accounting generally). It is a matter of opinion whether there is reasonable assurance that the hedge will be effective. There often will be an undesirable degree of flexibility in the choice as to which years' revenues are designated as a hedge. To make the accounting work over the term of the debt, monetary foreign currency assets have to be accumulated — in effect a sinking fund has to be set up — which may not be sensible from a business point of view. All in all, it is far from clear that revenue-stream hedge accounting is a good idea.

What then would be preferable accounting? It is strongly arguable that leaving the accounting alone would provide a more faithful representation of what is actually occurring. The fact of the matter is that revenue in any year ought to be translated at the exchange rate in effect in that year, not a rate in effect some time earlier. The gain or loss on exchange rate movements occurs when the rate changes, not some years later when cash is collected to pay off the changed liability. If there is concern about immediate income recognition of reversible exchange rate fluctuations, the *CICA Handbook* already provides a method (albeit one that is flawed) for dealing with that problem. There is no need to engage in the fantasy of revenue-stream hedges.

Translation of foreign currency financial statements for consolidation or equity accounting purposes

Many enterprises have investments in branches and subsidiaries that operate in foreign countries and prepare financial statements expressed in the foreign currencies. For purposes of preparing consolidated financial statements, it is necessary to "translate" those financial statements into the reporting currency of the parent. Likewise, when an entity has an investment position that gives it significant influence over a foreign company or when a entity is a participant in a joint venture operating abroad, it is necessary to translate the foreign currency statements of the investee for the purpose of performing equity accounting or proportionate consolidation in the financial statements of the investor. In each case, the translation procedure is governed by the same principles. For ease in explanation we shall concentrate on translation of the financial statements of subsidiary companies for incorporation in the consolidated financial statements of their parent. It should be understood that the same considerations apply to the translation of the financial statements of branches and investees.

Techniques for the translation of foreign currency financial statements developed over a long period of time without any very profound conceptual basis. It was clear that, from a parent company's point of view, operations abroad have risks not present in domestic operations. One risk is that of changes in the exchange rate for the currency of the country in which the subsidiary is situated. The questions pertinent to translation techniques were: (1) How should that risk exposure be measured? and (2) When should gains or losses from foreign exchange risks be considered realized?

In the turbulent state of the foreign exchange markets that developed after the collapse of the Bretton Woods system, the traditional bases for translation were seen to be inadequate. Today's accounting standards prescribe two different bases for translation to be applied in different circumstances — the temporal translation method and the current-rate translation method.

The temporal translation method

The "temporal" approach to translation was developed in Accounting Research Study No. 12 published by the American Institute of Certified Public Accountants in 1972.[13] The study looked at the problems of translation very much from the perspective of the parent company. The logical translation method would be derived, it was argued, if one asked a simple question. What would the accounts show if (1) all the transactions of the foreign entity had been conducted by the parent company itself, (2) it had recorded them in its accounts in its domestic currency equivalent at each transaction date, and (3) it subsequently had modified carrying values of foreign currency assets and liabilities recorded following the rules of generally accepted accounting principles? The answer also was simple. Under generally accepted accounting principles some assets, such as inventory, fixed assets, or deferred charges, would be carried most of the time based on the historical cost established when they were acquired. For these, then, the appropriate translation rule was this: translate historical cost shown in foreign currency accounts at the historical exchange rate applicable at the transaction date. Other assets, such as accounts receivable in a foreign currency, would be carried under generally accepted accounting principles at a realizable or market value at the financial reporting date. To express these at their equivalent realizable or market values in domestic currency, the current foreign exchange rate at the financial reporting date would be required.

From this the temporal principle was deduced. If an asset or liability is to be recorded under GAAP at historical cost, apply the historical exchange rate to its historical cost in foreign currency. If an asset or liability is to be recorded at current value, apply the current exchange rate to its current value in foreign currency. The rule was to be applied rigorously. Thus, since the generally accepted accounting basis for inventory is lower of cost and market, the historical cost and the current value, after translation into the domestic currency at the applicable exchange rate, should be compared to find the appropriate carrying value in the parent company's financial statements.

Under the approach as advocated, cash held by the foreign subsidiary was assumed (logically) always to be carried at current value and hence was to be translated at the current exchange rate. This thinking, however, was extended to all assets and liabilities denominated in foreign currency (that is, assets and liabilities customarily described as monetary). If the intention was not to change GAAP, this was an error. Generally accepted accounting principles do not require that monetary items such as certain long- term investments or long-term bonds payable be carried at current market value. Accordingly, the temporal theory should not have called for such items in foreign currency to be translated at the current exchange rate as it did.

Three principal criticisms were made of the temporal method in the form in which it was implemented.

- When a foreign country devalued its currency just before a fiscal period-end, the temporal method still required inventory held by a subsidiary to be translated at its acquisition cost using the historical exchange rate before the devaluation (unless net realizable value translated at the current rate was lower). In many situations, it was not possible to raise selling prices in the foreign currency immediately after the devaluation. Nevertheless, the inventory did not have to be written down so long as its historical cost could still be recovered by sales proceeds translated at the new rate. Consequently, in the first reporting period after the devaluation the profit margin on sales would appear much diminished, if not wiped out. Many people felt that in this situation there had been a real loss on inventory from devaluation and that this was, in error, being deferred to the next period and reported as an operating loss rather than as a loss on foreign exchange.
- Immediate recognition in income of the net gain or loss on translation of monetary items made net income reported very volatile under a floating rate exchange system. For example, if (1) short-term monetary assets and liabilities were in balance, (2) the long-term debt/equity ratio was one to one, and (3) the net income excluding foreign exchange translation adjustments represented ten percent of shareholders' equity, a five percent movement in the foreign exchange rate from one fiscal period to the next could result in an increase or decrease in profit reported for shareholders by fifty percent. Research undertaken after the temporal method was adopted in the United States showed that some managements were engaging in costly transactions, so-called accounting hedges, to neutralize this accounting effect.[14] The many people who believed that the temporal method did not properly reflect a firm's exposure to foreign currency risk considered this uneconomic activity a particularly unfortunate result of the method.
- Many believed the method was often actually perverse in its accounting for the effects of foreign exchange movements. An illustration often cited was that of an American parent company with an investment in a self-contained German subsidiary. If monetary liabilities in the German subsidiary exceeded monetary assets, as was usually the case, a strengthening in the West German mark vis-à-vis the American dollar would cause recognition of a loss on the net foreign currency debt exposure. Yet since future earnings in West German marks would now be more valuable in terms of American dollars, the real economic effect of the exchange rate change in most cases would be favourable. (It would not necessarily be favourable if the German subsidiary exported much of its product and the strengthening of the mark left it less competitive in its markets.)

Such criticisms as these were so telling that the FASB standard relying on the temporal method had to be modified within a few years of its adoption. (A Canadian standard following and largely copying the U.S. standard had to be suspended even before it became effective.)

The current-rate translation method

The chief alternative proposed in the 1970s was the "current-rate" method. This method was widely used by British companies and some other multinational companies outside North America and was recommended (with modification in some situations) in a Canadian research study.[15] The method was simplicity itself. *Every* asset and liability item in the balance sheet of the foreign subsidiary would be translated at the year-end rate of exchange. Revenues and expenses recorded in the income statement were either translated at the same rate or at the average rate for the year (to approximate the rate prevailing at the transaction dates). The effect of the method was that a gain or loss would be shown in the translated accounts every time the exchange rate changed. The amount of gain or loss would be equal to the percentage change in the value of the foreign currency (in terms of the domestic currency) applied to the net reported assets of the foreign operation. The amount of such gain or loss for a year was included in income or, in British practice, was taken directly to retained earnings or treated as a capital transaction.

The focus of attention under the current-rate method was on the subsidiary, rather than on the parent company. The subsidiary was viewed as an operating entity in its own right, whose earnings happened to be received in a foreign currency. To the parent, therefore, it was the net investment in the subsidiary that was at risk of changes in exchange rates, not just certain of the subsidiary's assets and liabilities. That overall risk, it was felt, could be properly portrayed by translating all assets and liabilities at the current exchange rate.

The current-rate method also had its critics.

- Many accountants did not like the idea that, in the parent company's statements, the same subsidiary asset would be shown at different amounts from one accounting period to the next. For example, a newly constructed building acquired by a foreign subsidiary and initially carried at $1 million in the parent company's statement would be stated at $1,100,000 the next year if the foreign currency appreciated by ten percent. It was argued that this was fundamentally inconsistent with historical cost accounting.
- This characteristic of the current-rate method resulted, in extreme cases, in the "disappearing asset" phenomenon. In a foreign country with a high rate of inflation and consequently a rapidly declining exchange rate, use of the current-rate method rapidly reduced the carrying value, when translated into the parent company currency, of all assets held over a number of years. For example, if the foreign currency was weakening at the rate of twenty-five percent a year vis-à-vis that of the parent company, an investment in land by the subsidiary at a cost equivalent to $1 million in parent-company currency would be reduced to a carrying value of approximately $11,000 in the parent company's statements after twenty years.

Clearly the current-rate method could also be inconsistent with economic reality. Where the temporal method assumed that changes in the amount of foreign currency cash flows from nonmonetary assets would completely compensate for changes in the value of the currency, the current-rate method presumed that cash flows in foreign currency from nonmonetary assets would remain completely static, no matter what changes occurred in the value of the foreign currency. In an economy suffering from rapid inflation, this assumption is clearly wrong.

The Canadian research study recognized this problem and suggested that the answer, where subsidiaries operated in a highly inflationary economy, would be to use price-level-adjusted accounts rather than historical cost accounts as the basic accounts for the subsidiary and translate them at the current-rate method.[16] This is the so-called "restate-translate" approach. The obvious difficulty would be deciding where to draw the line between "highly" inflationary economies and economies with a more moderate rate of inflation.

The lesson that emerges from this discussion is that all inflexible rules for translation are likely to be in error at least some of the time. Ideally, what is required is a set of translation methods from which one method can be selected in each case to fit the real economic exposure to exchange risk of the entity whose financial statements are being translated. Consider the possible differences in circumstances of a West German subsidiary of an American parent. If the subsidiary incurs all its costs in Germany and sells all its output in Germany with little competition from foreign suppliers, its business will be relatively unaffected by exchange rate movements. A weakening of the mark against the U.S. dollar would suggest that the investment in West Germany will show lower returns in U.S. dollars. Suppose, instead, that the West German subsidiary sold most of its output in the United States. With revenues in the stronger currency and costs in the weaker, the change in exchange rates would be highly beneficial to operating profits. Suppose, in the alternative, that the subsidiary sold most of its output in Italy in lira and that currency had weakened even more than the German mark. Then the subsidiary would be even worse off than it was in the first case.

This discussion far from exhausts the possible economic effects of exchange rate changes. One must also consider the cost performance of the subsidiary and its competitors. If, for example, the German subsidiary is competing with a Swedish company to sell its product in America and the Swedish costs have risen more slowly than the weakening of the krona against the U.S. dollar while German costs have risen faster than the rate of weakening of the mark, the loss in its competitive edge might well more than outweigh the apparent beneficial effect of the weakening of the mark against the dollar when viewed in isolation.

It seems that, in general, it will be hard to find a translation method that will regularly be consistent with the full economic impact of exchange rate movements. The reason is that the impact of movements in exchange rates between countries is interlinked with changes in exchange relationships with other countries and relative changes in prices in all countries concerned. This means there will be considerable ambiguity about the significance of "gains" and "losses" thrown up in translation of foreign currency statements, no matter what translation approach is utilized. Some writers believe that the problem of foreign currency translation cannot be solved without the adoption of current value accounting. With current value accounting all assets and liabilities could be translated at current rates. Even this solution depends upon the current values reflected in the accounts being good estimators of future cash flows from the assets and liabilities, which will not always be the case. (See further discussion in Part III.)

The 1980s standards for foreign currency translation

As has been noted, a FASB standard put into effect in the mid-1970s and a Canadian standard, both based on exclusive adoption of the temporal method, failed to win support and acceptance. As a result, compromise standards were issued in both countries in the early 1980s. These standards attempted to be more responsive to differences in circumstances — adopting the current-rate method for one set of circumstances and the temporal method for other circumstances.

The attempt was to base the choice of method on distinctions in the economic environment of the subsidiary. The FASB described the problem as one of determining the "functional currency" of the subsidiary, "the currency of the primary economic environment in which that entity operates." The CICA described it as distinguishing between "self-sustaining foreign operations" and "integrated foreign operations," by which is meant foreign operations whose exposure to exchange rate risk is similar to that of the parent company.

Considerable judgment is required in assigning foreign operations to one category or the other. The standards suggested these guidelines:

- Sales prices of a self-sustaining foreign operation are responsive primarily to local conditions. They are not determined primarily by international prices or worldwide competition which would make them sensitive in the short run to exchange rate changes.
- A self-sustaining operation has an active local sales market and, to the extent it exports, its markets are primarily outside the parent company's country.
- The labour, material, and other costs of a self-sustaining operation are primarily local in origin rather than originating in the country of the parent company.
- Apart from the parent company's basic investment, financing of a self-sustaining operation is carried on primarily in its own currency and is capable of being serviced by its own operating cash flow.
- A self-sustaining operation has a low volume of intercompany transactions with its parent; neither is there any other extensive interrelationship of their operations.
- As a result of all these conditions, the cash flows of a self-sustaining entity are primarily not in the currency of the parent company and are insulated from the parent company on a day-to-day basis.

If these guidelines, taken together, do not indicate that a foreign operation should be considered to be self-sustaining, it is to be treated as an "integrated foreign operation" — that is, it is to be considered to be more in the nature of an extension of the parent company's own operations.

When a foreign operation is self-sustaining, only the parent's net investment is considered to be exposed to foreign exchange risks. Accordingly, the current-rate method of translation is to be used. Because of the ambiguous nature of the debit or credit arising on translation, however, it is considered best to exclude it from the income statement. Instead it is treated as a separate component of shareholders' equity.

Should the parent company sell all or part of its investment in a self-sustaining foreign operation, a proportionate part of the translation adjustments accumulated in shareholders' equity would be transferred to income account and treated as part of the gain or loss recognized on disposition of the investment. A reduction in the equity of the foreign operation for reasons such as dividends, other capital transactions, or losses should also be accompanied by a transfer of a proportionate part of translation adjustments from shareholders' equity to income. (This is not called for under U.S. standards.) It would seem to follow in logic that, if the foreign subsidiary itself sold off its business operations and, say, reinvested its proceeds in securities, so that it was no longer a self-sustaining operation, the parent company should, in consolidation, transfer the accumulated deferred exchange gains and losses to income to be offset or grouped with the gain or loss on sale of its business operations shown by the subsidiary itself.

It would not normally make sense to hedge the exposure to foreign currency adjustments arising on translation using the current-rate method, since these may well not represent real economic gains or losses. Where it is important to maintain the debt/equity ratios shown by the consolidated financial statements, however, a hedge could be undertaken. The gain or loss on the hedge would offset the adjustment from translation treated as a component of shareholders' equity. The FASB indicates that the cost of the hedge may also be carried to that account.[17] The author believes that charging such costs to income would be more logical.

As already described, the current-rate method of translation becomes unsatisfactory when a high rate of inflation in the foreign environment causes a rapid weakening in the exchange value of its currency. Accordingly, the *CICA Handbook* states that the temporal method should be used in place of the current-rate method for self-sustaining operations in economies where the inflation rate is high relative to that in the economy of the parent company. No specific guidance is given as to the difference in inflation rates that would be considered high. The FASB suggests that the current-rate method should not be used when the cumulative inflation rate in the foreign economy (*not* the excess of the foreign inflation rate over that in the country of the parent) reaches approximately one hundred percent over a three-year period. (That would be equal to a level rate of twenty-six percent per annum.)

The temporal method of translation is to be used for integrated foreign operations as well as for self-sustaining operations in highly inflationary economies. Canadian practice has introduced one variation from the approach described earlier. Previously it was stated that all gains and losses on translation under the temporal method are recorded in income as they occur. To be consistent with its treatment of long-term foreign currency investment and borrowing transactions entered into by a domestic enterprise, the *CICA Handbook* directs that gains and losses on translation of long-term monetary assets and liabilities also be deferred and amortized over the remaining term of their life.

Other issues

Certain countries have a variety of foreign currency controls and also may have a variety of official exchange rates at which businesses may acquire or sell foreign currencies arising from foreign operations. Unofficial or free-market rates may also be in existence. Where this situation exists, any translations required to be made at the current rate encounter the problem of choosing which current rate is appropriate. The FASB suggests that, except in unusual circumstances, the rate selected should be that which would be available upon remittance of dividends to the parent company.[18]

Throughout most of the literature and throughout this discussion it has been assumed that an actual exchange rate — whether historical or current — must be used for translation. Some writers have suggested that this results from a fixation with currency and currency movements as though all the assets of a subsidiary were going to be returned to the parent company in the form of currency sooner or later. The fact is, to the contrary, that physical resources of the subsidiary are, in general, not going to be liquidated and the proceeds remitted but rather are going to be replaced. The objective, then, is to find a reasonable basis for measuring and translating, not the currency itself, but the physical resources of the foreign operation. For this purpose, it has been suggested, actual exchange rates may be a poor medium because of the many erratic short-term influences upon them. These ideas have not as yet received any very extensive exploration and development.[19]

Summary

The fact that an enterprise may conduct business in more than one currency results in several problems for accounting. First, when a significant proportion of the enterprise transactions is conducted in one or more currencies other than that of its country of domicile, the question is raised as to what currency the enterprise should adopt as a basis of expression in its financial statements. Once that is decided, it is necessary to consider how to account for transactions that are denominated in currencies other than the reporting currency and how to report gains and losses resulting from movements in exchange rates. Finally, when an entity has an investment in a branch, subsidiary, joint venture, or other investee over which it has significant influence and those entities report in a foreign currency, it is necessary to have a standard method for translating the statements of the other entities for the purpose of consolidation accounting, proportional consolidation, or equity accounting.

The choice of reporting currency is only occasionally difficult. Important considerations are: In what currency is most business done? What currency will be familiar to users of the financial statements? What is the relative stability of the various currencies that seem to be possible contenders? These indicators need not point in the same direction, so that the choice among them ultimately comes down to a matter of judgment.

Numerous questions arise relating to accounting for transactions denominated in a foreign currency. The general principles adopted to guide practice are set out below.

- A transaction denominated in a foreign currency is translated at the spot rate when first recognized in the accounts. This approach is generally satisfactory but can be criticized when it is applied to transactions resulting from commitments made at a significantly earlier date. Once a commitment expressed in a foreign currency is made, an enterprise is at risk of exchange rate movements from that date. That risk can be minimized by entering into a forward exchange contract or some other type of hedging instrument. If the risk is not hedged, it is strongly arguable that the change in the commitment price as a result of the exchange rate change over the period of the commitment ought to be reported as a gain or loss on foreign exchange, not as an adjustment of the cost reported in a purchase transaction or the revenue proceeds reported from a sale.

- The carrying values of monetary assets and liabilities expressed in a foreign currency that result from operating, investment, or borrowing transactions are continuously updated after their first recognition to their equivalent amount at reporting-date exchange rates. The resulting adjustment is written off as a gain or loss on foreign exchange in the United States. In Canada, an exception is made for gain or loss on long-term monetary assets and liabilities that have an ascertainable life.
- The amount of gain or loss deferred on long-term positions in Canada is to be amortized over the remaining life of the asset or liability. Should there be a renegotiation of the term to maturity of the position, the amortization rate is adjusted to the new term. These provisions are open to serious criticism. If one currency is showing progressive deterioration in relation to another, the instruction to amortize gains and losses over *remaining* life will pile up the adjustment in the years closer to maturity of the asset or liability. As for renegotiation, there is no theoretical justification for extending amortization of deferred gains and losses over the new term, since the act of renegotiation creates additional exposure to exchange rate risk and has no relation to the exposure under the previous term.
- The foreign exchange risk with respect to a foreign currency contract — a forward, futures, option, or swap contract — also carries risk with respect to movements in the exchange rate. If the effect of foreign exchange movements on obligations under such a contract is in the opposite direction (i.e., favourable or adverse) to the effect of foreign exchange risk on an existing asset, liability, or commitment, the two positions are said to be hedged. If a foreign currency contract is not hedged, it is speculative in character. That speculative character should be recognized by continuously valuing the effect of exchange rate changes on the contract and recording an asset or liability as a result of that valuation, carrying the adjustment to income as gain or loss on foreign exchange.
- When a foreign currency contract hedges a foreign currency monetary asset or liability, the same accounting as just described for a speculative contract has the appropriate effect. When both positions are continuously revalued at current exchange rates, and value adjustments are recognized in income, the adjustments to income will offset each other to the extent that the hedge is fully effective. If it is not fully effective, the net adjustment will properly show as gain or loss on the exposed risk.

- When one or both sides of a balanced hedge position are not recognized as an asset or liability in the balance sheet, the question arises how to recognize the effect of exchange rate changes. It is not the practice (unfortunately) to recognize a change in the value of a foreign currency commitment as an asset or liability and carry the adjustment to income. Accordingly, if a foreign currency contract, or some other position, hedges a commitment, it is necessary either to (1) ignore the effect of exchange rate changes on the hedging medium up to the time when the commitment becomes a recognized transaction, or (2) defer the foreign exchange gain or loss recognized on the hedging position. The second of these is the practice that is adopted. Because of the deferment of recognition of gain or loss in this situation, it is important that there be assurance that an effective hedge really exists.
- The *CICA Handbook* contains ill-thought-through suggestions with respect to treatment of nonmonetary assets or future revenue streams as hedges of positions exposed to foreign currency risk. Implementation of these suggestions will distort reporting of future profit on sale of the nonmonetary asset or future revenues. The proposal is also open to manipulation to avoid current recognition of foreign exchange loss.

A third area of difficulty caused by business done in a foreign currency is that of translation of the statements of a branch or investee that are maintained in a foreign currency. Two possible approaches to translation on consolidation are in use: the temporal approach and the current-rate approach. Consolidation by the use of either method will result in net debits or credits appearing upon translation whose significance can be hard to interpret. If the translation method were ideal, any such net debit or credit would represent a real economic loss or gain from movements in the exchange rates attributable to the exposure to currency risk of the subsidiary or investee. It is very doubtful, however, that any method of translation could be devised to measure these economic effects accurately in every situation. Certainly, it can easily be shown that both the temporal and current-rate methods are unrealistic in given situations.

Accounting standards have attempted to reach a compromise that will be broadly satisfactory, even though far from perfect. The basic idea is that if a foreign operation is relatively self-contained, the exchange risk of the parent company does not pertain to the individual assets and liabilities of the subsidiary but rather to the fact that the future cash flows from the subsidiary available for dividends or further investment will be in the foreign currency. Application of the current-rate method to translate all the assets and liabilities reported by the subsidiary ensures that, if the foreign currency weakens vis-à-vis that of the parent, there will be a debit adjustment on translation and vice versa (assuming the parent has some positive equity in the subsidiary). In view of the fact that there is no assurance that a debit adjustment is a real loss or a credit adjustment a real gain, these translation adjustments are not reported as gains or losses in consolidated income but rather are accumulated as a separate component of shareholders' equity.

Where a foreign currency is rapidly weakening because of inflationary pressures, the current-rate method, in effect, writes down every asset and liability. This is unrealistic with respect to nonmonetary assets held for a significant period of time (such as plant) because increased prices in the foreign currency will usually maintain the real value of the asset or at least slow its loss. Accordingly, the temporal method is to be substituted for the current-rate method for translation of all self-sustaining operations in highly inflationary economies.

The theory underlying the temporal method, however, has nothing to do with inflation. This method takes the perspective of the parent company and seeks to achieve the same result through translation as would occur if the parent company conducted all the transactions abroad itself, rather than through a foreign subsidiary. Thus, nonmonetary assets and liabilities of the foreign operation are translated at the historical exchange rate applicable when the assets were acquired or liabilities incurred (unless it is necessary to record them at market values, in which case current-rate translation of their foreign market value would be required). Monetary assets and liabilities are translated at current rates just like monetary assets and liabilities of the parent company itself that are denominated in a foreign currency. The adjustments arising from such translations at current rates on short-term monetary assets and liabilities are taken directly to income and on long-term items are deferred and amortized. If the assets and liabilities of the foreign operation are hedged, however, the treatment of exchange adjustments would be consistent with that described above for hedges of foreign currency transactions by a domestic company.

References

[1]See E.J. Richardson, "Currency Swaps — A Canadian Perspective," *Canadian Tax Journal*, March-April 1984, pp. 347-61.

[2]One exception is N.G. Rueschhoff, "U.S. Dollar Based Financial Reporting of Canadian Multinational Corporations," *International Journal of Accounting*, Spring 1973, pp. 103-9.

[3]CICA, "Foreign Currency Translation," *CICA Handbook*, Section 1650 (Toronto: CICA), par. 61.

[4]Ibid., par. 23.

[5]See P.D. Jackson and M.B. Meagher, "The New Foreign Currency Recommendations," *CAmagazine*, December 1978, pp. 46-53.

[6]*CICA Handbook*, Section 1650, par. 27.

[7]Ibid., par. 49

[8]See FASB, *Foreign Currency Translation*, Statement of Financial Accounting Standards No. 52 (Stamford: FASB, 1981), pars. 132-33.

[9]*CICA Handbook*, Section 1650, par. 50.

[10]Ibid., par. 51.

[11]Ibid., par. 48.

[12]Ibid., par. 53.

[13]L. Lorensen, *Reporting Foreign Operations of U.S. Companies in U.S. Dollars*, Accounting Research Study No. 12 (New York: AICPA, 1972).

[14]See T.G. Evans, W.R. Folks, and M. Jilling, *The Impact of Statement of Financial Accounting Standards No. 8 on the Foreign Exchange Risk Management Practices of American Multinationals: An Economic Impact Study* (Stamford: FASB, 1978).

[15]R.M. Parkinson, *Translation of Foreign Currencies* (Toronto: CICA, 1972).

[16]Ibid., chap. 10.

[17]FASB, *Foreign Currency Translation*, par. 20a.

[18]Ibid., par. 27b.

[19]However, see G.M. Scott, "Currency Exchange Rates and Accounting Translation: A Mismarriage?" *Abacus*, June 1975, pp. 58-70. Scott suggested several possible substitutes for actual exchange rates in a Position Paper presented at the FASB public hearings in December 1980 and urged further extensive research. One of these possibilities was advocated in D.H. Patz, "A Price Parity Theory of Translation," *Accounting and Business Research*, Winter 1977, pp. 14-24. The Winter 1978 issue of the same journal contained rigorous criticism of Patz's ideas in J. Flower, "A Price Parity Theory of Translation: A Comment," pp. 64-65, and F.L. Clarke, "Patz on Parities, Exchange Rates and Translation," pp. 73-77. It also contained a lengthy reply by Patz to Flower's comment — "A Price Parity Theory of Translation: A Reply," pp. 66-72.

Chapter Twenty-One

The Statement of Changes in Financial Position

There are two, and only two, basic kinds of financial statements. There are statements reporting stocks of resources and claims upon them at a single point in time (such as a balance sheet). There are also statements reporting flows of resources, designed to explain changes in the amounts of net resources held between two dates. The income statement is a flow statement. It explains increases in resources and consumption of resources associated with the earnings activities of the entity.

The income statement, however, does not tell the whole story about resource flows. First, it deals only with those resource flows that are part of earnings activity. It does not report changes in resources and claims resulting from investment and borrowing or raising capital. Second, it deals with resource flows in general. It does not distinguish, for example, between an expense consisting of consumption of cash and an expense consisting of the consumption of serviceablity of fixed assets. Both consumptions are expressed in monetary terms because money is used as the unit of account, but the resources consumed are different. Thus, there is room for statements of resource flows other than the income statement. There can be a statement that explains all changes in aggregate resources and claims over a period — a "statement of changes in financial position." And there can be one or more individual statements that focus on individual resources or specified groups of resources — such as a "statement of cash flows."

In the first section of this chapter we discuss the variety possible in statements of resource flows. In the second section we discuss the proposals of some accounting thinkers for changing the present make-up of financial reports to make a cash statement the principal financial statement. Although these proposals are outside the present accounting model, it is convenient to discuss them here because of their close relationship with other matters to be discussed in this chapter.

The possible variety in statements of resource flows

Business is undertaken with the objective of making a return. The income statement is designed to measure the entity's success in doing so. But income, measured in accordance with accrual accounting principles, is not always accompanied by a corresponding net inflow of cash. For example, consider a manufacturer of complicated equipment, each unit of which costs $50,000 in out-of-pocket costs. If that equipment can be sold for $100,000 a unit, one might think, correctly, that the business is profitable. But, if the customary practice is to sell the equipment for only $10,000 down with the remainder payable over ten years with interest, the entity will have paid out $40,000 more than it receives at time of sale for each unit.

In the long run, the cash will be more than recouped. But in the short run, especially if sales are brisk, the entity has an ever-increasing need for cash and, if financing is not available, may become insolvent even though it is basically a sound business.

This is only one example among many possible causes of financial difficulty. A business may become unable to meet its debts as they fall due because it overexpands in relation to its capital base, because it assumes heavy fixed operating costs in a venture whose revenues are volatile, or because it invests in illiquid assets with only short-term financing, trusting to refinance the debt as it falls due. The moral is simple: It is not enough to be profitable; one must be solvent as well.

Early desires for a statement of flows of cash or near-cash resources were, no doubt, greatly influenced by the need for a solvency perspective. The actual format of such "funds" statements, as their use became more widespread, tended to be geared to explain changes in working capital, rather than some more narrowly defined group of liquid resources. In part this may have been because bankers relied heavily upon working capital and working capital ratios in assessing creditworthiness of prospective borrowers. Thus it was logical to account for changes in the resources that the bankers were looking at. In part, also, it may have been because it was easier to construct a statement using working capital as the definition of funds than it was to construct one focussing on movements in cash alone.

An easy way to explain changes in working capital is to (1) take the figure of net income for the period, (2) analyze the changes in noncurrent assets and liabilities over the period, (3) adjust the net income figure for entries, such as depreciation, whose opposite side is a noncurrent asset or liability (and therefore do not represent a source or use of working capital), (4) eliminate from further consideration the effects of transactions that represent changes in long-term assets and liabilities only (such as the purchase of fixed assets for long-term debt), and (5) report any remaining transactions affecting long-term assets and liabilities as investing or financing transactions in the statement of funds. This was the method taught in influential accounting texts from early in the century.

The fact that this approach fails to report financing and investment transactions that do not involve a source or use of working capital was considered unfortunate by some accountants. It meant that changes over a period in balance sheet figures for long-term assets and liabilities were not always fully explained. Moreover, it could be deemed to be misleading, since a purchase of fixed assets in consideration for direct assumption of debt, for example, is hardly different in economic effect from a purchase of fixed assets using working capital coupled with a replenishment of working capital by borrowing. Thus a sentiment grew up in favour of including a report of all investing and financing activities in the statement, not just those that had an immediate impact on working capital.

Under this total resource perspective it was considered more descriptive to entitle the statement "Statement of Changes in Financial Position" (SCFP) rather than "Statement of Funds." The practice of producing a figure of working capital (or some other measure of liquid funds) from operations continued, however, so that the statement now had two objectives — to display the cause of changes in all resources and claims upon resources and, within this, to explain what subset of these causes represented the impact of operations on resources classified as funds. Precisely how this should be done, however, remained unclear, and the flexibility of authoritative accounting standards on the subject reflected that lack of clarity.

Some more detailed examination of possible objectives is therefore in order.

Objectives of the statement of changes in financial position

Some of the objectives for the SCFP are described briefly below.

- In the ultimate, the value of a business to an investor depends upon its ability to generate cash. Some think that an explanation of past cash flows, especially for a series of years, will be useful as a basis for prediction of future cash flows. There is a source of possible confusion in this. Cash flows are irregular in their incidence over the lifetime of an enterprise. The purpose of accrual accounting in the measurement of income is precisely to eliminate confusion caused by these irregularities — to assign revenues and expenses to the period giving rise to them rather than the period when the cash flow occurs. Why then is it desired to get back to actual cash flows?

  One explanation lies in the possibility that prediction of future cash flows may best be made by a two-stage process. Past years' reported incomes, because they are determined by an orderly process, may form a good basis (along with other information) for predicting future years' incomes. Then a separate prediction can be made of future years' cash flows based upon analysis and projection of items that reconcile income and cash flows. It is important, in the end, to get back to a prediction of actual cash flows per period because more distant cash flows are worth less than those soon to be received.

  A second explanation is that a comparison of cash flows from operations with the income reported for a year provides information about what is called "the quality of earnings." The simple thought is that if operations are producing significant cash flow in relation to the income reported, there is less risk than when income reported is accompanied by very little current cash flow. The explanation is related to the fact that some people mistrust accrual accounting. They feel that it is too flexible in its assumptions and requires too much judgment in its application to be reliable. Hard cash data are deemed less subject to errors in judgment and arbitrary procedures.
- A more obvious use of cash flow information is that of assistance in the prediction of the debt-paying capacity or solvency of an enterprise. Such a prediction requires information both from the financial position statement and a statement showing operating cash flows. The future cash requirements to meet existing liabilities and required future investment must be compared with projected realizations of existing resources and projected cash funds from operations within the forecast time frame. In tight situations, cash flow from operations may require prediction on a month-to-month or even day-to-day basis.
- Cash flow information is also one element in a somewhat broader assessment — that of financial flexibility. A firm may be able to pay its debts as they fall due but have little left over to expand or take advantage of opportunities to move in new directions. Financial flexibility comes not only from cash generated by the existing business and the ability to realize upon existing assets without disrupting the business, but also from the ability to raise new financing. Since the greater the amount of assets available to provide security the easier it will be to come by new financing, it is arguable that a somewhat broader definition of funds from operations is appropriate

for this purpose. Information as to unused lines of credit could also be pertinent.

- The title "Statement of Changes in Financial Position" implies a quite different objective for the statement than the foregoing. Under previous forms of the funds statement, investment and financing transactions were reported only if they resulted in changes in whatever was defined as "funds." If the definition of funds was working capital, as it usually was, this normally left only a few investment and financing transactions unreported. It proved relatively easy to extend the funds statement, therefore, to portray all transactions that had economic significance for any of the resources or claims upon resources that are reported in the balance sheet. Under this objective, very few items given accounting recognition would not be recognized in the SCFP. (Such items include mere rearrangements of reported shareholders' equity, such as appropriations to reserves or stock dividends or stock splits.)

This discussion of objectives suggests that the present SCFP is not clearly designed to perform a single function. Perhaps the significance of the statement would be clearer if it were divided into three: one statement recording investment activities, one statement recording financing activities, and one statement analyzing the effect on funds of operating activities.[1] That solution would still leave open the nagging question of what is the most useful definition of funds. It might also stimulate some additional questions. Why should it be considered, for example, that a purchase of fixed assets is an investing activity while purchase of inventory is an operating activity? Some of these questions will be discussed subsequently. It seems probable, however, that the long-standing tradition of having only one flow statement in addition to the income statement will continue, and there will continue to be compromises in its presentation.

Issues in the presentation of the SCFP

To a considerable extent, the SCFP simply recombines information that is already available in the balance sheet and income statement. Its value lies principally in the grouping of that information to highlight the results of management decisions on investment and financing as well as on operations, and to highlight relationships between them. Issues of presentation are extremely important to the success of the SCFP. They are also difficult to resolve in an unequivocal manner in view of the multiple objectives of the statement.

Statement format. Until recently the most common format for the SCFP was one divided into two categories — sources of financial resources and uses of financial resources. Under this structure the focus of interest — the bottom line — was on the net change in liquid funds (however they were defined).

When the proposition was accepted that the SCFP should account for *all* changes in resources and claims upon resources, there were two results. First, transactions that did not involve any source or disposition of funds had to be forced into those categories on the statement. This was accomplished by treating such transactions as though they involved a simultaneous source and use of funds. Thus a purchase of fixed assets financed by a long-term liability could be treated as a deemed use and source of funds.

Second, it became logical that the SCFP should be in balanced form. Since changes in all components of a balance sheet over a period were explained in the statement, the structure of the statement itself was naturally in balance. However, since each change in a resource was described basically in terms of its effect on funds — for example acquisition of fixed assets was described as a use of funds — a net *increase* in funds themselves had to appear under the caption "*use* of funds" to balance the statement. This was a source of potential confusion to readers.

The recent trend to presentation of a statement classified by financing, investing, and operating activities does not remove all possible causes of confusion. Financing and investing categories still contain figures relating to transactions that did not affect cash resources but that add up to subtotals described as net sources (uses) of cash from the financing or investing activities.

The reordering of the SCFP also creates a more serious potential for lack of comparability. Under the former statement format it was at least fairly clear into which category — source or use of funds — a transaction fell. There is not the same clarity to the semantic distinction between "operating," "investing," and "financing" activities. This is likely to be a significant source of noncomparability in the future that may well hamper a reader's interpretation of the significance of the SCFP.

Classification issues. One of the most fruitful sources of confusion will be the difficulty in interpreting what is meant by "operating." In previous practice it was customary to calculate funds from operations as being working capital resulting from all transactions other than those that involved noncurrent borrowing or the acquisition of noncurrent assets. In essence, the classification of operating, financing, and investing was governed by the "geography" of the balance sheet. Compare this with some other concepts of what is meant by the term "operating." In the classification of accountable events in chapter 5, a distinction was made between purchases and sales occurring in the conduct of the principal business carried on (called operating transactions) and passive investment transactions or financing activities. Under this definition, the purchase of a fixed asset required for the business carried on would be an operating transaction just like the purchase of inventory. On the other hand, receipt of income from investments would be an investment transaction, and payment of interest on borrowing would be a financing transaction.

The 1985 CICA recommendations on the SCFP do little to clarify this confusion.[2] The recommendations state that "...some may prefer to classify certain items, such as regular replacements of fixed assets, as an operating activity rather than an investing activity."[3] Nothing is said directly about interest income and interest expense, although one may infer that they are not regarded as investment and financing activities. As to dividends paid, it is said: "With regard to payment of dividends, while some view this as a financing activity, others view it as a normal part of operating activities; still others may prefer to classify dividends separately."[4] It appears that "as you like it" is the order of the day, and it will be up to statement readers to adjust figures if they wish to have comparability among reporting entities.

It is arguable that a statement user will wish to use the figure of funds from operations as an important element in the projection of future cash flows. If so, it would be helpful if cash inflows or outflows that are expected to recur on a regular basis were classified as operating. Such a criterion would suggest the following conclusions:

- Treat investment income received and debt interest paid as operating, even though the related purchase of investments and borrowing are treated as investment and financing activities respectively.
- Treat the purchase of operating fixed assets as an investing activity.
- If a regular dividend policy has been established, treat dividends paid as a deduction from operating funds.

The treatment of interest paid that has been capitalized as part of the cost of fixed assets is debatable. Under the traditional approach to interest capitalization, whereby only incremental interest cost attributable to construction is capitalized, there is a strong, although perhaps not conclusive, argument for classifying the interest capitalized as an investment cost, not as a deduction from funds from operations. Under the FASB approach to interest capitalization, which allows capitalization of interest on debt that was incurred before construction began, this argument is much less strong. If the income statement treatment of interest under the FASB method is also followed in the SCFP, interest on a given debt issue might be treated as a deduction from operating funds in year one, not as a deduction in year two, and as a deduction again in year three. One may question whether a statement of operating cash flows should be affected by allocations in this way.

Definition of funds. Achieving the objective of providing information that will help to assess and predict solvency and financial flexibility requires some definition of liquid funds that is best suited to this purpose. The definition used in most SCFPs for many years was working capital, but that has now fallen into disfavour. The following are the candidates:

- Cash. This is the ultimate liquid asset. Its meaning is unambiguous. Its disadvantage for this purpose is that leads and lags in cash flow can cause essentially meaningless fluctuations in net amounts of cash reported from one period to another.
- Cash and temporary investments. The inclusion of temporary investments that are used as a "parking place" for spare cash removes one possible source of fluctuation in actual cash balances. However, it requires a decision on what is meant by "temporary." Some investments that qualify as current assets under the customary one-year test may be too long-term to be considered truly temporary.
- Cash and temporary investments, less short-term borrowing. The immediate effect of short-term borrowing is to replenish cash, and that cash may possibly be used to purchase some temporary investments. This possible conection leads to consideration of the need to deduct short-term borrowing in the definition of funds. On the other hand, there are distinct objections to such a treatment. Short-term and demand borrowing are largely used to finance investment in accounts receivable and inventory. As such, they may often be an enduring part of the financial structure — not really short-term at all. If short-term borrowing is increasing without increases in assets financed, it is indeed a sign of deterioration in the liquid position. Even if such borrowing is accompanied by increases in such assets, there may be a deterioration in the liquid position if those assets are not liquid. Howver, an invariable rule that short-term borrowing must be deducted in the definition of funds may well lead to misleading inferences as to the deteriora-

tion or improvement of liquidity over a period. On balance, a better rule would be to deduct short-term borrowing only up to the amount of temporary investments included in the definition of funds.

- Net short-term monetary assets. This definition of funds would modify either of the two preceding definitions to include accounts receivable and accounts payable and accrued charges. The advantage of this definition is that it would eliminate the erratic effect of irregularities in straight cash flow, including irregularities possible as a result of deliberate delay in making payments. Its usefulness depends on an assumption that accounts receivable and payable will be liquidated over a short period — say, not longer than sixty to ninety days. Accordingly, longer-term accounts receivable and payable should be excluded. Because the allowance for uncollectible accounts is a judgment figure, a funds definition including accounts receivable would not be as "hard" as one based on cash alone, but the scope for variation in judgment seems too narrow to be a significant factor in this decision. The most serious objection to the inclusion of net monetary assets in the definition stems from the existence of inflation. If prices are generally rising, the dollar amounts of each of accounts receivable and accounts payable (as well as inventory) are likely to increase over a period of a year even though the volume of business done remains constant. As a result, much of the earnings shown by the historical cost accounting system is likely to be represented by the net increase in investment in these resources, and not by cash available for distribution. A more narrow definition of funds would show this; the broader definition would not.
- Net working capital. This definition of funds is the broadest of all. Provided all the elements of working capital will be turned into cash within a short period, it may serve as a satisfactory indication of liquidity and may well provide a more stable basis for prediction than other measures of funds. It has, however, been severely criticized. First, the inclusion of short-term borrowing under the conventional definition of current liabilities means that such borrowing does not appear as a financing activity — a suppression of information that some consider important. Second, inventory and prepayments are different in kind from other current assets. They do not represent cash or claims to cash; they represent outlays made with the hope of recoupment of their value. In a crisis there is considerably less assurance that they can be liquidated quickly for something near carrying value. Third, the inclusion of inventories in the definition greatly magnifies the danger under inflationary conditions that the funds statement will conceal the squeeze on cash that may be extracted from operations. Finally, because of differences in accounting conventions, the comparability of funds-flow figures between companies is reduced if this definition is used. For example, apparent funds flow for a period may be very different depending upon whether inventory is costed on a direct-costing or absorption-costing basis, or whether the FIFO or LIFO convention is used. Many people are attracted to the funds statement precisely because it need not be contaminated by the flexibility in accepted accounting principles. Achievement of that objective, however, requires that the definition of funds include only items that are measured on a consistent, unambiguous basis.

The CICA has recommended that the definition of funds — the indicator of liquidity — should be "cash and cash equivalents." These, it suggests, will normally be cash and temporary investments less short-term borrowings.[5]

Since there seems to be some flexibility in the CICA recommendations, it is desirable that financial statement preparers think through the definition of funds most suitable for their circumstances — in particular the policy they should follow in deciding just what should be considered temporary investments and short-term borrowings for this purpose — and disclose the components decided upon.

Statement presentation of funds from operations. Cash from operations for a period is, of course, ultimately derived from collections of revenues. A positive net cash flow from operations is shown if such collections exceed the total amount of operating payments of all kinds and interest and taxes.

The direct way to report the elements of cash from operations, accordingly, would be to list these various amounts, classifying collections by source and payments according to their nature. This listing would look very much like a statement of income. A principal difference would be that the income statement figures are measured by accrual accounting while the funds statement figures would report actual cash flows. Collections from customers would replace sales revenue; payments to manufacturing labour and suppliers of materials would replace the cost of inventory sold, and so on. The cash statement would be factual and should not be capable of misinterpretation.

In spite of these advantages, the direct method of presentation of funds derived from operations is hardly ever used. Instead, the traditional approach starts with the figure of reported income for the year and identifies elements therein that are not associated with funds flows, as well as gains and losses reported that should be classified as resulting from investment and financing activity rather than from operations. With this information in hand, the indirect method backs into a figure of net funds from operations by adding to or subtracting from the income figure those aspects of revenues, expenses, gains, and losses that should be classified as financing or investment or that do not represent funds flows at all.

This "indirect" or "reconciliation" approach has been sharply criticized. It is felt that a statement of operating funds flows should report actual flows, not consist of a reconciliation statement in which no single figure represents a funds flow. Beyond this, it is asserted (with considerable justification) that the format of the statement is positively misleading. For example, by starting with net income and adding back the depreciation and amortization figure, the statement makes it appear that depreciation is a source of funds or cash when it is nothing of the sort. Under the traditional form of funds statement in which funds were defined as working capital, the error was compounded by statement preparers or financial analysts who took the figure of funds from operations and described it as *cash* flow.

Against this criticism it has been strongly argued that the indirect form of presentation is valuable precisely because it highlights the difference between income and *cash* flow and because it pinpoints allocations (such as depreciation and deferred taxes) that represent somewhat arbitrary elements in the income statement.[6] A further practical advantage, not yet realized in practice, is that it permits reporting of different definitions of funds within one statement. For example, the reconciliation could be set up as shown in Table 21-1.

When funds have been defined as working capital, it has been fairly easy to derive the figure of working capital from operations from the figure of net income

Table 21-1

Explanatory Format for Reconciliation of Cash from Operations

Net income from operations	$XXX
Add (deduct) expenses (revenues) not affecting working capital in the year	
Depreciation and amortization	XX
Increase in long-term deferred taxes	XX
etc.	XX
Net increase in working capital as a result of operations	XXX
Add (deduct)	
Increase in inventory	(XX)
Decrease in prepayments	XX
Net increase in short-term monetary resources as a result of operations	XX
Add (deduct)	
Increase in accounts receivable	(XX)
Decrease in accounts payable and accrued expenses	(XX)
Net decrease in cash and cash equivalents as a result of operations	($ XX)

for the period. Now that funds are defined as cash and cash equivalents, the indirect method is more difficult. It requires that examination be made of movements in current assets and liabilities that are not regarded as cash and cash equivalents, as well as in noncurrent assets and liabilities, in order to see whether they involve operating, investing, or financing activities.

It is normally impractical to examine all non-cash current assets and liabilities in detail for this purpose. Instead, the cash flow statement is likely to treat the *net* change over the period in such accounts as a reconciling item between income and cash from operations. Such a treatment will involve an error if part of that net change is an offset to a change in a noncurrent asset and/or liability that is reported as a financing or investment activity.

For example, suppose fixed asset purchases in the year have been financed by accounts payable that are still outstanding at the year-end. The total of such purchases will show as an investment in the SCFP. The related accounts payable should be shown as financing in the year (and reduction in financing next year when paid off). If, instead, the total of all accounts payable at the end of the year is merely compared with the total of all accounts payable at the beginning and the net change is treated as a reconciling item in arriving at cash from operations, the financing will be understated and cash from operations will be overstated. Similarly, an account receivable with respect to the sale of an investment can result in misstatement of funds from operations. To avoid these errors it is necessary at least to scrutinize the balances of current accounts receivable and payable at each year-end to identify any material amounts that do not arise from operating transactions.

In a similar fashion, an increase in the accrual for interest or the liability for dividends over a reporting period means that the figures for cash interest and dividends reported in the SCFP will be different from those for interest expense and dividends declared reported elsewhere in the financial statements.

Some technical problems

A number of technical problems that are encountered in the preparation of the SCFP are noted below.

- The use of absorption costing for inventory valuation can cause confusion when the indirect method of portraying funds from operations is used. Suppose, for example, that depreciation of manufacturing plant for a year is $100,000 but that depreciation included in closing inventory is $5,000 higher than in the opening inventory. Thus, the actual non-cash charge against income for the year with respect to manufacturing depreciation is only $95,000. If in the SCFP the increase in inventory as shown by the balance sheet is treated as a use of cash, the actual use of cash to build inventory will be overstated by $5,000. To compensate, the add-back to income specifically with respect to depreciation must be stated at $100,000, not the $95,000 amount that was implicit in cost of sales for the year.
- Under equity accounting for an investment, the investor recognizes as income the increase in its equity in the investee. That income does not represent a cash flow. Some would treat it as such in reporting cash flow from operations, compensating by recording a notional outflow of cash as an investment activity. On this basis, any actual cash inflow from dividends would be recognized as realization of the investment. Such a presentation is of dubious merit, since the investor does not make a conscious decision to reinvest in the investee and does not have control over the amount of dividends. The preferable treatment is to recognize the equity in income of the investee as a non-cash item and pick up any dividend received as a cash flow from operations (so long as the dividend together with dividends previously received does not exceed the investor's share of income subsequent to acquisition of the investment).
- Similarly, alternative treatments are conceivable with respect to the minority interest share of consolidated income. That share could be reported as though it were a notional outflow of cash and a corresponding financing inflow of cash of that amount less dividends actually paid to the minority interest. Although the arguments for this treatment are not completely without merit, the alternative is customary — to treat the minority interest share in earnings as a non-cash item but treat actual dividends paid as an operating cash outflow.
- When constructing plant for their own account, public utility companies traditionally capitalize an "allowance for funds used during construction" (AFUDC), representing a return on all capital utilized for construction purposes, not just borrowed capital. As discussed earlier, it is debatable whether interest capitalized on construction ought to be regarded as an investment cost or as a reduction of net cash from operations. At the very least, however, the portion of such AFUDC that is applicable to equity financing ought to be treated as a non-cash credit to income. A significant number of Canadian utility companies do not make such an adjustment and thereby overstate the real cash flow from operations.
- Gains and losses on disposals of fixed assets and investments or on extinguishment of debt are reported in income. Practice shows some variation as to the treatment of these items in the SCFP. An argument could be

made that such gains or losses are simply an adjustment of the figures previously reported for income from the investment or cost of the debt. For example, if dividends are treated as part of operating income, one might say that gain on sale of the shares could be recorded as operating income also. On the other hand, this treatment means that investment disposal proceeds, or payments made to discharge debt, are reported in two separate places in the statement. An amount equal to the book value of the asset or debt is treated as a cash receipt or outlay related to an investment or financing activity. The difference between that figure and the actual investment proceeds, or cost of debt discharged, is treated as operating. Such a division seems rather arbitrary. In the interests of simplifying the presentation of the statement, however, pragmatic considerations favour not adjusting the reported income figure to remove such gains or losses, at least when they are not material.

- The reconciliation of net income and cash flow from operations begins with the figure of net income excluding extraordinary items. It is then necessary to ascertain the cash effects of any extraordinary items and report them as operating, investment, or financing cash flows according to their nature. Since extraordinary items are reported after any applicable tax effects, any consequential effect of the extraordinary item on actual taxes payable will be grouped with the cash flow consequences of the extraordinary item.
- If an ordinary gain or loss is removed from net income from operations and reported as an investment or financing activity, in principle any effect of that gain or loss on actual taxes payable should likewise be removed from the report of cash flow from operations. Ascertaining that effect on actual taxes payable, however, may require considerable effort in some cases because of its interaction with deferred taxes. That effort is likely to be rewarded by figures that have little information content. Consider, for example, disposal of some depreciable property for proceeds equal to its original cost. If that property constitutes the only depreciable property of the enterprise, all the capital cost allowance previously claimed for tax purposes will be recaptured and substantial actual taxes will be associated with the disposal. On the other hand, if the property belongs to the same class as other depreciable assets, the credit of the disposal proceeds against the class for tax purposes might result in a lesser amount of recaptured capital cost allowance or none at all. Hence, the immediate tax payable as a result of the property disposal might be substantial, something less than substantial, or nothing at all. Future capital cost allowance claims also will be affected by the fact situation, so that reported net cash flow from operations in future years after the adjustment for deferred tax will be correspondingly greater or less.

In the author's opinion there is little value in making a careful computation of actual cash effects in this situation. A possible alternative would be to assume a notional tax charge that would be appropriate to the profit recognized (at normal tax rates to the extent the profit was represented by recaptured CCA, and at capital gains tax rates beyond that) and to offset the differences between that notional tax charge and the actual tax charge through the reconciling item for deferred taxes in the presentation of funds from operations. Alternatively, it might be arbitrarily decided that all income taxes actually paid should be shown as deductions from funds from operations except in individual cases where the effect on tax of a gain or loss reported in the investment or financing section of the statement of SCFP is both obvious and substantial.

- Portraying the effect of a business combination understandably in a SCFP presents a practical problem. The acquisition of another business will result in increases in virtually all the asset and liability categories in the balance sheet. As a result, net changes between opening and closing consolidated balance sheets will be affected by both the acquisition and by the regular activities of the reporting entity. If the cash from operations is calculated using the indirect method, the adjustments of net income for changes over the year in balances of monetary assets and liabilities and inventories (for example) must take into account only the net change in these items from regular activities. As a result, readers may be confused if they attempt to compare the net change figure described in the SCFP with the net change shown by the opening and closing balance sheets. To help readers understand the reason for this lack of correspondence, the investment in the business acquired can be shown by individual asset and liability categories in the section on investing activity. This, however, is a cumbersome presentation which makes the statement more difficult to comprehend. Most statement users would understand the effect of the business combination better if it were shown in a very few figures only. To achieve this, the investment in the business acquired should be shown as one figure of total cost less the cash and cash equivalents acquired. The financing could also be shown as one figure, or details could be given if not too many types of financing are involved. To help the reader to an understanding of how the acquisition affected individual balance sheet categories, an "acquisition equation" is useful as supplementary disclosure. A hypothetical example of the SCFP presentation and supplementary acquisition equation is shown in Table 21-2.
- There may be occasions when a company embarks on a new activity that involves investment in plant and buildup of inventory and monetary working capital. It would not be illogical in such a case to treat the whole buildup of assets for the new activity in the same fashion as an acquisition of a business. That would mean that the initial increases in inventory and accounts receivable less accounts payable attributable to that activity would not be treated as deductions in arriving at cash flow from operations. It would obviously be necessary to have a clear and carefully controlled understanding of the buildup period to avoid abuse of this presentation.
- A sale of a segment of a business that has been included in the consolidated financial statements — a "decombination" — presents similar problems in reverse. The short-form presentation is normally preferred, as follows:

Proceeds of disposal of Subsidiary Limited	$XXX
Less cash and cash equivalents included therein	XX
Net cash from disposal	$XXX

- A company may engage in a variety of transactions that give rise to assets or liabilities denominated in foreign currency or may hold foreign currency cash balances. For accounting purposes all these balances of foreign currency assets and liabilities will be continuously adjusted to current exchange

Table 21-2

Illustration of Presentation of a Business Combination Supported by an Acquisition Equation

Statement of Changes in Financial Position

Operating Activities		$ XXX
Investing Activities		
Purchase of 100% of the shares of X Co. Ltd.	$25,000	
Less cash and cash equivalents acquired	2,000	
Net cash outlay		$23,000
Other investing activities (detail)		XXX
		$ XXX
Financing Activities		
Consideration given for purchase of X Co. Ltd.		
12% floating charge debentures	$20,000	
8% 2nd preference shares	5,000	$25,000
Other financing activities (detail)		XXX
		$ XXX
		$ XXX

Acquisition Equation

Assets acquired at fair value:	
Cash	$ 2,000
Accounts receivable	5,000
Inventory	6,000
Plant and equipment	7,000
Goodwill	5,000
	$25,000
Consideration given:	
12% debentures	$20,000
8% preference shares	5,000
	$25,000

rates, giving rise to the recognition of gains or losses in income if the assets and liabilities are current or to deferred gains and losses if the assets and liabilities are long-term (under Canadian practice). Such deferred gains and losses are subsequently amortized to income.

With respect to foreign currency assets and liabilities that are included in the definition of funds (i.e., cash and cash equivalents), gains and losses recognized as the exchange rate changes are properly treated as cash flows from operations since they represent changes in the carrying amount of cash and cash equivalents.

With respect to accounts receivable and payable in foreign currency that are classified as current, gains and losses recorded must be eliminated from the statement of cash flow from operations because they do not represent a change in defined cash and cash equivalents. The indirect approach to the calculation of cash from operations achieves this elimination automatically by adjusting net income from operations for differences between the opening and closing reported balances of such monetary assets and liabilities.

With respect to noncurrent monetary assets and liabilities in foreign currency, there is no such automatic adjustment. For these items, therefore, it is necessary to treat the amount of any amortization of deferred foreign currency gains or losses or any write-off on settlement of the asset or liability position as a non-cash adjustment to net income. The cash received or paid on ultimate settlement of noncurrent foreign currency assets or liabilities would appear in the investment or financing activity sections. These same rules apply for a foreign operating unit that is included in the consolidated financial statement whose accounts are translated using the temporal approach (see chapter 20).

- A different position applies for units that are translated on the current-rate method because they are "self-sustaining." Here a problem arises in reconciling opening and closing consolidated balance sheet figures because of the use of different translation rates for each of the opening balance sheet, the SCFP for the year (translated at an average exchange rate), and the closing balance sheet of the foreign unit (translated at the current rate). The problem is briefly illustrated below. Assume the domestic currency value of the foreign currency in question is $1.00 at the opening balance sheet date, $1.10 on average during the year, and $1.20 at the closing balance sheet date. The position in foreign currency and as translated into dollars is set out in Table 21-3.

During the year the parent company's investment, translated into dollars, has increased from $21,000 to $27,600. The net retained earnings shown by the subsidiary upon translation, however, is reported only at $2,200. Accordingly, a translation adjustment balance is carried forward in the reported consolidated shareholders' equity equal to $4,400. This can be analyzed as:

Opening investment — gain on translation at $1.20	$21,000 x 0.2 =	$4,200
Retained earnings for year		
— translated at closing rate $2,000 at 1.2 =	$2,400	
— translated at average rate $2,000 at 1.1 =	2,200	200
		$4,400

That translation adjustment can be partitioned among all the assets and liabilities of the foreign unit that are reported in the balance sheet. For example, the adjustment pertaining to cash can be calculated as follows:

Table 21-3

Statements of a Self-Sustaining Foreign Unit Translated for Purposes of Consolidation

	In Foreign Currency		As Translated	
	Opening	**Closing**	**Opening**	**Closing**
Balance Sheet				
Cash and cash equivalents	1,000 FC	200 FC	$ 1,000	$ 240
All other resources (net)	20,000	22,800	20,000	27,360
Equity of parent company	21,000 FC	23,000 FC	$21,000	$27,600
Income and Retained Earnings				
Net income for the period		4,000 FC		$ 4,400
Dividends paid		2,000		2,200
Retained earnings		2,000 FC		$ 2,200
Statement of Changes in Financial Position				
Cash flow from operations		6,700 FC		$ 7,370
Cash used for investment		(4,000)		(4,400)
Cash used in financing activity		(1,500)		(1,650)
Dividends paid		(2,000)		(2,200)
Net decrease in cash		(800) FC		($ 880)

Adjustment of opening balance	$1,000 x 0.2 =	$200
Cash flow for the year		
— translated at closing rate ($800) at 1.2 =	($960)	
— translated at average rate ($800) at 1.1 =	(880)	(80)
Net translation adjustment applicable to cash		$120

If one wishes to reconcile the opening and closing balance sheet figures for cash, this adjustment must be used, for example:

Opening balance of cash	$1,000
Net cash outflow (from SCFP)	(880)
	120
Translation adjustment	120
Closing balance of cash	$240

The question to be resolved is how to reflect this translation adjustment in the SCFP. There are several possibilities:

1. Ignore the translation as being essentially meaningless with respect to funds flow. Possibly present a separate schedule enabling the reader to reconcile opening and closing balance sheet figures if desired.
2. Insert one line in the SCFP described as "effect of exchange rate changes on cash and cash equivalents" so that the reader can reconcile cash balances at least. (In the above example, the figure to be inserted on this line would be $120.)
3. Build the analysis of translation adjustments completely into the SCFP.[7]

- Holding companies typically include a consolidated SCFP in their consolidated financial statements. Chapter 19 referred to the weaknesses of consolidated statements for the purpose of revealing the creditworthiness of the holding company. Those observations are of particular importance for the SCFP because its use is so closely associated with the evaluation of solvency and financial flexibility. Developing problems in the cash position of a holding company or in any of the subsidiaries may be masked by strong operating cash flows in other components in the group. Debt covenants or other impediments will often prevent the free transfer of cash between components. If this difficulty exists, the only real solution seems to be to present additional disclosure — possibly to the extent of providing an analysis of the SCFP by components or segments.

The best solution to each of the foregoing technical problems is often a matter of opinion. It is unfortunate that the latest CICA recommendations fail to address these issues. In fact, guidance provided in previous recommendations has been dropped. Part of the reason for this may be the notion that different solutions are appropriate in different circumstances. The problem with this proposition is that the theory underlying the SCFP is so vague that it is difficult to deduce just how a different situation should affect presentation. Observation of published SCFPs discloses a number of inconsistencies and many obscurities. In view of these deficiencies, accounting standard-setters need to make an extra effort to explain the theories underlying the SCFP and spell out their implications for specific issues.

Financial institutions and SCFPs

Certain special characteristics of financial intermediaries raise some doubts as to the relevance of the conventional SCFP to their situation.

- Cash and cash equivalents are nonearning or low-earning assets. As a result, most institutions will attempt to keep holdings of such assets to an absolute minimum. Consequently, emphasis in the SCFP on a bottom line of cash provided by or used in various activities is not the most useful format.
- Because the shareholders' equity in a financial institution will be small in relation to its deposit or policy liabilities, the net income and related net flow of cash from operations is bound to be relatively small in relation to receipts and disbursements associated with financing and investing activities. In one sense, receipt of funds from depositors or policyholders and the investment of those funds are operating activities. Thus the basic distinction in any analysis of cash flows might well correspond with the two sides of the balance sheet — cash flows associated with financing activities, including flows of deposit money, money for policy reserves and debt and equity

transactions, and cash flows associated with investment activities, including maturities, disposals, and new investments.

- A substantial part of the assets of a financial institution will be monetary in nature and reasonably liquid. As a result, insolvency is less likely to occur merely because of an excess of operating expenditures over operating revenues in the short term. Rather, the danger of insolvency comes more from such factors as mismatching of maturity dates of financial liabilities and invested assets, net reductions in deposit support because depositors have more attractive opportunities for use of their funds elsewhere, and declines in the quality of invested assets, reducing their liquidity and at the same time stimulating withdrawal of funds by depositors.

The foregoing suggests that a starting point in evaluating solvency of a financial institution and understanding its dynamics might be a simple analyzed statement showing cash in and cash out associated with each of the various types of financing (equity, debt, and deposits or policy reserves) and with movements in the various types of earning assets. Unfortunately, the gross cash flows in and out will be unavailable for the most active categories such as deposits and loans, so that one has to make do with net changes by category. That information is largely a recapitulation of totals that anyone could derive from comparative balance sheets but nevertheless provides a convenient summation of shifts that have taken place in available financing and the emphasis in investment policy over a period. It needs to be supplemented by information as to maturity dates of assets and liabilities in order to help project refinancing requirements. That information may also be tied in with disclosure whether interest rates on both sides are floating or fixed, and if fixed, when they are open to renegotiation. In brief, an SCFP for a financial institution may well take a different format from that used by other types of enterprise and is probably less useful, taken by itself, in assisting in the evaluation of solvency and financial flexibility. Additional information can be provided, however, that helps a knowledgeable analyst to assess these matters.

Cash flow accounting models

Some accounting theorists consider the statement of cash flow to be something more than just one of a number of possible flow statements. Rather, they consider it the preeminent flow statement that should be used to the exclusion of others, especially the income statement. They have two reasons for this, one positive and one negative. The positive reason rests upon the proposition that users of financial statements are interested in an entity's ability to generate cash. From this they reason that a statement focussing on cash will provide feedback on actual results achieved as compared with previous expectations and (possibly) will provide a better basis for assumptions as to the future. The negative reason rests upon their rejection of conventional income accounting because of its reliance upon allocations. Cash flow theorists believe accounting allocations are so arbitrary that measures of resource flows that are seriously affected by them must be meaningless.

The statement of cash flow (SCF) is considered acceptable as a substitute for an income statement because it largely avoids the allocation problem. It does so, however, only at the expense of creating another problem — that of presenting information whose usefulness is limited because its proper interpretation is not clear. If the cash balance is reduced over a period, for example, one must ask whether this is because of lack of profitability of the business or because of increased investment in inventory and plant attributable to growth. Attempts to deal with this problem include (1) broadening the definition of "cash flow," (2) interpretive classifications within the SCF, (3) provision of multiperiod data to reduce the impact of temporary fluctuations in cash flow, and (4) provision of supplementary information on assets and liabilities measured on an allocation-free basis.

Since the SCF dispenses with an income statement, it is clear that the indirect method of presentation, starting with net income and reconciling to a figure of cash flow from operations, cannot be used. The following comments should be considered in the context of a statement disclosing cash inflows and cash outflows directly.

The definition of cash flow

Cash flow theorists face a question equivalent to that discussed earlier under the heading "definition of funds," namely, what shall be the definition of "cash flow?" Similar considerations apply. Straight cash is completely factual, but it may be unduly affected in any reporting period by leads and lags in the cash impact of other transactions. To mitigate this impact, some theorists have suggested that legal claims to receive or pay cash should be treated as "unrealized cash flows." In effect, a "cash flow" is something different from a flow of cash. From the standpoint of the information value of the SCF, this approach is probably an improvement over a statement tied to cash movements alone, but it is not without problems.

- It would seem foolish to report an extremely temporary investment of cash — say a purchase of short-term deposit receipt — as a cash outflow. Yet, if one admits that some investment transactions should not be reported as cash outflows or cash inflows, the question arises as to what is the logical dividing line. It cannot be that no security investment transaction should be reported as cash outflow or inflow. An investment in a venture capital company, for example, might be as doubtful, if not more doubtful, of return as an investment in plant and equipment.
- If the creation of accounts receivable on sale is reported as unrealized cash inflow, should there be any limit to the maturity date of the receivable? One might well argue that if the period until the due date is longer than that which business normally allows for collection of the receivable without an interest charge, either the account should not be recognized as an unrealized cash flow or else its face value should be discounted. One may add that as soon as an uncollected account receivable is recorded as a cash flow, a form of allocation has taken place. A future real cash flow has been allocated to the present period. An allocation process is even more evident if the account receivable is discounted. Then the future cash flow is being allocated part to the present and part (as interest) over the period until the account becomes collectible.

Classification within the statement

The information value of any flow statement depends to a significant extent upon the classification of flows. For expenditures there are two fundamental bases of classification — by nature of expenditure and by purpose of expenditure. Thus expenditures may be classified as purchases of materials, merchandise, supplies, utilities, equipment, labour, and so on. Or they may be classified as spending on acquisition, manufacturing, and storage of goods, acquisition of equipment, repairs and maintenance, marketing, general and administration, research and development, and so on. To a considerable extent the latter classification system requires allocation. Labour and supplies, for example, may be manufacturing, marketing, administration, or research and development costs. They may even be part of the cost of a fixed asset acquired, if an enterprise is constructing on its own account.

Allocations are normally also required if there is any desire to report cash flows by different segments of a business. A further type of allocation often suggested is that of partitioning expenditures for plant investment among costs of maintaining existing productive capacity, investment for growth, and other expenditures that neither add to capacity nor to growth — for example, for pollution control devices. This partitioning, it is felt, would help the reader understand whether the business is consuming its capital base, something that is not apparent from a cash flow statement for short periods of time. Undoubtedly this would be valuable information if it could be obtained. Unfortunately it requires very uncertain estimates. If new plant substitutes for labour without any increase in physical output capacity, is that growth? Or if new plant can produce 150 % of the capacity of plant replaced at a lower cost per unit, how is the replacement portion of the expenditure to be measured? These questions are essentially the same as those that have arisen under current cost accounting for the purpose of measuring depreciation on a current cost basis — and have proven very contentious. (See Part III for more complete discussion.)

It must be conceded that the SCF does eliminate certain types of allocations. Once cash outflows are reported and classified, there is no further allocation, such as allocation of inventory cost to cost of sales or of plant costs as depreciation. In addition, the extent of allocation can be reduced, for example by assigning variable costs only to described purposes. Thus, if allocation-free accounting is the goal, cash flow accounting achieves it to a considerable degree.[8] The key question is whether, in so doing, it destroys much of its usefulness.

Multiple-period cash flow statements

G.H. Lawson's suggestion for overcoming the limited significance of a SCF for a single period is that such statements should be presented as a series covering a number of years.[9] This suggestion has a degree of persuasiveness since, over a long enough period, any going concern must replace the investment it starts out with, and over a period of time net cash flows will tend to approach net income. There are some difficulties with the idea, however.

- Cash flows over a series of years will be reported in dollars of different purchasing power, so that the series as a whole lacks internal comparability. The solution suggested to this is to use an index to restate the series to a constant dollar basis.
- An entity that has been in operation for a limited number of years only and is still growing may not provide a history long enough to provide a represen-

> tative picture of long-term cash flows. Even a long-established entity may be steadily growing or declining in real terms throughout the period covered by the series of cash flow statements. Since a cash flow statement, by definition, shows capital expenditures as an outflow and does not attempt to measure the growth or shrinkage in capital base, the proper interpretation of a series of cash flow statements, even for an extended period, may be in doubt.

Lawson proposes to meet the latter difficulty in the following fashion. First, he assumes that the market value of a company's securities should reflect its expectations for future cash flows. Thus, a statement that shows how that market value has changed in total over a period (when measured in constant dollars) should show whether the real capital base is increasing. If the capital base is relatively constant, then it may be assumed that the average net cash flows after capital expenditures, when expressed in real terms, fairly represent the basic profitability of the business. This test may be supplemented by examination of the real rates of return over a period on the debt and equity securities of the company based on their market prices. Inadequate rates of return would reinforce the implications of declining real net cash flows over the period, and vice versa. Egginton criticizes Lawson's proposals on the grounds that if the cash flow information is inadequate in itself to inform investors and creditors, the difficulty cannot be cured by introducing investor valuations based upon the presumably inadequate information.[10]

Supplementary information on assets and liabilities

A more direct way to cope with the failure of cash flow statements to disclose growth or shrinkage in the capital base is to provide supplementary information about assets and liabilities that are not treated as part of the cash position. Cash flow adherents take it as given that this information cannot be based upon conventional historical cost accounting valuations because such valuations depend upon allocations — the very procedures that cash flow accounting is trying to avoid. The only alternative is to adopt a market valuation approach to measures of assets and liabilities. Once the historical cost accounting model has been abandoned, it seems obvious that those market values must be values current at the reporting date. Moreover, to be consistent with cash flow accounting theory the valuations too must be allocation-free.

The most obvious allocation-free market values are exit prices — estimates of net amounts realizable for the assets.[11] Entry values — estimates of current costs of acquisition — can be allocation-free as well, but only if they are based upon second-hand market prices. In contrast, the usual approach in current cost accounting is to estimate the values for property, plant, and equipment by obtaining replacement costs new and deducting accrued depreciation therefrom. Since depreciation is an allocation, this approach is unacceptable. The problems in arriving at current valuations for assets will be explored in greater depth in Part III.

Summary

A financial statement focussing on changes in the liquid resources of an entity has a long tradition. Unfortunately, the objectives of that statement have not always been clear and there can be several variations in its form. The following are some of the statement's objectives:

- The statement may help assess the financial flexibility of an entity, its credit-worthiness, and whether its operations are contributing to its solvency.
- The statement may help predict future cash flows by showing how past operations have affected the liquid position of the enterprise.
- The statement, by reporting investing and financing transactions, helps explain changes in resources and claims that are not explained by the income statement.
- By reconciling net income with liquid funds from operations, the statement helps to enlighten the reader as to the extent to which profits are represented by liquid resources and also the significance of some accounting allocations to the figure of net income reported.

It is not clear that all these objectives can be well served in one statement. It might be simpler in the long run to have several statements of flows, each focussing on different activities — one on the effects of financing activities and increases or decreases in capital employed, one on the effects of management decisions on investment and disinvestment, and one explaining total changes in cash and cash equivalents over a period with particular emphasis on the effects of operations.

Several major questions must be addressed in settling the presentation of the single statement that is customarily provided at present.

- Should the primary distinction in the statement be between activities giving rise to liquid resources and those consuming them, or should all activities, both sources or uses of funds, be classified by the main decision areas of operations, investment, and financing? The new CICA recommendations have supported the latter form of presentation.
- Just what activities should be classified as "operating?" This has not been settled conclusively.
- What is the best definition of liquid funds for the purposes of the statement? The tendency is away from a broad definition such as working capital and towards cash and cash equivalents. The term "cash equivalents," however, is used loosely.
- Should liquid funds from operations be computed directly by reporting sources of cash inflows and objects of cash expenditures or indirectly by reconciliation of funds from operations with reported net income? Either approach is considered acceptable, but a large majority of statements adopt the indirect method.

There are numerous technical problems in drawing up a SCFP. Authoritative literature provides little firm guidance on these, and practice is far from consistent. This fact plus the flexibility possible in the choice of definition of liquid funds and in the division between operating and other activities ensure that SCFPs prepared by different enterprises will continue to be noncomparable.

The decision on the appropriate form of SCFP for financial institutions presents a distinct problem. The liquidity of the assets of a financial institution may depend more on their individual quality than on the class of asset. For example, a loan receivable may be extremely liquid or extremely illiquid, depending upon the financial health of the borrower. The primary function of a SCFP for a financial institution, therefore, may be to cast light on the effects of management decisions on financing and on allocation of funds for investment.

A small number of accounting theorists advocate cash flow accounting not as one component of historical cost financial statements but as a substitute for them. The problem for a reporting system focussing on cash flows is to make the statement of cash flow provide more information than one would obtain merely from reading a bank passbook. To achieve this objective, cash flow theorists have had to address many of the questions discussed earlier — how to define cash flows, how to classify them in an illuminating fashion, and how to give a clue as to expectations of future cash flows beyond those that are implicit in the balances of cash and cash equivalents reported.

Consideration of these questions leads directly to a conclusion that some disclosure of values of assets and liabilities that do not represent cash and cash equivalents is necessary. As a result, cash flow accounting cannot be looked upon seriously as a separate accounting model. It can be used as a means of providing a different perspective from the income statement in historical cost accounting, or it can be used as a component of a current value system. But a statement of cash flow cannot stand alone as an adequate financial report for any complex business.

References

[1]See L.C. Heath, *Financial Reporting and the Evaluation of Solvency,* Accounting Research Monograph No. 3 (New York: AICPA, 1978), chap. 7.

[2]CICA, "Statement of Changes in Financial Position," *CICA Handbook,* Section 1540 (Toronto: CICA).

[3]Ibid., par. 17.

[4]Ibid.

[5]Ibid., par. 03.

[6]See E.P. Swenson and R. Vangermeersch, "Statement of Financing and Investing Activities," *The CPA Journal,* November 1981, pp. 32-40.

[7]These possibilities are illustrated in A.H. Seed, III, *The Funds Statement: Structure and Use* (Morristown, N.J.: Financial Executives Research Foundation, 1984), chap. 4.

[8]For a more extended discussion, see B.A. Rutherford, "The Interpretation of Cash Flow Reports and the Other Allocation Problem," *Abacus,* June 1982, pp. 40-49, and T.A. Lee, "Cash Flow Accounting and the Allocation Problem," *Journal of Business Finance & Accounting,* Autumn 1982, pp. 341-52.

[9]A concise explanation of the suggestion may be found in G.H. Lawson, "The Measurement of Corporate Performance on a Cash Flow Basis: A Reply to Mr. Egginton," *Accounting and Business Research,* Spring 1985, pp. 98-108. A similar idea in concept is outlined in Y. Ijiri, "Recovery Rate and Cash Flow Accounting," *Financial Executive,* March 1980, pp. 54-60.

[10]See D.A. Egginton, "Cash Flow, Profit and Performance Measures for External Reports: A Rejoinder," *Accounting and Business Research*, Spring 1985, pp. 109-12.

[11]See T.A. Lee, "Reporting Cash Flows and Net Realizable Values," in *Cash Flow Accounting*, ed. B.E. Hicks and P. Hunt (Sudbury, Ontario: International Group for Cash Flow Accounting, and Research and Publication Division, School of Commerce and Administration, Laurentian University, 1981), pp. 215-37.

Chapter Twenty-Two

Statement Presentation and Disclosure; Interim Financial Statements; Analytical Data

The discussion to this point in Part II has concentrated on the measurement of assets, liabilities, revenues, and expenses. It is now time to consider how these measurements should be reported in financial statements. The selection of information to be presented and the manner of presentation are governed by accounting standards. To a considerable extent, these standards are designed to assist in the interpretation of the operations of the reporting entity. The user of the financial statements, however, will take the data presented therein, analyze them, possibly work out ratios or percentages considered significant, and look at trends. Thus, to some extent, there is an overlap in functions performed by the accountant and the financial analyst, and it is not clear just where the responsibility of one ends and the other begins. Within the last two decades, for example, accounting standards have been developed for the presentation of figures of earnings per share in financial statements — a calculation that one might think should be made by the analyst in whatever fashion seems appropriate to him or her.

Whatever the conclusion on this point, it is clear that accounting standards for presentation of financial information must take into account the need to communicate efficiently with statement users. In this chapter we discuss standards for presentation and disclosure in financial statements with primary emphasis on the user perspective. We then discuss interim financial reports prepared in the interests of timely communication. Finally, we turn to a discussion of information of an analytical nature that is also called for by today's accounting standards.

Statement presentation and disclosure

Since the purpose of disclosure standards is to improve communication of relevant information to users of financial reports, it is elementary that disclosure standards should be in tune with users' wants and needs for information. Nevertheless, that general proposition is open to several questions. Are there limits to what should be disclosed? Whose needs for information should be considered? Is it possible that too much information could be provided? How do we decide what is unimportant and therefore need not be disclosed?

Constraints on disclosure

Even though user needs are seen to be paramount in disclosure standards, most would concede that they are not absolute. An enterprise may suffer competitive disadvantage from too much disclosure. Knowledge that a business is exceptionally profitable in some areas may attract new entrants to that business. Knowledge of the cost structure of a successful enterprise may guide competitors to improvement of their own operations. Knowledge that an enterprise is weak in some area may lead to a vigorous competitive attack to force it out of business.

The need for some measure of confidentiality should be respected in establishing disclosure standards. Yet it is difficult to decide where to draw the line. Enterprises often argue that added disclosure will hurt their competitive position. The argument was made fifty years ago against disclosure of revenue figures and fifteen years ago against disclosure of information about separate segments of a company's business. Companies have survived the imposition of both these types of disclosure and many other types as well. It seems impossible to provide any specific guidance in this area. Authorities who establish standards for disclosure must simply be sensitive to needs for confidentiality considered legitimate.

The other general constraint on disclosure rests on the proposition that costs of disclosure should not exceed benefits. Once again it is difficult to make this advice specific. Benefits from additional financial disclosure may be small if the information disclosed is available in other ways. Even if it is not, it is notoriously difficult to measure the benefits of additional information. Secondary effects are hard to identify, and it is often not known what the result would have been without disclosure. Direct costs of disclosure may be easier to estimate, but again secondary costs (or benefits) may be difficult to identify. In the end, the balance between cost and benefit is very much a matter of opinion.

Identification of the user

To deduce what would be useful disclosure, one must have some mental image of the readers of financial reports. Potential readers of financial statements will have different abilities to understand them. It is very difficult to convey complete information about the financial position and performance of a complex business in financial statements that occupy only a few pages. Most would agree that some potential readers of financial statements will never understand them, no matter what effort is made to keep the statement simple. Beyond this there is disagreement. The FASB states that financial information "should be comprehensible to those who have a reasonable understanding of business and economic activities and are willing to study the information with reasonable diligence."[1] The image portrayed is that of an intelligent and motivated layman, but not that of a professional financial analyst.

Other writers argue that it is a mistake to worry about any particular class of user. They point to a large body of research that indicates that there is close to instantaneous reaction to information supplied to well-developed capital markets. If this is so, it is argued that it is fruitless for individual investors to attempt their own analysis as a basis for investment decisions. The important objective is to make information available to the market and, in general, the more information made available and the faster it is disseminated, the more efficient the market will be.

Still others argue that it is important not only to provide information that serious analysts can use but also to meet the perceived needs of other users, since not all markets are efficient.[2] Moreover, even in generally efficient markets it is possible that, for one reason or another, a particular stock is not "followed" by analysts. And, of course, analysts are concerned only with public companies.

It seems to be agreed that a minimum standard of disclosure calls for information that will be useful to a reasonably informed layman. The difficult question is whether disclosure standards should go beyond this and require information that can be used only by a sophisticated analyst.

The question of information overload

Depending upon the identification of the user to whom financial communications are directed, one may or may not have to deal with the problem of possible information overload. Studies of "human information processing" seem to suggest that people are limited in the amount of information that they can use as an aid in arriving at a decision. Beyond a certain point, more information does not improve judgment — in fact, it may make it worse — even though the information user is more confident of his or her judgment.

The implications of this research for disclosure remain to be worked out, and more research is probably needed. One possible conclusion might be that there should be "differential disclosure." That is, more disclosure might be made accessible to sophisticated statement users who are better able to use it. Such an approach is, in effect, supported by the U.S. Securities and Exchange Commission, which requires financial reports filed with it to be supplemented by more detail than is customarily given in reports to company shareholders. It is not clear, however, that professional analysts are able to use more information; it may be merely that they are better able to distinguish between what is relevant and irrelevant. Thus the real significance to disclosure standards of the phenomenon of information overload might be that every effort should be made to avoid meaningless "boilerplate" disclosure in whatever financial report is presented.

As well as making extensive additional information available to the professional analyst, it could be desirable to move in the other direction and present simplified accounts. These may well have merit from a public relations viewpoint but have their own pitfalls in terms of selection of information to be highlighted and changes required in terminology to make the simplified statements understandable.[3]

Materiality

The concept of materiality in accounting is firmly based on the orientation of financial statements to user needs. That is to say, there will be a failure in communication if the statements contain a material error, misrepresentation, or omission. The financial statement preparer uses the materiality criterion in fulfilling his reporting obligation, but it must be understood that the criterion is derived from user needs, not from the preparer's opinion. Likewise, the auditor uses the materiality criterion, but again the criterion is derived in principle from the user.

The auditor uses the materiality criterion in two ways. First, he or she must form some idea of what *amount* of error would be material in order to construct a program of audit tests, especially those using statistical sampling techniques. For this purpose, materiality must be expressed in quantitative terms. Then, at the conclusion of the audit, the auditor must consider how the financial statements must be presented to merit an unqualified opinion. For this purpose, there will be in hand conclusions based on the audit examination as to the amount of probable errors or omissions in the financial statements presented, together with firm knowledge of some actual errors, some of which knowledge conceivably could have been acquired by chance. In deciding on the need for corrections of errors and even more on questions of statement presentation, the auditor may well be influenced by certain unquantified assumptions as to user welfare as well as the quantitative criteria of materiality. We should be clear, however, that a program of audit testing can only be planned in terms of quantitative criteria.

The accepted concept of materiality is that some information or some aspect of statement presentation is material if its omission or misrepresentation could affect a decision by a reasonably intelligent reader of the financial statements. Although logical, this concept presents considerable difficulty in implementation. Since information that might affect one reader's decision could leave another completely unmoved, what financial statement reader are we talking about? Most definitions of the concept refer to decision making by "a reasonable person" or "the average prudent investor."

Unfortunately we do not have very concrete evidence explaining how people make investment or credit decisions. Thus, how can we know what they would consider material? Research has proceeded along various lines. Some research investigates the correlation between accounting data and significant economic events such as business failures, stock market performance, or changes in bond ratings. The hope is to identify key accounting variables and changes in variables that result in significant reactions or presage significant events.[4] In several studies a series of illustrative situations is presented to groups of financial analysts, credit grantors, auditors, academics, or statement preparers, and these groups are asked to express opinions on the materiality of specific information in the illustrations and explain how their opinions are arrived at.[5] Other research is exploratory, descriptive, and normative.[6]

The research suggests that (1) there can be considerable dispersion in opinions held by various observers as to what is or is not material, (2) enough consensus exists that some guidance can be given in broad quantitative terms, and (3) there are some factors that affect materiality judgments by statement preparers and auditors that can only be expressed in qualitative terms. In other words, the assessment by statement preparers and auditors of materiality to a reasonable user of financial statements ultimately comes down to a matter of judgment. Criteria that affect materiality judgments are discussed below.

Quantitative criteria. People tend to begin their consideration of the materiality of an item by looking at it in quantitative terms. Usually the quantitative expression relates the size of the item in question to some reference statistic such as net income. It has been asked whether an absolute test should be applied as well. That is to say, is there some amount — say $10 million or $100 million — that should always be regarded as material regardless of the size of the reporting entity? The majority answer appears to be in the negative. If a piece of financial information is small relative to its setting, it is not material just because it might be an enormous amount in relation to the wealth of an average individual.

What base should be used as the standard of reference against which materiality is judged? Net income is, not surprisingly, the most commonly used reference base. A large number of user decisions are influenced by the measurement of income or disclosure of components of net income. Given the emphasis upon income as an indication of financial well-being and performance, it is logical that it should be the primary standard against which materiality is measured.

Other bases of comparison may also appear logical depending upon the circumstances. For example, suppose a question concerns disclosure of a possible contingent loss which, if it occurred, would not be considered a recurring factor in any evaluation of the earnings prospects of the business. A comparison of the possible loss with the amount of shareholders' equity, rather than with income for a single year, might well seem more logical in such a case. In still another situation, if a company were suffering a liquidity problem one might judge the materiality of a particular question by the impact its treatment would have on the total of liquid assets disclosed or on the net working capital.

Finally, it is sometimes asked whether materiality should be judged by the relation of the amount in question to the particular line in the income statement or balance sheet that would be affected by its correction. For example, if research and development expense would be increased by fifty percent through correction of an error, might that be regarded as material even though the effect on net income reported for the year was well below the standard of materiality normally applied? There is no absolutely clear-cut answer to this. If the statement reader places particular emphasis on the item in question and might make a mistaken inference as a result of the error, it should be regarded as material. Frequently, however, common sense will suggest that such a possibility is slight. It would rarely matter, for example, whether prepaid expenses were reported at twice as much or half as much as their correct amount.

Certain questions follow from the predominant use of income as the reference base. Income will vary from one year to the next. Yet it makes little sense (assuming the business remains essentially the same) that the measure of materiality should vary correspondingly. It is generally felt that the reference base should be a representative income figure, perhaps as indicated by an average of net income for several years, rather than the current year's figure if it is abnormally low or high. Even this modification does not solve the problem if the enterprise has just broken even or shown losses for several years. In such cases the quantification of materiality may be based upon a notion of a normal level of profitability — which may be derived by applying a conservative target percentage return on equity to the amount of shareholders' equity reported in the balance sheet.

The question may be asked whether the reference base should be final net income for the year or net income before extraordinary items, taxes, and possibly other items. Most accountants would think it proper to exclude extraordinary items for obvious reasons. One might also argue that a figure of income before income taxes, and perhaps before interest as well, should form a more stable reference base than one that is after these items. On the other hand, users place heavy emphasis on net income after taxes and beyond that on earnings per share. On occasion, an item may appear to be more material on an after-tax basis, and this also lends support to the use of after-tax income as the reference base. For example, if the question at issue is whether a large gain on sale of securities should be disclosed as an unusual item, the gain after capital gains tax will be a higher percentage of after-tax income than the percentage of before-tax gain to before-tax income.

When materiality is based on income as a reference base, several studies have suggested the rule of thumb that an item over ten percent of normal income should always be regarded as material, while an item under five percent need not be regarded as material — subject to certain qualitative factors to be discussed subsequently. The existence of the intermediate zone emphasizes the need for judgment in assessing the impact of the item in question on users' decisions.

This rule of thumb applies in the context of annual financial reports. Interim financial statements present a problem. An item that represents only four percent of normal net income for a year is likely to be a much higher percentage of net income for the quarter in which it occurs. It does not seem reasonable that an item that is immaterial in the context of annual reporting should become material just because the report is for only part of the year. On the other hand, the possibility of giving a misleading impression of trends is enhanced in interim reports. The end result of this dilemma is that the quantitative criteria expand when applied to an income figure that is less than a full year, but not by a factor of four (for quarterly reports) nor to any very well-defined consensus figure. In interim financial reports, then, the scope for judgment seems even higher than it is in annual reporting.

The results of the application of quantitative criteria may depend upon whether materiality judgments are considered individually or in the aggregate. Several points may be at issue, each of which by itself is immaterial but which add up to a material amount. If the points at issue are questions of measurement, it is accepted that the aggregate is what counts and corrective action should be taken. On the other hand, suppose two errors are made, each of which is material but which have opposite effects on net income so that the net result is immaterial. For example, suppose inventory is understated and cost of sales overstated but that an omission of an account payable results in an understatement of some other expense. If the errors affect different lines in the income statement, it would seem far better (and little trouble) to make the correction in the interest of the user who is analyzing statement trends in detail.

Qualitative criteria. In assessing materiality a number of considerations exist that cannot be expressed in quantitative terms. These considerations influence decisions when the quantitative tests fall in the intermediate zone and may on occasion be sufficient to suggest that an item should be considered material even when it falls below the customarily recognized minimum level of materiality.

- Accounting measurements in certain types of industries are inherently less precise than in others. As a result, reported earnings may well fluctuate widely from period to period as specific uncertainties become resolved and settlements take place. It may well be felt that the materiality of an uncertainty requiring disclosure in such a situation may be higher than in an enterprise in a more stable type of industry.
- The precision with which assets and liabilities may be measured varies substantially according to their nature. Cash may normally be measured absolutely accurately, while estimation of cost or realizability of inventory, or realizability of fixed assets, may often be very difficult. It is generally felt that the materiality test may be less stringent in the latter cases than in the former.
- A particular type of event or contingency may have an isolated impact upon an enterprise or may promise a continuing impact. More stringent materiality levels apply in the latter situation than in the former.
- For a variety of reasons a business may face greater risk and uncertainty than the normal run of business. The economic environment for the business may be difficult, or the business itself may have a weak financial structure or be experiencing liquidity problems. Materiality is interpreted more stringently in such a case when considering known errors or questions of

statement presentation. Indeed, if a particular item in question could mean the difference between signalling or not signalling default on a debt covenant, the leeway for materiality consideration virtually disappears.

Finally, there are a limited number of situations in which quantitative criteria for materiality may not be relevant. There are certain conditions or transactions that a user of financial statements is entitled to know about if they exist. A good example is provided by transactions with related parties. These may be immaterial in their financial effect, but the statement reader is entitled to know that they have taken place, especially if similar transactions could become material in future.

User-oriented statement presentation and disclosure

Given the objective of communicating useful information to readers of financial reports, it is logical to put oneself in the shoes of the user and ask oneself what information is pertinent to his or her decisions, especially those concerning investment or the granting of credit. We have discussed earlier the problem of different levels of comprehension of different readers of financial reports. In the immediately following section our central concern is with what is *potentially useful*. For this purpose, it is appropriate to take the perspective of a skilled analyst so as to probe the limits of disclosure. The following ideas go beyond present requirements in some respects.

Direct estimation of value. Investment and credit decisions basically involve some notion of value of the reporting entity, present and prospective. There are a few types of entity whose value is highly correlated with the sum of the values of individual assets. The prime example is the entity whose sole function is to obtain returns through investing in a portfolio of readily marketable securities or other readily marketable investments. The single most important piece of information in a financial report of such an entity is the current market value of its assets. It would be highly useful to supplement that information with details of the assets held so as to disclose their risk characteristics. If the entity is expected to continue in existence under the same management, the past record of investment income and holding gains and losses on the portfolio (whether realized or unrealized) might also be considered some evidence of management capability.

Assessment of cash-generating potential. In the majority of cases a business enterprise is not in a position to realize upon its assets severally without reducing its overall value thereby. Rather, the value of the business today lies in the ability of the assets working together to generate net cash inflows in future. An analyst, therefore, is interested in information that is useful in assessing the amount and timing of future cash flows.

An analyst's forecast of the future will usually begin with a review of the past. That analysis forms one input to a judgment as to the extent to which future events are likely to resemble past events. The analyst will be assisted in this task if published financial reports clearly identify various components of the income reported.

First, there should be clear disclosure of any debits or credits that have little significance for future cash flows but rather represent adjustments of the past record — such as the effects of changes in accounting policy or changes in accounting estimates. Then there should be disclosure of gains and losses that are one-shot in character. (Some, but not all, of these will be characterized in financial statements as "extraordinary.")

The general aim should be to distinguish between the regular and irregular in revenue and expense flows. It will be helpful to distinguish between the results of the core business carried on and peripheral or incidental activities, including the realization of holding gains, because the latter are more prone to irregularity. Even within core operations, items that are inherently unstable should be identified, such as gains and losses on foreign exchange. Other items may need special disclosure because they occur infrequently or, in a particular year, are significantly different from their usual amount.

Identification of key variables. Simple projections of past trends and earnings are unlikely to produce satisfactory forecasts of the future. Every business is subject to a variety of influences, the effect of which can be estimated more reliably by looking at their impact on various types of revenues or costs individually. Some aspects of a business are more important than others to its overall success, so that a decomposition of figures to permit concentration on these key variables will be helpful. The following would be useful in this task:

- A basic classification of the balance sheet components as (1) operating assets and liabilities (including plant and equipment among operating assets), (2) more or less passive investments, and (3) financing liabilities, would assist in an appreciation of the basic structure of the enterprise. Segregation of revenues and costs by these same categories would assist in an appreciation of the key variables, especially if the regular and irregular were differentiated in each category as suggested above.
- Within the operating category it would be useful if changes in revenue from year to year were explained as resulting from changes in price, changes in volume, and the introduction of new products. Disclosure of the amount of credit sales would also facilitate calculation of accounts receivable turnover.
- Similarly, explanation of the behaviour of costs could be useful. A separation of expenses between those that vary with changes in production volume and those that are relatively fixed in amount would greatly assist user forecasts. It needs to be appreciated, of course, that it is rarely possible to make a clean categorization of cost as being one or the other, so that any overall division would be somewhat subjective.
- Classification of expenses by function served — as cost of sales, marketing, administration, and so on — is more useful for forecasting than classification by object of expenditure. Identification of cost of sales permits calculation of inventory turnover; for this purpose, costs identified as cost of sales should be the same costs that are recognized in costing inventory.
- Disclosure of amounts of expense in categories that are subject to a degree of management discretion would be useful. These would include, for example, costs of repairs and maintenance, advertising costs, and research and development costs.
- Similarly, disclosure of expenses that are incurred largely for future benefit even though written off currently would be useful. These would include, for example, costs of research and development and major product launch costs.

- Disclosure of some nonmonetary indicators could also be useful, such as the percentage of capacity utilization in the period, order backlog at the end of the period, and so on.

Exposure to risk. Risk is a key factor in any evaluation of an enterprise's prospects. Familiarity with a company's products and services provides an analyst with a basic understanding of risk. That understanding can be enhanced by financial disclosure broken down by segments of the business that may be subject to significantly different risks and different rates of profitability and growth. Segmentation by geographical area provides another helpful perspective on political, economic, and foreign currency risk. (See further commentary below on segmented reporting.) Improved assessment of risk and uncertainty is also the principal justification for disclosure of an enterprise's commitments and of contingencies.

Accounting variables. An analyst needs some understanding of the possible impact on figures reported of different available methods of accounting. Obviously, knowledge is also required of the accounting methods actually used in every case analyzed. Thus disclosure of significant accounting policies is now accepted as a required accompaniment of financial statements. Disclosure is to be made of all accounting policies that are significant to the reporting entity. Of particular importance is disclosure of the policies selected when alternatives are permissible, policies followed that are peculiar to the industry, and, even more important, policies adopted with respect to significant situations that are peculiar to the entity itself and are not clearly governed by a general accounting standard.

Obviously disclosure should be made of changes in accounting policies that have a material effect on figures presented or that potentially could have a material effect in future years. The disclosure should, where possible, indicate what revisions have been required to previous years' figures presented for comparison as a result of the adoption of the new method and what the current year's figures would have been had the new method not been adopted.

In the application of many accounting policies, judgments are required. When those judgments involve the future they are, by necessity, subjective. Disclosure should be made of any significant estimates of this kind. For example, estimates of useful lives and salvage that are used as a basis for depreciation rates, or of the rates themselves that result from such estimates, are required to be disclosed. Unfortunately, current disclosure relating to depreciation is often too imprecise to be useful. It does no good to know that the useful life of equipment has been estimated in the range of five to thirty years, unless one knows what type of equipment is being depreciated over each different period used and what is the dollar amount of investment depreciated over each different period.

Aids to analysis and forecasting. If enough is known about how the analysts use reported figures, it could be a great convenience if financial reports were to produce figures in the same format and to calculate statistics based thereon. For example, it is common for financial reports to include five- or ten-year summaries of earnings and other selected figures, thereby facilitating analysis of trends over time. Totals of current assets and current liabilities have been provided in balance sheets for many years, and considerable attention has been devoted in accounting standards to deciding just how assets and liabilities should be classified as current or noncurrent. The calculation of earnings per share is also the subject of a detailed accounting standard.

More could be done along these lines. Calculations could be provided of return on assets (especially pertinent if assets are divided between operating and investment as already suggested), debt/equity ratios, coverage of interest and preferred dividend requirements by earnings, and so on. Cooperation between accounting standard-setters and financial analysts would be desirable if extensions of disclosures in this way were contemplated.

Recurring suggestions have been made over the past two decades (with relatively little response) that management might provide short-term forecasts of revenues and earnings. Professional analysts make forecasts on their own account but might welcome the check on their opinions provided by management forecasts. It is also argued by some that management makes forecasts in any event; these are known to insiders and may be disclosed selectively to favoured analysts. Thus, general disclosure is urged to provide a fair game for all and help the efficient operation of the market. Against this, there is some concern that management forecasts could be biased and misleading or that unsophisticated readers might place too much faith in them.[7]

Other perspectives. As will be discussed in Part III, the historical cost accounting model has severe deficiencies under conditions of rapidly changing prices. Supplementary disclosure of figures at current cost levels or figures adjusted by an index of general purchasing power have been required or urged as voluntary disclosure in several countries. The majority of statement preparers have been hostile to this additional disclosure for a variety of reasons. Surprisingly, professional analysts who rely on financial information have been, at best, apathetic. Figures adjusted to current costs or current purchasing power levels require consequential adjustment in the significance attached to the various ratios that are used in financial analysis. The analysts appear to have been unwilling to make the effort to change their perspective, preferring to make intuitive adjustments to allow for the distortion in information derived from historical cost financial statements.

Current accounting standards respecting disclosure

Much of the disclosure suggested above as being useful for financial analysis is required by current accounting standards. In addition, information that is not required is often to some extent provided elsewhere in annual reports to shareholders. The principal shortfall in present Canadian practice lies in the area described above under the heading of "identification of key variables." Canadian standards do not require, for example, disclosure of a figure for cost of sales. As to other operating expenses, disclosure is required only of specific items associated with such accounting areas as accounting for leases and for government assistance. In the United States, accounting standards require more complete disclosure, and securities authorities require still more, including a Management Discussion and Analysis to accompany the financial statements. This discussion provides an opportunity to present information in approximate terms that might be too "soft" or imprecise to be included in audited financial statements. Extension of the idea that good financial reporting requires something more than the necessarily limited hard data in financial statements and extension of some efforts to add credibility to soft data short of audit verification seem to be consistent with present trends.

Means of disclosure

Information may be communicated in a variety of ways. There is a basic distinction between information conveyed within the financial statements and its associated notes and schedules and that conveyed outside. As suggested, information may be required outside the financial statement because it is desired to leave room for flexibility in the form of disclosure or because the information is more subjective and has a lower level of reliability. Accounting standards, of course, deal with disclosure in financial statements only. In Canada, any disclosure outside the financial statements results from the voluntary action of management.

Within the financial statements there are various ways to convey information.

- The classification of assets and liabilities in the balance sheet and of items of revenue, expense, gain, and loss in the income statement and statement of changes in financial position may be designed to enhance information. The description of each line item is itself information, and information may also be provided parenthetically. However, to avoid cluttered financial statements as a result of too much information, it is customary to remove much detail and explanation to notes or supplementary schedules to the statements.
- It is highly desirable to cross-reference notes and schedules to the particular items in the financial statements to which they relate. Notes should be in as simple, concise language as it is possible to achieve. Language that is filled with accounting jargon or couched in legalistic terms may utterly fail in its objective of communication. Disclosure is not a substitute for proper accounting treatment of an item in question, especially if the disclosure is obscure. A note also should not raise questions in the reader's mind (except when warning of some uncertainty); it should answer them.

Interim reporting

The usefulness of financial reports depends significantly upon their timeliness. Although annual reporting is the traditional norm, public companies have been required to provide interim reports to shareholders for some two decades, and many companies voluntarily supplied quarterly or semiannual reports long before that time.

Previous chapters have revealed the problems in assigning revenues and costs to annual periods for the purpose of measuring income. These problems are even more severe when the reporting period is less than a year. In annual reports, many costs are treated as expense when incurred, even though known to benefit the future, because expectations of the amount and timing of future benefit are too uncertain to permit reliable allocation. In the more confined perspective of interim reporting, the nonallocation is perceived to involve an even greater distortion of income measurement. The question is, should something be done about it?

Two different concepts of interim reports

The answer to the preceding question may depend upon one's concept of an interim report and its objectives. Under one possible concept, the description "interim report" is considered to be a misnomer. A report for a three-month period ought not to be considered interim. It is a report for a self-contained or "discrete" period of three months. As such, there should be no difference in accounting principles and procedures between a report for a quarter and a report for a full year. If certain procedures are not satisfactory for quarterly reporting, they should be changed — but the same changes should be made in annual reporting. The perspective of a short period provides a good test whether accounting procedures are satisfactory.

Under a completely different concept, a financial report for less than a year is considered an interim report on part of the year, not an independent report in its own right. The main idea underlying the so-called "integral" concept is that an interim report should help the reader predict what the annual report will show. It is appropriate to allocate the results of events between interim periods if, by so doing, prediction of the annual figures will be assisted, even though such allocation would not be permitted between annual periods.[8]

The limits of the integral concept should be understood. It is not intended that the net income reported for three months should be one-quarter of the net income expected to be reported for a full year. Operating revenues for the quarter, for example, will be measured on the same basis as for a full year and thus will vary from period to period. Rather, the general idea is that some operating expenses will be allocated in proportion to revenues so that the margin on sales for the interim period should be a better estimate of the margin obtainable for the full year. Thus, it remains necessary for the statement user to predict revenues for the full year in order to predict the year's net operating income. In addition, allocations are restricted to ordinary operating costs. Gains and losses on disposal of capital assets and investments or any items that would be classified as extraordinary or unusual in annual reporting are to be reported in the period when they occur, not "smoothed" over several interim periods within the fiscal year.

It is far from clear that the objective of assisting the prediction of annual results necessarily requires adoption of the integral concept. The integral method requires that both revenue and costs for the remainder of the year be accurately forecast by management in order that costs may be allocated so as to result in approximately level margins of operating profit in all periods. If a business is volatile, not only may the interim figures be poor predictors of annual results, they could also be a poor record of actual events, having been contaminated by the effect on allocations of estimation errors.

Neither has it been established that the discrete concept provides a poor basis for prediction. A policy of reporting expenses largely as costs are incurred, together with a history of quarterly experience in previous years, might well provide a serious analyst with a good basis for prediction. Unfortunately, there does not appear to be any accounting research that provides a basis for firm conclusions on these issues.[9]

On the surface, Canadian and U.S. standards are at odds as to the preferable concept. The *CICA Handbook* states: "Interim financial reports should present information with respect to the results of operations of a company for a specified period rather than a proration of expected results for the annual period."[10] In contrast, the U.S. standard says, "... each interim period should be viewed primarily as an integral part of an annual period."[11] Examination of the actual recommendations in the two standards, however, indicates that neither rigorously adheres to a single concept and they are not seriously at odds with each other. Each might be described as taking a compromise or "combination" approach. In addition, a U.S. research study has shown that actual practice does not rigorously adhere to the standard.[12] It seems probable that Canadian practice would exhibit similar inconsistencies if studied.

Allocations in interim reporting

Costs that are allocated in a special way for interim reporting purposes are of two types. First, there are those costs that are already allocated under accounting standards for annual reporting purposes but whose allocation pattern is considered to need further refinement for interim reporting. The prime example in this group consists of overhead costs allocated to inventory. Second, there are those costs that are written off as incurred in annual reports but which need some form of allocation for interim reporting. The need for allocation within a year arises because the costs in question are deemed to benefit interim periods other than those in which they are incurred (even though they are not deemed to benefit *years* other than those in which they are incurred).

Reallocation of inventory overheads. As described in chapter 10, absorption-costing procedures call for the allocation of manufacturing overhead costs to inventory at a predetermined rate based on some indicator of production activity such as labour hours, labour costs, or machine hours. The predetermined rate is often established by dividing estimated overhead costs for a year by an estimate of normal production for a year. As production actually takes place, overhead is charged to inventory (absorbed) at the predetermined rate in accordance with actual production. Since many overhead costs are incurred or amortized in a fairly level amount each year whereas productive activity may fluctuate for seasonal or other reasons, this procedure results in underabsorption or overabsorption of overheads at any interim period-end.

At a fiscal year-end such underabsorbed or overabsorbed amounts are not carried forward. For interim reporting purposes, however, they may be. The reason is that if production during interim periods varies, but in the manner anticipated in the estimate of annual production activity, the balances overabsorbed or underabsorbed at any interim period-end may be expected to be offset by the fiscal year-end. The carryforward of such balances at an interim period-end is only proper to the extent that it is expected they will be offset over the remainder of the fiscal year. If, for example, there is a significant underabsorbed balance at a period-end because of low production attributable to slack economic conditions, that balance should be written off. Likewise, efficiency variances identified under a standard cost system would ordinarily not be expected to be recovered.

Programmed costs. The U.S. standard lays stress on the ability of a particular cost to benefit periods other than that in which it is incurred as a justification for allocation among interim periods. The best example of such a cost is provided by advertising. Costs of a major campaign may certainly bring revenues over a number of months so that deferral on some reasonable basis seems justified. In some cases, accrual and expensing of future advertising costs may also be justified. For example, if the sales of a manufacturer to wholesalers or retailers are predicated upon a promise of support in a national advertising campaign to be carried out later in the year, accrual of some part of such advertising costs when the sales are made may well be justifiable.

It must be conceded that the criterion of benefit to several periods as justification for accrual or deferral of costs raises some questions. For example, if a cost is not deferrable at a fiscal year-end on the grounds of future benefit, why should it be deferrable at an interim period-end? The only logical explanation must be that the cost is considered material in the context of interim reporting but immaterial in the context of annual reporting. Even so, the criterion of benefit to more than one period can hardly be relied upon to give clear guidance since, in a broad sense, one can argue that almost any cost that is incurred at intervals greater than the reporting period must be considered to benefit more than one period. Looked at in this way, the test of multiple-period benefit simply leads to smoothing the write-off of irregular expenses. For example, an American study shows that almost half of companies surveyed allocated the cost of major repairs programmed for the fiscal year (especially those programmed for a shutdown period) on some basis other than a write-off as paid or incurred.[13]

Costs determined at the year-end. Certain costs incurred by a company (or cost reductions) may be based on formulas that are calculated only annually or at some period longer than a quarter year. In such cases, it is necessary to make estimates of the effect of the formula in order to make accruals at interim period-ends. Similarly, a company may have a policy of paying year-end profit-sharing bonuses. In such a case, the expected bonus rate with respect to the annual profits would be calculated and accrual made for interim reporting purposes by applying that rate to the interim profits reported.

Income taxes. Income taxes represent a special case of a cost determined by a formula at the year-end. Although the calculation may be more complex, the principle is the same as that just described. The general objective is to calculate an effective rate of tax for the year and apply it to the pretax income as reported for the interim period. Some detailed questions that arise in doing this are discussed below.

- If the business is eligible for the small business tax credit or the manufacturing and processing credit, the effective tax rate will be sensitive to the proportion of profit for the year not qualifying for the credit. The estimate, therefore, needs to be kept under review as the year progresses so that the assumed rate can be adjusted if conditions change. Similarly, estimates of the amount of any permanent tax/accounting differences need to be kept under review.
- Suppose different types of income are taxed at different rates. For example, suppose capital gains are included in income, or suppose consolidated income contains foreign source income taxed at different rates than domestic income. Should the pretax income reported at each interim period be disaggregated and different effective rates be applied to each component, or should the average effective tax rate for the year be calculated on a global basis and that rate applied to the pretax reported income of the interim period regardless of its components? The U.S. standard prescribes the latter approach except that tax with respect to unusual or extraordinary items is to be dealt with individually. In the writer's opinion, a disaggregation of rates so as to deal separately with each class of income taxable at different rates would be a better answer.

- If a business expects to break even over a full year, a problem is presented in calculating a tax for profits or losses shown with respect to interim periods since there is no apparent effective tax rate. What tax rate then should be assumed? Possibilities include the full statutory tax rate, some assumption of a "typical" effective tax rate for the business (based on recent experience), or an estimate of the effective tax rate that would be shown for the current year if only profitable interim periods were taken into account. Any choice is arbitrary; the last method cited has the greatest appeal to the writer since it is based on current-year conditions.
- If a business shows a loss in one or more interim periods at the beginning of the year and that loss is expected to be offset by profits in the remainder of the year and if a taxable profit also existed in previous years within the loss carryback period, an assumption must be made as to whether the interim period loss should be deemed to be carried back to previous years or offset by profits of future periods within the current year. The rate of tax applied in calculating the tax recovery might differ depending upon this choice. The *CICA Handbook* recommends assuming a tax recovery as though the loss were carried back to previous fiscal year(s).[14] If there is no taxable profit within the loss carryback period or if its amount is not sufficient to fully absorb the interim period loss of the current year, a potential tax recovery may be assumed from profits to be expected in the remainder of the current fiscal year or in future years, but only to the extent that such profits are virtually certain.
- If a loss carryforward exists from previous years and profits are expected in the current fiscal year, the *CICA Handbook* suggests two possibilities. The first is that no recognition of the tax loss recovery be made until the last quarter of the current year, on the grounds that the benefit from a loss carryforward is not realizable until a taxation year is completed. Alternatively, to the extent that the recovery is virtually certain from profits within the current year, the estimated recovery would be prorated over the interim periods.[15]

Presentation and disclosure

Standards for interim financial reports concentrate upon income statement data. Details of the required disclosure parallel those required for annual statements. No balance sheet information is specifically required, but significant changes in financial position should be disclosed. Many companies do provide condensed balance sheets and statements of changes in financial position. Supplementary disclosure by way of footnote is usually limited, but companies are requested to note significant changes since the date of the last annual report, such as changes in contingencies or commitments or changes in capital structure.

Analytical data

In this section we shall discuss three areas in which accounting standards have required information to be disclosed in financial reports in direct response to presumed user needs. In the first of these areas — that of segment reporting — users in general would not have access to the information if it were not required by accounting standards or provided voluntarily by issuers of financial reports. In the other two areas — calculation of earnings per share and the provision of totals of current assets and current liabilities — users are able to make their own calculations from the information normally supplied in the financial statements, so that the requirements for disclosure in the statements are justified (if at all) only on the basis that they impose uniformity on the calculation and save effort on the part of users who wish to have the information.

Segmented reporting

Segmented reporting had its genesis in the early 1960s with concerns over the trend among corporations towards diversification into a number of lines of business. With diversification it became less easy for financial analysts to make an intelligent assessment of a company's prospects, since distinctly different risks and prospects for growth and profitability among various segments of the business carried on could be concealed within consolidated financial statements. After much debate the U.S. Securities and Exchange Commission imposed requirements for "line of business" reporting upon registrants with the commission. These were followed within a few years by FASB requirements for "segmented" disclosure in financial statements (which requirements were restricted within two years to enterprises with publicly traded securities). In 1979, as so often happens, Canadian accounting standards were changed to follow the United States lead. Again the application of the new standards was restricted to public companies.[16]

Definition of a segment. Several practical problems had to be addressed in formulating a standard for segmented reporting. The first of these was to define just what was meant by a segment of an enterprise. The objective of segmented reporting was to identify segments subject to different risks and with different growth and earnings prospects. This objective did not lead directly to criteria for segmentation. Risks and growth prospects might vary, for example, according to the type of product, according to the industry to which the product was sold, according to the degree of concentration in the market for the product, or according to the geographical area in which business was done. On top of this, there could be serious practical problems in particular enterprises in producing figures for segment revenue and even more for segment profitability, depending upon the organizational structure of the enterprise. Often there was a conflict between bases of segmentation that were available and those that would be useful.[17]

The accounting standards adopted in the face of this dilemma represent a compromise. Two different perspectives are provided by calling for segmentation by "industry" and by the geographic area in which business is carried on. Segmentation by industry can be based upon the nature of the product, the nature of the production process, or the nature of the market served. The principal objective is to group operations with similar risks and prospects. Profit centres defined for internal management purposes are often usable for this purpose, but the organizational structure is not supposed to determine the definition of segments if the resulting segmentation does not meet the test of similarity of products and risks. Standard Industrial Classification codes may also be helpful as a starting point in suggesting the definition of segments but are not conclusive. Not infrequently the code structure indicates separation of what are essentially interdependent products or processes. The standards also recognize that even after logical segment definitions are adopted, it may be impractical to obtain the necessary data on a worldwide basis. In such cases, foreign data that are not disaggregated by segments may be treated as though they were derived from a single segment.

Geographic segmentation is based on the location of a company's operations. All operations in the home country are to be reported as the domestic segment. Foreign operations of a multinational company are to be grouped in segments by geographic areas. The standards are not specific as to which countries constitute separate geographic areas for this purpose. Rather, each company is to determine by common-sense tests what groupings of countries constitute a natural geographic segment of its operations, based on such factors as proximity of operations, interrelationship of operations between countries, and the degree of commonality in economic and political conditions.

Determination of reportable segments. Once segments are identified, the standards provide some quantitative guidelines to be applied so that only material segments are reported. For industry segmentation purposes, the segment is considered material (and therefore reportable) under any of three tests. If its revenue (including revenue from intersegment transfers) or its identifiable assets constitute more than 10% of the total of the company's revenue or identifiable assets respectively, the segment is reportable. In addition, if the operating profit or loss of any segment exceeds 10% of the greater of (1) the total of operating profits of all segments with profits or (2) the total of operating losses of all segments with losses, that segment is reportable. In the interests of consistent reporting there is flexibility so that a segment that usually would be reported (or not reported) under these tests will not have to be treated differently just because the tests so indicate in one particular year. Notwithstanding these guidelines, enough segments should be reported individually to account for 75% of a company's operations. If this would require the reporting of more than ten segments, an attempt should be made to group segments on some reasonable basis. Conversely, if one segment accounts for more than 90% of the revenue, profit or loss, and identifiable assets of the total company and no other segment is large enough to be reportable, the company may omit segmented reporting on the grounds that one segment is dominant.

The guidelines for determination of reportable geographic segments are somewhat different. Profitability is not normally to be considered a factor. Ordinarily, a segment is reportable if it accounts for 10% or more of the revenue from sales to outside customers or 10% of the identifiable assets of the company as a whole.

Determination of segment revenue. Since segment revenue reported includes both sales to outside customers and sales between segments, one might think that the basis of pricing of intersegment sales would be specified. One suggestion was that all intersegment sales should be priced at cost. On the other hand, some companies, particularly multinationals, use transfer prices between segments that are deemed to represent fair value. It would be costly to force another calculation of transfer prices upon them, and, in any event, profit computation based on fair value of output also has its attractions. In the end, it was concluded that no single basis of pricing intersegment transfers should be prescribed, but rather each company should report intersegment revenue using the transfer prices it uses for its own internal accounting purposes.

Revenue and expense allocation. Opinions have varied on the extent to which certain revenues and expenses should be allocated to segments. At one extreme, it might be argued that the most informative presentation would carry segmentation of revenue and expenses just as far as possible, right down to the bottom line of income after taxes on occasion. At the other extreme, it could be argued that allocations should be avoided so far as possible, so that it would be preferable to report only the "contribution margin" of each segment, that is, the margin resulting from the deduction from revenues of directly traceable expenses.

The segmentation standards have taken a compromise position. Revenue reported for a particular segment is to be only that directly attributable to its operations. Segment expenses are to be those operating expenses that are directly attributable to the segment or that can be allocated on a "reasonable" basis. Interest on intersegment loans is excluded from segment revenue unless a segment's operations are financial in nature. Interest expense is excluded from all segments except for a segment whose operations are financial in nature. Head office or corporate revenues and expenses are not allocated, nor is income or loss from investments that are accounted for on the equity basis unless the investee's operations are vertically integrated with those of a particular segment. Also excluded are income taxes, extraordinary items, and minority interest. In essence, what is reported is profit from operations (excluding financial activities and incidental gains and losses) before taxes. However, an enterprise is free to report some more refined measure of profitability for a particular segment if it considers that information useful.

Presentation and disclosure. In some cases segmented information may be incorporated in the body of the financial statements, but normally it is found in a supplementary note or schedule. Such disclosure should show separately for each segment the revenue from sales to outside customers and to other segments. Segment operating profit is also to be disclosed. In each case elimination of intersegment revenues or profits should be made so that the totals agree with figures in the consolidated income statement. The total of segmented operating profit after elimination should also be reconciled with the net income reported in the income statement. Identifiable net assets of each segment are also to be disclosed, and the total of these reconciled with the net assets shown in the consolidated balance sheet. Figures for capital expenditures and depreciation and amortization by segment are also to be disclosed for industry segments but are not required for geographic segments.

There should be sufficient explanation to make the segment report understandable. Thus, there should be a general description of the products and services of each industry segment and identification of the countries included in geographic segments. Accounting policies that are significant to a reportable segment should be disclosed, even though not sufficiently significant to be disclosed in the statement of accounting policies for the enterprise as a whole. Likewise, information should be given to explain the significance of segment figures when appropriate — for example, a description of the basis of pricing intersegment sales. Any change in the grouping of segments should cause restatement of prior period figures. Changes in the basis of transfer pricing or allocation of expenses should also be disclosed, along with the effect thereof. The impact of any change in overall accounting policies on segment information should also be disclosed.

Other matters. A company may rely on foreign markets even though it has no foreign operations. If geographic segmentation is required because of the risk attached to foreign operations, it is logical that any significant reliance of the domestic segment on export sales should also be disclosed. The standards require disclosure of the amount of sales to foreign customers if they exceed ten percent of sales to domestic customers, and encourage specifying the different geographic areas to which such export sales are made.

The U.S. standard also requires disclosure of the fact if a single customer accounts for ten percent or more of enterprise revenue, and identification of the segment(s) selling to that customer. For this purpose, all the agencies of a government (such as the Federal government) are to be taken as one customer. In Canada, the required disclosure of economic dependence may provide similar information, although not identified with segments.

Evaluation of segment reporting. It is evident from the foregoing description that the figures of segment revenues and costs reported by one company are unlikely to be comparable with those of any other company because of the flexibility possible in the basis of segmentation, the pricing of intersegment sales, and the allocation of expenses. Despite these limitations, analysts have generally been very much in favour of segment disclosure, since it improves their understanding of the reporting company itself. Empirical research indicates that segmented reporting has produced benefits in improving the forecasts of financial analysts, although it appears that disclosure of segment sales is more important for this purpose than disclosure of profits. Segment information apparently has had an impact on the market's assessment of enterprise risk, and there is some evidence that the perceived riskiness of companies has been reduced more frequently than it has been increased as a result of the information.[18] There have been some suggestions, however, that the compliance of companies with segment reporting requirements has not been wholehearted.[19]

The calculation of earnings per share

One of the most widely quoted statistics in financial analysis is that of earnings per share (EPS). In the decade of the 1960s many companies began issuing a variety of securities that provided a contingent interest in or claim upon present or future earnings that otherwise would accrue to the residual equity shares in the company (usually common shares). Such complex securities — sometimes dubbed "Chinese money" — were often issued as a major part of the consideration used by one business to acquire another. If the claim of those securities upon residual earnings was not reflected in the earnings per share figure of the issuing company, but the earnings of the acquired company were included, it was possible for an acquirer to show spectacular gains in quoted figures of EPS.

Types of securities giving rise to these problems included convertible debt or preference shares, various forms of rights to acquire common shares including options and share warrants, and residual equity shares issuable without consideration in future upon the resolution of some contingency. All these types of securities and rights will be called hereafter "contingent equity." Security authorities were alarmed by the possibility for abuse through pumping up the figure of EPS. The accounting profession was to some degree reluctant to become involved in what was essentially not a question of financial reporting but was eventually persuaded that a standardized calculation of EPS reported as part of the audited financial statements would be constructive.

The accounting standards on EPS. The essence of the problem in calculating EPS is to assess fairly the impact of contingent equity on the numerator and denominator of the EPS statistic — that is, the residual earnings accruing to the equity and the number of shares with a claim upon those earnings. The approach taken in the Canadian EPS accounting standard is as follows:[20]

- Calculate a figure of EPS based upon the hard facts as they exist at the financial reporting date — that is, based upon the number of fully participating shares actually outstanding at the financial reporting date and the actual earnings reported as reduced by interest or preferred dividends actually paid or accrued with respect to other securities, including contingent equity.
- Calculate a "fully diluted" figure of EPS on a "what if" basis. That is, calculate the EPS for the period as it would have been had the claims of the contingent equity been exercised at the first of the period (or at the date of their issue if after the first of the period). To do this, the calculation of EPS is revised to increase the number of residual equity shares deemed outstanding and to increase the reported earnings in the numerator for the estimated impact upon earnings if the contingent equity claims had been exercised. The calculation is to be subject to certain constraints — to be described below — the principal one being that a contingent claim should not be deemed to be exercised if it would have an antidilutive effect — raising EPS rather than reducing it. The theory is that the existence of antidilution suggests that the contingent claim will not be exercised.
- The essence of the proposal is to portray for the guidance of investors the limits of a range of possible EPS figures from the best case to the worst from the standpoint of existing residual equity holders.
- Fuller disclosure is to be made of both basic and fully diluted EPS on a pro forma basis if contingent equity is issued after the end of the reporting year but before the financial statements are issued.

The United States standard modifies the approach described above to some degree.[21] It is felt that some securities included in the contingent equity are so likely to exercise their rights to become residual equity that it would be misleading to calculate a basic EPS figure leaving them out. Accordingly, tests are devised for identifying securities that should be regarded as "common stock equivalents," and the best-case presentation of EPS is restricted to a calculation of diluted EPS recognizing both common stock equivalents and residual equity shares actually outstanding in the denominator of the calculation. This statistic is called "primary" EPS.

This U.S. modification has been heavily criticized in American literature. With respect to convertible securities, the test adopted for deciding whether they are common stock equivalents is based on their effective yield at the time of issue. If the yield is less than two-thirds of the average yield on Aa-rated corporate bonds at the time of issuance, the security is to be considered a common stock equivalent. This test is criticized on the grounds that convertible securities issued by less risky companies will have lower yields than those of more risky companies, and thus (illogically) will be more likely to be classified as common stock equivalents. A more serious criticism is that the security is classified as a common stock equivalent once and for all at its date of issue. Thus, the figure of primary EPS quoted subsequently will not necessarily reflect the likelihood of conversion at the reporting date. Empirical research has shown that the test adopted for identification of common stock equivalents does not perform well as a predictor of securities that will be converted.

The significance of calculated dilution. Concerns have been expressed about the significance of fully diluted EPS figures. In the first place, it is argued that diluted EPS figures are significant only if the claims of contingent equity on residual equity status actually will be exercised. Other than the prohibition against factoring in antidilutive securities to the figure of EPS, there is nothing in the calculation of fully diluted figures that can be said to attempt to estimate the probability that such claims will or will not be exercised. As to the prohibition of antidilution, it has been suggested that apparent antidilution may not be a good indicator of the probability of exercise of conversion rights. Basic EPS for any given year may be temporarily depressed without greatly affecting the probability that a convertible security will ultimately be converted. If so, presuming that the fully diluted EPS figure is looked upon as a forecast of the share position after conversion, it is arguable that it is proper to quote a figure ignoring the antidilution prohibition.

In the second place, the calculation of diluted EPS gives no recognition to the timing of possible exercise of the rights (other than to provide that rights need not be taken into account if they are not exercisable within ten years of the reporting date). For example, warrants and options will not be exercised until just before their expiry date in order to delay payment of the exercise price (except in the unusual case where the dividend on the stock provides a cash return that exceeds what could be obtained by investing the money for the exercise price elsewhere). Similarly, the conversion privilege on debt or preference shares will not be exercised before the date that the privilege expires or the conversion ratio is reduced, unless the cash dividend on the residual equity exceeds the interest or dividend payable on the convertible security.[22] The question then is: Given the time value of money, how useful is a calculation of dilution based on existing earnings in portraying an effect that may not occur for several years? Specifically, consider the case of a company that pays out a high proportion of its earnings in dividends to common shareholders. There is little dilution of current earnings for the common shareholders since they are paid out in dividends. It is only at some future date that the dilution becomes a matter of significance.

Concern has also been expressed about the calculation of the dilutive effect of outstanding warrants or options. Under the Canadian approach, the diluted EPS figure is calculated by (1) adding to the actual earnings for the year a notional return on the money that would be received upon exercise of the securities, and (2) dividing the total by the total number of shares that would be outstanding after exercise. The notional return represents a conservative estimate of the after-tax income that could be earned or the costs that could be avoided through the use of the funds received from exercise. Some writers have argued that there is no reason to assume a rate of return on such funds any different from that which could be earned on other capital. The U.S. basis of calculation — the so-called treasury stock method — is different from the Canadian but has also been questioned albeit on different grounds.[23]

Some technical issues. A number of technical problems must be dealt with in calculating EPS.

- If preferred shares are in existence that rank prior to the residual equity and dividends have not been declared upon them in the period, how is earnings (or loss) per share to be calculated? If the preferred shares are cumulative, an amount equal to the dividend to which they would be entitled at the prescribed rate is deducted from the earnings (or added to the loss), and EPS for the residual shares is based upon the adjusted figure. If the preferred share dividend is noncumulative, no such adjustment is made. To avoid confusion, however, special disclosure is given along with the EPS figure of the existence of a preferential claim to any dividends declared.
- When residual shares have been issued or reacquired during a period, the denominator of the figure of EPS is based upon a weighted average of shares outstanding during the period.
- After a stock dividend on common shares, a stock split, or a reverse split, basic EPS figures published subsequently (and fully diluted figures when published) should be based upon the new subdivision of share capital. This applies to figures published for a year just completed even if the change in stock took place after the year-end.
- Any shares with unlimited rights to participate in dividends are to be treated as common shares for the purpose of reporting EPS. If, however, fully participating preferred shares have different dividend rates from the common, it is necessary to apportion the earnings and calculate different EPS figures to reflect the difference in rights. Net income is first reduced by the actual dividends paid in the period together with any unpaid dividends for the period to which rights accumulate. Any remaining unallocated earnings are divided among the classes of shares in proportion to their rights to participate. EPS reported for each class of share is based on the total of its dividend rights and participation rights.
- If a number of potentially dilutive securities exist, the point at which a given security appears to have an antidilutive effect in the calculation of fully diluted EPS can depend upon the order in which each different type of security is taken into the calculation. Unless one security must be exercised before another or at the same time, the sequence of calculation of fully diluted EPS should begin with the security that has the most dilutive effect on a per-share basis, and the calculation should proceed, security by security, progressively reducing the figure of diluted EPS until one comes to a security that would not further dilute the per-share figure.
- When common shares are contingently issuable based on the attainment of earnings above the level of earnings for the year reported upon, such higher earnings are to be assumed for the purpose of calculating whether the issuance of the contingent shares would have a dilutive effect. If the number of shares contingently issuable is based on some external factor such as the market price of the common shares at some future date, the number of contingent shares deemed issued is to be based upon the share price at the end of the reporting period. (This guidance with respect to stock contingently issuable comes from U.S. standards. The *CICA Handbook* is silent on this point.)

Evaluation of EPS accounting standards. From the discussion above, it appears that the significance of EPS figures is open to some question. In view of this, it appears that Canadian standard-setters were wise to avoid some of the complications of the U.S. standard, including the somewhat arbitrary definition of common stock equivalents. The chief merit of an accounting standard on the calculation of EPS is that it requires disclosure to the statement reader about the potential dilution in the interest of common shareholders in a company's earnings and provides a range of EPS figures indicative of the potential dilution impact (even if the manner of calculation of the fully diluted figure is not completely free from question). It may be that a more complete tabulation, giving information individually on all the securities that have a potentially dilutive effect on residual equity, would be even more useful.[24] As it is, research has indicated that mandatory disclosure of fully diluted EPS did have an impact on the pricing of company shares.[25] Thus it appears that analysts have found the information to be of some value.

Current assets and liabilities

The idea of current assets and liabilities, or "working capital," may be traced to two sources. As recounted in chapter 3, nineteenth-century English accounting developed the idea of circulating capital as consisting of those assets that go through a continuing cycle of purchase, manufacturing, and sale together with the liabilities that finance them. The subdivision of the balance sheet between circulating capital and other long-term capital proved to be of some significance for credit-granting purposes as well. Bankers of early industries were interested in realizable assets available as security for their loans. Thus it was convenient to have a subdivision of assets between those that would be realized in cash in the normal course of operations and those that would not and a subdivision of liabilities between those that would be paid out of such realizations and those that would not.

Unfortunately, these two foundations for classification within the balance sheet are not perfectly compatible in concept. The first notion of circulating capital simply provides a basis for classification. It was designed to differentiate between different characteristics of assets held and not primarily designed to measure their liquidity. The distinction was based on whether assets would be consumed in carrying on operations or whether they would be sold. The relevance of this distinction to the use of financial statements, however, was not established. For example, manufacturing supplies are consumed in operations while raw materials are wrought into the final product. Yet each is necessary to production. Inventory costing procedures recognize that fact when overheads are accepted as part of the cost of inventory for balance sheet purposes. But if manufacturing supplies can be treated as overhead, so can depreciation on manufacturing plant. The economic facts are that all assets in some way contribute to future cash receipts from customers. The key question is, when?

The banker's perspective was much more obviously a liquidity perspective. But this was never made clear, simply because it was assumed that liquidity was indicated by the balance sheet description of an asset. Thus inventory was current, regardless of how long it might be in process. Plant and equipment was noncurrent, even though its contribution to cash flow might occur over at most two or three years.[26]

The confusion was not clarified when the accounting profession attempted to provide an authoritative definition of current assets and liabilities. The Committee on Accounting Procedure of the AICPA provided the most extensive consideration of the subject in its Bulletin No. 30 issued in 1947.[27] The committee introduced the idea of an "operating cycle," being the average period that elapses between the time materials are acquired for inventory and the time the product is sold and cash collected upon the sale. Thus the operating cycle is a cash-to-cash cycle.

This idea clearly stemmed from the notion of "circulating capital." All resources expected to be realized in cash or sold or "consumed" within the normal operating cycle represented current assets. The reference to "consumed" probably was made to allow for the case of manufacturing supplies, as discussed above. Unfortunately it raised the question why parts of assets, such as plant and equipment, that will be consumed within the operating cycle should not be classified as current under the same test.

In addition, the concept dealt only with classification of assets that were used in an operating business and did not cover investments. Perhaps for this reason and perhaps as a compromise with well-established tradition, the committee inserted a one-year test for current assets as well. Assets would be treated as current if they were expected to be realized within the operating cycle or within one year. Effectively the current asset standard became the longer of the operating cycle or one year — a standard that straddled two criteria. In most situations the one-year rule would govern.

Current liabilities were then defined as obligations that would require the use of existing resources properly classified as current assets or that would require the creation of other current liabilities. The committee went on to explain what sorts of liabilities it intended to classify as current and in the process made it clear that its definition was not operational. For example, a company might have no current assets whatsoever. Yet, under the definition, if its cash flow from operations was positive and was sufficient to meet obligations as they fell due, none of the obligations would be required to be classified as current. Such a result was not intended by the committee. Rather, it intended that any liability financing items entering into the operating cycle would be treated as current. Any other liability would be classified as current if it was expected to be liquidated within twelve months. This included the portion of long-term debt to be liquidated within one year, even though cash flow from operations before the next instalment was due would assuredly be sufficient to meet the obligation.

The result of all this in practice is that, for the most part, an asset is classified as current if it is expected to contribute to cash flow within twelve months. A liability is classified as current if it is expected to be liquidated within twelve months. The operating-cycle test becomes operative only when the cash-to-cash cycle with respect to goods sold (or services rendered) takes longer than twelve months. Under that provision, inventories in certain industries may be treated as current even though the investment in them will be tied up for much longer than one year. Instalment accounts receivable may also be classified as current if that is the normal basis upon which goods are sold. The twelve-month test could be considered to be moderately useful for the purpose of indicating solvency. The operating-cycle criterion considerably diminishes that utility.

The reference to assets expected to be sold or consumed also creates some difficulties. Under a strict application of the test, marketable securities not intended to be sold would be excluded from current assets. Yet, if it is desired to use the current asset figure as an indication of liquidity, holdings of marketable securities are certainly pertinent. As a result, it seems to be accepted that such securities may be classified as current. On the other hand, an intention test excludes from the current category short-term obligations that are intended to be refinanced. In this case, however, there is a question whether that intention can be fulfilled. Accordingly, accounting standards permit classification of such obligations as long-term only if contractual arrangements exist (before issuance of the financial statements) ensuring refinancing on a basis that pushes the maturity date beyond twelve months. In Canada, practice also permits certain debts that are short-term in form to be classified as noncurrent (for example, demand bank loans that are designated as term loans) provided the lender acknowledges its intention to permit the loan to remain outstanding beyond twelve months.

If one is concerned with the potential cash requirements to liquidate debt, there is another point of some significance. If an entity borrows $1 million at 10% maturing in ten years, it commits itself to the payment of $100,000 a year and $1 million at the end of the ten-year period. Customarily, no part of the $1 million is shown as a current liability until the end of the ninth year. Yet, at the issue date, the present value of the interest payments accounts for approximately $614,000 of the liability, and the present value of the payment on principal ten years hence is only $386,000. The present value of the first year's interest payment alone is $91,000. One can argue that current liabilities should include a figure of $91,000 or $100,000 with respect to such debt if the real desire is to portray its requirements for cash in the short term.[28]

In view of the confusion in the concepts of current assets and current liabilities and anomalies in their interpretation, it is questionable whether a requirement to present totals of current assets and current liabilities in a balance sheet is justified. If it is continued, it would be preferable to concentrate on its significance for the evaluation of entity liquidity and condense the rule into one that is based upon (1) expectations of cash realization in operations within a short time period, such as a year, and (2) capability of being realized upon within short notice. Even such simple criteria are open to objection.

- All assets represent expectations of future cash inflows in a sense, or they would not been shown as assets. Yet it would be difficult, if not impossible, to quantify realistically the contribution to cash over a year of such assets as fixed assets and goodwill.
- In any event, the picture shown by a statement of position is static. It tells very little about the cash flow from operations to be expected over the next year or period of years. What is important to the evaluation of solvency is the balance of cash flows over future periods, not the limited information provided by an analysis of cash expectations from individual assets and liabilities existing at just one point in time.

On balance, it would be more sensible if the classification of assets and liabilities between current and noncurrent were abandoned. As a substitute, more information could be given as to the maturity date of monetary assets and liabilities shown in the balance sheet, including disclosure of past-due amounts. This, together with cash flow predictions, would provide the analyst with a better perspective on the liquidity of the enterprise.

Summary

The communication of financial information is a two-way process. Information must be made available on the one hand. On the other, it must be used, understood, and acted upon. Both preparers of financial information and users of financial information have responsibilities if the effort at communication is to be productive.

Society has required the publication of financial information by public companies and others. It follows logically that the primary criterion for information to be presented in financial reports is its helpfulness to users. User needs, however, are not the sole consideration. Most would agree that reporting entities have rights to some degree of confidentiality. Also, one ought to consider whether costs of providing information may exceed possible benefits. Unfortunately, there is rarely proper evidence or clear criteria to guide decisions as to how much financial reporting is enough. In practice, accounting standard-setters must grapple with these questions almost on a situation-by-situation basis.

There is also significant uncertainty as to what are user needs for information. We do not know how investors and others make decisions. Even if we did, we would likely find that different people make decisions differently depending upon their degree of technical sophistication. There is a good argument that financial information should be aimed at sophisticated users because it is they who make the capital markets efficient. But that argument is limited by the fact that only a minority of reporting entities are public companies, and even then, professional analysts may not follow all companies closely. Compromises are necessary and some degree of differential disclosure for different classes of users is probably helpful — making full information available to the capital markets but producing less complex reports for shareholders in general.

The concept of materiality is a practical tool to assist in the selection of information to be disclosed in financial statements. The usual definition of materiality states that an item of information is material if it has the potential to affect a decision by an average prudent investor. To make the concept of materiality operational, it has been necessary to adopt quantitative rules of thumb. There seems to be a consensus that, in most cases, an item will be considered material if it is over ten percent of a representative net income figure, it will be considered immaterial if less than five percent of that figure, and possibly material depending on the circumstances if it falls in between. The rule is amplified and modified to fit special circumstances, also based on judgment.

Accounting standards for statement presentation and disclosure are, or ought to be, arrived at primarily by looking at issues through the eyes of the user. The list of possible useful information is virtually without limits. One principal question identifies information that is useful: Would the information help to predict the future progress of the entity?

Timeliness in financial reporting is assisted by interim financial reports. There are two theories as to the nature of interim reports. One holds that each period's report should stand on its own feet; the other is that accounting allocations should be managed so that the interim report helps the user to forecast what will be the financial results for the full year. Interim reporting practices represent a compromise. For the most part, they are based upon the same accounting methods as those adopted for annual reporting. However, refinements are made to allow allocations between interim periods that are material to the income reported for those shorter periods, even though immaterial for the full year, and expedients are adopted to allocate to interim periods revenues and costs that are accurately determined only once a year.

Today's accounting standards call for certain information to be included in financial statements, not so much because it is necessary for fair presentation, but rather because it is convenient for analysis.

- Segment data provide a breakdown of revenues, profits, and certain other financial figures by distinguishable industry segments and by geographical areas. The objective is to provide additional information on aspects of an enterprise's operations that are subject to different risks, growth prospects, and rates of profitability.
- An EPS statistic is provided for two reasons. First, it is so widely quoted and used that it is convenient for readers to have it provided routinely in financial reports. Second, it puts readers on notice of possible dilution in their interest in a company's earnings (even though the significance of the fully diluted figure is open to some question).
- Assets and liabilities have been classified as current or long-term for some one hundred years. In spite of this, the objectives and basis for classification are confused, and the significance of the classification is limited. It must be conceded that portrayal of the liquidity of an enterprise is important. That portrayal could be acomplished more efficiently by other means, however.

References

[1]FASB, *Objectives of Financial Reporting by Business Enterprises,* Statement of Financial Accounting Concepts No. 1 (Stamford: FASB, 1978), par. 34.

[2]For an exchange of views on this subject, see W.H. Beaver, "Current Trends in Corporate Disclosure," *Journal of Accountancy,* January 1978, pp. 44-52, and G.I. White, "More on Current Trends in Corporate Disclosure," *Journal of Accountancy,* August 1978, pp. 42-44. A reply by Beaver and additional comment by L.K. Newton follow White's article.

[3]For a review of the difficulties in preparing simplified financial statements, see P. Bird, "The Complexities of Simplified Accounts," in *External Financial Reporting: Essays in Honour of Harold Edey,* ed. B. Carsberg and S. Dev (Englewood Cliffs, N.J.: Prentice-Hall International in cooperation with London School of Economics and Political Science, 1984), pp. 16-24.

[4]For a review of such research, see M.C. O'Connor and D.W. Collins, "Toward Establishing User-Oriented Materiality Standards," *Journal of Accountancy,* December 1974, pp. 67-75.

[5]One of the most extensive studies of this kind is J.W. Pattillo, *The Concept of Materiality in Financial Reporting* (New York: Financial Executives Research Foundation, 1976).

[6]Two examples are Accountants International Study Group, *Materiality in Accounting* (Toronto: AISG, 1974) and D.A. Leslie, *Materiality: The Concept and its Application to Auditing* (Toronto: CICA, 1985).

[7]A thorough review of the issues and problems with respect to published management forecasts may be found in R.H. Kidd, *Earnings Forecasts* (Toronto: CICA, 1976).

[8]For an exposition of the theory, see D. Green, Jr., "Towards a Theory of Interim Reports," *Journal of Accounting Research,* Spring 1964, pp. 35-49.

[9]The issues are considered but firm conclusions are not reached in J.E. Kiger, "Volatility in Quarterly Accounting Data," *The Accounting Review,* January 1974, pp. 1-7, and D. Fried and J. Livnat, "Interim Statements: An Analytical Examination of Alternative Accounting Techniques," *The Accounting Review,* July 1981, pp. 493-509.

[10]CICA, "Interim Financial Reporting to Shareholders," *CICA Handbook,* Section 1750 (Toronto: CICA), par. 13.

[11]AICPA, APB, *Interim Financial Reporting,* APB Opinion No. 28 (New York: AICPA, 1973), par. 9.

[12]M. Schiff, *Accounting Reporting Problems: Interim Financial Statements* (New York: Financial Executives Research Foundation, 1978).

[13]Ibid., chap. IV. The significance of the results obtained concerning the treatment of other types of irregular expenses is obscured by some ambiguity in the survey questionnaire.

[14]*CICA Handbook,* Section 1750, par. 20.

[15]Ibid., par. 19.

[16]See FASB, *Financial Reporting for Segments of a Business Enterprise,* Statement of Financial Accounting Standards No. 14 (Stamford: FASB, 1976) as amended by SFAS No. 18 (1977), SFAS No. 21 (1978), SFAS No. 24 (1978), and SFAS No. 30 (1979), and CICA, "Segmented Information," *CICA Handbook,* Section 1700 (Toronto: CICA).

[17]For a review of possible bases of segmentation, see N.R. Yarian, "Segmentation for Reporting Purposes," *Management Accounting,* April 1975, pp. 16-20.

[18]A summary of the research may be found in R.M. Mohr, "The Segmental Reporting Issue: A Review of Empirical Research," *Journal of Accounting Literature,* Spring 1983, pp. 39-68.

[19]See L.F. Steedle, "Disclosure of Segment Information — SFAS #14," *The CPA Journal,* October 1983, pp. 34-47.

[20]CICA, "Earnings per Share," *CICA Handbook,* Section 3500 (Toronto: CICA).

[21]AICPA, APB, *Earnings per Share,* APB Opinion No. 15 (New York: AICPA, 1969) as amended by APB Opinion No. 30 (1973), SFAS No. 21 (1978), SFAS No. 55 (1982), and SFAS No. 85 (1985).

[22]See R.L. Vigeland, "Dilution of Earnings per Share in an Option Pricing Framework," *The Accounting Review,* April 1982, pp. 348-57.

[23]For an interesting discussion with some debatable points, see B. Barlev, "Theory, Pragmatism and Conservatism in Reflecting the Effects of Warrants on Diluted EPS," *Abacus,* June 1984, pp. 1-15. See also L.W. Dudley, "A Critical Look at EPS," *Journal of Accountancy,* August 1985, pp. 102-11.

[24]A tabulation containing several attractive features was suggested in an early article on the subject. See L. Spacek, "Umpiring the Earnings Per Share Results," *Management Accounting,* March 1969, pp. 9-14, 27.

[25]See S.J. Rice, "The Information Content of Fully Diluted Earnings Per Share, *The Accounting Review,* April 1978, pp. 429-38.

[26]The confusion is well described in L.C. Heath, *Financial Reporting and the Evaluation of Solvency,* Accounting Research Monograph No. 3 (New York: AICPA, 1978), chaps. 3 and 4.

[27]This bulletin was subsequently reproduced in American Institute of Accountants, Committee on Accounting Procedure, *Restatement and Revision of Accounting Research Bulletins,* Accounting Research Bulletin No. 43 (New York: AIA, 1953), chap. 3A.

[28]This point is convincingly made in R. Ma, "Liability Measurement: The Case of the Lessee's Obligation," in *External Financial Reporting,* ed. Carsberg and Dev, pp. 81-89.

Chapter Twenty-Three

Accounting for Oil and Gas Production Companies

Preceding chapters have covered most of the major issues in accounting standards and practice and their solutions under the historical cost theory. This chapter and the next two discuss three special situations in which the central ideas of historical cost accounting provide only limited assistance for the production of useful financial information. In this chapter we discuss the oil and gas production industry as a prototype of extractive industries generally. Occasionally specific references will be made to mining enterprises as well.

The facts of supreme importance for an enterprise in an extractive industry are its control over exploitable reserves of minerals and hydrocarbons and its ability to discover additional reserves. Historical cost accounting can, by somewhat arbitrary methods, produce a figure for cost of discovered reserves. But, unlike most other industries, cost is only by chance a close approximation to value. This fact, together with revenue recognition rules that require exchange transactions to justify recognition of changes in value, mean that the most important information about an enterprise in an extractive industry is poorly portrayed in its financial statements. Unfortunately, no other accounting model exists capable of solving this problem in a practical way.

The oil and gas production industry

The oil and gas production industry, as described in this chapter, refers to that branch that is devoted to exploration for, and development and production of, crude oil and natural gas (with some minor by-products). These activities are commonly referred to as "upstream" activities to distinguish them from the "downstream" activities of transportation, refining, and marketing products in a usable form. Certain features of the upstream segment of the industry have a significant impact on its accounting practice.

Since oil and gas are commodities in demand throughout the world, and since much of the technical expertise required is common to exploration and production wherever conducted, the industry is international in scope. Many companies, ranging in size from very large public companies to relatively small private companies, conduct exploration and production activities in more than one country. Significant differences exist in the political environments of the producing countries.

Traditionally, the costs of finding oil and gas reserves have been much greater than the production costs. As a result, comparatively little attention has needed to be paid to accounting for producing or "lifting" activities. This has changed somewhat in recent years for a number of enterprises that are involved in off-shore, frontier, heavy oil, and tarsands activities. In such activities, production costs can become a very significant element affecting the economics of production. (Because of the special characteristics of heavy oil and tarsands production, accounting practices in that segment may differ in some respects from the practices described in this chapter for conventional oil and gas production.)

Since oil and gas are finite resources, and since explorers tend to drill the best prospects first, there is an inevitable tendency for finding costs to increase as time passes. Also, since oil and gas are international commodities with an assured demand and (in the short run) an elastic supply, selling prices and ability to sell oil and gas are subject to significant variation.

Because oil and gas are nonrenewable natural resources, the industry attracts more government attention and regulation than most and in some jurisdictions may be subject to taxation beyond the taxes normally imposed on profits. Attempts to minimize the burden of tax can lead to complex business arrangements that may pose problems for fair accounting presentation.

The industry is highly capital intensive. Major risks are undertaken and costs incurred in the search for reserves. It is therefore common to conduct exploration and development projects in the form of joint ventures. In a joint venture, participants designate one party as the operator who conducts the development and operation of the property for the benefit of all participants. The operator is responsible for coordinating the work, including obtaining and paying for drilling, road construction, well servicing, and providing tangible equipment. The operator will also be responsible for billing the other participants for their shares of the development costs, operating the well once it commences production, distributing the net revenue to the respective participants, and in most cases paying royalties. Participants in joint ventures account for their share of joint venture activities as though they were their own. In essence they follow a proportionate consolidation approach (see chapter 19), rather than the equity accounting basis that is more common in most other industries.

Discovery value accounting

As already noted, the information of most relevance to the financial position and operations of an oil and gas producer concerns its producible reserves, proved and potential. If it were possible to recognize the value of reserves when discovered, there would be a much closer correlation between the economic fortunes of an enterprise and the operating results as expressed in its financial statements. However, the difficulties of such an accounting model, known as "discovery value accounting," are formidable. Experience indicates that quantities of oil and gas reserves cannot be measured with an acceptable degree of accuracy, nor can prices at which such reserves will be sold be determined until they are produced.

For a relatively few years beginning in 1979, the Securities and Exchange Commission in the United States required companies subject to its regulation to prepare data that displayed the results of operations in accordance with "reserve recognition accounting," a current value concept. This experiment lasted for a few years but was eventually dropped when it became generally accepted that the determination of reserve values was too unreliable.

As a result there appears little likelihood of any significant departure from historical cost accounting for this industry in the forseeable future. What has developed is a widespread acceptance of the need to provide supplementary information in addition to the information developed in accordance with GAAP. Such supplementary information tends to include reference to estimated physical quantities of reserves, additional detail as to the nature of finding costs, and, in some cases, certain value information with respect to reserves of oil and gas. These supplementary disclosures are more fully described later.

Accounting issues

Even given the continuation of the use of the historical cost accounting model, there are a number of accounting issues that are peculiar to the industry. These will be discussed below under the general headings of (1) accounting before commercial production, (2) accounting for production revenues and expenses, (3) capitalization of property costs and exploration and development costs, (4) depletion and depreciation, (5) impairment of unproved properties, (6) the full cost ceiling test, and (7) disclosure of supplementary information.Before these questions are addressed, however, it will be useful to describe two contrasting broad approaches to oil and gas accounting that influence the answers given to a large number of individual issues.

Successful efforts and full cost accounting contrasted

Once production begins and continuing through the primary recovery period, little exploration or development cost is required with respect to reserves being produced. (In this respect oil and gas production companies differ from mining companies.) Thus the crucial questions for oil and gas producers relate to their treatment of costs of exploration, finding, and development of reserves before production begins. The problem is to determine which costs should be written off as they are incurred and which costs may be deferred on the grounds they are applicable to reserves that have been or will be discovered and therefore should be matched with revenue from production.

Under the "successful efforts" method, exploration and development costs are classified by types of cost and then deferred or written off on the basis of two tests:

- Before results are known, the test is whether the costs are related to a capital asset.
- After results are known, the test is whether the cost outlays have been successful in finding and developing reserves. At this time, some costs previously capitalized — e.g., costs of drilling — may have to be written off.

Under a diametrically opposed accounting theory, the "full cost" theory, all costs related to exploration, no matter what their nature, and all costs of developing reserves, whether individually successful or not, are deferred as being necessary to the finding and development of the company's reserves. The only limit to this is that if the costs deferred exceed the estimated recoverable amount in respect of the reserves, the excess must be written off.

The major authoritative source on the application of successful efforts accounting is FASB Statement of Financial Accounting Standards No. 19.[1] At the time that SFAS No. 19 was issued, the FASB intended that the successful efforts method become the only acceptable method in the United States. Because of significant opposition, the standard was suspended before becoming operative except for its disclosure requirements. Nevertheless, insofar as it provides a uniform set of rules for implementing the successful efforts approach, it has received fairly broad support and acceptance, in Canada as well as in the United States. There is no comparable Canadian pronouncement as yet.

At the time of the suspension of SFAS No. 19, the SEC introduced Rule 4-10 into its Regulation S-X with which registrants subject to the regulation of the SEC must comply.[2] Rule 4-10 includes a methodology for the application of both successful efforts and full cost accounting rules. The successful efforts rules are compatible with those set out by the FASB. The full cost rules did not have any counterpart in existing accounting standards. The SEC methodology gained fairly broad acceptance in both Canada and the United States, although there are many variations in the way those rules are applied by enterprises not subject to SEC regulation. In 1986, the Accounting Standards Steering Committee of the Canadian Institute of Chartered Accountants authorized an accounting guideline that sets out a recommended methodology for the application of full cost accounting in Canada.[3] It must be remembered, however, that a guideline does not have the same authority as that carried by accounting recommendations included in Volume I of the *CICA Handbook*.

The successful efforts approach is inherently conservative. During the exploration stage and the development stage before results are known, all costs incurred are written off unless they can be associated with what are conventionally regarded as capital assets — property or property rights, a well, a structure, or tangible equipment. After drilling results are known, costs previously carried forward are subjected to a second hurdle — they must be seen to be clearly associated with producible reserves, or else they are written off. The application of this test requires interpretation of what costs are reasonably associated with the reserves and thus opens the way to further debate.

It can be argued that the first-stage test is inherently illogical. All costs incurred are expended with the objective of finding reserves. If reserves are not found, the wells drilled and the property rights are worthless, just as much as the geological and geophysical or other expenditures. In this situation, the traditional distinction between a capital expenditure and a revenue expenditure is irrelevant in economic terms. If the successful efforts method were true to its own logic, it would write off all costs incurred before results in terms of producible reserves are evaluated and (perhaps) at that time would retroactively capitalize the costs that could then be identified as having been successful in finding reserves.

The full cost method, in contrast, can be regarded as nonjudgmental. If costs are incurred for the purpose of finding and developing reserves, they are all to be carried forward equally. There is no limit to the carryforward except the ceiling value limit. The full cost method is criticized precisely because it is nonjudgmental. Because of this, it is said, costs may be carried forward even if current efforts are disastrously unsuccessful, so long as the accumulated deferred costs do not exceed the value ceiling. (As will be seen later, the application of the ceiling test itself is not without problems.) In addition, the full cost method does not identify costs with geologically differentiated areas of interest. Instead, it accumulates costs by large "cost centres" — such as a country as a whole. As a result, when it comes to writing off deferred costs against production revenues, the amount written off may represent an average of high cost and low cost reserves that bears little necessary relation to the cost of the reserves actually being produced.

It is possible to wonder why people become so exercised about the merits of one of these methods as against the other. The fact is that the criticisms of both methods are justified, and, beyond this, both methods produce irrelevant information. The information that matters is the physical quantities and qualities of the reserves, where they are situated, the extent to which they have been consumed and replenished over a reporting period, and some indication of their value. As we have seen, value estimates are considered too unreliable to be included in financial reports, but the desirability of providing information on reserve quantity estimates is increasingly recognized.

Perhaps the most that can be said in choosing between the two methods is that probably the amount carried forward as deferred cost in the balance sheet under the full cost method is closer, most of the time, to the value of the underlying reserves than the amount carried forward under the successful efforts method. (Considering the variation possible in the circumstances of individual companies, that is not saying very much.)

In the course of the controversy in the 1970s over which method should be adopted to the exclusion of the other, some concern was expressed that prohibition of the full cost method would have the result of hindering the raising of capital by smaller companies engaged in exploration and thereby would reduce the extent of exploration and the ability of companies to explore in more costly and riskier areas. Research on this question has produced some conflicting results. The FASB concluded, however, that restriction of accounting methods to the successful efforts method should not significantly affect the ability of companies to raise capital for exploration.[4] If this is so, as it may be, it raises the question why it is necessary to make a choice between the two methods. Beyond this, it raises the more fundamental question whether the problem could be solved by departing from the income accounting model in financial reporting for oil and gas producers, since it is that model that forces a decision on the question of method of write-off of exploration and development costs.

Accounting before commercial production

Since reserves must be found (or purchased) before production can take place, exploration is a major activity of most companies. For some, it may be the sole activity, and, if relatively unsuccessful, the company may never emerge from the preoperating stage.

Since companies in the preoperating stage have virtually no revenue, the ordinary accounting rules for revenue recognition and cost matching are simply inapplicable. The important questions for these companies are:

- To what extent should costs be deferred when incurred, and if deferred, at what point must they be written off?
- How should costs incurred be classified and described in the financial statements?
- When and on what basis does a company make the transition from accounting as a pure exploration enterprise to accounting as a producing enterprise or perhaps a mixed producing and exploration company?

Since all costs of a pure exploration company are incurred in the hope of gain and since there is no substantial revenue against which costs may be written off, it is standard practice to defer all costs initially, including general and administrative costs. Sundry income, such as interest earned on temporary investment of cash, is credited against the deferred costs. On this basis of accounting, there is no profit or loss account, but a statement of cash or cash-equivalent flows will show the flow of funds provided by the shareholders and others through to their use in the exploration program.

When the full cost approach is used (if the CICA guideline is followed), the net costs capitalized will be classified as between unproved properties, proved properties, and other costs. In mining exploration companies, costs identified with mining properties or claims are capitalized separately, while remaining costs are customarily lumped into one figure of preproduction costs for purposes of balance sheet display. Customarily, an exhibit is provided showing a breakdown of these costs according to their nature, analyzed by the several geographical areas in which the company is carrying on exploration.

In principle, the recoverability of costs deferred should be kept under regular review, and if considered unlikely to be recovered in future, they should be written off. That determination may be hard to make. If the likelihood of full recovery is uncertain, but loss is not recognized because the uncertainty is too great to allow reasonable determination of its amount, that uncertainty should be disclosed.[5] In mining exploration companies, the lapse or abandonment of claims will require a write-off of deferred property costs and any related costs of exploration associated with those properties. Not infrequently, exploration and other deferred costs should be written off before then if work has ceased, even though the claims are being kept in good standing on a speculative basis.

Preproduction stage accounting comes to an end when "commercial production" is achieved. In an oil and gas company that point will be reasonably clearly identifiable with respect to any particular reservoir or field. In a mining company, it may take some time from the beginning of ore extraction to the attainment of reasonable levels of production, so that the date of commercial production may be less clear-cut. Nevertheless, it will usually be apparent that the start date of commercial production falls within a reasonably restricted period of time. For accounting purposes, the significance of the date is: before commercial production, any sales proceeds are credited against accumulated deferred preproduction costs; after profit and loss accounting begins, revenue is recognized in the normal fashion, and it becomes necessary to begin amortization of the accumulated preproduction costs.

In order to begin amortization of preproduction costs against revenue, it is necessary to separate the costs incurred and deferred to date between those applicable to the project from which commercial production is being derived and those applicable to other projects still in the exploratory or development stage. There is little problem in doing this in the mining industry, since exploration and development efforts tend to be localized so that those applicable to an eventual producing mine can be fairly readily identified. The situation is different in the oil and gas industry. Some exploration costs may relate to a very large territory, so that there is a real practical question whether all preproduction costs should be regarded as applicable to the commercial production from the first commercial field, or whether some could reasonably continue to be deferred as a contribution to future potential recoveries.

Under the full cost accounting method, it has been decided that the boundaries of the "cost centres" used for accounting purposes shall be geographical country boundaries.[6] That means that the first time commercial production is reached within a country, amortization must begin of all the costs incurred in that country except those that are related to unproved properties (and with a further exception covered in the description of depletion below).

In contrast, under the successful efforts method of accounting the cost centre used is the individual property or an aggregation of properties covering a single reservoir or field. Whichever of these is adopted, the cost centre is much smaller than a whole country. In addition, under successful efforts accounting costs that cannot be identified with a capital asset, such as a property or a well, are written off when incurred. Thus, if a Canadian company were to adopt successful efforts accounting upon attaining commercial production, it would be faced with an immediate write-off of a very large portion of its preproduction costs. One may speculate, then, that a Canadian company is likely to adopt full cost accounting when it first emerges from the preproduction stage, adopting the successful efforts method, if ever, only much later after it has achieved significant success and growth. (In the United States, it may be noted, a company does not have the option of a separate basis of accounting in the preproduction period. It adopts either full cost accounting or successful efforts accounting from the first.)

The foregoing suggests one general observation. The larger a company is and the longer its record of past success, the more conservative its accounting methods are likely to be. Larger, long-established oil and gas production companies are likely to follow successful efforts accounting rather than full cost accounting. A somewhat similar phenomenon is found in the mining industry. A well-established producing mining company is likely to write off exploration expenses as it goes, treating them as a recurring cost of maintaining its business, and tends to defer property development costs only with respect to major projects that have received the green light to proceed to production.

Accounting for production

Apart from the problem of accounting for amortization of deferred costs of exploration and development (to be discussed in the next section), accounting for production revenues and expenses does not present serious problems and is not greatly different in its essentials from the accounting for any other industry producing a tangible product. The following paragraphs discuss a few questions peculiar to the oil and gas production industry.

Royalties and royalty interests. Holders of royalty interests in reserves that an enterprise has the right to produce have a legal entitlement to a share of those reserves. Commonly, this takes the form of an interest in the proceeds from the sale of production, and this is remitted to the royalty holder. The usual accounting for such payments of royalties is to net the royalties against the gross production and report only the net amount of production.

Royalty interests may vary for a number of reasons. Crown royalties typically are payable on a sliding scale with higher quantities of production. In the case of many royalty agreements, royalty percentages may increase or decrease depending on whether a royalty holder or a working interest holder has reached "payout," as determined by the terms of the agreements. The changing amounts of royalty are normally accounted for as they occur. A variation that would be sound in theory but difficult in practice would be to anticipate the total eventual royalty payments and to amortize them over the life of related production so that each unit of production might bear the same royalty burden. Because of the difficulties in forecasting production and future prices, such a refinement is seldom carried out in practice.

"Take-or-pay" receipts. It is not uncommon for gas sales contracts to contain a provision requiring that the purchaser take a certain minimum quantity of gas each year if not prevented by circumstances beyond its control and if the gas is available for delivery. If the purchasing company should fail to take the minimum quantity, it is nevertheless required to pay for that quantity at the current contract price. Usually, it is permitted to recoup the deficiency out of deliveries that exceed the minimum quantity in a subsequent period or periods. However, if the contract price should increase in the meantime, through an escalation clause or otherwise, the purchaser is frequently required to pay the difference between the price prevailing in the period when the minimum quantity was not taken and the price prevailing in the period (or periods) when the deficiency is made up.

Most companies treat the working-interest fraction of deficiency payments received (or receivable, depending upon the basis of accounting for gas sales) as unearned revenue, pending make-up or forfeiture by the purchaser. The cost of any make-up gas will not emerge until the later period when make-up occurs. Deferment of the credit is necessary to match the revenue with the costs incurred in its generation. If at a later date the purchaser loses its option to take delivery without further payment, the deferred amount is taken into income at that time. Until that time the amount received is more in the nature of a deposit.

The balance sheet classification of that portion of the take-or-pay deposit to be extinguished in the next year must be resolved. The *CICA Handbook* states that liabilities that will be settled from other than current assets should be excluded from the current liability classification. The liability created through gas prepayments is to be settled from future production from oil and gas properties, which is not a current asset. Therefore an argument can be made that the prepayments should remain classified as a long-term liability. Practice to date has been mixed, but most companies appear to be classifying the amounts due in the next fiscal year as current liabilities.

Inventory valuation. Oil and gas companies involved only in exploration and production generally sell at the wellhead. Thus they often do not own inventories of crude oil or refined products. If products are still owned beyond the wellhead, however, there can be a costing problem. Production from each different structure has its own qualities and production costs. However, after entering the pipeline crude oil is combined with crude from other fields, making it impossible to trace the cost of a specific barrel. Because of this difficulty, crude may be valued at the lower of average cost and net realizable value.

Crude may also be valued at net realizable value when production is guaranteed a fixed price. Such was sometimes the case prior to deregulation in Canada. At that time, production in Alberta from both freehold and crown lands was regulated by the Alberta Energy Resources Conservation Board, and prices were set by the Alberta Petroleum Marketing Commission. Since deregulation, this basis of inventory valuation is no longer possible.

For an integrated oil company, inventories of crude oil retained in the business for refining purposes are generally recorded at the lower of cost and net realizable value. Costs included in inventory valuations generally include those costs associated with the production and manufacturing or purchase of products, as well as transportation costs and government taxes or charges levied at the wellhead, refinery gate, or some other point in the production process. In practice, crude is often "sold" from the "upstream" component of the business to the "downstream" component. Accordingly, an adjustment to consolidated inventory values is required to restate that portion of inventory to cost and eliminate the unrealized profit included in the transfer price.

Linefill. Because a minimum quantity of product must be maintained in a pipeline, the initial production from a field connected to a new pipeline is referred to as linefill and capitalized as a fixed asset, not treated as inventory. Until discontinuance of use of the pipeline, an equivalent amount of product will continue to be so classified, valued at the original cost unless crude oil prices fall and it is written down to net realizable value.

Abandonment costs. Costs of the eventual abandonment of an operation that must be borne by the enterprise should be provided for on some rational basis in the producing period. (See chapter 9.) Costs of abandoning conventional wells are normally not provided in advance of the abandonment because such costs are usually not significant. In the case of off-shore wells and gas plants, however, abandonment costs may be significant.

In such cases, two practices exist. On the one hand, abandonment costs may be accrued over the life of the project by recording an accrued liability with an offsetting charge to operations. On the other hand, estimates of abandonment costs may be added to the total of incurred costs subject to depletion with the result that depletion expense is increased accordingly. This latter method is required under SEC Rule 4-10.

Enhanced oil recovery. The rapid escalation of oil prices in the 1970s and the high price of oil in relation to natural gas and natural gas liquids provided an incentive to undertake enhanced oil recovery projects. These projects involve the injection of fluids and/or natural gas into a crude oil reservoir to increase the recovery rate of oil in place. It is usually anticipated that the injected fluids or natural gas will for the most part be recovered.

As the objective of engaging in such activity is to increase the total value of reserves to be recovered, an argument may be made that the costs of injection should be capitalized and classified as fixed assets in the financial statements. These capitalized costs would then be written off on the unit-of-production basis, using production data and total estimated reserves of crude oil plus reserves related to the natural gas or natural gas liquids injected. Consistent with this view, full cost companies usually capitalize the cost of injected substances, although operating costs of injection facilities are usually treated as production expenses.

In contrast, many companies using successful efforts accounting charge costs of injected fluids to expense, in effect treating them as an additional cost of current production. This is particularly true for fluids injected in pilot projects. All the authorities prohibit taking into account reserves that are expected to be added through enhanced recovery until actual test results confirm the success of the enhancement program. It is consistent with this conservative outlook to write off program costs incurred, at least during that period.

Accounting for government assistance. Difficulties can be encountered when an attempt is made to account for government assistance in accordance with the principles described in chapter 14, because the form of the assistance may be different from its substance. For example, royalty reductions are often negotiated on a project-by-project basis for enhanced oil recovery projects. Are such reductions to be reflected in current income as a reduction of royalties in accordance with the legal form, or do they represent government grants in aid of a specific project? To date, the most common accounting for such reductions is to reflect them in income as reduced royalties, rather than crediting them against the cost of the recovery projects. One reason for doing so is that the actual amount of total government assistance becomes determinable only as a result of future production.

Sales of interests in production. Owners of oil and gas interests sometimes enter into arrangements whereby they sell rights to proceeds from production for a limited period of time. Such arrangements are described as the sale of a reversionary working interest or a "carve-out." The normal carve-out transaction is structured as a disposition of a property interest for income tax purposes. Because of guarantees, however, under the typical arrangement substantially all of the usual risks of production remain with the vendor. Such a transaction is more in the nature of a financing than a disposition of a property right, and practice has been to account for it as such.

Capitalization of property costs and exploration and development costs

The difference between successful efforts and full cost accounting in the treatment of exploration and development costs incurred has already been noted. Typical practices under the successful efforts approach are described below:

- Costs of exploration or drilling rights, including lease bonuses, legal costs, etc., are usually capitalized as representing a capital asset.
- Costs of land and leasing departments, carrying charges such as delay rentals, shut-in royalties, etc., are usually written off on the grounds that they do not add value to the capital asset.
- Costs of exploration work may be expensed in total as giving rise to no tangible capital asset, or part may be deferred where the costs relate to, or lead to, the acquisition of land rights.
- Costs of drilling wells are capitalized if the well is a producer, and not if it is a dry hole.

Practices of individual companies following the successful efforts accounting approach may vary considerably in detail — for example:

- Geological and geophysical costs may be entirely expensed, or some may be deferred if they can be identified with specific properties (particularly if the work is done by outside contractors).
- Some, but not all, companies will amortize acquisition costs capitalized with

respect to undeveloped properties on the grounds that some part of the properties will ultimately prove to be nonproductive.

- Some companies will capitalize the cost of dry holes if they are drilled as development wells to outline a known producing area. Others will expense the costs of all dry holes.
- The cost centre adopted for capitalization may vary. If the individual lease is used, all costs of nonproducing leases will be written off when drilling results are known and the property is abandoned. But if the cost centre is defined more broadly as a lease block, a field, or a wider area of interest, a greater amount of costs will be carried forward as associated with productive properties.

In contrast, under the full cost method all costs associated with property acquisition, exploration, and development are capitalized. Care must be taken to ensure that such costs do not include any ordinary production costs or general overhead. Overhead directly related to exploration and development activity, however, may be capitalized. Interest also may be capitalized with respect to unproved properties and major development projects, so long as their costs are not being depreciated or depleted.

Property acquired for shares. Companies often acquire properties that have no tax basis in exchange for shares. The result is that a certain portion of such a company's future depletion expense will not be deductible for income tax purposes. In accounting for such transactions, companies must be careful to value the properties and shares at an amount that properly reflects the lack of future tax deductibility.

Farmins/farmouts. Often risks are shared and financing obtained through an arrangement by which a "farmee" earns an interest in certain properties in consideration for undertaking work on the properties. These arrangements are called farmouts to the party giving up the interest and farmins to the party earning the interest. Although it could be argued that such a disposition or acquisition should be accounted for on the basis of the fair value of the interest given up or acquired at the time of the transaction, this is not normally done because of the difficulty in arriving at reliable values.

Such transactions are ignored at the date of the agreement. As costs are incurred by the farmee, those costs are accounted for according to their nature even though conceptually they represent the cost of acquiring an interest in a property. For example, a farmee earning an interest of, say, ten percent in a particular property by virtue of incurring certain seismic costs would account for the expenditure as a seismic cost, rather than as a cost of the property. Depending on the accounting method followed (that is, either successful efforts or full cost) seismic costs would either be capitalized or written off as incurred.

Unitization. Often, in the interests of economy, the operation of a number of wells in an area will be "unitized." Under such an arrangement, working and royalty interest holders in a number of leases within a particular area pool their respective interests to form a single operating unit. The result is that each owner ceases to have an interest in production from a particular lease but instead assumes an interest in production of the whole unit.

Normally, no gain or loss will be recognized by any of the participants at the time of the unitization agreement. However, since the participants' properties usually have various values and are in various stages of development, cash equalization payments will be made by some participants to others in order to equalize the investments of each party. In these circumstances, the cash paid is normally recorded as an additional investment in the unitized property, and cash received is normally reflected as a recovery of costs applicable to the project.

Depletion and depreciation (D&D)

Depletion is the method used to distribute the cost of capitalized oil and gas assets, less salvage value if any, over the estimated useful life of the assets in a systematic and rational manner. Whatever the basis upon which costs are capitalized, i.e., full cost or successful efforts, the costs must subsequently be written off against production revenues. Apart from the cost of tangible fixed assets, which may be written off by normal depreciation methods, the customary practice is to deplete costs on a unit-of-production basis. The depletion rate is subject to recomputation regularly as new costs are incurred, impairment in the value of properties is recognized, abandonment or sales occur, reserves are added, or previous reserve estimates are revised.

Under the successful efforts accounting basis, costs deferred at any time consist only of property costs and development costs that can be associated with individual properties. Depletion may be computed at individual rates developed property by property or on the basis of some reasonable aggregation of properties with a common geological feature or stratigraphic condition, such as a reservoir or a field. Normally the depletion rate on the unit-of-production method is calculated by dividing the total of costs incurred to date plus estimated costs for future development by the total of proved reserves. Sometimes, however, the depletion rate is based on proved *developed* reserves only, in which case it is appropriate to omit from the calculation the estimated future expenditures required to bring proved undeveloped reserves into production.

Under the full cost accounting basis, one depletion rate is calculated for each cost centre, and as noted a company has only one cost centre for each country. Thus the basis of the depletion calculation, in essence, consists of figures for total proved reserves in the country and total deferred property acquisition, exploration, and development costs for the country with two possible exclusions. Those exclusions are:

- all costs associated with the acquisition and evaluation of unproved properties
  - acquisition costs
  - geological and geophysical costs
  - carrying costs
  - drilling costs
  - capitalized interest, and
  - capitalized general and administrative costs; and
- costs incurred in connection with major development projects, such as offshore drilling platforms required to permit further drilling to ascertain the quantities of proved reserves attributable to the properties under development.

Continued exclusion of the foregoing costs from the depletion calculation is subject to the following conditions:

- inability to assign proved reserves to the properties
- the existence of exploration and development plans that are in progress or firmly planned for the near future
- an assessment that impairment in the value of the properties has not occurred.

Once proved reserves are established, there is no further justification for continued exclusion of costs from the depletion calculation, even if other factors prevent immediate production or marketing of reserves. However, costs of major development projects are permitted to continue to be excluded until a portion of the related property becomes capable of production.

The depletion method. Capitalized costs are most often depleted by the unit-of-production method. Prior to 1985, when economic circumstances in Canada warranted, depletion for a period could be based on the relationship of actual revenue for the period to the total of actual revenue and estimated future net revenue from proved reserves of oil and gas. This method was known as "revenue depletion." As a result of the deregulation of crude oil pricing in 1985 and a similar government proposal with respect to natural gas pricing, sufficient assurance of future revenues to permit the use of revenue depletion will rarely be present.

Under the unit-of-production method, costs are depleted based upon the relationship of actual quantities of oil and gas produced to total estimated quantities of proved reserves of oil and gas. Natural gas and condensate reserves are normally converted into a common oil-equivalent unit according to either their approximate relative energy content or their relative value based on current prices.

Costs to be depleted. Costs to be depleted on the unit-of-production basis using proved oil and gas reserves include:

- all capitalized costs in productive cost centres, less accumulated depletion (which may exclude, under the full cost method, costs of certain investments in unproved properties and major development projects, as explained earlier)
- estimated future expenditures, based on current prices, required to bring into production those proved undeveloped reserves that have been included in the depletion calculation
- estimated dismantlement and abandonment costs, net of estimated salvage values.

Both the estimated future development costs and estimated proved reserves included as components of the depletion calculation should reflect the costs and reserves related to the development method most likely to be adopted by the enterprise.

The reserve calculation is based on actual production for the period, expressed, in principle, as a proportion of proved reserves at the end of the period plus production for the period. As a practical matter it may be based upon the figure for proved reserves at the beginning of the period adjusted for major changes in estimates subsequently. The standards call for the calculation to be made on a consolidated basis. There seems to be a difference between SEC requirements and the CICA guideline with respect to the treatment of depletion in the figure of income from investees accounted for on the equity method. The SEC requires equity-accounted investees to be taken into account separately; the CICA guideline in effect requires a calculation of depletion for purposes of recording the investor's share of the investee's income as though the investee had been consolidated.

Related matters. Under both the full cost and successful efforts methods, it may be more appropriate to depreciate natural gas processing plants and similar tangible assets by a method other than the unit-of-production method, e.g., based on their estimated economic or useful physical life.

Property disposals

Under successful efforts accounting, sales of property are recognized in the same fashion as in any other industry, involving write-off of the carrying value of the property and recognition of gain or loss, so long as the sale is straightforward. However, as touched on earlier, if conveyances of property leave substantial risks with the vendor, are merely part of a plan for pooling of risks, or in other respects depart from unconditional dispositions, it is appropriate, depending on the particular situation, to (1) defer recognition of gain or loss, (2) defer recognition of gain only, or (3) treat the transaction as a financing rather than as a property sale.

When unproved property is surrendered or abandoned, capitalized costs should be written off against the related allowance for impairment (see below). To the extent the previous allowance for impairment is inadequate, loss is recognized. However, if only one individual well or item of equipment, or only one lease out of a group constituting the amortization base, is abandoned or retired, the cost is written off to accumulated depreciation or amortization, subject to the possibility that some abnormal event that causes the retirement indicates that loss should be recognized.

Under the full cost method, in contrast, proceeds from disposals of proved properties are normally simply credited to the pool of capitalized costs subject to D&D. The CICA guideline suggests an exception when the credit of proceeds to the pool would cause a change of twenty percent or more in the amortization rate. In such a case an allocation is to be made of the net book value of properties in the pool between the properties sold and the properties retained, based on valuations of each arrived at by estimating future net revenue for each and discounting it at ten percent. Gain or loss on the disposal is recognized by matching the calculated net book value of the property disposed of with the proceeds. Proceeds from disposal of unproved properties are normally also credited to the pool of costs subject to D&D and the book value of the properties is at the same time transferred into the pool. Again, the guideline suggests an exception if this accounting would alter the D&D rate by twenty percent or more. Gain or loss is recognized by allocating the balance of the pool (including the net book value of unproved properties transferred into it) between properties sold and properties retained based on the ratio of net sales proceeds to the sum of the estimated discounted future net revenue from the properties retained and the net proceeds from the sale. This description, based upon the CICA guideline, differs in points of detail from SEC guidance.[7]

Royalty interests received as sales consideration. A common business transaction in the industry is to sell certain properties but to retain a royalty interest in the properties sold. Normally, such royalty interests are not valued because of the difficulty of forecasting future production and prices. Consequently, related royalty income is usually recorded only as the royalty holder becomes entitled to receive its share of production proceeds following production.

Impairment of unproved properties

Unproved properties and costs incurred in connection with major development projects that are excluded from costs subject to depletion under full cost accounting should be regularly assessed to determine whether or not it is still appropriate to continue to carry the costs related to the property at their book value. If the results of the determination indicate that there has been an impairment in value, the amount of the impairment should be written off under successful efforts accounting and transferred to costs subject to depletion under full cost accounting. In the latter situation, costs transferred to costs subject to depletion become subject to the ceiling-test limitation.

There are several indications of an impairment in the value of the property:

- A dry hole has been drilled.
- Management has no firm plans to continue drilling.
- An inability to fund further exploration or development is apparent.
- Negative geological and geophysical findings are present either in the property or in nearby properties.
- The time frame to expiration of the right or licence to complete exploration or drilling activities is foreshortened.
- Other economic, financial, and management constraints exist that indicate the value has been impaired.

Exploration in frontier areas tends to require sophisticated and very expensive technology. As well, it is likely to be very expensive to provide facilities for production of reserves discovered and for their transportation to market. In these circumstances, assessment of impairment is both important and very difficult.

The full cost ceiling test

The full cost accounting method requires capitalization of all costs directly associated with exploration and development, whether successful or not. Inevitably costs are capitalized that do not increase the future revenues expected to be generated by the company. Because of this and because of variations in revenue prospects, it is possible that from time to time costs accumulated in the accounts may exceed expected future revenues. Accordingly, it is necessary to consider the need for a ceiling on costs deferred with respect to proved reserves, as well as the need to recognize impairment in value of unproved properties.

The manner of application of the ceiling test has been subject to considerable debate. As chapter 17 has indicated, GAAP is far from consistent in its approach to recognition of loss with respect to assets owned. Assets classified as current are subject to a ceiling value of current market value or net realizable value at the reporting date. Assets classified as long-term are written down only if the loss in value is considered to be other than temporary, and then it is not entirely clear whether the write-down should be to a "recoverable value" without discounting or to an estimate of economic value that requires discounting of future net revenues or proceeds.

The 1986 CICA guideline takes the position that the ceiling test for an oil or gas producer should be a cost recovery test, not an estimate of current fair market value.[8] In certain aspects, however — notably the use of current prices which may be depressed and the consideration given to future financing costs — it can be regarded as more conservative than the traditional recoverable value test recognizing long-term impairment. The use of a more tightly defined ceiling test in the CICA guideline is fully understandable in view of the extreme difficulty of judging long-term recoverable values or judging whether impairment is likely to be more than temporary.

The ceiling test is in two parts. The first part applies to costs carried forward, cost centre by cost centre, while the second part looks to the viability of the enterprise as a whole. Features of the first part of the test are as follows:

- Prices used in estimating future recoveries from proved reserves are based on prices current at the measurement date (subject to the effect of firm contractual commitments or regulation of prices). To avoid the effect of a very temporary price fluctuation, however, an enterprise is entitled to use average prices over a period up to twelve months ending on any of (1) the balance sheet date, (2) the date of public announcement of earnings, or (3) the date of issue of the financial statements. If an enterprise chooses to use such an average price, it must disclose what write-off would have been required if it had used the price prevailing at the balance sheet date.
- In connection with unproved properties and with major development projects excluded in the calculation of D&D, recovery may be assumed at their cost figures less allowance for impairment.

If costs deferred in a cost centre exceed the sum of net recoverable amounts calculated on the above bases, a write-off is to be made. That write-off is not reversed subsequently even though estimated values may recover. Such a write-off is to be reported as additional D&D, but disclosure of any material write-off as an unusual item may be necessary.

The second part of the test builds upon the estimates used in the first. Net recoverable amounts from proved reserves in all cost centres are estimated similarly (that is, based on net future revenues estimated at current price and cost levels), and to this is added the net costs of unproved properties and major development projects after deduction of an allowance for impairment. A deduction is also made for general and administrative costs (at current cost levels), and foreseeable financing costs and income taxes over the production period for the reserves being valued. Estimates of future financing costs are based on existing debt obligations, capital lease obligations, and preferred shares with characteristics (such as cumulative dividends and retraction provisions) that make them more like debt. To calculate the net interest obligation over the period, it is necessary to project the extent to which debt may be retired out of net cash flow within the period or the extent to which interest may be offset by earnings on net cash flow. Additional borrowing must be assumed if net cash flow is expected to be negative for a period. It is necessary to make allocations of financing costs in those cases in which proceeds of existing borrowing were used for activities other than oil or gas production.

The test is to be made on a consolidated basis. If there is an excess of recoverable value over costs deferred in a subsidiary and that subsidiary has a minority interest, the portion of the excess attributed to the minority interest should be excluded from the consolidated deficiency as otherwise calculated.

It is conceivable that a significant acquisition of proved oil and gas reserves might be made in which the recoverable amount determined under the foregoing rules is less than the acquisition cost. It seems likely that such a situation would be based on an expectation that a deficiency in estimated current recoverable value does not represent permanent impairment in value. If such can be shown, no write-off need be made under the ceiling test with respect to that acquisition for a period up to twenty-four months from the date of acquisition.

If a further write-off is required under this enterprise ceiling test, it also would be characterized as additional D&D. This write-off also would not be reversed subsequently if values recover. Since the write-off is based on after-tax figures, for purposes of balance sheet presentation it would be grossed up and used to adjust both the net book value of the oil and gas properties and any related deferred income taxes. The write-off would be allocated to cost centres on a judgmental basis.

This two-part ceiling test is different in some respects and somewhat more complex than that required by the SEC.[9] It is also possible to question if the second part of the test is completely logical. Consider a situation in which the net revenues calculated for all cost centres under the first part of the test are just sufficient to cover estimated future general and administrative, financing, and income tax costs. As a result, under the second part of the test, nothing is left over to cover costs deferred with respect to producing properties, and a complete write-off is indicated. But this seems overly severe. The estimate shows that the properties can produce some net operating cash flow before financing costs. Therefore they have *some* value (even apart from the possibility of a recovery in prices in future that is not factored into the calculation). In this situation, the more customary valuation approach of discounting estimated future net operating cash flows would provide a better indicator of value than does the second part of the test.

Disclosure of supplementary information

Because of the limitations of historical cost accounting and the divergence of practice within the industry, it has generally been felt that supplementary disclosure of information related to oil and gas operations and reserve estimates should be made. In the U.S., SFAS No. 69, requires disclosure of information as follows.[10]

Capitalized costs. The aggregate capitalized costs relating to an enterprise's oil and gas producing activities and the aggregate related accumulated depreciation, depletion, amortization, and valuation allowances shall be disclosed as of the end of the year. If significant, capitalized costs of unproved properties shall be separately disclosed. Capitalized costs of support equipment and facilities may be disclosed separately or included, as appropriate, with capitalized costs of proved and unproved properties.

Costs incurred. Each of the following types of costs incurred for the year shall be disclosed (whether those costs are capitalized or charged to expense at the time they are incurred):

- Property acquisition costs
- Exploration costs
- Development costs.

Results of operations. The results of operations for oil and gas producing activities shall be disclosed for the year. That information shall be disclosed in the aggregate and for each geographic area for which reserve quantities are disclosed.

Reserve quantity information. Net quantities of an enterprise's interests in proved developed reserves of (1) crude oil (including condensate and natural gas liquids) and (2) natural gas shall be disclosed at the beginning and end of the year. Changes in net quantities over the year are to be analyzed to indicate their source — discoveries, production, revisions in estimates, purchases or sales of reserves in place, and so on.

Standardized measure of discounted future net cash flows. A standardized measure as of the end of the year of discounted future net cash flows shall be disclosed. These estimated cash flows relate to an enterprise's interests in (1) proved oil and gas reserves and (2) oil and gas subject to purchase under long-term supply, purchase, or similar agreements and contracts in which the enterprise participates in the operation of the properties wherein the oil or gas is located or otherwise serves as the producer of those reserves. The standardized measure of discounted future net cash flows relating to these two types of interest in reserves may be combined for reporting purposes. The information shall be disclosed in the aggregate and for each geographic area for which reserve quantities are disclosed.

Enterprises shall disclose the total change in the standardized measure of discounted future net cash flows for the year. If individually significant, they shall present such changes relating to proved oil and gas reserves resulting from the following factors separately for the year:

- Net change in sales and transfer prices and in production (lifting) costs related to future production
- Changes in estimated future development costs
- Net change due to extensions, discoveries, and improved recovery
- Net change due to purchases and sales of minerals in place
- Net change due to revisions in quantity estimates
- Previously estimated development costs incurred during the period
- Accretion of discount
- Other — unspecified
- Net change in income taxes.

The CICA guideline recommends the following disclosures, for enterprises using the full cost method:

- Interest and general and administrative costs capitalized during the period
- Costs at the balance sheet date excluded from costs subject to D&D together with comparative amounts for the previous year

- The method used in converting gas and oil to a common unit of measure for purposes of calculating D&D
- Whether D&D was calculated using gross or net (i.e., before or after royalties) figures
- Prices used for the ceiling test.

The guideline indicates that additional disclosure is desirable. It suggests, however, that disclosure of reserve-based information should be considered supplementary, rather than part of basic financial reporting.

Summary

The oil and gas production industry is an industry whose financial performance is not well portrayed by traditional historical cost accounting. The basic reason for this is that the cost of the industry's most important asset — its reserves of oil and gas — is often not a good surrogate for the value of the asset, even at the time the reserves are discovered. The success of exploration activity cannot be predicted before it is undertaken, and the reserves discovered may be worth considerably more or less than the costs incurred to find and develop them.

Short of the adoption of full-scale current value accounting, the obvious way to improve this situation would be to value reserves discovered at their estimated worth at the time when they first become capable of estimation, writing off costs applicable to the reserves evaluated at that time, and deferring other costs whose outcome in terms of reserves discovered is not yet capable of evaluation. Such a basis of accounting could, in theory, provide a far better measure of enterprise performance in the crucial aspect of reserve discovery. It would also result in a more relevant balance sheet portrayal of assets.

A current value accounting approach was required for a few years as supplemental information by companies subject to the SEC requirements. It was concluded after this experience that the information was too unreliable to be useful. The requirement to present the information was abandoned, to be replaced by expanded disclosure of estimated quantities of proved oil and gas reserves and a standardized calculation of the present value of estimated future net revenues, together with an analysis of changes in that net present value over the reporting period. These data do not purport to be current value information since somewhat arbitrary bases are adopted for the present value calculation. Nevertheless, it is considered that such a common benchmark calculation has value for comparative purposes.

The adoption of supplemental disclosure requirements does not settle the question of the accounting procedures to be adopted for the basic financial report. Under traditional historical cost accounting, two sharply different methods evolved for dealing with costs of exploring for and developing reserves. The successful efforts approach follows familiar accounting procedures whereby costs capitalized are restricted to those that can be associated with a recognizable cost object, such as land rights, structures, or equipment. On this basis, substantial amounts of exploration costs have to be written off when incurred. In contrast, the full cost approach adopts the fundamental premise that the cost object consists of the reserves to be discovered, and that all exploration and development costs can be deemed to be costs of those eventual reserves, even if they consist of the cost of drilling dry holes, since the nature of the business is speculative. Not all bets pay off, but by placing a spread of bets the chances of success are greatly improved.

Both methods are subject to the fatal flaw that they do not measure the real success of an enterprise in finding reserves. Accordingly, both are easy targets for criticism, and it is virtually impossible to persuade adherents of one method of the superiority of the other method. The present state of accounting standards is that both approaches are accepted. Standard-setters have confined themselves to prescribing detailed procedures for the application of each method — a necessary development in view of the diverse methods of application that grew up in practice. Important aspects of the standards described in this chapter include: (1) determination of which costs may be capitalized and which must be expensed at the time they are incurred, (2) determination of a basis for defining a cost centre for the purpose of the depletion calculation, (3) prescribing the basis of depletion calculation, (4) prescribing rules for recognition of impairment of unproved property costs, and (5) prescribing rules for determining ceiling values for costs carried forward.

The standards are necessarily highly arbitrary. It may well be argued that figures of income based on such diverse and arbitrary rules for the treatment of costs have no value. Data restricted to showing the excess of production revenues over lifting costs, general and administrative expense, and financial expenses, together with supplementary information on reserve quantities and expenditures on exploration and development, probably contain all the relevant information that it is possible to produce. Unfortunately, such a restricted basis of accounting cannot easily be combined in the financial reports of enterprises with activities other than oil and gas production that must report a conventional income figure.

References

[1]FASB, *Financial Accounting and Reporting by Oil and Gas Producing Companies,* Statement of Financial Accounting Standards No. 19 (Stamford: FASB, 1977).

[2]"Financial Accounting and Reporting for Oil and Gas Producing Activities Pursuant to the Federal Securities Laws and the Energy Policy and Conservation Act of 1975," Rule 4-10, *Form and Content of and Requirements for Financial Statements,* Regulation S-X, 17 CFR Part 210.

[3]CICA Accounting Guideline, "Full Cost Accounting in the Oil and Gas Industry," August 1986, *CICA Handbook* (Toronto: CICA).

[4]See FASB, *Oil and Gas Producing Companies,* pars. 157-74.

[5]CICA Accounting Guideline, "Full Cost Accounting in the Oil and Gas Industry," par. 5(b).

[6]Ibid., par. 4(b).

[7]Ibid., pars. 22-26. For comparison see Rule 4-10 of Regulation S-X, par. (i)(6)(i).

[8]CICA Accounting Guideline, "Full Cost Accounting in the Oil and Gas Industry," par. 38.

[9]Compare with Rule 4-10 of Regulation S-X, "Full Cost Method," par. (i)(4).

[10]FASB, *Disclosure about Oil and Gas Producing Activities,* Statement of Financial Accounting Standards No. 69 (Stamford: FASB, 1982).

Chapter Twenty-Four

Accounting for Financial Institutions; Life Insurance Companies: A Special Case

This chapter discusses accounting and reporting problems encountered by financial institutions. Because of the nature of these entities, their accounting problems tend to be outside the normal problems of revenue recognition and cost matching that are dealt with by the historical cost model.

For example, accounting for investments of all kinds is a vital issue to a financial institution. As already observed in chapter 16, some different perspectives on investment accounting appear when one thinks in terms of portfolios held on a continuing basis rather than in terms of holdings that may be disposed of at any time. Accounting for loan portfolios also involves considerations not usually evident when dealing with trade accounts receivable in the ordinary business. To a considerable extent, the revenues of financial institutions represent a reward for risk bearing, and this adds a new dimension to revenue recognition questions (as touched on in chapter 8). In the life insurance industry it is even impractical to identify the portions of premiums received that are equivalent to earned revenue for another enterprise. Hence life insurance accounting necessarily revolves around questions of valuation of assets and liabilities, not around techniques for matching costs and revenues.

The first part of this chapter deals primarily with issues common to most financial institutions. The second part deals in greater depth with the challenge presented by accounting for life insurance institutions since, at the time of writing, consideration is being given in Canada to the adoption of standards for this industry.

Accounting issues in financial institutions

There are a number of types of financial institution performing a wide variety of functions. Certain characteristics distinguish financial institutions as a group from other types of enterprise, and these distinctive characteristics have, as a matter of history, led to distinctive accounting practices. It is often difficult to decide whether these distinctive accounting practices should be regarded as generally accepted because they are justified by the special character of the institutions or whether they are contrary to generally accepted accounting principles within the historical cost accounting system.

Characteristics of financial institutions

The key characteristic that sets a financial institution apart is that, because of the nature of its business, it is entrusted with substantial funds by parties other than its shareholders, and a significant part of its income is derived from the successful investment of those funds. In a financial institution the funds received from the public typically far exceed the amount of capital committed by the shareholders. Indeed, in the more stable type of institution the risk-taking function of ownership can be dispensed with completely, as it is in mutual insurance companies.

The maintenance of a pool of investable funds may be merely incidental to the business of the institution. For example, an investment broker requires a margin deposit as security for trades made as agent for others. A property and casualty insurer requires premiums in advance to provide coverage of insurable risks. A life insurance company requires premiums, often well in advance of need, both to cover risk and also to invest for ultimate repayment.

In other cases, financial intermediation — the receipt of deposits from the public for the purpose of investment — is the primary function of the institution. Thus, trust and loan companies raise money by the issuance of guaranteed investment certificates and debentures to make mortgage loans and other investments. Credit unions accept deposits from members for the purpose of making loans to other members. Chartered banks accept deposits from the public largely for the purpose of making commercial loans.

In some types of institution public funds are withdrawable on demand or on short notice. As a result, the institution's risk relates not only to the risk inherent in investments and loans but also to the risk of loss of confidence on the part of depositors and creditors. In these circumstances financial institutions have a heightened need for liquidity. In the ultimate, their status as a going concern depends not only upon their ability to obtain income from investments and loans in excess of interest on liabilities but also on their ability to escape serious net withdrawals of funds — a relatively unpredictable factor.

The large pools of investable funds within financial institutions give them credibility as guarantors of third-party risks. As a result, commitments of all kinds are likely to be far more important to the overall financial position of a financial institution than they are to the ordinary enterprise.

Because of the importance of the investment policy of financial institutions to the economy, the very large public stake in financial institutions, and the small margin of safety against loss inherent in their leveraged financial structure, government regulation or industry self-regulation under government oversight is inevitable.

Regulation of financial institutions

Regulation of financial institutions with a view to limitation of the risks taken on by them and control over the possibility of management fraud may take several forms.

- When agency business involves enhanced risk, regulators may require, as they do with stockbrokers, that clients who create that risk be asked to provide cash as a margin of safety against loss on their business.

- Controls may be placed over the quality of investments made by a financial institution to minimize the risk of serious loss.
- Controls may be placed over the types of investments that may be made by particular types of institutions. In part those controls are imposed to minimize interest-rate risk and protect liquidity. Thus an institution whose liabilities are predominantly short-term may be restricted in the amount of long-term lending it can undertake. In part also, the controls may be designed to encourage specialization by different types of financial institutions.
- There may be requirements to maintain "reserves" consisting of cash, deposits with the central bank, or short-term securities as a first line of defence against waves of withdrawals of demand deposits stemming from loss of confidence.
- Numerical limits may be placed on leverage in a financial institution, expressed in terms of the percentage that assets must form of liabilities or of the permitted ratio of liabilities to shareholders' equity.

In recent years there has been some tendency to liberalize the controls over types of investments that may be made by particular types of financial institutions, as the competition between types has increased. In any event, not all forms of regulation are applied to all types of institutions.

To be effective, regulation must be complemented by supervision, which is achieved by reporting requirements and periodic inspection. Reporting requirements include the frequent provision of financial statements together with detailed information and analysis about key aspects of the institution's operations. For ease of comprehension, reports are required on a standardized basis. The result is that the regulator almost invariably prescribes forms for reporting. In addition, the application of controls on leverage, such as the maximum permitted ratio of liabilities to equity, depends upon accounting measurements of assets and liabilities. This naturally leads to prescription of accounting methods by statute or by statutory delegation of the power to prescribe accounting methods to the regulatory agency.

For some industries, notably the insurance industry, such prescribed or "statutory" accounting methods have often been described as being designed with solvency in mind, rather than the normal financial reporting objective of fair presentation of financial position and results of operation. The description "solvency accounting" is not completely enlightening. Some prescribed accounting bases do emphasize readily realizable values as a test for asset valuation. Thus, it has been traditional in the insurance industry that assets such as furniture and equipment, leasehold improvements, amounts due from agents, inventories of supplies, and so on have not been "admitted" as assets. On the other hand, other rules have little to do with the measurement of solvency — such as the limitation on mortality tables and interest rates that may be used in valuing the policy liabilities of a life insurance company.

In general, statutory accounting methods have been designed in a rather judgmental way to provide a margin of safety — to make the financial position look worse than it is — almost as if it is desired to have a trip wire that gives a signal when an institution is heading for trouble, so that remedial action can be taken in good time. It is not clear that the margin of safety desired could not just as easily be provided simply by varying the permitted ratio of policy or deposit liabilities to the amount of capital and retained earnings measured using normal accounting principles

Important accounting issues

Even if this were accepted, however, there would remain the question of what ought to be generally accepted accounting in relation to many issues that are peculiar to financial institutions. A number of issues commonly encountered are discussed below.

Investment valuation. Investment valuation issues have been described in chapter 16. Under generally accepted accounting principles, investments are generally carried at cost or amortized cost (less allowance for other than temporary impairment), or lower of cost and market (LOCAM) when the investments are short-term in nature and classification. Some financial institutions find this basis of accounting satisfactory. Others find two of its aspects unsatisfactory: (1) its inhibiting effect on investment decisions when the current market values of securities, especially fixed-interest securities, are below carrying values, thereby requiring losses to be recognized when individual securities are sold, and (2) the failure to give any recognition before realization to appreciation in value of equity securities.

With the exception of investment companies, financial institutions generally do not find the market value basis for investment valuation a practical solution to these shortcomings (except for trading portfolios). The possible effect of fluctuations in market value on investment valuation and on the amount of reported income and shareholders' equity is too extreme. A few institutions have used deferral and amortization accounting for long-term portfolios of debt securities. That method has also been supported in CICA-sponsored research studies on trust and loan companies, property and casualty companies, and credit unions. As a result, it appears to be an acceptable alternative in Canada to the standard basis of investment valuation in the special circumstances for which the method is designed (a portfolio of fixed-interest securities held for the long term and generally stable or increasing in amount). It is also prescribed by regulatory authorities for use by chartered banks and life insurance companies. In the case of banks, rather than amortize all security gains and losses over the term to maturity of the securities sold (as the deferral and amortization theory calls for), an arbitrary five-year period of amortization is used, considered to be a reasonable approximation that saves detailed record keeping.

In contrast, there is not the same degree of support in practice for departures from cost-based accounting for equity securities. A smoothed valuation basis is prescribed for regulatory reporting purposes for life insurance companies. The carrying value of the equity securities portfolio is adjusted annually towards market value by recognizing fifteen percent of the difference between the carrying value and the current market value. Since it is acknowledged that life insurance companies do not follow generally accepted accounting principles, this method does not provide a precedent that carries weight with respect to what is acceptable for other financial institutions. The CICA research study on property and casualty insurance companies advocated a five-year moving-average market value basis of valuation for equity securities, but that suggestion was not supported in a subsequent guideline in the *CICA Handbook*.[1]

In the United States, deferral and amortization accounting is not considered generally accepted for debt securities owned by financial institutions. For banks and insurance companies, trading portfolios are carried at market. Other debt securities are carried at amortized cost less allowance for other than temporary impairment. Equity securities are to be valued at market value in the insurance industry and at the lower of aggregate cost and market in other financial institutions. Unrealized gains and losses are not taken to income but rather are treated as a separate component of shareholders' equity. Investment companies are different from all other financial institutions in that all their investments are carried at market value or estimated fair value where a market price is not available.

Accounting for loans and loan losses. A portfolio of loans represents a major part of the assets of many types of financial institutions. Loans vary considerably in character — whether they are long-term, short-term, or demand, how they are secured, and whether they are made to persons or to businesses. The risk associated with the loan portfolio may vary accordingly.

It is possible that loans or portfolios of loans may be sold. For example, a financial institution might sell a block of mortgages to a pension fund. (In the United States, "securitization" of mortgages and other income-earning assets, permitting unit interests to be sold to private investors, has gone much further than in Canada.) By and large, however, loans are held until repaid. Consequently, their collectibility, rather than their current market value, is the dominant factor to be considered in assessing the appropriate carrying value for them. Also, since amounts collectible may be less than the face amount of the loan but will never be more, the key problem in valuation is that of making appropriate provision for losses.

The problem of loan loss provision is often thought of as being equivalent to the problem of providing an allowance for uncollectible accounts receivable in a normal business enterprise. As such, it calls for examination of loans individually and an estimate of amounts not recoverable based on the current condition of the debtor. Sometimes reference is made to the accounting standard on contingencies (see chapter 9) to justify making provisions for losses on individual loans only when they are both probable and reasonably capable of estimation.

Such an approach is not satisfactory for a financial institution. Its practical effect is that loan losses will generally be recognized late. To begin with, if the contingency guidance is followed literally, no provision for loss will be made when a loss with respect to a given account is reasonably possible but yet cannot be called probable. Likewise, no provision may be made if the amount of loss is hard to estimate. Yet, from the viewpoint of a loan portfolio as a whole, a reasonable possibility of loss on a considerable number of loans may add up in a statistical sense to virtual certainty of some loss for the group of loans as a whole.

Beyond this, it is necessary to remember that in some situations — especially in commercial lending — once a line of credit is extended, a loan to the debtor may be on the books in varying amounts for a lengthy period or even indefinitely. The interest rate charged on loans will reflect an assessment of risk thereon. Suppose that a group of new loans of average risk is taken on. Over the whole period these loans are outstanding, there are bound to be some losses, and that is allowed for in the interest rate charged. Yet, for some time after the original advances an examination of the loans individually might not identify one on which loss appears to be probable. Nevertheless, it can be argued that a fair reporting of the income on those loans requires some recognition of the potential loss that is accruing and that, statistically speaking, is probable for the group as a whole. If that argument is accepted, a financial institution should make specific provision for uncollectible loans based upon individual examination of the loan portfolio, plus a general provision based on experience and judgment for portfolio losses that will not be apparent in an individual examination. Unfortunately, there is little precedent for this in the accounting of other industries, nor is there any generally recognized precedent or authoritative guidance to determine the amount of the general loss provision if it is made.

Certain specific questions also arise in loan accounting.

- If interest payments are not currently being made on loans, should the accruing interest be capitalized so that income continues to be recognized? One conceivable answer to this is that so long as the total amount recorded on a loan including capitalized interest is assessed for collectibility, it is proper to continue to capitalize interest. On the other hand, if there are doubts as to collectibility, the interest accrual should not be made. This complicates day-to-day accounting by requiring the special categorization of "nonperforming" loans with respect to which interest accrual is not to be made. In principle such categorization is judgmental but, for convenience, some financial institutions may adopt a standard rule, or some regulators may require a rule, such as that no interest is to be capitalized with respect to loans on which principal or interest payments are more than ninety days overdue.
- One objection to capitalization of interest that is not being paid currently is that the income reported is not represented by a current cash inflow. Ideally this would be shown in a statement of changes in financial position by excluding interest capitalized from the figures for cash flow from operations. Unfortunately, the amount of such interest capitalized would require a special analysis to obtain. (Its accuracy would also be hard to monitor, since additional loans could always be advanced to enable interest payments on previous balances to be paid in cash. See further comments on funds statements for financial institutions in chapter 21.)
- When a creditor and debtor enter into a "troubled debt restructuring" — that is, the creditor grants concessions that it would not make to a financially sound debtor — what accounting is required? The FASB has provided guidance with respect to such restructuring.[2] Restructuring may consist of modifications of the debt terms to ease the cash strain on the debtor or the acceptance of certain assets of the debtor in full or partial satisfaction of the debt. The FASB indicates that assets received to be applied against the debt should be recorded at fair value. Any remaining carrying value of the debt should be compared with future amounts estimated to be collectible, regardless of whether those amounts are designated as interest or principal. If a restructuring consists only of modification of terms of payment on the debt, the same test of collectibility applies. A loan asset is required to be written down only if future payments are estimated to be less in total than the asset carrying value.

  Implicit in the FASB recommendation is a broader point. The traditional assessment of collectibility of a loan has looked only to the recovery of the amount recorded on the books. The collectibility of future interest on the loan is not considered. The result is that a loan that is expected to yield collections just equal to its principal amount over a period of time (perhaps from realization on its security over an extended period) but from which interest payments are not expected does not require a specific loss provision. In essence, the loan continues to be carried at a figure above its real value.

Such a recoverable value test is consistent with that applied to long-term investments or other long-term assets held by ordinary business enterprises. It is unsatisfactory for financial institutions, however, where loan portfolios may represent a major part of the assets of the entity and where realizability of assets and liquidity are of such importance. A better basis for calculating specific loss provisions would be to limit the asset to the present value of future amounts estimated to be collectible, using a discount rate equivalent to interest rates currently applicable for the type of business in question. Even that basis could be argued to overstate the real value of the loan, since loans from debtors in difficulty are likely to be more risky than the typical business loan.

Cyclical accounting and reserves. It is often argued that losses in a financial institution, especially one engaged in commercial lending, tend to be cyclical. Loan losses are likely to be bunched when business conditions are bad. On the other hand, when demands for loans are increasing (so that interest rates are tending to rise) a bank may be required to realize losses on its investment portfolio to the extent that fixed-interest securities have to be liquidated to provide loanable funds. Of course, the cyclical incidence of losses or low profits is characteristic to some degree of many business enterprises. But the requirement to maintain public confidence in financial institutions has historically been considered to justify various expedients to smooth reported losses and income over a cycle.

The most direct way to achieve smoothing of losses is through the provision of "inner" or "secret" reserves. These reserves are created by arbitrary charges to income or understatement of realized income, with the credits being applied against the carrying values of investments or loans in such a way that readers of the financial statements cannot tell the amounts of such reserves. Varying the amount of inner reserves from one year to the next can offset the impact on income of actual losses recognized.

Inner reserves have always been subject to criticism because of the opportunity they afford to manipulate income reported and misstate the actual financial position. To meet that criticism, there has been a tendency first to disclose arbitrary reserves in the balance sheet (under some such title as "reserve for investments and contingencies") and then to exclude provisions for such published reserves from the income statement, reporting them rather as appropriations of retained earnings.

Over an extended period of time the use of undisclosed reserves in Canadian financial institutions has been eliminated, although it is still common in the financial reporting of banks and other financial institutions outside of North America. The most important vestige of cyclical and reserve accounting in Canada is found in the regulated accounting of banks. First, the provision for loan losses charged against income by banks is not the actual amount of specific provisions set up in the year but rather is a figure based on the average ratio of loss experience to loan portfolios outstanding over the last five years. In addition, the banks appropriate arbitrary amounts from retained earnings. These two amounts, the one charged against income and the other against retained earnings, are credited to

"Appropriations for Contingencies." Actual loan write-offs and provisions for specific reserves, net of reversals and recoveries, are charged against that account. The balance in the account is not treated as part of shareholders' equity, although it and shareholders' equity are both shown in the balance sheet under the heading "capital and reserves." In effect, the appropriations for contingencies represent general loss reserves in arbitrary amounts.

By normal standards this accounting is objectionable, for two reasons. First, it is not clear whether the balance in the reserve is an asset valuation allowance or part of the shareholders' equity. Second, even if one grants that loss experience charged against income should be smoothed out, the long-term average income reported is overstated if any part of the cumulative appropriations from retained earnings (which have not been charged against income) has been required to make adequate provision for real losses.

Recognition of fee revenue. Financial institutions receive a wide variety of fees. Their traditional practice has been to record such fees as earned revenue when they are received or become billable. Such a basis of revenue recognition is often not appropriate. Careful analysis of the reasons fees are received is required to suggest what would be preferable accounting.

- Fees may be received for a distinct service. For example, they may be received for appraisals of property in connection with a mortgage loan. Placement fees may be received for bringing together a lender and borrower. Fees may be received for performance of management functions in connection with estates, trusts, or investment funds. In general, fees for one-shot services should be recognized as earned when the service is completed. Fees for continuing services should be recognized as the service is rendered if performance can be measured so as to permit accrual, and on a time basis if measurement indicators are lacking but the service is rendered on a reasonably uniform basis.
- Fees may be received for providing guarantees of performance of third parties, such as that the financial institution will stand behind the third parties' obligations on financial instruments or swap transactions. There could be an argument for deferring recognition of such revenue until the risk period is over; at the least, revenue should not be recognized more quickly than in proportion to the expiration of the risk period.
- Fees may be received for undertaking commitments to provide financing at the going rate when it is required. Such a fee may be taken into income over the commitment period.
- Fees may also be received for undertaking commitments that involve risk. For example, a commitment to lend funds at a fixed interest rate exposes the enterprise to the risk of adverse changes in interest rates over the commitment period. It follows that the fee should not be recognized in income immediately. Different views are possible, however, as to the best treatment beyond that. One possibility is to regard the fee as equivalent to a premium received by someone writing an option on interest rates. It would be possible to account for such an assumed premium on a mark-to-market basis. A second possible treatment would be to record the amount of the fee, when received, as a deferred credit. Should changes in interest rates in the com-

mitment period reduce the apparent value of the future loan by more than the fee, loss would be recognized and the deferred credit increased. When the loan was issued, the deferred credit would be offset against the loan receivable to the extent necessary to reduce it to its then-current value, and any remainder of the deferred credit would be recognized in income. This treatment, in effect, would recognize possible loss, but not gain, in the commitment period.

A third possibility is the current U.S. practice of deferring recognition of the fee revenue until the commitment period ends and at that time taking it into income or using it to write down the loan, depending upon whether the change in interest rates over the commitment period has been favourable or adverse. A fourth possibility is to defer the recognition of the credit from the fee and use it to write down the loan (if any) when made, regardless of the change in interest rates. The FASB has expressed support for this approach based on the argument that the primary benefit to the borrower is the loan, and therefore the fee should be used to adjust the yield from the loan.[3]

Discounting of claim liabilities in property and casualty insurance. Companies writing property and casualty insurance are required to recognize liabilities for the estimated amount of claim payments and claim adjustment costs with respect to events giving rise to claims that have occurred up to the reporting date. That liability is to include estimates of amounts with respect to claims for events that have occurred, notwithstanding that the company has not yet received notification of claim. The amount of liability provided has traditionally represented the best estimate of actual amounts payable without discounting, except when the liability is in respect of a claim that will be paid in instalments over the long term. Some have argued, however, that such liabilities should be discounted to present fairly their economic effect, much as policy liabilities in life insurance companies are discounted.

This argument has a good deal of force. Since invested assets available to pay claims are valued at cost or LOCAM (i.e., they do not take into account future interest to be earned before they must be used to pay claims), it would seem that an equivalent basis of valuation for liabilities would be a discounted figure.

On the other hand, if specific recognition is to be given to the time value of money in this case, it is necessary to consider its consistency with other aspects of the accounting. Consider a $1,000 premium received in advance for a three-year policy and recorded initially as unearned revenue. The $1,000 can be regarded as the present value of revenue to be earned in future. If interest rates are 10% per annum, the $1,000 received in advance is equivalent to an annual payment of $402.11 at the end of each of the three policy years. Correspondingly, the unearned premium liability at the end of the first year is the present value of $402.11 payable at the end of the next two years, or $697.89. At the end of the second year the unearned premium calculated on the same basis would be $365.56. The amount to be recognized as earned premium in each of the years, therefore, would be the decrease in the calculated provision for unearned premium. That is, recognized revenue, allowing for time value of money, should be $302.11 in the first year, $332.33 in the second year, and $365.56 in the third year. What this tells us is that the conventional straight-line basis of revenue recognition tends to overstate revenue earned in the early years of a policy and understate the figure of unearned revenue correspondingly.

Another way of viewing this is to look at what happens to the cash premium received in advance. That cash will be invested until it is required to cover policy administration expenses and claims. As the cash is used up over the three years, investment earnings will fall. At the same time, premium revenue recognized on a straight-line basis will be constant. Thus, the total reported revenue derived from the policy will fall steadily over its term and so will its apparent profitability. Accounting recognition of premium revenue on a time-value adjusted basis, as outlined in the previous paragraph, would compensate for this effect.

Conventional accounting procedures generally ignore discounting for reasons of simplicity and convenience, trusting that apparent errors caused by the failure to recognize the time value of money will cancel out over time. If it is proposed to alter that situation for any aspect of accounting, it is logically necessary to look at the other accounting procedures for the entity. Specifically, if interest effects are to be taken into account with respect to claim liabilities, it can be argued that interest should also be recognized in the accounting for earned revenues from premiums.

Recognition of premium deficiencies. The figure recorded for unearned premiums by property and casualty insurers at any time should be sufficient (1) to absorb amortization of acquisition costs that have been deferred with respect to policies in force, (2) to meet charges for future expenses required to administer the policies, and (3) to meet claims arising in the remaining term of the policy and expenses connected therewith. (The obligation to meet claims that have already occurred should be covered by the separate liability provision.) If the unearned premium figure is not sufficient for all these purposes, a "premium deficiency" is said to exist.

It is accepted that a loss should be recognized when such a deficiency exists. (The loss is recognized first by writing off deferred acquisition costs and, if that is not enough, by recognizing a provision for loss.) Some argue in this case as well that the provision for premium deficiency should be discounted because it will be a long time before cash is actually required to meet the expenses not covered by premiums. This argument is essentially the same as that for discounting claims provisions, and the same comment applies. The argument is sound in isolation, but it conflicts with the failure to take interest effects into account in the valuation of all recorded assets and liabilities.

Balance sheet recognition of commitments. Canadian banks are required to show an asset and a liability of equal amount with respect to their guarantees of customers' acceptances. In ordinary accounting such a contingent liability would not be recorded in the balance sheet but would simply be disclosed. In addition, the practice seems to be inconsistent in that all sorts of obligations of somewhat similar character — such as those resulting from acting as intermediaries in swap transactions — are not given balance sheet recognition.

In modern commerce, financial institutions are taking on contingent obligations of major proportions in relation to financial instruments not dreamed of twenty or even ten years ago. There is a need for the most meticulous recording of these obligations and for disclosure in the financial statements of their nature and extent. At the same time, there needs to be some theory that does not now exist to explain which items, if any, should appear as assets and liabilities in a balance sheet and why.

Accounting for life insurance companies

Among all the various types of financial institutions, the life insurance business presents the most difficulty in reconciling its traditional accounting practices with those we are accustomed to under historical cost accounting. There are at least three significant reasons for this. First, life insurance companies enter into contracts extending many years into the future. Far more than in the normal business, accounting for these contractual transactions requires estimates of future events that are in some respects little more than guesses. For this reason, life insurance accounting has traditionally had a bias towards conservatism, rather than towards best estimates. Second, life insurance accounting is dominated by actuarial measurements. Actuarial measurements traditionally start from valuation of assets and liabilities, rather than from allocation of costs and revenues as is the case with more conventional accounting. Third, many of the valuations in a life insurance statement are based on discounting of future cash flows. In contrast, in traditional accounting discounting is avoided as much as possible in favour of allocations of known transaction results or, failing that, valuations based upon market prices.

The difference between traditional accounting approaches and life insurance accounting begins with the figure of revenue for a period. In traditional accounting, the revenue figure is the amount deemed *earned* in a period. In a life insurance business, the revenue reported has virtually nothing to do with earnings of the period; it is simply the amount of premiums falling due in the period. Thus, for a paid-up policy nothing is reported as premium revenue in the period, even though the policy does have an impact on the final figure of income for that period. It is clear from this that life insurance accounting cannot be described as a process of matching costs with revenues recognized. In this respect, life insurance accounting differs even from the accounting for property and casualty insurers. In the latter industry, the premium revenue reported is not the figure of premiums falling due in the period, but rather the portion of premiums on policies in force deemed to be applicable to coverage in the period in question.

The valuation of policy obligations

For the most part, a life insurance company writes off all costs incurred during a year as incurred — such as policy benefits paid or accrued, expenses of policy acquisition, expenses of policy administration, and investment management costs. Thus each of policy premiums, investment income, and expenses (with the minor exception of depreciation on recorded fixed assets) is reflected in income when due or incurred — that is, on a basis very close to cash accounting. It is the provision for change in policy liabilities that controls how much profit or loss is shown on the business for the period.

As calculated in accordance with standard actuarial practice, the provision for policy obligations with respect to a block of policies is a net figure consisting of the two components described below:

1. A liability component is based on a discounted valuation of estimated benefits to be paid in future on the block of policies.

2. An asset component is calculated as follows:
   a) An assumption is made concerning so-called "valuation premiums" assumed to be collectible in future on the block of policies;
   b) The assumed valuation premiums are reduced by an allowance for costs of acquiring and servicing the policies; and
   c) The net valuation premiums so determined are discounted to a present value.

As will be explained more fully below, the valuation premiums used in these actuarial calculations are frequently not equal in amount to the actual premiums collectible under the policy contracts.

Accountants are apt to find this actuarial basis of calculation difficult to understand because it is rather different from anything they are familiar with in other industries. To begin with, it is foreign to normal accounting to recognize amounts receivable that are not yet due (premiums receivable over policy lifetimes) based on estimates that include substantial allowances for cancellation of policies before maturity. Moreover, even if the basic idea were accepted, that is that the accounting should be influenced by estimates of lifetime cash flows on policies from their inception, accountants would probably go about things differently. In particular, they would be likely to account for the different cash flow elements separately — along the following lines:

1. Special consideration would be given to costs of policy acquisition and administration only to the extent that it was expected the costs would be significantly irregular in their incidence. In practice, this would mean that the heavy costs incurred at the inception of policies, such as salesmen's commissions, would be deferred and amortized over estimated policy durations. (This contrasts with the actuarial practice of deducting an allowance for total lifetime policy expenses from the valuation premiums.)
2. At the inception of policies, the present value of *actual* future premiums estimated to be collectible would be recognized as an asset. (This contrasts with the actuarial practice of recording the present value of valuation premiums, which can differ in amount from actual policy premiums.)
3. At the inception of policies, the credit resulting from recognition of the policy premiums receivable would be recorded as unearned revenue. Some basis would then have to be devised to recognize revenue as earned over the duration of the policies. The balance in the unearned revenue account, as it stood from time to time, would be considered to cover the obligation to pay future policy benefits, and, if at any time it appeared insufficient for this purpose, the balance would be increased and loss recognized. (In contrast, actuarial practice regards the valuation of policy obligations as a separate valuation from that of premiums receivable, right from the inception of the policies, and does not think of the policy obligation figure primarily as unearned revenue.)

If the accounting for a block of policies were performed in accordance with an approach understandable to accountants, as just described, no profit or loss would be recognized at the inception of a block of policies. The deferred costs would equal actual acquisition costs (at least ideally), and the unearned revenue account would equal the asset recognized for premiums collectible. In contrast, depending upon the approach taken to the valuations of the several components of the net policy obligations figure, an actuary could record a substantial loss or a substantial profit at the time policies are first written. Traditionally, under the influence of regulation, actuarial valuations have resulted in recognizing losses on new policies (often described as "reserve strain" from new business). This results from one or more biases built into the actuarial calculations:

1. An assumption may be made that policy benefits will be payable sooner than is actually expected (as a result of adopting conservative mortality tables, for example). The present value of the calculated future amounts payable may also be increased by using discount rates lower than the actual rate of return expected on investments.
2. The valuation premiums used in calculating the present value of future premiums may be less than actual premiums on the block of policies. A valuation premium is supposed to be calculated as the premium that would be required to make provision for policy obligations with a margin or "provision for adverse deviation" that an actuary, using professional judgment, considers "adequate and appropriate." It will often happen that such a calculated premium is less than the actual premium called for under a policy.
3. As noted earlier, an allowance for lifetime policy expenses is deducted from the valuation premiums. Under the "net level premium" approach, such lifetime expenses are deducted in equal amounts from each premium to arrive at a level premium each year. Since actual policy expenses are heavily weighted by policy acquisition costs, the assumption that they are level over a policy's life is unrealistic and has the effect of understating the net valuation premiums to be collected in future. The conservative bias caused by this treatment is often reduced by using a "modified net level premium" approach that omits or reduces the allowance for policy expense in the figures of valuation premiums for the first year or so of a policy. Even these modified approaches, however, may contain some conservative bias.

The foregoing describes the traditional conservative bias resulting from actuarial practices prescribed or permitted under regulation (sometimes described as "statutory accounting"). As already noted, however, actuarial methods, if free from regulatory constraints, might record a substantial gain rather than a loss at the time policies are written.

To understand this better, consider the problem of establishing premiums to be charged for policies. The premiums, together with income earned on premium proceeds before they are required to meet policy obligations, must be sufficient to meet the obligations and expenses as they fall due. The actuary therefore needs best estimates of the amount and timing of policy benefits and expenses and of the rate of return available on investment of policy proceeds in order to price the required premium. In actually pricing the premium, the actuary will provide margins for adverse deviation of experience from best estimates, usually calculated separately for each key element but occasionally established as an overall amount. A loading may also be added for extra profit if competitive conditions permit.

Given this situation, all that would have to be done to maximize profit reported at the inception of the policy is as follows:

1. Calculate the present value of policy obligations using *best estimates* of amounts and timing of future policy benefits and future expenses and using

the expected rate of return on investments as the discount rate. That is to say, do not make any allowance for possible adverse experience.
2. Recognize the present value of *actual* premiums collectible.
3. Give no recognition to policy acquisition costs — that is, write them off to expense at the time of acquisition.

On this basis, the entire expected profit shown on the policy would be recognized at its inception. Profit or loss recorded thereafter would result solely from the deviation of actual experience from original best estimates.

Since such a range in possible treatments exists, we must ask what is an appropriate basis for recognizing profit on insurance and what basis of calculation of policy assets and liabilities will achieve the appropriate result.

It seems intuitively obvious that the statutory basis of accounting, which often results in recognition of large losses when a policy is written even though the policy is expected to be profitable, does not provide what accountants would regard as a fair portrayal of financial position and results of operations. But what would be fair? Consider the functions that an insurance company performs. There are several. The first is that of risk bearing. The company receives funds by way of premiums and promises certain benefits. It takes an "underwriting" risk that policy obligations will be more onerous than those it allowed for in calculating the premiums required. Involved with this is an investment risk. Funds are collected in advance of need and invested until benefits become payable. The policy premiums are based on an assumption that certain rates of return can be obtained on funds before they are needed to pay benefits. Thus the company takes a risk with respect to investment returns as well as the underwriting risk. It also performs a service in managing the investments and in administering the policies. Premiums must provide some recompense for this function as well.

All these functions are performed over the lifetime of the policy. One might argue then that, from the viewpoint of the policyholder, profit is earned over the whole period of the policy. The accounting should let that profit emerge as the functions are performed and the period of risk expires. On the other hand, one might ask, should some of that gain be recognized when the policy contract is sold? The sale of policies is, after all, a significant part of an insurance company's activity.

The answer given to these questions in the United States has the following principal features:[4]

- The provision for policy liabilities is to be based on estimates of investment yields, mortality, morbidity, terminations, expenses, and participating policyholder dividends applicable at the time the insurance contracts are entered into. Those initial estimates will generally be continued for the duration of a block of policies being valued.
- The assumptions are to include a provision for adverse deviation from expected experience that is deemed adequate and appropriate in the actuary's opinion.
- The assumptions (including the margins for adverse deviation) upon which policy premiums were priced *may* be appropriate for use in the calculation of the present value of policy obligations. If, however, experience and the future outlook indicate that these assumptions are unduly conservative, less conservative assumptions may be used.
- The same assumptions that are used in valuing the policy benefits are used

in calculating the net valuation premium the present value of which is deducted from the liability to arrive at the net policy liability. Accordingly, no profit or loss should be shown at the inception of the policy.

- In the event that the assumptions (including the provisions for adverse experience) used in calculating the policy obligations and valuation premiums are less conservative than those used in pricing the actual premiums, the valuation premiums will, of course, be less than the actual premiums. The effect of this is that an amount equal to the difference between the actual premium received each year and the reduction in the year of the figure for the present value of future valuation premiums will flow into income of the year. In other words, in the event that actual premiums on a block of policies are greater than is thought to be required to allow an "adequate and appropriate" provision for adverse deviation, that excess or profit element will be recognized in income over the premium-paying period of the policies (which may be a shorter period than the entire lifetime of the policies).
- Acquisition costs when premiums are written will be identified and deferred, to be amortized in proportion to the expected receipt of premiums.
- The policy obligations will be recalculated year by year using the same assumptions. The amount of obligations recognized for each block of policies will steadily decrease as they are fulfilled. In effect, the decrease in policy obligations is credited to income, while the actual cost of meeting the policy obligations is recorded as an expense. Since the amount released from the provision for policy obligations will include the provision for adverse deviation with respect to that year, the actual cost of obligations will ordinarily be less than the amount released. Likewise, actual investment earnings should be greater than was assumed in discounting the amount of the obligations. Accordingly a profit should emerge that may be considered to be the reward for risk taking by the company and for investment management.
- The adequacy of the provision for policy obligations is to be kept under review. This requires for each block of policies an estimate of the present value of future policy benefits and costs, based on revised assumptions, less the present value of *actual* premiums expected to be received in the future. If the resulting net figure is greater than the net policy obligations recognized in the accounts on the basis described above, reduced by any remaining deferred acquisition costs for that block of policies, a premium deficiency exists. In that event, the deferred acquisition expenses are to be written down and the provision for obligations increased to the extent necessary to provide a breakeven over the remaining policy period.

Some of these provisions could be debated. For example, some might argue that the assumptions used in making provision for policy liabilities should always be the same as those used in pricing the premium. That is to say, less conservative assumptions should not be permissible in valuing policy obligations. If so, all profit inherent in a block of policies would be spread over the duration of the policy period, rather than some of it being reported over the shorter premium-paying period. On the other hand, some might argue that the sale of policy contracts with premiums that carry greater margins than are customarily required to make provision for adverse deviation in experience should result in separate profit recognition, but that it would be more logical to recognize *all* that profit at the time the policy is sold (when the important effort takes place), rather than spread it over the premium-paying period. Evidently, as in all allocation questions, there is room for some difference of opinion.

The supremely important element in this basis of accounting is the actuary's provision for adverse deviation included in the assumptions upon which the calculations are based. It is said that such provision is to be "adequate and appropriate" in the actuary's opinion. The degree of variation possible in opinions as to what is adequate and appropriate will determine whether results achieved for different companies using this criterion will be comparable. The author is not aware of any research on this point.

Other accounting questions

A number of other questions in relation to life insurance accounting are briefly reviewed below.

- It is sometimes argued that the cash surrender value established in policy contracts should set a minimum for the amount recognized as the liability for future policy benefits, even though a calculation based on probability of policy termination is lower. The opposing argument is that the actuarial estimate of policy terminations should be relied upon because the provision for policy obligations looks to the *probable* actual cash payments, not the minimum guarantees. The latter is the stronger argument in the context of accounting principles.
- Investment accounting issues have already been reviewed. The investment policy of life insurance companies is almost always of a long-term nature, and their policy liabilities will be valued using a long-term investment return assumption. Accordingly, the life insurance industry has a stronger argument than any other industry for the use of investment accounting methods that smooth the recognition of gain or loss in income. Even if such methods are not regarded as appropriate for business generally, there is a good argument that they should be accepted for insurance companies, just as a market value basis of investment valuation is accepted for investment companies, even though not accepted generally. Some might well argue that deferral and amortization of realized gains and losses on mortgage portfolios and a market-related basis of valuation for real estate should also be permitted, because of the similarity of characteristics of these types of investments to investment in bonds and common shares respectively.
- Life insurance companies usually argue that tax allocation accounting should be applied on a discounted basis in their case. If one accepts the accrual approach to tax allocation (which chapter 15 suggests is logical), a life insurance company has the strongest claim to discounting of any industry, inasmuch as all the monetary assets and liabilities of life insurance companies are accounted for on a discounted basis.
- Many life insurance companies have a significant foreign business. Usually foreign regulatory bodies require significant local investment to balance the liabilities on policies of local residents. As a result, the foreign activities can be regarded as relatively self-sustaining and independent of the domestic insurance operations of the company. The "current-rate" method of translation of foreign operations seems appropriate for life insurance companies.

It is questionable, however, that translation gains or losses should be excluded from income and treated as a separate component of shareholders' equity. Because of the relatively balanced position of foreign assets and liabilities, it is also questionable that the current-rate method needs to be abandoned when the foreign operations are conducted in a currency subject to a high rate of inflation. Thus some exceptions to the generally accepted basis of foreign currency translation seem to be justified for life insurance companies.

- Life insurance companies often have substantial blocks of business in what are known as "segregated funds." Although the company is the legal owner of the assets of these funds, in many cases it functions as little more than an investment manager, and the real risk and reward from the assets accrues to the fund beneficiary. There is a good argument that the financial position and results of operations of such funds should not be intermingled with those of the ordinary insurance business of the company, even though some aspects of segregated fund operations have some similarity to some aspects of insurance policies.
- In a stock life company that writes participating life insurance, income is allocated between an amount pertaining to the participating policyholders' funds and amounts deemed earned on nonparticipating business and on shareholders' funds. The shareholders are entitled to all the profits of nonparticipating business but are restricted, under the law, in the amount they may receive from earnings of the participating policyholders' funds. Transfers from the participating policyholders are limited to a small percentage of dividends actually paid to participating policyholders. No transfer is allowed if policyholder dividends are not paid. The question then arises: Should the earnings reported for the shareholders with respect to income derived from participating policyholder funds be restricted to the transfer actually made to the shareholders, or should they be reported as the maximum amount that could have been distributed to the shareholders out of participating policyholders' income for the year? Since the amount distributed as policyholder dividends may be unrelated to income actually earned in any particular year, it may be argued that basing the shareholders' reported income on that figure could be misleading. That is to say, it would be better to base income reported for the shareholders on their percentage interest in the participating fund earnings, whether or not they are paid in dividends. However, as the size of the participating policyholders' equity grows, the percentage of participating dividends that qualifies for transfer to the shareholders drops in a succession of steps. Thus, if it can be predicted that the participating fund will grow to a point where the lower percentage cuts in before policyholder dividends are actually paid out of a year's income, that lower percentage should be used in recording the shareholders' interest in that income.

Summary

Financial institutions have characteristics that set them apart from ordinary enterprises. Their business involves them in the receipt of large sums from the public and the investment of such sums until they are needed to fulfill obligations to the public or until withdrawal. The amount of public money entrusted to financial institutions typically far exceeds the shareholders' equity. Sometimes public funds may be withdrawable on short notice; hence it is vital that the financial institution retain public confidence and also maintain liquid reserves available to meet sudden surges in the level of withdrawals. The importance of financial institutions to the economy and their importance to the public makes government regulation and supervision inevitable. All these characteristics tend to have an influence on accounting by financial institutions.

- A financial institution is forced to be relatively fully invested at all times in order to pay competitive returns to depositors or to offer competitive premium rates. Accordingly, financial institutions tend to follow long-term investment policies for the majority of their assets, even though individual holdings may be short-term in character. They are therefore likely to consider investment accounting methods that provide a long-term measure of investment performance particularly suitable for them.
- A portfolio of loans represents a major part of the assets of many institutions. There can be losses on uncollectible loans, while the opportunity for gain on loans (apart from the interest charge) is small or nonexistent. Therefore, appropriate recognition of probable loan losses is an important accounting problem. Assessment of the probability of losses on an individual loan basis, while necessary, is not likely to make sufficient provision for loss. A debtor/creditor relationship is often a continuing one, and some loss is likely for any portfolio of loans (and will be allowed for in the interest-rate charged) even though an examination of individual loans indicates a low probability of loss with respect to any single loan. For this reason, there should be a general loss provision in addition to specific loss provisions, but little authoritative guidance has been provided on the basis of estimating such general provision. In addition, specific provisions for loan loss in accounting have traditionally considered only the ultimate amount collectible on the loan, following the precedent for allowances for bad debts in an ordinary business enterprise. Such a recoverable-amount test produces carrying values that are above the present value of future cash inflows on the loan.
- Financial institutions receive fees for providing a variety of services and undertaking a variety of obligations. These should be recognized as earned in accordance with their nature, rather than merely when they are received or due. Generally, revenue recognition should be based on the performance of the service or expiration of the risk involved in the obligation. If fees represent, in whole or in part, an adjustment in yield from some investment position, they should be credited to the carrying amount of the investment to be amortized over its term to maturity.
- Questions of measurement of assets and liabilities on a discounted basis arise more often in financial institutions than in other industries. A discounted basis of measurement of a monetary asset or liability normally provides a faithful representation of the economic significance of the item in question. The consistency of accounting for assets and liabilities as a whole, however, should be taken into account in considering the desirability of discounting for an individual asset or liability. In the life insurance industry, for example, discounting is consistent with virtually all its accounting prac-

tices and provides greater justification for following tax allocation accounting on a discounted basis than is found in other industries. In contrast, discounting of provisions for claims or premium deficiencies in property and casualty insurers may be considered inconsistent with the treatment of unearned premium liabilities.

It is more difficult to conform the accounting of a life insurance business to the concepts underlying generally accepted accounting principles than it is for any other industry. It is difficult if not impossible, for example, to identify what portion of premiums received on life policies are equivalent to sales and service revenue of other industries. In general, in life insurance accounting, profits emerge from the process of valuation of assets and liabilities, especially the liability for policy obligations, rather than from a process of matching costs against revenues recognized. The key questions in profit determination for a life insurance business relate to:

- the amount of recognition given to heavy policy acquisition costs in the form of a deferred acquisition cost asset or equivalent reduction in the amount of liability recorded for policy obligations; and
- the degree of conservatism (or "provision for adverse deviation") allowed for in valuing the policy obligations.

Depending upon the treatment of these two factors, (1) a considerable loss or a considerable profit may be reported at the time that insurance policies are initiated, and (2) the distribution of any remainder of profit on the policies among years will be affected. Because the principal function of a life insurance company is risk bearing, it is right that the provision for policy obligations contain some provision for adverse experience in future under policies in force. Such provisions are released over the lifetime of the policy so that (unless the adverse experience occurs) profits emerge as the risk bearing takes place. The key question is: What is the proper measure of the provision for adverse deviation?

References

[1]CICA Accounting Guideline, "Financial Reporting by Property and Casualty Insurance Companies," *CICA Handbook*, April 1986 (Toronto: CICA).

[2]FASB, *Accounting for Debtors and Creditors for Troubled Debt Restructurings*, Statement of Financial Accounting Standards No. 15 (Stamford: FASB, 1977).

[3]See FASB, *Accounting for Nonrefundable Fees and Costs Associated with Originating and Acquiring Loans*, Exposure Draft of Proposed Statement of Financial Accounting Standards (Stamford: FASB, 1985).

[4]See FASB, *Accounting and Reporting by Insurance Enterprises*, Statement of Financial Accounting Standards No. 60 (Stamford: FASB, 1982), and AICPA, Committee on Insurance Accounting and Auditing, *Audits of Stock Life Insurance Companies*, 2nd ed., Industry Audit Guide (New York: AICPA, 1979).

Chapter Twenty-Five

Accounting for Nonprofit Organizations; Accounting for Government

We come now to the third chapter discussing an accounting area in which the historical cost theory has little to say. The historical cost model has laid so much stress on the measurement of income that one could easily believe it has no relevance for organizations not seeking profit. Indeed, it is not infrequently asserted by accountants in nonprofit organizations and governments that their entities are different and therefore their accounting and reporting must be different. That may or may not be true. It is undeniable that these entities have different characteristics from profit-oriented entities. Whether that requires a different set of accounting principles, however, is a different question.

To answer that question we need some theory. Unfortunately, until recently accounting theory and accounting standards have largely ignored nonprofit entities and governments. That situation seems to be changing.[1] However, it must be conceded that, to date, generally accepted accounting principles for nonprofit entities and governments (if, indeed, there are any) have developed largely from practice and have been little influenced or controlled by theory. It is true that, for some types of nonprofit organizations, recommendations have been published by bodies with some authority (especially in the U.S.), but these have been largely procedural in character and have their roots in practice, not in a general theory.[2]

The description "nonprofit entity" might be considered to embrace governments as well as organizations formed for charitable, social, or recreational purposes. Indeed, the two sectors have important characteristics in common, including the facts that they do not have owners who benefit directly in a financial way from their operations and that earning a profit is not a primary objective for them. That is why they are dealt with together in this chapter. In the early part of the chapter we shall deal with a few accounting issues stemming from these basic characteristics that are important both to governments and nonprofit entities other than governments. Subsequently, for convenience, we shall discuss certain other issues that are peculiar to, or more commonly encountered in, one sector or the other. There will not be a hard-and-fast dividing line, however, and we shall find that issues encountered by charities, etc., will often find a parallel in government, and vice versa.

Fundamental conceptual issues

Any review of the accounting and reporting practices of nonprofit entities and governments will show that they are extremely diverse. They differ from one segment of nonprofit activity to another — for example, hospital accounting is different from university accounting. Substantial differences are also often exhibited between individual entities within one segment. For example, we will find significant differences between the financial reporting practices of different provinces in Canada. Some rationalization of practice has resulted from efforts by individual industry associations. Nevertheless, especially in Canada, diversity remains between segments and within segments.

There are two major conceptual issues common to governments and nonprofit entities. The first concerns criteria for determining what activities should be considered to be those of the reporting entity. That is to say, we have to define the boundaries of the entity before we can know what it should be reporting. The second concerns the selection of elements to be reported in the financial statements. That is to say, we must decide what assets and liabilities make up its reported financial position — in effect, what resources and obligations it is accountable for. These can be very contentious issues.

Definition of the accounting entity

As we saw in chapter 19, it is accepted in accounting for profit-oriented entities that we seek to report on the economic unit. We can ascertain the boundaries of an economic unit by looking to control relationships, and these, in turn, stem to a considerable extent from ownership. In nonprofit entities and governments we lack the test of ownership. Without a profit orientation we also weaken the power of the idea of an economic unit. Do two activities form an economic unit because they are supported by a common source of funds — for example, taxation or borrowing — or must there be some stronger relationship between them? Why is the concept of an economic unit important for a nonprofit entity anyway? Some competing concepts are discussed below.

The core activity. One concept that is sometimes apparent in practice, although not often articulated in accounting literature, might be called the "core activity" concept. Consider a university that carries on a large number of ancillary activities ranging from printing and publishing and the operation of hospitals and medical and dental clinics to the operation of athletic stadiums and parking lots. There is little doubt that the core activities of a university are teaching and research. One possible basis for financial reporting, therefore, is to include only the assets, liabilities, revenues, and expenses of those core functions in the financial statements of the university and treat the ancillary activities as separate entities, each of which would have its own financial report. Such a reporting basis may fit in well with the organizational structure, since it is quite likely that the activities will be administered in a decentralized fashion and will often have their own set of accounting records.

The core activity concept is also quite strong in government accounting. One instinctively feels that there is a difference between "governmental" activities such as police and fire protection, the administration of justice, etc., and quasi-commercial functions such as the distribution of electricity on a fee-for-service basis. Moreover, an argument can be made that it is desirable to exclude the assets, liabilities, revenues, and expenses of such dissimilar activities to avoid confusion. In particular, there is a different significance to the "bottom line" in commercial and noncommercial activities, and merging the two will possibly destroy that significance.

In brief, the argument for the core activity concept is that it will produce financial statements that are more understandable and more informative. This argument is reinforced by the belief, held by some, that an accounting basis appropriate for commercial-type activities differs from that which is appropriate for other activities. (The choice of basis of accounting is the next major issue to be discussed.)

There are also significant arguments against the core activity concept. There almost inevitably will be situations in which the boundaries of the core activity are uncertain. For example, in a municipality, what clear difference is there between garbage collection service (paid for out of general taxation, but conceivably something that could be charged for), provision of water (paid for by a special charge, but one that may not be determined on a cost-of-service basis and that is often accompanied by an arbitrary "sewer" surcharge), and the provision of electricity?

Exclusion of some controlled activities from a financial report is also objectionable because it can be used to "manage" results reported. For example, prior to the 1960s, provincial government grants to universities, whether for capital or operating purposes, were written off as expended. In the 1960s, when university capital spending was at a peak, some provinces set up crown corporations to "lend" money to the universities to meet their building programs. Government advances to the crown corporations were treated as assets. The corporations' loans to the universities, however, could be repaid only out of regular grants from the governments. Subsequently those assets were written off by means of extra grants to the universities to repay the debts to the crown corporations, enabling them to repay their debts to the governments. In effect, expenditures for university capital purposes were treated as amortizable assets, contrary to previous practice and contrary to the treatment of other capital assets.

These are practical reasons that suggest the core activity concept is unsatisfactory. There is also one significant theoretical reason. It may well be asked whether a nonprofit entity or government is fulfilling its accountability obligation if some activities for which it is responsible are excluded from its external financial report. Some will argue that this objection is unimportant if separate financial reports for the excluded activities are readily available. Indeed, they will argue that separate reporting is desirable because it is more understandable.

Others hold to the view that a recognizable entity should provide a financial report, in summary form if necessary, covering all the activities for which it is responsible. Only in this way, it is felt, can the full financial significance of the entity be appreciated. Understandability can be achieved by careful design of the report, additional detail as to segments of activity, and additional separate financial reports for segments, as desired. From the standpoint of reporting to parties external to an entity, this contention seems quite persuasive. From the standpoint of internal management, the separate reporting of activities is likely to be more useful. However, given an efficient accounting and reporting system, that need not control the form of the external report.

The concept of control. If it is acknowledged that an entity should provide accountability in its summary financial report for all activities for which it is responsible, some clarification of the idea of responsibility may be necessary. One might begin by suggesting that an entity is responsible for activities it controls. But are there some limits to the concept of control?

Control might be interpreted in an administrative or financial sense or both.

For example, suppose a government sponsors a charitable organization and, to this end, it provides an initial grant and appoints the first board of directors. Thereafter, the organization raises its own funds and a mechanism is in force for election of the governing board that does not provide or require that a majority be government appointees. Should that organization be included within the government entity up to the time that government funding no longer forms a majority of its revenues, up to the time that government nominees no longer control the board, or never?

Consider some even more significant examples. Both hospitals and universities are practically under the control of provincial governments since they could not continue without government financial support. Municipalities are also, in law, "creatures of the province," notwithstanding that municipal governing bodies are elected by their residents. It seems unlikely that many people would argue that details of the operations and financial position of any of these bodies should be included in the financial reports of the provinces. This suggests that for financial reporting purposes an activity should be considered to be controlled by a non-profit entity or government only if both (1) a majority of its governing body is subject to appointment by the entity, and (2) a majority of its operating funding is obtained from the entity. It could be argued that such a rule is less than pure since, realistically, the power of the purse is the power to control. It may nevertheless be a reasonable practical answer.

Such a compromise answer is capable of abuse in some situations. For example, some social organizations may, for various reasons, delegate some or all fund-raising responsibilities and perhaps certain other activities to a separately incorporated foundation or agency. Such fund-raising organizations may be set up with complete legal independence of the organization for which funds are raised, even though they have common objectives. It may be strongly argued that the financial position of the social service agency cannot be properly understood if significant resources held for its benefit by the fund-raising agency remain unreported. Indeed, someone interested in either agency needs the financial report of the other for complete understanding.

Ideally, then, the two agencies should issue an annual report in common, with their financial statements reported on a combined basis or at least side by side. Again there may be borderline cases, such as those where a fund-raising agency raises funds for more than one operating agency. It has been suggested that in situations where the desirability of combined financial statements is debatable, the following considerations may tip the balance in favour of combined reporting:

- The purpose of the separate organization is to solicit funds for the reporting entity and substantially all of the funds solicited are intended by the contributors to be transferred to the reporting organization for use at its discretion.
- The reporting entity has transferred some of its resources to the separate unit to be held for the benefit of the reporting entity.
- The reporting entity has assigned functions to a controlled entity that is not primarily funded by public contributions.[3]

Restricted-purpose funds. Some nonprofit entities receive contributions that are restricted by the donor or grantor to spending for specific purposes. In some cases the restrictions may create a legal trust. In other cases, there may be no trust, but the circumstances in which the money is collected — for example, a capital campaign for specific building purposes — create an implicit trust that the recipient will try to respect. Legal provisions may also require that government units use certain revenues only in certain ways. For example, a law establishing a parking authority might require that parking revenues be used only to meet operating expenses of the authority or to acquire additional parking lots and structures.

In all such cases it is necessary that the entity make a special record in the accounts of the balances of restricted funds unspent and the purposes for which they are held. Often the monies received for restricted purposes and the investments therefrom are segregated from other assets of the entity in a separate "fund." A fund, in accounting, consists of a self-balancing segment of the accounts, set up to show monies received for specific purposes, the income therefrom (if it is to be credited to the fund), expenditures for the specific purposes, and the assets still held to balance the unspent residual of original proceeds and investment income.

The existence of restricted-purpose funds poses a question for the financial reports of the entity that receives them. Some hold that when funds are restricted the reporting entity is the fund, not the organization as a whole for whose benefit the restricted-purpose funds were created. (Although the financial report of the organization will usually cover all funds in one form or another, that is a matter of convenience, rather than an acknowledgement that the organization is one entity.) Those who hold this view are doubtful of the propriety of presenting a combined statement of funds and especially presenting consolidated totals of all funds. Others strongly believe that some consolidation or combination is necessary to an understandable portrayal of the activities of the organization.[4] We shall comment further on the presentation of restricted-purpose funds later in this chapter.

Basis of accounting

If we pursue the idea of a financial report as a report demonstrating stewardship or accountability, we must soon ask what the entity is accountable for. Is it accountable only for the cash it has received, or has it a broader responsibility for all the resources with which it is entrusted? Examination of the financial reports of nonprofit entities and governments will soon convince us that different entities answer this question in widely different ways. The diversity that can be encountered, even among similar entities, provides evidence that little thought has been given to the goals served by summary financial reports of nonprofit entities and little consensus exists. Clearly some conceptual framework is needed. It may be helpful in working to that end to explore the reasons for the present diversity in practice.

Size of the entity. To some extent different bases of accounting simply reflect differences in size and complexity of reporting entities. We should not be surprised that an entity follows a cash basis of accounting if cash is its only asset. To such an entity a classified list of cash receipts and disbursements for a period, reconciling with the change in cash and bank balances between the beginning and end of the period, is the only possible basis of financial reporting. Even a small entity, however, will often invest a cash balance temporarily or even engage in temporary borrowing. Usually the results of these transactions are accounted for as separate assets and liabilities and are excluded from the disbursements and receipts reported for the period. Again such a report is perfectly satisfactory. It may be loosely called cash basis accounting, but in fact it is full accrual accounting for an entity whose only assets and liabilities consist of cash, investments, and borrowing.

For many entities the first real question as to basis of accounting comes when they begin buying on credit. Do they now set up a system for formally recording accounts payable, or do they stick to the cash accounting and reporting system? Often they stick with cash accounting for a time because it causes less work. Sometimes such an entity receives an unpleasant surprise because bills pile up unnoticed. As a result it switches to a "modified cash" basis of accounting, accruing for liabilities unpaid but continuing to recognize revenues on a cash basis.

Once accounts payable are recognized, however, it is hard to resist an argument that accounts receivable should be recognized as well. Once the accounting has reached this stage it is often described as "accrual accounting." (As noted in chapter 5, this usage of the term differs from that in business accounting.) Sometimes only certain major accounts receivable and payable are recognized, in which case the entity may be said to be using "modified accrual accounting." The assets and liabilities recognized under the foregoing definition of "accrual accounting" are sometimes described as "financial claims" because they consist of cash or rights to receive cash (although certain forms of investment do not entirely fit that definition). The statement of activity for a year on this basis of accounting will reflect "revenues and expenditures" rather than "receipts and disbursements," the latter being the terminology generally reserved to describe cash flows.

To this point, it has been suggested that differences in accounting basis result principally from the complexity and extent of transactions. There is no serious difference in principle. It probably is possible to get agreement that a nonprofit entity should be responsible for reporting all material financial claims and the net change in them in its financial statements. (There could, however, be some differences of opinion on specific questions as to what qualifies as a financial claim.) The real arguments begin when it is suggested that entities ought to be accountable for assets and liabilities beyond those that can be categorized as financial claims. Factors other than the size of the entity bear upon this question, as will appear in our further discussion.

The influence of sources of financing. In several types of nonprofit entities there is a strong tradition of separate accountability according to the source of funds — that is, distinguishing between funds received for "capital" and "operating" purposes. Sometimes this separation reflects the formal restriction of grants or donations for capital purposes. Sometimes it merely reflects the entity's own view as to how it should finance its activities. Two examples are mentioned below:

- A private club may have a policy that the cost of club premises and major renovations should be financed out of initiation fees from members so far as possible. Accordingly, initiation fees will be excluded from the report of operating activity, as will capital expenditures of the type described. Other capital expenditures of a minor nature, however, may be written off as operating expenditures when incurred. Depreciation on expenditures capitalized may or may not be recognized as an operating expense depending upon the directors' policy decision whether depreciation should be recovered from annual fees, a decision which may change from time to time.
- A university, public art gallery, museum, or similar institution may have

an understanding that major building projects will be financed by capital campaigns. Accordingly, campaign donations and the projects financed by them will be excluded from the report of operating financial activity.

This type of accounting may be said to provide accountability in accordance with policy decisions made by a governing body, presumably with proper authority. Unfortunately, it leads to inconsistent reporting of assets and expenses from one entity to another and over time for the same entity.

The influence of fee setting. An organization that charges a fee for service designed to cover costs may want its financial reporting to provide a summary of expenditures that is useful for predicting future levels of expenditure and thereby assisting the fee-setting decision. The "financial claims" test for recognition of assets may not be fully satisfactory for this purpose because it results in writing off when incurred all large irregular expenditures that do not give rise to financial claims.

To avoid this, the entity may follow normal business practice in recording prepayments, inventories of major supplies, and fixed assets so that the statement of operating activity will record expense as the benefit from these assets is consumed, rather than when they are acquired.

If major fixed assets have been acquired by a capital campaign, however, depreciation would not be recorded in the operating statement with respect to them. The argument usually made is that campaign contributors intend to donate these assets; hence depreciation should not be recognized because it should not be recovered from service fees.

It would be consistent with the rationale of this accounting approach to make (and fund) a systematic calculated provision for irregular major renovation and repair costs to buildings and plant. Such major expenditures usually are too unglamorous to serve as objectives for a capital campaign and therefore must be covered by fees. Unfortunately, governing bodies often do not have sufficient vision or discipline to make such a regular provision. Instead, a board will often wish to set aside an arbitrary reserve in prosperous years. Accountants generally consider it misleading to report such an arbitrary appropriation as though it were an expenditure.

The influence of the spending budget. In a nonprofit entity or government, a budget adopted for a year may be used as a device to control expenditures. Every purchase order placed or other commitment reduces the amount authorized, and any new commitment can be placed only if it does not exceed the remaining limit. With such a system in force, an entity may argue that amounts authorized by the budget for spending out of current year's resources and for which spending authorization is carried forward should be reported as liabilities at a period-end, so long as purchase commitments have been placed with suppliers. Thus, amounts reported as liabilities include both actual accounts payable and "encumbrances" — that is, unfilled commitments. As a result, expenditures reported include intended expenditures as well as actual. Where followed, this accounting basis can be used to manage results reported merely by varying the decision as to the extent to which unspent budgetary authority is deemed to have lapsed.

From the foregoing paragraphs we can see that nonprofit entities and governments may choose to account for financial claims only; may also account for various assets such as prepayments and supplies; may capitalize some or all fixed assets and record depreciation on some or all or none of them in the statement of operating activity; and may even recognize liabilities for commitments placed from which no benefit has yet been obtained. Explanations can be given for all these various treatments, usually in terms of their value for certain policy decisions or for control. What is lacking is any theory of what represents relevant reporting to users external to the entity. In the next two sections we shall look at various users of financial reports (internal as well as external), followed by some suggestions that have been made as to objectives for reporting.

Users of financial reports

It is possible to draw up a lengthy list of potential users of the financial reports of nonprofit entities and governments. The following covers the main categories.

- The operational management of the entity. Management uses summary statements of resources and transactions in their evaluation of the results of past effort, in the control of resources, in planning for the future, and in advising regulatory or governing bodies on these matters.
- Governing bodies. These include members of the cabinet in senior governments, the mayor and councillors in municipalities, and boards of trustees or directors in other nonprofit entities. Financial reports will be helpful if they assist these bodies to evaluate the results of past policies and predict the possible effect of present and future policies.
- Legislators. In senior governments, legislators who are not members of cabinet have a responsibility to evaluate and criticize past and proposed policies. Financial reports will be useful if they contribute to an understanding of the financial impact of policies.
- Oversight and regulatory bodies. Nonprofit entities are often accountable to funding agencies. Municipalities are subject to control by provincial governments. Even senior governments may be accountable to other governments with respect to cost-sharing programs.
- Lenders and creditors. Although investor interest is absent in nonprofit entities, lenders and creditors are interested in their solvency and borrowing capacity. Lenders to governments, especially senior governments, tend to be less concerned with apparent solvency because their chief reliance for repayment is upon the government's power to tax. However, lenders ought to be concerned about a government's economic performance since its impact upon such matters as inflation and interest rates is significant to the attractiveness of government securities as investments.
- Donors and grantors. Major contributors to nonprofit organizations are interested in their accounting for contributions received and would also find useful any possible indication of quality of performance for assessing an organization's claim to further support.
- Analysts. With the nonprofit sector now accounting for something in the neighbourhood of fifty percent of the gross national product, its economic and social impact is of considerable interest to economists, sociologists, experts in public finance, and the like. Senior governments, particularly, have such an impact on employment, interest rates, and exchange rates that reliable, timely, and frequent financial reports are of considerable significance.
- Employees, members, recipients of benefits, and other constituents. The

financial status of nonprofit entities financed by membership fees is of obvious interest to members. The significance of other nonprofit entities and governments to taxpayers and citizens is less direct but nevertheless important. The general public, however, tends to rely upon the media for analysis of policies and financial affairs of nonprofit entities, particularly of governments.

Lengthy lists of users of financial statements of business entities, not unlike the above, have been drawn up by a number of accounting researchers. The very length of such a list militates against its utility for the purpose of selecting criteria to govern information in financial reports. For business enterprises it has been necessary, as a practical matter, to zero in on a particular class of user — in this case, investors and creditors — to make some progress.[5] It is possible to reason that the interest of such users in the possibility of cash return to themselves from the enterprise leads to a concern for financial reporting that helps to assess the prospects for future cash flows for the entity itself.

Is there any parallel in the case of nonprofit entities and governments? We have said enough already to suggest that internal management uses have had a powerful effect on the form of reporting of these entities (and this has led to diversity in practice). But we do not need to provide standards for internal use. If we are talking about standards for external financial reporting, we logically ought to be addressing the information needs of external users.[6] Can we then identify one class or group of external user (as has been done in the case of business enterprises) to provide a focus for consideration of information needs?

In the case of governments, one possible answer is attractive. There is one group of external users (or potential users) of government financial reports that has a direct stake in the government's performance. That group consists of the taxpayers. In a business enterprise we identify investors as being important users because future cash inflows of the enterprise are expected to lead to cash inflows to the investors. In a government, we could identify taxpayers as an important interest group because future government cash outflows will have a direct impact on taxpayer cash outflows. The analogy between the information needs of taxpayers and investors is far from exact. But perhaps it leads to a useful conclusion — that an emphasis in government financial reports on data that would help prediction of future cash requirements would be valuable.

In contrast, the performance of nonprofit entities will not have the same direct impact on any external group of users. Several groups may be interested in the quality of service by a nonprofit entity. One group stands out, however, as being both interested in the service and in a position to do something about it. It seems logical, then, to think of that group — those who provide resources to the nonprofit entity — as the primary potential users of its financial reports.

Objectives of financial reporting

A number of assertions as to the objectives of financial reporting by a nonprofit entity can be found in the literature.

Stewardship. A frequent assertion is that the primary purpose of financial reports of nonprofit entities is to demonstrate stewardship or accountability. The entity has been entrusted with resources by contributors or taxpayers. It is expected to demonstrate that it has spent the resources in accordance with its basic purposes in a properly authorized fashion. This proposition has been interpreted to suggest, among other things, that (1) cash basis accounting for contributions and revenue is appropriate because the entity cannot be accountable for resources it has not yet received, (2) expenditure in accordance with proper authority represents a discharge of the entity's responsibility, and (3) financial reports must demonstrate accountability for restricted-purpose funds by reporting them separately from unrestricted funds.

These interpretations of the stewardship concept, although often encountered, are essentially negative. A more enlightened view is that "dollar accountability" is not sufficient to discharge a stewardship reporting obligation. The goal of every nonprofit entity is to provide some service. (The government objective to promote social welfare is more complex than that, but service is important among its goals as well.) To this end, an entity is entrusted with certain resources. Accountability does not end when cash resources are spent. Real accountability requires some indication of performance. Ideally, to discharge its accountability obligation an entity should report what it has accomplished both in quantitative and qualitative terms.

Anyone who has thought about it realizes that it is very difficult to measure and communicate the quality of service. Some might also question what such information has to do with a financial report. The answer is that if the goal of a financial report is to report on performance, it must provide some indicators of the entity's output. In a business entity the revenue of the enterprise from outside parties provides a positive indicator whether its output is satisfactory. The same is not true of nonprofit entities, except for those that operate on a fee-for-service basis. Therefore, indicators of service output are needed. But those indicators by themselves will also be insufficient. To enable proper assessment, indicators of quantity and quality of service output need to be compared with the cost of providing that service. Only in this way can a judgment be made whether the service is worthwhile.

We are a long way from having reports of stewardship that meet the ideals just expressed. Nor does it appear, in view of the intangibles in assessment of service quality, that we will ever reach that ideal. Experimentation is required to discover what is possible, and efforts are made from time to time to that end.[7] In the meantime, however, one limited measure of performance is possible. Apart from specific project activities, it is a goal of every service enterprise to maintain its ability to serve indefinitely. To do so the entity must maintain its long-run financial health. It must raise enough money to cover its program costs, or else it must tailor its programs to the resources available. A financial report can at least inform its readers whether this goal is being achieved.

Compliance. In government it is often asserted that the primary objective of government financial reports is to demonstrate that spending or other allocations of resources are in compliance with authorizations provided, following laid-down legal procedure. This idea is essentially the same as the dollar accountability interpretation of stewardship. In its extreme form it is assumed to impose certain requirements on the financial reports of government.

- Published financial reports must follow the organizational forms established in government legislation providing for specific activities. Thus, for example, if a special fund is set up to receive certain tax or other revenues and to finance certain activities, such revenues and expenditures must be excluded from the financial report of the government itself.

- Since the budget (or "Estimates" in the federal government) authorizes spending, the expenses must be reported using the classification system used in the budget, regardless of what classification basis might be considered most relevant for statement readers.
- The accounting basis used in the financial report must be consistent with that used in the presentation of the authorized budget. Since the principal purpose of that budget is to authorize spending, it is likely to be prepared on a pure cash basis, a financial claims basis, or a financial claims basis modified to recognize encumbrances (unspent commitments) as a liability. There is no room in such a system for recognition of assets such as inventory or property. System modifications are required to permit such recognition. For example, a capital and operating budget, implicitly authorizing some assets to be capitalized, may be presented. Or, whenever it is felt that full accrual accounting is desirable for a particular activity, an off-balance-sheet special fund may be authorized that will report as a separate entity from the government, using the accounting basis considered best suited to its needs.

The proposition that reporting compliance is a key objective for financial reports is open to severe question. The idea that legislators should be interested in knowing that actual spending has been properly authorized is, of course, beyond question. It is questionable, however, whether the financial statements are the best means for providing that assurance. Financial reports are usually at too high a level of aggregation to demonstrate compliance effectively. It is strongly arguable that assurance as to compliance is better obtained through a strong system of internal control, together with special reporting by the government auditor on the internal controls and on any lack of compliance discovered in the audit examination.

The compliance objective, as it has been interpreted, also undermines the potential of financial reports to communicate needed information. Budget authorization of spending is a decision for the here and now. If a government policy does not have a major impact on spending in the short run, a financial statement focussing only on short-run spending decisions will not say much about that government policy. Legislators and the public generally ought to think about long-run policy, and financial reports ought to help them to do it. Moreover, the expedient of creating special off-balance-sheet funds to permit selective application of full accrual accounting opens the way to the management of reported financial results. The treatment of advances for university capital spending in the 1960s, already referred to, provides an example.

Long-term cost of service. It was suggested above that dollar accountability is too narrow a concept of accountability. The statement reader is interested in the expenses of operation, not mere expenditure of cash. Full accrual accounting, including allocation of all costs incurred to the period in which their benefit is consumed, tends to show the long-term cash demands of the program carried on rather than the short-term cash demands. We say "long-term" because in some cases — for example, buildings and equipment — the current period feels the benefit of cash paid long ago, and in others — for example, employee pensions — the current period benefits because of promises to pay cash that will mature many years into the future. If one assumes that the entity will continue to serve indefinitely, with replacement of assets as needed, such a portrayal of long-term cash demands may be very significant. (We also say "tends to show" because an allocation of costs incurred some time ago provides only an imperfect measure of cash required at current prices to replace assets consumed.)

Often those who advocate full accrual accounting for nonprofit entities are accused of wishing to impose business accounting principles upon nonprofit entities without understanding their special nature and requirements. If users of the financial reports of nonprofit entities are interested in a long-term perspective on the financial consequences of their entities, that argument is unfounded. Nor is it an either/or proposition. The probability is that both long-term and short-term perspectives are useful. If so, one of the arguments in favour of full accrual accounting is that it is relatively easy to convert a statement based on full accruals into a statement portraying flow of cash or liquid resources. In contrast, it is impossible to convert cash accounting into full accrual accounting without supplementary information tantamount to accrual figures for assets and liabilities.

A measure of long-run cost of service is important for two reasons. First, the long-run cost of service can be compared with contributions, taxes, and other revenue for the period to see whether the current generation is absorbing the full cost of service, or whether it is, in effect, running down capital provided by previous generations or passing on a burden to future generations. In other words, knowing whether capital has been maintained in a nonprofit entity—that is, whether it has operated on a breakeven basis—requires full accrual accounting, just as does measurement of income in a business organization. Although the objectives are different, the means of satisfying them are the same.

Second, such a full accrual basis of accountability could be considered to be more relevant than cash accounting to contributors to a nonprofit entity, because it facilitates evaluation whether the service is worthwhile. It is true that it deals only with the cost side of any cost/benefit analysis. Indicators (usually nonmonetary) of service outputs need to be provided as well, to permit informed judgments as to the value of the service and the entity's effectiveness in meeting program objectives. Nevertheless, provision of cost data is the starting point if any program evaluation is to be made.

Usually, performance indicators are easier to develop in relation to individual programs or activities of an entity rather than in relation to its service as a whole (particularly if it carries on diversified activities). Thus, cost-based accounting could be valuable to administrators in planning programs and monitoring their success and to governing bodies in policy decisions whether to initiate or terminate programs. The use of cost-based accounting for internal program evaluation does not, by itself, mean that it ought to be used for external reporting. However, adoption of accrual accounting techniques across the board would probably increase the reliability of accrual figures developed for individual programs. Thus, arguments for the usefulness of full accrual information for external and internal purposes tend to support each other.

Multiple objectives. It should be observed that identification of particular information needs for one group of users and different needs for another group does not necessarily mean that one basis of reporting must be adopted to the exclusion of others.

Many groups of users could be interested in financial reports on more than one basis. For example, analysts interested in the economic impact of government are likely to be interested both in the long-run costs of programs in being and in short-run cash requirements in view of their significance to interest rates and foreign exchange rates. Lenders to senior governments are likely to be more interested in short-run cash requirements in view of their reliance on the general taxing power of the government, but lenders to municipalities or other nonprofit entities may well be more interested in knowing whether these entities are covering long-run costs.

Financial reports are capable of considerable flexibility in design. There could be different ways to present information in the financial reports of nonprofit entities and governments so as to provide perspectives on both long-run costs and short-term cash flows. The primary problem is to identify what information would be useful to report. Just how the report is constructed is a secondary problem that might well be decided based on consideration of what would be most understandable to users.

The accounting of nonprofit entities

In this section we take a closer look at accounting and reporting issues that crop up regularly in nonprofit entities.

Restricted-purpose funds

The receipt of funds to be spent for designated purposes only is characteristic of many nonprofit entities. The practical importance of the restriction may vary. The purposes of some restricted donations may be so much a part of the normal operations of the entity that the restriction is purely a matter of form. The entity meets the restriction simply by doing what it intended to do anyway. At other times, donations may be received for spending on purposes that the entity would not include in its program were it not for the special funding. These variations in circumstances make it difficult to draw hard-and-fast rules as to how restricted-purpose funds should be accounted for and reported.

As noted already, some people think that funds received for restricted purposes are not part of the reporting entity. Accordingly, the accounting for receipts, expenditures, and residual balances of such funds should be excluded from the financial report of the entity or at least separated from its accounting for unrestricted funds. Alternatively, such an exclusion might be considered appropriate whenever there is an actual legal trust requiring that assets held for restricted purposes be segregated.

Such a legalistic point of view is open to criticism. Usually, if an entity accepts funds spendable for restricted purposes, it may be assumed that those purposes are compatible with the service objectives of the entity. Often the restricted gift merely enhances the capacity of the entity to undertake or expand programs that it wants to do in any event. It would hamper the portrayal of the activities of the entity if spending on one program were reported in two or more different places depending upon whether the spending was funded by unrestricted or restricted donations.

It is suggested that, taking into account all the circumstances, the following principles should guide accounting and reporting with respect to funds received for spending on restricted purposes:

- Complete exclusion of restricted-purpose funds from the reports of resources and activities of an entity should not be permitted except in unusual circumstances when it can be demonstrated that the entity holds the funds only as a disbursing agent and has no interest in the activity benefiting from the support.
- Spending of restricted-purpose funds should be combined in the financial report with figures of spending of unrestricted funds or should be presented in such a way that the figures can be readily combined.
- Unspent balances of restricted-purpose funds should be disclosed or segregated from unspent balances of unrestricted funds. Assets held in trust for restricted purposes should likewise be segregated or identified.

Further comments on restricted-purpose funds and their statement presentation will be made in succeeding sections.

Board-designated restricted funds

In the past, some entities have appropriated funds from operating budgets for special purposes and reported such appropriations as though they were expenditures, with a corresponding receipt being shown in the restricted-fund category. Alternatively, they might dedicate certain unrestricted contributions to specific purposes and, for this reason, account for such contributions as though they were restricted, not unrestricted. The opportunity to manipulate the record of what has actually happened in this way is usually frowned upon in accounting literature. It is considered that the voluntary dedication of funds for restricted purposes should be shown as appropriations, rather than being allowed to affect the report of unrestricted revenues and expenditures in a period. Likewise, unspent balances of any such "board-designated" funds ought to be clearly disclosed as being distinct from true restricted funds.

Revenue recognition issues

Except for fees for service, most of the support for nonprofit entities comes from nonreciprocal transactions — that is, transactions in which there is not an exchange of value between two parties. Some would say that support received in nonreciprocal transactions — donations, grants, and the like — is not revenue since it is not earned. From this they argue that nonreciprocal support should not appear in the entity statement of activity but in a separate statement, thereby avoiding the necessity of showing a "bottom line" and implying that in some way there is a matching of revenue and expenditure for a period in a nonprofit entity. There is merit in this suggestion; the majority practice, however, is to use the term revenue loosely so as to include nonreciprocal support and to report revenue and expenditure in one statement. The nonreciprocal nature of support revenue, however, does raise questions as to how it should be recognized and when.

- The first question is whether all support should be treated as revenue, or whether some is equivalent to capital contributed in a business organization.

When support is received in the form of an endowment — that is, contributions that may not be spent but must be invested to produce income for the entity — the regular practice is to credit the contribution directly to the endowment equity account, more often than not in a separate fund grouping.

- If funds are received whose use is restricted to spending on plant, possibly as a result of a "capital campaign," such support is usually not reported together with operating support but rather is credited to a separate plant fund, never to appear in the statement of current activity. This treatment is not the only possibility, however, as will be discussed later.
- When support is received of a type that cannot be counted upon on a regular basis — for example, large bequests — some governing boards become concerned about the effect on the bottom line of reporting the support as revenue. There is a tendency in such cases to wish to earmark the support for specific purposes (there may even be a stated policy that all bequests shall be treated as endowment) and accordingly to exclude the proceeds from the regular statement of activity. This is essentially the same question as that discussed above in relation to board-designated funds, and the answer is the same. All support that is not restricted by the donor should be reported as received in the current statement of activity. Self-imposed restrictions should be reported as appropriations after the figure of balance of revenues and expenditures for the year, rather than be reported in the same fashion as externally imposed restrictions.
- Some nonprofit entities receive gifts in kind. Writers on accounting usually suggest that such gifts should be valued and recorded as part of the entity revenue so long as the gifts are (1) suitable for the entity's purposes, (2) capable of being valued objectively and without inordinate effort, and (3) material in amount.
- The work of many nonprofit entities receives major support from volunteers. A full portrayal of the scope of activity would require that the value of services donated by volunteers be recognized in the statement of activity. Doing so, however, would involve considerable work in keeping track and valuing services rendered. A Canadian research study has suggested that material amounts of donated services should be recognized (as both current revenue and expense) if (1) the service is essential and would be paid for if not volunteered, (2) the volunteer accepts direction much as an employee would, and (3) the value of the service is readily measurable.[8] It is doubtful that this recommendation has been accepted in Canadian practice as yet.

Fixed-asset accounting

Reference has already been made to the wide variation in accounting for fixed assets by nonprofit entities. Treatments found in practice include: (1) record all fixed asset acquisitions as expenditures that are written off in the statement of activity, possibly leaving $1.00 in the asset account as a reminder that fixed assets exist but are not valued; (2) capitalize all fixed assets financed by regular sources of support and record depreciation in the statement of activity; (3) record fixed assets financed by capital grants, contributions, or borrowing in a separate plant fund account, and write off all other fixed asset acquisitions as expenditures in the statment of activity; (4) leave fixed assets capitalized in the plant fund at original cost until disposed of (treating disposal proceeds as revenue of the current fund);

(5) depreciate fixed assets capitalized in the plant fund, by a charge against the fund balance; (6) depreciate the fixed assets in the plant fund, recognize the expense in the statement of activity, and fund the depreciation by a transfer from the current fund to the plant fund.

The following arguments are very commonly made against depreciation accounting:

- It is difficult to estimate useful lives. Whether this is true may depend upon the particular situation. In general, since obsolescence is less likely to be a factor affecting the assets of nonprofit entities, one would expect that estimation of useful lives would be easier than it is in business accounting, not harder.
- A charge for depreciation should not be made with respect to donated fixed assets because that would imply that the depreciation should be covered out of current donations or other revenue.
- Depreciation is meaningless unless it is funded. This argument implies that a long-run perspective on cost of operation has no significance for statement readers.
- A figure for depreciation based on the historical cost of assets will be meaningless because of changes in replacement cost of asset capacity and the purchasing power of the dollar. This objection has some strength, as it has in business accounting as well.
- Depreciation accounting will cost more than it is worth. This is a matter of opinion. Normally, depreciation accounting for external reporting is inexpensive. Greater costs would be involved if depreciation figures were to be allocated to programs, etc., for internal management purposes, but conceivably more value would be derived from such use. Initial conversion to a depreciation accounting system would entail some cost, which might or might not be significant depending upon the individual situation and the degree of insistence on precision in the figures.

The case for depreciation accounting rests upon the value of the long-run perspective on costs of operations, which may vary from one case to another. For example, it might be important for activities operated on a fee-for-service or cost-recovery basis. One might expect that whenever the use of fixed assets is significant the long-run perspective would be more important, so that greater accounting cost would be justified.

Investment accounting

A few types of nonprofit entities that receive substantial restricted-purpose donations and endowments may build up large pools of investments awaiting spending. This fact gives rise to issues as to (1) valuation of investments for reporting purposes, (2) measurement of investment income, and (3) allocation of pooled investment return among funds when investments for individual restricted-purpose funds are pooled.

The first two of these issues are interrelated. If investments held are carried on the customary basis of cost or amortized cost, irregular gains and losses on realization will increase the difficulty of budgeting for smooth spending of income and principal of the restricted-purpose funds. A market value basis of valuation will provide the best portrayal of financial position from time to time, but the recording of unrealized gains or losses would exacerbate the problem of income distribution. As a result, nonprofit entities with large investment pools are quite likely to wish to use accounting methods that smooth the recognition of investment income, such as those described in chapter 16. With respect to holdings of equity securities, some institutions use a "total return" concept in computing amounts to be distributed from the investment pools, whereby a "spending rate" is established based on an assumption as to capital gains that may be expected to be realized on average over the longer term.[9]

When monies received for many specific purposes are merged into one investment pool, some method must be adopted for allocating the income, however measured, from the pooled investments to the individual contributing funds. A common solution to this is to assign points to each participating fund at the time it enters the pool based on market values of the pool assets at the date of entry. For example, if the market value of an investment pool is $100,000 and existing participants hold 5,000 points so that each point is worth $20, a new fund contributing $20,000 in assets to the pool will receive 1,000 points, and that will entitle it to receive 1,000/6,000 of the pool income distributed thereafter, until the total number of points changes by further accessions to or withdrawals from the pool.

Statement presentation

There are two matters of concern in the presentation of financial statements for nonprofit entities. The first is the manner of classification of revenues and expenses. The second and more difficult is that of achieving proper disclosure with respect to restricted-purpose funds without destroying the understandability of the statements.

Classification issues. Nonprofit entities differ in their classification of revenues and expenditure (or expense). Revenues will usually be classified by type and source. Thus, they might be classified as revenues from sales and service, fees, contributions from others, investment income, and so on. Contribution revenue might be subclassified by source such as public donations, corporate donations, government grants, and so on.

A more fundamental division exists in the classification of expenditures or expenses. A frequent basis of classification, especially in smaller entities, is by object of expenditure, such as salaries and wages, employee benefits, supplies, utilities, and services. Another basis of classification is by purpose of expenditure. Expenditures may be classified broadly by function — as program activity, fund-raising, and administration — or more detail may be given for individual programs and activities. A third possible basis of classification is by centres of responsibility.

Each basis of accounting has its usefulness for management or external reporting purposes. If all are to be accommodated, the internal accounting system must be designed to provide a two- or three-way classification of expenditures as they occur. For external reporting purposes, it is generally thought that classification by function, program or activity is most valuable (especially if it is possible to relate the figures to indicators of program output and achievement). The AICPA also suggests the provision, as supplementary information, of a schedule of functional expenditures cross-classified by object of expenditure.[10] Accounting by centre of responsibility has lesser informational value for external reporting.

Treatment of restricted-purpose funds. When restricted-purpose funds are received, the accounting records must be set up so as to make sure the restrictions are observed. That means that the initial receipt must be credited to an identified obligation account and the funds, if required to be segregated from unrestricted funds, must be deposited in separate bank accounts and investments therefrom designated in the records. Thereafter there must be a system to control the release of segregated assets and reductions of obligations as spending on the restricted purposes takes place. In some cases an entity may have received funds for hundreds of separate special purposes. Although the accounting records must account individually for each fund, it is acknowledged that funds may be classified into a number of natural groupings for the purpose of financial reporting so that only totals for each group of funds are reported. Common fund groupings are endowment funds (funds whose capital may not be spent), plant funds (received for the acquisition of buildings and equipment), and funds received for other restricted purposes, subclassified as seems appropriate.

There are basically two ways in which restricted-purpose funds may be included in an entity's financial statements. The first is to present the statements of financial position and activity in columnar form, with one column for unrestricted funds and one for each of the groups into which the restricted-purpose funds have been classified. Total columns provide figures for the assets and liabilities of the entity as a whole and for all its revenues and expenditures (or expenses). A drawback to this basis of presentation is that it is usually too cumbersome to give comparative figures for previous periods except for the total column.

A second basis of presentation is known as a "layered" presentation because of the appearance of the statement of financial position. In effect, a separate balance sheet is recorded for the unrestricted funds and for each separate restricted-purpose fund group, one after the other on the page — hence the designation "layered." This form of presentation has the advantage that it is possible to present comparative figures fund by fund. On the other hand, it fails to provide totals for assets of all funds classified by types of assets (such as investments).

Revenues and expenses for a period are not usually presented in the same layered fashion. Rather, a full statement of operating activities is presented, and separate statements are provided showing movements in the balance of restricted-fund groups over the year. When this form of presentation is used, it is usually desired to provide a full report in the statement of operating activities for program spending for the year, whether or not some programs or parts thereof are financed by restricted-purpose funds. To achieve this, an amount equal to the restricted-purpose funds spent is reported as though it were another donation. In other words, the use of restricted-purpose funds is reported in the statement of operating activity both as a donation and expenditure.

One difference can occur in accounting for the use of restricted funds. Suppose funds are received and set aside for a given purpose in the amount of $100,000. Suppose further that the entity spends $150,000 for the purpose in a year, which has the effect of satisfying the restriction, but finances that spending entirely out of unrestricted funds — that is, its regular budget — rather than using any of the funds set aside. One school of thought holds that the donation of restricted funds should not be reported as current revenue in this situation because the money set aside has not actually been used. Another school of thought argues that once the funds become free of restriction, the receipt should be reported as revenue.

The latter point of view is preferable. The former basis of accounting is open to manipulation whenever an entity is in a strong enough financial position to pick and choose when it will take restricted-purpose money to meet its program costs.

Some accountants go even further and argue for the reporting of all donations as current revenues when received, whether or not they are restricted. Then, to the extent that restrictions have not been satisfied by spending in the year, an appropriation to the restricted-funds grouping is shown at the foot of the statement of activity. Assuming that restricted-purpose funds will only be accepted for purposes the entity considers worthwhile, it is argued that full reporting of donations in the statement of activity better portrays the entity's fund-raising performance.

The reporting of restricted-purpose funds as operating revenue when spending on the restricted purpose takes place is customarily used just for restricted donations that assist ordinary program expenditures. It is not used with respect to donations for capital expenditures, which, as previously noted, are normally credited directly to a plant fund. Suppose, however, that it was considered desirable to report expenses on a full accrual basis, including depreciation, in order to provide a measure of the long-run cost of operating at the present program level. It might be objected that this would be wrong if property subject to depreciation had been acquired from capital donations, because the receipt of the donation would have been excluded from the statement of activity while the depreciation is included. That objection would be met, however, if the capital donation were treated like any other restricted donation, so that a transfer to current revenue is reported at the time that the expense subsidized by the donation (in this case, depreciation) is recognized.

The accounting of governments

This section discusses commonly debated issues in government accounting.

The government entity

Definition of the reporting boundaries of a government entity presents more problems than it does for any other type of entity. Senior governments, particularly, have a variety of devices for structuring certain activities so that, under present permissive accounting practice, the activities may be effectively excluded from the principal government financial statements. The effect of such exclusion is that the assets, liabilities, revenues, and expenses of the unit excluded are not covered in the figures reported in the government's financial statements. All that is reported is the amount of investment in or advances to that unit (if such have not been written off) and dividends or interest (if any) received from it.

The following describes the means that may be used for exclusion of designated activities. A "special fund" may be created and financed by dedicating a given class of revenue to the fund or by appropriating cash. Similarly, a "special account" may be set up for a certain activity by charging government expenditure and crediting a liability. Thereafter, revenues and expenditures of that activity are recorded as increases or decreases in the liability figure rather than as revenues and expenditures of the government. "Revolving funds" are created by making advances (that may or may not be written off) to finance some activity that is usually more or less commercial in nature and that is expected to operate on a self-sustaining basis.

Crown corporations may also be used in a somewhat similar manner to hive off activities. Sometimes crown corporations operate commercial ventures so that there is some rationale supporting their segregation. In many cases, however, they carry on activities that otherwise would be carried on by the government itself. The creation of crown corporations thus can result in suppression of some information about government activity. Sometimes this disadvantage is overcome by consolidating the figures of crown corporations, but there is no recognized accounting standard that prescribes when consolidation should take place, and practice varies from one government to another.

If we wish to formulate criteria for determining what activities should be included or excluded from the government entity, we must address the questions discussed earlier in this chapter. The threshold question is whether any organizational unit controlled by a government (assuming control can be defined satisfactorily) is properly excluded from the government entity. At least some people would hold that there is a need for one overall summary report on government activity to indicate adequately its importance to and impact on the economy of the region governed. A summary report cannot be expected to provide much detail about individual activities of the government, but, if well designed, supplementary notes and schedules can lead serious analysts to sources of more detailed information.

If any activities are excluded, there ought to be an understandable rationale for their exclusion. The only intuitively appealing rationale is that the government's financial report should be confined to core "governmental" activities. Commercial activities should be excluded. As explained earlier, that idea gets us into severe problems of defining what is or is not commercial and of ensuring that the possibility of excluding some controlled entities is not used to manage results by accelerating or delaying write-offs and loss provisions that otherwise would be required.

Taken altogether, it seems probable that full consolidation of government controlled activities would leave less opportunity for management of reported results and thereby would make the financial reports more useful for disinterested users. The potential confusion caused by aggregation of results of dissimilar activity could be mitigated by supplementary reports of segments of activity on a basis somewhat similar to segmented reporting in the private sector.

Basis of aggregation. If a government entity is defined on a comprehensive basis, there can be questions as to the best way to aggregate the results of units of activity. Instead of full consolidation, one could consider equity accounting for investments in commercial-type entities or even the cost basis of investment accounting if a commercial entity is not expected to provide a return to the government on the investment in it.[11] Anything less than full consolidation of all units would raise the same sort of question as to definition of entities excludable from full consolidation as has just been discussed. On the other hand, the use of investment accounting on the equity or cost basis could provide a pragmatic answer to the problem of the use of different accounting bases for governmental and commercial units (if such differences persist).

Basis of accounting. The issue of the extent to which accrual accounting is adopted is one of the most debated issues among senior governments. In recent years there has been a trend in Canada to the financial claims basis of accounting. That is to say, recorded assets are limited to those that directly represent expected cash inflows or are convertible into cash. Recorded liabilities represent expected cash outflows. Assets that represent potential for service are not recognized even though some, such as real property, also have potential salable value.

There needs to be some clarification of the treatment of investments under this system. Earlier, reference was made to provincial governments making "investments" in crown corporations that simply re-lent the money to universities or other institutions that could never repay it without government grants. Such an investment had little or no potential for a net return in cash — yet it was carried as an asset under the financial claims or cash basis of accounting. Questions may be asked even about investments that are much closer to self-sustaining. Suppose a government invests equity in a crown corporation such as the Canadian National Railway Company or a provincial power commission. If it never receives a dividend on its investment, does it have an asset? The logic of the financial claims concept leads one to at least question the asset status of such investments.

Earlier, we reported the argument that a longer-term perspective provides justification for full accrual accounting for nonprofit entities as well as business organizations. Certain counter arguments are repeatedly heard in the context of senior government accounting. The first is that the greatest asset of a government is its taxing power. If that is not recorded, the argument runs, why should we bother with trivial matters like inventories or fixed assets? This argument is largely based upon the concept of an asset as something that is capable of producing cash to meet liabilities shown by the balance sheet. As such, it does not even touch upon the main grounds suggested for full accrual accounting — the informational value of a measure of program activities in terms of resources consumed rather than cash spent.

Even on its own grounds the argument is nonsense. To be recognized in a statement of financial position, an asset ought to exist, not merely represent future potential. A young person may have a great expectation of earning future income, but that does not entitle him or her to record future salary expectations in a personal balance sheet. If we were to recognize future taxes as an asset, we would also have to recognize future program expenditures as a liability. When we consider how difficult it is even to reduce the annual deficit, let alone produce a surplus to reduce the accumulated deficit from prior years, we must conclude that the notion of future taxation power as a present asset is ludicrous.

A second argument takes the approach of a *reductio ad absurdum*. If we capitalize purchases of fixed assets, it is said, why should we not capitalize expenditures on education, for example. The value of such an intangible may be far greater than the tangible asset acquired. This argument is misconceived. If we were attempting to draw up a balance sheet for the nation as a collective whole, we might well wish (if it were possible) to quantify the benefit from the superior educational status of the population. But we are not talking about a balance sheet of the nation as a whole. We are talking about the financial statements of the government of the nation, or of a province as a separate entity within the nation. The value of the superior education of a citizen belongs to the citizen — not to the government — and has no place in a government's balance sheet.

There are possible arguments — largely pragmatic — against full accrual accounting for governments, but these two red herrings do not belong among them.

Capital and operating funds

The accounting of municipalities is perhaps even more influenced by financing aspects than is nonprofit entity accounting. The result is a traditional separation between an operating fund whose expenditures are financed by taxation and other current revenue and a capital fund whose expenditures are financed by capital borrowing. It seems probable that this distinction originated with the idea of equity between generations. Expenditures with transitory benefits should be paid for by current taxation. The cost of assets with long-service lives should be paid for in a manner that spreads the cost over a long period — in effect the period over which the debt is liquidated.

Over time, however, strict adherence to the idea that the nature of the asset governed the financing evaporated. Now, current funds may be used to finance capital spending, and it is the source of financing that governs the accounting for the expenditure. If bought from current revenue, the asset is written off. If bought with capital financing, it is capitalized in the capital fund and thereafter may be written off in step with the liquidation of the debt financing it.

Capital borrowing by municipalities is controlled by provincial authorities. This adds some assurance that only real capital assets are recorded in the capital fund. The same is not true in other situations. At one time a few provinces also used capital and operating funds in their accounting. Since there were no standards governing provincial government accounting, it was only necessary to define an expenditure as capital in order to reduce the operating budget and apparent deficit. The opportunities for managed reporting were very great.

The overwhelming reliance upon financing considerations in an accounting system based on separate capital and operating funds reduces the opportunity for informative accounting. For example, many of the capital expenditures of a municipality — such as sewers, watermains, roads, and bridges — have very long lives, far longer than the period over which they are financed. As a result, a municipality that has established its basic infrastructure is likely to hit a period when its debt is paid down but major assets are not yet due for replacement. Then, as many American cities have discovered, there comes a time when much of the basic infrastructure needs renewal but the increases in taxes required to service additional debt are so major that they are politically very difficult to manage. Some municipalities have the foresight to start providing reserve funds in good years against future costs of this nature, but it is their own imagination and not their accounting that alerts them to the need.

Accounting for tax revenue

If revenues are accounted for on the accrual basis, the estimation of income taxes receivable presents problems. Since income taxes are self-assessed in the first instance, the government does not have good evidence of amounts due for a period until tax returns are filed, and even then changes will occur as a result of the examination of returns. Governments have traditionally accounted for such tax revenue on a cash basis rather than make (perhaps hazardous) estimates of the full amount of taxes receivable with respect to the fiscal year just ended. Such estimates are made by Statistics Canada for the System of National Accounts, however, so that estimation is not an impossible task. It is a matter of judgment whether the incorporation of such estimates, with their inevitable margin for error, is justified by the improvement in significance of figures in the summary financial statements.

A question with possibly greater significance is that of the reporting of "tax expenditures." It is a common practice of governments to provide incentives to the private sector by offering selective reductions of taxable income or tax contingent upon actions taken by the taxpayer. (See chapter 14 for discussion of the investment tax credit as an example.) Such reductions of taxes are equivalent in substance to conditional grants or subsidies by the government and for this reason have been described as expenditures through the tax system or, simply, tax expenditures. Such expenditures tend to be hidden from the public view, and it is often argued that government financial reports would be improved by suitable description of their existence and amount.

This proposal has a great deal of merit. There is a considerable problem, however, in deciding on just what should be deemed to be a tax expenditure. Most would agree, for example, that investment tax credits are similar in effect to outright grants. On the other hand, there could be considerable disagreement with a proposition that the tax exemption for marital status or the basic personal exemptions for everyone are equivalent to government subsidies rather than simply being elements of an equitable tax. There are many gradations between these two extremes. It would seem that there would need to be some consensus on just how a tax expenditure should be defined to permit what would be deemed significant disclosure.

Other hidden expenditures

The tax expenditure issue is part of a larger issue. Because a government's accounting is so tied to cash accounting, it is possible for noncash transactions to go unrecognized. For example, a provincial government may subsidize a corporation with a grant of valuable natural resources or with cash. The former is not accounted for; the latter is. Common sense suggests that the former subsidy in kind ought to be valued and recorded to achieve fair presentation.

Social program accounting and disclosure

There is one question in government financial reporting that has little or no equivalent in other nonprofit entities. It has been suggested that full accrual accounting helps the statement user appreciate the long-term spending impact of the present level of activity. That may be only partially true with respect to some important government programs. The reason is that a given program may require a given level of expenditure today but, because of changing demographics or other reasons, may show quite a different cost level in future.

For example, it can be predicted that the level of health care expenditures will show a marked increase on a per capita basis, if the present standard of publicly supported health care is maintained, simply because the proportion of elderly to the population at large will steadily increase over the next few decades. Is a forecast of such future effects pertinent to today's financial reports for governments? It is arguable that it is. Certainly, when governments are deciding upon new programs, such long-term forecasts of the costs of present programs are relevant information. Perhaps the best way to force consideration of long-term effects upon governments whose attention is concentrated upon winning the next election would be to require publication of long-term projections in budgets and annual financial reports for costs of major programs. The provision of multi-year reports on spending as part of, or supplementary to, the financial report would also be helpful in indicating long-term trends.

Summary

The financial reporting practices of nonprofit entities and governments have developed with relatively little guidance by way of theoretical discussion in accounting literature. The methods used in the financial reporting of such entities have grown out of practice. Accordingly, they have tended to be influenced by the thinking of preparers of financial statements and have been little influenced by perceived needs of users. In particular, the use of financial statements to assist in the preparation of budgets and to evidence compliance with spending authority has tended to bias financial reports towards the short-term objective of reporting the flows of cash or of financial claims.

Consistent with this, conceptual discussions of the objectives of financial reporting for nonprofit entities have focussed on stewardship, which is interpreted as "dollar accountability" — the demonstration that funds raised have been spent in accordance with the purposes for which they were raised. In government accounting particularly, the idea of dollar accountability has been elevated to suggest that demonstration of compliance with legal directions, in terms of spending authorization and forms of reporting, is the dominant objective of the financial report.

Latterly, considerably more attention has been paid to the possible uses of financial reports to provide information to parties outside the entity — contributors, members, oversight bodies, legislators, analysts, and the public generally. The idea of stewardship reporting has been expanded to suggest that financial reports should account for resources consumed in programs, not just money spent. In this way, a better perspective may be provided upon the long-term financial requirements of the entity than is offered by figures of short-term spending.

External users are also likely to find a classification of spending by function and by program more useful in evaluating stewardship than a classification merely by objects of expenditure. Of course, classification of expenditure by program does not provide much indication of program effectiveness unless some information is provided as to specific outputs of programs. The development and reporting of performance indicators is in its infancy but is necessary if financial reports of nonprofit entities are ever to have much meaning to outsiders not intimately acquainted with the entity in question. It is clear that performance indicators ought to be compared with resources consumed, rather than resources acquired, to permit a proper judgment of stewardship. Thus, this broader concept tends to lead to full accrual accounting and away from a short-run cash-based perspective. As is true of business organizations, however, a statement of flow of cash or liquid resurces has value in its own right.

There are a host of accounting issues related to nonprofit entities and governments upon which unanimity of opinion is lacking. The most important of these relate to bases of accounting and definition of the reporting entity. The question of basis of accounting — whether focussing on cash, financial claims, or all resources capable of rendering service — ties in with the question of objectives of reporting as just discussed. The entity question stems from the lack of ownership interest in nonprofit entities and the emphasis on compliance with donor wishes or legal requirements in the handling of resources. Unfortunately, the means taken to demonstrate compliance — fund accounting by entities receiving restricted funds or the completely separate reporting of activities by units of government — have the potential of obscuring the overall picture of the financial position and results of activity of the entity. Some form of consolidated or combined reporting is often necessary to provide a clear picture.

With the increased interest in financial reporting of nonprofit entities and governments in recent years, it seems probable that much clearer standards will be established in due course. In the meantime, in view of the diversity in practice in Canada, a reasonable observer may well conclude that well-recognized "generally accepted" accounting principles do not exist for most types of nonprofit entities or for governments.

References

[1]For example, the FASB has concluded that an independent conceptual framework is not necessary for any particular category of entity. See FASB, *Objectives of Financial Reporting by Nonbusiness Organizations*, Statement of Financial Accounting Concepts No. 4 (Stamford: FASB, 1980), par. 1. Consistent with this conclusion, the FASB has produced definitions of the elements of financial statements that pertain to both nonprofit and profit-oriented entities. See FASB, *Elements of Financial Statements*, Statement of Financial Accounting Concepts No. 6 (Stamford: FASB, 1985), especially par. 28. To focus on individual accounting and auditing standards for governments, the CICA has formed a new committee, the Public Sector Accounting and Auditing Committee; in the United States a Governmental Accounting Standards Board has been set up to parallel the work done by the FASB for the private sector.

[2]The AICPA has published the following Audit Guides in the years indicated: *Hospital Audit Guide* (New York: AICPA, 1972); *Audits of State and Local Governmental Units* (1974); *Audits of Voluntary Health and Welfare Organizations* (1974); *Audits of Colleges and Universities*, 2nd. ed., (1975); and *Audits of Certain Nonprofit Organizations* (1981). Minor revisions of recommendations in some of these Audit Guides are contained in Statements of Position issued by the Accounting Standards Division of the AICPA from time to time.

[3]See AICPA, *Accounting Principles and Reporting Practices for Certain Nonprofit Organizations*, Accounting Standards Division Statement of Position No. 78-10 (New York: AICPA, 1978).

[4]Research exists that shows a fund reporting format to be less understandable by readers than a statement that combines fund activity. See K.V. Ramanathan and W.L. Weis, "How to Succeed in Nonbusiness, Without Really Trying: A University Case Study," *Journal of Accountancy*, October 1980, pp. 46-52.

[5]See FASB, *Objectives of Financial Reporting by Business Enterprises*, Statement of Financial Accounting Concepts No. 1 (Stamford: FASB, 1978), especially pars. 28-30.

[6]This agrees with the FASB conclusion in *Objectives of Financial Reporting by Nonbusiness Organizations*, par. 10. The FASB concludes in this statement that the primary users whose information needs should be considered are those who provide resources to the entity.

[7]The recent interest in "comprehensive auditing" fits in with the concern for nonmonetary indicators of performance.

[8]See *Financial Reporting for Non-Profit Organizations* (Toronto: CICA, 1980), chap. 13, p. 16. Compare AICPA Statement of Position No. 78-10, *Accounting Principles*, par. 67.

[9]See M.J. Gross, Jr., "An Accountant Looks at the 'Total Return' Approach for Endowment Funds," *The CPA Journal*, November 1973, pp. 977-84, 1001.

[10]AICPA, Accounting Standards Division, *Accounting Principles*, par. 88.

[11]The possibilities are fully discussed in the CICA Research Study, *Financial Reporting by Governments* (Toronto: CICA, 1980), chap. 5.

Chapter Twenty-Six

Observations on Current Accounting Standards

Historical cost accounting has had remarkable staying power. It is over fifty years since it became the dominant paradigm of financial accounting. In that period, its fundamental premises and many points of detail have been challenged by many accounting theorists. In the inflationary 1970s that challenge was reinforced by representations of practical businessmen and government officials (although not so much by their actions). Yet the model survives. Although it is manifestly incapable of reporting important aspects of economic performance, no competing paradigm has succeeded in gaining recognition as clearly superior.

Various reasons may be suggested for this. There are some undoubted virtues in a transaction-based system of accounting. Reliance on transactions does introduce some measure of objectivity into the system — although a more limited measure than is generally supposed. Reliance on transactions also means that the figures required for the system are, for the most part, readily available in the basic records. This makes it economical. Even the weaknesses of the system have their attractions to some. Those responsible for financial reporting like flexibility in the choice of what to report and when to report it. A system that provides a more faithful portrayal of economic events might be less open to management of results through the choice of transactions engaged in. Finally, inertia and a reluctance to think through possibilities for improvements in reporting are powerful impediments to change.

We are forced to conclude that the historical cost model will be with us for some time to come. It is, therefore, worthwhile to spend some time considering how best to apply it. Previous chapters bear witness to many deficiencies in practice. To a large extent, accounting standard-setters must study these individually to arrive at standards that will improve the situation. That is a process that has gone on for many years and may be expected to continue. This chapter, however, is concerned with two broader points as well — the need to clarify the significance of general acceptance to standards and the need for a better expression of the theory of historical cost accounting.

The significance of GAAP

Earlier chapters have traced the inception of the historical cost theory to the 1930s. It was pointed out that the theory largely represented a rationalization of ideas that had gained ground as to preferable accounting practice. There was no formal professional adoption of historical cost theory as a framework of concepts that should control practice. Rather, it was felt that the ultimate test of good accounting was acceptance in practice. The historical cost theory, as propounded in the literature, merely represented an explanation of why accounting practices were what they were.

This has produced a confusing situation. From the pervasive references to GAAP in all audit reports and in accounting literature, a nonaccountant observer might justifiably conclude that acceptance in practice is the decisive test of an accounting standard. Yet, recommendations of standard-setters often prohibit accounting methods that are generally accepted and sometimes prescribe others that have no precedent in practice. On the other hand, those who set accounting standards sometimes reject proposals because they are considered too different from existing practice. It is not clear when GAAP governs and when it does not, and what does govern when GAAP does not.

There were several fundamental assumptions that underlay the original development of the notion that GAAP provided accounting standards. The first was that practice that comes to be widely accepted will be good accounting. A second was that one preferable practice for every individual situation will tend to emerge or become generally accepted through some sort of consensus process. A third was that, because all accounting practices are designed to portray some aspect of the real economic situation, they will tend to be consistent with one another, the consistency being achieved by their reflection of the underlying reality.

All these assumptions are false to some degree. The evidence for this lies in the numerous instances in which conflicting accounting practices for identical situations have become prevalent, with no sign of a tendency toward consensus. The standard-setting function has grown to its present-day extent precisely because of the shortcomings in the notion of general acceptance.

Accounting practice with respect to the recognition of obligations arising out of current operations provides an outstanding example of the inadequacy of general acceptance as a guide to good accounting. The income measurement goal in accounting absolutely requires that all costs incurred or to be incurred be recognized as expense as their benefit in terms of service potential expires. That goal applies regardless of whether the cost in question becomes due and payable before the time its service is rendered or after. The important point is that the ultimate cost, whenever payment takes place, must be recognized as expense not later than the time its benefit is felt in operations.

There have been recurring illustrations of the failure of accounting practice to observe this basic requirement of income measurement. Often these illustrations relate to promises to employees, express or implied, of future benefits in return for their services currently. A recent example is provided by grants by employers of health and dental benefits for retired employees. But the accounting principle in question is not restricted to the case of employee benefits — it applies to all future costs that arise from operations.

There are several possible explanations for this error in accounting practice. The first is mere oversight. It is easier to overlook accounting for a payment that has not been made than one that has been made. The second is the materiality consideration. When first encountered, the expense may be small and the unrecognized liability also small in relation to the total liabilities of the enterprise. The third is the possible misapprehension that a liability must be an indubitable legal obligation in order to be recognized. Sometimes an obligation assumed by an enterprise represents a moral obligation only, which may be cancelled under certain circumstances. Not everyone understands that such an obligation should be recognized, notwithstanding its quasi-voluntary nature, unless it is likely not be fulfilled. Finally, there can be reluctance to recognize the obligation because of uncertainty as to its amount. Not infrequently the amount of future payments required to liquidate an obligation will be uncertain, and acountants are instinctively reluctant to recognize uncertain estimates.

Numerous individual accounting standards have been necessary to deal with the recurrent failure of accounting practice to recognize future obligations. This example and many others raise the fundamental question as to what role acceptance ought to have in accounting standards. In the author's opinion, it is long past time that we abandoned the illusory criterion of general acceptance in favour of a well-reasoned theory of financial reporting.

Theory as a guide to practice

Accounting standard-setters frequently have to choose between alternative possibilities in accounting for specific situations. They must have some theory to guide their choice. As has been indicated, that theory tends to be the one we know as historical cost accounting. The trouble with this is that no authoritative written expression of the theory has been published. As business complexity increases, accountants and businessmen can be uncertain as to what principles should govern the accounting recognition of important transactions and events. Different accounting methods proliferate for the same types of transactions, and it is not surprising, given the advantages accruing to statement preparers of an optimistic report on operations and minimization of reported obligations, that developing practice may be something less than evenhanded.

The product of this situation is standards overload. In the absence of clear principles, many questions arise that have to be dealt with by detailed rule making. In the presence of diverse practice and vested interests in particular practices, any standard method prescribed has to be buttressed by highly specific instructions to ensure that the standard is applied in accordance with its intent. Auditors add to the demand for specific instructions, partly because of genuine uncertainty as to the intent of a standard, but more to minimize the possibility of conflicts with clients over the interpretation of standards. Highly specific instructions, however, invite legalistic structuring of transactions to evade the intent of the standard. Such evasions lead, in turn, to further detailed standards and technical interpretations. These contribute to the burden of standards overload and, incidentally, increase the likelihood that literal interpretation of the rules will, in particular cases, produce results that do not pass the test of common sense.

It is often suggested that the solution to the problem of standards overload lies in the substitution of professional judgment for detailed rule making. Standards should be couched in general terms indicating the objectives sought by the standard in each particular problem area and the criteria that govern how the accounting should be performed. Professional judgment should then be applied in particular cases in determining the extent to which criteria have been met.

This suggestion has much to commend it. It must be recognized, however, that professional judgment cannot function in a vacuum. There must be a broadly agreed conceptual framework if there is to be any hope that individual issues can be settled by judgment as to the applicable principle involved. The broad principles of that framework need to be stated in explicit terms if it is to be effective in guiding practice.

The following opinions and suggestions for further consideration are made in the light of this analysis. They are not intended to be a rethinking of a conceptual framework for accounting de novo. Such musings are reserved for Part IV. Rather, the observations here are based upon an assumption that the historical cost model is the closest thing to an operational conceptual framework that we have or are likely to have for some time. The objective is to consider how that model can be expressed more clearly in principles that will guide individual accounting standards.

In some cases, all that is required is a clear expression of the broad principle that already is fully accepted and deduction of the accounting standards that flow from it. In other cases, areas are identified where it is not clear that any broad principle is well understood or accepted. These are areas in which it is very difficult to arrive at accounting standards, in large measure because of the lack of agreement on principle. It may be arduous to reach such agreement, but the effort to do so will be worthwhile. In the absence of agreement, accounting standards in the area will run the risk of being ill-advised, will inevitably appear arbitrary, and (unless they cater to all vested interests) are likely to be contentious.

Fundamental principles of the historical cost model

Transaction recognition

An accounting model that depends basically upon transactions to provide input ought to be clear as to precisely when a transaction should be recognized by formal entry in the accounts. The emphasis on the balance sheet as the primary financial statement in the nineteenth century and the concept of the balance sheet as a listing of property and legal claims thereon have left us with a tradition of basing transaction recognition on legal tests such as transfer of title. On the other hand, more recent emphasis on income measurement and the matching of economic benefits and sacrifices tends to direct us to more practical business tests of whether the entity is effectively in a position to enjoy the benefits of its assets or has received consideration for obligations assumed. As indicated in chapter 6, it is difficult to discern one overriding principle. Different conventions appear to have evolved for different types of transactions. In general, these conventions are satisfactory, but it would be desirable to specify their underlying rationale more clearly. The more serious problems come with the initial measurement of transactions and with the principles for recognition of revenue and expense.

Unperformed obligations

The importance of clear principles governing the initial recognition of transactions in the accounts is emphasized by the increasing importance to business of long-term contractual arrangements. These arrangements mean that most businesses are subject to substantial unperformed legal obligations at any reporting date. No persuasive proposal has yet been made for the recognition of executory contracts in the form of assets and liabilities recorded in a balance sheet. Nevertheless, it has long been agreed that commitments are important to a proper appreciation of financial position. Frequently, accounting standards dealing with individual topics prescribe disclosure of related commitments. It would be useful to enunciate a general principle:

All existing contracts or conditions that are likely to have a significant impact on future cash flows should be disclosed in notes to the financial statements if capitalized values of such cash flows have not been recognized as assets and liabilities in the balance sheet.

This general principle places no restriction on the nature of contracts to be disclosed. Thus, contracts to be disclosed would include significant contracts for purchases of materials or sales of product, for labour and executive compensation, for capital equipment, for financing, and for future investment.

There would need to be the usual discussion of form of disclosure and what should be considered significant. In some cases, disclosure of minimum cash requirements in total and year by year for the next five years, as is now given for leases, would be appropriate. In other cases, disclosure of unit prices on purchase or sale commitments might be sufficient. Standards dealing with particular accounting areas would, as now, provide more specific guidance.

Initial measurement of transactions

Since transaction data represent the basic input to the accounting model, everything depends upon appropriate measurement of the transaction. If cash represents the consideration on one side or the other of a transaction, the amount of cash provides the measurement. When the transaction does not call for an immediate cash payment, the measurement clearly ought to be the current value equivalent of cash.

This principle is so obvious that it is amazing instances can be found where it is not followed. Sometimes accountants seem to be mesmerized by such factors as the face value of debt securities or shares issued in an exchange so that they forget to ask whether the real value in the exchange is equal to this face amount. Since the weakness in practice may be used to achieve a deliberate manipulation of the financial statements, there ought to be an explicit statement in accounting standards:

Transactions should be measured when initially recognized at the best estimate of the current cash value of the property exchanged.

This means that when property is exchanged in return for a promise to pay cash in future, that promise should be discounted at a market rate of interest appropriate in relation to the risk involved. This rule is ignored in practice for credit transactions maturing within a short period of time. It should be acknowledged, however, that such practice is justified solely by considerations of convenience and materiality. If interest rates were to rise sharply, for example, it would be less and less rational to ignore the discount factor even on short-term credit.

Barter transactions may also justify some exceptions to the general rule. If a cash-equivalent value cannot be estimated with sufficient reliability, either for the property given up or the property taken in exchange, it is accepted that the property acquired may be assigned the carrying value of the property given up. United

States standards also prescribe that treatment where property is exchanged under conditions that do not suggest culmination of an earnings process.

Allocation of initial measurements

A single transaction may involve the acquisition of more than one asset or the assumption of more than one obligation. In subsequent accounting, those assets and obligations usually need to be dealt with individually. Accordingly, not only must the transaction as a whole be measured at its transaction date cash-equivalent value, but that value must also be allocated among the asset and liability components of the transaction. The logical basis for allocation of the overall transaction value is in accordance with the relative value of each component.

> *The value of the consideration in a basket purchase should be assigned to individual assets in accordance with their relative values.*

The values of individual assets should be measured on a cash-equivalent basis just like the valuation of the transaction as a whole. In business combinations this means that the tax status of assets acquired and liabilities assumed *must* be taken into account.

Business combination standards do not allocate total consideration in a manner that is completely proportionate to estimates of fair value. Rather, when a discrepancy exists between the total consideration and the sum of the estimated fair values, the allocation is designed to allow for probable differences in the reliability of valuations of individual components. While this is sensible in general, situations are encountered in which the allocation of a negative purchase discrepancy might better include some recognition of a bargain purchase credit. (See chapter 18.)

The allocation of proceeds from the sale of securities is one area in which Canadian practice is deficient. This deficiency is becoming more and more serious as a result of the proliferation of security issues with special features that distinguish them from "plain vanilla" debt or equity. Failure to account separately for these special features can result in understatement of a realistic measure of interest cost and/or improper balance sheet classification of securities or rights under securities.

> *The consideration received in a sale of securities should be allocated among the various types of securities sold and the distinguishable rights sold, in accordance with their relative values.*

There can be serious problems in the valuation of particular forms of securities or security rights. It seems probable, however, that a degree of arbitrariness in their valuation will cause less error than does the failure to account for them separately. There are related issues in accounting for securities and security rights that also need to be addressed. At the time this is written, the FASB has just announced its intention to study all aspects of the accounting for financial instruments. This is a most important project.

Earned revenue recognition

The increase in complexity and variety of business activity is most evident in the increase in revenue recognition problems in the past two or three decades. When the historical cost accounting model originated, it was generally considered that revenue should be recognized at point of sale. This was regarded as particularly suitable because it represented the culmination of the earnings process, usually resulted in acquisition of a liquid asset, and usually was accompanied by removal of most uncertainties as to collectibility of revenues and the amounts of costs required to earn the revenues. Recognition of revenue on an accretion basis by long-term contractors was regarded as an exception to the general rule justified by special circumstances that would rarely be applicable in other cases.

These simple ideas have proved inadequate in the face of such developments as the increasing importance of the service sector in the economy and the variety of arrangements possible for sales of products and services. Revenue recognition at point of sale can no longer be considered the virtually invariable norm. Yet it is not clear what circumstance justify departures from it and what criteria exist for the application of other approaches to revenue recognition. There is a great need to think through a set of principles capable of sorting out the various situations encountered and prescribing defensible revenue recognition policies for each type of situation.[1]

The trend away from strict adherence to the realization rule over the past two or three decades suggests an underlying feeling that reporting the culmination of earnings activity should not be the primary objective of revenue accounting. Instead, there appears to be a desire to recognize revenue as earned in the course of productive activity. That is to say, it is felt that faithful representation of economic activity is achieved by recording its reward as work progresses, rather than upon its completion. It may be time for this basic principle to be acknowledged, together with safeguards to allow for uncertainty.

There are two possible ways to interpret such a basic principle. One interpretation would lead to revenue recognition in proportion to an entity's performance of activities that can be identified as associated with the receipt of revenue. The other interpretation would lead to revenue recognition by an entity only with respect to performance of those activities that give the customer satisfaction: that is, the activities producing the product that he or she is prepared to pay for.

To a large extent, activities giving rise to revenue recognition would be the same under these two interpretations, but they would not be completely identical. An example may clarify the difference. A finance company making a loan incurs certain costs in documenting the loan and taking security. If the first of these interpretations were followed, part of the revenue on the loan would be apportioned to those activities and only the remainder would be treated as interest revenue. Under the second interpretation, it would be reasoned that the customer is interested only in the loan. Therefore, all revenue would be recognized as interest over its term. The costs of setting up the loan could be deferred and amortized over its term but should not give rise to revenue recognition.

Opinions differ as to which of these bases is preferable. On balance, the idea of looking to the product or service that the customer is willing to pay for seems preferable as the basis for revenue recognition. Thus the revenue recognition principle could be expressed as follows:

> *Subject to certain conditions, revenue should be recognized as earned as work is accomplished for which the customer is paying or as service is rendered. Services rendered under this description include the loan of money to the customer or the bearing of risk on his behalf.*

It may be noted that if the customer buys a product with a warranty, under this principle some revenue would be deferred for recognition as the warranty obligation expires, rather than recording all revenue at the time of sale and merely accruing future warranty costs.

Revenue recognition has traditionally been affected by uncertainties. That presumably will continue, and therefore the principles need to be expressed to allow for uncertainty. Three types of uncertainty typically affect revenue recognition: (1) uncertainty as to price, (2) uncertainty as to collectibility, and (3) uncertainty as to cost to complete the work contracted for.

> *Revenue should not be recognized before there is reasonable certainty as to its amount. A contract of sale is normally required to provide such certainty. However, reasonable certainty may be present when there is an established customer relationship and an understanding as to basis of charging which experience confirms is reliable. Reasonable certainty may also be provided by the existence of markets for the product or service capable of absorbing all output at prices that can be known in advance.*

The requirement that significant price uncertainty be removed means that sale remains an important factor in revenue recognition. It is not, however, the justification for revenue recognition, but merely a condition normally necessary to provide reliable figures. In special cases, that reliability may be established in other ways. For example, an audit firm may have an established basis for setting fees that provides adequate assurance as to recovery. Also, in exceptional cases, an industry selling in a regulated market (such as the market for crude oil in Alberta in the early 1980s) may have the necessary price assurance.

> *Revenue should not be recognized as earned unless there is a sufficient degree of assurance concerning collectibility to permit the establishment of allowances for noncollection within a reasonable margin for error.*

> *Revenue should not be recognized as earned unless remaining costs to satisfy the commitment to the customer can be estimated within a reasonable margin for error.*

Accounting literature is not very helpful with respect to the degree of assurance as to collectibility or as to future costs that is required. It would seem reasonable, in making a judgment on these matters, to look to the possible effect of resolution of the uncertainty on the figures reported. It might be suggested, for example, that if there were considered to be a possibility as high as one chance in three that profits reported could be extinguished by noncollection or cost overrun, revenue should not be recognized.

Guidance would also be desirable as to the allocation of revenue when one price covers two or more quite different functions. For example, a fee for a financial service might cover both risk bearing and some other service. In such a case, it would seem desirable to allocate the fee between the functions on the basis of their relative value. Reference to market prices for similar functions performed individually would sometimes be helpful in making the allocation. If not, the various types of service rendered by an industry may be so specialized in character that individual study is required to suggest supportable bases for revenue allocation to functions.

When a single price covers several functions, revenue should be allocated among functions in proportion to their relative value.

On the other hand, where one price covers several successive activities, revenue should be recognized commensurate with progress.

Revenue should be recognized commensurate with progress achieved. Progress may be measured by percentage of output or percentage of total estimated cost incurred or some other basis, whichever is considered to best measure achievement.

Finally, principles are needed to guide the recognition of revenue from initial fees. When two or more types of charges are made to the customer but the customer must pay both to acquire the product or service desired, the danger, from the point of view of fair revenue recognition, is that the total charges may be compensatory for the service rendered, but too much may be loaded in one charge and not enough in the other in relation to the costs that are supposed to be covered. The following principle should apply:

Revenue from initial charges should be recognized in full only if the initial service represents a clearly distinguishable service and the continuing service charges are shown to be sufficient to cover future operating costs with a reasonable profit margin.

Recognition and measurement of obligations

We have already noted that in recent decades business has tended to take on increasing obligations to be liquidated in future and accounting practice has regularly failed to make proper provision for the obligations as they arise. Several accounting standards have had to deal with particular examples of this general shortcoming in practice. Pension accounting standards represent the most prominent example. It would be desirable to have a broad general statement of principle so that it would not be necessary to tackle the basic issue repeatedly in a variety of contexts:

Enterprises should recognize an appropriate measure of expense with respect to obligations to make future payments or equivalent sacrifices in consideration for services, assets, or other benefits received in the current period or with respect to obligations that are assumed as a necessary condition of the operations of the business.

Some attention needs to be paid to the measurement of the cost and obligation attributable to an accounting period. Depending on the circumstances, this can be a very complex question, as it is for pension cost accounting, for example. One conclusion follows from the general transaction measurement principle, stated earlier, to the effect that transactions should be measured at the best estimate of the current cash value of the exchange at the time the transaction is recognized:

An obligation for future payment arising out of current operations should be recognized at a discounted amount.

If it is possible to estimate the future amount payable in nominal dollars, the discount rate applied should be a market rate deemed appropriate to the nature and risk of the obligation. In at least some cases, however, the future amount payable in nominal dollars will vary substantially according to the rate of inflation that occurs over the period up to the discharge of the obligation. In such a case it may be easier to estimate what the payment would be if it had to be made at the reporting date — that is to say, in dollars having today's purchasing power — and discount that estimate at the assumed "real" rate of interest. The effect of inflation on costs would be ignored, but the effect of inflation on interest rates would be subtracted to compensate.

Identification of period costs

Costs that are not incurred to satisfy prior obligations are either recognized as expense when incurred or attributed to cost objects to facilitate their subsequent recognition as expense in some rational fashion. In theory, the difference in treatment depends upon whether the cost is deemed to benefit operations subsequent to the period in which it is incurred. Since future benefits from a cost are necessarily uncertain, in practice it is possible to be optimistic or pessimistic on this point. There seem to be no operational criteria to determine whether an optimistic or pessimistic point of view should be taken.

Whenever a significant cost is incurred on an irregular basis, there traditionally has been some tendency to assume that the cost must have some longer-term benefit, without there necessarily being any clear idea just how or for how long that benefit will be manifested. Thus various "deferred" costs have been carried in the balance sheet, representing the residue of the process of matching costs with revenues and time periods, without further evidence as to their value. On the other hand, traditionally little objection has been taken to the practice of expensing most costs when incurred in view of the generally favourable opinion in which conservative accounting is held.

Since the beginning of the 1970s, individual accounting standards appear to have become more inclined to the pessimistic point of view. SFAS No. 2 of the FASB exemplified this change, in its conclusion that research and development costs should never be carried forward as assets because of the lack of certainty as to future benefit from them. That attitude has not carried through in every standard, however, nor does it appear that standard-setters in Canada are quite as averse to deferment of costs of nebulous intangible assets as is the FASB.

The result of all this is a state of some confusion as to guiding principle. Something is required to improve overall comparability among enterprises, but it is not clear how that goal can best be accomplished. The easiest way to improve uniformity would be to provide that no costs should be carried forward as assets that are not traceable to tangible or identifiable intangible assets that are capable of being separated from the business and sold.

This solution would certainly be criticized as being overly conservative. On the other hand, to take the opposite extreme and require that all significant costs be carried forward provided they are incurred in the hope of future benefit, rather than to repair damages from the past, would unquestionably arouse opposition from the many enterprises that routinely expense all costs of intangibles. Moreover, it would require some better direction as to the manner in which such deferred costs should be written off against future income, a problem that is now handled in a highly arbitrary fashion.

A third and possibly the only feasible course of action in view of the conflicting opinions is to tackle the problem in a series of standards for individual industries, attempting to find a consensus that will improve comparability within each industry without necessarily achieving consistency in broad approach among all industries. Even this course of action is extremely difficult, as is proved by attempts to get agreement on the treatment of computer software costs.

Attachment of costs to cost objects

A lack of consistency is also evident in the approaches taken to costing of cost objects, ranging from situations in which only directly traceable costs are treated as part of asset costs, to cases where there is a full allocation of costs to the asset, including manufacturing overheads and interest during construction. The full-cost approach seems conceptually superior, provided there is some control against the inflation of cost of overstocked inventory as a result of the inclusion of fixed overhead that otherwise would be charged against income.

On the other hand, practical considerations often favour restricting costs deferred to directly traceable costs. When inventory is produced and sold on a regular basis, costing on something close to a direct cost basis is less expensive and usually will produce a figure of income little different from that shown using full costing. With respect to other assets, such as plant and equipment and intangibles, a restriction of costs to directly traceable costs avoids the danger that continuing costs of operations may be deferred during the acquisition or construction stage for such assets and fall back against income when the assets are completed.

It is not clear that noncomparable costing methods are a serious problem in current practice. If it were desired to achieve greater standardization, however, a practical answer might be to prescribe full absorption costing for inventory produced irregularly — to special order or in batches — and restrict the costing of other types of inventory and other assets to directly traceable costs.

Determination of cost of goods sold

The theory of historical cost accounting is that income for a period represents the excess of sales revenue over the actual cost of goods sold, minus other costs whose benefit has been consumed in the period. The actual cost of goods sold, however, is only known with complete accuracy in the unusual case when inventory is costed on the specific identification basis. Other costing conventions, such as FIFO and average cost, represent reasonable ways to approximate the results of specific identification that do not seriously affect the internal consistency of the theory. The LIFO method is another matter. In substance, it represents a different theory of income measurement — that income is the difference between revenue and a current or recent cost for the goods sold. Thus the unrestricted use of LIFO presents a problem if accounting standards are supposed to be consistent with the historical cost conceptual framework.

If it were desired to make accounting standards fully compatible with the historical cost conceptual framework, LIFO accounting for inventory would be proscribed or at least confined to a small minority of situations. In some ways that would be unfortunate, because LIFO accounting operates somewhat similarly to replacement cost accounting when there is no material reduction in inventory quantities held over a period. Replacement cost accounting can provide valuable information under conditions of rapidly changing prices. (See discussion in Part III.)

However, it is always open to any business to provide supplementary information when conditions warrant, and information as to the current costs of doing business is specifically encouraged by authoritative recommendations. Thus the elimination of LIFO should not result in the loss of valuable information, except in the case of an enterprise that is not complying with recommendations to supply current cost information.

Depreciation and amortization

The theory of historical cost accounting is that the cost of assets held for use should be written off as their utility is consumed. This is done in two steps: (1) estimation of the useful life of property, plant, and equipment, and other assets held for use, and (2) allocation of the difference between original cost and estimated salvage over that period in a pattern that is thought to be systematic and rational. As pointed out in chapter 11, there is no exclusive theory as to what would be rational. Moreover, even if there were such a theory, the information necessary to implement it — such as the pattern of decline in the asset's market value over its lifetime or the amount of its net revenue contributions over its lifetime — is rarely possible to obtain. Even estimates of an asset's useful life rely heavily on judgment, given the importance of obsolescence as a factor in ending an asset's utility. Observation of practice suggests that most enterprises follow customary norms for asset life estimates, rather than making efforts to see how these norms fit their individual circumstances.

It is conceivable that accounting research could improve the information available about useful lives of assets and provide an actual or simulated pattern of decline in value with life. Given the multiplicity of types of productive assets and the lack of much interest in this task, however, it seems probable that the present highly arbitrary patterns of depreciation and amortization and judgments as to useful life will continue for some time to come. In the light of this, those responsible for accounting standards might take a number of actions to improve the understandability and comparability of financial statements:

- The disclosure of the manner of estimation of depreciation of property, plant, and equipment, and amortization of other long-life assets, could be improved by more detailed analysis of the types of assets and more precise subdivision in the disclosure according to the amortization rates or asset lives assumed.
- Efforts could be made to obtain consensus by industries as to expected lives for different categories of assets and appropriate patterns for write-off.
- As an extension of this, a benchmark calculation of depreciation and amortization using published consensus rates could be required disclosure when companies choose to continue to use different rates.

Loss recognition — operating assets

It has always been understood in the historical cost model that an asset should not continue to be carried at a cost-based figure if that figure exceeds its value at the reporting date. There has been confusion in practice, however, as to precisely what is to be the basis for write-down in various situations. Accordingly, this question ought to be thought through and some general principles established. Those principles must be capable of adaptation to operating assets held for sale and for use in production, as well as for nonoperating investments.

The historical cost theory depends vitally on the idea that historical cost represents value at the date of acquisition. If there is to be a subsequent revaluation, it would seem logical that the revised carrying amount should represent value at the date of revision. There is one problem, however. One knows that historical cost was deemed to be value to the firm because the asset was acquired. At some subsequent date, there is no similar assurance that the asset is worth its market price to the firm. This suggests the adoption of something similar to the concept of "value to the firm," which is explained more fully in Part III. That is to say, a basic general principle could be:

> *Assets should be written down to their "value to the firm" when that value is below a carrying value based on historical cost.*

From the basic concept of value to the firm the following standards can be deduced:

> *Inventory should be written down to replacement cost, if the firm would replace it at the current market price. An exception to this rule applies if the net realizable, value of the inventory has not suffered a decline corresponding to that of its replacement cost. In such a case, there has been no loss in value of the inventory to the firm.*
>
> *If the firm would not replace the inventory even at the lower replacement cost, it should be written down to net realizable value. If that net realizable value is immediately realizable, it is the equivalent of cash and no further write-down is justified. The measure of net realizable value, however, need not assume a quick sale, possibly on a distress basis, if some other method of disposal would produce a greater present value. But if realization will take some time to achieve, the net realizable value should be discounted to assure that the valuation is a present value.*
>
> *Property, plant, and equipment should be written down to replacement cost if the firm would replace the assets at those prices. Again, an exception would be justified if there has been no reduction in the originally expected returns from the plant.*
>
> *Property, plant, and equipment should be written down to its "economic value"—the present value of estimated future cash flows — if plant would not be replaced but it is planned to continue operations. If it is planned to dispose of the plant, the write-down should be to estimated net realizable value allowing a discount for delay in realization.*

The above rules flow directly from the adoption of the concept of value to the firm. It is, however, usually very difficult to estimate replacement cost of plant in service, and estimation of economic value is even more subjective. An accounting standard might contain a proviso to the effect that a write-down need not be made unless it is strongly evident that the loss in value is enduring and not likely to be reversed. Indeed, it might even be considered desirable, when the estimate of replacement cost or economic value is considered highly uncertain, to permit postponement of any write-off until a firm decision to close or dispose of the plant is taken. The principle should be maintained, however, that if a write-down is made, it should be to the best estimate of a current value and not merely to an estimate of dollars recoverable disregarding the delays probable in recoverability.

Intangible assets contributing to operations should be written down to economic value when it appears the decline below carrying value is unlikely to be reversed.

In most cases, intangible assets are sufficiently individual in character that there will be no apparent replacement cost.

When operating assets have been written down, the written-down value is treated as though it represented cost so that subsequent write-ups are not to be made, even though the market price or estimated economic value recovers.

Loss recognition — nonoperating assets

The historical cost conceptual framework has been developed largely in relation to business operations — particularly those of a business engaged in manufacturing or distribution of a tangible product. Procedures for accounting for nonoperating assets, such as investments, are usually developed by analogy to operating assets without any particular reference to the individual characteristics of such assets. Such procedures include: initial recording at cost, recognition of income as realized, and revaluation of holdings to market when below cost. By reasoning from the precedent of operating fixed assets, it is held that write-downs to market value need not be made when the decline in value is considered likely to be temporary.

Forming an opinion whether a decline in value of an investment is other than temporary is an exercise of the imagination, since the future is unknowable. The literature suggests that a decline in value of an investment with a fixed maturity amount may be considered temporary so long as the entity is not likely to be forced to realize upon the investment while the market is depressed. One might extend this thought to suggest that a value decline for other investments that is merely in step with general market conditions need not cause concern, since it is in the nature of market values to fluctuate. However, one cannot ignore the possibility that a particular segment of the market may be depressed because characteristics of the industry make its expectations of recovery smaller. With respect to individual investments, the *CICA Handbook* suggests that when a condition suggesting value impairment has persisted for three or four years, there should be a presumption that the loss in value is other than temporary.[2] This has a decided air of locking the stable door after the horse has been stolen.

Accounting standard-setters ought to consider whether the historical cost accounting theory provides a good conceptual framework for nonoperating assets such as investments. The historical cost model, as noted, has in view a going business concern earning income from the excess of revenues over costs on a repetitive basis, whose productive assets are often specialized for the business, are rarely traded, and therefore have no ready markets. These characteristics generally do not apply to nonoperating assets such as investments. Return on investments is often likely to come as much from change in asset value as from regular income, and the assets are often readily marketable. An accounting system based on market values rather than historical cost and recognition of changes in market value as a component of income, suitably disclosed, makes much more sense. If that proposal is considered too radical, a compromise whereby investments are carried at market value in the balance sheet but fluctuations in value (that is, those considered to be temporary) are carried directly to a separate component of shareholders' equity, rather than to income, would have some merit.

The principal opposition to such proposals often comes from institutions holding large portfolios of securities which, to them, have more the character of operating assets than of readily disposable nonoperating assets. The reasons for these objections have been explored in chapter 16, along with possible specialized investment accounting methods to meet the objections.

Changes in estimates

Establishing a carrying value for assets and liabilities arising from operations often involves estimates of one kind or another. Thus, estimates of amounts collectible from revenue transactions, of amounts payable for employee benefits and many other expenses of operations, or of useful lives of depreciable assets are often tentative when made and subject to revision. The treatment of changes in such estimates does not appear to be consistent.

- Estimates of amounts collectible on revenues and payable on obligations arising out of operations (where the latter are provided — see earlier comments on the failure to accrue for some obligations) are made on a best-estimate basis.
- Revisions in estimates are made regularly so that assets and liabilities continue to portray best estimates. Revisions are usually charged or credited to income immediately. Revisions to recorded pension obligations, however, are amortized, usually over the average remaining service life of employees.
- The effect of revisions to estimated lives of depreciable plant is not generally reflected immediately, either in the asset carrying values or in income. Instead, the rate of depreciation is adjusted so as to arrive at the proper amount of accumulated depreciation over the remaining life of the plant.

It would be helpful if some rationale were provided to explain why immediate recognition in income is given to some changes in best estimates, while others are amortized. The apparent reason for the latter treatment seems to be that in some cases — such as those of pension obligations and depreciation — there is considerable uncertainty whether the new estimates will prove to be much more accurate than the old. When the ultimate target remains shrouded in uncertainty, it seems to be considered better to avoid sharp adjustments to income based on such unreliable evidence.

Recognition of unforeseen losses and gains

Not infrequently, an entity has to recognize a liability not previously expected or provided for. Somewhat less frequently it falls heir to an unforeseen asset. It may seem that losses or gains resulting from these unexpected events are different in character from the effects of changes in estimates referred to in the previous section. However, it can be argued that the difference is merely a matter of degree, not of kind. The possibility of a liability must have existed when the operations giving rise to it took place. Simply, the liability was estimated at zero because there was little or no basis for anticipating it.

If a basic similarity is acknowledged between changes in estimates and recognition of contingent losses and gains, the inconsistencies in their accounting treatment become puzzling.

- Loss contingencies are not recognized until they pass a threshold based on probability of occurrence and assurance as to amount, whereas ordinary business uncertainties are based on best estimates only.
- When a loss contingency is likely to occur and there can be reasonable assurance as to its amount within a range but no figure in that range is considered more likely than any other, the minimum amount of loss is accrued. On a best-estimate basis, the central figure in the range or some other figure considered the most likely error would be recognized.

The first question to be dealt with is whether there should be any different principles for what are called contingencies than there are for ordinary accounting estimates involving uncertainty. There may be one plausible basis for distinguishing between the two. It may be argued that a true contingency involves serious doubt as to whether a loss or gain will occur (event uncertainty). A "win-lose" situation exists. You either win the lawsuit or you don't. In contrast, in the ordinary operating estimate some cost or revenue is expected; the crucial question is how much.

We need to be very careful about this distinction. In looking at any individual account receivable, we might feel that we are in a win-lose situation; a loss will occur or it won't. However, even though every single account has a high expectation of collectibility, taken together there usually will be a high probability of some loss. In other words, we may be able to distinguish the contingency from the ordinary operating uncertainty only on the basis that the contingency is confined to a one-of-a-kind situation that may or may not involve loss or gain, while the ordinary operating uncertainty relates to a situation in which probability of loss or gain is high with respect to a mass of similar transactions, even though it may be quite low with respect to any one of them.

This is a very fine distinction and one that may even be considered artificial. For example, consider a publisher of a sensationalist newspaper. In its case, lawsuits might be almost a normal business risk, which would suggest that a liability should be accrued by it for statistically probable lawsuit losses, just as an ordinary business should accrue for warranty losses. Nevertheless, some distinction must be made if different accounting is to be prescribed for contingencies and ordinary operating uncertainties. The distinction between one-of-a-kind events and ordinary operating events will probably be workable in most cases.

Chapter 9 contains comments on principles that should guide accounting for estimates with respect to normal operating risks and accounting for contingencies.

Other matters

The broad principles of the historical cost theory are reviewed above with suggestions for possible clarification. Below we touch on one matter of concern in the application of the theory and then conclude with brief suggestions for improvement in, or reconsideration of, certain aspects of present accepted practice.

Reliance on transactions

The reliance of the historical cost system on transactions to provide the raw material for financial reports is one of its great strengths. At the same time, it is a weakness because (1) it does not report value gains and losses when they occur, but rather when they are realized (except to the extent losses are recognized before realization), and (2) it permits management of reported gain or loss by advancing or delaying realization.

The weaknesses of a transaction-based system have to be accepted with its strengths. Vigilance is required, however, to avoid magnifying its weaknesses. Certain observations follow from this.

- The requirement to value assets at the lower of cost and market provides at least a partial deterrent to attempts to avoid loss recognition by delaying realization. There is no such deterrent with respect to outstanding debt. Consequently, there may well be significant unrealized losses with respect to the debt position when interest rates change or foreign exchange rates move adversely. When debt is retired out of funds from operations or new equity, there is no alternative to recognition of such loss. The same is not true when debt retirement takes place out of the proceeds of another debt issue. It is then possible to make arguments that nothing has changed in substance and that the refunding is advantageous; therefore no loss should be recognized. In the author's opinion, there should be great reluctance to accept such arguments. It is bad enough that the losses have not been recognized when they occur. The integrity of a transaction-based system will be undermined if it is possible to pick and choose whether or not loss is recognized, even after realization, merely by structuring a new transaction apparently linked to the old.
- Conversely, when there is an unrecognized gain on a position, there can be a desire to accelerate recognition by simulating a real transaction. An example is provided by the procedure known as "debt defeasance." Again it may be argued that this undermines the integrity of the system. It may be unfortunate that the realization convention prevents recognition of gain when it occurs, but that situation is not improved by allowing entities to pick and choose when or if gain shall be recognized. If reliance is to be based on transactions, they should be real transactions.
- A requirement that transactions be genuine implies they should be irrevocable. That suggests that gain should not be recognized on sales with recourse to the vendor or other transactions under which risk is not completely disposed of, unless that risk is remote. Similarly, sales with strings attached, such as a requirement upon sale of some securities to repurchase the same or different securities, should be scrutinized carefully to make sure the transaction pricing is realistic. If it is not, the appropriate action may be to treat the sale as a financing or to recognize loss on the sale, as the circumstances indicate.

The general point here is this. The theory is that transactions are relied upon as the basis for accounting because they provide unbiased evidence of economic phenomena and events. That reliance can be justified only if care is taken to see that transactions are not orchestrated to produce desired effects on financial reporting.

Accounting practices in need of reconsideration

Set out briefly below are the author's personal opinions on some accounting standards or accepted accounting practices that need reconsideration or change.

- The standard on capitalization of leases requires calculations that are more onerous than most. It is not clear that the criterion for capitalization of leases—namely, that they be tantamount to purchase and sale of the property leased — is the most significant aspect of a lease. It can be argued that what is significant is that the lessee obtains the use of property in return for a commitment, and that this is similar to purchase of an asset and assumption of debt, whether or not the lease passes the entire risks and reward of the asset leased to the lessee. Even a short-term lease passes property risks and rewards for the period of the lease. On top of this argument, experience indicates that leases can be structured to avoid capitalization. Reconsideration of the standard might lead to a conclusion that lease accounting should go either forward or back. Capitalization of all lease rights and obligations (except for very short-term leases) would probably be more straightforward than capitalization of ownership-type leases and would be less subject to manipulation of the figures. On the other hand, inclusion of sufficiently detailed information in a note to the financial statements might be satisfactory from an information standpoint, without causing the difficulties that are caused by major changes in presentation of the financial statements themselves.
- The FASB standard on interest capitalization introduced a new accounting procedure to Canadian practice, which already permitted inconsistent accounting in this area. That alone suggests a need for a Canadian standard to regularize the situation. The FASB procedure is open to considerable criticism. Under it, interest that was being charged against income before the start of construction will temporarily be capitalized and when construction is complete will revert to a charge against income. When sufficient debt is outstanding, the effect is much the same as though interest on equity were being capitalized. In addition, the interest rate used, being based on debt outstanding in earlier years, may be quite inappropriate to current conditions. Once again it would be better to go forward or back. Either capitalization of an appropriate cost with respect to all capital tied up in construction should be called for (probably accompanied by exclusion from income of the credit on equity capital), or the previous Canadian practice (of capitalizing only increments in interest expense that can be deemed caused by construction) should be confirmed and be made a required, rather than optional, practice.

- There has been some tendency for the use of sinking-fund depreciation to spread in the past ten or fifteen years in Canada. At one time it was restricted to public utilities and used only occasionally by them. Then it was introduced in the real estate industry for income properties, which are usually leased for long periods and financed heavily by debt. These conditions provided greater justification for sinking-fund depreciation than is generally the case. Since then, the use of sinking fund depreciation has tended to spread to different types of commercial real estate. There is extreme danger of substantial underdepreciation under the sinking-fund method as a result of overstatement of the economic life of assets. Consideration should be given to limitations that ought to be placed upon its use.
- Carrying fixed assets at appraisal values is inconsistent with the historical cost theory. Appraisal values are now recognized only by a very small number of entities. It is time the *CICA Handbook* stated specifically that appraisal accounting is not appropriate in historical cost financial statements. If an entity wishes to report current values as supplementary information, nothing prevents it from doing so.
- Canadian treatment of identifiable intangible assets is inconsistent with the treatment of purchased goodwill. Although each may have indeterminable life, the latter is required to be amortized but the former is not. That situation is all the more unfortunate because so-called identifiable intangibles are often little more than goodwill to which a different name has been attached. The treatment of the two should be reconciled.
- As indicated in chapter 13, the Canadian 1987 pension accounting standard is completely inadequate in the disclosures required as to the key variables in the measurement of pension costs and obligations. Over two-thirds of the respondents to the exposure draft preceding the standard criticized this inadequacy. In the interests of fair financial reporting this shortcoming should be rectified.
- The subject of accounting for hedging instruments needs to be thought through again. A basic question is why an instrument, such as an option or futures contract, needs any different accounting when it is held as a hedge than it receives otherwise. The answer given is that if the hedging instrument is accounted for at market value and the position hedged is not, there will be a mismatch of recognition of gain or loss on the two positions, which is contrary to the fact that a hedge exists. That point emphasizes the basic fact that a risk that is hedged is a risk of changes in value. An effective hedge cannot exist if the value of the hedging instrument and the position hedged do not respond to the same forces (in opposite ways) *at the same time*. This effectively means that there can be no such thing as an "anticipatory hedge," nor can a nonmonetary asset or a *future* revenue stream provide a hedge of a monetary liability.
- Accounting standards have tried for years to define an "extraordinary item" so as to make clear what should and should not be reported as such in income. The result of this effort is that the accounting use of the term "extraordinary" no longer agrees with what the ordinary person considers extraordinary. Moreover, it often remains difficult to decide whether a particular item of gain or loss should be classified as extraordinary. It is time that accounting standards abandoned the attempt to draw fine classification lines on a basis not understood by the readers of the financial statements.

The requirement should be simply that all material items that occur infrequently, or are abnormal in relation to ordinary operations, be given special disclosure.

- Recent changes in the recommended format of the statement of changes in financial position (statement of cash flows) call for distinguishing operating, financing, and investing cash flows. Numerous questions of classification arise, to some of which, at least, the answers are arbitrary. It is already evident that classification practice is not consistent among companies. Precisely because classification decisions are arbitrary, the accounting standard needs to give guidance in the interests of obtaining comparable reporting.
- The recent change in the statement of changes in financial position emphasizing the movement of cash and cash-equivalents calls attention to the fact that the classification of assets and liabilities in the balance sheet between current and long-term categories has become relatively unimportant, except as a matter of tradition. Where classification in financial statements does not provide useful information, it should not be required, since borderline cases always cause difficulty. The *CICA Handbook* should move toward dropping the requirement for distinguishing between current and long-term and any accounting rules based upon that distinction.
- A more informative basis of classification, both in the balance sheet and the income statement, would be between operating assets and liabilities, investments, and financing. This basis of classification fits the new format prescribed for the statement of changes in financial position. Within these categories in the balance sheet, assets and liabilities should be listed in order of their liquidity.
- The traditional classification of the liability side of the balance sheet between debt and equity is losing its significance with the issuance of equity that behaves like debt and other securities that blur the dividing line between debt and equity. The best solution to this problem is to drop the separate classification of equity and list all securities outstanding in order of the date(s) when their repayment may be required. Ordinarily, retained earnings would be grouped entirely with the residual equity position, but allocation could be required for special cases, such as the existence of unpaid dividends with respect to cumulative preferred shares.
- Such a re-ordering of the liability side of the balance sheet suggests a corresponding revision to the income statement. One possibility would be to deduct all interest and dividends ranking prior to the residual equity within the income statement. The "bottom line" would then be the reported earnings for the residual equity, which would be stated on a basis consistent with that used at present in the calculation of earnings per share. Another possibility would be to break the income statement into two. The primary statement would come down to a figure of operating and investment income before tax. The second statement would report the claims upon that income from income tax and the various sources of financing.

References

[1]The section on revenue recognition added to the *CICA Handbook* in 1986 gave a formal blessing to most existing revenue recognition practices but utterly failed to provide a theory to explain the manifest contradictions among them. See CICA, "Revenue", *CICA Handbook*, Section 3400 (Toronto: CICA).

[2]See discussion in CICA, "Long-term Investments," *CICA Handbook*, Section 3050 (Toronto: CICA) pars. 29 to 35.

Part Three

Accounting for Changing Prices

Chapter Twenty-Seven

The Elements of Income Accounting Models

Part II has described the accounting system we use today, which is based on concepts and standards customarily known as generally accepted accounting principles (GAAP). For the most part, accounting data recorded under this system result from transactions between the entity and outside parties — financing transactions, investment transactions, and all sorts of exchanges arising in the course of operations. In the course of operations, also, resources may be transformed or consumed without the intervention of outside parties, as when labour is applied to raw material to turn it into work in process and then finished goods, or when equipment is consumed through use. These actions also are given accounting recognition in the system. That recognition, however, is given by means of cost accounting — rearrangement of costs incurred in external transactions — not by way of value accounting.

In general (with some exceptions), the value added by enterprise productive activity and value changes that occur merely because prices of various resources held change in the marketplace are not given recognition in the accounts until they are confirmed by an external transaction. Even then, there is no separation of the value change attributable to productive activity and that attributable to price changes in resources.

The omission of recognition of value changes not confirmed by external transactions results in some lack of realism in historical cost accounting. The value of an item of inventory does not suddenly jump when it is sold, nor is the resulting profit attributable in its entirety to the effort of sale or the time of sale. Even less is the gain or loss on disposition of an asset acquired for investment or speculation attributable solely to the period of sale. Thus, GAAP as we know it has deliberately departed from the goal of faithful representation of entity resources and changes in them. There are many reasons for this. Chief among them is the uncertainty attaching to any attempt to value many types of resources, particularly those — such as work in process or special purpose fixed assets — for which no regular markets exist. Also important is the fact that it is convenient to base accounting measurements on transaction amounts and not to have to look outside the accounts for them.

For many years accounting theorists have criticized this lack of realism in historical cost accounting. It is only when price changes become widespread and the rate of change becomes extreme — that is, under conditions of severe inflation or deflation — that businessmen join in these criticisms. Under inflation, historical cost accounting generally reports profits that are higher than the cash available for distribution. Businessmen find this disturbing, especially if the reported profits form the basis of taxation. Thus, throughout the high-inflation period of the 1970s there was intense interest in finding a solution to the inadequacies of historical cost accounting. In the early 1980s that interest evaporated as the rate of inflation declined. In Canada, CICA recommendations for supplementary disclosure of the impact of changing prices were made just as interest died away and were widely ignored.

Nevertheless, it would be rash to predict that significant inflation or deflation will never recur. Also, specific prices are always changing, even though there is no general price trend, and these changes may be important to some enterprises. It is still pertinent, therefore, to investigate the shortcomings of historical cost accounting and consider what might be done about them. In general, the problem with historical cost accounting is that out-of-date costs are matched with revenues to determine realized income, and unrealized holding gains (and occasionally losses) are ignored. The following simple fable illustrates the first of these shortcomings.

The fable of the Steady State Company

There once was a happy country whose economy had been characterized for many years by very stable prices. In that country lived a man who had operated the same business in a steady state (neither shrinking nor growing) ever since his youth. The operating conditions of that business can be simply described, as follows:

- The business was conducted entirely on a cash basis. It bought and resold one specific commodity. It had no expenses other than costs for goods purchased, and there were no taxes.
- Goods purchased were held on average three months before sale (i.e., inventory turnover was four times a year). Generally, the earliest goods in stock were sold before goods purchased later (i.e., the actual flow of goods was FIFO). There was no seasonal pattern in demand for the product, and buying for inventory was accordingly spread evenly over the year. The cost of the typical amount of inventory held was $100. Selling prices were set so as to obtain a margin over cost of 3%. This, given the four times turnover, yielded a return on investment (which was all represented by the owner's equity) of 12% a year. All profits were paid out in dividends.

Because of the stable conditions, the financial statements of the business showed little change from one period to another. Typical quarterly figures are shown in Table 27-1.

Table 27-1

Steady State Company
The Stable Price Period

	1st Quarter	2nd Quarter	3rd Quarter	4th Quarter	Total for Year
Cash sales	$103	$103	$103	$103	$412
Original cost of goods sold	100	100	100	100	400
Net profit	3	3	3	3	12
Dividends paid	3	3	3	3	12
Retained earnings	$ —	$ —	$ —	$ —	$ —
Average inventory held during year					$100
Return on equity			$12/$100	=	12%

All good things come to an end. After many years, for reasons no one clearly understood, prices began to rise throughout the country. The supplier of goods to the Steady State Company was quick to detect the trend and on January 1 of year 1 of the new era raised selling prices by 3%. Similar 3% price increases were introduced regularly at the beginning of each quarter thereafter.

Faced with this new situation the owner of the Steady State Company considered his pricing policy. He quickly realized that he must raise prices to cover costs. However, for the first quarter of year 1 he was filling orders from goods bought before the supplier's price increase, so he did not raise his selling prices until April 1. In the meantime, he found that he was somewhat short of cash in the first quarter, so he did not take any dividends out that quarter. Strangely, the cash shortage continued even after he started raising prices, so he refrained from taking dividends throughout the whole of year 1. His financial statements at the end of the year are shown in Table 27-2.

Table 27-2

Steady State Company
Rising Price Period — Year 1

	1st Quarter	2nd Quarter	3rd Quarter	4th Quarter	Total for Year
Cash sales	$103.00	$106.09	$109.27	$112.55	$430.91
Original cost of goods sold	100.00	103.00	106.09	109.27	418.36
Net profit	3.00	3.09	3.18	3.28	12.55
Dividends paid	—	—	—	—	—
Retained earnings	$ 3.00	$ 3.09	$ 3.18	$ 3.28	$ 12.55
Average inventory held during year					$106.28
Return on equity		$12.55/$106.28		=	11.8%

After a year of getting no cash out of the business, the owner concluded that something was wrong. His financial statements gave him little help in arriving at that conclusion. They showed his year 1 profit as being higher than during the previous stable price period even though his return on investment rate was very slightly down at 11.8%. So he decided to catch up on inflation. His supplier had been raising prices 3% a quarter (which was just about the rate of inflation shown by widely published price indexes). He decided to raise his prices in step with his supplier but to catch up on the price increase he missed a year earlier. Now, at last, it looked like he might have the cash to enable resumption of dividends. And he began paying out every penny collected from sales over and above the amount necessary to pay for replacement of inventory sold. His financial statements for year 2 are shown in Table 27-3.

By now the owner was disillusioned with his accounting. He thought it strange that profits were reported at $28.68 when all he could take out of the business was $14.55. Always, before inflation had started, his business was able to pay out dividends equal to its reported profit. Furthermore, he was certain he was

Table 27-3

Steady State Company
Rising Price Period — Year 2

	1st Quarter	2nd Quarter	3rd Quarter	4th Quarter	Total for Year
Cash sales	$119.41	$122.99	$126.68	$130.48	$499.56
Original cost of goods sold	112.55	115.93	119.41	122.99	470.88
Net profit	6.86	7.06	7.27	7.49	28.68
Dividends paid	3.48	3.58	3.69	3.80	14.55
Retained earnings	$ 3.38	$ 3.48	$ 3.58	$ 3.69	$ 14.13
Average inventory held during year					$119.62
Return on equity		$28.68/$119.62		=	24.0%

not making 24% on his investment when he had only been making 12% before. He didn't feel better off than before, and yet his statements made him look like a profiteer — the kind of person who causes inflation, not one who is merely trying to keep up with it. So he asked his accountant whether something wasn't wrong, and sure enough he found there was another way of figuring things — called LIFO inventory accounting — that could be used. Table 27-4 shows how the figures looked when recalculated on the LIFO basis.

Table 27-4

Steady State Company
Rising Price Period — Year 2

	1st Quarter	2nd Quarter	3rd Quarter	4th Quarter	Total for Year
Cash sales	$119.41	$122.99	$126.68	$130.48	$499.56
Cost of goods sold (LIFO)	115.93	119.41	122.99	126.68	485.01
Net profit	3.48	3.58	3.69	3.80	14.55
Dividends paid	3.48	3.58	3.69	3.80	14.55
Retained Earnings	$ —	$ —	$ —	$ —	$ —
Average inventory held during year					$112.55
Return on equity		$14.55/$112.55		=	12.9%

"That's more like it," thought the owner. "But what's that average inventory figure of $112.55? That's what it cost me at the beginning of the year, and prices have gone nowhere but up since then. That understatement of inventory explains why my return on equity looks so high at 12.9%. It should be the same as it always was — about 12%. I must ask him about it."

When tackled on this point, the accountant was adamant that the figures weren't wrong — for reasons that weren't entirely clear to the owner. Then the accountant was rash enough to say that if they had started LIFO accounting back in the stable price period, the inventory today would only have been valued at $100 and the return on equity would have shown as 14.55%. At this point the owner lost interest and decided that he'd just watch his cash balance from here on in. (This proved to be unfortunate in the long run. Two years later the supplier was unable to fill orders for two months during a strike. The owner of the Steady State Company spent all his cash and was out of business.)

The significance of concepts of income

The situation illustrated in this fable can be interpreted in (at least) three ways:

- The accounting based on the original cost of inventory sold was perfectly correct for all years. A factual and accurate measure of profit is obtained by comparing actual sales proceeds with actual costs incurred to make the sale. This comparison showed that earned profits were $12.00, $12.55, and $28.68 in the three years portrayed. The fact that there were variations in net *cash* flows simply indicated that the business had a *financing* problem. When prices are rising, naturally a business needs more financing, which in this case was correctly shown as coming from retained earnings. LIFO accounting was an incorrect application of original cost accounting since the costs matched against sales were not actual costs for the goods sold.
- The accounting based on the original cost of inventory sold was wrong because it was an imperfect application of the matching principle. Profit is correctly measured by matching costs with revenues, but there must be a proper measurement of "cost" to achieve the right result. The significance of a cost incurred in business is that it represents a sacrifice of general *purchasing power* involved in making the investment. If the results of the investment are to be properly reported, one must compare the purchasing power gained from the sale with the purchasing power given up when the investment was made. Since the purchasing power of money changes over time, a simple comparison of money amounts of costs and revenues at different points of time will not yield a proper measure of profit. The two must be expressed in terms of purchasing power of money at a common date to give a measure of gain in purchasing power — the only real test of profit.
- The accounting based on original cost of inventory sold was wrong because original cost is not a proper measure of the sacrifice involved in making the sale. That sacrifice is best measured by the cost of putting the business in the same position it was before the sale — i.e., by accounting for the *cost to replace* the goods sold. In this particular case LIFO accounting gave a correct measure of profit because, under the assumptions of the example, LIFO cost and replacement cost were identical.

Examination of these points indicates that the differences between them simply represent different views as to how income (or profit) should be defined. There has never been a formal attempt to obtain consensus on the definition of income for accounting purposes. Rather, the customary accounting notion of income as the residual resulting from the subtraction of expenses from realized revenues has evolved as a practical way to present financial information.

Concepts of income and capital

Since dissatisfaction with that practical answer under inflation largely stems from a popular perception that accounting income is overstated under inflation, it is pertinent to inquire into the ordinary person's understanding of what income is. In general usage, capital and income are interrelated concepts. Capital is a source of future benefits, which, in our business economy, usually take the form of inflows of cash. Income represents some part of those cash benefits, but not necessarily all. It is necessary to distinguish between benefits that represent a return *on* capital (that is, income) and those that represent a return *of* capital (that is, repayment of principal). Income is restricted to that portion of the return that can be consumed without reducing capital. The idea that capital should be maintained is deeply rooted in human experience. To consume the "seed corn" would be disastrous for expectations of future crops. That, in essence, is why the proper measurement of income — the amount consumable while maintaining capital — has traditionally been regarded as very important.

Capital maintenance is easy to visualize when we talk in elementary physical terms such as that of seed corn. It becomes more difficult to interpret when we think of the wide variety of business enterprises in our economy. Some general concept of capital that can be applied across the board is required. In view of the immense variety of productive assets, it is obvious that the omnibus term "capital" has to be expressed as an amount of money so that different compositions of capital can be compared one with the other or from one time period to another. A key question, however, concerns what that amount of money is supposed to represent. Instead of asking what is income, we have to ask ourselves what is the capital that is to be maintained.

Three different concepts of capital are found in the literature. First, capital to be maintained may be conceived of as simply a given amount of money. Second, it may be thought of as a pool of purchasing power. These two concepts are both known as financial capital maintenance concepts. Third, capital may be thought of as a pool of productive capacity. This is the concept that is closest to the notion of seed corn but also, in an exchange economy, the most complex and difficult to understand. This concept is generally described as a physical capital maintenance concept.

Financial capital maintenance — monetary basis. Under this concept, capital at any point in time is the cumulative total to that point of contributions less withdrawals of resources, each contribution and withdrawal being expressed as a monetary amount. (Retained earnings are regarded as capital contributions.) Income for a period is simply the increase in the monetary amount of net resources over the period after allowing for any increase received by way of capital contributions (not including retained earnings of the period itself) or any decrease caused by dividends, capital withdrawals, or other distributions in the period. On this basis, any change in asset and liability valuation that is recognized in the accounts, whether it results from productive activity or from changes in prices while held (i.e., holding gains and losses), forms part of the income reported. Because the accounting is conducted strictly in terms of units of money, a dollar of reported income is worth less and less under continuing inflationary conditions, and the reverse holds true under deflation.

Financial capital maintenance — purchasing power basis. Under this concept, capital is considered to be the *purchasing power* inherent in the net resources at any point in time. Income for a period is simply the gain in purchasing power of net resources over the period (again excluding the effect of capital contributions and withdrawals during the period). Changes in purchasing power are measured with the help of a general index of prices. On this basis, any change in valuation of an asset or liability within a period is compared with the change in the price index from the beginning of the period or from the time the asset or liability was acquired, if later, in order to measure the gain or loss in purchasing power.

Physical capital maintenance. A radically different concept is based on the idea that income cannot be earned until capital is maintained in physical terms. This is an intuitively appealing idea. In the final analysis, production of income depends on real factors of production. To pierce the veil of "the monetary illusion" and account for real things seems to get at the heart of the matter.

Unfortunately, there are severe difficulties in making the idea of physical capital maintenance work. Consider the simple agricultural homestead. Even if the amount of seed corn held at the end of the year is the same as at the beginning, there will be one more year's wear and tear on the farm equipment, the farm animals will also be a year older but some new ones may have been born, and so on. How do we decide whether capital in the aggregate has been maintained when some elements of capital are identical in quantity and utility at the beginning and end of the year, some are identical in form but one year nearer the end of their useful lives, and some new elements have been acquired? There has to be some common measuring stick or "numeraire" in order to compare the total of different capital elements held at the beginning and end of the year.

In a modern exchange economy, that numeraire obviously has to be money. But then we are forced to ask: If we attach money amounts to the various elements of capital and if we compare the total amount thereof at the end of the year with the amount at the beginning of the year, are we not adopting a financial capital maintenance concept? How do we measure physical capital maintenance in monetary terms? There are two possible solutions to this problem.

One possible solution is to develop a price index of physical goods making up the productive capital of the entity. Then the dollar amount of capital reported at the beginning of the period could be factored up by the *specific* price index, and the amount of that adjustment would be a charge upon income otherwise reported from productive activity and from price changes of assets held.

A more widely advocated way to achieve physical capital maintenance does not seek to express opening and closing capital in their equivalents in physical terms but rather seeks to ensure physical maintenance through the matching process in income determination. This is accomplished by expressing resources sold or consumed in the process of earning income in terms of their replacement costs at the time of sale or consumption. Assuming that revenues cover costs so expressed (and assuming that replacement expenditures do take place about the same time — see discussion in chapter 29), the remaining income reported should be distributable while still leaving the capital intact in physical terms. The difference between replacement costs of resources consumed in operation and their original acquisition cost (elsewhere called holding gains and losses) is *excluded* from income and, in effect, treated as a revaluation of invested capital.

There are two difficulties with these possible solutions:

- The physical assets involved in a modern enterprise are continually changing. Technological change may be considerable, so that assets replacing those sold or consumed in operations may be substantially different from those replaced. Also, conceivably there may be no replacement at all, and resources derived from the sale or consumption of existing capital may be redeployed in other lines of endeavour. Thus, the literal notion of physical capital maintenance becomes impossible to interpret. Because of this impossibility, the notion of physical capital maintenance is modified in practice to a notion of maintenance of "productive capacity" of the capital held at the beginning of the year. This modification, however, complicates the problem of creating an index to measure capital maintenance because of the somewhat vague character of the notion of productive capacity. Equally, it adds uncertainty to the estimation of replacement cost of capital sold or consumed if one is talking about the replacement cost of productive capacity and not the replacement cost of specific identifiable assets.
- Some components of capital in any modern business are financial in character, rather than physical. Consider cash, accounts receivable, marketable investments, and so on. It is not clear how an index should be constructed so as to measure whether the productive capacity of financial assets has been maintained. In the alternative, the method of income determination based on applying the replacement cost of assets sold or consumed against revenues clearly does nothing to provide assurance that the productive capacity of financial assets (which are not sold or consumed) is maintained.

These difficulties will be dealt with more fully in chapter 29 where accounting proposals based on physical capital maintenance are discussed.

Valuation of assets and liabilities

A capital maintenance standard is applied to the amount of net resources in the aggregate (although, as we have just seen in considering the physical capital maintenance approach, it may be implemented through the accounting for individual transactions). The notion of capital maintenance does not, however, prescribe how individual assets and liabilities shall be measured. This specification is required as well to provide a complete formula for income measurement.

Valuation of assets

Under historical cost accounting, the starting point in the measurement of assets acquired for the production of income is their original acquisition cost. That carrying value is affected by allocations of cost made subsequent to acquisition in the course of income accounting but remains rooted in original cost. This fact explains why holding gains and gains from productive activity are not reported in income under the historical cost system until realization occurs (with some exceptions when revenue is recognized before complete realization). On the other hand, if the carrying values of assets are to be restated to some more current basis of valuation, income reported will be affected because the expense recognized when assets are sold or consumed in operations will be different. Holding gains or losses from the changes in their measured amount will also be recognized in some form, although whether they are reported as part of income will depend on the particular model of income reporting that is adopted.

If we consider possible bases of measurement of assets in general terms, we can think of several approaches. One approach is to look to the value in exchange of an asset indicated by market prices. Such prices in turn might be taken from the buying side of the market — an "entry value" — or the selling side— an "exit value" — or a valuation might be based upon the average of the two. Another approach is to value an asset on the basis of discounting its future expected cash flow. Such a discounted cash flow (DCF) valuation is sometimes described as "value in use" or "economic value." A DCF valuation can be quite subjective because it depends both on uncertain expectations of future cash flows and a judgmental selection of an appropriate discount rate. It is a feasible basis of valuation in some circumstances, however, especially for monetary assets whose future cash flows are fixed by contract and where the appropriate discount rate can be assessed in relation to market yields on assets of similar risk. Each of these bases of valuation may also be subject to some differences in interpretation when they are applied. Such differences will be explored in our discussion of different income accounting models in subsequent chapters.

A given income accounting model may or may not apply a single basis of valuation to all assets. Some researchers believe that only one basis of valuation is appropriate for all assets, based on the argument that one cannot add apples and oranges and get a total that has real world significance. Others argue that in differing circumstances different measurement bases may be the most reliable or most efficacious way to arrive at useful valuations. In large measure the difference of opinion stems from differences in fundamental concepts.

For example, R.J. Chambers stresses the adaptivity of an enterprise as a fact of supreme importance to readers of its financial reports. The enterprise's ability to adapt advantageously (to new opportunities or challenges) depends upon the *current cash equivalent* of its resources, and thus the financial characteristic that is of the greatest importance to an asset is its realizable value — an exit price. *All* assets must be measured at their exit prices to arrive at a measure of the total adaptivity of the enterprise.[1]

Other writers contend that an important purpose of financial reports is to help readers *predict* future cash flows of the enterprise. It is not helpful for this purpose to report the current realizable value of an asset such as a special purpose piece of heavy equipment if that asset is not going to be sold but rather will continue in use indefinitely with far different consequences for future cash flow. Thus, it is argued, different bases of valuation may be appropriate to indicate the *desired* asset attribute — the present value of future cash proceeds expected to result from its possession.

Having described three possible bases of valuation, we can expand the number of possibilities by adding a time dimension. Values under any of three bases of valuation may conceivably be derived from information as to conditions existing in the past or the present or expectations of conditions in the future. Thus, we can discern nine valuation possibilities (even though some are rather unlikely choices) as set out in Table 27-5.

Table 27-5

Possible Approaches to Asset Valuation

Valuation Basis	Time of Valuation: Past	Present	Future
Entry price	Historical cost (HC)	Replacement cost (RC)	Future estimated buying price
Exit price	Past net selling price	Current net realizable value (NRV)	Future estimated net proceeds
Value in use	Past estimate of DCF	Present estimate of DCF, known as "economic value" (EV)	Future estimate of DCF

Note that the historical cost accounting model is among those models that use different bases of valuation in different situations. Those bases differ not only in approach — entry value or exit value — but also in the time dimension. Historical acquisition cost is a past entry value, but, in particular circumstances, certain assets may be valued at a present entry value (replacement cost) or a future exit value (recoverable value).

Accounting models proposed to provide a better portrayal of the effect of price changes on specific assets are forced by this objective to be more consistent in their choice of valuation basis. Clearly it is important for financial statement figures to be expressed in values that are current in the reporting period. What is the best approach to valuation for each type of asset, however, is still open to question and debate.

Considerable thought has been given to the creation of a decision rule for the selection of asset valuation bases that would correspond to the intrinsic value of assets to the enterprise. The resulting valuation approach has been variously called "deprival value," "opportunity value," or "value to the firm" (VF).[2] The reasoning underlying this approach runs as follows:

- The future cash consequences of any asset owned will be (1) the net proceeds from its sale, (2) the cash inflow attributable to its use, or (3) the amount collected if it is merely an account receivable.
- The present value of the higher of (1) the net proceeds available from disposition and (2) the cash inflow available from use represents the benefit accessible by the firm from possession of the asset. In the case of goods held

for use in the business, this higher value is normally EV. In the case of goods to be sold, the higher value is almost always NRV.
- Another way to measure the benefit from possession of an asset is to look at the sacrifice a firm would have to make were it deprived of the asset and wished to restore its position. That measure is RC.
- If RC is lower than one of the other two measures, it would pay the firm to replace the asset if it did not have it. Thus, RC becomes the appropriate basis of valuation.
- If RC is higher than both of the alternative measures, the asset would not be replaced if lost. In these circumstances, the higher of the other two measures indicates what probably will be done with the asset and the appropriate basis of valuation.

Since there are three different possible measures of value, there are six different ways in which the values could be ranked from the highest to the lowest. For a given type of asset, some of these value rankings are much more likely than others, as indicated below.

- The ordinary valuation situation for inventory:

  (1) NRV > RC > EV

- The common valuation situations for fixed assets:

(2) EV	> RC	> NRV	Asset will be replaced. Use RC.
(3) RC	> EV	> NRV	Asset will continue to be used but will not be replaced. Use EV.

- A situation encountered frequently with inventory, less frequently with fixed assets:

(4) RC	> NRV	> EV	Asset will be sold (or scrapped) and not be replaced. Use NRV.

- Less common valuation situations:

  (5) NRV > EV > RC
  (6) EV > NRV > RC

The great majority of valuation situations can be covered by two simple valuation rules derived from the above. These are: value assets held for sale at RC unless NRV is lower; value assets held for use at RC unless EV is lower.

This reasoning leads to a serious practical problem. Fixed assets are to be valued at EV when replacement is no longer worthwhile. The decision as to when this point is reached presumably must be made by management but will be, to a degree, subjective. The problem of subjectivity becomes worse once it is decided that the EV valuation basis is called for. Any estimate of the present value of future cash flows for a business must be subjective. When it comes to estimating EV of individual fixed assets there is an added complication. In most business situations a variety of capital assets is needed to achieve the final output. When this is the case, allocation of the final output among the individual contributing productive assets is arbitrary and hence cannot be verified. If the cash flows attributable to an asset cannot be ascertained, its EV cannot be measured — it can only be guessed at. In the face of this problem, a decision must be made whether to deviate from the conceptually correct application of the VF concept.

- It could be decided to accept the virtually complete subjectivity of management estimates of EV and determinations of when that valuation basis is appropriate. Such acceptance might be coupled with special disclosure of cases where the EV valuation option has been used.
- It could be decided that fixed assets should continue to be valued at RC until management makes a formal decision to discontinue a whole plant or line of business.
- It could be decided that the RC basis of valuation should be continued for all assets in operation until they are ready to be scrapped.

Valuation of liabilities

Much has been written concerning the measurement of assets in a current value accounting system. Very little, relatively, has been written about the measurement of liabilities. Yet, in a sense, the issues here are even more complicated. There is no question that assets must be revalued for the purpose of current value accounting — that is the whole object. There is a question whether liabilities must be regularly revalued in such a system or whether they should be left at their original transaction proceeds (amortized to maturity value where necessary). Several arguments have been made as to why revaluation of liabilities should or should not take place.

Some current value accounting models espouse the entity theory of accounting (see chapter 5). Under the entity theory, all liabilities are treated equally with the equity interest as claims on entity resources, and interest payments are regarded equally with dividends as distributions of entity income earned, not as deductions to be made in the measurement of income. An entity theorist, therefore, is interested in the current value of assets but not nearly so much in the current value of liabilities. Since liabilities and equity are both viewed as claims on assets, it is considered the function of the market place, not of accounting, to estimate their value. If the value of the equity claim is not recorded in the financial statements, it is considered equally logical, by this way of thinking, not to record the value of the debt claim.

The proprietary approach, in contrast, focusses on the claim of the equity, the residual left over after deducting liabilities from assets. If it is important to the portrayal of the net equity position to report assets at current values, one would think that the same would be true of liabilities. Some arguments are made, however, for differentiating the treatment of liabilities.

- First, an asset is acquired in order to be put to its most profitable use. Current values are therefore said to be important to show the result of the acquisition decision on an up-to-date basis. In contrast, a debt obligation is usually taken on as part of the financing plan of the enterprise with the intention of maintaining the debt position until maturity. There is no intention to trade in debt obligations. Thus, introducing changes in the value of debt would confuse the picture of management performance. (Not everyone would accept this. Decisions are required as to the timing of debt incurrence, whether the debt should be long- or short-term borrowing, and whether it should be incurred at all. Good or bad judgment can be displayed just as much in these decisions as in asset acquisition decisions.)

- Second, there is a difference in the flexibility of action available with respect to assets and to liabilities. Whether to sell or hold an asset is a perfectly unfettered decision (except when the asset is specifically mortgaged). In contrast, to pay off a liability requires cash which an entity may not have and which it may be precluded from borrowing by capital market conditions. Thus, it is felt that since the current value of debt may be irrelevant to any possible decision, it should not be used as the reporting basis for debt in the financial statements. (Some people are likely to dispute the contention that current values of debt are irrelevant. It is always possible that the business as a whole may be sold. If it is, the price arrived at by a rational buyer and seller will take into account the question whether debt assumed by the purchaser carries a favourable rate of interest.)
- Third, it is often remarked that the market value of an entity's debt is influenced both by the general level of interest rates and by the market's perception of the particular risks attached to the entity itself. If the entity is perceived to have become riskier, the market value of its debt securities will decline. It is intuitively repugnant to many that a decline in debt from this cause should be reported as an increase in equity (and that reported income also be increased if holding gains are treated as part of income).

Those who favour recording debt at current values must be prepared to answer a second question: On what basis is the current value to be determined? The possibilities may be listed as a sort of mirror image of the possibilities for assets, for example:

- Entry price — the amount that could be borrowed currently in return for a promise to pay the same amount as the outstanding debt in terms of interest and payment at maturity.
- Exit price — the amount required currently to pay off the loan. In the case of debt, two exit prices are possible:
  - the amount that would have to be paid in the market to buy in the outstanding debt in an orderly fashion; and
  - the contractual redemption price, if the borrower has the right to call the debt.

  The appropriate exit price would be the lower of these two amounts.
- Economic value — the present value of the payments that have to be made by way of interest and payment at maturity on the existing debt if it is not redeemed or replaced. This present value, of course, would depend on the discount rate assumed. Presumably the discount rate would be the current cost of debt funds to the entity, and thus the present value of existing debt would be the same as the amount that could be raised currently by committing the entity to the same schedule of debt payments (the entry-price alternative above).

The valuation alternatives for debt thus appear to be narrower than those available for assets. Following an approach like that used in estimating "value to the firm" of assets, one might estimate "burden to the firm" of debt along the following lines. Assume first that the firm has the flexibility to pay off the debt if it chooses or to borrow afresh.

- If there are no better uses for its money, the firm will buy in the debt. The burden cannot be greater than the repurchase price (exit value) of the debt. Even if there is a debt covenant prohibiting the entity from calling or repurchasing the debt, it would normally be possible to buy securities of equivalent risk and equivalent terms so as to provide cash to meet the debt obligation as it arises. Thus, an appropriate valuation would be based on a market price or market yield to a security purchaser, unless the debt could be redeemed at a lower price, which is relatively unlikely.
- If there are better uses for its money, the firm will leave the debt outstanding. In such a case, the loan cannot be more burdensome than the proceeds the entity would receive from a new loan upon engaging itself to make payments equivalent to those called for under the existing loan.

Thus, if the firm has the flexibility to choose whether or not to pay off the loan, the burden cannot be more than the repurchase price of the loan at the current market rate. Since the loan is still outstanding, however, in the absence of a repurchase intention the burden is better measured by the proceeds obtainable on a replacement loan carrying the same repayment conditions. The contractual redemption price is normally irrelevant.

If the firm cannot find the cash to pay off the loan and would not be able to raise money for a replacement loan on equivalent security, the situation is problematical. This would be the case of a company in financial difficulty. In such a case, the contractual redemption price would seem to be the best valuation basis, except in the unlikely event that valuation at the market rate of interest provides a higher figure.

Thus, the normal valuation rule might be: (1) use a replacement loan value if the entity has attractive investment opportunities and therefore little intention to pay off the loan; (2) use repurchase market value if it does have such intention; and (3) use the contractual redemption price if its financial position is such that it has little choice in the matter.[3] It may be noted that the application of this rule would eliminate the possibility mentioned earlier that gains might be recorded on debt because its current market is depressed by the risky financial position of the company.

Other elements in income accounting models

As just indicated, the old debate between the proprietary and entity viewpoints also carries over into income measurement models not based on historical cost. In some contexts, the attraction of the entity viewpoint is enhanced. For example, if the objective in measuring income is to maintain the physical capital of the enterprise, it may seem somewhat artificial to consider only the maintenance of physical capital attributable to the equity investment in the enterprise, rather than the total productive capacity of the enterprise.

Finally, there has to be a decision whether the realization test has any place in income reporting. The answer to this is largely a matter of preference. It may seem that an answer will be implicit in the choice of a basis of valuation for assets and liabilities. Thus, if all assets are recorded at current realizable values, the realization test may seem to have been bypassed. But this is not necessarily so. It is always possible to identify and segregate from reported income those gains and losses attributable to value changes in assets and liabilities still on hand.

Thus, there are four elements to any accounting model that aims to report income for a period: (1) adoption of a concept of capital to be maintained, (2) adoption of rules for the measurement of assets and liabilities that make up aggregate capital, (3) a decision as to whose income is being measured, and (4) a decision whether income reported is to be subject to a test of realization. The historical cost accounting model answers these specifications in this way:

- Capital maintenance concept — financial capital maintenance expressed in simple monetary terms
- Basis of valuation of assets and liabilities — generally, original transaction amounts with some exceptions (especially to recognize write-downs to market)
- Concept of the entity — the proprietary interest
- Realization test — applied with a few exceptions.

A very large number of accounting models could be built up depending on the decisions made as to these specifications. This fact contributed greatly to the confusion and controversy in the period from 1970 to the early 1980s over the modifications that might be made to historical cost accounting to better depict the consequences of changing prices. Different theorists adopted different specifications for their models, and as a result there was much argument at cross-purposes.

Summary

Because historical cost accounting is primarily based on transactions with external parties, it fails to portray some events that have real economic significance to an enterprise. It often fails, for example, to recognize gain from productive activity before realization. It also fails to recognize gains and to some extent losses attributable to changes in value of an enterprise's several assets and liabilities before realization. Then, when realization occurs in the course of operations, it fails to tell us how much of the profit or loss on the thing sold should be attributed to productive activity and how much could be considered merely to be keeping up with changes in acquisition prices for the thing sold or changes in the purchasing power of money since the acquisition date.

Many accounting theorists have criticized these inadequacies in historical cost accounting. Typically they have been unable to arouse much concern among businessmen and practicing accountants except in times of relatively high inflation. The specific prices of factors of production are always changing to some degree, even in the absence of a general inflationary or deflationary trend. Practical people appear to be unwilling to make the effort to formally incorporate such price changes in the accounts. Instead, when price changes affecting assets are particularly severe, they have resorted to patchwork expedients such as the adoption of appraisal values for property, plant, and equipment or base stock or LIFO accounting methods for inventory.

Under historical cost accounting, when prices change between the time that factors of production are acquired and the time they are sold, the costs that are "matched" with revenues in the process of income determination are outdated. If the general price trend is inflationary, most businesses will find that income determined in this way exceeds the cash available for distribution because of the need to buy replacement factors of production at higher prices. That is disturbing since most people traditionally and instinctively think of the income of a business as an amount that can be safely paid out to its owners. Thus inflation, more than deflation, leads to disillusionment with accepted accounting practice and attempts to improve the measurement of income in accounting.

In order to measure income from business or property, we must define income. The common notion of income for a period is that of an amount that can be paid out without infringing on capital — that is, that maintains the value of capital (net resources) held by the enterprise. This definition merely leads to the need for a further definition — of the capital to be maintained. Capital may be thought of as a stock of money. Capital is maintained under this concept if the amount of net resources (measured in terms of money) at the end of the period is equal to the amount of resources at the beginning of the period plus or minus the money amount of any capital contributed or withdrawn during the period. This concept of capital maintenance is known as a financial capital maintenance concept because it visualizes capital in monetary terms.

Such a concept of capital maintenance is unlikely to be considered satisfactory under inflationary conditions when money is steadily losing its value. A second concept of capital retains the basic idea of capital as a monetary measure of net resources but defines maintenance in terms not of the amount of money itself but of the purchasing power of the stock of money. Thus, it is the current purchasing power of the stock of net resources that is to be maintained, not simply a net amount of money. This concept of capital maintenance is known as financial capital maintenance in purchasing power terms.

A third concept of capital maintenance is rather harder to understand. It visualizes capital not as a stock of money equivalents but as a stock of physical productive capital. The capital of a business is not maintained unless its capacity to produce is maintained. This concept is known as a physical capital maintenance concept.

A theory of income measurement is not achieved merely by specifying the concept of capital maintenance. The capital consists of net resources, and these must be measured in some fashion to permit a comparison of their aggregate amount at the beginning and end of a period. Various attributes of assets and liabilities can be measured, including their exchange values in the original transactions by which they were acquired or incurred, their current costs to replace, their current realizable values, or some measure of future values. A decision on the appropriate basis of valuation is thus required for complete specification of a method of income determination.

A theory of income measurement must also specify whose income is to be measured. Thus, we meet an old friend, the theory of the accounting entity. Is income to be measured for the entity as a whole or merely for the proprietary interest in it? Finally, a decision has to be made whether gains to be reported as income must be subject to a test of realization.

The succeeding chapters will discuss various models that have been suggested for the purpose of accounting for changing prices and indicate what choices have been made in these models with respect to capital maintenance, basis of valuation of assets and liabilities, entity or proprietary approach, and recognition of a realization test.

References

[1]See R.J. Chambers, *Accounting, Evaluation and Economic Behavior* (Englewood Cliffs, N.J: Prentice-Hall, 1966; reprint ed., Houston: Scholars Book Co., 1974), especially chap. 9.

[2]This concept has been traced to J.C. Bonbright, *Valuation of Property* (New York: McGraw-Hill, 1937). It has also been propounded by (among others) D. Solomons, "Economic and Accounting Concepts of Cost and Value," in *Modern Accounting Theory,* ed. M. Backer (Englewood Cliffs, N.J.: Prentice-Hall, 1966), pp. 117-40, and E. Stamp, "Income and Value Determination and Changing Price-Levels: An Essay towards a Theory," *The Accountant's Magazine,* June 1971, pp. 227-92.

[3]Others have also attempted to arrive at a valuation rule for liabilities using reasoning analogous to that used in arriving at "value to the firm" for assets. See W.T. Baxter, *Accounting Values and Inflation* (London: McGraw-Hill, 1975), pp. 138-40, and D. Kulkarni, "The Valuation of Liabilities," *Accounting and Business Research*, Summer 1980, pp. 291-97.

Chapter Twenty-Eight

General Price-Level Accounting

In the 1970s, when inflation became too serious and too persistent to be ignored any longer, the initial proposal of the accounting profession in most countries was to adopt general price-level accounting (GPL accounting).[1] The techniques of this system of accounting had been fairly well worked out by 1970. It involved the adjustment of figures arrived at under the familiar historical cost system by a single well-established index, published independently by some authority. Thereby, it promised to retain the objectivity thought to be associated with historical costs. It also enabled avoidance of the uncertainties and difficulties always associated with attempts to measure the current values of individual assets and liabilities.

The crucial thing to appreciate about GPL accounting is that it aims to change GAAP in one respect and one respect only. That is, it aims to substitute a unit of common purchasing power (a constant dollar or "dated dollar") for money as the unit of account. The adjustments to the nominal dollar figures in the accounts are *not* revaluations of the assets, liabilities, or other figures affected. They are simply corrections so that all dollar figures shown will be expressed in terms of a dollar with a consistent purchasing power. The adjustments thus do not represent changes in the asset and liability attributes measured. If an asset is shown at historical cost before adjustment, it continues to be shown at historical cost, but that cost is expressed in terms of dollars having a base-date purchasing power. If the asset is shown at market value, it continues to reflect market value.

The grafting of the GPL concept onto the historical cost accounting model means that GPL accounting also embraces the financial capital maintenance concept. That concept, however, is expressed in terms of maintenance of purchasing power rather than maintenance of a stock of money. As just indicated, the attributes of assets and liabilities that are measured under historical cost accounting (usually historical cost, but sometimes market value) are also retained but are expressed in terms of dollars of constant purchasing power. Similarly, the proprietary emphasis is retained, and realization is required for profit recognized, on the same basis as in the historical cost accounting model.

The concept of accounting in purchasing power units

Accounts are kept in terms of money amounts for good reason. Originally, coins consisted of precious metal. As such they were valuable in themselves. Because coins were valuable in themselves they could be used as a medium of exchange, and because they were an accepted medium of exchange they represented purchasing power. Now that paper money and credit have largely supplanted coins (and coins themselves have been debased), money no longer has much value as a commodity in itself — whether paper or metal. But because it still is accepted as a medium of exchange, it still represents general purchasing power. That characteristic of having general purchasing power continues to make money useful as a unit of account. We can have two quite different types of assets, but if each can be priced in terms of money, we are able to add the two amounts to express our total wealth in terms of money. It is the fact that money represents a standard measuring resource that makes it useful as a unit of account.

In a sense, then, we can say that we are already accounting in terms of units of purchasing power when we use money as the unit of account. The trouble is that the purchasing power of money changes over time. If we do not change the monetary amount recorded as the purchasing power of money changes, we are not using a consistent standard of measure. Because the standard is not consistent, addition of two different money amounts — say, adding the cost of an asset bought in 1970 to that of one bought in 1985 — tends to become meaningless. It is as though in measuring a room we changed from a measuring stick calibrated in inches to one calibrated in centimetres. It is for this reason that GPL accounting seeks to transform dollar measures made at different times into measures expressed in a unit of constant purchasing power.

The problem is that general purchasing power is an abstract concept. None of us buys or sells things in general. We buy or sell specific goods and services, and for this we pay or receive money or promises to pay money. It appears we must start with prices for specific commodities in any attempt to measure purchasing power in general. If we know that commodity A has a price of $1.00 and commodity B has a price of $2.00, we say that each commodity is worth these respective amounts. Equally we could have said that $1.00 is worth one unit of commodity A or one-half unit of commodity B. That is to say, the worth or purchasing power of a unit of money in terms of a commodity is the reciprocal of the price of that commodity in terms of money. Thus, purchasing power is a function of prices, general purchasing power must be thought of as a function of prices in general, and to approximate it we must go through some sort of averaging process applied to prices.

In essence, this is what is done in the construction of a price index. Given quantities of commodities are priced at different dates. The aggregate of the value of those commodities at a base date is set at 100, and differences in aggregate values at different dates are expressed as higher or lower index figures correlating with the change from the base-date values. Some of the more commonly referred-to indexes in Canada are: the consumer price index (CPI) — an index of prices of goods and services bought by individuals and families for personal consumption; the industry selling price index (ISPI) — an index of prices of Canadian manufacturing output; and the Gross National Expenditure deflator — an index of changes in the prices of all goods and services produced in Canada.

There are problems in constructing an index that purports to measure pure changes in prices.

- Substitution. When relative prices of commodities change, people change their spending habits. Thus, if butter becomes more expensive, some people will switch to margarine. If beef prices go up, more chicken will be consumed. Thus, a price index that traces the changes in price of a "fixed basket" of goods with "fixed weights" assigned to the goods in the basket (as does the CPI, for example) may become less representative of prices of goods actually produced or consumed and overstate the rate of price change of goods actually being produced or consumed.
- Quality changes. Over time, technological innovation increases the quality

or desirability of many products. (In some cases the quality of a commodity can decline over time — consider local postal service, for example.) Some attempt is made in the construction of price indexes to factor out the cost of quality improvements, but it is admitted that no price index adequately adjusts for quality changes.

Because of these difficulties, it may be that some price indexes tend to overstate the real rate of price change. Thus, although price indexes offer a means of estimating changes in the level of prices, they are not perfect tools for that purpose.[2]

Some people argue that an index of prices in general has no meaning. It is well known, for example, that it can cost more to live in one locality of a country than it does in another, even though the same currency is used as a medium of exchange in both places. The best answer to this is that if a country itself has any meaning and if its currency is freely exchangeable, the concept of general purchasing power is useful, just as an average can be a useful measure in many contexts.

Despite these objections to the relevance of price indexes, it is strongly arguable that price-level adjustments for financial reporting purposes are likely to improve the relevance of figures based on prices established at different dates. Once this is acknowledged, it is necessary to choose the index to be used as a measure of the change in general purchasing power of money. The argument to this point has been that the objective of price-level accounting is simply to correct our measuring unit. Therefore, since money is exchangeable for any commodity, changes in its value should be measured in relation to changes in the prices of all commodities. That is to say, a broadly based price index, such as the GNE deflator, should be used. There are, however, some different views.

- Some have contended that it may be assumed that a business should maintain the purchasing power committed to it for business investment purposes. Therefore, an index of prices of goods in which the business customarily invests would be preferable to a completely general index for measuring the progress of that business.
- Others have argued that the index should be the CPI, since an important objective is that of reporting to shareholders and the shareholder is interested in the success of an enterprise in maintaining the purchasing power of the dollar for consumption purposes. In addition, the consumer price index is more convenient for practical use because it is published more frequently. The GNE deflator not only is published quarterly rather than monthly but also is subject to considerable revision for a long period thereafter, as preliminary figures are refined.

Whatever the index selected to measure the change in general purchasing power, its reciprocal will record the change in the value of money. That is to say, as prices rise the value of money falls. In principle, the procedure to restate the unit of account to a unit of constant purchasing power is as follows:

- In the absence of a defined unit of general purchasing power, we arbitrarily select the purchasing power of the dollar at a specific date as our standard of general purchasing power. Any date can be selected. An obvious choice is the date of the financial report, since it is relatively current and readers will have a good feel for the purchasing power of money amounts shown in the statements. (Another possible choice is to use a "dated dollar," such as one having the purchasing power a dollar had in the base year of the index used to translate the actual dollar figures.)

- All dollar amounts in the accounts are translated for reporting purposes into their equivalents in terms of the purchasing power of the dollar at the selected date. For example, if an asset were shown in the accounts at an historical cost figure of $100 and the price index was 120 when it was bought and 150 at the selected date, the historical cost would be recalculated as $100 x 150/120 = $125.

This procedure will now be illustrated based on the simple situation of the Steady State Company.

The GPL restatement process

Table 28-1 recapitulates opening and closing balance sheet and income figures that were developed in chapter 27 for the Steady State Company. The figures are for the second year of rising prices when FIFO accounting is used.

Table 28-1

Steady State Company
Rising Price Period — Year 2

	Opening Balance Sheet	Income Statement	Closing Balance Sheet
Assets			
Inventory	$112.55		$126.68
	$112.55		$126.68
Equity			
Opening	$112.55		
Sales		$499.56	
Cost of sales		470.88	
Net profit		28.68	
Dividends		14.55	
Retained earnings		$ 14.13	
Closing			$126.68
	$112.55		$126.68

This example assumes a rise in the general price level occurring at the rate of 3% every three months. A price index with a base of 100 on December 31 of year 1 would show the following figures at dates relevant to GPL calculations in this example:

Year 1		Year 2	
Nov. 15	98.53	June 30	106.09
Dec. 31	100.00	Nov. 15	110.90
		Dec. 31	112.55

The basic requirement of GPL accounting is to restate all money figures presented in terms of their equivalent in the purchasing power that the unit of money had at the selected base date. Suppose the base date selected is the close of the latest fiscal period being reported upon. In our illustration, that date is December 31 of year 2, at which time the general price-level index stood at 112.55.

For convenience in restatement, it is useful to translate our price index into a purchasing power index for the dollar, putting the base at 100 at December 31 of year 2. The index figures for purchasing power of the dollar at the relevant dates then will be:

Year 1		Year 2	
Nov. 15	114.23	June 30	106.09
Dec. 31	112.55	Nov. 15	101.49
		Dec. 31	100.00

To accomplish the restatement of financial statement figures, it is necessary to trace the dates of the transactions that gave rise to the assets, liabilities, revenues, and expenses reported in the financial statements. Since inventory is the sole asset in this illustration, let us trace the adjustment required to the figures for inventory and cost of goods sold. The inventory turns over every three months. It is a fair approximation, therefore, to assume that the inventory on hand at December 31 was acquired on average on the preceding November 15. The example also stated that buying for inventory was not seasonal. It is, therefore, a fair approximation to assume that purchases for the year were acquired on average at June 30 prices. With these assumptions, the historical cost figures for inventory and cost of sales can be adjusted to their equivalent in dollars having the purchasing power of December 31, year 2 dollars by using our purchasing power index, as shown in Table 28-2.

Table 28-2

Restatement of Historical Cost Figures

	Historical Cost Figures	Purchasing Power Index	GPL-Adjusted Figures
Opening inventory	$112.55	114.23	$128.56
Purchases for the year	485.01	106.09	514.54
	597.56		643.10
Closing inventory	126.68	101.49	128.56
Cost of sales	$470.88		$514.54

One generalization can be made from this. Whenever figures for assets or liabilities at the end of the year require an index adjustment, the impact of those figures on the income or funds statements (which explain *changes* in assets and liabilities over a period) must be specifically worked out using a continuity of change schedule similar to that illustrated in Table 28-2. This rule applies generally to assets and liabilities known as "nonmonetary."

Table 28-3

Steady State Company
Rising Price Period — Year 2
Restated Balance Sheets and Income Statement

	Opening Balance Sheet			Income Statement			Closing Balance Sheet		
	Original	**Factor**	**Restated**	**Original**	**Factor**	**Restated**	**Original**	**Factor**	**Restated**
Assets									
Inventory	$112.55	114.23	$128.56				$126.68	101.49	$128.56
	$112.55		$128.56				$126.68		$128.56
Equity									
Opening	$112.55		$128.56						
Sales				$499.56	106.09	$529.98			
Cost of sales				470.88	(Table 28-2)	514.54			
Net profit				$ 28.68		$ 15.44			
Dividends				14.55	106.09	15.44			
Retained earnings				$ 14.13		$ —			
Closing							$126.68		$128.56
	$112.55		$128.56				$126.68		$128.56

After working out the adjustments for nonmonetary items, attention is turned to other figures in the statements. In this case the restatement of figures for sales and dividends paid must be completed. Since the example stipulated that these transactions were spread evenly throughout the year, it is fair to assume that all such transactions took place at June 30 and can be restated by a factor based on the change in the price index between June 30 and December 31 of year 2. The complete restatement, then, is shown in Table 28-3.

It may be useful to pause and compare the GPL-restated figures with those shown by LIFO accounting in chapter 27 (which were identical, under the assumptions of this illustration, with replacement cost accounting). Both GPL accounting and LIFO accounting show that all profits were paid out in dividends. The LIFO version of historical cost, however, showed the actual cash amount of dividends, namely $14.55. In other words, historical cost accounting reports in units of money, disregarding the differences in the purchasing power of money at different points of time. GPL accounting reports in units of purchasing power at a stated date — in this case the end of year 2.

Readers of GPL statements must be able to grasp the concept of reporting in purchasing power. Opponents of GPL accounting argue that people naturally think in money terms since that is the medium in which transactions actually take place. (For example, the owner of our business will have actually received dividends totalling $14.55, not $15.44.) On the other hand, proponents of GPL accounting stress its power to cure the misleading nature of historical cost data when purchasing power changes over time. Suppose a history of sales figures were reported in the annual report of the Steady State Company for the second year of the rising price period. Table 28-4 shows the figures both under historical cost accounting and GPL accounting.

Table 28-4

Comparison of Sales Time Series

	Historical Cost Accounting	GPL Accounting
Year 0	$412.00	$529.19
Year 1	430.91	514.53
Year 2	499.56	529.98

The historical cost figures show substantial increases in the latter two years. That might well mislead anyone who did not accurately remember the declining value of the dollar in those years. That decline began towards the end of year 0 in our example, and the owner of the business did not adjust his prices so as to catch up until the beginning of year 2. The GPL figures correctly show that the owner's pricing failed to keep up with inflation in year 1 and clearly account for the zero profit that would be shown under GPL accounting for that year.

GPL adjustments of monetary assets and liabilities

The foregoing provides a broad explanation of the GPL restatement process. Now let us introduce our first complication. Let us continue the preceding example with only one change. The business held $10.00 as a cash float throughout year 2. Table 28-5 shows the opening and closing balance sheets restated by the appropriate purchasing power index factors.

Table 28-5

Steady State Company
Rising Price Period — Year 2
Restated Balance Sheets
(Including monetary asset)

	Opening Balance Sheet			Closing Balance Sheet		
	Historical Cost	Factor	Restated	Historical Cost	Factor	Restated
Cash	$ 10.00	112.55	$ 11.26	$ 10.00		$ 10.00
Inventory	112.55	114.23	128.56	126.68	101.49	128.56
Equity	$122.55		$139.82	$136.68		$138.56

Two observations should be made about the figures in Table 28-5:

1. The GPL closing balance sheet is expressed in terms of the purchasing power of the dollar at the closing date. It follows that actual cash balances at that date are translated at parity. On the other hand, the opening balance sheet is also translated in terms of the purchasing power of the dollar *at the end of the year.* Since a dollar could buy more at the beginning of the year than at the end, it follows that the $10.00 of cash held at the beginning of the year is translated into $11.26 in terms of the purchasing power of money at the end of the year.
2. The translation of the net income for the year and dividends paid shown previously (Table 28-3) showed no balance of retained earnings or deficit to be added to or subtracted from equity. The GPL balance sheet in Table 28-5 shows a decline in equity from $139.82 to $138.56 when expressed in equivalent end-of-year purchasing power terms. It is clear from this example that the cause of that loss was the decline in purchasing power of the cash held throughout the year from $11.26 at the beginning of the year to $10.00 at the end. Ordinarily, the cash balance of a business will fluctuate up and down over the year, and it will be impossible to compute the gain or loss in purchasing power from holding cash merely from a comparison of opening and closing balances. This illustration indicates, however, that if all the other restatements are made correctly, any difference in restated equity that is otherwise unexplained will represent the gain or loss in purchasing power from holding assets or liabilities that are fixed in terms of money.

Proponents of GPL accounting think that the disclosure of gain or loss in purchasing power associated with monetary items is one of the most important bits of information emerging from GPL accounting.

Cash represents general purchasing power today. It must be evident that any gain or loss in purchasing power with respect to cash holdings must be considered to have occurred the instant that the general purchasing power of the dollar changes. The same presumption is not quite so clear when we are talking not about cash balances but about promises to pay cash in future. Hence, let us expand our example to take in such a case. Let us assume that, at the close of business in year 1 the owner borrowed $25.00 for a five-year period with interest payable semi-annually at 16% per annum and reduced his equity by the same amount. Table 28-6 shows the year 2 statements adjusted for this assumption and following the same GPL restatement process.

Note that the restatement of the opening debt position shows it at a GPL-adjusted figure of $28.14. The closing debt position, however, remains at $25.00 because the liability is fixed in terms of money. The difference of $3.14 thus appears to be some sort of gain.

This illustration raises one of the most contentious issues in GPL accounting. What is the essence of the $3.14 gain on debt? Is it part of net income? Is it realized? A variety of arguments has been made concerning gain on debt.

- First of all, some proponents of the entity theory would not dispute that there was some sort of gain associated with the debt but argue that it should not be recorded in net entity income. In contrast, the purchasing power loss on cash held would be considered to belong in income because the cash is an asset of the entity required for its operation. Entity theorists argue that the purchasing power gain on debt is not a gain to the entity but rather a transfer of purchasing power from the debt holders to the shareholders. The assets for which the entity is accountable are not increased in either monetary or purchasing power terms because of the debt. Instead, the claim on entity assets by the debt holders has been decreased in purchasing power terms, and consequently the shareholders' claim has increased.
- Many people think that purchasing power gains and losses are unreal because they cannot perceive cash flows associated with such gains and losses. LIFO accounting or replacement cost accounting would have shown that the cash available from the business after paying interest of $4.00 was $10.55, not the $13.33 reported in the illustration. The concern of such people is that a gain in purchasing power cannot be spent. It seems irrational that the higher the debt position (which is often evidence of a shaky company), the greater will be the reported purchasing power gain on debt. As some have put it, a company could be showing substantial gains all the way into bankruptcy.
- Many people also are concerned that in some sense the gain is not "realized" until the debt is paid off. The general price level could reverse itself before the maturity date of the debt so that the present gain might be cancelled out by a loss. People who argue this way are thinking of realization of the gain in terms of it being finalized or fixed in amount by some terminating event.
- In contrast, the traditional position of GPL theorists is that the concept of realization has no meaning in relation to changes in purchasing power of

Table 28-6

Steady State Company
Rising Price Period — Year 2

Restated Balance Sheets
(Including monetary asset and liability)

	Opening Balance Sheet			Closing Balance Sheet		
	Historical Cost	Factor	Restated	Historical Cost	Factor	Restated
Cash	$ 10.00	112.55	$ 11.26	$ 6.00		$ 6.00
Inventory	112.55	114.23	128.56	126.68	101.49	128.56
	122.55		139.82	132.68		134.56
Debt	25.00	112.55	28.14	25.00		25.00
Equity	$ 97.55		$111.68	$107.68		$109.56

Restated Income Statement

	Historical Cost	Factor	Restated
Sales	$499.56	106.09	$529.98
Cost of sales	(470.88)	(Table 28-2)	(514.54)
Purchasing power loss on cash(b)			(1.13)(a)
Profit before interest	28.68		14.31
Interest	(4.00)		(4.12)(c)
Purchasing power gain on debt(b)			3.14
Net profit	24.68		13.33
Dividends	(14.55)	106.09	(15.44)
Retained earnings	$ 10.13		($ 2.11)

Notes:

(a) The loss on holding cash cannot be calculated solely from the opening and closing balance sheets because the cash balance was reduced by interest payments during year.

(b) In practice the purchasing power loss on cash is likely to be grouped with the purchasing power gain on debt. They are separated in this illustration on the grounds that purchasing power gains or losses on operating assets and liabilities, such as cash or trade accounts receivable and payable, are appropriately shown as an element of operating profit. In contrast, since the debt is a means of financing, the purchasing power gain is appropriately grouped with financing costs.

(c) The mid-year interest payment of $2.00 represents $2.12 in year-end purchasing power. This, added to the year-end payment of $2.00, totals $4.12.

monetary assets or liabilities. Such changes, by definition, occur when the price level changes and are measured by it. There can be no justification or rationale for assigning the result of a change in price level occurring in one period to some other period. The simple fact is that if the value of the dollar decreases, the burden of an obligation expressed in dollars decreases at the same time.

Even if one grants the technical correctness of this last argument, it may be instructive to consider just how the purchasing power gain manifests itself in terms of real assets. If there is a gain, it somehow must be evidenced by an improvement in the amount of the equity's claim on assets. Consider the illustration we have been dealing with. When the $25.00 was lent to the business, it gave the creditor a claim against $124.23 in assets, being $10.00 in cash together with inventory that had a replacement cost of $114.23 at the date of the loan. The creditor's claim therefore represented 20.1% of the value of the assets at that date.

A year later, even after all the cash flow from the business had been paid out in dividends, the assets had a current value of $134.56 and the debt claim represented only 18.6% of the increased value of the assets. Clearly, the value of the equity claim on assets had gone up *even though the entire cash flow from the business before interest had been paid to the equity by way of dividends.* Moreover, if the owner had merely refrained from purchasing inventory in any quarter of the year, all the assets at the end of the quarter would have been in cash form. (If the business assets had been equipment instead of inventory, of course, the length of time required to turn the asset into cash through operations would have depended on the useful life of the asset.)

Two conclusions follow from these observations:

1. From the viewpoint of the equity, the gain of purchasing power resulting from the debt position is a real provable gain *provided* the assets in which the debt proceeds are invested (largely inventory in our illustration) increase in value at least as fast as the rate of increase in the general price level.
2. If one is interested in knowing when that purchasing power gain is realized in cash, one must look to the realization period of the assets in which the debt proceeds are invested. When the debt is invested in inventory, the realization period is short. Of course, in a going concern inventory is regularly replaced so that the purchasing power gain on debt is not withdrawable unless the business shrinks its operations. This does not mean that the gain is not real. So long as one can assume that reinvestment will be accompanied by returns that are consistent with the higher nominal dollar value of the assets, the equity is still better off.

The first is the more significant of these two points. What guarantee is there that the assets in which the debt proceeds are invested will hold their purchasing power? Consider monetary assets first. Obviously they do not hold their purchasing power. However, GPL accounting will recognize a loss in purchasing power on such assets to offset any gain reported on the debt financing them, so that the net result is correct. Then consider inventory. If the inventory on hand at the end of the year expressed in terms of the year-end purchasing power equivalent of its cost is above market value, GPL accounting calls for the inventory to be written down to market under the standard market value test. Thus, one should be able to count on loss recognition to offset any purchasing power gain on debt when the debt proceeds have been invested in inventory.

Finally, consider fixed assets. As is shown in chapter 17, one cannot count on fixed assets being written down to their economic value in regular historical cost accounting, partly because the economic value of fixed assets is so difficult to measure. For the same reason, then, one cannot count on a write-down of GPL-adjusted carrying values of fixed assets. Hence, to the extent that debt proceeds have been invested in fixed assets, it is uncertain that the purchasing power gain on debt is realizable. This is a practical chink in the armour of GPL accounting theory.

Some implementation problems in GPL accounting

It will be evident from the foregoing that the distinction between monetary and nonmonetary assets and liabilities is very important in GPL accounting. This section will, therefore, first discuss this problem and then continue with a discussion of certain other conceptual and technical questions.

What is monetary?

Assets and liabilities need to be classified as monetary or nonmonetary for a simple reason. Consider money on deposit in a bank. The value or purchasing power of that deposit depends upon the purchasing power of the currency in which it is expressed. Consequently, when the purchasing power of that currency changes, there is a loss or gain in the purchasing power of the bank deposit that must be reflected under GPL accounting. Other types of assets are also affected by changes in the purchasing power of the currency, basically because they are denominated or defined in money terms. Thus, if a bond having a face value of $1,000 is acquired at par and held to maturity, the purchasing power invested in that asset will decrease or increase depending on what happens to the purchasing power of money. In contrast, the purchasing power obtainable from a nonmonetary asset is not governed by the purchasing power of money, at least not nearly to the same extent, because it does not consist of a claim to a fixed amount of money.

Whether an asset or liability should be classified as monetary or nonmonetary is not always clear. The essential characteristic of a monetary asset or liability is that it is cash or it is *like* cash in that it represents a claim to future cash proceeds that are rigidly and irrevocably set at a specific money amount and it must be held to maturity.[3] The consequence of the fixed and irrevocable nature of the claim and its lack of saleability is that its holders gain or lose purchasing power *solely* as a result of changes in the general price level. Few assets or liabilities meet this test completely. Consider a holding of a government bond. The market value of the bond may change and a holder may realize a gain or loss that is *not* merely attributable to the change in the general price level. Thus, a rigid definition of "monetary" based on essential characteristics could virtually confine the class of monetary assets and liabilities to actual cash holdings or claims to payment in money on demand.

Published descriptions of GPL accounting have not applied such a rigorous test for identification of monetary items. Rather, they identify as monetary all those assets and liabilities that represent a claim that is a fixed and determinable money amount at maturity. The fact that changes in the general level of interest rates or in the risk quality of the claim may make its current value deviate from its face amount is ignored. Even this expedient, however, does not deal with all instances where the value of an asset or liability may be affected both by changes in the purchasing power of money and by other factors. Some of these additional problems are discussed below.

Convertible debt. This item has some characteristics of a monetary liability. It carries fixed interest requirements and promises a fixed amount repayable at maturity. Its conversion privilege, however, also gives it some of the characteristics of equity. The question is, which characteristic should dominate in the accounting? Professional statements have suggested that it should be treated as monetary until it is converted. This seems to be a rule of convenience rather than one designed to reflect the essential nature of the item. An alternative suggestion has been to treat it as nonmonetary when its market price begins to follow changes in the market price of the stock for which it is exchangeable, rather than changes in the interest rate that otherwise would be applicable to debt securities of the company of similar quality. A third suggestion would treat the convertible debt as nonmonetary from the date of issue on the grounds that it is basically intended as a means of raising equity when outright sale of equity would be difficult. (Reversion to treating it as a monetary item might then be required at some future time should the prospect of conversion into equity become remote.)

Preferred shares. Dividends on typical preferred shares are payable only if declared and therefore do not represent a fixed and irrevocable commitment. In addition, redemption is only occasionally a fixed obligation. Under a strict interpretation of the definition, then, preferred shares are nonmonetary. On the other hand, the only claim that preferred shares have upon a company is for money and that at a rate that is fixed, in the sense that it cannot be higher than the stated dividend rate. These characteristics are much closer to those of a monetary obligation than to those of the ordinary nonmonetary liability. Certainly, under inflation, the preferred shareholder steadily loses purchasing power, other things being equal. A compromise procedure is to classify preferred shares as nonmonetary but to provide that the GPL-adjustment procedure shall not cause them to be carried above their call price. Normally, this would quickly result in their having all the essential characteristics of a monetary item.

The above conclusions do not necessarily apply to preferred shares with special characteristics. Convertible preferred shares are similar to convertible debt securities, and similar considerations would apply to them. Fully participating preferred shares are akin to common equity and would be treated in the same fashion.

Unearned revenue. There are some who argue that payments received in advance of service rendered are like negative accounts receivable or a form of temporary financing and therefore should be treated as monetary. The contrary argument is that unearned revenue stands for an obligation to deliver goods or service in future and therefore should be nonmonetary. Which of these arguments is correct depends upon the facts of the case. If the payment received is a mere deposit and the actual prices or quantities of goods or services can vary, the former argument seems appropriate. In the more usual case, however, where the obligation is to deliver specific quantities of goods or services in future, the answer is different. Cash paid today has a different purchasing power from cash that will be paid, say, several months from now. If one is accounting in terms of equivalent purchasing power, revenue proceeds received today must be adjusted for proper matching with costs expressed in terms of purchasing power several months from now. To achieve this, unearned revenue must be treated as nonmonetary.

Deferred taxes. Chapter 15 has discussed the concepts underlying tax allocation procedures. Under the "deferral" concept that has been adopted as a basis for today's accounting standards, deferred taxes cannot be described as representing fixed claims to money. Hence, it would be inconsistent to treat such balances as monetary in GPL accounting.

If deferred tax balances are treated as nonmonetary, the make-up of each balance deferred has to be attributed to a year of origin ("vintaged") in order to determine its equivalent in terms of purchasing power of the dollar at the base date selected for use in the GPL financial statements. To do this accurately, the accounts would have to be capable of showing the extent to which deferred taxes set up in each previous year have subsequently been drawn down. Under the "net change" basis of recording deferred taxes this is virtually impossible to accomplish. Thus, the treatment of deferred taxes as nonmonetary is, in most cases, impractical.

Fortunately, as has been argued in chapter 15, the assets and liabilities resulting from tax allocation procedures can be shown to represent expectations of future cash inflows or outflows. In a fundamental sense, therefore, it is justified as well as expedient to treat deferred tax balances as monetary. It must be conceded, however, that present-day deferred tax accounting procedures are not designed to produce balances necessarily equivalent to the expected future tax payments or receipts. Thus, the treatment of these balances as monetary can only be regarded as a somewhat pragmatic compromise.

Foreign currency items. Assets and liabilities denominated in foreign currency do not represent claims that are fixed in terms of the reporting currency. Thus, it cannot be said that the sole source of gain or loss with respect to such items will be changes in the purchasing power of the reporting currency. By definition, therefore, these items are nonmonetary. It is doubtful, however, that such a classification corresponds with common sense.

Consider two countries that are experiencing very similar rates of inflation. Suppose a company in country A issues long-term debt denominated in the currency of country B. Suppose further that there is very little change in the exchange rate between the two countries over the lifetime of the debt (a fairly reasonable assumption given the fact that inflation rates are similar in both countries). If the debt is treated as nonmonetary (and assuming the GPL statements are expressed in terms of the purchasing power of the dollar at the end of the latest reporting year), it will be restated each year to a higher figure to allow for the deterioration in purchasing power of the currency of country A during the year. Then, if the debt figure is translated at current exchange rates, it will be written down again from its restated amount to its face amount at the current exchange rate and "gain on foreign exchange" will be credited. Given the assumption that the exchange rate changed very little over the period of the debt, it is apparent that it is misleading to classify all this gain as gain on foreign exchange.

Consider another simple illustration. Company A borrows $1,000 in foreign currency dollars at a time when the exchange rate is one dollar of foreign currency (FC) equals one dollar of local currency (LC) and the price index in both countries is 100. One year later the exchange rate is $2 FC equals $1 LC, and price indexes are 400 in the foreign country and 200 in the home country of company A.

If the GPL financial statements are to be reported in terms of the purchasing power of the local currency at the end of one year, the first step in the preparation of the statements is to restate the original carrying amount of the debt of $1,000 LC to $2,000 LC, its equivalent in current purchasing power. Then:

1. If the debt is considered as nonmonetary, its carrying value would be initially left at $2,000 LC. However, if the accounting policy is to translate foreign currency assets and liabilities at the current exchange rate, the liability of $1,000 FC (face amount) would be valued at $500 LC, and the difference between this and the GPL-adjusted carrying value of $2,000 would be recorded as a $1,500 LC gain on foreign exchange.
2. If the debt is treated as monetary, the original issue proceeds of $1,000 LC at the beginning of the year would be equivalent to $2,000 LC in year-end purchasing power, and this would result in the recording of a purchasing power gain of $1,000 LC. Then, if the actual liability of $1,000 FC is restated at the current exchange rate to $500 LC, there would be a $500 LC gain on foreign exchange recorded.
3. A third possibility might be called the FC purchasing power/monetary method. Under this approach the opening foreign currency amount of $1,000 FC, would be updated to its *foreign currency* purchasing power equivalent at the year-end — i.e., $4,000 FC, and the difference between this and the fixed liability of $1,000 FC would represent a purchasing power gain of $3,000 FC. This gain would be translated to local currency units at the *year-end* exchange rate so that the purchasing power gain to be reported by company A would be $1,500 LC. Since the initial proceeds to company A were $1,000 LC and these were equivalent to a year-end purchasing power of $2,000 LC, the recording of a purchasing power gain of $1,500 LC would leave the debt on the books at $500 LC, which in this case would be equivalent to its foreign currency face value translated at the current exchange rate. No gain or loss on foreign exchange would need to be reported.

Method 3 has not previously been suggested in the accounting literature. It would seem, however, that either of methods 2 or 3 are preferable to method 1. Method 1 is internally inconsistent. It identifies the foreign currency item as monetary by the fact that it translates it at a current exchange rate but treats it as nonmonetary for GPL accounting. In addition, it seems unrealistic to show no purchasing power gain on debt when the value of the currency has declined in both countries.

It might be argued that method 3 is preferable to method 2 on the grounds that the relative price performance in the two countries has a major influence on the exchange rate. Therefore the purchasing power of the foreign currency and the gain or loss with respect to it should be regarded as the dominant variable to be reported.

Other conceptual issues

Translation of foreign subsidiaries or branches for consolidation. Chapter 20 has described the two methods of translation of financial statement figures of units included in the consolidated financial statements whose accounts are kept in a foreign currency. The "current-rate" method is to be used for relatively self-sustaining foreign operations. The "temporal method" is used when operations of the foreign unit are interdependent with those of the parent company or are dependent upon it for financing.

GPL accounting introduces a new step to be completed in the process of consolidating the foreign unit. Its historical cost figures must be restated in GPL terms. The question is whether this restatement should take place before the translation of its figures into the currency of the parent company — the so-called "restate/translate" approach — or after — the "translate/restate" approach. Under the restate/translate approach, the purchasing power index used in the restatement process is that applicable in the foreign country. Under the translate/restate approach, the purchasing power index used is that applicable for the parent company's currency since the foreign unit's figures would be translated into that currency before GPL adjustments are made.

The merits of each approach must be considered in conjunction with the choice that has been made with respect to the method of translation. It must be remembered that inflation (or deflation) in a country will have an impact on the exchange rate for its currency with other currencies as well as show up in the purchasing power index. One could argue, therefore, that if a current exchange rate is used for translation, it should be associated with price-level-adjusted figures at the reporting date, and if an historical exchange rate is used for translation, it should be associated with historical cost figures.

Current-rate translation method. Under this method all the assets and liabilities of a self-sustaining foreign operation are translated at current rates. The argument just made suggests the use of the restate/translate sequence in these circumstances. To see how this might work, consider the following simple illustration:

- A parent company invests $1,000 in a foreign subsidiary, and this is used to set up an operating business. The business acquires nonmonetary assets with $800 and holds monetary assets for the remaining $200.
- At the investment date, the parent company currency and the foreign currency are at parity. That is, $1.00 LC = $1.00 FC.
- In the first year of operation the subsidiary remits all earnings measured under the historical cost basis of accounting. At the end of the year, the composition of its assets is unchanged. That is, the net assets consist of $1,000 FC, of which $200 FC are monetary.
- The purchasing power index for a unit of FC is 121 at the beginning of the year, 110 at mid-year, and 100 at the end of the year.
- The purchasing power index for the parent company's currency is 113 at the beginning of the year, 106 at mid-year, and 100 at the end of the year.
- The exchange rate between the two currencies is $1.00 FC equals $1.00 LC at the beginning of the year, 95¢ LC at mid-year, and 90¢ LC at the end of the year. (Note that the exchange value of FC in terms of LC has weakened faster than would be suggested by the relative price performance in the two countries. If exchange rates had moved exactly in conformity with the purchasing power parity theory, the exchange rate would have been $106/$110 = 96.4¢ at mid-year and $113/$121 = 93.4¢ at the year-end.)

In this example the foreign unit's figures entering into the consolidation at the end of the first year under the restate/translate approach would be developed as follows:

	Historical Cost	GPL Restatement	Translation
Monetary assets	$ 200 FC	$ 200 FC	$ 180 LC
Nonmonetary assets	800	968	871
	$1,000 FC	$1,168 FC	$1,051 LC
Equity	$1,000 FC	$1,210 FC	$1,089 LC
Purchasing power loss on monetary assets	—	(42)	(38)
	$1,000 FC	$1,168 FC	$1,051 LC

The parent company thus records a purchasing power loss of $38 LC with respect to the net monetary assets of the subsidiary. However, there is a further problem. GPL restatement of the parent company's unconsolidated balance sheet produces a restated figure for the investment in the subsidiary of $1,000 LC x 113 = $1,130 LC. The net equity shown by the translated statements of the subsidiary *before* recognition of its GPL loss is only $1,089 LC. Therefore, the consolidated financial statements have to record a further loss of $1,130 LC – $1,089 LC = $41 LC. This results from the fact that the exchange rate for foreign currency at 90¢ LC has weakened faster over the year than would be suggested by its relative price performance (which, as noted, would have produced an exchange rate of 93.4¢ LC). Accordingly, it seems reasonable to recognize the difference of $41 LC as a loss on foreign exchange. If the practice adopted under historical cost accounting is continued under GPL accounting, this foreign currency adjustment would be treated as a charge to a separate category of shareholders' equity, rather than a charge against income.

It may be noted that if GPL accounting is applied, it is no longer necessary to have a rule that investments in "highly inflationary" economies should be translated using the temporal method even though the unit is self-sustaining. This exception under historical cost accounting to the standard treatment for self-sustaining investments is only an expedient to avoid the "disappearing asset" phenomenon (as discussed in chapter 20). As soon as GPL accounting is adopted, this expedient becomes unnecessary.

Temporal translation method. Now suppose that the foreign subsidiary is not self-sustaining, so that the temporal translation method applies. Given the same facts as before, the translate/restate sequence would provide the following figures:

	Historical Cost	Translation	GPL Restatement
Monetary assets	$ 200 FC	$ 180 LC	$ 180 LC
Nonmonetary assets	800	800	904
	$1,000 FC	$ 980 LC	$1,084 LC
Equity	$1,000 FC	$1,000 LC	$1,130 LC
Loss on foreign exchange		(20)	(20)
Purchasing power loss on monetary assets	—		(26)
	$1,000 FC	$ 980 LC	$1,084 LC

A comparison of these results with those shown under the restate/translate method example shows that the translate/restate method reports a total loss of $46 LC ($26 LC purchasing power loss and $20 LC foreign exchange loss) while the restate/translate method reports a total loss of $79 LC ($38 LC purchasing power loss and $41 LC foreign exchange loss). The difference of $33 LC in the total loss figure is attributable to the nonmonetary assets, which are shown at $904 LC under the temporal method and only $871 LC under the current-rate method. The difference reflects the fact that the temporal method will always carry the nonmonetary assets at their original historical cost translated at the historical exchange rate. The current-rate method carries nonmonetary assets at their GPL-adjusted amount (using the foreign currency purchasing power index) translated at the current exchange rate. If the movements in the exchange rate do not fully compensate or overcompensate for differences in the price performance of the two currencies, this sort of difference will arise. It is matter of opinion which method provides the fairer picture of the effect of economic forces.

In the above illustration of the temporal method, the translate/restate sequence has been used across the board. The argument noted earlier, however, suggested that the restate/translate method should be applied to all assets translated at a current rate. If this were applied to the temporal method, it would mean that the sequence would be translate/restate for nonmonetary assets and restate/translate for monetary assets. In this case, the holding of $200 FC at the beginning of the year would be adjusted to $242 FC in terms of purchasing power at the end of the year. Thus, there would be a loss of $42 FC attributed to the decline in purchasing power of the currency, and that purchasing power loss, translated at the year-end exchange rate of 90¢, would be equivalent to $38 LC.

However, the value of the holding of $200 FC suffered, in terms of the parent company currency, not only because of the purchasing power decline but also because of the weakening in the foreign exchange rate. The year-end exchange rate should have been 93.4¢ based on the relative price performance in the two countries. Therefore, a foreign exchange loss of $200 x 0.034 = $7 should be recognized. Thus, the total loss recognized under the temporal method could be reported as $38 LC as a purchasing power loss and $7 LC as a foreign exchange loss. These two together would equal the sum of the $26 LC and $20 LC losses shown in the illustration above, after allowance for rounding error. It will be recognized that the difference in basis of portrayal described here is the same difference in principle as that described earlier between methods 2 and 3 for translation of foreign currency assets and liabilities that are held directly by an entity.

Tax provisions when the accounts are restated. When GPL-adjusted financial statements are presented in terms of purchasing power current at the reporting date, the carrying values of all nonmonetary assets are restated in terms of their equivalent purchasing power at that period-end. Suppose an entity was formed to buy and hold a piece of property in expectation of its appreciation over a period of years. Assume further that the initial balance sheet was as follows: Land at cost — $500,000; Equity — $500,000. Assume further that the land was leased out for five years at a rental equal to municipal taxes, and that the general price level rose by 100% in that period. A GPL-adjusted balance sheet, expressed in terms of purchasing power at the end of the five years would show: Land — $1,000,000; Equity — $1,000,000. Then suppose, one day later, that the land was sold for $1,000,000. Immediately after the sale a balance sheet would show: Cash — $1,000,000; Liability for taxes (assuming a 23% capital gains rate) — $115,000; Equity — $885,000. The question is: Was the GPL-adjusted balance sheet one day earlier, which showed an equity of $1,000,000, fairly presented?

- Many people see this as a problem to which tax allocation theory applies. That theory states that income tax is a cost that should be recognized as expense in the period when accounting income equivalent to taxable income is reported. That is, if accounting income is reported before being taxed, deferred taxes should be provided. In this case, however, the GPL restatement of asset cost is never credited to income but rather to capital. Thus there is no accounting income equivalent to the taxable income, and therefore it has been argued this is a "permanent difference" which should not be subject to allocation.
- If tax were provided in the GPL statements, there would be a question whether the tax should be charged against income, notwithstanding that the asset restatement was credited to equity. The alternative would be to apportion the credit arising on restatement between a tax liability and a credit to equity. If one believes that the purpose of GPL accounting is to show financial position and changes in it after the purchasing power of the equity is maintained, the former is the better answer. In this case, then, year by year there would be a charge to income without any compensating revenue or gain being reported. It might look odd to see a regular tax provision year by year when no net income or gain was showing. Yet this presentation would report an important reality. An income tax system that is based on historical cost is, in effect, a tax on capital during periods when the general price level is rising.
- The argument for making the tax provision is pragmatic. GPL accounting aims to retain the merit of objective exchange value as the primary basis for recording assets and liabilities in the accounts but to adjust for distortion caused by the changing value of the unit of measure. If the changing value of the unit of measure has some significance to the incidence of income tax, it is telling only half the story to leave that out of the reckoning.

The foregoing discussion outlines several arguments on this question. The preferable answer seems to be a matter of opinion. A similar question arises in the context of current value accounting whenever unrealized holding gains exist. There, the argument for recognition of tax effects associated with future realization of value changes recorded is even stronger.[4]

Implementation of GPL accounting

Technical details on how to calculate GPL financial statements may be found in standard works on the subject and will not be reviewed here.[5] One comment is worth making, however. If GPL accounting were to become the primary basis for financial reporting or were to become regularly required as supplementary information, it might well prove to be convenient to keep the basic accounts and records in terms of dollars of constant purchasing power at an arbitrary base date. That is to say, all transactions recorded would be translated into the base-date purchasing power units at the time of their entry into the basic books of account. For monetary items, at least, it would be necessary to record the nominal dollar transaction values as well, and if historical cost financial statements were desired, all the accounts would need to be maintained in both base-date constant dollars and in nominal dollars. Although this extra recording might sound arduous, it is no more so than is now dealt with successfully by certain businesses that account in both dollars and quantity units (e.g., stockbrokers and custom metal refiners). The advantages of such dual recording would be twofold:

- GPL statements could be prepared directly from the books of account without the need for supplementary restatement of the historical cost figures such as was illustrated earlier. If statements were required to be reported in dollars of purchasing power at the latest year-end rather than in base-year constant dollars, one simple conversion factor could be applied to all the constant dollar figures from the accounts.
- The gain or loss on monetary items would appear directly from the accounts, rather than appearing as the end result of a restatement and reconciliation process that contains approximations and is subject to error. The gain or loss on any monetary item (say, cash) would be discovered by translating the nominal dollar balance at the end of the period into its base-date dollar equivalent and comparing the resulting figure with the base-date dollar balance. The difference would represent the purchasing power gain or loss expressed in base-date purchasing power.

If a full set of base-date constant dollar accounts is not kept, it would nevertheless be convenient to keep certain accounts (especially those for fixed assets and depreciation) in base-date dollars as well as nominal dollars.

As has been noted, the GPL-adjusted statements can be presented either in constant dollars of a base date or in dollars having the purchasing power they possess at the current reporting date. The advantage of the latter treatment is that readers of the financial statements are likely to understand the value of the dollar at a recent date better than its real value at some arbitrary earlier date. On the other hand, the use of the current purchasing power equivalent each year, rather than a fixed standard dollar from year to year, has a significant disadvantage in that comparative figures from previous years' financial statements have to be updated every time a new financial report is published. That is to say, when the 1988 balance sheet and income and funds statements are published, the 1987 figures previously published have to be revised to be truly comparable in terms of the 1988 purchasing power of the dollar. There is no doubt that this can be confusing to an unsophisticated reader. Extra care needs to be taken to explain the concept of accounting in terms of purchasing power units when such statements are presented.

Gains and losses of purchasing power through holding monetary items also will be hard for many to understand, particularly since those gains and losses cannot be associated directly with flows of cash. Again a clear explanation is necessary, as well as clear disclosure of such gains and losses in the income statement. In addition, under inflationary conditions the maintenance of business liquidity is made more difficult. A clear statement focussing on cash flows and liquidity is all the more necessary when purchasing power gains and losses are recorded in income or otherwise reported as part of shareholders' equity.

Summary

The shortcomings of historical cost accounting, as already noted, are most evident under inflationary conditions. The almost instinctive reaction of the accounting profession — particularly accountants in practice — to such pressure is to consider the adoption of GPL accounting. GPL accounting has the advantage that it builds upon the historical cost model. Its only change in concept is the substitution of a unit of general purchasing power as the unit of account in place of a unit of currency. Thus, it retains the objectivity popularly attributed to historical cost accounting.

The transformation of accounts maintained in units of money into units of purchasing power presents a problem because the concept of a unit of purchasing power is an abstraction. We do not buy or sell with units of purchasing power; we buy or sell with cash or promises to pay cash. To make the concept of a unit of purchasing power operational in accounting terms, we must adopt a price index and convert it into an index of purchasing power.

A wide variety of price indexes is published by governments and other agencies. In choosing between them, the theoretical objective should be to use the index most representative of the totality of spending in the economy. The production of price indexes contains some inherent problems, and the accounting profession would be well advised to seek the advice of experts in the field if an accounting system based on indexing were to be adopted for general use.

Certain issues are particularly important in the application of GPL accounting.

- Because all figures in GPL financial statements are to be expressed in a "dated dollar," that is, one that is based upon the purchasing power of money at a selected common date, the actual transaction amounts at which items are recorded in the accounts at different dates must be adjusted. For nonmonetary items, that presents little problem. If, for example, an item of inventory were bought for $100 when the price index stood at 200, and the index at the date of the balance sheet was 210, the item of inventory would be reported at $105. On the other hand, if $100 in cash were received when the price index stood at 200, it must still be presented at $100 in any subsequent balance sheet because its purchasing power has not increased in step with the index. Thus, GPL accounting reports gains and losses with respect to monetary items when price levels change. This means that the correct classification of assets and liabilities as monetary or nonmonetary is critical. Unfortunately, the basis for definition of items as monetary is not absolutely clear in all cases.

- Because the carrying value of nonmonetary items is adjusted upward under inflationary conditions, the chances that carrying values will exceed realizable values are greater than they are under historical cost accounting. Greater attention therefore needs to be paid to the need for write-downs when GPL accounting is used.
- This point is reinforced by the fact that GPL accounting results in recording gains on liabilities under inflation. If such liabilities finance the purchase of nonmonetary assets and if those assets do not succeed in holding the purchasing power invested in them, losses on the assets should certainly be recognized to offset the gains in purchasing power recorded on the debt.
- A variety of technical issues are encountered in implementing GPL accounting. Issues in connection with the translation of monetary assets and liabilities denominated in a foreign currency and the translation of foreign currency accounts for consolidation purposes are among the most difficult. There is also a question whether a tax liability needs to be recorded when the carrying value of a nonmonetary asset is written up, if tax would apply should the asset be sold at the written-up price.

References

[1]A number of other names have been applied to this accounting model. They include Constant Purchasing Power (CPP) accounting, Price-Level-Adjusted (PLA) accounting, and Constant Dollar (CD) accounting.

[2]It is beyond the scope of this book to discuss differences in methods of construction of price indexes and problems with each method. If GPL accounting were to be used generally, the advice of experts in the design of price indexes would be desirable as to the best choice among those available. For some discussion of the use of price indexes in accounting, see R.R. Sterling, *Theory of the Measurement of Enterprise Income* (Lawrence, Kan.: University Press of Kansas, 1970), pp. 331-50; G. Whittington, *Inflation Accounting: An Introduction to the Debate* (Cambridge: Cambridge University Press, 1983), chap. 4; and *Reporting the Financial Effects of Price-Level Changes*, Accounting Research Study No. 6 (New York: AICPA, 1963), App. A.

[3]For a good discussion, see L.C. Heath, "Distinguishing Between Monetary and Nonmonetary Assets and Liabilities in General Price-Level Accounting," *The Accounting Review*, July 1972, pp. 458-68.

[4]This argument is clearly made in W.L. Raby, "Tax Allocation and Non-Historical Financial Statements," *The Accounting Review*, January 1969, pp. 1-11.

[5]For professional statements on the subject, see AICPA, APB, *Financial Statements Restated for General Price-Level Changes*, APB Statement No. 3 (New York: AICPA, 1969), and Accounting Standards Steering Committee, *Accounting for Changes in the Purchasing Power of Money*, Provisional Statement of Standard Accounting Practice No. 7 (London: Institute of Chartered Accountants in England and Wales, 1974). Exposure drafts were also issued but never finalized by the FASB and CICA. For a more detailed "how-to-do-it" treatment, see A.D. Stickler and C.S.R. Hutchins, *General Price-Level Accounting: Described and Illustrated* (Toronto: CICA, 1975).

Chapter Twenty-Nine

Current Cost Accounting

The adoption of general price-level (GPL) accounting represented the solution preferred (with some lack of enthusiasm) by practicing accountants to the problem posed by inflation in the early 1970s. The proposal did not satisfy other interested parties. Many people criticized GPL accounting because the figures it produced for assets and liabilities did not represent values current at the financial reporting date. Even though the same was even more true of figures produced under the historical cost model, the feeling seemed to be that if historical cost figures were to be revised, the revision ought to be based on current values.

Academic accountants also did not support GPL accounting. Even though its basic ideas had been largely worked out in academic literature years earlier, by the 1970s academic accountants were interested in a more fundamental restructuring of the accounting model. Unfortunately, academic accountants were by no means unanimous as to the manner in which current values for assets and liabilities could or should be integrated with concepts of income. The plethora of ideas, each with its vociferous proponents, hindered general acceptance of any single proposal.

Finally, governments and government agencies played a part in the developing controversy. Just as accounting standard-setters were on the point of adopting GPL accounting, the United Kingdom government announced a committee of inquiry into inflation accounting, and the United States Securities and Exchange Commission pre-empted the FASB by requiring companies to publish certain information based on replacement costs. Subsequently, government-sponsored reviews were initiated in Australia, New Zealand, and Canada (by the Ontario government).[1] The effect of the government interventions was to preclude the adoption of GPL accounting and, in effect, force accounting standard-setters to pursue accounting models directed to the valuation of assets and liabilities at current prices. Unfortunately, the government reviews were no more successful than academic studies in achieving consensus.

We shall now proceed to a description of a variety of accounting models based upon the use of current values. We shall use the term "Current Value Accounting" (CVA) to embrace current value models of all kinds, and more specific terms to identify particular versions.

The value objective in current value accounting

When we start to think about accounting systems that report current values, our initial question may be: What is it that we are attempting to value? Is it the individual assets of the entity? Or is the entity itself? Here we hit upon what is known as the "aggregation problem." If the valuations of individual assets are performed independently, their individual values will not add up to the value of the enterprise (although there may well be some correlation, especially in the longer run). Commonly, the value of a successful enterprise as a going concern will exceed the net amount realizable from the sale of its assets individually (and liquidation of its liabilities) or the sum of the amounts that would be required to replace its assets. As chapter 12 has described, we call the difference between the value of the enterprise and the sum of the values of its net resources "goodwill."

From the viewpoint of investors (and perhaps most other external users of financial reports), it is the value of the entity that is of primary interest. Investors cannot dispose of the entity's assets. Instead, all that can be acquired or disposed of consists of securities representing part interests in the entity. Because of this it is sometimes said that the ideal value information would be the value of the entity as a whole and the ideal definition of income of an entity would be the change in its value over a period after allowing for capital contributions and withdrawals.

Nevertheless, it is universally acknowledged that such an approach would be impractical for general use in financial accounting. The problem is that the valuation of an enterprise as a going concern can only be approached on a discounted cash flow (DCF) basis. This requires subjective estimates of the amounts and timing of future cash flows for the entity as a whole and a judgmental choice of discount factors to be applied to arrive at their present value. That inherent subjectivity rules out the use of such an approach in accounting. In addition, it is sometimes argued that firms are not qualified to estimate the discounts for risk, etc., that are appropriate to valuations by the capital market. It is the investor's job to estimate the present value of the entity. It is the job of financial reporting to provide information concerning cash flows, segment results, new projects planned, market values of tangible assets, etc., that will assist the investor's estimates.[2]

It is agreed, then, that the only possible objective for accounting is to value individual assets and not the entity as a whole. An important corollary follows from this that is not always appreciated. *Goodwill cannot be objectively valued on a current basis*. That is to say, if it is impossible to value the enterprise as a whole other than subjectively, the valuation of goodwill — which can only be arrived at by subtracting the fair values of other assets from the value of the enterprise as a whole — must be equally subjective.

In short, the case for current values in accounting rests upon the simple idea that with current value information a user of financial statements will be better equipped to estimate amounts and timing of future cash flows and to evaluate management performance than he would be with information based on outdated historical costs.

The choice of current values

Chapter 27 has indicated that there are three possible bases for valuation of an asset — discounted cash flow, an entry market price, and an exit market price. Any proposed current value accounting model must choose between these. Alternatively, a model may choose different valuation bases in different situations. It then must specify a decision rule for making the choice, such as the value to the firm (VF) rule described in chapter 27.

Because of its subjectivity, DCF is impractical as a basis to be applied across the board. (However, it can sometimes be used as a proxy for current market price of a monetary asset when a reliable market price for the asset is lacking.) Current value accounting models, then, can be classified on the basis of whether they rely on exit values, entry values, or a situation-specific basis of valuation such as VF. The latter basis of valuation will use replacement cost (RC) much of the time, so that it is largely equivalent to an entry-value system. Hence, we can say that current value accounting systems are basically of two types — exit-value systems, which we shall call current realizable value accounting (CRVA), and entry-value systems, which are now widely known as current cost accounting (CCA). In this chapter we shall discuss several possible versions of CCA.

The Constant Company — a hypothetical manufacturer

We have already seen the equivalent of a simple CCA application in Table 27-4, where the income of the Steady State Company is shown in accordance with LIFO accounting. Under the restricted assumptions of that example, cost of sales on a LIFO assumption equalled cost of sales on a replacement cost assumption. The only difference between RC and LIFO cost lay in the balance sheet. Under the LIFO system, the inventory was carried in the balance sheet at its cost at the time LIFO was first adopted, since all purchases of inventory for replacement were treated as costs of goods sold. Under an RC assumption, in contrast, inventory on hand would have been continuously revalued upward as prices rose. Hence, for the Steady State Company, the average equity during year 2 would have been \$121.25 and the return on equity would have been \$14.55/\$121.25 = 12.0%. The use of replacement cost accounting (RCA) would have cured a major objection to LIFO, namely the showing of outdated costs in the balance sheet.

The problems that arise with CCA are more difficult in relation to fixed assets than they are in relation to inventory. Hence, it is preferable to provide a more realistic example that deals with both of these types of assets. The illustration that follows relates to a hypothetical manufacturing company, the Constant Company, that also operates in a steady state over the period examined. The steady state assumption means that nothing is assumed to change in terms of the volume of business carried on, the physical operations of the business, or its financial characteristics such as sales collection periods, inventory turnover, and so on. Although unrealistic, the steady state assumption is useful because it isolates the impact of changes in specific prices on the figures reported by the business and enables us to examine how different accounting approaches affect the figures.

The detailed assumptions as to the operating characteristics of the Constant Company are as follows:

- All sales are made on credit; the average collection period is two months.
- Inventory is costed on the FIFO basis; on average there are four months' purchases of raw materials in inventory and two months of labour and manufacturing overhead.
- All purchases are on credit. On average the company pays its bills for materials, factory overhead, and selling, general, and administrative costs in two months. Labour cost accruals represent one-half month on average. Income taxes are accrued monthly, and instalments paid one month after accrual, on average.
- Fixed assets have a useful life of ten years, and purchases have been evenly distributed with one-tenth of the total being replaced at mid-year each year. Depreciation is on the straight-line pattern. There is no net scrap value on retirements. Depreciation is not treated as part of manufacturing overhead for inventory costing.
- The interest rate on short-term debt is 6% and on long-term debt is 7%. Short-term debt interest is paid at the end of each month. Long-term debt interest is paid semiannually at the end of the sixth and twelfth months.

- The income tax rate is 50%. There are no tax deferrals. Investment income includes a small amount of nontaxable dividends.
- All cash available at the end of the year is paid out as dividends.

The price-change assumptions built into the illustration are as follows:

- The replacement cost of the company's fixed assets has been rising at the rate of 0.5% a month (6.17% a year) for the entire period since the earliest piece of equipment in use was acquired. Given the assumed ten-year life of the equipment, this means that the latest machine acquired cost 182% of the machine it replaced. (It is necessary to assume that prices have been rising during the lifetime of equipment on hand in order to properly simulate the understatement of depreciation in historical cost accounting during prolonged inflationary periods.)
- Prices of all other cost inputs begin rising at the beginning of year 1 at the rate of 0.9% a month (11.35% a year). Before that they were level.
- Selling prices are also raised at the steady monthly rate of 0.9% from the commencement of year 1. Before that they were level.
- Short-term interest rates are arbitrarily assumed to rise to 10% in year 1 and 12% in year 2. (A rise in interest rates is to be expected as inflation takes hold. The long-term debt interest rate, of course, does not change because it is locked in.)
- The investment portfolio is assumed to consist of stocks and long-term bonds. A small increase in dividends received is assumed in year 2.

The income statement and balance sheet of the Constant Company under traditional historical cost accounting are shown in Tables 29-1 and 29-2. Market values of investments (not shown) declined with inflation, but no write-down has been made because the decline has been deemed to be temporary.

Certain analytical ratios drawn from Tables 29-1 and 29-2 are set out in Table 29-3, namely the operating margin (percentage of net operating profit to sales revenue), the return on operating assets (percentage of net operating profit to average net operating assets), and the return on equity (percentage of net profit reported for the year to average shareholders' equity).

The results in Table 29-3 seem to be very favourable. Yet, one may ask, what is the source of the apparent improvement in years 1 and 2? The model built in an assumption of a constant volume of business; therefore, the improved results are not attributable to growth. Selling prices and cost prices were assumed to change at the same rate except for fixed asset costs upon which depreciation is based. The lower rate of increase in depreciation expense cannot, however, explain all this improvement. Had the cost of fixed assets begun to increase at the beginning of year 1 at the same rate as selling prices and other cost inputs, there would only have been a minuscule increase in depreciation.

Therefore, relative price changes accounted for only a small proportion of the reported improvement in operating margin. What caused the remainder? An analysis of the causes of difference between net profits reported under historical cost accounting and cash available for dividends may be instructive.

It was an assumption of the model that dividends paid were restricted to free cash from operations. Table 29-4 is a statement showing cash available for dividends. Table 29-5 explains the causes of the difference between reported profits and available cash.

Table 29-1

Constant Company
Statement of Income
(Historical cost accounting)

	Year 0			Year 1		Year 2	
Sales			$360,000		$380,068		$423,210
Cost of sales							
Opening inventory		$ 61,000		$ 61,000		$ 67,006	
Purchases							
Raw materials	$96,000						
Labour	84,000						
Overhead	90,000	270,000		285,052		317,407	
		331,000		346,052		384,413	
Closing Inventory		61,000	270,000	67,006	279,046	74,613	309,800
Gross profit			90,000		101,022		113,410
Depreciation		16,434		17,447		18,523	
Selling, general, and administrative expenses		42,000	58,434	44,341	61,788	49,374	67,897
Net operating profit			31,566		39,234		45,513
Investment income			1,450		1,450		1,550
Net profit before interest and income tax			33,016		40,684		47,063
Interest — short-term		1,800		3,000		3,600	
— long-term		3,500	5,300	3,500	6,500	3,500	7,100
Net profit before income tax			27,716		34,184		39,963
Income tax			13,658		16,892		19,732
Net profit			14,058		17,292		20,231
Dividends paid			8,659		3,924		4,459
Addition to retained earnings			$ 5,399		$ 13,368		$ 15,772

Table 29-2

Constant Company
Balance Sheet
(Historical cost accounting)

	Year 0		Year 1		Year 2	
Assets						
Accounts receivable		$ 60,000		$ 66,216		$ 73,732
Inventory		61,000		67,006		74,613
		121,000		133,222		148,345
Accounts and income taxes payable		42,638		47,224		52,661
Working capital (net)		78,362		85,998		95,684
Fixed assets						
Cost	$169,254		$179,693		$190,776	
Accumulated depreciation	76,321	92,933	81,028	98,665	86,025	104,751
Net operating assets		171,295		184,663		200,435
Investments—cost		25,000		25,000		25,000
		$196,295		$209,663		$225,435
Liabilities						
Debt — short-term	$ 30,000		$ 30,000		$ 30,000	
— long-term	50,000	$ 80,000	50,000	$ 80,000	50,000	$ 80,000
Shareholders' equity						
Capital	60,000		60,000		60,000	
Retained earnings	56,295	116,295	69,663	129,663	85,435	145,435
		$196,295		$209,663		$225,435

Table 29-3

Constant Company
Selected Financial Ratios

	Operating Margin	Return on Average Operating Assets — Before Interest and Tax	After-Tax Return on Average Shareholders' Equity
Year 0	8.77%	18.72%	12.38%
Year 1	10.32%	22.04%	14.06%
Year 2	10.75%	23.64%	14.71%

Each source of difference is described in Table 29-5 from two perspectives — first from the perspective of the revenue and expense components of reported income, and second from the perspective of the figures in an historical cost balance sheet. It is apparent that net cash flow tends to diverge from historical cost reported profits for two main reasons.

First, in any going concern, commodities sold or consumed in the course of business are generally replaced. When the prices of items replaced are tending to rise, historical costs matched against revenues will be less than replacement costs. The difference means that over a period of time some portion of the excess of revenue over reported costs must be held back to finance the higher cost of assets replaced, unless financing is provided from external sources. If prices are tending to fall, of course, the opposite is true.

Second, accrual accounting records revenues and costs not at the time of cash receipt or payment but rather when the basic sale or purchase transaction takes place. Sale transactions usually precede cash collection and purchase transactions usually precede cash payment. This lag in the cash effect means that the cash throw-off from operations will not equal profits recorded on the accrual basis whenever the prices applicable in credit sales or purchases are changing.

The effect of this on the net cash available from operations depends upon the precise fact situation. If sales and purchase prices are rising at the same rate and accounts receivable and payable are approximately the same in amount, the lag effect will be offsetting. If, however, accounts receivable exceed accounts payable, net cash flow will lag behind profits reported, and vice versa. If sales prices and purchase prices are rising at different rates, this too will have an impact. Thus there is no invariable rule. In many situations, however, rising prices will mean that net cash flow from operations is below profits reported on the accrual basis.

It would be grossly simplistic to suggest that in the general case cash generated from operations each period ought to equal profits reported. But remember that in this case the basic assumptions were that there were absolutely no changes in the operating characteristics of the business over the course of a year. In such a case, one instinctively feels that profit reported ought to be available for distribution in cash. If it is not, perhaps there is something wrong with the reporting system.

We now turn to discussion of current cost accounting illustrated by the case of the Constant Company. The basic concept of CCA has several versions. We shall begin with its simplest form and add complications.

Table 29-4

Constant Company
Statement of Sources and Use of Cash

	Year 0		Year 1		Year 2	
Profit reported		$14,058		$17,292		$20,231
Add depreciation (an expense not requiring an outlay of cash in year)		16,434		17,447		18,523
		30,492		34,739		38,754
Deduct increase in investment required:						
Increase in working capital						
Increase in accounts receivable	—		$ 6,216		$ 7,516	
Increase in cost of inventory	—		6,006		7,607	
	—		12,222		15,123	
Increase in accounts and taxes payable	—		4,586		5,437	
Net increase in working capital	—		7,636		9,686	
Purchase of replacement fixed assets	$21,833		23,179		24,609	
Total investment requirements		21,833		30,815		34,295
Net cash available for dividends		$ 8,659		$ 3,924		$ 4,459

Table 29-5

Reasons Why Profits Reported under Historical Cost Accounting Are Not Represented by Cash When Prices are Rising

	Year 0	Year 1	Year 2
1. Replacement costs exceed historical costs:			
Depreciation of historical cost is less than cost to replace capacity of equipment consumed in operations. The excess of replacement cost is added to the asset account even though physical capacity to serve has not increased.	$5,399	$ 5,732	$ 6,086
The cost of goods sold under the FIFO inventory costing assumption is lower than the costs of replacing such goods at date of sale. The cost of goods in inventory increases as prices change even though the quantity does not.	—	6,006	7,607
Additional cash required for asset replacement	5,399	11,738	13,693
2. More *monetary* working capital is required at higher prices:			
Cash received lags revenue recorded for credit sales when selling prices are rising. The amount of accounts receivable rises even though the volume of credit sales remains constant.	—	6,216	7,516
The opposite effect occurs with goods, etc., bought on credit. Cash payments lag amounts recorded for materials and services purchased. Consequently, accounts payable rise even though the volume of purchases stays constant.	—	(4,586)	(5,437)
Profits retained in increased monetary working capital	—	1,630	2,079
Profits reported not represented by cash	$5,399	$13,368	$15,772

Simple replacement cost accounting (RCA)

The simplest form of CCA is one in which amounts charged against income for assets sold or consumed in use are stated at their replacement cost. Changes in asset prices while held ("holding" gains or losses) are treated as direct credits or debits to equity. A condensed income statement and balance sheet for the Constant Company on this basis are shown in Table 29-6. The cumulative total of holding gains is shown in shareholders' equity under the title "capital maintenance adjustment."

This accounting model is based on the physical capital maintenance concept, which is implemented by charging replacement costs against revenues at the time that transactions are recognized and by exclusion of holding gains or losses from income. It adopts the realization convention, and some writers would say that it adopts the entity concept since the capital maintained pertains to all the physical assets of the entity.

Table 29-6

Constant Company
(Replacement cost accounting)

Statement of Income

	Year 0	Year 1	Year 2
Sales	$360,000	$380,068	$423,210
Cost of sales	270,000	285,052	317,407
Gross profit	90,000	95,016	105,803
Depreciation	(21,833)	(23,179)	(24,609)
Selling, general, and administrative expenses	(42,000)	(44,341)	(49,374)
Current operating profit	26,167	27,496	31,820
Investment income	1,450	1,450	1,550
Net profit before interest and income tax	27,617	28,946	33,370
Interest expense	5,300	6,500	7,100
Net profit before income tax	22,317	22,446	26,270
Income tax	13,658	16,892	19,732
Net profit	8,659	5,554	6,538
Dividends paid	8,659	3,924	4,459
Addition to retained earnings	$ —	$ 1,630	$ 2,079

Balance Sheet

	Year 0	Year 1	Year 2
Assets			
Accounts receivable	$ 60,000	$ 66,216	$ 73,732
Inventory	61,000	67,924	75,636
	121,000	134,140	149,368
Accounts and income taxes payable	42,638	47,224	52,661
Working capital (net)	78,362	86,916	96,707
Fixed assets	112,481	119,416	126,783
Investments — cost	25,000	25,000	25,000
	$215,843	$231,332	$248,490
Liabilities			
Short-term debt	$ 30,000	$ 30,000	$ 30,000
Long-term debt	50,000	50,000	50,000
Total debt	80,000	80,000	80,000
Shareholders' equity			
Capital	60,000	60,000	60,000
Capital maintenance adjustment	40,605	54,464	69,543
Retained earnings	35,238	36,868	38,947
	135,843	151,332	168,490
	$215,843	$231,332	$248,490

This model could be turned into a financial capital maintenance model in nominal money terms merely by including holding gains and losses in reported income, rather than excluding them. It could be further turned into a financial capital maintenance model in purchasing power terms if the holding gains and losses on nonmonetary assets were measured from a price-level-adjusted cost base and if losses or gains in purchasing power were included in relation to monetary assets and liabilities.

The merits of RCA

Supporters of RCA in its physical capital maintenance form see several advantages in it.

- A system that reports income only after full provision for physical maintenance of the resources of the entity is considered to provide a good measure of performance. The exclusion of holding gains from income eliminates the fortuitous effect of changing prices from the record of performance. The resulting income figure shows whether the enterprise is able to recoup its costs from revenues when prices change.
- Since amounts charged against revenues for resources sold or consumed are stated at RC, it is considered that income reported provides a good basis for prediction of future profitability of the enterprise. If business conditions are the same next year, the income reported will be the same rather than being confused by less predictable holding gains or losses resulting from charging outdated costs in determining income. Of course, business conditions will not be the same next year, but the record for a period of years under RCA may show trends that help predict how costs and revenues respond to changing economic conditions.
- Since the charge for resources consumed is stated at RC, it is argued that the net income figure represents an amount that can be distributed while leaving the "substance" of the business intact.

The meaning of replacement cost

One of the crucial issues in the application of RCA is that of interpretation of the meaning of replacement cost. We shall begin with a minor point and then proceed to a more serious question.

Consider the sale of a manufactured product. The materials wrought into the product might have been acquired four months before the date of sale, and the labour applied in manufacture perhaps one to three months prior to the date of sale. Is the replacement cost of these factors of production to be taken as their cost at the date of sale or at the several dates they would have had to be acquired in order to be incorporated in the goods actually sold? If we assume that a certain quantity of inventory has to be on hand to carry on business on a continuous basis, then it is the sale that triggers the need for replacement, and therefore one concludes that it is the sale-date RC that is relevant.

The more serious issue in the interpretation of replacement cost is the question whether the RC assumed is to be that for an identical asset or is to be based on the cost of replacing the asset service in the most favourable way. Business conditions change and technology improves. Thus, we cannot assume that resources consumed will be replaced with identical assets when the time comes for replacement. This problem is particularly acute with respect to fixed assets.

- Notwithstanding the possibility of changes in business conditions and technology, the simplest approach is to interpret RC to mean the replacement cost of an asset identical to that which is being sold or consumed. Such RC may be more descriptively called "reproduction cost." Such an approach has the merit that expenses will be reported on an internally consistent basis. We will not, for example, report expenses for labour, supplies, power, etc., as actually incurred in the operation of an "old-tech" machine but report a cost for consumption of the machine service based on the cost of a different "new-tech" machine. Thus, the use of reproduction cost could be said to report performance on a factual basis. Income reported will be the result of the investment and operating decisions actually made in the past. By the same token, however, the reported income statement may be less useful as a predictor of what may be expected in future. If replacement, when it occurs, will be based on a different configuration of factors of production, it seems likely that such configuration will be more profitable than that obtainable with the existing configuration.[3] On top of this, there is the practical point that there may be occasions when a reproduction cost for existing fixed assets is hard to find because the assets are no longer being made and markets for used equipment of the same type are not active.
- An alternative approach is to estimate RC in terms of the replacement cost of equivalent capacity for physical service. This could be argued to be more realistic in that it does not base a charge to income for resource consumption on the RC of assets that will not be replaced. On the other hand, it can also be accused of being "what if" accounting — basing the allowance for resource consumption on costs of assets not even owned. In addition, it encounters the problem that actual operating expenses reported will have been incurred in conjunction with the use of the old-tech, presumably less efficient, assets. To cure this, it is accepted that if RC is based on an assumption of replacement with a more efficient asset, an estimate of the operating cost savings possible with the use of that asset must be made, and the capitalized value of those savings must be deducted from the RC of the new asset for the purpose of arriving at an estimate of RC for the assets actually owned.
- There is one further question on the basis of estimating RC. Should it be assumed that whole plant will be replaced in one stroke assuming the most efficient replacement configuration currently achievable, or should it be assumed that the replacement decision will be looked at on an individual asset basis? The sum of the cost of replacement of individual assets in a plant will probably not equal RC for the whole plant replaced at one time. There is no universal answer to this question. The common-sense solution is to choose one or the other basis of estimating RC in accordance with the way in which replacement is likely to take place. In most cases, this probably means making estimates on the basis of piecemeal replacement.

Professional recommendations on implementation of CCA take the view that RC should be estimated based on the decisions the enterprise would take if it were replacing its assets. That is, if it would replace with an identical asset, it should estimate RC on that basis; if not, it should estimate it on the basis of the new improved asset.[4] These hypothetical decisions can be avoided, however, if satisfactory used market prices are available for the asset actually owned. In that case, RC can be taken simply as the buying price of assets of the same age and condition in the market. Even if technologically advanced assets are available, it may be presumed that the used market price will compensate for any operating advantages held by them.[5]

Some implementation problems in RCA

Estimation of the RC of goods sold can encounter severe problems. Generally, the problem occurs when the nature of the business is such that inventory sold is not immediately replaced or replacement purchases are not the same types of goods. For example, when goods sold are seasonal in nature, identical replacement goods simply may not be available. Or when the inventory consists of fashion goods, replacement with identical goods may not be planned even if the goods are available. In such circumstances, the concept of current replacement cost becomes problematic if not imaginary. To achieve the aim of holding back enough from revenue to finance restocking, one might construct an index to show the annual rate of change in prices of goods dealt in by the enterprise and use this index to revise the actual figures for cost of goods sold. The procedure is obviously artificial but might be the only way to report results on a basis roughly comparable with other enterprises using RC accounting.

Estimation of the RC of fixed assets may present considerable practical difficulties.[6] "Direct pricing," under which current buying prices of assets actually held are determined, is the most accurate technique but is expensive. If the RC of technologically improved plant is to be estimated, it may be possible to take shortcuts based on generally known costs for units of size (for example, cost per square foot of buildings) or units of capacity for certain processing industries. Otherwise, estimation of the current cost of a modern equivalent plant and adjustments to allow for differences in capacity and efficiency of existing owned plant can be arduous.

There is some tendency in practice to rely on indexes applied to historical cost to produce current cost figures. When indexes are used, care needs to be taken that they are appropriate for the type of asset to which they are being applied. In particular, inquiry should be made as to the extent to which the index makes an allowance for technological change. If such an allowance is made, the application of the index to the historical cost of the asset will not yield reproduction cost (if that is the figure desired). On the other hand, if such an allowance is not made or is made to an insufficient degree, the application of the index to historical cost of the asset held will not yield a figure appropriate as an estimate of RC of service capacity.

Possible objections to simple RCA

There are a number of points at which it is possible to take issue with simple RCA. The first relates to a certain ambiguity in its concept of capital maintenance. We have already seen the problem in identifying physical capital maintenance when assets in a going concern are not replaced with identical assets. That problem is dealt with by shifting our concept to replacement of the equivalent service capacity — still a concept that is expressed in physical terms, although not relating to identical assets.

It seems, however, that there must be limits to the distance to which this idea can be pushed when the whole business environment is changing. For example, in 1935 most people crossed the Atlantic by ship. In 1965, most people crossed by air. A company in the passenger shipping business in 1935 is likely to have phased out much of its transatlantic business by 1965, in which case physical maintenance of its assets was irrelevant, no matter what technological improvements had been made to ships. (Had it been possible to instantly convert the ships to cruise traffic, this would not have been true, but that development came later.) Alternatively, a farsighted company, considering itself in the passenger transportation business rather than the shipping business, might have set up as an airline. Even so, it requires a considerable feat of imagination to visualize an income statement reporting the results of operations of the last remaining ships based upon replacement costs and operating conditions of airplanes.

In general, we can say that a physical capital maintenance concept will be hard to implement when assets are not going to be replaced with identical assets, and the greater the difference between the assets in which new investment take place and the superseded assets, the greater will be the difficulty in implementation.

A further difficulty with the concept of physical capital maintenance lies in the fact that the total investment in any going concern is likely to contain nonphysical as well as physical assets (trade accounts receivable as an example) and will be financed in part by trade credit. Thus, the net investment in a business entity is likely to be different from the sum of its physical assets. Simple RCA has no concept for maintenance of the net investment in nonphysical assets, because it is implemented by means of replacement costing of assets consumed, and monetary assets are not consumed.

It has been argued that for certain purposes this is unimportant.[7] A different response is to broaden the concept of physical capital maintenance to that of maintenance of "operating capacity." Thus, if the actual operations of a firm depend upon investment in monetary assets as well as physical assets, we must take into account a requirement to maintain the capacity of the monetary assets as well. This leads to the idea of an allowance for maintenance of monetary working capital to be discussed in a subsequent section. This is a slippery slope, however. Monetary assets obviously do not have a physical output. Thus, their "service potential" lies not in physical results but in their ability to contribute to cash inflows. When operating capacity maintenance is thought of in terms of ability to maintain cash inflows, it tends to merge with the idea of financial capital maintenance.

Although the concept of operating capacity maintenance can solve some problems, it leaves others unsolved. Consider the capital that produced the RCA income figures shown in Table 29-6. The capital invested in physical assets is maintained by charging income with their RC. The capital investment in monetary working capital required for operations may be maintained by adding an allowance for that. The capital dedicated to portfolio investments, however, has no device to ensure maintenance when prices change. Some proponents of physical capital maintenance have conceded this point.[8] The suggestion then is that nonoperating capital be treated differently. Holding gains and losses on such capital should not be excluded from income, and thus a financial capital maintenance concept should be adopted for them. Thus, the application of capital maintenance is situation-specific — different applications are considered appropriate for measuring income from different segments of the entity.

Even if attention is confined to business operations, there may be a problem with the physical capital maintenance concept in some situations. Most business operations dealing with tangible property operate in two markets. They buy material and labour and they sell in the finished goods market, or they buy wholesale and sell retail. In these circumstances, there is normally a significant spread between buying and selling prices which is unlikely to disappear completely under changing price conditions. In contrast, a few businesses operate in the same market — they are commodity traders or dealers. For them, buying prices and selling prices are equal, apart from transaction costs. Thus, RCA applied literally will always show zero profit.

This anomaly is recognized by most writers. The solution usually proposed is to include gains and losses in income and to adjust them by a capital maintenance allowance. This may be achieved directly by factoring up historical cost by a general price index in calculating gain and loss or indirectly by recording gains and losses on the basis of historical cost but treating the balance sheet carrying value of such inventories as though they were part of monetary working capital subject to an allowance to maintain its operating capacity.

The problem under RCA in dealing with the commodity trader is similar in some respects to a problem often raised in relation to an ordinary business. It is not uncommon for a business to vary its buying patterns for basic materials with the aim of buying at the most advantageous price. Good buying, in effect, is a managerial skill that is rewarded by holding gains. If a business speculated by buying or selling commodity options or futures contracts, there would be no doubt that gains would be part of operating income. If it takes equivalent risks through its purchasing policies for materials, however, any gain or loss is excluded from income by virtue of the fact that replacement cost is charged against revenue when revenue is recognized. Although this anomaly is widely recognized, no practical solution has been suggested to the problem of separation of gains and losses attributable to good buying and holding gains and losses from fortuitous price changes.

Apart from this specific situation, a number of objections are often made against the complete exclusion of holding gains and losses from reported income.

- Under one point of view, income is regarded essentially as the result of ventures undertaken (which may be reported on a realization basis or include unrealized gains, depending upon the system). It may be legitimate to analyze reported income between holding gains and operating profit based on the application of replacement cost at the date of realization. But, it is argued, it is not legitimate to measure income *solely* by the excess of the selling price over RC at the date of sale, because the use of RC mixes up the cost that is relevant to a succeeding venture (if it is undertaken) with the income of the venture just completed.[9] If one follows this argument through, it seems to be saying that physical capital maintenance is an improper test of income measurement because it mixes future events with the record of events that have actually occurred.
- A further criticism of the complete exclusion of holding gains from income is that it may understate the amount that can safely be distributed to shareholders in times of rising prices. If the amount charged against income

with respect to physical assets sold or consumed equals their replacement cost, there will be no need for debt financing for those replacements, assuming they take place promptly and regularly. Now, consider a company whose replacement costs are steadily rising. If percentage profit margins on replacement cost are maintained, the company will experience an ever-increasing net cash flow from operations, even after absorbing the full cost of asset replacements. As a consequence, the existing level of debt in nominal dollars will form an ever-shrinking percentage of the maintained capital of the entity, even though its "debt capacity," as evidenced by its rising cash flow and the current value of its assets, is increasing. In these circumstances, it is argued that the shareholders' position is improving as a result of the holding gains, and this should be reflected in reported income. The so-called "financing" or "gearing" gain to be discussed subsequently provides for this.

- Some researchers oppose such an adjustment. Those who believe the entity theory should be applied rigorously naturally believe that the benefits that accrue to shareholders from holding gains should not be reflected in entity income. They will agree that in some circumstances an entity may properly borrow and use the borrowed money to increase shareholders' distributions. But such distributions should not be regarded or reported as a distribution of entity income. Others argue that when replacement costs are rising, an entity may be unable to maintain its percentage margins over RC. This possibility provides a different reason for exclusion of holding gains from income.[10]
- Some researchers argue that while there may be some rationalization for the exclusion of holding gains from income on the grounds they are needed for capital maintenance, there cannot be the same rationalization for exclusion of holding losses. Upon examination, this contention seems to be based on the instinctive reaction that capital cannot be maintained when it shrinks in financial terms. But this is merely another (perhaps more vivid) way of objecting to physical capital maintenance as a satisfactory foundation for financial reporting. In rebuttal, it has been argued that if physical capital is maintained at a lower investment cost, a business may well be better off because the entity may be more profitable as a result of increased volume associated with lower prices.[11] No doubt this will be true in some cases — and false in others. However, the argument is fundamentally irrelevant. One cannot justify a *physical* capital maintenance concept in terms of future profit prospects.
- There is a different point that bears upon recognition of holding losses on fixed assets. Depreciation is an allocation of cost over the useful life of the asset to allow for its loss of utility. That loss of utility may be caused by obsolescence as much as or more than wear and tear. Obsolescence, if it existed, would be evidenced by a decline in replacement cost of the asset, at least in a used condition. (It might also result in discontinuance of production of the asset so that a reproduction cost becomes unavailable.) If depreciation is supposed to include loss in value from obsolescence and a decline in value occurs from this cause, such decline should have been anticipated in the depreciation provision. If it was not anticipated, the correction presumably should be treated as an adjustment of past depreciation expense, not a holding loss excluded from income. Thus, we are left to ask ourselves what decline in RC would not be evidence of obsolescence or expiration of

useful life and thus might reasonably be treated as a holding loss. One can visualize a situation in which the identical asset is still being produced, there is no competitive improved asset in production, and the reproduction cost has gone down. In those circumstances it would seem probable that the change in reproduction cost is not attributable to obsolescence of the asset but rather to economies in its production. Thus, this would be a situation in which a holding loss might legitimately be recorded. But, in general, it is hard to distinguish holding losses from adjustments of depreciation.

Finally, some questions have been raised about the claim that simple RCA provides a good measure of cash distributable from operations.

- It has already been noted that simple RCA makes no allowance in income for any increased investment required in monetary working capital. This can be shown from our tables. Table 29-4 shows the maximum cash distributable from operations. Table 29-6 shows that RC accounting reports profit larger (in this illustration) than the cash available. Table 29-5 shows that the difference is attributable to the increased investment in monetary working capital (the excess of accounts receivable over accounts payable) caused by the increases in selling and purchasing prices.
- Many writers have talked about the "backlog depreciation" problem. Backlog depreciation may be illustrated as follows. A three-year life asset is bought for $100 and is expected to have no salvage value. During its three years of service, average RC is $120, $150, and $180, so that current cost depreciation is reported at $40, $50, and $60 in successive years. When the time comes for replacement, the RC of the asset is $195. Accumulated depreciation written (assumed to be equal to cash held back from operations) is only $150. The total "backlog" over the period is $45. Although this phenomenom is usually illustrated, as here, by depreciable fixed assets, the problem is actually more general. The problem is that a charge against income based on RC withholds sufficient cash from distribution to replace the asset *at the transaction date.* If, however, that cash is not spent on replacement immediately and prices go on rising, the cash will be insufficient when the asset comes to be replaced. Of course, the cash itself may earn a return which could be enough to provide the higher amount required at the time of replacement. However, if that return is included in reported earnings and if those earnings are distributed, then the cash will not be available at the replacement date. On the other hand, the cash held back at the transaction date may be invested in physical assets. If there are holding gains on those assets equivalent to the increase in RC of the asset to be replaced, the exclusion of those holding gains from income will maintain the physical capacity of capital in the aggregate and there will be no backlog depreciation problem.[12] A number of researchers have proposed to cure the apparent problem by calculating backlog depreciation regularly and charging it against income. For reasons just indicated, this is in error. The best answer to this problem (which unfortunately has not been suggested in any authoritative recommendation on current cost accounting) is to make sure some capital maintenance allowance is provided with respect to *all* the assets of the entity on hand whether they be operating or nonoperating, monetary or nonmonetary.

- It has also been pointed out that the physical capital maintenance system will not ensure retention of sufficient cash to replace *physical* capacity when the replacement cost of assets actually held is based upon the replacement cost of a technologically improved asset of the same capacity but the latter figure has been discounted to allow for the capital value of operating savings that would be associated with the new asset. Suppose, for example, that a new asset with exactly the same volume capacity as the existing asset has an RC today of $100,000, but because of the lower efficiency of the actual asset owned, the latter is rated as having an equivalent RC of $60,000. Only $60,000 will be withheld from distribution over the lifetime of the asset (ignoring future price changes and backlog depreciation). Thus, there will not be enough cash at the time of replacement to buy the improved asset even though it offers no increase in volume capacity.[13] What this suggests is that the term "physical capital maintenance" cannot be taken too literally. What is being maintained is a physical asset of a certain quality. If an enterprise proposes to replace existing assets with assets having either a greater volume capacity or a higher quality with the same capacity, it must be expected to raise additional capital for the improvement.

The monetary working capital adjustment (MWCA)

One of the presumed advantages of CCA stated earlier was that it showed the amount of cash generated in a period that should be distributable. It was an assumption of the Constant Company model that all cash generated from operations not required for replacement of investment was distributed in dividends. Table 29-7 summarizes the profits reported under the simple RCA system and the dividends paid.

The reason for the shortfall in distributable cash in years 1 and 2 is evident from Table 29-5 and has already been explained. Simply, it is that accrual accounting is not cash accounting. Hence, if it is desired to report a profit figure that is distributable *in cash,* one must not only report costs at figures that allow for replacement of assets consumed, but one must also adjust the profit reported for changes in

Table 29-7

Constant Company
Summary of Profits and Dividends
(Replacement cost accounting)

	Profits	Dividends	Difference
Year 0	$8,659	$8,659	—
Year 1	5,554	3,924	$1,630
Year 2	6,538	4,459	2,079

the monetary working capital required by the business on account of changes in prices.

This idea is not easy to understand intuitively. The explanation commonly given is that, under conditions of rising prices, a given amount of monetary working capital loses part of its "operating capacity" — its capacity to finance a given volume of business. The more straightforward explanation is the one given earlier — that cash flows tend to lag accruals. If income is defined as *cash* distributable while maintaining capacity to operate at the same physical volume of business (and it is assumed that credit terms must be maintained to do that volume of business), then this monetary working capital adjustment to the reported profit figure must be made. Of course, some writers do not agree that income must be based on a pure distributable cash concept. They argue that an entity *is* better off if its monetary working capital increases. Therefore, the MWCA, if calculated at all, should be shown in the statement of cash flow, as an item reconciling reported profit and cash available from operations.

There is a superficial similarity between the concept of the MWCA and the idea of purchasing power gains and losses on monetary items in GPL accounting. In fact, if specific selling and purchasing prices of an enterprise were changing at a rate identical to the general price level, the MWCA would be exactly the same in amount as the GPL gain or loss computed with respect to the assets and liabilities defined to be part of monetary working capital. The basic rationales of the two adjustments, however, are quite different. The MWCA proceeds from a physical capital maintenance perspective and applies only to monetary items required to conduct operations. The other proceeds from a financial capital maintenance perspective and applies to all monetary items.

The actual calculation of the MWCA requires some approximation since it is only the change owing to changing prices that is to be included, while actual monetary working capital figures change both because of price changes and changes in the volume of business done. The latter amounts should not be treated as an adjustment to reported profit since they effectively represent changes in scale of investment, just as much as does an increase in investment in plant. Changes in the amount of monetary working capital owing to changes in the lag in cash flows — e.g., resulting from greater efficiency in collection — might also be deemed an adjustment of scale of investment.

Calculation of the MWCA, in theory, also requires application of different rates of price change according to the particular item of monetary working capital involved. For example, the adjustment for accounts receivable should be based on the rate of change in selling prices, while the adjustment for accounts payable should be based on the rate of price change for goods and services purchased. Some statements have erroneously referred only to the rate of price change in cost inputs for the purpose of making this calculation. (The use of a general price index has also been suggested as a practical expedient instead of making a refined calculation using actual rates of price changes in the items affected.)

Finally, there is some difference of opinion as to just what should be treated as operating monetary working capital. For example, some would treat all bank loans as a part of the financial structure of the entity. Others regard short-term bank loans as so intimately related to accounts receivable and inventory as to represent part of the *net* operating investment in the business. Thus, the concept of the MWCA has proved to be somewhat fuzzy.

The financing adjustment

One consequence of the CCA system is illustrated by the Constant Company. Table 29-6 presents the balance sheet under the simple replacement cost accounting described so far and shows that the ratio of debt to equity has declined from year to year. The absolute amount of debt is unchanged over the period because the calculation of distributable profits allowed for full replacement of all assets consumed in operations. Accordingly, since the assets as a whole have risen in price, the claim of the equity has increased relative to the fixed debt amount.

This is the result of the complete exclusion of holding gains on assets from reported income. As already indicated, many writers question that exclusion. They question why a business that is maintaining the real value of its total capital under rising price conditions should be required or influenced to reduce the extent of its reliance on debt financing. They conclude that, to the extent that holding gains have occurred on assets financed by debt whose claim on the assets is fixed in nominal dollars, that portion of the holding gains may properly be reported as income to the equity.

Against this, it is argued that holding gains, when defined as increases in RC, may not represent real improvements in the well-being of the entity. This point has to be conceded. However, if higher replacement costs have been charged against income with respect to assets consumed in operations, the holding gains on them must be considered as being realized. Thus, it is felt that it is proper to report income for the equity at least with respect to the debt-financed portion of realized holding gains. Some would go further and report income with respect to unrealized holding gains as well.

The incorporation of a "financing" or "gearing" adjustment into reported income changes the specification of the accounting model. The proprietary concept supersedes the entity concept as its basis. Physical capital maintenance remains as the capital maintenance concept, however, even though one could argue that financial capital maintenance is more properly associated with a focus on the proprietary interest. Finally, the model, as we have just stated, may or may not impose a realization test on income recognition.

The calculation of financing adjustments for the Constant Company is illustrated in Table 29-8. The following assumptions are made for the purposes of this calculation:

- Dividends paid by the Constant Company are increased by the amount of the financing adjustment related to realized holding gains only.
- Cash to pay those dividends is borrowed.
- The additional borrowing carries an interest rate of 12%.

The full income statement and balance sheet are shown in Table 29-9. It will be noted that, although the absolute amount of debt is increasing, the percentage of debt to total capital is tending to decline very slowly. This is because the unrealized holding gains recognized in the RC valuation of assets have not entered into the calculation of the financing adjustment used in this table..

The chief conceptual criticism of the financing adjustment lies in this restriction to realized gains. If one accepts the view that increases in the current cost

Table 29-8

Constant Company
Financing Adjustments

	Year 0	Year 1	Year 2
Realized holding gains			
Cost of sales — at replacement cost	$270,000	$285,052	$317,407
— at cost (Table 29-1)	270,000	279,046	309,800
Realized re cost of sales	—	6,006	7,607
Depreciation — at replacement cost	21,833	23,179	24,609
— at cost	16,434	17,447	18,523
Realized re fixed assets	5,399	5,732	6,086
Monetary working capital adjustment	—	1,640	2,104
Total realized holding gains	5,399	13,378	15,797
Increase in unrealized holding gains	1,138	2,121	1,386
Total holding gains — realized and unrealized	$ 6,537	$ 15,499	$ 17,183
Percentage of debt to total capital			
Debt — beginning of year	$ 80,000	$ 82,064	$ 87,016
Equity — beginning of year	129,306	133,779	144,326
Total capital — beginning of year	$209,306	$215,843	$231,342
Debt percentage	38.2216%	38.0202%	37.6136%
Financing adjustments			
• Realized holding gains *times* debt percentage	$ 2,064	$ 5,086	$ 5,942
• Total holding gains *times* debt percentage	$ 2,499	$ 5,893	$ 6,463

of assets held usually do represent real gains, then it is argued that it is inconsistent not to recognize the income element of all such gains. This criticism is reinforced by the observation that the realization restriction distorts the timing of recognition of holding gains. The rise in prices is recognized through the financing adjustment, not when the prices change but when the asset is charged off against income. Increases in the replacement cost of land held for productive purposes, for example, never get recognized unless the land is sold and not replaced. Increases in the replacement cost of depreciable assets are recognized in step with future depreciation and not when the price changes occur. Under persistent inflation this postponement can create a consistent understatement of income.[14]

Other criticisms or comments that have been made about the financing adjustment are as follows:

Table 29-9

Constant Company
(Current cost accounting with monetary working capital and financing adjustments)

Statement of Income

	Year 0	Year 1	Year 2
Sales	$360,000	$380,068	$423,210
Cost of sales	270,000	285,052	317,407
Gross profit	90,000	95,016	105,803
Depreciation	(21,833)	(23,179)	(24,609)
Selling, general, and administrative expenses	(42,000)	(44,341)	(49,374)
Monetary working capital adjustment	—	(1,640)	(2,104)
Current operating profit	26,167	25,856	29,716
Investment income	1,450	1,450	1,550
Interest expense	(5,300)	(6,748)	(7,942)
Financing adjustment	2,064	5,086	5,942
Net profit before income tax	24,381	25,644	29,266
Income Tax	13,658	16,768	19,311
Net profit	10,723	8,876	9,955
Dividends	10,723	8,876	9,955
Addition to retained earnings	$ —	$ —	$ —

Balance Sheet

	Year 0	Year 1	Year 2
Assets			
Accounts receivable	$ 60,000	$ 66,216	$ 73,732
Inventory	61,000	67,924	75,636
	121,000	134,140	149,368
Accounts and income taxes payable	42,638	47,214	52,626
Working capital (net)	78,362	86,926	96,742
Fixed assets	112,481	119,416	126,783
Investments — cost	25,000	25,000	25,000
	$215,843	$231,342	$248,525
Liabilities			
Short-term debt	$ 32,064	$ 37,016	$ 42,512
Long-term debt	50,000	50,000	50,000
Total debt	82,064	87,016	92,512
Shareholders' equity			
Capital	60,000	60,000	60,000
Capital maintenance adjustment	38,541	49,088	60,775
Retained earnings	35,238	35,238	35,238
	133,779	144,326	156,013
	$215,843	$231,342	$248,525

- Some people argue that it is fundamentally incorrect to assume a direct connection between debt financing and gains on assets. Money that is borrowed cannot usually be traced to specific uses. Hence, it is arbitrary to assume that assets on which holding gains have been experienced have been financed proportionately by debt and equity or in any other fashion. (In fact, some proposals for financing adjustments have called for specific deemed association of certain debt with certain assets — for example, mortgage debt with property mortgaged.) Accordingly, rather than assume that gain or loss associated with debt depends upon the experience of assets bought with the debt funds, such people would account separately for gains or losses on assets and gains or losses on debt. The latter might be measured by using a general price index applied either to the book value of the debt or to its carrying value after recognition of gains or losses to bring it to current market price. Such a partial application of a general price index, however, seems awkward and undesirable.
- The application of the financing adjustment is also debatable in another respect. It has been noted that there is some disagreement whether bank overdrafts and short-term bank financing should be treated as part of monetary working capital. This distinction affects the financing adjustment calculation also, since total debt (other than that specifically assigned to non-operating assets) must be accounted for in one way or another. Both the figures for the monetary working capital adjustment and the financing adjustment are affected by the decision on this point and the final income figure reported is affected as well.

Use of the "value to the firm" approach

As already discussed, RC can become a very nebulous or perhaps impossible concept when obsolescence sets in. Put more starkly — there is no such thing as RC when assets are not to be replaced. Even if this were not so — if replacement costs could be found for assets that are obsolete — most people feel uncomfortable with the idea of reporting RC figures in financial statements that exceed the current economic or realizable values for the assets in question. For these reasons, current cost accounting advocates have virtually universally embraced the concept of "value to the firm" described in chapter 27. As there stated, the valuation approach boils down in most situations to two rules:

- Value assets held for sale at the lower of RC and NRV.
- Value assets held for productive use at the lower of RC and economic value (EV).

Chapter 27 has explained the extremely subjective character of estimates of EV. Quite apart from this, however, there are problems in fitting VF concepts into CCA theory.

In the first place, consider the practical problem of separating the change in EV from one year to the next into something equivalent to depreciation and price change elements. Since EV is not a market price, it is impossible to measure any price change effect. Since this is so, there can be no amount credited to capital maintenance with respect to assets valued at EV, and the notion of maintenance of operating capacity is simply nonoperative.

A similar statement can be made for inventory carried at NRV. When NRV is below RC, it will no longer be profitable to trade in the goods in question. Hence, a decision by management not to replace a product or product line should signal the need to change from an RC valuation basis to an NRV basis. Once NRV is adopted, changes in NRV before sale will presumably be reflected in the operating profit figures. But there will be no revaluation of the inventory item to reflect changing costs of production. Hence, the notion of maintenance of operating capacity is nonoperative in this case also.

Finally, one must consider the consequences when all or most of the productive plant is carried at EV. By definition, EV is the discounted amount of estimated future cash flows. If the estimates are correct, the decline of EV for the remaining life of the plant (that is, the depreciation recorded) will result in a reported profit percentage on the invested capital at the beginning of each year that is equal to the discount rate used in calculating the EV. In other words, the accounting ensures (if EV is correctly estimated) that future profits will be reported at a predetermined rate. It is evident that in these unusual circumstances CCA does not come close to achieving its stated objective of reporting income only after provision for maintenance of operating capacity. Instead, it becomes a subjective valuation system, pure and simple.

The conclusion from the foregoing is that the adoption of the VF basis of asset valuation is incompatible with the concepts of physical or operating capacity maintenance when the latter concepts are implemented by exclusion of all or some holding gains from income. Only a straight RC basis of valuation can ensure physical capital maintenance on that basis. An alternative approach, however, is conceivable. A price index might be found or developed to track the changes in prices of a representative collection of productive assets. That index could be applied to the aggregate value of a firm's assets at the beginning of a period (valued on the VF approach or any other approach considered relevant), and income reported could be based upon the increase in aggregate value over the year (including holding gains) less the increase in value that the index indicates was required to maintain the productive capital at the beginning of the year. The same form of income statement presentation could be converted to a financial capital maintenance approach merely by changing the price index from one based on the prices of the firm's productive goods to one based upon prices of consumable goods or goods in general. Such a form of presentation will be illustrated in the next section.

Current cost accounting with capital maintenance based upon a price index

In order to illustrate the presentation of a current cost income statement using a one-line capital maintenance adjustment in place of the exclusion of holding gains from income, let us construct a price index that might be appropriate for the Constant Company. Such an index can be developed from the assumptions given in the example as to the rates of price increase and the current cost valuation of assets shown in Table 29-9 at the end of year 1.

	Balance Sheet Valuation	Rate of Price Increase	Product
Monetary working capital	$ 19,002	11.35%	$ 2,157
Inventory	67,924	11.35	7,709
Fixed assets	119,416	6.17	7,368
Total	$206,342		$17,234

Weighted average rate of price increase: $17,234/$206,342 = 8.352%

It was pointed out earlier that the physical capital maintenance concept made no provision for maintenance of the capital invested in portfolio investments. To provide comparability with the figures previously presented, we must exclude investments from the amount of capital to be maintained. To be consistent with the assumption made in applying the financing adjustment, we calculate that the $25,000 in portfolio investments was financed to the extent of 37.61% by debt. (See debt percentage at the beginning of year 2 reported in Table 29-8.) Accordingly, the portion deemed financed by equity is 62.39% of $25,000 = $15,597. The equity capital maintenance adjustment for year 2 is, therefore, 8.352% of ($144,326 − $15,597) = $10,751.

Table 29-10 provides a comparison of income statement figures for year 2 on three different bases:

- Column A shows the figures on the basis of the inclusion of realized holding gains only in income and deduction of a one-line capital maintenance adjustment. It will be noted that this shows a slightly lower net income figure than that shown in Table 29-9. The reason is that the income figures do not include the increase in unrealized holding gains during the year, but the capital maintenance adjustment is applied to the entire equity invested in operating assets and does not allow for the fact that some part of the increase in equity may be unrealized. It may be concluded that the use of a full capital maintenance adjustment in an income statement that recognizes realized holding gains only is somewhat illogical.
- Column B provides figures that are more defensible in logic. Unrealized as well as realized holding gains are included in income, so that a full capital maintenance adjustment is justified.
- Column C shows the figures as they would be if a financing adjustment were calculated on the basis of both unrealized and realized holding gains. Table 29-8 shows that realized holding gains plus the increase in unrealized holding gains in year 2 amounts to a total of $17,183. Application of the debt percentage in the opening capital structure (37.61%) yields the financing adjustment of $6,463. Because of the inclusion of unrealized gains in calculating the financing adjustment, this presentation is consistent in concept with that in column B. That is evident from the fact that the two bases of presentation result in almost identical figures of net income. (The small difference between them is attributable to the fact that a price index used in calculating a capital maintenance adjustment can rarely capture all the elements making up net investment. In this case, it does not take into account the fact that taxes payable, being based on the historical cost system, do not increase at the same annual rate, 11.35%, as do other expenses.)

Table 29-10

Constant Company
Comparison of Income Statement Figures for Year 2
Prepared on Three Different Bases
(Based on opening balance sheet figures in Table 29-9)

	A Realized Holding Gains with One-line Capital Maintenance Adjustment	B Realized and Unrealized Holding Gains with One-line Capital Maintenance Adjustment	C Financing Adjustment Calculated on Basis of Both Realized and Unrealized Gains
Sales	$423,210	$423,210	$423,210
Cost of sales	317,407	317,407	317,407
Gross profit	105,803	105,803	105,803
Depreciation	(24,609)	(24,609)	(24,609)
Selling, general, and administrative expenses	(49,374)	(49,374)	(49,374)
Monetary working capital adjustment	(2,104)	(2,104)	(2,104)
Current operating profit	29,716	29,716	29,716
Investment income	1,550	1,550	1,550
Interest expense	(7,942)	(7,942)	(7,942)
Holding gains — realized	15,797	15,797	—
— unrealized	—	1,386	—
Capital maintenance adjustment	(10,751)	(10,751)	—
Financing adjustment	—	—	6,463
Net profit before income tax	28,370	29,756	29,787
Income tax	19,311	19,311	19,311
Net profit	$ 9,059	$ 10,445	$ 10,476

The "dichotomization" of the income statement

The basis of presentation commonly suggested under the current cost accounting model calls for a separation in the income statement of current operating profit (COP) and realized holding gains. Several reasons have been advanced for this.[15] First, it is stated that different types of decisions may be involved in operating the firm and in acquiring and holding assets. Thus, separating the reported results of each type of decision helps in evaluating management performance. Second, it is argued that COP is a better indicator of distributable income to be expected over the long term. Third, it is argued that separation of the holding gain element should improve comparability of reported income figures among firms. Under conditions of changing prices, one firm will show different holding gains from another simply because its productive assets were bought at different times. Separation of this price change element, therefore, should make the remaining operating profit figure more comparable from one firm to another.

The first of these reasons has been severely criticized.[16] It is pointed out that for the most part it is impossible to conduct business operations without some minimum investment in assets. Thus, to a considerable extent the business operation decision and the asset acquisition decision are not two decisions but rather different aspects of a single decision. Moreover, even where a separable asset acquisition decision is made (suppose a business overstocks its inventory of materials in anticipation of a price rise), the subsequent holding gain does not completely measure the result of that decision. The reason for this is that the overstocking will cause some carrying costs that otherwise would not have been incurred. These costs will be buried among other operating costs and would need to be dug out for matching with the holding gains to permit a proper evaluation of the speculative overstocking decision. Thus, the performance evaluation argument for separation of holding gains lacks persuasiveness.

The second argument is that the figure of COP, separated from the confusing effect of price changes, should form a better basis than historical cost profit figures for prediction of some future event or variable such as future income or future distributable cash flow. Empirical research has generally not borne out this proposition.[17] The research, however, has generally been somewhat limited in design and scope and therefore may be inconclusive. In addition, the research generally assumes that prediction would take the form of a mechanical extrapolation of actual figures for COP or of trends in actual figures. Judgmental predictions, taking into account reported firm data while also taking into account forecasts of external factors (such as the state of the economy), cannot be tested in this way.

The third argument, namely that the COP figures will be more comparable from one firm to another, seems more persuasive if reasonably comparable replacement cost figures for different firms can be estimated. However, to the extent that speculative holding gains have been obtained at the expense of increases in expenses deducted in computing COP, the COP figure for one firm may become less comparable to that for another.

A final consideration favouring the separation of holding gains from COP is that this separation provides additional information as to sources of gain even if the sources are interdependent. This additional information may well be useful to anyone analyzing the financial statements and making estimates of future expected results. In the author's opinion, this potential analytical usefulness is the major justification for the separation of COP and holding gains.

Summary

GPL accounting as described in chapter 28 represents only a modification of the historical cost accounting model. When we account in terms of current values, we adopt an entirely new model. The exact specification of that model has been the subject of sharp debate. A choice has to be made as to the precise form of current value to be reported — whether an entry price, exit price, or economic value. Different versions of current value accounting also differ in their prescriptions of a capital maintenance concept, their choice of perspectives (entity or proprietary), and the decision whether to include unrealized holding gains in income determination.

In general, authoritative recommendations for the presentation of current value information have been based on entry values of assets rather than on exit values. (The concept of value to the firm calls for valuation at replacement cost — an entry value — most of the time.) A current value system based on entry values is popularly known as current cost accounting. In contrast, a current value system based on exit values may be called current realizable value accounting — to be discussed in the next chapter.

The point of departure of current cost accounting is the proposition that the RC of assets sold or consumed should be charged against revenues. The thinking is that any income reported after absorbing a charge sufficient to replace the assets represents a genuine improvement in well-being that can be distributed if desired. Proper measurement of RC is fundamental to this system and presents a number of conceptual and practical issues.

- Assets are frequently not replaced in identical form because of changes in technology. Also, even if they were to be replaced in the same form, the RC might vary depending upon whether the assets were replaced piecemeal or as an integrated operating unit. Depending on the assumptions made as to form and manner of replacement, the estimate of RC could vary considerably. Professional recommendations on this point are that estimates of RC should be based on the way in which a business would probably replace its assets. If it would replace them with technologically improved assets, the estimate of RC should be based on the prices of such assets, with a deduction to allow for the operating disadvantages of the assets actually owned. Likewise, if it would replace assets piecemeal, RC estimates should assume such a mode of replacement. In some cases, however, markets for used assets similar to those held can be used to provide figures for RC directly.
- Sometimes assets sold are seasonal and there is no RC for them. In other cases, it may be evident that assets will not be replaced. Such situations raise questions as to the applicability of accounting based on replacement cost.

- A variety of practical problems that make the estimation of RC difficult and/or costly may present themselves.

In addition, the technique of charging RC of goods sold against income falls down in the situation of a trader in commodities. In that situation, RC will always equal selling price (except for transaction costs), so that income calculated on a RC basis is not very meaningful. In somewhat similar fashion, if an ordinary business overstocks inventory in order to take advantage of expected price movements, any resulting gain will be excluded from reported income under RC accounting.

Simple RC accounting as just described has been subject to two major criticisms. First, capital maintenance is intended to be achieved through the device of charging income with the RC of resources sold or consumed and excluding from income the change in their RC since the day they were acquired. Obviously, this only maintains capital that is invested in assets that are sold or consumed. (The capital of most enterprises is partly invested in other assets as well as tangible assets held for sale or use. Most enterprises, for example, require some net monetary working capital as well as inventory and fixed assets. In addition, many enterprises hold non-operating investments.) Second, some people argue that simple RC accounting does not adequately portray the impact of changing prices on proprietary equity. The exclusion of all holding gains from income maintains all the capital that is invested in operating assets to be sold or consumed. Some of the capital invested in those assets, however, is supplied by debt, not by proprietary equity. If there are holding gains on assets financed by debt, the benefit from them accrues to the equity, but this is not in any way displayed under simple replacement cost accounting.

Two expedients have been suggested to alleviate these criticisms:

- A "monetary working capital adjustment" could be charged against income in an amount estimated to allow for the change in monetary working capital required to carry on the existing volume of business at current price levels.
- A "financing adjustment" could be calculated and credited to proprietary income to represent the portion of holding gains recorded that have been financed by debt.

There are some technical definitional problems that require resolution if these two modifications of simple RC accounting are adopted. It will be noted, as well, that these expedients do not compensate for the failure of RC accounting to maintain capital invested in non-operating assets.

Although current cost accounting rests very heavily upon the use of RC as the basis for valuing assets, there are obviously occasions when certain assets are not worth RC. For this reason, the application of CCA is normally modified by adoption of the concept of "value to the firm" for the determination of carrying values. On this VF basis, assets are valued at RC unless RC is above both NRV and EV. In the latter event, the assets are reported at the higher of NRV and EV — almost always NRV for inventory and EV for fixed assets.

This modification of the basic approach of CCA has serious consequences for its basic objectives. As already described, capital maintenance is supposed to be achieved under CCA by charging income with the RC of assets sold or consumed. If something less than RC is charged, clearly capital is not maintained in any meaningful sense. Fortunately, a solution to this problem is ready to hand. The solution is to abandon the idea of maintaining capital by excluding holding gains (and losses) from reported income. Instead, the gains and losses should be included in income, but a capital maintenance adjustment should be charged, calculated by applying an appropriate price index to the current value of the capital recorded as invested in the entity.

This expedient solves more than just the problem caused by adoption of the VF valuation basis. It also allows for maintenance of the net investment in monetary working capital, and it makes provision for maintenance of capital invested in non-operating assets. As well, if it is desired to adhere to the proprietary point of view, the capital maintenance adjustment is applied to the equity capital only, thereby obviating the need for the financing adjustment.

The principal problem with the use of the one-line capital maintenance adjustment lies in the selection of an appropriate price index. It may be that an index can be discovered or devised that reasonably reflects the changes in prices of assets specifically held by the entity, in line with the idea of maintaining operating capacity. Many, however, feel that the use of a general price index, as called for by the objective of maintaining financial capital, is more suitable.

To be logically consistent, the income figure against which a one-line capital maintenance adjustment is charged should include unrealized as well as realized holding gains and losses. For example, if a company's sole asset were its investment in land, it would be illogical to charge a capital maintenance adjustment of, say, ten percent against income from the land and yet ignore an unrealized gain in land value of an equivalent or larger percentage. Alternatively, if it is desired to exclude unrealized holding gains from income, consideration should be given to reducing the capital maintenance adjustment on some reasonable basis.

Finally, there has been some debate about the presentation of the income statement under CCA. The whole development of the idea of RC accounting has tended to lead to a split in presentation between current operating profit measured on the basis of the RC of assets sold or consumed and the holding gains and losses arising from changing prices. A number of theorists have questioned the significance of the separation of the two aspects of performance; it is arguable, however, that the refinement in information is likely to have some value to the analyst, as long as its basis is understood.

References

[1]The several government-sponsored studies in order of publication are: *Inflation and Taxation: Report of Committee of Inquiry* (Canberra: Australian Government Publishing Service, 1975); *Inflation Accounting: Report of the Inflation Accounting Committee* (London: Her Majesty's Stationery Office, 1975); *Report of the Committee of Inquiry into Inflation Accounting* (Wellington, N.Z.: Government Printer, 1976); and *Report of the Ontario Committee on Inflation Accounting* (Toronto: Ministry of Treasury, Economics and Intergovernmental Affairs, 1977).

[2]See K.V. Peasnell, "The Present Value Concept in Financial Reporting," *Journal of Business Finance & Accounting,* Summer 1977, pp. 153-68.

[3]See E. Petri and J. Gelfand, "The Production Function: A New Perspective in Capital Maintenance," *The Acounting Review,* April 1979, pp. 330-45.

[4]See FASB, *Financial Reporting and Changing Prices,* Statement of Financial Accounting Standards No. 33 (Stamford: FASB, 1979), par. 180.

[5]See L. Revsine, "Technological Changes and Replacement Costs: A Beginning," *The Accounting Review,* April 1979, pp. 306-22.

[6]Detailed investigation of these difficulties is beyond the scope of this book. For a more complete discussion, see *Estimating Current Values: Some Techniques, Problems and Experiences* (Toronto: CICA, 1979), and C.S.R. Drummond and A.D. Stickler, *Current Cost Accounting: Its Concepts and Its Uses in Practical Terms* (Toronto: Methuen, 1983).

[7]For example, Revsine argues that a capital maintenance concept appropriate for national policy decisions need be concerned only with physical assets because only "real" assets are of significance to the welfare of the nation as a whole. See L. Revsine, "Physical Capital Maintenance: An Analysis," in *Maintenance of Capital: Financial Versus Physical,* ed. R.R. Sterling and K.W. Lemke (Houston: Scholars Book Co., 1982), pp. 75-94. Revsine argues that different capital maintenance concepts are legitimate for different purposes. This contention, however, suggests that either financial reports should present a variety of income measures deemed appropriate for different purposes or we must pick the most widely useful basis for general purpose reporting. Revsine stopped short of making such a choice.

[8]For example, see Revsine, "Physical Capital Maintenance: An Analysis," p. 91.

[9]See comments by J.A. Milburn in *Maintenance of Capital: Financial versus Physical,* ed. Sterling and Lemke, pp. 97-100.

[10]Merrett and Sykes argue this point vigorously, citing a study showing that expenditures at higher replacement costs in Britain in years prior to 1975 earned no additional return compared with the lower cost assets they replaced. See A.J. Merrett and A. Sykes, "Seven Answers Looking for a Question," *Accountancy,* December 1979, pp. 74-78. See also Revsine, "Physical Capital Maintenance: An Analysis."

[11]See comments of J.R. Hanna in *Maintenance of Capital: Financial versus Physical,* ed. Sterling and Lemke, pp. 272-73.

[12]This was demonstrated in the so-called Sandilands Committee report — *Inflation Accounting: Report of the Inflation Accounting Committee,* pp. 142-45.

[13]See K.W. Lemke, "Financial Versus Physical Capital Maintenance: A Review of the Arguments," in *Maintenance of Capital: Financial versus Physical,* ed. Sterling and Lemke, pp. 295-96.

[14]See C. Kennedy, "Fixed Assets and the Hyde Gearing Adjustment," *Journal of Business Finance & Accounting,* Winter 1978, pp. 393-405.

[15]The most influential exposition of this idea of income dichotomization is the seminal work by E.O. Edwards and P.W. Bell, *The Theory and Measurement of Business Income* (Berkeley and Los Angeles: University of California Press, 1961).

[16]Critical articles include D.F. Drake and N. Dopuch, "On the Case for Dichotomizing Income," *Journal of Accounting Research,* Autumn 1965, pp. 192-205; P. Prakash and S. Sunder, "The Case against Separation of Current Operating Profit and Holding Gain," *The Accounting Review,* January 1979, pp. 1-22; and R.A. Samuelson, "Should Replacement-Cost Changes be Included in Income?" *The Accounting Review,* April 1980, pp. 254-68.

[17]See, for example, Prakash and Sunder, "The Case against Separation of Current Operating Profit and Holding Gain," and Y.M. Mensah, "The Usefulness of the Holding Gains and Losses Disclosure," *Journal of Accounting, Auditing & Finance,* Winter 1983, pp. 130-41.

Chapter Thirty

Current Realizable Value Accounting; Price Changes and Specialized Industries; Evaluation of Current Value Accounting

This chapter completes our consideration of new accounting models or amendments to the historical cost accounting model that have been proposed to respond to the problem of rapidly changing prices. In chapter 29 we discussed a number of current value accounting models based principally upon entry values of assets. These are collectively referred to as current cost accounting (CCA). We begin this chapter with a consideration of an accounting model based entirely upon exit values. This we have denoted by the generic term "current realizable value accounting" (CRVA). (A prominent exponent refers to this model as continuously contemporary accounting — or CoCoA for short.) We continue with some discussion of specialized assets and industries to see how different price-change accounting models might apply to them and conclude with an evaluation of several current value models discussed in these chapters.

Current realizable value accounting

The foundations of the CRVA model may be summarized as follows:[1]

- A balance sheet portrays the wealth of an entity. It is an important statement in its own right because, unlike the income statement, it is capable of verification by reference to external evidence. That is to say, assets can be observed, physically verified by counting, weighing, etc., or may be confirmed with outside parties.
- The total entity wealth shown by a balance sheet is meaningless unless the individual components of measures of wealth are "additive" — that is, unless their character is homogeneous so that any addition is of like to like. This means the model must select a single asset attribute to be measured in monetary terms and reported in the balance sheet.
- For reasons set out below, the most significant asset attribute is its realizable value — an exit value.
- Income for a period is the change in wealth over the period after allowance for capital contributions and withdrawals. It thus consists in essence of

changes in realizable value of resources owned. If so desired, the income statement can be analyzed by matching costs against revenues (using either historical costs or replacement costs in the analysis) so long as all holding gains and losses are reflected somewhere within the income statement.
- The real value of money lies in its purchasing power. Since the purchasing power of a unit of money changes over time, any measurement of income must take that into account. A one-line capital maintenance adjustment may be made to reported income to maintain the purchasing power of the equity at the beginning of the year. Alternatively, the original carrying amounts of assets and liabilities may be continuously adjusted to their current purchasing power equivalent. On this basis, holding gains on nonmonetary assets and liabilities will be measured from a price-level-adjusted base, and purchasing power gains and losses will be shown with respect to monetary assets and liabilities whose exit value in nominal terms does not change over time.

In short, the CRVA model sees capital maintenance in financial terms, adopts exit value as its sole basis of valuation, has a proprietary perspective, and does not embody a realization constraint.

The merits of CRVA

The preeminent feature of CRVA is its adoption of exit value as the sole value attribute to be measured in the model. Both pragmatic and conceptual reasons are given for this. On the practical side, it is argued that exit value is virtually the sole value attribute that is capable of being independently observed. Discounted cash flows cannot be observed because the cash flows lie in the future and the choice of discount rate is subjective. Historical cost can be verified by observation at the time of acquisition, but, with minor exceptions, historical cost is only the point of departure for asset valuation in historical cost accounting. Both inventory and fixed asset carrying values are subject to allocations and reallocations after acquisition. These allocations are arbitrary and result in carrying values that cannot be related to any real world evidence. Replacement costs as customarily calculated are based upon replacement costs new, possibly with estimated deductions for capitalized operating cost savings, and with an allowance for depreciation that is an allocation just as much as is depreciation in historical cost accounting. Such replacement costs cannot be related to real world phenomena either. (It is conceded, however, that if replacement cost is estimated on the basis of used market prices, it will be based upon the same quality of evidence as exit values.)

The conceptual justification for the use of exit values lies in their significance for decision making. Decision making involves a choice between alternative courses of action based upon prediction of the consequence of each course of action and the preference of the decision maker for one consequence over the other. As an example, many business decisions relate to buying or selling assets. If one is considering selling an asset rather than holding it, the relevant comparison is between the estimated discounted value of future cash flows if the asset is held and the present realizable value (and perhaps also the discounted value of reinvestment opportunities). The exit value is pertinent to that decision. If one is considering purchase of an asset, the relevant comparison is between the estimated discounted cash flow of the new asset and its entry price. Even here, however, the exit prices of existing assets provide information as to the availability of resources or borrowing capacity to make the purchase, assuming that purchase of a new asset is attractive.

Supporters of the exit value basis of valuation argue that what is true of individual buy/sell/rent decisions is true at the level of the firm as a whole. Realization of the individual assets of the firm in a liquidation, for example, is an alternative to continuation of the business or sale of the business as a going concern. In general, it is argued that the sum of realizable values for a firm's assets is a measure of its "adaptivity" — its ability to take a variety of beneficial actions. A decline in that total realizable value means that an entity is subject to greater risk, and this is of significance in assessing its solvency. An increase in realizable value gives the entity the flexibility to pay off debt, to increase borrowing, to switch from one business to another, and to take advantage of new investments to increase profitability. The argument is not that other value information would not be relevant — especially the discounted cash flow of various possibilities. Rather, the contention is that realizable values are relevant to most decisions and therefore should take priority as the basis for financial reporting.

Questions in the application of CRVA

There are some unclear points in the application of CRVA. Two principal issues will be mentioned here.[2]

- Chambers has described exit values as "current cash equivalents" — a description that is appropriate to the objective of CRVA, namely, to display the ability of the entity to adapt. Sterling interprets an exit value as an immediate market selling price. Since it is immediate, that selling price must necessarily be for the asset "as is." Thus, for example, the exit value for a retailer's inventory is not the sum of the amounts for which he could sell his goods individually, but rather the price he could obtain for quick disposition of the whole inventory — which may be approximated by the wholesale price in carload lots less incidental costs.[3] Chambers, on the other hand, speaks of resale prices in the short run and in the ordinary course of business. In this way he avoids the charge that his system is liquidation accounting, rather than accounting for a going concern. His concept, however, does seem to introduce some ambiguities. First, one could argue that a sum collectible in the ordinary course of business may not really be a "current cash equivalent" either literally (because it is cash in the future not cash currently) or in value terms (because it is not discounted to its present value). For example, Chambers would record collectible accounts receivable at face value without even an allowance for cash discounts that are likely to be taken.[4] Second, there are some assets whose sale is simply not in the ordinary course of business. Work in the course of manufacture is the obvious example. Chambers' reply to this objection would probably be that if there is no such thing as a sale in the ordinary course, no sale price can be found and the asset must be valued at zero.
- What is the current cash equivalent for debt? Sterling regards debt as a negative asset to be recorded at the amount required to discharge it at the reporting date. That amount may be market value if the firm is permitted to buy in its own debt.[5] Chambers, in contrast, would show debt at the

amount legally recoverable by the creditor, usually its nominal face amount. This, too, hardly seems consistent with the notion of a current cash equivalent.[6]

Debatable issues in CRVA

The concepts of CRVA seem simpler and easier to understand than those that underlie the various CCA proposals described in chapter 29. Notwithstanding, the exit-price model was everywhere rejected in favour of entry-price models when standards for the publication of price-change-adjusted information were published in several countries in the late 1970s and early 1980s. The principal criticisms made of CRVA are as follows:

- The first criticism stems from the "aggregation" problem. Most people, including supporters of CRVA, acknowledge that the sum of exit values of individual assets will be less than the selling price of the firm itself in a very large number of cases. The question then is asked whether exit values based on individual assets are relevant information — particularly for small shareholders of a company who are not in a position to make sell-or-hold decisions with respect to individual assets. The answer is likely to be pragmatic. There are no markets for firms as a whole (stock market prices are *not* equivalent to a market price for the firm, although they may be indicative). Any estimate of the exit value of the firm therefore is likely to be too subjective to be used in financial reporting. However, there will be some situations where the sum of exit values of the assets of the firm is above the value of the business itself (implying that the firm should be liquidated), and in every case the sum of exit values will indicate a floor value of the firm, which has some significance. Proponents of CRVA also point out that the sum of replacement costs of assets will not equal the replacement cost of the firm either, so that both current value models suffer from this defect.
- The second basis of criticism is related to the first. Often it takes the form of a question: Why should we report selling prices of assets that are not going to be sold? In essence, the question asks why exit values should take priority as the sole basis of valuation. That question in turn is based upon lack of acceptance of "adaptivity" and changes in adaptivity as the primary objective for balance sheet and income statement measurements. The charge is made that to take the measurement of exit values as an objective is to make an assumption of liquidation — an assumption that is unwarranted unless there are indications that liquidation is in prospect. Critics who hold this view are likely to think of income measured on an RC basis as a better basis for prediction of future income to the going concern, and a valuation basis such as VF as a more appropriate basis of balance sheet valuation because it reflects expectations whether individual assets will be sold or retained. In rebuttal, supporters of exit-value accounting point out that liquidation of firms is not uncommon. No one disputes that exit values are the relevant figures if liquidation is expected, but how are financial statement readers to know that liquidation is the most favourable prospect if exit values are not supplied?
- A third criticism of exit-value accounting is that it anticipates income not yet earned as a result of using resale prices as a basis of valuation for assets

not yet sold. Whether this criticism is valid depends upon the way in which exit values are estimated. As already indicated, there does not seem to be complete agreement on this. Sterling's suggestion that the immediately realizable price be used as the basis of valuation is not open to this criticism. Chambers' contention that prices used should be those obtainable on disposal in the normal course of business does suggest that the profit attributable to the effort in selling the product is being recognized before sale.

- A final major source of disagreement with exit-value accounting in essence may be traced to different concepts of income. The disagreement usually comes to a head in a dispute over the balance sheet valuation of "nonvendible durables." The CRVA model works on the presumption that if you cannot find a selling price for an asset in its present form, it should be reported at zero in the balance sheet. Thus, work in progress in inventory would often be carried at no value. Any fixed assets that do not have a resale market — for reasons such as that they were built to the special specifications of the purchaser or that it would cost too much to rip them out and resell them — are also to be reported at no value. CRVA theorists readily concede that such assets may have a very substantial "value in use" — as measured by discounting expected cash flows from their use. They do not accept this as a measure of the asset value, however, because it is not a resale value and therefore is not a cash equivalent. The CRVA view is that the difference between acquisition cost of an asset and its resale value is a "sunk cost" that has no significance to the solvency or adaptivity of an enterprise. To the extent that an enterprise has taken cash or cash equivalents and sunk them into assets that are not saleable, it has taken on risk. This should be evidenced by writing off the sunk costs.[7] This result is unacceptable to many accountants and businessmen. The reason is simple: they do not have the same concept of income as that adopted by CRVA theorists. Specifically, they do not accept that a business is worse off as soon as it formally takes on a risk that the business was set up to undertake. In their view, a decline in liquidity is a fact that is important and should be reported, but no recognizable loss has occurred (and may never occur) until the outcome of the risk taking becomes known. There is no way to reconcile this disagreement unless a particular concept of income becomes generally accepted or legislated. At present, anyone is free to define income any way she likes.

Price changes and specialized industries

In the course of drafting standards for CCA in the period around 1980, standard-setters spent much effort in considering how CCA should be applied to a wide variety of specialized industries and specialized assets. The difficulties encountered provide enlightenment on the validity and workability of various ideas for accounting for price changes. The following brief discussion provides some highlights.

The case of severable assets

Current cost accounting, as we have seen, lays great stress on matching a current cost at the transaction date against revenue recognized. That emphasis tells us something about the kind of business that is implicitly contemplated in the CCA model. It is a business that is engaged in continuing operations and one that is likely to be replacing resources sold or consumed. Although many businesses fit this description, others do not. We may ask, then, how appropriate CCA is for other types of business whose character is such that individual assets may be disposed of and replaced by other assets without significantly damaging the value of the entity.

Investment holding companies. As reported in chapter 16, many investment holding companies carry their assets at market value. That practice has become generally accepted for primary financial reports even though accounting principles generally accepted for most other industries adhere to the historical cost basis. What does this tell us? It tells us, at the least, that when assets are individually severable from an entity and there are good market prices for them, most people are prepared to concede that a current value is more significant than historical cost. It does not tell us whether that current value should be an entry price or an exit value. The latter certainly measures the cash accessible by the entity if this is considered the most important attribute to be reported. The fact that the asset has not been sold at that price, however, indicates that management would rather hold the asset than the cash, so that the exit value is a lower limit to its estimate of value. On the other hand, one cannot assume that management would buy the asset if it did not have it at any price above that lower limit. Thus, exit value is the conservative basis of valuation. Mid-market price could also be regarded as a reasonable indication of intrinsic value, being an average of the prices at which people are willing to buy and sell. In a good market the difference between the mid-market price and an exit value (net realizable value after transaction costs) should be small.

Income-producing real estate. The real estate industry performs various functions. The comments below relate to the accounting for properties held by developers or investors for the production of income.

Although there may be some economies in management of a portfolio of investment properties, individual properties can be bought and sold with little disruption to the activities of the entity. Operating cash flows are identifiable with individual properties to a high degree, and financing is often on an individual property basis without recourse to the owner. Individual properties are also unique in location and other characteristics. Thus, even though an investor in property may intend to hold it for long-term income, sale of any individual property at a favourable price is always a very real possibility. In addition, companies can and do make policy decisions from time to time to dispose of entire portfolios of properties of a certain type or in a certain location to free up resources for investment elsewhere.

Thus, it can be concluded that estimates of net realizable values of properties are always pertinent information. Because of the unique characteristics of individual properties, estimates of market values are not as reliable as those for actively traded securities. Nevertheless, when the operating cash flows of a property are reasonably predictable for some period of time (predictability is often enhanced by the existence of long-term leases with fixed minimum rents), valuation formulas generally used in the industry provide reasonable indicators of values realizable on the property.

Estimates of replacement cost can be used to provide a cross-bearing on estimates of realizable values. Estimates of replacement cost would begin with the current market value of land comparable in location and other characteristics to the property owned. To this would be added the estimated cost of construction, using modern construction methods and materials to provide the same capacity in terms of quantity and quality of rentable space. The cost of capital tied up during construction would also be an element of replacement cost.

It is possible, therefore, to adopt the CRVA model or one of the CCA models in financial reporting for such assets. A CCA model would display a figure of current operating profit after depreciation, together with whatever treatment of holding gains, realized or unrealized, is called for by the particular model adopted. The CRVA model would report revenues less operating costs excluding depreciation, together with changes in the exit values of assets regardless of whether they were realized.

Which is to be preferred? The real estate industry has traditionally argued that depreciation is not relevant to it. The major reason usually given is that "our properties don't depreciate, they appreciate." Since buildings do wear out and become obsolete, this assertion, taken literally, is incorrect. A more precise statement of what is intended would probably be something like this: "Our buildings do wear out over a very long period, but the decline in utility of the building is typically outweighed by the gain in land value. Therefore depreciation is not a factor that we pay any attention to as such in our decision making." In essence, the industry is arguing that realizable values are more relevant information than unamortized costs, and this argument is adhered to regardless of whether the costs in question are historical costs or replacement costs.

Conclusion. The examples of these two industries suggest that where net realizable values are obtainable and when the assets are individually severable from the entity without disrupting operations, the CRVA model is preferred to CCA.

The case of financial institutions

An argument is sometimes made that financial institutions, especially those that take in deposits from the public, are sharply distinguishable from other types of enterprise because the vast majority of their assets and liabilities are monetary in character. It follows from this that (1) the carrying values of assets and liabilities under historical cost accounting do not depart greatly from their current values, (2) as a result, no adjustment needs to be made to the present form of income statement to place it on a current value or current cost basis, and (3) a purchasing power adjustment based on the equity in the business is sufficient to give recognition to general inflation.

In other words, a result equivalent to current value accounting could be obtained simply by reporting the historical cost income figures and then deducting a one-line capital maintenance adjustment based on applying a general purchasing power index to the equity shown in the balance sheet at the beginning of the year plus any additions during the year. Alternatively, if it were felt that there were sufficient nonmonetary assets — such as property and equipment used in operations — GPL accounting would be a satisfactory approximation to current cost accounting.

This argument has attractions because of its simplicity in application. Whether it is satisfactory, however, depends upon the validity of its assumptions — especially that nonmonetary assets are negligible in the total asset structure of the entity. In this connection, the leverage in the financing of a financial institution should not be overlooked. If the equity represents only four percent of the total financing, nonmonetary assets equal to two percent of total assets will equal fifty percent of the equity. In this context, variations in their current value appear to be more material.

Banks and other deposit-taking institutions. The argument just described rests upon an assumption that the earning assets of the financial institution are almost all monetary. The accuracy of that assumption is doubtful. It may be close to being true in a bank; it is less true for other deposit-taking institutions. For example, two types of investments that are nonmonetary are investments in common stock and investments in income-earning real estate. Both these investments are of a type that we have just concluded are best reported at net realizable value or mid-market prices. One might argue, then, that these at least should be recorded at current values, with holding gains and losses included in income before the capital maintenance adjustment.

Such a suggestion immediately raises a question as to the basis of valuing portfolios of monetary assets bearing a fixed rate of return, such as bonds and debentures. One might argue on grounds of consistency that these also must be valued at a current market value or their market value equivalent based on current levels of interest rates. If this is done, however, it is clear that consistency would require valuation of interest-bearing liabilities carrying a fixed interest rate at a current market equivalent as well. In the absence of an actual market price for liabilities, that market equivalent would be calculated by discounting the liability at the current interest rate applicable to similar obligations. Such calculations could be onerous.

Any full application of CRVA as just described would probably be strongly opposed. Recognition of unrealized gains and losses over the whole portfolio of assets and liabilities could cause sharp swings in income reported from year to year and might be sufficient to overwhelm the equity, given the leverage in the financing structure. The usual arguments would also be made that the accounting is unrealistic because the entity is not in a position to trade in and out of its assets, and because quoted market values could not be realized in any event if a sizable financial institution were to liquidate its holdings. The essence of this argument is that a financial institution is a going concern by its nature and thus does not have the option of realizing on substantial blocks of its portfolio even though, individually, each and every asset in it is readily marketable. Although these arguments carry a degree of conviction, they raise two important questions. First, what assurance can there be that an entity can remain a going concern? That is to say, if it encounters liquidity strains and cannot realize upon large blocks of assets so that its solvency is in question, what warning is provided in the accounts? Second, if current value accounting is not the most useful basis of reporting, what is? These are difficult questions.

Insurance companies. Much of what has been said about deposit-taking institutions applies to insurance companies as well. It only remains to add that the valuation of liabilities represents the central problem in insurance accounting. In casualty insurance companies the estimated provision for future claims determines the underwriting profit or loss reported. Chapter 24 has described how the valuation of policy obligations in the life insurance business in effect controls the release to profit of any margin that was built into contractual premiums to cover risk and profit. Estimation of a current value for the policy obligations would seem to require a theory to govern the appropriate degree of risk provision. It would then require a decision whether the interest rate assumed in discounting policy obligations should reflect current rates attainable for re-insurance or whether it should represent some long-term (and arbitrary) guess at future investment earnings rates. Only after these questions were solved could one begin to address the question of what would be a consistent basis of asset valuation.

Conclusion. Examination of the situation of financial institutions indicates some severe problems in the way of selecting a current value accounting model for these entities. Theories of current value accounting have paid relatively little attention to the question of accounting for liabilities. Yet the issues in accounting for liabilities loom large in financial institutions, because of their highly leveraged financial structure and because of the highly individual character of liabilities in the case of life insurance companies. It seems clear that valuation of assets and liabilities ought to be internally consistent. In the simple case of interest-bearing assets and liabilities, the interrelationship between market values and changes in interest rates must be borne in mind. A revaluation of an interest-bearing asset on the basis of current market values implies some change in interest rates (in the absence of a change in the inherent security of the asset). To be consistent, changes in interest rates must be taken into account in valuing liabilities if the accounting is to make sense.

The leverage in the capital structure of financial institutions magnifies the impact on equity of any change in asset values not hedged by an opposite change in liability values. In the extreme, the equity could easily appear to have been wiped out or to have doubled in size in a very short period. Many would be concerned that this is somehow an unreasonable portrayal of changes in the financial position of the firm, so long as it is going to continue in business and not be liquidated. So long as the firm can survive, one may speculate that the fluctuation in its value as a whole will be of smaller amplitude than the fluctuation in the sum of the values of its net resources. That consideration leaves us with questions but no answers. It suggests that, notwithstanding the fact that net realizable value seems the most relevant information for a severable asset taken by itself, a thoroughgoing valuation of all assets and liabilities at a current cash equivalent may not be an acceptable basis for reporting the resources of a firm that is not practically in a position to liquidate.

The case of irreproducible assets

Chapter 29 has touched on the difficulties under CCA in arriving at a RC for an asset that is not to be replaced. Two industries of great importance in Canada that are exposed to this problem are the oil and gas producers and the mining industry.

Oil and gas producers. The principal assets of an oil and gas producer consist of the reserves of oil and gas in the ground and rights to share in additional reserves that may be discovered on certain lands. Under historical cost accounting, mineral rights are carried at their original cost so long as their reserve potential has not been proved or disproved. Thereafter, the costs are included in costs of discovered reserves or are written off in accordance with the accounting method used by the entity. (See chapter 23 for a description of these methods.) As reserves are produced, depletion expense is recognized so that the remaining reserves are carried at their original cost less accumulated amounts written off for depletion.

Sales and auctions of property rights provide a basis for estimating a current value for potential producing property rights. Considerable judgment is required in translating such market data into estimates of current values for property rights actually owned because of (1) possible changes in value that take place between the dates of actual market transactions and the financial reporting date, and (2) the need to make sure that actual exchange prices apply to property of equal desirability or to make allowances for differences in desirability.

Occasional bulk purchases and sales of oil and gas reserves also occur. It is doubtful, however, that such transactions provide a sufficient basis for valuation of reserves generally. In the first place, the value of reserves depends considerably upon their location and quality. Lifting costs, processing costs, and transportation costs to market all may vary so that actual price data would have to be adjusted to allow for this. In the second place, assurance as to the quantity of reserves may differ from one situation to another. Thus, sale situations where reserves are mainly in the "proved" category could be noncomparable to situations containing a significant amount of reserves that are merely "probable." In the third place, significant sales of reserves are not frequent; thus, the lapse of time since a previous sale may make its significance as an indicator of current value suspect.

It thus seems unlikely that current value accounting could be based on market data for oil and gas producers. How about replacement cost? Two approaches are possible to the estimation of RC of reserves in place. A company may accumulate its current costs of exploration and development for a period or it may obtain data on industry costs. These can be compared with figures for reserves proved in the period to develop a unit cost for the reserves to be taken as replacement costs. There are serious objections to this procedure, including (1) the fact that finding costs per unit vary from one region to another and the available data may be for regions not comparable to those containing the reserves to be valued, and (2) it is difficult to relate reserves developed to expenditures in a particular period, since some expenditures in any time period will always relate to reserves yet to be developed. A second possible approach is to examine the company's past costs of developing its reserves and express them in current prices, perhaps with the help of price indexes, and then reduce those accumulated cost figures for production to date.

Even it were possible to obtain good figures for the current RC of reserves owned, one might still question the worth of the information. Since the easiest reserves are likely to be found first, the expectation must be that RCs of oil and gas reserves will follow a long-term rising cost curve quite apart from the effect of changes in prices of the elements in that cost. In addition, any individual company may have experience that is much better or much worse than the industry's generally or than its past experience would indicate. In these circumstances, the significance of RC for existing reserves is quite limited.

In the absence of an ability to rely on actual market transactions, estimation of the NRV of reserves also becomes problematic. One might consider reporting a DCF calculation as an indicator of likely NRV. This would be open to all the subjectivity in estimation of future cash flows and in the selection of a discount rate that has been referred to already. The difficulties in the calculation for oil and gas producers would be even greater than for most other industries because of the unpredictable swings possible in prices for basic commodities such as oil and gas, and because of the fact that estimates of reserve quantities are so uncertain. In addition, it would have to be remembered that a DCF valuation will theoretically produce an estimate of value of all the producing assets, not just the reserves in isolation from other assets.

FASB standards require public companies to provide a DCF calculation for proved reserves based upon the year-end price of oil and gas and the application of a standard ten percent discount rate.[8] Also to be disclosed is a detailed explanation of the causes of changes from the previous year-end in the calculated DCF figure. Because of the restriction to proved reserves and the standardization of price and discount rate assumptions, this DCF calculation can definitely *not* be deemed the equivalent of a value calculation. Rather, it represents only a benchmark, considered to have some value for the purpose of making comparisons between companies. The fact that the board chose not to attempt a value calculation but rather chose a standardized calculation of limited significance, casts considerable doubt on the feasibility of CRVA in this industry.[9]

Thus, neither CCA nor CRVA has been shown to be of great value in the unique circumstances of the oil and gas industry. FASB standards for supplementary disclosure of the effects of changing prices cling to the CCA model but permit the use of GPL-adjusted historical costs for mineral resources as a substitute for an attempt to measure RC.

Mining. Virtually everything that has been said about the difficulties of applying either CCA or CRVA to oil and gas producers applies to the mining industry as well. Indeed, the problems may be even more severe. Mining properties are bought and sold less frequently than are oil and gas reserves so that market value information is even harder to come by. In addition, it is not unusual that the extent of an ore body (the equivalent of oil and gas reserves) has not been sufficiently delineated to provide a measure that is equivalent to an estimate of proved reserves of an oil and gas producer. Consequently, CRVA is just not feasible, and CCA is possible only by updating historical costs previously incurred and making a deduction for minerals already produced. Such a calculation may be extremely speculative because of the lack of good data on the full extent of the ore body.

Conclusion. Current value accounting for unique or irreproducible assets is likely to be extremely difficult. If the asset is irreproducible, RC can only be estimated on the basis of markets for the asset or an updating of historical costs actually incurred. Markets for the asset, if they exist, are likely to produce prices of limited relevance because of the unique or at least highly individual characteristics of the reserves. Updated historical costs are even worse. They are essentially meaningless if the asset cannot be reproduced.

CRVA also depends upon the existence of markets for the assets, which, as indicated, are likely to be limited. The use of a DCF valuation as a substitute would probably be considered invalid by pure CRVA theorists who emphasize the importance of cash today. Even if that were ignored, DCF valuations are unreliable because of their subjectivity and are particularly so in the special cases discussed of the extractive industries.

Other cases

Forest products. An important asset of companies in the forest products industry is their supply of standing timber. Under historical cost accounting, even in the absence of changing prices, the value of that supply is greatly understated because historical cost accounting gives no recognition to values added by growth.

Current value accounting in the industry, as in other specialized industries, is hampered by the lack of good markets for the company's productive assets. It is conceivable that sales of timberlands could provide a basis for valuation in certain regions. Often, however, regions are too widely separated and sales too infrequent to permit reliance on this source.

In the absence of transaction data, the application of CRVA is confined to a DCF calculation, with all the objections already noted. Such a calculation would necessarily be based on revenues after considerable processing of the timber in sawmills or pulp and paper mills. Hence, it would provide a valuation of the operations as a whole, not just of the timber assets. Once again, it may be noted that this is inconsistent with the pure CRVA model. The notion seems unlikely to be generally acceptable.

CCA is more feasible and should have some relevance since the asset — standing timber — is reproducible. The calculation could be directly tied to the company's experience by ascertaining all the expenditures and forest management costs over the past number of years that were required to bring existing timber to its present stage of maturity. Those costs could then be repriced at current cost levels.

Two issues would arise in so doing. Many of those costs are written off when incurred under historical cost accounting. It has to be decided whether CCA should aim to be fully comparable to the historical cost accounting model except for the effect of changing prices or whether it should attempt a more accurate reflection of full costs of the assets.

The second issue deals with the inclusion or exclusion of cost of capital. The emphasis in CCA is upon matching current costs of assets sold or consumed in operations against revenues in order to display current operating profit and margins. Costing procedures for inventory normally do not contain any allowance for cost of capital tied up in inventory. Usually such allowance would be immaterial. In the case of timber, however, cost of capital tied up during the growing stage is material.

Should cost of capital be included in the calculation of current costs? If not, the carrying value of the asset in the balance sheet is likely to be understated in relation to its economic value. If it is included, however, the income reported logically should reflect not only the higher cost of timber consumed in operations but also the credit for cost of capital that has been capitalized. That result would occur automatically if holding gains (including unrealized gains) were fully included in current cost income reported, but not otherwise.

Public utilities. Current value accounting for regulated public utilities cannot ignore the method by which revenues are determined under regulation. Often that determination is based on the use of historical cost accounting figures. Rates are set that are estimated to produce revenues to cover (1) out-of-pocket operating expenses, taxes, and historical cost depreciation, and (2) a return for capital calculated as a rate of return applied to the amount of the investment (rate base) in the utility. The rate base also is based largely on historical cost figures. The rate of return awarded is typically calculated so as to cover actual interest payable in a year on debt financing the plant in service (that is, excluding interest capitalized on construction) and a rate of return on equity that is considered to be fair based on such factors as the market cost of capital for enterprises of comparable risks, the need to attract capital, and so on. The composite return requirement is expressed as a percentage of the historical cost rate base.

The fact that the amount recovered through rates with respect to depreciation in plant is based upon historical cost depreciation means that the recoverable value of the investment is effectively limited to original cost. However, since the rate of return for shareholders is higher under inflation than it would be in the absence of inflation and the same is true of interest rates covered by the rates, the rates established do provide some approximation to the recovery of capital consumed at current price levels — but part of that recovery is called interest expense and profit for shareholders, instead of recovery of capital.[10] The effect of this is that if all reported earnings were paid out to shareholders,the company would have to raise new equity (and also additional debt) to be in a position to finance replacement of plant at higher price levels.

As noted, the effect of this method of regulation is that recovery of the investment in plant in future will be limited to the historical cost amounts included in the rate base. Having received an approximate compensation for the effect of price changes on their capital investment through the rate of return, the shareholders and bondholders will not receive additional compensation in future. The significance of this for a system of price-change accounting is obscure. The FASB has suggested that if a utility is likely to replace plant when the time comes, it should present a figure of current cost income after depreciation calculated on the basis of replacement cost. Such a presentation could be accused of double counting, because the impact of higher prices is given full recognition in the amortization of capital cost but expectations of such changing prices will also have increased the nominal interest expense.

To avoid this inconsistency, a complete portrayal of income on a current cost basis would logically include (1) current operating profit before interest after amortization of the replacement cost of plant, (2) to be consistent, the full amount of the write-up of the plant to a replacement cost basis — the "holding gain," (3) a countervailing write-down of the depreciated replacement cost of the plant to its depreciated historical cost at the year-end because the recovery is limited to that amount (in effect, the plant has been turned into a monetary asset by restricting recoveries to its historical cost carrying value), (4) a deduction of interest at its actual amount because that is what is allowed to be recovered from revenues, and (5) application of a one-line capital maintenance adjustment to equity capital at the beginning of the year to reduce equity income reported to real terms.

It may be noted that in this presentation the difference between the amount of the write-up of plant in the year to the RC basis and the countervailing write-down to its recoverable historical cost amount (items 2 and 3 above) would be equal to the excess of depreciation on the RC basis (item 1 above) over the figure that depreciation would have been on the historical cost basis. This being so, it appears that the current cost presentation just described arrives at the same reported net income as an historical cost presentation with a one-line capital maintenance adjustment for the equity. It could be argued that the latter presentation would be desirable because it conforms to the way the entity's revenues are established. It should be emphasized, however, that this conclusion holds only because the system of regulation has, in effect, turned the plant and equipment into an asset whose current value from the standpoint of investors cannot appreciably vary from its book value. Such a form of CVA would not be appropriate for unregulated industries. Only when book value equals current value is a simple capital maintenance adjustment applied to the book value of the equity legitimate.

Evaluation of current value accounting

Efforts to cope with the effect of price changes require a new theoretical framework for financial reporting. Four assumptions are necessary to provide an income accounting model: a choice of a standard for capital maintenance, a choice of the attribute to be measured in reporting assets and liabilities, a choice of focus of interest (entity or proprietary), and a decision whether to include unrealized holding gains and losses on asset and liability positions in income. Different proposed models have been founded on different combinations of these elements. This diversity has engendered controversy and made it difficult to obtain general acceptance of any one CVA model.

The description and analysis in this chapter and the preceding one suggest that there are implementation difficulties with every CVA model. That should not surprise us. Much of Part II was taken up with a description of implementation difficulties in historical cost accounting, many of which are still debatable even after fifty years' use of the model. If some other model is to be adopted for financial reporting, it is to be expected that practical expedients will need to be developed to make it work. Conceptual questions in individual areas also remain to be solved, but this too is true of historical cost accounting.

The analysis and discussion in these chapters suggest a number of observations.

Capital maintenance concepts

Maintenance of operating capacity. The concept of maintenance of physical or operating capacity is seriously inadequate as a foundation for measuring income at the level of an individual enterprise. First, it provides no answer to the problem of maintenance of capital invested in nonoperating assets such as portfolio investments. Second, it is difficult to apply when operating assets are not of a type that are sold or consumed in the course of operations. Since this includes virtually all the assets of institutions such as banks, it seems particularly hard to apply it to them.

Even on its own territory, the operating capital maintenance concept is difficult to implement because it is essentially a static concept founded on an implicit concept of continuing replacement of productive assets. When an entity is likely to replace existing productive assets with improved assets, it is necessary to make allowances for differences in "service capacity" between the new assets and the assets to be replaced. Beyond this, enterprises are continually changing their business operations, disposing of assets in one line of business and investing in others. When such a change in direction occurs it is hard to know what maintenance of productive capacity means. Professional statements have suggested that when an asset consumed in operations is not to be replaced, it may be charged against income on the basis of its recoverable value. There is no way in which the recoverable value of an obsolete asset can serve as a standard that shows whether productive capacity has been maintained.

It is usually suggested that the operating capacity maintenance concept be implemented by charging replacement cost for resources sold or consumed in measuring income from operations and by excluding all holding gains from income. This is ineffective in maintaining the productive capacity of monetary working capital and, as already indicated, does absolutely nothing to achieve maintenance of capital invested in nonoperating assets. An alternative approach that could provide for maintenance of the total capital invested in an entity would recognize all holding gains in income, whether realized or unrealized, but deduct a one-line allowance for capital maintenance based on the change in prices shown by an index applied to the amount of the invested capital.

If such a price index were constructed based on the weighted average of prices of operating assets held by the entity itself, the income reported would, insofar as operating assets are concerned, approximate that obtained under the more customary approach of achieving capital maintenance by not recognizing holding gains in income. If the index were broadened to be representative of price changes in broader categories of business investment, it would help to meet the objection that a physical capital maintenance standard is too tied to the operating assets of the business in which the entity is currently engaged. It would still be debatable, however, whether the use of such an index makes sense from the standpoint of reporting to investors.

Financial capital maintenance. A financial capital maintenance concept expressed in constant purchasing power could also be implemented by a one-line capital maintenance adjustment based on a general price index or an index of consumer prices. The use of the financial capital maintenance standard has at least two advantages. First, it is arguable that the price index used will be of greater relevance to investors than an index of change in purchasing power for business investment. Second, the display of revenues, expenses, gains, and losses during the year can be made on whatever basis seems most useful. If it is considered useful to show a figure of current operating profit based on matching revenues with replacement costs of goods sold or consumed, that can be done, but it does not have to be done.

Valuation of assets

Objective evidence as to current value can come only from markets. The alternative to the use of market values is to estimate a value in use or economic value of an asset by estimating the future cash flows it will produce and discounting them to a present value figure. Usually this is a highly subjective valuation, because both the cash flows and the appropriate discount rate will be uncertain. As a result, discounted cash flow has little role to play in asset valuation. (An exception is possible in valuing monetary assets whose cash flows are fixed by contract if an appropriate discount rate can be deduced from market yields.)

Readily marketable assets. Some entities buy and sell in the same market. The difference between buying and selling prices in the same market will consist of dealers' commissions and transaction costs and will tend to be minor if the market is active. Most business entities, however, buy and sell in different markets. In these cases the business adds value to the thing bought and sold, and buying prices and selling prices are commonly far apart as a result. It is usually important, therefore, in applying current values to specify whether the valuation should be based on buying or selling prices.

The situation of a dealer in standard commodities provides the strongest possible case for the use of exit prices — net realizable values. Since the dealer does not add intrinsic value to the commodity dealt in, there is no question of "value in use" of his assets being different from market value (with the unimportant possible exception of office equipment, etc., with which he carries on business). Since you cannot buy an asset you already own but you can sell it, the market value that is relevant to a dealer's decision is the exit price.

The situation of the investment-holding entity is slightly different. Its choice lies between selling individual assets or holding them for the production of income. Since management did hold any assets recorded in its balance sheet at the end of the year, it may be presumed that it considered such investments worth more than their exit price. A neutral basis of valuation for such assets held at the end of the period would be their actual market price without deduction of transaction costs. The exchange price ignoring transaction costs represents, in a sense, an average of buyers' and sellers' estimates of ownership value. Of course, an investor might feel that management's performance is better measured by valuing assets at the amount of cash immediately accessible — that is, the market price less incidental cost of selling. The difference in valuation, however, would not be very large when there are good markets for the assets.

One can generalize from these examples that where organized markets exist for trading a commodity, a market price or a market price less selling costs represents the most obviously useful basis of valuation. These market conditions apply most often to nonoperating assets of a entity — assets that can be sold individually without disrupting operations. In some cases, however, they apply to operating assets as well. For example, the vehicle fleet of many companies consists of vendible units. Also, active markets exist for used machinery and equipment of certain types. Where this is so, these markets could provide data for estimating current costs and for calculation of depreciation under a current cost system. Such a basis for estimating replacement cost would be preferable to the use of estimated replacement cost new, because the latter requires the calculation of depreciation using allocation patterns comparable to those used in historical cost accounting.

The question whether CCA or CRVA should be used for an operating business is very much interrelated with that of the availability of organized market prices. The real estate company investing in income property for which there are relatively good markets illustrates the issue. Many consider the current market price figure to be the more relevant information in the real estate industry. Others, however, take a contrary view based on the proposition that the company's business is to invest in income properties for the long term. If this is so, it is argued that fluctuations in market values from time to time are largely irrelevant. The proponents of reporting market values seem to have the better of this argument. Replacement of properties lies in the future, and it is normally highly speculative whether the same type of development will take place when the property is redeveloped. Current market values, in contrast, represent relevant information because they help the statement reader appreciate the outcome of a possible course of action — disposal of the properties.

Operating assets. We now come to the situation where organized markets do not exist for the majority of the productive assets of an entity. It buys from suppliers, produces its product, and sells in a completely different market. A significant portion of its assets are bought not for resale but for use, and it is expected they will be scrapped or disposed of for relatively little after their usefulness is exhausted. In these circumstances, should the current values used in accounting reflect the buying market or the selling market?

The case of the nonvendible durable highlights the question. A highly specialized piece of equipment is obtained from a supplier and is transported and installed at considerable expense. If it were to be resold, it would realize very little because it is specialized and because of the costs of removal to a new location. It seems that such a resale would take place only in an extreme situation. Should the resale value be used in current value accounting? In particular, should the difference between the low resale value and the buying cost be charged to income in the year of acquisition?

Advocates of CRVA think the resale price should be used because of the importance of measuring the adaptivity of the firm. In contrast, most businessmen instinctively think it undesirable (1) that the balance sheet value should represent a value based on the unlikely event of sale, and (2) that income reported should suffer when management makes an investment in specialized equipment based on a capital budgeting analysis that indicates the purchase should be profitable. Instead, there is considerable support for the value-to-the-firm basis of valuation, whereby the balance sheet carrying value will be based on replacement cost if the asset is expected to be replaced and the higher of its net realizable value or economic value if not.

Value to the firm and the reporting of COP. Unfortunately, it is hard to blend the VF approach to asset valuation with the division of the income statement between a figure of COP and holding gains and losses. Consider a hypothetical example. A unit of inventory is bought for $1,100. Shortly thereafter, at the next period-end, its RC has risen to $1,200, but its NRV is estimated at only $1,000. On the VF basis it will be valued in the balance sheet at $1,000, and an unrealized holding loss of $100 will be recognized. Assume that in the next period it is sold for $1,000 at a time when the RC is still $1,200. If cost of sales is recorded at $1,000, no gain or loss will be recognized. In that event, COP will not be a particularly good report on management performance or a particularly good indicator of future operating profit if the entity is going to continue to stock the same item (as it might in order to carry a full line of product). On the other hand, if the cost of sales is recorded at $1,200, COP will report a loss of $200 but a realized holding gain of $200 will also be reported. Since no price change at all took place in the period, this could be considered an unreasonable presentation of holding gains. A possible compromise procedure would be to charge cost of sales at historical cost, showing a loss of $100 only in COP and a recovery of the write-down charged to income in the previous period.

Authoritative recommendations with respect to CCA have taken the position that when VF valuations are below RC they should form the basis for recognition of the charge to income with respect to the assets sold or consumed. This has a strange result. Suppose all the assets were inventory carried at NRV which is below cost. Assuming that the NRV correctly anticipated ultimate proceeds upon realization, the COP would always show a break-even. Suppose, alternatively, that the only assets were fixed assets carried at EV. Again if the estimate of EV were accurate, charging depreciation based upon that estimate would, in the long run, result in reporting a COP profit which, as a percentage of asset values, would equal the discount rate assumed in calculating the EV of the assets. In other words, if the VF approach is adopted, COP theoretically would never show a loss. At the same time, there could be few or no holding gains reported, even if prices were rising. It is a matter of opinion what would be the best course in this situation.

- A compromise might be adopted whereby the valuation of an asset sold or consumed would be shown at RC if it was to be replaced, but at its VF valuation if it was not to be replaced.
- If it was mainly in the fixed-asset category that VF values were below RC, it might be desirable to show the operating margin before, rather than after, depreciation.
- If a substantial portion of all assets to be sold or consumed were valued below RC, one might well question whether it was worthwhile reporting a split between COP and holding gains at all. Instead, income reporting could be left on the historical cost basis (under which the operating profit figure includes realized holding gains and losses). Unrealized holding gains and losses resulting from changes in the valuations of assets recorded in the balance sheet would be shown separately in the income statement, and a one-line capital maintenance adjustment would be deducted.

The above discussion confirms one conclusion already stated in chapter 29. When assets are valued below RC using the VF principle, so that holding gains recognized with respect to them are low or nonexistent, the exclusion of holding gains from income has the result that operating capacity is not maintained, at least with respect to those assets. Once again, it is apparent that a better way to measure whether capital is maintained is to (1) include all holding gains or losses in income (rather than exclude them) and (2) deduct from income one capital maintenance adjustment based on application of a suitable price index to the net amount of capital employed at the beginning of the period (modified for any capital contributions or withdrawals within the period).

The lack of a perfectly satisfactory answer suggests that some degree of flexibility in presentation of the income statement under CCA is desirable.

Specialized industries. Specialized industries emphasize the difficulties in applying one current value accounting model across the board. The most difficult problem is posed by the extractive industries. Markets for their principal assets — reserves of oil and gas and minerals in the ground — do not appear sufficiently developed to provide values of an acceptable reliability for inclusion in an income reporting model. The best that seems possible is to provide extensive supplementary quantitative data on reserves, explaining the reasons for changes in estimated amounts over the year such as new discoveries, production during the year, and revisions to previous estimates. In other words, in the extractive industries it seems impossible to implement a satisfactory current value income accounting model.

At the other extreme, commodity dealers and investment holding companies provide the strongest possible case for adoption of a CRVA accounting model. The strength of this conclusion rests on two factors. First, the reliance of CRVA on realizable market values is completely compatible with the nature and objectives of the business carried on. Second, good organized markets usually exist to supply reliable data for implementation of the model.

Financial institutions, in contrast, have several features that make the case for CRVA less compelling, even though valuation of their assets, or some of them, at realizable values is not significantly more difficult than it is for investment holding companies. The most important feature is that large financial institutions, unlike investment holding companies, do not realistically have the option of discontinuing their enterprise or even of selling off portfolios of assets very quickly, given the consequent depressing effect on market prices.

Focus of interest

Any version of CVA can be adapted to embrace either the entity or proprietary focus. There is nothing in the idea of CVA that logically leads to the choice of one focus over the other. What is the preferable basis remains a matter of opinion, as it does under historical cost accounting. There is some misconception that adoption of the operating capital maintenance goal is consistent only with the entity concept. That misconception is based on the version of CCA in which all holding gains are excluded from income, thereby maintaining the operating capacity of total entity resources. However, the proprietary focus can be combined with the capital maintenance concept in two ways. First, a financing adjustment can bring into income the debt-financed portion of holding gains. Alternatively, all holding gains can be brought into income, to be reduced by a capital maintenance adjustment based on equity capital only.

Unrealized holding gains

It is also a matter of opinion whether unrealized holding gains should be excluded from reported income under CVA as they are under historical cost accounting. There is one point, however, that should be made when capital maintenance is provided through the one-line capital maintenance adjustment. Such an adjustment, based on the application of an index to capital employed in the period, shows how much the net resources should appreciate in nominal value for capital to be deemed maintained. Such appreciation can be realized or unrealized. Hence, it is somewhat illogical to use a one-line capital maintenance adjustment in an income statement that does not recognize unrealized holding gains.

Consider the example of an entity whose only asset is vacant land which increases in value by twenty percent over a year while the general price level increases by only ten percent. If that real gain is to be reported, the unrealized increase in current value must be included in income. It would be wrong in logic to charge a ten percent capital maintenance adjustment against nonexistent operating income from the land and show a loss for the year. It is probable that many accountants will instinctively wish to adhere to the realization rule on the grounds of conservatism. If the amount of unrealized gains is not greatly different at the beginning and end of a year, their omission from income determination will not be serious. If the rate of price change is rapid, however, it could be.

Some conclusions

One dominant conclusion emerges from these observations. No single model for current value accounting is suitable for all situations. In the case of the extractive industries it is even questionable that we should attempt to impose a closed model in which the income statement and balance sheet articulate. In other situations, a closed model is possible, but details of the way it is applied should be permitted to vary in accordance with the nature of the enterprise. The following principles seem best adapted to the provision of useful information with some measure of comparability across the board.

- The financial capital maintenance concept should be adopted to the exclusion of the operating capital maintenance concept.
- Capital maintenance should be implemented by making a one-line adjustment to income reported. That adjustment should be calculated by applying a purchasing power index to capital at the beginning of the year as modified by any contributions or withdrawals during the year. For this purpose, the capital must be measured on the basis of current values, not historical cost book values (except for a public utility company when regulation ensures that the historical cost book values are approximately equal to discounted recoverable values).
- The use of a one-line capital maintenance adjustment means that all other financial statement figures would be presented in units of money, not units of constant purchasing power. Accounting in units of money is likely to be more understandable to both statement preparers and users. If desired, however, a supplementary analysis of holding gains and losses could be presented on a price-level-adjusted basis. Such an analysis would reveal holding gains and losses on monetary assets and liabilities.
- Assets that are capable of disposition without disrupting the activities of the entity — that is, usually all nonoperating assets — should be valued at a current fair value, generally based on market prices.
- When substantially all of the assets are valued using market-based fair values, liabilities should also be valued at the estimated cost to discharge them or to provide a fund capable of meeting all the obligations related to them.
- Assets held for use or for sale in an operating business should be valued on the VF basis. Generally, that will mean the use of RC except when both NRV and EV are lower for particular assets.
- Some degree of flexibility is necessary in the presentation of the income statement. When CCA is followed, separation of COP and realized holding gains may be desirable for the purpose of a better portrayal of factors affecting business profits but should not be required in all cases.
- Ideally, both realized and unrealized holding gains should be included in income. If unrealized holding gains were excluded, it would be desirable to reduce the capital maintenance adjustment, at least with respect to assets such as land, whose real worth may be expected to be protected by unrealized appreciation.

It is evident that it is very difficult to provide a simple set of rules for current value accounting that will be applicable in all situations. The diversity encountered in the nature of activities accounted for and the practical difficulties in attaining what might be ideal in theory (as in the extractive industries) prevent simple answers. This creates what has, so far, proved to be an insuperable problem for accounting standard-setters. The normal accounting standard is designed to reduce alternatives in a fairly narrow area of financial reporting. We are not experienced in dealing with situations that require what is equivalent to writing and obtaining acceptance of a wholly new textbook on financial reporting.

As this is being written, interest in modification of accounting standards to take into account the effect of changing prices is at a low point. It is probably impossible to obtain support for further advances while the rate of inflation remains low. One may hope that this condition will continue indefinitely; it would be foolish to count upon it.

References

[1]CRVA has received significantly less attention from accounting practitioners than have the various versions of CCA. As a system, it is more homogeneous than CCA, lacking the variety of different versions that have been described in chapter 29. For a more complete understanding of CRVA and its rationale, the reader is referred to the works of Chambers and Sterling cited in the bibliography.

[2]For a more complete description of the points of debate that exist even among supporters of the general concept of CRVA, see E.R. Iselin, "Chambers on Accounting Theory," *The Accounting Review*, April 1968, pp. 231-38; R. Ma, "On Chambers' Second Thoughts," *Abacus*, December 1974, pp. 124-28; and R.J. Chambers, "Third Thoughts," *Abacus*, December 1974, pp. 129-37.

[3]See R.R. Sterling, *Toward a Science of Accounting* (Houston: Scholars Book Co., 1979), pp. 111, 117, and 220n.

[4]R.J. Chambers, *Accounting for Inflation*, Exposure Draft (Sydney, New South Wales: Department of Accounting, University of Sydney, 1975), par. 25.

[5]See Sterling, *Toward a Science of Accounting*, p. 159 n.

[6]Chambers' view has its vigorous supporters. See, for example, S. Henderson and G. Peirson, "A Note on the Current Cash Equivalent of Liabilities," *Abacus*, June 1980, pp. 61-66. See also Chambers' own defence in "Edwards and Bell on Income Measurement in Retrospect," *Abacus*, June 1982, pp. 3-39. The reader may judge for himself or herself whether the arguments therein are convincing.

[7]Sterling devotes an appendix of his book to the case of the nonvendible durable. See Sterling, *Toward a Science of Accounting*. He discusses an example of a drilling rig in the Sahara Desert that has no recoverable value by itself. Sterling calls this an extreme case and implies that if it can be defended, the exit value case for income reporting is conclusive. The author believes that the case is not as extreme as it could be because Sterling has chosen a situation where the outcome of the purchase of the asset is highly speculative. A more extreme case (from the standpoint of questioning CRVA) would be one in which the purchase has a high expectation of a profitable outcome. Consider a remote paper mill with a well-established customer base that invests in new paper-making equipment, the purchase being completely justified by demand and cost projections. That is to say, the speculative element has been reduced to a minimum. If the amount realizable from dismantling and transporting that equipment elsewhere for resale would be very small, CRVA would write off its "sunk cost" and charge it to income in the year of acquisition of the equipment. Most accountants find this difficult to accept as a reasonable way to measure income.

[8]See FASB, *Disclosure About Oil and Gas Producing Activities: An Amendment of FASB Statements 19, 25, 33 and 39*, Statement of Financial Accounting Standards No. 69 (Stamford: FASB, 1982).

[9]Further doubt is cast by the abandonment by the U.S. Securities and Exchange Commission of the requirement to report a supplemental earnings summary using "Reserve Recogni-

tion Accounting." That accounting was also based on a standardized DCF calculation relating to proved reserves only.

[10]Some disconcerting results of this method of regulation are explored in R.N. Morrison and R.J. Schultz, eds., *Pipeline Regulation and Inflation: An Evaluation of Tariff Levelling* (Ottawa: National Energy Board, and Montreal: Centre for the Study of Regulated Industries, McGill University, 1983).

Part Four

A Conceptual Framework and Standard-Setting

Chapter Thirty-One
A Conceptual Framework for Financial Reporting

Much has been written in the past three decades about a conceptual framework for accounting and financial reporting. And much effort has been expended, particularly by the FASB, to discover and propound such a framework. What is meant by a conceptual framework? Essentially, it is an interrelated structure of propositions and observations that helps us explain financial reporting practices or deduce what they ought to be. Such a framework can help us, when we are faced with a conflict in practice or a new problem, to arrive at which accounting policy is to be preferred.

Two kinds of conceptual framework

A conceptual framework may be arrived at in two ways. The first approach is descriptive. Accounting practices are observed and hypotheses are developed as to why they take the form they do. Some generalizations are then made about the goals of practice that are consistent, so far as possible, with observed practices and the hypotheses explaining them. This was the approach normally taken by accounting writers up to about 1960. The resulting accounting literature was generally described as accounting theory, rather than as a conceptual framework. Part II of this book contains elements of this approach as it explains current accounting practices in terms of the historical cost accounting framework.[1]

The usefulness of such a descriptive framework, if it is widely known and accepted, is that it provides guidance to accounting practice. The solutions to new reporting problems may be found by deduction from the concepts of the framework. Auditors may use it to provide criteria for fair presentation of financial reports. Standard-setters may refer to it to help choose preferable accounting policies where alternative practices exist, thereby promoting greater comparability in reporting. Proposed answers to new problems may also be tested by application of the concepts of the framework.

On the other hand, a purely descriptive framework has inherent limitations. If some well-established practice is inconsistent with the framework, there is always a basic question whether it is the practice that is at fault or the framework. Should the practice be prohibited, or should the framework be patched to rationalize the practice? Too much of the latter can lead to a formless structure that not only loses its power to guide practice but also loses respect. Moreover, a descriptive conceptual framework suffers from too great a reliance on the existing environment. If economic and social conditions change, the existence of a framework tied to practice under previous conditions may reinforce resistance to needed adaptation of accounting practice.

The second type of conceptual framework is the type normally meant when we refer to a conceptual framework today. What makes this type different is that it does not start with practice and attempt to describe and explain it. Rather, it begins with an examination of the objectives of financial reporting. From these, it attempts to reason forward based on observations and postulates as to such matters as the domain of financial reporting, the nature of phenomena to be reported, user information needs, qualities of useful financial information, and limitations on what it is possible to know and practical to report. A process of deduction from all these concepts suggests accounting policies that ought to be adopted.

Thus, this type of framework is prescriptive rather than descriptive.[2] This does not mean that it is wholly normative. On the contrary, like any good theory, it must be firmly grounded on factual premises. Empirical investigation is required to see that we have our facts straight before any conclusions can be drawn with respect to specific issues.

The great virtue and at the same time a potential source of weakness of this type of conceptual framework is that it is not bound by existing practice or existing ideas. Ideally, at least, each building block in the framework is researched and discussed on its own merits. As the framework is constructed, each block rests upon and is interrelated with the previous one.

There are difficulties with this. If one goes astray at an early stage in building the framework, that fact may not become evident until near the end of the structure, resulting in much wasted effort. Perhaps because of this, many people are uncomfortable about agreeing to generalized statements — for example, about objectives — unless they can foresee what conclusions will be drawn from them. This can force initial statements in the framework to be rather abstract to obtain acceptance. That quality of abstraction can reduce their strength as a foundation for further statements. It is not clear that it is possible to have a profitable discussion and debate about the merits of a conceptual framework before it is completed and its implications are clear. Unfortunately, at that stage vested interests and the natural human resistance to change are likely to arouse vocal opposition, which may drown out reasoned discussion.

It should be realized, as well, that any conceptual framework is valid only for its place and time. A highly socialized country, for example, would not place much emphasis on the importance of providing information to facilitate private investment decisions. Thus, as social and economic conditions change, the conceptual framework must change, as well as individual accounting standards. There is the same danger of rigidity with this type of framework as with one that merely rationalizes existing accounting practice. However, if a successful effort were made to arrive at an explicitly stated normative conceptual framework and the relationship between the conceptual premises and standards of practice became well understood, the habit of reasoning conceptually might make the whole structure more adaptable to change.

Is a conceptual framework necessary?

Some researchers argue that there is no need for either a conceptual framework or accounting standards. The content of financial reports could be the subject of private contract between those who manage entities and interested parties outside the entities, such as creditors and investors. If so, the content would be governed by what the contracting parties decide they want in their own best interests and are prepared to pay for.[3]

There are reasons to be skeptical of this proposition. First, many investors have too small and too transient an interest in any particular entity for it to be economical to enter into such contracts and to monitor their performance. Contracting intermediaries would have to be formed to buy the information and resell it. Second, it would be very difficult to control the dissemination of information in such an arrangement, but if it were not controlled few would be prepared to pay for it. Hence the idea of a market for information tends to break down.

Another area of active theoretical speculation stems from the observation that accounting standards and practices have specific economic, social, or political consequences. From this, it is argued that various types of political action will be taken to influence accounting standards when a standard-setting body exists. Some authors see managements of large companies as playing a central role in this political action because their self-interest is most highly involved in accounting reports. This research purports to offer evidence that leads to the relatively cynical conclusion that there never will be agreement on a theory or theories of accounting.[4] Accordingly, the search for a conceptual framework is a waste of time.

The skepticism of other writers is more broadly based. An agreed conceptual framework is regarded as a technical impossibility as well as being politically impossible. Any conceptual framework, it is argued, will conclude at the highest level of abstraction that financial reporting must aim to be useful. To follow this up, it is necessary to know who uses financial reports and how they use them — that is, how they make decisions based upon them. At present we have little knowledge on these points. Even if we did, we probably would find that different people seek different information. One can generalize that decisions are based on predictions, so that predictive power is a desirable characteristic of accounting information. But then, in the real world of uncertainty, how do we know what information is best for prediction? Because of such difficulties, these writers suggest that a conceptual framework leading to conclusions as to preferable accounting policies is at present out of reach. The best that can be achieved by conceptual thinking is to create an agenda for research.[5]

Finally, the CICA research study *Corporate Reporting: Its Future Evolution* argues that an "axiomatic approach" as taken by the FASB is not appropriate for Canada. It criticizes particularly the attempt to define elements of financial statements such as assets and liabilities. This criticism rests partly on the grounds that the definitions must be framed at such a high level of generality they will not be operational, and partly out of fear that, to the extent they are operational, there is danger they will be arbitrary. The major concern apparently is with the lack of flexibility and responsiveness to user needs that is thought to result from such an "axiomatic" conceptual framework. The axiomatic approach is compared to the legal framework in civil law jurisdictions such as France, which attempts to write down all legal rules and definitions in a code. It is argued that such a process is too rigid in its result for accounting. The preferred approach is said to be analogous to the legal process in common law countries. Statutes (or accounting standards) are enacted to govern actions in a particular area. Case law develops as a result of judges (management and auditors) applying the appropriate statutes (accounting standards) in specific circumstances.[6]

The trouble with this analogy is that it leaves completely unresolved the question of what basis there is for deciding upon accounting standards. Statutes are enacted by governments to serve some perceived social purpose or, at the least, because the law will be popular with the voters or influential pressure groups. Who is voting for accounting standards? The fact of the matter is that accounting standard-setters must have some framework of ideas, no matter how simple, in order to arrive at conclusions. The real question is whether the conceptual framework should be implicit, unwritten, and variable from one individual to another or whether there should be an attempt to make some consensual framework explicit.

In the following discussion we shall explore ideas that might be embodied in a conceptual framework. Although most of these ideas will be found in previous studies, particularly in the FASB Statements of Financial Accounting Concepts, the attempt here is not to provide a complete review of the literature. The possible permutations and combinations of ideas are too great for a work such as this. Instead, the author will attempt a personal statement of a structure of thought that seems plausible to him and see how far it leads.

A prescriptive conceptual framework

The domain of accounting

Most conceptual frameworks begin with a statement of objectives. It is of equal importance, however, to establish what accounting is about and to clarify its domain.

First, accounting is about recognizable entities. The issues in defining boundaries of a reporting entity were explored in chapters 5 and 25 and will not be repeated here. An entity is the focal point for accounting reports because it can be seen to be in possession or control of economic resources.

Economic resources and claims on them form the subject matter of accounting. The modifier "economic" as used here implies that the resources in question are both desirable and not freely available. Thus people must make sacrifices to acquire resources — that is, resources command a price. We focus on economic resources because no one needs information about free goods. It is only economic commodities — scarce commodities — about which we can use information. We are interested in information about resources because we want to keep track of them — we suffer a loss in the means of satisfaction of our wants if we lose economic resources. We also are interested in information about resources because we want to increase our wealth by trading in them or by processing them so as to add value.

A report on an entity's economic resources could consist merely of a description of assets, tangible and intangible, and of amounts owed. For reasons of economy in communication, however, we normally express resources in terms of money — a numeraire. Our shorthand expression for a report on economic resources expressed in money terms is a financial report. A financial report, thus, is a report expressed in monetary terms about an entity's resources and claims upon them at a specified reporting date and about the changes in net resources over a specified period ending on that date.

Although financial reports are expressed in monetary terms, much of the information content in them comes from the descriptions, classifications, and order of reporting of resources and resource flows within the report. From these details, for example, we learn much about the liquidity of resources and the likelihood of recurrence of resource flows. In general, however, the information is bounded by the point of view of the entity itself. We are able to describe the assets and services we get in exchange for payment. But we are not able to describe the consequences of the exchange on parties outside the entity.

This situation is not unsatisfactory in a commercially oriented entity where the consequences of exchanges with other parties will be evidenced in revenues, but it does limit the information value of financial reports of entities that are not commercially oriented. The money spent by a welfare organization, for example, is not expected to earn future revenue, nor is it intended primarily to give employment to social workers. Rather, the organization is intended to provide service to others, usually without recompense. The success of such an organization is therefore not reflected by its monetary exchanges, and a report restricted to financial matters leaves out much important information. It is an open question whether the domain of financial reports should be deemed to include nonmonetary indicators of the achievement of nonbusiness organizations. If its boundaries were to be expanded in this way, accountants would need to acquire skills beyond their traditional field of competence, or persons with different skills would need to share responsibilities for financial reports.[7]

Let us now examine the concept of a resource — an asset — and a claim upon resources — liability or equity — more thoroughly. At this point we have to make an initial decision whether we aim for one conceptual framework for accounting or have in mind distinct frameworks for different classes of entity — distinguishing, for example, between entities carrying on business and nonbusiness organizations. The choice must be made because conceptual definitions must be sufficiently broad to be applicable in all situations encountered.

The author's view is that one comprehensive conceptual framework is possible. The remaining discussion will be based on that assumption. The reader should note also that definitions, such as the following, attempt to reach the *essence* of the concept defined. There is no attempt at this stage to limit the definition so that it is possible to implement it in accounting practice.[8] The need for such limitations is left for consideration later in the framework.

The concept of an asset. There is a familiar saying: "You cannot eat your cake and have it too." The dictum implies a fundamental truth. The source of value to assets other than cash always lies in the future. Present value exists because of expectations of future proceeds from sale or future service value (or in the case of cake, consumption utility). But whatever the nature of the satisfaction furnished by an asset, it lies in the future.

An entity, of course, is likely to receive many benefits in the future. Many of those benefits do not represent assets today. The reason is that they will have their origin in future activities. Financial statements contain a record of the financial consequences of events that have taken place and conditions that exist. Measurement of the results of those events requires estimates of their future consequences but *not* forecasts of entirely independent events. Thus, Janus-like, the concept of an asset is both backward-looking and forward-looking.

Finally, the entity must be in a position to control the receipt of that future benefit for it to qualify as an asset. Thus we can define an asset as follows:

> *An asset is a potential future economic benefit obtainable by a particular entity resulting from past transactions or events.*

This definition differs from that of the FASB in one respect. The FASB used the word "probable" instead of the word "potential" used above. A simple example explains the reason for the substitution. Suppose you hold a ticket in a lottery promising five prizes totalling $1 million, and 200,000 tickets have been sold. Your chances of winning anything are extremely small, but they are not zero. Your assets and mine may be identical in all other respects, but if you hold an unexpired ticket and I do not, you are slightly better off than I am. That is not to say that accounting should record the lottery ticket as an asset (although perhaps it should). Further development of the conceptual framework is necessary to settle that point. However, the broadest possible definition of the concept of an asset will treat that lottery ticket as an asset because it is owned today and has potential for future benefit.

For a business enterprise, the future economic benefit will normally take the form of an inflow of cash (although occasionally it may be represented by the receipt of some other economic benefit or the reduction of a liability). In a nonbusiness organization, that future economic benefit often consists of the capacity to render service in furtherance of the entity's programs without requiring a further expenditure of economic resources. It seems quite reasonable to regard such potential service capacity as an asset to a nonbusiness entity, given its dedication to a service objective. However, we must consider the objectives of a financial report on a nonbusiness entity before we can conclude on this point. If no possible purpose is fulfilled by defining as an asset something that will not produce a future inflow of cash or its equivalent, then the definition has to be modified. The result would be that we have a different conceptual framework for nonbusiness organizations.

Three further points should be noted about the definition of an asset. First, although we tend to think of assets as tangible objects or legal rights, the common characteristic that gives them their economic significance, as already noted, is the fact that they represent a source of future economic benefit. Second, since the future is not observable, the essential characteristic of an asset for financial reporting purposes is not directly observable (except in the case of cash itself) — it is only an expectation, not a certainty. The source of virtually all the difficulties in accounting is this uncertainty as to the future. Third, since the factors that give rise to expectations of cash flow (i.e. the existence of land, buildings, equipment, a trained work force, etc.) generally operate together, the essential asset characteristic—expectation of future economic benefit—cannot be allocated to particular sources of that expectation. For these reasons, particularly the last, this definition of an asset ordinarily cannot lead without modification to operational rules for recognizing, measuring, and recording assets in accounts. The conceptual framework has to be extended and refined to accomplish that end.

The concept of a liability. A liability may be regarded as a negative asset. Its definition is like a mirror image of that of an asset.

> *A liability is a potential requirement on the part of the entity to sacrifice economic resources in future because of past transactions or events.*

Again this definition differs from that of the FASB in the substitution of the word "potential" for the word "probable". The degree of probability is a consideration in deciding whether to recognize a liability or how to measure it, but not whether a liability in its broadest definition exists. If this is accepted, any originating transaction and event that may result in a future sacrifice creates a liability. There is no need for a distinction in definition between ordinary liabilities and contingent liabilities. The problem is merely one of framing recognition, measurement, and disclosure rules to take account of the probabilities of future sacrifices arising from past events.

Dependent definitions. Given the fundamental definitions of assets and liabilities, it is possible to move on to dependent definitions.

> *Equity is the residual interest in the assets of an entity that remains after deducting the amounts of its liabilities.*

It is convenient to have a name to describe the excess of assets over liabilities. It is important to note, however, that equity cannot be observed or measured directly. It is merely a name given to the results of a mathematical operation comparing the amounts of assets and liabilities.

The FASB points out that "equity" is customarily used in connection with profit-oriented enterprises and less commonly used by nonprofit organizations. The term "net assets" is suggested as a neutral equivalent.

An important function of financial statements is to explain changes in assets and liabilities over an accounting period in addition to reporting their existence at the end of the period. For this purpose the following definitions are convenient:

> *Revenues are inflows or enhancements of assets (or settlements of liabilities) during a period that are in consideration for products or services created in the course of the ongoing major or central operating activities of the entity. Donations and contributions raised by major fund-raising activities of nonprofit entities and taxes raised by governments are nonreciprocal transfers from others that may also be called revenues.*

> *Expenses represent outflows of assets, or consumption of their capacity to serve, or incurrence of liabilities as a result of the ongoing major or central operations of the entity.*

Revenue is a gross concept — that is, it is a measure of the total inflow of assets from operations (such as cash or accounts receivable from sales) and is not reduced by a figure of assets given up in exchange (such as the goods sold). Expense likewise is a gross concept.

> *Gains represent increases in net assets resulting from transactions that are peripheral or merely incidental to the main activities of the entity and from all other transactions and events affecting the entity except for revenues, contributions by owners, or restricted donations to a nonprofit entity.*

> *Losses represent decreases in net assets resulting from transactions peripheral or merely incidental to the main operations and from all other transactions or events affecting the entity except for expenses or distributions to owners.*

Gain and loss are net concepts. Gain represents the excess of assets received (or liabilities liquidated) over assets given up (or liabilities incurred) in such transactions. Loss is the reverse.

Donations accompanied by restrictions on their spending present certain problems for the interpretation of the foregoing definitions. A donation given on terms that prohibit the spending of principal (an endowment) is somewhat akin to a capital contribution by an owner in a profit-oriented enterprise and thus is a direct credit to equity rather than either revenue or gain.

A donation that is temporarily restricted — for example, until the entity spends an equivalent amount on a specific program — could be deemed to be a liability until that spending takes place and at that time become earned revenue. The FASB, however, suggests that the fiduciary obligation to spend the money in a given way is normally different in character from an ordinary liability incurred for specific consideration in an exchange transaction. The board's preferred solution, therefore, is (1) to subclassify the net assets (equity) of a nonprofit entity as permanently restricted, temporarily restricted, and unrestricted balances, (2) to credit restricted donations to restricted net assets (equity) when received, and (3) to reclassify temporarily restricted donations as unrestricted net assets when the restriction is released. The effect of this suggestion is that unrestricted donations are recorded as revenues, and restricted donations (even those whose only restriction is as to time of spending) are treated as "reclassifications" when the restriction is lifted. At this point the choice of definition appears somewhat arbitrary.

The foregoing definitions cover all the transactions and events that lead to changes in net assets over an accounting period. If we wish to cover all changes in individual assets or liabilities, however, we have to add exchanges of assets for assets (as in collection of accounts receivable or purchases of assets for cash), acquisition of assets by incurring liabilities (purchases on credit, or borrowing), exchanges of liabilities for liabilities (as in borrowing long term to repay the bank), and settlements of liabilities with assets (as in cash payments to liquidate debt).

The definitions of assets and liabilities — the elements of the accounting domain — go to their substance: (1) future *economic* benefits or sacrifices (2) controlled by the reporting entity and (3) arising from the activities of the entity and events affecting it that have taken place up to the reporting date. The dependent definitions are essentially matters of classification. Classifications are always debatable to some degree and thus are less fundamental. They are nevertheless important because it is they that convey a picture of financial position and activity to the statement reader.

A conceptual framework geared to portrayal of assets and liabilities and explanations of changes in them seems stronger than one founded on measurement of income — defining assets and liabilities merely as the residual from the income measurement process. The reason is that income is an artificial construct — a name given to an idea that has never been expressed in a completely operational form. But we must not overstress the superiority of the asset and liability foundation for a conceptual framework. Our observation that the significance of assets and liabilities lies in the future means that they can never be measured with absolute certainty. Surrogate measures must be found, and therein lies the essential problem of accounting.

The objectives of financial reporting

Every study of objectives of financial reporting comes to the primary conclusion that financial reports are intended to be useful. It is conceivable that financial reports might, in fact, be a mere customary ritual. It hardly seems likely, however, that a mere ritual would have persisted as long as financial reports have or would generate so much heated argument as they sometimes do, if they were not thought to have important practical uses. An assumption that financial reporting is a purposive activity, therefore, seems justified. But that assumption leads only to questions as to whose interests it serves and how it helps their interests.

Stewardship and accountability. As we have seen in Part I, the use of financial reports developed with the growth of larger scale enterprises requiring the provision of capital from outside sources to supplement the resources of those running the enterprise. The institution of the limited liability corporation involved the intervention of the state, resulting in the beginning of regulation of accounting activity.[9] The purpose of the government intrusion was essentially to ensure fair dealing between the managers of a corporation and its shareholders and creditors, who had limited access to information about it.

In this, the early corporations law was influenced by the old-fashioned stewardship idea that a financial report was required simply to hold managers accountable for resources entrusted to them. In other words, it was intended as a control mechanism. The idea that the capital of a limited liability corporation constituted a fund for the protection of creditors also reinforced the concept of capital maintenance, a concept that could provide guidance for accounting practice. Unfortunately, as we saw in Part I, the courts rendered this idea ineffectual in the dividend cases towards the end of the nineteenth century. Thus, in practice, the concept of stewardship has proved to a weak objective for financial reporting.

The concept of accountability is sometimes taken as merely another name for stewardship accounting. Rosenfield, however, regards the former term as preferable because of the vagueness and ambiguity of meanings attached to "stewardship" and consequently its use in several senses.[10] He noted the narrow interpretation of the stewardship reporting responsibility as being merely an obligation to report on safe custody or proper disposition of assets entrusted. A broadening of the view of the stewardship obligation leads to a requirement to report on efficient, economical, and effective use of resources. Still further broadening requires a report on the steward's (management's) success in achieving goals expected of the enterprise. The significance of the shades of definition may be illustrated by the consequences thought to flow from the concept. The narrow definition of stewardship reporting—that is, reporting on custody and disposition of assets—is often taken to justify continued reliance on historical costs in financial statements. A broader definition that embraces reporting on management performance arguably calls for reporting on changes of value of assets while held, so long as the management has effective discretion whether to buy, sell, or hold.

The term "accountability", in contrast to the term stewardship, focusses attention on identification of those parties *entitled* to an accounting and the purposes for which they are presumed to use the accounting. The obligation to report is created by law or custom, which changes from time to time. Correspondingly, the people deemed entitled to receive entity reports change, and with them the purposes served by the reports. English corporations law gave shareholders the right to receive reports. Securities legislation created a new dimension. The interests of prospective investors as well as existing shareholders is to be given weight in the reporting. Currently, many people argue that an extended public is entitled to some form of reporting from larger corporations, at least, in view of the significant influence of such corporations in society. To date, however, "social responsibility accounting" (part of which should, no doubt, consist of reporting in other than financial terms) has not been given systematic recognition in legislation, at least in North America.

Promotion of social welfare. Some accounting theorists argue that accounting is a social choice mechanism and must be consciously designed to serve social welfare.[11] It is a social choice mechanism because accounting policies make some people better off and others worse off. As a simple example, additional disclosure requirements impose costs on preparers of financial statements, the benefit, if any, being received by those who use the information. Changes in risk assessments by users of financial statements may increase the cost of capital to some entities and lower it for others. This must be so, it is argued, because if such effects were not present, there would be no reason for regulation of financial reporting (and, we may add, no reason for financial reports). If this is true, the argument runs, accounting standards must be designed with the objective of enhancing social welfare.

The obvious question concerns how social welfare is to be enhanced. One criterion suggested is that an accounting standard should be "Pareto-efficient," which means that no one should be made worse off by it but a potential should exist for benefit to someone. Since people do have conflicting interests in an entity and various entities are in competition with each other, it seems most unlikely that this criterion could ever be met. A second possible criterion is that total benefits of a standard should exceed total costs, even though some might gain and some might lose.

It should be apparent that these or other criteria of social welfare are essentially ethical in character. Those who argue for the social welfare objective stress that the setting of accounting standards cannot be regarded as solely a technical process. There is enough truth in this to give one pause for thought. For example, an accounting standard that requires that contingent liabilities must be disclosed, even though disclosure may increase the likelihood of the claim being asserted, favours the interests of potential investors in an entity over those of existing investors. Government-imposed requirements for fair presentation justify such a standard. But there must be grave doubts that private-sector standard-setters have the legitimacy to make decisions on social welfare grounds in the absence of governmental direction.

A serious objection to the social welfare objective stems from doubts as to its feasibility. Measurements of costs and benefits are notoriously difficult to make, and this would be the simplest criterion to apply. Attempts to combine individual preferences into an expression of social preference are generally considered to be impossible.[12] There might be greater confidence in the feasibility of a social welfare objective to guide financial reporting if one observed such an objective functioning as a guide to the deliberations of our legislatures.

If one does believe that social welfare considerations are effective in guiding legislative and governmental actions, it may be argued that a clear signal has been given to guide accounting standards. Corporations and securities legislation requires that financial statements be fairly presented or yield a "true and fair view." Such wording implies a conclusion that social welfare is served by unbiased financial disclosure, even though the disclosure may not benefit all individual interests. The existence of securities legislation, in particular, attests to the importance of the belief that efficient capital markets will be socially beneficial and therefore should be a fair game. With this authoritatively established objective, it becomes much more possible to view accounting standard-setting as an exercise in which technical competence should be an overriding concern.

Facilitation of contracting. A comparatively recent adaptation of the traditional stewardship reporting objective (control over the steward) is provided by "agency theory."[13] Agency theory views a firm as a nexus of contracts. In particular, there will be a class of contracts (implicit or explicit) that will govern the sharing of the uncertain outcomes (profits) of the firm's activities. Such contracts include contracts between the firm and providers of capital, as well as management incentive contracts. The contracts entail (1) agreement on actions to be performed by the parties, (2) a system that reports on outcomes of entity activities, and (3) agreement on sharing of results depending on outcomes (that is, payment of interest, dividends, and management incentive bonuses). Those parties who perform management functions under the contract are designated "agents." The passive partners — those who provide capital — are designated "principals."

The theory reasons that the agent has some personal incentives (desire for personal leisure, desire to avoid risk) not to perform as agreed in the best interest of the principals and may also wish to manipulate the reporting system to his own advantage (to obscure poor performance or to gain unearned incentive compensation). The reporting system suitable for contracting must have certain characteristics to mitigate these dangers. It must be objective (be based on hard data). The process of reporting must be reliable — that is, given a set of events, the accounting alternatives to report those events must be narrowly circumscribed. Finally, disclosure must be adequate for the purposes of the contracting parties.

At its present, still exploratory stage of development, agency theory has little to say about what should be the information content of financial reports. One suggestion has been that, to be useful for contracting, the accounting results to be expected from events and transactions should be predictable, the accounting methods should be well understood by contracting parties, and accounting measurements should be hard — that is, should not be open to wide variation depending upon individual judgment. It has been argued that the observed durability of the historical cost model of accounting may be attributed to the desire, perhaps unconscious, for hard data for contracting. It hardly seems that history bears out this interpretation, considering the limited evidence of contracts between principals and agents to establish accounting methods, the arduous struggle to eliminate purely arbitrary aspects of accounting such as the use of secret reserves, and the much publicized inability to make the allocations required in historical cost accounting anything but arbitrary.

Nevertheless, the proponents of the contracting theory may well be right that agreed-upon, highly reliable accounting rules are valuable for contracting purposes. The difficulty is that hard-and-fast accounting rules may produce unintended results if something in the economic environment changes. Consider a management incentive contract based on reported accounting profits. Such a contract might be eminently fair and satisfactory while price levels are stable and absurdly unfair and unreasonable under conditions of rapid inflation (for reasons fully explained in Part III). One may be skeptical that flexibility in contract terms or the possibility of renegotiation of contracts when conditions change can provide an adequate answer to this problem. More thought is required to answer the question of how accounting methods that produce hard data for contracting can be made adaptable to changed conditions.

Usefulness for decision making. Given the basic assumption that financial reports should be useful, the obvious question is, useful for what? The equally obvious answer is that reports will be useful if they make a difference to decisions taken by users of the reports. Thus, the goal of decision usefulness has been accepted as the primary objective in many explorations of possible conceptual frameworks. Acceptance of that goal immediately begs two questions: Who are the potential users of financial reports, and what financial information would be relevant to their decisions? The answers to these questions are far from easy.

Typically, conceptual framework studies produce a long list of actual or potential users of financial reports. This immediately poses the problem of what to do when different types of users are anxious to have different types of information. If a wide variety of decisions potentially would be facilitated by financial information, is it possible to meet the needs of all? In essence, this question asks whether truly general-purpose financial statements are a practical possibility. If they are not, then there somehow must be some ranking of the decision needs of various types of users, requiring what are virtually social choice judgments on the part of those who set standards.

The FASB, in its conceptual framework statements, chooses to concentrate on the use of business financial reports for investment and credit decisions. The board suggests, plausibly but without evidence, that information for these purposes will serve most other purposes as well. To the extent it does not, however, a value judgment has been made to give primacy to the decision needs of capital market participants.[14] In view of the existence of securities legislation this seems a reasonable, if not inescapable, conclusion. As argued already, only constituted political authority has the legitimacy to make such social welfare choices.

A second problem is that we know very little about how decisions are actually made. There may be a wide variety of decision models calling for different information inputs. Even if we were aware of the whole range of decision models, we might find difficulty in conveying the information required for all possible models without making it hard for individual users to select and work with the specific information they want. We also face the probability that some decision models may be unreasonable and must ask ourselves whether there is any obligation to supply information upon which it would be irrational to base decisions.

So long as there is any limitation on the quantity of data supplied (and the volume of activities engaged in by sizable complex entities suggests that there must be), some choices must be made. That being so, it would seem that accounting standards should at least seek to segregate the rational from the irrational decision models and concentrate upon the former. For this purpose, attention needs to be paid to the findings of finance and economic theory, and perhaps additional research is needed. In the meantime, the FASB suggests as a working supposition with respect to business financial reports that most users are interested in information that will help in assessing the amounts, timing, and uncertainty of prospective cash inflows to the reporting entity.

It may be possible to lessen concerns about the variety of decision models by focussing on the decision maker and the process gone through in making a decision. Any decision consists of three operations: (1) outlining all the feasible actions in a given situation, (2) evaluating the outcome of each possible action, and (3) making a choice of action based on the outcome desired.[15] Since the choice in question is an economic choice, it is likely to be made in the relatively simple terms of maximizing reward and minimizing risk. Evaluation of outcomes is likely to be the most crucial operation in the process, and this involves prediction. Most successful predictions rest to some degree on knowledge of the past. Hence one can say that one test of the relevance of accounting information is its value in assisting prediction. (This is not to say that predictions consist merely of extrapolation of past trends. Rather, a good understanding of the reasons for past results is necessary to enable adjustment of predictions to take account of changes in underlying conditions.)

In the actual event, of course, any prediction is likely to be in error to some degree. Knowledge of the reasons for error has the potential for improving further predictions. Accounting information that provides feedback to compare with previous predictions is therefore also relevant to user decision making. Feedback on entity performance, of course, may to some degree be directly relevant to decisions having to do with quality of management as well as being indirectly helpful in improving predictive judgment.[16]

Understandably, the decision-usefulness objective leads to quite a different chain of reasoning in the case of nonbusiness organizations. The FASB identifies resource providers, constituents (members or service beneficiaries of the entity), governing and oversight bodies, and managers as the principal groups interested in the financial reports of these entities. The decisions that may be influenced by financial reports include decisions as to allocations of resources to these organizations which may, in turn, rest upon assessment of the services provided by an organization, its ability to continue to perform those services, and the manner in which its managers have discharged their stewardship responsibility.

Although the FASB perceives quite different decisions being assisted by the financial reports of business and nonbusiness organizations, it comes to remarkably similar conclusions as to the information needed in their respective financial reports. In essence, it is information about economic resources, claims to those resources, and the effects of transactions, events, and circumstances that change the resources and claims over a period. In the case of nonbusiness organizations, ideally reports would also provide information about service accomplishments in terms of goods and service outputs and program results. Since all these have already been identified as within the domain of accounting (or just at its boundary in the case of nonfinancial indicators of achievement), the decision-usefulness objective seems to add little to what existed before thought was given to a conceptual framework. It is possible that research into just how users make decisions and what makes for predictive ability might provide more original insight, but at this stage the decision-usefulness objective remains barren of results.

Representational faithfulness. The FASB has coined the phrase "representational faithfulness" as one characteristic of useful accounting information. Representational faithfulness is defined as correspondence or agreement between a measure or description and the phenomenon it purports to represent. In accounting, the phenomena represented are assets and liabilities and the transactions and events that change them. The term "isomorphism" — which means identity in shape or form — is sometimes used as a synonym for representational faithfulness. The term captures the idea of a portrayal that is in scale, in balance, or "in the round." A more colloquial expression of the same idea is "tell it like it is." Yet another expression of the idea, widely found in accounting literature, is that accounting should portray "economic reality."

Portrayal of economic reality as a goal has lost status in the past little while, especially among academics. Some think that adherents to that goal hold a naive belief that there is some Platonist ideal of reality or truth that we can hope to approximate in practice. In particular, these critics suggest that adherents mistakenly believe there is something that can be called "true income" and that accounting policies can therefore be evaluated by the criterion of whether they reflect income or distort it. This criticism is misdirected as a criticism of the goal of representational faithfulness here described. That goal does not even require that a concept of income be adopted but rather requires concentration on the underlying phenomena of assets, liabilities, and changes in them.

A more weighty objection to the concept of representational faithfulness or economic reality is that reality is multifaceted. The implication is that it is impossible to express economic reality — one has to pick and choose. That choices have to be made is undeniable. But a basic choice is made for us when we say that we are seeking the objectives of *financial* reports. That means that the report is basically in monetary terms, and this itself eliminates from consideration many aspects of reality that might otherwise be reported. That is to say, we need not be concerned that we are not reporting the volume or weight or aesthetic appeal of assets because those facets are outside the domain of accounting. This conceded, the problem is reduced to much more manageable proportions. Within the domain of financial reporting there are only two variables that need to concern us in relation to multirealities. One is the aspect of monetary expression — what we call measurement or valuation. The other is the aspect of description and classification in the reports.

The problem in the first of these is to choose an attribute to be measured. In chapter 27 we laid out a matrix of nine possibilities for valuation based on entry prices, exit prices, and value in use and on three time periods — past, present, and future. Many combinations of these can be rejected with little consideration so that we are really only talking about a few candidates for reporting — considerably fewer than nine.

As to description and classification, we may also ask how many possibilities there are. For example, we can categorize assets as tangible or intangible, as operating or nonoperating, or on a scale of liquidity. We can classify expenditures by object of expenditure, purpose of expenditure, or by organizational division responsible for spending. Present financial reports manage to provide classifications on more than one basis quite handily. Critics of the goal of representational faithfulness may be too glib when they reject it on the grounds of its undoubted multifaceted nature.

One of the advantages of the representational faithfulness goal is that it can be argued, a priori, that its achievement will contribute to the achievement of other goals. It is hard to believe that biased reporting of information will contribute either to good decision making by users or overall social welfare. It is less easy to reconcile the goal of representational faithfulness with the goal of facilitating contracting if it is accepted that contracting parties only want hard accounting measurements. Since the real measure of assets and liabilities rests upon future benefits and sacrifices and the future is always uncertain, faithful representation cannot be confined to hard-and-fast measurements. However, since any representation, to be faithful, should in some manner convey the range of uncertainty, it is conceivable that information required for contracting could be accommodated as one end of the range of measurement required to be reported to achieve the goal of representational faithfulness.

The real problem with the goal of representational faithfulness lies in the observation that the essence of resources and obligations lies in the future. We cannot measure the future. The best we can do is measure and report expectations about the future, so that the goal of faithful representation must be interpreted in that light. Since it is expectations about the future that influence market prices, it is inevitable that market prices will form an important element in the portrayal of representational faithfulness. The problem is that markets are incomplete — a fact that takes on increasing importance as we move from the formulation of abstract goals for financial reporting toward more concrete concepts to guide recognition and measurement.

Conclusion. Consideration of the objectives of financial reports does not appear to provide much guidance for specific reporting policies. It is hardly debatable that accounting should be useful, but there are many questions as to who uses accounting information and how it is used—or, even more important, could be used if better information were available. The answers to these questions quite conceivably could suggest such a multiplicity of possible uses that it might be concluded that general-purpose financial reporting is impossible in the absence of a judgmental hierarchical ordering of users and user needs.

There is a strong tradition in accounting history to the effect that the purpose of accounting is to report upon the stewardship of management. That purpose implies one information use — the use of information to assist assessment of performance of management. As an extension of this, it has been suggested that such information is vital to the operation of control devices — the contracts between owners of an entity and its management, between the entity and creditors, and between management and subordinates. The evidence that financial accounting reports are actually designed in the most effective way to facilitate contracts is sparse, but it is nevertheless possible to argue that it would be desirable that they be so.

Any report on stewardship and any report used for contracting, to be successful, must have some correspondence with what is actually taking place within the accounting entity. The goal of faithful representation of the financial position of the entity and of the transactions and events that have affected its financial position is attractive because it seems likely to be useful, if not essential, for any other conceivable purpose.

It should be noted that these objectives are not fundamentally in conflict with one another. Each of the stewardship and contracting objectives represents one specification of decision usefulness. The faithful representation objective represents an interpretation of what will be decision useful. What seems to be lacking is a strong connection between any of these objectives and a set of accounting policies designed to achieve them. As previously noted, some regard this as suggesting that, in our present state of knowledge, a conceptual framework that is not inductively derived from practice can serve only as an agenda for research. Others draw a different conclusion — that accounting is a service activity and service activities do not need grandiose statements of theory, all that is required is some identified need or set of needs, which may be on a quite mundane level.[17]

Qualitative characteristics of useful information

The FASB has suggested a number of characteristics of accounting information that contribute to its usefulness. To some extent, these merely expand upon the usefulness objective and have been covered in the discussion above. Other qualities primarily represent exhortations to good practice or descriptions of practical limits on the usefulness of information. For the most part these represent common sense and need be referred to only briefly.

Relevance. The primary qualitative characteristic mentioned is that of relevance to users. This merely emphasizes the decision-usefulness objective. Information to be supplied should ideally be relevant to some decision. The corollary is that information that is not relevant need not be supplied even if it is true. The notion of relevance is sharpened by suggesting that two criteria of relevant information are predictive value and feedback value, both of which have been referred to above.

Timeliness. The predictive value of given information trickles away as time passes. Every event can be traced to a variety of antecedent conditions, some in the recent past, some in the more distant past. The farther away one gets from a particular date, the less likely it is that conditions at that date have any influence on what is happening currently or is about to happen. Consequently, timeliness is a necessary characteristic of information that has predictive value or current relevance.

Timeliness in financial reporting has two aspects. First, timeliness requires a certain frequency of reports. If a financial report were issued only every five years, for example, the information about transactions in the early part of the five-year period might have little relevance for decisions to be taken after the report was issued. Second, timeliness requires that financial reports be issued as soon after the reporting date as is reasonably possible. (There is a practical constraint here, however, in the work required to gather and organize information for the report. An attempt to issue reports too quickly could create risks of errors that would nullify information usefulness.)

Reliability. The other primary qualitative characteristic mentioned by the board is reliability. The board suggests that, to be relied upon, information must be representationally faithful, neutral, and verifiable. All three characteristics are necessary to reliability as that term is used by the board. As has been indicated, the author suggests a higher status for representational faithfulness, at least until the concept of relevance becomes more operational as a result of more definite knowledge of user decisions and information needs.

Neutrality. Neutrality is a necessary characteristic of representationally faithful information. As applied by the board, its principal significance is to indicate that there should be no bias in the choice of information or the manner of its presentation in order to achieve some intended consequence.

This point is particularly important because of the marked increase in interest in recent years in the economic consequences of accounting standards.[18] If accounting does have information content and hence does affect decisions, it clearly will influence human behaviour with, upon occasion, noticeable economic impact.

There are those who would have standard-setters take economic consequences on interested parties into account in establishing accounting standards. Should they do so? The answer is yes and no. If it is suggested that standard-setters should tailor their conclusions to favour the interests of one party over another or to avoid potential damage to someone now benefiting from inadequacies of information publicly available, the answer must be no. Repeated examples of such action would, in short order, destroy the credibility of the standard-setters and of the accounting profession.[19] On the other hand, if the suggestion is that standard-setters should try to be aware of potential economic consequences of their actions and should monitor actual consequences, the answer must be yes. If some interests may be damaged by a new accounting standard, it had better be right and defensible. It is only prudent for standard-setters to be aware of possible reactions to their actions.

Verifiability. While neutrality is a necessary component of representational faithfulness, verifiability is a constraint upon its achievement. In essence, information is verifiable if several qualified measurers would arrive at approximately the same measure for it. The adoption of verifiability as a characteristic of useful accounting information requires some consideration of the conditions that may detract from the likelihood of duplication of an accounting measure or estimate, namely, lack of precision of the estimate and the possibility of bias.

Absolute precision is not possible in any measure. Even repeated measurements of physical attributes using a scientific instrument are likely to vary somewhat, because no matter how fine the calibration of the instrument, the object measured may fall between the marks. Accounting measurements (or estimates) are obviously much less precise. The essential question then is what is the meaning of verifiability if independent measurers are likely to differ. One could argue that lack of precision should not, by itself, be considered to negate usability of information. For example, if two observers agree not on the measure itself but on the probable range of precision, the individual measure arrived at by either one of them, when accompanied by disclosure of the range of precision, could be said to convey useful information. This suggests that verifiability could be interpreted as agreement among independent measurers on the range of precision, provided that range is disclosed.

The situation is different when the range of precision is wide, not because of measurement difficulties but because of the use of different measurement methods. For example, it is an offense against logic that an inventory could be reported at two very different figures, each being described as "at cost." The requirement of verifiability does not deal with this situation, since independent verifiers might attest that each figure is quite a precise representation of "cost" simply by following the original measurement methods. The general problem here is that the inventory is not faithfully represented when it is simply described as "at cost" and cost can be measured by different methods having widely different results. A more complete description of the cost method followed is required for accurate portrayal. (There may also be a question whether the portrayal is as relevant as possible if alternative measurement methods are acceptable.)

Verifiability of information is reduced and the possibility of bias increased to the extent that the accounting measurement depends upon judgment and estimation, rather than on observation. On the other hand, relevance and representational faithfulness may indicate a need for information that is difficult to verify.

A good illustration is provided by the case of a producing oil company. The major asset of any producing company is likely to be its reserves of oil in the ground. The value of that asset is obviously highly relevant to investment and credit decisions relating to the company. Yet with so many unknown variables, the range of possible estimates is very wide, and the estimates cannot be verified in any meaningful sense. As a result, as described in chapter 23, accounting standard-setters have shied away from requiring value estimates of oil reserves in spite of their undoubted relevance and the fact that a statement of financial position cannot be fully representationally faithful without them. On the other hand, quantity estimates of reserves are being required in spite of the fact that they also are difficult to verify. Thus, trade-offs between relevance, representational faithfulness, and verifiability have been made, with the actual information to be produced falling short of the ideal on all three counts.

This discussion leads to one important point — that in an uncertain world information cannot be perfect. No conceptual framework can make it perfect. There have to be practical trade-offs between representational faithfulness and measurability or verifiability. At the point trade-offs become necessary, we pass from the conceptual framework to the real world of compromise. That suggests that when we come to discuss recognition and measurement, the importance of concepts becomes diluted and generalizations become even more debatable.

Recognition and measurement

Let us recapitulate the salient points of the preceding discussion as a foundation for considering the significance of the conceptual framework to practical issues of recognition and measurement.

- Financial reports are intended to communicate information. The subject matter of these reports consists of economic resources held or owned by identifiable entities and claims upon them. The information conveyed in financial reports consists of a report on the status of resources and claims at a given point of time and an account of changes in the resources and claims over a stated period ending at that point of time. To facilitate communication, financial reports classify into categories resources and claims upon them and the events that give rise to changes in them. The information is also quantified through the use of money as a measuring unit.
- The essence of a resource or asset is that it is capable of providing future satisfaction. Resources accounted for are limited to economic resources. That means the resources are not available in unlimited quantities for the asking; they are valuable because they are scarce. An entity accounts for those resources the benefits from which it is entitled to enjoy to the exclusion of others. In its statement of financial position at a given point of time, it accounts for those resources to which it has become entitled as a result of transactions and events up to that time. It does not account for assets to which it expects to become entitled as a result of future events. Thus a financial report is historical in nature. A liability is the reverse of an asset. It represents an obligation to sacrifice valuable resources in the future as a result of past transactions and events. The equity of an entity at a point in time consists of the excess of its assets over liabilities at that time. Changes in equity over a period may be classified as revenues, expenses, gains, and losses.
- Financial reporting is intended to be useful. This general objective is capable of several interpretations. Reports will be useful if they help readers to make better decisions. For example, reports may help assess the performance of

management. Reports on past results should also help investors and creditors predict future progress of the entity and thereby evaluate potential risks and rewards from investment or lending. Rights and obligations expressed in contracts between the entity and parties interested in it may use reported financial indicators as bases for sharing of rewards or as controls over actions of one of the contracting parties. The most ambitious interpretation is that financial reports should be useful in serving social welfare objectives. Standards for financial reports, it is argued, affect the interests of different people in different ways. Conflicts between these interests should be resolved in a manner consistent with social welfare.

- The problem for those who set accounting standards is to link these various objectives with specific standards for financial reporting. It is argued here that private sector standard-setters do not have the legitimacy to make social welfare decisions, particularly if such decisions are venturesome. Fortunately, corporations and securities legislation has already made the decision that it is in the public interest that the capital markets receive information that fairly presents the financial position and results of operations of reporting entities. This implies that financial reports must aim to faithfully present the significant economic data about a reporting entity. This goal is compatible with the goal of decision usefulness, since neutral reporting of significant figures surely seems required for usefulness. It is also not incompatible with the goal of facilitating contracting, since contracting parties are likely to want to base their agreements on data that fairly reflect the economic position and progress of the entity. The need for hard data for contracting, however, could conflict with the need for standards that leave room for judgment in reporting under conditions of uncertainty. This suggests the need for expansion of information reported to provide information on more than one basis.
- Indeed, the central problem in financial reporting is the need to reconcile the conflicting demands of faithful representation and reliability of measurement. The basic subject matter of financial reports consists of assets, liabilities, and changes in them. The essential character of assets and liabilities is that they represent *future* benefits and sacrifices. Since the future is unknowable, we cannot know with absolute certainty whether we have faithfully represented assets and liabilities. Standards designed to achieve that aim, therefore, require great judgment and are likely always to be open to some debate.

This exposition of a conceptual framework suggests that even complete agreement on the framework will not lead to perfect agreement on accounting standards addressing particular issues in financial reporting. Nevertheless, a conceptual framework can suggest directions in which reporting should move. The following represents some conclusions as to standards for recognition and measurement that might be drawn from the line of thinking set out here.

- The goal of faithful representation clearly implies that we cannot ignore an entity's commitments, even though they are unperformed. Possible treatments of executory contracts have already been discussed in chapters 6 and 26 and need not be repeated here.
- Given the fact that the essence of assets and liabilities consists of future

benefit or sacrifice and given the inevitable uncertainty about the future, standards for recognition must revolve around considerations of probability of realization of those benefits and sacrifices and considerations of measurability. General standards should focus on improving the specification of probability and measurability beyond present vague terminology such as "likely" and "remote" and "reasonably measurable." More detailed standards would then concentrate on the necessary evidence of probability and measurability in the context of individual issues.

- Even without extended consideration of problems of measurement, one may speculate that internally generated goodwill will never be measurable with sufficient precision to warrant recognition. It follows from this that the overall well-offness of an entity can never be fully reported. Consequently, a definition of income in terms of the change in well-offness over a period cannot be implemented either. Any report on entity performance must be partial, at least to some degree.
- Questions of measurability interact with questions as to the attribute to be measured—whether it is historical cost, current value in exchange, or something else. It is hard not to conclude that a current value is more relevant than a past value in a report on present financial status.[20] On the other hand, an actually experienced past acquisition cost may be subject to less difficulty in estimation. Also, comparisons of realized sales proceeds with original acquisition cost may sometimes be useful as a basis for contracting. If information is to be reported in financial statements on one basis only for each asset and liability category, trade-offs will be necessary between these considerations. However, the goal of faithful representation will be seriously compromised if current values are not reported in some fashion. Thus, if it is decided to retain cost as the primary foundation for financial reporting, estimates of current values should be provided to the extent possible, at least as supplementary information. In addition, as chapter 26 has suggested, there would be merit in adopting current market value as the standard basis for reporting assets (such as passive investments) that are both marketable and disposable without affecting the value of other assets of the entity.
- The apparent inevitability of trade-offs when only one value-attribute for each category of assets and liability is reported naturally leads to speculation whether faithful representation could be improved by expanding the extent of supplementary reporting or by alternative bases of reporting. For example, the resources in a statement of financial position might be presented on the following alternative bases:
  - A listing of only those assets that are individually disposable by the entity (thus excluding goodwill, for example) valued on the basis of the lower of historical cost (amortized where appropriate) and "value to the firm."[21]
  - A listing of those assets that are individually disposable valued at a current cash value determined on the basis of "value to the firm." Some indication of ranges of possible value would be desirable when valuations are more speculative in character.
  - A listing of all assets of the entity — the disposable assets being valued as in the basis immediately above and other assets being reported but not valued unless management is prepared to provide subjective estimates of value.

- If considerable weight is given to the need for hard data for contracting, even carrying values reported under the first alternative above may not be fully satisfactory. The chief reason for this is the variability in figures that may be reported under historical cost accounting owing to the arbitrary nature of allocations. Consideration could be given to making figures more comparable among entities by specifying standard methods and assumptions for such allocations as depreciation (i.e., specifying depreciation patterns and estimated asset lives) and pension obligations (i.e., specifying standard economic assumptions).
- Although assets and liabilities represent the basic phenomena to be reported, the utility of financial reports depends as much or more upon the explanations given for changes in assets and liabilities over a period as it does upon the report of their status at the end of a period. We are accustomed to acknowledging this under present accounting by speaking of the importance of the income statement. We ought to realize, however, that because of the impossibility of measuring goodwill, we cannot measure income under any ideal definition of that term. If we think, instead, in more mundane terms of explaining changes in reported assets and liabilities over the reporting period, we can conclude that it is not necessary to do so entirely within one statement. We might, for example, provide one statement reporting operating profit, one statement of recognized value changes, one statement of the distribution of interest, income tax, and dividends to stake-holders, and so on. Two advantages could accrue from this greater flexibility in reporting. First, the explanation of reasons for changes in assets and liabilities could be more clearly displayed. Second, the ill effects of overstressing the importance of one "bottom line" for a short period of time might be minimized. It would, however, be necessary to be careful to reconcile the several statements with the total change in equity over the reporting period, to avoid losing sight of important components of that change.

Evaluation of the normative conceptual framework

Several reasons have been advanced for the development of an explicit, agreed-upon conceptual framework. First, it can help the process of setting accounting standards if fundamental premises do not have to be thought through afresh each time a problem is considered. An agreed framework should help those making representations on a proposed standard to identify and address issues that ought to be considered. It can help the standard-setters identify where empirical research is required with respect to a particular issue. Standards arrived at that have been considered and tested against the background of an agreed framework should be consistent. A well-thought-out, agreed-upon conceptual framework should make accounting standards more defensible against politicial pressures, an increasing feature of standard-setting in recent years. Finally, an agreed-upon conceptual framework should reduce the need for detailed standards. If the conceptual logic is apparent, it may be hoped that practice will often adapt to it without the need for detailed guidance.

These are the reasons for a conceptual framework. Does it appear they can be realized? The discussion in this chapter certainly raises some doubts. The principal problem lies in the fact that we live in a world of uncertainty. It is all very well to reason that accounting is about wealth and that the essence of wealth consists of expectations of future benefit. If we cannot foresee the future, we are going to have difficulty measuring wealth. When we seek surrogate measures in terms of market prices of individual resources and obligations, we immediately shift from a goal of measuring the wealth of an entity as a whole to the lesser goal of measuring individual identifiable assets and liabilities. When we seek market prices for individual assets and liabilities, we encounter further major difficulties. These are likely to lead to yet further compromises and turn accounting more into the art of the possible rather than the implementation of a tightly reasoned logical structure. For these reasons it seems likely that difficulties in framing rules for recognition and measurement will persist; standards dealing with individual issues will to some degree be arbitrary and therefore will continue to require at least some detailed rules; and the conceptual framework will not be strong enough to prevent lobbying and political pressure.

On the other hand, this does not mean that a conceptual framework is without value. Consider the tentative conclusions on recognition and measurement issues described earlier. Undoubtedly some, perhaps many, accountants would disagree with those conclusions or at least some of them. In the past, such disagreements have emerged when particular standards for recognition or measurement were under discussion. If a disagreement has its roots in different fundamental assumptions as to the objectives of the financial report, it cannot be resolved at the level of a particular issue, and it is likely to emerge time after time as additional issues are tackled. For example, many accountants will say that a primary purpose of financial reporting is to demonstrate stewardship. Yet there can be considerable disagreement as to the precise meaning of that term. Unless we make clear to ourselves the significance of such fundamental assumptions, we shall continue to disagree. And the only way to achieve that clarification is to make the framework explicit, research it, argue about it, and interpret it in a variety of situations. Eventually, perhaps, a measure of consensus will emerge.

In the meantime, it appears that attempts to state conceptual frameworks are unlikely to result in great flashes of illumination that instantly resolve areas of controversy in financial reporting. It is only if standard-setters are prepared to take an explicit conceptual framework seriously and allow its influence to guide their resolution of individual issues that it will, little by little and from precedent to precedent, gain in power and utility.

References

[1]Significant examples of attempts to build conceptual frameworks that describe and explain practice include W.A. Paton and A.C. Littleton, *An Introduction to Corporate Accounting Standards*, Monograph No. 3 (AAA, 1940); *Accounting and Reporting Standards for Corporate Financial Statements and Preceding Statements and Supplements* (AAA, 1957); P. Grady, *Inventory of Generally Accepted Accounting Principles for Business Enterprises*, Accountng Research Study No. 7 (New York: AICPA, 1965); AICPA, APB, *Basic Concepts and Accounting Principles Underlying Financial Statements of Business Enterprises*, APB Statement No. 4 (New York: AICPA, 1970); and R.M. Skinner, *Accounting Principles: A Canadian Viewpoint* (Toronto: CICA, 1972).

[2]Examples of attempts to propound this type of conceptual framework or elements of it include the AICPA Accounting Research Studies Nos. 1 and 3: M. Moonitz, *The Basic Postulates of Accounting* (New York: AICPA, 1961), and R.T. Sprouse and M. Moonitz, *A*

Tentative Set of Broad Accounting Principles for Business Enterprises (New York: AICPA, 1962); *A Statement of Basic Accounting Theory* (AAA, 1966); W.J. Kenley and G.J. Staubus, *Objectives and Concepts of Financial Statements* (Melbourne: Accounting Research Foundation, 1972); *Objectives of Financial Statements*, vol. 1 (New York: AICPA, 1973); *The Corporate Report* (London: Accounting Standards Steering Committee, 1975); *Corporate Reporting: Its Future Evolution* (Toronto: CICA, 1980); and the six Statements of Financial Accounting Concepts published by the FASB from 1978 to 1985. Some of the proposals for changes in accounting to better reflect the impact of changing prices also effectively represent normative conceptual frameworks, although their authors pay relatively less attention to discussion of objectives and premises and relatively more to the practical working out of their proposals. See especially the works by Chambers, Edwards and Bell, and Sterling cited in the bibliography for chapters 29 and 30.

[3]For a thorough review of the research and arguments supporting this point of view, see E.R. Brownlee, II and S.D. Young, "Financial Disclosure Regulations and Its Critics," *Journal of Accounting Education*, Spring 1986, pp. 113-26.

[4]See R.L. Watts and J.L. Zimmerman, "The Demand For and Supply Of Accounting Theories: The Market for Excuses," *The Accounting Review*, April 1979, pp. 273-305. A criticism of the research and interpretation in this article may be found in C. Christenson, "The Methodology of Positive Accounting," *The Accounting Review*, January 1983, pp. 1-22.

[5]See R. Macve, *A Conceptual Framework for Financial Accounting and Reporting: The Possibilities for an Agreed Structure* (London: Institute of Chartered Accountants in England and Wales, 1981).

[6]See *Corporate Reporting: Its Future Evolution*, especially pp. 85-96.

[7]For an exchange of views on this subject, see M.E. Francis, "Accounting and the Evaluation of Social Programs: A Critical Comment," *The Accounting Review*, April 1973, pp. 245-57; T.W. McRae, "Social Auditing Questioned," *Journal of Accountancy*, December 1973, pp. 92-94; M.H. Granof and C.H. Smith, "Accounting and the Evaluation of Social Programs: A Comment" and E.L. Sobel and M.E. Francis, "Accounting and the Evaluation of Social Programs: A Reply," *The Accounting Review*, October 1974, pp. 822-25 and pp. 826-30, respectively; and A.L. Thomas, "Evaluating the Effectiveness of Social Programs," *Journal of Accountancy*, June 1976, pp. 65-71.

[8]Confusion on this point led the author of the Canadian study *Corporate Reporting: Its Future Evolution* to criticize the FASB definition of an asset on the grounds that it did not specify whether something must be severable to be deemed an asset or the level of aggregation of separate items that are to be considered an asset. See pars. 53 to 59 in chap. 9 of this study.

[9]It will be remembered that we have confined our attention to the accounting tradition in English-speaking countries. Government regulation of accounting activity both occurred earlier and is more pervasive in some European countries.

[10]See P. Rosenfield, "Stewardship," in *Objectives of Financial Statements*, vol. 2, ed. H. Cramer, Jr. and G.H. Sorter (New York: AICPA, 1974), pp. 123-40.

[11]For a lucid exposition of the argument, see J.E. Boritz, "Accounting Standard Setting: From Plato to Robin Hood," *CAmagazine*, June 1982, pp. 30-36. See also "Report of the Committee on Concepts and Standards for External Financial Reports," *The Accounting Review*, Supplement 1975, pp. 41-49, and R.G. May and G.L. Sundem, "Research for Accounting Policy: An Overview," *The Accounting Review*, October 1976, pp. 747-63.

[12]See, for example, J.S. Demski, "The General Impossibility of Normative Accounting Standards," *The Accounting Review*, October 1973, pp. 718-23, and May and Sundem, "Research for Accounting Policy."

[13]For readable expositions of this point of view, see C. Robb and C. Robinson, "Theories of Standard Setting: The Simplest is Best," *CAmagazine*, April 1983, pp. 22-29, and J.E. Butterworth, M. Gibbins, and R.D. King, "The Structure of Accounting Theory: Some Basic

Conceptual and Methodological Issues," in *Research to Support Standard Setting in Financial Accounting: A Canadian Perspective,* ed. S. Basu and J.A. Milburn (Toronto: Clarkson Gordon Foundation, 1982), pp. 2-65.

[14]For a criticism of this approach, see N. Dopuch and S. Sunder, "FASB's Statements on Objectives and Elements of Financial Accounting: A Review," *The Accounting Review,* January 1980, pp. 1-21.

[15]For a fuller discussion of the decision-making process, see G.J. Staubus, *Making Accounting Decisions* (Houston: Scholars Book Co., 1977), pp. 82-85, and R.R. Sterling, *Toward a Science of Accounting* (Houston: Scholars Book Co., 1979), pp. 95-98.

[16]All this is rather oversimplified. For a more careful analysis of the adoption of predictive ability as the practical criterion for decision usefulness, see B. Carsberg, J. Arnold, and A. Hope, "Predictive Value: A Criterion for Choice of Accounting Method," in *Studies in Accounting,* 3rd. ed., ed. W.T. Baxter and S. Davidson (London: Institute of Chartered Accountants in England and Wales, 1977), pp. 403-23.

[17]See K.V. Peasnell, "Statement of Accounting Theory and Theory Acceptance: A Review Article," *Accounting and Business Research,* Summer 1978, pp. 217-25.

[18]See S.A. Zeff, "The Rise of 'Economic Consequences,'" *Journal of Accountancy,* December 1978, pp. 56-63.

[19]The arguments here could not be better expressed than they are in FASB, *Qualitative Characteristics of Accounting Information,* Statement of Financial Accounting Concepts No. 2 (Stamford: FASB, 1980), pars. 98-110.

[20]An interesting progression of ideas is provided in three stimulating articles by G.J. Staubus. In the first, "The Measurement of Assets and Liabilities," *Accounting and Business Research,* Autumn 1973, pp. 243-62, Staubus describes different types of evidence for amounts of assets and liabilities and evaluates their utility for representing cash flow potential using the qualitative criteria for useful information. In the second, "An Induced Theory of Accounting Measurement," *The Accounting Review,* January 1985, pp. 53-75, Staubus argues that measurement methods actually in use under GAAP are crude attempts to simulate market prices. They are crude because they usually (but not always) ignore discounting of future cash flows and the substitution of current market prices for old prices. Several approaches may be taken to the simulation of market prices, and the choice of approach taken in each case appears to be influenced by the goals of stabilizing figures in the income statement, conservatism, and the flexibility provided to management to control income measurement. In the third article, "The Market Simulation Theory of Accounting Measurement," *Accounting and Business Research,* Spring 1986, pp. 117-32, Staubus extends his argument to suggest that the simulation of setting-specific market prices based on principles of market economics should be adopted as a goal.

[21]For discussion of this idea, see FASB, *Conceptual Framework for Financial Accounting and Reporting: Elements of Financial Statements and Their Measurement,* Discussion Memorandum (Stamford: FASB, 1976), pp. 69-75.

Chapter Thirty-Two

The Establishment of Accounting Standards

We began this book with a description of the emergence of the financial reporting function in the nineteenth and twentieth centuries. We described how financial reporting is carried out today using the historical cost accounting model as a framework and delved into the many issues encountered in applying that model. We considered possible alternatives that might capture the economic effects of changing prices more effectively than does historical cost accounting and chronicled the failure of any one model to gain sufficient support to date to supplant it. In the immediately preceding chapter, we considered the possibility of a generalized approach to thinking about financial reporting that could provide a framework within which we could seek solutions to individual financial reporting issues.

It has been evident through this history that any but the most simple financial report — that is, any but one that is confined to reporting cash received and paid and cash balances — involves difficult choices. It must be decided what is the reporting entity, what types of resources and claims shall be reported, how they shall be measured, what forms of statements shall be presented, and what supplementary information shall be provided. The history of financial reporting for the last two centuries is the history of the evolution of ways of making these choices and of the standardization of financial reporting practices, at first through custom and increasingly over time through a formal standard-setting process. In this chapter we concentrate on that process.

Parties interested in financial reporting

Let us begin our inquiry by considering who is interested in or affected by financial reporting. Since financial reporting is a communication process, there are obviously two major interested parties or groups — those whose responsibility it is to prepare the financial reports and those who use them directly or indirectly. A third party at interest is added when auditors are given a responsibility by law or contract to attest to the fairness of the information communicated.

The degree of homogeneity of these groups varies. Auditors constitute a relatively homogeneous group, sharing a common training and discipline. Financial statement preparers have somewhat less in common. The financial reports they prepare may be for a business organization, a nonbusiness organization, or a government. There are wide variations in risk among various industries that furnish financial reports. Even within one industry, there may be sharp differences in viewpoint between a well-established successful company and a new enterprise that is pressing on the limits of its financial resources.

The third group — the users — is even less well defined. Some providers of capital may be able to exercise significant influence on financial reports as a condition of providing capital. Others with a financial stake in the enterprise may be in a much weaker position, being entitled to only as much financial information as the law requires. Still others may have no rights to receive financial information directly but may yet have some interest in the financial health of an entity because they are employees or potential investors or creditors. We may note also a distinction between those users who have a direct financial interest in an entity in their capacity as suppliers of debt or equity capital and those whose interest is indirect, such as financial analysts or agencies that gather, collate, and publish statistical information. In spite of this considerable diversity in the composition of parties interested in financial reporting, it may be useful to make some generalizations that have some significance for the activity of standard-setters.

Preparers of financial statements. The managements of reporting entities have an interest in providing sufficient information to reassure those who provide resources needed by the enterprise. Thus, we would expect to find financial reporting of some sort, even in the absence of standards for reporting.

It is important to ask whether the preparers' self-interest in rendering financial reports is sufficient to result in satisfactory reports without outside intervention or the imposition of standards.[1] There are reasons to believe that it is not. So long as people save, they will wish to invest for a return somewhere. Even in the absence of good financial information, investment in business enterprises will be attractive so long as the return offered is higher on average than that in other, perhaps less risky investments (such as government bonds) and so long as a desirable measure of liquidity is offered (such as is provided through the operation of stock markets). In addition, investors may minimize risk by diversification of their portfolios. As a result, investors are probably willing to accept a less than optimal degree of information (from the standpoint of the most efficient allocation of their resources) rather than forgo investing in corporate enterprises altogether. In these circumstances, the power of individual users to bargain for desired information is quite small.

Of course, highly successful enterprises have some incentive to encourage full disclosure because efficient capital markets should reward them with a lower cost of capital relative to their less successful brethren. One might think, then, that competition for capital would tend to force all enterprises to match the standards of the more successful. On the other hand, even successful enterprises have some reasons to limit disclosure. Too much flaunting of success may attract competition and possibly unwelcome attention from government regulatory agencies. Also, it is commonly thought that a smooth record of progress is preferable to the ups and downs of normal business, so that even the managements of successful companies have some incentive to retain flexibility in financial reporting — which effectively means something less than full and unbiased reporting of events as they occur. Managements are also judged (sometimes unfairly) on results shown by financial reports in the short term. It is, therefore, quite natural for them to wish to retain some degree of control over how information is reported.

It must also be remembered that financial reporting is not without cost. External reporting of information that is routinely available from the accounting records or that is developed for purposes of internal reports to management does not entail significant incremental cost. Going beyond this may do so. This fact may help to explain the frequent emphasis by managements on cash-oriented information and managements' resistance to standards that require additional computations or valuations such as those involving tax allocation accounting, lease capitalization, and reporting the effects of changing prices.

In the final result, it is observable that those responsible for financial reports generally desire that accounting standards be flexible and be stated in general terms, leaving considerable scope for judgment in the precise method of application of the general principles.[2] Typically, management will argue that this approach is necessary to avoid a stultifying uniformity in financial reports that is not responsive to real differences in circumstances.

Users of financial reports. Users of financial reports are so diverse that it is difficult to make general statements as to their preferences. Only financial analysts are vocal on accounting matters, and their interests may not necessarily coincide with those of users in general. Financial analysts have an interest in accounting methods that are consistent from one company to another since such a condition greatly facilitates their work of analysis.[3] They also tend to prefer accounting standards based on hard figures even though that may create a significant conservative bias (and occasionally bias in the other direction). They tend to be suspicious of financial information based on management judgment as to future economic benefits and sacrifices. Although financial analysts are often critical of accounting standards, experience shows that it is relatively difficult to obtain significant participation and assistance from them in the process of establishing standards.

Auditors. Auditors stand between the preparers and users of financial reports. They are charged with the responsibility of attesting to the fair presentation of financial statements. It is in their self-interest that the financial statements be fairly presented and be seen to be so presented, because otherwise their attestation loses credibility. But they can face great difficulties in achieving this objective. In the first place, there is the inevitable uncertainty in business affairs. Things may turn out to be worse (or better) than has been expected. Second, there is the difficulty of judging what is fair presentation when well-established practice does not clearly cover a particular situation. Third, there is the fact that the audit appointment is usually greatly influenced by management even when it is nominally made by the shareholders.[4]

The auditor is thus subject to contradictory forces. A well-understood conceptual framework for financial reporting and well-recognized broad principles of application are clearly in the self-interest of auditors. Some auditors are inclined to stop there, trusting to professional judgment to arrive at reasonable solutions to particular reporting problems that may arise in the ordinary course. Other auditors feel a need for a much more detailed formulation of accounting standards in view of the possibilities for differences of opinion on complex issues and the consequent inevitability of inconsistent practice without rigorously defined rules of application.

These remarks are not intended to be critical. The opinions held by various parties interested in or affected by financial reporting stem naturally from the positions in which they find themselves. But certain conclusions follow that are pertinent to the process of establishing accounting standards. First, there will be many situations in which a generally accepted accounting treatment will not emerge by consensus. It is not even to be expected that preparers as a group — auditors or users — will be unanimous as to the preferable treatment. Second, it is not to be expected that a requirement to have an audit will result in a satisfactory degree of consistency among entities in their methods of financial reporting. In the absence of a high degree of underlying consensus, auditors will be unable to discriminate between acceptable and unacceptable practice within quite a wide range. Third, for competitive reasons, bad accounting practices will tend to drive out good ones among companies dependent on the public capital markets. Managements of companies are unlikely to report lower earnings than they might, if they feel that their performances will be in any way judged by the reported results.

The ultimate conclusion is that voluntary accounting standards are an unrealizable dream. Standards must be backed up by some authority. In the remainder of this chapter we shall explore various models for standard-setting, the goals to be sought in accounting standards, the nature of effective standards, the content desirable in a standard, the process of establishing standards, and certain collateral matters.

Models for standard-setting

In this section we consider possible mechanisms for arriving at financial accounting standards. This involves consideration of who should be entrusted with the responsibility for setting standards and the ultimate source of legitimacy for the standards.

Free-market standards. We have already suggested that voluntary standards will not prove satisfactory. For the sake of completeness, however, let us consider how voluntary standards would be arrived at. This is, in fact, the situation that prevailed up until the 1930s in the United States and until still later in other English-speaking countries.

The foundation of recognized standards would be practice. Preparers of financial statements would be influenced in their choice of accounting method by observation of what other reporting entities were doing. Guidance would also be provided by textbooks on accounting theory and discussions in professional journals. The law might require that financial statements be "fairly presented" or give "a true and fair view." If not required by law, an assertion of fairness could be inferred from the very fact that a financial report is published. (To deliberately publish a misleading financial report could be considered fraud.) It would be believed that (1) the overriding requirement of fairness, (2) the power of precedent, and (3) the guidance given in accounting literature by authorities on the subject would combine to produce a consensus or "general acceptance" as to best method of accounting in given circumstances.

While it would be believed that the vast majority of enterprises would publish fair financial reports, a control over misleading reporting would exist through the medium of the audit. The auditor would be guided by the same understanding of theory and accepted practice as management. If the auditor were unable to issue an unqualified report, the financial statement reader would be made aware of possible questions concerning the integrity of management representations.

Associations of auditors might stimulate the process of general acceptance by providing studies of difficult questions and publishing recommendations as to the best practice. Although these recommendations would not be mandatory, their publication would be a step in the direction of imposed standards, since auditors generally would be under some pressure to form their opinions having regard to these authoritative independent views.

Certain advantages can be claimed for this model.

- Management would have considerable latitude for selecting accounting methods it considered best suited to its circumstances. Accordingly, there would be little likelihood that management would be forced to use different methods for external reporting than those it considered best for internal management reporting. In this way, accounting costs would be minimized.
- Enterprises would be free to experiment with new methods of accounting in new or changed economic circumstances. General acceptance would not become an inhibiting factor until such time as it became apparent that other entities did not consider the innovative accounting to be appropriate.

On the other hand, experience has shown serious problems with this model.

- Accounting theory has not provided unequivocal guidance to the resolution of a large number of important issues. Relatively straightforward examples of this lack include the issues of accounting for the investment tax credit and for the effect that timing differences have on income tax expense.
- General acceptance has not emerged to compensate for the lack of persuasive theory. The result has been continuance of conflicting accounting practices among entities when there are no obvious differences in economic circumstances to justify the different accounting.
- Even when accounting measurements are not in dispute, the degree of disclosure can vary, with substantial impact on the significance of the financial statements. The strong resistance encountered from time to time to proposals for disclosure of important information (such as the resistance over several decades to disclosure of sales) suggests that optimal financial reporting is unlikely to be achieved when responsibility is left solely in the hands of statement preparers.
- It also seems clear from experience that, in the presence of wide diversity in generally accepted practice and the absence of mandatory standards, the auditor has little ability to impose improved accounting methods and disclosure upon clients.

Government-mandated standards. At the other extreme lies the possibility that accounting standards might be, in effect, legislated by a government or a government agency. This would be in dramatic contrast to the situation in which accounting standards are controlled largely by those who have the obligation to report. A simple line of argument could be proposed in favour of such a shift. The reason for government interference in the first place would be the belief that fair financial disclosure is in the public interest (for reasons such as promotion of efficiency of the capital markets or the importance of reliable financial information for public policy). It would be further believed that adequate financial reporting would not be achieved by placing on managements the responsibility for reporting on their own performances, subject to the concurrence of auditors who subsist on fees from the preparers of the statements.

The chief advantage of government-mandated standards would lie in their enforceability. If a particular standard or its application were ambigious, it presumably would be possible to obtain an authoritative interpretation. The possible objections to government-established standards include the following:

- While a government would be independent of excessive influence from financial statement preparers, it might be overly open to pressures from other sources. The government itself might wish to bias accounting standards to attain certain ends. Such efforts have been made in the past and would be more likely to be made if standards were set by a government agency rather than a professional body. If the agency were to set standards for financial reporting by governments themselves, the possibility of political pressure would be even greater. To avoid these pressures, it would be necessary to give a governmental standard-setting agency the sort of independence that is granted to such bodies as the Bank of Canada, Statistics Canada, or the Auditor General of Canada.

- There would be considerable danger that the standard-setting function would be underfunded and, as a result, would fail to command the best talents available. The status and independence of the agency would be factors in determining the importance of this difficulty.
- In maintaining independence from pressures from the private sector, the staff of a government agency might tend to become cut off from first-hand experience with accounting issues, thereby losing some degree of competence.
- A bureaucratic organization might fail to be sufficiently sensitive to the costs associated with its reporting requirements and to the possibility that costs might exceed benefits.
- A bureaucratic organization might tend to protect itself through the adoption of rigid rules, thereby limiting innovation and the exercise of judgment. It might also be reluctant to change a position once taken and might leave rules outstanding that have outlived their usefulness.

These objections are possible but not inevitable, especially if a conscious effort were made to guard against them. In Canada, however, there appears little support for the setting of accounting standards by government at the time of writing. A cost to the government would be involved that is now borne by the private sector. In addition, if the responsibility for standard-setting were split among the provinces, as is securities administration at this time, the danger of underfunding and its attendant evils would be greatly multiplied.

Mixed government/private-sector standards. Various compromises are feasible by which responsibility for establishing accounting standards might be shared by the government and the private sector. One such compromise is found in the United States. The Securities and Exchange Commission is empowered by law to establish accounting standards for companies whose securities are publicly traded. It has never exercised that power to the full. It has directly established standards for disclosure in financial statements required to be filed with it. But, by and large, it has relied upon the private sector — first the accounting profession and latterly the FASB— to establish standards for accounting measurement. The distinction between disclosure and measurement does not have a great deal of intrinsic logic since both are necessary for fair presentation of financial information. Neither is the distinction inviolable in practice. The SEC not infrequently has provided its interpretation of what accounting measurements ought to be or has indicated that it does not support standards for measurement arrived at in the private sector.

There are practical advantages to this sharing of responsibility. The SEC is relieved of a great deal of cost and gains access to a great deal of expertise through its reliance upon the private sector. For its part, the private sector is able to feel that accounting standards are, for the most part, set in a forum in which the interests of all are represented, rather than being handed down by fiat from an autocratic authority.

There are also disadvantages. Chief among these is the fragility of the arrangement. Because the APB was the creature of the accounting profession, it had a solid basis of financial support. The FASB, in contrast, is nominally independent. That means it must obtain its funding from parties interested in financial reporting. Effectively, its efforts must satisfy most contributing parties most of the time. In view of the substantial differences of opinion possible over accounting standards, that is not easy to do. Indeed, one suspects that it is only by persistent reference to the need to retain standard-setting in the private sector that support is maintained. Moreover, the board's efforts can be undermined in other ways. Those dissatisfied with standards or proposed standards are sometimes able to lobby the SEC or U.S. Congress for relief — a process that is inordinately harmful to orderly standard-setting. The result has been excessive politicization of the United States process for establishing accounting standards.

Private-sector standards. In several countries, a private-sector standard-setting body has evolved out of efforts by the accounting profession to encourage good reporting. The difference between standards set by such bodies and those described earlier as voluntary or free-market standards lies solely in the greater authority of the standard-setting bodies. The development can be a gradual one, as epitomized by the Canadian experience.

Early Canadian accounting recommendations purported to be no more than guides to good practice. Unless a recommendation became accepted as the sole accounting method to fit the circumstances or auditors were persuaded that they should qualify their reports unless the recommended method were used, a recommendation might have little practical influence. Chapter 4 has recounted how that condition gradually changed. The most notable event was the adoption of National Policy No. 27 by Canadian security administrators in 1972. Under that policy and subsequently under corporations legislation of the federal and several provincial governments, the term "generally accepted accounting principles" was interpreted to mean the recommendations in the *CICA Handbook*. The recommendations thereby became accounting standards required by law for most corporate financial reports.

The resulting position cannot be described simply as a state in which accounting standards are set in the private sector, since the support rendered by the governmental recognition is an essential element. Nevertheless, the formulation of the standards themselves has remained the prerogative of a private-sector institution — the CICA. There are several advantages to this situation. Standards are established without cost to the government. Standards are largely free from political interference. The CICA has ready access through its membership to the advice and service of volunteers with a wide range of experience in financial reporting problems. A substantial budget permits funding of research and employment of staff, although there is always a question whether resources are sufficient to meet needs.

This historical development in Canada has occurred without a great deal of conscious thought as to its implications. In their early days, the membership of provincial institutes of chartered accountants and of the CICA consisted largely of *public* accountants. The institutes were formed to create qualifying standards for service to the public and to promote recognition of the special skills of their members. There was a strong tendency to equate accounting as a profession with public accountancy. (Members who took employment with a company sometimes described themselves as "leaving the profession.") It was natural for an association largely composed of auditors, much of whose work lay in giving opinions on fair presentation of financial statements, to be especially concerned with criteria for fair reporting. And it was well within the rights of the members to consult together and provide recommendations or even rules binding on the membership as to the terms upon which members should be prepared to express unqualified opinions on financial statements presented to them for audit.

The auditor's role in financial reporting is to add credibility to the information conveyed in financial statements. In so doing, the auditor stands between the statement preparer and the statement user and must have regard to the interests of both. Since the user is in the weaker position by virtue of not having access to the detailed accounting records, the natural tendency for the auditor is to represent the user. When the auditor deals with the management of his client directly, the possibility of pressing the user viewpoint vigorously is limited by the fact that the auditor has a practical need to retain the goodwill of the management. When auditors act together through their professional association, however, a better balance is possible. It is arguable that a strong motivation behind the formation of professional committees to make recommendations on financial reporting questions was the desire of auditors to find some way to counterbalance preparer control of financial reports and the resulting potential bias.

To the extent that standard-setting is controlled by auditors, one needs to ask what bias they are likely to have on their own account. It has been suggested that their responsibility to report on fair presentation must predispose them to look at matters through the eyes of users. On the other hand, the fact that they have greater contact with preparers than with users almost certainly makes them sensitive to the preparers' point of view. Their own situation leads to a possible bias — that is, a bias toward hard data, conservatism, and uniform reporting methods, since all these reduce the risk in giving an audit opinion. Fortunately, as we have seen, that bias is not inconsistent with preferences often expressed by users and may be a worthwhile counterpoise to the overoptimism, deliberate or otherwise, of some issuers of financial statements.

On balance, recommendations made in the *CICA Handbook*, largely upon the initiative of auditors, have been both progressive and reasonably evenhanded in reflecting the views and needs of both statement preparers and users. It is this fact that justified securities administrators and legislators in giving special place to the *Handbook* in the scheme of regulation of financial reporting. But such reliance implies that it must be acknowledged by the CICA and its membership that the standard-setting function entrusted to it is in the public interest. That means that the function must be performed efficiently. It also means that the self-interest of members must be subordinated should it conflict with the public interest in standard-setting.

One question that could be raised is whether it is legitimate to entrust a public function — standard-setting — to a private body. That question is capable of becoming more troublesome than it has been in the past. In Canada, in some contrast to the United States, a high percentage of accountants and financial managers business and government have obtained their CA qualifications before entering employment. Happily, they have valued their CA designations sufficiently to retain their memberships. The presence of chartered accountants among senior financial managements of reporting entities has helped to retain support for standards set by the CICA. Such support might be more difficult to achieve if it were a body dominated by auditors, as is the AICPA in the United States.

This position in Canada is changing and seems likely to continue to change. It seems probable that in future a higher proportion of financial executives will reach their positions without first qualifying as CAs. In addition, there are other accounting associations in Canada that have their own qualifying requirements and that regard their members as professionals, even though they may have had no experience in public practice. It is possible for such accountants to feel that they are unreasonably excluded from the standard-setting process. Sensitivity to these concerns has led the CICA to reserve some positions on its Accounting Standards Committee for nominees of other bodies, including representatives of users and government as well as other accounting associations. An Accounting Research Advisory Board, composed mainly of nonaccountants, also provides advice on the committee's agenda and other matters. These moves have not fully satisfied other accounting associations.[5]

There is some danger that recognition of accounting standard-setting as a public-interest function will lead to the notion that different parties interested in financial reporting are entitled to have their interests "represented" in some sort of voting procedure. Nothing could be more mistaken. Standard-setting in the public interest should be performed by disinterested (unbiased) parties, not interested parties. Ideally, the standard-setter should be able to separate himself or herself from the point of view of a statement preparer, auditor, or statement user. One test the standard-setter could apply would be to ask: If I did not know whether I would subsequently be in the position of a preparer, user, or auditor of financial statements, what standard would I consider appropriate in this situation?

Competent standard-setting requires ability and a variety of experience. Because of this, it makes sense to ask a variety of organizations to nominate "representatives." But representatives, as just indicated, should be chosen for the wisdom they can bring to the standard-setting process, not as representatives sent to bargain for a particular point of view.

A final question concerns who should cover the cost of standard-setting. Even with a substantial amount of voluntary effort, establishing accounting standards in a modern economy is costly. Research, staff support, and extensive exposure of the process to the views of interested parties is required. The membership of the CICA bears the whole cost of this work now. This is an historical accident. As has been noted, accounting standards are of direct assistance to auditors. Thus, when the CICA was dominated by auditors, it was entirely natural to devote some of its resources to encouragement of improvements in financial reporting. Governmental reliance on CICA efforts represents a form of free ride that continues to be possible only so long as the membership continues to consider the burden worthwhile. With a steady or increasing demand for accounting standards in an ever more complex economy and the declining percentage of auditors in the membership (who have the greatest stake in good accounting standards), it is conceivable that the membership at large could become unwilling to continue to bear the entire cost of what needs to be done. Such a condition would call for reconsideration of the place of the standard-setting function within the CICA or even within the private sector.[6]

Conclusion. The foregoing does not suggest hard-and-fast conclusions as to the best model for developing accounting standards. Each possible model has some advantages and some problems or possible problems. Certain generalizations can be made, however, concerning prerequisites for successful standard-setting.

- There must some external medium to encourage or require reporting entities to observe the standards. Audit qualifications by themselves do not appear to be adequate for this purpose. Legal support is much the most effective means.
- Standard-setting is costly in both money and effort. It can be accomplished within the accounting profession provided the profession has enough cohesiveness. The danger is that those who are not members of the profession or of the particular standard-setting body may feel excluded and be tempted to undermine that body.
- An independent foundation for research and standard-setting could also work. Funding the activity would be more difficult in such a situation. The need to satisfy all parties, especially those counted on for financial support, carries with it some danger of greater politicization of standard-setting.

On balance, the Canadian model in which standards are developed by the profession and supported by governmental authority has worked well, without some of the stress and controversy experienced in other countries. It is not clear, however, how long this model can continue without some modification of present arrangements. Standard-setting has become more difficult as its scope has widened and the complexity of business, finance, and the economic environment has increased. There is a question whether volunteers can spend the time to become sufficiently familiar with all aspects of these complex issues. There is a need for more and more expert staff and increased research support. There is a question whether a body such as the CICA will be willing to continue to bear the increasing burden of doing what needs to be done. This, together with political pressures for a more widely representative standard-setting body, could force a change, perhaps in the direction of the FASB model or perhaps in the direction of an agency funded, or partially funded, by government.

Goals of standard-setting

The primary goal of standard-setting is to facilitate achievement of the goals of financial reporting. These were discussed in the previous chapter. There it was suggested that faithful representation of real economic phenomena and events in a cost-effective manner provides the most satisfactory goal for financial reporting in the present state of accounting theory. Also discussed in chapter 31 was the more ambitious goal of promotion of social welfare. Some advocates of that goal consider that it has important implications for standard-setting. Some further discussion is therefore in order at this point.

The argument runs as follows. An accounting standard will probably favour some parties in society and harm the interests of others. Therefore the imposition of a standard is, in effect, a social choice. One of two possible conclusions follows from this.

- Standards should be consciously selected so as to promote social welfare. It is not very clear how this should be done. One possibility is that the probable effects of an accounting standard should be compared with national policies to see whether they are compatible. (Thus the United States accounting profession's preference for a standard treatment of the investment tax credit was frustrated by the supposed incompatibility of that treatment with the stimulative effect intended by the government in creating the investment tax credit.) A less directive conclusion might be that accounting standards should be appraised in terms of their probable economic consequences. This, however, merely leads to more questions. Since an important purpose of accounting is to give assistance in decision making, an effective standard ought to be expected to have economic consequences. The real question is whether the consequences are good or bad. That is a value judgment that few are qualified to make. Moreover, one should be skeptical of one's ability to truly assess economic consequences. Immediate consequences may be capable of being perceived, but secondary effects usually are not. In general, it appears that judging specific accounting standards by a social welfare criterion is likely to be impossible or completely lacking in objectivity. If it were possible, however, a serious question would be posed as to the legitimacy of any non-elected standard-setting body.[7]

- The other conclusion drawn from the social choice line of thinking is that standard-setting should be a political process. Those interested in or affected by proposed standards would lobby for their own interests. Standard-setters would be expected to find some accommodation that all could accept. The test of a good standard would not lie primarily in its relevance to users or its faithful portrayal of economic events but simply in the fact that it facilitated orderly reporting. It is not hard to see that under this philosophy the wishes of organized forces with money behind them would prevail.

In the author's opinion, acceptance of the conclusions from either of these two lines of thinking would be disastrous. Nothing could undermine the credibility of financial reporting among users more than knowledge that the amount of information released in financial reports has been determined by political horse trading or that the information itself may have been biased by standard-setters' opinions as to what is good for people to know. Rather, accounting standards must be neutral to be believable.[8]

To say that accounting standards should not be politically motivated is far from saying that standard-setters should not be aware of political influence. On the contrary, standard-setters must be concerned with what has been called "the marketing of accounting standards." No matter how competently standards have been drawn up, there are bound to be those who disagree with them. If standard-setters do not explain the standards sufficiently to make them defensible against attack and make sure that supporters of the standards as well as detractors are heard from, there is danger that particular standards or the standard-setting authority itself may be upset.

Various means are available to build support for particular accounting standards or the standard-setting body.

- A persuasive conceptual framework with which individual standards can be shown to be consistent would be extremely valuable. Unfortunately, as chapter 31 has indicated, efforts to produce a conceptual framework capable of providing strong support to individual standards have, to date, been disappointing.
- Thorough research of all aspects of an issue and publication of the results help prepare the way for a standard. Research studies sponsored by standard-setting bodies have facilitated some standards, but much more

could be done. In particular, there is a need for exploration of the possible significance of other disciplines to accounting. For example, could economic theory concerning currency exchange rates have helped the accounting standard on foreign currency transactions and translation? Can finance theory dealing with evaluation of options help accounting measurements related to risk bearing? Can research in human information processing help in questions relating to the display of financial information? The challenge is both to make clear the practical application to accounting standards of such theory and research and to make that application known to those responsible for accounting standards.

- Standards should be issued only after "due process" allowing ample opportunity for interested parties to submit their views. (A subsequent section will discuss the standard-setting process.)
- The reasoning underlying standards arrived at and the reasons for rejecting major alternatives should be explained as clearly and incisively as possible. On those occasions when a standard prescribes some degree of arbitrariness in measurement in the interest of greater comparability, that should be frankly admitted. Where a standard requires complicated procedures unfamiliar to present practice, illustrations should be provided. Briefings and educational seminars may also be necessary.

The standard-setting body should also consider to what extent standards can be framed to minimize problems in implementation without impairing their effectiveness. The nature of the standards themselves is discussed in the next section.

The nature of accounting standards

The word "standard" can be used in several senses. In one meaning it refers to agreed-upon or legislated units of measure or specifications which, when applied to describe an object, provide assurance that it is what it is represented to be. Thus, because a standard description has been provided for a kilogram and a metre, we can know what we are getting when we buy something measured in one of those units. Or if we buy some piece of mechanical equipment approved by a standards association, we are provided with some assurance that it will perform in accordance with the specifications (or standards) of that association. In a similar way, the purpose of accounting standards is to provide the reader of a financial report with some assurance as to the significance and reliability of the information conveyed in the financial statements. Unfortunately, because of the uncertainty inherent in economic affairs, it is much more difficult to create effective accounting standards than it is to define physical measurement standards or standards of physical performance.

Accounting standards and professional judgment. In the presence of uncertainty, the application of judgment is inevitable. But since accounting standards are intended to minimize uncertainty in accounting presentation, there must be a question where the boundary lies between those matters that are best covered by a standard and those that are best left to professional judgment. Surprisingly little is found in accounting literature on this point.

We may begin by observing that every accounting standard is a substitute for individual opinion or judgment. That is the point of having a standard. It is to get away from a chaotic situation in which each person's opinion is as good as the next person's. It is an attempt to substitute the *collective* judgment of the standard-setters (who, it is to be hoped, will reflect the best thinking and evidence available) for that of individuals. The key question is: When should a collective judgment be embodied in a standard and when should the matter in question best be left to the judgment of preparers and auditors?

To cast light upon this and related questions, let us digress to consider possible applications of judgment in financial reporting.

- We talk in accounting about "measurement." As we use the term, measurement can rest upon factual information such as original cost or a current market quotation or upon an estimate involving the future such as that of an asset's economic life. Estimates are inherently a matter of judgment. Ordinarily a judgment estimate is highly dependent upon the facts of the situation in which it is made. There is a very strong case that situation-specific estimates should be left to the individual judgment of preparers and their auditors. There may, however, be exceptions. For example, suppose it were observed that, within a particular industry, estimates of useful lives of similar depreciable assets varied quite widely. Suppose, also, that investigation revealed little or no evidence of differences in circumstances justifying the differences in estimates. The varying estimates simply reflected varying degrees of optimism on the part of those making the estimates. In such a case, it would not be unreasonable for standard-setters to demand that individual estimates be based on better evidence or, failing that, that some consensus or average estimate be used.
- Often accounting standards call for action based on such words as "likely," "reasonably estimable," "adequate," or "significant." These words imply that an estimation judgment is to be made. They also require an additional judgment, however. The preparer or auditor must come to a conclusion as to what the words themselves mean before they can be applied. The requirement for the latter type of judgment is questionable. Statement preparers and auditors are not experts in semantics. Every effort should be made in accounting standards to avoid the necessity for readers to guess at the meaning of words. In practice, this suggests that the estimates called for should be described in more concrete, quantitative terms.
- Standards often use words such as "material," "understandable," "meaningful," or "self-evident." These words usually refer to user reactions to information supplied. When the words are used, they typically require the statement preparer and auditor to form a judgment as to possible user reaction. Since human behaviour is often situation-specific, it seems reasonable to allow for some individual judgment when standards deal with communication of information. However, research into human behaviour can improve judgment in this area and probably should be emphasized more in accounting education. Research and experience may also result in conclusions that are sufficiently general to be incorporated into accounting standards.
- Occasionally a standard suggests that something be done when "practicable" or "practical." These words obviously call for an individual judgment, but the basis of such judgment is far from clear. It would usually be desirable to be more specific as to the considerations deemed to influence the judgment, such as cost/benefit tests or a test of political acceptability. Even so,

the words are capable of so wide an interpretation that they effectively make a standard optional. They should be used sparingly, if at all.

- Again, standards may use such phrases as "alternative acceptable methods," "proper accounting treatment," "most appropriate in the circumstances," or "which most fairly match revenue." Phrases such as these again ostensibly call for judgment. The judgment called for is a conclusion as to what is GAAP (for example, in the reference to "acceptable") or what is in accordance with accounting theory (for example, the references to proper accounting or to fairly matching revenue). Such calls for judgment are essentially circular. It is the function of accounting standards to indicate what is good financial reporting. To instruct that preparers or auditors should exercise judgment as to what is acceptable or fair says nothing and, in effect, negates the objective of standard-setting.

What do these examples tell us? They tell us that the primary role of accounting standards is to express a collective judgment as to the best accounting theory and its practical application. Standards for application are developed chiefly for accounting problems that can be categorized as having common characteristics. The more individual the characteristics of a problem, the less likely it is that standards, inevitably worded in general terms, can deal with it. The preeminent role of individual judgment lies in making estimates under uncertainty that are applicable in a specific situation and in that situation only. Standard-setters often signal an intention that individual judgment be used through their choice of words. While this is legitimate, care is necessary to see that the objective sought by the standard is clearly specified. There may be some temptation for standard-setters to avoid controversy by failing to make clear the objective of the standard and by using wording vague enough to admit several interpretations, under the guise of allowing individual judgment.

The allocation problem and professional judgment. Part II of this book has emphasized in a number of places that the allocation of costs to periods in which their benefit is consumed — that is, accounting recognition of expense — is arbitrary to some degree. We may say, for example, that depreciation should be systematic and rational, but we have no strong theory to tell us what is rational; neither do we have the means to measure the rational amount, even if we knew what theoretically was the best method. Professional judgment is largely inoperative in this situation. The result is variation in practice without any very visible connection to differences in circumstances. It may be argued that accounting standards should step into this void in the interests of comparable financial reporting.

Broad versus detailed standards. Often the issue of the role of professional judgment is stated in terms of making a choice between broadly stated standards — assumed to leave room for the exercise of professional judgment — and highly detailed rule making. In view of the previous discussion, this issue may be stated in more black and white terms than it should be.

Consider the most commonly cited example of detailed rule making — that is, the standard on capitalization of leases. The broad principle in that standard is that leases that are in substance purchases of assets should be capitalized. Unfortunately, such a broad standard would never have been operational. There was too much scope for variation in opinion as to what made a lease "in substance" a purchase. The standard had to provide criteria to indicate what ought to be considered an "in substance" purchase.

In the United States these criteria were expressed as hard-and-fast quantitative rules that have had to be expanded as the concept was tested. In Canada, essentially the same criteria were expressed only as aids to judgment. The result was not greatly different; the criteria tended to become rules (except that they could be bent a little). The indication is that, in a complex matter, it is difficult for standard-setters to say clearly what they intend without producing what may be taken as rules.

Standards overload. Accounting standards may be classified as standards governing the presentation of financial information and disclosure in financial statements and standards governing measurement of magnitudes portrayed in the financial statements. In recent years both measurement and disclosure standards have been issued at an increasing pace. There are several reasons.

- The course of economic events has revealed weaknesses in theories underlying accounting practices. For example, the instability in currency exchange rates since 1970 emphasized the lack of any good rationale for traditional foreign currency translation procedures.
- The course of economic events has raised new challenges to existing accounting models. The challenge of inflation in the decade of the 1970s is the preeminent example.
- Some business arrangements now common have more lasting consequences for financial position and consequences less easy to measure than did business transactions previously. Employee pension plans, with their uncertain long-term costs, represent a primary example.
- New financial instruments blur the distinction between debt and equity and provide facilities for assumption and shedding of risk that raise entirely new questions.
- Government policies have affected business arrangements, providing benefits contingent upon actions whose full costs may not be easy to measure.

These developments have inevitably meant proliferation of accounting standards. Moreover, standards issued have tended to become more complex, mirroring the complexities in the transactions and the events they have to deal with. The result has been complaints that accounting standards are imposing an increasing burden on financial statement preparers. That charge is pressed most vigorously in relation to small business. It is argued both that (1) the relative cost of complex accounting standards is greater for small business than for large because the small business may not have the skills in-house to make the computations that are necessary to implement complex standards, and (2) the benefit from complex standards is less or even nonexistent for small business because owner-managers don't understand them.

In passing, one may note that complaints tend to be directed at the standards, not the underlying conditions that give rise to them. For example, accounting standards did not cause exchange rate instability; rather they had to adjust so as to continue to provide realistic figures under the unstable conditions. A complaint concerning increased complexity in accounting standards is not logical unless the standards themselves fail to capture the essence of the economic phenomena being accounted for (as sometimes they do). Nevertheless, exasperation with accounting standards is real and very human.

Several expedients may be considered to lessen the problem associated with more complex standards. The first is to try to simplify the standards notwithstanding the more complex economic environment. The second is to introduce "differential standards" — that is, standards that are less demanding upon small entities than upon large. The third is to free some entities entirely from the requirement to provide financial reports based on recognized accounting standards. If either of the latter two solutions were attempted, of course, it would be necessary to define which entities qualified for the lightening of the burden and to rationalize the distinction.

A movement toward simplification of standards probably would mean a movement away from accrual accounting and toward cash accounting. Such a movement has some attraction in the face of uncertainty. For example, reduction of uncertainty was a motive in the standard for treatment of R&D costs. Unfortunately, in a complex economic environment such simplification tends to run counter to faithful representation of economic events. Thus there are likely to be distinct limits to such simplification, and opinions are likely to differ sharply on how far it can be carried.

Another possible form of simplification consists of reduction of the degree of disclosure required in financial reports. It might be argued that if the standards for accounting measurement are sound, there is little need for extensive disclosure as to how the measurements were made. Unfortunately again, the economic situation in which an entity finds itself often needs explanation. Also, there is so much scope for judgment in the application of accounting standards that disclosure of what has been done is necessary to facilitate user evaluation and comparison with other entities. Unless measurement procedures are standardized much more than they are currently, substantial disclosure remains necessary in the interests of faithful representation.

If the opportunities for simplification of standards are limited, what are the possibilities for differential standards — standards that are different for different classes of entity? The immediate problem with a proposal for differential standards is that of providing defensible criteria for distinguishing between different classes of reporting entity. One possible criterion could be that of size. The problem with this lies in justifying the criterion of size. Quite small entities may enter into complex transactions that require careful accounting. Also, there is no strong evidence that users of financial statements of small entities do not need the same quality of information as is required from larger entities, and the existence of differential standards might well be confusing to some users.

Another possible criterion might be based on the degree of outside interest in the entity. Thus entities that do not have publicly traded securities outstanding might be permitted to follow less onerous standards than companies with a public interest. This proposal could also be questioned on the grounds that users of the financial statements of closely held companies, if not insiders, may well have a need for information of the same quality as that provided by public companies. In addition, some would argue that the financial health and performance of large, closely held entities is of such importance to society that their financial reports should meet accepted standards for public reporting and be freely available even though a widespread ownership interest is lacking.

If a satisfactory basis for distinguishing between classes of entity were found — perhaps based upon a combination of size and public involvement — it would still be necessary to decide which standards should apply to each class of entity. It is often argued that it is reasonable that disclosure standards should be less demanding for closely held entities where financial statement users may be more familiar with the entity or may be in a better position to obtain information from management as needed. On these grounds, for example, it is felt that such entities may be released from the necessity of providing a statement of changes in financial position or supplementary information on segments of the business or on the effects of changing prices.

In contrast, some feel that there is no justification for different measurement standards between classes of entity. If, for example, the standards are well designed to measure the performance of a large entity, it is not obvious why different standards should be selected for another entity simply because it is small. There is some suggestion that cost/benefit considerations may justify the distinction. If the small entity is not already making the calculation on its own account and needs to obtain outside help to implement a standard, the relative cost of so doing may be considerably greater than for a larger entity. If, in addition, there are few report users for whom the information would make a difference, it may carry little benefit. This thinking has been followed to suggest that tax allocation accounting and lease capitalization might not be required for smaller entities. Beyond this, however, there does not seem to be a strong demand for measurement standards different from those generally applicable.

It may be that it is not necessary to specify different standards for smaller, non-public companies. The key problem is to arrive at some practical definition of entities whose financial reporting is unimportant from the standpoint of society at large. If such a definition could be framed, it would be possible to dispense with all but a very minimum financial reporting responsibility for such entities. It would then up to those having financial or other dealings with such entities to contract with them for financial reports in whatever form is mutually satisfactory. For example, a bank extending credit might require a financial report prepared so as to meet normal standards, might be satisfied with a simplified statement, or might accept the statements prepared for taxation purposes. If the public interest in the financial report is minimal, there is no reason why the contracting parties should not make their own decisions on the form and extent of reporting. For this approach to be feasible in Canada, it would, of course, be necessary to amend corporations legislation to permit such freedom for defined classes of entity.

The content of an accounting standard

As noted earlier, many people believe that standards should be stated in terms of broad principles in order not to impede the exercise of professional judgment. This seems generally desirable provided that, in a given situation, the conclusions of a representative sample of professionals on the issues involved would fall within a reasonably narrow range. If they do not, the standard will be ineffective. In practice, this will often happen with broadly stated standards. It then becomes necessary to make the guidance within the standard more specific, laying it open to a charge of being a mere mindless set of rules.

This suggests that it is unproductive to argue the merits of broad standards against detailed standards. The important question is what sort of standard will be effective. It is suggested that every standard ought to contain material that explains how its conclusions flow from the conceptual framework, explicit or implicit, and thereby the intention of the standard should be made clear. In addition, most standards need to contain some guidance as to how they may be implemented in typical situations. The former material, the explanation of the theory and intent of the standard, may be regarded as embodying the broad principles — hence being the essence of the standard. There could even be some merit in separating this explanation of theory and intent from the guidance to implementation. However, both are likely to be necessary in any complex area if the standard is to be effective.

The logical makeup of a standard and the difficulty of separating its elements are illustrated in the following discussion of the 1987 Canadian standard for accounting for pension costs.

- Our implicit conceptual framework calls for current recognition of obligations that are caused by activities and probably will involve future payments. A pension plan, whether explicit or implicit, imposes such an obligation.
- The objective of the standard is to recognize the cost and obligation currently as plan members earn their entitlements to future benefits. Since an employer receives no benefit from payments after an employee retires, it is an objective of this standard to recognize the cost of benefits over the working career of the employee.

This might be described as the essence of the standard. Much more guidance is required, however, to make the standard effective.

- The accrual of cost should be made based on best estimates of future events. That instruction is necessary because best estimates were not invariably used in practice before 1987. What are best estimates is left to professional judgment. However, it is specified that best estimates should be made in the context of expected long-term experience and not be unduly influenced by recent events. This elaboration is necessary to clarify the meaning of "best estimates." It remains to be seen whether this clarification will lead to application of judgment in a consistent manner.
- The cost to be recognized in a year with respect to future benefits payable could be determined in a wide variety of ways. Since professional judgment provides no basis for selecting a single recognition method, the standard prescribes such a method for each broad type of plan in the interest of comparability between reporting entities.
- Professional judgment could vary widely as to the methods to be used in accounting for and presentation of pension plan investments. The standard essentially makes the choice that the amount of plan assets is to be netted from the amount of plan obligations and investment income is to be netted from pension costs recognized for the period.
- The standard also deals with the special problems of past-service cost associated with plan amendments, experience gains and losses, and adjustments resulting from changes in actuarial assumptions. Professional judgment again could vary widely as to the appropriate treatment of these.

> Accordingly, the standard provides direction but nevertheless leaves some room for judgment without clearly indicating the factors that should affect judgment.

This example, because of its complexity, is not typical. Nevertheless, it illustrates the impossibility of having accounting standards couched only in very broad terms and the considerable necessity of what may be regarded as relatively arbitrary rule making. A standard should be based upon a principle. But it must also be clear and workable. The standard should be structured so as to bring out its intent. Also, it should make clear when it is making arbitrary choices in the interest of promoting comparability and when it is relying on judgment to fit the circumstances of the situation being accounted for. In the latter case, it would be most helpful if those who write the standards were able to indicate what considerations they believed should affect judgment.

The standard-setting process

Considerable variety is possible in arrangements for setting standards. The following comments will therefore not be exhaustive.

Due process. At one time the making of accounting recommendations was regarded very much as a technical matter. Now that recommendations have become virtually binding standards and their public-interest character has been recognized, the need for "due process" in setting standards is accepted. Due process means simply that adequate publicity has been given to the deliberations and intentions of the standard-setters and all interested parties have had an opportunity to be heard.

There could be some variation in emphasis in due process procedures. If standard-setting is still largely regarded as a system for arriving at the best possible technical answer, the primary objective would be to make sure that all information and data relevant to the issue were available to the standard-setters. On the other hand, if standard-setting is regarded as being largely a political process designed to arrive at compromise answers acceptable to all affected parties, more emphasis would be placed on giving free expression to all possibly conflicting opinions and having an open decision-making process to avoid any suspicion that the conclusions of the decision makers were subject to undue influence.

From previous remarks it will be apparent that the author believes the former emphasis is preferable. Indeed, it can be argued that Canadian statutory references to fair presentation of financial statements imply that reporting standards must be neutral. Thus the important objective is that they be technically competent, not that they simply represent acceptable compromises. This having been said, it must be conceded that a large measure of openness in the standard-setting process is desirable, for the simple reason that it may result in eliciting information bearing on the subject under consideration that otherwise would not be available.

What represents satisfactory due process will vary from time to time and place to place depending upon the complexity of the issues to be addressed. Several features of the Canadian process are designed to promote well-considered standards.[9]

- The twenty-two member complement of the Accounting Standards Committee (ASC) is drawn from a wide variety of backgrounds. Thus, at least

some members will normally have first-hand experience relevant to issues under review. The time commitment of each member is substantial.
- Each member is entitled to name a number of "associates" who receive draft material on projects underway before the exposure-draft stage. The views of associates can help to enrich and broaden a member's participation in the committee's work.
- When the necessary majority of the committee are prepared to endorse a proposed standard, an exposure draft is published which is widely disseminated both inside and and outside the accounting profession. A special effort is made to reach persons or entities that may be assumed to have a particular interest in the subject of the standard being proposed.
- Invariably, changes are made to the exposure draft as result of comments received. If these changes represent changes to important principles of the draft or introduce new principles, a revised exposure draft is published.
- A final standard is adopted only with the approval of at least two-thirds of the members of the committee.

The CICA has adopted the commendable practice of formally reviewing procedures for setting standards every five to ten years. The latest such study, by the Special Committee on Standard-Setting (SCOSS), was issued under date of December 1980.[10]

Although these procedures seem quite exhaustive, it is possible to question whether they are good enough. In 1978 a standard dealing with foreign currency translation was issued after full due process, only to be suspended before it became effective. Most commentators on this embarrassing incident use it as an illustration of the proposition that standard-setting is a political activity and the CICA suffered the penalty of failing to appreciate that fact. The author's explanation is different. The standard had to be abandoned because it signally failed to provide a faithful representation of the economic situation in a significant number of cases. It thus was indefensible. Of course, there are few financial reporting problems as difficult as that of accounting for foreign currency translation. However, other criticisms outlined in Part II raise the question whether the standard-setting process is fully adequate to cope with financial reporting challenges today.

The most important question for the standard-setting process is whether it is successful in eliciting responses to exposure drafts that are (1) sufficiently representative of all points of view and (2) likely to uncover all potential pitfalls and problems not foreseen by the standard-setting committee. Additional measures could be taken to this end, and the possible additional cost should be balanced against the possible gain in information. The FASB extends its public exposure two ways. For major projects a discussion memorandum is prepared by the staff with the assistance of an advisory task force and made public. This discussion memorandum provides an organized and comprehensive review of issues relating to the particular topic and permits a linkage of possible provisions in the standard with underlying theory or reasoning that is much better than that found in the typical exposure draft. Public hearings are held after the issuance of discussion memorandums and after some exposure drafts to increase the dialogue between standard-setters and interested parties. By these means the FASB unquestionably broadens its exposure to different points of view. The question is whether the additional cost involved is justified by the more thorough public airing of the issues and consequent improvement in the final standard.

SCOSS concluded that public discussion should be stimulated in Canada before the exposure draft stage and recommended earlier publication of "issues papers" or "discussion documents" in the case of controversial or difficult subjects.[11] An additional possibility would be to make a document available to interested parties at the time an exposure draft is prepared, outlining the principles upon which the committee rested its conclusions, the alternatives considered, and the reasons for their rejection. Traditionally, exposure drafts and the subsequent standards have tended to provide a listing of arguments in relation to each recommendation, followed by an indication of the committee's preference without providing much by way of linkage between the preferences expressed and a coherent theory.

Research. Since standards should be based on informed judgment of the standard-setters it is natural to consider what research support should be available. Research for this purpose may take several forms. First, there is empirical or descriptive research designed merely to discover and report factual information on how business is carried on, how calculations are made, or how the economy works. For example, considerable factual knowledge of leasing arrangements, the working of options and futures markets, actuarial methods for calculation of pension costs and accrued liabilities, and workings of the foreign exchange markets are necessary before accounting standards in these areas can be intelligently considered.

Second, there is what may be called analytical research. The relationship between the problem area under consideration and general accounting theory is traced. Based on this and on the specific characteristics of the problem, issues are identified that need resolution in an accounting standard, and possible paths of reasoning are worked out leading to different possible solutions.

Third, SCOSS suggested there should be research into the costs and benefits of standards and their possible economic impact.[12] In the author's observation the results of such research, particularly with respect to estimates of benefit and economic impact, should be treated with some skepticism. Nevertheless, the information, if available or attainable, is certainly pertinent to standard-setting.

If much original empirical or analytical research is required, it may be desirable to commission one or more research studies before attempting to consider accounting standards in particular areas. In many cases, however, it will be possible to draw upon prior research. If so, a library search and summarization of results may be sufficient to permit consideration of the standards to begin.

All this is stated in rather idealistic terms. In practice, it seems quite difficult to utilize research to influence accounting standards. Research is time-consuming and therefore expensive. It rarely covers all aspects of a problem area and often does not lead to clear conclusions. Considerable vision is required to commission research that will provide answers when they are needed. Skill is also required in communicating the results of research in an understandable manner. We cannot say that such vision and skill are always available in support of the standard-setting process.[13]

There is much accounting research, particularly that carried on in the universities, that does not fit the categories of research described above. The implications of such research for standard-setting are usually indirect, rather than direct, and often lie in the future, rather than being relevant to current issues. For this reason, reference to such research in this book has been limited. That does not mean that it is unimportant, merely that it needs to be evaluated from a perspective beyond that of the formulation of standards for current accounting practice.[14]

Collateral matters

Once it is accepted that standards are necessary to assist fair financial reporting and a system is in place for producing such standards after due process, we must ask: Is the mere production of standards sufficient? What else is required to produce the results hoped for? Several aspects of these questions need consideration.

Completeness. When a process for issuing recommendations was first adopted by the accounting profession, the principal objective was to reduce areas of difference in practice — to deal with particularly difficult and contentious questions. The intention was not to write a framework for accounting practice that would permit deduction of appropriate standards for all questions. Rather, it was thought that the broad principles of financial reporting were in existence or would emerge through general acceptance, and guidance was needed only in cases of special difficulty or controversy. The *CICA Handbook* is the outcome of this process. Even though its treatment of topics is organized in a logical and more or less sequential fashion, it does not purport to address every aspect of financial reporting.

Whether such an ad hoc approach is satisfactory in the long run depends upon the extent to which broad areas of agreement exist as to the framework of financial reporting. If individual standards proliferate over a period of time to address numerous controversial issues, there is a danger of conflict between individual standards, and there will be a greater perceived need for an overall theory. On the other hand, an increase in topics covered by standards will make more evident any implicit theory that is accepted by the standard-setters. Thus it may become easier to fill in gaps if it is desired to do so. For example, the *CICA Handbook*, although originally merely a compendium of a series of unrelated bulletins, has through time become much more all-inclusive in its coverage. The adoption in 1986 of a standard on revenue recognition filled in a major gap in topic coverage, and it would not be too difficult to cover the remaining gaps, at least in broad general terms.

A difficult question concerns the extent to which standard-setters should address questions that are peculiar to specific industries. There has been a strong feeling that standards should not be written for special industry situations. It is thought that general principles should apply to all industries; all that is required is their adaptation to fit any special circumstances. Although this view has a degree of persuasiveness, it encounters the practical difficulty that specific industry situations often disclose an absence of general principle or weaknesses in the general principles. For example, practices in the real estate and franchising industries in the relatively recent past forced recognition of weaknesses in long-established tests for revenue recognition. Similarly, the questions encountered in the several financial services industries have little in common with those encountered in industries dealing with tangible products, and it is difficult to see what general principles cover both situations.

A considerable part of the problem lies in the fact that our accounting theory is rooted in the 1930s and 1940s and was developed to fit the circumstances of commercial and industrial enterprises manufacturing or handling tangible products. It is unrealistic to think that this theory or standards derived from this perspective will always be adaptable to other types of enterprise — extractive industries, agricultural enterprises, and service enterprises of all kinds — without a good deal of thought. Standard-setters, therefore, cannot ignore special industry situations. Either special standards have to be written to take care of their special circumstances, or broad general standards have to be rethought to make sure they can be applied to all situations.

As a practical matter, an interactive process is desirable. It is useful to prepare research studies for highly specialized industries, describing the kinds of businesses they carry on, ascertaining the various procedures adopted in practice for accounting for those businesses, and assessing the extent to which such practices are consistent with general standards as normally stated. To the extent that inconsistencies exist or that general standards do not cover the special industry situation, standard-setters can consider the need for amplification of the general standards. There may also be a few instances, such as that of the life insurance industry, when the situation encountered is so individual in character that it is more effective to prescribe accounting for the industry separately rather than strain the wording of the general standards.

Timeliness. Difficult reporting questions often arise very suddenly. A government action or change in legislation may have financial implications for business or certain types of business, and consideration is required as to how that impact should be taken into account. As well, some new form of business arrangement or some new form of financial instrument may raise questions as to the substance of the arrangement — for example, whether a transaction represents a sale or financing, or whether a financial instrument has the characteristics of debt, equity, or an option. Standard-setters have to exercise judgment as to whether guidance should be provided on the consequential accounting issues. If guidance is desired, two problems have to be addressed. There has to be some means of becoming aware of emerging issues. There also needs to be some facility for giving timely guidance. That means, as a practical matter, that full "due process" is impossible.

The first problem should not be difficult to solve. In the first place, an informed accountant who is alert to the possibility can discern potential accounting problems merely by keeping up on current affairs. A careful reading of the financial press is important, together with such occasional documents as government budget papers and other material dealing with legislative proposals. Second, the public accounting firms and securities commissions become aware of new accounting issues fairly early and can be requested to point out problems that may become troublesome. The chief requirement is that standard-setters or someone delegated by them should be actively looking for emerging accounting issues.

The second problem is more troublesome. The CICA permits the steering committee of the accounting standards and auditing standards committees to issue "guidelines" as (1) interpretations of existing *Handbook* recommendations or (2) expressions of views on other issues of concern to the profession when the normal standard-setting process does not appear to be appropriate or cannot be proceeded with on a timely basis. SCOSS expressed concern that such guidelines might be regarded as carrying too great a degree of authority for documents issued without due process. Accordingly, it recommended that guidelines should be issued sparingly and should be physically separated in a separate volume of the *CICA Handbook* so that they would not be confused with authoritative standards that had been subject to due process before issuance.[15]

The author agrees that it is reasonable to emphasize the opinion character of guidelines but does not agree that they necessarily should be few in number. Guidelines should be issued when needed, and no one can predict the degree of frequency of that need. In the author's opinion, accounting practice to date would have been improved if guidelines had been issued more frequently. Too often undesirable accounting practices with respect to novel types of transactions take root and are subsequently hard to eradicate, simply because of the lack of prompt attention.

The United States has two means of addressing emerging problems. Staff accounting bulletins of the SEC frequently nip undesirable accounting practices in the bud. In addition, the Emerging Issues Task Force of the FASB appears to be playing a useful role in providing nonauthoritative opinions on the substance of new forms of business arrangements and financial instruments and the appropriate accounting for them. In the author's view, provision of less formal guidance by the CICA needs to be strengthened, not limited. Since some of this guidance would consist of interpretations of existing standards and some would not, further discussion will deal with both these aspects.

Interpretations and guidelines. At present a CICA guideline may represent an interpretation of an existing standard or may discuss matters not apparently covered by standards. It may deal with a problem that is new or one that has been in existence for some time. There seems to be no strong concept as to what is or is not a proper subject for a guideline. In essence, a guideline is issued whenever it is deemed useful to provide some guidance on a subject without going through the formalities of due process. The resulting statement lacks the authority of a standard but may well carry weight in some quarters merely as a result of its association with the CICA. Some fuller consideration of the role of guidelines seems desirable. Let us think first about their role as interpretations.

There may be different meanings attached to the term "interpretations" of standards. One kind of interpretation may be required simply because the wording of the standard appears to be ambiguous when applied to actual situations. SCOSS suggests (and the author agrees) that such clarifying interpretations should be made through the medium of a guideline, but that as soon as possible the standard itself should be amended so that the guideline can be withdrawn.[16]

A second kind of interpretation may be illustrated by the guideline issued in February 1982 with respect to the petroleum incentives program of the government (PIP) and the petroleum and gas revenue tax (PGRT). In that guideline the opinion was expressed that PIP incentives were government grants and therefore should be accounted for in accordance with Section 3800 of the *CICA Handbook*. The PGRT, in contrast, should be reflected in income in step with the revenue that was taxed. This example differs from the type of interpretation previously described in two ways. First, there was no suggestion that the wording of the standard on government assistance was ambiguous. There was simply a statement of opinion that the PIP incentive was a government grant and accordingly that standard was applicable to accounting for PIP incentives. Second, an opinion was given on the appropriate accounting for PGRT that was not based on standards within the *Handbook* but simply represented the steering committee's opinion as to the general governing principle. It is worth thinking about this illustration.

- The statement that Section 3800 governed PIP incentive accounting represented what SCOSS referred to as a "ruling." It was not an interpretation of meaning in the abstract, but rather an application of the standard to a specific case. In this case the ruling was issued as a response to what was perceived as an emerging problem. But it was not different in character from the situation that would exist if a company or an audit firm or a securities commission had come to the CICA and said: "Here is a fact situation; what accounting is called for by accounting standards?"

- SCOSS expressed serious reservations about the issuance of rulings.[17] In essence, these reservations rested upon the belief that, in many situations, a relatively wide range of alternative presentations can be supported in the exercise of professional judgment. It was argued that if a ruling is given on a stated question before the situation is accounted for, the result is merely the substitution of the judgment of the person(s) giving the ruling for that of the preparer of the financial report. On the other hand, if a ruling is given after publication of the financial report — perhaps upon referral by a third party — the professional judgment of those responsible for the financial report is impugned.
- The portion of the guideline dealing with PGRT was not based on written accounting standards at all. Some might question even more strongly the intervention of the CICA in such a situation, unless the answer to the question submitted was arrived at after due process.

Although the answer to the question of the desirability of rulings is not black and white, the author questions the position taken by SCOSS. The concern of SCOSS was that there are many situations in which legitimate professional judgment could lead to relatively widely divergent accounting treatment. The author doubts this. Instead, he is concerned that (unhappily) there are many situations in which divergent accounting may be adopted when diversity is *not* justified by legitimate differences in professional judgment.

However much we deplore the fact, in the real world statement preparers on occasion have powerful reasons for preferring one accounting treatment over another, and these reasons have nothing to do with what is sound accounting in a technical sense. In such situations, any ambiguity in the wording of a standard or any wording that seems to offer a loophole for arguing the merits of the desired position may be exploited. Such ambiguities or loopholes will often exist, since no committee can write flawless recommendations, nor is it possible, when drafting a standard, to foresee every situation to which the standard may need to be applied.

Indeed, one can argue that if standards are to be worded in general terms, as most people desire, the need for an interpretation facility is all the greater. Moreover, if there are *not* genuine grounds for differences in professional judgment on a question, surely it is in the public interest for the standard-setting body to say so. In the case of the PIP grant, for example, if the steering committee was correct in its interpretation (as the author believes it was), it could be considered to be an abdication of responsibility on the part of the profession not to have acted to prevent the confusion that would have followed from conflicting accounting treatments by different enterprises. In short, if the CICA is acting in the public interest to promulgate standards, it must be in the public interest to make their application clear.

Further exploration as to the significance of this generalization may be useful.

- By no means will every emerging issue or every question that might be referred to the CICA be covered by an existing standard. It would therefore be useful to separate statements that are made into two series — interpretations and other guidelines.
- Interpretations will inevitably take on the authority of the underlying standard. That being so, it would be desirable to add some formality to their issuance. Perhaps interpretations should be issued only when approved unanimously by a highly qualified panel — such as one consisting of the chairman of the standard-setting body, the previous chairman, and the chairman-elect.
- If the panel members were unanimous as to the best interpretation but they nevertheless considered that the opinions of unbiased observers could reasonably differ, then an interpretation should not be issued. It might be appropriate in such cases to initiate a standard-setting project to answer the question. Alternatively, an informal expression of preference could be given in a guideline, *provided* it is not represented as being authoritative or prohibiting alternative treatments.
- Some might question whether it is appropriate to issue guidelines that do not represent interpretations of existing standards. The argument would be that once a process exists for issuing authoritative standards, there is no room for issuance of less authoritative recommendations, because of the possibility of confusion as to their status. Although such concern is not groundless, the prohibition of publication of any recommendations that have not been subject to due process seems extreme. It would mean that no guidance could be given on emerging issues unless the issue in question were covered by an existing standard. It would also preclude the possibility of the profession providing advice on subjects too specialized to be embodied in a standard or too minor to justify being made subject to the standard-setting process. Nevertheless, there is enough substance in this concern to suggest that every effort should be made to distinguish mandatory standards from such informal guidance. Except for emerging issues that need to be dealt with promptly, informal guidance should be given sparingly and, if concerned with a substantial topic, would be better dealt with either in the form of a research study or by initiating a full-fledged standard-setting project.
- Several concerns may be felt about the practice of making rulings: (1) that preparers will feel impelled to seek rulings in all situations requiring judgment for fear that a subsequent ruling on a similar situation may differ from their decision and thereby lay them open to criticism, (2) that the body making interpretations will be overwhelmed with requests for assistance, and (3) that the making of interpretations will be exceedingly time-consuming because of the care required and hence will be costly. While these concerns cannot be dismissed out of hand, they may be less serious than this description suggests. In the first place, if preparers and their auditors can readily agree on the best answer, there should be little possibility of a subsequent contradictory ruling in a similar situation. Ordinarily it will only be when a preparer and auditor have some difference of opinion that reference will be desirable. Second, a request for interpretation should not automatically result in a ruling. Interpretations or rulings should be issued only when it is clear that the case falls squarely under an existing standard or can be

> dealt with under an accepted criterion such as that of "substance over form" and the circumstances of the case do not admit of a range of answers within the proper exercise of professional judgment. If these conditions are not met or insufficient information is provided to judge whether they are met, the request for a ruling should be refused. If rulings are given only under these restricted terms, their numbers should be limited and the costs involved in dealing with them minimized.

In brief, this discussion leads to the following conclusions. If authoritative standards are desirable in the public interest, it seems also desirable that there be a facility for providing interpretations indicating how the standards would apply in specific situations. In addition, the broad framework or theory governing present accepted accounting practice is sufficiently well-established that interpretations can often be provided even though a specific standard governing the case is not stated in the *Handbook*. An interpretation that is, in effect, a ruling should be given only when the application of the standard or established practice is clear. An interpretation facility should be careful not to provide interpretations in cases where professional judgments could legitimately differ or the situation is not clearly covered by existing standards or established theory. If an interpretation cannot be provided for a situation likely to be encountered commonly, a need for a standard-setting project may be indicated.

The fact that the CICA has responsibility for providing authoritative standards should not prevent it from providing less authoritative guidance in areas where standards are lacking. Such guidance may be useful to meet new situations, specialized situations, or questions that are too unimportant to justify disposition through the normal standard-setting process. It is important that such less formal guidance be clearly distinguished from standards arrived at after due process because of its lesser authority. In essence, its influence, like that of arguments in a textbook or magazine article, should rest upon persuasiveness, not authority.

Accounting standards and change. One concern often expressed about accounting standards is that they may stifle innovation. The charge has some substance. One of the main purposes of standards is to reduce confusion by limiting diversity in methods of accounting for similar situations. This necessarily involves prohibition of some methods that could be considered innovative.

In spite of the need to minimize confusion by standardizing financial reporting, there is a case to be made for allowing some diversity. Changes in the economic environment may create a need for new information not provided under existing accounting standards. Standards may not change to provide this information as quickly as is desirable. For example, accounting information to illustrate the effect of price changes was desirable long before accounting standard-setters were able to come to agreement on what might be provided. Experimentation with new accounting methods may be worthwhile. For example, it is possible to make a strong argument for the merits of discounted deferred taxes (although the method of discounting needs careful consideration), but present accounting standards prohibit any such presentation. New forms of presentation may also have merit. For example, a statement of value added provides interesting insights. The problem, in general, is how to encourage or permit some innovation, without compromising the objective of maintaining comparability between enterprises.

- One possibility is to allow alternative presentations but make sure that those that conflict with generally accepted standards are clearly segregated. Thus, a statement of value added could be included with the primary financial statement since it merely represents a different form of presentation of data drawn from the regular accounts. On the other hand, an income statement based on accounting incorporating price change information or based on discounting deferred taxes would have to be presented as supplementary information since the measurement principles would differ from those used under accepted accounting. This possibility of making supplemental presentation has existed in the past and has been little used. The problem may be that statement preparers are unwilling to present figures on two bases — they want changes in standards or nothing.
- SCOSS suggested that from time to time in a new situation a "preliminary" standard might be issued following the normal due process. The standard would express preferences in a given situation but allow the use of competing methods in published financial statements — presumably with adequate disclosure of the methods used.[18] It may be that the issuance of such a preliminary standard would have a useful practical result. It would force statement preparers to consider their own preferences carefully and publish what they consider appropriate in the circumstances. This would contrast with the present situation in which respondents to exposure drafts are free to criticize the proposed standards but are not forced to take a firm stand on what they believe is the best solution. Unfortunately, such a preliminary standard might elicit a mass of conflicting practice in a complex situation and thereby make an ultimate resolution even more difficult.
- A possible way to lessen this problem in some circumstances might be to publish an exposure draft offering two or three possible choices for accounting for the area under consideration. For example, a standard requiring supplemental disclosure of price change information might have been issued much earlier if the standard-setters had not tried to arrive at a single basis for reporting figures. Rather, the standard might have said, in effect: "Something needs to be reported with respect to changing prices. Here are three possibilities. Choose the one you consider most appropriate and cost effective, but report something."

Unfortunately, both of these last two possibilities seem likely to be appropriate only relatively infrequently.

Possibly the most effective contribution to innovation that can be made by a standard-setting body is to review existing standards regularly in order to evaluate their continuing acceptability and usefulness. SCOSS suggested such a review every five years. In this connection it made sensible suggestions concerning monitoring compliance with standards and problems in their application.[19]

The challenge of international and U.S. accounting standards. Accounting standards have typically been developed in a national setting. The standard-setting agency is often stimulated by government pressure, and the standards themselves are often influenced by local laws and institutions. Uses of financial reports, however, are not confined within national borders. In particular, capital flows across boundaries. It is obviously in the interests of efficient allocation of capital on an international basis that reporting standards be harmonized internationally to the extent possible. Acceptance of that goal has led to the formation of the International Accounting Standards Committee. That committee has issued a series of concise international standards. There is some tendency for a larger number of alternatives to be permitted because of the desire not to have significant conflicts between the international standard and the national standards of influential participating countries. This tendency dilutes the impact of the international standards somewhat. Nevertheless, they make a worthwhile contribution to improved financial reporting in many countries.

A Canadian representative participates in the work of the IASC. A Canadian Advisory Group consisting of representatives of the sponsoring accounting bodies in Canada and of the Financial Executives Institute reports on differences between Canadian standards in practice and international standards as they are developed. It also recommends changes that might be considered in the *CICA Handbook*. The CICA has also published a looseleaf comparison of the international standards with Canadian practice. These arrangements seem well designed and desirable. The chief impact of international standards on Canadian standards has probably resulted from the interaction when the same subject is being studied by both Canadian and international standard-setters. Apart from this, the impact of the international standards on Canadian practice is not very noticeable. On a cumulative basis there are a fairly large number of minor differences between the recommendations of international standards and Canadian practice. A number of these differences represent worthwhile elements in the international standards, so that at this time a project to eliminate the differences would have merit.

A much more important challenge to Canadian standards is provided by U.S. accounting standards. Historically, U.S. literature and U.S. practice have been recognized as authoritative support for practices in Canada. Indeed, many innovations in Canadian accounting practices have had their origins south of the border. In effect, "general acceptance" in the United States has been taken as equivalent to general acceptance in Canada. This situation has continued, even though changes in U.S. accounting practice now normally originate in FASB and SEC pronouncements, rather than as a result of spontaneous development. The result has been that the FASB and SEC have a very considerable impact on Canadian accounting practice.

Although there are some positive elements to this fact, there are some distinct disadvantages. The practical situation is that any new U.S. standard automatically becomes acceptable in Canada unless the area covered by the standard has already been dealt within the *CICA Handbook* and the Canadian standard clearly precludes the American position. A good example of the importation of American practice is provided by SFAS No. 34 on the capitalization of interest. The procedures required by the FASB in that standard had no precedent in Canadian practice, and their merits are at best doubtful. After the standard was issued, however, it became possible for Canadian companies either to continue their previous accounting practice or to adopt the new U.S. recommendations. In this way, U.S. standards lead to an increase in diversity of accepted accounting practice in Canada. Worse, entities are able to pick and choose which U.S. standards they will adopt, and there may even be occasions when it is not clear whether it is possible to adopt some aspects but reject others of a single U.S. standard.

It is long past time that Canadian standard-setters addressed this problem. The answer is not simply to prohibit changes in practice to conform with U.S. standards, since (1) U.S. standards are often very desirable, and (2) Canadian companies registered with the SEC should not be barred from adopting a desirable accounting practice that will at the same time reduce the special disclosure and explanations they must make in reports to shareholders as to the effects of differences between Canadian and U.S. standards. It seems inescapable that managing this problem will require case-by-case examination of U.S. standards as they are issued to determine the best possible Canadian reaction, even though this requires some expenditure of limited Canadian resources. Based on such an examination, the Accounting Standards Committee might make one of several possible statements:

- The subject of the U.S. standard is on the agenda of the ASC or will shortly be placed upon it. No change should be made in Canadian accounting practice until a Canadian standard is issued.
- The U.S. standard will be used as a basis for an accelerated standard-setting project in Canada. Because of the possibility of differences in final recommendations, however, changes in Canadian practice should not be made until that project is completed. (On occasion a U.S. standard may be relatively uncontentious. If so, there might well be a "fast track" procedure, whereby the U.S. standard could be utilized as a "statement of principles" in the Canadian standard-setting process and shortly be issued as an exposure draft with relatively little change in wording.)
- The U.S. standard provides a reasonable interpretation of accepted accounting theory, and its recommendations may be regarded as being within generally accepted accounting principles in Canada. (On occasion it might be advisable to state that the U.S. recommended position should be adopted only if it is adopted in its entirety, including the required disclosures.)
- The U.S. recommendations are too different from generally accepted accounting principles in Canada and should not be adopted.

The last of these statements is the one most likely to draw criticism. However, if the ASC is to control its own agenda and priorities and yet stem the proliferation of accounting practices resulting from the leakage of U.S. standards across the border, some such action must be considered. It goes without saying that Canadian standard-setters should keep fully informed of work proceeding in the United States and should consciously try to tailor their own projects so as to avoid unnecessary conflicts with American standards.

Monitoring the effectiveness of standards. The preceding pages have suggested the need for a somewhat broader view of the standard-setting function. Such a broader view would place additional demands upon standard-setters. It is questionable whether all that needs to be done can be accomplished by volunteers alone, assisted by CICA staff. SCOSS has provided a balanced discussion of the possibility of having full-time standard-setters.[20] Few believe that a full-time standard-setting board modelled on the FASB is desirable in Canada, even if it could be successfully financed, which is doubtful. The use of two or three full-time standard-setters is, however, more possible. Two or three full-time members would facilitate greater responsiveness to emerging issues and the provision of interpretations and other guidance. SCOSS expressed some concern that a mixture of full-time and volunteer standard-setters would create first- and second-class citizens. The author feels less concern about this, considering the generally high quality of volunteers now recruited and the fact that their first-hand familiarity with accounting issues would continue to be a vital element in the success of the standard-setting function.

Summary

In this chapter it is argued that standards for financial reporting are necessary. No well-established simple theory exists to provide answers to the many questions that can arise in the complex business of compressing a faithful representation of financial position and results of operations within a few pages of narrative and figures. In addition, there is a conflict of interest between financial statement preparers and users of information, and the latter are not generally in a strong enough position to demand and enforce full and fair financial presentation. A public interest in financial reporting is evidenced by corporations and securities legislation. Standards of financial reporting are a natural extension of that public concern.

It is often said that standards rest upon general acceptance. In a broad sense that is true. But it is a mistake to think that standards must please everybody and that standard-setting is a political process designed to achieve that end. The achievement of fair financial presentation is a demanding technical process that must, if it is to be effective, be conducted in an unbiased fashion. The public interest calls for neutral, unbiased standards. It is essential that standard-setters have enough authority to achieve that objective, without in the process becoming an insensitive, bureaucratic machine. Various combinations are possible for achieving that balance. The Canadian situation in which the accounting profession musters private-sector expertise to establish standards that are granted a measure of legal status seems to represent a structure at least as good as that in any other country.

Several conditions are necessary or desirable for competent standard-setting. The standard-setters themselves should have wide experience so that they are knowledgeable about the conditions accounted for. Research is often necessary to provide additional factual information about the subject matter of a standard, practice in handling the problems involved, and the economic background to the problems. A realistic broad theory of financial reporting is helpful in formulating specific standards. Finally, the process of standard-setting should be open and designed to elicit responses that will uncover problems and pitfalls and indicate the possible advantages and disadvantages of potential versions of the standard.

The complaint is often made that accounting standards are too numerous, too complex, and too detailed. These conditions are said to inhibit professional judgment, lay an undue burden on reporting entities, and invite attempts to circumvent the intent of the standards by loophole picking. There can be some truth in these charges, but it is overly simplistic to think that the situation can be cured by reverting to broadly expressed standards that merely outline governing principles. The fact is that many legal and business arrangements are complex, so an explanation of how they ought to be accounted for must itself be complex. Nevertheless, it is incontrovertible that effective standards should make clear the principles upon which their recommendations rest.

A fully effective system does not end with the establishment of standards. No matter how carefully standards are expressed and particularly if they are expressed in broad terms, questions of interpretation will arise. It is not logical to suggest that standards are desirable but that once they are issued no guidance should be given as to their application to specific situations. On the contrary, a standard-setting body should contain a facility for providing interpretations. In so doing, it must be careful not to make new standards by the back door without due process. A standard-setting body should also monitor compliance with its standards to bring to light any need for modification or additional interpretation. Standard-setters should also systematically and periodically review standards to identify those that are obsolete or no longer required.

On balance, standard-setting under the aegis of the CICA has served the public well. That does not mean that it should be exempt from criticism. If one primary shortcoming were to be identified, it would lie in the system's failure to react to emerging issues quickly. Improvements could also be made in monitoring the application of standards, coping with the overflow of U.S. practice, and utilizing research to support standards. There is a serious question whether significant improvement can be achieved without a full-time dedication to standard-setting of a few highly qualified individuals. Whether the membership of the CICA will be able or willing to bear the cost increases inevitably associated with additional functions and improvements to the process is also a question. If there is doubt on this score, it may become necessary to seek a broader base of public support.

References

[1]A relatively small group of scholars believes that statement preparers' needs to retain the confidence of the capital markets provide sufficient incentive for the provision of adequate financial reports. See, as an example, H. Kripke, "Would Market Forces Cause Adequate Securities Disclosure Without SEC Mandate?" in *Government Regulation of Accounting and Information*, ed. A.R. Abdel-khalik (Gainesville, Fla.: University Presses of Florida, 1980), pp. 202-24. The arguments of this group would not be pertinent to financial reporting by nonbusiness organizations and governments.

[2]The generality of this observation may be illustrated by literature from two countries. See E.H. Flegm, *Accounting: How to Meet the Challenges of Relevance and Regulation* (New York: A Ronald Press Publicaton, John Wiley & Sons, 1984), and I.N. Tegner, "British Accounting Standards — A Finance Director's Assessment," in *British Accounting Standards: The First 10 Years*, ed. Sir R. Leach and E. Stamp (Cambridge: Woodhead-Faulkner, 1981), pp. 223-30. C.T. Horngren, a one-time APB member, once said, "... financial executives in the aggregate will oppose almost anything that a standards group comes out with." See R.R. Sterling, ed., *Institutional Issues in Public Accounting* (Lawrence, Kan.: Scholars Book Co., 1974), p. 309.

[3]See M. Gibbs, "Accounting Standards and Investment Analysis," in *British Accounting Standards: The First 10 Years*, ed. Leach and Stamp, pp. 149-57.

[4]For a vividly stated exposition of this problem, see R.R. Sterling, "Accounting Power," *Journal of Accountancy*, January 1973, pp. 61-67.

[5]The Society of Management Accountants of Canada urged an expansion of its representation on the Accounting Standards Committee from one member to three members (out of twenty-two members) in a submission to the CICA Special Committee on Standard-Setting. The Certified General Accountants' Association of Canada incorporated an Accounting Standards Authority of Canada in 1981. The association proposes that the new body issue standards for management accounting as well as financial accounting and that

it be directed by a board of thirty-one members drawn from some twenty-one different organizations.

[6]A former chairman of the CICA Accounting Research Committee has argued that any expansion of CICA efforts would need independent support from the business community. See R.W. Park, "Is *Corporate Reporting* Asking Too Much?" *CAmagazine,* December 1981, pp. 34-37.

[7]However, one does not have to be overly skeptical to have serious doubts as to the competence of an elected standard-setting body.

[8]See D.J. Kirk, "Concepts, Consensus, Compromise and Consequences: Their Roles in Standard Setting." *Journal of Accountancy,* April 1981, pp. 83-86. See also two articles by D. Solomons, "The Politicization of Accounting," *Journal of Accountancy,* November 1978, pp. 65-72 and "The Potential Implications of Accounting and Auditing Standard Setting," *Accounting and Business Research,* Spring 1983, pp. 107-18.

[9]For a more complete description, see R.D. Thomas, "Studies and Standards: The Processes and the Products," *CAmagazine,* May 1985, pp. 76-80.

[10]CICA Special Committee on Standard-Setting, *Report to CICA Board of Governors* (Toronto: CICA, 1980).

[11]Ibid., p. 88.

[12]Ibid., pp. 100-102.

[13]See J.W. Buckley, ed., *The Impact of Accounting Research on Policy and Practice* (Reston, Va.: The Council of Arthur Young Professors, 1981), especially the papers by M.O. Alexander and B. Carsberg and by R.M. Skinner.

[14]Three books, among many, conveying the flavour of academic research are: W.H. Beaver, *Financial Reporting: An Accounting Revolution* (Englewood Cliffs, N.J.: Prentice-Hall, 1981), R. Mattessich, ed., *Modern Accounting Research: History, Survey and Guide,* Research Monograph No. 7 (Vancouver: The Canadian Certified General Accountants' Research Foundation, 1984), and R.L. Watts and J.L. Zimmerman, *Positive Accounting Theory* (Englewood Cliffs, N.J.: Prentice-Hall, 1986).

[15]See CICA Special Committee, *Report,* pp. 20-21, 37-38.

[16]Ibid., p. 22.

[17]Ibid., pp. 23-25.

[18]Ibid., p. 18.

[19]Ibid., pp. 106-7.

[20]Ibid., pp. 82-85.

Selected Bibliography

Part I: The Historical Development of Accounting

Chapter 2

The Record-Keeping Function of Accounting

Brown, R., ed. *A History of Accounting and Accountants*. London: Frank Cass & Co., 1905; reprint ed., New York: Augustus M. Kelley, 1968.

Chatfield, M. *A History of Accounting Thought*. Rev. ed. Huntington, N.Y.: Robert E. Krieger Publishing Co., 1977.

Littleton, A.C. *Accounting Evolution to 1900*. New York: American Institute Publishing Co., 1933.

Littleton, A.C., and Yamey, B.S., eds. *Studies in the History of Accounting*. London: Sweet & Maxwell, 1956.

Scott, W.R. *The Constitution and Finance of English, Scottish and Irish Joint-Stock Companies to 1720*. 3 vols. Cambridge: Harvard University Press, 1912; reprint ed., New York: Peter Smith, 1951.

Chapter 3

Emergence of the Financial Reporting Function

Brief, R.P. *Nineteenth Century Capital Accounting and Business Investment*. Ph.D. dissertation, Columbia University, 1964. New York: Arno Press, 1976.

________. ed. *The Late Nineteenth Century Debate over Depreciation, Capital and Income*. New York: Arno Press, 1976.

Chatfield, M. *A History of Accounting Thought*, Rev. ed. Huntington, N.Y.: Robert E. Krieger Publishing Co., 1977.

________. ed. *Contemporary Studies in the Evolution of Accounting Thought*. Belmont, Calif.: Dickenson Publishing Co., 1968.

French, E.A. "The Evolution of the Dividend Law of England." In *Studies in Accounting*, pp. 306-31. 3rd ed. Edited by W.T. Baxter and S. Davidson. London: Institute of Chartered Accountants in England and Wales, 1977.

Hunt, B.C. *The Development of the Business Corporation in England, 1800-1867.* Harvard Economic Studies, vol. 52. Cambridge: Harvard University Press, 1936.

Littleton, A.C. *Accounting Evolution to 1900*. New York: American Institute Publishing Co., 1933.

Littleton, A.C., and Yamey, B.S., eds. *Studies in the History of Accounting*. London: Sweet & Maxwell, 1956.

Wells, M.C. *Accounting for Common Costs*. Monograph 10. Urbana, Ill.: Center for International Education and Research in Accounting, 1978.

Yamey, B.S. "Some Topics in the History of Financial Accounting in England, 1500-1900." In *Studies in Accounting*, pp. 11-34. 3rd ed. Edited by W.T. Baxter and S. Davidson. London: Institute of Chartered Accountants in England and Wales, 1977.

Chapter 4

Financial Accounting in the Twentieth Century

American Accounting Association, Executive Committee. "A Tentative Statement of Accounting Principles Underlying Corporate Financial Statements." *The Accounting Review,* June 1936. Reprinted in *Accounting and Reporting Standards for Corporate Financial Statements and Preceding Statements and Supplements,* pp. 59-64. AAA, 1957.

Boockholdt, J.L. *Influence of Nineteenth and Early Twentieth Century Railroad Accounting on Development of Modern Accounting Theory.* Working Paper No. 31. Academy of Accounting Historians, 1977.

Chatfield, M., ed. *Contemporary Studies in the Evolution of Accounting Thought.* Belmont, Calif.: Dickenson Publishing Co., 1968.

May, G.O. *Twenty-Five Years of Accounting Responsibility, 1911-1936.* Edited by B.C. Hunt. 2 vols. New York: Price Waterhouse & Co., 1936; reprint ed. (2 vols. in 1), Houston: Scholars Book Co., 1971.

Paton, W.A., and Littleton, A.C. *An Introduction to Corporate Accounting Standards.* Monograph No. 3. American Accounting Association, 1940.

Previts, G.J., and Merino, B.D. *A History of Accounting in America.* New York: John Wiley & Sons, 1979.

Ripley, W.Z. *Main Street and Wall Street.* Boston: Little, Brown & Co., 1927.

Storey, R.K. "Revenue Realization, Going Concern, and Measurement of Income." *The Accounting Review,* April 1959, pp. 232-38.

———. *The Search for Accounting Principles: Today's Problems in Perspective.* New York: American Institute of Certified Public Accountants, 1964.

Part II: Accounting Standards Today

Chapter 5

Historical Cost Accounting

Alexander, S.S. "Income Measurement in a Dynamic Economy." Revised by D. Solomons. In *Studies in Accounting Theory,* pp. 126-200. Edited by W.T. Baxter and S. Davidson. Homewood, Ill.: Richard D. Irwin, 1962.

Alexander, S.S.; Bronfenbrenner, M.; Fabricant, S.; and Warburton, C. *Five Monographs on Business Income.* New York: American Institute of Accountants, 1950; reprint ed., Houston: Scholars Book Co., 1973.

Anthony, R.N. *Tell It Like It Was: A Conceptual Framework for Financial Accounting.* Homewood, Ill.: Richard D. Irwin, 1983.

Dewhirst, J. "Dealing with Uncertainty." *Canadian Chartered Accountant,* August 1971, pp. 139-46.

Hicks, J.R. *Value and Capital: An Inquiry into Some Fundamental Principles of Economic Theory.* 2nd ed. Oxford: Oxford University Press, 1946.

Lee, T.A. *Income and Value Measurement: Theory and Practice.* Baltimore: University Park Press, 1975.

May, G.O. *Financial Accounting: A Distillation of Experience.* New York: Macmillan

Co., 1943; reprint ed., Houston: Scholars Book Co., 1972.
Meyer, P.E. "The Accounting Entity." *Abacus,* December 1973, pp. 116-26.
Study Group on Business Income. *Changing Concepts of Business Income.* New York: Macmillan Co., 1952; reprint. ed., Houston: Scholars Book Co., 1975.
Thomas, A.L. *The Allocation Problem in Financial Accounting Theory.* Studies in Accounting Research No. 3. American Accounting Association, 1969.
________. *The Allocation Problem: Part Two.* Studies in Accounting Research No. 9. American Accounting Association, 1974.

Chapter 6

Initial Recognition and Measurement of Accountable Events

Accountants International Study Group. *Related Party Transactions.* Toronto: AISG, 1978.
Arnett, H.E. "APB Opinion No. 29: Accounting for Nonmonetary Transactions—Some New Perspectives." *Management Accounting,* October 1978, pp. 41-48.
Burns, J.S.; Jaedicke, R.K.; and Sangster, J.M. "Financial Reporting of Purchase Contracts Used to Guarantee Large Investments." *The Accounting Review,* January 1963, pp. 1-13.
Flaherty, R.E. "Historical Cost and Business Combinations." *The CPA Journal,* November 1972, pp. 948-51.
Ijiri, Y. *Recognition of Contractual Rights and Obligations: An Exploratory Study of Conceptual Issues.* Stamford: Financial Accounting Standards Board, 1980.
Johnson, L.T., and Storey, R.K. *Recognition in Financial Statements: Underlying Concepts and Practical Conventions.* Stamford: Financial Accounting Standards Board, 1982.
Mason, A.K. *Related Party Transactions.* Toronto: Canadian Institute of Chartered Accountants, 1979.

Chapter 7

Accounting for Leases

Abdel-khalik, A.R. *The Economic Effects on Lessees of FASB Statement No. 13, Accounting for Leases.* Stamford: Financial Accounting Standards Board, 1981.
Basu, S. *Leasing Arrangements: Managerial Decision-Making and Financial Reporting Issues.* Hamilton, Ont.: Society of Management Accountants of Canada, 1980.
Canadian Institute of Chartered Accountants. *CICA Handbook,* Section 3065, "Leases." Toronto: CICA.
Dieter, R. "Is Lessee Accounting Working?" *The CPA Journal,* August 1979, pp. 13-19.
Financial Accounting Standards Board. *Accounting for Leases.* FASB Statement No. 13 as amended and interpreted through May 1980. Stamford: FASB, 1980.
International Accounting Standards Committee. *Accounting for Leases.* International Accounting Standard No. 17. London: IASC, 1982.
Thornton, D.B. "An Application of Current Value Accounting to Lease Assets." *CAmagazine,* June 1976, pp. 32-41.

Chapter 8

Income and Revenue Recognition

Accountants International Study Group. *Revenue Recognition.* Toronto: AISG, 1978.

American Institute of Certified Public Accountants, Construction Contractors Guide Committee. *Construction Contractors.* Audit and Accounting Guide. New York: AICPA, 1981.

Canadian Institute of Public Real Estate Companies. *Recommended Accounting Practices for Real Estate Companies.* 2nd ed. Toronto: CIPREC, 1980.

Financial Accounting Standards Board. *Accounting for Certain Service Transactions.* FASB Invitation to Comment. Stamford: FASB, October 23, 1978.

________. *Recognition and Measurement in Financial Statements of Business Enterprises.* Statement of Financial Accounting Concepts No. 5. Stamford: FASB, 1984.

Jaenicke, H.R. *Survey of Present Practices in Recognizing Revenues, Expenses, Gains and Losses.* Stamford: Financial Accounting Standards Board, 1981.

Chapter 9

Expense Recognition; Accrued Liabilities; Contingencies; Non-cash Executive Compensation

American Institute of Certified Public Accountants, Accounting Principles Board. *Accounting for Stock Issued to Employees.* APB Opinion No. 25. New York: AICPA, 1972.

Brown, C.S., and Wyatt, A.R. "Liabilities Belong in the Footnote — Or Do They?" *Georgia Journal of Accounting,* Spring 1983, pp. 1-15.

Financial Accounting Standards Board. *Accounting for Stock Appreciation Rights and Other Variable Stock Option or Award Plans: An Interpretation of APB Opinion No. 15 and 25.* FASB Interpretation No. 28. Stamford: FASB, 1978.

Moonitz, M. "The Changing Concept of Liabilities." *Journal of Accountancy,* May 1960, pp. 41-46.

Ross, J.A. "Accounting for Hazardous Waste." *Journal of Accountancy,* March 1985, pp. 72-82.

Staunton, J.J., ed. *Liabilities in a Theory of Accounting.* AFM Exploratory Series No. 13. Armidale, New South Wales: Financial Management Research Centre, 1982.

Chapter 10

Inventory and Cost of Sales

Barden, H.G. *The Accounting Basis of Inventories.* Accounting Research Study No. 13. New York: American Institute of Certified Public Accountants, 1973.

Fremgen, J.M., and Liao, S.S. *The Allocation of Corporate Indirect Costs.* New York: National Association of Accountants, 1981.

Johnson, C.E. "Inventory Valuation: The Accountant's Achilles Heel." In *Financial Accounting Theory: Issues and Controversies,* pp. 89-101. Edited by S.A. Zeff and T.F. Keller. New York: McGraw-Hill Book Co., 1964.

Jones, R.C. "Some Aspects of Cost." In *Financial Accounting Theory: Issues and*

Controversies, pp. 60-70. Edited by S.A. Zeff and T.F. Keller. New York: McGraw-Hill Book Co., 1964.

Liao, S.S. "The Matching Concept and Cost Allocation." *Accounting and Business Research*, Summer 1979, pp. 228-35.

Sorter, G.H., and Horngren, C.T. "Asset Recognition and Economic Attributes — The Relevant Costing Approach." *The Accounting Review*, July 1962, pp. 391-99.

Wells, M.C. *Accounting for Common Costs*. Monograph 10. Urbana, Ill.: Center for International Education and Research in Accounting, 1978.

Chapter 11

Fixed Assets and Depreciation

Baxter, W.T. *Depreciation*. London: Sweet & Maxwell, 1971.

Bennett, A.H.M. "Depreciation and Business Decision Making." *Accounting and Business Research*, Winter 1972, pp. 3-28.

Biedleman, C.R. *Valuation of Used Capital Assets*. Studies in Accounting Research No. 7. American Accounting Association, 1973.

Bierman, H., Jr., and Dyckman, T.R. "Accounting for Interest During Construction." *Accounting and Business Research*, Autumn 1979, pp. 267-71.

Brief, R.P. "A Late Nineteenth Century Contribution to the Theory of Depreciation." *Journal of Accounting Research*, Spring 1967, pp. 27-38.

Egginton, D. "Fixed Assets: Costs, Lives and Depreciation." *Accountancy* (England), November 1984, pp. 138-44.

Johnson, O. "Two General Concepts of Depreciation." *Journal of Accounting Research*, Spring 1968, pp. 29-37.

Lamden, C.W.; Gerboth, D.L.; and McRae, T.W. *Accounting for Depreciable Assets*. Accounting Research Monograph No. 1. New York: American Institute of Certified Public Accountants, 1975.

National Association of Accountants, Committee on Management Accounting Practices. *Fixed Asset Accounting: The Capitalization of Costs*. Statement on Management Accounting Practices No. 4. New York: NAA, 1972.

________. *Fixed Asset Accounting: The Allocation of Costs*. Statement on Management Accounting Practices No. 7. New York: NAA, 1974.

Wright, F.K. "Towards a General Theory of Depreciation." *Journal of Accounting Research*, Spring 1964, pp. 80-90.

________. "An Evaluation of Ladelle's Theory of Depreciation." *Journal of Accounting Research*, Autumn 1967, pp. 173-79.

Chapter 12

Accounting for Intangibles

Bierman, H., Jr., and Dukes, R.E. "Accounting for Research and Development Costs." *Journal of Accountancy*, April 1975, pp. 48-55.

Catlett, G.R., and Olson, N.O. *Accounting for Goodwill*. Accounting Research Study No. 10. New York: American Institute of Certified Public Accountants, 1968.

Charlebois, L.R. "Deferred R&D Costs: Who Are They Really Fooling?" *CAmagazine*, November 1982, pp. 44-47.

Courtis, J.K. "Business Goodwill: Conceptual Clarification via Accounting, Legal and Etymological Perspectives." *The Accounting Historians Journal,* Fall 1983, pp. 1-38.

Crooch, G.M., and Collier, B.E. "Reporting Guidelines for Companies in a Stage of Development." *The CPA Journal,* July 1973, pp. 579-88.

Erickson, N., and Herskovits, D.H. "Accounting for Software Costs: Cracking the Code." *Journal of Accountancy,* November 1985, pp. 81-96.

Gellein, O.S., and Newman, M.S. *Accounting for Research and Development Expenditures.* Accounting Research Study No. 14. New York: American Institute of Certified Public Accountants, 1973.

Gynther, R.S. "Some 'Conceptualizing' on Goodwill." *The Accounting Review,* April 1969, pp. 247-55.

Hughes, H.P. *Goodwill in Accounting: A History of the Issues and Problems.* Research Monograph No. 80. Atlanta: Business Publishing Division, College of Business Administration, Georgia State University, 1982.

Lee, T.A. "Goodwill: An Example of Will-o'-the-Wisp Accounting." *Accounting and Business Research,* Autumn 1971, pp. 318-28.

Stivers, B.P.; Kertz, C.L.; and Beard, L.H. "What's Proper Accounting for Software Development?" *CAmagazine,* January 1985, pp. 28-33.

Chapter 13

Accounting for Pension Costs and Obligations

Archibald, T.R. *Accounting for Pension Costs and Liabilities (A Reconciliation of Accounting and Funding Practice).* Toronto: Canadian Institute of Chartered Accountants, 1980.

Dankner, H.; Glinksy, M.P.; Grady, J.H.; Hirsch, M.B.; and Steinberg, R.M. *Employer Accounting for Pension Costs and Other Post-Retirement Benefits.* New York: Financial Executives Research Foundation, 1981.

Ezra, D.D. *The Struggle for Pension Fund Wealth.* Toronto: Pagurian Press, 1983.

Gewirtz, P.A., and Phillips, R.C. "Unfunded Pension Liabilities ... The New Myth." *Financial Executive,* August 1978, pp. 18-24.

McGill, D.M. *Fundamentals of Private Pensions.* 5th ed. Homewood, Ill.: Richard D. Irwin, 1981.

Pesando, J.E., and Clarke, C.K. *Economic Models of the Labour Market: Their Implications for Pension Accounting.* Studies in Canadian Accounting Research. Canadian Academic Accounting Association, 1983.

Report on Survey of Pension Plans in Canada. 6th ed. Toronto: Financial Executives Institute Canada, 1983.

Rue, J.C., and Volkan, A.G. "Financial and Economic Consequences of the New Pension Accounting Proposals: Is the Gloom Justified?" *Journal of Accounting Auditing & Finance,* Summer 1984, pp. 306-22.

Schipper, K., and Weil, R.L. "Alternative Accounting Treatments for Pensions." *The Accounting Review,* October 1982, pp. 806-24.

Skinner, R.M. *Pension Accounting: The Problem of Equating Payments Tomorrow with Expenses Today.* Toronto: Clarkson Gordon, 1980.

———. "Research and Standard Setting in Financial Accounting — An

Illustrative Case." In *Research to Support Standard Setting in Financial Accounting: A Canadian Perspective*, pp. 154-202. Proceedings of the 1981 Clarkson Gordon Foundation Research Symposium. Edited by S. Basu and J.A. Milburn. Toronto: Clarkson Gordon Foundation, 1982.

Trowbridge, C.L., and Farr, C.E. *The Theory and Practice of Pension Funding.* Homewood, Ill.: Richard D. Irwin, 1976.

Winklevoss, H.E. *Pension Mathematics: With Numerical Illustrations.* Homewood, Ill.: Richard D. Irwin, 1977.

Chapter 15

Accounting for Income Tax Expense

Baines, R.A.; Dieter, R.; and Stewart, J. "Tax Allocation Revisited." *CAmagazine,* March 1984, pp. 69-73.

Beaver, W.H., and Dukes, R.E. "Interperiod Tax Allocation and Delta-Depreciation Methods: Some Empirical Results." *The Accounting Review,* July 1973, pp. 549-59.

Beechy, T.H. *Accounting for Corporate Income Taxes: Conceptual Considerations and Empirical Analysis.* Toronto: Canadian Institute of Chartered Accountants, 1983.

Beresford, D.R.; Best, L.C.; Craig, P.W.; and Weber, J.V. *Accounting for Income Taxes: A Review of Alternatives,* Stamford: Financial Accounting Standards Board, 1983.

Bierman, H., Jr., and Dyckman, T.R. "New Look at Deferred Taxes." *Financial Executive,* January 1974, pp. 40-49.

Black, H.A. *Interperiod Allocation of Corporate Income Taxes.* Accounting Research Study No. 9. New York: American Institute of Certified Public Accountants, 1966.

Bullock, C.L. "Reconciling Economic Depreciation with Tax Allocation." *The Accounting Review,* January 1974, pp. 98-103.

Drummond, C.S.R., and Wigle, S.L. "Let's Stop Taking Comprehensive Tax Allocation for Granted." *CAmagazine,* October 1981, pp. 56-61.

Milburn, J.A. "Comprehensive Tax Allocation: Let's Stop Taking Some Misconceptions for Granted." *CAmagazine,* April 1982, pp. 40-46.

Watson, P.L. "Accounting for Deferred Tax on Depreciable Assets." *Accounting and Business Research,* Autumn 1979, pp. 338-47.

Chapter 16

Accounting for Portfolio Investments, Options, Futures, and Swaps

Accounting for Portfolio Investments. Toronto: Canadian Institute of Chartered Accountants, 1984.

Beaver, W.H. "Reporting Rules for Marketable Equity Securities." *Journal of Accountancy,* October 1971, pp. 57-61.

________. "Accounting for Marketable Equity Securities." *Journal of Accountancy,* December 1973, pp. 58-64.

Bonen, T.K., and Kolber, P.B. "Hedging Can Reduce Corporate Rate Imbalance." *Financial Executive,* February 1983, pp. 20-30.

Clarkson Gordon. *Interest Rate Futures in Canada: A Reporting Guide.* Toronto: The Toronto Futures Exchange, 1984.
Mackenzie, M.A., and Playfair, J.L. "Interest Rate Futures — Not for Idle Speculation." *CAmagazine,* November 1981, pp. 40-49.
Morris, W.J., and Coda, B.A. "Valuation of Equity Securities." *Journal of Accountancy,* January 1973, pp. 48-54.
Schrott, A.N.; Casciani, W.P.; and Bernstein, J. "Interest Rate Futures Trading, Parts I and II." *The CPA Journal,* April 1980, pp. 16-21, and May 1980, pp. 27-31.
Storey, R.K., and Moonitz, M. *Market Value Methods for Intercorporate Investments in Stock.* Accounting Research Monograph No. 2. New York: American Institute of Certified Public Accountants, 1976.
Walther, L.M. "Commodity Futures: What the Accountant Should Know."*Journal of Accountancy,* March 1982, pp. 68-82.

Chapter 17

Recognition of Gains and Losses; Statement Presentation of Gains and Losses and Other Accounting Adjustments; Accounting for Capital

American Institute of Certified Public Accountants, Task Force on Impairment of Value. *Accounting for the Inability to Fully Recover the Carrying Amounts of Long Lived Assets.* Issues Paper. New York: AICPA, July 15, 1980.
Arnett, H.E. "The Distinction Between Ordinary and Non-Ordinary Gains and Losses." *New York Certified Public Accountant,* April 1967, pp. 267-78.
Chottiner, S., and Young, A. "A Test of AICPA Differentiation Between Stock Dividends and Stock Splits." *Journal of Accounting Research,* Autumn 1971, pp. 367-74.
Deming, J.R. "New Guidelines for Extraordinary Items (A Review of APB Opinion No. 30)." *The CPA Journal,* February 1974, pp. 21-26.
Eisenman, S.; Akresh, M.S.; and Snow, C. "Reporting Unusual Events in Income Statements." *The CPA Journal,* June 1979, pp. 23-28.
Friskhoff, P. "Consistency in Auditing and APB Opinion No. 20." *Journal of Accountancy,* August 1972, pp. 64-70.
Jaenicke, H.R. *Survey of Present Practices in Recognizing Revenues, Expenses, Gains and Losses.* Stamford: Financial Accounting Standards Board, 1981.
Klink, J.J. "The Net Realizable Value Controversy." *The CPA Journal,* June 1984, pp. 7-8. (Excerpt from *Real Estate Update* [Price Waterhouse], December 1983.)
Melcher, B. *Stockholders' Equity.* Accounting Research Study No. 15. New York: American Institute of Certified Public Accountants, 1973.
Nichols, D.R. "The 'Never-to-Recur Unusual Item' — A Critique of APB Opinion No. 30." *The CPA Journal,* March 1974, pp. 45-48.
Pusker, H.C. "Accounting for Capital Stock Distributions (Stock Split-Ups and Dividends)." *The CPA Journal,* May 1971, pp. 347-52.
Sheldahl, T.K. "Reporting Treasury Stock as an Asset: Law, Logic and Economic Substance." *The Accounting Historians Journal,* Fall 1982, pp. 1-23.
Walker, R.G. "Asset Classification and Asset Valuation." *Accounting and Business Research,* Autumn 1974, pp. 286-96.

Warner, S.E., Jr., and Whitehurst, F.D. "A Graphical Approach to Lower of Cost or Market." *The Accounting Review,* July 1982, pp. 631-37.

Chapter 18

Accounting for Business Combinations

Byrd, C.E. *Business Combinations and Long-Term Intercorporate Investments: The Canadian View.* 2nd ed. Hamilton: Society of Industrial Accountants of Canada, 1976.

Chapter 19

Accounting for Intercorporate Investments

Accountants International Study Group. *Consolidated Financial Statements.* Toronto: AISG, 1973.

Baxter, G.C., and Spinney, J.C. "A Closer Look at Consolidated Financial Statement Theory, Parts I and II." *CAmagazine,* January 1975, pp. 31-36, and February 1975, pp. 31-35.

Ludwick, A.M., and Simpson, K.W. "The Case of the Missing Property Or When Does 50% = 1/2?" *Canadian Chartered Accountant,* April 1973, pp. 17-29.

Neuhausen, B.S. "Consolidation and the Equity Method — Time for an Overhaul." *Journal of Accountancy,* February 1982, pp. 54-66.

Chapter 20

Foreign Currency and Financial Reporting

Aliber, R.Z., and Stickney, C.P. "Accounting Measures of Foreign Exchange Exposure: The Long and Short of It." *The Accounting Review,* January 1975, pp. 44-57.

Hall, T.W. "Inflation and Rates of Exchange: Support for SFAS No. 52." *Journal of Accounting Auditing & Finance,* Summer 1983, pp. 299-313.

Heywood, J. *Foreign Exchange and the Corporate Treasurer.* London: Adam & Charles Black, 1978.

Jacque, L.L. "Management of Foreign Exchange Risk: A Review Article." In *International Accounting and Transnational Decisions,* pp. 361-84. Edited by S.J. Gray. London: Butterworth, 1983. (First published in *Journal of International Business Studies,* Spring-Summer 1981, pp. 81-101.)

Patz, D.H. "The State of the Art in Translation Theory." *Journal of Business Finance & Accounting,* Autumn 1977, pp. 311-25.

Rodriguez, R.M. "Measuring and Controlling Multinationals' Exchange Risk." *Financial Analysts Journal,* November-December 1979, pp. 49-55.

Vézina, P. *Foreign Currency Translation.* Toronto: Canadian Institute of Chartered Accountants, 1985.

Chapter 21

The Statement of Changes in Financial Position

Arnett, H.E. *Proposed Funds Statements for Managers and Investors.* New York: National Association of Accountants, 1979.

Heath, L.C. *Financial Reporting and the Evaluation of Solvency.* Accounting Research Monograph No. 3. New York: American Institute of Certified Public Accountants, 1978.

Henry, E.J. "A New Funds Statement Format for Greater Disclosure." *Journal of Accountancy,* April 1975, pp. 56-62.

Hicks, B.E., and Hunt, P., eds. *Cash Flow Accounting.* Sudbury, Ont.: International Group for Cash Flow Accounting, and Research and Publication Division, School of Commerce and Administration, Laurentian University, 1981.

Lee, T.A. *Cash Flow Accounting.* Wokingham, Eng.: Van Nostrand Reinhold (UK), 1984.

Rosen, L.S., and DeCoster, D.T. " 'Funds' Statements: A Historical Perspective." *The Accounting Review,* January 1969, pp. 125-36.

Seed, A.H., III. *The Funds Statement: Structure and Use.* Morristown, N.J.: Financial Executives Research Foundation, 1984.

Swanson, E.P., and Vangermeersch, R. "Statement of Financing and Investing Activities." *The CPA Journal,* November 1981, pp. 32-40.

Chapter 22

Statement Presentation and Disclosure; Interim Financial Statements; Analytical Data

Backer, M., and McFarland, W.B. *External Reporting for Segments of a Business.* New York: National Association of Accountants, 1968.

Bloom, R. "Functional Fixation and Information Overload Applied to Financial Statement Users." *Cost and Management,* July-August 1980, pp. 43-45.

Burton, J.C. "The Changing Face of Financial Reporting." *Journal of Accountancy,* February 1976, pp. 60-63.

Financial Accounting Standards Board. *Criteria for Determining Materiality.* FASB Discussion Memorandum. Stamford: FASB, March 21, 1975.

________. *Interim Financial Accounting and Reporting.* FASB Discussion Memorandum. Stamford: FASB, May 25, 1978.

________. *Reporting Earnings.* FASB Discussion Memorandum. Stamford: FASB, July 31, 1979.

Heath, L.C. "Is Working Capital Really Working?" *Journal of Accountancy,* August 1980, pp. 55-62.

Hicks, E.L. "Materiality." *Journal of Accounting Research,* Autumn 1964, pp. 158-71.

Landsittel, D.L., and Serlin, J.E. "Evaluating the Materiality of Errors in Financial Statements." *Journal of Accounting Auditing & Finance,* Summer 1982, pp. 291-300.

Leslie, D.A. *Materiality: The Concept and Its Application to Auditing.* Toronto: Canadian Institute of Chartered Accountants, 1985.
Mautz, R.K. *Financial Reporting by Diversified Companies.* New York: Financial Executives Research Foundation, 1968.
Shank, J.K. "Case of the Disclosure Debate." *Harvard Business Review,* January-February 1972, pp. 142-58.

Chapter 24

Accounting for Financial Institutions; Life Insurance Companies: A Special Case

Accounting for Trust and Loan Companies in Canada. Toronto: Canadian Institute of Chartered Accountants, 1971.
American Institute of Certified Public Accountants, Accounting Standards Division, Accounting Standards Task Force on Investment Companies. *Financial Accounting and Reporting by Investment Companies.* Statement of Position 77-1. New York: AICPA, 1977.
________. The Banking Committee. *Audits of Banks.* Industry Audit Guide. New York: AICPA, 1983.
________. Committee on Finance Companies. *Audits of Finance Companies.* Industry Audit Guide. New York: AICPA, 1973.
________. Committee on Insurance Accounting and Auditing. *Audits of Stock Life Insurance Companies.* 2nd ed. Industry Audit Guide. New York: AICPA, 1979.
________. Committee on Investment Companies. *Audits of Investment Companies.* Industry Audit Guide. New York: AICPA, 1973.
________. Committee on Savings and Loan Associations. *Savings and Loan Associations.* Rev. ed. Audit and Accounting Guide. New York: AICPA, 1979.
________. Stockbrokerage Auditing Subcommittee. *Audits of Brokers and Dealers in Securities.* Rev. ed. Audit and Accounting Guide. New York: AICPA, 1985.
Financial Reporting for Credit Unions. Toronto: Canadian Institute of Chartered Accountants, 1984.
Financial Reporting for Property and Casualty Insurers. Toronto: Canadian Institute of Chartered Accountants, 1974.
Keith, D.M. "Valuation of Policy Liabilities under GAAP." *Proceedings of the Canadian Institute of Actuaries.* Vol. XIV, No. 3, 1982-1983. CIA, pp. 377-400.
Report of the CICA/CIA Joint Task Force on Generally Accepted Accounting Principles for Life Insurance Companies. Toronto: Canadian Institute of Chartered Accountants and Canadian Institute of Actuaries, December 1, 1982.

Chapter 25

Accounting for Nonprofit Organizations; Accounting for Governments

Anthony, R.N. *Financial Accounting in Nonbusiness Organizations: An Exploratory Study of Conceptual Issues.* Stamford: Financial Accounting Standards Board, 1978.
Beedle, A. *Accounting for Local Government in Canada: The State of the Art.* Research

Monograph No. 2. Vancouver: The Canadian Certified General Accountants' Research Foundation, 1981.
Bolton, W.B. "A Critical Look at Governmental Accounting." *CAmagazine,* May 1973, pp. 35-41.
Federal Government Reporting Study: Detailed Report. Ottawa: Office of the Auditor General of Canada, and Gaithersburg, Md.: U.S. General Accounting Office, 1986.
Figlewicz, R.E.; Anderson, D.T.; and Strupeck, C.D. "The Evolution and Current State of Financial Accounting Concepts and Standards in the Nonbusiness Sector." *The Accounting Historians Journal,* Spring 1985, pp. 73-98.
Financial Reporting by Governments. Toronto: Canadian Institute of Chartered Accountants, 1980.
Financial Reporting for Non-Profit Organizations. Toronto: Canadian Institute of Chartered Accountants, 1980.
Freeman, R.J., and Shoulders, C.D. "Defining the Governmental Reporting Entity." *Journal of Accountancy,* October 1982, pp. 50-63.
Local Government Financial Reporting. Toronto: Canadian Institute of Chartered Accountants, 1985.
"Report of the Committee on Nonprofit Organizations, 1973-74." *The Accounting Review,* Supplement 1975, pp. 1-39.

Part III: Accounting for Changing Prices

Chapter 27

The Elements of Income Accounting Models

Chasteen, L. "A Taxonomy of Price Change Models." *The Accounting Review,* July 1984, pp. 515-23.
Lemke, K.W. "Asset Valuation and Income Theory." *The Accounting Review,* January 1966, pp. 32-41.
Rosenfield, P. "A History of Inflation Accounting." *Journal of Accountancy,* September 1981, pp. 95-126.
Seed, A.H., III. *Inflation: Its Impact on Financial Reporting and Decision Making.* New York: Financial Executives Research Foundation, 1978.

Chapter 28

General Price-Level Accounting

Stickler, A.D., and Hutchins, C.S.R. *General Price-Level Accounting: Described and Illustrated.* Toronto: Canadian Institute of Chartered Accountants, 1975.

Chapter 29

Current Cost Accounting

Baxter, W.T. *Accounting Values and Inflation.* London: McGraw-Hill, 1975.

Carsberg, B., and Page, M., eds. *Current Cost Accounting: The Benefits and the Costs.* 4 vols. Englewood Cliffs, N.J.: Prentice/Hall International in association with The Institute of Chartered Accountants in England and Wales, 1984.

Dean, G.W., and Wells, M.C., eds. *Current Cost Accounting: Identifying the Issues.* Lancaster, Eng.: International Centre for Research in Accounting; and Sydney, New South Wales: Department of Accounting, University of Sydney, n.d.

Edwards, E.O., and Bell, P.W. *The Theory and Measurement of Business Income.* Berkeley and Los Angeles: University of California Press, 1961.

Revsine, L. *Replacement Cost Accounting.* Englewood Cliffs, N.J.: Prentice-Hall, 1973.

Skinner, R.M. *Memorandum on the Significance of Debt Financing During an Inflationary Period and the Implications Thereof to a System of "Inflation Accounting."* Supplementary Paper No. 2 prepared for the Ontario Committee on Inflation Accounting. Toronto: Ministry of Treasury, Economics and Intergovernmental Affairs, 1977.

Sterling, R.R., and Lemke, K.W., eds. *Maintenance of Capital: Financial versus Physical.* Papers from the Clarkson Gordon Foundation Symposium held under the auspices of the Faculty of Business Administration and Commerce, University of Alberta, August 1981. Houston: Scholars Book Co., 1982.

Chapter 30

Current Realizable Value Accounting; Price Changes and Specialized Industries; Evaluation of Current Value Accounting

Bell, P.W. *CVA, CCA and CoCoA: How Fundamental are the Differences?* Accounting Theory Monograph No. 1. Melbourne: Australian Accounting Research Foundation, 1982.

Chambers, R.J. *Accounting, Evaluation and Economic Behavior.* Englewood Cliffs, N.J.: Prentice-Hall, 1966; reprint ed., Houston: Scholars Book Co., 1974.

________. *Accounting for Inflation.* Exposure Draft. Sydney, New South Wales: Department of Accounting, University of Sydney, 1975.

________. "Edwards and Bell on Income Measurement in Retrospect." *Abacus,* June 1982, pp. 3-39.

Kirkman, P.R.A. *Accounting Under Inflationary Conditions.* 2nd ed. London: George Allen & Unwin, 1978.

Sterling, R.R. *Theory of the Measurement of Enterprise Income.* Lawrence, Kan.: University Press of Kansas, 1970.

________. *Toward a Science of Accounting.* Houston: Scholars Book Co., 1979.

Sterling, R.R., and Thomas, A.L., eds. *Accounting for a Simplified Firm Owning Depreciable Assets: Seventeen Essays and a Synthesis Based on a Common Case.* Papers from Accounting Researchers International Symposium held at Jesse H. Jones Graduate School of Administration, Rice University, May 1978.

Whittington, G. *Inflation Accounting: An Introduction to the Debate.* Cambridge: Cambridge University Press, 1983.

Part IV: A Conceptual Framework and Standard-Setting

Chapter 31

A Conceptual Framework for Financial Reporting

American Accounting Association, Committee on Concepts and Standards for External Financial Reports. *Statement on Accounting Theory and Theory Acceptance.* AAA, 1977.

Amernic, J.H., and Lemon, W.M. "Do We Need a Canadian Conceptual Framework?" *CAmagazine,* July 1984, pp. 22-27.

Carsberg, B. "The Quest for a Conceptual Framework for Financial Reporting." In *External Financial Reporting: Essays in Honour of Harold Edey,* pp. 25-39. Edited by B. Carsberg and S. Dev. Englewood Cliffs, N.J.: Prentice/Hall International, in cooperation with London School of Economics and Political Science, 1984.

Corporate Reporting: Its Future Evolution. Toronto: Canadian Institute of Chartered Accountants, 1980.

Cramer, J.J., Jr., and Sorter, G.H., eds. *Objectives of Financial Statements.* Vol. 2. New York: American Institute of Certified Public Accountants, 1974.

Financial Accounting Standards Board. *Objectives of Financial Reporting by Business Enterprises.* Statement of Financial Accounting Concepts No. 1. Stamford: FASB, 1978.

———. *Qualitative Characteristics of Accounting Information.* SFAC No. 2. Stamford: FASB, 1980.

———. *Objectives of Financial Reporting by Nonbusiness Organizations.* SFAC No. 4. Stamford: FASB, 1980.

———. *Recognition and Measurement in Financial Statements of Business Enterprises.* SFAC No. 5. Stamford: FASB, 1984.

———. *Elements of Financial Statements: A Replacement of FASB Concepts Statement No. 3 (Incorporating an Amendment of FASB Concepts Statement No. 2).* SFAC No. 6. Stamford: FASB, 1985.

Kahn, N., and Schiff, S. "Tangible Equity Change and the Evolution of the FASB's Definition of Income." *Journal of Accounting Auditing & Finance,* Fall 1985, pp. 40-49.

Macve, R. *A Conceptual Framework for Financial Accounting and Reporting: The Possibilities for an Agreed Structure.* London: Institute of Chartered Accountants in England and Wales, 1981.

Objectives of Financial Statements. Vol. 1. New York: American Institute of Certified Public Accountants, 1973.

The Corporate Report. London: Accounting Standards Steering Committee, 1975.

Chapter 32

The Establishment of Accounting Standards

Abdel-khalik, A.R., ed. *Government Regulation of Accounting and Information.* Gainesville, Fla.: University Presses of Florida, 1980.

CICA Special Committee on Standard-Setting. *Report to CICA Board of Governors.* Toronto: Canadian Institute of Chartered Accountants, 1980.

Denham, R.A. "Standard Setting Under Pressure." *CAmagazine,* May 1985, pp. 36-45.

Laughlin, R.C., and Puxty, A.G. "Accounting Regulation: An Alternative Perspective." *Journal of Business Finance & Accounting,* Autumn 1983, pp. 451-79.

Leach, Sir R., and Stamp, E., eds. *British Accounting Standards: The First 10 Years.* Cambridge: Woodhead-Faulkner, 1981.

Mosso, D. "Standards Overload — No Simple Solution." *The CPA Journal,* October 1983, pp. 12-22.

Stamp, E. *The Future of Accounting and Auditing Standards.* ICRA Occasional Paper No. 18. Lancaster, Eng.: International Centre for Research in Accounting, 1979.

Index